BLACK

N

Ephesus

Antioch

Damascus

AN

SEA

Jerusalem

Alexandria

A

N

e LOWENSTEIN

# THE INTERPRETER'S BIBLE

# THE INTERPRETER'S BIBLE

## IN TWELVE VOLUMES

VOLUME XI

The Epistle to the
PHILIPPIANS

The Epistle to the
COLOSSIANS

The First and Second Epistles to the
THESSALONIANS

The First and Second Epistles to
TIMOTHY
and
The Epistle to
TITUS

The Epistle to
PHILEMON

The Epistle to the
HEBREWS

# THE
# INTERPRETER'S BIBLE

—

## *The Holy Scriptures*

IN THE KING JAMES AND REVISED STANDARD VERSIONS

WITH GENERAL ARTICLES AND

INTRODUCTION, EXEGESIS, EXPOSITION

FOR EACH BOOK OF THE BIBLE

IN TWELVE VOLUMES

VOLUME

## XI

Ἐν ἀρχῇ ἦν ὁ λόγος

NEW YORK *Abingdon Press* NASHVILLE

ISBN 0-687-19217-X

Library of Congress Catalog Card Number: 51-12276

The text of the Revised Standard Version of the Bible (RSV) and quotations therefrom are copyright 1946, 1952 by Division of Christian Education of the National Council of the Churches of Christ in the United States of America. Scripture quotations designated "ASV" are from the American Standard Version of the Revised Bible, copyright renewed 1929 by the International Council of Religious Education. Those designated "Moffatt" are from *The Bible, A New Translation*, by James Moffatt, copyright in the United States, 1935, by Harper & Brothers, New York; copyright in countries of the International Copyright Union by Hodder & Stoughton, Ltd., London. Those designated "Amer. Trans." or "Goodspeed" are from *The Complete Bible, An American Translation*, by J. M. Powis Smith and Edgar J. Goodspeed, copyright 1939 by the University of Chicago.

S

SET UP, PRINTED, AND BOUND BY THE PARTHENON PRESS, AT NASHVILLE, TENNESSEE, UNITED STATES OF AMERICA

# ABBREVIATIONS AND EXPLANATIONS

## Abbreviations

Canonical books and bibliographical terms are abbreviated according to common usage

Amer. Trans. — *The Bible, An American Translation,* Old Testament, ed. J. M. P. Smith
Apoc.—Apocrypha
Aq.—Aquila
ASV—American Standard Version (1901)
Barn.—Epistle of Barnabas
Clem.—Clement
C.T.—Consonantal Text
Did.—Didache
Ecclus.—Ecclesiasticus
ERV—English Revised Version (1881-85)
Exeg.—Exegesis
Expos.—Exposition
Goodspeed—*The Bible, An American Translation,* New Testament and Apocrypha, tr. Edgar J. Goodspeed
Herm. Vis., etc.—The Shepherd of Hermas: Visions, Mandates, Similitudes
Ign. Eph., etc.—Epistles of Ignatius to the Ephesians, Magnesians, Trallians, Romans, Philadelphians, Smyrnaeans, and Polycarp
KJV—King James Version (1611)
LXX—Septuagint
Macc.—Maccabees
Moffatt—*The Bible, A New Translation,* by James Moffatt
M.T.—Masoretic Text
N.T.—New Testament
O.T.—Old Testament
Polyc. Phil.—Epistle of Polycarp to the Philippians
Pseudep.—Pseudepigrapha
Pss. Sol.—Psalms of Solomon
RSV—Revised Standard Version (1946-52)
Samar.—Samaritan recension
Symm.—Symmachus
Targ.—Targum
Test. Reuben, etc.—Testament of Reuben, and others of the Twelve Patriarchs
Theod.—Theodotion
Tob.—Tobit
Vulg.—Vulgate
Weymouth—*The New Testament in Modern Speech,* by Richard Francis Weymouth
Wisd. Sol.—Wisdom of Solomon

## Quotations and References

Boldface type in Exegesis and Exposition indicates a quotation from either the King James or the Revised Standard Version of the passage under discussion. The two versions are distinguished only when attention is called to a difference between them. Readings of other versions are not in boldface type and are regularly identified.

In scripture references a letter (*a, b,* etc.) appended to a verse number indicates a clause within the verse; an additional Greek letter indicates a subdivision within the clause. When no book is named, the book under discussion is understood.

Arabic numbers connected by colons, as in scripture references, indicate chapters and verses in deuterocanonical and noncanonical works. For other ancient writings roman numbers indicate major divisions, arabic numbers subdivisions, these being connected by periods. For modern works a roman number and an arabic number connected by a comma indicate volume and page. Bibliographical data on a contemporary work cited by a writer may be found by consulting the first reference to the work by that writer (or the bibliography, if the writer has included one).

## Greek Transliterations

| | | | | | |
|---|---|---|---|---|---|
| α = a | ε = e | ι = i | ν = n | ρ = r | φ = ph |
| β = b | ζ = z | κ = k | ξ = x | σ(ς) = s | χ = ch |
| γ = g | η = ē | λ = l | ο = o | τ = t | ψ = ps |
| δ = d | θ = th | μ = m | π = p | υ = u, y | ω = ō |

## Hebrew and Aramaic Transliterations

### I. HEBREW ALPHABET

| | | | | | |
|---|---|---|---|---|---|
| א = ʼ | ה = h | ט = ṭ | מ(ם) = m | פ(ף) = p, ph | שׁ = s, sh |
| ב = b, bh | ו = w | י = y | נ(ן) = n | צ(ץ) = ç | ת = t, th |
| ג = g, gh | ז = z | כ(ך) = k, kh | ס = ş | ק = q | |
| ד = d, dh | ח = ḥ | ל = l | ע = ʻ | ר = r | |

### II. MASORETIC POINTING

| Pure-long | Tone-long | Short | Composite *shᵉwa* |
|---|---|---|---|
| ָ = â | ָ = ā | ַ = a | ֲ = ª |
| ֵ = ê | ֵ = ē | ֶ = e | ֱ = ᵉ |
| ִ or ִי = î | | ִ = i | |
| וֹ or ֹ = ô | ֹ = ō | ָ = o | ֳ = ᵒ |
| וּ = û | | ֻ = u | |

NOTE: (*a*) The *páthaḥ* furtive is transliterated as a *ḥaṭeph-páthaḥ*. (*b*) The simple *shᵉwa,* when vocal, is transliterated ᵉ. (*c*) The tonic accent, which is indicated only when it occurs on a syllable other than the last, is transliterated by an acute accent over the vowel.

# TABLE OF CONTENTS

## VOLUME XI

### THE EPISTLE TO THE PHILIPPIANS

### THE EPISTLE TO THE COLOSSIANS

### THE FIRST AND SECOND EPISTLES TO THE THESSALONIANS

# THE INTERPRETER'S BIBLE

## THE FIRST AND SECOND EPISTLES TO TIMOTHY AND THE EPISTLE TO TITUS

## THE EPISTLE TO PHILEMON

## THE EPISTLE TO THE HEBREWS

## MAP

The Epistle to the

# PHILIPPIANS

*Introduction and Exegesis by* Ernest F. Scott
*Exposition by* Robert R. Wicks

# PHILIPPIANS

## INTRODUCTION

Seven of the epistles attributed to Paul were written in prison—Philippians, Ephesians, Colossians, Philemon, I and II Timothy, and Titus. It is more than doubtful that the so-called Pastoral epistles (I and II Timothy and Titus) are the work of Paul, although they may contain short notes by him, expanded by a later writer. His authorship of Ephesians has been called in question, on grounds which are not altogether convincing. Philippians, Colossians, and Philemon may safely be accepted as letters by Paul, and in all of them he describes himself as a prisoner.

Philippians, however, stands apart from the other epistles of the captivity. Colossians, Philemon and, if genuine, Ephesians were all sent by the same messenger, Tychicus, who was making a journey into Asia Minor. They were written presumably during the month or so before his departure, and largely repeat each other, as letters of the same date are wont to do. Philippians was sent by Epaphroditus, on his return to the Philippian church, of which he was a member. It makes no reference to the subjects discussed in the other letters, and reflects a different mood and situation. Whether it was earlier or later than the letters carried by Tychicus can only be conjectured. Its allusions to Paul's trial as then imminent might seem to point to the final days of his imprisonment, but he may have expected the crisis long before it came. Nothing can be gathered from the letter except that he was in prison, and had been so for some time, and was anxiously awaiting the verdict on which his life depended.

### I. Destination and Occasion

The letter is addressed to the church at Philippi, an ancient and historic city of Macedonia. Philippi took its name from Philip, the father of Alexander, who founded a new city on the site of an early settlement known as "The Springs." The position, he perceived, was of high strategical value, and there were mines in the neighborhood and a fertile stretch of country. This Macedonian town came into worldwide prominence when it was the scene in 42 B.C. of the great battle between Brutus and Cassius on the one side, and Antony and Octavian on the other. It was this victory of the avengers of Julius Caesar which marked the beginning of the Roman Empire, and when Octavian became head of the state, under the title of Augustus, he rebuilt Philippi, and peopled it with his old soldiers. It henceforth held the rank of a "colony," a military outpost of Rome, endowed with special privileges. Lying as it did at some distance from the sea it never became a commercial center. Even in Paul's day, when it was most flourishing, it was only a small city, and gradually it fell into obscurity; only a few vestiges of it now remain. But its people were proud of their connection with Rome, which was more than a sentimental one. The city was laid out as a miniature of Rome, and all Roman customs and municipal arrangements were faithfully observed. Many inscriptions have been unearthed on the site, and a full half of the names mentioned in them are Latin. The Egnatian road, the great highway connecting the Eastern provinces with Rome, ran through the city, and by means of it this provincial town was in daily communication with the capital. Perhaps there was no city in the empire which was more conscious of its dignity and importance than this outpost of Rome in Macedonia.

It was at Philippi that Paul made his first acquaintance with Europe. Most probably in A.D. 52 he crossed the Aegean Sea from Troas, in consequence, Luke tells us, of a dream in which he saw a man of Macedonia calling to him, "Come over and help us." That he had such a dream is itself evidence that a Western mission was in his mind. We cannot doubt that he had long been planning it, and he accepted the dream as a token of divine approval. He sailed in company with Silas and Timothy, and apparently Luke, whose "travel diary." in the book of Acts, begins at this point; and made a straight course to Neapolis, the nearest seaport of Macedonia. Philippi was only a few miles inland, and Paul there opened the mission which was to plant Christianity in Europe. This, as he himself suggests, was one reason why Philippi had a special place in his affection. It was associated in his mind with "the beginning of the gospel" (4:15) —the raising of the Christian flag in the great world of the West.

Luke seems to have been one of Paul's companions on this first visit to Philippi, and his account of it in the book of Acts is particularly graphic. He tells us that at Philippi, as in most cities of the empire, there was a Jewish community, but this one was not large enough to maintain a synagogue. The Jews held their service at a "praying place," apparently in the open air beside the river, and Paul went there on the sabbath and proclaimed his message. He won several converts, most notably Lydia, a native of Thyatira in Asia Minor, who dealt in the purple fabrics for which that city was famous. Perhaps she used the name Lydia—"the Lydian woman"—for purposes of trade, and she may be mentioned under her proper name in the epistle. She was not a Jewess but a "worshiper of God," one of the earnest pagans who were impressed by the lofty character of Jewish religion and attached themselves to the synagogue. Evidently she was a woman of some wealth and standing, and threw her house open to Paul and his companions as a center for their work.

We do not know how long he stayed in the city, but it must have been for at least some weeks, for a church was formed which was able to hold its own after the missionaries were gone and which they left well grounded in the Christian faith. The end came abruptly. In Philippi, as in other Roman cities of the time, the arts of soothsaying were in high repute, and the local practitioners owned a slave girl who was specially gifted as a medium. She had been moved by Paul's teaching and followed the missionaries about, declaring to everybody that they spoke for the true God. Paul did not wish for testimony from this doubtful quarter, and quieted the hysterical girl, who recovered her senses at the cost of her magical gift. Her owners brought an action against Paul, accusing him of introducing a religion which was subversive of Roman practice and tradition. On a point of this kind the magistrates of a Roman colony were highly sensitive. Paul and Silas were arrested and scourged and thrown into prison, but during the night there was an earthquake which terrified the jailer and convinced him that his prisoners were indeed from God. The main fact is certain, that after they had been beaten and imprisoned, Paul and his companion were set free. This change of front on the part of the magistrates was not due to the earthquake or the jailer's conversion but to their discovery that Paul and Silas, whom they had scourged without trial, were both Roman citizens. Such treatment of citizens was a criminal offense, and the magistrates were anxious to make peace with their victims and get them away from the city before they could openly protest.

It was not till five years afterward that Paul had a second opportunity of visiting Philippi. For part of the interval he had been occupied with his work in Greece; then he had to make a journey to Jerusalem, returning overland to Ephesus, where he was engaged for three years in strenuous labor. After this he went back to Greece by way of Macedonia, and seems to have stayed for some time at Philippi, where he probably wrote II Corinthians. He repeated the visit in the following year on his way from Corinth to Jerusalem—the last journey he was destined to make as a free man. During all these years the Philippian church had been steadily growing. It had remained faithful to Paul through the troubled period when most of his churches were turning against him. It had distinguished itself by its liberality, taking a foremost place in Paul's scheme for a collection in behalf of the poor in Palestine. He himself had owed much on several occasions to the generosity of the Philippian Christians, and he was to be put in their debt again.

After Paul's death the church at Philippi drops out of sight. The Christian cause was now centered in metropolitan cities—Antioch, Ephesus, Alexandria, and Rome—and the records are silent on this small community in a provincial town. We have one welcome glimpse of it, however, in the letter addressed to it by Polycarp, sixty years after Paul's last visit. The Philippians had written to him concerning Ignatius who had passed through their city on his way to martyrdom at Rome, and Polycarp answered them in the one writing of his which has been preserved. We learn from it that after two generations the Philippian church was still standing firm, and that it cherished the memory of its great founder. For Paul's sake it had honored Ignatius, and had made every effort to render him help and sympathy. What it had done for Paul it was eager to do for his successor.

As we turn from the Philippians to the letter which Paul wrote to them, it is necessary to bear in mind that this is the most intimate of his epistles, and cannot be understood without some knowledge of the circumstances which called it forth. These are made sufficiently clear, at least in a general way, by allusions in the letter itself. Paul was in prison, and the Philippians had sent Epaphroditus, one of their number and apparently a trusted leader, to bring him a gift of money, and also to stay beside him and render him any services he could. Their messenger, not long after his arrival, had fallen seriously ill, and had lain for some time between life and death. News of his illness had reached his friends in Philippi, who were greatly concerned about him, and when Epaphroditus had learned of this after his recovery he was in much distress. The Philippians were troubled even more about Paul himself, whose trial was drawing near, and whose prospects, by all accounts, were very dark. He therefore sent Epaphroditus back to them to relieve their anxieties and also to convey this letter, in which he thanked them for all their kindness and explained the true state of his affairs.

## II. Place and Date

The conditions under which Paul wrote are thus known to us more fully than in the case of any other epistle, but the most important question is left unanswered. Where was he when he wrote the letter? It was taken for granted until recent years that he was at Rome, awaiting trial before the supreme court, in consequence of his appeal to Caesar. This assumption seemed to be placed beyond all doubt by the express reference to the *praetorium* (1:13) and by the final greeting from "those of Caesar's household" (4:22). Inscriptions, however, have come to light which prove that these allusions do not necessarily point to Rome. The government quarter in every important city was known as the *praetorium*, while "Caesar's servants" was a name attached to all who were employed in administrative work—clerks and police and janitors as well as high officials. When once these facts were established, the question of where Paul wrote his letter was thrown open, and it was seen that there were difficulties in the view that he was in Rome. The chief one was that Rome was far distant from Philippi, nearly eight hundred miles, and yet several notices in the epistle imply frequent communication. The Philippians heard that Paul was in prison, and sent Epaphroditus with a gift. News came back to them that their messenger was sick, and he in turn got news of their concern. Four distinct journeys are thus involved, and how could they have taken place,

under ancient conditions of travel, between cities so far separate as Rome and Philippi?

Again, Paul assures the Philippians that if he is set free he will come at once and visit them again. We know from the Epistle to the Romans (15:23-24) that his plan was to go on from Rome to Spain, and begin a great new mission in the West; perhaps it was largely with this object that he had claimed a trial which would secure him a passage from Palestine to Rome. In Philippians there is no hint of this projected Western mission. He has no plan in his mind but a continuance of his work in the familiar field.

Once more, and this is a weighty objection, the epistle is similar in character to those which Paul wrote at an earlier period. In a number of its phrases and ideas it recalls the Epistle to the Romans. Parallels to much of its teaching may be found in Galatians and in the two Corinthian epistles. From several allusions it might appear that Paul was still faced with the opposition of those Jewish teachers who were bent on wrecking his work during his sojourn in Ephesus. If there had been no tradition that he wrote Philippians at Rome, and this letter had to be dated simply by comparison with the others, it would be assigned most naturally to the same period as Romans and Galatians. On all these grounds, and on several others of a less cogent kind, it has been held that while undoubtedly he wrote the letter in prison, the imprisonment was a good deal earlier than the Roman one, and that he suffered it in a city which was much nearer to Philippi than Rome was.

According to one view which has found favor with many scholars this city was Caesarea. Paul was a prisoner there for two years, and it has often appeared strange that we have no letter dating from this time when he had ample leisure and the needs of his churches were still fresh in his memory. Philippians, it is argued, is just such a letter as he might have written then. But the difficulty of distance, which tells so heavily against Rome, can be urged with equal force against Caesarea. We know, moreover, that in Caesarea he was not in serious danger. He was detained by a corrupt governor in hope of a bribe, and at any moment could free himself, as he finally did, by appealing to the higher court. The Caesarean imprisonment was tedious and irksome, but would not justify the tone of martyrdom which pervades the Epistle to the Philippians.

The view most commonly put forward is that which connects the epistle with Ephesus. Little is told us in the book of Acts of Paul's three-year sojourn in that city, although he was then at the height of his powers and accomplished his greatest work, both as a missionary and a writer. He tells us himself, however, that in Ephesus he underwent much suffering. He was "pressed out of measure, above strength, insomuch that we despaired even of life" (II Cor. 1:8-10). In this same passage he indicates that at one time he was under sentence of death. He says in I Cor. 15:32 that he had fought with wild beasts at Ephesus, although it is clear from the additional words "after the manner of men" that the statement is not to be taken literally. He had been attacked by beasts in human shape, or perhaps the meaning is that if men had had their way he would have been thrown to the lions. It cannot be doubted that all this ill-usage included imprisonment, and in Rom. 16, which is almost certainly a note addressed to the Ephesian church, he greets two of its members as "my fellow prisoners." Here then, it is argued, we are to find the true setting of the Epistle to Philippians. Ephesus was the capital of a province and would have a *praetorium* and a staff of "Caesar's servants." It was only a few days' sail from Philippi. We are told definitely that after he had ended his stay at Ephesus, Paul departed for Macedonia (Acts 20:1), which is just what he promises to do in the epistle. Before going himself, he sent Timothy (Acts 19:22), which is also in keeping with the plan outlined in 2:19. So when it is assumed that he writes from Ephesus, everything appears to fall into place. Paul was in terrible danger but was hopeful of deliverance, and events proved that he was right. Messages went to and fro between two cities which were in easy distance of each other. No mention is made of a mission to the West, for the project of such a mission was not yet formed. Add to all this that the letter agrees in thought and language with the epistles which certainly belong to the Ephesian period and there would seem to be little doubt that Ephesus was its place of origin. Many scholars would now regard this as almost self-evident.

The new theory, however, is open to grave objections. For one thing, there is no definite proof that Paul was in prison at Ephesus, and a reasonable assumption must not be treated as a fact. If an imprisonment took place, it cannot have been of long duration. The time spent at Ephesus was the most active in Paul's whole career, and we cannot strike off a large part of it as passing idly in prison. Any imprisonment at Ephesus must have been of much the same character as that which the two apostles suffered at Philippi. In consequence of a popular outcry Paul would be arrested and placed under guard, with a view to summary trial and execution. His enemies would be in no mood to leave him a prisoner until a long routine of legal proceedings had run its course. A long captivity, however, is plainly implied in the Philippian letter. Again, Paul describes his acquaintance with the Philippians as one of old standing, and indicates that at various times he had been present with them. He reminds them of what they had done for him "in the beginning of the gospel," as if those early events were now in a distant past. But when he was in Ephesus, the Philippian church had been in existence only three or four years. He had never revisited it since his first departure, and all the expressions of warm affection, of which the epistle is full, could mean very little either to the Philippians or to Paul himself. Again, he speaks in disparaging terms—almost bitterly—of the people who are with him as he writes. Timothy alone, he says, had shown himself a true friend; as for the others "all seek their own, not the things which are Jesus Christ's" (2:21). If this was written at Ephesus, it was surely ungenerous in the last degree. All his best friends were there in his company, among them "Priscilla and Aquila, my helpers in Christ Jesus, who have for my life laid down their own necks" (Rom. 16:3-4). Once more, he tells how the church around him is divided into factions, some of which regard him as an interloper and exult over his misfortunes (1:15-16). This does not answer to the conditions at Ephesus, where the church had been founded by Paul and was subject to his control.

Thus the old view that the epistle was sent from Rome is still by far the most probable. It is certain that Paul there endured a long imprisonment as he waited for his trial before the emperor's court, and was distracted for several years together between hopes and fears. The references to the *praetorium* and to Caesar's household are most natural in a letter written from the capital by a prisoner whose chief associations were with soldiers and officials. The account of rival parties taking sides for and against the famous missionary who had come among them applies most fittingly to the Roman church, which had arisen independently of Paul and could not but regard him with some misgiving. His feeling toward the Philippians can be understood best when we think of him as looking back, near the end of his life, to those first friends he had made in Europe, with whom he had sojourned on three separate occasions, and who had remained loyal to him through all that had come and gone.

The arguments against Rome are by no means unanswerable. It is true that Paul says nothing of a Western mission, and promises, if he is set free, to return at once to Philippi. But some years had now passed since he had planned a journey to Spain. In the interval he had been continually a prisoner and had become an aging man, broken in health and spirits, with the one desire to spend the remainder of his life among old friends. Again, it is possible to make too much of the distance between Rome and Philippi, and of the frequent communications which are assumed in the epistle. Ephesus was indeed much nearer, as measured in miles, but may well have taken as long to reach or even longer. Philippi was a Roman colony and had regular connections with the capital. It lay on one of the great highways which afforded overland travel in all seasons. Half a century later, when Ignatius was sent under guard to Rome, he passed through Philippi because this was chosen by his escort as the most expeditious route. On any hypothesis the number of journeys indicated in the epistle is remarkable, and must have involved a considerable time. But Paul's imprisonment at Rome was a long one, much longer than any he can have undergone at Ephesus. Its conditions, moreover, were far more stable, and the Philippians could be reasonably certain that each new message would find him in much the same circumstances, while at Ephesus his position would be critical, and anything might have happened at any moment. Those many communications on which the Ephesian theory is mainly built may be said to furnish the strongest argument against it.

From the teaching of the epistle nothing can be inferred as to the place and time of its origin. If the ideas expressed in it are in harmony with those of earlier epistles, this proves nothing more than that Paul had long arrived at convictions which he never changed. Time and experience had only strengthened his hold on what he now considered the essential Christian truths. From this point of view it may fairly be argued that Philippians belongs to a later period than Galatians and Romans. In those epistles Paul finds himself obliged to make sure, by elaborate reasoning, that his interpretation of the gospel is the right one. In Philippians he takes it for granted. He gathers up in a single sentence (3:9) all that he contends for in the long theological discussion of Romans. The conclusions to which he is there feeling his way have now become an integral part of his thinking, and need only to be stated.

One point which has generally been overlooked provides a striking evidence that the epistle was written from Rome. Paul is anxious, above all things, that the new religion should be talked about and known (1:12-18). He wel-comes his approaching trial because it will bring publicity to the gospel. He is willing that his ill-wishers should contradict and malign him because this at least draws attention to his message. The one thing that matters is to have Christianity brought before the world. If men can only be made aware of its existence they will be drawn to it as by a magnet, and will come to realize its saving power. From the outset Paul had planned his mission in this confidence that if the gospel was proclaimed in a number of central cities, it would diffuse itself by its own intrinsic power. Rome was the very heart of the world. If by any means an interest in Christianity could be awakened in Rome, all men would come to hear about it before long. It was shortly after the date of this letter that the Roman Christians, accused by Nero of setting the city on fire, were massacred in a spectacular fashion on the Vatican Hill (A.D. 64). Up till then only a few people here and there had even heard of Christ, but now his name was sent ringing through the empire, and everyone was curious to know what it stood for. The attempt to destroy it had proved the grand advertisement of the new religion. Paul speaks of his own affliction as making Christ manifest (1:13-14), and his words lose half their significance unless we assume that he wrote from Rome. To acquaint the world's capital with his religion was to his mind a triumph well worth martyrdom.

He writes, then, when his trial is still in its preliminary phase, and the outcome uncertain. We are nowhere informed on what charge he was formally indicted. It cannot have been that of teaching Christianity, for as yet there was no legal ban on the new religion. The accusation can have been only some general one of disturbing the peace, with special reference to the riot he had occasioned at Jerusalem. Subsequent events had thrown an ever darker color on this offense. Judea was now plainly on the edge of revolt, and his judges would take a grave view of a commotion aroused in the Judean center. It was not the prosecution but Paul himself who made Christianity the issue. This, he indicates, was his defense—that he was not a political rebel, but a Christian, and was in bonds for the sake of the gospel. He was trying to make this clear to the soldiers who guarded him, and to all who were concerned in his case. For his own communities there was no question that he was venturing his life as the champion of their faith, and the Philippians had sent their gift not merely to relieve his need but to assure him that they made his cause their own. He speaks to them throughout the epistle as his fellow sufferers, partaking with him in his confession of Christ.

It was a settled principle with Paul to accept no payment for his services as a missionary. He was fully convinced that churches ought to support their teachers, bestowing material things in return for spiritual benefits (I Cor. 9:11), but for his own part he preferred to work for nothing. By following this rule he refuted his enemies, who accused him of self-seeking motives; he also asserted his inward freedom by doing willingly, without any thought of wages, the work to which Christ had compelled him (I Cor. 9:16-18). His churches were sometimes offended by his refusal to accept their gifts, but he held firmly to his independence, and earned by his own labor as a tentmaker enough for his simple needs. From the outset, however, he made an exception of the Philippians. They stood in a special relation to him, and their friendliness was not open to any misunderstanding. From time to time when he was in difficulties they had come to his assistance, and when he was in prison, unable to do anything for his own support, they could not but feel that their help was needed.

The date of the epistle must remain uncertain in view of the dispute as to its place of origin; and whatever theory is held on this point is subject to doubt. Alike in Ephesus, Caesarea, and Rome, Paul's sojourn extended over several years, and we can only conjecture at what stage in any of the three periods he may have written the letter. He worked in Ephesus, so far as we can determine, from A.D. 54-57; and if he wrote during that time, it was probably near the end. If he wrote from Caesarea, the date of the letter might be approximately A.D. 59. If the letter belongs to the Roman imprisonment, as seems on every ground most likely, we have three years to choose from, presumably A.D. 60, 61, and 62. According to one view, he wrote quite early in this three-year period, when he was still hopeful of a speedy trial and expected a favorable verdict. Time must be allowed, however, for all the communications between Philippi and Rome, as well as for the spread of interest in the prisoner and the formation of parties for and against him. The letter would thus fall into the later days of Paul's sojourn at Rome, when he was under the very shadow of the end. This would fit in with the gloomy forebodings which he cannot conceal, even when he tries to comfort the Philippians with a promise that he will soon come back to them. Such a date would also give a fuller meaning to his lofty confidence that whatever happens to him all will be well,

"For to me to live is Christ, and to die is gain" (1:21).

### III. Authenticity and Integrity

The authenticity of the epistle cannot reasonably be questioned. Doubts have been thrown on it from time to time, chiefly because of the reference to bishops and deacons in the opening verse. It is argued that in Paul's time church leaders were referred to only in general terms—"the outstanding men," or "those who rule among you." They were separated into orders and given specific titles only at a later time. The notice in Philippians is indeed peculiar, but it may well have been that the names which were in common use a generation later had already been adopted at Philippi. They were natural designations for the chief overseers and their assistants, and we know that Paul took care to appoint such officers in every church he founded. The titles appear suspicious only when we read into them the significance they came to acquire in the later ecclesiastical system. Apart from this one difficulty, which cannot be regarded as a serious one, the epistle bears all the marks of Pauline authorship in a pre-eminent degree. Its teaching is unmistakably that of Paul. It is everywhere in keeping with all we know of his life and character. In its language and sentiment and manner of thought it carries the signature of Paul in every verse. Besides the internal evidence, we have the express testimony of Polycarp, who himself wrote to the Philippian church half a century afterward. It may be confidently affirmed not only that the epistle is by Paul, but that it is one of the most characteristic of all his writings.

There is more ground for questioning whether it is all a single letter. Several of Paul's epistles appear in their present form to be composite, with fragments of one incorporated by accident in another. Rom. 16, for instance, is pretty certainly a note by itself, addressed to the church at Ephesus. II Corinthians is made up apparently of two separate letters, and also may include a short passage from a third. It still happens occasionally that leaves of correspondence get mixed together, and the possibility of some similar confusion must be allowed for in the letters of Paul. He doubtless wrote more than once to a church so dear to him as that of Philippi, and Polycarp speaks in the plural of the "epistles" which the Philippians had received from their great teacher. May it not be that the epistle which we now have contains a stray portion from another? The view is held by some scholars that ch. 3, or at least the earlier part of it, belonged to a letter which Paul had written at a previous time, when his controversy with the Judaizing teachers was at its height. In this chapter the tone of the epistle appears suddenly to change. After speaking of his opponents with splendid magnanimity in the first chapter, Paul now denounces them in violent terms. He raises controversial issues which he has hitherto been careful to avoid. He starts his letter again when he is in the very act of saying farewell. Thus it is held that the first part of ch. 3 is out of place, and must be assigned to an earlier, polemical letter which has otherwise been lost.

But there is no sufficient ground for this assumption. It rests on the idea that Paul denounces fellow Christians who think differently from himself; but the context would seem to make it plain that he speaks of hostile Jews, who were seeking to pervert the Philippians from their faith in Christ. That he should be indignant with them and call them hard names is no reproach to his Christian charity. Moreover, the chapter is all of one piece, and the invective with which it opens leads up to the great confession of faith which is one of the most moving and elevated passages Paul ever wrote (3:8-14). One cannot draw any dividing line in the chapter. It is equally difficult to separate the chapter as a whole from the rest of the epistle, which from beginning to end is pervaded by the same ideas and would be impoverished if any portion of it were left out. Paul may indeed have written other letters to the Philippians, and may have them in his mind when he apologizes in 3:1 for so often repeating the same things. If those other letters had survived, they might have thrown light on much that is perplexing in that which we now possess. But they have disappeared, and all attempts to recover any fragments of them are hopeless. None of them, we may be sure, was comparable in beauty and pathos to the one which now stands in our New Testament. This was apparent to the Philippians themselves when they guarded Paul's last letter to them as their chief treasure, and bequeathed it to the church at large.

The epistle is written in the two names of "Paul and Timotheus, the servants of Jesus Christ"; but this does not imply that the younger man had any part in composing it, or even that he acted as Paul's secretary and wrote down what he dictated. After the opening verse Paul speaks consistently in his own person, and rests his whole appeal on what he himself was experiencing. In the course of the letter he has occasion to speak of Timothy as one of his assistants, and praises him in glowing words which Timothy could not have written even to dictation. We know from the other letters of

Paul that it was his practice to include one or more of his companions when he wrote to a distant church. In this manner he acknowledged the help of those who worked with him, and at the same time added weight to the letter by making himself the spokesman for the missionary cause. There were also special reasons why he conjoined the name of Timothy with his own in this epistle. They had both taken part in founding the Philippian church. He was planning also to send Timothy as his representative, and wished to suggest to his readers that they must regard this messenger as his other self.

## IV. Purpose

It is commonly assumed that the Epistle to the Philippians is Paul's letter of thanks for the money they had sent him by their messenger Epaphroditus. This, it has been suggested, is the reason why the "bishops and deacons" are particularly mentioned in the opening verse. Paul is writing his acknowledgment for money received, and naturally addresses himself to the officers who administered the funds of the church. But if this is the purpose of the letter, Paul certainly proceeds in a curious way. He never mentions the gift until near the close, and then in a kind of postscript, as if this were a minor matter which he had half forgotten. This procedure has sometimes been put down to his delicacy of feeling. He wishes to show the Philippians that what he really prizes is the Christian spirit which had prompted their gift, and if he had dwelt on the money itself he would have struck a jarring note. But would he not have shown a truer delicacy if he had magnified the gift? The Philippians had raised that sum of money with much trouble and self-denial; they were proud of their effort and would wish to know that it had been appreciated. When his letter was opened they would look first for some reference to the gift, but he makes them wait till he has disposed of other matters, and then only touches on it by way of afterthought. Again—and this is even stranger —he has let some months go by before he acknowledges their gift. The impulse of every right-minded person who receives a sum of money, even in payment of a debt, is to answer immediately, and in the ordinary courtesies of life Paul was never wanting. But if the present epistle is his letter of thanks, he certainly took his time; and this delay cannot have been due to lack of opportunity. The news of Epaphroditus' arrival and of his later sickness had been carried to Philippi, and Paul, if he had chosen, might have availed himself of the same messenger. The probability is surely that he had done so. He had thanked the Philippians as soon as he received their gift, and he now writes for a different purpose. He indeed makes mention of the gift in terms of exquisite feeling, but this is an addition to what he had said already.

The epistle, therefore, is not primarily a letter of thanks; but it may be well to look first at this aspect of it. While thanking the Philippians, Paul takes care to assure them that he is not in dire need, as they had feared. He tells them, indeed, that the money itself was not strictly necessary, although he values beyond all price the love behind it. From the material point of view he has all things and abounds. Perhaps he says this merely to allay the anxiety of his friends, but it may be that his words should be taken literally. It is an interesting suggestion of Sir William Ramsay that Paul in his later days had come in for a small legacy from one of his wealthy relations at Tarsus. For the greater part of his career he had lived from hand to mouth on his scanty wages, but toward the end his circumstances appear to have changed. Felix had reason to expect a bribe from him; he undertakes to pay back out of his own purse the money which Onesimus had stolen; he was able to live at Rome in his own hired house. The Philippians would not know that his position had altered, and he could not directly tell them that there had been no call for their liberality. But he appears to hint to them, as delicately as he can, that they need not deny themselves again.

What, then, was the main purpose for which the epistle was written? It was sent, we know, by Epaphroditus, who was returning to Philippi after his recovery, much earlier than he was expected. The Philippians had meant that he should remain in Paul's company to assist him; and now at Paul's own desire he was on his way back. He carried with him this letter, and its immediate purpose, we can hardly doubt, was to ensure him a good reception. The Philippians were to know that he came to them at Paul's behest as his representative, and were therefore to take him fully into their counsels. This, we may surmise, is why the bishops and deacons are specially addressed. They were the officers of the church, and Epaphroditus was to place the letter in their hands as the credentials of his mission.

The task of Epaphroditus in the first place was to report on Paul's circumstances and prospects. Rumors of every kind had reached Philippi, and Paul wishes his friends to know what his situation really is. He sends them a messenger who will describe all the outward conditions at firsthand, while in the accompanying letter he tells them of his state of mind.

While admitting that he is in danger and has much to suffer, he is not depressed, and the Philippians must not be too anxious about him. He is confident that everything will turn out well, and he looks forward to seeing them again. Meanwhile he is comforted to know that they are thinking of him, and that his imprisonment has proved helpful to the cause of the gospel and to his own soul. This strain of hopefulness in the letter may well be genuine. Nothing had yet been decided, and since there was no real case against him, Paul had no reason to despair. Yet we can see, as we look more closely, that he was prepared for the worst. His faith was not in human probabilities but in Christ, whose passion he felt himself to be sharing. He seeks to inspire the Philippians, who are sorely troubled on his behalf, with the same faith. Throughout the epistle he keeps saying in various language, "Have no fears about me; do not think of my distress at all, but only of Christ, who will use me for his own purpose as he sees best."

The view has recently been put forward that a double motive runs through the epistle. Paul is conscious while his own life is threatened that the Philippians are exposed to the same danger, and his object is to encourage his fellow sufferers by his example. The epistle is thus to be read as a martyr's exhortation to other martyrs. It is indeed true that several times he speaks of his readers as in the same situation as himself, "Unto you it is given in the behalf of Christ, not only to believe on him, but also to suffer for his sake, having the same conflict as ye saw in me, and now hear to be in me" (1:29-30). Such language, however, may be taken in a general sense. All true Christians are in their own degree martyrs. They stand for the truth and cannot do so without incurring the enmity and hardship which have their supreme type in the martyr's death. Paul knows too that he has the perfect sympathy of his friends at Philippi. They have made his cause so much their own that they may be said to be suffering along with him. He is able to open his heart to them in this knowledge that they are much more than spectators of his struggle. But there is no indication that they were themselves passing at this time through the fires of persecution. If this had been so, Paul would not have confined himself to one or two vague allusions. At Philippi, as elsewhere, Christians were no doubt subject to dislike and injustice, but they could not be punished for their religion since it was not yet regarded as a crime. So far indeed from facing a great danger, the Philippians, when Paul wrote to them, seem to have entered on a time of prosperity. He congratulates them on this happy change which had enabled them at last to come forward with their gift (4:10).

Nonetheless he is aware of troubles at Philippi, and here we may discover the underlying purpose of his letter. He loves the Philippians, and admires the noble spirit which has expressed itself in new kindness to him. But for this reason he is afraid of certain influences which menace the well-being of this devoted church. As yet they have caused no serious harm and may be arrested, and he is anxious to have them dealt with while there is still time. He cannot come himself, although he hopes that before long this may be possible, but he is arranging to send Timothy, his most trusted assistant, as soon as he can spare him. The Philippians all knew and honored Timothy, who had been one of the founders of their church, and they would be ready to give heed to his counsels (2:19-24). Meanwhile Epaphroditus is coming. He will be Paul's ambassador and will act as Paul has directed him, and the Philippians must welcome him for Paul's sake as well as his own. He will present this letter, which will convince them that he speaks for Paul himself.

The troubles which Paul has in mind are clearly indicated, although he touches on them gently and tactfully. In the first place, the church had become divided, not by doctrinal issues as in Galatia and Corinth, but by personal animosities. Philippi was a small city, and the Christians in it were a small community, in which every individual was conscious of his own importance. It is evident that women took a very prominent place in the Philippian church. The first convert had been a woman, and in her house, where the church held its meetings, she would gather other women of her circle. Paul gladly acknowledges his debt to those Philippian women who "labored side by side with me in the gospel" (4:3), and we can well believe that they were the chief inspirers of the loyalty and generosity which distinguished this church above all others. But the church was broken into cliques, and was vexed with petty questions of precedence. Instead of all working together in the great cause, the Philippian Christians were distracted by feuds and rivalries. Paul pleads with them again and again to have done with personal ambition. It is in this connection that he introduces the sublime passage on the example of Christ, who was of divine nature and yet humbled himself and took on him the form of a servant.

Again, the Philippians are warned against the delusion that anyone in this life can consider himself perfect. Whatever you accomplish there is always a further goal toward which you must strive; this never-ending sense of shortcoming belongs to the very essence of the Christian life. It can hardly be doubted that Paul here deals with a question which was warmly debated in the Philippian church; he expressly refers to those of his readers who "are otherwise minded." There have always been Christians who maintain that a state of perfection is attainable, and who claim to have reached it. They argue that Christ came to redeem us and that redemption cannot be a matter of degrees. If you are a Christian you must be a perfect one, or you cannot have been redeemed at all. This position had apparently commended itself to not a few of the Philippian converts, all the more so as they had proved faithful through many trials. They felt that they had done everything that Christ required of them, and were standing on a height from which they could look down on others and condemn them. Paul was convinced that this frame of mind was utterly wrong. He instances himself as one who to all appearances had lived up fully to the Christian standard. His faith was absolute; he had sacrificed everything for Christ; he was now lying in prison awaiting possible martyrdom. Nevertheless he knew that as yet he had done little, and was still reaching forward to a fulfillment which was far distant. He declares that all true Christians must feel in the same way, or they do not know the meaning of Christianity.

Once more, the Philippians were exposed to a constant danger from the side of Judaism. It does not appear that the emissaries from Jerusalem who had disturbed the church in Galatia, and perhaps in Corinth, had found their way to Philippi. Paul's references are not to Jewish Christians, but to Jews who, as a nation, had now become actively hostile to Christianity. We know from the account in Acts that Paul had met with a Jewish community in Philippi, and that he had first proclaimed his message at its place of worship on the riverbank. The community he founded was closely related to this Jewish one, and the Christians would daily be encountering Jews who would try by argument and ridicule to shake their faith. Paul reminds them (3:1) that on many occasions he had warned them against this danger, and he does so again in the most forceful language. Judaism, he says, is seductive because it offers visible tokens of God's favor; but this is precisely the reason why it leads astray. It calls on men to put their confidence in earthly things—social privileges, rites and ordinances, mechanical obedience to a written law. Religion, however, means the apprehension of things not seen. It is rooted in the sense of a higher world, known only to faith. Paul again makes use of his own experience for the guidance of his converts. He had himself possessed in the fullest measure all that Judaism prized most—purity of descent, consecration by hallowed rites, faithful performance of every command of the law. All this he had discarded, and had asked for nothing more than the knowledge of Christ. The gain he had thus secured had infinitely outweighed the loss, and so it would be with everyone who exchanged the material things for spiritual. In the Christian religion there must be no divided loyalty. You must submit yourself entirely to the higher rule or take your place among the enemies of the cross of Christ.

Paul writes, then, with a view to the special dangers which overhung the church at Philippi. He never employs the language of rebuke, as he freely does in other epistles. The nearest he comes to it is in his admonition to the two women who had broken the harmony of the church by their private quarrel, and at once he qualifies his censure by words of praise and gratitude to both of them. His feeling for the Philippians is one of unstinted affection. He is proud of them, and asks for nothing better than to have his work judged by the record of this one church (2:16; 4:1). The epistle has sometimes been read as if it were only the outpouring of his love for the community which had always stood by him and had now comforted him by a generous gift as he lay in prison; but this, when we look more closely, is a one-sided view. While he thanks the Philippians, he is also concerned about them, and these two feelings, his gratitude and his anxiety, are blended in the letter and give it a character of its own. It is the most beautiful of Paul's letters; and this is due in no small measure to his consciousness of grave faults in those whom he loves. He implores them in this message, which he feared with good reason might be his last, to rise above all littleness and doubt and self-complacency. He tells them what Christ has done for him, and is now doing, as he lies in prison. By their kindness and sympathy they have shared in his suffering, and he seeks to impart to them something of the grace which has sustained him.

### V. Character and Contents

Attempts have often been made to trace a logical sequence in the letter, but this is unnecessary. Paul writes out of a full heart, putting down his ideas as they come to him, and personal notices, outbursts of tenderness and thanksgiving, warnings, profound reflections, are all mingled together. Several of Paul's greatest religious utterances are to be found in this epistle, most notably the passage on the self-humiliation of Christ, which is cardinal for all the Pauline theology. But the epistle is not meant to be theological. Instead of arguing about his beliefs, Paul is content simply to state them, and to show how they attest themselves in actual living. But although it has no formal plan, the epistle is all in harmony. It gives expression in almost every verse to the same mood of feeling. Its thought revolves around two or three dominant themes which are always recurring, as in a musical symphony.

For one thing, it has been remarked that the word "joy," with its various equivalents, is found more often in this short letter than in all the other writings of Paul put together. This is strange when we consider the tragic circumstances in which he wrote, but it is the background of tragedy which gives significance to his use of the word. He tells in the closing chapter that by the vicissitudes of his life he has "learned the secret" of contentment; and he might have said even more truly that by suffering he had learned the secret of joy. Now that all earthly comforts had been taken from him, he had discovered the one happiness he could never lose, and he seeks to communicate his secret to the Philippians. They were complaining of their various troubles, many of them hardly worth the naming, but in their knowledge of Christ they could always rejoice; and in this inward joy they would find power to endure and overcome. Paul gives them this assurance, and impresses on them that they cannot doubt it since he writes to them from a martyr's prison.

Another word which is constantly repeated, sometimes twice or thrice in the same verse, is "all" or "always"; and this word also had acquired a new meaning for Paul. He had trusted in Christ and worked for him in his years of hope and activity. During his happy visits to Philippi, on which he now looked back, he had often spoken of God's goodness, and it was not difficult in those days to believe him. He now tells his readers that under the changed conditions he can still offer them the same message. Christ is ever-present to every one of them, and his gospel is valid for all times and circumstances. So, as he brings his letter to a close, he sums up the meaning of all that he has written: "Therefore, my brethren dearly beloved and longed for, . . . stand fast in the Lord" (4:1). Whatever may be their troubles and fears, they must hold to the truth as they have learned it, assured that they can rest in it amidst all changes. In most of his writings Paul has to deal with specific problems, and tries to find some answer which will be sufficient for those needs. He writes this epistle in the immediate prospect of death, and his mind is set on those things in the Christian message which will be always the same. They have become clear to him now, when he has done with time and is face to face with the eternal.

Once more—and this is part of the same thought—he declares ever and again that the Lord is at hand. Everything he has to say is brought into the light of that "day of Christ" when all the purposes of God will reach fulfillment. He forgets his own afflictions as he looks forward to that approaching day. He desires the Philippians to be always thinking of it, so that they may be ready to meet the Lord when he appears. It may seem that in this epistle there is much less of the apocalyptic element than appears in Paul's thought elsewhere, and in some respects this impression is true. He no longer expects that Christ will return almost immediately on the clouds of heaven and that he will himself be caught up, while still living, "to meet the Lord in the air" (I Thess. 4:17). He is reconciled to death, and hopes only "to depart, and to be with Christ; which is far better" (1:23). Yet his mind is occupied, as never before, with the vision of a great day in the future. In other epistles he relies on theological argument, while in Philippians he never seeks to explain and justify what he believes; but it may be said that in this epistle the thought of the coming day takes the place of argument. He calls on his readers to look beyond the confusions of the hour to the final issue. When they stand at last in the Lord's presence, this earthly life, with its pride and ambitions, its troubles and apprehensions and sufferings, will seem as nothing. They must try to measure life now as they will see it hereafter, on the day of Christ. So although he attempts no proof of the Christian message, Paul nowhere presents it so convincingly as in this letter. His one aim is to put his readers at the right point of vision so that they will apprehend the truth for themselves.

As he refrains from theological argument, so he has little to offer in the way of ethical teaching. His practice is to close each of his letters with a series of practical counsels, in which the principles he has laid down are applied to the conduct of life. In Philippians there is no such catalogue of moral precepts. In place of it he sums up all in one comprehensive verse (4:8), which says in effect: "Whatever things are true and honorable and just and pure and lovely, consider such things." The suggestion is that in the Christian life it is unnecessary to draw up an ethical code, with all the rules of behavior carefully marked out. We need only have our minds directed always to "the things which are excellent," acting on every occasion in the right and noble way. One perceives what that way is by a power of insight which springs of its own accord out of one's religion. The Christian will "abound more and more, with knowledge and all discernment" (1:9). The Christian ideal of goodness becomes ever more clear, and one's single effort is to follow it out more faithfully. Paul compares himself to a runner who looks neither to right nor left but only to a goal which is ever in front of him, and he desires the Philippians to pursue the highest ends with the same singleness of purpose. Of special instruction in the right mode of living he has little to give them, for they will not need it if only they have the Christian frame of mind.

It is hardly possible to gather up the contents of Philippians in a formal outline. More than any other epistle of Paul, with the exception of the personal note to Philemon, it is a genuine letter; and the writer passes from one topic to another without any thought of arranging his ideas in regular sequence. Moreover, there is much in the letter which needs to be read between the lines. Paul has misgivings about the Philippian church which he does not care to express in so many words. He has fears concerning his own future which are only suggested in what he actually says. From any bare outline of the letter it would be difficult to form anything but a dim conception of its real purport. At the same time it falls naturally into a number of sections, distinct from each other but closely connected by the mood of thought which is common to all of them. In the Exegesis these sections are considered separately, but it must always be remembered that the epistle has to be studied as a whole. Each part of it serves to illuminate the others, and all must be taken together before we can rightly understand the message which lies behind them.

VI. Final admonitions (4:1-9)
VII. The gift from Philippi (4:10-20)
VIII. Final salutations (4:21-23)

### VI. Selected Bibliography

BIGGS, C. R. D. *The Epistle of Paul the Apostle to the Philippians* ("The Churchman's Bible"). London: Methuen & Co., 1900.

DIBELIUS, MARTIN. *An die Thessalonicher I, II. An die Philipper* ("Handbuch zum Neuen Testament"). Tübingen: J. C. B. Mohr, 1937.

DUNCAN, G. S. *St. Paul's Ephesian Ministry*. New York: Charles Scribner's Sons, 1930.

JONES, MAURICE. *The Epistle to the Philippians*. London: Methuen & Co., 1918.

LIGHTFOOT, J. B. *Saint Paul's Epistle to the Philippians*. London: Macmillan & Co., 1894.

LOHMEYER, ERNST. *Die Briefe an die Philipper, an die Kolossen, und an Philemon*. Göttingen: Vandenhoeck & Ruprecht, 1930.

MICHAEL, J. HUGH. *The Epistle of Paul to the Philippians* ("The Moffatt New Testament Commentary"). London: Hodder & Stoughton, 1928.

VINCENT, M. R. *A Critical and Exegetical Commentary on the Epistles to the Philippians and to Philemon* ("International Critical Commentary"). New York: Charles Scribner's Sons, 1897.

# PHILIPPIANS

## TEXT, EXEGESIS, AND EXPOSITION

Any interpreter of Paul should welcome this letter to the Philippians as our most unlabored, spontaneous expression of the Christian way, in all its heights and depths, by one who had lived it out, fought it out, and thought it out under the severest pressure to the bitter end.

Here is an intensely human and personal document which was never intended to be the material for either a theological system or an ecclesiastical theory; and certainly was not designed for a neatly ordered series of expository sermons. It cannot be divided into logical headings that trace a development of the thought; nor is it a storehouse of moralistic platitudes that are the bane of all preaching. Above all it is not a deposit of sweet comfort for easy Christians.

It is rather the utterance, written not long before his death, of the supremely great Christian who had "suffered the loss of all things" at the hands of his fellow men and had come through unembittered to face his final martyrdom with serene confidence and with the "peace of God, which passeth all understanding" still steadying his mind and heart. It contains only a few reverberations of the controversies which Paul waged over contemporary issues that seem remote to us. The rabbinical text-twisting arguments with which he countered legalistic minds are conspicuous by their absence, and there is a happy freedom from Paul's overworked illustrations which, so unlike the clarifying parables of Jesus, often confuse rather than illumine the argument.

With good reason Christians of later times, who have suffered in life's tragedy and felt the force of man's ageless perversity, have cherished this letter as a rigorous antidote to human pride and a fortifying corrective for all the excuses of self-pity. And all ministers of the gospel should read and reread these words of the apostle as a withering indictment of the dull and deadly type of preaching which has well earned the excoriating criticism that Anthony Trollope years ago leveled at the church in *Barchester Towers:*

> No one but a preaching clergyman has, in these realms, the power of compelling an audience to sit silent, and be tormented. No one but a preaching clergyman can revel in platitudes, truisms and untruisms, and yet receive as his undisputed privilege the same respectful demeanour as though words of impassioned eloquence, or persuasive logic, fell from his lips. . . . Let a barrister attempt to talk without talking well, and he will talk but seldom. . . . We desire, nay, we are resolute, to enjoy the comfort of public worship; but we desire also that we may do so without an amount of tedium which ordinary human nature cannot endure with patience; that we may be able to leave the house of God without that anxious longing for escape which is the common consequence of common sermons.[1]

No doubt Trollope may have wanted the wrong kind of comfort in his worship, with no prophetic disturbance, but still his diatribe needs to be pondered and inwardly digested by all who today would be partakers with Paul "in the defense and confirmation of the gospel."

[1] New York: Modern Library, I, 252.

1 Paul and Timotheus, the servants of Jesus Christ, to all the saints in Christ Jesus which are at Philippi, with the bishops and deacons:

1 Paul and Timothy, servants[a] of Christ Jesus,
To all the saints in Christ Jesus who are at Philippi, with the bishops[b] and deacons:

[a] Or *slaves.*
[b] Or *overseers.*

## I. INTRODUCTION (1:1-11)

### A. SALUTATION (1:1-2)

**1:1.** The epistle opens, after the manner of ancient letters, with the names of the writer and the persons addressed, followed by a few words of greeting. While adhering to the conventional forms, Paul makes them expressive of Christian ideas. Although he is the sole writer of the letter, he conjoins the name of Timothy with his own. Timothy had assisted him in founding the Philippian church and shared his interest in it. They were now together and had discussed the situation at Philippi, and to this extent they were both responsible for the letter. In most of his epistles Paul takes care to state at the very outset that he is an apostle, duly appointed; but at Philippi his title has never been disputed, and in any case the title does not apply to Timothy. So he describes himself and Timothy simply as **servants of Christ Jesus.** The word he uses (δοῦλοι) means literally "slaves," and implies that Paul and Timothy not only worked in Christ's service but belonged to him, body and soul. This idea of utter devotion to Christ strikes the keynote of the whole epistle.

It is addressed **to all the saints in Christ Jesus who are at Philippi.** They were saints in the sense that as Christians they were set apart from other men and dedicated to the new life, and Paul assures them that he has all of them in his mind. Later on he has to

---

**1:1-2. Salutation.**—The opening of this letter, patterned after the formal letters of that day, illustrates the ultimate contribution of Christianity, which is to Christianize everything it touches; not supplanting the routine proceedings of life, but helping to transform them. The customary form of greeting is here turned into a highly condensed expression of the Christian view of life, which crops out again and again in every incidental topic throughout the letter.

**1. Paul and Timothy.**—In passing, one cannot overlook this thoughtful inclusion of Timothy as coauthor of a letter that was to be read publicly at a church meeting. Since the two men had worked together to found this church, the senior partner did not forget to recognize his assistant in all that he did. In human relations it is always a serious difficulty for an older and abler man to work in harness with a young subordinate and not allow the distinction between superior and inferior to spoil the teamwork. As noted in the Exeg. (see on 1:1), the word "servant" or "slave" means that these men "not only worked in Christ's service but belonged to him, body and soul." That common feeling of belonging to something greater than themselves had within it ample living room for all human distinctions.

The simple principle of two unequal personalities working happily within a higher loyalty that keeps self in second place is basic to all free co-operation. It applies first in the life of a good family, and runs out through all the larger relations of a tolerant society. In this connection Lincoln's famous sentence, as quoted by Lord Charnwood, reveals its Christian rootage: "As I would not be a slave, so I would not be a master. This expresses my idea of democracy. Whatever differs from this, to the extent of the difference is no democracy." [2]

Jesus rebuked the rivalry among his disciples by saying, "You know that those who are supposed to rule over the Gentiles lord it over them" (Mark 10:42). How that illumines the fierce contentions of the modern world! Jesus implied that when men belong to God they feel that they belong to people in need, and the most exalted are those most completely given to fulfill the lives of their fellow men. In ch. 2 Paul runs this principle back to the Creator himself, whose nature is to come down to the lowest level of human need.

The unique truth of the whole O.T. lay in this idea of a sovereign God involved in all the relations of human history. The later psalms made this human interest of God apply not only to the national life, but to individual persons, "O Lord, thou hast searched me, and known me" (Ps. 139:1). "If I make my bed in hell, behold, thou art there" (Ps. 139:8). And Second Isaiah's

[2] *Abraham Lincoln* (New York: Henry Holt & Co., 1917), p. 456.

2 Grace *be* unto you, and peace, from God our Father and *from* the Lord Jesus Christ.

2 Grace to you and peace from God our Father and the Lord Jesus Christ.

---

speak of their divisions, and he wishes to make clear from the start that he favors no one party. But while he writes to all the church, he addresses himself especially to **the bishops and deacons** (ἐπισκόποις καὶ διακόνοις). This is the only place in Paul's writings, apart from the doubtful Pastoral epistles, where these officials are mentioned. But the Greek words mean nothing more than "overseers and assistants," and we must not read into them the more definite significance which they acquired at a later day. Philippi was a Roman colony in which the Jewish term "presbyters" would be unfamiliar; and the church may well have preferred to call its leading men by names which were in general use. Why Paul makes particular reference to these church officers is difficult to say. If he means his letter to serve as a receipt for the money sent to him, he may feel it necessary to address those who took charge of the finances. More probably he wishes to indicate that he is writing more than a mere friendly letter. He has counsels to offer which the church leaders must take note of and carry into practical effect. Thus construed, the reference to them at the outset throws a light on the whole purpose of the epistle.

2. The formal opening is followed by the customary greeting. In Greek and Latin correspondence this was conveyed by a single word, "joy" or "prosperity"; the Eastern peoples preferred, as they still do, the word "peace" (*shālôm*). Paul combines the two forms of salutation, and changes them into a Christian blessing: **Grace to you and peace from God our Father and the Lord Jesus Christ,** i.e., the joy and peace which can come only from above.

---

picture of the suffering servant (Isa. 53) numbered among the transgressors is the last link in the chain that binds the O.T. to the N.T.

2. *The Way.*—Paul's salutation contains a view of life which is the complete antithesis of our modern secularism, so often infecting our Christianity and reducing it to the simple human effort to do good. When modern man is told that the early Christians called their religion "the Way," he is apt to interpret this as a *way to behave.* Salvation by behavior seems to be within his own will power, and is unencumbered by the perplexities of belief in God.

Paul had found through great tribulation of soul that the effort to make oneself righteous was not the end but the beginning of the problem, and he learned also that self-made righteousness ended in self-righteousness which concealed a hidden selfishness that remained unredeemed. Deliverance from self was something that could not be accomplished by the self alone. At that point of despair Paul discovered untapped resources beyond will power, which could make over human nature like a complete surprise.

The Way by which this transformation is accomplished is described in highly condensed form in the opening lines of the letter.

(a) First, there is absolute commitment of one's personality to the greatest Personality ever given to the world. Alfred North Whitehead has well said that growth of personality depends on a continuing "vision of greatness," but Paul went beyond mere admiration of greatness, which is not enough in itself, and committed himself in costly action. With his passionate nature he went all out to make his personality an utterly willing "servant," a veritable "slave" to a greater individual. That is a highly dangerous thing to do except to one Personality, who is a perfect revelation to man of the love of God which can remake our nature into his likeness. To be completely under the power of such love would make any man totally himself, and yet his uniqueness would not be lost (absorbed in divinity), but fulfilled and glorified.

(b) Again, the Way involved relation to a unique community: "All the saints in Christ Jesus." Saints, as is explained in the Exeg., are imperfect people who, like Paul, "set themselves apart," gave themselves up, with all their imperfections, to be refashioned by the power that takes possession of them through Christ.

This familiar and much-studied phrase of Paul's, "in Christ," will come again and again to our attention in this letter, and it should be understood not as some mysterious and mystical absorption into divinity, but as being "in the power" of another. We all know how the spirit of one person can take possession of the very center of another individual's whole being, and transform him without violation of his freedom or uniqueness. Christian personality never exists and grows in complete separation,

3 I thank my God upon every remembrance of you,

3 I thank my God in all my remembrance

---

B. Thanksgiving and Prayer (1:3-11)

**3.** In ancient letters the salutation was followed by one or two pious sentences in which the writer gives thanks to heaven for the health and good fortune of his friend, and prays that they may continue. Paul keeps to the usual form but gives it a higher meaning. He takes this opportunity of telling the Philippians how fervently he prays for them, and how much he rejoices in their kindness to him and their progress in the Christian life. His thanksgiving is offered to **my God,** and this phrase, used almost

---

but always through this community or "body" of imperfect people, who are ready to be forgiven and to forgive. Through all who have offered themselves to be continually remade in unforeseen ways, the Spirit of God extends his operation from Christ into the world, spreading from one individual to another, from one family to another, from one generation to another, from one nation to another, by underground routes that defy all divisions of age or race or class or sect.

(c) And finally, the Way stresses a gift of power over and above whatever men can do for themselves: **Grace to you and peace from God our Father and the Lord Jesus Christ.** Anyone who has felt inside him the power of love from someone who has trusted and suffered for him knows from firsthand evidence that something stronger than his weak will has given him what he could not achieve. Kierkegaard has somewhere said that we are thus redeemed "back through" near friends and loved ones, to Christ whom we can see, to God whom we cannot see.[3] Thus the redemption of man from himself can be achieved only by this givenness, this "grace" from God through Christ and the communion of "saints."

The function of an interpreter today is to lift this way of dealing with sinful nature out of the situations in which Paul used it, and reapply its insights to the human conditions, personal and social, which beset each new generation. For the problems of human nature remain always the same. They are met with on new levels, in more complex situations of modern life, on a wider stage, and in more momentous crises. As the world becomes more closely related in all its parts, the possibilities of good and the possibilities of evil go hand in hand.

The mere mention of the ecclesiastical terms "bishops and deacons" would scarcely warrant a discourse on the nature of the organization of the early church. Lightfoot, in his commentary on Philippians, has an essay of many pages

treating the controversial subject suggested by the word "bishop." Whether or not there can be a true church without a "bishop" in the proper apostolic succession is a question for historical investigation far beyond the bounds of this Expos. Of one thing we can be certain: Paul did not look forward to a church in this world such as we know it, for he expected with his contemporaries that the end of the world was fairly close at hand. What he, like Jesus, was primarily interested in was the saving power which acted in individuals in community to deliver them from self into union with the life of God.

**3-11. Thanksgiving and Prayer.**—In this rather formal paragraph the interpreter of Paul may find many hints revealing the winning power which was the secret of the apostle's ability to get along with people and make lasting friends. In a world where bluster and bluff have become prevailing traits in men's approach to one another, where insincerity and self-seeking are dressed up by a science of public relations, and where managing other people's minds for self-centered purposes has become the technique of clever propaganda on all sides of all questions, it is highly important to notice in some detail the personal craftsmanship in this Pauline masterpiece of human understanding.

In this same paragraph there are also rich nuggets of thought, containing insights of universal application, which can well be lifted out of their context and considered for their wider significance. Again and again, in a passing sentence, Paul throws out a suggestion which is the ripe fruit of his whole Christian experience. The flashes of truth are perhaps the more suggestive just because they are not set forth in any formal pattern of teaching, but are rather tossed off in a crisp phrase, in confidence that his friends will be reminded of much that is left unsaid. First we will consider the paragraph as a whole as a lesson in the way to meet persons.

The most obvious peculiarity of this letter to the Philippians is its extremely personal na-

---

[3] Walter Lowrie, *Kierkegaard* (London: Oxford University Press, 1938), p. 180.

| 4 Always in every prayer of mine for you all making request with joy, | of you, 4 always in every prayer of mine for you all making my prayer with joy, |
|---|---|

unconsciously several times, reflects his mind all through the epistle. In his present loneliness he has been communing much with God, and his sense of dependence on God has been growing ever closer and more personal. He has also been thinking much of old friends, and very specially of his beloved church at Philippi. **In all my remembrance of you** may refer generally to his happy memories of their life together; but in view of I Thess. 1:2, where the same phrase is used in connection with thanksgiving, it probably denotes the mention he makes of them in his prayers.

4-5. Paul tells his readers in emphatic language that he prays for them incessantly, and that he never fails to include all of them. His feeling, as he thus remembers them

---

ture. Paul felt himself the spearhead of a movement that embraced mankind, and yet he knew his universal gospel could spread only through channels where persons met with persons. Such interrelation is a timeless problem, for, as has been well observed, "all life is meeting."

Growth and creation in the human sphere take place in relations where lives enter into each other, interpenetrate, and become members one of another. There is no individual growth, or salvation, for a person is a social being. No one is self-made, because he starts life in a community of at least three, with his life deriving from others, and his children's lives deriving in turn from his. All are forever in a social bundle of unlimited extent, while the creative, saving, and judging action of God takes place through all this interrelatedness. The channels are sometimes observable, sometimes forgotten, always extending into the unseen, where influence comes and goes like a contagion which we cannot perceive. The interpenetration of persons is the chief wonder of the whole creation, more mysterious than cosmic space or the electrons which constitute the bulk of the universe. Evolution, reaching limits in the natural world, expands into infinite possibilities in this area of shared life.

Providence is evidently bent on the extension of relations which are needed both to gain a living and to increase the meaning of life. Even against our plans the world moves toward more intricate alliances. Every invention, every competition of interests, all discoveries, the uneven distribution of resources—all things work together to bring men into a state of unity. Now for the first time in history we have "one world," interdependent in all parts which once were strangers to each other. Tyranny anywhere affects freedom everywhere.

It follows therefore that where men fail to meet, and gulfs of misunderstanding exist, there we find the beginnings of disintegration which proceeds apace in an atmosphere of ignorance,

suspicion, and hate. Should these points of non-meeting be multiplied by thousands and millions, they become the areas of those demonic forces of evil which set men against themselves contrary to their own best intentions. Just for lack of meeting, men deprive themselves of the life that is in store for them, and society thus tends to commit suicide. History seems to indicate that broken-down civilizations were conquered by outside foes only after they had been so inwardly divided that they were already committing suicide.

Paul was profoundly aware that all the incalculable resources, developed and undeveloped, which are stored up in the underground chambers of men's lives can be unlocked only when the key is turned from the inside. Our human problems finally boil down to one: Are we going to have available the worst or the best in man?

Before noticing Paul's technique, a word needs to be said, by way of contrast, about the modern science of manipulating people. One reason why psychology is having such a vogue in the colleges and in business is the yearning for facility in overcoming human balkiness, or sales resistance, or whatever the obstacle may be, in order to induce people to do what another wants. Nothing is more sought after among us than the skill to make another man will our will.

Up to a point such skill is essential for getting things done in a complicated age in which we are all so dependent on each other's services; but we must be on our guard against its grave and deceptive deficiencies. To read or listen to the modern ballyhoo of advertising is to be battered by appeals to the less worthy motives of pride, greed, envy, and the passion to buy happiness. Propaganda has become a science of pushing people's minds around, when they are but slightly aware of what is happening. Ideas are repeated so often and so unctuously that careless folk take them for granted without thought. It is possible that the modern age, by

5 For your fellowship in the gospel from the first day until now;

5 thankful for your partnership in the gos-

---

before God, is one of joy. The sentence is loosely constructed, and it is hard to say whether he states, in the words which follow, the reason for his thanksgiving or his joy. Presumably he speaks of his thanksgiving, since this is the main subject of the passage, but a reference to his joy is also implied. He gives thanks "for all your fellowship with regard to the gospel"; and the thought of it fills him with gladness. The word "fellowship" (κοινωνία) is used in the N.T. in a variety of senses, and we can seldom be quite certain in which of them it should be taken. Literally it means "participation," and it may denote (a) the fellowship of Christians with one another; (b) the communion with Christ or the

---

its machinery of communication, is cultivating a growing multitude who do not want to think or know the truth. In mass control we have developed an art of confusing people by contradictions, so that they hesitate to make difficult decisions and prefer to trust those who make the loudest noise and promise the most lucrative rewards. Half-truths are used to obliterate finer distinctions, until it seems that saints are oppressed by devils.

Worse than lying is the warborn ingenuity of using virtuous appearance to conceal evil ends, playing upon men's most sacred obligation to their loved ones in order to force acquiescence to tyranny, and appealing to the fiercest hates and prejudices to generate action for the public good. No one ever dreamed that even unregenerate human nature could descend in the twentieth century to such abysmal depths of evil in the business of manipulating fellow men. Our modern methods have exalted the strong-willed man who can dominate his fellows and impose his will with ruthless efficiency. Business has come perilously near worshiping the man of power who can threaten and bully all to come to terms with him. Collective action tends to favor the more heartless type of leadership, operating impersonally. Police states justify the pitiless dictator. The initial advantage is with the effective tyrant, but in the long run he has human nature against him, for he leaves untapped the passion of man to be himself, and the invaluable resources of inner willingness which cannot be commanded or bribed. Mutual lust for power, and mutual fear, may hold a hierarchy together for a time, but the best in human response remains out of reach, and selfish rivalries tend in the end to eat each other up.

Paul's approach to people, as exemplified in the verses under consideration, is a far cry from secular manipulation. His was an art of winning men to a cause into which they could not be pushed. In the audience to which the letter was to be read were some true friends, and some who had been true but were now tempted to

"look after their own interests, not those of Jesus Christ" (2:21). That subtle corruption has been the curse of the church in all ages. The apostle had to reprimand the offenders, while at the same time he allowed for the fact that they had once faithfully labored side by side with him as true yokefellows. In other words, this church presented the perennial human mixture of faithfulness and selfishness.

A man who knew that all "fall short of the glory of God," including himself, was prepared to treat people as though all needed forgiveness because all were in the state of becoming; none had attained perfection and none was totally depraved.

Paul instinctively begins by *grateful recognition of the good* the Philippians had done him: **I thank my God in all my remembrance of you** (vs. 3). Imagine these common folk being told that the man who bore the whole burden of the first churches on his heart was grateful every time he remembered them. It is a great thing for any of us to know we have been remembered for some unconscious influence. Such remembrance, instead of ministering to our petty pride, tends rather to awaken a grateful humility, out of which new courage and aspiration arise.

Another principle of Paul's approach was his *readiness to care for people regardless of their deserts*. In this one paragraph (vss. 3-11) he repeats over and over the inclusive word "all." No matter how some had behaved, he took them all under his concern: **Every prayer of mine for you all** (vs. 4); **to feel thus about you all** (vs. 7); **I yearn for you all** (vs. 8). We recognize that there was nothing studied about this emphasis, for it sprang spontaneously from his belief that there was much in himself and in all men that needed to be forgiven. If God takes the just and the unjust under his universal benevolence, and seeks us out while we are yet in our sins, and invades our contrite hearts with his new spirit before we have proved we deserve the gift, then what is man that he should make himself a standard of judgment?

Spirit; (c) the sharing of possessions. In this last sense it is sometimes used specifically for a gift, and some have found an allusion in the present verse to the money which Paul had lately received from Philippi. But however welcome this gift may have been, it would not account for the heartfelt gratitude and joy to which Paul here gives expression. He is thinking rather of all the co-operation in the work of the gospel which the Philippians have shown. They have joined willingly with him and with one another; they have been

---

Paul knew the grace of God through his conversion from being a fanatic who was ever ready to condemn and kill those who differed from his rigid legalism as a Pharisee. That fierceness which so often infects orthodox people and hardens their self-righteousness, so that they judge others with the absoluteness of God, had been almost wholly cleaned out of the apostle's life; though once or twice an "anathema" slips from him, as an echo of the former self that had been tamed. He confessed in another letter that he felt disinclined to judge others finally because he was not even wise enough to judge himself: God was his judge (I Cor. 4:3-4). Such inclusion of oneself with all others under the superior judgment of God was the secret back of the little word "all." We have to make judgments of people in order to live with them, to guard against their weaknesses, and to place them in responsibility; but our judgments are safe only when, over against our discrimination and incriminations, we can see the judgment and mercy of God that includes "all."

A third principle in handling other minds appears in Paul's *positive recognition of worth that is mingled with unworthiness.* In this instance, again, his unspeakable gratitude for having been made an ambassador of the faith after he had been a virulent persecutor made him wary of critical generalizations against those who disappointed his expectations. He himself had been an egregious disappointment to the God whom he was serving with such self-righteous zeal. There were signs of the depravity of pride among the Philippians, but not of total depravity. He never ceased to be thankful for their **partnership in the gospel from the first day until now** (vs. 5). People can take criticism with more or less grace, provided the critic gives full credit to their good points and does not assume his own record to be without its liabilities. Willingness in men is elicited not by condemnation, which may be deserved, but by trust in their worthy qualities, which, in the Christian view, are the fruit of the spirit of God amid the frailties of the flesh.

Praise with discrimination alongside of correction, from one who considers himself also under judgment, is a winning combination. "Brethren, if a man is overtaken in any trespass, you who are spiritual should *restore* him in a spirit of gentleness. Look to yourself, lest you too be tempted" (Gal. 6:1). First, strictness with self, then leniency in appraising others in the interest of restoration. No reprimand without a deserved compliment.

Another characteristic evident in the opening of this letter is Paul's *freedom from any private "ax to grind."* There are occasions when we try to secure the help of other people for our purposes, which is a proper thing provided the purpose is understood and the profit of others is considered in the bargain. This is plain business, a kind of tit-for-tat mutual aid. But influencing another person to correct his ways is quite another matter, for everything depends then on how far the motive is removed from self-interest and the holier-than-thou attitude. The effort to improve others begets resentment because the improver seems to "think himself righteous" and appears to be ready to enforce his pattern of goodness on a different personality, thus failing to reflect the unique character of the working of God's Spirit in each individual. If we waited to be perfect before dealing with transgressors, evil would have a clear field. Somebody has to step in where angels might fear to tread; and even humility is a menace when used as an excuse for inaction.

Paul illustrates the only possible solution. He is enthusiastic about what the grace of God had done with his mistaken ambitions, and he wants others to be **partakers with me of grace** (vs. 7). What a far cry from the attitude of the conventional uplifter! As one needy man to another in the same need, he pleads for the contrition that opens the way again to the divine power which **began a good work** in them (vs. 6) and which, he was sure from his own experience, was always ready to complete what had been begun. He claims the right to make his plea, not on the basis of his own superior worthiness, but because the love that was in Christ had stirred up in his own spirit a yearning for all who were having a battle with themselves. Vss. 9-11 go on to describe the good he hoped might come of his prayers.

These principles of handling people are exemplified in every paragraph, indeed in almost every sentence of this whole letter. Pleading, rebuke, and confidence go hand in hand: "As you have always obeyed . . . in my presence . . . [so now] much more in my absence" (2:12). He wants to be certain that he did not labor in

**6** Being confident of this very thing, that he which hath begun a good work in you will perform *it* until the day of Jesus Christ:

pel from the first day until now. 6 And I am sure that he who began a good work in you will bring it to completion at the

---

in sympathy with Christ himself. It has to be noted that the secondary meanings of "fellowship" are always combined with the idea that Christians share with one another, in virtue of their common faith, their inward fellowship with Christ. The Philippians, Paul says, had given all they had, materially and spiritually, for the gospel. They had proved this noble disposition **from the first day until now.** We know from the book of Acts that Paul had scarcely begun his mission at Philippi when ardent helpers had rallied around him, and this enthusiasm had not been due to a passing impulse. After all these years the Philippians were still the same as they had been at first.

**6.** Paul is confident, therefore, that God **who began** [or "initiated"] **a good work in**

---

vain, and assures his friends that even if he becomes a "sacrificial offering," he will still be "glad and rejoice" (2:17). He sends Timothy to bring news of them, for he is "genuinely anxious for [their] welfare" (2:20), and dispatches Epaphroditus to relieve their anxiety (2:25 ff.). He includes himself in his exhortations: "Let those of us who are mature" (3:15). At the climax of the letter he finally entreats Euodia and Syntyche, the troublemakers, to agree; and bids Clement to "help these women, for they have labored side by side with me in the gospel" (4:3). At the end of ch. 4 he is glad to tell them that he is grateful for their gift, even though he has no need of it—a triumph of tact and affectionate ingenuity.

A profound student of the life of Lincoln has reviewed the private papers of the president, so long unpublished, and demonstrated how these same principles which Paul followed gave Lincoln a "craftsmanship in the art of human relations" that was unique.[4] He attributes this skill to no clever artfulness or utilitarian purpose, but to a deep inner honesty and sincerity of intention. From his contemplative nature there developed a persuasive and kindly manner, informal, full of human and native courtesy, and highly disarming. Again and again he wrote indignant letters and then, realizing how they might hurt another, tore them up. When a general wanted a commission dated to give him precedence over a rival, Lincoln refused but told him that the general's victories in battle would always be remembered whether or not he outranked Grant *on paper.* He always avoided humiliating people, tried to forestall misunderstanding by writing a letter *in time.* He would turn a reprimand of an officer into a friendly interview: "Although what I am now to say to you is to be, in form, a reprimand, it is not intended to add a pang to what you have al-

[4] J. G. Randall, "The Great Dignity of 'the Rail Splitter,'" *New York Times Magazine,* February 8, 1948, p. 7.

ready suffered. . . . You have shown too much of . . . promise as an officer, for your future to be lightly surrendered." [5]

Nothing thus far said about the method of persuasion should obscure the fact that when persuasion fails, there remains the human problem of restraint, regulation, and compulsion. No perfect balance can be kept between the two approaches, and a recovering of balance will be a constant requirement. Christianity offers no support for humility that is not coupled with force of character. Gentleness that lacks firmness becomes sweetness that has no light.

In studying the winning technique of Paul it is well to read, along with Philippians, the more controversial letters where the apostle has a real fight on his hands: Galatians, I and II Corinthians. The combination of sternness and affection, criticism and love, is everywhere in evidence. Paul was able to keep an honest pride in his mission together with real humility because he first gave credit to the grace of God for being the man he was. He knuckled to no one and allowed no questioning of his apostolic authority, saying, "Our boast is this, . . . that we have behaved in the world, . . . not by earthly wisdom but by the grace of God" (II Cor. 1:12).

William Blake speaks of a "cringing" Christ as the common picture which completely misrepresents the real person of the Master. His gentleness and humble patience, which so upset the popular notions of a powerful Messiah, stemmed from a personality of such stubborn force that the combined powers of political and religious authorities beat upon him in vain. He calmly "went his way," and no earthly might was able to prevent the nonviolent movement he started from surviving the fall of the mightiest empire in the ancient world.

**6.** *And I Am Sure That He Who Began a Good Work in You Will Bring It to Completion.*—Good old religious terms like "conver-

[5] *Ibid.,* p. 54.

**you** will perfect it. He employs two words which would convey a special meaning to readers converted from paganism. Those who were admitted to the mysteries had first to be "initiated," i.e., to qualify by preparatory rites; they then passed on to the higher revelation which was supposed to "perfect" them. So God, who has manifestly begun his regenerating work in the Philippian Christians, will advance it stage by stage until **the day of Jesus Christ,** the day when Christ will return. In his earlier epistles (cf., e.g.,

---

sion," "salvation," "justification," and "sanctification," which denoted the mystery of divine assistance, are now almost unintelligible to multitudes both outside the church and inside it. Merely to repeat these phrases, which are themselves a source of doubt for modern man, is to preach the gospel in vain.

The proposition which is set forth in Paul's words here is a universal principle: *man cannot complete his own life.* Over against all secularism, which puts man's salvation in his own hands, there stands the inescapable fact that neither the beginning nor the end of anything is in our hands.

Jesus illustrated this familiar truth in the parable of the rich man who tore down his barns to build bigger ones, and said to his soul, "Soul, thou hast much goods laid up for many years; take thine ease." So the higher voice answered, "Thou fool" (Luke 12:19-20). This is a subtle parable because most people would like to be in such a rich man's shoes. The catch is that human life cannot be completed within natural limits. We would all admit that the strongest factor in our nature is an urge to completeness, and yet we can never complete our own life, try as we will. This paradox is presented in various forms in the Philippian letter.

The bald statement of such a predicament sounds pessimistic and frustrating; and so it is, because it states only half of the truth. Paul added the other half by affirming that *God* would complete what he had begun. In other words, we were never designed to be self-sufficient, for we live, move, and have our being under the all-sufficiency of the Creator who completes what he begins.

The actual picture of man's situation would give the following pattern: (*a*) Before we do anything, we are supplied with "our creation, preservation, and all the blessings of this life." The source of everything we live by is not in our hands. Creation as a going concern preceded us, even if we can offer no more of a definition than an ancient Chinese thinker who asserted that before creation there existed "a presence." There is no escape from this precedence of the Creator over the creature. (*b*) The completion of everything is hidden in the future, and is always in the power of the Creator who alone knows the future and has the last word about the meaning of life. The outcome of the present is always unpredictable, and no event can be wholly understood, because we never see the end of it. (*c*) With the beginnings and endings in the hands of God, we occupy the little area in between. The present is partly ours, along with the powers and resources that have been given us. To use our gifts, answering each moment to the call for our best, and leaving the outcome for God's correction and completion— this is the true formula for human existence. Even when men cannot define God, they can follow this design for living.

The modern mind, which holds belief in human self-sufficiency, may be helped to recognize its dependence by the analogy of the forces of nature, which are not produced by man. Everyone takes for granted, when he plants a seed, that growing power will be supplied; a sailor with a stranded boat waits for the tide to supplement his strength; the scientific machinery of an industrial civilization, so evidently man-made, depends entirely on nature's powers which, like the sun, are bestowed "on the evil and on the good." Because God completes what he begins, man's possibility is always greater than his ability.

The same dependence extends into the world of persons, with its network of relations making one life a part of all other lives in a "field of force" of another kind. An unpredictable factor operates in and through all our relations with each other. Our experience is therefore ambiguous, i.e., we cannot quite tell what it signifies at any moment because something more is done with everything we do. History has turning points which are seen only as we look back to where the unexpected began. In our private lives some minor incident, some incomprehensible misfortune, may bring on consequences which reveal a larger context. Living is like rowing a boat, moving forward while looking backward to gain the perspective of our course. So long as we cannot know the future, we must depend upon a purpose that began before we came and goes on after we are through.

A modern interpreter of our congenital incompleteness should recognize the points at which our generation has drifted farthest away from the biblical position.

Certainly one point is where the ideal of

**7** Even as it is meet for me to think this of you all, because I have you in my heart; inasmuch as both in my bonds, and in the

day of Jesus Christ. **7** It is right for me to feel thus about you all, because I hold you in my heart, for you are all partakers

---

I Thess. 4:15; I Cor. 15:51) Paul had expected to be living himself when that day arrived. He has now given up that hope, but has no doubt that the day is soon coming, and that some of his Philippian converts will witness it, fully prepared by that time to meet the Lord. He is **confident of this very thing** because of their unwavering fidelity.

**7. It is right for me,** he says, **to feel thus about you all, because I hold you in my heart.** He is separated from them and cannot actually see how they are progressing, but all through his trouble he has had the inward sense that they were with him and were supporting him. Many a sufferer has known this companionship of absent friends. They may not be near him in bodily presence, but he is absolutely sure of their mindfulness and

---

"freedom from want" lures us on to the proverbial pot of gold at the end of some political rainbow. There is no way to satisfy our desires completely because they are limitless, and there is no way to eliminate the desires because they are the driving force that gives thrust and vitality to the life of society.

Desires remain limitless because we can never catch up with our imagination. As soon as some desire has achieved its goal, imagination makes the mouth water for more that is out of reach. Our mind begins to minimize objection and create new excuses for having a little more. Pride urges us to "keep up with the Joneses," not because we need a bigger house on a better street, but because we want to outshine somebody, like the poor woman in a tenement who purchased a piano which she could not play, just to have something that her neighbors could not have.

This brings us to another point at which modern people have drifted away from the biblical view of human insufficiency. We take it more or less for granted that we can complete our own goodness. The popular notion of human character suggests that we could be good if we really wanted to be, though strangely enough we seldom want to be all we ought to be. To a certain extent, if it suits our interest, we can make ourselves good; but the temptation is to stop at some respectable level simply because we like ourselves too well at that point. A student once asked, "How can one make himself want to be unselfish?" Intelligence can make unselfishness reasonable, but there is no intelligence that can convert self-will because we were never designed to complete our righteousness by will power alone. This was Paul's great moral discovery, which will come up for further discussion in ch. 3.

Paul's teaching is best understood when we see the consequence of denying it. All sorts of ways have been tried to dodge the issue of man's

moral impotence without God, and they all stem from the optimistic effort to believe in man by himself. If one is going to believe in man, he starts by asserting that man is naturally good, for this is the normal reaction from the teaching that man is naturally bad—which is the popular impression of the religious view. Old theological words are in part responsible for this misunderstanding, since they seem to say that our human nature is utterly "corrupt" and "depraved," and totally incapable of good. Such phrases are taken to mean that we are morally rotten through and through, whereas the biblical teaching is far more searching. Like psychology, it claims that the element of self-love in all our righteousness is what makes it fall short of the glory of God. Overcoming self-love requires more than our will power.

In contrast to this profound insight, all modern attempts to make man naturally good prove to be superficial and deceiving, for after we say that we are by nature good, then some explanation has to be offered for our behaving as badly as we do. These explanations are familiar to all:

(a) "We are naturally good, but we are spoiled by environment or by people with whom we have to live." In the back of our minds we know there is some fallacy here. Imagine a father's reaction if his son should say, "Father, I can't help being what I am after living so long with you." The son might believe that, but not the father. We are, to be sure, conditioned by environment, but not totally conditioned. We are not helpless victims, else we would never rise above environment and try to change it.

(b) "We are naturally good, but we are corrupted by hidden forces in our subconscious." The psychologists try to explain our behavior by analysis of the secrets that lie beneath the conscious level of thought; and such exposure of the obscure causes of human perversions is

defense and confirmation of the gospel, ye all are partakers of my grace.

with me of grace, both in my imprisonment and in the defense and confirmation of the

---

sympathy, and can feel that they are sharing his burden. Thus the Philippians had been loyal to Paul in past days when he was in their company, and he is no less conscious of their affection now, **in my bonds, and in the defense and confirmation of the gospel.**

These are technical terms, the first (δεσμοῖς) denoting that a man is held prisoner; the second (ἀπολογία), that he pleads his innocence before the judges; and the third (βεβαιώσει), that he supports his plea by convincing evidence. So it has been inferred that Paul here reports a series of actual events: after long imprisonment his trial has begun and is in full process; he has made a speech in his defense; he has proved by every means he could use that the charges against him were unfounded; now he is awaiting the verdict, with good assurance that he has made out his case. But his words, when we examine them, cannot bear this construction. He was not to be tried as a Christian missionary, and a

---

invaluable as far as it goes. Bringing to the conscious mind the buried troubles of our life is a priceless help toward a cure, provided we will not turn explanations into excuses, as though behavior were determined for us without any choice on our part. When the father of a little girl tells her to study, she throws the book in his face and says she will not. Is little daughter bad? Not at all. She is just maladjusted; something has been wrong with her parents or with the family life. Everything is to blame except the native cussedness in the child.

(c) Revolutionists believe that "we are naturally good, but we are spoiled by oppression." Free men from tyranny and they will become good. But history teaches that the oppressed, when freed, can become the worst oppressors.

(d) Most of us feel that "we are naturally good, but not yet." We pray that we may be pure, loving, unselfish, but not until we have had our indulgence. Educators have been trusting this "not-yet" explanation, and have tried to persuade us that self-love is cured by education. All too often enlightened selfishness may be a more vicious, deceptive, and dangerous thing than open wickedness.

What Paul discovered was not merely a Christian truth, but the ageless truth about human nature: that it is good only when our natural self is made over into a new nature under the power of God's self-giving love. There is no way adequately to convey this truth in words or doctrines, for it is a living truth, transferred alive from life to life.

**9. And It Is My Prayer That Your Love May Abound . . . with Knowledge and All Discernment.**—In this sentence we have a statement of the kind of truth which Christianity offers for all men to know. It is not scientific knowledge, important as that is. It is not mathematical truth, or abstract truth arrived at by the logical processes of the mind. Paul Tillich describes it

as a "something which is *done*." [6] It is known when it is acted out, and it attracts us when we see it performed by a person, and it is realized inside of us as we do it. It is personal truth transmitted only through living persons. Reason can clarify it, relate it to other truth, and guide its application, but reason cannot make it, for this truth is a life.

Our most familiar illustration of this is friendship. We are little moved by an explanation of friendship, and no scientific analysis can make it effective. Intelligence may prove that it is a reasonable obligation, but such proof does not make us love our friends, and certainly not our enemies. If reason should entice us with advantages to be gained, it begets only a counterfeit friendship that seeks its own ends. No, we are won over by friendliness when we see it enacted as a selfless spirit that seeks us out while we are yet in our selfishness, suffers for our ingratitude, takes upon itself our troubles, and lives for our sakes. What thus approaches us from outside is made our own inside after it has exposed our self-love, to make us hate it and yield ourselves willingly to the living power revealed through those who befriend us.

Our religion identifies this selfless spirit of love with the truth of God which once actualized itself in a historical person who denied all claims of self. The extension of that revelation in a body of people is known to us as the Holy Spirit, actively proceeding from life to life as the one redeeming force in the world. Thus love abounds and spreads a kind of knowledge which is revealed through living.

We shall defer some exposition of this Christian truth to the discussion of 4:1, and draw attention here only to the dependence of such truth upon revelation. For modern man tends to be suspicious of revelation as some magical

[6] *The Shaking of the Foundations* (New York: Charles Scribner's Sons, 1948), p. 116.

8 For God is my record, how greatly I long after you all in the bowels of Jesus Christ.

gospel. 8 For God is my witness, how I yearn for you all with the affection of Christ Jesus.

---

speech "in defense of the gospel" would not serve his purpose. No confirmation he might offer of the truth of his teaching would answer the charge that he had caused a riot at Jerusalem (see Vol. IX, pp. 292-306). Therefore, he must be thinking here, not so much of his approaching trial, as of all the hardships he had been suffering. It was his work for Christ which had brought him to prison; and by all his conduct he was seeking to show what the gospel meant, and how it afforded hope and courage to those who believed in it. Whatever might be the formal indictment, it was the cause of Christ which was really on trial; and Paul was called on to prove in his own person that it was a noble and inspiring cause. In this task the Philippians, by their understanding and sympathy, were helping him. They were his companions in prison, **partakers of my grace.** This final word gives a beautiful turn to the whole passage. Paul would naturally have said "of my affliction," but he refuses to think of his experience in that way. He feels that by allowing him to suffer in defense of the gospel, God has bestowed on him a high privilege in which the Philippians are sharing.

8. He assures them that in thus regarding them as his comrades he makes no pretense. **For God,** who knows the minds of men, **is my witness, how I yearn for you all with the affection of Christ Jesus.** This may mean simply that he has an intense desire to see them again; but in view of the context the thought must be taken more comprehensively. As

---

method of bringing knowledge which we accept without thinking. After generations have been trained in the painful search for truth which science pursues, taking nothing for granted save that which can be proved step by step, it is difficult for man to understand how special knowledge is given to be accepted on faith. Yet there is a widespread hunger for some certainty which transcends our uncertain opinions.

The difficulty has been greatly increased by vague knowledge of historical criticism of the Bible. If revelation has to be interpreted by fallible creatures, if some parts of the Bible are of questionable authority, there seems to be no refuge for the simple credulity which likes to assume that God dictated certain propositions which man must blindly accept.

We can only hint at some points that need clarification for the confused mind of our contemporaries concerning the contribution of revelation.

(a) All "discovery" in any field of knowledge is a revelation of truth that was already prepared by God. The discovery is simply the sudden moment when the God-given truth "comes" to the human mind, after that mind has been properly educated to the point of reception. We describe the impact of truth by saying, "It struck me," "It occurred to me," "It dawned on me." Man has a part to play, without which nothing happens, but the new always "comes" as a surprise, as though we were in

a living universe ever bent on self-disclosure. It is necessary to recover this lost awareness— that all finding of truth is a movement of God, the author of truth, "striking us," "wakening us," "opening our eyes."

(b) Confidence in the power of pure reason by itself to reach the truth we need, has, in the classic religious tradition, been seriously questioned. Rationalists have argued that intelligence has laws of logic as rigid as the laws of nature, and if reason follows its true nature, it can arrive at truth that is absolutely trustworthy. The difference of opinion through the ages has centered around that little word "if." Our reason, like our will, is always connected with self, and it is perverted by self-interest just as frequently as our will is corrupted by it. If that self-interest is ever left behind, as the later discussion will emphasize, it is always "by the grace of God"; for self cannot deliver itself from itself, either by reason or by will, for both are infected with the interest of self.

Thomas Aquinas taught that reason "unaided by revelation" could acquire in certain areas a large amount of real truth. We ourselves have learned that in the realm of science, where personal interest is farther in the background, intellect can operate more accurately. But science does not have anything to do with purposes and goals, and when we turn to the area where human purposes and ambitions are dominant (in private life, economic life, political life), the effect of interest on the action of

9 And this I pray, that your love may abound yet more and more in knowledge and *in* all judgment;

9 And it is my prayer that your love may abound more and more, with knowledge

---

he remembers them in his prayers his heart goes out to them in a great love. He associates them with his devotion to Christ, and feels that his love for them is inspired by Christ, and is the same in quality as Christ's love for his people.

**9.** Paul has dwelt on the sincerity with which he prays for the Philippians, and now he indicates some of the things for which he prays. This section (vss. 9-11) furnishes the clue to the epistle which follows. With all his affection for his readers—and he has sought to convince them that it is deep and genuine—he is not blind to their shortcomings. There are some things of which they stand in need if they are to be worthy of their calling; and he now foreshadows the warnings on which he is presently to enlarge. **And it is my prayer that your love may abound more and more, with knowledge and all discernment**, i.e., that it may not only become ever greater but may be accompanied with more insight and

---

the mind increases without our knowing it. In these important realms more perversion occurs, so that the keenest reason may produce false and biased judgments.

Wherefore, in the practical realm of ordinary living there are three causes for our suspicion of "unaided" reason: (i) most people are too busy or stupid; (ii) mature thinking takes a long time and requires mature minds which are scarce; (iii) and private interest is always twisting reason to its own ends.[7]

(*c*) The same classic tradition that suspected "pure reason," as Karl Marx also did in modern times, has insisted that without the "grace" of God no part of us functions according to our true nature. For our true nature demands that our natural self be caught up and transformed by a new Spirit from God, who comes to us through death to self. Man cannot by his own efforts justify (i.e., make absolutely right) either the action of his will or of his mind. This is basically good psychology, confirmed by everything we have learned about the subconscious influences that affect our behavior. To be on guard against man's subtle ways of deceiving himself by overconfidence is just as important as recognizing the undoubted capacity of his creative intelligence.

(*d*) Biblical revelation has to do with truth that is "done" in life, and centers in a special movement of God toward man in the strand of history described in the Bible. The special light which was there given reached its fullest illumination in one event in a particular god-given person.

Some people feel that they can blunder along toward truth by trying everything; some think that only so much as is scientifically proved can be relied on; some say we can trust

[7] Alan Richardson, *Christian Apologetics* (New York: Harper & Bros., 1947), p. 246.

what works; some through tragedy and crushing of all selfish aims find a way to God. Christianity invites us, whatever way we follow, to take a clue which *God gave* through Christ, so that we can then use reason and experiment to confirm the clue and apply it to all the problems of human nature. The knowledge which comes after our nature has been possessed by the love of God is the knowledge without which no other knowledge can save us.

While all knowledge of truth is from God, only through the clearest revelation in Christ do we see what all knowledge is for in its relation to the final meaning of life. Likewise, the revelation through Christ subjects all our partial attainments to a test which reduces the pride of even the noblest souls, and so begets the ceaseless humility that permits the grace of God to win our more complete submission. Whatever we learn naturally from the constant revelation of all kinds of truth, this revelation in Christ abides to illumine and lend significance to everything we know, while it acts as the everlasting corrective to all premature human pride. It reminds us that "we live, and move, and have our being" in a vast "givenness" that precedes and follows all our knowing, supplying all there is to learn as well as the urge to learn it.

The Gospel of Jesus Christ . . . tells us of a God who not only satisfies our desire for truth but Himself is the source of that desire, who is not only the answer to our questions but the author of them within us, the end of our quest for goodness and also its origin.[8]

**9. And . . . All Discernment.**—The Exeg. explains the varied meanings which have been proposed for this clause. The shades of difference, however, are little more than aspects of

[8] *Ibid.*, p. 249.

10 That ye may approve things that are excellent; that ye may be sincere and without offense till the day of Christ;

11 Being filled with the fruits of righteousness, which are by Jesus Christ, unto the glory and praise of God.

and all discernment, 10 so that you may approve what is excellent, and may be pure and blameless for the day of Christ, 11 filled with the fruits of righteousness which come through Jesus Christ, to the glory and praise of God.

---

understanding. Love, as Paul insists in I Cor. 13, is the spiritual gift which includes all others; and it is at once love to God and love to our fellow men. But he here warns his converts that it must not be indiscriminate. Nothing perhaps is more harmful than the easy good nature which is willing to tolerate everything; and this is often mistaken for the Christian frame of mind. Love must fasten itself on the things which are worth loving, and it cannot do so unless it is wisely directed.

**10.** Paul goes on to define what he means. **That you may approve what is excellent,** literally, "that you may test the things that differ." This may imply what is good in contrast to what is evil, but more probably it means things which are good in the highest degree. The term is sometimes used by Greek philosophical writers to denote essential qualities, as opposed to those which are secondary, and this is most probably the idea in Paul's mind. Christians, with their hearts set on that which is highest, will not be misled by any appearances or side issues, but will always fix, with a sure instinct, on what is absolutely the best. Paul makes this clear when he states the object of his prayer in another form: **that you . . . may be pure and blameless** [literally, "not stumbling"] **for the day of Christ.** Two images are here joined. One is that of a precious material from which all the dross has been strained or burned out. The other is that of a traveler who has met with no blocks or accidents, and arrives in good time at his journey's end. The goal which believers have set before them is the **day of Christ;** and their present life is all a preparation for that hour when Christ will appear and claim his people. They must so live that he will find nothing in them to condemn.

**11.** Not only so, but they must meet him **filled with the fruits of righteousness.** It is not enough to be faultless in a negative way, but a Christian life must result in all kinds of noble activity; it must manifest itself in a rich harvest consisting of righteous deeds. Paul is careful to add, in accordance with the central principle of his gospel, that men cannot grow this fruit through their own effort. It comes **through Jesus Christ,** i.e., through the faith in him which changes us into new men; and the motive out of which it springs is **the glory and praise of God.** Righteousness is not something of one's own which one can boast of, but is the gift of God in Christ.

---

the power to make distinctions, without which life loses its vital sense of proportion.

With the decline of clear faith in God, who transcends all human opinions and judgments, the modern world has in large part become detached from any fixed truth or eternal verities by which to estimate the purely relative outlooks of our human minds. The final word about everything is with the Creator and not with any man, and therefore, unless all our views are held subject to correction from the source of all truth, we have nothing left but conflicting opposites.

What men want women to be, and what women want to be on their own, is decided on the basis of passing fashion, as though God had no higher purpose of his own for the unique personality of each. The decision as to

what fulfills the whole of life, and what does not, is left to shortsighted human opinion. Why one man should be worthy of more trust and respect than another becomes a question decided by power. Right and wrong become partisan cries, with the distinction determined by might. Everything tends to be resolved into a quest for power, which hungers for more power, which as it becomes inordinate corrupts all who share it until "absolute power corrupts absolutely" and leads to mutual destruction.

The love of God in Christ, which Paul prayed might take possession of his friends, may never be practicable where all men are selfish; but the possession of our nature by that nature of God is the absolute fulfillment to which all our relative achievements and comparative estimates must be brought for final judgment.

**12** But I would ye should understand, brethren, that the things *which happened* unto me have fallen out rather unto the furtherance of the gospel;

**12** I want you to know, brethren, that what has happened to me has really served

---

## II. PAUL'S LIFE IN PRISON (1:12-30)

After the preliminary greetings and good wishes, Paul enters on the main business of his letter. He has first to inform the Philippians of his own circumstances and plans. They know that he is in prison awaiting his trial, and will be anxious to learn how he is bearing up under his troubles, and what is likely to be the outcome. Conflicting rumors will have reached them, and they have probably written to him, asking what they should believe; and he now tells them the facts, although he has to confess that he cannot speak of them with any certainty. All he can do is to describe his situation in a general manner, and to tell them something of his state of mind. His vagueness is also due to his desire to say nothing that will unduly alarm his readers. They are terribly concerned about him, and he wishes as much as possible to relieve them; but it is evident that he actually fears the worst. The main reason, however, why he tells so little is plainly that he is not so much interested in his own prospects as in the possible effects of his imprisonment on the Christian cause. He is facing his great ordeal, but on this he touches lightly; he considers only how his mission is being helped or retarded. From a historical point of view this is unfortunate, for a little more detail in this passage would have cleared up many difficulties regarding the life of Paul and the position of early Christianity. It would also have answered some of the questions—e.g., its place and date— now presented by the epistle itself. But we are given to understand something of the great soul of Paul when we find him in this crisis of his life so little concerned about his own troubles. All his anxiety is for his work, and so long as it goes forward he cares nothing for himself.

**12-13.** So he begins at once: **I want you to know, brethren, that what has happened to me has really served to advance the gospel.** It might have been expected that the

---

**12-30.** *Paul's Life in Prison.*—We come in this section to a revealing glimpse of the inner mind of the apostle, who is trying to steady his apprehensive disciples by stating frankly his own feelings about the disasters that have befallen him. Apparently he is a completely defeated man: at the end of a strenuous career, confined to prison, awaiting his probable execution, with only a faint hope of release. What must his followers think about their new faith when their leader has come to a hopeless end, caught in the ruthless power of an all-conquering state? He is facing a terrifying ordeal; but he says little of it in his letter, and refers to it only to reassure the Philippians that the cause is invincible, no matter what happens to a representative of it.

The Letter to the Philippians has in the course of time come to be one of the favorite sections of the whole Bible, and has been cherished as a message of comfort and consolation to people in trouble. It must be remembered, however, that it offers no easy comfort to smooth the roughness of life. This passage is from a man who is not looking for an easier life, but from one who has found what to live for

because he has found what to die for. Many of our modern cults of happy thoughts are using religion to minister to men's selfish aspirations for success, to their desire for escape from hard life, and to their craving for an inner peace of mind that will pull down the blinds on the fierce gloom and woe of masses in a world of universal tragedy. To Paul the chief issue was not how an individual or a nation won happiness and security, but what faith one can live and die for, whichever way the winds of fate should blow. What is there to be certain about amid vast uncertainty? That to Paul was more important than his own fate.

At this point we may see the relation of Paul's approach to that of great psychologists like Freud. Their aim has been to uncover the *unnecessary* sources of interference, buried at subconscious levels, in order that the patient might be more free to meet the real necessities which condition all human existence and which permit of no escape.

**12.** *What Has Happened to Me Has Really Served to Advance the Gospel.*—Paul found some certainty given in Christian faith that became more certain the more it was opposed. He

13 So that my bonds in Christ are manifest in all the palace, and in all other *places;*

to advance the gospel, 13 so that it has become known throughout the whole praetorian guard[c] and to all the rest that my

[c] Greek *in the whole praetorium.*

---

withdrawal of its chief apostle would be a fatal blow to the Christian enterprise; but instead of that it was proving a benefit. The result of it has been **that my bonds in Christ are manifest.** Two ideas seem to be fused here. On the one hand, Paul's captivity has become a matter of public interest. People are all talking about this prisoner, and wondering how his case will go. On the other hand, it is becoming evident that his misfortune has something to do with his religion. He believes in some new divinity called "Christ," and has brought trouble on himself by his devotion to this strange faith. Who was this Christ who inspired his followers with such willingness to suffer? It means

---

felt about it like a scientist who grows more sure that vitamins are vital as he watches any life that tries to live without them.

The craving for certainty was never so strong and so dangerous as it is today. People want something absolute to live by, and are discontent with a mere "perhaps." Yet it is obvious that the human mind cannot attain absolute certainty about the meaning of life, and therefore all man-made philosophies or ideologies are no more than a "perhaps." To stake life on a "perhaps," as though it were finally so, is to court divisiveness, hate, war, and destruction. Christianity, according to Paul, affirms that final certainty cannot be *attained* by man, but *it can be given.*

The church has not always made clear what this certainty is that can be given, or how we can be as sure of it as Paul was. All through history Christians have made exaggerated claims about the kind of knowledge given them infallibly through the Bible. They have overestimated the amount of detailed information supplied us about a picturesque hereafter. Oriental imagery of the Bible, suggesting truth in pictures, has often been taken as literal, scientific description of spiritual truth—which can never be humanly described except in symbols. The assumption that religion has given us a complete explanation of the universe, its origin, purpose, and its end, brought on the unnecessary conflict between science and theology. All the divisions of Christendom have originated in the claim that some human interpretation of the Bible was the actual, dictated word of God. What crimes have been committed in the name of religious certainty!

Paul asserted that Christ revealed a certainty which is learned inside by obedience. In Christ, God came nearest to man in human form, to lift man out of self into the life of God for which he was created. To Paul that was not at the start a doctrine, but an effect experienced inside his life when he went all out in obedience,

regardless of his past sins and mistakes. Christ affected him not as a very good man to imitate, but as an act of God, an act of creation, doing more to him than he could possibly do by trying to imitate an example and follow rules.

Paul's experience was a psychological and religious discovery about a miraculous change in human nature that can be tested anywhere by anybody. Elsewhere in this Expos. this "gospel" of certainty will be enlarged upon again and again, but its bare outline can be set down in five points which Paul is always repeating.

(*a*) He was absolutely sure that all the righteousness which he produced by adding virtue to virtue fell pitifully short of the glory of selfless love that showed itself "in the face of Jesus Christ."

(*b*) He became increasingly certain that he could not attain that glory by will power and by any outward observance of a code. The distance between what he was and what Christ embodied only grew wider with trying.

(*c*) The more effort he made, the more his natural egotism rebelled against yielding to a goodness that would be the death of it, as a man's laziness rebels against getting out of bed on a cold morning and clings to the comfortable warmth.

(*d*) Furthermore, he was sure that the self-giving love he had seen in Christ's first followers, whom he persecuted, had reached out to him. When on the road to Damascus he finally gave up to it in utter willingness ("What wilt thou have me to do?"), the love that was in Christ took charge of his frustrated nature and made it into a new nature, as when a self-centered man becomes a self-giving friend.

(*e*) Finally, he was certain that what had happened inside of him could happen in every human being, and so create a fellowship of kindred spirits, a community of God, where there were no longer any distinctions of race, color, position, or age. In Christ, therefore, **the**

14 And many of the brethren in the Lord, waxing confident by my bonds, are | imprisonment is for Christ; 14 and most of the brethren have been made confident in the Lord because of my imprisonment, and

---

everything to Paul that the name of Christ, known hitherto only to a few, has through him become known to many. He had thought at first that his captivity, withdrawing him from his active work, would retard the Christian mission; but it had helped it forward by awakening this interest in Christ, whose message, when once it was known, would speak for itself.

Paul can say little of the city generally but he can answer for his immediate surroundings. The name of Christ is now familiar "in the whole *praetorium*." This word originally signified the general's tent in the encampment of a legion; then it was applied to the military headquarters in Rome itself and in the provincial capitals; then the local name, as often happens, was transferred to the group of men who were stationed in the place. If the present verse had stopped with the word *praetorium*, the reference might have been to the barracks, or the military district; or to the **palace**, as in the KJV, for the civil ruler was also commander of the forces. But Paul adds the words **and to all the rest**, indicating that in the previous clause also he had thought of a body of men—the so-called **praetorian guard**. The soldiers assigned to watch him would be always changing, and one man would talk about him to his comrades, so that Paul can say quite truly that the whole guard was now aware of why he was a prisoner—and not only the guard but **all the rest**. This last phrase must refer to all who in any way were connected with the military establishment, civilians as well as soldiers. To all of them Paul had become an object of interest, and he could be sure that through them some knowledge of him and his gospel would be diffused.

**14.** He goes on to speak of another result of his imprisonment. There was a Christian church in the city, and through his presence most of its members had been stirred into

---

kingdom of God and the expected age of the Messiah had come.

Further discussion of this conflict of man with himself will follow in the Expos., of ch. 3, but at this point special emphasis needs to be laid on the unique kind of certainty which is *given* and not *gained*. Our age has tried to supplant this inner spiritual certainty by reason, with the result that multitudes of our youth have found that reason kills the spirit by its analysis. Reasoning is not living, and it cannot make anyone love, even though it may prove that love is reasonable. The argument of a finite mind can never give us final truth about the infinite. It may make God plausible, but it cannot bring us to God, just as it may make immortality reasonable without bringing the experience of the eternal within us.

Christian certainty can be seen in living form even in a child, for there come moments in childhood when behavior suddenly becomes free, requiring no restraints and no orders. An inner willingness has done away with rules and directions, so that obedience is the fruit of a new inclination and goes beyond anything that could be commanded. Self-love has given way to love that is joyful and free. Perhaps these moments are rare; but when they come, their transforming quality is the most certain thing in the world.

Paul testified that such certainty was made stronger in him by opposition. When he landed at Philippi a possessed girl was healed, and Paul was put in jail for interfering with her exploiters' business, which had been profitable. That imprisonment gave him his chance to make a friend of his jailer by saving his life, and the incident served to advance the gospel. At the end of his career he was again in prison in Rome, and he wrote to his friends that it gave him opportunity to make friends with the soldiers in Caesar's household, and that his very suffering had become a challenge to all disciples to speak more boldly. Even unfortunate Christian factions, which he deplored, were calling attention to Christ. No wonder that nothing could stop this man who was so sure that Christ could be honored in his body, whether by his life or by his death (vs. 20). It was this assurance which gave the drive and invincibility to the apostle's mission, and furnished power to endure all suffering.

Without understanding this kind of certainty that is given us, our modern world is groping in increasing confusion. We never have had so much knowledge in our possession, and never

| much more bold to speak the word without fear. | are much more bold to speak the word of God without fear. |
| 15 Some indeed preach Christ even of envy and strife; and some also of good will: | 15 Some indeed preach Christ from envy and rivalry, but others from good will. |

fresh activity. He is careful to say only "the greater number" (most), for there were some who thought little about him one way or another. The words in the Lord cannot be taken with brethren, as in the KJV; for when he speaks of "brethren" Paul always means Christians, and no addition is necessary. This phrase must be taken with confident, as in the RSV. Thus Paul says, in effect, that he has not only brought the knowledge of Christ to many pagans but that most of the Christians also, "made confident in the Lord by my bonds, dare more fearlessly than ever to speak the message of God." His captivity has roused them to new zeal for their religion. They had already spoken out for it courageously but were now even bolder in their confession. The meaning seems to be that while hitherto they had confined themselves to the more earnest heathen who were well disposed to them, they now spoke openly to everybody. Paul's imprisonment had given them the opportunity to proclaim what they believed.

**15.** He makes a distinction, however, among the brethren who had been thus emboldened by his coming. Some of them were unfriendly. While acknowledging that he was a Christian like themselves, they held that he did not teach the genuine message. They used him as an object lesson for denouncing the type of Christianity for which he stood,

have we been so uncertain as to what it all means. All sorts of philosophies are bidding for attention, and people feel like students in a professor's philosophy class who, as they hear a dozen theories explained, believe each one in turn, only to be surprised by another. Which one should they believe?

Some try to avoid the issue by assuming the typical business cockiness that thinks it has the sure answer to everything. Some are intrigued by the so-called "dialectical" theory, which presumes to move toward certainty by a sort of mental walking process, throwing the weight on one idea until the emphasis is over-balanced and so making a shift of weight on some opposite idea. This theory is of course true to a degree, but it overlooks the fact that we do not have to step ahead to regain balance—we may step sideways or even backward. The mere business of keeping balance does not guarantee progress. Communists have trusted the dialectical opposition of classes to move society toward the millennium, but they have forgotten that the elimination of the exploiting class does not stop the conflict of opposites. No final certainty lies at the end of that road—in a supposedly classless society.

Others have given in to a despairing acceptance of the anguish of uncertainty, and this resigned acceptance brings a certain peace which men in all ages have toyed with. Everyone has shared the anguish of living out his brief span in the indifference of infinite time and infinite space, with no knowledge of how or why he happens to be here. All we seem to have is our freedom to make our way about in fear and trembling, deriving a subjective impression of innumerable pieces of life. No spinning of theories or systems can bring these endless pieces into unity. Such a view of our existence is not just a modern fad; it is the recurring bewilderment of man in all ages when he tries to depend on the certainty acquired by the finite mind. Paul had plenty to say about the ultimate futility of the "wisdom of this world" when it is separated from the certainty which is given through Christ, and known inside by obedience.

In this connection certain familiar phrases of the apostle take on living significance. "When I came to you, brethren, . . . I decided to know nothing among you except Jesus Christ and him crucified. . . . And my speech and my message were not in plausible words of wisdom, but in demonstration of the Spirit and power" (I Cor. 2:1-2, 4). "Where is the wise man? . . . Where is the debater of this age? . . . We preach Christ crucified, . . . Christ the power of God and the wisdom of God" (I Cor. 1:20, 23-24). And in another letter there is a fine description of a Christian as a living epistle: "You yourselves are our letter of recommendation. . . . You are a letter from Christ delivered by us, written not with ink but with the Spirit of the living God, not on tablets of stone but on tablets of human hearts" (II Cor. 3:2-3).

**15-18. Some Indeed Preach Christ from Envy and Rivalry.**—In these words Paul raises searching questions which have always perplexed mankind: How can the perfect be expressed through the imperfect; how can the unconditional use

16 The one preach Christ of contention, not sincerely, supposing to add affliction to my bonds:

17 But the other of love, knowing that I am set for the defense of the gospel.

16 The latter do it out of love, knowing that I am put here for the defense of the gospel; 17 the former proclaim Christ out of partisanship, not sincerely but thinking to

---

and for showing, perhaps, that it was bound to lead to misfortune. It is sometimes assumed that these enemies of Paul were Jewish Christians, and that once again he was meeting the opposition which had nearly wrecked his work at an earlier time. Of this there is no evidence. From all that Paul says they appear to have been members of the local church who were there before he arrived, not enemies from abroad who had followed him. These **preach Christ from envy and rivalry.** They were Christians, but denied the name to all who were outside of their own circle. They turned the gospel into a battleground of rival doctrines. By **others from good will** Paul does not mean friendliness to himself, though no doubt he implies it. The good will of these **others** consisted in love for the Christian message, apart from any theories which might be held about it. They were able to see that however it was interpreted, it was God's word to men. Paul says that both these classes of believers had been more active since his coming, although from different motives.

**16-17.** Those of the one party were standing up for their religion **out of love** [i.e., out of sympathy with the purpose of Christ], **knowing that I am set for the defense of the gospel.** They might not agree at every point with Paul, but they were able to see in him a true apostle, in whose person Christianity itself was being tried. Instead of criticizing, they did all they could to strengthen his hands, seeing that the cause for which he suffered was that of all who called themselves Christians. The others—to translate literally— "proclaim Christ in a partisan spirit, not purely." While they preached the Christian message, they made it secondary. Their real interest was in their own peculiar views, which were at variance with those of Paul. They cared little for what might happen to him so long as they made out that he was wrong and they were right. The apostle hints,

---

the conditional as its agent; how can the eternal be involved in the temporal? These questions bring us to the very heart of the gospel of Christ, which is the final answer to the inescapable imperfection or sinfulness of the natural man.

The subject is particularly pertinent to preaching, but it has a far wider reference to all areas of life. Emphasis will be laid all through this Expos. on the fact that the human can never be equal to the divine; yet the divine, as we know it in Christ, can be manifested only in the personalities of fallible persons like ourselves. The secular struggle for a material living cannot be other than secular, and yet it must be the field where creative power can work in the making of personality. Perfect love cannot be a practical method in a world dominated by the forces of self-interest, and yet the leavening force of love can change the way the secular works. In other words, everything in this world has to be thought and achieved by people who are conditioned by their culture, limited by heredity and temperament, secretly biased by their interests, equipped with only partial knowledge, and so constrained by self that they use reason to escape doing what they

know they ought to do. This is the everlasting predicament of man, known as his "sinful state," quite apart from any sinful deed. "All . . . fall short" (Rom. 3:23), says Paul, not only because we cannot know it all, but because we fail to live up to what we do know.

**What then?** says the apostle. He was spreading a new truth with all the sincerity and selfless energy of a devoted life, and his converts had already begun to mix their devotion with motives of **envy and rivalry.** While some were working with **good will . . . out of love,** others were proclaiming Christ out of partisanship and insincerity. And Paul's answer was to let the gospel be proclaimed **whether in pretense or in truth.** That is a dangerous doctrine, subject to perilous perversions.

Some will infer from it that the **ministries** and sacraments of the church can be carried on regardless of the character of those who are responsible. Some will interpret the gospel according to a rigid fundamentalism, and others according to a liberalism which has very loose foundations. Some will make the gospel a purely individual matter, and some will generalize on the social gospel.

People in the churches will like to identify

18 What then? notwithstanding, every way, whether in pretense, or in truth, Christ is preached; and I therein do rejoice, yea, and will rejoice.

19 For I know that this shall turn to my salvation through your prayer, and the supply of the Spirit of Jesus Christ,

afflict me in my imprisonment. 18 What then? Only that in every way, whether in pretense or in truth, Christ is proclaimed; and in that I rejoice.

19 Yes, and I shall rejoice. For I know that through your prayers and the help of the Spirit of Jesus Christ this will turn out

---

indeed, that they were glad to see him in trouble. They sneer at him and condemn him, thinking **to add affliction to** [his] **bonds.** The word he uses means literally "friction," and a vivid image is implied. His fetters were hard to bear but these people would have them gall and chafe him. It seems almost incredible that there were Christians who took advantage of Paul's helplessness to vex him still further, but the same thing has often happened. Nothing is more stupid and cruel than the partisan spirit.

**18-19.** Paul has described the attitude of others, for and against him, and now in a very noble passage he speaks of his own reaction to them. **What then? Only that in every way, whether in pretense or in truth, Christ is proclaimed.** He does not accuse his opponents of only pretending to be Christians. He recognizes that in their own way they believe the gospel, but the gospel is not their first consideration. They use it only as a means for bringing forward their own theories. They criticize Paul's statement of the message, and are far more interested in their criticisms than in the message itself. The others declare the gospel "in truth," with the sincere desire that men should understand and accept it. They perceive that this is Paul's motive also, and therefore support him, even when they differ from him on this point or that. Both parties, however, are at one in this, that they speak about Christ, and so make him known to those who have never heard of him. **In that,** says Paul, **I rejoice. Yes, and I shall rejoice.** By the repetition he makes it clear that he is not merely uttering a magnanimous sentiment, but has fixed on the line of conduct which he will follow. So long as he remains in prison he will allow friends and enemies to say what they will about him without offering any protest. The discussion of his case, whether in his favor or against him, will at least spread the knowledge of Christ his Master, and this is all he cares for.

Vs. 19 contains a quotation from Job 13:16 (LXX). How does Paul apply the O.T. words to his own case? **For I know that . . . this will turn out for my deliverance** (literally, "salvation"). Does he use the word "salvation" in its religious sense, or is he thinking only of **deliverance** from his present troubles? Since he is quoting from an ancient book,

---

the gospel with what they think it is, and will desire to hear only what they like to hear. Church officials will love to hold power, and to keep the institutions in line with their prejudices; parishioners will bring pressure, financial and otherwise, to have things their way; Catholics will continue to think Protestants are not closely connected with God and his saving power, and Protestants will continue to protest against a hierarchy, self-appointed, which claims to speak with the voice of God in a church whose history has been involved in politics in every country where it has gone.

The important thing is to accept the fact that human nature, whether it is inside the church or out of it, will be affected by **envy, rivalry, and partisanship** to the end of time on earth. We are all born self-centered in every generation, and we like ourselves too well until the

day of our death. There is no use expecting perfection, and no use sitting scornfully in glass houses and throwing stones. There is also no point in letting evil alone because no one is good enough to correct everybody else, just as there is no reason to abandon the struggle for peace when, after a war, the victors are not good enough to tell the rest of the world how it should behave.

Paul had the only way out: Keep right on making the gospel known, and rejoice that it is held by every means before men's minds. Even when the church exploits the state or the state exploits the church, the gospel will forever breed the men who revolt against its perversion. For behind it is the living God, with all the power of creation bringing on the inevitable consequences of man's presumption, and standing ever ready with tireless mercy to do a new

20 According to my earnest expectation and *my* hope, that in nothing I shall be ashamed, but *that* with all boldness, as al-

for my deliverance, 20 as it is my eager expectation and hope that I shall not be at

---

no very definite significance can be forced into the statement. He says, in effect: "I believe, as Job did, that the end of my present affliction will be some great good. I am in prison and exposed to enmity and misunderstanding, but God always protects those who put their trust in him." He is confident that all will be well **through your prayers and the help** [literally, "a rich provision"] **of the Spirit of Jesus Christ.** The suggestion is that God will answer their prayer by supplying him in still fuller measure with the Spirit, enabling him to bear up through all troubles. The Spirit in Paul's thought proceeds from God, but is given in answer to faith in Christ, and may thus be regarded as his Spirit. Paul relies on this divine help but does not forget that he must do his own part.

20. The Spirit will work in accordance with **my eager expectation and hope.** Paul uses a word which means literally "stretching out the head" in order to descry an object in the distance. He lives with his eyes fixed constantly on the day when Christ will appear; and in this hope he sees beyond the afflictions which are only for a moment. He can feel

---

thing whenever his judgments have brought sinful men to their senses.

So long as the world can be made aware of this double truth that the "wages of sin" will be some kind of death, and that new life from God constantly waits on human repentance, there is hope of renewal through tragedy and loss. The power of the Spirit can always make a new beginning out of every ending—even after death. **And in that I rejoice,** concludes Paul.

20. *As It Is My Eager Expectation and Hope.* —Everybody likes to be hopeful, and we have all sorts of dodges and tricks for keeping optimism alive; but it seems that there are times when it is unwise to be too hopeful, lest we be disillusioned and overcome by the craftiness of men. There are also times or situations so despairing that hope seems like whistling in the dark. Prudent men advise us to be optimistic with moderation, so that we may not be swept away by enthusiasm. Worldly wisdom is very cautious about being too hopeful, lest an unwise expectancy prove itself to be based on a false premise; and yet the worldly wise have encouraged many unfounded hopes:

(*a*) The nineteenth-century optimism which trusted in automatic progress was a case of unwise hopefulness, which was no more than wishful thinking with no foundation in reality.

(*b*) There has been a false hope at the heart of the protracted struggle between individualism and collectivism, free initiative and socialistic control. It has been assumed that freedom of the individual is a privilege granted by a materialistic society, and that such liberty given to self-centered persons or groups would issue in social harmony. Freedom essentially belongs to the spirit of man, and can be only a precarious and limited affair on the material level.

(*c*) Long and sad experience has shown a secularized world again that there is a false hope in the doctrine that "economic man" needs no purpose beyond making a living. In pursuing more and more costly happiness on the material level we have landed in the unhappiness of world chaos. In place of a continual disclosure of the deeper meaning of life as an inward and spiritual affair, we have been enticed by futile worldly utopias which promise a heaven on earth. It was a vain supposition that increasing control over nature would solve the problem of human nature.

Yet the Western world spread these philosophies as though they were the hope of the world. Totalitarianism was fashioned out of this same delusive optimism which has no need of God. It claims that the only sovereignty over man is man himself, that the individual is less important and valuable than some general good of the group, and that moral considerations must give way to expedient methods of controlling society by terror and force. For many generations we will be fighting the results of the deceitful and antihuman hope that we have bequeathed to mankind. It will not be a struggle of saints against sinners, but it will be basically a struggle for all of us to recover the whole truth about the spiritual nature of man, against which we have all sinned.

Now, in what sense can we have a hope that is always hoping? Instead of anticipating moderate results that prudence might reasonably calculate as possible, Paul had some kind of unlimited optimism which stayed alive even when everything appeared hopeless. **I shall not be at all ashamed.**

At least we can distinguish this attitude from certain kinds of hope that are quite legitimate

ways, *so* now also Christ shall be magnified in my body, whether *it be* by life, or by death.

all ashamed, but that with full courage now as always Christ will be honored in my body, whether by life or by death.

---

confident **that in nothing I shall be ashamed,** i.e., he cannot possibly fail; in spite of all hindrances he will come out triumphantly and will complete the task he has undertaken. **But that with all boldness**—the word means literally "freedom of speech," although in Paul's day it was applied generally to the attitude of a freeman. It may here retain something of its original meaning. Paul thinks of himself as speaking for Christ, not only in words, but in all his actions and through his brave endurance of all misfortune. **As always, so now also Christ shall be magnified in my body** [i.e., "in my person"] **whether it be by life, or by death.** Paul has spoken previously of his indifference to what men say about him, either in praise or blame, and now he gives a grander sweep to this idea. He has ceased to regard himself as anything but an instrument of Christ. His one ambition is that he may serve as the means whereby Christ may be glorified. To this end he dedicates both soul and body; he can therefore be certain that he will never fail in his purpose, for whatever disaster may befall him personally, the cause of Christ will go forward, and he exists only for that.

---

and useful as far as they go. The hopefulness of some people is in part a by-product of a healthy extrovert temperament. Much of Robert Browning's rugged optimism came from this source. A study of some of his poems, such as "Rabbi Ben Ezra" and "Saul," would yield instances of this most enviable buoyancy which goes along with the "wild joy of living."

The hopefulness of youth is proverbial, and without its continual challenge of the conventional the life of the world would die of dullness imposed by those who are distrustful of change. But we are not always youthful, and youth itself may not have the wisdom to make its confidence worthy of trust.

The restlessness of the masses, who are *in* society but not *of* it (Arnold Toynbee's definition of the proletariat), is a source of disturbance where the contented classes of society would stall further creation. This mass discontent can be trusted to disturb society where it has tucked itself in, but the wisdom of the masses cannot always be trusted as the way of redemption.

There is also some limited hope which comes from a calculation of prevailing conditions. Cleverness, being "wise as serpents," holds a far more reliable promise than sheer idealism that is blind to practical realities. A businessman once said that he would rather hire a man who was clever, though crooked, than a man who was good but dumb. Some of us would feel that this was a choice between bad apples, but the world has suffered as much from respectable dumbness as from clever crookedness. In fact, the latter has flourished because of the futility of the former. In the long run we cannot depend on clever manipulation of conditions to

keep us constantly hoping. Kierkegaard was right when he said, "For practical purposes it is at the hopeless moment that we require the hopeful man. . . . Exactly where hope ceases to be reasonable, it begins to be useful." [9]

Certainly it was at the most desperate point of Christ's career, the Cross, that an eternal trust in the invincibility of the spirit was given a new start in the world.

Paul's power of hoping through all apparent hopelessness derived from his own inward experience of a new life suddenly coming into being within him after the death of his old life of self-regulation. Here we are back to the constant theme song which runs through all that he wrote. There is always a possibility that this new life of the spirit may revive in any man, no matter how desperate his past, and regardless of the state of the world. It appeared in Paul just when he despaired of making himself good by obeying rules, and at a time when a mighty civilization at the zenith of its power was about to collapse into disintegration. The movement which was transmitted through Paul to the Western world survived the death of Roman civilization and all crises of the social order ever since. Paul spoke from an experience of hopeful change that can occur in man always to the end of time, a universal and timeless fact. It is a new beginning that is always possible when the forgiving love of God is so transmitted that it comes to life in our human flesh. Whenever self is put to shame, and constrained and conquered by that life of the living God which "came down" to our human level in Christ,

[9] *Works of Love* (tr. David F. and Lillian Marvin Swenson; Princeton: Princeton University Press, 1946), pp. 199-213.

21 For to me to live *is* Christil, and to die *is* gain. | 21 For to me to live is Christ, and to die is

**21-22.** He is thus led to speak of his approaching trial. He considers it not improbable that he will be acquitted, but warns the Philippians that he may be taken from them. If so, they are not to be distressed on his behalf, for it will be well with him whatever happens. **For to me to live is Christ, and to die is gain.** He means that his life, even while he possesses it, is not his own but is wholly devoted to the service of Christ, and death therefore will only bring his life to fulfillment. The words are not to be read as if he

anyone may become free from the world. The boldness of Paul's hope came from his assurance that **Christ will be honored in my body, whether by life or by death.**

This new life which Paul found inside himself extended his hope to all men in line with Jesus' admonition to love others as ourselves.

Every man loves himself; every man has hope for himself. . . . We, therefore, do not cease to love ourselves when we fail of a certain degree of self-development; and hence love for ourselves is *always* hopeful: it always lays hold expectantly on *another* possibility for good. Christianity desires simply to reverse all this and requires us to love our neighbor as unswervingly as we love ourselves. . . . We will not cease to love them on account of any kind of setback in their improvement. And hence love for neighbor is *always* hopeful; it always lays hold expectantly on *another* possibility for good.[10]

The life of Jesus, as Paul would say, can be unexpectedly manifest in any man's "mortal flesh."

**21. *For to Me to Live Is Christ.*—**It may not be easy for the secular mind of modern man to understand the mysticism of Paul expressed in these familiar verses. His absolute devotion to a supreme personality (cf. on vs. 1) gave him his reason for living; and vestiges of such an experience are known to all Christians, whatever terminology is used. Through the personality of Christ there still can be conveyed to us a reason for living that alone can fulfill our life, because it gives us something to live for of which we need never be ashamed as we honor it in our body, "whether by life or by death."

Different approaches may be made to this question of what we are to live for. If Paul's mystical description sounds strange to some ears, other words must be found to show modern man the relation between religious belief and the reason for living.

A counselor of souls, distressed by the tensions and strains of modern life, tells his patients to remember the steadiness of an old clock, doing its duty one moment at a time, as a symbol of

[10] Paul Ramsey, "A Theory of Virtue According to the Principles of the Reformation," *Journal of Religion*, XXVII (1947), 196.

a well-ordered life. It is a good symbol. A grandfather clock, two hundred years old, has a reason for existence that is still good after all that has happened in a changing world. With its wheels and weights and pendulum it is a human instrument that uses the eternal force of gravity to prove God's time to man. With no hurry or worry it has met the unknown future by doing each second of each day just what its reason for living required. Nobody has had to write books on worry and peace of mind for such a clock. Amid family anxieties and festive seasons, through sun and storm, in war and peace, it has pursued the reason for its existence—ticktock. Of course a clock has a rather dull life, but all men need some reason for existence that "makes them tick."

Once a student said: "The trouble with me is that I have no reason for living. Many seem to do well without one, earning money to have a good time, but a man needs a reason, and I haven't one." Sooner or later, events drive everyone back into a corner, and demand if he has a reason for living.

**For to me to live is . . .** —what? That is the question which is as searching as Hamlet's "To be or not to be?" We are living in a time when secular success has outrun our quest for a meaning; and although we have never before known or possessed so much, we also have never been more confused about making sense out of life.

Paul had a religion that "made life into sense" under all conditions—even where it might seem senseless. Modern man may be led back to this experience by way of an important distinction: through our senses we gain everything we need for living—except the *reason;* through religion we get the reason we need to make it worth while to live—no matter what happens. And what we make out of our existence depends finally on that reason.

What reason can religion give us? Obviously it cannot give us the total purpose for the whole creation, simply because our minds are too small. Edison once said that we do not know a millionth part of anything, and yet we are not dismayed. Man is finite and must live a

22 But if I live in the flesh, this *is* the fruit of my labor: yet what I shall choose I wot not.

gain. 22 If it is to be life in the flesh, that means fruitful labor for me. Yet which I

---

were contrasting life and death. They are both the same, except that death will bring him in larger measure all that he has been seeking throughout his life. His whole aim while he lives is to yield himself to Christ, and in death he will complete this surrender. Of this he is so certain that now, when the event may turn either way, he is in a difficulty. Ought he not to desire an end to this present life which excludes him from the full attainment toward which he has been striving? His language at this point is broken and obscure, reflecting the perturbation of his mind as he turns from one alternative to another and cannot arrive at a decision. Literally rendered, it reads, "But if life in the flesh—this is fruit of work to me, and what I shall choose I do not know." The fragmentary verse has no doubt to be filled out in this manner: "But if continued life in the flesh is to be my portion, this will mean more fruit of my work, and between that and a longer life I cannot choose."

---

finite existence, always subject to correction and open to more light.

Obviously also, a childish religion cannot give a grown-up reason. A small child of three was teasing her mother all afternoon for grapes. At bedtime she watched her small cousin saying her prayers, and asked for an explanation of these unfamiliar proceedings. The mother said that the cousin was talking to God, asking him to bless her family and make her a good girl. Immediately the child went into her own room and shut the door, to say *her* prayers. Upon emerging she said to her mother, "I talked to God and he said I was a very good girl—and I could have a grape." The whole history of primitive, immature religion is condensed in that incident where a child's reason for living was herself, while she used God to make her happy. Plenty of grown-up people try to live with a child's religion, and come to disillusionment. A popular writer on religion has suggested the dilemma which confronts such persons: God is good and wants to make his children happy. God is all-powerful to do what he wants to do, but not everybody is happy. Therefore God is either not good or he is not all-powerful—or there is no God.

Our senses and our capacities were given us to obtain what we need from all that has been supplied on earth, and we must not expect God to take the place of anything we can do. In Russia superstitious and childish religion was accused of being an opiate, just because it substituted God for all that man was supposed to learn through his senses by scientific methods. It has proved easy all over the world to accept what science and the senses can bring us as a substitute for religion.

A grown-up religion, though it cannot give the total meaning for everything, yet can give

us as much reason as we need for our human life. If it is difficult to grasp Paul's affirmation **For to me to live is Christ,** we might get his intention from other words of his in two sentences brought together from different letters: "Eye hath not seen, nor ear heard, neither have entered into the heart of man, the things which God hath prepared for them that love him" (I Cor. 2:9). "Therefore, brethren, by the mercies of God, . . . present your bodies a living sacrifice . . . that ye may prove what is that good, and acceptable, and perfect will of God" (Rom. 12:1-2). We were born to *prove* something, not merely to get what we want.

Unlike the clock, proving the time, we were created to prove that more which is true and good can become real for all of us. We are born self-centered creatures with a capacity to be transformed into creators who can prove in new situations what is the inexhaustible will of the Creator—a will that is partly known in what has happened, and mostly concealed by the unknown future.

**For to me to live is . . .** —what? There is no escape from that question. It is not only inescapable, but it calls for a reason that is inexhaustible and never finished. In 3:12-15 we shall see how Paul felt that one always falls short of the perfect will of God revealed in Christ for our redemption. A good sermon could be preached on the way people try to *stop living* to get comfort and peace and content by attaining some neat finish. It is very easy to will not to live, resting with what is good enough, with what "gets by," with the conventional that is expected and approved. Life is limitless because the will of God is never finished, always leaving more to be proved.

**22. Yet Which I Shall Choose I Cannot Tell.** —The sentences immediately following state a

23 For I am in a strait betwixt two, having a desire to depart, and to be with Christ; which is far better:

24 Nevertheless to abide in the flesh *is* more needful for you.

25 And having this confidence, I know that I shall abide and continue with you all for your furtherance and joy of faith;

shall choose I cannot tell. 23 I am hard pressed between the two. My desire is to depart and be with Christ, for that is far better. 24 But to remain in the flesh is more necessary on your account. 25 Convinced of this, I know that I shall remain and continue with you all, for your progress and

---

**23-24.** For many years he had been carrying out his great missionary enterprise, which was just beginning to show results. Like a good husbandman he wants to see the trees he has tended bearing fruit, and is loath to go while as yet there is so little to show for all his labor. So he can only say, **I am hard pressed between the two,** i.e., "I am shut in on two sides"; he is at a fork in the road and cannot tell which way to take. **My desire is to depart,** literally, "to break up my tent." Life is transitory at the best; and he feels that here he has stayed long enough and should now be moving on **to be with Christ; which is far better**—so much better that he strains the grammar and says "more better by far." If nothing were in question but his own wishes, he would not hesitate for a moment to break away from this troubled, imperfect life. **But to remain in** [or "to stand fast by"] **the flesh is more necessary on your account.** The idea is that of a soldier holding a position which he must not quit. Paul has been appointed to a work which requires his continuance on earth, and he must choose to stay rather than depart. This is necessary for the good of others, but he thinks in the first instance of his own duty. The soldier does not ask why he has been assigned his station, though he knows that it is for the general good; the necessity laid on him is that of obeying orders.

**25.** Paul, we cannot doubt, is here stating what he really felt. He was tired of life and longed to get away, and if he wished to remain, it was only from a sense of duty—duty to those he worked for and above all to Christ, who had placed him at the post he held. **Convinced of this I know that I shall remain** [in this life] **and continue with you all,** i.e., he will not only survive the present danger but will pay another visit to Philippi. He seems just here quite certain of his acquittal, and reasons have been sought for his false assurance; but the only ground for it, as he has just said, was his inward feeling that his life was necessary. Apart from this he never hints at any human probability that he will be set free. His immediate plan, if he won his liberty, was to return for a time to Philippi, **for your progress and joy in the faith.** There might seem here to be two ideas—**your progress** and also **your joy**—but these two are evidently meant to go together. The measure of progress in Christianity is the ever deeper joy one finds in it. Paul may appear to use the word "faith" ($\pi\iota\sigma\tau\iota\varsigma$) in the general sense of "religion," which it was to bear afterwards. More probably he thinks of faith in the manner he always does, i.e., as the

---

problem which was peculiarly Paul's own. He was divided in his mind as to what was the best use of his life, at the very consummation of his career. He was quite willing to go to his death for his faith, knowing, as he had said (vss. 12-14), that whatever happened to him would "serve to advance the gospel." If by his imprisonment the brethren had "been made confident in the Lord," and were "much more bold to speak the word of God without fear," surely his martyrdom would stir even greater devotion. And death would be a welcome release from his prison, for he was old and had suffered long, and was ready to go.

**24-30.** *But to Remain in the Flesh Is More*

*Necessary on Your Account.*—Here is no morbid longing after death such as has so often found voice in our hymns, and in the ultrasaintliness of the "religious." So long as there was any uncertainty as to what to choose, the only safe rule for Paul was to hold himself at God's disposal for the needs of people—no matter how welcome another outlet might be. Like his Master, he faced every choice with the reservation, "Nevertheless, not my will, but thine, be done."

This question of the use of one's life, short of the decision between life and death which does not always confront us, is often a very perplexing problem, especially in youth. We do

26 That your rejoicing may be more abundant in Jesus Christ for me by my coming to you again.

27 Only let your conversation be as it becometh the gospel of Christ: that whether I come and see you, or else be absent, I may hear of your affairs, that ye stand fast in one spirit, with one mind striving together for the faith of the gospel;

joy in the faith, 26 so that in me you may have ample cause to glory in Christ Jesus, because of my coming to you again.

27 Only let your manner of life be worthy of the gospel of Christ, so that whether I come and see you or am absent, I may hear of you that you stand firm in one spirit, with one mind striving side by

---

trust in Christ and his redeeming work. This faith is capable of advancement inasmuch as it can always grow stronger and more sure.

**26.** The meaning here is: "In order that your pride in me may abound in Christ Jesus." The Philippians made no secret of their pride in Paul, whom they regarded as in a special sense their own apostle; and they had doubtless said something to this effect in the messages they had sent him. He touches on this half playfully, at the same time reminding them that his Master and not himself must be the subject of their boasting. He tells them that any pride they have in him will be enhanced **because of my coming to you again.** When he is actually present with them he will be able to help them in their spiritual life as he cannot do at a distance.

**27. Only** [whether I come or not] **let your manner of life be worthy of the gospel of Christ.** The verb means literally "behave as citizens" (πολιτεύεσθε). It had come to be applied to all moral conduct, though always with the idea of fitting one's action into social requirements. In the ancient world a man's duty was hardly conceivable apart from the tribe or city to which he belonged. This was especially so in a place like Philippi, where the civic consciousness was highly developed. Paul may be thinking of the city when he uses the word here. The Philippians are to do their part as citizens in such a manner as to do honor to the gospel, showing everyone that it makes men just, and kind, and ardent in all good causes. This social effect of the new religion was one of the chief causes of its progress in early days. At the same time Paul thinks not so much of the earthly city as of a higher community of which all Christians have become members. Later on in the epistle (3:20) he employs the noun to which this verb corresponds: "Our citizenship is in heaven." So he impresses on his readers here that they are members of the heavenly community, and must so order their lives.

**That whether I come and see you:** This clause has no sequel in the Greek. Paul says nothing of how he will feel when he sees them, and speaks only of what he hopes to hear. This may be due only to the loose construction which is natural in a letter, probably dictated, but it may well be that Paul here betrays his real conviction. To comfort his readers he has spoken cheerfully of a visit which he is planning to make, but he doubts in his heart whether it will ever take place. Most likely he will never see his friends again; and all he can expect is that while **absent, I may hear of you that you stand firm in one spirit, with one mind** [literally, "soul"] **striving side by side.**

We know from Paul's teaching elsewhere that he thought of man's nature as compounded of three elements: the body, the soul which animates it, and the mind or "inner man," which is peculiar to man as a rational creature (see Vol. IX, pp. 369-71). Sometimes, as here, he conceives of the soul and the mind as together constituting the higher nature of man. He believes, however, that a new element enters into the Christian man.

---

not know what God has prepared for us to prove; yet we are here to fit ourselves to prove something worth while with the one life given us to live.

In making this important choice the first step is to make an estimate of oneself. One way for

a modern man to do this is to make a list of all that he likes most to do. To see the longings, interests, leanings, and capacities all set down in black and white is a revealing experience. The list may be reduced to a few outlets which would give satisfying expression for one's

28 And in nothing terrified by your adversaries: which is to them an evident token of perdition, but to you of salvation, and that of God.

29 For unto you it is given in the behalf of Christ, not only to believe on him, but also to suffer for his sake;

side for the faith of the gospel, 28 and not frightened in anything by your opponents. This is a clear omen to them of their destruction, but of your salvation, and that from God. 29 For it has been granted to you that for the sake of Christ you should not only believe in him but also suffer for

---

The Spirit takes possession of him, and is henceforth part of his own being, so that even on earth he becomes a child of God. Thus when Paul speaks of the Spirit, it is often difficult to make out whether he refers to the divine Spirit or to man's own transformed nature. In the present verse both meanings seem to be implied. Renewed by the Spirit of God, the Philippians are to work harmoniously together, since they are all controlled by the one power from above. Although they are separate persons, they can feel that in their inner nature they are one. The same idea is present in the benediction with which the epistle closes.

They are to work also "with one soul," i.e., with a common ardor, so that the life-giving energy in each one of them may be gathered into a single force, directed to one end. As a result they will be **striving side by side** [literally, "joining in wrestling"] **for the faith of the gospel.** Here again "faith" is almost equivalent to "religion"; not in the later sense (as, e.g., in the Pastoral epistles), but as defining the peculiar character of the Christian religion, which teaches that faith is the essential thing in man's relation to God. To assert this great principle the believers must put forth their utmost strength. Paul writes for people in a Greek city, and in this passage, as in others that follow, he employs the language of the athletic games, which counted for so much in the life of the Greeks.

28. He uses the same athletic imagery in the next words, "at no point swerving." The word applies properly to a startled horse—the RSV renders it **not frightened**—and some have inferred that Paul has a chariot race in his mind; but in view of his previous language ("take a firm stand," "unite in striving") it seems more natural to suppose that he is thinking of a band of combatants, swordsmen or pugilists, engaged in conflict. The Philippians are never to turn aside, even for a moment, from this engagement. Their antagonists will try to distract them by force or trickery; but they must fix their eyes on the one object. This will be an **omen to them** [their enemies] **of their destruction, but of your salvation.** For Christians these words had a religious significance; but they could also apply to defeat and victory in a contest, and Paul avails himself of the double meaning. By their firmness and self-possession his friends at Philippi would show to everyone that theirs was the winning side, and in proportion to their confidence their enemies would be discouraged. And success in the earthly conflict would foreshadow the salvation on which they would finally enter. They will conquer and their enemies will fail, **and that from God**—i.e., this will be proof that God himself is with his people, and will save them in the future as he is doing now.

29-30. **For it has been granted to you that for the sake of Christ:** The verb (ἐχαρίσθη) is one which denotes a high privilege; and Paul goes on to show that it is the double one—

---

cherished capacities, so that the whole self could be poured out and be fulfilled.

The second step, which Paul felt so deeply when he was wondering whether to live or die, is to make an estimate of needs to be met. This can be done by making another list of those things which one feels are *most* needed in the world around him, and then eliminating those for which he is least fitted, until he can recognize a connection between what he wants to do

and what is waiting to be done. Advice can then be sought and experiments made. Particular capacities tied to a great need make for the richest expression of a man's whole being.

A third step, implied in Paul's statement about his choice, is a complete readiness to have life "worked through" without too much interference by one's own preferences. This final step is a hard order, but to a degree everyone has experienced this joyful abandonment of self

**30** Having the same conflict which ye saw in me, and now hear *to be* in me.

**2** If *there be* therefore any consolation in Christ, if any comfort of love, if any fellowship of the Spirit, if any bowels and mercies,

his sake, **30** engaged in the same conflict which you saw and now hear to be mine.

**2** So if there is any encouragement in Christ, any incentive of love, any participation in the Spirit, any affection and

---

**you should not only believe in him but also suffer for his sake.** The Philippians have attained to the knowledge of Christ and are thus far stronger than those to whom Christ means nothing; but besides that, they have been called on to suffer for him. God has so favored them that they are placed in circumstances which enable them to test their faith and learn more of its meaning. Paul had found in his own experience that faith becomes more real through suffering; even as he writes, this truth is being driven home to him. And the Philippians are now granted an experience similar to his own, **engaged in the same conflict which you saw and now hear to be mine.** They had witnessed his trials while he was with them, and they know by report what he is suffering now. They are engaged in a like contest. Again the word is taken over from the athletic games, carrying out the imagery of the verses before.

The comparison of the Philippians to him has sometimes been pressed too literally. It has been inferred that they were enduring a persecution like his own, and the whole epistle has been explained as a message of comfort from one martyr to others who were facing the same perils. But there is no evidence that the Philippian Christians were being actively persecuted. They had to struggle for their faith against powerful opposition, as all Christians had to do at that time. Perhaps the pressure on them was more severe than elsewhere, since Philippi was a Roman colony, and it was known that their apostle was under grave suspicion at Rome. But all that Paul says of their hardships might apply to Christians generally at that time and in many times since.

### III. The Christian Life (2:1-18)

Paul has spoken of his imprisonment as it affected the Christian mission. He has told the Philippians that it has a special significance for them, since by their love and sympathy they are partakers in his suffering. As his comrades they can share in the faith that sustains him, and make it a power in their lives. He now enlarges on this idea, with particular reference to conditions in the Philippian church. Of its kindness and loyalty he cannot say enough, but it is threatened by dangers which have made him anxious. He deals with them very gently, but his chief motive in the epistle is to warn his converts against errors, apparently trivial, which might have the gravest consequences unless they are corrected.

---

in the nearest duty, leaving the outcome and the next opportunity to God. Somehow, the man who is faithful in the little things that lie next to him can demonstrate a thoroughness and a faithfulness that make him wanted without pushing himself. The need seeks him out and draws him on from one opening to another, until his life may not seem to be his own. However, this leading may not bring a man to prosperity; it may mean a risk of life through suffering, regardless of any practical calculation.

In the early stages of a man's career he seems to be passing simply from one task to another. Then he begins to feel the relation of his effort to the effort of others. His best stimulates the best in others who can do more than he can, so

that he starts more life going than he can live himself. His faithfulness and sacrifice appear to be part of all the devotion which God has used to keep all goodness fighting and triumphing over evil. As older lives drop out and newer ones come along to take vacant places, the sense deepens that each life is a charge given by God to be used to prove more and more of the Creator's will.

It is a pitiful thing to go through the motions of life and prove nothing. The chief end of man is to give his will to the will of his Creator and enjoy him forever.

**2:1-30. If There Is Any Incentive in Love.—** In the previous chapter, at the end, Paul used his experience of imprisonment as a testimony

## A. The Need for Self-Effacement (2:1-4)

**2:1.** He begins with a solemn adjuration, four times repeated. **So** [i.e., in view of my desire that you should stand fast and work harmoniously in the cause of the gospel] **if there is any encouragement** [literally, "support"] **in Christ,** i.e., if you can count on his power assisting your own, as of course you can. The word translated "support" (παρά-κλησις) is that which appears in the name "Paraclete," applied in the Fourth Gospel to the Spirit and in I John 2:1 to Christ himself. This name means literally "one whom you call to your side," and was translated into Latin as *advocatus,* a counsel for the defense. In some modern English versions of the N.T. it is therefore rendered "Advocate"; but the Spirit, as described in John's Gospel, instead of merely pleading for the believer, actively helps him. So the best translation of the name is the familiar one "the Comforter"; only this word must be understood in its original sense of "helper" or "strengthener" (it is

to the faith that sustained him. He knew that he represented a cause of which he would never be ashamed, and since his disciples shared his interest and his sufferings, they could be supported by an unconquerable assurance in all troubles which might befall them. Now, in the present chapter, with the utmost skill and sensitivity, Paul turns the argument on his friends, and seeks to enlist their loyalty and faithfulness against the divisions that had arisen within the Philippian church.

The transition from praise to rebuke is a delicate problem of human relations wherever it occurs, in a family, in a business, or in a political situation. The Philippians had stood up well against outside opposition, but now some rather trivial rivalries had arisen within their church, with such consequences that Paul feared for the future of this first missionary enterprise on the European continent. From that day to this, in the work of the church and in every kind of human organization, this age-old danger of personal rivalries has had to be faced. It can corrupt secretly the very religion which is supposed to be the greatest bulwark against it; and it has been the bane of the Christian church from the time when Jesus' disciples questioned who would be first in the kingdom of God, down to the church squabbles, small and great, which curse us still.

Unfortunately the victims of this ancient disease seldom know they have it, for their attention is mainly directed to signs of the disease which they see in their opponents. We all can see the sins of others more clearly than we can see our own. Ch. 2 of this letter to the Philippians, therefore, which we might think to have been concerned with faraway issues which have little interest for us, actually has a vital bearing on all that we are doing today.

**1-11. The Need for Self-Effacement.**—The everlasting trouble we have in trying to get along with people roots back in one continuous cause. It is the perversity of man that he allows self to get in his own way, and that in trying to

save self he constantly defeats himself. This is the paradox of all human existence, and on a world-wide scale it has reached its most tragic denouement when our boasted civilization, with all its education and scientific resources, brings us to an impasse where we might well say that humanity is now arrayed against itself.

It should be instructive to see how Paul approaches the issue of self-effacement from a religious angle, which seldom enters into the calculations of contemporary man.

To well-grounded Christians this famous passage conveys one of the profoundest insights of our faith. It has been one of the controversial portions of scripture, and it stands as a bulwark against all oversimplified and superficial interpretations of Christ's revelation. Such passages in the Bible maintain the reality of an ultimate mystery at the root of all that is finest in human personality, against all modern attempts to reduce the life of the spirit to easy explanations of enlightened and calculating self-interest.

Anyone who deals with the secularized minds of this age must remember that a great gulf separates them from the style of thought which Paul here employs. For them, Paul is guilty of introducing the complex discussion of theology into the simplicity of Christian living. Whether the Messiah pre-existed with God before his appearance on earth seems an irrelevant question, forever beyond the compass of the human mind. The modern man, trained in a world of physical and social science, hardly knows what a messiah is—some product of religious superstition, perhaps—and he is completely unaware that in Paul's day the notion of a suprahuman person coming down from God's home in heaven to this world of evil was as current in people's thought as scientific views are common property with us. So quite naturally Paul could talk to his contemporaries about the eternal fact that the divine has a way of coming down and penetrating the human with redeeming and transforming power.

In the Exeg. it has already been shown that

2 Fulfil ye my joy, that ye be like-minded, having the same love, *being* of one accord, of one mind.

sympathy, 2 complete my joy by being of the same mind, having the same love, be-

---

derived from the Latin *confortare,* "to give fortitude"). Paul thus means here "You must not say that the effort required is beyond you, for you have the strength of Christ to fall back upon." He emphasizes and defines this idea in the words which follow. **If there is . . . any incentive of love,** i.e., any sense of Christ's love to you, reviving you when you grow weary. If there is **any participation in the Spirit,** i.e., the power bestowed by Christ on those who put their trust in him. If there are **any affection and sympathy:** Paul meant evidently to express himself in a different way, for his "any" here is singular in number and both "affection" and "sympathy" are plural in form (KJV: **bowels and mercies**). Apparently he was at a loss for a word, for the idea he sought to convey was altogether new. He believed that Christ, although of the same nature as God, has a human heart and can sympathize with human weaknesses. Men can rely on him because he understands their difficulties and will give them just the help they need.

**2.** Thus Paul reminds the Philippians of all the grounds they have for confidence, and so appeals to them: **Complete my joy.** While he is proud of them and rejoices in all the progress they have made, there is something more they can do to complete his joy. It consists in this, **being of the same mind,** i.e., working together harmoniously because in all of them there is the same disposition. Paul is presently to tell how Christ himself is the grand example of this disposition of mind, but he shows first how it will manifest itself in the life of the church. They will all be in harmony, **having the same love, being**

---

this section of the letter is not as casual as the rest of the writing, but is more like a carefully wrought bit of poetry. As a matter of fact, the only way to talk about "the spiritual life" is in poetical and picturesque language. Artistic living pictures and poetic images talk to us by suggestion, rather than by definition and explanation. The best things of life that lie "too deep for words" cannot be put in physical, accurate terms. In recent years even scientists have come to realize that they themselves are using symbolic language to talk about the mysterious energies of the physical world; and it is therefore not unscientific for religious people to use picturesque figures to suggest what lies ever beyond the reach of precise description.

Orientals who wrote the Bible were always thinking in pictures. All ages understand pictures, which suggest more than can be said. The one thing to do with them is to *let them talk* to the mind, without trying to reduce them to some logical analysis or philosophical abstraction, or even to a theological formula to be presented to men's minds as though it were a literal chip off the block of absolute truth. In religion we are not trying to escape mystery, but to maintain it and to enter, like little children, into its unfathomable suggestiveness. It is always the part of life that is "past understanding" that we care most about.

*1-5. Have This Mind . . . , Which You Have in Christ.*—Whoever divided this letter of Paul's into chapters must have noticed that the writer

waxed fervent and emphatic in four places as the intensity of his feeling grew upon him. In ch. 1 he gives a very personal expression of the confident, consuming faith that dominated his life, so that he could only say, "For to me to live is Christ." In ch. 2, in a supreme bit of poetic expression, he brings the deepest implications of this faith to bear upon the petty quarrels of the church at Philippi. In ch. 3 he contrasts his old life of legalism with his new life in Christ; and in ch. 4 he gives us an unconscious testimony to his prayer habits which he found necessary to sustain a Christian's commitment.

Since the Exeg. has treated these eight verses in full detail, suggesting the controversies that have raged over them and the scholarly difficulties which they have created, it is better here to treat the passage as a whole; for, as has already been said, it is a dramatic picture, full of Oriental imagination, having direct reference to the practical problem of keeping people working together where personal rivalries disrupted relations.

It is unfair to Paul to turn this poetic passage into a theological answer to speculative questions with regard to the relations of divine and human nature.

To stand outside Paul's experience of conversion from law to spirit, and use his words as literal and rational explanations of the mystery of the Incarnation, is to ignore his own motive in using this picture. He was intent on dealing

43

**in full accord and of one mind.** There will be a common love, a common ardor, a common purpose. This perfect unity will come about only when all the different people who make up the society have in them the same disposition.

We have here one of the first efforts to define the essential mark of all who call themselves Christians. Our religion exists in so many different forms that often it seems impossible to say what it is essentially. Some would hold that it is a matter of belief; unless you assent to a particular creed you cannot be a Christian. According to others it is a matter of worship, and they would rule out all who will not take part in certain acts and ceremonies. By others the emphasis is laid on moral behavior; the law of Christ requires that we should perform a number of duties, and by our practical obedience, not by our beliefs and piety, we prove ourselves to be his disciples. Paul offers a test which is not so definite as any of these but is far more searching. Christianity, he says, is a condition of mind. However far those who profess it may differ from each other, they must have the same attitude to life, the same desire to know God and serve him. Thus, amidst all their differences they can understand one another and feel that they are united. So in this passage, where he pleads for harmony in the church, he dwells on the "mind,"

---

with the partisan jealousies and private ambitions which are the perennial foes to every effort of men to work together. The Philippian church, the pioneer of the Christian movement in our Western world, threatened to break up because of some party split precipitated by two jealous women, Euodia and Syntyche. Doubtless some election to office was coming up.

In passing, let it be noted that the perpetuation of harmful divisions in the church, local, denominational, and interdenominational, is due mostly to persons in places of some power who do not want to yield to rivals. To be sure, some divisions in the church are essential when they spring from healthy and robust difference over issues that are crucial; for in all great matters the truth is best disclosed, not by authoritative declarations of a superior group alone, but by the free and bold difference of strong opinions. But how often some people with influence based on wealth and position hold a church in a strangling grip; how many mergers of struggling institutions are blocked by officials who like to keep their offices; how many reforms are nipped in the bud by those whose interest is vested in the *status quo;* how much is left undone in relating our middle-class churches to the world of labor by supporters who want sermons without disturbing implications and only those policies pursued which they approve and to which they have been long accustomed. These are delicate personal matters, but they are exactly the same as those which Paul criticized in one of the most gracious Christian letters that was ever written.

Nothing is intended here to belittle the kind of theological speculation which has always been a requirement of the human mind. Religions have degenerated either into form or emotion when divorced from those severe intellectual disciplines which to the common man often

seem so far removed from the realities of life. It is very easy for unthinking people to reduce the Incarnation to an example set by a very, very good man, which is only half of the truth, and which fails to deal with the mysterious fact that the life "in Christ" is not attainable by man but has the quality of a divine gift received through renunciation of self.

However, when we grant the need for intellectual formulations, which add the "metaphysical" to the "physical" aspects of life, it is still true that Paul's famous picture of Christ "emptying himself" in order to come to earth can hardly satisfy our minds as an explanation of the relation of Christ to God. It is a question whether it was ever so used until modern minds seized upon it as a possible way of expressing two sides of an inexpressible mystery. If Christ, the Second Person of the Trinity, set aside his divine attributes of omnipotence and omniscience, that seemed to make it possible for him to be a true human being, subject to the slings and arrows of our outrageous human lot, with all its limitations. Such a theory fell in with our modern emphasis on the historical Jesus; but as an account of what happened in the Incarnation, it simply deepens the mystery. It oversimplifies the matter by using a purely temporal figure of speech to define what Paul expressed in a picture of an eternal event. To say that Christ was once God and that he left behind him in some remote place both the divine wisdom which holds within it the total possibilities of our life and the superhuman power on which everything depends for existence, and that after his career on earth he left his humanity behind and became equal to God again, creates more difficulties for the mind than it tries to explain.

On the one hand, it practically leaves the universe unsustained for the period of Christ's

**3** *Let* nothing *be done* through strife or vainglory; but in lowliness of mind let each esteem other better than themselves.

ing in full accord and of one mind. **3** Do nothing from selfishness or conceit, but in humility count others better than your-

---

the inward disposition which should be in all Christians, and is the one essential mark of their religion.

**3. Do nothing from selfishness or conceit,** i.e., try to rid yourselves of all selfish motives—zeal for your party or your own advancement. These two things usually mean much the same; you join a party because it represents your interests and will bring you some personal advantage. As a Christian you must look to the larger good, leaving yourself entirely out of account. The right attitude, therefore, is one of **humility** (literally, "lowly-mindedness"). Paul had here to coin a word, for the idea he wished to express was one which had hitherto found no place in Greek thought or language. It had been taken for granted that everyone ought to *assert* himself, and that no one but a fool or a coward would yield of his own accord to any rival. Paul tells the Philippians that as Christians they must have a humble disposition: **count others better than yourselves.** He can hardly mean that Christians should be always depreciating their own merits and abilities, for this kind of humbleness is never sincere, and, as a rule, is nothing but a cover for vanity. He is thinking rather of claims to outward distinction. When honors are in question, you are not to push yourself forward; each man must be willing to give way to his neighbor, as worthier than himself.

---

life; and on the other hand, the everlasting humanness of God is confined to that brief period now twenty centuries distant from us. Such a statement does not do full justice to the profound thinking behind this attempt to combine the eternal and the temporal, but it may serve to relieve this passage of Paul's from bearing too great a theological burden, and set it free for the practical purpose for which it was originally written.

The premise to all that follows in this chapter begins with an "if": **If there is . . . any participation in the Spirit** (vs. 1). To be "in Christ" (i.e., in the power of Christ as though possessed by his life), to have the spirit of Christ or the "mind" of Christ, to have the spirit of God—all are one and the same thing to Paul, and these terms stand in complete contrast to *our* spirit. Yet our spirit can participate in the reality called the Spirit of God, which is given to us and not made by us.

So foreign to our modern thought is this talk about the Spirit of God and the spirit of man that we must come back to it again and again. The contrast is drawn out fully in the letter to the Galatians. "The *works* of the flesh are plain." Then follows a list of what our natural self can produce under its own steam (Gal. 5:19-23). It can drive us in the pursuit of inordinate desire—"immorality, impurity, licentiousness." It can erect some limited thing into an absolute, make a human idol that is worshiped as though it were God—"idolatry, sorcery." It can, by absolutizing its own limited view, create all the dissensions that pull men

apart and destroy unity—"enmity, strife, . . . party spirit, envy," etc. In other words, "our spirit" can push to the limit both our endless desires and our lust for power, and work for these ends under the guise of respectability. Paul would no doubt admit with the Greeks that since we are God's offspring, "our spirit," our creative intelligence, and all our natural powers, can be a creative force. The whole scientific movement in our day bears testimony to what "the works" of the human spirit can be. They are so overwhelming that they have blinded us to what our spirit cannot of itself perform.

The "fruit of the Spirit is love, joy, peace, patience, kindness, goodness, faithfulness, gentleness, self-control" (Gal. 5:22-23). Everyone knows that such things cannot be forced by will or created by reason. Argument and calculation never furnish the power which makes this life of the spirit possible. Will power can make a show, put on an appearance, but that is all.

In the passage under consideration in this Philippian letter Paul emphasizes these same fruits that come from **participation in the Spirit: Encouragement** in the sense of the power to endure, **incentive of love, . . . affection and sympathy.** Our natural mind, our impulses, emotions, and will cannot create any of these things because our spirit is a servant of self.

Strangely enough we find, as Paul did, that there is an actual strife going on between our spirit and this Spirit from God. Paul speaks of an enmity here, a "warring against," as though it split our nature into factions (Rom. 7:21 ff.).

4 Look not every man on his own things, | selves. 4 Let each of you look not only to
but every man also on the things of others. | his own interests, but also to the interests of
5 Let this mind be in you, which was | others. 5 Have this mind among yourselves,
also in Christ Jesus:

---

**4.** From this point of view we have to understand the words which follow: **look not every man on his own things, but every man also on the things of others.** This might mean "considering the interests of others as well as your own" (so apparently the RSV), but Paul is speaking not of justice or fair-mindedness, but of humility. He admits that one may have a good claim to precedence, but one is not to insist on it. Other people also have their fine qualities, and one must not grudge them the honors which go to them. The whole passage has to be explained in the light of what was happening at Philippi. Paul has learned to his deep sorrow that the church he loved so much, and which had earned such a lofty place, was in danger of going to pieces, all through petty jealousies over honors and rewards. He seeks to impress on his readers that they must have more of that new disposition which is the essential characteristic of the Christian. One of the marks of it is the readiness to efface oneself.

### B. The Humility of Christ (2:5-11)

It is in this connection that Paul introduces the great passage which is the chief glory of the Epistle to the Philippians. Nowhere in his writings does he rise to a loftier height of eloquence, or afford us a deeper insight into his Christian beliefs. At the same time the passage is involved in peculiar difficulties, and needs to be considered as a whole before it is examined in detail.

The first problem is that of its literary character, in which it is quite different from the rest of the epistle. Philippians is a personal letter, and is written freely and spontaneously. Paul sets down his thoughts as they come to him, with little regard to fine language or logical sequence. Many of the sentences are hardly grammatical. The one aim of the writer is to get close to his readers and talk to them informally, as he might do in private conversation. This passage, however, is constructed with the utmost care. Each clause is balanced against another, and this principle can be traced even in the choice of each particular word. In form, as in substance, the passage has all the characteristics of a hymn or poem, and must have been composed deliberately with this end in view. It has been argued, therefore, that Paul has here inserted a Christian song with which his readers would be familiar, and which expressed his own ideas more forcefully

---

Our love of self is so strong that it actually resents this contrast with another spirit which contradicts our infinite desires and the urge for power.

From the most ancient times God's will has appeared as a law that man knows he ought to obey, while he also knows that he cannot perfectly fulfill the requirements. Hence the obstinate resistance to what is required. A child rebels the moment his will is crossed by a parental requirement, even when it is imposed for his own good. So long as the goodness of God appears not as a Spirit seeking to possess our life, but as a duty imposed contrary to our natural disposition, we either revolt or find some self-deceiving way around it. Just because we are no worse or better than millions of others, we do not notice the betrayal of the best. In fact, it has been well said that the wickedness

which has overwhelmed the world in the twentieth century was possible because so many people are no better or worse than each one of us.

The drive of Paul's amazing career came from the certainty, within his own life, that our spirit may be united with the Spirit that was in Christ, to be changed (sublimated) into a new reality altogether, with the enduring power of love, and the humility that is at the opposite extreme from **selfishness or conceit.**

This redeeming mystery of the Spirit Paul brings to bear upon the troubles that had arisen at Philippi. "If" all this is so about the Spirit, then **Do nothing from . . . conceit, but in humility count others better than yourselves. Let each of you look not only to his own interests, but also to the interests of others.** Here we have that strange mixture of human effort and

and beautifully than he could do himself. Against this view, however, we cannot but observe the absolute fitness of the passage to its context. It has not been dragged in but rises naturally out of what has been said before, and prepares the way for all that follows. The main thought, moreover, is one which Paul expresses elsewhere in different words, e.g., in II Cor. 8:9, "Ye know the grace of our Lord Jesus Christ, that, though he was rich, yet for your sakes he became poor." It may be doubted whether any other teacher had yet arrived at this conception of the work of Christ, and a passage which expresses so grandly the conviction of Paul may safely be ascribed to Paul himself. Among his other gifts he had that of a poet, as we know from a number of splendid outbursts in his epistles.

Again, it has been objected that the passage is out of all proportion to the subject with which Paul is dealing. He is anxious about the personal quarrels which have disturbed the harmony of the Philippian church. Some admonition was no doubt necessary, but the occasion hardly justified the tremendous comparison between Christ's divesting himself of deity and the ambition of little cliques at Philippi. A few gentle words of reproof, it is held, would have been enough. This, however, is to miss Paul's whole intention. He wishes to make clear that in Christianity the disposition is everything, and it is the same in quality however great or small the issue may be. The Christian temper must always be that of Christ, and we must ever keep before us how he himself acted when he made his great decision.

Once more, it has often appeared strange that in this crucial instance of an appeal to the example of Christ, Paul leaves the earthly history out of account, and falls back on something which he thinks of as happening in a heavenly pre-existence. In the recorded life, he might have found many illustrations of how Jesus had denied himself and had chosen the lowly road when a more splendid one seemed open to him. The most powerful motive in the Christian life has always been the example of Christ, as set before us in a manner there can be no mistaking by the actual story of the Gospels. Why does Paul make nothing of the opportunity which lay so obviously at his hand? His reason may have been partly theological. He had determined, as he himself tells us, not to know Christ after the flesh, and to think only of the Lord risen and exalted; but this statement in II Cor. 5:16 must not be taken literally. He never forgets how Jesus had lived and suffered. In the passage before us the whole emphasis is laid on that obedience to the death of the Cross by which Christ had won for himself his sovereign place. So when the apostle looks back on what Christ had been in eternity, he does not ignore the earthly history but seeks only to explain it. Why was it that in all his action Christ had been so entirely free from personal ambition? His life must be viewed against the background of what he had always been.

---

divine participation which is discussed below (vs. 13), and which is never oversimplified in Paul.

Any moment when we are prompted to love, we know something is moving us (an "incentive") which is not like the force of our will, yet when the incentive moves us to act, it is our will that has to perform the act. This mixture of motive powers can never be analyzed and divided distinctly into its differing parts, because our spirit was created on purpose to be possessed by God's Spirit. The Spirit "bloweth where it listeth," and where it blows from is not always plain, because its sources may be in memories of those who long ago captured our imagination by the spirit which possessed them.

In an interview Somerset Maugham advised young writers that the character material which they could interpret best would be found in people they knew in their childhood. "You never see any characters for the rest of your life as clearly as you see the ones you associated with when you were a child." [1] The theological net can never catch in its doctrinal meshes the vestiges of the Spirit that reach us from the fellowship of those possessed even in a small way by its winning power. The effect of a good family, holding us in the bonds of affection while giving us freedom to make our own choices, is one of the prime illustrations of a power stronger than our own will at work within us. An economics professor, completely agnostic in religion, confessed that his faith in the "scale of values" which determined his life came from living with his mother and with others who were in the Christian tradition.

Having developed his premise concerning the

[1] *New York Times Magazine*, June 23, 1940.

| | |
|---|---|
| 6 Who, being in the form of God, thought it not robbery to be equal with God: | which you have in Christ Jesus, 6 who, though he was in the form of God, did not count equality with God a thing to be |

In his character as a man he displayed that utter self-forgetfulness which had ever been the law of his being.

**5-6.** Paul thus implores his readers, **Let this mind be in you, which was also in Christ Jesus.** He has impressed on them in the previous verses that what they require as Christians is an inward disposition which will direct them in all they do without their knowing. They will possess it by taking their example from Christ, who had acted by it before he ever appeared in this world. Vs. 6, literally translated, reads, "Who being in the form of God did not consider equality with God a thing to be seized." The whole passage turns upon this clause, which is exceedingly difficult, and has been interpreted in many different ways.

Almost every word in it has to be examined with the closest attention. (a) The word for "being" (ὑπάρχων) is a philosophical word which denotes the underlying nature, as opposed to chance variations. Something which we call humanity is inherent in men, but Christ, in his fundamental attributes, was divine. (b) This is expressed by "in the form of God." The Greeks, with their keen analytical sense, had two separate words for "form." One of them applied to mere shape and appearance, as when a bank of cloud takes the form of a mountain. The other suggests that the form of the object is the expression of what it really is. The reality discloses itself in the form. It is this word which Paul employs here (ἐν μορφῇ). When he says that Christ existed in the form of God, he implies that Christ was of the same nature as God, that the principle of his being was essentially divine. (c) Since he had this affinity with God, he might have aspired to "equality" with him; he might have claimed an equal share in all the powers which God exercises and in all the honors which are rendered to him by his creatures. Standing so near to God, he might have resented his inferior place and thrown off his obedience. (d) Yet he never attempted the **robbery** which might have raised him higher.

This term, rendered in the RSV by **a thing to be grasped** (ἁρπαγμόν), is the crucial word in the verse, and the meaning of it has been much contested. In the Greek of Paul's time it was often used in the general sense of a prize or a windfall—something one lays hold of at once when it comes his way. The suggestion may thus be that Christ was not tempted by a chance which no one else could have resisted. "He did not think it a prize to be equal with God," for his mind was set on a quite different aim. But in Greek, as in English, the word "robbery" involved the idea of violent seizure, and what Christ resisted was not merely the prize but the means of obtaining it. He refused to seize for his own the glory which belonged to God. It is more than probable that when he thus describes how Christ had withstood temptation, Paul has a contrast in his mind. Some have seen a reference to the story of man's fall in Genesis: Adam and Eve had been tempted by the serpent's promise "ye shall be as gods," and had given way. Here, however, there was no question of robbing God of his supremacy, and Paul must be thinking of someone who was in a position comparable to that of Christ. In various mythologies we hear of a rebellion on the part of an inferior divinity against the sovereignty of God. A

participation of the divine Spirit with our spirit, Paul proceeds to his great exhortation: **Have this mind among yourselves, which you have in Christ Jesus.** The Exeg. points out that in this passage we have the first definition of the test for a Christian: *a disposition of mind.* Not creeds, sacraments, rites, or correct morals, and certainly not any beliefs in economic or political systems, but a disposition of mind. In this letter before his death, after all that he had argued and explained in other writings, the apostle puts the final emphasis on a phrase that is one more of his synonyms for the Spirit of God.

**6-11. *The Servant Supremely Exalted.*—** When he tries to describe this disposition, Paul's language turns from prose to poetry as he pictures the revelation of it in one **who, though he was in the form of God, did not count equality with God a thing to be grasped,**

7 But made himself of no reputation, and took upon him the form of a servant, and was made in the likeness of men: | grasped, 7 but emptied himself, taking the form of a servant,[d] being born in the like-

[d] Or *slave*.

---

myth of this kind may underlie the magnificent chapter of Isaiah which tells of the fall of Lucifer (Isa. 14). The author of Revelation conceives of a war in heaven, in which Satan with his host had been overthrown. Gnostic speculation in the second and third centuries was based on the idea that an original harmony had been broken by the false ambition of one of the aeons who made up the divine fullness. It was from myths of this kind that Milton derived the framework of *Paradise Lost,* and they were doubtless familiar to Paul. He sets the obedience of Christ over against that old conception of a heavenly being who had sought by violence to make himself equal to God.

**7.** Thus Paul proceeds to tell how Christ, because of the "mind" that was in him—the humble, obedient spirit—had put aside all temptation, and had descended, instead of climbing higher. Being in the form of God, he **emptied himself** (ἑαυτὸν ἐκένωσεν). This is what Paul says, and the KJV rendering **made himself of no reputation** is only an attempt, and not a very intelligent one, to explain what he means. The translators, no doubt, were influenced by the theological debate of their time, which turned largely on the question of how far Christ had ceased to be God when he became man. Did he strip himself entirely of the divine nature, or merely forgo certain attributes of majesty? But Paul is here not primarily concerned with any theological problem. He says only that Christ **emptied himself;** instead of aspiring to a higher status he gave up that which he had. He abdicated his divine rank and assumed **the form of a servant** (literally "a slave").

Here, as in the previous sentence, Paul uses that word for "form" which implies a form corresponding with the substance. Christ did not merely disguise himself as a servant but *became* one, expressing in his action and appearance what he had become in fact. As a slave had no rights of his own, so Christ's attitude to God was one of absolute submission. It has sometimes been supposed that Paul is glancing here at the lowly circumstances of Jesus' life. He not only became a man but a poor man, laboring with his own hands. But a thought of this kind would here be quite irrelevant. The contrast in Paul's mind is the infinite contrast between the heavenly nature of Christ and his condition as a man, subject to all human weaknesses and limitations. If he had appeared on earth not as a carpenter, but as high priest or Roman emperor, the distance between this and his former station would not have been perceptibly less. In so far as there is a special significance in the word **servant,** it lies in the suggestion it carries of Isaiah's prophecy of the "servant of the Lord." The prophecy of the servant, who would suffer and die and would finally be "exalted and extolled, and be very high" (Isa. 52:13) has clearly influenced Paul's thought in the present passage.

He himself defines what he means by **the form of a servant.** He says that Christ took on him this form having become (by his own voluntary act) **in the likeness of men.** This phrase was used in early controversy to support the strange Docetic view that while Christ appeared to be a man, his human body was only a kind of mask or disguise in which an essentially divine being walked the earth. The same theory has been put forward with various modifications in many subsequent doctrines of the Incarnation. Paul's view,

---

**but emptied himself, taking the form of a servant, being born in the likeness of men. . . . He humbled himself and became obedient unto death, even death on a cross.**

What a picture! After all that scholars have done to explain the meaning of this language, it is certainly best understood as an Oriental picture of eternal reality. There are elements in it that seem like echoes from the ancient myth, which Milton revived in *Paradise Lost,*

that some highly placed being in the heavenly host had aspired to be equal with God and was cast out because of that pride which is the chief sin against God and the source of "all our woe." Here Paul holds up a contrasted figure who, with the nature of God, became a servant to the lowliest on earth, whom we would consider beneath us; and who, by enduring all that the typical sins of men can do, revealed how respectable people (with whom we would feel

8 And being found in fashion as a man, he humbled himself, and became obedient unto death, even the death of the cross.

9 Wherefore God also hath highly exalted him, and given him a name which is above every name:

ness of men. 8 And being found in human form he humbled himself and became obedient unto death, even death on a cross. 9 Therefore God has highly exalted him and bestowed on him the name which is

however, is entirely different. His purpose is to emphasize the full identity of Christ with the race of men. He holds, with the writer to the Hebrews, that "in all things it behooved him to be made like unto his brethren" (Heb. 2:17), so that he might act on their behalf.

**8. And being found in fashion as a man:** Paul here uses the other word for "form" (σχήματι), that which denotes shape and appearance, as distinguished from substance. Perhaps his reason is that he now puts himself at the point of view of those who beheld Christ as he lived on earth. The mystery of his being was hidden from them. They could judge him only externally, and all that they saw was a man like themselves, subject, as they were, to human frailty and suffering. This was how they "found" him, and they treated him with scorn and hatred, never guessing who he was. But to all that befell him as a man he submitted patiently. **He humbled himself,** laying aside entirely all the privileges which were rightly his. Not only so, but he carried his humiliation to the uttermost. Vs. 8*b* means "He became obedient to the point of death, the death of the Cross"— the most terrible and ignominious of all modes of death. The emphasis is on the word "obedient." He gave up all personal ambitions, all self-seeking impulses, and surrendered himself without reserve to the will of God.

Paul thus draws two pictures which he puts side by side in their marvelous contrast. On the one side, Christ in his original glory, of the same nature with God, so near to God that he might have dared to usurp his sovereignty; on the other side, Christ as he chose to be. Instead of aspiring higher, he abandoned everything which he rightly possessed. He exchanged the form of God for that of man. He suppressed himself so utterly that he died at last on the Cross.

**9.** Now, however, a third picture is held up before us. As a result of his humiliation, he was raised to a yet higher place than he had before. **Wherefore God also hath highly exalted him.** If he had sought equality with God by "robbery" he would have failed, like the rebellious angels in the ancient myths. The way he took was that of self-denial and entire obedience, and by so acting he won his sovereignty. God bestowed on him **the name which is above every name.** Paul is presently to say explicitly that this transcendent name was "Lord," but he prepares for the mention of it by telling what it was to signify. It needs to be remembered that in ancient thought a peculiar value was attached to a name. The person himself was supposed to be somehow present in his name, so that in uttering it one brought oneself under the other's influence. A soldier took his oath in the name of Caesar, and thereby became Caesar's man. A Christian convert was baptized in the name of Jesus, and thus yielded himself to Jesus' will and secured his protection. So Paul assumes that the new name bestowed on Christ carried with it an active power, in virtue of which he had a divine authority.

quite at home) may be the chief enemies of the living God who seeks their liberation.

The thing to do with a picture is not to analyze it, but to let it talk, as Paul wanted it to talk to those in Philippi who were exalting themselves. It suggests that God the creator, who "eternally gives himself that we might exist," has had in his nature from all eternity this outgoing, self-giving disposition of mind; which became visible by one supreme revelation in Christ, reaching down to individuals in

order to lift each one out of self into a new union with the selfless life of God, for which our spirit was created. Once this revelation was made in a deed, there was nothing more that could be added to it.

There is dynamite in this picture of the Creator's eternal interest in each human personality. It blasted the social climbing which had showed its ugly head at Philippi. And down through the ages it has been the heart of a continuous revolution; for the forces of

10 That at the name of Jesus every knee should bow, of *things* in heaven, and *things* in earth, and *things* under the earth;

11 And *that* every tongue should confess that Jesus Christ *is* Lord, to the glory of God the Father.

above every name, 10 that at the name of Jesus every knee should bow, in heaven and on earth and under the earth, 11 and every tongue confess that Jesus Christ is Lord, to the glory of God the Father.

---

**10-11.** This idea is developed in the words that follow: **That at the name** [literally, "in the name"] **of Jesus every knee should bow.** The translation **at the name** is inadequate, suggesting, as it does, that whenever the sacred name is uttered everyone should bend in reverence. Paul might have approved this custom, but he certainly meant much more. He believes that now, when he bears the name of Lord, Jesus has come to exercise a constraining power. The man who had become obedient to death was now the world's sovereign. In his name, i.e., acknowledging his authority, all will submit to him because they cannot do otherwise. Paul's words are an echo of Isa. 45:23, "I have sworn by myself . . . that unto me every knee shall bow, every tongue shall swear." The prophet speaks of God, and Paul transfers the words to Christ, indicating that Christ has now obtained by his obedience that equality with God which he refused to seize by robbery. At the same time the prophet's idea is carried out to its full extent. Every knee shall bow of beings **in heaven and on earth and under the earth,** i.e., in the higher world and in this world and in the world of the dead. The thought is similar to that of Eph. 4:10, "He that descended is the same also that ascended up far above all heavens, that he might fill all things." So Paul continues the prophetic saying and applies it in a new sense to the rule of Christ: and that **every tongue** should **confess** from the heart **that Jesus Christ is Lord.** Here at last he reveals the new name which is above all others. Christ, by way of his humiliation, has won his place as universal *Lord.* Three times in the course of his epistles Paul quotes the formula "Jesus is Lord," and each time with a special solemnity (Rom. 10:9; I Cor. 12:3; and here). There can be little doubt that he repeats the confession which every convert made at his baptism. As yet there was no formal creed to which assent was necessary. Nothing was required but the affirmation that one accepted Jesus as one's Master. The later creeds all grew out of this baptismal confession, which was not a creed but simply an oath of loyalty. Paul reminds the Philippians of the declaration they had all made, and wishes them to realize what was implied in it. In calling Jesus "Lord" they had acknowledged that he was supreme. A day would come when all things in God's creation would join with the church on earth in submitting to this Lord, **to the glory of God the Father.** The one purpose of Christ had been the fulfillment of God's will. He had been utterly obedient to God, and the lordship to which he had attained was that of God himself.

At first sight the passage might seem to be nothing but a glorious speculation. The work of Christ is thrown into a mythological framework. His earthly life is linked up with a celestial drama, for the truth of which there could be no evidence, and the gospel, as thus presented, has only a visionary foundation. Objections of this kind have often been raised, but they are valid only when the passage is taken by itself, without regard to its

---

change always start, like the "vengeance of God," from just those distressed areas where human personality is being exploited and suppressed.

And Paul says there was something so final and supreme about this great act of creation that God exalted this lowly Man and gave him **the name which is above every name, that at the name of Jesus every knee should bow, . . . and every tongue confess that Jesus Christ is Lord, to the glory of God the Father.** When

dogmatists have used these words to exalt their own human interpretation of Christianity, endeavoring to prove superiority over all other religious doctrine, their spiritual pride has been identified with the will of God, to the shame of the church and not to the **glory of God.**

The enduring supremacy of Christ's revelation will not depend on the support of theologians or the vote of the churches. It will rest on the simple fact that to the end of time no one can show us any power other than the

| 12 Wherefore, my beloved, as ye have always obeyed, not as in my presence only, but now much more in my absence, work | 12 Therefore, my beloved, as you have always obeyed, so now, not only as in my |
|---|---|

context. Paul's motive in introducing it is not mystical or theological. He is dealing with the feuds and jealousies which had arisen in the Philippian church, and seeks to show his readers that they must rise above this littleness. As Christians they must have in them the mind of Christ, and he illustrates his meaning by the example of all that Christ had sacrificed. He does his utmost to impress on them the greatness of the sacrifice. Possessing everything, Christ had been willing to surrender everything in his unlimited obedience to God. How can his followers cling to their small ambitions when they profess to have Christ as their Master? It must be noted, too, that while he speaks of matters beyond man's knowledge, Paul's interest in them is not speculative. He thinks of those transcendental events in their moral significance. The very secret of Christ's nature, in heaven as on earth, had been his complete unselfishness, and it was by this road and no other that he had arrived at his sovereign place. This is the thought which occupies Paul's mind all through these verses, and it is one of the central truths of the Christian religion. In this poetical passage Paul has given it sublime expression.

### C. The Obligations Laid on Christians (2:12-18)

**12.** The apostle now draws the practical inferences from his appeal to the example of Christ. **Therefore,** i.e., as men who serve Christ and have his mind in them. It is

love that stooped to earth in him, which can win over our human spirits from enslavement to self. This power unto salvation contradicted all the expectations of authorities, religious and secular, in Jesus' own day. And it will forever contradict every way of imposing on the human will from outside which tries to supplant *this inside persuasion and constraint. Nothing else can save man from himself and at the same time leave him his freedom.*

All kinds of saviors will promise to change the world from outside, and they can bestow certain external benefits; but at long last man must be freely won away from self if he is to know the true "liberty of the children of God."

Even the greatest in power and wisdom could not more fully reveal the Heart of God and the heart of man than the Crucified has done already. Those things have been revealed once for all. "It is finished." In the face of the Crucified all the "more" and all the "less," all progress and all approximation, are meaningless. Therefore, we can say of Him alone: He is the new reality; He is the end.[2]

**12-17. The Obligation Laid on Christians.—** Immediately following the great passage on the "self-emptying" of Christ, Paul turns the force of his high argument upon the rivalries of pride among his old friends in Philippi, saying they need to be concerned for their salvation **with fear and trembling.** In a following section the implications of this startling phrase will be discussed, but at this point something should be said about certain common dispositions of mind

that tend to breed indifference to "the mind of Christ." We will not let ourselves be given over to that mind until we want it desperately; and so long as we can get by with some other contemporary attitude, there is no desperation to intensify desire for any new life. The society known as Alcoholics Anonymous has rediscovered the truth that the working of God begins when self-sufficiency reaches the end of its rope. Victims of drink find a renovation of life only at the point where the weakness of their human will becomes truly desperate. So long as they think they have everything under control, they remain incurable. And we do not have to be confirmed drunkards to recognize certain self-sufficient dispositions which today make many persons, perhaps including ourselves, religiously unreceptive.

First there is *the psychological mind.* Where our fathers were religiously minded, our generation grows more and more psychologically minded. The two types of mind need not be opposed, for they are really complementary; but a popularized psychology has confused self-analysis with self-excuse. Men turn to psychology to understand why people behave as they do—including themselves. No one would deny the contributions which have been made by thoroughgoing analysis of the quirks and twists and reactions that occur in the subconscious levels of our minds. However, this explanation of behavior and a change of heart through self-surrender are not one and the same thing. Without the latter, explanations are often used as excuses that shirk responsibility and evade

[2] Tillich, *Shaking of the Foundations,* p. 148.

always a delicate matter to intrude on household quarrels, and Paul is anxious to avoid all suspicion of rebuke or criticism. He addresses his readers as **my beloved,** and assures them that they **have always obeyed,** i.e., they had proved by their conduct in the past that they had understood the meaning of Christ's example. Formerly, however, they had

the mood of honest repentance in which real healing begins.

A newspaper reported a biochemist as saying, "Hereafter, when we deal with a criminal we will not say he is vicious and bad, we will say that he has too much pyruvic acid in his thalamic cells." No doubt the acid is there, which is good to know, and the overdose will doubtless condition the man's conduct; but to make this into a final excuse is to avoid the crisis of repentance without which the human spirit is never open to the transforming Spirit of God, and is left as much involved as ever in the same old self.

The superficiality of such an attitude is shown by our abandonment of excuse and analysis where the trouble is not deemed serious. We hear much explanation of the superiority complex and the inferiority complex, but who ever talks about a mediocrity complex? That is the affliction with most of us—self-satisfaction. We are not even trying to excuse the fact that we are neither extraordinary nor subordinary but just ordinary. We are so like the majority that we cause no disturbance in society; we leave the average where it is. We are like Peter standing outside the judgment hall where Christ was on trial, just "warming himself." We become spectators, looking down at evil people and bungling people, complaining of their stupidity, as though everybody were betraying the good cause but ourselves. "I only am left."

Another obstacle lies in *the self-coddling mind.* Our world is full of people who are upset because they are not as happy as they wish they were. A book has been published under the title: *Florida—How to Be Happy in It.* There are many good people in Florida who would not need such a book; but evidently there are many there who become bored with having everything they want, and who need advice on how to be happy amid idleness and luxury.

Multitudes who cannot escape to places like Florida are troubled by a world full of tension and strain and fear and disappointment. They have heard that wrong thoughts in the mind create trouble, and by introducing happy, confident thoughts, a more comfortable frame of mind will result and unguessed success will follow. There is an abundant literature on how to push oneself, improve oneself, "sell" oneself, and comfort oneself. The advice is a combination of psychology, religion, and common sense

—and mostly the last. Whenever religion is at a low ebb, this kind of practical common sense becomes exposed, like the deep channels in a shallow bay when the tide goes out. The book of Proverbs is a sample of this practical wisdom which appeared when the fervor of prophetic religion had subsided. There is an age-old sameness about these practical ways of avoiding worry and making the most of happy patches in a rather meaningless existence.

Such undisguised hunger for help for a troubled life is a sign that conventionalized religion has failed to meet a need. True religion will not deny any of this common sense, but it will furnish a healthy antidote to the self-sparing emphasis which is characteristic of a merely sensible life.

A professor who had suffered from nervous exhaustion was given a book on thought control for the sake of health and peace. He found much that was helpful, but he also found himself being told not to work too hard, not to undertake too heavy a burden, not to bother himself with disturbing situations; and he came to the conclusion that he was being subtly drawn into a self-sparing life which was not what he wanted to live.

Christianity is not devised to keep the natural self peaceful, happy, and content. Its real intent is to disturb self and make us so sick and ashamed of self that we will want to stop thinking about it, until something of the self-forgetful disposition of our Creator can take command of our self-tormented souls.

Still another contemporary attitude which breeds unreceptiveness toward God is *the business mind.* Our civilization depends so much upon the ingenuity of this type of mind, and all of us are so affected by it under the pressure of making a living that it has become a sort of "sacred cow" among the democracies. So far from being a bad mind, it is a highly necessary and efficient mind, but it is extremely limited in its scope; for, like the political mind, it is devoted to what is possible in the present, and it is also infected with a perverse view that man is merely an economic animal. Such a view for most people is a rather unconscious assumption that somewhere ahead man will be better as he becomes better off financially. This materialism is characteristic of capitalism and socialism and communism alike. Some say that more private property and prosperity will solve our problems; others in the opposite camp affirm

| out your own salvation with fear and trembling: | presence but much more in my absence, work out your own salvation with fear and |
|---|---|

been supported by Paul's own help and influence, and now they must learn to stand alone. **Not as in my presence only, but now much more in my absence.** Thrown on their own responsibility, they must put forth a greater effort, for the very test of a Christian is

that less private property and more public property will bring an end to human selfishness and create harmony in a classless society.

The United States has become peculiarly addicted to this business mind, despite the crimes that have been committed in its name. Ministers are often slow to attack it because they hesitate to bite the hand that feeds them. Once President Coolidge proclaimed that "the business of America is business," and long before him, at the very beginning of the nation, de Tocqueville observed that nowhere in the world were there "so many ambitious people with such low ambitions."

Under the business mind's domination, vast corporations have been treated under the law as persons, with their inordinate desires protected from government interference on the principle that persons cannot be deprived of property without due process of law—a principle once used to protect the institution of slave property. Labor unions have tended to follow suit, as they have achieved power, arguing that what was good for the goose is good for the gander. The bigger the enterprise, the less personal and more inhuman it inevitably becomes, through no one's fault; and private conscience is desensitized by bigness of organization. Men will do in big aggregations what they would never do as individuals to their neighbors.

From Paul's poetic flight into the sublime mystery of the relation of the divine to the human, he now comes down to earth again; and with that one word **therefore** he seeks to bring the resources of supernatural power to bear upon the quarrels and rivalries of human self-love. In this case, feminine rivalries of the most petty nature are the point at issue; but the rivalries of self-love, petty as they most often are, can be magnified into national and class competitions.

Paul never loses sight of the fact that the natural self-centeredness of our human nature in small and great affairs is the root of all our woes, and never in this letter, or in other letters, does he let us forget that it takes more than prudence and will power to save us from *self*. What Euodia and Syntyche were quarreling about two thousand years ago in the Philippian church is of supreme indifference to us, but that sort of severing of human relationships so that

people *fail to meet* is everywhere and always the chief obstacle in the way of the Creator who created us "on purpose to be together." The saving operations of creation require the interrelatedness of lives in community; and salvation, as Paul treats it, is not like snatching "brands from the burning" one by one. The Holy Spirit always deals with us in and through relations.

**12-13. Work Out Your Own Salvation . . . ; for God Is at Work in You, Both to Will and to Work.**—To help a modern man understand and experience the truth back of this admonition is a major difficulty, because the familiar words have lost much of their force when human self-sufficiency is so much to the fore as it is in the world today. To speak in the same breath about saving yourself and being saved, working and being worked in, sounds like double talk; but such paradoxical double talk is the only language in which all sides of the gospel can be expressed.

The words that preface the admonition to **work out your own salvation** bear unconscious testimony to factors in the saving process that play a hidden and undefined part.

(a) **My beloved.** Real affection had been brought to bear on these people at Philippi, in a person who never spared himself. No dogma can ever convey such an influence. Some living mediator must usually transmit the love of God to man, because mere words, however orthodox, have no saving power. The address "dearly beloved brethren" in a service of worship is a conventionalized term which has lost the impact of the original, but imagine sitting in a room and talking face to face with a personality like Paul, whose selfless devotion has been a byword for twenty centuries! It used to be said in the old Jerry McAuley Mission in New York that no down-and-outer was ever saved there who had not had somewhere in his life a mother or friend who had loved him.

(b) **As you have always obeyed.** Before men can be changed they must obey. Obedience is the one form of self-surrender that hurts enough to prove that self has really given up some of its own will. It may be forced, and lack the true spirit, but it is the first step in putting a man where the work of God can be done through him. None of the forces given in this universe, personal or impersonal, can be effective for man until he has rendered up some measure of obedience. Thus only can he release far more than he himself can supply, but he must give his bit.

(c) **As in my presence.** The immediate presence of someone who loves us and is beloved moves us with a power that is past our understanding. Certainly for children a personal presence carries more weight than God himself, probably because God's Spirit is most effectively transmitted to us in such living nearness. There was nothing irreverent in a small child who in his attic room was frightened at night by a thunderstorm, and who, after being assured by his mother that God would take care of him, replied, "Well, you come up here and stay with God, I want to come down and sleep with father."

(d) **In my absence.** Obedience, in the absence of friends, can still be stimulated by memory. Augustine's great treatise on the memory was no doubt prompted by the recollection of his beloved mother, whose love for him while he was yet in his youthful sin played some vital part in his salvation. Memory can refresh the influence of those who have moved or inspired us. Whether our connection with people is direct or indirect, and regardless of distance in time or space, the interrelationship of persons which memory reopens may channel the life-changing power of love which has its source in God. Man can be acted upon by love so that he permits it to pass through him to others, but no man by sheer strength of mind or will can produce love to order.

Consider, then, the mystery of unselfishness and the equally mysterious working that creates it in us. Once Albert Einstein was brought to a Christian church by a friend. As he listened to the preacher saying rather uncomplimentary things about selfishness, he whispered to his friend, "Oh, I love selfishness." We find it easy to talk against selfishness, but we all love it. We were born in it, as any parent knows when an infant with the colic howls through the livelong night, completely oblivious to the feelings of others. We know as we grow up that we ought to be unselfish; we admire unselfishness above all, and know that love is the greatest thing in the world; yet we love selfishness.

There is no simple solution of this predicament. A student once said, "I know one ought to be unselfish, but how do you make yourself want to be?" Of course the answer is, *"You cannot."*

Paul's insight is profound when he combines inextricably the working of man and the working of God, **both to will and to work** in the saving process. There are numerous expressions of this complex experience in the apostle's letters: "For to me to live is Christ" (1:21); "Not having a righteousness of my own . . . but . . . the righteousness from God" (3:9); "I worked harder than any of them, though it was not I, but the grace of God which is with me" (I Cor. 15:10); "For I am the least of the apostles. . . . But by the grace of God I am what I am" (I Cor. 15:9-10). Down through the centuries theologians have tried, in perplexing language of paradox, to say that God makes moral demands and then by his Spirit gives what is demanded.

Everything would be simple if we could neatly assign a certain area to God's operation, and another to the work we ourselves must do; but such a clear-cut division would be like trying to separate the influence of a good mother from the willing response of her son. She both invites it and creates it, while he also wills it. All Paul's letters center around his discovery of this twofold working of the will of man and the will of God. Like all his forebears, and multitudes of his successors, he first thought of morality as rules of behavior or laws, imposed upon us by a moral ruler who required obedience and administered punishment to those who disobeyed. Then it dawned on him in a conversion that God is always trying to give us his life, his Spirit, if we would only put self out of the way and make room. God's so-called requirements are simply the demands of our own nature, which he created to receive his Spirit and be transformed by it. Sin is separation from a life-giving God, and its punishment is merely the consequence of shutting out God and trying to live with an unredeemed self.

To modern man, whose religion has become so largely moralistic, the high demands of the ethics of Jesus, expressed in the Sermon on the Mount, and in all his "hard sayings," seem to be too difficult for any practical use. This judgment is quite correct if Christianity offers no more than a perfect moral code for imperfect man to obey; but "the grace of God" is much more than a mere moral command.

Unfortunately, "grace," as the Bible uses the term, has been crowded out of our vocabulary by much psychological analysis that presumes to be more scientific. "Grace" means more than "graciousness." It means a gift added to our life, which we cannot do without, which we cannot supply ourselves, and for which we can only be grateful.

In one sense all the powers of nature are the grace of God—i.e., they are given us and not made by us. I sail my boat, yet not I but the winds of God that are with me; I grow my vegetables, yet not I but the growing power which nature supplies; I start my car, yet not

I but the electrical power that was here before cars were invented. In all these ways we work, and yet the working is not all ours—but we must work.

Something like this "givenness" is also found in our personal lives, in the moments that border on the unselfish. Few of us ever experience pure unselfishness; but whenever we approximate it, we know that the good we do seems to be done through us rather than by us, and yet we choose to do it. We are prompted to say, "Don't thank me; I claim no credit; it was just one of the things one could not help doing." Obviously, calculation cannot generate such actions. Reckoning on the future effects spoils the spontaneity which is the very essence of self-forgetful love, venturing forth regardless of hope. Furthermore, making unselfishness seem reasonable does not supply the motive power; for mere thinking does not create life, and all the intelligence in the world cannot produce love. So long as love appears to us as a moral command laid upon us, or as a strategy for success and security, it is not love. Nor can will power alone force us to be unselfish. In our best moments our will power itself becomes reinforced and carried along by a power other than itself. It is like a swimmer supported by a strong tide. I swim, yet not I but the tide that is with me—yet I must swim.

Even children experience this mystery of grace long before they can possibly understand it. In certain stages they may make themselves a nuisance to everybody, obeying their elders with grudging reluctance, exhibiting a self-will that seeks only its own. There come times when a totally new spirit possesses them. The love they have seen in others outside, patiently bearing their bothersome faults, trusting without much reward, becomes a force inside their own life. They act like new persons altogether; they do not even *want* to bother; their obedience is changed into a free and joyful inclination. As Jesus said, this childlike way of entering the kingdom of God (or having the kingdom of God within one's life) is the one way for all of us, for we are most free, most ourselves and most responsible, in these rare moments when the good is done in us rather than by us.

A Scottish theologian has suggested that these familiar experiences are the modern man's best clue to the age-old experience of "grace": "I labored—yet not I but the grace of God that was with me." [3]

To sum up this discussion on the work of man and the work of grace, one might say that the self-giving Spirit of God cannot be made by man, simply because man cannot make God.

[3] D. M. Baillie, *God Was in Christ* (New York: Charles Scribner's Sons, 1948), ch. v.

This Spirit belongs to God before it is made our own, just as surely as gravity and wind and electricity belong to the Creator before we work with them and they with us. Christ was the perfect instance in history when God was so free to work in all the acts of a man that the nature of man revealed once for all the nature of God, and yet the man was just as human as all of us. His mission was not to set an impossible ideal before us, but to win us into union with his Spirit so that we might the more often say, "I labor—yet not I but the Spirit of God that is in me."

There are many aspects of the mystery of unselfishness which need to be clarified for people who have grown away from the Bible's idea of "grace."

First, we must always be loved before we are moved to love. God took the initiative in sending Christ to suffer for the typical sins of men, and once that revelation took place nothing afterward could be the same with mankind. Furthermore, there can be no separation of Christ from those who went before and those who have come after. He was not a lone flash of light in complete darkness. He was a light that was a life from God, seeking from the foundation of the world to win its way into the lives of his creatures. The Gospel of John, which reflects, as Paul did, the influence of the Gentile world and its current manner of thought, puts the initiating effect of Christ's coming in these familiar words: "The true light that enlightens every man was coming into the world; he was in the world, and the world was made through him, yet the world knew him not; he came to his own home, and his own people received him not. But to all who received him, who believed in his name, *he gave power to become children of God*"—i.e., children who had the Spirit working through their actions (John 1:9-12).

This initiation from God is "technically" known as "prevenient grace," or the grace that comes before and prompts the movement of mind and will. A modern interpreter of this prevenience should realize that the most realistic illustration of it is in the relation of every man to the home and family from which he has come. Our life is derived from other lives in a mystery that forever remains beyond any scientific understanding.

A young man who was very vague about religion was once asked what kept him at his best when circumstances were against him. He replied that he had back of him a family which he did not want to let down, and he also felt that there were many back of his family whom they had not wanted to let down. There was something like an "endless conspiracy" which

to remain one when he is left entirely to himself. **Work out your own salvation;** i.e., without any assistance from Paul they are to follow out the Christian life. Several times in his epistles Paul uses the phrase **fear and trembling** (e.g., I Cor. 2:3; II Cor. 7:15) to indicate a humble frame of mind. So here he does not mean that the hope of salvation,

---

added a peculiar power to his life before he made decisions. No matter how often he betrayed it, it never let him go.

In the light of this old doctrine of prevenient grace we are able to see how God instituted marriage and the family as the primary channel through which the power of his love could enter human society afresh, to meet generation after generation of children as soon as they were born. Inevitably we begin life in a society where we are first loved before we are moved to love. Families may fail in their function, or ungrateful children go against the best of families; but no matter how many the exceptions, they all prove the rule. We must first see love in action, giving itself away without payment, suffering for indifference and ingratitude before it strikes through our selfishness to win entrance to our hearts. From then on, if we respond, the love that enters our lives from others works through us from life to life in the endless interrelation of human beings. Intellectual doubt of God may often exist alongside our experience of the love of God within us.

It is not surprising that those who have an unfortunate family life seem to lose some steadying power that ordinarily supplies strength at the very times when the human will is wavering or meeting with frustration.

The dean of a great university reported that nearly 80 per cent of the serious trouble with maladjusted students comes not only from broken families, but also from homes where selfishness creates a strained relationship between parents, thus forcing children to take sides with one of their loved ones against the other. This same college official affirmed without any reservations that the best preparation for a successful college life—or any career for that matter—is a good home where parents know how to live together happily.

The true depth of all social problems is never sounded until everything in our society is judged from the point of view of its effect on the home life of the people.

Another aspect of the mystery of unselfishness which troubles the skeptical and secular mind is its resistance to analysis. Our addiction to psychological practice inclines many people to reduce all behavior to motives easily understood.

A very widespread tendency, especially among young people, is to describe all unselfishness in terms of selfishness. All good, it is claimed, is done for our own pleasure; therefore it is selfish. Logically this leaves no distinction between a murderer who shoots his pal and a man who lays down his life for his friends. The satisfactions are, to be sure, on different levels, but they are selfish nevertheless. Not only intellectuals use such arguments, but common folk who have known little but the seamy side of life are inclined to discount all disinterested action. Some sailors on a train were once arguing loudly that all people are selfish and that nobody can be trusted. This conclusion was proved by the experience of one boy who had been cheated out of one hundred dollars by a man whom he took to be his friend. They knew no friends who were not looking for their own selfish interests. In an age of collective action, which is a technique for self-interest, such a personal influence as selfless love is hard for many to take seriously.

There are two fallacies in this reduction of all behavior to selfishness:

(a) All the neurotic difficulties which have called the profession of psychiatry into being come from being wrapped up in self, "like a porcupine rolled up the wrong way in his own prickles." Self-indulgence is slow death to the finer feelings that give life its enduring satisfaction; self-absorption is a major foe of good health; self-consciousness spoils all effectiveness; self-pity begets the inferiority complex and self-defeat. Living for self alone is self-torture, because we discourage ourselves by comparisons that hurt, and wear ourselves out by nursing needless grudges and protecting false pride. The tensions of keeping up with the procession are more than our ordinary nervous systems can stand. Our deepest longing, after all is said and done, is to be released from self, even while we love selfishness. This is the deep cleavage in human nature.

(b) The other fallacy lies in the fact that doing good to another for our pleasure violates the other's personality. In each one of us there is a unique and hidden worth, an unknown potentiality, placed there by the Creator, with a "natural right" to fulfillment. To use another for the fulfillment of our personality is to overlook and perhaps frustrate the uniqueness in his life. We are sure of this frustration when the situation is reversed, and someone tries to do us good for his own pleasure and imposes on us his idea of what is best for us. We have a native dislike for having good done us in this way. Such patronizing benevolence is the source of all tyranny and inevitable rebellion. One might write a book on "How to Make Friends and Alienate People"—by doing them good for our own purposes.

Another aspect of the mystery of unselfishness is that humanly speaking it is an impossible achievement. The meaning of the grace of God, participating in our acts, begins to be understood *after* we recognize that we possess no power to make self unselfish. All our natural powers belong to the self, and they are in the service of self, like politicians on the pay roll who always vote to keep their boss in office. All our interior life, from our emotions, impulses, and will, up to our creative intelligence, is at the disposal of self-defense.

Reason is ready to do the wishful thinking for our unlimited desires and our inexhaustible will to power. Our will can only put on a show of unselfishness, for which we take the credit, like a rich family who once built a church in memory of the father, moving the church from a poor district where it was most needed to a residential section where it would be more convenient for the well-to-do. Someone suggested that the dedicatory inscription should read: "This church was built for the glory of our wealthiest citizen, and in loving memory of God."

Practical considerations often would identify mutual aid, which we can produce by force of will, with unselfishness which cannot be so willed. Serving other people for the sake of one's own business; being honest and square to keep a good credit; treating labor fairly to prevent labor trouble that interferes with profits— all this and more is good business, and is far better than bad business. However, it may have nothing to do with unselfishness, though no one can tell from outside observation whether some unselfish motives may or may not be mixed with such practical procedures.

Middle-class respectability has often concealed its impotence in transforming selfishness by using a pretense of brotherhood to cover a canny profit motive. It was the mission of Karl Marx to point out this subtle hypocrisy, and to declare that financial interest in making our living had more effect on our character than did our professed ideals. The opposition which his declaration has met has been vicious in proportion as it has struck home to a hidden sin.

Nevertheless, the Marxians, curiously enough, have always been confused by an opposite error. Suspicion of middle-class virtues like disinterested friendship and brotherly love has always been part of their revolutionary propaganda.

But they have believed that these unselfish virtues would blossom like the rose when the proletariat came to power, and a classless society had been made secure by the abolition of private property. Under the utopian rule of the workers, with no class exploiting another, there would be no meanness, no running after profits, no betraying of one another.

Something, however, seems to have gone amiss. The classless state has been in existence and put to the proof. The hardness and cruelty of a police regime, which was excused at first as part of the revolutionary stage, has become even more ruthless as an official policy, while love and sympathy and forgiveness and truthfulness are looked upon as bourgeois weaknesses. This same disillusionment occurred under the Nazi regime which claimed that it served the people. Two other considerations must conclude this treatment of vss. 12-13.

(*a*) When we are driven by human events to see that *selfishness is a permanent factor* in society, which by ourselves we are powerless to overcome, then we are in a position to see that *the grace of God is also a permanent factor*, "wearying out evil," as the Quakers say. The self-giving spirit from God works amid human selfishness like leaven in a lump of dough. The dough remains, but it is a very different thing to use for food when yeast has been at work within it.

A good family is made of selfish people; but it holds together because just enough of the self-forgetful spirit is at work there to renew affection and forgive mistakes and preserve trust.

In society, if there were nothing but selfishness, Hobbes would have been right when he said that a leviathan state would be required with absolute power to keep peace between warring parties. A democratic country is saved from such statism only so long as there are enough people who, before they know how others will respond, go more than half way to furnish the trust that begets trust where it did not exist before. A minority may thus be a very real leaven in the dough. We are surprised that so much can be done for so many by so few. Out of despair hope may be ever reborn, because God can work through a few to the many, to transmit his own Spirit which makes new experiments of trust possible.

(*b*) Another consideration is added here to guard against a common misunderstanding. Unselfish love is not a strategy. It is something more than a means for ironing out social difficulties and gaining practical results. In Christ the Spirit of God did not bring an earthly success; but—and this was more important—that supreme personality demonstrated that union

even for the best of men, is something precarious, about which men need always to feel anxious. The very essence of faith, as Paul conceives it, is the certainty that Christ will save. His idea is rather that one must never lose the sense of one's own weaknesses, and must endeavor constantly to trust Christ more and to serve him better.

---

with the self-giving Spirit of God is union with the eternal life which is the gift of God and the final meaning of our temporal existence. "What does it profit a man, to gain the whole world and forfeit his life?" (Mark 8:36.) "There is great gain in godliness with contentment; for we brought nothing into the world, and we cannot take anything out of the world. . . . For the love of money is the root of all evils" (I Tim. 6:6-7, 10).

Paul never allows us to lose sight of the fact that the end of our natural life is on the new level of the spiritual, where we are not dismayed that everything earthly comes to an end. "So we do not lose heart. Though our outer nature is wasting away, our inner nature is being renewed every day. For this slight momentary affliction is preparing for us an eternal weight of glory beyond all comparison, because we look not to the things that are seen but to the things that are unseen; for the things that are seen are transient, but the things that are unseen are eternal" (II Cor. 4:16-18).

**12. With Fear and Trembling.**—What can be said to the modern man that would put the fear of God into him again? Something of the sort is badly needed, but the "fire and brimstone" method can no longer produce the desired effect. When we are disastrously affected with an easygoing, good-natured Christianity which deceitfully favors an easy conscience and Pharisaic complacency, the soul-searching gospel that strips away all pretense and lays open the hidden self in awe and dread before the Creator should be the order of the day, for now as always "the fear of the Lord is the beginning of knowledge" (Prov. 1:7).

The persistent popular notion of "the fear of God" refers to something that scares the life out of a man so that he will be good. Such fear could be the beginning of caution, but there is no way to scare people into being good or great or wise.

Being afraid of God cannot mean that our actions make God mad, so that he vents his wrath upon his creatures in human fashion. Certainly no anger of man can be a good simile for the wrath of God. Yet there is a truly frightful side to the working of Providence in a sinful world. Whenever we set our partial view over against the way of the universe, we separate ourselves from the good possibilities that are eternally provided, and we have to take the consequences which are the opposite of good.

That sort of separation from the inevitable ways of God, embedded in the very order of life itself, is indeed hell. Practically speaking, separation from God (which is sin) results in a hellish separation from the life we were created for. That is a fearful thing.

A modern scholar [4] has pointed out that in the writings of Paul there is no statement that God becomes angry. "The wrath" is an impersonal phrase, apparently indicating the impersonal working out of consequences, like the fall of a house built on sand when the nature of things called for a foundation of rock. Whenever we take anything in the universe contrary to its nature, we have to pay for it. All evil has to be paid for, somewhere, somehow, and the innocent will be involved with the guilty; for the laws of life cannot be retracted to spare the family in that falling house, though they may not have been to blame for the choice of the foundation.

This negative aspect of fear can be the beginning of caution and restraint, but it can never be the beginning of wisdom that understands the spiritual values which constitute the meaning of life.

The classic biblical illustration of the man who lives by the positive fear of God is found in the primitive story of Abraham, who "went out, not knowing whither he went" (Heb. 11:8). This phrase has been remembered through the ages, because it eternally suggests the person whose greatness is that he moves into the unknown fearing lest he be unfaithful, and "having no other fear."

That fear of being unfaithful is not an intellectual attainment at the end of a rational argument. It is a deep-seated, inexplicable passion which we receive by contagion, if we receive it at all, through the whole company of faithful people. It is something that cannot be taught rationally; we are caught by it when someone silently bears witness to it in his life; and we can pass it on, just in so far as our own life in turn becomes a witness.

In the sense just described this real person works with "fear and trembling" because our Creator alone knows and provides the total possibility of life and meaning. All we ever know is a partial possibility limited by our interest. At the beginning of everything we do we face

---

[4] C. H. Dodd, *The Epistle of Paul to the Romans* (New York: Harper & Bros., 1932; "Moffatt New Testament Commentary"), pp. 20 ff.

13 For it is God which worketh in you both to will and to do of *his* good pleasure.

trembling; 13 for God is at work in you, both to will and to work for his good pleasure.

---

**13.** So far from being anxious about salvation, one can be sure of it, **for it is God which worketh in you both to will and to do.** It has often been assumed that Paul here contradicts or corrects himself. He has said that men must work out their own salvation, and immediately adds that they cannot do so, since they must depend wholly on God. But when he speaks of "your own salvation," he is only contrasting the unaided effort of the Philippians with that which they formerly made when he was present with them. And so far from saying that they can do nothing since it is God alone who works, he

---

three roads: (*a*) There is the way our interest makes us view the possible. (*b*) There is the way other men's interest makes them view the possible. (*c*) And there is the way to the total, inexhaustible possibility which God has provided eternally. Since our interest is always special, the total can never be included in our specialty. Since our power of expression in thought or deed is always limited, the whole meaning can never be in our representation. What we might become aware of, and what we might express, has no known limit; hence the fear and trembling experienced by a man like da Vinci whenever he undertook a great work of art, or by a more ordinary but no less sincere man when he undertakes a heavy responsibility. The fear of being unfaithful to the infinite source of truth and meaning, the fear of not giving one's best, is the continuous beginning of unpredictable possibilities.

Every man has set before him a door into the infinite "that no man can shut." One approaches it without questioning or asking "to see the distant scene." Like a traveler with both hands full of the burdens he must carry, coming to an entrance watched over by an "electric eye," he walks into what looks like a closed path. The opening appears just when hope seemed to be a dead end.[5]

Perhaps the best way to interpret the fear of God to a modern mind is to contrast it with the fear of man, which in our time has almost usurped the place of God. All that man can do to us is to increase our fear for self. Such intensification of self-centeredness results in the worship of safety, which today receives the emphasis which our fathers gave to salvation.

Fear for self is obviously not the beginning of wisdom, for it puts the wrong things in first place. A few typical instances of this perversion can easily be noted.

To get an education so that one can secure a better job, with more money to support a family in a home on easy street, may seem a

[5] Robert R. Wicks, *What Is a Man* (New York: Charles Scribner's Sons, 1947), p. 159.

first demand in the struggle for existence today; but it is not the beginning of wisdom.

Again, it seems that the first thing is to please people, win friends, be popular, and get ahead; but however essential this ambition, it is not the beginning of wisdom.

Even the desire to have influence and to do good, however acceptable in society, is not the beginning. The worst political crooks and tyrants of all kinds cultivate this influence derived from doing good where it pays in the quest for power.

Many today who are beset by fears for self are looking first for peace of mind through comfort. Men need, God knows, some protection from frustration; but self-protection and self-satisfaction were never meant to be the primary consideration.

How this purely human fear has stolen the primacy from God can be seen from a poll taken by the *Ladies' Home Journal* to gauge the religious temper of the American people. The answers to the questionnaire were submitted to three scholarly representatives of the Protestant, Catholic, and Jewish faiths, who furnished the following analysis: (*a*) 95 per cent said they believed in some kind of God—which is hopeful; but only 26 per cent thought that God had any personal relation to their daily behavior—which is not so hopeful; (*b*) 91 per cent said they were trying to lead a good life—which is encouraging; but 82 per cent admitted that the struggle seldom interfered with what they wanted to do—which is not nearly so promising; (*c*) 90 per cent believed that the problems of human society would be solved by following the law of love, and 80 per cent felt they were attaining a high average in following that law—which certainly sounds optimistic; but since the problems are more acute than ever, it appears that 80 per cent of the population are blaming somebody else for the failure. The scholars were agreed that the poll seemed to prove that the American people are obsessed with self-satisfaction instead of the fear of God.

gives this as the very reason why they can do everything. They can feel that God is behind them. He will create in them the will to be ever pressing forward. He will also supply the power by which they will overcome every difficulty. All this he does "on account of the good will." Some would refer this to the Philippians themselves: they are

When people are satisfied with themselves, they are not at the beginning of new wisdom or receptive to change, and are thus their own worst enemy.

In contrast to this fear of man we can better understand the quality of the fear to be unfaithful: (a) First of all, it cannot be in itself a practical plan of operation. Unquestioning faithfulness can give only the *direction* for strategy. Like love, it can be affecting everything, even when no immediate result may be achieved. A sailor might want to sail his craft straight into the teeth of a north wind, obeying absolutely the needle of his compass. But if he is laboring under adverse wind, he cannot move directly where he ought to go. However, his very life depends on observing the compass while he uses human skill to keep his boat in the wind without losing his direction.

(b) Again, the fear to be unfaithful is felt at its true depth only at the limit of self-renunciation. If we could imagine all our fondest wishes packed into one and then see ourselves called upon to renounce that, what would be left? The modern answer is to jump out of a tenth-story window, which only proves there was nothing left to live for.

The psychology of these spiritual depths, when the limit of surrender is faced, cannot be comprehended from an outside point of view. The so-called objective "scientific" approach of the disinterested psychologist cannot fathom the inner struggle. We know about it from the witness of those who have walked alone through their valleys of dark shadow.

The ancient story of Abraham pictures the experience of the ultimate fear of God, tested in complete self-renunciation. The story has it that God "tempted" Abraham to sacrifice the son he loved best, to prove his final devotion to God alone. To modern ears this sounds like a strange thing for God to ask of a man; but we are dealing here with a tale from a very primitive time, when men took it for granted that devotion to God was shown by sacrificing upon the altar that which one valued most. In that setting Abraham becomes a profoundly interesting study.

Here was a man in the grip of an absolute obligation to give up everything, to withhold nothing. He was like Luther, saying, "Here I stand, I cannot do otherwise." Since no reasonable arguments could explain his fear to be unfaithful, he could not make himself understood. He rose up early in the morning to escape from the house before his wife could ask any questions, for how could he ever bring himself to say to her, "Excuse me, Sarah, but I have to go away to sacrifice Isaac, our son"? What good would words do? So in the early dusk he saddled his ass, took two servants and his son, gathered a supply of wood, stored some live coals in a pot, and equipped himself with a *knife!* That knife must have been the last straw. There was no sudden, hasty impulse in this venture, for he was three whole days plodding along afoot toward the land of Moriah; and when he saw the mountain, he left the two men and the ass, while he and Isaac proceeded alone up the mountain *"to worship."* How outside of it all those two men were who stayed behind!

Naturally Isaac himself began to be curious about the mysterious proceedings. There was the wood and the fire and the *knife,* but where was the lamb for the burnt offering? "God will provide"—that was all he could learn from this silent father. Finally they reached the place, and Abraham built stones into an altar—every stone with a heartache—and he laid on the wood, and he bound his beloved son on the pile, and *lifted up the knife.* In that upraised hand the last limit of self-renunciation was expressed; and just at that moment a voice said, "Lay not thine hand upon the lad, . . . for now I know that thou fearest God, seeing thou hast not withheld thy son." Nearby he saw a ram caught by his horns in a thicket, an unforeseen substitute for his son (Gen. 22:1-13).

These ancient stories of the Bible are without equal for dramatizing even to modern minds the mysteries of spiritual conflict which can hardly be defined in words.

Kierkegaard, whose thought has now after one hundred years regained wide attention, wrote his book *Fear and Trembling* on the theme of Abraham's faith and fear. In a similar crisis of his own life the Danish thinker perceived in the old story meanings which became real in the depth of his own suffering. His crisis occurred when the woman he loved became engaged to another man, and Kierkegaard, dreading lest his disappointment mar the happiness of the one he loved, made himself out to be unworthy of her. At that outermost reach of self-renunciation, with its seeming contradiction of moral principles, he saw the finality of the fear to be unfaithful, which has no other

earnestly meaning to do right, and God, recognizing their pure intentions, will lend them his aid. But whenever Paul speaks of "good will," he has in his mind the gracious purpose, the **good pleasure,** of God. It is his will that men should be saved, and what we must rely on is not our own deserving or poor endeavor but this redeeming will of God.

---

fear. One could go on alone with that, leaving the disclosure of the unexpected to God. Sometimes the unexpected may be the beginning of some far-reaching change in the earthly condition; sometimes it may be a unique turn in individual fortune; sometimes it may be, as with Christ, a deepening of that union between the soul and God, which is the chief end of man. In any case, the one thing needful is to go out of self, not knowing where the faith will lead, obeying and trusting, which is "safer than any known way."

(c) In a secularized age it is peculiarly hard for people to understand the unconditional quality of this fear to be unfaithful. We are habituated to judging everything by practical results, which is always a necessary judgment, for without it all practical strategy would break down into futility. However, the final faithfulness we have been describing precedes results. It comes first in order (at the "beginning"), and results come second, in time. The very greatness of this devotion is attested by its lack of all calculation. It is absolute, requiring no reason outside itself. No human relation can be compared with this ultimate relation of the creature to the Creator—it is in a class all by itself. At this point man encounters a claim that cuts across all human wishes. Sometimes the surest proof of what God wants is that self does not want to do it.

Incidentally, one common difficulty must be faced before going further. How can we do effectively what we do not feel like doing? Obedience that is forever against the grain proves reluctant and short lived. One can hardly imagine people like Christ or Paul, or any heroic souls, surrendering self in sacrificial action without feeling like it. In the last analysis we have to do what we feel like, or the power and drive of emotion is not behind our act. This means simply that not only our minds and wills, but our feelings also, need to be trained or developed. Some feelings must be subordinated, restrained, and harnessed to a better purpose, or sublimated into feelings of a higher kind. One might feel like exploring the contents of a tank of gasoline with a lighted match, but the end would be the abolition of all feelings whatsoever. According to Paul's view, the kind of faith that surrenders all in faithfulness to God is a consuming passion that gathers into itself a man's whole nature, mind, will, and feelings. It is often necessary to act, give oneself

away, before one's emotional nature is constrained by the new devotion. God is the author of this magnificent constraint; and our part is the self-renunciation, which is most often against our inclinations. One might say that as self moves out, the spirit of God moves in— as a gift, to create in us a new life altogether. But that is not an accurate description, because life shows no such clear division between our action and the action of God. Surely the constraint which reaches us from God through the company of faithful people works in and through the effort required to renounce self.

This analysis of a familiar difficulty serves to emphasize the nature of faithfulness which requires complete commitment before any results can be calculated. The mothers who have won our lasting loyalty did not know how their care for us would turn out. They persisted even when it turned out badly. So it is with all the heroes we hold in reverence. Though we look back at them now with the results of their sacrifice before us, they had to act in the dark, so to speak, before the verdict of history had been turned in.

In the case of Christ himself we are apt to measure his greatness by the amazing effect of that one lowly life that set all history on a new road. But he saw so little effect that he cried out in his agony, "My God, my God, why hast thou forsaken me?" (Matt. 27:46.) He had previously countered his own doubts with the words "Yet not what I will, but what thou wilt" (Mark 14:36). To view that total surrender in the light of its influence through twenty centuries is to see only half of the picture. The danger is that we find ourselves admiring the reputation of a man who lived long ago, who paid a price we never intend to pay; and we end in a fruitless sentimentality instead of in a costly commitment of will.

The whole discussion has been elaborated at some length because the battle for God in every generation centers in this distinction between the fear of God and the fear of man. Which of these two fears shall be put at the top of our list of preferences remains at every moment a life-and-death decision.

The decisiveness of this order of preference is relatively clear in the individual's life, but becomes more obscure in the complexities of social life. Every individual has a scale of values which reveals itself not so much in his words as in his choices. Everything depends on what

| 14 Do all things without murmurings and disputings: | 14 Do all things without grumbling or |
|---|---|

**14-15.** Paul therefore exhorts his readers to put forth their best effort, knowing that God himself is with them. **Do all things without grumbling or questioning.** It is evident from the words which follow that he is thinking of the Israelites in the wilderness, who so often missed God's help because they refused to trust him. They murmured against him openly and doubted him in their hearts. Paul tells the Philippians that they must have in them the spirit of simple obedience: **that you may be blameless and innocent** [literally "unmixed," right actions arising from right motives], **children of God without blemish in the midst of a crooked and perverse generation.** These words are suggested by the farewell song of Moses, in which he laments the errors of the people he had been

---

choice is at the top of the list. On the one hand, when first place is given to prosperity, safety, and self-satisfaction, integrity and the fear to be unfaithful will still have their claim recognized, but only when it suits our purpose and does not get in the way of what we want most. We will not be very conscious of the subordination because our dominant interest can always persuade reason to justify it; and so long as we still hold integrity as an ideal, we persuade ourselves that possessing an ideal is the same thing as living up to it. Almost everyone thinks that his ideals determine his conduct, while his interest may be subtly persuading him to betray the ideal. In making a living where we deal with investments, income taxes, business operations, and labor relations, are our attitudes affected more by our ideals or our income? Which will sway our decision more?

On the other hand, if integrity really has the dominant claim, the fear for self will be in second place, and the enjoyment of being utterly faithful in everything we do (as unto God and not men) will ordinarily bring what is best for our interest without our giving it much thought. *Ordinarily*—but by no means always. In a sinful society the faithful are often the victims of the predatory. Individuals cannot be made safe separately when the social life on which they depend is ordered according to the jungle principle of the survival of the fittest to devour. There is no escape from social responsibility in the endless battle to change the outside order so that the inside worth of every man may have a better chance. We were created, for better or worse, to be together, and to take the consequences of each other's lives. The question is: Whose soul is more fit to survive the struggle and contribute to its true end—the man who is dominated by fears for self, or the man who fears to be unfaithful, regardless of all that scares the rest of us?

**14-16.** *Children of God Without Blemish.*— What does it mean to be blameless children of God in a crooked and perverse generation?

To take that problem out of the environment of the first Christians and relate it afresh to the Christian's predicament in the present generation is the sternest duty laid upon a modern interpreter of our faith. Paul was looking for the end of the world in the near future, and was not envisaging the intensification of social problems through centuries of "progress" on this earth. The converts at Philippi, who were to work out their own salvation "with fear and trembling," had no way of participating in the policies of the government of their Roman overlords, or of sharing in what we call political and social change. To survive as a tiny community of a new religious sect in an overwhelming sea of paganism was their trial, and they met it well, so that we inherit today the faith they defended.

Now, we must understand what it implies to be a "blameless" Christian in the midst of a modern paganism that is just as crooked and just as perverse as anything the Philippians faced.

It might appear, on first reading Paul's admonitions, that he had slipped back into his old Pharisaism, bidding his friends to be more righteous than other men; but the context and the apostle's whole point of view should clear him of this charge (see Expos. on 3:17).

According to Paul, Christians are to avoid blame, and furnish light amid darkness by **holding fast the word of life.** This "word" is the gospel's message to the self-centered nature of man, with its continuous need of judgment and of transformation into a new life. The crookedness and perversity of our generation have come very largely from losing hold of this profound insight, and substituting for it what seem to be more cheerful and confident views of man. In the fight for freedom, ever since the French Revolution, earnest thinkers have tried to find answers outside our religious tradition.

One foremost source of error has been a widespread and almost unconscious belief that

**15** That ye may be blameless and harmless, the sons of God, without rebuke, in the midst of a crooked and perverse nation,

**15** that you may be blameless and innocent, children of God without questioning,

---

leading. "They have corrupted themselves, their spot is not the spot of his children: they are a perverse and crooked generation" (Deut. 32:5). Paul hopes that the opposite may hold true of the Philippian Christians. Living in a corrupt heathen society they are to stand out as God's children, showing by their lives to the people around them that

---

natural self-interest can be made so farsighted that it will be sufficient to achieve a united, harmonious society. Somehow if men could only see that the common interest is the best interest of each, the brotherhood of man would follow as day follows night.

The fallacy of such an assumption appears when we examine a statement of pure secularism that explains everything in terms of self-interest pursuing happiness. A bold exposition of this view can be found in the writings of an eighteenth-century philosopher, Helvetius, who feared that the freedom sought by the revolution was being sold out to tyranny. "Corporeal sensibility is . . . the sole mover of man, he is consequently susceptible . . . of two sorts of pleasures and pains, the one are present bodily pains and pleasures, the other are the pains and pleasures of foresight or memory." Helvetius would bemoan the loss of a friend, who "exposed his life and fortune to save one from sorrow and destruction," only because the friend would no longer be present to "help relieve his disquietude and the disagreeable sensations of the soul." Other people seemed to exist to preserve his happiness. No doubt Helvetius, like all unconscious hedonists, had "moments of grace," when the memory of such self-giving friends would shame his selfishness and permit the self-giving spirit in their lives to take over the control of his will and make him a better man than his theory.

Helvetius shows the dangerous conclusion of this gratification of desire when it leads him to an *interest in power*. Every modern man who trusts a self-interest which fears men alone has been caught in the same deception.

It is because I esteem power as the most sure means of increasing my happiness. . . . Men love themselves: they all desire to be happy, and think their happiness would be complete, if they were invested with a degree of power sufficient to procure them every sort of pleasure.[6]

Words so complacently uttered in the eighteenth century show us how the catastrophic rise of the will to power in our time was completely unforeseen. We are reminded of the ugliness which has come into our social life when man fears only for himself. In the light of the trend that emerged from this way of thinking, we need to reread Machiavelli's *The Prince* to see how man actually deals with his fellows when only the fear of man is his guide.

The argument runs as follows: Man is like an animal. He must be governed for his own good by force and fear. Since law is insufficient, force must be used as with a beast. The leader must be clever like a fox to recognize traps, and strong like a lion to scare lesser brutes. No one need keep faith against his interest, because others are bad and will not keep faith. The state must always act as though all men were animals ready to display their vicious nature.

Such a condensation of *The Prince* pretty well describes our **crooked and perverse generation**. The truth is that human nature works just this way—when we fail to reckon with the Christian view that our self-centeredness was designed to be under judgment and then transformed continuously into a new nature which subordinates the fear of man to the fear of God.

A second source of our error and confusion springs from too great trust in *understanding* as a means for controlling the dangers of self-interest. A representative of this misconception is Jean Condorcet, one of the leading political figures of the French Revolution, and an apostle of the optimistic age of the Enlightenment. He had no use for Christianity, and put his trust in reason. Science and reason would together save mankind. Despite the fact that his colleagues in the revolution, against all reason, became tyrants and sent him to the guillotine, nevertheless, while waiting for his execution he wrote his famous dissertation on *The Progress of the Human Mind*. After reviewing the long progress of man from the Stone Age, he says,

Man . . . is a being . . . capable of reasoning upon and understanding his interests, and of acquiring moral ideas. . . . Do not all the observations . . . prove, that the moral goodness of man . . . is, like all his other faculties, susceptible of an indefinite improvement?[7]

---

[6] Claude Adrian Helvetius, *Treatise on Man* (tr. D. I. Eaton; London: Albion Press, 1810), I, 124-30.

[7] *Introduction to Contemporary Civilization of the West* (New York: Columbia University Press, 1946), I, 864, 874.

| among whom ye shine as lights in the world; | blemish in the midst of a crooked and perverse generation, among whom you shine |

they belong to God. This is a favorite thought of Paul—that Christian men are the best evidence of the truth of the Christian religion. He illustrates it by a fine image, **among whom you shine as lights in the world.** The word he uses means "light-givers," and his thought may be simply that every Christian carries a lantern by which others may be guided. But the Greek word is one which is always applied to the heavenly bodies, and

---

In other words, as we go on understanding more and more, trusting more and more science, we shall be infinitely better in the future. All fear for self in the face of our fear of man will be cured by *understanding*. After all we have endured from increased knowledge, a leading psychiatrist has been led to observe in a magazine article:

Many . . . serious scientists [and we are all sitting at their feet today] really believe that greater intellectual understanding of life and living will make people *better*. . . . To understand means to be good.[8]

One needs only to reread ch. 2 of Paul's letter to the Romans to see how surely he recognized the tragic gap between knowing and doing.

Another crooked trend in our thinking was illustrated in the American Revolution by Alexander Hamilton, before the Constitution was adopted. While Jefferson tended toward Condorcet's optimism about the individual man in freedom, Hamilton feared any easy trust in the people. In forming a government, "*every man* ought to be supposed a *knave;* and to have no other end, in all his actions, but *private interests.*"[9] Orthodoxy never laid a stronger emphasis on the sinful self-centeredness of man as opposed to all literal belief in man's natural goodness.

Thus in America began the struggle between fear of the people and fear of government, which is the eternal fight for freedom everywhere on earth. With Hamilton the question was, Whose self-interest was least reliable?

All communities divide themselves into the few and the many. . . . The first are the rich and well born, the other the mass of the people. . . . The people are turbulent and changing. . . . Give, therefore, to the first class a distinct, permanent share in the government. They will check the unsteadiness of the second; and as they cannot receive any advantage by a change, they therefore will ever maintain good government.[1]

[8] Gregory Zilboorg, "Psychoanalysis and Religion," *Atlantic Monthly,* CLXXXIII (1949), 49.
[9] Quoted in V. L. Parrington, *Main Currents in American Thought* (New York: Harcourt, Brace & Co., 1927), I, 298.
[1] *Ibid.,* I, 302.

The chief executive, in his opinion, should "have so much power that it will not be his interest to risk much to acquire more."

This notion that self-interest would be good, provided it was rich enough and powerful enough, did not originate with Hamilton nor end with him. It has been a growing curse in the entire world, blessed by Nietzsche and cherished by all totalitarian tyrannies. The twentieth century has been a hideous tale of the corruption of self-interest by power.

Another variation in our crooked thinking can be seen in the person of Herbert Spencer, who felt we could be saved by applying to man the same scientific procedure which proved so fruitful in dealing with nature. This view was another version of the idea that mere scientific understanding can make men better.

All the various perversities in these secular views of human nature and its control bore fruit in the political systems which have arisen in opposition to Western democracy. One of them distrusted moral values from the start, made the interest of the state absolute, trusted in an elite class that held the common man in contempt (fit only to be an instrument of the elite), and ended with the master race which was to save the world by its power. The other traced the source of evil not to the corruptions of egoism, but to the institution of private property which divided society into warring classes. The fear of a propertied minority was the final fear. To abolish an evil institution that made men sinful, to create a classless society that should possess the common wealth, would bring a utopia of harmony in which there would be no fear of government, because all government would cease to be needed. A temporary dictatorship would be a mere fly in the utopian ointment during the transition period.

That the corruptions of power would develop as they did in these rival political systems should have been recognized as a foregone conclusion, for the fatal development has been the direct outgrowth of the crooked ideas that have circulated so long in all our unsuspecting minds. Since we were not prepared to believe that the self-interest of man, unredeemed by the spirit of God, was capable of such ruthless and hellish brutality, the menace caught us

16 Holding forth the word of life; that I may rejoice in the day of Christ, that I have not run in vain, neither labored in vain.

17 Yea, and if I be offered upon the sacrifice and service of your faith, I joy, and rejoice with you all.

as lights in the world, 16 holding fast the word of life, so that in the day of Christ I may be proud that I did not run in vain or labor in vain. 17 Even if I am to be poured as a libation upon the sacrificial offering of your faith, I am glad and rejoice with you

---

Paul doubtless intends it in this sense. Christians are children of God, and the light they diffuse is from a heavenly source, like that of the stars. Looking on them men become conscious of a higher world, since in this one they are living in the spirit of Christ.

**16.** This thought is carried out in the next words, **holding forth the word of life,** i.e., making their actions a constant proclamation of the message which brings a new life to those who receive it. Into this appeal for conduct worthy of the gospel Paul throws the personal note which is the special charm of this epistle. He loves the Philippians and knows their deep affection for him. He is aware that now while he lies in prison, it may be at the point of death, their hearts are with him as never before. So he calls on them to be steadfast in their faith **so that in the day of Christ I may be proud that I did not run in vain or labor in vain.** He thinks of the coming day when Christ will make his awards to his servants, like the master of the games at the close of a strenuous race. What place will be assigned to him Paul cannot tell, but he can at least be sure, if his Philippians remain steadfast, that he will not be disgraced. He will have proof to show that he ran well, and that his hard training had not been wasted.

**17-18.** Then the thought comes to him that he will not live to see that day of Christ's return, for which he had looked so ardently; and the image of the race is merged in a

---

unawares. We are not yet fully conscious that the things we hate in systems opposed to our own arise from the thoughts we have helped spread through the earth; and we are still using the sins of our opponents to blind us to what is wrong with ourselves.

A telling and positive illustration of how we must guard ourselves against the persistent perversity of human nature can be found in the political thought of James Madison, whose influence was peculiarly potent in framing the Constitution of his country.

> If men were angels, no government would be necessary. If angels were to govern men, neither external nor internal controls on government would be necessary. In framing a government which is to be administered by men over men, the great difficulty lies in this: you must first enable the government to control the governed; and in the next place oblige it to control itself.[2]

Madison saw that society would always be a conflict of interests, corruptible by power, and that government's task was to arrange checks and balances that would help hold the self-interest of parties in the direction of the public good, constantly correcting inordinate forms of power wherever they threatened to arise. There

was to be no end to this battle with human self-interests.

> Wherever the real power in a Government lies, there is the danger of oppression. . . . This is a truth of great importance. . . . Wherever there is an interest and power to do wrong, wrong will generally be done.[3]

Thus the Christian view of human self-interest (the **word of life**), is brought to bear on practical strategy to supply the "eternal vigilance" which is the price of liberty.

This rather extended dissertation in the relations of a Christian to the crookedness of the generation of which he is a part is based on quotations selected by two teachers in the secular fields of history and English. The selection is significant because it shows how much material for real religious understanding is available to any alert teacher in the interpretation of great literature and in the analysis of human events. Much preaching would gain in depth and relevance to current life if ministers could draw fresh insights from these sources which the younger generations of teachers are beginning to exploit.

**17-18. Be Glad and Rejoice.**—Seeing, as we do now from a long perspective, what happens

---

[2] James Madison, *The Federalist*, No. 51, February 8, 1788. Quoted by Carl Van Doren, *The Great Rehearsal* (New York: Viking Press, 1948), p. 51.

[3] Quoted in C. A. Beard, *An Economic Interpretation of the Constitution of the United States* (New York: The Macmillan Co., 1935), p. 158 n.

18 For the same cause also do ye joy, and rejoice with me.

19 But I trust in the Lord Jesus to send Timotheus shortly unto you, that I also may be of good comfort, when I know your state.

20 For I have no man likeminded, who will naturally care for your state.

all. 18 Likewise you also should be glad and rejoice with me.

19 I hope in the Lord Jesus to send Timothy to you soon, so that I may be cheered by news of you. 20 I have no one like him, who will be genuinely anxious for your

---

more solemn one. **Even if I am to be poured as a libation upon the sacrificial offering of your faith:** The idea is that of a priestly ceremony in which a victim is laid on the altar and the sacred rites are duly performed; by way of a final consecration a drink offering is poured out. The faith of the Philippians is conceived of as the sacrifice they are making to God. They have performed all the preliminary service but something more is needed to make the offering complete. This is the libation, which will consist of Paul's own life-blood; and he will not grudge it. On the contrary, **I am glad and rejoice with you all.** They will have the gladness of knowing that their sacrifice is a perfect one, and they must not grieve because it has cost him his life. He is glad to feel that he will make their sacrifice acceptable, and as he rejoices with them, **likewise** [they] **also should be glad and rejoice with** [him].

### IV. The Sending of Timothy and Epaphroditus (2:19-30)

The letter has now taken a personal turn, and Paul speaks in detail of the arrangements he is making for the church at Philippi. He would fain come himself, but as yet this cannot be; so he is sending two trusted assistants to represent him, both of them as dear to the Philippians as they are to him. In a way this is the central part of the epistle, though it is concerned only with personalities and not with religious principles. Paul writes the letter in order to prepare the way for these delegates, and he wishes to impress on his readers that they will act with his full authority. From the fact that he so commissions them, we can gather that he takes a very serious view of the situation at Philippi. This is the church he loves best, and he is immensely proud of it, but he feels that it is in danger, and that something must be done to set things right before the mischief has gone too far. The whole epistle must be read against the background of this anxiety for the Philippians which is mingled with his affection for them.

**19-20. I hope in the Lord Jesus** [i.e., if the Lord favors my plans] **to send Timothy to you soon.** Timothy had been one of Paul's companions on his first visit to Philippi (cf. Acts 16:1 ff.) and had gone there in advance of him when he paid his second visit (I Cor. 16:10). He was thus well known to the church, and had endeared himself to all its members by his personal qualities as well as by his close association with Paul. If the apostle could not go himself, he could find no better substitute. He refrains from stating his full reason for this mission of Timothy and puts it on the general ground **that I may be cheered by news of you.** He had sent them news of himself to relieve their anxiety, and from Timothy's visit he expects a report which will put his own mind at rest. But more must be implied than appears on the surface. By many channels Paul might have got word from Philippi which would assure him that his friends were well and that the church was flourishing. If he sent a special messenger, it must have been for a special

---

to men when they lose hold of the "word of life" in the gospel, we can well understand how the apostle was ready to have his life **poured as a libation** in sacrificial offering to make this life-view known for the first time in history. If it was his lot to "complete what remains of Christ's afflictions" (Col. 1:24), he had learned in whatsoever state he was "therewith to be

content," and he could say to his friends: **I am glad and rejoice with you all. Likewise you also should be glad and rejoice with me.**

**19-30. The Sending of Timothy and Epaphroditus.**—In this section of ch. 2 we come to the main purpose of Paul's letter. He is writing to pave the way for two of his most trusted friends to exert an influence on the troubled relations

21 For all seek their own, not the things which are Jesus Christ's.

22 But ye know the proof of him, that, as a son with the father, he hath served with me in the gospel.

23 Him therefore I hope to send presently, so soon as I shall see how it will go with me.

24 But I trust in the Lord that I also myself shall come shortly.

welfare. 21 They all look after their own interests, not those of Jesus Christ. 22 But Timothy's worth you know, how as a son with a father he has served with me in the gospel. 23 I hope therefore to send him just as soon as I see how it will go with me; 24 and I trust in the Lord that shortly I myself shall come also.

---

purpose—to make inquiries about matters which were not apparent on the outside and yet were highly important. For this object he has chosen Timothy, for he has no one "equally minded." This may mean "of the same disposition as Timothy," but more likely Paul is comparing Timothy with himself: there is no one who sees eye to eye with Paul as Timothy does. **Who will be genuinely anxious for your welfare:** The word for **genuinely** is one that suggests kinship (thus KJV **naturally**) and might be translated "like a brother." Timothy will look into all their troubles with genuine sympathy and understanding.

21. Paul says that he has no one else, meaning that among his present associates Timothy is the only one he can rely on, for **they all look after their own interests, not those of Jesus Christ.** This is the only word of complaint in the whole letter, and it comes strangely from Paul, who always speaks generously of his fellow workers. In the previous chapter he has acknowledged his debt even to these who preached the gospel with a desire to injure and discredit him. It may be that under the long strain of imprisonment he was growing disheartened, and had begun to feel like Elijah, "I only, am left." Or perhaps the Roman Christians, without intending it, had made him realize that he was not one of them. They were wrapped up in the welfare of their own church, and cared little, in his judgment, for the Christian cause at large. In many good Christians of all times the missionary spirit has been sadly lacking. We can gather from the verse that when he wrote, Paul's old comrades, with the one exception of Timothy, were not with him; and this alone would seem to be sufficient evidence that he was not in Ephesus, where he was the center of a devoted band of helpers (see Intro., pp. 5-7).

22-24. With regard to Timothy he can say confidently **ye know the proof of him.** The word (δοκιμή) was used of gold and silver which had been tested and could be accepted as current coin. He reminds the Philippians that they themselves had tested Timothy, and that he had rung true every time. **How as a son with a father he has served with me in the gospel:** In the opening salutation he had described himself and Timothy as "slaves" of Christ, and here he repeats the same idea, except that now he makes it clear that Timothy worked under him, though his service was a willing one, like that of a son helping his father. **I hope therefore to send him just as soon as I can see how it will go with me:** Paul indicates that just at present all his plans must be vague. He could not tell when his trial might come on; his health was precarious, and he had undertaken what

---

in the Philippian church, and what he says carries a universal significance: the power from God which alone can redeem men from divisive selfishness and create unity can be transmitted alive only through human personality. Everything in Christianity was first and best expressed in this world through the deeds of an utterly surrendered life.

The world cannot be saved by talk, not even talk about the most perfect ideals, nor can people be finally changed and moved by reason-

ing, however persuasive, except as the reasoning comes from some person whose life is itself a persuasion. Sinful humanity is not corrected by advice, save as the advice comes from one whose winning power is felt before his words are heard. Religious principles, moral ideals, theological beliefs, written and spoken words, all have their place; but all power that remakes persons must be conveyed alive through a human personality. That is the meaning of the Incarnation: saving power from God, unlike

25 Yet I supposed it necessary to send to you Epaphroditus, my brother, and companion in labor, and fellow soldier, but your messenger, and he that ministered to my wants.

25 I have thought it necessary to send to you Epaphrodi′tus my brother and fellow worker and fellow soldier, and your

---

work he could in connection with the local church. Time was needed for careful consideration—the word he uses (ἀφίδω) means literally "to look away," i.e., to exclude everything else and concentrate on the one matter. When he has satisfied himself that he can dispense with Timothy, he will send him at once. **I trust in the Lord,** he adds, **that shortly I myself shall come also.** He can only promise this provisionally, for his future lies in the Lord's hands. Perhaps he makes the promise more to encourage the Philippians than with any hope that he will be able to fulfill it. The sending of Timothy was itself a confession that there was little prospect of his ever coming in his own person.

**25.** Timothy might not arrive for some time, but meanwhile Paul sends a deputy who will be with them right away, bringing with him this epistle. **I supposed** [better, "considered"] **it necessary,** or rather, "I *do* consider it." In ancient letters it was customary to use the past tense where we would use the present. The writer put himself in the position of the reader, for whom his present thoughts and doings would be matters of the past. Paul deems it necessary, then, **to send to you Epaphroditus.** This was the man, as we learn later (4:18), who had conveyed a gift of money from the Philippian church. His name was a longer form of Epaphras, and in the Epistle to the Colossians we hear of a man so named who also had occasion to visit Paul in his imprisonment. It is a natural conjecture that the same man is intended in both epistles; but this is hardly possible. Epaphras was the founder of the church at Colossae, and all his interests were there. Epaphroditus was one of the leading men of the Philippian church, and was so much identified with it that he had been chosen for a highly responsible task. The name, in both its forms, was not uncommon, and two men who were both prominent in the Gentile mission may quite probably have borne it.

The Philippians had evidently sent Epaphroditus not merely to carry their gift, but to stay with Paul in his captivity and to assist him in every way he could. Paul speaks of him as representing them. They would all have liked to be near their apostle, and in the one man he was to see the whole church. He is lavish in his praise of Epaphroditus, describing him as **my brother and fellow worker and fellow soldier**—not only a Christian like himself, but one who had labored for the cause and suffered for it. "Soldiers of Christ" was one of the favorite names assumed by the early Christians, and it carried with it the suggestion of fighting for Christ in face of the enmity and persecution of the heathen world. We know nothing of any occasion on which Epaphroditus had fought by Paul's side in one of his many battles. It may have been when he was in danger at Philippi, or more recently during some conflict at Rome. He speaks of him also as **your messenger and minister to my need.** The first word is literally "your apostle," though it is obviously used in its original sense of messenger. It is significant, however, that Paul chooses the word which had a special meaning to Christian ears. This man had been "sent out," in the service not only of the Philippian church, but of Christ himself. **Minister to my need** is also meant to have a wider reference. Epaphroditus had come to relieve Paul in his financial need, but he had also helped him by his counsel and sympathy and companionship.

---

the powers of nature, is revealed and activated through the channel of personality. Timothy and Epaphroditus were sent by Paul to implement the gospel in Philippi.

Making biographical messages from sketchy materials left us concerning biblical characters

is to be carefully guarded. Too much imagination is often used to read into faraway persons more than we really know. Just because they are characters who are mentioned in the Bible may not today commend them as the most effective examples. It is often better to take such **hints**

26 For he longed after you all, and was full of heaviness, because that ye had heard that he had been sick.

27 For indeed he was sick nigh unto death: but God had mercy on him; and not on him only, but on me also, lest I should have sorrow upon sorrow.

28 I sent him therefore the more carefully, that, when ye see him again, ye may rejoice, and that I may be the less sorrowful.

29 Receive him therefore in the Lord with all gladness; and hold such in reputation:

messenger and minister to my need, 26 for he has been longing for you all, and has been distressed because you heard that he was ill. 27 Indeed he was ill, near to death. But God had mercy on him, and not only on him but on me also, lest I should have sorrow upon sorrow. 28 I am the more eager to send him, therefore, that you may rejoice at seeing him again, and that I may be less anxious. 29 So receive him in the Lord with all joy; and

**26.** Paul now proceeds to tell why he is sending back this associate whom he valued so highly. **For he has been longing for you all, and has been distressed because you heard that he was ill.** His illness had been followed by a depression of spirits, aggravated by the news that his Philippian friends were all anxious about him. This account of why Epaphroditus was going back is by no means satisfactory. If he had been ill some months before—for there had been time for messages to pass to Philippi and back—he was presumably well again. A fit of homesickness, moreover, was not sufficient excuse for leaving the post which had been assigned to him; and Paul was the last man who would tolerate such an excuse. We know from the book of Acts how he regarded Mark's desertion, apparently for a similar reason (Acts 13:13; 15:37-39). It might seem almost as if he was tired of Ephaphroditus, and was glad of any pretext to get rid of him; but we cannot doubt from the whole tenor of the passage that he had a real affection for the man, and made a sacrifice in letting him go. Behind the reason he states he probably had another, which he does not care to mention explicitly. He has some doubt as to how things are going at Philippi. As soon as possible he is to send Timothy to inquire into conditions there. Meanwhile he sends Epaphroditus, out of this same concern. He feels that this trusted worker in the Philippian church is needed at home, where things had been going wrong for the want of a guiding hand.

**27-28.** He prefers, however, to lay all the stress on the health of Epaphroditus, which requires that he should be back among his friends. For **indeed he was ill, near to death. But God had mercy on him, and not only on him but on me also.** He makes it clear in this delicate way that he would gladly have kept Epaphroditus. He had come to love the man, and his death would have added a grief to the many he was bearing, so that his recovery had been a special mercy to him. Vs. 28 means: "I send him therefore much earlier than I meant, that seeing him you may get back your joy, and that I also may be less grieved." His appearance would ease the minds of the Philippians, and Paul also would be freed from an anxiety when he was no longer responsible for detaining a sick man. It may be that he is trying to forestall any ill-natured criticisms of Epaphroditus for returning so much sooner than he was expected. He had indeed been seriously ill, and the Philippians had cause to be thankful that they saw him again.

**29-30.** Paul dwells on this note, and impresses on them that they must welcome their messenger. **Receive him in the Lord** [i.e., as a true servant of Christ] **with all joy; and honor such men.** He wishes that Epaphroditus should not only be welcomed, but treated

as are given as to vital qualities of character and illustrate them in lives more familiar to the modern mind. The worth of good co-operators and fellow workers is marked, as in these men, by genuine anxiety for others in forgetfulness of private interests, by ability to work with a superior as a son with a father, by complete sharing of hardships, by capacity to be distressed by human trouble, by willingness to risk life unto death.

**30** Because for the work of Christ he was nigh unto death, not regarding his life, to supply your lack of service toward me.

**3** Finally, my brethren, rejoice in the Lord. To write the same things to you, to me indeed *is* not grievous, but for you *it is* safe.

honor such men, **30** for he nearly died for the work of Christ, risking his life to complete your service to me.

**3** Finally, my brethren, rejoice in the Lord. To write the same things to you is not irksome to me, and is safe for you.

---

with high respect. Here it is implied that weight should be attached to his counsels when he speaks of any matters that concern the church. For because of the work of Christ he **nearly died, . . . risking his life to complete** [literally, "fill up the lack in"] **your service to me.** The sentence is rather obscure, and has sometimes been taken as reproaching the Philippians for not having done enough. This would indeed have been an ungracious response to a generous gift; but Paul's meaning, which is clearer in Greek than it can be made in English, is just the opposite. He says that there was only one thing wanting in the kindness the Philippians had shown him, and that was their own presence. This was what he most desired; and since they could not give it, Epaphroditus had made up for the want. He had acted on behalf of them all, and had endangered his life in order to do so. Nothing is told us of the cause and nature of his sickness, but it was evidently the consequence of his difficult journey, or of the hardships he suffered after his arrival. He had attested his fidelity by incurring the risk of death, and Paul says that such men should be honored above all others.

This declaration was to prove a momentous one in the history of the church. The age of persecution was now opening, and Paul seemed here to sanction the principle that those who suffered martyrdom in any form were thereby vested with authority. In the century that followed, wise counsels were often overridden by the veto of a martyr, perhaps ignorant or fanatical, who was allowed the final word. This could not be foreseen by Paul, whose idea was only the natural one that the man who has suffered in a cause has more right to speak for it than those who have done nothing but acquiesce. It seems clear, however, that he wishes Epaphroditus, on the ground of his suffering, to have a prevailing voice in the counsels of the Philippian church, and that he sends him for this purpose. He cannot come himself, and Timothy's coming may be delayed. Something must be done immediately to meet a dangerous situation, and he sends Epaphroditus, fortified by this letter, to act in his stead.

### V. Paul's Apologia (3:1-21)

### A. Warning Against Judaism (3:1-3)

This third chapter, at least in its opening section, is different in character from the rest of the epistle. Paul has written hitherto in terms of warm affection. He is aware of weaknesses in the Philippian church, but touches on them gently, and is careful to avoid all appearance of rebuke. He speaks tolerantly even of those teachers in his neighborhood who are working against him. All at once he changes his tone and breaks out into angry remonstrance. The view has been held by many scholars that we have here a passage from another letter, which has strayed into the present one. It is more than likely that Paul had written on previous occasions to the Philippians, and Polyc. Phil. 3:2 expressly speaks of the "letters" from him which they possessed. A leaf from one of these lost letters might easily have found its way into the one we have.

---

**3:1-4. The Struggle of Paul with the Judaizers.** —Taking this chapter as a genuine and necessary part of the letter (see Exeg.), we can sense here a flare-up of the bitter fight with his own people which left its scars on Paul's life to the end. The gentle, winning effect of this epistle

issues from an almost fanatic nature which had been tamed and redeemed; but the old persecutor in Paul, ready to kill those who differed from him, and ever bursting with hate that was mistaken for righteousness, was never perfectly converted. This fervent soul is brought near

The subject has been dealt with in the Intro., but it may be repeated that ch. 3 connects so closely with the others that the epistle would be incomplete without it. It may be noted, too, that the whole chapter is of one piece, so that no one part of it can be detached and assigned to a different letter. The opening verses are indeed polemical, but they run without a break into the great passage in which Paul gives utterance to his personal faith, and this leads to a new plea that the Philippians also should believe in Christ and serve him. No one can doubt that ch. 4, dealing as it does with the Philippian gift of which nothing has hitherto been said, is integral to the main epistle. Ch. 3 prepares the way for ch. 4, and it is not possible at any point to draw a line of division.

**3:1.** The one real difficulty is the abrupt transition in the middle of the first verse. Paul has begun: **Finally, my brethren, rejoice in the Lord.** In the course of the letter he has spoken much of joy, and he now desires that his readers should find their true joy in Christ. The word "rejoice" was also the Greek for "farewell," and by introducing it with "finally" he shows that he has this meaning in his mind. His Christian admonition is blended with the conventional "good-by." So we might have expected the letter to close at this point, with the addition perhaps of a few greetings and affectionate words. But in the very act of saying farewell Paul starts denouncing certain enemies of whom his readers must beware. It cannot be denied that the new subject is brought in very awkwardly, but it does not follow that there is no connection with what has gone before. We are only reminded that Paul is not writing a studied essay, but a letter in which his mind moves freely. Something has occurred to him which he has overlooked, and now he hastens to set it down. It may be that he has purposely kept back one of his gravest warnings until he seems to have finished, just as in letters today the important thing is sometimes to be found in the postscript. There is some dispute as to whether the words of farewell ought not to close the previous chapter instead of beginning the new one. On the whole they are better where they stand, since the rest of the epistle is like the continuation of the farewell.

Before he closes, then, Paul repeats a warning which he had often given before. **To write the same things to you is not irksome to me, and is safe for you.** He compares himself to a schoolteacher going over the same lesson again and again; the task is a weary one but he does not mind it, since this is the only way of thoroughly grounding his pupils. According to one view, he refers to what he has written in the earlier chapters, and apologizes for ringing the changes on a few simple ideas—joy, faith, harmony. But thus far he has written only two or three pages, and they do not contain a single word of needless repetition. The reference is clearly to what he is now about to say. He is going to reiterate a warning they have often heard from him, and they must not take it amiss, for they can have no security in their Christian life until they have taken it fully to heart. He seems to imply that he has already given the warning in written form, and if so, he is reminding them of previous letters now lost. This may well be; but perhaps he is expressing himself loosely to the effect that he will put into writing what he had often said when he was present with them.

---

to us by the very fact that glimpses of his old life break through his struggle to keep himself committed to his new life "in Christ."

All the doctrines which Paul had elaborated in his letters to the Galatians and the Romans are here condensed in a deathbed declaration, so to speak, against the subtle deceitfulness and ultimate futility of a religion that puts the main emphasis on externals. It matters not whether these are external obedience to moral rules, or external observances of religious rites and traditions. The true inner life of the soul, no longer centered in self, is the creation of an act of God, even though co-operation of the human will is involved in it. With his final breath Paul combines warning and hope in his insistence that man cannot make himself righteous without ending in self-righteousness.

That the Judaizers wanted to hold Christian converts subject to the Jewish law is only of historic interest to us. It is not our conflict today, and sounds very remote to the casual reader of Paul's writing; but the history of this whole struggle in Jewish history between the spirit of the legalist and of the prophet, between those who stressed external requirements

| 2 Beware of dogs, beware of evil work- ers, beware of the concision. | 2 Look out for the dogs, look out for the evil-workers, look out for those who muti- |

---

**2.** He states at once, in the most forcible terms he can think of, the danger against which he had often warned them: **Look out for the dogs, look out for the evil-workers, look out for those who mutilate the flesh** (literally, "for the mutilation"). The three reproaches are all aimed at the same people, and are expressed differently only that they may be driven home in a manner there can be no mistaking. Paul has in mind those who are trying to seduce the Christians into a Jewish type of religion. Each of the terms applied to them carries several meanings. The first one may be suggested by the familiar notice, *Cave canem,* set up to caution the wayfarer against a dangerous dog. But no doubt Paul thinks of the opprobrious term by which the Jews spoke of the heathen, indicating that they were hardly to be regarded as human beings. Perhaps it had a special reference to their eating everything, like dogs at a garbage heap, without any discrimination of clean and unclean meats. Paul turns the contemptuous name against them; they are the dogs, always looking downward in their scent for mere rubbish. He calls them also **evil workers,** again with a twofold suggestion. They are intent solely on the futile works enjoined by their law; they are mischief-makers, and in this work they are incessantly active. Our word "busybodies" serves to bring out something of the idea. Lastly he describes them by making a bitter pun on the Greek word for circumcision—just as he does in Gal. 5:12. Their sacred rite is nothing but a mutilation of the body, and can have no spiritual value whatever.

The violent language of the verse is certainly out of keeping with anything else in the epistle, and this is one of the chief reasons put forward for assigning the whole passage to a different letter. It is assumed that Paul here attacks the Judaistic party in the church, much as he had done in Galatians and somewhat less vehemently in Romans. The verses therefore must belong to the period when the Judaistic controversy was at its height, and if integral to the present epistle, must be taken as evidence that Paul wrote from Ephesus, about the time when he was engaged on those other epistles. Otherwise it must be detached from a letter in which his chief aim was to reconcile all contending parties.

But it is a pure conjecture that his attack is directed against the Jewish Christians. All that he says has reference to Jews as distinct from Christians. His argument hinges on the conviction that in Jewish ritualism there is no place for Christ, and that those who cling to it are intent on destroying the Christian faith. The Judaizers, who had sought to combine the law with the gospel, had now ceased, apparently, to be a serious menace. For that matter, they had never caused much trouble at Philippi, for Paul rejoices that this church has remained faithful to him from the very first. Probably at Rome there were not a few who leaned to the Judaistic side, and they may have been among those who were hostile to Paul, although he freely acknowledges that they "proclaim Christ" (1:17). The

---

and those who focused on the internal transformation of human nature, has become a classic illustration of the eternal human conflict between legalism and the power of an inner spirit. The one has tended to kill freedom, originality, and creativeness, while the other has been the source of new life, fresh revelation, and free growth.

**2.** *Look Out for the Dogs.*—We may not know exactly what Paul meant by this epithet, but certainly our understanding of how a dog keeps on the trail of his enemy is very suggestive of the way legalism "dogs" religion to this day, bent on killing its disturbing creativeness. We have seen in our history how it dogged the

Puritans and such great leaders as Calvin, all of whom were brought up on Paul's writings. They knew that man cannot make himself righteous by will power, and they explained this inability, this flaw in the will, as corruption that entered human history with the fall of Adam. They were deeply convinced that all our human powers, including reason, were untrustworthy apart from the miracle of regeneration by the grace of God, but they clung to a truth which later generations lost sight of: that man's natural self-centeredness is only the first, never the final stage in his creation. To improve self-centeredness, educate it, and enlighten it, to make it behave by imposing restrictions upon

3 For we are the circumcision, which worship God in the spirit, and rejoice in Christ Jesus, and have no confidence in the flesh.

late the flesh. 3 For we are the true circumcision, who worship God in spirit,[e] and glory in Christ Jesus, and put no confidence

[e] Other ancient authorities read *worship by the Spirit of God.*

real enemies of Christianity were now the Jews themselves, who stood for the law and nothing but the law. Paul is aware of the mischief they are doing, not only in shaking the faith of ignorant Christians, but in exciting the Gentiles against the new message. All this must be remembered before we condemn the violence of Paul's criticism. He is not speaking of misguided friends, but of declared enemies, menacing the cause which he has at heart. At Rome they would come forward as the chief witnesses against him at his approaching trial. In Philippi, and everywhere else, they were trying to poison the minds of his converts against all he had taught them to believe.

3. Paul insists, then, that the sacred rite of Judaism is only an external one, a mere "mutilation." **For we are the circumcision,** i.e., we Christians, not only the party which

it, cannot really change its nature. However respectable, educated, and powerful self-interest becomes, it remains a corrupting and defeating factor in human life simply because it was never meant to be complete in itself.

3. *For We Are the True Circumcision, Who . . . Put No Confidence in the Flesh.*—This sentence is the key to all that Paul has to say about the gospel as a resource beyond anything man can do by his own will. Unfortunately the significance of the whole statement is concealed behind two words that make either a wrong impact or none at all upon the ordinary man of today: **circumcision** and **flesh.**

The first word has no relation to our life; but it symbolizes all *external* performances and rites which cannot be trusted as proof of a right inner life. Over against all forms of outward behavior, no matter how important they may be, Paul insists, as Jesus did, that a change in the heart and affections is all that satisfies God, and man by his own efforts cannot render this satisfaction. What is done to us to change our hearts is always something more than we can do ourselves. Such a psychological fact any modern man can recognize when he tries to force himself to love. Love is not man-made. All legalistic religion and all legalistic moralism, which emphasize external regulations and observances, are finally impotent by themselves alone to transform selfishness into unselfishness. Paul's fight against the sufficiency of any legalism that would put man's salvation largely in his own hands is still a major battle in our secular age, for many of the tragedies which have overtaken us were due to the blindness of overconfidence in the perfectibility of man by his own works.

The other word, **flesh,** means to our minds the physical body. The Greeks considered this material flesh as the source of evil, entangling

man's immortal spirit. But Paul, as a Hebrew, did not believe that sin came wholly from the body. In his commentary on Romans, C. H. Dodd suggests that **flesh** symbolizes the whole bundle of natural desires, together with our natural reason, which constitutes the self-centered personality known to our forefathers as "the natural man."[4] However, there are occasions when Paul uses **flesh** as a physical term for the material body which is morally indifferent. These two connotations should be kept distinct.

With such explanations we can take the words **put no confidence in the flesh** as a disclaimer of final trust in any purely human thought or achievement. Such a pessimistic view is distasteful to the optimistic mind which for a century or more has been trying to uphold a belief in the natural goodness of "the natural man."

Ways must be found to reinterpret this traditional mistrust of man apart from God. Human incompetence is the crucial issue of civilization, and there is no irreligious answer to it.

Certainly no one in his right mind can question the imperfection of all things human. A man of prominence once remarked that the greatest help he received from his education was contained in an oft-repeated saying of his history professor: "Nothing human is ever exactly right."

At first sight that is a very discouraging statement; for it means that most of us, nay all of us, can be quite wrong because we think we are quite right. Only a few people in our circle go wrong intentionally and like it. Whenever we think others wrong, we find that they feel they are right; and when we are accused of being wrong, we in turn are heartily sure that

[4] *Epistle of Paul to Romans,* pp. 112-13.

he himself represented, but all who have put their faith in Christ. Circumcision at the best was a poor symbol of inward consecration; and we Christians have the reality. We **worship God in spirit.** The Jews claimed to practice the true forms of worship, prescribed, according to the Scriptures, by God himself. Christians had given up the ancient forms, but believed that the Spirit was with them in their meetings, enabling them to serve God aright. Paul develops this thought in Rom. 8:26-27. It finds supreme expression in

---

we are right. The truth of the matter is that nothing human is ever exactly right.

Our inevitable imperfection is partly our fate and partly our fault. Through no fault of our own, our finite minds cannot comprehend all sides of the whole truth before we form opinions and make decisions. Finiteness itself is therefore not a sin, unless our pride tries to make our relative truth into an absolute, i.e., identical with God's truth.

Since we have to make decisions and act before all the facts are in mind, we "make a stab at it," as we say. But our judgment is always biased by our interest, and our reason tends to defend our bias because we like our interest better than the other man's. We know it better, and can never see another's point of view as clearly as our own. Likewise, the public good is very hard to distinguish from our own prosperity. Soon self-interest leads to wishful thinking that is a mixture of truth and falsehood.

In such a condition other people are needed, with their particular biased interest, to conflict with and correct us; and then, in turn, they will stand in need of similar correction.

All totalitarians in any sphere try to believe that their type of society can correct everybody without being itself subject to correction.

Liberal-minded people, especially Americans, are tempted to be cynical about trusting any group or system whatsoever. Political parties that live in glass houses deceive no one as they throw stones at each other in an election. Everybody seems to be ready to confess the sins of other people. A cynical electorate, like cynical churchmen, may take refuge in self-righteous indifference, while the less worthy elements take over the responsibility. The so-called "middle class" of people, the "bourgeoisie," have always been lulled into a complacent attitude by their relative security, becoming blind to their own shortcomings and afraid of the ruthlessness of groups who disturb the peace. Most of the revolutionary shocks which have befallen our modern world owe much of their violence to the listless conservatism of those who identified their respectable way with the way of God.

Paul's admonition against putting confidence in the natural man is in line with the biblical view of human incompetence, which is a combination of negative and positive aspects. The negative aspect is expressed in a characteristic

O.T. phrase: "My thoughts are not your thoughts, neither are your ways my ways, saith the LORD. For as the heavens are higher than the earth, so are my ways higher than your ways, and my thoughts than your thoughts" (Isa. 55:8-9). Modern thinkers express this wide separation by the word "discontinuity," which designates the complete "otherness" of God, while still admitting a certain "likeness" between the Creator and his creatures who are made in his image. The likeness is not identical with the otherness. The human mind must hold these two opposites together in order to complete its picture of man's dependence upon God.

The positive aspect is trenchantly expressed in a sentence from the book of Revelation: "For the former things have passed away. . . . Behold, I make all things new" (Rev. 21:4-5). Here is a recognition of the continuous nature of creation, forever doing a new thing, bringing new consequences out of old consequences, and realizing new possibilities, new "styles of life" where old orders have passed away. Paul experienced this truth in his conversion, and described its effect in a typical sentence: "Therefore, if any one is in Christ, he is a new creation; the old has passed away, behold, the new has come" (II Cor. 5:17).

The two aspects put together constitute a universal formula like this: Nothing we can conceive corresponds fully with the idea of the Creator, whose understanding is "unsearchable." When we admit that anything which falls short of reality must pass away, we become receptive to the eternal "promise" that new doors are still open for the Creator. From the things that pass away we can never predict the new life which may come from the future's margin of surprise. This formula is the only one known to man that is repeatedly verified by the centuries, as they speak to correct the impressions of some passing hour.

In his book *The Protestant Era* Paul Tillich calls this negative-positive formula "the Protestant principle." Over against our human judgments there is always an everlasting "No"—"my thoughts are *not* your thoughts." When we humbly and contritely admit the negation, we are met by the everlasting "Yes," with its promise of an unpredictable new thing to all who are willing. "The Protestant principle" is not identical with any form of Protestantism,

John 4:23:"The hour cometh, and now is, when the true worshippers shall worship the Father in spirit and in truth." That the Christians and not the Jews are God's people is further proved by this: that they **glory in Christ Jesus, and put no confidence in the flesh,** i.e., they trust in no outward performance of their own, but only in what God has done for them through Christ.

This for Paul is the distinctive thing in Christianity, marking it off as the true religion. Judaism, and other religions even more, build wholly on acts and privileges which are plainly of a material nature, which have nothing to do with spiritual reality, and cannot, therefore, contribute to the higher life. Christianity takes its stand on what God himself has done. Paul develops this idea all through the rest of the chapter, illustrat-

---

and brings every other "ism" under the final judgment of God. No human way can confine the freedom of God. Everywhere we need the constant protest against every Tower of Babel that pretends to be as absolute as God, so that life may be left open to everything.[5]

Interpreters of the N.T. might retranslate the biblical notion of justification in terms of this universal principle of protest. When we accept the divine judgment as ever superior to ours, life becomes like a trial where the case is never closed. When we evade the correction from above and try to close the case by our opinion, some fatal shock is bound to occur to reopen it and make way for the new, for man cannot stop creation at any point. It is told in connection with the famous Quebec cantilever bridge that a young engineer discovered a mistake in the figures estimating the strains and stresses. No one took his discovery seriously, so when the long arms of the bridge, stretching out in the air from either shore, reached that point where the human mistake was made, the bridge fell into the river. Wherever a human construction falls short of reality, reality always wins out in the long run.

A most suggestive statement of this perpetual issue of justifying human nature was made to a college class by a professor of politics. It ran something like this:

(a) If we distrust people, how can we check a government that does not serve the people?

(b) If we depend on the people, how can we control the consequences of their ignorance and special interests?

(c) If we fight for minority rights, how can we counteract those minorities that acquire inordinate power which endangers the public good?

(d) If we suppress minorities, how can we escape the inhuman practices of the police state?

(e) If we exalt the individual, how shall we handle the corruption of selfishness which threatens to disintegrate the unity of the state?

(f) If we exalt the state, how can we recognize and preserve personality when a state is too big to know the peculiar needs of individual persons?

[5] Chicago: University of Chicago Press, 1948, chs. xi and xiii.

Such an exposition of the insoluble human problem points up in concrete situations the truth that man can never justify himself. No method will be equivalent to the thought of God; and yet to a degree it may serve until it begets conditions that require a fresh revamping of the method.

The imperfect situation must constantly be kept open and fluid, whether it is in a home, a school, a business, a union, or a state. For God designed human nature to be fulfilled neither under complete freedom nor under control, but under constant remaking through sharing responsibility. No human will is good enough to be imposed on the hidden possibilities of other individuals or groups. And no victory of a country in war proves that that country is good enough to manage the affairs of the world, or of its former enemies. All remains "under God," and his correcting and renewing operation takes place where men are not separate selves but "members one of another."

In bringing up children the wise and truly religious parent knows the eternal correction that stands over his knowledge of his child's life. Children must begin with their wills under and within older wills. Then by a mixture of control and freedom they are gradually brought up, not to mere liberty, but to become responsible in their own right.

And what is it to be a responsible person, which is God's intention for all of us? He is one who is *able to respond,* on the one hand to God who has new meanings still to disclose that are not yet realized by us, and on the other hand to people who require help peculiar to their own characters. What spoils such ability to respond is "self," keeping first place where it is a trespasser, and so preventing us from the experience of being worked through, "controlled," by a will greater than our own which is concerned with the unknown worth of each and all of us.

Jesus once proclaimed this idea of human control when he said: "You know that those who are supposed to rule over the Gentiles lord it over them, and their great men exercise

4 Though I might also have confidence in the flesh. If any other man thinketh that he hath whereof he might trust in the flesh, I more:

in the flesh. 4 Though I myself have reason for confidence in the flesh also. If any other man thinks he has reason for confidence in

ing from his own experience how Christianity does really what Judaism and all other types of faith can only pretend to do. His object is to show that men are inwardly renewed by the Christian message; and he therefore takes himself as an example, since he is the one person whose inward life he can fully know.

## B. PAUL LOOKS BACK ON HIS OWN LIFE (3:4-16)

**4-6.** Paul tells first how he had been born to all the privileges of which Judaism makes so much: "Although I am one who may place confidence even in the flesh." It is easy to mock at outward advantages, such as wealth or position, when one does not have them. Paul wishes to make it clear that this cannot be the reason why he disparages

authority over them. But it shall not be so among you; but whoever would be great among you must be your servant" (Mark 10:42-43). What does it mean to be a servant of someone's human nature? It does not mean to be a lackey, a bootlicker, or even a patronizing benefactor who likes to do good provided he can keep the doing of it entirely in his own control, as if he were as wise as God, and as if God were not at work in others to induce them to care for themselves.

We serve human nature by obeying the laws of personality, just as we serve nature by obeying natural laws. We have learned in agriculture that when men have imposed their selfish wills upon the soil for private exploitation, they have brought ruin to the soil of a whole country, until the tragedy of erosion and depletion has become a national menace. The judgment of the Creator is making itself known in the threat of world famine. In the new agriculture men are answering to the laws of the soil, serving them to allow the soil to build up its fertility and productiveness. There seems to be no end to what is possible.

Such a lesson is harder to learn in the human realm because we have to start afresh with every generation. When a little child first discovers that it has a will of its own, it rebels against every command with the cry, "I don't want to." But when sent outdoors to join other children, the situation is reversed. "Now I will be the mother, and you must do what I say." Under the sweet disguise of motherly benevolence a child's will seeks to control other wills, and from the other children comes the protest, "I don't want to." From one generation to another the problem of human control is renewed. There is no solution, but a continuous creation of situations in which people are led to be responsible in some group where they feel like members one of another.

Democracy is a form of human control that accepts the fact that no single group or set of individuals can be good enough to close the case of conflicting interests. While there are groups left out of power, or new groups coming up to taste power, there will be continuous contention between the "outs" and the "ins," between the "haves" and the "have-nots." A government of the people must therefore furnish wide room for difference, experiment, contest of opinion and rivalry of interest. Imperfect as such a scheme must be, it can provide for continuous revelation through opposition and partnership. Many minds may thus appreciate more truth than can the minds of some dominant group. The controlling principle is God, who forever corrects and forever remakes.

**4-16. Paul Looks Back on His Old Life.—** Paul's description of his past life from which he was converted affords light for understanding the pertinence of the apostle's insights for today. To know what a man has reacted from is essential for interpreting his final point of view.

Paul's training at home and in the school of the Pharisees prepared him to be an extremist in his devotion to a legalistic religion. All through the O.T. the prophetic strain in Judaism was in tension with the legalistic; but the legalistic had the predominant place in Paul's day. Much that is associated with Paul came from this pre-Christian heritage, and should be distinguished from his Christian convictions, for it was the raw material to be transformed by his religious conversion.

Paul the apostle was a Pharisee *made over*, but with some of the elements of his original character and some of his points of view carried into his new life without much modification. Many ideas of the first century current among the Jewish people no longer appeal to the minds of our generation, but they were the

5 Circumcised the eighth day, of the stock of Israel, *of* the tribe of Benjamin, a Hebrew of the Hebrews; as touching the law, a Pharisee;

the flesh, I have more: 5 circumcised on the eighth day, of the people of Israel, of the tribe of Benjamin, a Hebrew born of He-

---

Judaism. He had possessed in the fullest measure all the benefits which it estimates so highly. **If any other man thinks he has reason for confidence in the flesh, I have more.** He, of all men, has the right to boast of every hereditary title to God's favor. In two other passages in his epistles he speaks of his high standing as a Jew in much the same terms as he does here, although with different motives. His aim in Rom. 11:1 is to assure his countrymen that as a Jew himself he is in heartfelt sympathy with them. In II Cor. 11:22 he dwells on his unblemished descent as one of the reasons why his Jewish opponents must pay him due respect. Here he insists much more emphatically on his Jewish antecedents in order to show that they mean nothing to him. As a Christian he has come to see that the distinctions on which he had once prided himself are utterly worthless. First of all he puts the purity of his descent beyond all question. **Circumcised the eighth day,** i.e., born into Judaism and not a proselyte. **Of the people of Israel,** i.e., not of a mixed stock, like many of the conglomerate population which now occupied Palestine. **Of the tribe of Benjamin:** This was the little select tribe which had given Israel its first king, and which held the prerogative of marching in the vanguard on a day of battle. "After thee, O Benjamin" had been the ancient war cry. **A Hebrew born of Hebrews:** This

---

atmosphere of the apostle's thought. Since comprehension of moral and spiritual truth is quite distinct from any changing views of the world, we have to lift out Paul's experience from the immediate problems of his ministry and from the world view he shared with his generation, so that we can discover how timeless and universal was the inner, transforming experience through which he passed.

At this point we are concerned with only one struggle which Paul had with his Pharisaic upbringing. Once and for all he learned through bitter experience that no legalistic religion could save a man from himself. He was particularly concerned with Jewish law, but what he learned about the inadequacy of a religion centered in a law or moral code is vital still for all of us.

To a Pharisee the law was the heart of religion. The temple at Jerusalem, with its altar and sacrifices, was rivaled by the synagogue, because Judaism had become a religion of a book, and interpreters of this book were the leaders of religious life. The young man Saul was trained in the rabbinical method of interpreting scripture, seeing its prophecies being fulfilled in present events, turning its stories and teachings into types or examples of life everywhere, and using allegory to prove almost anything from passages taken at random out of their context. Paul's arguments and illustrations in his more controversial letters seem often far-fetched and involved, as compared with Jesus' parables, simply because of this rabbinical habit of extracting intricate meanings from a

given text. They appealed to many of Paul's listeners who were Jews, but they sound strained to us. However, we can tolerate this strangeness in Paul's way of writing because it leads straight to the crisis of frustration to which legalistic religion is bound to lead.

Let us translate into modern terms the dangers which lie along the path of anyone who associates religion with law:

(*a*) External observances inevitably gain the pre-eminence over a true spirituality because external acts can be performed whether or not there is any sincere spirit supplying the motive force. The most selfish considerations can move a person to live up to the outward appearance of religious respectability, and even charity and self-denial can become outward acts with no inner reality. Only after a radical conversion was Paul able to say, "If I give away all I have, and if I deliver my body to be burned, but have not love. I gain nothing" (I Cor. 13:3).

(*b*) Furthermore, when religion becomes a matter of living up to rules and following a set pattern, the minor observances can easily be substituted for the major duties. Tithing of "mint and anise and cummin" can soothe a conscience that condones lovelessness and failure in all the weightier matters of justice and human understanding. Every clergyman in a parish should realize that this deceptive habit is the chief battle with his parishioners and with himself, for to both alike the temptation is ever present to find some conventional way of protecting an easy conscience. Because God is the great "Disturber," a preacher must be a

6 Concerning zeal, persecuting the church; touching the righteousness which is in the law, blameless.

brews; as to the law a Pharisee, 6 as to zeal a persecutor of the church, as to righteous-

---

name was now commonly used to denote those who clung to the national language, and Paul's family had continued to speak it, although settled in a Greek city. He himself, when he was mobbed in Jerusalem, was able to address the people "in the Hebrew tongue" (Acts 21:40).

From the question of descent Paul passes to that of religious standing. **As to the law a Pharisee**—one of the strict sect who made it their whole vocation to obey the law in every detail. **As to zeal a persecutor of the church**—not only a Pharisee but an active one, determined to suppress any heresy by main force. **As to righteousness under the law blameless.** Paul reserves this as the crowning proof that his Judaism had been irreproachable. The ambition of every pious Jew was to secure, by unfailing observance of the law, a righteousness which would make him perfect in the sight of God. Few could ever claim to have come anywhere near that ideal, but Paul could feel, after incessant self-discipline, that he had become truly a righteous man. No one who examined his life could accuse him of any shortcoming.

---

disturber of whom his people may well say as years pass, "What we remember now about him are the things he said and did that upset our equilibrium." No man can fulfill this function unless he includes himself with his parishioners, for he is far more like them than he is like Christ or Paul. In the church, above all places, it has ever been the religious, cultured, respectable, and educated people who have opposed all the radical changes in our life which later proved to be of greatest benefit to society. The bourgeois character of church membership in our time has a tendency to produce a deadly complacency which is uncreative just because it tends to identify an easily attained mode of life with Christian living.

It would be well for ministers to reread regularly such books as Trollope's *Barchester Towers*, Archibald Marshall's *Exton Manor*, Thackeray's *Vanity Fair*, and Mark Twain's *Tom Sawyer* and *Huckleberry Finn* just to see how the world of real people look at the church religion which has grown self-righteous and superior with no justification for its form of righteousness.

(c) Again, legalistic religion always divides people into superior and inferior categories, where the purists set themselves apart from the life of ordinary men and women. The Pharisees were the purists of their day, the strict observers of the law, with the inevitable result that they thought themselves "righteous" and "despised others." Masses of people who have to earn a living, businessmen and politicians who have to live by compromise, and all the rest of us who accept our living from the hands of business and politics, become so used to moral compromise in daily living that Christian life, so-

called, is not to be distinguished from the average standards of the world.

(d) When religion is oversimplified into a moral code, doing good gradually takes the place of God. A student once said that he saw no reason why a child could not be brought up as a Christian without God, because he felt that the essence of Christianity was a perfect moral code exemplified in Christ. This is the modern way of relapsing into legalistic religion. The phrase in the Lord's Prayer, "thy will be done," separated from the idea of the "kingdom" that *comes* from within, suggests to the ordinary man a line of behavior which we are to follow. If we *do* God's will, we surreptitiously ignore God and shoulder the whole responsibility ourselves. The fallacy in this procedure is that human beings decide what the "good" is that God wants done. Inevitably we make a pattern, follow it long enough to approximate it, and then assume that little more can be expected.

(e) Living up to an ideal code becomes a snare and a delusion for the unwary and uncritical. We talk about ideals so glibly that we unconsciously assume our belief in the ideal is equivalent to achieving it in our conduct; or we fool ourselves into thinking that we will achieve the ideal a little later, with more education, as though human beings could be saved from their self-centeredness by education, or induced to do good by mere information. In other words, we rely on human reason, leaving God in the remote past as the originator of the laws of life. Since education does not do all we claim for it, we generally rest back on the conviction that some pattern of life which seems difficult to change is all that God expects of us.

7 But what things were gain to me, | ness under the law blameless. 7 But what-
those I counted loss for Christ. | ever gain I had, I counted as loss for the

---

**7-9.** But he turns from what he had been to the change he had undergone through his conversion. **Whatever gain I had, I counted as loss for the sake of Christ.** Paul uses the language of a man who reckons up his wealth and finds that by some error he has put to the credit side what had been his losses, and under this delusion has been hastening toward ruin. So Paul has discovered in the light of the gospel that all his racial privileges, all his scrupulous observance of the law, had stood in the way of his true spiritual life. And it was not the law only from which he had shaken himself free. **I count everything**

---

(f) The moralism which characterizes legalistic religion may lead to the tragedy of helplessness. Strict moralists (or sentimental idealists) are tempted to sit on the side lines as critics of the compromises which imperfect people make in doing the business of the world. Advice from the spectators can degenerate into such a futile platitude as the familiar slogan, "If everybody had the spirit of Christ, all our problems would be solved," affording no strategy for the actual situation where almost no one has the spirit of Christ. When the moral people are thus helpless in a practical crisis, those who are less moral take over the running of worldly affairs. In fact, if matters become really desperate for the masses, they throw morals and ideals to the winds and trust the man of power who can *get something done.*

(g) All moralistic religion has one tragic blind spot. Its followers fail to see that human beings are not completely rational and that often they fail to do exactly what they know they ought to do. No amount of information can catch up with this human perversity. In his letter to the Romans Paul puts a searching question to those who boast of knowing the law, "While you preach against stealing, do you steal?" (Rom. 2:21.)

The worst consequence of moralism is the self-deceit which it generates. Hypocrisy is always a disease unrecognized by the person infected by it. Everybody knows he cannot live up to a perfect ideal in a selfish world, but he may pretend that it can be done and that he has approximated the ideal as nearly as his class of people expect, thus persuading himself that he is good enough to take charge of doing good to others. Thus is born the conservative who wants to be a benefactor to the less fortunate, but who will decide how and when the good is to be done, completely ignorant of the feelings of the people. He cannot comprehend that his paternalism is resented, that others do not feel he understands their need, and that members of his class cannot possibly sense how life looks to those in the class "below." He fails to realize that people develop their capacities neither by being helped nor by being paid, but through sharing common effort in interesting work on which their very existence depends.

Here are three samples of this insensitiveness of the successful—those who equate material success with moral worth and take their pattern of moral intentions as something not to be questioned. Alexander Hamilton believed that the most successful people in the business sense should be the controllers of government, because they were the right ones to judge what was right for everybody. In his *Report on Manufactures* he glibly states:

It is worthy of particular remark, that, in general, women and children are rendered more useful, and the latter more early useful, by manufacturing establishments, than they would otherwise be. Of the number of persons employed in the cotton manufactories of Great Britain, it is computed that four-sevenths, nearly, are women and children; of whom the greater proportion are children, and many of them of a tender age.[6]

Fancy a standard of goodness which left a man utterly unaware of the effect of this commercial usefulness upon the mothers and children of the working class! Without underestimating the value of modern industry in raising the living standard, we can now look back at the tragic exploitation of women and children in industry and wonder how it ever could have been condoned as a benefit to society.

Nearer our own day, at the turn of the last century, Andrew Carnegie preached the gospel of wealth, holding up the wealthy man as the hope of the world. He can be expected to do his duty in "becoming the mere agent and trustee for his poorer brethren, bringing to their service his superior wisdom, experience, and ability to administer, doing for them better than they would or could do for themselves." [7]

In 1900 Bishop William Lawrence of Massa-

[6] Quoted in Parrington, *Main Currents in American Thought*, I, 306.
[7] Ralph H. Gabriel. *The Course of American Democratic Thought* (New York: Ronald Press Co., 1940), p. 151.

**8** Yea doubtless, and I count all things *but* loss for the excellency of the knowledge of Christ Jesus my Lord: for whom I have suffered the loss of all things, and do count them *but* dung, that I may win Christ,

sake of Christ. **8** Indeed I count everything as loss because of the surpassing worth of knowing Christ Jesus my Lord. For his sake I have suffered the loss of all things, and count them as refuse, in order that I

---

**as loss because of the surpassing worth of knowing Christ Jesus my Lord.** With this knowledge he had learned to look with new eyes on everything this world could give him. He had been like a prisoner whose whole interest for years has been in some toy which he has tried to make out of the sticks and straws he has found in his dungeon, but which, once he is free, he never thinks of again. This is the only place where Paul speaks of **my Lord.** The revelation he describes is that which had come directly to himself when he accepted the Christian message.

**For his sake** [i.e., for the sake of possessing him] **I have suffered the loss of all things:** The words mean literally "I had all things confiscated"; to secure the priceless thing he had to give up all the rest. One is reminded of Jesus' parable of the man who found the matchless pearl and sold all that he had to buy it; the parable had become fact in the experience of Paul. **And** [I] **count them as refuse,** literally "thrown to the dogs"—scraps only fit for the rubbish heap. He had come to think in this way of all the things he had once prized—Jewish privileges and worldly advantage of every kind—and he now tells what he had got in exchange: **that I may gain Christ and be found in him.**

Two things appear to be in his mind—his present fellowship with Christ and his future deliverance. Throughout the epistle he looks forward to the "day of Christ," believing that when it comes he will have his place among Christ's people. He has already said "to me to live is Christ, and to die is gain" (1:21), and the same thought is now repeated in another form; only he expands it, and goes on to define what he means by being "found in Christ." **Not having mine own righteousness, which is of the law, but that which is through the faith of Christ,** i.e., the faith which Christ made possible, and which is the only means of obtaining righteousness. Paul touches here on his cardinal doctrine of justification by faith. He is not writing a theological epistle, and does not

---

chusetts gave his episcopal blessing to this ideal of the wealthy man:

In the long run, it is only to the man of morality that wealth comes. . . . Godliness is in league with riches. . . . Material prosperity is helping to make the national character sweeter, more joyous, more unselfish, more Christlike. That is my answer to the question as to the relation of material prosperity to morality.[8]

In these illustrations there is much truth, but it is vitiated by the deceptive assumption that Christianity gives us a code of moral behavior which can be quite satisfactorily attained. So accustomed have we become to the transformation of religion into a moralism to be acquired that we have almost forgotten that this age-old problem of the frustration of legalistic religion was the heart and core of Paul's gospel. The forms of the old perversion are new and various, but the same attitude of mind is present throughout.

**8-10. *For His Sake I Have Suffered the Loss of All Things . . . in Order That I May . . .***

[8] *Ibid.,* pp. 149-50.

*Be Found in Him.*—Here is Paul's testimony to "the mysterious reserves of life" that lie out beyond the suffering and tragedy of human existence. These reserves are never fully revealed save in those who have indeed suffered the loss of all things. We envy those who attain a comfortable life in this world, but we keep our final admiration for those suffering and crucified lives that manifest the invincibility of spirit which is never disclosed in an easy life.

This realm of experience is hardly glimpsed by conventional Christians who live in the tame areas of respectability. Emerson, living in the smugness of Concord society, where the ugliness of evil seldom raised its head, could define evil as absence of good—just a moral vacuum. Herman Melville, on the other hand, could not abide this interpretation, so oblivious to the terrifying power that evil can let loose in the world. It seemed to him that Emerson was so complacent that, had he been present at the Creation, he might have offered the Creator a few valuable suggestions. In his life at sea with many loathsome characters he dis-

9 And be found in him, not having mine own righteousness, which is of the law, but

may gain Christ 9 and be found in him, not having a righteousness of my own, based

expound the doctrine, as he does at full length in Romans. The Philippians were well acquainted with his teaching, and did not question it; so he feels it enough to remind them as briefly as he can of the principle on which it rested. In Christianity God had offered a new way of salvation. Men had trusted hitherto in their own righteousness, which consisted in strict performance of all the works prescribed in the law. They had now learned that all this was useless, and that nothing was required of them but faith in

covered that disgust could suddenly become an infinite pity for all lost souls. As he felt life giving forth a strange new power through suffering with others in evil, he realized that such saving, forgiving love interpreted for him the love of God in Christ that came down to be involved in sin to achieve redemption.

**9. *Not Having a Righteousness of My Own.***—Here is a phrase which can be so used as to baffle the modern mind. It seems to suggest that no one can acquire virtue or character on his own responsibility. To say that man was so totally depraved by "the Fall" that he is completely incapable of any right thinking or right living is more likely to confuse than to enlighten our contemporaries.

Paul's assertion is made to emphasize a contrast. After he had known the new life of the Spirit, with its *given* quality, all the righteousness which he had acquired by the severest discipline of will seemed like nothing at all in comparison. However severely Paul deprecated "whatever gain" he had (i.e., acquired righteousness), however he counted it as "loss" and "refuse" when it stood in the way of a different sort of life altogether, nevertheless he gave that zealous moral effort a real place in his life. He said it was like a "tutor" preparing him for the new that was as yet beyond his reach. Consequently from his best and most conscientious moral effort he turned away in humility, for at that extreme limit of self-discipline he saw the eternal difference between two kinds of righteousness. There is the righteousness we attain by trying, and there is the righteousness we catch through contact of life with life (as the grace of God is mediated). Often from the outside these two look exactly alike, but their motivations are utterly different, and the truth about life always lies in just such fine distinctions.

(a) Self-made righteousness is produced by adding one virtue to another, and by restraining selfishness, lust, and other vices. Benjamin Franklin disciplined himself by keeping a moral ledger, with lists of the virtues he sought to attain and the evils he hoped to avoid. Every night he checked up his accounts and reckoned

his moral achievements or failures for the day. Paul had worked on himself like that, fanatically, and it was that severe discipline which brought him to the despair which opened his eyes to life that came by the grace of God.

(b) The righteousness that is caught or given comes from seeing the best *done*. The revelation of God in Christ was first of all an act. Words could describe the act, but they could not convey its power. When we become receptive, the new spirit takes command of us; we do not own it, but it possesses us, while leaving our wills free. What was outside attracting us, occurs inside as a reinforcement to our will. Faith, in Paul's sense, is something like the sheer receptiveness which allows the constraining power of personality to have its effect within us. And faith in God would then be the same sheer receptiveness toward all creative action that is operative beyond our power to see or understand.

Jesus insisted that the test of this inner life possessing us is its capacity to be absolutely secret, not "to be seen of men." What is God-given cannot lead to self-glorification. It persists regardless of publicity, like the widow giving her mite unobserved, in contrast to the Pharisee, forever blowing his own horn to attract attention.

To many, or rather to the great majority, in modern times the question whether we are saved by our own "works" alone or by "faith" in Christ alone, seems like a dead issue, but it is really a very live one in concrete situations. The pendulum is always swinging between hopelessness and hopefulness about man's power to reason rightly, between a feeling of helplessness and a feeling of confidence about his power to live rightly. That pendulum swings in our private lives, from hours when we are disgusted with ourselves to times when we are pleased with ourselves. It swings in all our judgments of other people and of the human race. Through the entire history of the church there has been this vacillation between extreme despair and extreme optimism.

We often forget that one root cause of contrasting estimates of human nature is the *un-*

that which is through the faith of Christ, | on law, but that which is through faith in
the righteousness which is of God by faith: | Christ, the righteousness from God that de-

what God himself had done for them through Christ. If the Philippians would only
bear this in mind they would be fully armed against all Jewish efforts to mislead them.
But while the passage is only a condensed summary of ideas which he sets forth elsewhere,
it is of the utmost importance for the understanding of Paul's doctrine.

He says much in other epistles of the "righteousness of God," and the phrase, taken
by itself, is an ambiguous one which can be variously interpreted. Here he tells definitely

---

*evenness* of human experience. Sometimes children are very, very good, and sometimes they are horrid, and the switch between the angelic and the devilish is all part of the day's work in the best-regulated family. Some days we are easy to live with, and again we will crucify the thing we love; if we go to bed like a lamb, we may get up like a lion—"on the wrong side of the bed." We like to think of ourselves, as we think of our skill in a sport, when we are on our best behavior, but we are ourselves when we are also at our worst.

In the long history of religious thought some have said that man had an "original righteousness" which he lost in "the Fall," so that he is totally incapable of right thinking or acting and is wholly dependent on the grace of God. Some have always replied that the original image of God was marred and perverted but not totally destroyed. And there have been all grades of thought in between.

Something very human and continuous must underlie this ancient difference of opinion which has become central again in all judgments about the nature of man today. Obviously all the goodness in the world did not begin with faith in Christ, nor is it confined to Christianity or any form of it. Paul admitted that not the Jews alone, but also the Gentiles had some natural inclination toward and perception of what is right. Saints have described this original disposition as a kind of handle by which God takes hold of us and draws us toward himself. The Society of Friends has emphasized the divine spark within us, and modern humanists have felt that we could keep the Christian virtues without the Christian faith. All secret intimations that we belong to some goodness and truth that are quite beyond man's codes and systems are signs of the "prevenient" grace of God, as though God was forever finding us before we find him. Certainly the Creator "came before" his creatures, whom he created with a capacity to share his life. Wherefore Christians are not to be so jealous of faith in Christ that they would try to monopolize all goodness in the world for the sake of maintaining the finality of their religion.

The debate between "original righteousness" and "original sin" finally comes down to very practical questions.

What is wrong with an acquired righteousness of our own? It is certainly better than having an unrighteousness of our own; we can be certain of that. Nevertheless, our own style of goodness tends to become a "closed morality," as Henri Bergson once described it. We make a type of goodness that suits us and our condition and our class, then like the Pharisees, we begin looking for a place to stop. What people are our neighbors? How many times should we forgive? We draw a circle and leave out those whom we would like to forget. Then unconsciously we come to like one type too well, think ourselves righteous and despise others, or at least discount them heavily in our favor. If all speak well of us we are satisfied before we deserve to be, and become blind to what others find so obvious in us. Thus we become static.

Our self-loving ego tends to invent its own standard of goodness by which we condemn all others to inferiority. There is the "white" style of righteousness that looks down its nose at people of color who outnumber the whites seventeen to one. There is the free enterprise kind of righteousness that denounces all social planning as governmental tyranny, and accepts the sort of men who, through interlocking directorates, may control the largest corporations in a nation and plan everybody's economy. And there is the totalitarian police state kind of righteousness that would dominate the world in place of God; and in between is the do-nothing kind of righteousness of ordinary citizens who see what is wrong with all parties and just look out for number one.

What is good about acquired righteousness?

(a) It can at least stand guard against the notion of "easy salvation" which assumes that all we have to do is to believe in Christ and so be saved without deserving it and without effort. We can see plenty of people who make glib use of conventional clichés about salvation from their sins, who nevertheless seem to need much more saving. They are often the con-

what he means. Over against the righteousness which we can earn for ourselves by obedience to the law he sets "the righteousness which is from God on the ground of faith." By their own effort men could never obtain the righteousness without which they must stand condemned, but God bestows on them the righteousness they lack, accepting faith alone as a substitute for laborious fulfillment of all the demands of the law.

---

spicuously self-righteous people, judging others by themselves, and unable to work with any save their own kind.

(b) Furthermore, the emphasis on human effort can preserve the mystery of personality which includes both our own effort and something more that is done to us, with no neat line to be drawn between the two (see on 2:12-13).

(c) Again, it is by effort that we realize the limits of "trying." An athlete trying not to be nervous before a game, a speaker trying not to be embarrassed, all of us trying not to be self-conscious only to become more so, give proof that self-conscious effort increases the self-consciousness. Psychiatrists make their living from people who are literally tired out trying to escape from themselves and from their fears. And we all know moments when we lose ourselves in action, and experience a deliverance from self which no amount of trying could achieve.

Paul, by trying to be righteous, discovered that self-conscious effort increases the self-centeredness and self-righteousness, and at his wit's end realized that God through Christ supplied a "given" element that was a new thing altogether. It was a life of rigid self-discipline in Paul that was transformed into a new discipline of commitment to the Spirit of God. A lax and easygoing moral character is often converted into a lax and easygoing Christian character—which is a counterfeit. So long as a person is subject to vagaries of feeling and mood, he is an "unstable character" under any name. The new life in Christ can transform a self-centered discipline into a self-giving discipline which has no mercy on passing moods.

(d) Finally, effort can set going more than it can accomplish by itself. Mere wishing, believing, admiring, are not enough; something must be *done*. The spirit of God waits upon our self-surrender, but only a costly deed can demonstrate that we have given ourselves away and made ourselves available to the power of the Spirit. It is a familiar psychological principle that we must act the way we want to feel before we feel that way. Writers start writing to make themselves feel like it; artists practice in order to get into the mood of it; we must all act as if we were interested in others to awaken the interest. It is often necessary to act without an inclination before the inclination arrives—though, of course, a mere show of righteous works can thus be used to cover an unregenerate self, and this is why our forefathers were so suspicious of mere "works" as a sign of conversion.

What can this special revelation in Christ add to our moral effort and bring for our salvation? How our effort is fulfilled and transformed into a new life through Christ is discussed under many sections of this letter, but here we would stress the function of the Christian revelation in precipitating a predicament. Kierkegaard[9] suggested that Christ is the absolute pattern which we must follow, if only to discover that we have no power in our "self" to attain it, thus being made ready for an understanding of grace and redemption. After we endeavor self-consciously to produce as many good works as possible, we discover they are not selfless, as goodness should be. There is always some compromise with private interests by which we are bound.

Christ detached himself from everything we are attached to, like family obligations, patriotic ties, and the necessities of making a living, in order that he might serve only the will of God, and manifest it as crucified by so much that we assume is good enough. If such a perfect revelation was needed for our compromising world, this extreme detachment and final Crucifixion was the price that had to be paid; no cheaper, halfway revelation could purchase our salvation. Then at last it became clear that our nature was created for the Spirit of God, and that it rebels against surrendering itself to give God possession. We try to justify ourselves by reducing the requirement, and making Christ more sensible, reasonable, and practical until we remake him in our own image.

Christ's revelation remains the final correction of all human efforts, because it forever reminds us that "men knowing the right everywhere do that which is wrong, and human idealism itself, by becoming the occasion of sinful pride in man's ability to save himself, so easily turns into the daemonic force which brings human life to the brink of destruction."[1]

And such eternal correction of our partial successes preserves a positive, open, creative at-

[9] *For Self-Examination and Judge for Yourselves* (tr. W. Lowrie; Princeton: Princeton University Press, 1944), pp. 161-220.

[1] Richardson, *Christian Apologetics*, p. 129.

10 That I may know him, and the power of his resurrection, and the fellowship of his sufferings, being made conformable unto his death; | pends on faith; 10 that I may know him and the power of his resurrection, and may share his sufferings, becoming like him in

---

**10-11.** Paul now goes on to speak of what is involved in this saving faith in Christ. **That I may know him:** The word "know" as Paul uses it has almost always much more than an intellectual meaning. In true knowledge the will and the heart must be active as well as the mind. This holds good for almost every kind of knowing, and most of all where religion is concerned. To know Christ is to love and to serve him and to identify our lives with his. Paul dwells on this in the words that follow. **That I may know him [i.e.], the power of his resurrection, and the fellowship of his sufferings.** The belief that Christ rose from the dead must so work in us that we shall ourselves rise to a new life. The knowledge that he suffered must enable us to suffer, utterly resigned, as he was, to the will of God. We must feel, whatever the burden laid on us, that he is bearing it along with us. It may seem strange that the Resurrection is mentioned before the sufferings, but this is no accident. First one must rise to the new life which Christ has entered, and only then will one be able to suffer with him.

---

titude of life which has been well summed up in three abiding convictions, which Richard Niebuhr considers as basic in the Christian understanding of man: (a) The most common source of all our wrong thinking is self-defense. We try to justify a partial view as though it were God's whole view, and so close our eyes to new truth that might disturb us. (b) The chief source of evil is the attempt to make some relative opinion or interest an absolute, putting it in first place where God alone belongs. When anything human is exalted to a divine level, it becomes a devilish source of confusion and terror. (c) The one source of hope is the Christian belief in continuous reconstruction and re-creation. Once we know that we cannot make anything human absolutely right, we are in a position to see that our Creator is forever ready to take us as we are, and provided we are completely willing, do some new thing with our life.[2]

**10. That I May Know Him and the Power of His Resurrection.**—Paul here discloses his characteristic way of referring to eternal life. It is knowing a "power," which he associates with knowing a person and sharing a love that suffered even unto death.

We are reminded of what he says in ch. 1 about a kind of knowledge that is actually love. All the truth which Christianity offers was revealed in a deed. Such truth can be uttered only by living it, and can be *known* only as it lives again in us. This way of knowing lies on a different level entirely from scientific knowledge, which is knowledge *about* objects or forces or facts that can be studied without any personal commitment. What a specialist knows

[2] *The Meaning of Revelation* (New York: The Macmillan Co., 1941), p. viii.

about chemistry, or what a businessman knows about the market, and what they both know about loving their family and friends, are certainly two different kinds of knowledge, each with its own importance.

The modern mind, steeped in knowledge *about* things, tries to bring eternal life into this familiar sphere of knowing, as though the finite could grasp the infinite and the temporal comprehend the eternal.

To Paul resurrection was just the continuation of a mystery that runs all through life. How does one pass from the level of materialistic self-preservation to a new level where self-preservation is forgotten and swallowed up in a victorious devotion? That is a mystery story which Paul calls the "mystery of the gospel," and he identifies this transformation with resurrection as the same miracle.

Jesus, as reported in the Gospel of John, associates this miracle with friendship. When anyone who is absorbed in looking after himself becomes a true friend who gives himself away, "lays down his life" in action that cannot be paid for, there is the eternal and irreducible miracle. Knowledge inside one's own life of this power that transforms is knowing the power of the resurrection—in a small degree. Out of death to self comes a rebirth of life which is new, not self-made, but *given* before it is earned.

Paul never ceases to glorify this miracle which had occurred in him, which was not complete, and which ever enticed him to know more.

Certain facts about this eternal kind of life are open to anyone's knowing, right here and now in this world of death.

(a) It is not like a change in the old, natural, selfish life, but rather like an exchange of the

11 If by any means I might attain unto the resurrection of the dead.

his death, 11 that if possible I may attain the resurrection from the dead.

---

Vss. 10b-11 may be rendered: "Being conformed to his death, in the hope that I may attain to the final resurrection from the dead." Paul here touches on his great doctrine, expounded in Rom. 6, of the dying and rising with Christ. It has been maintained that on this side of his thought he was influenced by the so-called mystery religions, which turned on the idea that the initiate, by taking part in given rites, passed through the experience of a divine being who had been slain and miraculously restored to life. He was "conformed" to this divinity, making himself one with him, so that he too passed through death into a new life. It is not improbable that in the statement of his belief Paul availed himself of ideas and phrases which were current in the religious thinking of the time, but the belief was rooted in his Christianity. This is evident from the present passage in which he manifestly speaks of a profound experience of his own. He had realized so intensely the meaning of Christ's death on his behalf that he had died to

---

old for a new kind altogether, with another sort of driving power. To put it another way, it is different from improving ourselves, dressing up an old self to look better, in an effort to be nicer, sweeter, wiser, more efficient, or more polite. For some of the nicest, sweetest people can be as loveless as a steel trap when something threatens their income, or disturbs their accepted way of life, or attacks their prejudice. Whenever the miracle of transformation occurs, the old life seems so different that we wonder how we ever felt it was life at all.

(b) It is not merely a future matter. We are always aware of a self which has no power to transform itself into what God designed it to be. This self is a perpetual reminder of our curious predicament. It drives us farther into self-torture and despair, or drives us the other way toward that death to self which opens the way for God to give us his Spirit, which is a power and a convincing presence that cannot be produced by argument. To Paul the Spirit of God, the Spirit of Christ, and the Spirit in us is eternal life. By him we can be made into more than potential children of God and brought into an actual union with our eternal meaning. In a sense we live in two worlds, or on the border of two worlds—one is the world where self is forever unable to fulfill itself, and the other is the world where that miraculous and inexhaustible life of the Spirit tells us we are one with the eternal Creator of our souls.

(c) Another characteristic of this power of eternal life is its intimate association with suffering. Some of this suffering is related to times of utter loneliness, when man feels forsaken and even separated from God. Christ experienced this when all his life seemed to be ending in frustration, with no sign of help from God or man. But just in these times of forsakenness the Spirit of God is somehow there, working upon us in the very emptiness, and using

our own helplessness to deepen our dependence upon the Spirit—with no other support. Perhaps Paul meant this when he said "when I am weak, then I am strong" (II Cor. 12:10).

Men have tried to make out that such suffering is really good, and that bearing it shows the independence of the soul—but suffering is not good or bad in itself. It may teach or defeat us. Others try to refer it to error in the mind, and seek to deny its existence. Cynics may take it as proof of the meaninglessness of life. But to Christ, and in like manner to Paul, suffering was the final point where all self-will gives way. No explanation, no calculations, can help. All we can do is to make no effort to ask why it is here or how we can stand it for the days ahead. We may pray for deliverance, and then immediately comes the "nevertheless not my will, but thine, be done." Only at such points where self-will can do nothing have men known and shown to us that perfect resignation where the human spirit is committed finally to the eternal Spirit of God, trusting his power of transformation to make new life from the very depth of suffering.

(d) Again, the power of the eternal may appear in the midst of imperfection, in hints and vestiges which are not even given a name. Wherever we have turned, through a mixture of motives, from what is good for us to what we are good for, we have tasted the power of resurrection. Wherever the claim of human beings summons us out of self-absorption to be part of something greater than ourselves, to be swallowed up in purposes valuable to everybody, we know a little of what it means to rise from death to life. The feeling that our suffering is somehow at one with all suffering by which good has survived all evil, is another taste of union with the eternal. Thus we come, piece by piece, to know that we are children of the infinite and eternal, bound together in

12 Not as though I had already attained, either were already perfect: but I follow after, if that I may apprehend that for which also I am apprehended of Christ Jesus.

12 Not that I have already obtained this or am already perfect; but I press on to make it my own, because Christ Jesus has

---

his old self and risen into a new state of being. The one object which he now set before himself was "to attain, if possible, to the full resurrection." He uses a compound word (ἐξανάστασιν) to denote not merely the inward resurrection of which every Christian is conscious even in this life, but the ultimate rising from the dead. Here on earth, as he says in Rom. 8:23, "We . . . groan within ourselves, waiting for the adoption, to wit, the redemption of our body." For this Paul must continue to strive, so as to make certain that he will attain.

12. In the verses which follow (vss. 12-15) Paul enlarges on this idea that the present life at the best must be a period of struggle and aspiration. He himself knows how little he has accomplished; and so it must be with every Christian. It can hardly be doubted that he has a special reason for this confession that as yet he is only striving toward an end which is still far beyond him. There are those, he says a little later, who are "otherwise minded," and he implies that some of them were in the Philippian church. They held that perfection was possible in this life, and were convinced that they themselves had attained to it. This apparently was one of the errors which made Paul anxious about his converts at Philippi. Too many of them had fallen into a mood of self-complacency. They argued that since Christ had saved them, there was no need for any

---

the community of the Spirit which is in all communities but not identical with any.

A skeptical professor once found that there was something lacking in his explanation that reduced all virtues to survival virtues. He had no answer to a man who brought up the instance of a beloved mother who, outside of the time she gave to eat and sleep to keep herself going, never seemed to be concerned with preserving herself for one moment. She never had to visit a psychiatrist to have her neurosis treated, her inhibitions unraveled, and her complexes unscrambled. There was a serene and quiet effectiveness about her which lifted her above the things that bothered most people. She did not even have to drink every time something went wrong—like people in the movies who in all tribulation seem to think first of their bottle. She had her imperfections, her human failings; yet by the grace of God the love that lost itself could be transmitted through her.

Here is the very core of the truth of the Incarnation, that the divine can be revealed through the human. We can be reconciled to exchanging the old self for the new life only when we are shown in the flesh, in living form, the divine love foregoing all self-concern and suffering for the typical sins of our self-centered lives. Something of that sort has to happen right in the continuing stream of life, where the grace of God operates through witnesses, to induce us to let self die and to welcome the

life which God would give in all its transforming power. The miracle occurs "while [we] are yet in [our] sins," independent of any merit of our own. "The gift of God is eternal life"— here and hereafter.

12. *Not that I Have Already Obtained . . . but I Press On.*—Compressed into these few sentences we have one of the best expressions in all literature of the one way to be right in a world where nothing can ever be wholly right. Here is the final word of the greatest Christian who ever lived, spoken in the face of death, concerning the only inexhaustible satisfaction amid all that is transitory and imperfect.

This continuous conviction of more life to be created was to Paul the abiding secret of becoming more and more alive, down to the very end. In the moral sphere this conviction marks the difference between the "closed morality," always looking for some place to stop, and the "open morality," which sees that the ways of expressing a good life are endless in variety and infinite in scope. To the question "Who is my neighbor?" Jesus gave an answer in the story of the good Samaritan, whose spirit of neighborliness led him to do an original and unprescribed service where both the priest and the Levite, trained in rules, did not realize that it was the thing to do (Luke 10:29-37).

In the scientific sphere this humble conviction of falling short is the indispensable condition of endless ambition to pursue the truth, and all scientific progress depends on respond-

13 Brethren, I count not myself to have apprehended: but *this* one thing *I do*, for-

made me his own. 13 Brethren, I do not

further effort. They were now in full possession of the Christian life, and nothing was required of them but to remain as they were. Paul declares that he himself was not under this delusion. **Not that I have already obtained this or am already perfect.** This last word means literally "full-grown," and Paul applies it elsewhere to mature Christians, as distinguished from those who had newly entered the church and were still in need of elementary instruction (e.g., I Cor. 2:6).

But the word also signifies a state of fulfillment, when something has become in fact what it was ideally meant to be. In this sense Paul uses it here. He aims at the complete salvation which Christ has promised, but knows that it is not yet within his grasp. One may translate: "Yet I follow on, in hope that I may apprehend that for which also I was apprehended by Christ Jesus." The latter part of this sentence may also be rendered "seeing that I was apprehended," and this idea is certainly involved. His power to go forward depends on what Christ has done for him. But he speaks in the verse of something definite to which he is aspiring, and the sense would be incomplete if this were not indicated. What he desires is the final redemption, and Christ has laid hold of him for the one purpose that he may at last gain it. Paul never fails to insist that the action of Christ must precede any action of our own. We know as also we are known (I Cor. 13:12). We forgive one another as we have been forgiven (Eph. 4:32). All work that we do is made possible by the work of Christ on our behalf. So we can look forward to a full redemption because Christ has been before us and has determined that we should obtain it.

**13.** Yet that redemption is still in the future. "I, brethren, do not yet consider myself

ing to a sense of wonder that is absolutely inexhaustible.

Whenever groups or individuals try to live and work together, the forgiving and tolerant attitude required becomes possible only as all parties recognize that nobody can possibly be totally right. New truth appears where partial views meet.

In the whole complicated business of living we have all noticed a rather vague line between the limitations of mere existence and the boundlessness of real living. A modern professional man skilled in engineering says we can make a chart of our life to show the distinction between the things we do to keep going or to hold our place, and the things which yield all degrees of meaning as we become more and more alive to their immeasurable worth. Mere existence deals with everything that comes to an end, but real living revels in the glory of an endless life.

And the span of possibility is from zero to infinity; at any given moment our life is what we are alive to—and no more. The shortest biography ever written is contained in a sentence from the O.T. describing Methuselah: "And all the days of Methuselah were nine hundred sixty and nine years: and he died" (Gen. 5:27). In all his nine-hundred-odd years he had never achieved anything which seemed worth remembering. Some animal contentment

made him unaware of all that could be done with that much time. Plenty of people with a shorter span are missing most of the possibilities that could be theirs, filling their days with insignificant occupations, and so leaving no time for what is most worth while. A newspaper once declared that most young people never use more than one tenth of their minds. Anyone can remember a time when he thought he knew the measure of his own mind, only to have his calculations upset as he read for the first time some truly great book, which suddenly expanded his own mental horizon beyond his power to foresee. In fact, we continue to know more of our own intellects as we expose them to a variety of greater ones, and this exposure is the essence of a broad education.

Our whole civilization tends to confine our lives by its obsession with the satisfaction of producing *things* that perish, until, like the rich man in the parable with bigger and bigger barns, we hear that disturbing whisper, "Fool! . . . Your soul is required of you" (Luke 12:20).

The continuous conviction of not having attained perfection is simply the sign that something which might be a part of us is knocking at our door when we are asleep. There is no limit to this "open life," provided we do not think we have attained it.

**13. *One Thing I Do.*—**In the perpetual condition of a finite man who falls short, Paul sees

getting those things which are behind, and reaching forth unto those things which are before,

consider that I have made it my own; but one thing I do, forgetting what lies behind and straining forward to what lies ahead,

---

to have apprehended." The meaning depends on the strong emphasis on himself, which is apt to disappear in an English translation. He is addressing people who differ from him, believing that perfection may be attained in this life. They must judge of their own condition; he can speak only of himself, and knows that he is not yet a perfect Christian man. The Philippians looked on him, he is aware, as the typical Christian; more than ever now, when he was offering his life for his religion, he stood out as their great example. Yet he confesses that when he examines his own life, he finds that he has still a long way to travel. **But one thing:** These words stand by themselves without any explanatory verb, and are on that account the more impressive. One thing only, **forgetting what lies behind**

---

one thing to do. The core of his thought is best appreciated in a paraphrase: "I do not believe that I or anyone else can exhaust the possibilities of creation, so I detach myself from what has been imperfectly known or done (never clinging to it as though it were the end), holding myself ready under God for everything to be corrected and made over, stretching forth toward the things that are ahead, and pressing on in answer to an infinite call from beyond, that I may lay hold of that which has already laid hold of me." This formula of man's response to a divine impact is applicable in every field of human growth. We are always first laid hold of by more than we have already made our own. The initiative comes from the Creator, and the outcome depends on the humble and willing response of his creatures.

Before any doctrines were formulated, the living power of Christ to reduce human pride and open the way for a divine re-creation had come as a "free gift" to men. A student at the end of his college course came to a chaplain to say that he had lost all faith and wanted advice. There was no time for a long argument, so the chaplain asked this question: "Do you see anything in the personality of Christ which so commands your imagination that you feel sure it would be worth giving yourself to it, no matter what came of it?" "Of course," the student replied, "but that has nothing to do with religion." Unconsciously he had come upon the very heart of the truth of the Incarnation, that "God was in Christ reconciling the world to himself" (II Cor. 5:19). The popular notion of Christianity reduces it to a perfect moral code which human beings seek to imitate by sheer effort of will, but the gospel is just the opposite of that. In Christ is revealed a kind of life *unattainable by will power,* which "comes down" as from an illimitable height, laying hold unconditionally upon our imagination and moving us from outside, as it were. Its

effect is to wake us up inside, make us feel how little alive we really are, and to convince us that a new creation could occur within us before we deserve it, if only we would put self aside and commit our life obediently to the "high calling."

The process of salvation always begins from an encounter outside, and then is experienced inside. Paul as a persecutor had seen Christians, like Stephen the martyr, *in action* under the severest conditions. Before Paul became a Christian there was in existence this company of people transmitting Christ's spirit *alive,* and this Christian community first confronted Paul from outside, troubling his conscience until finally he found himself inside the community and sharing the power which worked through its imperfect members.

Much reinterpreting is necessary to bring this gospel of a divine life completing our natural life into real contact with a world that has been so generally secularized. The "sense of sin" has become associated mainly with moral degradation and indecency, as though there were nothing serious about the self-centeredness and self-love that are characteristic of very respectable people who do not call themselves "sinners." Furthermore, the legal view of God as moral governor has lost much of its force, and men no longer receive the early training which made John Fiske say that he had first pictured God sitting behind a great book, writing down the bad deeds of John Fiske. The reality of the judgment of God, finding out man's shortcomings through the inevitable consequences, is as vital as ever, but legal pictures of the severity of God, inducing men to cry for mercy and salvation, have lost their appeal for multitudes.

We can see the redeeming power of God in a new setting when we think of God as a *continuous creator.* His difficulty is with finite and imperfect creatures who like themselves and their own ways too well, whose private and

| 14 I press toward the mark for the prize of the high calling of God in Christ Jesus. | 14 I press on toward the goal for the prize of the upward call of God in Christ Jesus. |
| --- | --- |

**and straining forward to what lies ahead:** He has spoken of a single aim, and now he imagines a race in which every faculty is concentrated on the one object. The runner is lost if he turns to see what is happening behind him; his eyes must be fixed steadily on the course he has still to cover.

14. Literally, Paul says here: "In line with the goal I follow toward the prize." The image of a race is carried out in all its details. It was customary to set the prize in a conspicuous place at the very point where the race was to end. The sight of it roused the competitors to strain every nerve, and to forget everything but their one object. Paul describes himself as looking solely toward the prize, which consists not of any material reward, but of "God's heavenly calling in Christ Jesus." Two ideas are blended. The

social patterns of behavior, premature convictions, and desire for comfort get in the way of more life that can be created. To break down human obstinacy some severe shocks have to be administered to those who will not listen to reason, and whose wishful thinking would rationalize the *status quo.* The consequences of stagnation must work out to present a new challenge that may awaken men. The whole process of correction is not punishment from an angry God, but a means of making men open to the gift of more and more life. Humility is the condition of new revelation, and only out of humility can anyone be remade for new opportunity.

Such a view of continuous re-creation fits our situation where no human problems are susceptible of a final solution, whether they are racial, social, political, or family problems. Every partial solution may open up fresh opportunity for new adjustments under new conditions, provided there is no expectation of a neat end to human difficulties. We are never through renewing our relations with each other, and God is never through remaking human personality. He is not apart from the conflicts of individuals and groups, but in the midst of the constant give and take of some community.

Many suggestive lines of thought can be followed from this new emphasis on God as a loving creator, refusing to let alone any unfulfilled life, and ready always to be involved in making all things new where man responds in humility and penitence.

(a) We need to associate the conviction of falling short with the creative attitude, not with the traditional attitude of the cringing sinner bent on saving himself. What we require is to be saved from our old selves so that our productive and creative powers can be released for the ever-fresh challenges that confront us. Only so can we integrate the conflicting elements within us, extend our relations

with other men, and unite our human will with the all-sufficient will of the Creator.

(b) Furthermore, it is important to stress the radical nature of creation. There seems to be no way to separate creation from continuous destruction, i.e., we cannot have what is new and still keep old familiar ways just as they were. Only through the perishing of one form of life is the way cleared for some unpredictable new life. The spirit of God cannot be born in us merely through improvement of the old self, but only through death to the self. Such a truth is not easy to state because some elements of old life are taken up and transformed into the unexpected developments.

Human history as a whole may be looked upon as a constant remaking of various styles of life that "have their day and cease to be." We always think of our own age or style of civilization as the peak of development from a less satisfactory past, but this need not necessarily be so. We may be living at a point where our order of life has outlived its usefulness and has declined rather than advanced. Before a new form can come alive we must be ready to recognize what has ceased to be vital and creative. What a tragedy to live one's life trying to defend what is condemned to death in God's creation!

Just here we can see the pertinence of the historian's view that when some creative minority in a civilization becomes a dominant minority and ceases to be creative the inventive power becomes active in some proletariat whose first impulse is to destroy the uncreative that is holding back society.[3]

(c) Again, people who have lost the magical idea of the supernatural must be helped to see today that there is a suprahuman, incalculable factor forever involved in all our living. It is

[3] Arnold J. Toynbee, *A Study in History,* Abridgement of Vols. I-VI by D. C. Somerwell (New York: Oxford University Press, 1947), chs. xvi, xviii.

prize was for those who had listened to the higher call, and it would take the form of God's summons to inherit eternal life. The victor would hear the voice which says, "Well done, good and faithful servant; . . . enter thou into the joy of thy Lord." In both senses it is **in Christ Jesus:** he issues the call to his people, and their reward for obeying it will be to share in his exalted life. The passage closes with a direct appeal, and to this the whole chapter has been leading. Paul had begun by warning the Philippians against a type of religion which rested, like Judaism, on outward performance. He has shown that through Christ they have access to a higher world, they rely on spiritual motives and seek a new kind of righteousness. So as Christians they have before them an endless field of endeavor, and can never assume, while they live on earth, that their task is finished. All that talk of "perfection," in which many of them were indulging, must therefore be meaningless, for it belongs to the very nature of a spiritual religion that there is always a height which has not yet been attained. Paul had found it so in his own life, which is the only one he can really know, and he believes that what is true of him must likewise be true of every Christian man.

---

hidden, just as all the forces of growth are hidden, but unceasingly active, and always emerging as a surprise which could not be foretold. For instance, everyone has noticed how children grow by stages that can never be predicted. New stages emerge out of the passing of former stages. A grandfather was considerably disturbed by the way a granddaughter had changed from an innocent infant into a perpetual nuisance. She bothered her elders, and acted like a sadistic tyrant over those of her own age, but suddenly she became so different that she was asked, "Why have you stopped bothering people as you used to do?" To which she gave this inexplicable reply, "I don't seem to want to bother anyone anymore." Her family had endured her truculence, continued to love and trust her (as a kind of human illustration of the love of God that was so perfectly revealed in Christ), and just when no one could foresee it, the new life was born in her. Such sudden emergences from unpleasant to pleasant stages come like a godsend to parents, who could scarcely survive without them, but no stage is ever final. After a sadistic period may come the show-off, the deceitful, and the adolescent stages, and so on. Life does not develop evenly and steadily as an escalator rises from floor to floor, but by these "breaks" where men

> rise on stepping-stones
> Of their dead selves to higher things.[4]

No one can ever say when the present may blossom into a new meaning. We live along in a certain stage as though it were our natural permanent life but new potentialities gather with experience which require more room. They cannot be contained in old ways, and restlessness increases because so much is unex-

[4] Tennyson, *In Memoriam*, Part I, st. 1.

pressed. Then some new acquaintance, a new book, or an unsettling experience creates a shock which shatters the enclosing walls, so that some new thing can be done with us. However, the new never arrives until we are prepared to let go the old and give ourselves "costingly" to the new possibility that has laid hold of us.

Thus, individuals may have firsthand information of the creative power always concealed in the events of existence. Whenever some potentiality has disturbed us from the outside, and comes alive within us through humility and obedience, we understand a saving power (more than our own will) which can break the grip of the past and make a fresh kind of existence possible. This is our best proof of an all-pervading power which we can trust in the long run to break up old ways everywhere and turn the consequences in the direction of new creation.

(d) Finally, this view of the persistence of creation can be helpful in explaining why Christ cannot be made a practical ideal for a sinful world. While the love made manifest from God in Christ must always be the final measure of all human action which is forever falling short, it can never be contained (made to work perfectly) in any human situation. The reason is that every situation needs to be re-created to admit more of the life of God into this world. Wherever individuals are radically transformed, unforeseen outward changes in the world become possible where we assumed that they were impossible; though it is also true that many outward changes must be effected by us before there is a "highway for our God." Any successful way of life, by its very success, outgrows the methods that created it, and may become an obstacle to the will of God. To be forever ready for God to work his wonders out is to be linked with the eternal, confident that

15 Let us therefore, as many as be perfect, be thus minded: and if in any thing ye be otherwise minded, God shall reveal even this unto you.

16 Nevertheless, whereto we have already attained, let us walk by the same rule, let us mind the same thing.

17 Brethren, be followers together of me, and mark them which walk so as ye have us for an ensample.

15 Let those of us who are mature be thus minded; and if in anything you are otherwise minded, God will reveal that also to you. 16 Only let us hold true to what we have attained.

17 Brethren, join in imitating me, and mark those who so live as you have an ex-

---

**15-16.** So he concludes, **Let those of us who are mature be thus minded.** The suggestion is that the only perfection possible to a Christian is to be always striving toward something better. To stand still, in the fancy that one has now reached the goal, is only stagnation, and proves that one is not yet truly a servant of Christ. At the same time Paul will not wholly condemn those who differ from him. **If in anything you are otherwise minded,** i.e., if you cannot agree with me on this matter of perfection, **God will reveal that also to you.** Believe the truth as you see it, and God will lead you eventually to the larger truth. The man who is trying earnestly to serve God, perhaps in a mistaken manner, will discover where he has been wrong and will change his mind. One thing, however, is necessary, and Paul here expresses himself in language so condensed that his precise meaning is doubtful, although the general sense is clear. "Only, whereto you have attained, walk by the same." In some ancient MSS the word "rule" is added: "Keep following the rule of conduct by which you have arrived at your present condition." But Paul is speaking of a revelation, not of the rules of Christian living. Much in the revelation may still be obscure, but there can be no doubt of the essential things. Let Christians be faithful to the light they have, and then they may hope for further light.

### C. The Need for Moral Consistency (3:17-21)

**17.** In this closing section of the chapter Paul follows out his warning that there can be no progress without fidelity to what we already know. At the same time he brings to a

---

neither disaster, disappointment, destruction, nor death can ever have the last word.

**15-16. *Let Those of Us Who Are Mature.*—** The KJV has the word **perfect** in this sentence, which seems a contradiction to Paul's insistence that he has not been made perfect. However, Paul is simply saying that the attitude of mind just described in the previous sentences is the only attitude that could be perfect: ready to admit shortcomings, susceptible to correction and fresh revelation, willing to be refashioned in mind and heart. The whole question of perfection needs a thorough restatement from the standpoint of a limitless creation. Paul remarks that if people do not have the right attitude, God has his ways of revealing the mistake through drawing the conclusions which we refuse to draw. The "time of troubles" in which we are now living is the direct revelation of mistaken attitudes which have been accepted as right.

There is of course a danger in the view that every human conclusion is partly erroneous and inadequate, for it is easy to conclude that no-

body can be sure of anything, nothing can be rightly done, and not all of us together can know what we ought to know. This moral defeatism is characteristic of an age that has been disillusioned about ideals that are never attained. Men feel that if all is tentative, nothing much is worth doing. In such a mood we should take heed of Paul's advice, **Let us hold true to what we have attained.** This admonition in the moral realm is exactly what the scientist follows so successfully when he realizes he *can never know* all the truth, and that all his opinions are tentative. By living with what has been discovered, however incomplete, he is put in the position where he can be corrected and given fresh insight. There is no other way for incomplete life to be given further completion.

**17-21. *The Need of Moral Consistency.*—** In these closing words of ch. 3 Paul essays the precarious business of telling other people how to behave. The urge to improve the moral consistency of our fellow men has been a devastating curse throughout Christian history,

point his protest against the radical error of Judaism. It magnifies the external instead of the inward and spiritual, and when religion is thus bound up with outward things, the whole conception of life is materialized. Men are aware of nothing beyond this world, with the result that they live for it wholly, and cease to be guided by moral

despite the fact that morals everywhere need checking up. We cannot let moral degeneracy continue on the broad and easy road to destruction, but who are to be the "improvers"? Who of us is so morally consistent that he can safely set himself up as an example?

Lynchers who take the law into their own hands—are they fit to be final judges of their fellow men? Church people whose moral views are biased by their economic interest—how can they be the examples of an impartial social conscience? Every one of us has his moral blind spot; every one favors some partial interest that corrupts his impartiality. All of us see the sins of others more easily than we see our own; but how can we set out to appraise, judge, criticize, and improve those who in turn can see our faults better than they can see their own? We have to judge others and try to do them good, but how can this be done without falling into the danger which Jesus likened to a man who with a floor beam jammed into his own eye tries to extract a tiny mote from his neighbor's eye? We need to re-examine this duty of setting oneself up as an example, which we so glibly urge upon our children and young people as though we would make them the kind of righteous prigs which they so rightly hate.

Moralism, with all its advice and exhortation and inevitable presumption, is the very antithesis of Christianity, but all through the ages there has been a fatal confusion of the two.

At the end of almost all of Paul's letters there appears a series of moral directions and exhortations, often in much detail. This seems like a return to his old Pharisaism, with its readiness to lay down the ethical rules for a good life. In the Philippian letter there are no moral precepts offered in detail, but on the other hand, we have an unforgettable illustration of the right psychological attitude required in dealing with the moral inconsistencies and shortcomings of sinful human beings.

17. *Brethren, Join in Imitating Me.*—How can a person who acknowledges his imperfections set himself up as an example? This question has been ignored by superficial Christians, and by all who have tried to substitute morals for religion. Most of our minor and major tragedies have arisen from a mistaken notion of setting an example. And yet how many people carry in the back of their minds the vague impression that a Christian is a good person who does other people good by offering his own

goodness to be admired and imitated. At the same time, a youthful distaste for such an attitude has remained unspoiled by all exhortations to the contrary.

It cannot be that Paul is referring to his own righteousness as worthy of imitation, because he has distinctly stated that he looked on himself as "not having a righteousness of my own." What he wanted others to imitate was the sense of falling short, which keeps one committed to the Creator's infinite purpose that is stronger than any man and worthy of all men. A man is right when he feels he is so far from exhausting the meaning of a good life that he always holds himself open for more of the Spirit of God to refashion and work through him. Jesus put his blessing on the state of mind that was humble enough to "hunger and thirst after righteousness" so that life could be given more and more abundantly. "Woe to you, when all men speak well of you" was Jesus' warning against enjoying the deceptive sense of being an acceptable example (Luke 6:26). That phrase "woe to you" is none too strong, for all sorts of tribulation come from forgetting that more life than we can dream of is yet to be created. What moral damage in human relations has derived from those who considered themselves good examples!

In 1800 an unknown publisher issued a small pamphlet entitled *Excerpts from the Memoirs of Caroline E. Smelt.* This Miss Smelt as a young woman was an insufferable prude, but she thought she was a model of propriety. On her deathbed she sent a message to her cousin, "Tell her never to enter a theatre, never to play cards, never to attend tea parties. For if any one of these is evil, they all are; and of this I am absolutely certain." God speaking through Caroline E. Smelt, telling everybody how to be good! What inquisitions have been set up in the world by people like that who would judge others by themselves! The eternal Pharisee is in all of us, as a continual temptation to favor our own goodness, to underestimate and despise other men, and to close our minds to the unguessed possibilities which only God knows. For these possibilities forever demand more of us by far than we are ready to give up, and their higher reaches do not lie within the natural limits of a worldly life.

The whole question of how to influence people has become central in community life everywhere today, for so many of our ills spring

instincts and principles. It is necessary, even for purposes of daily conduct, that Christians should always be mindful of the higher nature of their religion. Paul has spoken of himself to show how everyone falls short of the Christian ideal. He again offers himself as an example, in so far as he has honestly tried to act out in his life the things which he

from the everlasting difficulty of getting on with other people. It is important that we should reinterpret the issues involved in this age-old perplexity. There are several basic truths which call for fresh emphasis.

First is the fact of an inescapable predicament. To exert moral influence by example is not a simple matter, for there is a hidden presumption that we are sufficiently superior to do good to our inferiors. That in itself is a bad example to begin with, and it is so recognized by others and interferes with our effectiveness. Superiority condescending to be benevolent is the beginning of all tyranny.

This hidden false pride begets resentment in those to whom it seeks to do good. Among American writers none has seen more clearly than Herman Melville the evil of pride that may enter in to defeat human influence. In *White-Jacket,* one of his lesser-known novels, he points up the weakness and danger of all Pharisaism in the character of the commodore on a man-of-war:

It beseemed him . . . to erect himself into an ensample of virtue, and show the gun-deck what virtue was. But, alas! when Virtue sits high aloft on a frigate's poop, when Virtue is crowned in the cabin a commodore, when Virtue rules by compulsion, and domineers over Vice as a slave, then Virtue, though her mandates be outwardly observed, bears little interior sway. To be efficacious, Virtue must come down from aloft, even as our blessed Redeemer came down to redeem our whole man-of-war world; to that end, mixing with its sailors and sinners as equals.[5]

The second truth is that responsibility for evil cannot be ignored. While it is true that none of us is perfect enough to be a corrector of others, we cannot wait to be perfect before doing anything about the evil that we see in others. Certainly parents cannot wait to be faultless before disciplining the faults of their children. Citizens who may be as selfish as the worst politicians must nevertheless influence the politicians lest the worst go unrestrained. Somehow it is necessary in society to rely on the good intentions of very faulty people to rally strength enough to combat evil.

The third truth that offers a way out of the predicament is the need of commitment to a common obligation in which both parties might have an interest. To a Christian such a purpose

⁵ Ch. liv.

is the will of the Creator, who seeks to create more life for all his faulty creatures. There is no presumption in promoting mutual interest and co-operation in such an inclusive and endless purpose as that.

The fourth truth is that the spirit of the Creator is at work underground in all men, even in the worst, to win their self-will over to the Creator's will for all men. By this truth we can distinguish two ways of doing good:

(*a*) The patronizing way, which is characteristic of the more conservative elements in a community, seeks to do others good by taking charge and control of the good that is to be handed out. There is generally a hidden threat of withdrawing benefits if the recipients do not accept the domination of the benefactor.

(*b*) The creative way is apt to be present among the more radical or revolutionary elements of a community. In this approach there is more readiness to trust the Spirit of God at work in other men, transforming them through responsibility which is entrusted to their hands. There is a risk involved because no one can tell beforehand what response will be made. However, if any real change is to be effected, it must come only by this creative way which releases the inventiveness of God himself. This is the method of influence in all good families.

The fifth truth is that loss of faith in a Creator, above and beyond human powers, ends in an unconscious degradation of influence. In our modern world the techniques of psychology have tended to take the place of religion in human relations. A student who was asked the reason for the immense popularity of courses in psychology, replied, "Most of us do not know what calling we intend to pursue, but we are sure that in every calling we will have to deal with people." The indispensable contribution of psychology in this field often puts to shame the sentimental and ignorant bungling of so-called religious people, and we need more, not less, of this thorough study of human motives and reactions. However, this modern "science of human management," divorced from a religious background, can easily degenerate into mere manipulation of human beings as though they were things—instead of spiritual personalities, with an inner, unique worth known only to God. Advertising may become a clever psychological method of inducing people to want what they do not need, and this skill in molding the minds of men can be

believed. **Brethren, join in imitating me, and mark those who so live as you have an example in us.** Addressing the whole church, he calls on its members to join as one in living as he does. His apparent egotism in this and similar appeals has often been misunderstood. We need to remember that his readers were Gentiles to whom the Christian ethic was alto-

perverted into propaganda which has reached hideous proportions in totalitarian states. Without a deep sense of God's secret intention for the dignity and value of each individual in his own right, multitudes in our secular civilization will devour books on how to win friends and influence people without realizing that such an effort is at the opposite pole from real friendship, which does not seek to use others for its own purposes. The tricks of human management often reveal a callous disrespect for another man's soul.

Before leaving this subject of being an example, attention should be called to the recurring problem of Pharisaism in every generation of Christians. Religion, by its very moral enthusiasm, has a subtle way of reverting to the legalistic moralism from which it aimed to deliver men.

An illuminating illustration can be seen in the way Puritanism betrayed itself. The original Puritans were strong believers in original sin, and felt that man could not be made trustworthy by mere self-improvement. Improving self-centeredness made it more respectable, but not less dangerous. But the very fact that only the redeemed man could be trusted reopened the door to Pharisaism among those who felt themselves redeemed by the grace of God. They believed that they, by their reason and judgment, were best fitted to rule in a community. They presumed to make a moral plan for others' lives, forgetting that their human idea of a good life was not identical with God. They acknowledged the supreme authority of God, but for practical purposes in church and state, some people had to represent God. Who should be the divine representative? John Cotton clarified this position in the following words:

Now if it be a divine truth, that none are to be trusted with public permanent authority but godly men, who are fit materials for church membership, then from the same grounds it will appear, that none are so fit to be trusted with the liberties of this commonwealth as church members. For, the liberties of this commonwealth are such, as require men of faithful integrity to God and the state, to preserve the same.[6]

Thus, church members presumed to declare who should be citizens with voting power, and the magistrates became moral censors for the

entire community. In the economic realm they tended to believe that prosperity came by God's favor to those who were diligent in business, and that poverty was the judgment assigned to those who were shiftless. By this convenient moral judgment on social conditions the well-to-do established their position, and looked upon any disturbing movements from the common man as dangerous to the order of society which God had arranged. Thus, prosperity has always bred the spirit of tyranny.

This presumption of man in judging *what God wants for others* can be further illustrated in its twisted social implications by certain quotations from John Calvin's *Institutes:*

Wherefore it ought not to be doubted that God here lays down a universal rule for our conduct; namely, that to everyone, whom we know to be placed in authority over us by his appointment, we should render reverence, obedience, gratitude, and all the other services in our power. Nor does it make any difference, whether they are worthy of this honour or not (II. viii. 36).

[Another] rule will be, That persons whose property is small should learn to be patient under their privations, that they may not be tormented with an immoderate desire of riches (III. x. 5).

Lastly . . . the Lord commands every one of us, in all the actions of life, to regard his vocation. . . . He has appointed to all their particular duties in different spheres of life. . . . No one will be impelled by his own temerity to attempt more than is compatible with his calling, because he will know that it is unlawful to transgress the bounds assigned him (III. x. 6).[7]

Such Pharisaism has been the temptation of all people who have "arrived" in the struggle for existence. The successful would presume to be judges of who should hold authority and who should obey, who should strive to get ahead and who should know his place, who should be ambitious and who should be content with what he happens to have. Most of our social ills and group strife run back to this unconscious presumption of the well established who would prescribe the bounds beyond which the less privileged should not go. The collective efforts of the masses, so inconsiderate of others, have been occasioned by the blind conservatism of all of us who presume that the *status quo* which

[6] Quoted in Parrington, *Main Currents in American Thought*, I, 34.

[7] *A Compend of the Institutes of the Christian Religion,* ed. Hugh Thomson Kerr, Jr. (Philadelphia: Board of Christian Education of the Presbyterian Church in the U.S.A., 1939), pp. 67, 107. Used by permission.

18 (For many walk, of whom I have told you often, and now tell you even weeping, *that they are* the enemies of the cross of Christ:

18 For many, of whom I have often told you and now tell you even with tears, live as enemies of the cross of Christ.

---

gether new. They could make nothing of it unless they saw it in action, and Paul considered it one of his chief duties to exemplify in his own person the things he taught. He required of his converts that they should model their behavior on his, and thus stand out on their own part as living illustrations of the Christian mode of life.

**18-19.** This was the more necessary "for there are many who live"—one would expect him to say—"in a very different manner"; but he gives another and more emphatic turn to the sentence: men **of whom I have told you often, and now tell you even weeping,**

---

favors us is the arrangement prescribed by God himself.

The moral blindness of lives that have lost their endless sense of falling short in a continuous creation is still as dangerous as the violence and open wickedness which it stirs up in opposition. Public disasters in our own day should always be analyzed from the point of view of this blindness of those who overestimate their own righteousness. In his book *Peacemaking 1919,* Harold Nicolson says that Woodrow Wilson inherited from his Covenanter background something of the moral arrogance that accompanies all forms of "hard religion." It made him "impervious . . . to . . . shades of difference . . . as incapable of withstanding criticism as of absorbing advice," and it was his "spiritual and mental rigidity which proved his undoing." [8]

How different such an attitude was from the way Lincoln approached human problems. For him neither the South nor the North was altogether right, nor was he himself totally right. Only God possessed the total view, and therefore let no one set himself up as the standard, but let all acknowledge their shortcomings so that "with malice toward none; with charity for all" they could work together to finish the task so nobly begun on the American continent.

In this twentieth century Americans especially are in danger of precipitating tragic misunderstandings by assuming that the so-called "American Way of Life" is an example for the whole world, with God's blessing upon it. We can easily be blinded by our own achievements on a virgin continent. If we are not aware of the faults of our democratic way, faults which make our influence weak with masses of people everywhere, then our failures give opportunity for some other alternative like communism to take over. For communism may be partly a reaction from the failure of Western religion and industrialism to meet the problems of the people. In the United States the system of individ-

[8] Boston: Houghton Mifflin Co., 1933, p. 198.

ual initiative and free enterprise has been a great success in developing capable individuals who could rise out of the masses, but this same system ignored the multitudes who were incapable of rising to the top. They were left to find their own way through collective action to create a life of their own. Capitalism and communism, both materialistic philosophies, are competing for the allegiance of the neglected multitudes. The neglects of democracy are, under God, being revealed by the success of police states, which in turn will meet judgment at the hands of those who learn to bring masses into a partnership of free men under law, to share responsibility for the common good. Both forms of materialistic civilization, so proud in their own might, have come into a time of troubles, because both alike have planned life mainly for "economic man" and have subordinated the life of the spirit to the insistent demands of the body.

**18-19. For Many . . . Live as Enemies . . . of Christ, . . . with Minds Set on Earthly Things.** —Who the people were of whom Paul had often spoken **even with tears** we do not know. But these two verses describe a human condition which is forever recurrent in all civilizations, and which confronts us now in our civilization at a time when we had assumed that we were at the peak of progress.

There are many today who have become **enemies . . . of Christ** unconsciously, and we are all more or less in their company. For it has become a modern habit to ignore belief in God in favor of belief in our senses.

It is perhaps extreme to say literally of the majority that **their god is the belly,** as though they were sensuous gluttons. Plenty of the intemperate are with us, of course; but a far vaster number of respectable people are living quite unaware that they represent **minds set on earthly things,** for in a scientific age it becomes a habit to trust what the senses tell us about life, as though our senses were God.

The fact is that we have all been swept along

**that they are the enemies of the cross of Christ.** He may refer to unworthy members of the Philippian church, but if it contained many such people, he could not have dwelt, as he does repeatedly, on his love for all who were in it. More likely he speaks in a general way of professing Christians who had disgraced the name. He had mentioned

blindly in a movement away from God that began some three hundred years ago under the leadership of science. We have transferred our trust to scientific knowledge, which comes through our senses, because from this source we gained the immeasurable benefits, conveniences, and luxuries which are the essence of modern life. At the same time, the whole area of religious meaning and spiritual value, which lies beyond the senses, tended to become less and less real, and the self-sufficiency of man grew so large as to overshadow the all-sufficiency of God. The means became a substitute for meaning, while our civilization drifted into confusion and bewilderment. Paul's words about **minds set on earthly things** have now assumed a world-wide significance, and have reference to many issues more complex than the worldly-mindedness of some individuals.

Interpreters of religion must acquaint unsuspecting people with the far-reaching effects of this secular "mind set." If "God is dead," as Nietzsche said in the nineteenth century, it is real tragedy for man, for then there is nothing left but to take what our senses tell us as the final gospel. Because of this practical atheism, which may still talk vaguely of God while ignoring him in action, religion loses its power not by opposition but by default.

The early scientists were not irreligious. Newton believed in God, but he could study gravity without reference to God or a moral purpose. This method was called disinterestedness, "objective" thinking, and created a popular impression that God was being crowded out of his place in the universe. Since God was not subject to scientific proof, he made less of an appeal to the modern mind.

A simple parable illustrates the strange development. Suppose a man endeavored to understand a machine like a newspaper press. From what his senses could tell him he would learn that every wheel and gadget set other wheels and gadgets moving, so that every part was determined by some other part; and the whole was driven by some natural, impersonal force like steam which had no moral purpose whatsoever. All this information could be gathered without knowing the purpose in the minds of the editorial staff. No study of the machinery by itself could reveal such a purpose, and a man might assume it did not exist. However, if from some other source he became acquainted with the editor's intentions, he could see how

an impersonal machine might have a hidden purpose working through it. He could proceed from the editor to interpret the machine, but he could not go the other way around and interpret the editor from the machine. If a worker by accident were caught in the wheels and killed, no one could say, "That shows what a heartless man the editor is."

In some such way the scientific movement led men's minds away from God without any campaign of opposition. Nonhuman nature could be explored without reference to God or his moral purpose. And since no analysis of nature (apart from man) revealed a clear purpose running through it, there was gradually built up in the popular mind an imaginative picture of a purposeless universe, of such vast dimensions and stupendous age that man appeared hopelessly insignificant, alone and unbefriended amidst titanic forces. Not all scientists believed this, but the idea took hold in the popular mind, especially in countries like Russia, where a highly superstitious popular religion was being maintained by the powers of reaction. And churches everywhere were too slow to reinterpret religion to meet this needless threat of scientific knowledge.

**Their end is destruction.** The conclusions that have been drawn from this way of picturing the universe—for it is just a human picture and no more—are legion. Many other factors entered into the stream of causation, but back of and underneath all was this mind **set on earthly things,** conforming itself to what the senses revealed. The more serious thinkers of today are discerning these conclusions in the signs of the times. Some consequences can be mentioned here as topics which deserve much elaboration.

(a) When nonhuman nature appears no longer to be subordinate to some purpose of the Creator, man takes over nature and exploits it for his own purposes. The commercial waste of natural resources, regardless of the ultimate effect on human destiny, the defrauding of future generations by mistreatment of the earth's soil, the prodigal spending of irreplaceable material wealth in total wars, all have a direct relation to an irreligious view of nature, as though there were no other purpose beyond man.

This analysis should make plain that an industrialized machine civilization, in which we are all inescapably involved, is actually a mean-

persons of this kind during his visits to Philippi, and he has now to confess that they had grown steadily worse. He cannot speak of them without shame and sorrow. They are **enemies of the cross,** not merely in the sense that by their evil lives they have set the world against it, but because they are themselves opposed to it in their hearts. Pretending

---

ingless construction which almost overnight can be converted into a war machine equipped with the atom bomb, enabling man to extinguish himself from the earth. Certainly it is fitting to contemplate in this connection, **even with tears,** the fateful words of Paul: **their end is destruction.** And the irony of our worldly success, of which we are so proud, is well described in the phrase **they glory in their shame,** or as the KJV has it, **whose glory is in their shame.**

(*b*) Another result of trusting our senses alone is a conception of human nature that ends in nonsense. The atomic scientist has pronounced the judgment that each of us has enough atomic energy in his body to blow up the city of London. Not long ago, before this last analysis, we were told that we were just a bag of skin full of water in which millions of infinitesimal bugs were swimming about, utterly indifferent to our thoughts about ourselves. That is enough to give one the creeps, but it is nothing compared with the most recent discovery: "I am just a bomb, full of sound and fury, signifying nothing." What a reason for living! We are here to blow up London or, short of that, to keep alive a bag of Infusoria.

Lest this illustration seem facetious, another might bring this nonsense into a practical situation. At a rocket plane factory in which are constructed planes to surpass the speed of sound, a pilot was offered $50,000 to make the first test flight. Because the wings of the plane were too small to lift it off the ground, it had to be taken up by another plane and dropped at thirty thousand feet, with enough fuel to last only for two minutes at top speed. When the pilot was dropped off, he turned on only part of the power and shot straight up in the air at 650 miles per hour until he nearly blacked out. At that point he abandoned his reward, dumped the rest of his fuel, glided to earth and lived to tell the tale. When a member of the company was asked what sense there was in such a tale, he replied, "We are in the kind of civilization where you either keep ahead of others or they will get ahead of you." From which one might well conclude that a civilization which for three hundred years has put final trust in the senses is now headed for an abyss of nonsense. The hopeful sign in this dark picture is evident in the growing feeling that "we have ceased to be men with a meaning," for out of such a feeling may come the promise of redemption.

It is meaningful . . . to make as many people as possible realize where they are; what they are missing; what has happened to them; what they have lost; why they are lonely, insecure, anxious, without ultimate purpose, without an ultimate concern, without a real self, and without a real world. Men are still able to feel that they have ceased to be men. And this feeling is the presupposition of all spiritual reconstruction.[9]

There is no salvation for a sinner until he knows and admits that he is a sinner. And the sin above all sins is to put our human senses in a higher place than God.

(*c*) Again, the ignoring of God has engendered an overconfidence in human reason. Reason, working with such facts as sense can furnish, tries to understand the self-operating constitution of nature. If our hearts have no relation to anything beyond what we can analyze with reason, then we are tempted to confine thinking to the business of explaining how nature operates. Thus reason, dealing with sense material, yields only explanations of how everything works—including our own human constitution.

This overemphasis on reason has led to a disillusioning view of human history. How many idealists have assumed that history moves in a logical way, and that what ought to be will naturally come about—by some process of evolution! It seems logical that humanity must unite in one world; therefore one might expect that all men would move in the direction of their best interest. Thus the problem of human perversity, which Christianity makes a central issue, is sidestepped. For self-interest can corrupt reason more often than reason can control self-interest. Reason can always find or invent a good excuse for doing what we want to do. So long as "self" is left untransformed by the Spirit of God, it remains the great corrupting force in society. There is always needed the rough, catastrophic shock of judgment—which is not in the hands of man—to bring reason to book and reduce self to humility before the promise of new life can be realized. All social programs that would create a new society without any redemption of man from the slavery to self, and without reckoning on superhuman judgment, are doomed to disillusionment. While still exalting the high office of a disciplined mind, we must recover the gospel's insight that

---

[9] Tillich, *The Protestant Era*, p. 267.

**19** Whose end *is* destruction, whose God *is their* belly, and *whose* glory *is* in their shame, who mind earthly things.)

**19** Their end is destruction, their god is the belly, and they glory in their shame, with

---

to believe in it, they detest everything for which it stands. **Their end is destruction**—this, and not eternal life, is the goal toward which they are traveling. **Their god is the belly, and they glory in their shame.** We have here a terrible description of what is the real religion of many men. They conceive of no higher good than the satisfaction of their

---

self-centeredness cannot be self-improved or self-educated without the intervention of the surprising judgment of God, showing up our unsuspected shortcomings and their unforeseen consequences, followed by the mercy of God which redeems the consequences where men are contrite and willing.

(*d*) Once more, abandonment of devotion to God is followed by a purely human religion of devotion to humanity. Of course this religion of humanity is half of real religion, and need not be among the **enemies of the cross of Christ.** In fact, humanists and religionists have so much in common that everything today depends on their learning to work together. Most humanists who have consciously decided to trust man instead of God are unconsciously living by standards of value and a view of life which they have carried over from the religious heritage of their civilization.

But devotion to man degenerates when it is long separated from devotion to that which is forever above and beyond man. Paul saw this when he wrote to the Romans: "Therefore God gave them up in the lusts of their hearts to impurity, to the dishonoring of their bodies among themselves, because they exchanged the truth about God for a lie and worshiped and served the creature rather than the Creator" (Rom. 1:24-25). It was Dostoevski's message one hundred years ago that whenever men stopped believing in God they tended straightway to deify man. This not only happened in Paul's day when emperor worship arose in the empire, but it has happened in our own day, beginning with Nietzsche's theoretical superman. When masses of people are left in desperation, they throw moral considerations overboard and trust the most powerful man in sight. Thus we have a modern type of leader who is not devoted to God against the mob, but devoted to the wants of the desperate mass regardless of God and his moral law.

Everywhere, under stress, the worship of the strong man, who is soon corrupted by the very power which invites the trust, works out toward tyranny. Condescending help of the mighty toward the weak is the very essence of tyranny—though in disguise. Christianity and the condescension of superiors in any situation are forever enemies. How little this is realized by patronizing Christians who identify their self-pleasing condescension with the spirit of God!

Furthermore, devotion to humanity apart from God ends in man's becoming a victim of his own society. For devotion to mankind in general always begins with some group. So-called devotion to the good of others may thus become the chief divisive force among nations. And since no one in any society knows what is the good of the whole group, some dictator is trusted to decide what is best for everybody. Those who differ from the decisions of the few are suspected of treason. Regimentation grows apace until men and women become a means to perfecting a total organization, unable to call even their souls their own. They exist for the state, instead of the state existing under God for the service of the people.

(*e*) It is plain also that minding the things of sense leads straight to all forms of practical materialism. The materializing and dehumanizing of modern society affect all of us, even though we do not call ourselves materialists. By a natural step the success of science, dealing with the world of sense, was taken over into business to produce the commercialism of our machine mass production. More and more man was taken as a being who is moved only by economic causes. History was explained in terms of material interests pushing and pressing individuals. Big business, the bigger it became, grew more dehumanized, leaving undeveloped the better possibilities in the field of personal relations, and failing to discover individual capacities through shared responsibility. The individual conscience was overwhelmed in the actions of great corporations fighting for survival and expansion. Because of the impersonal nature of business for business' sake, the masses of men responded with equally impersonal mass pressure. In collective action men have done to others what as individuals they would never be inclined to do.

For so long this process of dehumanizing society has been eating its way into modern life that we should not expect some panacea that will suddenly humanize it again. But every-

**20** For our conversation is in heaven; from whence also we look for the Saviour, the Lord Jesus Christ:

minds set on earthly things. **20** But our commonwealth is in heaven, and from it we await a Savior, the Lord Jesus Christ,

---

bodily appetites. The things they are most proud of are the miserable successes of which they ought to be ashamed. Their **minds [are] set on earthly things.** This is the sum of the indictment. No error is so fatal as to look only to material good. When this is the one aim, a man's whole nature is gradually debased until he is himself nothing but an earthly clod, like the things he honors. Paul had known many, even among Christians, who had suffered this degradation, so that now he cannot speak of them without tears.

**20.** Over against these he sets those who have understood the Christian message and have tried to live by it. "For our country is in heaven" is perhaps the best translation of

---

where now the pioneers of a new world are those who seek ways to make industrial relations more human and implement the ancient truth that the sense of partnership is basic to personality. The state is too big an agency to cherish the individual with his unique capacities. The large community must create within itself small communities where ordinary men can share responsibility. There is a profoundly religious aspect of all secular activity that is concerned with restoring personal interest where it has been overpowered by an impersonal bigness, thus re-creating local self-government inside the over-all control of the state.

(f) Another destructive result of the unconscious abandonment of religion is in the moral confusion which besets us. Where men no longer strongly believe in God with an overruling moral purpose, they inevitably feel that morals are their own creation. Every interpreter of religion has a major task in explaining the inadequacy and the peril of merely human morality. The bias of self-interest inevitably enters in to pervert it to partial ends until universal convictions disappear and it becomes almost impossible to maintain community. The point is that all human morals are *relative*—they are developed to fit some situation, to maintain the welfare of some particular state, or to foster the prosperity of some special class within the state. The temptation is to make this relative morality absolute and suppress all its enemies.

It is for the good of religion to admit this relativity of every human code, for thus only can we see the need of universal principles by which all human codes are judged for better or worse. Here the revelation of the love of God in Christ becomes the universal norm, given to us and not created by us, never completely expressible in any imperfect condition in this world, but ever remaining the final test of such relative justice as we can attain from time to time. That human nature, with all its native

self-centeredness, can be transformed and fulfilled only by that love which goes out of self and enters into the lives of others for their sakes is a universal fact that is true to life in all places and can be verified only through obedience that costs. But such individual conversion must be related to social reconstruction or it will have little appeal to masses of men.

(g) Finally, the abandonment of God has resulted, strangely enough, in the restoration of belief in "blind fate." Ordinarily men are not brought to such a conclusion by logical thought; but when God goes, there seems to be nothing left but "chance." In practical life this is expressed in the familiar *laissez faire,* which means "let things rip and see what happens." Then, when the unplanned for and unexpected happens, it appears not as a divine providence nor as a human achievement, but as the inexplicable action of a blind fate. Determinism as an intellectual creed, abolishing free will, affects comparatively few; but whole populations are caught in the vague feeling that we are being pushed around in this world by forces that we do not control and which determine our destiny against our will. We are drawn into the industrial machine, or tossed out of it, dragged into depression, or swept into world wars, in ways that make our human wills feel helpless and afraid. Only from a religious view can men look upon the frustrations of life as having a meaning. That meaning can never be read accurately and clearly; but most wisdom is found where the frustrating events of human society are looked upon as the conclusions drawn (not by us) from some violations of the laws of life, like judgments of God which reduce human pride as a prelude to correction and renewal.

**20. But Our Commonwealth Is in Heaven.—** No phrase could better illustrate the gap which exists between modern man and the traditional expressions of religious truth. To approach people who have lost the meaning of ancient phrases by mere repetition of those terms which

the peculiar word (πολίτευμα) which is here employed. It was sometimes used in the abstract to denote a way of living which was associated with a given city—Athens, Rome, Alexandria. Paul has himself used the verbal form of the word in this sense in a previous chapter (1:27: "Conduct yourselves worthily of the gospel"), and here he may have the same idea in his mind. "Our citizenship," the pattern of life we must follow as Christians, "is in heaven." But the word had also a concrete, local meaning, indicating the city or state to which a man belonged. In this passage Paul appears to speak locally. He thinks of a commonwealth which exists in heaven, and goes on to say that Christ will come forth from it. So he reminds the Philippians that although they live on earth, their real country is elsewhere. His words would have a special significance to the people of a Roman colony, who proudly called themselves Romans (Acts 16:21), though they lived in a city far away in Macedonia. Paul impresses on them that they had still another country, of which they were citizens, and to whose laws and customs they must be faithful. It was not for them, as members of that heavenly community, to be intent on earthly things. And

---

make no appeal is to alienate them, or turn them into "gospel-hardened sinners," of whom we have more than enough. What can it mean to the secular mind to speak of a "commonwealth" in "heaven"? Is this the old other-worldliness that made men endure life here in order to attain the hereafter?

We need to bring down to earth, so to speak, this familiar description of God in heaven, and restate in everyday language the idea behind Paul's reference to citizenship in a spiritual commonwealth.

The most obvious connotation of the word "heaven," which we can share with the ancient world, is its unreachableness. The distance between earth and heaven is so immeasurable that it has always been a symbol of that which is out of reach of man's senses and even of his power to think. Belief in our senses confines us to things we can see, hear, touch, and measure, and such belief seems the easier course because it keeps our feet on the ground. Hence its popularity. But the end thereof, as we have seen, is "destruction" and nonsense.

Now, religion is frankly betting one's life on the unreachable, beyond our senses and our reason. In the letter to the Ephesians there is an excellent statement of this extraordinary attitude of man, "Now to him who by the power at work within us is able to do far more abundantly than all that we can ask or think, to him be the glory . . . for ever and ever" (Eph. 3:20). In the nineteenth century Tolstoy brought himself out of skepticism by clinging to the inescapable fact that more is being done with us and through us than we can ever account for.

The Creator's activity is not limited to our understanding. We modern people are sophisticated, and hold ourselves within the understandable areas of life. We ignore any final mystery which we cannot reduce to an explanation the size of our mind. We are like a man in the navy who, being asked in an examination how far the sun was from the earth, replied, "I don't know, but it is far enough off so that it will not interfere with anything I want to do in the navy." But there is no sense in thus shying off from remote mysteries, for there are at least two very natural ways by which we all make contact with the unreachable. Both ways are mysteries, but they are so normal that we take to them early, as a duckling takes to water before he has been formally taught to swim.

First, there is the mystery of an inexhaustible preparation. Whatever we learn was already prepared to be known, beyond our knowledge. Who prepared it? Where was it kept in store as a possibility before we discovered it? No human mind has ever found an answer to these questions because to a finite mind they are absolutely unanswerable; and it is only begging the question to say that everything is as it is. Some ordering of possibilities has existed before us, and will continue after us. Every action that leads to new knowledge confirms this mystery, even when we cannot describe it in a mental picture.

In another letter Paul says, "Eye hath not seen, nor ear heard, neither have entered into the heart of man, the things which God hath prepared for them that love him" (I Cor. 2:9). We know what he means without any explanation. There is nothing magical about this "supernatural" preparation, nor do we make it any simpler by dismissing the word "supernatural" in favor of some substitute like "the transcendent."

We naturally take to the supernatural beyond our reach because we were endowed by our Creator with a unique capacity to rise outside of what we now are and where we are, to be connected with something still greater and better than we can dream of. All growth

21 Who shall change our vile body, that it may be fashioned like unto his glorious body, according to the working whereby

21 who will change our lowly body to be like his glorious body, by the power which

---

**from it we await a Savior, the Lord Jesus Christ.** It is remarkable that the name "Savior," by which we now commonly speak of Christ, hardly ever appears in the N.T., perhaps because it was originally a pagan title applied to kings who were supposed to have saved the state in a time of crisis. This may be the very reason why Paul makes use of it here. He thinks of the church as an outpost of the mother city in heaven. It looks in that direction for the deliverer, the true Lord to whom it owes allegiance, and who will not forget it in its distress.

**21.** Not only will Christ save his people, but "he will transform the body of our humiliation." For Paul man is essentially a spiritual being, and his present condition as an earthly creature, clothed in a body of flesh, is alien to him. In consequence of the sin into which he has fallen he has been thus humbled, and will not recover his true freedom and dignity until he has escaped from the earthly body. We can well conceive how Paul, with his magnificent soul obstructed at every turn by an ailing body, was sensitive, more than other men, to the "humiliation" he had constantly to suffer. He declares that Christ at his coming will **change** [literally, "refashion"] **our lowly body to be like** [literally, "of

---

and discovery depend on this capacity. It makes each person more significant than the contents of his body. It gives man a central place in the universe as the unique creature through whom the Creator reveals the latent possibilities of his creation. It gives us the only constructive attitude in the face of adversities and frustrations, enabling us to say, "I can rise out of myself, look back at myself to see how unworthy I am compared with all I ought to be, and then look forward to being re-created unpredictably by all that I pass through." No one understands how we can thus get above and beyond ourselves, but we do it. Through this God-given capacity of the soul the unreachable has a way of reaching us, disturbing us, using us, and confronting us with an unconditional call toward more that could be true and more that is good to be. Classic religion has always insisted that we never would have tried to find God if he had not already found us.

Even people who consider themselves irreligious may have this devotion to the unreachable without seeing its religious implications. A young colored man who had suffered from the race prejudice of so-called Christians lost not only his faith in God but also his faith in man. He assumed he was a complete skeptic, but he said in a letter, "I believe there is a goodness higher than any human code." Where was that goodness located? He could not tell, yet he used it to judge all human codes that fell short. So we all know that our truth is never the whole truth, for "we know in part." Our meaning is good so far as it goes, but it is never the total meaning. The last word about the truth and

meaning of life is always with the Creator, and never with his creatures. It is better to accept this mystery of infinite preparation, and bet our life upon it, than to explain it by explaining it away. For then nothing is left but what our senses tell us, and the wide-open temptation to hold some relative truth as though it were absolute.

Christianity makes the affirmation that the unreachable has come down within our reach in the personality of Christ, not indeed to show us all there is of God, but to reveal supremely the redeeming love of God seeking every man among us, while enduring the consequences of our sin, that we might no longer live unto ourselves but unto God.

Second, we also have contact with the unreachable in the mystery of conclusions. We cannot draw the conclusions of what we do or think, but we leave them to be drawn beyond our control. Thus our living becomes a healthy combination of fear and hope when we stake our life on the proposition that wherever we leave conclusions to be drawn, they will be drawn—but not by us. Up to a point we are free to decide and act; but from there the consequences take over, to create a new situation that presents us with a new challenge demanding a response.

This mystery of conclusions is fearful because we lose the control of our own life. A young minister in his first parish was making friends with the boys on his street by kicking a football in an open lot between houses. Once he made a most satisfactory kick, but the moment the ball left his toe he felt in his bones that it was

| | |
|---|---|
| he is able even to subdue all things unto himself. | enables him even to subject all things to himself. |

one form with"] **his glorious body.** The two Greek words for form (cf. 2:6) are both used in the present passage. On the one hand, Christ will "change the appearance" (μετασχηματίσει) of the existing body; what it will look like we cannot yet tell, but it will be a different kind of body altogether. On the other hand, its outward appearance will correspond to its inner nature (σύμμορφον). Men will enter on a new state of being, and their bodies will be similar to that of the exalted Christ, and will manifest that higher life on which they have now entered.

The whole passage must be read in connection with I Cor. 15:42-53, where Paul expounds at length the ideas which are here only suggested. He believes that the dead will rise, not with the corruptible bodies which are laid in the grave, but with "spiritual bodies," woven apparently out of an ethereal substance of the nature of light. Many will be alive when Christ returns, but they also will exchange their earthly bodies for these "bodies of glory"—"We shall not all sleep, but we shall all be changed." Christ has been the "first fruits" of this change, but they who are Christ's will be made like him. Paul has the final drama in his mind, but he here adds the idea that Christ himself will effect the transformation. He will make the bodies of his people like his own, "according to

---

headed straight for a window at which one of his old parishioners was sitting. He longed to have that ball back in his control, but it carried on relentlessly to a foredoomed conclusion, smashing the window and showering his parishioner with glass.

Life is like that—letting go pieces of our life to break into other lives where conclusions are drawn out of our reach. One is free to neglect to fit himself to enter other lives in order to make some real contribution there, and he himself will not see the conclusions of that neglect; but somewhere down the line they will be drawn where some door of opportunity is shut in his face. Napoleon felt free to ignore God and impose his own will on the world, with no universal principle behind him. The conclusions of his proud ambition were drawn in so many countries and in so many surprising ways that he could not keep track of them; but they kept track of him. *Sic semper tyrannis!*

Winston Churchill in his book *The Gathering Storm*[1] aptly describes the fateful nature of human decisions when confronted by the mystery of unforeseen conclusions. "How little can we foresee the consequences either of wise or unwise action, of virtue or malice! Without this measureless and perpetual uncertainty, the drama of human life would be destroyed." He points out that Hitler's genius taught him that victory could not be achieved anywhere by a process of certainty. Decisions always had to be made before everything could be known, and before everything could be completely ready, for to wait too long "was probably to wait till

all was too late." Indecision is itself a decision that leaves conclusions to be drawn, as was illustrated by the inability of the government to make up their minds in the crisis while events moved relentlessly on to unavoidable situations demanding new decisions. "They go on in strange paradox, decided only to be undecided, resolved to be irresolute, adamant for drift, solid for fluidity, all-powerful to be impotent." What a picture of the incalculable peril of all human indecisiveness everywhere!

However, not all conclusions are fearful. There is a hopeful side to the fearfulness, for every noble act also leaves conclusions to be drawn far beyond our knowledge. One Man on a cross has proved how irresistible are the conclusions of life in the hands of God.

The reconstruction of the world centers around this hopeful mystery. We are being driven back from all particular purposes of our own to a universal purpose of saving the meaning of personal life. Our salvation is not in recovering some golden past, nor in attaining some earthly utopia of the future, but in this universal purpose of God, which is neither new nor old, but timeless. Any human being who is loyal to the final mystery of infinite preparation and is ready with his best to answer the call of conscience and leave the conclusions for the Creator to draw is the most creative factor in the world scene. Here we are back to the biblical view that God participates in human history, and is known in those through whom his timeless purpose is working in time. The redeeming power that stoops to understand and save is the only kind of power that has nourished and

[1] Boston: Houghton Mifflin Co., 1948, pp. 201, 215, 260.

the working of his power even to subdue all things to himself." Being now the Lord he has a universal power, and will put it forth in the great act of bestowing his own nature on his people. The closing words are an echo of Ps. 8:6. The psalmist speaks of the majesty which God has conferred on man, putting all things under his feet. We know, however, from Heb. 2:6-9, that in early Christian thought the psalm in honor of man was regarded as a prophecy of Christ, and in this sense Paul also interprets it. Christ was the unique Man, to whom everything in the end would be subject.

It will be noted that the lofty conclusion of the chapter is linked by a natural train of thought with the opening verses of denunciation. Judaism is false because it ties religion to outward and material things. Christianity is a spiritual religion. It releases men from their bondage to things of this earth. It makes them citizens of a higher world and brings the assurance that this life in the body will be merged at last in that heavenly life which the believer will share with Christ.

---

transformed personality from the beginning of time. Apart from that divine activity within, no life can fulfill itself by itself, and no group is secure by itself; and all progress in control over nature leads to a devilish conclusion.

The hopeful meaning of our life is this: We are never perfectible, always corruptible, but always convertible from self into union with God's timeless purpose. And the company of people who are united in that purpose are in the "commonwealth" of "heaven," here and hereafter. To have citizenship in that "company of all faithful people" is to be part of a vast community from which our life draws strength and continuity. Each one must choose his place, either among the minority who would make the world, or with the majority who come along to live in it, exploit it, and make it nonsense.

From it we await a Savior. This traditional word "Savior" has taken on fresh meaning as we live among the signs of a disintegrating civilization. For the ancient question has again arisen: Are we trying to save a civilization, or are we trying to save people who are caught in one that perhaps ought not to be saved? No matter what happens to a civilization, whether it disintegrates or comes to new birth, *people* go on and have to live their lives, while new styles of life are gradually created.

The symbolic picture of a Savior coming out of a spiritual commonwealth ("coming down from heaven"), to save people from an earthly commonwealth that is temporal, has many suggestive implications for the interpreter of biblical truth today.

For instance, we now see that Rome at the peak of her power was stricken with the same disease of meaninglessness which now afflicts our own world. Just when the empire was apparently growing in strength, the fatal disease was present. But people carried on, and some there were who began to be saved from that dying commonwealth. They were only a few,

and they were scarcely mentioned by contemporary historians. They believed that through Christ they were given a new principle of interpretation for the meaning of existence. Christ embodied that living interest in the inner quality of every individual which roots back to the Creator himself. From the foundation of the world this interest has been a fact, and will be from everlasting to everlasting. The mystery of man is that the Spirit embodied in Christ can come to birth, like new life, at any time and in anyone where self is willing to give over. Crucify that Spirit, and it continually comes alive; for it is timeless as God, and only through death to self may our human nature be transfigured and rise into the commonwealth of the Eternal.

Such a new life is validated in history. For from what looked like a hopeless defeat of Christ on a cross, new conclusions have been drawn through the rebirth of that kind of life inside a continuous company of people. And wherever the Spirit in men is renewed, it prompts them to create new forms for its expression—in families, schools, business, social systems, and world affairs.

Every social system becomes corrupted, involving all citizens in the corruption, and must be re-created around the timeless purpose of fulfilling personality in single human beings in a limitless community. Inside the church and outside of it, in secular organization and with secular ingenuity, in all callings and fields of work and in all countries, the faithful few act like a "leaven in the lump." They make beginnings from which new conclusions begin to be drawn beyond their sight. They cannot change the world at once, indeed they may seem to fail; but they have a single mind to answer the divine call for their best in each situation, leaving conclusions in the hands of God, whose endless business is the reconstruction of his creation where men spoil it, that he might reconcile men to his eternal purposes.

4 Therefore, my brethren dearly beloved and longed for, my joy and crown, so stand fast in the Lord, *my* dearly beloved.

4 Therefore, my brethren, whom I love and long for, my joy and crown, stand firm thus in the Lord, my beloved.

## VI. FINAL ADMONITIONS (4:1-9)

It is Paul's custom to close each of his epistles with a section made up of practical counsels and of personal notices and greetings. This is not necessary in the present epistle, for it has been personal throughout, and has dealt with practical issues in the Philippian church. At the same time the closing chapter is more definite in its character than those which have gone before. Paul turns to matters of immediate interest which he has hitherto touched on only in general terms.

**4:1.** The opening verse may be meant to conclude the preceding section: **Therefore, my brethren, whom I love and long for, . . . stand firm thus in the Lord:** Paul has reminded them that through Christ they have part in a kingdom which is not of this world, and as citizens of heaven they must hold firmly to their allegiance; no specious

**4:1-9. Final Admonitions.**—Paul's winning appeal comes to a climax in the closing sentences of his letter. It is more than a play on words to say that all the tactics of human relations depend finally on tact. The effective person is one with a genius for "getting the good out of us" for some purpose bigger than himself. He is the opposite of the improver who seeks to do others good, thus unconsciously showing his pride in his own goodness. One has only to read a very human book like Mark Twain's *Huckleberry Finn* to see how the improver tends to intensify in youth the very deviltry he desires to suppress. Certainly the chief reason why Sunday-school teaching has often become an unfortunate memory is its obnoxious tendency to moralize. In dealing with human beings the main question is whether we "bring out" the best or the worst side of their nature.

In this last chapter of the letter Paul brings all he has been saying to bear upon the best instincts of his friends in Philippi. He has taken his time before coming to grips with the particular trouble that has worried him, and he has revealed his deep and affectionate interest in "all" of them. He has reminded them that the gospel for which he has suffered is a truth which is advanced by anything that can possibly happen to its followers, and he has brought the condescension of the love of God into comparison with petty rivalries that spoil human fellowship. He has disclaimed any superior righteousness of his own making, and pounded home the mystery of a new life that can be created in men by the grace of God alone, for which no one can take credit upon himself. What a disarming and subtle approach!

**Therefore, my brethren, . . . stand firm . . . in the Lord.** Paul liked this figure of speech, taken from the familiar act of standing. It occurs

also in the letter to the Ephesians, "Having done all, to stand. Stand therefore" (Eph. 6:13-14). These letters were written in the days when Nero was looming on the horizon, like Hitler in the twentieth century, when the necessity of decision might prove fatal.

How inexorably we are always confronted with the demand for self-commitment is illustrated by the daily act of standing on our feet. In walking we deal with the inescapable force of gravity that is actively at work on us all the time so that we must decide to commit our weight somewhere. We may choose to stand first on one foot and then on the other, but we cannot keep both feet off the ground in indecision, for that amounts to a decision to sit down.

In the first part of ch. 4 Paul reveals very informally and almost casually some of his own methods of keeping his life committed. His religion was what all right religion should be, a constantly renewed quest for the truth to which he could commit his whole life without any reservations. Once he had discovered that salvation from self was not to be found in mere trying to be righteous, but rather in a persistent sense of falling short and of utter surrender to the new life of the Spirit, which is the gift of God, he found it was not easy to *stay committed*. He is ever repeating his warning against slipping back to respectability, and resting on the oars of acquired self-righteousness. Here we have the perennial religious problem, not the single act of committing oneself, but the practice of renewing the commitment. In conventional language this procedure is known as the practice of devotion.

Lest "devotions" should smack to the ordinary man too much of artificial piety, it is necessary to show how naturally such practice fits into everyday living. For we are ever beset by solici-

105

2 I beseech Euodias, and beseech Syntyche, that they be of the same mind in the Lord.

2 I entreat Eu-o'dia and I entreat Syn'-

---

arguments, from the Jewish side or any other, must seduce them from their faith in Christ. It seems better, however, to take the verse by itself as gathering up the purport of the whole epistle. Paul has had occasion to warn the Philippians of dangers which have made him anxious, and now he would have them know that all this fear is due to his great love for them. His one desire is that they should continue to be Christ's people, as they have been in the past. Into the word **therefore** we have to read everything he has said of the kindness and fidelity of his readers, and the hopes he has set on them. When he describes them as **my . . . crown** we are not to think of the diadem worn by a monarch. He uses a word which means simply a wreath, such as was assumed by a victor in the games and also by guests at a banquet. He wishes it here to carry these two suggestions of triumph and of festivity. The Philippians were the convincing proof that he had "not run in vain." They were also his chief cause for rejoicing. The thought of them filled him with gladness, as if he were sitting at a feast instead of lying in prison.

2. As Paul exhorts them to be steadfast, he desires them to remain in concord. This has been one of the underlying motives of the letter, and now it finds concrete expression.

---

tations to give a piece of life here, a little of our time there, and a portion of our strength elsewhere; and without some over-all loyalty to hold us together we may literally go to pieces. The wisdom of our ancestors and of all the saints is in the periodic habit of renewing the devotion that is worthy of all there is in us. Plenty of human tragedy warns us that life disintegrates when it has no purpose that is sovereign above all human purposes, and that deserves the devotion of all kinds and conditions of men in all ages, from everlasting to everlasting.

If we thus take religion as devotion, it divides men into religious types, according to the attitude they take. (a) A thoroughgoing atheist (not a merely intellectual one) would be one who felt there was nothing worth while to which he could commit himself. Logically this attitude would put a man in the impossible position of keeping himself entirely to himself. It took the German submarines along the American coast in World War II to prove that there were plenty of people in the country who almost corresponded to this self-serving type. The southbound ships along the shore at night were silhouetted against the glow of light over Atlantic City and Miami Beach, so that submarines could pick them off like sitting ducks. When a blackout was ordered, a cry went up all along the Atlantic seaboard that the tourist season would be ruined, though the purpose of the blackout was to save mariners from drowning at sea. That illustration might well halt thoughtless people (like all of us) with the question: "How much of the time are we just helping ourselves at our own tea party, as

though the rest of our fellow men were our servants?" For in a machine age we are tempted to reduce human relations to what can be paid for.

(b) Akin to the practical atheist is what might be called the "drifting" type, in whom the "sense of sin" has been replaced by a "sense of drift." The feeling of being lost and at loose ends is characteristic of multitudes whom two world wars have left in complete confusion about any fixed truth to which they could be attached.

Adolescents often fall into this class, even without wars. Before some central and commanding purpose has laid hold upon them, they are inclined to try anything once. They desire to learn by doing; but without any clear idea of ends and purposes, they may proceed toward the questionable to see what the harm might be, only to find the answer when it is too late to avoid the harm.

A kind of adult adolescence has caught many people in postwar times, people disillusioned with everybody and everything. The intellectuals in this group call themselves "existentialists," but many who do not know what this term means are afflicted by the same state of mind. They have a vague and "anxious" feeling that since we created neither ourselves nor the universe, we cannot possibly know what ultimate purpose calls for our devotion. We can know only *what we do*, each by himself in his freedom taking a step in some direction. This inviolable freedom, with its individual responsibility, tends to generate a highly individualistic point of view, as though each had to fight his lone battle in a brief time in the face of the

3 And I entreat thee also, true yoke-fellow, help those women which labored

tyche to agree in the Lord. 3 And I ask you also, true yokefellow, help these women, for they have labored side by side with me

---

He has heard of quarrels which had broken out in the church, due apparently to those personal ambitions which he had condemned in ch. 2, in the light of the great example of the humility of Christ. One quarrel in particular had grieved him, since the two women concerned in it were both very dear to him. **I entreat Euodia and I entreat Syntyche to agree in the Lord,** i.e., to consider their dispute in a Christian spirit and so come to an agreement. Only the names of these women are known to us; but it is evident from the manner in which Paul speaks of them that they were among the most active workers in the church, and had been so from the beginning. One of them may possibly be the "Lydia" of whom we hear in the book of Acts (cf. Vol. IX, p. 219) for this appears to be only a surname, indicating her place of origin.

3. Paul appeals to a third person to assist in composing the quarrel, and here we meet with a singular difficulty. "Yes, and I ask you, genuine comrade, to lend a hand to them," i.e., to act as intermediary. Who is this "comrade" (literally, "in the same yoke") on whose help Paul relies? The word gave rise at an early date to the wild conjecture that Paul was married to a woman at Philippi, most probably to Lydia. This absurdity

---

ultimate frustration with which death overtakes us all.

Christianity accepts this truth of knowing by doing, but gives it a goal and a guide. Kierkegaard fathered "existentialism" within the Christian context; but when devotion to this experimental drifting is taken out of that context, it is little more than grown-up adolescence. It is safe to say, however, that comparatively few people can break themselves loose completely from values which have been bred into them by tradition.

Trying everything until one sees what fails him might be likened to a man on a fishing trip who decided to walk across a log jam near a dam in the river, while his friends trusted themselves to a path on solid ground. After a few steps, a light log let him down; and being required to find another footing, he tried a big log which rolled and forced him to leap to the small end of another log that sank under him. On he plunged amid rolling, splashing timber, until he fell through and hung by his armpits while his friends came to fish him out, a wetter and wiser man. His friends had taken a clue from past generations who had found a way through the alders around the pool, and used their freedom to prove to themselves by walking that it was worthy of their trust. The problem of the world today, amid widespread bewilderment, is to relate on ever-new levels the originality of a creative person and the tested experience that speaks through tradition.

(c) An improvement on the above types is found in those who call themselves "humanists." Most who belong to this class are not aware of this rather academic title, but feel much like a

social-minded businessman who confessed he could understand the second great commandment about loving one's neighbor, but was quite in the fog about loving God first. When men become vague about God or disillusioned with conventional religion, they consider it adequate to devote themselves to human relations. Up to a point this decision parallels the teaching of religion, for human nature, created in the image of God, can find fulfillment only by entering into the lives of others.

But no one can devote his whole self to mankind in general without being as futile as the man who wanted to show his love of all men by smiling kindly at his fellow passengers in the subway train.

We have to begin caring for mankind in some concrete situation, and our personal interest selects some people ahead of others, with the result that devotion to our favorite human beings may lead to the deadliest conflicts. All kinds of prejudice—racial, class, and religious—all partisanship, and the fiercest nationalisms, arise from a devotion to humanity that becomes sharply limited by interest. So long as life on earth lasts, this original tendency of man to be conditioned by his special concern for himself and his group will cause strife among us. But that strife may become creative instead of destructive when the local attachment is always held under that final attachment to God, from which comes humility and a willingness to be corrected and a readiness to share life in common effort. Popular religion may be too anemic and uninformed to mitigate the struggles between man and man; it may even intensify the oppositions; but the only answer to immature

| with me in the gospel, with Clement also, and *with* other my fellow laborers, whose names *are* in the book of life. | in the gospel together with Clement and the rest of my fellow workers, whose names are in the book of life. |
| --- | --- |

may at once be set aside, for the adjective which accompanies the noun is masculine. There have been many guesses as to the identity of this man, whom the Philippians would recognize at once without mention of his name. Sometimes it has been supposed that he was Epaphroditus, but it would be strange that Paul should thus address his messenger in the letter which he was himself carrying. The most likely solution of the riddle is that Σύζυγος, which meant comrade, was also a proper name, and this would give point to the adjective "genuine." With a very obvious play on words Paul says, "I ask you, Syzygus, whose character answers to your name." The one objection is that Syzygus is found nowhere else as a proper name, but this only proves that it was somewhat uncommon. This man, then, is asked to make the two women friends again, **for they have labored side by side with me in the gospel,** i.e., they had stood by Paul when his missionary task was hard.

As he remembers their past struggle he cannot but mention others who had likewise taken part in it: **together with Clement and the rest of my fellow workers, whose names are in the book of life.** Clement was the name of a Roman Christian, the author of an epistle which still survives—the earliest Christian document outside of the N.T. There is no evidence, however, that he came from Philippi; and Clement, in the early centuries, was a favorite name. Paul adds that there were others whom he might mention; but this is needless, for their **names are in the book of life.** This is a phrase taken over from apocalyptic thought, and it appears several times in the book of Revelation. An ancient city kept a register of its citizens, and it was conceived that in heaven also there was a book in which the names of God's true servants were inscribed. This was the **book of life**— the list of those who had a title to eternal life.

religion is the cultivation of high religion, which can reduce the pride of men so that they may begin to see each other as limited creatures of a common Creator.

Christianity offers a unique answer to this persistent requirement of our nature to commit ourselves. It affirms that there is a known, fixed truth to which we can devote all there is in us with no reservations. This particular truth, as was pointed out in 1:9, can be recognized only when it is acted out in the life of a person. Our religion first presented the truth of God in a *deed,* through one who was sent by God. His coming was an act of God, an event in the divine initiative. Before there were any doctrines, or churches, or rites, there was this Great Deed, in which the divine kind of life was actualized in man, and thence became further realized in a company that has spread to the ends of the earth, having kinship with all people in any religion and in any age who have responded in any degree to that Spirit which eternally seeks to live in man.

There is no way to appreciate Christianity and its promises apart from this living current of life, from God as an infinite source, through Christ and the whole activity of the Spirit in the interrelation of all responsive people. Here

is a known, unchanging, life-giving Spirit entering into self-centered people like a new creation, always doing a new thing, and seeking to make a bad consequence into a better one. Constantly crucified, it forever rises with deathless power like an eternal thing—which it is.

Paul's plea for commitment centered in this personal truth revealed in a life which, he never forgets, is not a human achievement, but a gift from God to men, and which can be confirmed inside the life of anyone. Thus we can see why the problem of staying committed has always been the continuous element in the practice of "religious devotions."

For our self-commitment is a very spotty affair, occasional at best. A charming woman of the old school, being complimented on a new dress, said to her small grandchild, "You know, grandmother always tries to look just as nice as she can." "Yes," replied the child, "and *sometimes* you succeed." Few of us do better than that—we do our best sometimes. We need to realize that the practice of devotion is designed to improve the rest of the time when we forget God and serve ourselves.

After setting forth in this chapter the appeal to **stand firm,** and after an entreaty directed to the quarreling factions at Philippi (for an

| 4 Rejoice in the Lord always: *and* again I say, Rejoice. | 4 Rejoice in the Lord always; again I will |

---

**4-5.** At the beginning of ch. 3 Paul had begun to say farewell, and to this point he now returns. **Rejoice in the Lord always; again** [as I have already done] **I will say, Rejoice.** It must be remembered that the Greek word for rejoice was also used by way of good-by, and Paul avails himself, as he had previously done, of this double meaning. His idea is similar to that in the Fourth Gospel (14:27) : "Peace I give unto you: not as the world giveth," i.e., "I do not say farewell in the merely conventional sense." Paul emphasizes his deeper meaning by adding "always." Joy, in all circumstances and under all trials, should be the mood of the Christian man, and Paul goes on to show how this habit of joy may be obtained. **Let all men know your forbearance:** The word implies fair-mindedness, a willingness to give and take instead of standing rigidly on one's rights. The Christians were surrounded by a heathen population to whom their conduct and

---

extended treatment of the mixture of praise and censure in vss. 2, 3, see on 1:3-11), Paul reveals rather indirectly the practices of devotion (of commitment) which he evidently followed himself. The elements in this practice are not set down in orderly fashion, with successive steps neatly following one another. The apostle is simply passing on his passionate zeal for self-commitment which constantly absorbed him.

**4. Rejoice in the Lord Always.**—Paul persistently reminded himself that his new life **in the Lord** (i.e., in the power of) was not a product of his uncertain will, but a new creation from God himself. It was as though he always said to himself: "When I really live, it is not I but the grace of God in me, and I take no credit for it—I simply rejoice that I am being worked through, without having to ask how or why or to what end. And whenever I fail, I remind myself that by myself I always fall short, and then I forget the failure as I recommit myself for God to renew his work in me." By such a habit of dismissing failure in the joy of a new commitment, the past becomes a spur to further and more complete offering of self.

The habit of an ordinary man—such as we all are—is to feel self-satisfied with the credit of a good deed, thus revealing that the action was largely motivated by some concealed self-love. Paul evidently battled with this familiar temptation, for he often urges others not to think of themselves more highly than they ought to think—which, by the way, leaves ample room for a proper self-estimate. But to Paul every true act of self-giving was prompted by the grace of God and empowered by the Spirit of God; so that on every occasion he rejoiced to give the credit where it belonged, and thus enticed himself, as it were, into more and more of the joy of a totally surrendered life.

In this connection it is noticeable that in his continuous rejoicing Paul included a past of

which he was deeply ashamed. During his fanatical younger years he had murdered Christians under the blind conviction that he was absolutely right and they were absolutely wrong. He had presumed to say just how God wanted people to be religious. He had his pattern of morality so fixed that he judged all others by it, and condemned all who differed. The hateful sin of hard orthodoxy, which through all the ages has led to persecutions and inquisitions, rested heavily upon Paul's soul. His sense of guilt was deep and ineradicable.

Such a sense of unresolved guilt has been attacked by modern psychologists as a fruitful source of neurotic disorders; and often our modern treatments are aimed at lightening or dismissing the sense of guilt. Paul would agree that a sense of guilt should not be left to fester in the subconscious. What he did was to use it with rejoicing to increase his zeal as an apostle. To remember himself as a persecutor in order to double his effort as an advocate was a positive and essential practice. It was the gospel's answer to all human souls caught in the irrevocable results of a bad past.

One easy way out is to forget as soon as possible those we have hated or hurt. No use crying over spilled milk, we say. We are repelled, and rightly so, over the morbid consciousness of sin with which some conventional Christians have afflicted themselves, but we need those memories that sting our easy conscience and deflate our self-protecting pride. We need them not to brood helplessly over them, but to make us contrite, to keep us grateful for the forgiveness that offers us a new chance at self-surrender, and to deepen our earnestness to prove that God can have whatever is left of life. When anyone, from Paul down to our own day, is resolved that God shall have all there is of him —faults, failures, virtues, the whole past and the whole future—the sense of guilt can always be sublimated in a joyful self-abandonment.

5 Let your moderation be known unto all men. The Lord *is* at hand.

say, Rejoice. 5 Let all men know your for-

---

beliefs appeared strange. They were to be patient under misunderstanding, so that their enemies might see that they were no mere hotheaded fanatics. Such patience might often be difficult, but they are reminded, **The Lord is at hand.** This was the watchword of the early Christians, sometimes expressed in the Aramaic form *māranā thā.* The hope which

---

**5-6. The Lord Is at Hand. Have No Anxiety About Anything.**—We are living today in an anxious and worried world, and multitudes of people are seeking comfort for troubled minds and tense nerves and worn-out spirits. There is no end to books concerned with the destructive effects of fear and worry on human personality; and psychiatry has become the rival of religion in ministering to the tortured soul.

Much of the advice that ministers to this widespread hunger for comfort and peace is highly practical and basically true. It runs something like this: Do not think about things that may not happen; take life an hour at a time, a day at a time, and do not borrow trouble from the future; analyze what it is that causes your worry; ask yourself if there is anything you can do to remove it; then make the most of your opportunity to improve what cannot be removed. Probably everybody needs to have these simple rules repeated over and over, for they are excellent *if* we can follow them. On the border of religion new discoveries have been made concerning the power of mind over body, and there has grown up a popular literature that promises almost miraculous results by the simple act of changing the thoughts that control attention. The connection between this power of the mind and the power of faith is buried too deep in our nature to be explained. Where the two are combined, changes in bodily health, mental serenity, and all-round effectiveness may occur beyond all calculation.

Sometimes secular advice is mingled with religious teaching, which gives to the patient the assurance that God is ready to bring healing and comfort where trust makes one ready to receive. Just as the forces of nature are ever ready to serve us, so the healing, peacemaking forces of God are ever surrounding us, waiting only for us to give them a chance. We are told to do what we can, and entrust the rest to an ever-working God.

There are three dangers in this modern quest for happiness through comfort. The first is the temptation to overlook the disturbing effect of the divine impact which the Bible insists is the initial effect of God. There must be some painful breaking down of human pride which bars the entrance of the Spirit. A second danger lies in the "self" which remains at the center, ever ready to inject its fears and its hurt pride into any peace that is temporarily attained. Third, the whole practice of self-healing is apt to be too confined to individual anxiety, with no intelligent concern for the world's future which is the major source of fear for everybody.

As a protection against these dangers we need the deeper understanding of life represented in the words of Paul, "Rejoice in the Lord. . . . Have no anxiety about anything." Here is the ageless wisdom of religion asserting that we can deal rightly with an uncertain future only when we have something more than the future and more than ourselves that we care about.

Modern man has been trying for nearly three hundred years to substitute faith in the future for faith in God, but the result is not making sense. When the prospects are rosy, man is hopeful; but when they are black, man is in despair. This vacillation between hope and despair shows that we have habitually worshiped a future which is precarious, instead of God who is the same yesterday, today, and forever. Nothing is more disconcerting to youth today than the way our faith in the future has been shattered by the colossal stupidity of man. Veterans of the wars do not like to be told that this blind and staggering world is the golden age for which they and their friends risked their lives. The fact is that there is no future which man can make on this earth which man with his pride and lust for power cannot unmake. To live for a spoilable tomorrow as the chief end of life is to spend our days fooling ourselves.

Paul combines his joy "in the Lord" with deliverance from anxiety, and adds a familiar phrase that means almost nothing to a modern reader, **The Lord is at hand.**

Christians of Paul's time had come to believe that the new age, when the kingdom of the Messiah was to be established on earth, had actually arrived in Christ. He had brought into the earthly sphere the redeeming power of the Spirit, and initiated a fellowship of people who lived and moved in a new sphere of life, which was still in the world but not of it. The satisfaction and inner joy of this unearthly life of the Spirit, with its deep serenity past all under-

sustained them was that of the Lord's return, and they assured each other whenever they met that the hope was certain. Paul here repeats the watchword as supplying the grand motive to patience. Injustice and derision might be hard to bear, but all these little troubles would soon be over. The Lord was coming.

standing, meant more to those within the fellowship than any earthly future whatsoever.

The full significance of such a view appears in connection with the whole historical background from which Paul derived his religious outlook. Biblical religion was born and reared on that "dangerous edge of things" where human existence faced extinction, and it originated as no fair-weather, easygoing faith. The great prophetic leaders arose at a time when the Hebrews were in the midst of the breakdown of their civilization and at the end of their national existence. In our tragic age we are in a mood to appreciate this religion which rose triumphant in a "time of troubles."

The call of the prophet Isaiah, described in visionary terms (Isa. 6), may be taken as a universal symbol of the great reversal from the worship of the future to the worship of God. The vision came "in the year that King Uzziah died," which marked the beginning of national collapse. Right there on the edge of doom the prophet saw "the Lord, . . . high and lifted up."

That impact of God came like a blow which demolished the last vestige of any egoistic view that earthly happiness was the chief end of life. God was realized primarily as the great disturber, who shook all human foundations in order that men might realize what is unshakable and eternal.

With the overwhelming impression of the absolute majesty and holiness of God came a profound awareness of the "unclean" (i.e., the unconsecrated) nature of the national life, in which prophet and people shared alike. "Woe is me! for I am undone."

From the depths of this humbling and searching experience there came next the voice of conscience, "Whom shall I send, and who will go for us?" There was the unconditional summons that is the voice of the Creator calling man to give his best, blindly and rashly if need be, and become God's partner in creative actions.

To the unconditional call there came the human response of utter willingness, "Here am I; send me." From then on this prophet was to find that the sense of duty in a prescribed task was the law of life, whatever the future.

George Adam Smith, in commenting on Isaiah's call, gives an interesting parallel in the career of Mazzini to show how this spiritual pattern belongs to all men in all ages. Mazzini

fought to liberate Italy, only to find himself deserted and misrepresented by those he set free. Just when every last hope was blasted he wrote, "I felt that I was indeed alone in the world. . . . Perhaps I was wrong and the world right." Then one morning he awoke with his mind tranquil and his spirit calm and with one thought uppermost, *"Your sufferings are the temptation of egotism."* He suddenly realized how he shared with his people the misconception that life was a search for happiness, and recognized there was such a thing as "love without earthly hope," like the eternal love of God. From then on, when duty had become the law of life, he could say, "I learned to suffer without rebellion, and to live calmly and in harmony with my own spirit." [2]

Incidentally, it should be noted how different such prophetic leaders are from many leaders of the masses today. In a biography of Columbus the author points out that the great navigator was not a leader chosen by the multitudes to accomplish their desires, but "a Man with a Mission, . . . alone with God against human stupidity and depravity." He did not reach the Indies, as he hoped, but by his faithfulness he was used to open up America. [3]

The Bible remains a best seller today because it records the supreme demonstration of this life which is independent of the future. Christ allowed himself to be completely stripped of all that men feel is necessary for happiness, and out of his final crucifixion there was revealed the glory of a triumphant spirit that proved stronger than anything that could happen to it. Such a perfect revelation could not have been made in some easier way. The love of God, in its amazing self-sufficiency and its complete contradiction of all respectable life that men accept as good enough, could be shown to us only in one who was crucified by the typical sins of this world. Christ bore witness to a life for every man, a life that lies above and beyond the natural like a new creation, a new nature. Christ's disclosure was so rooted in reality that it survived all contradictions and all evil, deathless and eternal.

Paul's way of meeting anxiety is of course in direct line with Jesus' admonition and practice,

[2] *The Book of Isaiah* (New York: A. C. Armstrong & Son, 1901; "The Expositor's Bible"), I, 86.

[3] S. E. Morrison, *Admiral of the Ocean Sea* (Boston: Little, Brown & Co., 1944), p. 46.

"Be not anxious." We need to relate such confident faith with practical problems in a world of fear. Three lines of thought particularly merit repeated elucidation.

(a) **Have no anxiety** should not be taken as a counsel of perfection. Spiritual freedom of the inner life will not, for most of us human beings, put an end to all worldly anxiety, but it may *put it in second place* where it is more readily handled. When given first place, it can be literally the death of us.

So long as we have to make a living and keep "body and soul together," we have to be more or less anxious about our job and our future, our families, social injustices, and a better future for everybody. There is anxiety in our waiting for future possibilities to show themselves, but when such concern is in second place, it will not dominate our whole life and interfere with what we care most about.

William Lyon Phelps, who lived his life with students, used to say that before young people attain a sense of mission they have to be anxious about their outward appearance, for if they were fat and wrinkled and baldheaded we could not bear to have them around. But people with the most interesting thoughts are the most satisfied and satisfying persons, and when they are *really* interesting, they prove acceptable regardless of how they look from the outside.

In far more important matters it will always be the man with something inwardly fine to live for who can most wisely meet the perplexing anxieties of practical existence.

(b) When the sense of duty becomes the law of life, that life is never anxious about devotion to duty, no matter what else there may be to worry about. Therefore the man of faithfulness is most free to prove what hidden possibilities are waiting to be realized; and his deep sense of mission under God liberates the mind from limited practical expectations. Who knows how many times he ought to be patient, how kind or honest he ought to be? Who knows what love can do, or how far the influence of integrity may go? Only one who is unconditionally faithful before he can know the consequences can be the instrument for an unwearied Creator.

The place of sheer faithfulness is best understood when we remember that there are always two ways of looking at any task that we confront. We must needs have an eye on the future effect of our action on the human level. It is necessary to calculate, gauge the conditions of success, the chances of defeat. Politics and business constitute together the "science of what is possible now." The religious sense of duty cannot take the place of such common sense scanning of the landscape; but on the other hand, we must look away from men to God, beyond all practical considerations, toward what ought to be. For God's possibilities are never exhausted by any human plan. The only key to the unknown is the unconditional call from God, to be faithful, truthful, creative, "with unlimited liability" for persons in their own right. We cannot substitute practicality for such faithfulness, nor vice versa—the two must be kept together in a continuous tension.

(c) The biblical way of facing an uncertain future is a correction to earthly views of progress. History is not like an escalator moving steadily and inevitably away from evil toward a happier (or shall we say easier?) order of life. Every success is corruptible by human pride that comes before a fall. All complacency is a stoppage in creation, inviting catastrophe.

Going back to our biblical history we can see that the spiritual insights of our race are the permanent assets, while civilizations rise and fall. Out of the dim past Babylon rose to its peak of splendor, and then fell. Rome reached the summit of material power and glory, and went down. Another high peak was reached in the Middle Ages, but the pride of the church and of a feudal society tried to prevent a new future, and once again an end came. Now our modern world, after reaching the highest peak of material glory, has descended through two world wars to an unprecedented depth of disaster. But through all the ups and downs the emergence of the Spirit in the lives of great men and common men abides as the true end of man's being. Without that, men do not become more significant, no matter how they acquire the wealth of this world that ever becomes one with Nineveh and Tyre.

Once more let us quote from America's greatest literary interpreter of human nature, Herman Melville. In *Moby Dick* he gives a sermon of the preacher in the sailor's bethel in New Bedford, containing these unforgettable words:

Jonah did the Almighty's bidding. And what was that? To preach the Truth in the face of Falsehood. . . . Oh! shipmates! on the starboard side of every woe, there is a sure delight; and higher the top of that delight, than the bottom of the woe is deep. . . . Delight is to him . . . who against the proud gods and commodores of this earth, ever stands forth his own inexorable self. Delight is to him, . . . who acknowledges no law or lord, but the Lord his God, and is only a patriot to heaven. . . . And eternal delight . . . will be his, who coming to lay him down, can say with his final breath—O Father! . . . I have striven to be Thine, more than to be this world's, or mine own. . . . I leave eternity to Thee.[4]

[4] New York: The Modern Library, 1944, pp. 47-48.

6 Be careful for nothing; but in every thing by prayer and supplication with thanksgiving let your requests be made known unto God.

bearance. The Lord is at hand. 6 Have no anxiety about anything, but in everything by prayer and supplication with thanksgiving let your requests be made known to

**6.** They not only had this hope for the future, but they could feel in the strength of it that all was well in the present. **Have no anxiety about anything, but in everything by prayer and supplication with thanksgiving let your requests be made known to God.** Continual prayer will be the safeguard against all anxiety, and Paul describes in a compressed sentence the nature of true prayer. It involves first the attitude of waiting upon God; then it means that in our weakness we ask his help; then it requires that we state clearly what we want from God, believing that he will give it. But along with all this there must be the spirit of thanksgiving. We cannot ask God for new mercies unless we are mindful of those he has bestowed already. The unthankful man cannot pray, for he has no real sense of the goodness of God.

**6.** *In Everything by Prayer and Supplication.* —This admonition would seem to suggest that a man must pray all the time, no matter what he is doing. But most of us find it hard to think of God and mind our particular business at the same time. One reason why the old practices of devotion insisted on taking time out to concentrate on God was to offset this absorption of our attention by the world. The devotional writers also have much to say about "ejaculatory prayers," brief utterances in the midst of our busyness, to keep our wills committed.

Perhaps the psychological basis for Paul's use of prayer **in everything** might be expressed in the rather naïve habit of a beloved mother who, whenever a serious decision had to be made, always "asked God first." Jesus in the crisis of his life wanted the cup to pass from him, but first he wanted the greater will of God to be done. To want the greatest, wisest will of the Creator to be done before we insist on what we want is certainly no vain and pious submission, but rather a highly aggressive aspiration like that of a scientist when he wants the truth to be known "though it blister one's eyeballs."

**With thanksgiving.** There is prevalent among us what is known as the "Pollyanna" philosophy, ever grateful for the bright side of everything. It is of course a one-sided philosophy, and is very widely practiced because it refuses to face up to the black side of things which is just as much a part of the picture, and just as instructive, as the bright side.

Here again Paul's practice of increasing his gratitude was always with one end in view—to deepen his commitment. The more grateful he was, the more eager he became to consider his whole life as an obligation. An interesting study could be made of the kind of conduct that springs from utter gratitude, as contrasted with

that which all other motives can generate. Basic with Paul, of course, was gratitude for God's justification of a life that could not justify itself by its own imperfect works. This affected him even more deeply than gratitude to God "for our creation, preservation, and all the blessings of this life." Above all was gratitude for the gift of Christ, and for the new life of the Spirit mediated to man from God through him and all who received him.

**Let your requests be made known to God.** This sentence can hardly lend support to the idea that we need only to ask for what we want and God will give it to us. What we want can generally be distinguished from what God wants by some frustration of desire, for God's purpose is something infinitely greater and more worthy than the satisfaction of any man's selfish wants. Even one's unselfish wants may be in the larger necessity quite impossible. Since God's will began and continues in infinite time, our particular preferences must be subject to the qualification, "Not my will, but thine, be done."

But such qualification should not limit the practice of opening inner chambers of our lives to let every desire hidden there be made known in the presence of God. In that larger setting our human wishes are seen in a true perspective. Since our desires act on us unconsciously to determine our decisions and even deceive our reason into wishful thinking, they must be constantly exposed. The peril of living an unexamined life, determined by suppressed desires acting on us through the subconscious, has been abundantly exploited by modern psychology, which stresses in no uncertain terms the necessity of bringing to consciousness the concealed concerns that are really dominating us. Any family with many children knows the struggles that go on daily to keep a good ap-

| | |
|---|---|
| 7 And the peace of God, which passeth all understanding, shall keep your hearts and minds through Christ Jesus. | God. 7 And the peace of God, which passes all understanding, will keep your hearts and your minds in Christ Jesus. |

**7.** Paul then dwells on the effect of true prayer, even when the particular request may seem to be unanswered. **And the peace of God, which passes all understanding** (literally, "surpasses all thought") : This has been variously explained. According to

pearance in the front hall where visitors enter. Some convenient hiding place where all the clutter can be thrown under the stairs when company approaches is part of the equipment of any well-ordered home. To all appearances the guest finds a neat house, but we would not have him see the disorder in the closet.

We all have something like a hall closet, where we conceal what we do not want company to see. We have ingenious ways of trying to forget what is in that closet—we keep very, very busy; we never take time to think; we seek continuous distractions and stay with the crowd. That is why Paul insists on making everything known to God in moments when we are alone and still with our decisions.

Such prayer is nothing more or less than putting ourselves in a position where "there is no place to hide." For inside each of us is that secret place where no human being can ever enter. Only God shares that. And the consciousness of being absolutely alone there is in reality the "eternal consciousness of being an individual," finally responsible to his Creator.

**7.** *The Peace of God, Which Passes All Understanding.*—There is a singular parallel between the final words of Paul and of his Lord in the presence of death. Each had endured persecution and suffering from the hands of men they sought only to help. Each was rewarded with ingratitude, misunderstanding, and blind opposition. One was confronting crucifixion, the other was in prison awaiting a fatal verdict. Both speak of an unutterable joy and peace, which, since it is not given by the world, cannot be taken away by the world.

The author of John, out of his experience of the Spirit, recalls the comforting words of Christ in the closing hours of the great tragedy, "These things I have spoken to you, that my joy may be in you, and that your joy may be full" (John 15:11). "Peace I leave with you; my peace I give to you; not as the world gives do I give to you. Let not your hearts be troubled, neither let them be afraid" (John 14:27). And Paul's last injunctions are almost an echo of these words of Christ: "Rejoice in the Lord always; again I will say, Rejoice. . . . And the peace of God, which passes all understanding, will keep your hearts and your minds in Christ Jesus."

It is important to remember that these words were not addressed to people living on Easy Street to make their life still easier. They were spoken by one who had been stripped of everything in the world that human beings naturally want, and they were directed to a handful of disciples defending a new faith against a hostile ruling class. Such a message can be fully understood only as men become matured by the inherent tragedy of this earthly life. And the promise stands the same in all ages: when we are finally stripped of self, there comes to us from God a life which is a joy in itself to live, and which carries with it a satisfaction and peace that are "out of this world."

What the world means by peace and what the Bible means are two different things altogether. The peace of this world is deliverance from tribulation; the peace of God is the result of deliverance from self. Worldly peace is manmade, religious peace is God-given. Neither one is supposed to take the place of the other, and neither is to be identified with the other.

Since the peace of God is best understood against the background of earthly peace, we must first consider the latter's advantages and limitations.

The quest for peace is the major preoccupation of mankind in our age. Everything depends on relief from violence equipped with all the destructive power that lies in nature. In our personal lives, quite apart from the troubles of civilization, we require relief from tribulation. When a mother of many children finally after a hectic day has them all tucked in bed, she settles down for a little blissful peace. Parents could not survive without such release; but it is short-lived, for children always wake up to act and to grow by the very strife that drives their elders to distraction.

Industrial peace and international peace must be sought at all costs, for violence must be reduced to a minimum in human affairs, but when it is eliminated, life is still strife minus the violence. All secular hopes delude us when they aim at some utopia free from want, where all tribulation will cease. Neither in private nor public life is there any permanent and conclusive way to separate ease from disturbance, joy from pain, security from change, or life from death. Worldly peace is good to a certain ex-

one view, accepted in the familiar English translation, the meaning is that the peace of God is unfathomable: we are conscious of it but it is beyond our comprehension. Others would take the Greek word for "mind" in its restricted sense of "cleverness" or "ingenuity." Paul would thus say, "The peace of God will do far more for us than any careful

---

tent, but change and decay and death warn against it as a final hope.

The peace of the world is inevitably linked with self-interest, which creates strife as naturally "as the sparks fly upward." God created each of us as a "particle of creation," with a will of his own and with a basic concern for his self-preservation which by its very nature brings us into conflict with others who are equally concerned for themselves.

Every person views life from his own angle, which is different from every other man's standpoint, and no one can see the whole view. Each must "draw the Thing as he sees It for the God of Things as They Are," but whenever that reference to God is left out, then the way each "sees it" conflicts with what others see; and truth is best found not where someone pretends to be impartial, but where ideas of many meet head on and are allowed a hearing. What comes out of the struggle of many views freely argued is likely to disclose more truth than can be known by any one man or group of men however wise. What students call a "bull session" suggests that a little bullying is necessary to break the grip of complacent and obstinate conviction.

All our best learning comes through strife that creates disturbance and upsets equilibrium. The conservatism of an older generation would hold the world in outworn ways, save for the unsettling power of a new generation. We learn to co-operate where rivalries and conflicting interests confront us with problems we cannot solve alone. Our own personal character is the product of a perennial struggle with our self-centeredness. Love that had not triumphed over self would not be love. Life is always strife.

Self-interested peace may degenerate into dullness when survival is assured. The advertising business, knowing that satiety bores people, invites desires for something new, with no boundaries set. Prosperity begets restlessness because possession allays neither pride nor ambition nor fear. Some with more than they need pursue the "game" of business for the satisfaction of doing the dramatic thing which is beyond the power of others, often with altruistic ends as a sop to conscience.

Pride prompts men to lord it over others, which requires power, and once men enter upon the quest for power they come under limitless temptation, for their control creates resentment which threatens their security. This drive for unlimited security beyond the need of survival is in most cases mixed with a variety of good motives. Even self-interest finally compels one to consider others' security for the sake of his own, for without some transfer of interest from self to the community there is no mitigation of the consequences of the will to power.

Collective forms of the will to survive seem on the surface to be entirely beneficent, claiming to be devoted to the common good and the peace of the world. Nevertheless, we have learned that group pride, group fear, and lust for power, equipped with technology and with control of information, may become Frankenstein's monster devouring its creator. What the Bible calls "principalities and powers" we experience in these impersonal aggregations of social pressures which are out of our personal control and which are not God's creation. We call them demonic forces, as though they were neither man's nor God's but the Devil's. The forces of evil are not entirely accounted for by personal wickedness.

It is easy for collectivism to prove that by serving others we really serve ourselves. Certainly our good is wrapped up in the public good, and it is quite true that in seeking our own welfare we may contribute to the welfare of all in ways which we do not plan. Totalitarians hold that the public interest is just everybody's interest collected in one big lump, as though the harmony of all is simple, logical, and inevitable. Idealists argue that we need only to sacrifice a little of our private concern for the sake of the community, and then induce the local community to yield some of its prerogatives for the sake of the national community, and finally persuade the national groups to sacrifice some of their autonomy for the world community, and lo, the dove of peace will be hovering over us all.

Summing up the case for the pursuit of earthly peace, we must say it is both necessary and unlimited, but the degree of its success depends on our understanding of another kind of peace altogether. With the saving work of God in the constant remaking of the human spirit left out of account, man by himself defeats himself. For reason assumes the place of savior instead of God. This creative intelligence, highest of human capacities, is ever susceptible of being seduced by some personal or group bias leading to strife. To restrain the rivalries

planning of our own." But in the light of the context the idea of the verse would seem sufficiently clear: Paul has just said that we should think of our special needs and so offer our petitions, but now he declares that God will give us something infinitely better than any benefit we can conceive. He speaks elsewhere (Eph. 3:20) of him "that is able to do

of groups within the state, government must take a hand. Then the question of who shall control government begets continuous struggle for power within the nation. Where the acquisitive interests of powerful states conflict, logic seems to demand a world state which has authority to maintain world peace. Forgetting that a world state cannot arise save as we have first learned to work together as a practical world community, we trust history to be made by logic; and when events do not prove to be logical, we are tempted to put final hope in more education and more time. We trust the Future with a capital "F," and Evolution with a capital "E." But History, however it is capitalized, has not the saving power.

Revolutionists who would transform the earth without reckoning on a change in human nature transfer the capitalization to a Classless Society, which will so condition men that love, kindness, and fairness will prevail.

Nietzsche, instead of putting faith in a class of ordinary men, felt the world's hope lay with a company of Supermen, with a capital "S."

It [the aristocracy] should . . . accept with good conscience the sacrifice of a legion of individuals who, *for its sake,* must be suppressed and reduced to imperfect men, to slaves and instruments. . . . [Society exists] only as a foundation and scaffolding, by means of which a select class of beings may be able to elevate themselves to their higher duties, and in general to a higher *existence:* like those sun-seeking climbing plants of Java which encircle an oak so long and so often with their arms, until at last, high above it, but supported by it, they can unfold their tops in the open light, and exhibit their happiness.[5]

As pure theory, Nietzsche's idea had its promise, but when the Nazis appointed themselves the supermen, the world was not convinced that the peace of mankind was assured as they "unfolded their tops and exhibited their happiness."

We see on every side the ancient quest for "peace of mind" in a world of strife. If Paul were alive today, he would probably say of the modern technique for self-conquest, as he said of the law, that it is a kind of "tutor" preparing us for the "peace of God."

Much of the psychological advice offered to

---

[5] *Thus Spake Zarathustra.* Reprinted from *Introduction to Contemporary Civilization in the West,* II, 839. Copyright 1946 by Columbia University Press. Used by permission.

troubled souls is common sense merging into religion. Self-analysis, to find hidden sources of evil, is akin to the old self-examination leading to confession. Learning to replace defeating thoughts by thoughts that bless and heal is not far from the old practice of prayer. The use of one case to help another case is employing the principle of contagion, which was so popular in revival campaigns and testimony meetings.

Through all the tragic limitations of worldly peace we are prepared for an appreciation of the peace of God so desperately needed in addition to the peace we make for ourselves. It "passes all understanding" because it is something given to us as a fruit of self-surrender. Just as the righteousness of God is not a product of our effort of will, but a gift of the Spirit, so there is a serenity which keeps our "hearts" and "minds," which is due not to relief from trouble but to relief from self.

From Paul's life we can recognize its characteristics. (*a*) It is a peace of humility. Once one feels that the new spirit within is nothing he can boast about, pride and all its vexing troubles that wear and sour the spirit are swallowed up in gratitude. Out of deep thankfulness for new life there springs the desire to give away one's best, without caring what others say or without asking for gratitude.

(*b*) It is a peace of singleness of mind. With all life committed to a purpose greater than itself, there is no part of life left on the side lines watching for effects and calculating returns. No one of us ever attains such a singleness in perfection, but we have had moments when all the diverse activities of life seemed to be included in the effort to "will one thing." Paul summed it up in his phrase "One thing I do."

(*c*) It is a peace of a justifiable life. No one can know all he ought to know, or be all he ought to be. By no effort can we finally make ourselves completely right, i.e., completely justified. But God can recognize an imperfect person as right when he has the right attitude which opens the way for God to enter his life, remake him, and use him for greater purposes than he can know. William Booth resolved "that God should have all there was of William Booth," and that was all that God required. God is different from a judge laying down a law; he is a self-giver, waiting to give the fullness of his own Spirit to those who really give all of themselves to him. Anyone who has tasted even

exceeding abundantly above all that we ask or think"; and here he tells the nature of this blessing, which surpasses all that we can ourselves imagine. God bestows his peace, the knowledge that he is with us and that we can rest on him. This **will keep** [or "guard"] **your hearts and your minds in Christ Jesus.** The image is that of an armed escort protecting the traveler from all possible danger. With the peace of God encompassing

---

a moment of the peace of self-abandonment has found release into a bit of the "liberty of the children of God."

(*d*) Again, it is a peace of final judgment. There is an unspeakable relief in the thought that our worth is judged finally by God and not by man. To live subject to the correction of God is to feel that one is picked out and recognized for what he thinks and does, as though his life really mattered to the Creator. There is nothing to hide, no public reputation to keep up; only loyalty and willingness are the objects of concern. Here again, no one attains perfection, but ever and again we sense the meaning of this utter readiness to be corrected.

(*e*) It is also a peace growing out of forgiveness. Those who, like Paul, felt themselves forgiven, i.e., put to a new use despite a mistaken past, have power to forgive others. Self-righteousness, defending itself, seeking its own, has no forgiving power—except in words. The free inclination to be magnanimous and forgiving comes by the grace of God, if it comes at all, out of actual experience of new beginnings in our own lives after many failures that put us to shame. To be delivered from the endless wear and tear of nursing grudges and remembering offenses unprofitably is to be set free for understanding others who, like ourselves, do wrong when they do not quite know what they do.

This deliverance is far different from the selfish comfort of not bothering about others, or the stoic endurance of ill-treatment. We have heard much of dictators who never forget a wrong done their people, and who promise vengeance to the bitter end; and we are apt to compare this fierceness unfavorably with some easygoing, weak-kneed liberality which we call Christian forgiveness. The comparison is misplaced. In this world evil always has to be paid for, and human agents are used in collecting the payment. For better or worse we have to judge each other and bring evil to book, but we are safe in this business only when we remember that both the judge and the judged are under the judgment of God, whose sole aim is to reconcile men to his higher purposes and to give them the new life of his own Spirit. The peace of God can dwell in us only when, like Paul, we confront our fellow sinners in humility as though God, through our forgiven life, had

"given to us the ministry of reconciliation" (II Cor. 5:18).

In passing, it may be added that what defeats all reconciliation is malice, for malice is a fiercely contagious and devastating thing. It multiplies itself beyond all calculation. Its source is in the unabandoned self, which is ever driven into blind rage by whatever rivals its claim or stirs its envy. Malice is the curse that brings all broken relations, private and public, back to the doorstep of each one of us. It disperses the crowd, and puts each individual squarely under the final judgment of a long-suffering God. Abraham Lincoln, under deep concern for an enslaved race and the unity of the whole nation, insisted that the issues were too great for "malicious dealing."

(*f*) Another aspect of the peace of God is contentment with *being*, as contrasted with *having* or *doing*. Paul in prison was at the point of life where having possessions availed nothing, and where further action was denied him. His final relation with God was in being himself. No matter what we have or what we do, the ultimate rest for a human soul is in the union of one's spirit with the Spirit of God, for that is union with the Eternal; and this experience is as much a social as it is an individual experience. For Paul to be "in Christ," an intensely private matter, is also to be in the "body of Christ," i.e., one of the company of people who embody in greater or less degree the new humanity of which Christ is the chief representative (Rom. 12:5). Paul's Christian mysticism is a very different thing from the ineffable union of the "alone" with the "Alone." His sense of union with Christ and God in the Spirit was conditioned from beginning to end by his life in a society controlled by the Spirit. Paul indeed knew something of an indescribable mystical ecstasy that was individual (II Cor. 12:2-5), but supremely he cherished what he knew of love, generated in and sustained by an active fellowship with the members of a body of people who lived in a "new sphere of life." The Spirit of God is always mediated to us through an undefinable community of persons, past and present.

Finally, a word must be said about the relation of peace and memory. Our memories can harry us to the end of life by recollections of those moments when we were free to do the better or the worse, and chose the irrevocable

8 Finally, brethren, whatsoever things are true, whatsoever things *are* honest, whatsoever things *are* just, whatsoever things *are* pure, whatsoever things *are* lovely, whatsoever things *are* of good report; if

8 Finally, brethren, whatever is true, whatever is honorable, whatever is just, whatever is pure, whatever is lovely, what-

---

us we have nothing to fear. No outward troubles can assail us since we have perfect tranquillity in our own souls. This peace, Paul says, will be ours, when we trust in God as we know him in Christ.

8. The main concern of the Christian is with this peace of God; but how shall one deal with the countless minor concerns which press daily on every man? About these Paul is thinking when he says, **Finally** [or "for the rest"], **brethren.** All that is necessary, he says, is to have a few settled principles on which one always acts. He uses an expressive word which is not adequately rendered by the English **think on** or **think about.** This translation implies that one's mind ought always to be occupied with pure and elevated thoughts; and such a condition is no doubt highly desirable. But Paul's whole point is that thoughts are not enough. Mere contemplation of what is excellent often weakens a man, leading only to romantic fancies which correspond to very little in his actual life. The word used by Paul means properly "calculate," as when a workman takes careful

---

worse. Psychologists have warned us about the peril to personality of an unrelieved sense of guilt, buried deep in the subconscious, working like a cancer in the healthy tissues of moral life. However, it is equally dangerous to let pass easily the occasions when we have used our freedom "for an occasion to the flesh" and not to gain increased freedom from self in the larger purposes of our Creator.

The pain of the spirit when we make self rather than God our chief end is a healthy and not a morbid pain, just as healthy as the pain that warns us of a tooth's decay. As children, we remembered that a toothache meant a visit to the dentist, and we contrived ways to avoid the remembrance as long as we could. So, in all our shortcomings, we like to get over the memory of them as fast as we can. There is a moment of "feeling sorry," and then we try to leave the "guilty thing" behind and act as if it had never occurred.

But our past never is left behind. It is always a part of the present, conditioning it both in ourselves and in others whom we have influenced or hurt. Paul could not take back the lives he had murdered in his mad career as a persecutor, and the memory of that fanatical mistake never left him. He speaks of it in his letters again and again, as though he did not want to forget it. For it stood in his mind as a measure of God's forgiveness that so grave a sinner could be made into an apostle by the grace of God. Passing regrets over our past doings have little effect. But the persistent regret that issues in a constantly renewed desire to put one's whole life, consequences and all,

in the hands of God is what the Bible means by "godly sorrow," so very different from being sorry for one's foolish self.

> It is not gain that guilt should be wholly forgotten. . . . But it is a gain to win an inner intensity of heart through a deeper and deeper inner sorrowing over guilt. . . . When consequences even become redemptive . . . this is the older, the strong and the powerful repentance.[6]

Thus can the peace of God transform all sense of guilt into an unsparing sense of responsibility for all misled and misunderstood and frustrated lives.

The conclusion of this whole matter of the strife of life was given us in the Prince of Peace, who found no peace for himself on earth. He stood against the full force of malicious evil, so that he was hated by the authorities and ruling classes, misunderstood by the masses, deserted by his friends, with no apparent help from God, until the waves of calamity submerged him completely. Only after the deadliest thing had happened did it become plain that there is a unity between the Spirit of God and the spirit of man that remains "beyond tragedy," and survives all the accidents of life or death. "Therefore let those who suffer according to God's will do right and entrust their souls to a faithful creator" (I Pet. 4:19). And that really is the conclusion of the whole matter.

**8-9. *Finally, . . . Whatever Is True, . . . Think About These Things.*—**In the Exeg. the

---

[6] Søren Kierkegaard, *Purity of Heart* (New York: Harper & Bros., 1938), pp. 17-18.

*there be* any virtue, and if *there be* any praise, think on these things.

ever is gracious, if there is any excellence, if there is anything worthy of praise, think

---

measurements before he sets about his task. Paul seeks to impress on his readers that they must have certain right standards of action, and consider on each occasion how these should be applied.

**Whatsoever things are true:** This is the first requisite—to make sure that one is not mistaking some error for the truth. It is a melancholy reflection that most of the world's mischief has been caused by well-meaning people who act conscientiously by rules and convictions which are entirely wrong. **Whatsoever things are honest** (or **honorable**), literally, "worthy of reverence" (σεμνά). The word carries with it a religious suggestion. Much in our codes of honor is stupid and artificial, but there are modes of action which we know by our deepest instincts to be right. To act contrary to them is to offend against God. **Whatsoever things are just:** Paul here employs his word for saving righteousness in its ordinary sense. Every man can resolve that in his daily business and in all his social relations he will at least deal justly. **Whatsoever things are pure:** This is a comprehensive term. Besides actual vices there are many habits and actions which degrade a man in his own eyes and in those of others. He must purify himself of all these meannesses. As he keeps his body clean, he must wash away everything that debases his soul. **Whatsoever things are lovely:** This is an exact translation of the Greek word, only it must be understood in its original meaning of "worthy of love." There are some ways of acting and types of character which have a charm about them. What it is we may not be able to explain, but we are attracted and wish that we could act in that manner and be like that. **Whatsoever things are of good report** (or "are well spoken of") —i.e., what men have always agreed should be held in honor—cannot be set aside. Paul thus enumerates the

---

word **think** is translated as equivalent to "calculate," i.e., one is not simply to think about **these things,** but to think about them as though he were calculating the cost of committing himself to them in action. Commentators have often suggested that this list of abstract virtues and principles which reason should ponder is an indication of Greek influence upon the apostle. A final judgment cannot be made on such issues, but it is important to connect this paragraph with the whole Christian position that moral or spiritual truth with which Christianity is concerned *must* be expressed in living persons. It cannot be abstracted from action, put into words like purity, honor, loveliness, excellence, and have power to move the will to action. All **these things** to which Paul refers are qualities of life known only when lived by persons. Such an interpretation is confirmed in the sentence that follows, where Paul says: **what you have . . . seen in me, do.**

All the great devotional writers of the church have stressed, as part of prayer or as introduction to it, the discipline of bringing before the mind those living personalities who at some time or other have moved one to action, put one to shame, and saved one from clinging to self. To renew this moving power which reaches us through persons, and to commit ourselves

over and over again to that power, is a normal part of the practice of keeping ourselves committed to God.

That it must be a discipline should be plain to modern man, whose mind is battered with suggestions from morning to night, over the radio, in advertisements and by the hectic struggle of everyone to make a living, asking him to commit himself to *these* things. It is a law of psychology that when unconscious suggestions come into conflict with the conscious suggestions, the unconscious almost always win control of our wills when we are not looking.

Just because we respond so automatically to unrecognized suggestions, we require some discipline which delivers the automatic part of us from the power of the world to the power of God's Spirit which is manifested to us in "mortal flesh," alive and seeking us.

Underneath the whole practice of commitment we must realize the central intent to *deny self.* Many rather smug Christians try conventional ways of giving up the tea and cake they have been serving themselves through the year in order to observe Lent. To a degree this has justification, even in its limited usefulness, for it may help a person to develop the habit of saying "No" to himself in preparation for more important occasions. Certainly anyone who

**9** Those things, which ye have both learned, and received, and heard, and seen in me, do: and the God of peace shall be with you.

about these things. **9** What you have learned and received and heard and seen in me, do; and the God of peace will be with you.

---

moral standards by which conduct should be tested, and he summarizes in the clause that follows all that he has in mind: **If there be any virtue, and if there be any praise.** The word "virtue," on which all pagan morality turned, occurs only here in the writings of Paul, and the idea of "praise" is likewise a pagan one. For Christianity the only judgment which mattered was that of God, and very often it condemned the things praised by men. So Paul does not intend that what he has been saying should include the whole Christian rule of life. He has spoken rather of normal goodness. There are some things which men as moral beings have always found to be necessary, and the Philippians are not to think that they can now dispense with the old requirements. These will never cease to be valid, and the Christian morality must rest on this foundation, given in the very constitution of man.

**9.** For Christians, however, the good life consists in this and something more, which is indicated in the following verse: **What you have learned and received and heard and seen in me, do.** Again Paul offers himself as an example, for his effort had been not only to teach Christianity, but to exhibit it in his own person. Since it was not merely a set of rules but a new life altogether, it could be presented only through a living man. He carefully defines, therefore, how he had imparted the Christian knowledge. He had done so first by instruction in the principles of the faith; then by handing down the tradition of how Jesus had lived and died; then by all the counsels he had given to those who sought his guidance; then by his personal actions. The Philippians had seen for themselves, while he lived among them, how he had followed the Christian teaching in spite of weakness and temptation and persecution. They must keep his example before them and act as he had done; **and the God of peace will be with you.** Here he returns to what he has already said, that the grand safeguard of the believer is the peace of God. His readers may be sure of this protection when their one aim is to do what is right, and to hold steadfastly to their Christian faith.

---

never practices saying "No" to self will never be ready for any great obligation if and when it comes along. He will probably be blind to its coming. The practice of self-denial can make one aware more and more of the opportunities that are customarily overlooked. However, to both Jesus and Paul denying self was a positive practice of giving oneself away to God and to men in need. We may sometimes be put into the mood for self-giving by performing an unselfish deed just when we do not feel like it. Psychology confirms the truth that the finest feeling follows the finest doing—not the other way round.

A note might be added at this point to indicate the importance to a free world of beginning from within individuals where commitment occurs. Outward schemes of organization in secular society and in the church are necessary for the promotion of every human good. But these external arrangements require continuous renovation and remaking, and creative

change is made less violent by the multiplication of devoted individuals who are not just serving themselves. Those who are more or less detached from their own concerns can help men trust each other to reach working agreements. The real object and dominant aim of the Philippian letter becomes evident at the end, where Paul entreats Euodia and Syntyche to *agree*, and calls on others to help restore unity. Even such a selfless, dedicated man as Paul could not prevent dissension in his churches, but nevertheless it was his singlehanded influence that held those earliest groups together at a time when disintegration and persecution threatened on all sides. Though it is impossible to prevent disagreements, growth and freedom are maintained by the tireless capacity to reach new agreements where the old ones have failed.

From the practice of self-committal outlined above Paul derived two enduring benefits: deliverance from anxiety and inward peace. One is mentioned in vs. 4, the other in vs. 7 (see Expos. on these verses).

10 But I rejoiced in the Lord greatly, that now at the last your care of me hath flourished again; wherein ye were also careful, but ye lacked opportunity.

10 I rejoice in the Lord greatly that now at length you have revived your concern for me; you were indeed concerned for me,

## VII. The Gift from Philippi (4:10-20)

Before he closes the letter, Paul takes occasion to thank the Philippians for the money they had sent him by the hand of Epaphroditus. As yet he has not touched on this subject, except in one or two vague allusions, and this has often seemed surprising. It is assumed that the main purpose of the epistle was to acknowledge the gift, and yet nothing is said of it except in these final paragraphs. Various explanations have been given for this neglect. One is that Paul was dissatisfied with the amount of money sent to him, which was less than he had expected and had come too late. This would be quite inconsistent with the character of Paul and with the whole tenor of the letter; also with the present passage of thanks, when it is rightly understood. Others have here detected one of the many instances of Paul's delicacy of feeling. He avoids speaking of the gift until the very last because any mention of money would have struck a jarring note. He dwells rather on all the claims the Philippians have on his affections, and casually at the end alludes to this one, although it had been constantly in his mind. But his delicacy would rather have prompted him to speak at once of the gift, and make much of it. The Philippians had made a real sacrifice on his behalf, and would wish to know, before anything else, how it had been appreciated. There is no difficulty, however, if we assume that Paul had already thanked them for their gift. If he had not done so, he must have allowed some months to pass before he even acknowledged it, although messages had been passing freely between Philippi and his place of imprisonment. Paul, of all men, could never have been guilty of such discourtesy. The present epistle is not to be regarded as his letter of thanks. This had been sent already, but at the end of another letter, written for a different purpose, he thanks his friends again. When it is thus understood, the passage falls at once into its natural place.

**10. I rejoice in the Lord greatly** [i.e., my joy is not so much in the gift as in the Christian love which inspired it] **that now at length you have revived your concern for me.** The image is that of a plant flourishing again after a time of drought, and the verb may be taken either in a transitive or an intransitive sense. If it is used intransitively, Paul would say, "I am glad that you have flourished again, so that you can be thoughtful about me." He would thus imply that the Philippians had been passing through hard times and were in no position to help others; now they have got back to prosperity. The other construction (see RSV) is the more probable; but even so, Paul hints at an improvement in the circumstances of the Philippian church. It might seem at first sight as if he were complaining; "Now at last, and it is high time, you have remembered my

**10-20. The Gift from Philippi.**—This closing reference to a gift of money which Paul had received from his converts in Philippi furnishes an introduction to one of the greatest utterances in the Bible concerning the inviolable independence of the inner life of the Spirit. The best that our religion has to say about the providence of God is concentrated in these few famous sentences. No doubt Paul had previously thanked his friends for the gift he received (see Exeg.). Here he is expressing an attitude toward money which seems a long sea mile away from the feelings of anyone who

has to struggle for a living in our materialistic civilization. Under the pressure of trying to make both ends meet, our reaction to a sudden windfall from an unexpected quarter would not be likely to turn our thoughts in a spiritual direction.

Our first impulse would be to spend part of this unearned increment on some luxury, and deposit the rest in government bonds against the inevitable rainy day. Money is so important in meeting our immediate needs that it does not naturally remind us that "life consisteth not in the abundance of the things which [a

11 Not that I speak in respect of want: for I have learned, in whatsoever state I am, *therewith* to be content.

12 I know both how to be abased, and I know how to abound: every where and in all things I am instructed both to be full and to be hungry, both to abound and to suffer need.

but you had no opportunity. 11 Not that I complain of want; for I have learned, in whatever state I am, to be content. 12 I know how to be abased, and I know how to abound; in any and all circumstances I have learned the secret of facing plenty and

---

need." But his object plainly is to assure his readers that he quite well understands the cause of their delay and is sorry for it: "Now at last you have shown your kindness, as you could not do before." That this is his meaning is evident from the words that follow: **You were indeed concerned for me, but you had no opportunity.** They had long been anxious to assist him but had hitherto lacked the means.

**11-12. Not that I complain of want** [i.e., like a man in desperate need]; **for I have learned, in whatever state I am, to be content** (literally, "self-sufficing"). Paul here borrows a word from the Stoic philosophy, though it had now passed from the lecture room into common speech. It was one of the maxims of Stoicism that a man's real life was in his own soul, and that he must not depend on outward accidents but should be "sufficient

---

man] possesseth," but this truth is never fully appreciated except at points where money can do nothing for us.

Paul is speaking from just such a point. He was an old man, at the time of life when people begin to realize that "we brought nothing into this world, and it is certain we can carry nothing out." The older we grow, the more we tend to turn to things that do not fail, which no amount of money can buy. Furthermore, Paul was in prison facing a sentence of death—after a long life of pioneering in a cause for which he had sacrificed a settled family life, given up the ordinary business of making a living, and literally "suffered the loss of all things." Such a man can speak with authority to us about the obscured truth that "the things which are seen are temporal," while "the things which are not seen are eternal."

**12. *I Have Learned the Secret of Facing Plenty and Hunger, Abundance and Want.*—** This affirmation is a very personal expression of a universal paradox of human life: we are driven by necessity to acquire things to live with, but our real life does not consist of the things we need.

For our modern age the most convincing illustration of this eternal paradox came in the life and tragic death of Mahatma Gandhi. With no wealth, no permanent office, no material power, no security, this strange little man showed us that the inner life is the real measure of a man. Against the whole temper of a materialistic age, he bore witness to the fact that true progress and security are found in the transformation of the outward into the inward life.

Even the scientists are being led by the logic of their discoveries beyond the confines of the world of sense. Once it was supposed that matter was a hard substance moved by external pressure, which made the universe look like a vast machine driven by physical force. But later matter was dissolved into electrical particles, so that hard substance became intangible, as though the ultimate thing was energy. When it was found that this all-pervasive and invisible energy could be described only in a mathematical formula, men began to say that the universe was not so much a great machine as a great thought. If there were a God, he must be a mathematician. But finally it became clear —and the atom bomb made it perfectly clear— that none of our knowledge about energy, however refined, can give us any meaning for life. That has to be found where the life of the spirit appears in the activities of man, transforming the outward into an inward life, and bearing witness to spiritual power, which is more significant than all material power because it alone fulfills the character of man.

Scientific logic cannot lead us to God, but it can bring us to the revelation of Christ as the highest demonstration that the forces which reach us from the Creator through human personality are rooted as deep in reality as any force in the natural world.

We are so obsessed with other kinds of progress and safety, good in themselves, that it is hard to believe with Paul that there is a secret way to live beyond the reach of either abundance or want. There is some kind of detachment which radically affects our attachment to worldly things.

to himself." Paul says that his experience has taught him this lesson. In his troubled career he has undergone all kinds of vicissitudes, and is now able, whatever the conditions are, to put up with them and be content. **I know both how to be abased, and I know how to abound:** One day he might be destitute, and another he might have means to spare, but he could adapt himself without any difficulty to either lot. **In any and all circumstances I have learned the secret** (literally, "I have been initiated"). As he has taken one word from the philosophy of his day, he takes another from its religion. In all the pagan cults there was a higher discipline to which only the select few were admitted. Anyone might join in the public worship, but the "mysteries," the inner secrets of the cult, were reserved for the initiates, who were obliged by solemn oath not to divulge their knowledge. So Paul had acquired a secret which no man ever learns except by hard experience, "both to feast and to go hungry, both to have too much and to have too little." In all the ups and downs of life he could now find himself equally at home.

---

Half a century ago Charles Cuthbert Hall, in his Barrows Lectures before educated groups in the Far East, won a great hearing when he pleaded with Orientals to understand Christ, who was an Oriental himself, and reinterpret to the West the religious depths of his teaching. The mystical East had much to give the practical West, which had tended to water down religion to the ethical precepts of the great Master. Gandhi has fulfilled that plea.

It is expected that after the West has overwhelmed the East with its modern ways, there should come a return influence from those who have been dominated. Gandhi learned from his own religion the discipline of mystical withdrawal of the mind from all worldly suggestions, in order to recover the ultimate union with and attachment to God, who is the beginning and end of our being and the final source of the life of the Spirit. From reading the N.T. with its story of Christ as the representative of God dying on the cross for the sins of men, he glimpsed the idea that union with God, who is creative love, requires both a withdrawal from the world and a return to the world, to be involved as Christ was in the remaking of human life, especially at its lowest levels. Gandhi stood for the double practice of detaching himself from the world to renew his relation with his Creator, and then coming down to earthly attachments that he might serve the redemptive purpose of creative love.

We all have been impressed by vestiges of this kind of life in ordinary people. We piece together our impression of it from the impacts of many who have affected us.

It is very easy for us, who seldom give God five minutes' thought between Sundays, to forget that the secret of this inner life of the spirit depends at long last upon a constant renewal of our final relation to God alone.

There are at least two deathless reasons for this alternation between attachment and detachment.

(a) One is to keep ourselves creative. Human perversity inclines us to accept some way of our own as though it were good enough for creation to stop there. In other words, we take some human creation as though it could be equal to God. We level off in our efforts where we have measured up to this expectation of our particular society, and can thank God we are not like some others who have not. Whenever we stop being creative, we are trying to peg creation at that point. The fact is that everything requires renewal: friendship, integrity, love, sympathy, as well as all our opinions about our achievements. God's creative power will take away life where it ceases to grow, and will destroy all stoppage in the way of his inexhaustible purpose.

Keeping ourselves creative is particularly important today in the world of human relations. There it is constantly necessary to create new partnerships out of old dictatorships. For we all are dictators by nature, and we love to impose our will on the world around us. The hardened businessman is always marked by his pride in getting what he wants when he wants it. The patronizing elements of society anywhere are incipient tyrants, for their native self-love likes to lord it over others under pretense of doing them good.

During the great coal strike in the United States in 1902, the head of the coal operators wrote a famous letter to a correspondent who had pleaded with him to stop the strike. He said:

You are evidently biased in favor of the right of the working man to control a business in which he has no other interest than to secure fair wages for the work he does. . . . The rights and interests of the laboring man will be protected and cared for—not by labor agitators, but by the Christian men to whom God in his infinite wisdom has given control of the property interests of the country.[7]

[7] H. F. Pringle, *Theodore Roosevelt* (New York: Harcourt Brace & Co., 1931), p. 267.

| 13 I can do all things through Christ which strengtheneth me. | hunger, abundance and want. 13 I can do all things in him who strengthens me. |

**13.** "I have strength for all things in him who gives me inward power." Up to this point Paul has used the language of Stoicism, and this was no accident. Even in ancient times resemblances between Stoic thought and that of Paul were noted; and these have appeared more and more numerous in the light of modern inquiry. Paul's native city of Tarsus was one of the chief homes of the Stoic philosophy, and clearly he had been attracted by many things in its teaching. His speech at Athens, as reported in Acts 17, is

That smug, man-made "gospel of wealth" was not only a bad prophecy but it was also a fallacious psychology.

When workers in large-scale business were left with no interest in the enterprise save their own profit, they tended to feel less and less responsible for anything in an impersonal corporation except their wages and working conditions. They finally learned to organize themselves, to guard their rights against the power of absentees who controlled the very sources of their living. They wanted no longer to remain objects of charity; they intended to be major factors in creating change. As they gained power, they too fell under the temptation to dictate to everybody, until the dictatorial powers had the public at the mercy of their rivalries.

Now the best men on both sides are trying in official or informal ways to bring to pass some kind of responsible partnership. Without extending responsibility to those incapable of assuming it fully, tentative efforts are appearing everywhere to introduce the principle of partnership in business, education, social welfare—and the home. Let it be repeated again and again that people grow, not in assurance of prosperity, and not under dictation, but through shared responsibility in a partnership.

It is not enough for democracy to be against the dictation of a police state in its various forms. For the power of a free society lies in its genius for continuous experiments with new partnerships where old forms of dictatorship have become oppressive. Just as the family begins with domination of an older over a younger generation, and at its best develops toward a free partnership, so in the community, in business, in education, and all movements for human welfare, domination must constantly be converted into participation by creating situations which favor such conversion. There are no final rules or solutions because no problem of living together is subject to a final resolution through the observance of a law. What can happen to people as they become partners in new situations and on an even wider scale is known only to God.

(b) Another abiding reason for the alternation between attachment and detachment is to keep ourselves creatable. Our lives are never finished, they are not even half-done. After all we can do there still remains the question of what can be done with us. Our ability is never the measure of our possibility. Baron von Hügel once wrote his daughter in college that the mere endurance of grim or dull experiences was not enough, because on all occasions she was either being "done good" or "done harm."

Looking back over the years we all become aware that the making and remaking of life occurred where growth could not have been predicted. Moments there are when the burden of insistent self-concern is tossed aside, and we find ourselves being refashioned in some unaccountable way—often by some experience which we dreaded, and from which we would have escaped if we could. All of which is a familiar proof that we cannot create our own lives, and must needs keep ourselves open for creation where we least expect it may occur.

Too many people think that following Christ is simply an effort of will to make themselves duplicates of his personality. Imitation of Christ is most effective when we think of it as following his example of permitting oneself under every circumstance to be used and shaped by a will greater than one's own, like clay in the hands of the potter. No one knows how radical such remaking may be, especially when it is a matter of transforming the outward into the inward life.

Psychology has taught us that keeping ourselves creatable requires that we locate the unconscious stoppages. If we are at all normal, we can analyze ourselves and find what holds us back. If we become abnormal, unable to understand a sick mind, we may need expert help to uncover what is hidden in the unconscious levels of our personality.

A member of the Society of Friends, who believes that there is a vestige of the Spirit of God at work in every one of us, was helped by psychology to realize that our "ego" really wants to unite with that divine Spirit but is separated from it by some wall of its own creation—some

14 Notwithstanding, ye have well done, that ye did communicate with my affliction.

14 Yet it was kind of you to share my

---

Stoic throughout, alike in thought and language. Yet beneath the superficial agreements there is a profound difference between Paul and the Stoics, and the nature of it is strikingly brought out in the present verse. The Stoics maintained that in man, as a fragment of the universal soul, there is an intrinsic force which can resist and overcome all outward pressure. Paul was convinced that man by himself can do nothing, but is in hopeless bondage to the evils of this world. That was why God had sent us a deliverer, and all human effort must forever be futile unless we have the power of Christ to help us. So when Paul tells here how he had learned under all conditions of life to be self-sufficient, he takes care to add that he does not rely wholly on himself. He is conscious of the inward presence of Christ, who at all times supplies him with the needful strength.

**14-15. Yet it was kind of you to share** [literally, "make common cause with"] **my trouble.** Paul feels that his readers might misunderstand him. He has spoken as if their generosity had been wasted, but he has indeed been grateful for the gift, and still more for the sympathy behind it. This new kindness is all of a piece with many others he has received from them. He looks back on his earliest connection with the Philippian church. Even then, when he had newly founded it and was on his way from Macedonia to Greece, he had learned its generous disposition. He describes this period of his work as **the beginning of the gospel**, although he had then been a missionary for many years; but he writes from the Philippian point of view. Up to that time his readers had been ignorant of the gospel, but as soon as the light had dawned on them they had shown a sense of their obligations. **No church entered into partnership with me in giving and receiving**

---

"artifact," as the experts would say. Before the union can take place to renew life unpredictably, some crisis must smash the wall.

A man in public life broke down from fatigue, lost control of himself, and went for help to a doctor who knew the ways of the human mind. Knowing that the patient had broken down some thirty years before, the doctor told him that the memory of that bitter experience had been lingering in the subconscious mind as a subtle suggestion that it might occur again. Through overwork some signs of the dreaded feelings were now returning. Each sign was exaggerated by fear, which, being overstressed, begot still other symptoms which produced more fears. The doctor had a collection of 325 symptoms that could be created out of such nervous disorder, and reminded his patient that he had surrounded himself with such a wall of fears that his sympathetic nervous system revolted. Not one of the fears was real. All were created out of feelings which come to all people when they are tired, and which they let pass without much thought. If any man grabs each fear, holds on to it, and builds a wall with it, no help can become available.

So the doctor told the patient to go back to his normal duty which made demands on him, fix a rigid schedule of work and play to be gone through daily regardless of feelings. He was to act like every other person who has a hard job to do, and who answers daily calls to give

himself away. In no time at all the fears began to melt away, and just where the man was utterly helpless to handle himself, he found some God-given supply of energy working all through his life, converting a semi-idiot into a useful and satisfied man.

Not everyone need go through such a crisis to learn that all men have some clutter of private creations walling off their egos from the Spirit of God within. Brick by brick they go on making the wall, shutting themselves in by moss-grown habits, bitter resentments, cherished grudges, selfish indulgences, dread of change, false pride, envy, laziness, self-pity, indifference, or comfort that makes cowards of us all. Most people could plead guilty to fixed opinions, held against any alteration in the economic scene, each one defended as though it were a chip off the block of absolute truth. Many can remember how the economic crash after World War I helped multitudes discover their souls after their money was gone.

Each man on the spot where he stands is either stopping creation or letting it through. No one else can take that individual place. Others might do better if they could be there. But each man is on some spot where no one else is, and he must do the best he can and let God make of him what he will.

**14-23. The Final Message of Gratitude and Greeting.**—We best understand the close of a Pauline letter when we remember that it was

15 Now ye Philippians know also, that in the beginning of the gospel, when I departed from Macedonia, no church communicated with me as concerning giving and receiving, but ye only.

16 For even in Thessalonica ye sent once and again unto my necessity.

17 Not because I desire a gift: but I desire fruit that may abound to your account.

18 But I have all, and abound: I am full, having received of Epaphroditus the things *which were sent* from you, an odor of a sweet smell, a sacrifice acceptable, well-pleasing to God.

trouble. 15 And you Philippians yourselves know that in the beginning of the gospel, when I left Macedo'nia, no church entered into partnership with me in giving and receiving except you only; 16 for even in Thessaloni'ca you sent me help*f* once and again. 17 Not that I seek the gift; but I seek the fruit which increases to your credit. 18 I have received full payment, and more; I am filled, having received from Epaphrodi'tus the gifts you sent, a fragrant offering, a sacrifice acceptable and

*f* Other ancient authorities read *money for my needs.*

---

[literally, "debt and credit"] **except you only.** Half playfully he uses the technical language of business. Philippi was the only church which had thought of keeping an account with him. Over against what they had received they put their estimate of what they ought to give. Elsewhere (I Cor. 9:11) Paul states his opinion on the payment of missionaries in explicit terms, saying literally, "If we have sown unto you spiritual things, is it a great matter that we should reap your carnal things?" But although this was his principle, he waived his own right in the case of all his churches except that of Philippi. With this church he had stood on a special footing from the outset.

**16-17. For even in Thessalonica you sent me help once and again.** On his first visit Paul had gone straight from Philippi to the Macedonian seaport of Thessalonica, and had there apparently found himself in difficulties of which we are told nothing in the book of Acts. Perhaps there was no opening for him in the craft by which he earned his livelihood and he was in dire poverty, which was likely to bring his mission in Europe to an end. The Philippians had come to his rescue more than once, and for this timely help in a critical emergency he owed them a lifelong gratitude. He is grateful also for what they have done now, but tells them that the money itself has been only a secondary matter. **Not that I seek the gift; but I seek the fruit which increases to your credit.** "Fruit" was a word commonly applied to the increment produced by money, and Paul plays again with financial terms. "I do not want the capital but the interest; and it accrues to your account, not mine." The meaning is that from every generous gift the giver obtains more than the receiver. The giver grows in his capacity for human sympathy; he breaks away from his little self and enters into a larger life. Apart from anything they had done for Paul, the Philippians had done far more for themselves.

**18.** It is with this thought in his mind that Paul comes back to the recent gift, saying in effect, "But I am paid in full, and have more than enough." Among the papyri which

---

written to be read aloud to a congregation of Christians gathered for worship, people who were not like the Sunday morning attendants in a comfortable middle-class church today. Unfortunately most so-called Christians—including ourselves—are so like the rest of the world that their religion—including our own—is not likely to be a disturbing factor in society. It has been streamlined, so to speak, to glide through the surrounding community with the least possible resistance. Moreover, church people, especially among Protestants, consider their religion as an individualistic private affair, self-made and self-sustained. Custom has

reduced to a minimum the feeling that our Christian life and faith were created through an age-old community, and that it needs to be forever fed out of the whole life of the past to keep it from merging into the worldly life about us, as a raindrop sinks into the sea. We talk of church unity as though it were a mere matter of bringing official organizations together for the sake of efficiency and to reduce the shame of ecclesiastical divisions.

These early Christians to whom Paul spoke needed to keep together, and to feel united with something greater than themselves, because they were up against real hostility, and were in

19 But my God shall supply all your need according to his riches in glory by Christ Jesus.

20 Now unto God and our Father *be* glory for ever and ever. Amen.

21 Salute every saint in Christ Jesus. The brethren which are with me greet you.

pleasing to God. 19 And my God will supply every need of yours according to his riches in glory in Christ Jesus. 20 To our God and Father be glory for ever and ever. Amen.

21 Greet every saint in Christ Jesus. The

---

have lately come to light in Egypt there are many receipted bills dating from Paul's time, and the word written on them is that which Paul employs here (ἀπέχω). Still imitating the terms of business, he puts down "paid" on his account with Philippi. He adds, however, that besides the full amount they have given him something over—the sympathy and affection which are more in value than the material gift. This idea is expressed more fully in the words that follow. **I am filled** [i.e., all my desires have been satisfied], **having received from Epaphroditus the gifts you sent, a fragrant offering, a sacrifice acceptable and pleasing to God.** The gift has been made to him, but he regards it as a sacrifice offered to God, since it tells of self-denial and hearts renewed by the love of Christ. One is reminded of David when water was brought to him from the well at Bethlehem, at the peril of brave men's lives. "He would not drink thereof, but poured it out unto the Lord" (II Sam. 23:16). The imagery of sweet-smelling incense also reminds one of the anointing at Bethany, when "the house was filled with the fragrance of the ointment" (John 12:3).

**19-20.** So the Philippians have made a sacrifice to God, **and my God will supply every need of yours** [as you have satisfied mine]. The phrase **my God** has here a special significance. Paul cannot repay them himself, but he throws the debt on God, whose servant he is. God will take charge of this, as of all Paul's other obligations, and will give the recompense **according to his riches.** By their gift the Philippians have won the favor of God, and he will reward them out of his infinite wealth, **in glory in Christ Jesus.** By what they have done with their earthly possessions they have laid up treasure in heaven. The effects of their kindness will appear when they have entered through Christ into the coming glory. As he thinks of this consummation, Paul breaks into a doxology. This is his custom at the close of every epistle, but in the present instance the ascription of praise springs naturally out of the thoughts he has just expressed. **To our God and Father be glory for ever**—literally, "for the ages of the ages," i.e., an age which will consist of countless ages. All through the epistle, and especially in these closing verses, Paul's mind has been full of God's goodness to himself and to all Christ's people; so he describes him here as "God our Father," the eternal One whom we worship and whom we can also love. The doxology is of the nature of a prayer, and is followed by an **Amen,** which serves also to mark the end of the epistle.

## VIII. Final Salutations (4:21-23)

**21.** Paul has now said everything he intended, but a letter is not complete without some words of personal greeting. We might have expected that in writing to Philippi, where he had so many dear friends, he would send a large number of greetings, and we cannot but feel regret that he has failed to do so. A few brief notices of the people

---

danger either of yielding to the popular trend or of being extinguished by persecution. That is why Paul makes his final plea for unity where personal rivalries, and differences that make no real difference, threaten the sense of belonging to the "company of all faithful people."

**Yet it was kind of you to share my trouble.** The closing sentences are the most gracious in all this gracious letter. They are the words of

a man who is beyond the help of his friends, and yet who says that their effort to share his trouble has filled him with comfort. They had sent him money, as they always had, but money was of no use to him now. Nevertheless, their generosity served to remind him of the affection and support they had offered him from the beginning, and he accepted the money because it was one more testimony to the fruit of the Spirit in them. He saw in them something of

| 22 All the saints salute you, chiefly they that are of Caesar's household. | brethren who are with me greet you. 22 All the saints greet you, especially those of Caesar's household. |

would have made us far better acquainted with this church, which he loved above all others. As it is, he speaks of nobody by name, and his reason no doubt is that he wishes his readers to feel that they are all equally dear to him. He limits himself, therefore, to a comprehensive greeting: **Salute every saint** [i.e., each member of the church, omitting none] **in Christ Jesus.** These last words must be taken with **salute,** as in other epistles where the same formula is used (e.g., Rom. 16:22; I Cor. 16:19). The affection conveyed by the greeting has its motive in the common faith in Christ. It is remarkable that instead of saluting his friends directly, Paul desires some others to do it for him. Who are these others? Perhaps he means that all the members of the church, after hearing the letter, should salute one another in the name of their absent apostle. More likely he expresses himself as he does because the letter is to be presented in the first instance to the bishops and deacons. They will read it themselves and then have it read out at the public meeting, and so convey the salutations.

21-22. Along with his own greetings Paul sends those of the **brethren who are with me,** i.e., his immediate group of associates. One of them was Timothy, whose name he had joined with his own at the beginning of the letter. Who the others were we do not know. In 2:20 Paul spoke of them disparagingly, and if he now includes them, it must be more by way of courtesy than because they had any lively interest in the Philippians. Not only his actual companions but **all the saints salute you.** All the members of the local church send their greetings to their sister church. It was one of Paul's chief concerns to bring Christians everywhere to a feeling of their unity. As yet each little company stood by itself and was jealous of its independence, but Paul, with his statesmanlike mind, seems already to have cherished the idea of a federated church. By every means he could think of he encouraged the scattered communities to join hands in one Church. So whenever he writes a letter, he takes care to assure the church at a distance that the church where he now is has its welfare at heart, and that Christ's people everywhere are a united body.

To the general salutation he makes the singular addition **especially those of Caesar's household.** These words have given rise to many conjectures. According to the old view, Paul refers not without pride to members of the imperial family. There is good reason to believe that before the end of the first century Christianity had made converts among the near relations of the emperor, but this was at least thirty years after Paul wrote his letter, and in his day the new movement was still making its way with difficulty in the humbler quarters of the great cities. Modern research has made it certain that "Caesar's household" was a general term for those who worked in the government service. Many of them were slaves; others held minor offices in the civil and military administration.

the "disposition of mind" that was in Christ, and it warmed his heart in a hopeless situation: **I have received full payment, and more.**

There is something unforgettable in this poignant sentence about being kind, assuring us that what people want most is to have their troubles and their joys *shared.* Sometimes we help by what we do, and when we cannot see what good we can do, we do nothing. There is a time for the simple token, whatever suits the occasion, to show another that his life is shared.

22. *All the Saints Greet You, Especially Those of Caesar's Household.*—What a challenge lay in that final greeting! There were committed disciples even in the household of Caesar! The

underground movement had penetrated to the very centers of power, and the nonviolent force of a new community of the spirit was demonstrating its divine capacity to survive the downfall of the mightiest empire the world had known.

Those saints under Caesar speak still to our time. They were powerless to change the political tyranny under which they lived; they had no voice in the government; "not many mighty" were among their numbers, which were few at best. But they did not succumb to the historic fallacy that environment is lord over men, determining their whole existence, and shaping even the thoughts in their minds. They were

23 The grace of our Lord Jesus Christ *be* with you all. Amen.

¶ It was written to the Philippians from Rome by Epaphroditus.

23 The grace of the Lord Jesus Christ be with your spirit.

It has been proved, too, that this "household of Caesar" was not confined to Rome. In the provinces for which the emperor made himself directly responsible there were large staffs of officials who drew their pay from him and counted as his servants. It is partly on this ground that many modern scholars have rested their argument against the Roman origin of the epistle. At Ephesus or Caesarea Paul would be in contact with members of the imperial service no less than in Rome itself. This must be granted, and the assumption that the letter was written during the Roman imprisonment must be confirmed by other evidence than that of the present verse, though it is still the most probable.

But a further question arises: Why does Paul lay such particular stress on the greetings from one small section of the church? It cannot be that he is boasting of his high connections, for the rank of government servant, then as now, was often a very humble one. The circumstances are now unknown to us, but apparently there were Christians in that employment who were interested in Philippi, and when they learned that Paul was writing to the church there they asked him to convey their good wishes. We are here reminded again that Philippi was a Roman colony, and its population was largely made up of former soldiers and government servants. They would have friends and relations in foreign cities, and especially in Rome itself, who were engaged in similar work.

23. The epistle ends, like all Paul's letters, with a benediction: **The grace of the Lord Jesus Christ be with your spirit.** We have evidence here that the letters were meant to be read out, in place of the usual address, at the church meeting. Paul thought of himself as speaking to the assembled people, and pronounced the blessing over them before they parted. This is doubtless the reason why he uses the singular **your spirit**, although he has a number of persons in his mind. He knows that when they listen to him, they will be gathered in a single company, all of them sharing in the one Spirit.

conditioned, but not mastered by the conditions. The freedom of the Spirit was there, for these disciples had learned that not even crucifixion could destroy its surviving power. The early Christians proved to the hilt that what goes on within the souls of men is the end toward which the whole creation moves: "The revelation of the sons of God." A rebirth of the Spirit might influence the direction of outward reform, but it is not the product of reform, nor is it forced to wait until environment is ready for it. The Spirit "bloweth where it listeth" because it is always a "beginning from within."

The Epistle to the

# COLOSSIANS

*Introduction and Exegesis by* Francis W. Beare
*Exposition by* G. Preston MacLeod

# COLOSSIANS

## INTRODUCTION

The epistles to the Colossians, to the Ephesians, and to Philemon form a little group of their own within the Pauline corpus. In this group Colossians holds the central position: it is linked to Philemon by the long series of personal references which are common to the two epistles; and to Ephesians by the remarkable parallelisms in language and in ruling ideas which are not represented, or at the most are barely shadowed forth, in the other epistles which are commonly ascribed to the apostle. In all three Paul appears as a prisoner in chains (Philem. 9; Col. 4:18; Eph. 3:1; 4:1; 6:20).

### I. Colossians and Its Companion Epistles

There is unfortunately no general agreement among scholars touching the authenticity of these epistles. The Tübingen school, from Baur to Weizsäcker, took the position that all three were pseudonymous writings of the second century. Among the great critical scholars of the present century, on the other hand, a fair number—F. C. Burkitt, C. H. Dodd, A. E. J. Rawlinson, E. F. Scott, and others—have found themselves inclined to accept all three as genuine works of the apostle whose name they bear. It may be said, however, that the opinion now most prevalent among the few who are competent to judge of such matters is that Philemon and Colossians are from the hand of Paul, but that Ephesians is the work of a disciple of the second generation. It can scarcely be doubted that if Colossians had been lost, no serious scholar would attempt to defend the authenticity of Ephesians; and if Colossians were not already suspected, no one would question the authenticity of Philemon. In this respect also Colossians stands in the middle position. Phile-mon, which is really unassailable in spite of the perverse attacks of the Tübingen critics,[1] is the chief support of the authenticity of Colossians; and Colossians in turn forms a bridge between the other epistles and Ephesians.

The relationship among the three epistles is understood in varying ways in accordance with the different judgments on the question of authenticity. If all three are authentic, it is clear that they must have been written at about the same time, to take advantage of the projected trip of Tychicus to the region of Colossae (4:7-8; Eph. 6:21-22) in company with the returning slave Onesimus (4:9; Philem. 10-12). If Philemon and Colossians are acknowledged, while Ephesians is ascribed to a later writer, it will appear that Ephesians has been composed in close dependence on Colossians—giving a broader and more general application to the ideas of Christ, of the church, and of the divine dispensation of salvation which have been advanced in Colossians in a particular context of controversy. And if we take the position that Philemon alone is genuine, we shall find offered to us a further variety of solutions for the problem of the relationship between Colossians and Philemon on the one hand, and between Colossians and Ephesians on the other. The relationship with Philemon will then be regarded as artificial and wholly external, amounting to no more than a borrowing of the personalia of the authentic letter by the author of Colossians; or else it may be held, with H. J.

---

[1] Curiously enough, the authenticity of Philemon was assailed in some quarters during the fourth century; it is defended by Jerome, Chrysostom, and Theodore of Mopsuestia, in terms which suggest that the attack came from theologians of the orthodox party, not from Arians.

Holtzmann, C. R. Bowen, and others, that Colossians rests upon an authentic letter written at the same time as Philemon, but that in its present form it has been largely interpolated by a later writer. The relationship with Ephesians may still be regarded as consisting simply in the dependence of this letter on Colossians; or the two may be regarded as independent productions of the same writer or school; or they may be seen in the light of the elaborate theory of Holtzmann, that Ephesians was first composed in dependence on the shorter original letter to the Colossians, which was subsequently expanded into its present form by interpolations made by the author of Ephesians. The full discussion of the questions of integrity and authenticity will be undertaken later in this Introduction (pp. 142-45).

Philippians, which was also written from prison (Phil. 1:7, 13-14, 17), is quite different in tone and in content from these three. It may have been written during the same period of imprisonment, but one would be inclined to feel that some months, if not years, must have elapsed between it and Colossians. The Pastorals, once reckoned among the "imprisonment epistles," do not enter into any consideration of interrelationships among the Pauline letters, for they are no longer regarded as authentic. Even if it can be shown that they contain some genuine fragments of Paul's writings, these cannot be attached with certainty to any particular period of the apostle's life.

## II. Origin and Destination

The Epistle to the Colossians was called forth by the necessity of guarding the truth of the gospel against an insidiously attractive perversion of its fundamental principles—a syncretism of Judaic and pagan doctrines and practices which tended to obscure and diminish the glory of Christ while professing to set forth a higher knowledge and a more severely ascetic morality. The nature of this sub-Christian teaching will be discussed more fully later (pp. 137-40).

Colossae was not an important city in itself. It was situated on the Lycus River, a tributary of the Meander, ten or twelve miles above the twin cities of Laodicea and Hierapolis and some hundred-odd miles from the famous city of Ephesus, the capital of the Roman province of Asia, where Paul had carried on a long and successful mission (Acts 19). It lay just within the western border of the ancient region of Phrygia, always a spawning ground of enthusiastic cults and wild prophets of new forms of religion. Under Roman rule the district was incorporated at first into the province of Asia; later it was transferred to Cilicia; and after

several such changes of jurisdiction it was finally left in its original attachment to Asia, which was maintained through the first four centuries of the Christian Era.[2]

Paul himself had not visited the Lycus region; Colossae and its neighboring cities appear to have been evangelized by his colleague Epaphras. Paul was dependent for his knowledge of the Colossian church upon the report brought to him in his prison by Epaphras, who came to tell him of the success of the mission and to bring him tokens of the love which was borne to him by the Colossian Christians who had never seen his face (1:8). The letter before us was written in the light of this report, to confirm the truth of the gospel as preached by Epaphras and to expose the errors of the more pretentious "philosophy" which his converts were now being invited to adopt.

It is interesting to speculate that the famous Stoic teacher Epictetus may have met Epaphras or heard his preaching of the gospel in his native city of Hierapolis. When the Christian missionary first came into that region, Epictetus, a slave, was just coming into young manhood; and the gospel of freedom must have run like wildfire through the slave population of all these cities, and can hardly have failed to stir the blood and quicken the imagination, especially of the younger slaves. Though his fundamental doctrine is founded upon Stoic tenets, the writings of Epictetus show some remarkable coincidences in language with the epistles of the New Testament; and it is tempting to think that he had some personal acquaintance with the teaching of the Christians, which was certainly accessible to him in his formative period.

## III. Time and Place of Writing

Where could Paul have been imprisoned when such a letter was written? To this question three answers have been given—Rome, Caesarea, or Ephesus.

This much at least is clear: we must think not of a temporary detention in jail, such as that which the apostle suffered at Philippi (Acts 16:22-40); but of a relatively long imprisonment such as he underwent at Caesarea (two years—Acts 24:27) or at Rome (also two years —Acts 28:30-31). It might be observed that Paul was never released by the Roman authorities after they had once taken him into custody at Jerusalem to save him from death at the hands of the mob (Acts 21:31-36); so that he could have described himself as a "prisoner" (Philem. 1, 9), if not as actually "in bonds"

[2] On the early history of Christianity in the region see especially J. B. Lightfoot, "The Churches of the Lycus," in *Saint Paul's Epistles to the Colossians and to Philemon* (London: Macmillan & Co., 1875), pp. 1-72.

(4:3; cf. 4:18), at any time over a period of five years (including the winter's voyage from Caesarea to Rome—Acts 27:1–28:16). This was really a single period of imprisonment, and there is no way of determining with certainty whether Paul wrote Colossians during the first two years or during the last two. The period of the voyage is ruled out by two considerations: first, that the runaway slave Onesimus could not have accompanied Paul on board ship (4:9; Philem. 10); and second, that only by the merest chance could Epaphras have encountered Paul en route. Besides, the letter implies that Paul is settled in some one place, where he is able to have regular converse with his friends, to receive reports from his mission fields, to make converts, and to write letters.

A. *The Case for Rome.*—The assumption of all the ancient commentators that Rome was the place where the "imprisonment epistles" were written was undoubtedly suggested to them in the first instance not by anything in Philemon, Colossians, or Ephesians, but by two phrases in Philippians—"my bonds in Christ are manifest in all the palace" (Phil. 1:13), and "all the saints salute you, chiefly they that are of Caesar's household" (Phil. 4:22). But these phrases cannot sustain the weight thus attached to them. The πραιτώριον (translated in the KJV as "palace," and in the RSV as "praetorian guard") most often means the military headquarters in a provincial capital or garrison town; and "Caesar's household" is a technical term for the slaves and freedmen attached to the imperial service, who were to be found in all parts of the empire. It is certain, at least, that they would be found as part of the administration in the provinces which were under the direct authority of the emperor; it is much more doubtful whether they would be found in the senatorial provinces. Syria (with Palestine) was one of the former group, and there would certainly be some of "Caesar's household" in Caesarea, and also a "praetorium." Asia, on the other hand, was a senatorial province; and it is not to be taken for granted that there would be either men of "Caesar's household" or a permanent military headquarters there. In any case, Philippians cannot be used to determine the date of Colossians, since it is quite different in style and in thought, and it cannot be lightly assumed to date from the same period of imprisonment. The question of time and place must therefore be decided solely on the basis of the internal evidence of Colossians itself and its companion piece, the letter to Philemon. Ephesians, even if it is regarded as authentic, adds nothing specific to the data of Colossians.

The case for Rome, as against any possible earlier imprisonment, rests substantially upon the fact that the thought of Colossians, especially in Christology, marks an advance far beyond anything that we find in the other Pauline letters, apart from Ephesians; foreshadowing indeed, as is recognized by critics of all schools, the Christology of the Epistle to the Hebrews and of the Johannine writings. Even if we grant that there are passing indications of this "cosmic" Christology in some other epistles— though no one has been able to find it suggested except in I Cor. 8:6—and that Paul was compelled to bring this always latent thought into the foreground in order to meet the specific problems of the Colossian heresy, it is still hard to imagine that once he had developed and elaborated his thinking along these lines it would again recede to the back of his mind, to leave no trace in such a masterwork as Romans. We have, therefore, a good deal of justification for feeling that this is the latest of the extant epistles. If it is dated in the period of Paul's Ephesian ministry, we should then be compelled to conclude that he had written no letters during the whole five years of enforced inactivity—or comparative inactivity—that set in with his imprisonment at Caesarea; or else that none was preserved. Seeing that this was just the period during which Paul would be most anxious to maintain by correspondence "the care of all the churches" (II Cor. 11:28) which he could no longer exercise by personal visitation, it is inconceivable that his literary activities were suspended for all that time. It is true that in any case the handful of letters which we have in our New Testament represents only a fragment of the apostle's correspondence: far more letters have been lost than have been preserved. But even so, it would be a strange accident of literary survival if all the extant letters were written before his final visit to Jerusalem. It would seem reasonable to assume, on the contrary, that when the letters came to be collected some years after his death, the later ones would more probably be accessible than those of his earlier period—not only because less time had elapsed in which they might perish, but also because the increasing greatness of his name among the churches would cause them to set increasingly high store upon his letters and to be more careful to preserve them.

Moreover, if we look carefully at the way in which Paul speaks of his "imprisonment for the gospel" (Philem. 13) and bids his friends "remember [his] bonds" (Col. 4:18), we shall begin to feel that he no longer thinks of imprisonment as a passing vexation, but as the settled state of his existence. It is not as if he wrote: "I, Paul, who am for the moment in prison"; but "I, Paul, who am called to exercise my apostolate as a prisoner." If this impression is justified, then we must certainly think of these words as written in Rome, since this is the only period in which imprisonment had been his lot long enough for him to think of it as a lasting condition. Even in Caesarea, if the account of Acts is true, he might have obtained his deliverance at any time if he had been able or willing to find a bribe for Felix (Acts 24:26). Only after his appeal to Caesar would he be certain that he must face a long period of detention still, for he could not entertain hope of a speedy hearing at the court of Nero.

**B. The Case for Caesarea.**—The assumption that Colossians and its companion letters were written from Rome was not seriously challenged until the nineteenth century, when it was attacked in 1829 by D. Schulz, who appears to have been the first to favor Caesarea. He has since been supported by a number of scholars, including Ernst Lohmeyer.[3] The case for Caesarea, as against Rome, rests upon a number of considerations, light enough in all truth, which may be summarized from Lohmeyer's argument. Some of the arguments to which earlier critics made appeal rest upon the assumption that "Ephesians" is addressed to Ephesus. As this assumption has been universally abandoned, the arguments which are based upon it no longer demand consideration.

(a) Lohmeyer considers that he has demonstrated with reasonable certainty that Philippians was written from Caesarea; and he thinks that there are sufficient points of contact between Philippians and Colossians to justify the conclusion that both were written at about the same time. The remark in Col. 4:11, that only three men "of the circumcision" have been a comfort to Paul is taken to indicate the very situation which underlies Phil. 1:15-17. In fact, however, the remark tells rather against Caesarea. As Theodor Zahn[4] has pointed out, Paul had been entertained in the home of Philip the Evangelist in Caesarea not many months earlier, on his way to Jerusalem (Acts 21:8); and it is scarcely conceivable that this tried and approved preacher of the gospel, the first man to break the barriers of Jewish exclusiveness by preaching the word in Samaria, should not be reckoned among the few who were "a comfort" to Paul.

(b) In Philem. 22, Paul indicates that he hopes to visit Colossae; he asks his friends to keep a lodging ready for him. Likewise, he tells

the Philippians that he hopes to visit them shortly (Phil. 2:24). Lohmeyer points out that during his stay in Caesarea, Paul had his heart set on getting to Rome; and that it would be in accordance with his custom, before entering upon a new field of labor, first to travel through the territories which he had already occupied for Christ, to encourage and strengthen his churches. If he were once set free by Felix, he would be inclined, in keeping with his general policy, to visit the Christians of Asia and Macedonia as he made his way westward to Rome. On the other hand, once he had got as far as Rome, it would be impossible to return east for such a visit to Colossae without postponing indefinitely the cherished project of a mission to Spain (Rom. 15:23-24). It might well be, however, that the great danger presented to his Asian churches by the kind of teaching which had made its appearance at Colossae would lead the apostle to subordinate his desire to break new territory for the gospel to the necessity of dispelling by personal intervention the threat of syncretic corruption in the older field.

(c) Great stress is laid upon the names of Paul's associates who are mentioned in Colossians and Philemon—Timothy, Luke, Aristarchus, Tychicus, Epaphras, and Onesimus. In recent years the mention of this group has been alleged as one of the strongest reasons for favoring Ephesus (see below); but it has also been argued that the presence of all these men is more easily imagined at Caesarea than at Rome. Luke—if he is the author of the so-called "we-document" in Acts—accompanied Paul on the voyage to Rome and may have been with him also during his detention in Caesarea. Timothy, Tychicus, and Aristarchus had gone up to Jerusalem with Paul (Acts 20:4) and would probably follow him to Caesarea after his arrest; it is not certain that any of them followed him to Rome. Aristarchus began the voyage with them (Acts 27:2) and there is really no reason to suppose that he did not go on to Rome; but it is conjectured that he may have left them at Myra (Acts 27:5) where they changed ships. As for Onesimus, the fugitive slave, it is represented that he could more readily have found his way to Caesarea than to the more distant Rome, and that Paul could have more readily arranged to send him back to his master. Yet it is hard to tell why Onesimus should have made for Caesarea of all places, whereas Rome, with its huge slave population, was a veritable mecca for runaways; and if Paul had once persuaded the slave that it was his duty to return to his master, the distance to be traveled would not affect the decision in the slightest degree. As far as Mark is concerned, his presence tells rather

[3] *Die Briefe an die Philipper, an die Kolosser und an Philemon* (Göttingen: Vandenhoeck & Ruprecht, 1930; "Meyer's Kommentar").

[4] *Introduction to the New Testament*, tr. John Moore Trout, *et al.* (Edinburgh: T. & T. Clark, 1909), I, 443.

in favor of Rome, with which he is connected by early tradition; while of the other associates of Paul who are mentioned in Colossians—Jesus Justus and Demas—nothing is known one way or the other.

C. *The Case for Ephesus.*—The hypothesis that the "imprisonment epistles" were written at Ephesus is "a novelty of twentieth-century criticism." [5] It has little to commend it. Though it may be granted, in spite of the silence of Acts, that Paul suffered imprisonment in Ephesus perhaps more than once, there is nothing to show that any such imprisonment was of long duration or that it was the kind of *libera custodia* in which the apostle was kept at Caesarea (Acts 24:23) and at Rome (Acts 28:30-31), which alone would permit the opportunity for literary activity and for converse with friends which is presupposed by the epistles.

There is some plausibility in the arguments (*a*) that a fugitive slave from Colossae would be more likely to seek refuge in the nearby metropolis of his own province than in the distant city of Rome; (*b*) that it is natural to think of Epaphras, faced with the threat of a subtle heresy in the city which he had evangelized and unable to deal with it himself, going to his mentor Paul in Ephesus to invoke his counsel and assistance, while the journey to Rome would have involved an absence of several months from the threatened congregation at the very time when it could least afford to dispense with the services of a sound and sober teacher; and (*c*) that the request to prepare a lodging for Paul at Colossae (Philem. 22) would be more intelligible if Paul were only a few days' journey away than if he were in Rome or even in Caesarea.

These considerations do not carry conviction. It is true that Colossae is a long way from Rome; but Rome was full of Levantines, all of whom had had just as far to travel; and a fugitive slave, liable to flogging and even to crucifixion if he was recaptured, would be likely to put as great a distance as possible between himself and his master. As for Epaphras—if he was worried about the inroads of the new teaching at Colossae, he might well feel that he must communicate with Paul at all costs, even if it meant undertaking the long journey to Rome. The request for a lodging needs to be examined a little more narrowly. It should be observed that Paul uses the present imperative, not the aorist; this suggests that we should render "keep a guestchamber ready," rather than "prepare a guest room" (Philem. 22). It means little more than "keep the welcome mat

[5] George S. Duncan, *St. Paul's Ephesian Ministry* (New York: Charles Scribner's Sons, 1930), p. 6.

at the door, for I shall be along someday." The words do not seriously suggest that an *early* visit to Colossae is contemplated.

It is further alleged that nearly all of the associates whom Paul mentions are known to have been with him in Ephesus. But, in fact, only Timothy and Aristarchus are known to have been with him during the great three-year mission in that city, and both of them accompanied him to Jerusalem on the journey which led to his arrest and imprisonment. Aristarchus was on shipboard with him at his departure from Caesarea, and there is nothing to show that he left the party en route. If Timothy did not accompany Paul on that ship, it is surely not unlikely that he would follow his old master to Rome as the months of his imprisonment lingered on into a second year. It is of no significance that "Acts gives no hint" that Timothy was ever in Rome,[6] for Acts ends with the arrival of Paul in the capital and a description in the most general terms of the conditions of his detention. If Timothy had arrived six months— or six days—afterward, the narrative of Acts would have no place to mention him.

There is, in short, no cogent reason for abandoning the traditional hypothesis that Colossians was written in Rome. Indeed, a demonstration, if it were possible, that the external circumstances envisaged in the letter are incompatible with a Roman origin, would at the same time end all hope of defending its authenticity (see above, p. 135).

The whole discussion is relevant only if the Pauline authorship of the epistle is admitted. If Paul did not write it, we shall of course have to date it some years after his death; and it will then be conjectured that it originated in Pauline circles in Asia, possibly in one of the cities of the Lycus Valley, where the type of teaching represented by the "Colossian heresy" was first perceived to be a really dangerous threat to the sound doctrine of the gospel.

### IV. The Colossian "Heresy"

The system of religious teaching which is combated in Colossians is usually called a "heresy," but this is not altogether a proper description. At this period the word could be used only by a kind of prolepsis, for until something in the way of formal standards of orthodoxy have been established, there is no basis for defining any particular variety of teaching as heretical. Even the great Gnostic schools of the second century are called heretical only in relation to the standards of orthodoxy which were established in the very effort to discredit them. In the apostolic age no such standards

[6] *Ibid.*, p. 80.

existed; Christianity was characterized by an extraordinary freedom of spirit and variety of activity and thought;[7] and as new interpretations of the gospel were offered by different teachers, they had to be judged on their merits, not dismissed out of hand as "heretical." There was no external basis of conformity. More important, it is not certain that the advocates of the system professed to be disciples of Christ; it is equally possible that they merely sought to make a place for Christ in a framework of thought which had been created without reference to him, and then tried to persuade the Christians of Colossae that their system embraced in its fullness all that Christianity had to offer, and set Christ in a more or less subordinate position among the ranks of angelic powers. Some such relegation of Christ to an inferior place seems to be implied in the words "not holding fast to the Head" (2:19).

The epistle itself gives nothing in the way of a direct account of the tenets of the Colossian philosophy (2:8); we are left to reconstruct it as best we may from a number of allusions which would be much clearer to the readers than they are to us. Paul was writing to people who knew at first hand what the heretical teachers had been saying. There was no need for him to set it forth for their benefit in order to refute it; they would understand perfectly well the point of every allusion and would recognize at once every catch phrase which he introduced. But for us, lacking their advance knowledge of the matter in hand, it is no easy task to weave out of the stray references which Paul makes in passing a coherent account of the system with which he has to deal.

The teaching was described by its proponents as a "philosophy"; Paul suggests that it would be better styled "vain deceit" (2:8). They made appeal in some sense to "tradition"—probably claiming for their system the support of a secret tradition handed down from remote antiquity, giving it the glamour of an immemorial wisdom stemming from some ancient seer.[8] The system itself seems to have rested

[7] Notice Paul's insistence on the "varieties" exhibited in the church, all of which he recognizes as legitimate manifestations of one and "the same Spirit," based on loyalty to "the same Lord," and deriving ultimately from "the same God who inspires them all" (I Cor. 12:4-6). For a general treatment of the subject see E. F. Scott, *The Varieties of New Testament Religion* (New York: Charles Scribner's Sons, 1943).

[8] Such claims were frequently put forth in connection with the older mysteries; cf. Plato's reference to people who hawked the books of Orpheus or of Musaeus in the Athens of his own day (*Republic* II, 364E); and the belief that the Eleusinian rites had been ordained by Demeter herself and preserved by tradition in the family of the Eumolpids from prehistoric times (Homeric *Hymn to Demeter*).

upon a doctrine of angelic beings, called "the elemental spirits of the universe" (2:8), who were to be worshiped (2:18). These spirits were held to be organized in a celestial hierarchy, with titles to denote their several ranks—"thrones . . . dominions . . . principalities . . . authorities" (1:16). They are taken to have important functions as mediators between man and the highest divinity, which is, as it were, unfolded in them; in their totality they constitute the pleroma ("fullness," 1:19; 2:9)—the full complement of divine activities and attributes. They offer men redemption, but in some sense not compatible with the Christian gospel—neither consisting in the forgiveness of sins (1:14) nor mediated through Christ in his passion and resurrection.

On the practical side this transcendental doctrine issued in an artificial asceticism, coupled with the bondage of a Pharisaic legalism. Here we meet with traces of Jewish influence. The leaders of the new cult judged men "in respect of eating and drinking, and in the matter of festival, new moon, and sabbath" (2:16). It imposed dietary obligations which went beyond the requirements of the Jewish code, since they applied not only to food but to drink; and it prescribed ritual observance of the sacred seasons of the Jewish calendar. Further, it had codified some of its legal requirements in a set of taboos—"Do not handle, Do not taste, Do not touch" (2:21)—which again go far beyond any of the prohibitions of the Jewish law. It seems likely also that it required its adherents to be circumcised; this is implied by the language of 2:11.

Finally, it has some of the aspects of a mystery cult, though the precise nature of these is even less clear than anything else about the matter. The leader of the group goes about "entering into the visions that he has seen" (2:18). This baffling phrase is not explained, but its connection with the mysteries has been established by some Anatolian inscriptions (see Exegesis on the passage); and the frequency with which the epistle speaks of Christian truth as a "mystery" (1:26; etc.) is a further indication that the "philosophy" was integrally connected with a mystery cult.

On the basis of these data, little more than hints and suggestions, it is not possible to identify the Colossian heresy with any system known to us from other sources; but it is easy to see that it is a local manifestation of certain widespread general tendencies in religious thought and practice. It reflects in its own way the typical Hellenistic interpenetration of philosophy and cult, which springs from the desire to find and to give effect to the true relation between the inward life of man and the universe in which his lot is cast. The place of the *individual* in the *cosmos,* rather than the place of the *person* in a *social order,* was the fundamental problem of the contemporary schools. The explanation of this emphasis lies in the fact that the meteoric career of Alexander the Great had destroyed all the old focuses of social order—the city-states of the Greek world and the empire-states of the ancient Orient alike—and nothing had yet been devised to replace them. With this disintegration of ancient society the old gods, the divine guardians of the historic communities, fell from their place of reverence and esteem which derived from the society in which they were worshiped; the old religions lacked a sphere in which to function and could survive at all only by a radical transformation in the direction of universalism. Thus the very concept of divinity was recast from the foundations, so that the individuality of the old gods was lost in the notion of a universal divine power of which Zeus, Serapis, and Helios were merely particular manifestations or popular symbols; and worship was paid less to them than to minor figures—"heroes" and deified men, such as Heracles, Asclepius, Attis—who functioned as "saviors" and offered men the hope of immortality. In the philosophical schools the same tendencies led inevitably to a nature pantheism, with the feeling that the cosmos was instinct with divinity and that this same divine principle was likewise latent in the individual human soul.

But the individual, thinking of himself *as an* individual in the cosmos, with no significant relation other than that which he bears to the cosmos, is a lonely figure. He is not naturally at ease and at home in the universe by himself; he needs the support of a social order in which he may have a settled place and a useful function in fellowship with others. A few strong souls made the vain attempt to satisfy themselves with the resources of philosophy—to learn the Stoic *autarkeia* ("self-sufficiency") or the Epicurean *ataraxia* ("impassivity"); just as the ideal Buddhist sage "wanders lonely as a rhinoceros." But though these philosophies have elements of nobility, they are ultimately the outcome of an effort to seek in the mind itself a refuge from deep-seated despair. They brought men neither joy nor hope, but only a certain power to endure—and even this endurance was limited, as the Christian patience was not, by the ever-open gate of escape through suicide. Besides, for the masses of mankind the air of the philosophical heights was too rarefied for comfortable breathing. They sought and welcomed a doctrine which brought divinity near

to them in a more accessible form than in the vast unity of the cosmos; and this they found in the various "Gnostic" schools which flourished all through this period. In them the physical speculations of philosophy were interwoven in an incredibly complex amalgam with odds and ends of cult practices borrowed without discrimination from many sources, compounded with large elements of magic and astrology; and the whole fabric was commended by the pretense of a secret tradition going back to immemorial antiquity. For the "knowledge" of which the Gnostic boasted was invariably a revealed knowledge; not the accumulated results of observation and reflection upon the data of experience, but a *revealed* doctrine of God, man, and the world, and of the means by which man is to achieve his destiny or—more accurately—to realize his potentialities.

It might seem that all this sort of thing would have little appeal for Jews, who possessed in their scriptures and in their national tradition a knowledge of the living God and a conception of his rule over the world, beside which all these Hellenistic myths and speculations would seem but feeble and distorted reflections of divine truth. But in fact we know that even in Palestine, Judaism was not immune to this Hellenistic syncretism; and in the Diaspora, less restrained by the conservative power of the temple cult, by the constant discipline exercised by the official classes, and by the jealous watchfulness of scribes and Pharisees, it found itself powerfully moved by these trends. On the philosophical side we see the Old Testament and the whole system of observances of Judaism reinterpreted in terms of Platonism by such men as Philo of Alexandria; all over the Roman Empire there were to be found Jews addicted to the practice of magic (Acts 13:6; 19:13 ff.); and in several of the mystery cults—notably that of Sabazios, who was identified with Yahweh-Sabaoth, "the Lord of Hosts"—there are clear evidences of Jewish influence, with a reciprocal influence of the mysteries upon Jewish circles.[9] Now it happens that in Phrygia there were thousands of Jews; their settlement in the area contiguous to Colossae dates from at least as early as the second century B.C. Moreover, this colony was transported there in the first instance from Mesopotamia, where its ancestors had been in touch with Iranian religion for centuries and could hardly have maintained their Judaism unimpaired; in fact, they could never have been directly subjected to the rigorous Judaism

[9] See especially Charles Guignebert, *The Jewish World in the Time of Jesus,* tr. S. H. Hooke (London: Kegan Paul, Trench, Trübner & Co., 1939), Bk. IV, ch. ii, "The Judaeo-Pagan Syncretism," pp. 238-52.

of the second temple at all. Such a group would be particularly amenable to the prevailing syncretism of Hellenistic times, and we can hardly go wrong in attributing to them at least a share in the peculiar Judaeo-pagan fusion which threatened to seduce the converts of Epaphras at Colossae.

The doctrine of "elemental spirits" (2:8, στοιχεῖα) has a double background in philosophy and astrology. In the language of the Ionian hylozoists and the early physical philosophers in general, *stoicheia* was used of the ultimate components of matter, in the sense in which modern chemistry speaks of "elements." [10] It must not be forgotten, however, that these early schools did not think of "matter" as inanimate; for them the stuff of the universe was endued with life, and the primary substances were accorded many of the attributes which were later predicated of deity.[11] The word maintained itself in this sense throughout the history of Greek philosophy and is one of the technical terms of the post-Aristotelian schools, particularly of the Stoics and the Neo-Pythagoreans. The type of teaching which is in evidence at Colossae is several stages removed from the great systems of the Hellenistic masters, and stands on a far lower level of thought, but it is a product of the same mental climate. From the conception of these primary constituents of matter as instinct with life there was an easy transition on the popular level to the conception of the same "elements" as spiritual essences ("elemental spirits"), to which the whole life of man within the cosmos was necessarily subject.

In astrology *stoicheia* was used of the heavenly bodies; and these were taken to be the abodes, or more literally the bodies, of celestial spirits as the human frame is the body which clothes the human spirit. This astral aspect of the doctrine does not appear distinctly in the epistle, though a number of the Apostolic Fathers find it implied in the demand for the observance of festivals, new moons, and sabbaths; and it is not improbable that they have hit upon the truth.

The *worship* of these spirits (2:18) suggests the intermingling of a third strand in the conception of their nature—that is, their identification with the Amesha Spentas ("Immortal Beneficent Ones") of Iranian religion, who are hypostatizations of the attributes of the supreme deity Ormazd. In the long interpenetration of Iranian and Babylonian cultures the Amesha Spentas came to be identified with the great astral deities of the Semites, as the masters of events and of individual destiny. It should be kept in mind that the whole doctrine of angels in later Judaism, at least as regards the conception of an angelic hierarchy with defined classes and categories, each with its proper sphere and functions, also stems from the Iranian religion.[12]

It is impossible to say which particular parts of this bewildering complex belonged to the doctrine of the Colossian teachers; but it is not hard to imagine that simple minds would be impressed, perhaps we should say overwhelmed and beguiled (2:4), by the very pretentiousness of the teaching, and would imagine that it must be much more profound than the simple doctrine which they had been taught by Epaphras. In fact, it had little to commend it to a clear and penetrating intelligence. It was a product of the mental and spiritual instability of the times, and it was bound to perish with the contemporaneous state of mind which begot it. We may be thankful that a great Christian thinker was moved to deal with it in the moment of its first attempt to capture the Christian imagination, and to provide the church with the weapons to defeat it in the greater struggles of the second century.

### V. Character and Contents

The teaching of the epistle is governed by the necessity of exposing the errors and weaknesses of the so-called philosophy (2:8) which threatened to make inroads on the ranks of the Colossian Christians. As the philosophy rested upon a doctrine of angelic mediators, and prescribed ritual observances and ascetic practices by which men might keep themselves in the proper relation to these "elemental spirits" and through them to the cosmos itself, the apostle is compelled in his counterattack to bring out the implications of the gospel in respect of the person of Christ in such wise as to show that Christ alone embraces in himself all the functions that are falsely ascribed to these lesser beings, and that he freely bestows all the blessings of redemption which men vainly seek to win through cultic rites and by ascetic observances. The depth and power of the thought will begin to appear only as we study the epistle itself, verse by verse and almost word by word; for "every sentence is instinct with life and meaning" (Lightfoot) and does not yield its treasures to a cursory glance. But we may here gather together the main lines of the

[10] It is interesting to note that in some of these thinkers στοιχεῖα ("elements") was used as a synonym for ἀρχαί ("first principles"); in a different context the ἀρχαί ("principalities") appear in Colossians as one of the classes of the στοιχεῖα ("elemental spirits").

[11] See James Adam, *The Religious Teachers of Greece* (Edinburgh: T. & T. Clark, 1908), Lecture IX, "From Thales to Xenophanes," especially pp. 189-90.

[12] Guignebert, *op. cit.*, Bk. II, ch. ii, "Angels and Demons," pp. 96-105.

teaching and attempt to set forth a summary view of the whole.

Following the salutation to the readers (1:1-2), the apostle offers thanks to God for the response which the Colossians have made to the gospel as preached by Epaphras, assuring them that the very same gospel which has given proof of its living power among them is likewise manifesting its power of growth and increase in all the world (1:3-8). This is followed by a prayer of supplication for their advance toward the fullness of knowledge and insight; which, however, is to be found in the knowledge of God's will for their lives, in spiritual growth and fruitfulness in good works, in the constant increase of inward strength, and in thankfulness to God for the benefits which he has bestowed upon them in Christ (1:9-14). There is here an implicit repudiation of the vague mystical "fullness" promised by the Colossian propagandists, together with the firm assurance that all the fulfillment which they can desire is already at their disposal in Christ.

The prayer of supplication merges almost imperceptibly into a formal statement of the doctrine of the person of Christ. As "the Son of God's love," the ruler of the kingdom of love into which God has translated us (1:13), Christ is set before us as (a) the sole Mediator of creation, and (b) the sole Mediator of redemption. God made the universe through him and for him, and God redeems the universe through him. Through him it comes into being; in him it is sustained as an ordered whole; and by him it attains its destined perfection. As "the first-born of all creation" (1:15) he stands incomparably high above all ranks of angels, whether they are called "thrones or dominions or principalities or authorities" (1:16), for they themselves are part of the creation, which exists for his sake, derives its being from him, and depends upon him for its continuance and coherence. As "the first-born from the dead" (1:18) he stands likewise at the head of the new creation, the redeemed body of the church; so that in every respect the first place belongs to him alone. All the fullness of the Godhead has its permanent abode in him alone (1:19); it is not distributed among a host of mediators. The cosmos, disordered and alienated from God through the rebellion and persistent disobedience of man, is restored to its true harmony through the act of sacrifice by which Christ makes atonement for sin. In this cosmic reconciliation the Christians of Colossae are assured of their part if they stand steadfast in the truth of the gospel which they have been taught (1:15-23).

The apostle now speaks of his own ministry.

The sufferings which he undergoes as a prisoner are, like the sufferings of Christ—as a kind of supplement to the sufferings of Christ—endured vicariously for the sake of the church, which he serves "according to the dispensation of God" (1:25) which was given to him for their benefit. God has entrusted him with the task of bringing his word to fulfillment. This word too is a "mystery" (1:26), but it does not depend for its authority upon an ancient tradition—it has "been hid from ages and from generations." But God himself has now revealed it, making known "to his saints" his hitherto secret purpose to break down the barriers of race and religious privilege by extending to Gentiles as well as to Jews the glorious blessing of the Christ who was promised to Israel. Paul's life is now devoted to bringing all men without distinction to the full and perfect enjoyment of the grace that is proffered to them in Christ. His care extends not only to those whom he has himself evangelized, but also to the Christians of the Lycus region who have never seen his face; he is concerned lest they should be victimized by the specious pretensions of a doctrine which really falls far short of the wisdom and knowledge that are hidden in Christ (1:24–2:5).

Out of this concern the apostle, as present with them in spirit, urges them to hold fast to Christ as he has been made known to them, and to make him the foundation of their lives. He now gives his first direct warning against the seductions of the *stoicheia* doctrine, which exalts the "elemental spirits" to the place of Christ. Repeating his theme, that "in him dwells the whole fullness of deity bodily" (2:9), he drives home in a series of affirmations the lesson that they already possess in Christ all that is falsely promised them as the reward of worshiping the angelic powers; as (a) he is the head of all such powers, and the fulfillment promised through them is already possessed in him alone; (b) in him Christians have been set apart for God by a *spiritual* circumcision which does not need to be supplemented by the physical operation; (c) this spiritual circumcision is symbolized by baptism, wherein they were buried with Christ to the old life of earth and risen with him to the new life of heaven, the sins of the past freely forgiven; and (d) in this forgiveness Christ has canceled the old indebtedness, freed them from subjection to external ordinances, and broken the tyranny of the elemental spirits, stripping them of the weapons which they once wielded for the control of men (2:6-15).

In the following paragraphs the whole system of taboos and cultic observances is attacked at the roots. None of these things has any value except as shadow of a truth yet to be revealed; and the substance of this truth is now given in Christ. The leader of the new cult makes much ado about his mystic visions; but all this is only the inflated pomposity of a mind that is not truly spiritual, and is divorced from living contact with Christ the Head, on whom all that is spiritual depends for its vitality and for the attainment of its true ends.

Taboos and prohibitions of every kind create an impression of wisdom, superior piety, and praiseworthy self-denial; but in reality they do not check the gratification of the self, and they belong to that lower level of the moral life which was under the dominion of lesser beings —the elemental spirits. To that life Christians are dead through their mystical participation in the death of Christ; its artificial rules do not apply to them any more than to him. Risen with him to a new life, they are to have their minds and hearts fixed on heaven, where he is; and their moral life is to be governed by the sense of its hidden, heavenly nature, and by the hope of the coming revelation of Christ in glory—a glory which will be manifested also in them (2:16–3:4).

The apostle then sets forth the application of these principles of religious experience in character and conduct. They result in the transformation of the whole inward character and consequently of its whole outward expression. The vices of the earth-centered life are made to perish—both the impurities that defile the man himself and the enmities that set him at odds with his neighbor. For the Christian is a new man, made over in the image of his Creator. All the old distinctions of race and class are done away. The new life flowers in the graces and virtues that befit the people of God —gentleness and humility, patience and forbearance, forgiveness as free as the forgiveness of Christ; and above all, the crown and consummation of all—love. Such a life is filled with peace and joy, and overflows in thanksgiving (3:5-17).

These general principles of conduct are now applied specifically to household relations—of husbands and wives, of fathers and children, of slaves and masters (3:18–4:1). The main part of this section is that which is addressed to the slaves; and it has been conjectured that the occasion for the introduction of a table of domestic duties (*Haustafel*) in this epistle— unique in this respect among the Paulines—was afforded by the apostle's concern with the case of the slave Onesimus.

The body of the letter is completed with injunctions to watchfulness and prayer, especially prayer for the furtherance of the apostle's own work (4:2-4); and a brief reminder of the need for a wise demeanor toward non-Christians (4:5-6).

In conclusion the writer introduces his friend Tychicus, who is to carry the letter; and Onesimus, who is to return to Colossae in his company (4:7-9); he sends greetings to the church from a number of his associates (4:10-14); bids them greet and exchange letters with the church in Laodicea (4:15-16); invites them to encourage Archippus to fulfill his ministry (4:17); and ends with a personal greeting in his own handwriting (4:18).

The general structure of the epistle may be indicated as follows:

I. Introduction (1:1-14)
    A. Salutation (1:1-2)
    B. Thanksgiving (1:3-8)
    C. Prayer of supplication (1:9-14)
II. Polemic against the doctrine of angelic mediators (1:15–3:4)
    A. Primal significance of Christ (1:15-23)
        1. In the universe (1:15-17)
        2. In the church (1:18-20)
        3. In application to the readers (1:21-23)
    B. The apostle's ministry (1:24–2:5)
        1. Ministry of suffering (1:24)
        2. Propagation of the gospel (1:25-27)
        3. Cure of souls (1:28-29)
        4. The apostle's interest in the readers (2:1-5)
    C. The vital center of the Christian's life: the victorious Christ (2:6-15)
    D. Ascetic and ritual regulations condemned as alien to the Christian life (2:16-23)
    E. The true sphere of the Christian life (3:1-4)
III. Moral instruction and exhortation (3:5–4:6)
    A. The transformation of the Christian in character and conduct (3:5-17)
    B. Table of household duties (3:18–4:1)
    C. Exhortation to prayer (4:2-4)
    D. On Christian behavior toward pagans (4:5-6)
IV. Introductions and personal greetings (4:7-18)
    A. Introduction of Tychicus and Onesimus (4:7-9)
    B. Greetings from Paul's associates (4:10-14)
    C. Greetings to Laodicea and final instructions (4:15-18)

## VI. Integrity and Authenticity

The authenticity of the Epistle to the Colossians has been subject to question since before the middle of the nineteenth century. By some critics it has been treated as a pseudonymous work in its entirety; others have taken the position that the groundwork is Pauline, but that in its present form it includes interpolations introduced by a later writer. The question is complex and difficult, and only the main lines of discussion can be indicated here.

# COLOSSIANS

**A. External Evidence.**—The external attestation to Colossians is hardly equal to that of the greater epistles; nevertheless, it must be regarded as strong. There is no certain evidence of its use in the Apostolic Fathers or in any of the writers of the second century before Irenaeus (*ca.* A.D. 190); and this is the more surprising in that it appears to be fitted above all other writings of the apostle to give the necessary answer to the errors of the great Gnostic schools. On the other hand, it certainly was included in the collection of Pauline letters from the time that they were first brought together, and was known to the author of Ephesians; it is listed in the Muratorian fragment on the canon (Rome; *ca.* A.D. 200); and it is included in the Chester Beatty codex of the Pauline epistles (p[46]), which was made in Egypt toward the end of the second century. Irenaeus and Tertullian quote from every chapter; Clement of Alexandria and his greater successor Origen both cite it as Paul's; and the heretic Marcion, who made his own canon of Christian scriptures about the middle of the second century, also recognized it as the work of the apostle. There is nothing to indicate that it was ever suspect in any quarter in the ancient church.

**B. Modern Criticism.**—The genuineness of the epistle was first questioned in 1838 by E. T. Mayerhoff on grounds of vocabulary, style, and theological content; on the ground that the heresy combated could be identified with that of Cerinthus (*post* A.D. 90); and on the ground that it was a secondary working over of Ephesians, which Mayerhoff took to be genuine. A few years later W. M. L. De Wette turned the latter argument into reverse, defending the authenticity of Colossians and regarding Ephesians as the work of a later writer who drew heavily on the former epistle. The entire Tübingen school rejected both letters, chiefly because they identified the heresy in question with the Gnostic movements of the second century; F. C. Baur even found traces of a polemic against Montanism! H. J. Holtzmann, as mentioned above (p. 134), put forward the complicated theory that a genuine letter of Paul to the Colossians was first used by a later Paulinist as the basis of Ephesians, and subsequently interpolated by the same person with matter drawn from his own composition of Ephesians. This theory was subjected to a close examination by Hermann von Soden, who admitted interpolation but reduced it to a few passages; in his commentary, published some years later,[13] the only interpolation which he admitted was 1:16*b*-17. An excellent review by William Sanday[14] of the course of German criticism is still the best defense of the authenticity of the epistle available in English. Since the publication of Sanday's article, the majority of New Testament scholars have accepted Colossians as authentic, whatever view they have taken of Ephesians. Nevertheless, the verdict of scholarship is not unanimous, and the question must be regarded as open.[15]

**C. Elements of the Problem.**—Authentic or not, the substantial integrity of the epistle is almost beyond dispute; the various theories of interpolation have proved convincing to few but their own creators. It is impossible to imagine an editor capable of such ingenious dovetailing as Holtzmann's elaborate theory requires; for he has left no seams or breaks to betray him, and as Adolf Jülicher remarks, "Suspicion of such interpolation . . . would never have arisen but for the presence of the Epistle to the Ephesians beside it."[16] The christological passage in 1:15-20, which has been suspected by critics who alleged no other instance of interpolation, is in fact necessary to the argument, providing the essential doctrinal foundation on which it rests. It has, indeed, no real parallel in any other Pauline letter, but it cannot for that reason be excised as an interpolation: if it falls, the whole body of the epistle falls with it.

Granting the integrity of the letter, it remains to inquire whether it is indeed the work of Paul or a writing issued under his name by a later Paulinist. On this issue it must be said at the outset that some of the arguments brought against the authenticity of the epistle by earlier critics have fallen to the ground as we have acquired a clearer knowledge of the religious movements of the first century. All the aspects of the "heresy" to which Colossians makes reply were to be found in pre-Christian speculations; there is nothing in the nature of the doctrines combated to compel us to assign them to the second century. Again, many of the objections formerly raised on the score of vocabulary were invalidated when it was perceived that most of the significant words which do not occur elsewhere in the Pauline epistles are borrowed from the terminology of the Co-

---

[13] *Die Briefe an die Kolosser, Epheser, Philemon* (Freiburg: J. C. B. Mohr, 1891; "Hand-Commentar zum Neuen Testament").

[14] In his article on the epistle in the *Dictionary of the Bible*, ed. W. Smith and J. M. Fuller (2nd ed.; London: John Murray, 1893), Vol. I, Part 1, pp. 624-31.

[15] The most complete presentation of the evidence ever to be published will be found in the dissertation by Ernst Percy, *Die Probleme der Kolosser- und Epheserbriefe* (Lund: C. W. K. Gleerup, 1946); with a formidable linguistic and theological argument in support of the authenticity of both epistles.

[16] *An Introduction to the New Testament*, tr. Janet P. Ward (New York: G. P. Putnam's Sons, 1904), pp. 137-38.

lossian teachers. Likewise, the absence of a large number of familiar Pauline words (including "justify," "justification," "fellowship," "believe," "salvation," "law"), upon which the critics of the last century laid great stress, appears less significant—though still worthy of attention, it may be remarked in passing—when we observe that a formidable list of equally familiar Pauline terms is missing from Galatians, or from any one of the epistles in which a similar search is made.[17]

The rebuttal of these objections does not, however, dispose of the whole case against the authenticity of the epistle. At least three major difficulties still confront us: (a) the striking differences between the style of Colossians and that of the generally accepted epistles; (b) the affinities of the thought, especially in Christology, with such post-Pauline works as the Fourth Gospel and the Epistle to the Hebrews; and (c) the nature of the relationship to Ephesians.

*1. Question of Style.*—All commentators recognize the peculiarities of style in this epistle. The features which help to cast doubt upon the authenticity of Ephesians are present here also, though less pronounced—the long and involved sentences; the concatenation of genitives; the measured liturgical cadences; the absence of the quick and eager dialectic. The characteristic differences will be perceived in a moment by anyone who takes the trouble to read in Greek such a passage as I Cor. 2:6-16, and to compare it with the treatment of substantially the same theme in Col. 1:25-27. The nervous vigor of I Corinthians has entirely disappeared in a cumbrous, overweighted sentence in which it is hard to recognize the working of the same mind.

Differences of style are indeed to be observed in all writers, in works composed at different periods of their lives and under differing circumstances; and it is difficult to decide how great the differences must be before they compel us to deny identity of authorship. Moreover, Ernst Percy has brought forward, to counterbalance these differences, certain distinctive similarities of style between Colossians and the acknowledged epistles.[18] It can therefore be granted that the matter of style is not sufficient in itself to settle the question; but it remains a significant factor in the making of the decision.

*2. Question of the Affinities of the Thought.*—It is admitted by critics of all schools that the thought of Colossians exhibits marked differ-

[17] Theodor Zahn, *Introduction to N.T.*, Vol. I, sec. 29, n. 10, pp. 521-22.
[18] *Die Probleme der Kolosser- und Epheserbriefe*, pp. 36-46.

ences from that of the acknowledged epistles of Paul. It may be said that the center of interest has shifted from the work of Christ to the person of Christ. The doctrine of the saving, life-giving effects of his death and resurrection is still brought forward, but it is now subordinated to a doctrine of his place in relation to a system of transcendental reality; the soteriological interest is subordinated to the cosmological. For those who seek to defend the Pauline authorship of the epistle this particular difficulty is sufficiently met by the reflection that Paul is compelled to enter the field of cosmological speculation because the debate has been carried there by his opponents. At the same time, it is recognized that for true parallels to the cosmic Christology of Colossians we must turn not to Paul's other epistles, but to Hebrews and the Fourth Gospel—works of the second Christian generation. Again, though Paul elsewhere tells us that he has a higher wisdom to unfold among those who are prepared to receive it (I Cor. 2:6 ff.), he repudiates the use of such speculations for the establishment and support of the Christian faith (I Cor. 1:18-25); yet the whole argument of Colossians rests upon precisely the kind of "wisdom" which Paul has declined to use in his teaching at Corinth.

But it is not only in Christology that the difference in the thinking makes itself felt. The Pauline doctrine of justification by faith and freedom from law is clearly brought forward in this epistle also, but in new and unfamiliar language. The word νόμος ("law") does not occur, nor does δικαιόω ("justify") or any of its cognates; nor the verb πιστεύω ("believe"); and the noun πίστις ("faith") appears to be used in the sense of the body of doctrine which is to be believed, rather than in the sense of personal trust and confidence. Again, the insistence of the earlier epistles that the law is not voided, but established, by the gospel of grace and faith (Rom. 3:31) seems to be controverted by the assertion that God has "canceled the bond which stood against us with its legal demands; this he set aside, nailing it to the cross" (2:14). Above all, the doctrine of freedom is not associated with the doctrine of the Spirit; nothing is said of "the law of the Spirit of life in Christ Jesus" as the *positive* power which "has set [us] free from the law of sin and death" (Rom. 8:2). In fact, the Holy Spirit is not so much as mentioned in the epistle from beginning to end. Even in the noble passage on the transformation of the inward and outward life (3:5-17), no place is given to the sanctifying power of the Spirit; and the familiar conception of the warfare of "spirit" and "flesh" within man is replaced by the contrast of "the old man" and "the new man" (3:9-10). In this we have an intermediate step toward the Johannine doctrine of the new birth, just as the Christology throws out a bridge toward the Johannine doctrine of the Logos.

We must also note what might be called the "catholicizing" aspects of the defense of the gospel—the appeal to apostolic authority and to the universality of the proclamation (see Exeg. on 1:6, 23), and the exhortations to stand by that which has been delivered (1:23; 2:6-7). Here is a distinct foreshadowing of the notion of safeguarding a deposit of faith, of maintaining a tradition unaltered, which becomes still more explicit in the Pastoral epistles and is destined to develop into the sense that the gospel is transmitted in the form of a fixed and unalterable tradition, resting upon the authority of those to whom it was first committed.

Again, it will be felt by many that these differences, which may be ascribed at least in part to the particular circumstances which occasioned the writing of this epistle, are not sufficient in themselves to compel us to reject the Pauline authorship; but they do reinforce the doubts which are raised by the differences of style already noted.

*3. Question of the Relationship to Ephesians.* —It is clear to every reader that Ephesians and Colossians stand in a particularly close relationship to one another, alike in language and in thought. Theologically, the cosmic Christology of Colossians is the foundation of the doctrine of the church expounded in Ephesians; and in respect of language Edgar J. Goodspeed is able to claim with justice that "three-fifths of Colossians is reflected in Ephesians." [19] The two epistles agree in the use of a number of technical words of theological vocabulary which are not elsewhere used by Paul; again and again they exhibit verbally identical phrases; still more often a passage used in the one reappears with only slight modification in the other. Even in style there are elements of resemblance; the long liturgical cadences of Ephesians appear only less conspicuously in Colossians.

The question which arises, therefore, is whether the relationship between Ephesians and Colossians can be satisfactorily explained in terms of the dependence of the one upon the other, or whether they must stand or fall together. Most scholars now adopt the position that the parallels are to be accounted for as simply reflecting the use of Colossians by the writer of Ephesians. In Goodspeed's theory this position is modified only by the claim that the writer of Ephesians has made similar though

less extensive use of all the other Pauline epistles as well.[20] Many others, however, feel that the problem is not so simple, and claim that the phenomena of resemblance tell rather for than against unity of authorship. For them, if Colossians is once accepted as the work of Paul, there is no sufficient reason for rejecting Ephesians; or conversely, if the objections to the acceptance of Ephesians are felt to be overwhelming, it is scarcely possible that Colossians, so closely related to it, can be authentic. The case against the authenticity of Ephesians is certainly very strong, and throughout this Commentary it is treated as deutero-Pauline. Once that view is accepted, the closeness of the relationship between the two epistles must be regarded as adding to the doubts which are felt concerning Colossians on internal grounds.

If Colossians is not authentic, two possibilities confront us: (a) that Colossians is an earlier work from the hand of the writer of Ephesians, in which he adumbrates in a particular context of controversy the fundamental christological ideas which are developed in the later work into a general *gnosis* of redemption; or (b) that the two epistles are from two different writers of the same school, both alike disciples of Paul and impregnated with his spirit and outlook; and both representing, each in his own way, a later development of theology on Pauline foundations.

It is clear, at all events, that we cannot accept the tradition of Pauline authorship of this epistle without reservations or misgivings. At the same time, it can hardly be claimed that the argument against its authenticity has anything like the force of a demonstration. The question remains open. Under the circumstances, it does not seem necessary to keep continually reminding the reader of the element of doubt in the matter; in the Exegesis the author will be mentioned regularly under the name of Paul, but no attempt will be made to draw upon his career or personality as an aid in the understanding of the thought.

### VII. State of the Greek Text

The text of Colossians has been preserved with great fidelity, yet it must be said that it presents more uncertainties than that of any other epistle of the Pauline group. Nearly all witnesses, both manuscripts and versions, show a measure of corruption by assimilation to the text of Ephesians in the parallel passages; as, for instance, in the addition of "and the Lord Jesus Christ" at the end of the salutation (1:2 KJV; cf. Eph. 1:2), or in the still more

---

[19] *The Meaning of Ephesians* (Chicago: University of Chicago Press, 1933), p. 8.

[20] *Ibid.;* and see the exhibit of "other Pauline Parallels," pp. 83-165.

extensive corruption of 3:16 by assimilation to Eph. 5:19. Textual problems of this type, however, carry with them the key to their solution, and it is nearly always possible to distinguish the true text with certainty.

But there are other instances of textual variation which do not permit equal confidence in the possibility of recovering the true text. In 1:7, where the KJV renders "for you" and the RSV "on our behalf," the variation amounts to only a single letter in the Greek text, and the evidence of manuscripts and versions is fairly evenly divided. In 1:12, where the Beatty papyrus (p[46]) now supports Codex Vaticanus in the addition of ἅμα (omitted from all other witnesses), this small but formidable combination compels us to consider the reading seriously, and with it the question of whether the participle εὐχαριστοῦντες ("giving thanks") refers to the readers for whom the prayer is made, or to the writers who make the prayer (vs. 9).

In ch. 2 more serious difficulties of text are presented, sometimes leading us to fear that the true text is not to be found in any extant witness. In 2:2 the phrase τοῦ Θεοῦ Χριστοῦ is the reading of only two Greek manuscripts (p[46] and Codex Vaticanus) and one Latin commentator; but all critics agree that it is the reading which underlies the whole bewildering variety of other readings (eleven in all) which are represented in the other manuscripts and versions. Yet it remains doubtful whether a still more primitive error does not lurk in this primary reading to which the comparison of the witnesses leads us. Again, the closing phrase of the chapter is transmitted without variant of any kind; yet it seems quite unintelligible as it stands, and it is probable that here also the true reading has been lost beyond all possibility of recovery, unless through the discovery of some new and very early manuscript.

These examples will suffice to illustrate the different types of textual problem which are presented in this epistle.

### VIII. Selected Bibliography

ABBOTT, THOMAS KINGSWELL. *A Critical and Exegetical Commentary on the Epistles to the Ephesians and to the Colossians* ("The International Critical Commentary"). New York: Charles Scribner's Sons, 1897.

DIBELIUS, MARTIN. *An die Kolosser Epheser an Philemon* ("Handbuch zum Neuen Testament"). Tübingen: J. C. B. Mohr, 1927.

LIGHTFOOT, JOSEPH BARBER. *St. Paul's Epistles to the Colossians and to Philemon*. London: Macmillan & Co., 1875.

LOHMEYER, ERNST. *Die Briefe an die Philipper, an die Kolosser und an Philemon* ("Meyer's Kommentar"). Göttingen: Vandenhoeck & Ruprecht, 1930.

RADFORD, LEWIS BOSTOCK. *The Epistle to the Colossians and the Epistle to Philemon* ("Westminster Commentaries"). London: Methuen & Co., 1931.

SCOTT, E. F. *The Epistles of Paul to the Colossians, to Philemon and to the Ephesians* ("The Moffatt New Testament Commentary"). London: Hodder & Stoughton, 1930.

# COLOSSIANS

## TEXT, EXEGESIS, AND EXPOSITION

| | |
|---|---|
| 1 Paul, an apostle of Jesus Christ by the will of God, and Timotheus *our* brother, | 1 Paul, an apostle of Christ Jesus by the will of God, and Timothy our brother, |

### I. INTRODUCTION (1:1-14)

### A. SALUTATION (1:1-2)

On the problems of authorship and destination see Intro., pp. 142-45, and 134.

The salutation is couched in the characteristically Pauline style, recalling to the readers the authoritative office which lends weight to the message and also reminding

**1:1. An Apostle of Christ Jesus.**—Paul's claim to this title and function was repeatedly challenged. Interested in the function more than in the title, he defended and constantly advanced his claim to the title in order to safeguard his exercise of the God-given function, to be the commissioned representative of Christ by the will of God.

them of their own commitment to Christ, which imposes on them the duty of heeding the words of Christ's apostle. His whole approach to them is determined by the relationship to God into which they have been brought through Jesus Christ.

The phrase **and the Lord Jesus Christ** is not represented in the best MSS and is therefore omitted in the RSV. It is usually found in the Pauline greetings (Rom. 1:7; I Cor. 1:3; II Cor. 1:2; etc.) and has been introduced here by later scribes to bring uniformity with the more familiar phrasing.

**1:1. An apostle of Christ Jesus by the will of God:** Paul "magnifies his office" (Rom. 11:13); in addressing a church with which he has had no personal contact, he makes appeal to the divine appointment which has conferred teaching authority upon him. The title "apostle" itself conveys the thought of a commissioned representative; the message which he has to deliver is not his own, but is committed to him by God. So in II Cor. 5:20 he describes his work as that of an ambassador, saying in effect, "We function as ambassadors on Christ's behalf, as though God were exhorting you through us." Christ has chosen Paul to be his apostle; and behind Christ's administration stands the divine decree which governs all things—**the will of God.**

**Timothy our brother:** Paul's young associate, born of a Greek father and a Jewish mother, of a family in Lystra in Asia Minor, which probably embraced the faith of Christ

---

The original twelve apostles were first disciples, i.e., learners. They had come through a process of "Christian education." They passed from the stage of being learners to that of being men "sent forth," with authority to proclaim what they had learned of Christ. It is interesting to note that Paul was never a disciple of Christ in this sense. The violent nature of his conversion telescoped the gradual process of learning through which the others had been led to their apostolic work. Yet he was not unprepared. All the mental and moral equipment of his pre-apostolic life and training became serviceable resources for the ambassador of Christ. God has a place for both kinds of men and perfects his spiritual leaders through both types of experience. In both cases the reality of apostleship rests not in personal merit or attainment, but in the claim of God on the soul.

**By the will of God.** This ultimate conviction of a call and commission of God to his lifework undergirded all Paul's thinking, teaching, and acting. "I was not disobedient unto the heavenly vision" (Acts 26:19). "The love of Christ constraineth us" (II Cor. 5:14). "Necessity is laid upon me; yea, woe is unto me, if I preach not the gospel!" (I Cor. 9:16.) "The God of our fathers hath chosen thee" (Acts 22:14). This conviction makes distinctive the life of every creative Christian. It animates not only the apostle, but also "the saints and faithful brethren in Christ" (vs. 2). It is the distinguishing mark of the Christian ministry, which without it becomes only another profession. It turns the work of every Christian in every walk of life into a Christian vocation.

It is one thing to say, "I have decided to lend my support to Christian causes; I am going to add my influence to the agencies of social right-

eousness; I have chosen to throw my weight behind the church for the saving of civilization." It is another and deeper thing to acknowledge and accept one's lifework as committed and entrusted by the will of God. We speak of "career diplomats" and "career men" in government service. There are no "career men" in the divine service, but men commissioned by the will of God.

Alexander Whyte, preaching at the induction of a young minister, drew a picture of the divine purpose, shaping the universe from pristine chaos, fashioning the earth, creating man, working his sovereign will through the long centuries of human history, sending Christ, founding the church, bringing that particular congregation of Christian people into existence, guiding its development, preparing it for a man who should lead it into greater fulfillment of the divine will; and at the same time preparing and maturing the man who should become that leader. Then, pointing to the minister who had been "called," Whyte declared dramatically, "And now, punctually, he is here!" Calls do not always reach this magnificent pitch of conformity to the divine will. The choice of any Christian's vocation may fall far below it, or miss it entirely. But the possibility is always there. The "sense of mission" is open to every Christian.

All is, if I have grace to use it so,
As ever in my great Taskmaster's eye.[1]

That was Paul's commissioning as an apostle. In all the diversities of skills, talents, functions, and opportunities that make up our life in community, that is the commission of every

[1] Milton, "On His Having Arrived at the Age of Twenty-three."

2 To the saints and faithful brethren in Christ which are at Colosse: Grace *be* unto you, and peace, from God our Father and the Lord Jesus Christ.

2 To the saints and faithful brethren in Christ at Colos'sae:
Grace to you and peace from God our Father.

---

during the first journey of Paul and Barnabas (Acts 14:6 ff.). He joined Paul soon after the latter's separation from Barnabas, as he was again passing through Lystra on his way west, and had been his right-hand man ever since. **Brother** does not mean "fellow apostle," but "fellow Christian"; here, however, it is more than a conventional term—it suggests the warmth of Paul's personal regard for his companion (cf. Phil. 2:19-23).

**2. Saints and faithful brethren:** It would probably be better to translate "holy and faithful brethren." The word ἁγίοις may indeed be taken as a noun, but the form of the phrase here makes it more natural to take it as an adjective, in parallelism with πιστοῖς. The meaning is essentially the same in either case: the word in all its forms conveys the basic thought of dedication to the service of God, and only secondarily the thought of the moral character which befits the life so dedicated. The adjective πιστός may mean "believing," or "trustworthy"; it combines the thought of "those who have faith" and "those who are true to the Master in whom their faith is placed." The word **brethren** is not used lightly. Those who are dedicated to God and faithful in their allegiance are members of one family, bound to one another in the strong tie of brotherhood by virtue of their common relation to God as Father. The phrase **in Christ** governs all three

---

faithful brother in Christ. Our choice of Christian vocation is no arbitrary selection on our own terms. At the deepest level it is our acceptance of the will of God for our lives.

**2. The Saints.**—Throughout the N.T. "the saints" is a term which embraces all Christians. Today the average Christian and the average church member would never permit himself to be classed among the saints. He thinks of the saints as those who have attained a supreme degree of Christian perfection. But Paul would have classified this ordinary Christian with the saints because he belongs with those who have been pledged and dedicated to Christ. He may be a "sorry saint," or a "feeble saint." He may be far from "holy," in the sense of being entirely sanctified, but he belongs by baptism and his own profession of faith with those who are pledged to the maturing discipline of the long process of sanctification. However unworthy, he is "in Christ." "I'm on my way up there, to my Father's house." It is the privilege and the obligation of every Christian to make that his watchword.

In the more robust words of Bunyan's *Pilgrim's Progress:*

> There's no discouragement
> Shall make him once relent
> His first avowed intent
> To be a pilgrim.

Far from degrading the quality of sainthood, or lowering the standard of the ideal Christian man, this conception extends the obligation to every Christian to measure his living by "the measure of the stature of the fulness of Christ" (Eph. 4:13). O. C. Quick points out in a penetrating passage [2] that in the O.T. the conception of "holiness" was one of increasing exclusiveness and separateness from the common life. The holy nation became the holy remnant, until finally Jesus alone fulfilled and sustained in his own personality the qualities of "the chosen" of God. Then, at Pentecost and after, the movement of exclusion becomes reversed, and the "common," heretofore considered "unclean," becomes the sphere of the sanctifying work of the Holy Spirit. The whole church and all its members are held in unity by the "common" possession of the "Holy" Spirit. The exclusive conception of "holiness" gives place to the inclusive and universal gospel of Christ, whose redemptive work is "to reconcile to himself all things, whether on earth or in heaven" (vs. 20). Although the Holy Spirit is mentioned in Colossians only in 1:8, his presence and work in the church are implied throughout the entire argument.

In short, while no one would claim sainthood for himself, and while normal people shrink from the thought of such self-exaltation, nevertheless no Christian has any right at all to turn his natural modesty into an excuse for renouncing his obligation to live toward, and increasingly up to, God's will for him. The recognition of being "no saint" must not be allowed to soften the force of every Christian's commitment as one who is pledged to Christ.

[2] *Doctrines of the Creed* (New York: Charles Scribner's Sons, 1938), pp. 284-85.

3 We give thanks to God and the Father of our Lord Jesus Christ, praying always for you,

3 We always thank God, the Father of our Lord Jesus Christ, when we pray for

---

elements in the description of the Christian readers. It is **in Christ** that men experience the new relationship to God which transcends all other relationships: setting them apart from the world, binding them in trustful fidelity to him, and incorporating them into one spiritual family.

**Grace . . . and peace:** Paul himself seems to have created this form of salutation, which combines the familiar Semitic greeting, "Peace be with you," and a kind of play on the common Greek greeting, χαῖρε (in letters, χαίρειν) —giving to both a higher significance. The conventional greeting becomes a prayer that the God whom his readers know as Father may bestow upon them that peace which the world cannot give and that grace which is the outflow of his own love and power; the inward peace that comes from the consciousness of sins forgiven and undisturbed communion with God, and the inward grace that issues in beauty of character and the power to do God's will.

### B. THANKSGIVING (1:3-8)

Ancient Greek letters nearly always begin with a prayer or an expression of thanksgiving for the good health of the person addressed, and Paul usually follows this convention. Among pagans the practice was prompted by a superstitious desire to begin every message with a word of good omen; in the same spirit a herald always took care that his first words should be good, even when his message was full of unpleasant things. No such need of placating unknown powers moves the mind of the Christian writer; the convention is transformed by him into a heartfelt expression of gratitude for the goodness God has manifested to his people. At the same time it enables the apostle to approach his readers in a spirit of good will, with the assurance that he recognizes in them the fruits of divine grace; it gives him the means of establishing a tie of sympathy and mutual confidence. If he has criticisms to offer, the hostility which they might provoke is disarmed in advance by warm words of praise and regard.

In this letter Paul introduces into the thanksgiving a word to confirm the truth which the Colossians have heard from his colleague Epaphras, assuring them that it is the

---

**Brethren in Christ.** The goal of Christ's redemption is all-inclusive:

> In Christ there is no East or West,
> In Him no South or North,
> But one great fellowship of love
> Throughout the whole wide earth.[3]

The words are ridiculously and tragically false, except for the opening phrase. The only possibility of such brotherhood is "in Christ." The actuality is depressingly far from the divine possibility. The world as it is is simply not "in Christ." If one were to substitute for the phrase "in Christ," the phrase "in the church," the actuality is still far from what it ought to be. And yet there is a great difference. In the church there is an acknowledgment of Christ and a commitment to him that simply is not in

[3] John Oxenham, "In Christ There Is No East or West," *Selected Poems of John Oxenham*, ed. Charles L. Wallis (New York: Harper & Bros., 1948). Copyrighted by Erica Oxenham, 1948, used by permission of the publishers.

the world. While the world remains uncommitted to Christ, those who *are* committed to him become a distinct and distinguishable brotherhood, set apart from the world, like the leaven in the dough, in order that they may the more convincingly win the world, and the more effectively transform it. In the Roman Empire the Christians came to be called the "third race," to distinguish them from Jews and pagans. Their inclusive purpose required an exclusive loyalty. This is the setting of all that follows. Paul is speaking not to foreigners and strangers, but to "fellow citizens with the saints" (Eph. 2:19). They are within the family of committed men. They are under special obligation to realize the full possibility of that commitment. God can do things with committed men that he can never do with the uncommitted. To this responsibility Paul calls them. He has something special to lay upon those who are **brethren in Christ.**

3. *We Always Thank God, the Father of Our Lord Jesus Christ, When We Pray for You.*—

very same gospel which is being proclaimed with effective power everywhere in the world; the tacit assumption is that the new doctrines which have been introduced locally are unheard of elsewhere, and are not worthy of attention.

**3. God and the Father:** The best MSS here read τῷ θεῷ πατρί. The same phrase is repeated in 3:17, but is not found elsewhere in the Pauline epistles. There is no apparent reason for the slight alteration in the usual form of the phrase. The thought remains the same: that the God to whom we give thanks is the God whom Jesus Christ reveals to us in his character of Father.

**Our Lord:** *Kyrios*—"Lord"—is the primary title applied to Christ among the Gentile churches. For them the word "Christ" (Hebrew, "Messiah") had no significance as a title. "The Anointed One" meant a great deal to Jews, but had no such weighty associations for Gentiles. Thus "Christ" quickly became, among the Gentiles, not a title of office, but a proper name, used with or without the name Jesus. *Kyrios*, on the other hand, struck a responsive chord. This title was in general use in the pagan cults, especially when the god was approached in his capacity as healer and savior of men. It was applied to Zeus, Serapis, Asclepius, and numerous other divinities; and to the Roman emperor. Its application to Christ, therefore, was a challenge to every other religious allegiance of the time. Paul affirms that the confession of Jesus by this title leads to salvation. Rom. 10:9 may be translated: "If thou shalt confess with thy mouth, 'Jesus is *Kyrios*,' and shalt believe in thine heart that God raised him from the dead, thou shalt be saved." Only the Spirit of God can prompt a man to make such a confession: "No one is able to say 'Jesus is *Kyrios*' but by the Holy Spirit" (I Cor. 12:3). Acts traces the use of this title to the very commencement of the Gentile mission (Acts 11:19-20). And in a great passage, Paul declares that Christians concede this high title to no other: "For although there may be so-called gods in heaven or on earth—as indeed there are many 'gods' and many 'lords'—yet for us there is one God, the Father, . . . and one Lord [*Kyrios*], Jesus Christ" (I Cor. 8:5-6). On the history of the title see W. W. Baudissin, *Kyrios als Gottesname im Judentum und seine Stelle in der Religionsgeschichte* (Giessen: Töpelmann, 1929); and with particular reference to early Christian usage see Wilhelm Bousset, *Kyrios Christos* (Göttingen: Vandenhoeck & Ruprecht, 1926), especially ch. 3, "Die heidenchristliche Gemeinde."

The phrase **for you**, attached in both versions to the participle, is better taken with the main verb, the participle being used absolutely—"We always thank God for you in our prayers."

---

Paul is led by the spontaneity of love and an overmastering creative purpose to approach the Colossian heresy from the positive and not the negative side. He begins by stressing not what is wrong, but what is right in the people whom he is about to guide. This sound psychological principle is uniformly present in all the epistles. Only in Galatians, where he is contending with opponents who challenge his right to be heard at all, does he begin with a direct attack. "I am astonished that you are so quickly deserting him who called you in the grace of Christ and turning to a different gospel" (Gal. 1:6). Elsewhere he accentuates the positive. Apprehension of truth, and the acceptance of it when apprehended, flow from the intercourse of minds united in friendship—as Paul himself, or one who was steeped in his spirit, wrote in Ephesians (4:15), "speaking the truth in love."

"If God is love, it is only among people animated by mutual love that understanding of

him can be advanced. To admit acrimony in theological discussion is in itself more fundamentally heretical than any erroneous opinions upheld or condemned in the course of discussion." [4]

The attitude of thanksgiving is a great deal more than one of the niceties of human intercourse. It is a factor in creative influence. Only the grateful and appreciative guide can draw the best out of those whom he seeks to lead. This is because the spirit of thanksgiving reveals the dominant attitude of one's own life toward others. Nothing could so effectively evoke in Paul's hearers the faith, hope, and love to which he longs to win them as a convincing demonstration of the same great qualities in his own bearing toward them. A glance at a concordance

[4] *Doctrine in the Church of England. The Report of the Commission on Christian Doctrine Appointed by the Archbishops of Canterbury and York in 1922* (London: Society for Promoting Christian Knowledge, 1938), p. 23.

4 Since we heard of your faith in Christ Jesus, and of the love *which ye have* to all the saints,

you, 4 because we have heard of your faith in Christ Jesus and of the love which you

---

**4.** The participle ἀκούσαντες may be taken as *causal* (**because we have heard,** RSV), or as *temporal* (**since we heard,** KJV). In any case, it reflects the fact that Paul had never had any personal contact with the church to which he is writing (cf. 2:1); he knew of their state only at second hand. **Faith in Christ Jesus:** The preposition ἐν ("in") marks out Christ not as the *object* of their faith, but as the *sphere* of spiritual experience within which faith lives. They are **in Christ Jesus** and through this union with him they look to God with the faith which he awakens and sustains.

**The love which you have for all the saints:** Here, as frequently, the thought of faith leads Paul on to the thought of the love which is the fruit of faith (cf. Gal. 5:6, "faith which worketh by love"). Here he thinks particularly of the love which is the bond of Christian brotherhood, created by the mutual relationship of all to Christ, not dependent upon natural sympathy or mutual interest or ties of race or kin; the love which dissolves animosities and forgives injuries and forges a true fellowship of the spirit. Such a faith and such a love necessarily look beyond the present circumstances to a time and a sphere in which they will come to perfection; the contrast between the

---

will show that the great majority of the instances of thanksgiving recorded in the Bible occur in the words and deeds of our Lord and of Paul. This persistent note of deep and genuine thanksgiving which characterizes the introduction to most of Paul's epistles, and indeed runs all through them, affords an important clue to the secret of his amazing influence.

**Always.** It is one thing to see the value of appreciation as a technique of persuasion and to take pains to use it when one wants to make a good impression. It is quite another thing to express thanksgiving and appreciation as a sincere and spontaneous attitude, out of an over-mastering passion for souls. There is no trace of the former calculating tactics in Paul. Signs of the latter consuming desire are seldom absent. It is said that Dwight L. Moody could not sit for twenty minutes in a barber's chair without making the man aware of his intense personal concern for him as a person, and as a potential and actual son of God. Certainly Paul, even when words of rebuke and correction are to come, or rather especially then, first draws love's circle which takes the other man in. **We always thank God . . . when we pray for you.** It is the expression of a habitual attitude.

**4-5.** *Your Faith, . . . the Love, . . . the Hope.*—This well-known triad, apparently originated by Paul, occurs much more frequently in the N.T. than is realized by the ordinary reader who is chiefly acquainted with I Cor. 13. A comparison of some of the passages discloses a wealth of meaning in the familiar words.[5] In

[5] See L. B. Radford, *The Epistle to the Colossians and the Epistle to Philemon* (London: Methuen & Co., 1931; "The Westminster Commentaries"), pp. 151-52.

the present passage they are set in a temporal sequence. Faith is directed to Christ—a reference to what has been done in the past, the "finished work" of salvation; love is directed to the Christian brethren—life in the present; hope is directed to the eternal spiritual destiny which awaits those who are in Christ—anticipation of the future.

In I Cor. 13:13, the three are set in the order of spiritual value. Faith leads into a life of hope, and both undergird a life of love, which is the supreme mark of the Christian. I Thessalonians stresses the practical effects. In I Thess. 1:3 they are set forth as the means of a spiritual offensive on life. Faith inspires service, love energizes it, hope perpetuates it. The same idea is repeated in II Thess. 1:3-4. In I Thess. 5:8 they are portrayed as the Christian's armament for spiritual defense against the attacks of cynicism, unbelief, and the insidious, unceasing pressure to conform to the ways of the pagan world; faith and love become a breastplate, and the hope of salvation a protecting helmet for the fight.

An extended comment in I Pet. 1:3-9, 21-22, puts hope first. It represents the Christian world outlook—the philosophy of history and view of man's life, duty, and destiny—which makes all who hold the Christian hope citizens and heirs of one spiritual kingdom. Faith in Christ binds the Christian to the eternal world in face of all the trials, temptations, and compromises which this world thrusts upon him. Love emerges as the necessary and only true expression of the new life in Christ.

Running through these passages is the thought that the Christian world view (hope)

5 For the hope which is laid up for you in heaven, whereof ye heard before in the word of the truth of the gospel;

have for all the saints, 5 because of the hope laid up for you in heaven. Of this you have heard before in the word of the truth,

---

ideal and its imperfect realization in this life is such that they can have full meaning only in the light of the Christian hope, which is thus the "anchor of the soul" that believes and loves.

**5. For the hope:** The connection is not clear. So far as the syntax goes, the phrase may be taken as attached directly to the preceding words—**the love which you have for all the saints, because of the hope laid up for you in heaven.** It is not clear, on the other hand, how the "hope . . . laid up . . . in heaven" can be regarded as the *cause* of the "love . . . for all the saints." It is perhaps better to treat "since we heard of your faith and love" as parenthetical, and to attach the "hope" phrase more closely to the main verb, "We give thanks for you . . . because of the hope which is laid up for you."

**Laid up for you:** The verb ἀπόκειμαι, which is used here, is a common business term, frequently found in storage receipts, of grain "stored" in a granary, books "housed" in a library, treasures "kept" in a temple. The **hope,** then, is here used in the concrete sense of "the object of hope," "the promised blessing," which is represented figuratively as a treasure stored in a heavenly treasure house, hidden from the world's view, inestimably precious, and forever secure.

**Whereof ye heard before:** The antecedent of "whereof" is "hope." Hope, in this concrete sense of the heavenly blessing which God has promised, is now treated as the substance of the gospel which was preached to them. **Before:** The προ of προηκούσατε may mean "before you received this message from me"; but more likely it means "before this complicated new doctrine was introduced." The gospel which they received in the

---

underlies both faith and love. So Paul thanks God for the Christians in Colossae, whom he has never seen, **because of the hope laid up for you in heaven.** If the **hope laid up for you in heaven** is regarded as the cause of the Colossians' faith and love, it is also in this same sense that it affords the basic outlook on life in this world from which Christian faith and love flow. Without a Christian world view—"If in this life only we have hope in Christ, we are of all men most miserable" (I Cor. 15:19) —individual efforts of faith and love become sporadic gestures in a universe which can neither support nor encourage them.

The Christian hope is not man-made, but God-given. It is not the product of a resolute spirit, nor of a naturally happy and buoyant disposition. It rests on what God is eternally, on what he has done in Christ, and on what he will do when "the kingdoms of this world are become the kingdoms of our Lord, and of his Christ; and he shall reign for ever and ever" (Rev. 11:15).

Two things follow: (*a*) Salvation is assured because God has underwritten it in Christ. Man is not to think of himself in the haunting but hopeless mood of Bertrand Russell as compelled to "sustain alone, a weary but unyielding Atlas, the world that his own ideals have fashioned despite the trampling march of uncon-

scious power." [6] (*b*) In every man as a child of God there are unlimited potentialities. Paul is about to say some forthright things about the devotees of the Colossian heresy. Christians were being beguiled by a religion of Pharisaic legalism and superstitious speculation which obscured and perverted the simple clarity of Christian faith and life. Yet even those who would feel most rebuked by Paul's message could not but sense from beginning to end Paul's confidence that the creative faith and love and hope of which he writes are in his hearers when they are at their best, and is in his own attitude to them always. He criticizes not to condemn, but to create; not to denounce, but to develop; not to reject, but to reclaim. His purpose is to make Christians, not to unmake them. Contending for the faith becomes contention about the faith unless our striving for religious truth rises above mere defense of a theological position, or mere attack upon a "school of thought." To see the possibilities in immature Christians, to lift disappointing Christians to their best, to encourage stubborn and troublesome Christians to rise to their full capacities in the fellowship of the kingdom; never to be content merely to rebuke what is at fault, always to be eager to make men see that one's deepest concern is

[6] *A Free Man's Worship* (Portland, Maine: T. B. Mosher, 1923), p. 28.

6 Which is come unto you, as *it is* in all the world; and bringeth forth fruit, as *it doth* also in you, since the day ye heard *of it,* and knew the grace of God in truth:

the gospel 6 which has come to you, as indeed in the whole world it is bearing fruit and growing — so among yourselves, from the day you heard and understood the

---

first place was the truth; it told them of the hope laid up for them in heaven. The false doctrine of the Gnostic teachers, as binding their thoughts and aspirations to earthly things, tended to rob them of this heavenly hope.

6. The construction as found in the true text weaves back and forth upon itself; in the late "received text," which lies behind the KJV, it has been simplified. The true text (somewhat freely rendered in the RSV) would run literally: "Which has come to you, as also in all the world it is bearing fruit and increasing, as it also does among you," etc. The "received text" has dropped the second participial phrase καὶ αὐξανόμενον, and has added a καί before ἔστιν. The true text, though it leaves an external awkwardness, has a verve and vigor which suggests the atmosphere of living speech; the reciprocal "as it also does among you" is introduced in passing, as if to throw in a note of appreciation of the progress which the Colossians have made.

**In all the world:** Not so much a hyperbole, boasting of the wide spread of the gospel message, as an assertion of its uniformity: the same gospel is preached, wherever it is preached. Here for the first time we have introduced into Christian apologetic the fateful theory that catholicity is a warrant of truth, the seed of the canon enunciated by Vincent of Lérins, *quod semper, quod ubique, quod ab omnibus.* Instead of an appeal to first principles, we have what amounts to an appeal to the use and wont of the churches generally. The new teaching at Colossae is condemned by implication on the ground that it is not taught anywhere else; the gospel preached by Epaphras is commended on the ground that it is preached everywhere in the world.

**Bearing fruit and growing:** To the test of universality is added a pragmatic test; the gospel which was preached to them in the first place is effective—it brings forth fruit wherever it is preached, and it keeps extending its influence more and more widely.

---

not with what they are, which may be at fault, but with what in Christ they may become— this is the creative Christian attitude toward others. So Paul thanks God for the Colossian Christians and prays for them **because of the hope laid up for you in heaven.**

**6. In the Whole World.**—Here is the grand sweep of the gospel. "God so loved the world . . . that the world through him might be saved" (John 3:16-17) ; "that the world may believe that thou hast sent me" (John 17:21) ; "God was in Christ, reconciling the world unto himself" (II Cor. 5:19) ; "Go ye therefore, and teach all nations" (Matt. 28:19). The universality of the gospel runs through all the N.T. witness. This is of the essence of the new covenant to which the whole N.T. bears witness. E. F. Scott characterizes this claim that the gospel was bearing fruit and growing in all the world as a wild exaggeration, because the church comprised only little handfuls of people in a vast pagan empire.[7] Yet, though rudimen-

tary and weak, centers of Christian teaching and influence were already established in every major quarter of Roman civilization. L. B. Radford points out [8] that the gospel had already been proclaimed in most provinces of the empire. He mentions Palestine, Syria, Cilicia, Galatia, Phrygia, Asia, Pontus, Bithynia, Macedonia, Achaia, Italy, with strong probability also of Egypt, Africa, and perhaps Gaul. A glance at a map of the ancient world, with a little reflection on the laboriously slow means of communication and the absence of almost all modern methods of mass education and propaganda, cannot fail to raise a thrill of wonder and gratitude for the romance of first-century missions. Though the church was as yet established in only a few centers, and though many localities had not yet heard the evangel, nonetheless Christian claims had been staked out in every major quarter of Roman civilization, and the lordship of Christ over all mankind was already a settled principle of the church's teaching.

In modern times, when other movements are not backward in their claim to embody the

[7] *The Epistles of Paul to the Colossians, to Philemon and to the Ephesians* (London: Hodder & Stoughton, 1930; "The Moffatt New Testament Commentary"), p. 16.

[8] *Op. cit.,* p. 153.

7 As ye also learned of Epaphras our dear fellow servant, who is for you a faithful minister of Christ;

grace of God in truth, 7 as you learned it from Ep′aphras our beloved fellow servant. He is a faithful minister of Christ on our[a]

[a] Other ancient authorities read your.

---

It has been suggested that this double phrase is "a regular Gnostic catchword," seized upon by Paul from the vocabulary of the Colossian "philosophy" and given a new application (W. L. Knox, *St. Paul and the Church of the Gentiles* [Cambridge: University Press, 1939], p. 149, n. 5).

**Heard and understood the grace of God in truth:** Χάριν ("grace") is the object of both verbs, in zeugma. "Grace" has a double sense: with the first verb it means the content of the gospel message; with the second, the divine favor which is communicated to those who hear and believe. Ἐπέγνωτε ("you understood") is the ingressive aorist—"you came to know," "you discerned" the blessing of the gospel for what it truly is. "You heard the message of God's grace and came to know the gracious blessing of the gospel."

**7.** Epaphras is mentioned in the letter to Philemon as Paul's "fellow prisoner." Here it is affirmed that he had evangelized Colossae under Paul's direction (reading ὑπὲρ ἡμῶν,

---

"wave of the future" for all mankind, notably the fascist and communist philosophies, Christianity cannot be advanced as the ultimate truth on less than a universal scale. The point is not that catholicity establishes truth, but that truth is by its nature catholic and universal. It is "the word of the truth of the gospel" (vs. 5) that inspires and compels Paul, not some fashion of thought that for a time may claim general attention.

Furthermore, the vision of the church universal, with the accompanying sense of participation in the empire of Christ, challenges allegiance in a vastly more vital way than the intriguing peculiarities of some local interpretation of the faith, such as the Colossian heresy, could ever do.

> How grandly hath thine empire grown,
> Of freedom, love, and truth! [9]

Local and parochial expressions of the Christian faith are broadened, deepened, and intensified through their relationship to the gospel for all the world. The "romance of modern missions," the new concern for the world outreach of Christianity, and the ecumenical fellowship of a reuniting church are true revivals of first-century Christianity in the church of the twentieth century. The gospel is still **bearing fruit and growing,** intensive cultivation (bearing fruit) going hand in hand with extensive development (growing).

**7. *Epaphras Our Beloved Fellow Servant.*—** At the heart of all progressive movements and achievements there is a man or a group of men. Surrounding these spiritual giants of a creative era there is always a corps of lesser associates

[9] Samuel Johnson, "City of God, how broad and far."

whose contribution is vital and indeed indispensable. A study of such minor characters in the N.T. church adds fresh insight into the life of the early Christian communities. Furthermore, the effort to piece together, from the scattered references in the books of the N.T., biographical sketches of the less prominent leaders, of whom little is directly known, will prove to be both fascinating and rewarding. Much can be learned by searching out the probable stories of Barnabas, Mark, Luke, James the brother of our Lord, Aquila and Priscilla, Timothy, and others like them. Among this group is Epaphras.

The Colossian church did not just grow. The Holy Spirit did not by-pass human agents in establishing the church in Colossae. Having thanked God for this community of believers, Paul mentions the man who brought the gospel to them. Epaphras was used of God to bring into being a new Christian community, though his name is preserved only in a few scattered references in Paul's letters.

Probably his first contact with Paul, and his subsequent conversion, took place during the latter's long mission in Ephesus, *ca.* A.D. 53-55. Paul seems to have remained in Ephesus during this time (Acts 20:18, 31), but his influence spread throughout Asia (Acts 19:10, 26), and Christian communities were founded, "the churches of Asia" (I Cor. 16:19). Some of those who, either under Paul's direction or at least inspired by his influence, carried the gospel to the towns and cities of the Lycus Valley, which Paul had never visited, are mentioned in his epistles, Nympha, Archippus, Philemon, and Apphia (4:15, 17; Philem. 1, 2), and, outstanding among them, Epaphras.

Epaphras was a Colossian—"one of yourselves" (4:12). Whether he was a presbyter,

8 Who also declared unto us your love in the Spirit.

behalf 8 and has made known to us your love in the Spirit.

---

"for us," in place of ὑπὲρ ὑμῶν, "for you," which is not so well attested). During his long mission in Ephesus the apostle apparently sent his associates from place to place throughout the province of Asia (Acts 19:10), and the cities of the Lycus Valley were assigned to Epaphras. Paul here supports him without qualification.

**Fellow servant:** Σύνδουλος, literally "fellow slave"—partner in that voluntary bondage to Christ in love, in which Paul delights as the only true freedom.

**8. Declared to us your love:** Paul would not have the Colossians think that Epaphras has come to him filled with complaints and criticisms about them. Δηλώσας really means "manifested"; the thought seems to be that Epaphras has brought to Paul in his imprisonment some practical token of the affection which the Christians of Colossae have felt "in spirit" for the great apostle whom they have never seen. Note that this is the true sense of ἐν πνεύματι here (as in 2:5, "I am with you in spirit"); not "in the Holy Spirit." The Spirit of God is never mentioned in this epistle.

---

deacon, or layman we are not told, but he was clearly the original evangelist of Colossae, possibly also of Laodicea and Hierapolis, which were close by (1:7-8; 4:12-13). This **beloved fellow servant** of Paul, and **faithful minister of Christ,** was a true pastor and shepherd of his flock (4:12-13), constantly exercising a deep concern for them.

In addition to founding the church in Colossae, Epaphras figures in another important event in Christian history. He had a share, though indirect, in producing one of the books of the immortal Christian Scriptures. Less than a decade after the founding of the Colossian church, the Colossian heresy, a strange doctrine, half Jewish asceticism and half Oriental speculation, threatened to supplant the authentic Christian emphasis on simple ethical goodness inspired by complete reconciliation to God through Christ. Epaphras journeyed to Rome. Whether or not his anxiety concerning this increasing threat to the life of the Colossian church, and his desire to seek the guidance of Paul in combating it, was his sole motive in coming to Rome, in any case it must have been a dominant one. He gave Paul a full account of the new perversion of the faith. Paul's letter to the Colossians, now a part of the Christian Scriptures, is the result of Epaphras' visit to Rome and of his report to Paul.

Epaphras did not return with the letter (4:12). He may have had other business to attend to in the capital. Possibly his Christian witness there had got him into trouble. Paul calls him a "fellow prisoner" (Philem. 23), though this may imply simply a voluntary decision to remain and support Paul in his trials. At all events he was the direct means of evoking from Paul, in this letter to the Colossians, the noblest and fullest interpretation of the

centrality of Christ to be found in the N.T., and also indirectly of prompting the great exposition of the divine nature of the church which is found in Ephesians. For this latter letter seems to have been written at about the same time, and to have been inspired by reflection on the message to the Colossians (see Intro., p. 145).

In the chain of events that lead to lasting achievements such is the service of lesser men in the church, without whom the "spiritual giants" could not have reached or maintained their prominence.

Of Epaphras' subsequent history nothing is known. Colossae and its neighboring cities, Laodicea and Hierapolis, became important centers of Christian thought and influence, but later declined. The persistence of the Colossian heresy may possibly be seen in the lukewarmness and compromise with the world for which the writer of Revelation so scathingly rebukes the Laodicean church (Rev. 3:14 ff.). Colossae itself, never as important as its two neighbors either as a city or as an ecclesiastical center, lost its importance much earlier than they. "Not a single event in Christian history is connected with its name; and its very existence is only rescued from oblivion, when at long intervals some bishop of Colossae attaches his signature to the decree of an ecclesiastical synod." [1]

Nevertheless, the faithful life of Epaphras was not thrown away. His steadfast witness, even in a Christian center whose importance was later to disappear, led to the great affirmations of the letters to the Colossians and the Ephesians, which are now sacred scripture, to the permanent enrichment of Christendom.

[1] J. B. Lightfoot, *St. Paul's Epistles to the Colossians and to Philemon* (London: Macmillan & Co., 1875), p. 68.

9 For this cause we also, since the day we heard *it,* do not cease to pray for you, and to desire that ye might be filled with the knowledge of his will in all wisdom and spiritual understanding;

9 And so, from the day we heard it, we have not ceased to pray for you, asking that you may be filled with the knowledge of his will in all spiritual wisdom and under-

---

## C. Prayer of Supplication (1:9-14)

This whole passage centers about the prayer that the Colossians may be **filled with the knowledge of his will in all spiritual wisdom and understanding.** The idea of "fullness" recurs again and again in the epistle; it appears that the false teaching in Colossae boasted that it offered the "fullness" of the truth and the spiritual blessing, while Epaphras had taught them only the first steps. Paul now affirms that he and his friends have always asked God in their prayers to give this "fullness" of blessing to the new converts, and he here indicates what the true "fullness" is. The fullness of knowledge for which he prays is not a speculative understanding of some abstruse mystery, but "the knowledge of [God's] *will"*; it issues in a life "worthy of the Lord" who rules it; it brings forth the fruit of good works; it shows its inward power in endurance and patience; it expresses itself in joyful thankfulness to the God who has manifested his transforming power.

**9. In all spiritual wisdom and understanding:** The two nouns (σοφία and σύνεσις) are to be taken together, "spiritual" qualifying them both. Aristotle groups σοφία, φρόνησις, and σύνεσις together as "the intellectual virtues" and carefully distinguishes the specific nature of each. Σοφία may mean excellence in a particular art or craft; in its general application it means the capacity to apprehend first principles. Φρόνησις is practical, having to do with a clear perception of one's own true interests. Σύνεσις is critical and derivative, enabling a man to form a sound judgment under another's guidance. "The σύνετος *qua* σύνετος does not initiate policies, or schemes of conduct, but has the intelligence to recognize good ones when they are put before him" (John A. Stewart, *Notes on the Nicomachean Ethics of Aristotle* [Oxford: Clarendon Press, 1892], II. 84). But the nice distinctions of philosophical analysis of the ethical life do not really enter into the question here. The double phrase is derived from the LXX, where the two nouns (and the two corresponding adjectives) are frequently found in conjunction; as, for instance, in the famous story of Solomon, "Give me now wisdom and knowledge" (II Chr. 1:10 ff.). In this conjunction the primary idea appears to be that of practical wisdom, good sense, clear discernment of right and wrong; not the idea of profundity; cf. Jas. 3:13-17, especially the concluding verse, "The wisdom [σοφία] that is from above is first pure, then peaceable, . . . full of mercy and good fruits, without partiality, and without hypocrisy." Such "wisdom and understanding" is "spiritual" in the sense that it belongs to the life of the spirit; it is acquired through devotion, not through rational speculation.

---

God uses a man not because of the prominence of the situation in which his lot is cast, but because of the faithfulness of his life, even though his immediate work does not endure. Being **a faithful minister of Christ,** Epaphras fulfilled his God-given destiny. Colossae is no more, but the Epistle to the Colossians remains. Epaphras had his part in that.

**9. Filled with the Knowledge of His Will.—** The key to this section of the epistle is the stress on the will—our wills in relation to God's will for us. Paul's purpose in writing is to deal with an incipient Gnosticism, a highly speculative and dubious philosophizing, which tended to supplant, and even pervert, the life of simple Christian love and practical moral obedience. He does not depend on theoretical argument and debate, setting up one system of cosmic speculation against another. He changes the climate of discussion with an invitation and a prayer, that his readers may be led to find the full and satisfying answer to their quest for knowledge by being willing to come to terms with God's will for them.

10 That ye might walk worthy of the Lord unto all pleasing, being fruitful in every good work, and increasing in the knowledge of God;

standing, 10 to lead a life worthy of the Lord, fully pleasing to him, bearing fruit in every good work and increasing in the

---

**10. Unto all pleasing:** Ἀρέσκεια has a bad sense in classical Greek usage, suggesting an undue obsequiousness, a degree of self-abasement that no man should show toward another. This sense appears later in the epistle (3:22) in the compound ἀνθρωπάρεσκοι, "men-pleasers." In Hellenistic times, however, the word usually has the sense of either popular or divine favor that is well deserved; it is used, for instance, in laudatory inscriptions. Examples of the use of the word in this sense are given in J. H. Moulton and G. Milligan, *Vocabulary of the Greek New Testament* (London: Hodder & Stoughton, 1914-19).

The two participles καρποφοροῦντες and αὐξανόμενοι ("bearing fruit" and "growing") must not be separated here, any more than in vs. 6. The phrase **in every good work** modifies both. The following dative—τῇ ἐπιγνώσει—is difficult. The difficulty of the construction has led a few scribes to insert ἐν, and others to alter to εἰς τὴν ἐπίγνωσιν. The true text must be rendered *"by* the knowledge of God" (instrumental dative). The basic thought is that spiritual growth is fostered by the knowledge of God and manifests itself in an abundance of good works.

The double participial phrase "bearing fruit and growing," used of the gospel in vs. 6, is here used of those who through the gospel have come to the knowledge of God. The image of the vine, familiar to readers of the O.T. as a symbol of the people of God (Isa. 5:1-7; Ps. 80:14 ff.), lies behind these words also. The vine that is healthy will both grow, putting forth new shoots and branches, and bear fruit for its owner. So in the Christian life, growth in spiritual stature and fruitfulness in good works must proceed together; the true knowledge of God will promote both.

---

**10. A Life Worthy of the Lord.**—In the conflict between Greek intellectualism and the Hebrew stress on the will Paul was always "a Hebrew of the Hebrews." It is Kant's distinction between the "pure reason" (rational speculation) and the "practical reason" (moral integrity). The same controversy runs through the First Epistle of John, "He that loveth not his brother whom he hath seen, how can he love God whom he hath not seen?" (I John 4:20.) The same thought is in the words of Hosea, "Then shall we know, if we follow on to know the LORD" (Hos. 6:3); and in the great saying of Jesus in the Fourth Gospel, "If any man will do his will, he shall know of the doctrine, whether it be of God, or whether I speak of myself" (John 7:17).

A striking characteristic of the great visions recorded in Scripture is perhaps little noticed. The vision, representing an insight into reality not disclosed to mundane sight, is always climaxed by the hearing of a voice—the will of God appealing to the human will; cf. Jacob's dream, "And, behold, the LORD . . . said . . ." (Gen. 28:13). Moses sees the burning bush, symbol of the spiritual meaning that underlies common events, but the significance of the vision is in the voice, "God called unto him out of the midst of the bush" (Exod. 3:4). Elijah, in spiritual flight, sees the portents of wind, earthquake, and fire, and senses the divine sovereignty behind the elemental forces of the world, "But the LORD was not in the wind" (I Kings 19:11). The message of God to his immediate problem came in the "still small voice." "What doest thou here, Elijah?" (I Kings 19:13.) The cure of the prophet's doubt and despair was found in the moral response of his will. Isaiah, in the temple, saw the Lord, but the full meaning of what he saw broke upon him when he heard and heeded the appeal of the divine will to his own will, "Also I heard the voice of the Lord, saying, Whom shall I send?" (Isa. 6:8.) Paul, on the Damascus road, had his blinding vision (strange paradox) of Christ, but the understanding came with the hearing of a voice, the challenge of the divine will to him, and the surrender of his will to the divine, "Lord, what wilt thou have me to do?" (Acts 9:6.)

Paul puts his controversy with the Colossians in that high setting from the start, "We have not ceased to pray for you, asking that you may be filled with the knowledge of his will" (vs. 9). Even salesmen and advertisers are taught not to argue, but to affirm and persuade. How much

11 Strengthened with all might, according to his glorious power, unto all patience and long-suffering with joyfulness;

12 Giving thanks unto the Father, which hath made us meet to be partakers of the inheritance of the saints in light:

knowledge of God. 11 May you be strengthened with all power, according to his glorious might, for all endurance and patience with joy, 12 giving thanks to the Father, who has qualified us[b] to share in the inheritance

[b] Other ancient authorities read *you*.

---

**11. Strengthened:** The present participle (ἐνδυναμούμενοι) suggests a steady accession of strength—"continually growing stronger." This growing strength is the gift of God, the effect of his working within us, "according to the power of his glory." The "glory" that he has manifested to us in Christ is imparted to us in increasing measure in the power to do and to endure. **Glorious power** (KJV) or **glorious might** (RSV) waters down the phrase "power of his glory." The "power" which strengthens Christians is a reflection of the "glory" of God; it brings into human life something of the radiance of the divine. There is a redundancy about the language here which seems liturgical, like the act of adoration which opens the Epistle to the Ephesians; the prayer takes on the roll and rhythm of music as the mind is swept up in contemplation of the wonders of divine grace.

**Unto all patience and long-suffering:** The strength that God supplies is manifested above all in endurance; it is not the kind of strength that seeks an outlet in domination or in self-assertion of any kind. Ὑπομονή (**patience**) is the capacity to see things through; to stand fast against affliction and disappointment and long trial; μακροθυμία (**long-suffering**) is the capacity to endure wrongs without being provoked to retaliation or to bitterness, even as God is long-suffering toward us, "not willing that any should perish, but that all should come to repentance" (II Pet. 3:9). Very instructive is the use of this noun and its cognate verb in Jas. 5:7-11.

**12.** Paul's final petition for the Colossians is that they may acknowledge God's goodness to them by their joyful thankfulness. The full knowledge of God's will, manifesting itself in good works, in growth in moral stature, and in steadily increasing inward power, leads us to offer perpetual thanks to the God whose grace makes this spiritual progress possible; indeed, the spirit of joy and thanksgiving is itself the final mark of spiritual progress. It is worth noting also that the giving of thanks is related particularly to the filial consciousness; in the blessings which we receive from God we recognize the bounty of "the Father" and know ourselves for his sons.

The Chester Beatty codex of the Pauline epistles (p⁴⁶) has the interesting reading, "and giving thanks at the same time to the Father"; Codex B omits "and" but retains "at the same time." With this reading εὐχαριστοῦντες would have to be construed in parallelism with αἰτούμενοι (vs. 9), "We do not cease to pray for you, and to ask . . . and to give thanks at the same time."

---

more the advocate of Christ. Men will resist the attempt to dominate them in argument, and will marshal their forces to counter an intellectual attack, but they cannot forever evade the influence of a man who prays for them out of a deep concern that their wills may be attuned to the knowledge of God's will.

The Exeg. brings out fully how a life so rooted "in all spiritual wisdom and understanding" (vs. 9) progressively unfolds—"bearing fruit . . . and increasing, . . . strengthened with all power, . . . . for all endurance and patience, . . . giving thanks to the Father" (vss. 10-12).

**12-14.** *The Inheritance of the Saints.*—The N.T. stress on the life of practical loyalty in

the brotherhood never becomes mere moralism. The moral stems from the theological. Noble living is rooted in high doctrine. Great conduct is the expression of great belief. While the word "grace" is seldom used in this epistle, in comparison with its frequent reiteration in Romans, Corinthians, and Ephesians, the idea and reality of complete salvation by the grace of God are central in the whole exposition. This is at the heart of the answer which Paul gives to the Colossian heresy, a heresy which implied the insufficiency, or at best only partial sufficiency, of Christ for complete salvation.

See the Exeg. for the force of the words **has qualified, has delivered,** [has] **transferred, and**

13 Who hath delivered us from the power of darkness, and hath translated *us* into the kingdom of his dear Son:

of the saints in light. 13 He has delivered us from the dominion of darkness and transferred us to the kingdom of his beloved

---

**Qualified us to share in the inheritance of the saints in light:** Our Father has made us worthy of the high destiny to which he calls us. The verb ἱκανόω ("qualify") is formed upon the adjective ἱκανός—"suitable, capable, competent"; cf. II Cor. 3:5-6, "Not that we are sufficient (ἱκανοί) of ourselves, . . . our sufficiency (ἱκανότης) is from God, who has qualified us (ἱκάνωσεν) to be ministers of a new covenant." Our share in the glories of heaven is not a reward for our merits; God in his grace has made us worthy of entering into his presence by forgiving our sins and transforming our nature. Theodore of Mopsuestia takes the verb in the sense of "count worthy, pronounce worthy"—"He pronounced you worthy to be of the company of his saints, when you were aliens from true devotion and worshipers of idols"—but this interpretation does less than justice to the vigor of the expression. Chrysostom draws a comparison with the action of a king who can give high office to whomever he will, but cannot make a man fit for the office which he is to hold: "The honor makes such a man a laughingstock"; but God "not only bestowed the honor, but made us fit to receive it."

Some Western MSS, with a number of versions, have the reading καλέσαντι ("has called us") in place of ἱκανώσαντι; in B, the two readings are conflated. B and ℵ read ὑμᾶς in place of ἡμᾶς, reading, "has made you fit"; the text of p⁴⁶ is missing.

**To share in:** Εἰς τὴν μερίδα is literally "for the part," i.e., the part which is assigned to us, our part. The phrase suggests the thought that each individual has a particular place in the corporate destiny.

**The inheritance of the saints:** Better, "the lot of the saints." Κλῆρος, here translated "inheritance," properly means "lot." At first the meaning is the lot that is cast; then that which is distributed by lot—the allotment; finally, the idea of "lot" practically disappears in the sense of "assigned portion." In the O.T. story the Promised Land was divided by lot among the tribes of Israel (Josh. 14–19); and a part of a tribal allotment might be assigned to an individual, "Unto Caleb . . . he gave a part among the children of Judah" (Josh. 15:13). Now the idea is spiritualized; the "lot of the saints" is no earthly territory, but an eternal abiding place in the presence of God. Κλῆρος was also used of the holdings assigned to veteran soldiers who were settled on the land after their fighting days were done. In this sense also it might appropriately be used of the abode of those whose spiritual warfare is accomplished. The whole phrase brings forward in a new figure the thought of "the hope which is laid up for you in heaven" (vs. 5).

**In light:** Literally, "in the light." This phrase might be taken closely with ἁγίων, "the saints in the light," which would then refer to the blessed dead who dwell in the light of God's presence; or it might be taken with κλήρου, "the lot in the light which is apportioned to the saints." The latter is preferable as it allows us to retain the usual N.T. significance of the word "saints" (all who are set apart by and for God).

**13.** This "lot in the light," for which God has fitted us, is now contrasted with **the power of darkness** from which he has delivered us. "Power" (ἐξουσία) has here the sense

---

**we have redemption.** Christians often neglect or fail to grasp, as these Colossian Christians were failing to grasp, the reality of "the finished work of Christ"—a new relationship between God and man already accomplished through Christ, a liberation won by redemptive love, and freely offered to us through him. It is true that men have still to make that **inheritance of the saints in light** their own, but there could be no possibility of accepting it unless the in-

heritance were there and actually offered to them. It is possible to say,

'Tis done: the great transaction's done!
I am my Lord's, and he is mine,[2]

only because a prior transaction has taken place, and a prior event has transpired. Christ has established the kingdom of God as a reality,

[2] Philip Doddridge, "O happy day, that fixed my choice."

| 14 In whom we have redemption through his blood, *even* the forgiveness of sins: | Son, 14 in whom we have redemption, the forgiveness of sins. |

---

of the sphere in which power is exercised; God has delivered us from the realm in which darkness holds sway. The words suggest a change of spiritual environment—rescue from the realm of darkness; translation into the kingdom of God's dear Son. The inward change that makes us fit for our place in the light is accompanied by an equally radical change in the conditions under which we live.

**Transferred us to the kingdom of his beloved Son:** Literally, "the Son of his love." This appears to be a variant on the more familiar expression "beloved Son," which we find in the story of the baptism of Jesus (Mark 1:11 and parallels). It stems originally from the messianic interpretation of Ps. 2, which speaks of the triumphs of the king, whom God hails as his Son (vss. 6-9). **Transferred** (μετέστησεν) is almost a technical term for the mass deportations which the Assyrian monarchs made a feature of their policy, as Hitler did in modern times. With these arbitrary tyrants it was a matter of uprooting people from their beloved homeland; here it is God who delivers his people from a dark tyranny which held them captive, and brings them into his kingdom of light and love, where "the Son of his love" holds sway. This thought brings out the full force of the novel turn given to the well-known expression in the preceding phrase. "The Son of his love" means more than **beloved Son;** it means not so much "the Son whom he loves, in whom he is well pleased," as "the Son who is the perfect embodiment of his love"—the Son in whom his love is manifested and made the basis of his rule over the hearts of men.

**14. In whom we have redemption, the forgiveness of sins:** The words **through his blood** (KJV) are not represented in the best MSS; they are introduced through assimilation to Eph. 1:7. **Redemption** in the N.T. has almost wholly lost its primary sense. It originally meant the regaining of an article put in pledge by repayment of the loan for which it was given in pledge; or the taking title through payment of a stipulated sum to a piece of family property which was in danger of being alienated; or securing the release of captives or of booty in return for a money payment. In Jewish usage, however, it had come to mean the deliverance of God's people, whether the storied deliverance from Egypt in the days of Moses, or the deliverance from Assyrian or Babylonian captivity which the prophets had proclaimed; looking beyond these historic events, it was used of the messianic deliverance for which the nation hoped. In this usage the idea of ransom on payment of a price all but disappeared; the thought is of a deliverance accomplished by a mighty act of divine power. In our passage the historic deliverances of Israel are treated as types of the moral and spiritual deliverance which God has accomplished for

---

both in human history and in personal experience. It is not merely an idea in the mind of God, not merely a human dream of what might be, nor merely a

> far-off divine event,
> **To which the whole creation moves.**[8]

It is a present reality. "The kingdom of God is in the midst of you" (Luke 17:21). Those who are in a living relationship with Christ actually are members of **the kingdom of his beloved Son.** This is true whatever unattained possibilities may yet lie before them "in Christ." Their Christian heritage is not the reward of

[8] Tennyson, *In Memoriam*, Epilogue.

personal achievement, nor even an arbitrary or unconditioned gift, but a right which inevitably accompanies their new relationship with God through Christ. The Colossians had been delivered from the darkness of heathenism when they put their faith in Christ. So is every Christian when he does likewise. Far from rejecting them as heretics, Paul calls them to realize their full Christian potential in the rank and status of Christians which is already theirs.

Furthermore, lest any should think of redemption in Gnostic terms of mystic formulas, secret initiations, and ceremonial rites (see 2:8, 16-18), Paul forcibly reminds them that redemption is a moral relationship, effected by the power of reconciling love. It is not attained by

us in Christ—deliverance which can be summed up as **the forgiveness of sins.** For the sins of men are the chains which keep them imprisoned in "the realm of darkness"; and these chains are broken when God "translates us into the kingdom of the Son of his love."

It is to be noted that in these verses the apostolic writer speaks of the saving acts of God as already accomplished. The kingdom of his Son is a present reality; our rescue from the realm of darkness and our translation into Christ's kingdom of love are not matters of expectation but realized facts. God *has rescued* us; *has translated* us; we *have* the redemption. In part, at least, this emphasis is a necessary corrective to the error which was being propagated at Colossae, which would have led Christians to believe that they had still to propitiate some kind of higher powers, and were still under the dominion of superior beings who controlled the physical universe. Against this it is emphasized that God has rescued his people from the domination of every power but his own, and has admitted them into the kingdom in which no writ runs but that of the Son who rules by love.

Behind all this language there lies a kind of "popular science" which is now as dead as the gods of ancient Egypt, but which was a part of the general outlook of people in the first century and was shared inevitably by the Christians of the time. Today we do not speak of "the realm where darkness holds sway," or of "the world rulers of this present darkness" (Eph. 6:12); or of "thrones, or dominions, or principalities, or powers," in the sense of mighty spirit-beings who control our destinies. But we have a popular science of our own which gives us the same sense of enslavement to forces which we cannot control and against which it is vain to strive. Catchwords like "economic determinism," "dialectical materialism," "behavior patterns," "complexes" of all descriptions, and the like—these are the dark tyrants which hold our spirits in thrall; and we still need to learn that in Christ we are really made *free*—rescued from the power of these blind forces that we find at work in history and in human society, and admitted to the kingdom of divine love wherein we may fulfill our lives according to the will of God.

Vs. 14 effects the transition to the great christological passage which now meets us. It tells us that it is in "the Son of God's love" that we have this deliverance. Christ is the key figure in our redemption. The passage which follows teaches that Christ holds this key place in the economy of redemption because of the unique relationship in which he stands to God and to the created universe; in every respect the Creator and the creation are linked together in him. Thus the knowledge of Christ as Redeemer unfolds itself in the understanding of his place as "first-born of all creation." No lesser view of his person is adequate to the greatness of the salvation which God has accomplished in us and for us through him.

---

intellectual speculation, nor by the mastery of some secret theosophy. It is imparted by God, who loves the unworthy and reconciles the unreconciled to himself. Whatever mystery there is in redemption is the mystery of the Cross, the way God takes to win men to accept his forgiveness of their sins.

It is easy to write off men as heretics, and so put them outside the bounds of our Christian duty to love them. It is a greater thing to draw love's circle that takes them in, and then to lead them on to their full possibilities in Christ. In taking the latter course Paul was dealing with the erring Colossians as Christ had once, and once for all, dealt with him. The passage is a magnificent declaration of the creative Christian attitude to win men to God's best for them.

While there are passages in the N.T. which warn against the live possibility of falling away from the state of grace (cf. Heb. 6:4-6; 10:36-39; II Pet. 2:20-22; and also vs. 23 below—"provided that you continue in the faith"), yet this particular passage rings with the utter assurance of salvation from which sprang the Calvinistic doctrine of the perseverance of the saints.

They whom God hath accepted in his Beloved, effectually called and sanctified by his Spirit, can neither totally nor finally fall away from the state of grace; but shall certainly persevere therein to the end, and be eternally saved.

This perseverance of the saints depends not upon their own free will, but upon the immutability of the decree of election, flowing from the free and unchangeable love of God the Father.[4]

[4] *Westminster Confession of Faith,* ch. xvii, arts, i-ii.

| 15 Who is the image of the invisible God, the firstborn of every creature: | 15 He is the image of the invisible **God**, |
|---|---|

## II. POLEMIC AGAINST THE DOCTRINE OF ANGELIC MEDIATORS (1:15–3:4)
### A. PRIMAL SIGNIFICANCE OF CHRIST (1:15-23)

The relative pronoun which opens this passage carries us back to vs. 13; the antecedent of ὅς is υἱοῦ. It is the *Son* who is **the image, the first-born, the beginning, the head.** This is by no means fortuitous; as in Heb. 1:2 ff., it is the idea of the divine sonship which is unfolded in the description of the person and work of Christ. The parallelism of the two passages is striking:

| *Colossians* | *Hebrews* |
|---|---|
| God has translated us into the kingdom of the Son of his love | God has spoken unto us in his Son |
| (1) in whom we have redemption, . . . the forgiveness of sins | who . . . by himself purged our sins |
| (2) who is the image of the invisible **God** | who being the brightness of his glory, and the express image of his person |
| (3) the first-born of all creation | appointed heir of all things, . . . the first-born |
| (4) for in him all things were created | by whom also he made the worlds |
| (5) and by him all things consist | upholding all things by the word of his power |

There is also an underlying parallelism in the exaltation of Christ over every kind of angelic being. Whether they are called "angels," as in Hebrews, or classified in ranks as "thrones, or dominions, or principalities, or powers," as in Colossians, they are all *created,* and are not to be compared in dignity with the Son, through whom and for whom they were created.

In the earlier Pauline epistles only one passage can be cited (I Cor. 8:6—"one Lord Jesus Christ, by whom are all things"—δι' οὗ τὰ πάντα) which even faintly suggests that the apostle ever indulged in speculation about the cosmic significance of Christ. True parallels to this Colossian passage are to be found only in Hebrews and the Fourth Gospel, i.e., in works of the *second* Christian generation. This fact has led some critics to regard the section (or part of it) as interpolated, inserted by a second-generation editor; to others it has seemed to afford sufficient ground for denying the Pauline authorship of the whole epistle. The former view is clearly wrong; this passage is no interpolation, for it "is integral to the whole argument and indeed supplies its philosophical groundwork" (E. F. Scott, *The Epistles of Paul to the Colossians, to Philemon and to the Ephesians* [London: Hodder & Stoughton, 1930; "The Moffatt New Testament Commentary"], p. 12). The latter view is not so easily dismissed; certainly the passage is sufficiently strange in Paul to compel us to raise the question of authenticity. But it is not sufficient of itself to settle

**15. *The Image of the Invisible God; the First-born of All Creation.*—**In his earlier epistles Paul makes little mention of the relation of Christ to the cosmos. He was dealing then with men whose basic ideas were drawn from a less abstract sphere—Jewish history and tradition, Hebrew ideas of sacrifice and atonement, of the law and sin, of the Messiah and the messianic kingdom.

But the gospel is for all men and all minds, and when Paul is faced with the task of making the evangel convincing to those whose world outlook has been influenced by the current philosophical speculation, he speaks to their condition. He finds a point of contact with their minds, relates the Christian revelation to their "natural theology," presents God's unique revelation of himself in Christ in the categories

the matter. Scholars who defend the authenticity of the epistle point out (a) that Paul is compelled to enter the field of cosmic speculation because the Colossian teaching which he is refuting has based itself upon a false cosmic theory; and (b) that the materials with which the passage works were available even before Paul's time in the speculations of Alexandrian Judaism and in the later wisdom literature. Dibelius even suggests that some of the formulas which Paul here applies to Christ are not of his own framing, and are not even specifically Christian, but were originally used in relation to logos or sophia. "Thus the first part of the Excursus may rest upon formulations which Hellenistic Judaism framed" (*An die Kolosser Epheser an Philemon* [Tübingen: J. C. B. Mohr, 1927; "Handbuch zum Neuen Testament"], p. 7). It is still open to question whether these logos or wisdom speculations had been applied to the Messiah in any pre-Christian Jewish circles; or to Christ himself in any Christian thinking before Paul; and except for this passage, there is no clear evidence that Paul so applied them. We may say, therefore, that if we have other grounds for suspecting the authenticity of Colossians, this passage will reinforce them; but in itself it is quite capable of defense as an authentic expression of the mind of the great apostle.

## I. In the Universe (1:15-17)

**15. Image of the invisible God, first-born of all creation:** J. B. Lightfoot (*Saint Paul's Epistles to the Colossians and to Philemon* [London: Macmillan & Co., 1875], p. 142) writes: "The Person of Christ is described *first* in relation more especially to Deity, as εἰκὼν τοῦ Θεοῦ τοῦ ἀοράτου, and *secondly* in relation more especially to created things, as πρωτότοκος πάσης κτίσεως." This division is quite wrong; in both phrases it is Christ's place in the universe as Son of God that is in question; both **image** and **first-born** are titles of sovereignty, and are related not to metaphysical doctrines of absolute reality, but to ancient conceptions of the kingship. In Egypt, where the classic idea of kingship was formed and elaborated, the Pharaoh is called again and again "the living image" of the supreme god; e.g., the name Tutankhamen means "living image of Amen"; and on the Rosetta Stone the youthful Ptolemy is called in the Greek text "living image of Zeus" (translated from a parallel Egyptian phrase). Within the same circle of ideas the living Pharaoh is equated with Horus the Son of (the unseen) Osiris, who rules forever in glory in the world beyond. The writer of our epistle, of course, whether Paul or another, does not draw immediately upon Egyptian sources but upon the transplanted and transmuted forms of the conception as it was taken up in Israel and applied first to the house of David and then to the ideal king, who is to be called the Son, not of Osiris, but of the God of

---

of thought with which they are familiar. In common with the later writers of the N.T. he does not mince words in dealing with those who beguile people "by philosophy and empty deceit, according to human tradition" (2:8). Nonetheless, he is quick to exalt Christ in terms that they will understand. His ranging mind never neglects an opportunity to reach men at the level of their own reasoning and so "take every thought captive to obey Christ" (II Cor. 10:5). To the intellectuals he could be as an intellectual that he might win the intellectuals. The relative failure of his sermon to the philosophers on Mars' Hill at Athens (Acts 17) may have led to his determination at Corinth, "not to know any thing among you, save Jesus Christ, and him crucified" (I Cor. 2:2), but he was so sure of the ultimate reality of "Jesus Christ and him crucified" that he did not fear or hesitate to present the Christian faith in the wider con-

texts of human speculation. One may surmise that Paul would have been an interested and formidable commentator upon the modern Gifford Lectures on natural theology had he lived in the twentieth century, and that in a scientific age he would have been a most convincing exponent of Christian theology as the "queen of sciences," not in spite of his consuming passion for evangelism but because of it. However baffling the effort to relate Christian belief to reasoned knowledge, the responsibility to pursue that effort is upon all men whom the Creator has endowed with reason. It is of the utmost importance that our conception of the world and its ultimate meaning shall be in terms of the spiritual ends which have been clarified and confirmed in God's self-revelation in Christ.

The pseudophilosophical speculations that were the fashion in Colossae are very remote from modern thinking, and of no great impor-

Israel, the Lord of heaven and earth. As **image of the invisible God** the Son is God manifest, the bearer of the might and majesty of God, the revealer and mediator of the creating and sustaining power of the Godhead in relation to the world. It is in these ancient forms of religious thinking that we must look for the roots of the thought, rather than in the abstractions of Philo or of the Stoics (for background material see G. van der Leeuw, *Religion in Essence and Manifestation* [tr. J. E. Turner; London: George Allen & Unwin, 1938], chs. xii-xiii).

In the O.T. the king is never called the "image" of God. The phrase has nevertheless O.T. associations of the first importance, in the creation story of Gen. 1. Here the primal man is created in God's "image" and "likeness"; and, let us note, is given *dominion* over the rest of the creation. We have therefore the triple association of creation, sovereignty, and the divine image, which we have found in our passage in Colossians. Only Christ is not *made* "after the image" (κατὰ τὴν εἰκόνα—LXX) of God; he *is* the image of God. Thus he is the embodiment of true humanity, as he is the embodiment of true kingship—the reality in whom all ideals and aspirations are fufilled.

The phrase **first-born of all creation** is likewise a title of dignity and function; it has nothing to do with relations of *time*. It certainly does not imply that Christ is himself a part of the creation, even the first part; the ancient church fathers rightly insist that he is called πρωτότοκος (first-born), not πρωτόκτιστος (first created). The word is undoubtedly to be interpreted in the light of the royal psalm, "I will make him my firstborn, higher than the kings of the earth" (Ps. 89:27); and more generally, in the light of the idea of the primacy of the first-born which is consistently assumed in the O.T. Among the nations, Israel is God's first-born (Exod. 4:22; Jer. 31:9); the first-born is the heir and destined ruler of all. As **first-born of all creation**, Christ is accorded in respect of the created universe that place of honor and of sovereignty that belongs to the eldest son in the household or in the kingdom.

---

tance now, but the underlying issues are the same. Paul's concern to proclaim the eternal purpose of God in Christ to minds steeped in that particular system of ideas leads him straight into this inspired passage on the centrality of Christ in the whole universe. While he makes use of current thought forms, the basic conception is of abiding significance.

The Exeg. gives in some detail the historic origins of the terms **image** and **first-born**. It is inevitable that men should think of Christ in the context of ideas which they possess. As men in Egypt had called the Pharaohs "the Living Image" of the supreme God, so the Christian, convinced in his own experience and by the witness of the Christian community that Christ was the real representation of the divine in a human life, appropriated the title for Christ. He is the true **image of the invisible God**. If the ideal king of Israel was given the title "Son of God," and even the tyrant emperors of Rome claimed it for their own, how much more truly was that title Christ's. If the nation of Israel was God's "first-born," how much more Christ crucified and ascended. If Messiah was the rightful title of God's expected deliverer, was not Jesus himself God's anointed—the Christ? If the deity of the pagan cults was addressed as "Lord" and "Savior"—Christians in all parts of the empire must have been familiar with this use of the words—surely, argued the early Christians, the only real "Lord" and "Savior" is Jesus the Christ. One who had opened the gate of new life to them as only he had done could be described only by the highest and most exalted titles that they knew. It may not at first have been reasoned theology, but rather the spontaneous, inevitable tribute of those who knew the transforming love of God in Christ.

Whatever term might be used for the highest revelation of deity was claimed for Jesus. No name that could be used of anyone was too high to belong to him. For men were struggling to interpret his absolute significance for faith. . . .

In viewing these religious evaluations of Jesus, we must recognize that they expressed the language of devotion rather than of systematic intellectual reflection. Theories of the person of Christ were not formulated. . . . These problems of formal Christology remained for the future. The earliest Christians were only intent on expressing the significance of Jesus for their faith. Amid all of the variety of interpretations which were followed one belief was constant: Jesus occupied a unique function in the revealing and redeeming activity of God. No one else could stand beside him. He was the "only begotten Son of God." [5]

[5] C. T. Craig, *The Beginning of Christianity* (New York and Nashville: Abingdon-Cokesbury Press, 1943), pp. 201, 210. See all of ch. xv for a revealing analysis of the various titles that Christians early came to apply to Jesus.

**16** For by him were all things created, that are in heaven, and that are in earth, visible and invisible, whether *they be* thrones, or dominions, or principalities, or

the first-born of all creation; **16** for in him all things were created, in heaven and on earth, visible and invisible, whether thrones

---

**16. In him all things were created: In him** (ἐν αὐτῷ)—not of *agency* (expressed below by δι' αὐτοῦ—"through him"), but of *spiritual locality*. The created universe, with all the physical and spiritual existences which it contains, is an unfolding of the mind of God in Christ. The same underlying thought is given expression in John 1:3-4, "That which was made, in him was life" (ὃ γέγονεν, ἐν αὐτῷ ζωὴ ἦν). This is the division of the text in Westcott and Hort and in the early versions and church fathers. **All things** (τὰ πάντα) means "the sum of things." The philosophical term τὸ πᾶν ("The All") is not found in the biblical writers; probably, as Lightfoot suggests, because of its pantheistic connotations. In Christian thought the universe is not self-contained or self-existent; it does not include God, but is dependent on him for life and order and motion. In the *Timaeus*—the most difficult, perhaps the least valuable, but by far the most influential of the dialogues—Plato speaks of the universe as a "second god," "son of God," "this one only-begotten universe," "a perceptible image of the God who is apprehended only by thought" (εἰκὼν τοῦ νοητοῦ θεοῦ αἰσθητός—*Timaeus* 92c). There is a relation, though it is not immediate, between these words and the language of Colossians; in cosmology, as in many other respects, Plato provided materials which were subsequently built into the lasting edifice of Christian thought. But for the Christian thinker the world becomes intelligible only as it is seen to be created "in Christ."

The comprehensive phrase **all things** is now elaborated in a series of classifications. This serves two purposes. First, it tacitly repudiates the notion of a fundamental division between the spiritual and the material—the pernicious dualism which lay at the root of all the "Gnostic" systems. It asserts that matter and spirit are alike of divine origin and have part alike in the divine economy. Second, it leads up to the particular insistence that spiritual existences of every order, no matter how exalted, are included in the totality of things that "were created in Christ." The Colossian angel worship (2:18) is thus condemned by implication as a worship of things created—"professing themselves to be wise, they became fools, . . . and worshipped and served the creature more than the Creator" (Rom. 1:22-25). The details of the classification are not significant in themselves: "in the heavens and upon the earth" is the familiar Jewish division of the universe (Gen. 1; etc.); **things . . . visible and invisible** is Platonic in origin. These terms represent

---

In like manner John Newton, exhausting all thought forms in the effort to express what Christ meant to him, wrote his great hymn on the name of Jesus.

> Jesus, my Shepherd, Brother, Friend,
> My Prophet, Priest, and King,
> My Lord, my Life, my Way, my End,
> Accept the praise I bring.[c]

**16-17. Christ and the Created Universe.**—**In him all things were created.** The quest of the ages has been for a principle of unity and continuity that will interpret the universe. This is primarily the task of philosophy and natural theology. While Paul never gives philosophical speculation a central place in his exposition of the new faith revealed in Christ, he does not shirk the responsibility to relate the gospel to

our whole conception of the world in the widest sense. In addition to the practical necessity of meeting the Colossian theorists on their own ground, he regards this as an obligation and privilege, since the Creator has endowed men with capacities of reason and ordered thought. He shows no trace of the dogmatic view that revelation should suppress and cancel out reason. In Romans (1:18-32; 2:15; 8:19-23) he makes his appeal to natural theology, as he does here, and as do the writers of the Fourth Gospel and of Hebrews in their opening chapters. What he opposes is the error of attempting to explain the ultimate meaning of things without taking into account the unique revelation of the nature and destiny of man and of God's relationship to the world that has been given in Christ.

Philosophic conceptions have changed greatly

---

[c] "How sweet the name of Jesus sounds."

powers: all things were created by him, and for him:

or dominions or principalities or authorities — all things were created through him

---

different modes of thinking about the universe, the one naïve, the other intellectual; but they are not used with philosophical exactitude. The double phrase simply emphasizes the thought that every kind of existence, however it may be conceived and wherever it may exist, exists in Christ as created in him. The classification of the angelic orders— **thrones . . . dominions . . . principalities . . . powers**—need not be regarded as expressing Paul's own notions; more likely he takes them over from the language of the heretical teachers. Similar classifications are found here and there in the literature of later Judaism; however, they are not a Jewish invention but a borrowing from Oriental astrological theosophy of Iranian and Babylonian origin.

The clause which follows is not a mere recapitulation; it introduces new and weighty thoughts: **All things were created through him and for him.** The words do not yield themselves to translation. We must observe the change of tense in the verb, and we must look closely at the prepositions. For ἐκτίσθη in the first clause of the verse, we find here ἔκτισται—the perfect instead of the aorist. The perfect turns the mind from the thought of creation as an *act,* to the thought of it as a *resultant state.* All things "stand created" through him and for him. As they had their origin ("were created") in him, so they owe their settled state, as a created universe, to his mediation, and move toward him as toward their goal. The three prepositional phrases—ἐν αὐτῷ, δι' αὐτοῦ, εἰς αὐτόν—"in him, through him, unto him"—set forth three aspects of the relationship of Christ to the creation. On ἐν αὐτῷ comment has been made above; δι' αὐτοῦ expresses *mediation,* as of a free co-operating agent; we find it again in the great "hymn of the Logos" in John 1 ("All things were made through him"—vs. 10). More frequently it is used of Christ's mediation between God and man: "Through him we . . . have access . . . to the Father" (Eph. 2:18); "God hath . . . appointed us . . . to obtain salvation by our Lord Jesus Christ" (I Thess. 5:9); and scores of like passages could be cited. We are not accustomed to think of the entire life of the universe as mediated from God through Christ in the

---

since the days of Paul and his controversy with the Colossians, but thinking minds must still come to terms with the Christian revelation. In one sense this task devolves anew upon each succeeding generation. The perennial attempt to relate science and religion has not been a wasted or unnecessary effort, and the natural mind still finds its moral and spiritual illumination in "the mind of Christ."

In this passage Christ is related both to God and to the universe. In the first place, he is **the image of the invisible God,** i.e., he resembles, represents, and reveals the invisible God in and to the world. "He that hath seen me hath seen the Father" (John 14:9). In the second place, he is the source, the channel, and the goal of creation, **in him all things hold together.** He makes the universe a cosmos instead of a chaos. He sustains it and moves it toward its destiny. In the end it shall return to him as its head and consummation.

Christ is the end, for Christ was the beginning,
Christ the beginning, for the end is Christ.[7]

[7] F. W. H. Myers, *St. Paul* (4th ed.; London: Macmillan & Co., 1923), p. 53.

When one has grasped the centrality of Christ, all things are seen in relation to him. In the language, not of logic but of devotion, a poet put it thus:

I see His blood upon the rose
    And in the stars the glory of His eyes,
His body gleams amid eternal snows,
    His tears fall from the skies.

I see His face in every flower;
    The thunder and the singing of the birds
Are but His voice—and carven by His power
    Rocks are His written words.

All pathways by His feet are worn,
    His strong heart stirs the ever-beating sea,
His crown of thorns is twined with every thorn,
    His cross is every tree.[8]

The fact that Paul uses the phrases "through him" and "to him" both of God and of Christ (see Rom. 11:36) means that it is the very God who comes into direct relationship with the world in Christ. This is the answer to the

[8] From *The Collected Poems of Joseph Mary Plunkett.* Used by permission of the publishers, The Talbot Press, Ltd., Dublin.

**17** And he is before all things, and by him all things consist:

**18** And he is the head of the body, the church: who is the beginning, the firstborn

and for him. **17** He is before all things, and in him all things hold together. **18** He is the head of the body, the church; he is the

same sense as our highest spiritual experiences are mediated through him; but that is because we are obsessed with a mechanical view of the universe, and the result is an impoverishment of our thinking. Our physical sciences could not be divorced as they are from our religion if we realized sufficiently that they too deal with a sphere of being in which God manifests himself through Christ; nor could we allow theology to reject "natural religion." The third phrase, **for him** or "unto him" (εἰς αὐτόν), speaks of Christ as the end of the universe, the goal toward which all existences seek to rise. He is not only the Alpha but also the Omega, "the beginning and the end" (Rev. 22:13). The world was made for Christ; this is the ultimate meaning of things for Christian discipleship. In the words of a Greek Father: "He Himself is the End. Thus while among the Greeks men debate about the End, whether it is pleasure, or speculation, or virtue, or indifference, or whatever the philosophical schools may say, it is enough for us to say that the End is Christ" (Cramer, ed., *Catenae in N. T.,* under I Pet. 4:7).

**17.** The **he is** of this passage is a declaration of absolute pre-existence; it is the counterpart of the "I am" which introduces so many of the great sayings of Christ in the Fourth Gospel. **Before all things:** Of time, but also of precedence in dignity; the phrase paves the way for the idea of headship (vs. 18; 2:19).

The verb συνέστηκεν (**consist, hold together**) is another perfect, expressing the state of the universe as an ordered *system* (σύστημα—from the same root as the verb). The thought is that the unity and order of the universe are not accidental or mechanical, but derive from its vital relationship to Christ.

### 2. In the Church (1:18-20)

**18.** With this verse the apostle moves from the consideration of Christ as the maker and mediator of the created universe with all its spiritual inhabitants to the complementary thought of Christ as the maker and mediator of the new creation, which forms around the nucleus of a redeemed humanity—the Christian church. This thought of

Colossian heresy. Only error and confusion can flow from the idea that the invisible God must be approached through a supposed hierarchy of subordinate beings, whether angels or thrones, dominions, principalities, or powers. Such speculations might be harmless, except that they obscure, and in effect deny, the full self-imparting of God to the world and to each human soul in Christ. We know God fully when we know and believe in Christ. And when we know Christ, we are in vital union not with an agent or intermediary only, but with God himself.

**18-20.** *Christ and the Church.*—**He is the head of the body, the church.** Paul now turns to the second part of his exposition of the cosmic significance of Christ—the place of Christ in human life and human history. When man became endowed with freedom, he became in a real sense a free agent. Henceforth he must be either a partner or a foe of the divine will. In fact, even the most thoroughly converted Christian plays both these contradictory roles at the same time. The responsibility for

human destiny, both the eternal destiny of the individual life and the destiny of mankind on this planet, is in human hands. God's purpose for humankind can now be realized only through the submission of human wills to the divine will. The responsibility is man's. The salvation is of God, working through men.

So "the first-born of all creation" (vs. 15) comes into human history to redeem to himself, and to launch into the stream of human history, the church, the community of redeemed persons. The church begins in history when the Christ incarnate lives through the tragedy of our human lot in utter depth and fullness of self-giving, and in love outlives the utmost that sin and death can do, to become **the first-born from the dead.** The earthly life and mission of Jesus is given its true place when it is seen in its cosmic setting as **the beginning** of a new relationship of redeemed humanity to God. The theme and scope of the gospel is "the redemption of the world by our Lord Jesus Christ," as the noble words of the general thanksgiving of

correspondence between creation and new creation is not peculiar to Colossians or to Paul, but lies implicit in nearly all the books of the N.T. It operated with great power on the Christian imagination, and became very fruitful in the later development of theology, being given especial prominence in the doctrine of Irenaeus. The words βίβλος γενέσεως, "The Book of the Genesis" (of Jesus Christ), which open the Gospel According to St. Matthew, take up the title of the first book of the O.T. (from the LXX); and both the ἀρχή of Mark 1:1 and the ἐν ἀρχῇ of John 1:1 reflect the "in the beginning" of Gen. 1:1. For all these Christian thinkers the coming of Christ was an "event in eternity," as wide in scope as the creation, destined to fulfill the divine purpose in creation; and that, not merely as canceling the ruin wrought by sin, but as introducing a new divine element of positive significance, which was required for the fulfillment of the eternal purpose of God even apart from the need of undoing the effects of sin. In this conception the Incarnation was not merely the prelude to the Atonement, nor was it primarily necessitated by the Fall. Even apart from sin man could not attain to his divine destiny, nor the universe be brought to its predestined perfection, until the Son of God should take upon himself our nature, the uncreated entering into vital union with the created. The "living soul" imparted to man at the creation required to be supplemented by the "life-giving spirit" of the Redeemer (I Cor. 15:45-49). A great vista of theological speculation is opened here, which has been explored only sporadically. (On this see the suggestive essay of B. F. Westcott, "The Gospel of Creation," in *The Epistles of St. John* [London: Macmillan & Co., 1883], pp. 273-315.)

The ἔστιν is again to be taken not as the copula, but in its full true sense of *being*—he is (as above). The three predicates which follow—κεφαλή, ἀρχή, πρωτότοκος, **head,**

---

the Prayer Book put it. He is the **first-born,** not only as the first in time to live out this new spiritual relationship of man to God, but as the one who effects and makes possible this new relationship for the multitudes who will follow him. He is **the head,** sovereign over mankind, and over all natural and spiritual powers and beings (including the supposed hierarchy of spiritual rulers who supplanted Christ in the Colossian heresy), and he is **the head of the body, the church.**

The church in this ultimate sense is not a body of people, self-organized to perpetuate the teaching and practice of Jesus, but a living organism of which he is the life and animating spirit. As Radford points out, the church is not a body of Christians, but the body of Christ. In the case of the church his leadership involves a measure of identity.

He is supreme over creation but supreme in the Church; distinct from creation but identified with the Church. . . . Its life is fed by "a communion (participation) of the Body of Christ." . . . As in the human body the afferent nerves communicate to the head the sensations of every organ, and the efferent nerves originate and control the movements of every organ, so in the mystical body of Christ the Head is conscious of the experience of every member, and prompts and guides the action of every member, unless it be paralyzed or dislocated by sin.[9]

[9] *Epistle to Colossians and Epistle to Philemon*, pp. 181-82.

**Preëminent.** It is in connection with the Resurrection and Christ's leadership in the church that the cosmic supremacy of Christ is (*a*) revealed in human history, and (*b*) realized in the experience of the individual soul. See Exeg. (vs. 18) for the force of the interpretation "that he might show himself preëminent," and (vs. 19) for the force of the interpretation that the fullness of God has "permanent abode," not merely "temporary sojourn" in Christ. The Colossian heresy may have included the view, prominent in later Gnosticism, that the divine could have no essential union with what is earthly and human, could not suffer and die as Jesus had done, and that therefore the divine nature could have dwelt in Jesus only for a time, entering into him at his baptism, and leaving him before he underwent the humiliation of human suffering and death on the Cross. This view is specifically repudiated in I John 5:6-9. The Apostles' Creed was formulated so as definitely to refute it. "Born, . . . suffered, . . . crucified, . . . dead, and buried, . . . ascended." Paul is here declaring that the nature, purpose, and power of God are fully disclosed and imparted to the world in the *whole* redemptive life of Jesus on earth, and in his risen and ascended life as head and Lord of the church.

Christianity is a historic religion. In complete contrast to the Colossian religion of intellectual speculation and philosophizing, Paul stresses the acts in human history by which God revealed

from the dead; that in all things he might have the preeminence.

beginning, the first-born from the dead, that in everything he might be preëminent.

---

**beginning, first-born**—all have *cosmic* significance; when they are applied to Christ in respect of his relation to the church, they point toward the thought that the church too has cosmic significance as the nucleus of a redeemed universe. In the church a redeemed humanity, now endowed with incorruption and immortality, begins to form about its center, the risen and exalted Christ.

**The head of the body:** This phrase is not found in earlier Pauline letters. Paul does indeed employ the analogy of the body (Rom. 12:5; and especially I Cor. 12:12 ff.) in relation to the church, but it is to illustrate the diversity of functions in a single organism; and he stresses rather the interdependence of the members than the sovereignty of Christ. In this analogy, indeed, he is clearly not thinking of Christ as the head in distinction from the members, since he speaks of the ear and the eye as among the interdependent members (I Cor. 12:16-17, 21). Here in Colossians, however, he thinks not of the several members with their variety of functions and dignities, but of the organism as a whole, deriving its vital powers from the head. To us the idea of the head suggests primarily the powers of intelligence and will—the figure prompts us to think of Christ as the mind which directs and the will which governs all the life of the church; but this would probably not fully represent the thought of the apostle. For him Christ as head is the unifying principle and the source of life, not only guiding and governing but also vivifying (see also on 2:19).

The term **body** (σῶμα) as used here is not an independent development of the analogy that Paul had used in I Corinthians, but a new approach to the whole concept of the church. In all probability the apostle takes over in σῶμα a technical term of the Colossian "philosophy," as he certainly does with πλήρωμα ("fullness") in the next verse. We cannot tell precisely how the Colossian Gnostics used σῶμα in the framework of their cosmic theory; whatever it meant to them, Paul affirms that it is realized in the church. The genitive ἐκκλησίας is epexegetic rather than a simple apposition—"the body, by which I mean specifically the church."

It remains a question whether by "the church" in this context he means the empirical institution, the visible society which exists within time and history; or whether he is thinking in transcendental terms, as of an eternal, heavenly "body," which would include ideally not only the redeemed from among mankind, but all "in heaven and in earth" that is or shall be subject to God (see Lohmeyer's note on the verse).

The second predicate, ἀρχή—**beginning**, is closely related in thought to the first. In Hebrew and other Semitic languages the words for "head" and for "beginning" have the same root; in Aquila's translation of Gen. 1:1, κεφαλή is substituted for ἀρχή. But the ideas are not identical: the thought is rather that the headship of Christ follows naturally from the fact that he initiates the redemptive process. As Abbott suggests, ὅς here has

---

the fullness of his nature and love in Christ and by which he perpetuates the saving influence of that self-revelation through the historic church, of which Christ is **the head, . . . the beginning, the first-born.** The following points are to be noted:

(*a*) A cosmic redemption is being effected through Christ. The Christ through whom creation took shape becomes the incarnate Christ, the Christ of human history, who creates the new spiritual community, the church. It is through his redemptive work wrought out in the history of man, the highest order of creation, that the whole disordered world, and the universe itself, will be brought

back to him as its center and goal (see I Cor. 15:27-28).

(*b*) The focus of Christ's redemptive action is in the life of man, not in the physical universe considered apart from man. It is not cosmic forces, nor natural and physical processes—the modern equivalent of the Colossian belief in the "elemental spirits of the universe" (2:8)—that will turn the world back to God, but the redemptive operation of God's love in Christ on the minds and wills of men. The order of creation was first the universe, then man. "In him all things were created, in heaven [first] and on earth" (vs. 16). The order of redemption is the reverse of this. The redemp-

| 19 For it pleased *the Father* that in him should all fulness dwell; | 19 For in him all the fulness of God was |

practically the force of the classical ὅς γε—not merely "who is the beginning" but "in that he is the beginning." And this thought is made concrete in the third predicate, **first-born from the dead.** It is specifically in his resurrection that Christ makes, in his own person, the beginning of the new creation; which is not, like the old, subject to dissolution and death. This predicate at the same time points the correspondence between the place of Christ in the creation and his place in the new creation; the "first-born of all creation" is likewise the **first-born from the dead.**

The title **first-born from the dead** recalls the words of I Cor. 15:20, "Now is Christ risen from the dead, and become the firstfruits of them that slept" (ἀπαρχὴ τῶν κεκοιμημένων). In that passage also the thought of the sovereignty of Christ follows upon the thought of the pledge and guarantee given in him of the final harvest, the general resurrection. It is to be noted that in neither context is the resurrection of Christ equated in any sense with the miracles of raising the dead which we find reported in the Gospels and elsewhere. In all such miracles the subject is restored to life, his mortal body reanimated for a further period of existence under the same conditions. But "Christ being raised from the dead dieth no more; death hath no more dominion over him" (Rom. 6:9). Thus his resurrection inaugurates for man a new life, a life that has passed through death and emerged victorious, life eternal.

In the final clause the change of verb is to be noted, though neither the KJV nor the RSV brings it out. Ἵνα γένηται . . . πρωτεύων is not simply **that . . . he might be preëminent,** but "that he might become" or, perhaps better, "might show himself preeminent." The thought moves no longer in the realm of absolute being, but in the realm of the contingent; it is the *experience* of the incarnate Christ, in the concrete fact of the Resurrection, that marks his universal pre-eminence. Note the parallel expression of Rom. 1:4: "Declared [or designated] . . . Son of God with power . . . by the resurrection from the dead." The clause emphasizes the unity of creation and redemption; **in all things** Christ has the pre-eminence. Again there is an implied repudiation of the limitation set upon the sphere of Christ's action in the cosmic theory of the Colossian teachers; no place is left for the activity of mediation which they ascribed to "the elemental spirits of the universe."

**19.** In this verse there is some doubt concerning the construction, whether the phrase πᾶν τὸ πλήρωμα is to be taken as subject of the main verb or as subject of the infinitive. The RSV reflects the former view; the KJV, the latter. To the majority of commentators, ancient and modern, it seems best to take εὐδόκησεν as having the subject ὁ θεός understood—"God was pleased," "it was his will"; then πλήρωμα will be the subject of κατοικῆσαι, in the accusative and infinitive construction. "God willed that the whole

---

tion of human life and society is the crucial task which must precede, and when once achieved, will inevitably lead on to the restoration of the disordered universe to harmonious union with God (see Eph. 3:10). Some commentators see this significance in the reverse order (as compared with vs. 16) of the words **to reconcile to himself all things, whether on earth** [first] **or in heaven.** To put it in another way, it is not the philosophers and scientists who can lead man to redemption, but the prophets and evangelists of God's love in Christ. The ultimate problems are spiritual, not material. The church is in the front line of battle in God's ongoing campaign to redeem the world. Man,

when he is brought into harmony with God, is to become God's agent and servant in directing the forces of nature to the fulfillment of the divine purpose.

(c) The universe is redeemable. The world and human life are not in their essential nature alien from God and necessarily evil. Redemption is the restoration of an original good relationship that has been distorted and lost. God is dealing with that which is his own. (See Exeg. for the meaning of **reconcile.**)

(d) Peace, the restoration of true community in society and of order in the world, cannot be achieved apart from a right relationship with God. It is in reconciling men to God that Christ

pleroma should take up its abode in him." For "the pleroma" cannot be regarded as an alternative expression for "God"; a modern theologian may profess himself willing to substitute the phrase "the totality of values" for "God," but this is unlikely to have occurred to any early Christian writer, whether Paul or another.

The word pleroma is undoubtedly a technical term of the Colossian "philosophy"; it is one of the key words in all the Gnostic systems. The classic discussion in English is Lightfoot's note "On the meaning of πλήρωμα" (Colossians, pp. 323-39), though a modern philologist would not insist so firmly on the passive force of the termination -μα in the Greek usage of the period (see the complementary note of J. A. Robinson, "On the Meaning of πλήρωμα" in St. Paul's Epistle to the Ephesians [London: Macmillan & Co., 1903], pp. 255-59).

In the Hermetic writings pleroma is used of God in a context of pantheistic immanence; he is "the Lord and Maker of all [τῶν ὅλων] being both All [τὰ πάντα] and One, . . . for the Pleroma of all things is One and in One" (Corpus Hermeticum XVI.3). The sense here is certainly not active ("that which fills all things"), but passive ("the totality of things"). In the great Gnostic schools of the second century the pleroma is the whole body of emanations. It would seem that the Colossian teachers used it of the whole array of the στοιχεῖα, the "elemental spirits of the cosmos," and imagined the various attributes of God to be distributed among them; or they may have conceived the στοιχεῖα as the attributes themselves, hypostatically existent. It is scarcely worth while to inquire into the particulars of such a fanciful system.

Taking the term ready-framed from the current philosophy of religion, Paul nowhere explains the sense which it holds for him. In some degree, then, he must assume that it has a fairly well-defined theological content which his readers will at once appreciate. In 2:9 he adds to it the phrase τῆς θεότητος—all the pleroma "of the Godhead," or "of deity": and the same phrase is to be understood in this first occurrence. He rejects the doctrine that the powers of divinity are distributed among a throng of mediating spirits of any kind—"thrones, dominions, principalities, powers"; and claims for Christ that the entire complement, "the aggregate of the Divine attributes, virtues, energies" (Lightfoot), resides in him alone. We find ourselves here moving in a world of ideas that is utterly strange to us, in which we can never feel entirely at home; but we can at least recognize the fundamental conclusion: that "God was in Christ," not in a limited or partial manifestation (that might be claimed of all the great teachers of mankind), but in his plenitude.

We have still to ask what is meant by the *dwelling* of **the fullness of God** in Christ. The scriptures, both of the O.T. and the N.T. when they speak of God as "dwelling" among men, always apply the idea in a particular, not in a general sense; the thought is not of his universal immanence, but of his living presence in a personal relationship of love and trust: where God "dwells," he manifests himself as God, bringing salvation. If, then, it is the good pleasure of God that "all the fullness should dwell in Christ," this means that in Christ God is made known to us in his saving power, awakening our love and enabling our worship. Compare the words of Christ in the Fourth Gospel (14:9), "He that hath seen me hath seen the Father."

---

restores right relationships between man and man, making peace by the blood of his cross.

(e) It is a divine act which initiates and accomplishes peace between man and God, and peace between man and man. The initiative of God's sacrificial love in Christ effects what man cannot do for himself or for his fellow man. Men become peacemakers only by sharing and living the divine love and forgiveness imparted to them in Christ. He *makes* peace by **the blood of his cross.**

(f) Man has a necessary part to play in the salvation of the world. This follows because man has the freedom to accept or reject the divine redemption. The Colossian system of thought with its ranks of angels, thrones, dominions, principalities, and authorities, conceived as spiritual beings sharing rule of the cosmic order, is, as has been noted, quite alien to modern thought, but we have our own popular science that gives a kind of rough equivalent of these (see Exeg. on vs. 13). We speak of

**20** And, having made peace through the blood of his cross, by him to reconcile all things unto himself; by him, *I say,* whether *they be* things in earth, or things in heaven.

20 pleased to dwell, 20 and through him to reconcile to himself all things, whether on earth or in heaven, making peace by the blood of his cross.

---

It is not easy to see how this affirmation is related to the kenosis doctrine of Phil. 2:5-7, "Christ, . . . who, though he was in the form of God, . . . emptied himself (ἑαυτὸν ἐκένωσεν), taking the form of a slave." Both thoughts clearly refer to the Incarnation, for κατοικῆσαι is most naturally taken as the *ingressive* aorist, "that the fullness should *take up its abode* in him." It is possible that Paul thinks of this in connection with the Ascension, and that he is here expressing in other terms what he affirms in Phil. 2:9-10, that "God also hath highly exalted him and given him a name which is above every name: that at the name of Jesus every knee should bow, of things in heaven, and things in earth."

Lightfoot points out that κατοικεῖν is contrasted with παροικεῖν as "permanent abode" over against "temporary sojourn"; and he suggests that Paul may be refuting a Colossian notion that the powers of the divine have only a passing and incidental association with Christ, while the apostle insists that they *abide* in him permanently. But it would seem that if such an emphasis were intended, it would have been made more distinct. The πᾶν is certainly emphatic, and it is in this that the real emphasis lies—*all* the divine pleroma abides in Christ, not partitioned or distributed.

**20.** The Son, the ruler of the kingdom of love, the effective agent and the appointed end of the whole creation, has been revealed in his office and function as head of the church and bearer of the whole pleroma of the Godhead. In this capacity, and with this endowment, he is now revealed as the effective agent of God in the reconciliation of the universe, in the making of a cosmic peace. The need of reconciliation implies a prior alienation of the universe from God; the need of peacemaking implies that the cosmos is rent with conflict. Nothing is said here of the how or why of this alienation; it is sufficient that this is the actual state of the world, and that Christ is appointed to effect the remedy. It is, however, of the utmost importance to Christian thought—which is here in fundamental opposition to the postulates of the contemporary philosophy, even in its highest forms—that this alienation from God is not inherent in the creation, but is somehow a departure of the creation from its true relation to God. God is not dealing with an intractable stuff, which is in origin and essence independent of him and incompatible with his nature, but with a frame of things that he himself has brought into being "in, through, and for" Christ. Its alienation is therefore neither inherent nor permanent; and it is his good pleasure to restore it to its true relationship with him and to its true internal harmony; and this ultimate purpose is to be accomplished through Christ, who acts as God's agent in reconciliation as in creation. The double compound ἀποκαταλλάσσειν here replaces the καταλλάσσειν of the earlier epistles (Rom. 5:1; II Cor. 5:18 ff.; etc.)

---

"blind forces" at work in history and human society, of "demonic influences," and the like. On a more constructive but still secular plane we look to human powers of organization in science, education, politics, and culture to lift mankind to a nobler life. Modern man has vastly increased his understanding of natural and social forces, and his power to use them for good or ill. He has become increasingly an agent in the process of creation, but he is still far from being a servant of the divine purpose for creation. He sets up his own "thrones or dominions or principalities or authorities." Often he worships these as the Colossians worshiped the angelic powers. But who shall control man, the maker of the systems, values, and governments which he sets up in the world? It is the task of the church to cast down "imaginations, and every high thing that exalteth itself against the knowledge of God," and to bring "into captivity every thought to the obedience of Christ" (II Cor. 10:5). Man's growing mastery of the forces of nature must be freely surrendered and dedicated to Christ, the Lord of life, that human society, and ultimately the whole creation, may fulfill its destiny in him for whom it was created. Man, destined to return to God the worship of his freedom, has this necessary part to play in his salvation; the responsibility is laid upon him to surrender

21 And you, that were sometime alienated and enemies in *your* mind by wicked works, yet now hath he reconciled

21 And you, who once were estranged

---

to emphasize that this is the restoration of a good relationship that has been lost; that God is dealing with that which is his own. The "peace" which is made means perhaps peace between God and the alienated universe, but more probably it is meant to suggest the restoration of peace *within* the cosmos, which is filled with internal conflict as the result of its alienation from God.

Peace is made **through the blood of his cross.** The mention of **blood** brings out the sacrificial aspect of Christ's death. Lohmeyer, who treats this entire section of the epistle (somewhat fancifully) as a kind of Targum on the ritual of the day of Atonement, suggests that the abrupt introduction of this phrase is intelligible only if it is put in the place of a more familiar image; and he thinks that this is to be found in the symbolism of the lamb which was offered in sacrifice on the day of Atonement. But could it be assumed that the Gentiles of Colossae would make this connection of thought as readily as Paul? It is in fact not clear in the context that the idea of atonement for sin is involved; and it is probably better to see in the words rather the idea of the blood as the seal of the covenant of peace—as having a mystic power, the power of a life liberated through sacrifice to become a living link of communion between the deity and that for which the sacrifice is made. Such an idea would not be peculiarly Jewish, but would be a commonplace of all ancient conceptions of the efficacy of a sacrifice that involved the shedding of blood. See Knopf's excursus on ῥαντισμὸν αἵματος (I Pet. 1:2) in his commentary *Die Briefe Petri und Judä* (Göttingen: Vandenhoeck & Ruprecht, 1912; "Meyer's Kommentar").

### 3. IN APPLICATION TO THE READERS (1:21-23)

The reconciliation of the cosmos is now viewed in its application to the readers of the epistle. Here again we must take note of the contrast between Christian and pagan doctrines of reconciliation and redemption. In all pagan thinking the physical cosmos is a lower form of being, inherently and irredeemably contrary to the spiritual; association with it degrades and defiles the soul, which can rise to its high estate only by shaking off the bonds of matter and penetrating through the planetary spheres, purging its defilements as it passes, until it rises to a purely spiritual existence, removed far above all the stages of its descent through the material realm (on this descent and restoration of the soul see P. Wendland, *Die hellenistisch-römische Kultur* [Tübingen: J. C. B. Mohr, 1912; "Handbuch zum Neuen Testament"], pp. 170 ff.). In Christian thinking, as this epistle makes clear, man is not saved *from,* but *with* the material creation; there is no fundamental dualism, but all, physical and spiritual alike, comes from God through Christ and returns to God through Christ. The redemption and reconciliation of man become the key to the redemption and reconciliation of the cosmos; cf. Rom. 8:20 ff., where "the creation itself" is depicted as sharing the same bondage and grief, and awaiting the same liberation as "the children of God."

**21.** The former state of the Colossian Christians is described as one of alienation and

---

the growing areas of his freedom to the rule of Christ; and Christ, in whom **all the fulness of God was pleased to dwell,** has shown himself **preëminent** in all things, and especially in his power **to reconcile to himself all things, whether on earth or in heaven, . . . by the blood of his cross.** The emphasis is not on the principle of self-sacrificing love, but on its demonstration in the historic Jesus and the risen Christ.

**21.** *The Cosmic Reconciliation Applied to Mankind.*—And you . . . he has now reconciled.

Paul never fails to make his teaching personal. He is always the evangelist. The gospel of Christ is an evangel. The first task of the church is evangelism. If life is shallow without "deep theology," "deep theology" is sterile apart from life. The magnificent flight into the ultimate through which Paul has just carried his readers sprang from his concern for their souls. Now he returns to his primary and very practical purpose to make stanch Christians of the confused and wavering converts of Colossae. Yet

22 In the body of his flesh through death, to present you holy and unblamable and unreprovable in his sight:

and hostile in mind, doing evil deeds, 22 he has now reconciled in his body of flesh by his death, in order to present you holy and blameless and irreproachable before

---

enmity. As **alienated**, they are represented as having part in the general alienation of the cosmos from God; as **hostile in mind, doing evil deeds**, they are represented as bearing a personal responsibility in thought and act. **Hostile:** Primarily to God, secondarily to one another; in those that are alienated from God the whole disposition of the mind is hostile.

**22.** The present condition of the readers is sharply contrasted with their past estate of alienation and enmity; and the sharpness is accentuated by a glaring anacoluthon. Both our versions adopt the reading of the received text (ἀποκατήλλαξεν), which undoubtedly has in its favor the weight of textual authority, both in MSS and versions (though in a textual problem of this type, the value of the evidence of the versions is doubtful) ; but the reading of Codex B, ἀποκατηλλάγητε, unquestionably preserves the true text, though it is supported only by p46 and a single minuscule (33—"the queen of the cursives") . Grammatically, the accusatives of vs. 21 would require the active, and this has led to the alteration which has found place in nearly all the witnesses. In the true text these accusatives are left hanging; and with an abrupt change of construction the apostle writes "Now, you were reconciled." The aorist passive emphasizes that the reconciliation, for them, is *accomplished;* cf. the strong aorists in vss. 12 and 13 above (noted in Exeg. on vs. 14) .

---

what has gone before is no mere irrelevant excursion into cosmic speculation. Theology does illuminate life. It is only by helping them "to comprehend with all saints what is the breadth, and length, and depth, and height; and to know the love of Christ, which passeth knowledge" (Eph. 3:18), that Paul is able to lead them to view the immediate problems of their personal faith *sub specie aeternitatis.* The cosmic salvation, viewed in its widest context, focuses down and takes immediate effect in Christ's transformation of their own lives. The "you" is emphatic. This cosmic salvation is no idle speculation, no mere far-off dream, no wistful surmise. It is going on now. Christ is at work in the life of mankind. More than that, he has wrought a saving change in your own experience: **You . . . hath he reconciled.**

Perhaps two things were dominant in Paul's mind when he put this emphatic and arresting "you" at the very beginning of his affirmation of the true Christian discipleship into which his hearers had already entered:

(*a*) In the thought which he states when he speaks of the Colossians as **once . . . estranged and hostile in mind, doing evil deeds,** he is appealing to what they know to be true of themselves. Christ had radically changed both their outlook on life and the quality of their living. **Estranged,** having drifted out of right relationship with God, or having never been in true relationship with him, they found themselves by inevitable consequence **hostile in mind,** deliberately and willfully opposed to his

will. The result was corrupt living, **doing evil deeds.** Christ had changed this, bringing them into a new relationship to God.

(*b*) The thought which he may have implied, which underlies all that he has to say to these Colossian Christians: You who have been looking elsewhere than to Christ, foolishly thinking that you have found a fuller and more effective guidance than Christ can give into a life well-pleasing to God; you who are substituting mystic ceremonials and dependence upon supposed angelic mediators of redemption for a frank and full reliance upon the spiritual energizing and the moral direction of Christ in your lives—*you* have been reconciled to God, not by speculations, nor mystic ritual, nor by fancied rulers of some supramundane sphere, but by Christ. It is he—who lived in the terms and under the limitations of a human life—who confronts moral evil and breaks its power, and wins wrong wills to right ways by the divine potency of God's self-giving love.

The sole and sufficient reconciler is Christ.

Christ! I am Christ's! and let the name suffice you,
    Ay, for me too He greatly hath sufficed:
Lo with no winning words I would entice you,
    Paul has no honour and no friend but Christ.[1]

**22. *In His Body of Flesh by His Death.*—**The cosmic Christ became incarnate. If you want to understand the nature and method of God's saving work, to realize the depth and efficacy

---

[1] F. W. H. Myers, *St. Paul,* st. i.

23 If ye continue in the faith grounded and settled, and *be* not moved away from the hope of the gospel, which ye have heard,

him, 23 provided that you continue in the faith, stable and steadfast, not shifting from the hope of the gospel which you heard,

---

This reconciliation is accomplished **in his body of flesh, by his death** (ἐν, διά). The prepositions "in" and "by," thus contrasted, represent respectively the *sphere* and the *means* of the reconciliation; it is accomplished in the sphere of the Incarnation, not in some purely spiritual, transcendental act; and it is accomplished "through death," as the means of deliverance from the life which was lived under the conditions of alienation and enmity. The efficacy of the Passion is here declared, but not explained.

The infinitive παραστῆσαι (**to present you**) is epexegetic rather than final; it defines the nature and effect of the work of reconciliation rather than its purpose. The subject is not expressed, but "Christ" is probably to be understood (not "God," as Lightfoot takes it). The words are frequently taken as having reference to the appearance of men before God on the Judgment Day; but it is better to interpret them more generally. In reconciliation to God the Christian stands in God's presence, no longer as unhallowed, marked with the blemishes of his sin, and bearing the burden of his guilt; but "holy, unblemished, guiltless"; cf. I Cor. 6:11—"Such [evildoers] were some of you. But you were washed, you were consecrated, you were justified in the name of the Lord Jesus Christ and in the Spirit of our God." To the new relationship with God there corresponds the inward transformation in those whom Christ now brings before him. The words belong to the vocabulary of sacrifice. Christ presents us before God, and we freely offer ourselves, as "a living sacrifice, holy and acceptable to God, which is [our] spiritual worship" (Rom. 12:1).

**23.** This is a warning against apostasy and the seduction of false doctrines. God has brought Paul's readers the fullness of blessing in Christ; it rests with them to stand firm

---

of his forgiving love, to know in your own lives his reconciling power, learn of him, who "became man for us men and for our salvation." This is what Paul is affirming here. To the Corinthians he wrote, "I determined not to know any thing among you, save Jesus Christ, and him crucified" (I Cor. 2:2). The thought is not that Paul would close his mind to any area of truth, but that he must view all life, all truth, all reality in the light of the crucified Christ. Reconciliation to God is not effected by thinking one's way to a new philosophical position, but by Christ's challenge to the evil wills of men, and by his conquest of the moral will of those whom he enables to believe in him and love him. Reconciliation was wrought **in his body of flesh by his death**; not in the realm of speculation, but in the experience of men. The Atonement is inseparable from the Incarnation. In the sphere, and under the conditions, of man's sin and failure, the divine life was lived and the divine redemption wrought.

The result is a new status of human life in relation to God and a new character in those who are brought into it, **holy and blameless and irreproachable before him.**

**23. *Provided that You Continue in the Faith.*** —This is the main theme of the epistle—a right faith in Christ, with emphasis on the rightness

of their faith. An examination of the great "ifs" of the Bible makes a very profitable study. Some of them point to the necessary conditions which must be fulfilled to attain or retain a desired result—as here. **And you . . . he has now reconciled, . . . provided that you continue in the faith** (see John 7:17, "If any man will do his will, he shall know of the doctrine").

In other cases the stress is on the further consequences which must flow from a desired condition which has already been accepted, as, "If ye then be risen with Christ [as you claim and acknowledge], seek those things which are above (3:1). See also the following: "If any man will come after me [as they had consented to do], let him deny himself, and take up his cross, and follow me" (Matt. 16:24); "If there be therefore any consolation in Christ [as they claimed and believed], . . . fulfil ye my joy, that ye be like-minded [the consequence]" (Phil. 2:1-2).

The promises of the gospel always place this twofold responsibility on those to whom they are proclaimed: (*a*) to fulfill the conditions of attainment, and (*b*) to exhibit the consequences of attainment. Both senses may be understood in the present instance. **You . . . he has now reconciled, . . . provided that you continue in the faith.** But also, since he has reconciled you,

*and* which was preached to every creature which is under heaven; whereof I Paul am made a minister;

which has been preached to every creature under heaven, and of which I, Paul, became a minister.

in the truth. Again Paul confirms that the gospel which they have already heard from Epaphras is the true and only gospel; it has been proclaimed everywhere in the world; Paul himself proclaims it. As in vs. 6, the appeal to the universality of the proclamation is not so much a boast of the wide extent of its progress as an assertion of its identity with that which Epaphras has preached.

Paul's mention of himself as a **minister** of the universal gospel paves the way for his account of himself and his mission, which follows. We might observe the nontechnical use of διάκονος, which in later usage was reserved for a lower order of ministry ("deacon"). Here it is purely functional, not official; it is as appropriate to Paul as to Epaphras (vs. 7); in both cases it is used specifically of preaching.

---

you must continue in the faith. The bestowal of grace is a divine operation. But the responsibility of the believer is neither violated nor waived (see the paradoxical statement of this truth in Phil. 2:12-13, "Work out your own salvation with fear and trembling: for it is God which worketh in you both to will and to do of his good pleasure").

A further thought is suggested here, viz., Paul's consistent purpose to stress the positive (see above, vs. 4). He does not call his readers heretics and then denounce them. He affirms what he wants them to affirm. They are "in the faith." Let them continue in it. Underlying this reminder is the further assumption that they *will* continue in the faith. He anticipates the best of them, and thereby encourages the best from them. Emphasizing the necessity of continuance in the true faith which brought them into the essentially Christian transformation of their lives, he imparts to them his own confidence that this is what they will actually do.

**Stable and steadfast** carries a double meaning. **Stable** means having a sure foundation, like the house built upon a rock (Matt. 7:24-29). **Steadfast** has the added meaning of persistently and consistently remaining on it. Heretical teachers were putting pressure upon them to rebuild their faith on shifting foundations.

**The gospel which you heard,** etc. Paul summons to support his appeal a threefold witness to the true faith. First, their own knowledge and experience. Second, the world outreach of the faith in Christ. This involves two things: (*a*) the essential universality of the Christian message, the ideal and goal of Christian evangelism as given in the Great Commission (Matt. 28:19, 20; Mark 16:15), and (*b*) the actual historical spread of Christian missions to every major part of the empire even at the time when this epistle was written (see on vs. 6 above). The appeal to share and uphold a common faith

with the world-wide community of the church is a powerful incentive to Christians immersed in local concerns, and also a sound corrective of local peculiarities and aberrations in belief. Paul could have enumerated an impressive total of cities, towns, and communities on the three continents of Asia, Europe, and Africa, in fact, in most major areas of the empire, where the faith had already been proclaimed and the church had already taken root. In like manner, and on a vaster scale, a modern teacher and advocate of the faith, by a simple enumeration of the centers of Christian activity on every continent, or even of those of which he himself has some general knowledge, can mightily impress his hearers with the consciousness that they are the heirs and custodians not of a parochial faith, but of a gospel for all mankind. A bare recital of the achievements and enterprises of the modern ecumenical movement can hardly fail to convey an equally telling challenge to those whose Christian outlook and concern are confined within the bounds of the local community. The faith which we are called to proclaim and extend is the universal gospel. The third witness to the true faith which Paul advances is his own personal testimony.

**Of which I Paul became a minister.** The "I Paul" is emphatic. All that he himself is, believes, has done, and is resolved to do is brought in willing tribute to the service of this universal gospel, of which the Colossians have already heard, and in which he bids them to remain steadfast. The greatest argument for the faith is a living example of it. The clinching verification of his reasonings and persuasions is the Christian character of the man himself.

Note also that the word here translated **minister** (διάκονος) is the humble word denoting not ecclesiastical rank, but simple service gratefully given. It is the word used in the great saying of Jesus, "Whosoever will be great among you, shall be your minister" (Mark 10:43-44).

24 Who now rejoice in my sufferings for you, and fill up that which is behind of the afflictions of Christ in my flesh for his body's sake, which is the church:

24 Now I rejoice in my sufferings for your sake, and in my flesh I complete what is lacking in Christ's afflictions for the sake

---

## B. THE APOSTLE'S MINISTRY (1:24–2:5)

In this passage the apostle seeks to justify his intervention in the affairs of a church which he has not founded and to which he is personally unknown. He has already reminded them that Epaphras, who brought them the gospel, came to them under his direction (vs. 7); and has suggested that he is simply confirming the truth of the message that they have already heard. He is not seeking to win them to a new loyalty. Now he makes appeal further (a) to his sufferings, endured for their sake, for the sake of Christ's whole church; (b) to his divine commission, which is not limited, but world wide in scope; and (c) to his personal interest in and care for them, and for all Christians, known to him and unknown alike.

### 1. MINISTRY OF SUFFERING (1:24)

**24.** In what sense does Paul mean that his sufferings are **for your sake;** and what are the implications of his assertion that he (to render literally) "fills up the deficiencies of Christ's afflictions for the sake of his body, which is the church"? These words are commonly applied by Roman Catholic theologians to the doctrine of the "treasury of merits" (first defined in the bull Unigenitus, issued by Clement VI in 1343, and made the basis of the theory of indulgences). In reaction against this false doctrine Protestant exegetes have often taken undue liberties with the clear meaning of the passage. Paul certainly does not suggest here that by his sufferings he lays up a store of merits which are available for the account of the church at large; there is not the least indication that he regards his sufferings as an atonement for the sins of other Christians; questions of sin and atonement do not enter into consideration here at all. He suffers **for your sake, . . . for the sake of . . . the church,** in the sense that his sufferings have come on him in consequence of his apostolic labors. He cannot look upon them as disastrous, or even as unfortunate, since they are the necessary consequence of the high service in which he is engaged. But more than that, by them he enters into a deeper fellowship with Christ. In the letter to the Philippians he tells us that he has sacrificed everything that once was dear to him, "That I may win Christ, . . . that I may know him, and the power of his resurrection, and the

---

Paul was sure of his apostolic calling, and when the occasion demanded it, he did not hesitate to assert his claim to apostolic authority. When challenged or repudiated, he could be very strenuous in defense of his right to be heard in the church (see Gal. 1–2; II Cor. 11–12). His fundamental integrity is seen in the fact that when not under necessity of vindicating his calling in the face of critical attack, he is content to identify himself with all who labor faithfully in the gospel as a humble servant of Christ.

**24. I Rejoice in My Sufferings for Your Sake.** —Paul cites elsewhere the severe and repeated sufferings that he has endured in the service of Christ as giving moral authority to his leadership in the church (II Cor. 4:7-12; 11:23-30). When a man has staked his life for a cause he cannot stand aloof from anything that threatens it, nor can his right to speak be challenged or

ignored. If Paul is able to rejoice in his sufferings, it is not because of an ascetic exaltation of suffering as an absolute virtue. That note is absent from the N.T., and notably from the life of Jesus as recorded in the Gospels. There is no unnecessary and arbitrary suffering in Christianity, no pain simply for the merit of enduring pain. Suffering is enjoined, and to be accepted, only as the necessary price that must be paid to achieve a higher and enduring good. A soldier once said, when a sympathizer had expressed sorrow that he had lost his leg, "I did not lose it, I gave it." So Paul rejoices in his sufferings, looking ahead to the Christian results that only sacrificial Christian living can bring to pass. It is because his sufferings are **for your sake,** and **for the sake of . . . the church** that he is sustained by an inner and holy joy even in enduring them. "For we which live are always delivered unto death for Jesus' sake, that the

fellowship of his sufferings" (Phil. 3:8-10). This ambition is now being realized—he "is filling up the deficiencies of Christ's sufferings." His sufferings, like the sufferings of Christ, are vicarious; they are not a punishment for sin, but are endured in the interest of others. This by no means implies that they are in any sense a satisfaction for the sins of others. The thought is rather that suffering belongs to the Christian vocation; the servant is not greater than his Lord, and the hostile world will treat the Christian as it treated Christ. But one may bear another's burdens; or may, as the apostle does here, rejoice that a great part of the weight falls on his shoulders, which the church must somehow bear with him or without him. In this experience he stands in the place of Christ: that is the force of the prefix ἀντ- in ἀνταναπληρῶ. The apostle now himself bears the cross; he drinks of the cup that Christ drank, and is baptized with the baptism that he was baptized with (Matt. 20:22-23).

The phrase "the deficiencies of Christ's afflictions" still requires explanation. The words do not imply that the sufferings of Christ were insufficient to accomplish their purpose of redemption; the economy of redemption is not in view. The underlying thought is that the afflictions of the church are also "Christ's afflictions." He who persecutes his church, persecutes him (cf. Acts 9:4); the sum of his sufferings includes both what he suffered in the flesh, and what he continues to suffer in his "body," the church. Thus the sufferings of Christians as Christians continually supplement the sufferings of their Master; they "fill up the deficiencies" in what now becomes an experience common to Master and servants. In the words of Lightfoot (*Colossians*, p. 164):

It is a simple matter of fact that the afflictions of every saint and martyr do supplement the afflictions of Christ. The Church is built up by repeated acts of self-denial in successive individuals and successive generations. They continue the work which Christ began. . . . But St Paul would have been the last to say that they bear their part in the atoning sacrifice of Christ. . . . These ὑστερήματα will never be fully supplemented, until the struggle of the Church with sin and unbelief is brought to a close.

---

life also of Jesus might be made manifest in our mortal flesh. So then death worketh in us, but life in you" (II Cor. 4:11-12).

We do not pity the parent who sacrifices himself for his child or the patriot who sacrifices himself for his country, if he does it with open eyes, aware of the risk he is taking. Secretly, we envy him, and wish we had the courage to follow in his train. Why, then, should we pity those who make the uttermost venture of faith, and live and die for an unseen Beauty, rooted in the heart of the universe, but not yet made manifest? Theirs is the greatest risk, but theirs is the greatest reward.

I confess that as I think upon the life of that supreme Lover and supreme Sufferer "who for the joy that was set before him endured the cross, despising the shame," I am never for one moment tempted to pity him for the faith in God that led him to his death. Rather I am disturbed with an uneasy sense that we sophisticated modern folk, with our pitiful timidity and our persistent self-seeking are living in darkness and misery when we might follow him through suffering into light and joy.[2]

**In my flesh I complete what is lacking in Christ's afflictions.** The Exeg. brings out the

[2] W. M. Horton, *Theism and the Modern Mood* (London: Student Christian Movement Press; New York: Harper & Bros., 1930), pp. 178-79. Used by permission.

important point that there is no suggestion here that the Atonement wrought by Christ is incomplete, or that his followers can add anything to "the sufficiency of Christ." The underlying purpose of the whole epistle is to refute the heresy that Christ is insufficient for salvation, and that other mediators of redemption are needed. On the contrary, it is the Atonement wrought by Christ that causes and empowers his followers to live out his sacrificial spirit in fresh applications of the life of love.

By the light of burning heretics Christ's bleeding
   feet I track,
Toiling up new Calvaries ever with the cross that
   turns not back.[3]

The phrase **in my flesh** gives the clue to the thought here. Paul frequently develops the idea of a mystical union between Christ and the soul and between Christ and the church. "I am crucified with Christ: nevertheless I live; yet not I, but Christ liveth in me: and the life which I now live in the flesh I live by the faith of the Son of God, who loved me, and gave himself for me" (Gal. 2:20). This identity with Christ cannot be complete until the Chris-

[3] James Russell Lowell, "The Present Crisis."

25 Whereof I am made a minister, according to the dispensation of God which is given to me for you, to fulfil the word of God;

of his body, that is, the church, 25 of which I became a minister according to the divine office which was given to me for you, to

---

## 2. Propagation of the Gospel (1:25-27)

The nature of Paul's ministry is now defined as (a) a high trust—**the divine office ... given to me for you;** (b) a propagation of the gospel—**to make the word of God fully known;** and (c) a cure of souls—**warning . . . and teaching . . . , that we may present every man mature in Christ.**

**25.** The **divine office** or **dispensation** (οἰκονομία) is the office of the steward (οἰκονόμος) ; so Paul speaks of himself and his associates elsewhere as "stewards of the mysteries of God" (I Cor. 4:1). It is exercised for the benefit of others (**for you**) under responsibility to God. The gospel is given to him in trust, imposing upon him the duty, and at the same time conferring upon him the right, to address the Colossians. The infinitive πληρῶσαι is epexegetic—it defines more precisely the task which is entrusted to Paul. The same verb is used in a similar context in Rom. 15:19, which may be rendered, "Thus from Jerusalem and around as far as Illyria I have made the gospel of Christ fully known." The sense is perhaps rather "to make fully effective," to "fulfill the word of God" by bringing in the full complement of those for whom it is destined.

---

tian expresses in his own experience and action a life in full conformity with his Lord. While evil remains in the world, an inevitable part of Christ-centered living is to share "the fellowship of his sufferings" (Phil. 3:10).

Furthermore, while such sacrificial living adds nothing to the fullness of Christ's reconciling life, yet it does extend his reconciling power in the world in new and multiplying victories of faith and love. The work of atonement goes on unendingly till the world is won. Christians share in it, and pay the price of it, in and sometimes with their own lives, but always because they have become willing agents and instruments of the indwelling Christ. They do not repeat the Atonement, nor add to its efficacy. They become the means through which the atoning Christ extends his kingdom in the world in ever fresh instances of the power of redeeming love. So Paul rejoices in his sufferings and presses on to complete in his own unfinished life (**in my flesh**) the total of afflictions and achievements that remain for him to accomplish for the sake of Christ's body, the church, in order that the spiritual pilgrimage of his life may end in full conformity to his Lord.

**25-27.** *Paul's Divine Commission.*—The word translated **dispensation** (KJV) and **office** (RSV) has a twofold meaning: (a) the divine plan and purpose for the world, and (b) the specific office and stewardship to which God calls his specially chosen servants. It is in the latter sense that the word is used here. Paul is not on his own, pursuing a self-chosen career.

He has responded to a divine call. He is "apprehended of Christ" (Phil. 3:12). He must speak wherever the kingdom is concerned. He must declare his message to these friends in Colossae who have never seen him. He trusts that they will recognize the constraint of Christ in what he has to say to them.

**To make the word of God fully known, the mystery hidden for ages and generations but now made manifest to his saints.** Christ is the revealer and bringer of God's redemption. Paul is the evangelist, the herald of that gospel. In common with the whole church he is commissioned to evangelize the world, and to make God's self-revelation in Christ effective in the minds and wills of men everywhere. He goes on to mention the special task and mission to which God has uniquely called him, i.e., to make the gospel known **among the Gentiles.** The Colossians, in the heart of Gentile Asia Minor, were in the particular sphere of service to which God had committed Paul.

**The mystery** is the Christian gospel in its fullest realization, which involves not merely knowledge about Jesus, his teaching and his way of life, but also and supremely the experience of the living Christ in the lives of all who believe, including the Gentiles. This personal union with Christ brings the believer into a saving relationship with God in the present, and it is the guarantee of a saving relationship with God eternally—**the hope of glory.**

It is a **mystery** in several senses: (a) It is a secret, a hitherto unknown truth, a way of living in God which, in all the previous history

26 *Even* the mystery which hath been hid from ages and from generations, but now is made manifest to his saints:

make the word of God fully known, 26 the mystery hidden for ages and generations[c]

[c] Or *from angels and men.*

---

**26-27.** These two verses are a kind of digression on **the word of God.** It is described as a **mystery.** This word comes from the same root as the verb "to initiate," and its first sense appears to be "a rite of initiation" or "a secret to which initiation is the key." In the common language of the time it is sometimes weakened to mean "a secret" in the most general sense; but in the vocabulary of religion it stands for the whole complex of initiation, cult, and secret doctrine on which the numerous private religious brotherhoods of the time were based. Paul, then, is seeking to present the gospel in terms that would be familiar to his readers, strange though they are to us. The gospel, too, is a **mystery,** to be known only by revelation. It has been kept secret from the beginning of time, but it has pleased God now to make it known **to his saints.** Again, as in vs. 22, the apostle resorts to anacoluthon to emphasize the fundamental change, the radical difference between the hiding (ἀποκεκρυμμένον) of the mystery in all past time and its revelation (ἐφανερώθη) in the present. (In the second clause a finite verb is substituted for the

---

of the world, men, for all their ingenuity and knowledge, had never been able to discover for themselves, much less achieve. It was unknown and unattainable until God revealed it in an act of history, the life, death, and resurrection of Jesus. It is revealed truth. (*b*) It is the true way of salvation, in contrast to the spurious ways of salvation offered by the mystic speculations and the "mystery religions" of the ancient world, which were beguiling the Colossians. It is in Christ that God imparts the salvation which the cults spuriously claimed to bestow with their "secrets," "initiations," and ceremonials. Throughout this epistle Paul is constantly taking the language and conceptions of the heretical teachers and reinterpreting them in the light of Christ. (*c*) It is a mystery in the modern sense, a reality which outstrips human understanding. Rational analysis cannot fathom it. But faith can appropriate it, live by it, and know its benefits. Perhaps this thought did not occur to Paul as he wrote to Colossae, but it is of the utmost importance to the modern reader of the Scriptures.

This mystery, God's revelation in Christ, has been **hidden for ages and generations.** The cults were always dealing with "hidden wisdom," and claiming to make it known to an exclusive community of "initiates." The gospel was hidden, but not in this exclusive sense. The idea that God arbitrarily withholds the truth that makes men free, arbitrarily conceals it through the long centuries, and then arbitrarily discloses it to an arbitrarily chosen few, must be ruled out. That idea belongs with the primitive belief in hostile gods, and with the myth of Prometheus, who had to steal fire from heaven. It finds a parallel in the modern skeptical attitude that man must wrest his freedom and

progress from an indifferent, if not an unfriendly, universe. The Christian faith affirms that God is our Savior "who desires all men to be saved and to come to the knowledge of the truth" (I Tim. 2:4). If mature belief leads to assurance that God is like that, then it must follow that God has always been like that. Why the gospel was **hidden for ages and generations** cannot be explained by attributing to God less worthy motives than the highest motives of men. Insofar as an explanation is attainable it must be found in other directions.

(*a*) It is a matter of simple historical fact that men did not know, and could not find, the Christian God in all his fullness until Christ revealed him in a Godlike life. This fact must be accepted, whatever the explanation.

(*b*) It was the divine initiative that manifested Jesus to the world. "God so loved the world, that he gave his only begotten Son" (John 3:16). It would be impossibly contradictory to think of Jesus as outstripping the divine love and, as it were, forcing the hand of a God who was more reluctant than Jesus to grant a full disclosure of himself. God is always more willing to give than men are willing to ask or receive.

(*c*) God did not reveal himself in Jesus in earlier ages and generations because mankind had not been brought to the level of moral and spiritual maturity necessary to understand and respond to the gospel in Christ (see Acts 17:30; Heb. 1:1). As it was, the generation to which Jesus came rejected him. He won to himself only a very small remnant through whom he founded the church and sent it forth to "make the word of God fully known."

(*d*) What holds back the kingdom is not the "delaying tactics" of God, but the unresponsive

**27** To whom God would make known what *is* the riches of the glory of this mystery among the Gentiles; which is Christ in you, the hope of glory:

but now made manifest to his saints. **27** To them God chose to make known how great among the Gentiles are the riches of the glory of this mystery, which is Christ in

participle; the accompanying change of tense makes the difference still more emphatic.) The content of the mystery is twofold: it lies in (*a*) the extension of the saving knowledge of God to the Gentiles; and (*b*) the mystical indwelling of Christ—**Christ in you, the hope of glory**—a revelation of the divine purpose which was as unknown to Jews as to Gentiles. This mystery is **made manifest to his saints**—to those that have been consecrated to him, not to the world in general; but unlike the pagan mysteries, it is not to be jealously concealed, but to be made known far and wide.

The presence of Christ in our hearts—**Christ in you**—is **the hope of glory.** The **glory** of the heavenly inheritance cannot become actual, or is at least not fully realized in us, so long as we are in the body. In the nature of things the present experience of communion with Christ can but point to "the glory which shall be revealed in us" (Rom. 8:18), which therefore remains a **hope** (cf. also Rom. 8:24-25). A kindred thought appears in the conception of the Spirit as "the earnest of our inheritance" (Eph. 1:13-14; II Cor. 1:22). Note again how in this epistle Christ himself occupies the sphere that Paul elsewhere assigns to the Spirit.

wills of men. Saving and liberating truth awaits those who are willing to fulfill the conditions of receiving it and living in it. "Behold, I stand at the door, and knock: if any man hear my voice, and open the door, I will come in to him, and will sup with him, and he with me" (Rev. 3:20). "He came unto his own, and his own received him not. But as many as received him, to them gave he power to become the sons of God, even to them that believe on his name" (John 1:11-12).

The whole stress of the passage is on the heralding of the gospel to all mankind. God has found the way to make known to the world his nature and his agelong purpose of redemption. The long process of increasing disclosure of his will through lawgivers and prophets had reached the point where at least a minority could understand and accept his supreme self-revelation in Christ. "In the fullness of time" Christ had come. By living in terms of our common humanity a divine life in complete identity with the will of God, by his death and resurrection, he had brought our humanity into a new and reconciled relationship with God. He had called and won his followers unto this new relationship, and now was sending them forth to be interpreters to the world at large of his saving gospel. Christ is the focal point of **the mystery hidden for ages and generations but now made manifest.** O. C. Quick points out [4] how through sacred history a process of increasing selection and exclusion seemed to be taking place—from Abraham in whom all nations were to be blessed, to the "chosen people," excluding the

Gentiles, to a faithful remnant, excluding the majority of Israel, until finally the faithful remnant is reduced to one, Christ, who alone and in a human life fulfilled the divine will. These rejections must be understood not as arbitrary choices by God of those whom he would favor, but as human rejections of the opportunities for moral advance which God extended. Finally, Christ alone fulfilled the conditions of perfect conformity of human character to the divine purpose, and that by God's own act and initiative ("God was in Christ"). From that point in history the movement of successive exclusion becomes a movement of increasing inclusion. "By his resurrection Jesus has become the head of a new redeemed humanity and people of God, who in him receive the promises, and are destined to bring blessing and salvation to the whole human race previously rejected by its sin." [5]

It may be noted that the KJV has **hid** *from* **ages and** *from* **generations.** The probable meaning is, as in the RSV, **for ages and generations,** i.e., during all previous time. Some interpreters, however, see here a reference to the "ages" and "generations" of the Colossian heresy, and later of the Gnostic teaching, which were regarded as spiritual beings, having a place in the hierarchy of the "elemental spirits of the universe."

If this interpretation is permissible, Paul's statement that the secret of the gospel is hid from them would mean that they have no clue to the true way of salvation, i.e., do not look

---

[4] See also Expos. on 1:2, above.

[5] Quick, *Doctrines of the Creed,* p. 279; see also pp. 278-86.

28 Whom we preach, warning every man, and teaching every man in all wisdom; that we may present every man perfect in Christ Jesus:

you, the hope of glory. 28 Him we proclaim, warning every man and teaching every man in all wisdom, that we may present

---

### 3. Cure of Souls (1:28-29)

**28.** The threefold repetition of **every man** is meant to emphasize the Christian rejection of the Gnostic exclusiveness of spiritual privilege, which made distinctions between men according to their spiritual potentialities and reserved the highest teaching for the few **mature** or **perfect** (τέλειοι) who were capable of assimilating it. Paul admits differences of spiritual attainments, but not of spiritual *potentialities;* he labors to **present every man mature;** he seeks to train **every man in all wisdom.** The double function of "warning" and "teaching" corresponds to the twofold training of the Christian, in conduct and in advancing knowledge.

---

for a way to God in idle and misleading speculation; you will find God in Christ and in the fellowship of the church which derives its inspiration and power from him.

**Manifest to his saints.** Though the secret of life in Christ is available to all men, nevertheless there remains a principle of selection and exclusion. It is not based on race, tradition, and heritage, as the Jews claimed. **How great among the Gentiles are the riches of the glory of this mystery.** It is not based on knowledge of occult lore or theosophical speculation, nor on secret initiation into an exclusive cult, as the Colossian heretics taught. It is based on conditions that may be fulfilled by any man, anywhere. As elsewhere in the N.T., so here "the saints" are not those who have attained supreme spiritual excellence, but all Christians, all who have accepted Christ as Lord, and dedicated themselves to be his followers, whatever their moral attainment or lack of it. "Whosoever will" is the gospel invitation. That is the only principle of selection or exclusion. Only those who will, but all who will, may know **the riches of the glory of this mystery, which is Christ in you, the hope of glory.** Moffatt translates "mystery" as "open secret." It is a secret. A necessary condition must be fulfilled before it can be known, viz., the moral choice, the willing assent to learn of Christ.

> The love of Jesus, what it is
> None but his loved ones know.[6]

But it is an open secret—open to all who will fulfill that condition, which all may fulfill.

**1:28–2:5. Paul's Personal Dedication to His Mission.**—**Him we proclaim** (RSV) stresses the urgency of the Christian witness more strongly than does **whom we preach** (KJV). The advocacy of Christ is no mere argument in the

[6] "Jesus, the very thought of thee."

realm of philosophical speculation. It is an announcement of what God has done in history, a testimony of what Christ has meant in personal experience, a promise of what he can do in the lives of those who hear. It is "preaching for a verdict." The "we" includes all Christians. To know Christ is to commend him that others may know him too. The whole church is charged with a mission to the world. Its many varieties of service and function must contribute to this overmastering purpose to proclaim Christ **that we may present every man mature in Christ.** The repetition of **every man** is an emphatic challenge to the idea, apparently to the fore at Colossae, that salvation was the exclusive privilege of the devotees of a secret cult. That notion is now generally repudiated, but the positive side of Paul's declaration of the universal mission of the church is still too often ignored and neglected. It is easier to "preach to the sheep," and to nourish those already in the fold, than to go out to win the pagans, especially if they are without a sense of sin or even a sense of need. It is easy for comfortable Christians to abandon responsibility for the secular and irreligious masses on the tacit assumption that they are constitutionally incapable of understanding and responding to spiritual truth. This is the modern way of making the faith the exclusive possession of a privileged cult. Paul's emphasis on the gospel for "every man" is as salutary a corrective for this error as it was for the spiritual snobbery which he detected at Colossae.

**In all wisdom** and the later phrases **all the riches of assured understanding and the knowledge of God's mystery, of Christ, in whom are hid all the treasures of wisdom and knowledge** (2:2-3) are obvious reference to the claims of special spiritual understanding on the part of the devotees of the Colossian heresy. Paul is again affirming that everything necessary for a

29 Whereunto I also labor, striving according to his working, which worketh in me mightily.

every man mature in Christ. 29 For this I toil, striving with all the energy which he mightily inspires within me.

---

**29.** The insistence with which Paul dwells upon his exertions—**I toil, striving;** cf. "How greatly I strive for you" (2:1)—seems at first sight to be incompatible with the enforced inactivity of his life in prison. The words which he uses imply the most strenuous activity of which a man is capable, the sustained efforts of an athlete in competition. Both κοπιάω (**toil**) and ἀγωνίζομαι (**strive**) belong to the vocabulary of the games of track and field; so in I Tim. 4:10—"to this end we toil and strive"—they again occur coupled together in an analogy drawn directly between training in godliness and bodily training (I Tim. 4:7-8). Though Paul's body is confined, his spirit is free, and his spiritual activities continue undiminished. The dangers of his own situation do not lessen his care for others; the restraints of imprisonment do not cause him to suspend his labors for Christ and the church. Κοπιάω is used by him elsewhere of his general missionary labors (as in I Cor. 15:10—"I labored more abundantly than they all"; while ἀγωνίζομαι is used more particularly of prayer (Col. 4:12; Rom. 15:30).

Like the athlete in the arena, Paul puts forth a sustained, strenuous effort, drawing upon all his powers. But unlike the athlete, Paul is not dependent upon his own natural endowments; he has unlimited reserves in the spiritual power of Christ which is active in him. As he can say, "It is no longer I who live, but Christ who lives in me" (Gal. 2:20), so he can also say in effect, "I do not strive in my own strength; Christ's 'energy' is at work within me" (cf. also I Cor. 15:10). For that reason his work is effectual; laboring in the strength of Christ, he labors **mightily,** or literally "in power" (ἐν δυνάμει). The last phrase should be construed with the main verb, not with ἐνεργουμένην. Elsewhere we find ἐν δυνάμει explicitly contrasted with ἐν λόγῳ ("not in word, but in power"—I Cor. 4:20; I Thess. 1:5); here the same contrast is implicit.

Lohmeyer suggests that ἀγωνίζομαι and ἀγών had already come to have a technical sense in specific reference to martyrdom. Certainly the second-century literature of martyrdom constantly represents the sufferers as athletes wrestling on behalf of Christ and in the strength of Christ against the evil powers that animate the persecutors; martyrdom is never viewed as an ordeal of passive endurance. It is not clear, however, that such a thought is in the apostle's mind here.

---

saving relationship with God is to be found in Christ, that this "open secret" is within the reach of every mortal who is willing to fulfill the conditions, and that the conditions to be fulfilled—to be a humble learner of Christ—are within the grasp of everyone who desires to fulfill them. However impervious to a Christian appeal, and however limited he may be in capacity to understand, every man needs Christ, and is capable of being made "wise unto salvation through faith which is in Christ Jesus" (II Tim. 3:15). "I look upon the world as my parish," said John Wesley. The goal of evangelism, which is an open possibility in the grace of God, is to **present every man mature in Christ** (see also Eph. 4:13).

**1:29–2:1. For This I Toil, . . . I Strive for You.**—One can contemplate the world-wide mission of the church, and also advocate it with great conviction, without boring in to do something about it at the point of one's own responsibility, in the sphere where one's own life is

lived. "Everybody's business is nobody's business." Paul affirms, "This is my business." He always brings the general task into vivid focus on the particular duty. Having drawn with bold strokes a sweeping panorama of the cosmic significance of Christ and of the world mission of Christianity, he flings himself into this mighty movement with unreserved personal abandon—**For this I toil.** Furthermore, his effort is not diffuse and vague, like a general expression of interest and good will. It is concentrated in a definite issue, a problem that lies immediately at hand, and it is directed toward particular individuals and groups who need his counsel and help—**I strive for you.** The titles of the epistles indicate this basic principle of effective evangelism to which Paul adhered with unerring insight—"To the Romans," not "A Treatise on Law and Gospel"; "To the Corinthians," not "Sundry Observations on the State of the Church"; "To the Colossians," not "A Refutation of Certain Heresies." Being aware

2 For I would that ye knew what great conflict I have for you, and *for* them at Laodicea, and *for* as many as have not seen my face in the flesh;

2 That their hearts might be comforted, being knit together in love, and unto all riches of the full assurance of understanding, to the acknowledgment of the mystery of God, and of the Father, and of Christ;

2 For I want you to know how greatly I strive for you, and for those at La-odi-ce'a, and for all who have not seen my face, 2 that their hearts may be encouraged as they are knit together in love, to have all the riches of assured understanding and the

---

### 4. The Apostle's Interest in the Readers (2:1-5)

**2:1.** The ἀγωνιζόμενος of the preceding verse is taken up here in ἀγῶνα ἔχω (literally, "I have a contest"). Paul assures the Colossian Christians that in his pastoral labors he is working for them and for their fellows in Laodicea; he seeks to do service to all Christians everywhere, not only to those whom he has evangelized in person. This universal scope of his office is his justification for addressing them. He would not have them think that he is intruding where he has no right. Laodicea is mentioned particularly because the letter is meant to be read there also (4:16); the nearby city of Hierapolis was perhaps not threatened by the false teaching which had begun to make headway in Laodicea and Colossae.

**2-4.** Paul now states the object of his "toiling and striving." It is that through his instruction, imparted in the spirit of love, immature believers may develop the inward strength and power of discernment which will enable them to reject false doctrine, even when it is most persuasively presented. The phrasing of these verses is very difficult and the Greek text is corrupt; the general sense is clear, but the interpretation must remain dubious in details.

**That their hearts may be encouraged:** Neither **encouraged** (RSV) nor **comforted** (KJV) is satisfactory in this context as a rendering for παρακληθῶσιν. The verb may also mean "strengthen," and this appears to be the sense here: "that their hearts may be strengthened"—i.e., that they may be confirmed in affectionate loyalty to Christ. "The heart has its reasons which the mind knows not"; and the true heart, strong in its loyalty, will not be overpowered by the intellectual pretensions of a doctrine which fails to honor Christ above all else.

**Knit together:** The chief justification of this rendering is that συμβιβάζω certainly has this sense in vs. 19. There, however, it is used in a metaphor drawn from the physical constitution of the body. Here it seems better to adopt the interpretation of the Vulg. (*instructi*), giving the verb the sense which it always bears in the LXX, of "instruct" or "teach." Taking συμβιβασθέντες to mean "instructed," we must interpret the phrase **in love** as of the spirit in which the instruction is given and received. Paul instructs them **in love,** not as a spiritual dictator, but as a friend and partner (cf. II Cor. 1:24); and he trusts that they will receive his instruction in the spirit in which it is offered, not in resentment at his intervention.

The next phrase indicates the issue of the instruction. Εἰς πᾶν πλοῦτος is coupled with ἐν ἀγάπη in a kind of zeugma; with the second phrase the force of the participle must be extended; rather, a new thought is tacitly substituted, as "instructed in love and so led on to appropriate all the riches," etc. The genitive πληροφορίας defines the content of the "riches"; what Paul desires for his readers is that inward wealth which consists in

---

of great issues, he was most intensely aware of the persons whom those issues most concerned. What Colossian, hearing this letter read, could fail to say, "This man is speaking to my condition; all this was meant for me"? What Christian preacher or teacher can afford to neglect

a like personal dedication to persons for Christ's sake?

**2:2-3. *That Their Hearts May Be Encouraged as They Are Knit Together in Love.*—**(See also Expos., 1:28.) Again, it is not by detached speculation, nor by impersonal wrestling with

3 In whom are hid all the treasures of | knowledge of God's mystery, of Christ, 3 in
wisdom and knowledge.                   | whom are hid all the treasures of wisdom

---

"the fullness of discernment." Σύνεσις is here used in its proper sense (see on 1:9), not of **understanding** in general, but of the practical capacity to distinguish the better from the worse. Εἰς ἐπίγνωσιν (**to the acknowledgment**, KJV) is parallel in construction to εἰς πᾶν πλοῦτος, stating in fresh terms the end to which Paul's instruction will lead them— **the knowledge of God's mystery.**

We are now confronted with a textual difficulty of the first magnitude. It will be seen at a glance that the text behind the KJV (**the mystery of God, and of the Father, and of Christ**) is very different from that which lies behind the RSV (**God's mystery, of Christ**). In the Moffatt translation still another Greek text is followed—the "open secret [Moffatt's translation of "mystery"] of God, the Father of Christ." Still more variants are offered by different groups of MSS and by early versions. An important group gives "the mystery of the God and Father of Christ"; a few reduce it to "the mystery of God," and a few others to "the mystery of Christ"; and these are by no means all of the variations.

This multiplicity of variants is the result of the extreme difficulty which the Greek scribes and scholars of the early centuries themselves found in the phrase τοῦ μυστηρίου τοῦ θεοῦ Χριστοῦ. This is the form of the text as printed in all modern critical editions (except von Soden) and as rendered by the RSV. The authority for this reading is very slender; it rests upon only two Greek MSS (B and p46), and the Latin rendering of Hilary (*in agnitionem sacramenti Dei Christi*). There is, however, no doubt that this is the reading which has given rise to all the others (see Lightfoot, *Colossians*, pp. 318-19).

It still remains doubtful whether this is the true text; the difficulties which baffled the Greek scribes and scholars and led them to attempt so many emendations still defy solution. As the text stands, the only natural interpretation which it can bear is that given by Hilary—*Deus Christus sacramentum est* ("The God Christ [or "God the Christ"] is the mystery"); i.e., Χριστοῦ is construed in apposition to θεοῦ, and this genitive defines μυστηρίου. Such an exegesis would not trouble a theologian who had been through the fires of the Arian controversy; but it is utterly unthinkable in the first century.

Modern interpreters, therefore, generally take Χριστοῦ in apposition to μυστηρίου: this relationship is indicated to the reader of the printed text by the insertion of a comma after θεοῦ. But it is more than doubtful whether the reader of an unpunctuated Greek MS could ever have made such a connection. For him τοῦ θεοῦ Χριστοῦ would appear to be a formation precisely analogous to τῷ θεῷ πατρί (see 1:3; 3:17); if the one means "God the Father," the other would mean "God the Christ."

Von Soden, regarding it as impossible to take Χριστοῦ in apposition with either θεοῦ or μυστηρίου, proposes to treat it as a dependent genitive—"the God of Christ." The genitive could be either a simple possessive, "Christ's God"; or better, subjective, "the God whom Christ reveals." This is grammatically possible, but again it seems to make an unbearable demand on the ingenuity of the reader.

The difficulty of interpretation is greatly lessened if we adopt Lohmeyer's conjecture that Χριστοῦ is an early gloss. (As it appears in the text in p46 it must go back to the second century.) The removal of the gloss would leave a quite acceptable sentence, "The mystery of God, in whom are all the treasures of wisdom and knowledge hidden"— with the implication that in Christ these treasures are brought to light. But since the epistle is concerned primarily with the fact that Christ is the sole mediator of the divine to man, it is not altogether natural that this thought should here be conveyed merely by implication. It would seem, therefore, that we must reconcile ourselves to admit that the text as it lies before us is corrupt, and that we are unable to recover the true text of the passage.

Retaining Χριστοῦ, and taking it (with Lightfoot and most other modern commentators) in apposition with μυστηρίου, we must likewise follow Lightfoot in taking it closely with the relative clause which follows. We may then say that the "mystery,"

4 And this I say, lest any man should beguile you with enticing words.

and knowledge. 4 I say this in order that no one may delude you with beguiling speech.

---

which in 1:27 was defined in *mystical* and *eschatological* terms as "Christ in you, the hope of glory," is now defined in *Gnostic* terms as "Christ in whom are all the treasures of wisdom and knowledge hidden." The language of the apostle is again pointed in reference to the immediate controversy. The Gnostic philosophy disturbing the church at Colossae is making its appeal as offering initiation into a "mystery" as the gateway to a secret lore. To Paul this is nothing but an attempt to **delude** believers **with beguiling speech** (vs. 4); for Christ himself is the depository of all truth. Emphasis is again laid on the comprehensiveness of Christ; all the treasures are in him, and there is no true secret lore which is not already available to Christians in him alone.

It is difficult to bring out the proper sense of ἀπόκρυφοι (**hid**), which is given great emphasis by its position at the end of the sentence. In what sense are **the treasures of wisdom and knowledge** which are in Christ said to be **hid**? The construction is not clearly indicated in either of our versions; it is not **in whom are hid all the treasures** (KJV), but "in whom are all the treasures, hidden." We are bound to ask why this emphasis is laid on the "hidden" nature of these stores of truth, when we should expect rather the affirmation that in Christ these things are *revealed*. The thought is certainly not that these treasures remain hidden in Christ, hidden even for those whom he enlightens. The words suggest rather that in Christ we have access to unlimited stores of truth, which are by their nature "secret," not the public property of the human race, but belonging to "the deep things of God" (I Cor. 2:10). The adjective is not equivalent to the perfect participle passive ἀποκεκρυμμένος (1:26; cf. I Cor. 2:7); it suggests not that these treasures are kept hidden by some decree of God, but that they are in their essential nature "hidden" or "secret," inaccessible to man except by revelation. The Colossian heretics boast of a secret lore, perhaps calling it ἀπόκρυφος; Paul agrees that there are indeed **treasures of wisdom and knowledge** which are ἀπόκρυφοι; but he affirms that these are all to be found in Christ.

The language of the clause is derived in part from Isa. 45:3 (LXX), "I shall give thee hidden treasures of darkness." The words are addressed to Cyrus, who is regarded by the prophet as the chosen agent of God. Paul may be consciously giving the words a secondary application to Christ, with a change of sense; but it is more likely to be an unconscious reminiscence of the language with which his mind is stored. It is also possible that the ἀπόκρυφοι of our passage is a gloss introduced through the recollection of the Isaiah passage.

4. Paul's aim in so addressing the Colossians is to keep them from falling victims to a clever propaganda: **that no one may delude you with beguiling speech**. The verb (παραλογίζομαι) means to "lead astray by false reasonings"; it implies that the danger of the new teaching lies in its appeal to the reason through a superficially plausible but fundamentally unsound dialectic. The term πιθανολογία (**beguiling speech**) has something of the same connotation; people are "talked into" accepting the teaching. In classical writers the word has the sense of a chain of argument falling short of mathematical demonstration, but affording good grounds for a given conclusion. In colloquial usage, however, it had come to have a bad sense, as in our expressions "fast talk" or "smooth line." It is well illustrated in this sense in a papyrus which speaks of thieves who "are trying to keep possession of their booty through πιθανολογία."

---

the problems of belief in the abstract, much less by acrimonious debate which puts the mind on the defensive and closes it to new truth, that understanding grows, but in "the fellowship of kindred minds." See Expos., 1:25-27 and also the Exeg., 1:26-27 for the sense in which **the knowledge of God's mystery, of Christ** may be

said to be **hid.** Spiritual maturity comes by growth, and growth comes by sharing in the loving relationships of a believing and serving Christian community. Remember the words of Jesus to the disciples, "I have yet many things to say unto you, but ye cannot bear them now" (John 16:12).

5 For though I be absent in the flesh, yet am I with you in the spirit, joying and beholding your order, and the steadfastness of your faith in Christ.

6 As ye have therefore received Christ Jesus the Lord, *so* walk ye in him:

5 For though I am absent in body, yet I am with you in spirit, rejoicing to see your good order and the firmness of your faith in Christ.

6 As therefore you received Christ Jesus

---

5. Paul concludes his justification of his intervention by assuring his readers that he does not feel himself a stranger or an outsider to them; and that far from accusing them of apostasy, he is eager to believe that they are standing firm in the faith. **Good order,** and **firmness** are terms of the military vocabulary; he compares the Colossian church to an army under attack, keeping its lines unbroken, showing the firmness which derives from confidence in the commander. Πίστεως **(faith)** is best taken as a subjective genitive; the thought is not of a firm faith, but of the firmness of life and conduct which results from faith in Christ.

One of the Church Fathers comments as follows: "He speaks of στερέωμα as if addressing soldiers who are posted firmly and in good order—no wile, no temptation shakes their ranks."

### C. THE VITAL CENTER OF THE CHRISTIAN'S LIFE: THE VICTORIOUS CHRIST (2:6-15)

This section of the letter resumes the theme of 1:15 ff., which was interrupted to allow Paul to justify his intervention by explaining the nature and scope of his ministry. He now begins to show his readers the consequences which follow from their participation in the cosmic work of reconciliation accomplished by Christ. Vs. 6 is connected in thought with the affirmation and the warning of 1:21-23: "You, who once were estranged, . . . he has now reconciled . . . in order to present you holy and blameless and irreproachable before him, provided that you continue in the faith, stable and steadfast." Now he urges them to this very stability and steadfastness, reinforcing his plea with a fresh statement of the pre-eminence of Christ and the vital relation with him into which they have entered. Once they have received him as Lord, Christ becomes the foundation and vital center of all existence for them; the **elemental spirits** to which they are invited to subject themselves are in fact subordinate powers whom Christ has overthrown by the victory of his death and resurrection, freeing his followers from their domination.

6. **As . . . you received Christ:** Παραλαμβάνω is used elsewhere in the N.T. in the sense of "receive as transmitted," "receive from teachers" (Gal. 1:9; Phil. 4:9), or more generally, "receive by revelation" (I Cor. 11:23). This is part of the meaning here—the words are an appeal to the Colossians to hold fast to the teaching about Christ as they

---

5. *Rejoicing to See . . . the Firmness of Your Faith in Christ.*—Paul returns again to the underlying note of confidence in his hearers, which inspires them to confidence in him, and encourages them to press on to the maturity of faith and soundness of doctrine which he desires and anticipates for them (see Expos., 1:3-4, 23).

6-7. *As Therefore You Received Christ Jesus the Lord, so Live in Him . . . Just as You Were Taught.*—This is the practical application of all that has gone before and of all that is to follow. The spirit of warm approval and commendation, a characteristic feature in all of Paul's letters, is never allowed to gloss over and obscure his dominant purpose in writing—to warn, correct, and inspire to fuller Christian

maturity. Sometimes it can be said of a good man that he is friendly but not influential. Paul could be friendly; he never failed to be influential. Now he is about to bear down. None of his readers is going to miss his meaning, or escape its challenge, by dwelling on the courtesies of social communication in which the letter abounds. It is a great thing to be able to come to the point.

**So live in him.** Note Paul's concern for spiritual nurture, as distinguished from an initial decision for Christ. The greatest evangelists give no less concern to the organization, instruction, and Christian enrichment of those who have already been brought into the faith than they give to the task of winning the unconverted.

7 Rooted and built up in him, and stablished in the faith, as ye have been taught, abounding therein with thanksgiving.

the Lord, so live in him, 7 rooted and built up in him and established in the faith, just as you were taught, abounding in thanksgiving.

---

have received it from Epaphras, and to found their whole life upon it; this thought is reinforced by the phrase "just as you were taught" in the next verse. But with the personal object here, the verb must include the further thought of "receive into the heart," so that the words become an appeal to the *experience* of the presence of Christ, which was the beginning of a new spiritual life for the Colossians. They have received, not a system of ideas that might become a subject of debate, but a person to whom they must now be loyal. **Live** or **walk**—περιπατεῖν in the sense of the Hebrew הלך—refers to the whole tenor of the moral life. The maintenance of this personal fellowship with the Christ whom they have received in the gospel is the sure protection against the allurements of a false doctrine that would bring them into subjection to other spiritual powers.

**7. Rooted and built up in him:** Taken with the verb of the preceding verse, we have at first sight a triple metaphor: the Christian life is treated as a pilgrimage ("walk"); a growing plant (**rooted**); a building in process of construction (**built up**). The metaphorical sense of περιπατέω ("to walk"), however, has practically vanished; and ῥιζέομαι ("be rooted") is often used of the sinking of the foundations of buildings and cities. Indeed, the mixture of metaphors would be intolerably violent if the literal meaning of these two verbs were retained; that which is "rooted" cannot be thought of as "walking." The two participles of vs. 7, therefore, must be taken as developing the injunction to "live in him," in terms of a single metaphor—that of a building under construction. Its foundations are to be sunk deep and firm in Christ as the solid rock on which the building stands; its superstructure is to be built up in the atmosphere of Christ's presence. Note that the first participle is a perfect: the laying of the foundations of life is not a process, but an established condition; the second participle is a present, denoting a continuing activity. Βεβαιούμενοι (**established**) is another present, again conveying the thought of a progressively increasing firmness. All three participles retain the imperative force of the governing verb, "Live in Christ: have the foundations of your life sunk deep in him; keep on building the whole structure of your life in him until it comes to completion; make it more and more firm." Τῇ πίστει (**in the faith**) may be taken as a dative of reference, as in both our versions; but it is probably better to treat it as a dative of instrument—"by the faith" which links you to Christ. This dative would then be attached to all three participles, not to βεβαιούμενοι alone; it is "by our faith" that we are enabled to found our lives upon Christ, to build, and to grow stronger.

---

Think of Francis of Assisi, Ignatius Loyola, Wesley—and Paul. It is one thing to sow the seed. It is another to cultivate the soil and raise a crop (see the parable of the sower, Matt. 13). A little of Paul's evangelistic preaching is recorded in Acts, and the glorious story of his first missionary impact on the Mediterranean world is related there. But all his epistles are addressed to those who had already been brought into the church. Every one of them deals with a crucial problem of belief, conduct, or Christian service, which if not solved, or if solved in the wrong way, might have undone, and certainly would have seriously frustrated, the work which had been so magnificently begun. One is tempted to elaborate, but the Christian teacher can make his own series of

studies on the misconceptions of Christian belief and practice which each epistle was written to correct. Such a series can be made to enrich greatly the thinking of the average church member. Even a cursory reading of the Pauline epistles, and indeed of all the N.T. epistles, will make abundantly clear the immense amount of time, thought, and care which Paul and the other leaders of the church devoted to the "sanctification" of the saved. Spiritual nurture is an essential part of evangelism. Note that to be **established in the faith** implies a continuing development and progress—being **built up in him.**

**Just as you were taught.** One of the most humbling and heart-warming experiences in life is to reflect on the best that one has learned

8 Beware lest any man spoil you through philosophy and vain deceit, after the tradi-

8 See to it that no one makes a prey of you by philosophy and empty deceit, ac-

---

**Just as you were taught:** A fresh assurance that Epaphras has imparted the whole truth to them, and that Paul is not interfering with his colleague's work, but merely seeking to consolidate it. The same scrupulous respect for the labors of others which made Paul always seek out untouched fields, where Christ had not been named, "lest [he] build on another man's foundation" (Rom. 15:20), leads him to affirm again and again his unqualified support of Epaphras.

**Abounding in thanksgiving:** This epistle lays repeated emphasis on thanksgiving as the unfailing mark of a healthy spiritual life (1:12; 3:15, 17; 4:2). The apostle may feel that the new doctrines can be a temptation only to those who are not sufficiently grateful to God for his gift of Christ, and therefore seek for something further.

**8.** Paul now begins his direct attack on the heretical teaching. Put forward under the proud banner of **philosophy,** it really lacks the substance of truth; it is a system of **empty deceit.** Its boasted antiquity is nothing more than **human tradition.** It leads men to revere **the elemental spirits of the universe,** at the expense of losing **Christ, . . . who is the head of all rule and authority** (vs. 10), including these very spirits whom God has **disarmed . . . and made a public example of them, triumphing over them in him** (vs. 15).

---

from great teachers. It may be assumed that Epaphras, because he based his witness on the enduring Christian verities, stood head and shoulders above the beguiling teachers of Colossae in intrinsic worth, though their occult lore and mystical rites may have had more publicity value at the time. Paul is not appealing for a slavish acceptance of what they have been told, but for a discriminating judgment under the guidance of trusted leaders.

**You received Christ Jesus the Lord.** The wonderful Christian message was not new and strange to them. Epaphras had brought it to them. They had heard it and accepted it. Paul is saying, as he said to the Christians of Thessalonica, "Prove all things; hold fast that which is good" (I Thess. 5:21). And, he adds in effect, do not fail to express gratitude for the new outlook, and the new life, which you have found in Christ—*abounding in thanksgiving.*

**8.** *See to It that No One Makes a Prey of You.*—Only after Paul has established confidence between himself and his readers in the bonds of Christian love does he come to the gravamen of his message to them. The long noncontroversial introduction has dwelt upon the common Christian faith which the Colossians hold with him and with Christians everywhere. Their minds have been elevated to inspiring contemplation of the pre-eminence of Christ in the whole universe, his reconciling and peacemaking power through the Cross, and his living presence in the church and in the experience of every believer. Then, but only then, Paul concentrates on the issue between them. If one must criticize, let his purpose be to persuade, not to denounce. If the purpose is to

persuade, let him first achieve mutuality with those whom he would correct. This is more than the art of persuasion. It is the wisdom, born of love, which wins to fuller wisdom. If all Christian controversy were on the high plane of this letter, truth would not suffer from its defenders.

The heretical Colossian teachers must have been very plausible and intriguing in their approach. Erroneous ideas can have a high degree of fascination, especially where they offer a short cut to truth for undisciplined minds, or an assurance of knowledge beyond human reach. They can be especially fascinating when they are sincerely believed by those who teach them.

To make a **prey of you** (RSV) or **spoil you** (KJV) has been variously translated—"getting hold of you" (Moffatt), "exploits you" (Goodspeed), "victimized" (Exeg.). E. F. Scott[7] pictures the Colossian teachers as "man-stealers," and the Exeg. describes them as "kidnapers." The word is emphatic. The Colossian church, at least a considerable number of its members, was being "taken in." L. B. Radford[8] suggests that the illusion was robbing them not only of their faith, but also of their intelligence, "stealing their brains," and making them incapable of discriminating judgment. A completely closed mind often characterizes those who have found a spurious security in the antirational dogmas of some fanatical religious sect. One cannot discuss truth with them because all evidence is distorted into conformity with the twisted perspective of their fixed ideas. One can get

[7] *Epistles of Paul to Colossians, Philemon, Ephesians,* p. 41.

[8] *Epistle to Colossians and Epistle to Philemon,* p. 223.

And Paul reminds his readers of all they have in Christ, which the **elemental spirits** cannot supply—**fulness of life** (vs. 10), and all the benefits which flow from Christian baptism.

The meaning of vs. 8 is: "Do not allow yourselves to be victimized by humbug masquerading as philosophy." The term translated by the RSV, **makes a prey of you,** is almost equivalent to "kidnap." The language reverts, as it were, to the figure of 1:13; the heretical teacher is pictured as a marauder who makes a foray against the kingdom of God, and seeks to carry off its inhabitants as spoil. **Philosophy,** in this single occurrence of the word in the N.T., is used in a bad sense, paired as it is with the phrase **empty deceit.** In classical writers the word appears always to have a good sense, as, literally, "love of wisdom," or more technically, "scientific pursuit of knowledge," or again as designating a particular body of philosophic doctrine—"the Ionian philosophy" or "the philosophy of the Academy." In later Christian writers contrasting attitudes are seen. Such men as Tatian and Tertullian denounce all philosophy, even in its highest forms; Justin Martyr, on the other hand, couples it with εὐσέβεια (piety), and Clement of Alexandria declares

---

through to them only (a) by the indirect approach of an attitude of Christian love and fairness, which Paul both teaches and practices throughout this epistle, or (b) by presenting truth in a coherent system of ideas that is close enough to their own thought patterns to make contact with them, and so provide a bridge by which their thinking can move into true Christian focus. It is the possibilities in this latter method which prompt Paul to use so many of the ideas and phrases of the Colossian heresy in his great summaries of the true Christian faith (see below). The Colossian teaching is strange to modern ears, but the lesson in these methods of approach is of perennial value.

Paul makes use of both approaches. He does not depend on love alone, on the assumption that the love which he has bestowed upon them gives him a kind of paternal right to control their thinking. "Mother knows best" is an attitude which aggravates and antagonizes those whose minds are reaching for an honest maturity. Nor does he depend on reason alone, as if anyone could be argued into a closer relationship to Christ. He respects their integrity, and approaches them with love guided by intelligence, and with intelligence illuminated by love.

**Philosophy and empty deceit.** Paul was not hostile to all philosophy. He has himself just concluded a noble statement of the centrality of Christ in the universe, using the terms and concepts of the current philosophy (1:15-20). What he repudiates is any philosophy that does not take into serious account the moral and religious contribution of the Christian revelation to the understanding of life (see Expos., 1:15). The phrase **empty deceit** need not imply insincerity and charlatanism in the Colossian teachers. They were more probably trying to harmonize Christianity with the prevailing religious outlook of the pagan culture which had molded their own thinking before the gospel came to them. They may well have been un-

aware that their attempted synthesis of Christian and pagan ideas was destroying the unique and liberating power of the new faith in Christ. But good intentions do not cancel out the bad effects of false ideas. The heretical teachers possibly thought that they were improving Christianity. They may have despised simple and unlearned Christians, and may have undertaken to give the new faith a wider appeal to the educated classes by reinterpreting it to the sophisticated minds of the intelligentsia. With their purpose Paul might sympathize, but with their errors he must deal plainly. Had their views prevailed, Christianity would have been absorbed into the prevailing culture. That is what was wrong with their philosophizing tendencies. Christianity is a revelation of the nature and purpose of God which transforms every merely human culture. Christians are not called upon to despise knowledge, nor the love of knowledge, nor the search for wider knowledge. But they are called upon to approach all knowledge in the light of Christ. "Avoid the godless chatter and contradictions of what is falsely called knowledge, for by professing it some have missed the mark as regards the faith" (I Tim. 6:20).

The immediate danger was that Christianity would become entangled with one of the fantastic, superstitious, and somewhat fanatical religious systems that abounded in Asia Minor.

Cosmological speculation, mystic theosophy, religious fanaticism, all had their home here. Associated with Judaism or with Christianity the natural temperament and the intellectual bias of the people would take a new direction; but the old type would not be altogether obliterated. Phrygia reared the hybrid monstrosities of Ophitism. She was the mother of Montanist enthusiasm, and the foster-mother of Novatian rigorism. The syncretist, the mystic, the devotee, the puritan, would find a congenial climate in these regions of Asia Minor.[9]

[9] Lightfoot, *Colossians,* pp. 95-96.

tion of men, after the rudiments of the world, and not after Christ.

cording to human tradition, according to the elemental spirits of the universe, and

---

boldly that it is the gift of God to the Greeks, conducive to piety, a schoolmaster to bring the Hellenic mind to Christ (*Miscellanies* I. 5).

It is not to be supposed that Paul is here showing himself hostile to all philosophy, but only to the fantastic angelology which is dignifying itself by that name at Colossae. In one of the Hermetic writings "philosophy" and "magic" are paired together as twin means of nourishing the soul. It is this lower kind of "philosophy" which calls forth Paul's scorn—not the kind of truth that has been apprehended by the severe discipline of investigation, but the mysterious lore which claims the sanction of ancient revelation. For Paul, mere antiquity is not a warrant of truth; **human tradition** carries no weight in comparison with the complete revelation of God in Christ.

Paul now comes to the cardinal error of this "philosophy": it teaches men to propitiate **the elemental spirits of the universe** instead of giving their allegiance to Christ. The word στοιχεῖα has a very wide range of meaning (see Intro., p. 140), but in this context only two senses need be considered. The word may be taken (*a*) in the sense of "the elementary things," the "A B C's"—in scornful belittlement of a doctrine put forward as something recondite; and τοῦ κόσμου will then introduce a further element of deprecia-

---

While such "fancy religions" still rise up to claim their devotees in modern times, the popular mind of today is more generally influenced by the skepticism and agnosticism which stem from serious philosophical inquiry, and by the humanistic worship of material science which characterizes a secular age. In any case, the cogency of Paul's warning remains. Whether the philosophy under consideration is the pseudo philosophy of Colossae, or the excursion into the occult of some present-day speculation, or the learned philosophy of modern rationalism and humanism, its interpretation of life will prove to be illusory and disappointing— **empty deceit**—if it fails to come to terms with the spiritual interpretation of life **according to Christ.**

**Human tradition.** Paul did not neglect the value of tradition as a steadying force, preserving the best from the experience of the past. His teaching is steeped in the religious traditions of his own people (see I Cor. 10:1-11). His letters to the Romans and to the Galatians cannot be understood without a sympathetic knowledge of the history and religious teaching of the Hebrews, which are preserved for us in the O.T. His philosophy of history includes all the past, finds the fulfillment of the quest of the ages in God's self-revelation in Christ, and gives significance to every stage of the agelong process of redemption in the final consummation of God's kingdom.

Furthermore, he frankly sought to establish and perpetuate a new tradition—the Christian tradition. "Just as you were taught," he admonished the Colossians. "I have received of the Lord that which also I delivered unto you"

(I Cor. 11:23), he wrote to the Corinthians, establishing the true tradition of the Communion. And again, "I delivered unto you first of all that which I also received, how that Christ died for our sins according to the Scriptures" (I Cor. 15:3), setting forth the authentic tradition of Christian teaching concerning the Resurrection. The Scriptures themselves, and the main line of Christian belief and practice based on them, became an authoritative tradition, correcting subjective misinterpretations of the leading of the Holy Spirit, and defending the church against numerous distortions of the faith, like the Colossian heresy.

As in the case of knowledge, so also in the case of tradition, what Paul bids Christians to repudiate is not knowledge and tradition as such, but spurious knowledge and **human tradition** which, whether explicitly or implicitly, depart from their soul and center in God's self-revelation in Christ. The word of God is not the product of human speculation, nor the creation of human culture. In Christ the word of God invades human culture to transform and redeem it.

Finally, Paul was not bound by tradition. Though he appeals here to the true Christian tradition—already established in Christ and in process of being verified in the experience of the church—as a means of correcting the erroneous compromises of the Colossians with pagan beliefs, he was no mere "traditionalist." In the fellowship of the living Christ, and in the creative presence of the Holy Spirit in the church, he found the divine power breaking through the hardening crust of human traditions, leading men of faith into new applica-

tion—"of the world," i.e., "belonging to the material realm; not heavenly, not spiritual." The phrase would then describe the Colossian teaching as based on "the rudimentary doctrines which belong to the world, not on Christ." This interpretation, though it has the weighty support of Lightfoot, does not appear to take sufficient account of the contrast κατὰ τὰ στοιχεῖα . . . οὐ κατὰ Χριστόν ("according to the στοιχεῖα, . . . not according to Christ"), which (b) indicates that Paul is here speaking of the στοιχεῖα as rivals of Christ, objects of human allegiance who are set in the place that belongs to him alone. There is, moreover, a good deal of evidence for the widespread use of the word in this sense in the vocabulary of the Hellenistic religious syncretism which is represented in one of its protean forms in the Colossian heresy. Here again Paul has seized upon one of the key terms of his opponents. In their "philosophy" the στοιχεῖα are related to the elementary substances of which the physical world is formed (earth, air, fire, and water; perhaps with the Empedoclean addition of love and strife), which are likewise the

---

tions of the truth in Christ, and liberating them from the dead hand of the past for fresh adventurings of love and brotherhood. See his treatment of the traditions of the Mosaic law in Romans and Galatians, and also our Lord's strictures on the scribes and Pharisees who obscured the divine guidance in the moral law under a heavy overburden of "the tradition of men" (Matt. 15:1-9; Mark 7:1-13). Paul's concern for the Colossians was that the tradition to which they adhered should be the *Christian* tradition. A similar concern should be ours when we speak with pride of "our tradition."

**The elemental spirits of the universe.** The Intro. and the Exeg. explain the origin and contemporary meaning of this conception in the Colossian theosophy. If one were to ask why Paul took so serious a view of this fantastic philosophy, instead of tolerating it as an unnecessary but harmless embellishment of plain Christianity, the answer must be that its moral effects were far from harmless. It involved a double peril.

First, it undermined man's belief in his freedom, and therefore also his sense of moral responsibility before God. The Exeg. describes the Colossian teaching as "astrological determinism." If man's nature and destiny are determined by the elements that make up the physical world, including the structure of the human body, whether these are considered simply as natural substances, or as natural substances controlled by spiritual beings and powers, then human personality is not spiritually free and self-determining, but the product of the interaction of these natural and amoral elements. This fatalistic doctrine has had a very modern recrudescence in the view that character and personality are determined not by moral choices, but by the particular combination of genes, hormones, and glandular secretions that make each individual human body what it is. On any such view, whether ancient or modern, both the sense of guilt and the

experience of forgiveness vanish with the lost conviction of moral freedom and responsibility. Instead of saying, "I have sinned," man learns to quip, "Don't blame me; it's my glands."

Second, carrying the Colossian teaching to what was apparently its further stage, if the elements of nature are assumed to have their counterparts in the stars and planets, and these in turn are believed to influence human life and destiny under the rule of the masters of the spheres—**the elemental spirits of the universe** —the same paralyzing fatalism casts its baneful pall over all human effort and moral aspiration. The superstitious fears of the forces of the universe, which plagued the pre-Christian Greek world, return, and man seeks a spurious salvation, striving to put himself into right relations with the powers that control his fate by cult practices that are likely to be devoid of moral quality. Salvation ("fullness of life") is promised through superstitious and puritanical cult rules—asceticism, taboos, angel worship, and festival celebrations related to the seasons and the ascendancy of the moon or the stars—which were supposed to bring the devotee into harmony with the natural and spiritual forces that ruled his life (see vss. 16-23). Such practices are without moral content and without moral result. At best they can give the devotee a subjective *feeling* of being in right relations with the universe, but such a feeling can be entirely divorced from reality. Since it is possible by such methods to achieve the feeling of "fullness of life," even when one's moral relations with God and one's fellow man are quite wrong and unworthy, the very quest of salvation along that road can literally demoralize the soul.

To revert to the modern parallel in the belief that genes, hormones, and glandular secretions make one's character what it is—this belief has also its counterfeit parallel to the spurious way of salvation which was taught in the Colossian heresy. Disciples of this modern naturalism are inclined to expect that pills, injections, and

9 For in him dwelleth all the fulness of the Godhead bodily.

not according to Christ. 9 For in him the

constituents of the human frame (a microcosmos in relation to the macrocosmos); and they are related at the same time to the great constellations, and conceived as astral divinities which control the spheres and are thus masters of human fate. The doctrine which Paul combats, then, appears to involve (a) an exposition of the nature of the physical world and man's place within it in terms of astrological determinism; and (b) instruction in the cult practices (asceticism, taboos, angel worship) which will propitiate these astral spirits and enable the devotee to attain fullness of life.

9. Paul finds the refutation of this false doctrine in the true apprehension of the surpassing greatness of Christ. This he had already unfolded in general terms in 1:15-20; now he takes up the central phrase of that passage (vs. 19) and draws out its consequences in direct relation to the Colossian doctrine of angelic mediators. **Bodily** (σωματικῶς) may be taken to mean "incarnate" (Lightfoot); but it is not so understood by the ancient fathers, and it is probably better to interpret it as meaning "genuinely" (i.e., not figuratively; so Cyril), or "in a body," "as a *corpus*, not as *disjecta membra*," in contrast with the distribution of divine attributes among the στοιχεῖα.

serums will do for the "patient" what Christ and the prophets once did for the soul. A balanced personality and wholesomeness of life are sought by means of physical, biological, or psychological "adjustments." One must have the greatest respect for the immense contribution of medical science and psychology to the improvement of physical and mental health. This is great gain. But the assumption that right *moral* relations with God and one's fellow man will *automatically* spring from physical and mental changes is an ancient illusion which outdates the Colossian heresy itself. A man may be healthy in body and well enough integrated in personality to get along famously in this world and yet be an unregenerate character, engrossed in self-centered pursuits, and living away from God. Moral salvation consists in the response of the moral will to the righteous purpose and the forgiving love of the living God. It is imparted to those who are brought into vital relationship with Christ, by first learning of him, and then committing their lives to him. "Be not conformed to this world: but be ye transformed by the renewing of your mind, that ye may prove what is that good, and acceptable, and perfect will of God" (Rom. 12:2).

9-10. *In Him the Whole Fulness of Deity Dwells Bodily, and You Have Come to Fulness of Life in Him.*—The stress is on the reiterated phrase **in him.** It is Christ—not "the elemental spirits of the universe," nor any speculative system for achieving a supposed harmony with the universe, but Christ—who provides the clue (a) to right relations with the world outside us in the widest sense (**fulness of deity**), and (b) to right relations with oneself, true integration of the personality (**fulness of life**). He is

the source, and he provides the spiritual dynamic of right living, both in the contemporary context of our lives and in the eternal context of our relationship with God.

As has already been stated, the danger in these schemes of mystical speculation is a moral danger. In addition to their unreality, they tend toward a primitive type of religion in that they make religion a quest for harmony with sources of sheer power, in disregard of the insistence of all prophetic religion that the power behind the universe is a *moral* power, loving righteousness and hating iniquity. Christ in his human incarnation (**bodily**) has fully revealed the moral nature and the loving heart of God, and by his spiritual presence imparts the power to live a life of moral rectitude in loving obedience toward God, and in unselfish good will toward one's fellow man. This is "the liberty wherewith Christ hath made us free" (Gal. 5:1). In no other way has God so identified himself with his sin-shackled world, and so imparted the forgiveness of divine love and the power to live the good life, as he has done in and through Christ. And no condition, circumstance, or power in all the universe can frustrate the saving work in the soul of "the grace of the Lord Jesus Christ and the love of God and the fellowship of the Holy Spirit" (II Cor. 13:14), except one—man's deliberate exercise of his own God-given freedom to refuse the new life which God offers. It is in this sense that Christ is **the head of all rule and authority.** The Colossian Christians had nothing to fear and nothing to hope from "the elemental spirits of the universe," in which they were being persuaded to place their confidence to the neglect of Christ. Nor has any Christian, however overawed he may be by his

| | |
|---|---|
| 10 And ye are complete in him, which is the head of all principality and power: | whole fulness of deity dwells bodily, 10 and you have come to fulness of life in him, who is the head of all rule and authority. |

**10. You have come to fulness of life in him:** More literally, "you have been fulfilled," "you are fulfilled" in him. The perfect (πεπληρωμένοι) indicates that the fulfillment which is promised in return for worshiping the "elemental spirits" is already realized in Christ. Πληρόω in this sense is doubtless a technical term of the new teaching, interpreted in relation to the idea of the ascent of the soul through the spheres, over which the elemental spirits hold **rule and authority.** For Paul the Christian believer is already in communion with God; no spheres or spirit rulers bar his way; his "life is hid with Christ in God" (3:3). It remains for him to live and act on the assurance that Christ has brought him fulfillment, not to seek new ways of access to a goal already attained.

This fulfillment is realized in Christ because he is the **head of all rule and authority,** i.e., every rank of spiritual being is subordinate to him and derives from him whatever powers it is able to exercise. The "elemental spirits," as inferiors, cannot offer men anything that is not given by their head. **All rule and authority** is again to be taken in

seeming utter dependence upon the impersonal "laws" of the natural world, or by his seeming helplessness before the demonic forces at work in human society, provided he is in vital personal relationship with Christ.

**Fulness of life.** Man needs to be saved not only from his fears, but also from false hopes. He is constantly seeking fullness of life in what cannot give fullness of life. An example of this error is the Colossian quest for salvation by identity with the "powers" of the natural universe, to the neglect of the righteous and loving God revealed to the world in Christ, who is the real power at the heart of the creation. There are numerous other instances, both ancient and modern. Man is prone to seek power rather than goodness, and often to the neglect of goodness. We even crave spiritual power while ignoring the moral conditions of spiritual power. We want to live successful lives, but pay less attention to our duty to live good lives. Simon the magician was mightily impressed by the *power* of the Holy Spirit which made Peter and John so influential in the early church. He tried to buy that power, offering them money and saying, "Give me also this power" (Acts 8:19). He might have thought to use it for his own ends, or he might have intended to employ it beneficently, but his chief aim and ambition was to possess power. Peter shamed him with a ringing declaration of the moral conditions of spiritual power, "Thou hast neither part nor lot in this matter: for thy heart is not right in the sight of God" (Acts 8:21).

In one disguise or another Simon the magician is still with us. The Colossians were offered by pseudoreligious teachers a technique for reaching "fullness of life" through harmony with "the elemental spirits of the universe." Mod-

erns, afflicted with fears, anxieties, inferiorities, and frustrations, are offered, and eagerly seek, psychological techniques for tapping the spiritual forces of life in order to correct faults of personality, and so achieve skill, efficiency, power, and success. These counsels are frequently put forth with the authority not only of psychology, but of religion. The Bible is brought to witness, and the great principles of living recorded in Scripture—confidence, faith, trust, prayer—are cited in corroboration of these rules for achieving mental poise in the interests of successful living. Now all this may be right and sound, but it may be grievously wrong. It is right if the purpose and goal of such teaching is to assist troubled people to lead more Christlike lives in fuller acceptance of the will of God for them and for the world. It is dangerously wrong if the purpose and goal of such mental and spiritual training comes subtly to be the achievement of power to live successfully for one's own self-centered ends. One writer cites the tributes of certain psychologists and psychiatrists to the supreme wisdom of the psychological laws to be found in the Bible.[1] In reference to the ability to shake off regret and remorse over the irrevocable past so as to prevent it from frustrating constructive living in the present, Paul is quoted: "Forgetting those things which are behind, and reaching forth unto those things which are before, I press toward the mark" (Phil. 3:13-14). What mark? The question needs to be asked. For the psychiatrist the rule may apply to any mark, including the goal of personal security and power. For the Christian there is only one mark, "the high calling of God in Christ Jesus." Paul

[1] Norman Vincent Peale, *A Guide to Confident Living* (New York: Prentice-Hall, 1948), pp. 117, 125-26, 152.

the sense of "every principality and power" (cf. 1:16)—two of the classes of στοιχεῖα being put for the whole array in all its gradations. At first sight it appears strange that Christ should be declared to be the head of an array of spirit powers which are uniformly regarded in this epistle as holding men in thrall. But it must be remembered that Christ remains the sovereign Lord of the whole creation, even when it is alienated from God. The στοιχεῖα, like men, are created beings; they are not independent of God, and such powers as they are permitted to exercise are derived from God through Christ. But their dominion over human life, such as it is, does not extend to those who believe in Christ. It is not necessary to suppose that Paul himself believes them to have any such dominion even over unbelievers; he simply does not stop to argue that point; for his immediate purpose it is sufficient to affirm that believers have nothing to fear and nothing to hope from them, since they are in any case subordinated to Christ.

thought it important to add that. For without that latter phrase the rule for achieving mental power may be "according to the elemental spirits of the universe," but it falls far short of being "according to Christ," and may even miss that mark altogether.

Another psychiatrist cited the great words in Ephesians, "having done all, to stand" (Eph. 6:13), as the wisest psychiatric statement ever made. Do the best you can. Do all you can. When there is nothing further to be done, stand. Stop fretting. Let the matter rest. Trust God to work it out. This is all very true in the biblical context. Perhaps the psychological law will work, subjectively at least, in any context, even in the quest for personal success and prosperity. The apostle of Christ evidently thought it important to state the purpose and goal for which the stand is to be made and the cause which it is to serve. "Wherefore take unto you the whole armor of God, . . . truth, . . . righteousness, . . . the gospel of peace, . . . faith, . . . salvation, . . . the sword of the Spirit, which is the word of God, . . . prayer and supplication in the Spirit" (Eph. 6:13-18). Apart from this context the psychological rule may work, but there is no guarantee that it will work "according to Christ."

A third instance is the saying of Jesus, "All things, whatsoever ye shall ask in prayer, believing, ye shall receive" (Matt. 21:22). A psychiatrist commended this as a great statement of the healing and power-releasing force of faith. True again, but entirely false if any should think, as many are prone to do in a success-worshiping age, that prayer is a wonderful means of enlisting the forces in the universe to fulfill one's own self-centered desires. Note the qualifying moral condition, the spirit of forgiveness, that follows Mark's version of these words (Mark 11:24-26); also Luke's statement that what the Father shall give to those who pray is the Holy Spirit (Luke 11:13); and the tremendously significant condition which invariably accompanies the statements of this

promise of Jesus in the Fourth Gospel, "in my name" (John 14:13-14; 15:16; 16:23).

**In him.** Paul repeats the phrase four times in this paragraph (vss. 8-15), and the parallel phrase, "with him," he reiterates three times more. All men seek "fullness of life." Many follow false hopes. It is Christ in whom the divine nature comes right into the welter of human life and human history so that all men can understand and know what God is really like; in whom real "fullness of life," as it is in God, dwells **bodily**, i.e., in the Incarnation, or in the concentrated unity of one unique personality—it is Christ who brings men to true "fullness of life." Without Christ what did union with the "elemental spirits of the universe" amount to, or what will modern techniques for the adjustment of personality achieve?

The Colossians had been beguiled by the thought of a more developed spirituality and a broader based salvation than could be found in Christ—a mystical identity with cosmic energies to be achieved by the fanatical disciplines of self-centered cult worship. Their motives may have been to find a more assured release from the fears and anxieties of life than they believed to be offered in the gospel, or to achieve power and success in their own undertakings, of a sort that the Christian stress on right relations with the righteous will of God did not seem to guarantee. Perhaps both motives were present. But they were following a false hope.

**You have come to fulness of life.** The Colossians had already been brought into the freedom of spiritual union with the one transcendent God. They had tasted true "fullness of life" in Christ—in the moral purity of his teaching; in the joyful experience of the divine forgiveness; in the assurance of complete reconciliation to God, whose love in Christ "endured the cross, despising the shame" (Heb. 12:2) to lift mankind into a new redeemed relationship with himself; in the enduring spiritual fellowship with him—"alive together with him" (vs.

11 In whom also ye are circumcised with the circumcision made without hands, in putting off the body of the sins of the flesh by the circumcision of Christ:

11 In him also you were circumcised with a circumcision made without hands, by putting off the body of flesh in the cir-

---

**11.** Paul now enlarges upon the benefits that Christians already enjoy by virtue of their faith in Christ; he draws out the particulars of "fulfillment." The physical circumcision which the false teachers require of them is needless, since Christian believers have already received a spiritual circumcision. The mention of circumcision suggests the inclusion of a Jewish element in the Colossian syncretism. The demand for circumcision, however, has not the same basis as in the Galatian dispute. There it involved the relation of Christianity to Judaism and arose out of the attempt to keep Christianity permanently a Jewish sect, to compel all Christians to become members of the national community. At Colossae there is no suggestion of nationalism. Circumcision is required as an act of dedication; as the rite, or part of the rite, of initiation into the "mystery" of the στοιχεῖα cult. Paul affirms that such a rite is meaningless for a Christian who has already received **a circumcision made without hands,** i.e., an effectual dedication of his whole being to God, carried out in the realm of the spiritual, the ultimately real. "Made with hands" and "not made with hands" (χειροποίητος, ἀχειροποίητος) are frequently contrasted thus in the N.T. in the sense of "the material" as against "the spiritual," "the symbolic" over against "the real." Thus in Heb. 9:24: "Christ is not entered into the holy places made with hands, which are the figures of the true; but into heaven itself." A circumcision "made with hands," then, could at best be only figurative; Christians have already experienced the spiritual reality which the physical operation symbolized; cf. Rom. 2:25-29; and especially Phil. 3:3: "We are the true circumcision, who worship God in spirit, and glory in Christ Jesus, and put no confidence in the flesh."

The spiritual circumcision is now contrasted with the literal in respect of its effect, which consists in **putting off the body of flesh.** Σάρξ (flesh) is used here in the peculiar ethical sense which it frequently has in Paul's writings; it means not the physical nature as such, nor yet the carnal passions, but the corrupt personality as a whole—what man is in himself apart from the regenerating grace of God. Σῶμα (body) is used in the sense of "sum total" (not of the human body, which has not been "put off" in any sense). The

---

13)—which Christ achieved for human beings, as never before, by living one unique human life of complete love and perfect goodness, which he bestows upon all who open their lives to his Spirit. All this they had already known and accepted.

In the light of all this their return to pagan speculation, at least the possibility of their return under the spell of misguided teachers (Paul never abandons his confidence that apostasy is a peril which they will surmount), would be a superstitious error, a lapse from the free spiritual religion into which Christ had brought them, back to the poor lower level of selfish and misguided salvation-seeking from which Christ had set them free. It would be a decline to the former unregenerate nature—"the body of flesh" (vs. 11)—enslaved by false fears, beguiled by false hopes, and engrossed in false desires, which had been put off when they had by their own choice been baptized into the life

of identity with Christ, for the high adventure of Christ-centered living, as servants of their fellow men in the spirit of Christian love.

In short, the moral salvation which Christ has achieved and which he imparts to the believer is the absolute and ultimate salvation, and the rich fruits of that salvation in creative living attest the identity of the believer with the real Power behind the universe, in contrast to the spurious and morally irrelevant identity with "the elemental spirits of the universe." There simply is no fuller life for man, no greater security in all the universe, than the spiritual integrity of a Christian life, irrevocably pledged to Christ, and meeting the uncertainties of this world in the free self-offering to God of a moral and spiritual faith.

**11-15. The Victory of Christ.**—The reader is referred to the Exeg. for the interpretation of the typical Pauline thought forms in which the fullness of the salvation wrought by Christ is set

12 Buried with him in baptism, wherein also ye are risen with *him* through the faith of the operation of God, who hath raised him from the dead.

cumcision of Christ; 12 and you were buried with him in baptism, in which you were also raised with him through faith in the working of God, who raised him from the

---

phrase **body of flesh,** then, has nothing like the same meaning it has in 1:22, where it is used of the physical human body of Christ. Here it can mean only "the whole of our lower nature," which is "put off" and "cast away" (this would give the force of the double compound ἀπεκ-), discarded as a filthy garment. There is no suggestion in the N.T. that the physical in itself is depreciated or regarded as a source of defilement (see I Cor. 6:13-20).

The spiritual circumcision is further described as **the circumcision of Christ.** The genitive Χριστοῦ is subjective; it is Christ who effects the circumcision, dedicating us to God.

**12. Buried with him in baptism** (KJV); not **and you were buried** (RSV) but "in that you were buried." The participle is epexegetic; it does not introduce the thought of an additional experience, but defines in fresh terms the content of the idea of "spiritual circumcision." Not baptism itself, but the spiritual experience represented in baptism is the "spiritual circumcision." Paul is not glorifying one external rite in order to depreciate another; for that reason, perhaps, he avoids the usual technical term βάπτισμα in favor of βαπτισμός. (Both βαπτίσματι and βαπτισμῷ are well attested; but the former is clearly the easier reading; and the latter enjoys a strong combination of Alexandrian and Western support [p46 B with D and G].) Elsewhere in the N.T. βαπτισμός is not used of the Christian sacrament, but of ceremonial lustration or "washing"—"washing of cups and pots and vessels of bronze" (Mark 7:4). Here, however, the apostle clearly thinks of Christian baptism. As in Rom. 6:3 ff., he assumes it to be common Christian knowledge that the experience symbolized and made effective in baptism is a mystical participation in the death and burial of Christ.

The clause **in which you were also raised with him** may be taken, as in both our versions, as dependent on **baptism,** continuing the exposition of the idea of a "spiritual circumcision"; or it may be taken in parallelism with "in whom also ye are circumcised" (vs. 11) as a second line of interpretation of the "fulfillment" of vs. 10. The former connection is probably the simpler; the thought of mystical participation in the death and burial of Christ leads naturally to the thought of participation in his resurrection. It should be observed, however, that while in Rom. 6 the Christian's participation in the resurrection of Christ lies in the realm of eschatological expectation (note the futures in vss. 6, 8), here it is regarded as already realized. If we are convinced of the authenticity of the letter, we shall be obliged to see an indication here of a trend in Paul's thinking—a lessening of his absorption in the future consummation and a deepening of his appreciation of the benefits which Christians have already realized in Christ (see also on 3:3-4). This change of emphasis might well be hastened by the controversy with a party which taught that the work of Christ needed to be supplemented by angelic powers.

---

forth—spiritual circumcision, baptism into Christ, death to sin and resurrection to new life, the transcendence of the law, and victory over the powers of this world. A word may be added about the last two of these.

The victory of Christ is complete and decisive. (*a*) **Having canceled the bond which stood against us with its legal demands.** He overcame man's helpless bondage to the moral law, his hopeless involvement in the guilt of

his failure to fulfill its absolute demands. These "counsels of perfection" stood over against man, requiring his obedience, and therefore condemning his disobedience. Christ has supplanted their negative authority over us—**nailing it to the cross**—with the creative authority of his sacrificial love. He removes the guilt and the power of sin, both of which shut us out from moral freedom. He brings us into a new life of free and forgiven union of spirit with himself,

13 And you, being dead in your sins and the uncircumcision of your flesh, hath he quickened together with him, having forgiven you all trespasses;

14 Blotting out the handwriting of ordinances that was against us, which was contrary to us, and took it out of the way, nailing it to his cross;

dead. 13 And you, who were dead in trespasses and the uncircumcision of your flesh, God made alive together with him, having forgiven us all our trespasses, 14 having canceled the bond which stood against us with its legal demands; this he set aside,

---

Paul now makes it clear that he does not think of baptism as a magic rite; the spiritual transformation which the Christian experiences in baptism is made effective **through faith in the working of God** (cf. Rom. 10:9). 'Ενέργεια **(working)** conveys the thought of God's power as active within the Christian. Believing that God raised Christ from the dead, we believe that the same life-giving power is exercised with us.

**13.** The "death" from which God has raised them is now defined not in terms of the symbolic dying to sin which is represented in baptism, but of their former spiritual state—they were **dead in trespasses and the uncircumcision of** [their] **flesh.** The datives (παραπτώμασιν, ἀκροβυστίᾳ) are causal—"by reason of your trespasses," etc. The strange expression **uncircumcision of your flesh** cannot in the context be taken in the literal sense of their condition as Gentiles (cf. "uncircumcised in heart and ears," of Jews, in Acts 7:51). Their outward "uncircumcision" is merely the token of their unregenerate nature, as not dedicated to God, which has expressed itself in transgressions of his law.

**Having forgiven us all our trespasses:** Their former state is considered under a double aspect: it was a state of spiritual death, from which they have been raised to the new life which they share with Christ; and it was marked by transgressions, offenses against God, which he has graciously forgiven. The tense of the participle is best taken as the aorist of coincidental action; forgiveness does not precede the awakening to new life but accompanies it; it is in fact the same act of divine grace viewed under a different but complementary aspect. Cf. Rom. 5:21, and indeed the association of the two groups of thought in the whole passage (vss. 12-21)—sin, condemnation, and death on the one hand; grace, forgiveness, and eternal life on the other.

**14.** Not only are our past transgressions forgiven, but the legal ordinances themselves are no longer in force against us. Paul uses a vivid metaphor. **Having canceled** (ἐξαλείψας, another aorist of coincidental action) means literally "rubbing off," as the ink would be rubbed off a sheet of papyrus. Χειρόγραφον **(bond)** may be used of any document written by hand; but in ordinary business usage it means a "note of hand" —an acknowledgment of debt given in the handwriting of the debtor. Probably this technical sense should not be insisted upon too strongly; like γράμμα (II Cor. 3:6-7), it represents simply the law as a written code. The dative τοῖς δόγμασιν—**with its legal demands** (literally, "in decrees")—depends on the idea of writing contained in χειρόγραφον. The new life is not governed by legal ordinances, by obedience to an external code, but by its own inward relationship to God in Christ. We have here a new expression of the fundamental thought of Paul, that Christians "are not under law but under grace" (Rom. 6:14-15).

The canceling of the bond is now represented under a different figure which has never been clearly explained. **God set** [it] **aside, nailing it to the cross.** It has been sug-

---

a life in which "love is the fulfilling of the law" (Rom. 13:10).

All this is the work of God, not of man. It does not arise from man's efforts of propitiation. It springs from the initiative of the divine love. (*b*) **He disarmed the principalities and powers.** He completely sweeps away man's moral sub-

servience to the impersonal or evil powers of the universe. When one is brought into loving fellowship with the God who is really in control of his universe and free to work his sovereign will, and when one is committed to use his own freedom so as to serve the good purposes of God in this world, then all the powers in the

COLOSSIANS 2:15

15 *And* having spoiled principalities and powers, he made a show of them openly, triumphing over them in it.

15 He disarmed the principalities and powers and made a public example of them, triumphing over them in him.[d]

[d] Or *in it* (that is, the cross).

---

gested that in some areas of the ancient world, when decrees were nullified, a copy of the text was nailed up in a public place. No evidence has been discovered for such a custom, but the words certainly suggest a reference to some familiar procedure of cancellation. Whatever the origin of the figure, the underlying thought remains the same—that the abrogation of the law is effected through the death of Christ. Paul does not stop to explain precisely how he understands this result to have been effected; the context would suggest that he thinks of the sacrifice of Christ as a full payment of the indebtedness which mankind has incurred to God through sin.

**15.** The thought now returns to the point from which it started—the futility of hoping for anything from angelic mediation. The work of Christ, which has been shown to mean for us resurrection, forgiveness, and emancipation from the bondage of legal ordinances, is now represented as breaking the dominion of all other spiritual powers which have reigned in our lives. In keeping with the conception of these spiritual powers as personal, Paul depicts the breaking of their dominion under the figure of a military defeat, and the parade of the vanquished in the triumphal procession of the conqueror. God has stripped them of their arms, displayed them in public as his trophies of victory, leading them in captive chains at his chariot wheels (θριαμβεύσας). As the forces in conflict are spiritual and invisible, the theater of this display must be taken to be in the invisible world. In the Cross the heavenly and the earthly meet; and the historical event has suprahistorical significance, being conceived as the decisive act in a cosmic drama of redemption (cf. on I Cor. 2:6-8). The mighty spirits which once held men in their "dominion of darkness" (1:13-14) are now reduced to impotence. The concluding **in him** ends the paragraph as it began, with the assertion that all the blessings of God come to man in Christ.

For Paul the government of life by legal ordinances belongs solely to the condition of man as unredeemed, as still in subjection to the elemental spirits. Once we are brought into the kingdom of God's Son, the laws of the old order are not applicable; in that kingdom life is not governed by "legal demands" (vs. 14) but by love. This association of ideas is now made the basis for Paul's repudiation of the ascetic and ceremonial requirements laid down by the heretical teachers. As Christian believers are not subject to the spiritual powers, now dethroned, they are under no obligation to submit to artificial regulations of conduct or of worship.

---

universe, both natural and moral, personal or impersonal, can neither frighten him, nor tempt him, nor can they paralyze his resolve to serve God in the creative obedience of a morally free life.

In vs. 8 the veneration of the "elemental spirits of the universe" appears to be a cultivation of powers which will aid the devotee and assist him to "fullness of life." In vs. 15 they appear to be hostile powers which were dreaded because they held man under an evil influence. Both views prevailed in the ancient world, and, as we have seen, the cult which was infiltrating the Colossian church probably sought favorable relations with the powers of the universe in the spirit of the times, both because of false

fears and because of false hopes. God's revelation of his real nature in Christ sweeps away the moral paralysis which this congeries of ideas inflicts on the mind of man. By the sheer moral magnitude of his life, and by the dominance of creative love, Christ has conquered fear, sin, death, and the demoralizing influences of human insecurity. The Christian need no longer think of himself as the impotent product of the forces of nature, nor as a helpless cipher in the operations of impersonal law. Through the free spirit of Christ indwelling his life he becomes a responsible and creative moral force, the transformer of the material world, a master of circumstance, a molder of his environment, a builder of brotherly relations among men, a

199

| 16 Let no man therefore judge you in meat, or in drink, or in respect of a holyday, or of the new moon, or of the sabbath *days:* | 16 Therefore let no one pass judgment on you in questions of food and drink or with regard to a festival or a new moon |

## D. Ascetic and Ritual Regulations Condemned as Alien to the Christian Life (2:16-23)

Paul now comes to a devastating criticism of the δόγματα or "legal demands" (vs. 14) of the Colossian heresy. These ascetic and ritual regulations are a mere shadow of the truth; they are the product of human vanity and disregard of the living sovereignty of Christ over all areas of life (vss. 16-19); they belong to the worldly order, to which Christians died when they were baptized into Christ, and cannot help us to overcome the impulses of our lower nature (vss. 20-23).

16. The **questions of food and drink** are probably requirements to abstain from eating flesh and drinking wine. **Festival, . . . new moon, . . . sabbath** denote yearly, monthly, and weekly cultic rites respectively. There are clear indications here of a strain of Jewish influence in the Colossian syncretism; but these prohibitions and ritual observances are not harnessed to a Pharisaic legalism or even to the worship of the one God, but to the propitiation of "the elemental spirits." The prohibitions go beyond anything in the Jewish law in touching drink as well as food; and it is probable that these requirements were not based upon any distinction of "clean" and "unclean" foods, but on principles of asceticism. No such principles enter into the Jewish food laws.

sharer in Christ's redemptive purpose to transform "man's world" into God's kingdom. When the disciples returned from their mission to herald the gospel of spiritual freedom in Christ, our Lord said, "I beheld Satan as lightning fall from heaven" (Luke 10:18).

The words anticipate Paul's vivid testimony to "the finished work of Christ." He [God] disarmed the principalities and powers, . . . triumphing over them in him [Christ].

16-23. *Therefore Let No One Pass Judgment on You, . . . Disqualify You.*—Having dealt with the doctrinal basis of this strange heretical cult, Paul turns to (a) their code of conduct—ascetic rules and regulations; and, (b) their forms of worship—the worship of supposed angelic powers.

They could be disqualified in two ways: by deliberately following these false teachers, expecting to find moral and spiritual guidance from a source that was spiritually bankrupt; or by being so overawed by the arbitrary claims to a higher spirituality that were being advanced by the devotees of this fanatical and semipagan cult that they would begin to doubt either the reality or the adequacy of their spiritual relationship with Christ, and so be lured back into the religion of externalism and superstition from which Christ had set them free.

There must have been something pathetic to Paul in the spectacle of timid and wistful, or gullible and misguided, Christians seeking a higher spiritual security than they had already found in the liberating gospel of our Lord. Even more than the Galatians, these Phrygian Christians were in danger of being "entangled again with the yoke of bondage" (Gal. 5:1).

Sheer pity and compassion for these people who were "as sheep not having a shepherd" (Mark 6:34) must have awakened in him a sense of spiritual outrage that men should so misunderstand Christ. Outrage must have aroused him to a great resolve to declare and proclaim, with such ringing testimony that none could fail to understand, the whole truth as it is in Christ. Paul's perennial passion was to commend Christ so convincingly that the hesitant, the half persuaded, and even the deluded and beguiled could not fail to find in the faith and fellowship of the church not less force of conviction than they could find in the superstitious cults and sects, but more; not less assurance of faith, but more; not less wisdom and understanding of life, but more; not less joy, happiness, helpfulness, brotherhood, and wholesome fellowship, but more—in short, not less real spirituality, as the Colossian heretics claimed, but more (see I Cor. 9:19-23). Is it so with a modern church, with its leaders, with its members?

Perhaps this explains why Paul's references to the Colossian cult are so allusive and fragmentary. They are incidental to his main concern. Paul would never be content just to dissect, analyze, and pillory this Colossian doctrine with the systematic thoroughness of a devastat-

17 Which are a shadow of things to come; but the body *is* of Christ.

18 Let no man beguile you of your reward in a voluntary humility and worshipping of angels, intruding into those things

or a sabbath. 17 These are only a shadow of what is to come; but the substance belongs to Christ. 18 Let no one disqualify you, insisting on self-abasement and worship of

---

**17. Shadow of things to come:** These words refer particularly to the sacred seasons which are kept by the heretics. Paul suggests that these observances had meaning only as foreshadowing symbolically a reality that was still to be revealed; as this reality is now present in Christ, the observances have no longer any meaning. **Things to come** means, of course, things which lay in the future when the observances were ordained; not things which still lie in the future. The **things to come** have come with Christ.

**18. Let no one disqualify you:** The verb καταβραβευέτω (**disqualify**) belongs to the figure of the race for the prize of "an incorruptible crown," under which the Christian life is often represented (I Cor. 9:24-27; Heb. 12:1; etc.). It expresses more picturesquely the same thought as "let no one pass judgment on you" (vs. 16); the sense is, "let no one impose upon you his arbitrary standards of Christian conduct; do not feel yourself inferior because your own life is not governed in the way that he declares to be necessary." Tender consciences are often needlessly disturbed by the condemnations pronounced by the "unco guid," who make profession of a superior piety. The verb may indeed be taken to mean "deprive you of the prize of victory"—**beguile you of your reward**—as the judge of the games might rule the victor in the race ineligible to receive the prize; but surely in this sense only God could be the author of such a disqualification. It does not seem possible to interpret the words as a warning that the acceptance of this artificial way of life will in fact render them ineligible for "the prize of the high calling of God in Christ Jesus."

**Insisting on self-abasement:** It is doubtful whether θέλων ought to be taken, as here, in the sense of "insisting on," "delighting in"—a sense for which few examples can be cited, and those poor and doubtful (see Dibelius' note); or whether we should connect

---

ing argument and then drop the matter. Nothing much is accomplished by proving that a man's faith is wrong unless he is led "to find a stronger faith his own." [2] Paul knew the stronger faith. He refers to the mistaken faith in only a few swift comments which expose its shallowness and falsity in order to go on to confirm his readers in the confidence of their full salvation in spiritual union with Christ. The constructive critics of religion are those who can offer a truer faith to replace the beliefs which they deride and expose.

One may deplore the false gospels in which wistful or willful people misguidedly seek salvation today. It may be important and very necessary to denounce secularism, paganism, humanism, the intellectual worship of science, the moral worship of success, or the worship of the false gods of race, state, and power by which the human ego seeks to fulfill and perpetuate itself. One may view with scorn, or with pitying condescension, the superstitious and strange beliefs by which multitudes still seek to unite themselves with the ultimate forces of the universe in quest of the spiritual security which all

men need—astrology, numerology, pyramidism, spiritualism, soul culture, and a host of other cult doctrines and practices which still win converts in our day. But when all is said and done, no one will come even within sight of making his words and influence, as it were, a modern "Epistle to the Colossians," unless he stands where Paul stood, and can persuade, as Paul persuaded, misguided men out of empty spiritual wandering into the maturity of positive and personal faith in Christ.

The confident assurance which Paul enjoins upon wavering and uncertain Christians, **Let no one disqualify you,** is no mere appeal to individualism. It goes far beyond the modern idea of spiritual autonomy, that every man has an inalienable right to believe anything or nothing, as he chooses, provided that he does not interfere with the exercise of a similar right by his fellow men. Freedom of worship is an essential right of man, but it is only the precondition of a positive faith. The principle on which Paul stands is not the illusory doctrine that freedom will automatically lead men to truth, but the biblical principle that the truth will make men free (John 8:32).

[2] Tennyson, *In Memoriam*, Part XCVI, st. v.

the participle closely with the imperative, giving it the well-established sense of "willingly," "gladly"—let us say, "at the prompting of his own will," "arbitrarily." The whole construction, if we adopt this latter sense for θέλων, will then parallel the construction in vs. 16, ἐν indicating the ground of the arbitrary condemnation—"let no one disqualify you as he wills [not at all as God wills], in questions of humility [self-abasement] and worship of angels." The apostle here seems to have in view the leader of the new cult, though he does not name him. This individual makes much ado about the virtue of humility, on which all Christian teachers insisted; and he seems to have taught that a proper humility would prompt men to show due respect to the angels, i.e., "the elemental spirits" of the cosmos, by offering them worship. He apparently supported this teaching by an appeal to his own attainment of mystic insight which had come to him through initiation—he was **taking his stand on visions.**

The phrase which is so translated—ἃ ἑώρακεν ἐμβατεύων—is not entirely clear; it means, literally, "entering into what he has seen." Many later copyists inserted a negative,

---

That is why his words **Let no one pass judgment on you** are preceded by the all-important **therefore** (vs. 16), which bases the spiritual independence, in which he bids his readers stand, on the great affirmations (vss. 8-15) of the fullness of truth and spiritual freedom which they have found in Christ and have received from him. It is truth, not freedom, which can disarm error of its power to delude and destroy. Freedom is but truth's opportunity.

The Colossian mysticism is rejected on three counts: First, it enforced a false asceticism which was held to be the necessary means of purifying the life from mundane influences so that the devotee could ascend to supposed higher realms of the spirit. This teaching involved a repudiation of the faith of other Christians who did not accept and follow the prescribed ascetic rules. It therefore encouraged the deadly sin of spiritual pride. These arbitrary rules had an **appearance of wisdom** (vs. 23). They required a puritanical self-discipline, and produced in those who practiced them a **rigor of devotion** (vs. 23) and even **severity to the body** (vs. 23), but they were entirely arbitrary and artificial—**according to human precepts and doctrines** (vs. 22)—and therefore quite devoid of any real relation to true moral and spiritual living, which is essentially an expression of the spirit of Christian love in the material and personal relationships of life. The Hebrew element in the Colossian teaching is seen here. Some of these ascetic practices seem to have been taken over from Judaism. Like the scribes and Pharisees, the Colossian cultists incurred our Lord's condemnation of the legalism which made the strict observance of external rules, whether negative prohibitions or the positive requirements of outward ritual, a substitute for true spiritual morality. "Whatsoever thing from without entereth into the man, it cannot defile him; because it entereth not into his heart. . . . For from within, out of the heart of men, pro-

ceed evil thoughts" (Mark 7:18-19, 21). Such morally irrelevant practices are spiritually stultifying because they delude the devotee into the false assurance that a spiritual result will flow from a material cause (see Isa. 29:13).

In addition to this, the Colossian asceticism went beyond anything prescribed in the Jewish Law. It probably contained elements of the Greek and Oriental belief—which was quite foreign to Jewish thought—that the material world is inherently evil, and that the sphere of salvation is not in this world at all, but in the realm of pure spirit. This delusion contained a double danger. (a) It fostered the idea that a positive spiritual life would inevitably follow from the negative practice of renouncing the things of this world. Withdraw from the material and you will automatically be absorbed into the spiritual. This is far removed from Christian spirituality, which is a positive self-dedication to Christ in every relationship of life, both material and spiritual. "Know ye not that your body is the temple of the Holy Ghost which is in you, which ye have of God, and ye are not your own? For ye are bought with a price: therefore glorify God in your body, and in your spirit, which are God's." (I Cor. 6:19-20.) (b) Paradoxically this view that the material world is inherently evil produced a disguised but deadly materialism. Excluding the material from the sphere of salvation, it encouraged in the first place the antinomian belief which the early church had constantly to repudiate, i.e., the belief that one could achieve harmony with the spiritual powers of the universe in complete disregard of his conduct in the material and physical world. Provided that one was "spiritually" saved, he could do anything he liked in this material world, a doctrine which often encouraged gross sensuality and extremely materialistic living in practical human relationships. This does not seem to have been the chief fault in the Colossian practice,

| which he hath not seen, vainly puffed up by his fleshly mind, | angels, taking his stand on visions, puffed up without reason by his sensuous mind, |

feeling that the apostle must have denied the reality of the visions to which the heretic made appeal; and thus the text took the form which is rendered in the KJV, **intruding into those things which he hath not seen.** But Paul is not yet turning to the criticism of this man's position; he is merely stating it. Unfortunately the precise meaning of ἐμβατεύω in this context cannot be determined. It was, however, shown to be a technical term in the language of the mysteries by its use in some inscriptions from Asia Minor, in association with μυέω—"initiate"; it refers to an act of entry which follows initiation (Wilhelm Dittenberger, *Orientis graeci inscriptiones selectae* [Lipsiae: S. Hirzel, 1903-5], Vol. II, No. 530: θεοπρόποι ἦλθον . . . οἵτινες μυηθέντες ἐνεβάτευσαν—"messengers came who received initiation and entered in"). By "entering in" to the inner sanctuary, which was forbidden to the uninitiated, the inquirers received a revelation from the god at first hand, as it were. But it remains doubtful whether the verb can properly take for its object ἃ ἑώρακεν—"what he has seen"; in the inscriptions, at least, the thought is not that of "entering into visions," but of entering into the place of vision. Perhaps Paul had heard

which tended rather toward a burdensome asceticism. But in the second place this conception of the essentially evil quality of material things produced another kind of materialism that was very much in evidence in the Colossian doctrine. Their teaching, interest, and major concern concentrated on material things. Their ascetic prohibitions focused the attention of the devout on **things which all perish as they are used** (vs. 22). They sought spiritual salvation by really concentrating their attention on the material things which they professed to despise. Furthermore, their preoccupation with material things was negative and repressive. Their attitude showed little or nothing of the creative Christian dedication of material things to the service of the ethical goals of love and brotherhood. They were failing to grasp the essential meaning of the Incarnation, that through the grace of God in Christ the spiritual can invest, transform, and glorify the material conditions of life. They were really still engrossed in the material, for all their pretensions to high spirituality, and were not experiencing the moral dynamic which faith, and hope, and love, when centered in Christ, can impart to life in this world.

E. F. Scott comments that

it has often been observed that the same type of religion which runs to asceticism may fall, just as easily, into the opposite extreme. When the attitude to the bodily life is essentially morbid, it is pretty much a matter of accident whether you practice an ascetic rigour or a gross sensuality.[3]

This is the interpretation of the difficult and variously translated last clause of ch. 2 that is

implied in the RSV: **They** [the ascetic rules] **are of no value in checking the indulgence of the flesh** (vs. 23) .

Contrast this asceticism as an end in itself with the rigorous self-discipline to which Paul subjected himself in order that he might attain a Christian character by fulfilling a Christian purpose in this world (I Cor. 9:27). Note also the morally wholesome ascetic rules which Jean Frédéric Oberlin drew up to discipline his will when, at the age of twenty, he set down on paper a formal declaration, yielding his will to the purposes of God.

I shall compel myself to do always the opposite of what my sensual inclination would require of me.
I shall eat and drink but little . . .
I shall try to master the temper that sometimes sways me . . .
I shall fulfill the duties of my condition with the utmost exactness and the greatest punctuality.
I shall always keep separate some part of my earnings, to give to the poor.[4]

Paul rejected the Colossian mysticism for a second reason. Its worship of angels was a mystical construction of the merely human imagination which (a) like the asceticism already mentioned, fostered a false spiritual pride toward those who did not join in the esoteric cult practices, and which (b) offered a pseudo-spiritual salvation by uniting the worshiper with the nonmoral forces of the universe. The ascetic practices were linked with the occult quest of union with the supposed heavenly rulers. The holy days, festival, new moon, and sabbath, taken over from Judaism, were associated with the periods of the year which were

[3] *Epistles of Paul to Colossians, Philemon, Ephesians,* p. 61.

[4] Marshall Dawson, *Oberlin, A Protestant Saint* (Chicago: Willett, Clark & Co., 1934), p. 20.

19 And not holding the Head, from which all the body by joints and bands having nourishment ministered, and knit

19 and not holding fast to the Head, from whom the whole body, nourished and knit

---

the jargon of the cult without concerning himself greatly about its precise application; perhaps he is simply breaking out into scornful ejaculations, and the two parts of the phrase should be taken as disconnected from each other, so that Paul is saying in effect: This man, with his talk of "what he has seen," his "entering in." Whatever uncertainty remains in the details of interpretation, the words reveal clearly enough that the Colossian angel worship has some of the aspects of a mystery cult, and that its leader boasts that he has been himself admitted to the highest degree of initiation and has seen the mystic vision.

In the apostle's view this sort of thing is no proof of spiritual excellence, but quite the reverse; the man is **puffed up without reason by his sensuous mind,** and has lost contact with Christ (vs. 19), from whom all true spiritual health and progress derive.

Neither **fleshly** (KJV) nor **sensuous** (RSV) seems to convey accurately the true meaning of the Greek τῆς σαρκός. Here again σάρξ has the peculiar ethical sense which Paul seems to have created for it by his own usage; it stands over against πνεῦμα ("spirit"), not as that which is gross or low in human nature, but as signifying the whole of human nature in its unredeemed state at all levels. The "mind of the flesh," then, is not so much a mind dominated by sensuousness as a mind which lacks spiritual enlightenment. The apostle is affirming that all the mystical experiences of which the Colossian teacher boasts, all his vaunted revelations and elaborations of secret lore, are nothing but the products of his own mind, working with its own resources in alienation from God.

**19.** In this verse Paul reverts to the thought of Christ as the Head of every principality and power. Taking the word **Head** figuratively, he develops the idea of the functions of

---

held to be under the special influence of various heavenly bodies, and the heavenly bodies were regarded as being under the control of angelic powers, "whether thrones or dominions or principalities or authorities" (1:16). By some kind of mystical initiation the worshiper sought a vision of the angelic realms, as a result of which he would achieve union with the heavenly beings, and so be brought into harmony with "the elemental spirits of the universe," with consequent assurance of their guardianship over his life. The whole thing was a presumptuous and valueless pretense to supernatural knowledge. It had no relation whatever to the ethical faith and spiritual fellowship for which Paul never ceased to pray on behalf of his Colossian brethren, "that you may be filled with the knowledge of his will in all spiritual wisdom and understanding, to lead a life worthy of the Lord, fully pleasing to him, bearing fruit in every good work and increasing in the knowledge of God" (1:9-10). Christ was lost from sight in a supposed hierarchy of angels. The devotee laid claim to a superior spirituality, but this was only human pride—**puffed up without reason** (vs. 18). The **humility** (KJV)—**self-abasement** (RSV)—which he assumed toward the angelic powers was accompanied by a most unworthy arrogance toward his fellow men and even toward his fellow

Christians. (See I Cor. 8:1, " 'Knowledge' puffs up, but love builds up." Contrast the use of the same word in I Cor. 13:4, where we are told that "charity [or love] . . . is not puffed up.") Furthermore, the higher spirituality of which the cultist boasted was really a materialistic desire for personal security through a supposed self-identity with the forces and powers of the material universe. It was the product of a **sensuous mind**—not a sensual mind, although, in view of the warning in 3:5, one wonders what the ethical condition of these Colossian sectarians may have been, but a mind obsessed by material considerations (see the Exeg.).

**Taking his stand on visions** (vs. 18). The Expos. of 1:9-10 stresses the essentially ethical nature of the great visions which are recorded in the Bible. The visions of the Colossian cult were of an entirely different kind—secret experiences of mystical contemplation, fantastically speculative, and completely subjective. There is no evidence that would liken them to the visions of the great mystics of Christian history, which came spontaneously to crown the culminating response of sensitive and disciplined souls to God, the ultimate reality, and which produced great Christian characters. The Colossian visions were restricted and bound to the deliberate practice of a prescribed ritual. Not

together, increaseth with the increase of God.

**20** Wherefore if ye be dead with Christ from the rudiments of the world, why, as though living in the world, are ye subject to ordinances,

together through its joints and ligaments, grows with a growth that is from God.

**20** If with Christ you died to the elemental spirits of the universe, why do you live as if you still belonged to the world?

---

the head in relation to the body, in an elaborate physiological metaphor. In ancient physiology (see Lightfoot's citations from Hippocrates and Galen) the head was regarded as the center and source of all the vital forces, supplying the body with all that it requires for health and growth, and not merely the seat of the directing intelligence. In Eph. 4:16, the same metaphor is used with reference to the co-operative functions of the body and of its several parts, in dependence on the head. Here the thought is concentrated on the absolute predominance of the head, and on the fact that in separation from the head there can be no life or growth in the body at all. As the Colossian teacher is **not holding fast to the Head,** it is impossible for him to contribute to spiritual growth—**a growth that is from God.**

**20.** Paul here reverts to the significance of Christian baptism (vs. 12) as effecting the transition of the believer from one sphere of life to another. The rule of "the elemental spirits" extended only over the old life, to which the Christian has died through his mystical participation in the death of Christ. With the abandonment of the old life, the **regulations** which belong to the cult of the elemental spirits have ceased to be valid; they have force only within the sphere of "the world" (κόσμος—translated "universe" in the first clause, and "world" in the second), not in the invisible realms of the spirit, which are the sphere of the new life. **To submit to regulations** is to fall back into the conditions

---

only were they incommunicable and indescribable, but they lacked verification in the higher qualities of ethical and spiritual living which authentic visions always inspire. One might ask concerning the visions of this cult, "So what? What came of them?" The chief result, according to Paul, was a man **puffed up without reason by his sensuous mind.** The real content of the vision seemed to be a self-centered indulgence of feeling, emotionally elating, ego inflating, and, worst of all, brother berating (vs. 18).

Paul, who seems to have had a sympathetic understanding of all sorts and conditions of men, and of all types of religious experience, knew about visions. He also knew how to put them in their proper place in a full and rounded Christian life. His account of "visions and revelations of the Lord" at the close of II Corinthians ends on this high note, "I will very gladly spend and be spent for you; though the more abundantly I love you, the less I be loved" (II Cor. 12:15). His speech in vindication of his lifework before the hostile mob in Jerusalem contains an account of the vision of the Lord which came to him while he prayed in the temple. Note his description of it. Paul "saw him *saying unto me,* Make haste, and get thee quickly out of Jerusalem, . . . for I will send thee far hence unto the Gentiles" (Acts 22:18,

21). That vision brought him face to face with the divine moral imperative for his life. In it he got his marching orders for that great career of pioneering Christian service. Similarly, in the account which Paul gave to King Agrippa of his vision on the Damascus road, the compelling summons of Christ to consecrated action simply towers over everything else in the experience, "Rise, and stand upon thy feet: for I have appeared unto thee for this purpose, to make thee a minister and a witness" (Acts 26:16). "Whereupon, O king Agrippa," says Paul in that immortal testimony, "I was *not disobedient* unto the heavenly vision" (Acts 26:19).

Did any Colossian devotee get from his vision that kind of directive for practical Christian action? Did the mystical experience send him forth to live a life for Christ, "in journeyings often, in perils of waters, in perils of robbers, in perils by mine own countrymen, in perils by the heathen, in perils in the city, in perils in the wilderness, in perils in the sea, in perils among false brethren; in weariness and painfulness, in watchings often, in hunger and thirst, in fastings often, in cold and nakedness" (II Cor. 11:26-27)—or to any comparable equivalent in terms of his own circumstances and opportunities? Apparently not.

One can select from the biographies of great Christians his own list of truly creative visions.

21 (Touch not; taste not; handle not; 22 Which all are to perish with the using;) after the commandments and doctrines of men?

Why do you submit to regulations, 21 "Do not handle, Do not taste, Do not touch" 22 (referring to things which all perish as they are used), according to human pre-

---

of the old life from which Paul's readers have been delivered in their baptism. Notice that the if-clause is not so much a condition as an assumption, which is made the basis of the appeal. The real sense is: "Knowing that you died with Christ, why do you allow others to impose upon you regulations which are not relevant to the life of the redeemed?"

**21.** Samples of the regulations are quoted. Chrysostom comments: "See how he mocks them." The prohibitions probably apply to food and drink (cf. vs. 16); possibly also to the opposite sex (cf. I Tim. 4:3: "who forbid marriage and enjoin abstinence from foods which God created to be received with thanksgiving").

**22.** Paul has two grounds of objection to these prohibitions: they **perish as they are used**, and they are based on **human precepts and doctrines**. There is no justification for the intrusion of the phrase **referring to** (RSV). The clause is difficult, but the relative ἅ does not refer to the things prohibited, but to the prohibitions themselves. The thought is simply that legal ordinances of whatever kind have no permanent validity. The clause sums up the doctrine with which Paul wrestles in Galatians and Romans, that the whole system of law is not fundamental to the religious life, but is a discipline for the immature.

---

Francis of Assisi's mystic experience of Christ, to the point of self-identification with the "stigmata," does not stand alone, but in vital relationship with that joyous life of loving service as Christian brother of the common man. Albert Schweitzer is not given to mystical visions, but he relates the moral nature of the intuition that shaped his career:

While at the university and enjoying the happiness of being able to study and even to produce some results in science and art, I could not help thinking continually of others who were denied that happiness by their material circumstances or their health. Then one brilliant summer morning at Günsbach, during the Whitsuntide holidays—it was in 1896—there came to me, as I awoke, the thought that I must not accept this happiness as a matter of course, but must give something in return for it. Proceeding to think the matter out at once with calm deliberation, while the birds were singing outside, I settled with myself before I got up, that I would consider myself justified in living till I was thirty for science and art, in order to devote myself from that time forward to the direct service of humanity. Many a time already had I tried to settle what meaning lay hidden for me in the saying of Jesus! "Whosoever would save his life shall lose it, and whosoever shall lose his life for My sake and the Gospel's shall save it." Now the answer was found. In addition to the outward, I now had inward happiness.[5]

E. Stanley Jones has disclosed the remarkable spiritual experience that lifted him out of a

series of seemingly incurable nervous collapses to set his feet on the road of strenuous Christian service which he has followed from that day to this. After his first eight years in India he was convinced that his health was shattered:

It was one of my darkest hours. At that time I was in a meeting at Lucknow. While in prayer, not particularly thinking about myself, a Voice seemed to say, "Are you yourself ready for this work to which I have called you?" I replied: "No, Lord, I am done for. I have reached the end of my rope." The Voice replied, "If you will turn that over to me and not worry about it, I will take care of it." I quickly answered, "Lord, I close the bargain right here." A great peace settled into my heart and pervaded me. I knew it was done! Life—abundant Life —had taken possession of me. . . . For days after that I hardly knew I had a body. I went through the days, working all day and far into the night. . . . I seemed possessed by Life and Peace and Rest—by Christ himself.[6]

Note the predominance of the voice, claiming the response of the will in practical Christian service. Recall also the significance of the voice which came to John R. Mott in his early days, saying, "Seekest thou great things for thyself? seek them not" (Jer. 45:5), to confirm him in the choice of that career which has meant so much to the cause of Christ in all the world.[7]

The Christian does not take his stand on mystic visions, but on the message of the divine

⁵ *Out of My Life and Thought, An Autobiography*, tr. C. T. Campion (London: George Allen & Unwin; New York: Henry Holt & Co., 1933), pp. 84-85. Used by permission.

⁶ *The Christ of the Indian Road* (New York and Nashville: Abingdon-Cokesbury Press, 1925), pp. 23-24. Used by permission.

⁷ George C. Pidgeon, *The Indwelling Christ* (New York: Oxford University Press, 1949), p. 58.

23 Which things have indeed a show of wisdom in will-worship, and humility, and neglecting of the body; not in any honor to the satisfying of the flesh.

cepts and doctrines? 23 These have indeed an appearance of wisdom in promoting rigor of devotion and self-abasement and severity to the body, but they are of no value in checking the indulgence of the flesh.*e*

*e* Or *are of no value, serving only to indulge the flesh.*

**Human precepts and doctrines:** As in Matt. 15:9, the words are taken from a well-known passage of Isaiah (29:13—LXX), but they are applied in a quite different sense. In the gospel passage the thought is that the plain intent of the law is evaded by casuistical elaborations—the Pharisees "nullify the word of God for the sake of their tradition." Here the thought is that the prohibitions themselves are of human framing, entirely lacking divine sanction.

**23.** This verse is full of obscurities. Paul again appears to be picking up key terms of his opponents, only to deny that the things of which they brag are really marks of a higher religion and morality. They claim for their cult three aspects of superior excellence. First, it is a "voluntary worship" (**will-worship**), probably in the sense that each devotee accepts it willingly for himself in glad personal adhesion. Second, it lays stress on **humility** (cf. vs. 18). Third, it imposes a severe physical asceticism (**severity to the body**). It is possible, however, to take all three expressions as Paul's own description of the cult, and thus expressions of disapproval. **Will-worship** would then have the sense of a cult devised by the devotees at their own fancy, not as willed by God; the idea of willfulness would extend into the **humility**, giving it the bad sense of a needless **self-abasement**; and the ἀφειδίᾳ σώματος would be taken to mean a fanatical **severity to the body** or a shameful **neglecting of the body**, implying on either interpretation a failure to give to the body the honor due to it as sanctified by the presence of Christ (cf. I Cor. 6:15 ff.).

voice to his life, directing and guiding him in paths of moral obedience and loving service. The fault and delusion in the visions of the Colossian cult lay in that whatever the initiate saw or thought he saw, no divine voice sounded through the mystery; the word of God laid no moral imperative upon his soul. Long on the selfish privileges of self-centered contemplation, their visions were short on the all-important matter of Christ's summons to moral obedience in a life of practical service.

Paul's third reason for rejecting the Colossian heresy was the most important of all. Instead of interpreting Christ it obscured him, and beguiled men away from their real moral and spiritual dependence on him

**Not holding fast to the Head** (vs. 19). Here was the root cause both of their false asceticism and of their false mysticism. They were looking to the wrong source for moral and spiritual salvation. Christ was subordinated to a hierarchy of supposed spiritual powers who were believed to exercise the real control and guidance of human lives. And in those powers, mere constructs of the speculative human mind, the revelation of the personal nature of God, his moral purpose, his redeeming love, and his

everlasting mercy, was simply not to be found. Nor could the joy of reciprocal fellowship with the living personal God be experienced in the worship of these vaguely conceived and largely impersonal beings.

There are many ways of **not holding fast to the Head.**

(*a*) When Christianity is presented as a system of religious ideas and moral principles, a "way of life," or a type of civilization, to the neglect of the source of these ideas in a vital experience of the power of Christ in one's own life, we are **not holding fast to the Head.** Christianity is more than a moral code. It is a living fellowship with Christ.

(*b*) When the correct doctrines about the "headship of Christ" are held and proclaimed, without knowing Christ as the Lord of our own lives, we are **not holding fast to the Head.** Christianity is more than a theology. It is union with Christ.

(*c*) When men are persuaded to accept the church, its teaching, fellowship, and program, as the source and goal of all Christian living, we are **not holding fast to the Head.** In and by itself, as a human institution, the church, or any branch of it, can become, as the Colossian

3 If ye then be risen with Christ, seek those things which are above, where Christ sitteth on the right hand of God.

3 If then you have been raised with Christ, seek the things that are above, where Christ is, seated at the right hand of

---

The former interpretation is preferable in that it allows us to give to ταπεινοφροσύνη (humility) its normal sense of a Christian virtue. Part of the seductive power of this new teaching lies in the fact that it does not challenge the validity of the Christian moral ideal in principle, but professes to bring it to a higher degree of perfection. Its ascetic doctrines can be said to have an appearance of wisdom in the appeal which their key words—"voluntary worship, humility, severity to the body"—have for Christian ears. In spite of this adoption of Christian terminology, however, they are profoundly anti-Christian. Paul evidently intends that his concluding phrase shall convey a devastating criticism of the practical effects of the system, but unfortunately the words as they stand are not clear; probably the text is corrupt. The KJV renders them literally—not in any honor to the satisfying of the flesh. The phrase not in any honor must be the counterpart to appearance of wisdom—above; the general sense is, "These seemingly wise precepts are really a form of nonsense, undeserving of respect." It is very difficult, then, to take πρός in the sense of "to remedy" or in checking (RSV); the examples from medical treatises, which are adduced by Lightfoot and others to justify such a force, are not really applicable. The only possible sense here is "to promote" indulgence of the flesh. The grammatical connection is not clear; but there can be no doubt that Paul's last word on the subject is the affirmation that the subjection of life to such a system of rules and regulations is nothing but an inverted form of self-indulgence. The alternative rendering of RSV is the better—are of no value, serving only to indulge the flesh.

### E. The True Sphere of the Christian Life (3:1-4)

The apostle here turns from the negative side of the argument to the positive. In 2:12 he set forth the double aspect of Christian baptism as representing, or rather as sacramentally effecting, the participation of the believer with Christ in death to this world and resurrection to the life of the world to come, life eternal. As dead with Christ,

---

teachers were threatening to make the church of Colossae, a purveyor of its own ideas, an apostate church, teaching a code of conduct and a way of salvation that depart more and more from God's revelation of his will and purpose in Christ, without the moral perspective, or the spiritual dynamic, to rise above the outlook of contemporary human society. Christianity is more than the church. It is Christ. The church by itself is a headless body. He is the head.

Christianity as a law of life, a way of living, or a "fellowship of kindred minds" is an emasculated Christianity. The living Christ is the Lord of thought, the Lord of the soul, the Lord of all life, and the church's Lord.

The whole body. Cf. the parallel passage in Eph. 4:15-16. The Colossian sectarians were a splinter movement, individualistic, self-centered, divisive, in danger of departing more and more from the faith which was "bearing fruit and growing" in the whole world (1:6). Paul called them back to their unity in Christ. The modern churches are reaching after their lost unity in Christ. As in the body, there must be diversity in unity, but not divisiveness. What holds all in

unity is Christ, as he was, is, and ever shall be. Furthermore, the church derives from its vital union with Christ not only its unity, but also its growth, its spiritual dynamic, its moral guidance, its capacity to fulfill increasingly God's redemptive will for the world. In vital union with Christ the church grows with a growth that is from God. Two things are implied: (a) It is God, not the human membership or the human leadership of the church, who supplies the life and power by which the church grows. (See I Cor. 3:6-7, "I have planted, Apollos watered; but God gave the increase. So then neither is he that planteth any thing, neither is he that watereth; but God that giveth the increase.") (b) The growth is not mere growth in numbers, prestige, influence, or activity, according to any merely human standard of progress. In vital union with Christ the growth of the church will conform to the divine nature and will, fulfilling God's purpose for his church.

3:1. If Then You Have Been Raised with Christ, Seek the Things that Are Above.—The discussion is now raised to higher ground. The problem is put in its eternal context. The pass-

the Christian, he argued, is forever removed from the sphere of the elemental spirits, and the ascetic regulations which their service imposes have no further validity for him. Now he sets forth the converse truth: as risen with Christ from death to a new and heavenly life, the Christian is to focus all his thoughts and desires upon heaven, the sphere of his risen and exalted Master. The whole tenor of his existence upon earth is to be transformed in the light of this new relationship. Instead of seeking (vainly) to win his way to heaven through an earthly discipline, he must seek to give effect in all earthly relationships to the heavenly nature which he shares with Christ. Thus Paul expounds in a new context the doctrine which occupies so large a place in Galatians and Romans and indeed in all his thinking—that the moral life of the Christian believer is not the *means* by which he seeks to win salvation, but the necessary *consequence* of the new relationship to God in Christ, into which he enters by faith.

**3:1. If then you have been raised with Christ:** The particle οὖν **(then)** indicates that the apostle is taking up, under a complementary aspect, the great change accomplished

---

ing references to the inadequacy and downright error of the earth-bound Colossian quest of salvation have been made. True to his unwavering principle never to be content just to refute error, always to be eager to establish men in the truth, Paul quickly returns to the positive and persuasive proclamation of the gospel. If, on the face of it, it seems to be wishful thinking to believe that "We needs must love the highest when we see it" [8]—the Colossians, who had been won to Christ, were turning again to a lower and mistaken faith; at least there was a live possibility of their doing so—nonetheless, we never shall love the highest unless we do see it. A Christian whose aim is to persuade and win rather than to denounce and reject will win nobody unless he presents the highest in so clear, convincing, and satisfying a way that his readers or his hearers must come to life's inevitable moral choices in full knowledge of what the highest is.

Though all the winds of doctrine were let loose to play upon the earth, so Truth be in the field, we do injuriously . . . to misdoubt her strength. Let her and Falsehood grapple; who ever knew Truth put to the worse, in a free and open encounter? [9]

One must admit that men can love darkness rather than light because their deeds are evil, but even then the darkness does not overwhelm the light and put it out (John 1:1-5; 3:19). Paul lifts their thoughts from earth-bound speculation to fix them in steady focus on Christ, who is "the way, the truth, and the life" (John 14:6). The best way to commend Christ is to proclaim him, not to become entangled in endless arguments about what is not Christ. So Paul breaks into one of those great declarations of the truth in Christ in which the N.T. abounds.

It is worth pausing to note how many of the immortal passages of Scripture were called forth by just such a situation as this. One might expect that the most inspired expressions of Christian truth, and the most creative moments of Christian witness, would come only when the human environment was most favorable. This is sometimes true, as when the Holy Spirit descended on a prepared and expectant company at Pentecost, though it must not be forgotten that the wider context of their meeting was a world that had just crucified Christ. It is always true in the sense that God cannot declare himself without dedicated lives to be the channels of his will. Without Paul, the consecrated servant of the Lord, there would have been no Epistle to the Colossians. Basically, however, the gospel is not the crown and flower of a wholesome civilization that moves inevitably toward it. The gospel is God's invasion of a sinful and lost world. The strongest kind of evidence of the power and love of God in this world is found in the events of history which show how God, working through devoted Christians, has released into the most unpromising and discreditable human situations creative influences for good. There is a toughness in the gospel that can outface the opposition of the world. Truth can stand up to error.

I cannot praise a fugitive and cloistered virtue, unexercised and unbreathed, that never sallies out and sees her adversary, but slinks out of the race, where that immortal garland is to be run for, not without dust and heat. Assuredly we bring not innocence into the world, we bring impurity much rather; that which purifies us is trial, and trial is by what is contrary.[1]

Christ took the measure of sin. The divine love shines forth most gloriously from the Cross. And when the human situation is most unfavorable, those who count as the mightiest factor

[8] Tennyson, *Idylls of the King*, "Guinevere," l. 652.
[9] Milton, *Areopagitica*.

[1] *Ibid.*

2 Set your affection on things above, not on things on the earth.

God. 2 Set your minds on things that are above, not on things that are on earth.

---

through baptism, which was advanced by him in 2:20 as the ground of his appeal for the rejection of the disciplines imposed by the heretical teachers. If baptism marks the end of life in the realm of darkness where the elemental spirits hold sway, it also marks the initiation of life in the kingdom of light and love where the sole ruler is Christ. It remains for the Christian to direct his aspirations toward that unseen realm in which the resurrection life is centered, to **seek the things that are above.** Though we think of this realm figuratively as **above,** it is not to be defined spatially, but in relation to the presence of Christ. **Above** means for us the sphere in which Christ lives and reigns. As **seated at the right hand of God,** Christ is enthroned as the universal king, entrusted with all power in heaven and on earth. We are released from all lower allegiances in order that we may acknowledge him alone, and govern our lives in accordance with his will.

**2. Set your minds:** The imperatives ζητεῖτε and φρονεῖτε are in the present tense to indicate a continuing attitude, in contrast with the aorist συνηγέρθητε, which refers to the accomplished experience of resurrection with Christ. The thoughts of our minds, like the aspirations of our hearts, are to be kept fixed on the heavenly realm into which our life has been transferred.

---

in their environment the influence of Jesus Christ can turn a negative situation into an occasion of great good for the world.

Consider three of the best-known and best-loved passages of Scripture that occur in quick succession in I Corinthians. One might expect them to have arisen from an atmosphere of peace and joy and faith, where kindred minds kindled one another in love. But the human situation was all against them. Paul's great summary of the Holy Communion, which has hallowed that sacred feast throughout all Christendom, and is the earliest written account of the Communion that we have—I Cor. 11:23-26 —what prompted him to write that? A most unseemly, snobbish, and degrading misuse of the Communion in the Corinthian church. Paul's noble hymn on the supremacy of Christian love—I Cor. 13—what human situation evoked those inspiring words? A discreditable and love-destroying dispute, born of human pride, as to who could claim the highest spiritual attainments. Paul's magnificent affirmation of the life everlasting, which has lifted the hopes of the bereaved into eternity in every Christian generation—I Cor. 15—what led him into that immortal declaration of immortal life? A barren intellectual dispute over human theories of the life beyond.

So here, in the Epistle to the Colossians, a materialistic distortion of Christian truth into endless confusions of earth-bound fancy is the utterly unpromising human situation into which one man, whose life was "hid with Christ in God," was led to inject deathless affirmations of the deathless life in Christ. The Colossian heresy is forgotten. The Christian affirmations

remain. The Christian life which they affirm is still lived. It is still the way of salvation, still the world's hope, and still available to all. One of these great affirmations is the passage under consideration (3:1-4). Two others have already been considered (1:12-20; 2:9-15).

**You have been raised with Christ.** The reference is to baptism, as is the previous and complementary statement, "with Christ you died to the elemental spirits of the universe" (2:20). Both refer back to the summary of Christian salvation in 2:12. Paul did not carry his emphasis on the inner and spiritual nature of faith to the point of rejecting the outward aspects of the Christian sacraments. He recognized the value of baptism, both as making distinct the Christian's separation from the ideals of the world on his entrance into the fellowship of the church, and as confirming and accompanying the spiritual change to new life in Christ. However, his references to baptism are never in terms of the outward rite alone, as is so common in Christian practice today. He always describes baptism so as to emphasize the spiritual reality which alone gives significance to the external act. So in 2:20, and in 3:1, 3, and 10, he does not even use the word "baptism," though that is what he is talking about. Instead, he talks about baptism by giving vivid expression to the nature and reality of the new life in Christ into which his readers have already entered—a striking example of "holding fast to the Head" in his thought and teaching, as well as in his own devotional life.

**2. Set Your Minds on Things that Are Above, Not on Things that Are on Earth.—** Christian "otherworldliness" is often misunder-

3 For ye are dead, and your life is hid with Christ in God.

4 When Christ, *who is* our life, shall appear, then shall ye also appear with him in glory.

3 For you have died, and your life is hid with Christ in God. 4 When Christ who is our life appears, then you also will appear with him in glory.

3-4. These verses reflect the remarkable modification, amounting to a transformation, in the Pauline eschatology, which is imposed by the theological trend of this epistle. The Jewish conception of a succession of ages has substantially given way to the Hellenic conception of realms or orders of being, for which succession in time is irrelevant. The parousia of Christ is now conceived not in terms of the inauguration of a new age, but in terms of the manifestation of the invisible. The beginnings of a conflation of these two essentially incompatible modes of thinking can be traced in the earlier epistles, especially in II Corinthians; indeed, it is to be found wherever we meet with the idea that the powers of the kingdom of God are already effective in our midst. But in Colossians the mind of Paul is moving fundamentally in the framework of the Hellenic conception, and little more than a vestige of the Jewish "historical" eschatology remains. The great transformation is no longer awaited with eager longing; it has already taken place. The Christian has been raised from the dead with Christ (see on 2:12); this mortal nature has put on immortality; mortality is here and now swallowed up of life. Only the life is not to be perceived and known as part of the visible universe; it is **hid with Christ in God;** its essence is Christ himself, and it will be manifested when Christ is manifested in glory.

stood by critics of Christianity, and sometimes misconceived by Christians themselves. It is misunderstood when it is considered to involve a flight from reality, an escapist withdrawal from the strains, stresses, and duties of this world. Religion has been called "the opiate of the people." It is misconceived when it is held to imply a belief that this world cannot be the sphere of salvation, that the conditions of secular society are no concern of the Christian, and that he need take no responsibility for "Christianizing the social order." But Christian "this-worldliness" soon loses its Christian quality if its inspiration and guidance are not constantly sought in the realm of spiritual realities and values "where Christ is." The Colossian heretics were seeking salvation by a pseudo spirituality, which in reality did not break their involvement in the material world of material forces, material interests, and material values. Their method of spiritual progress was by an earthly, and morally pointless, asceticism which, even in its negative attitude to material things, limited their aspirations to **things that are on earth.** Paul lifts their minds from the "things which all perish as they are used" to rest on Christ. In him they will find the creative personal Spirit who sustains the universe, moves it toward good, and can transform secular life, and the material world itself, to the service of enduring spiritual ends.

Only those who live in the realm of the spirit, whose "life is hid with Christ in God" (vs. 3), can find any such meaning in the life which we live on this earth. Only such can invest material existence and secular society with the creative Christian purposes. Upon such Christ lays the great responsibility and the supreme privilege of expressing and extending in this world for which he died the transforming fellowship of the kingdom of God. Christian "otherworldliness" and Christian "this-worldliness" are two aspects of one life—the life that is in Christ. It is therefore of the utmost importance to note that instead of repudiating this world, and regarding as of no spiritual significance the way a Christian lives in it, Paul devotes the rest of the letter to showing what a really Christian life must be in every earthly and human relationship.

3. *The Mystery of the New Life.*—This new life is **hid with Christ in God.** The word **hid** implies two things. First, the new life is a mystery. We cannot understand or explain how God creatively indwells our personalities to transform them and infuse them with cleansing and re-creating power. But we *can* experience and know the fact of his indwelling. Second, the new life is secure. It is protected and guaranteed against the strains and stresses of secular life and against the moral corrosions of evil because it does not depend on human defense, or personal resolution, but on God.

4. *You Also Will Appear with Him in Glory.* —Whether conceived in Hebrew terms, as the final triumph of God's kingdom at the end of history, or in Greek terms, as the timeless world of eternal realities, God's redemption will at last

5 Mortify therefore your members which are upon the earth; fornication, uncleanness, inordinate affection, evil concupiscence, and covetousness, which is idolatry:

5 Put to death therefore what is earthly in you: immorality, impurity, passion, evil desire, and covetousness, which is idolatry.

---

There is no attempt to define what "manifestation" may mean in this context; the mind of the apostle rests satisfied in the conviction that in the end, as in the beginning, the Christian believer is one with Christ.

For true parallels we must turn not to the earlier epistles, but to the Johannine writings (I John 3:2; and for Christ as "the life," John 14:6, "I am . . . the life") .

### III. MORAL INSTRUCTION AND EXHORTATION (3:5–4:6)
#### A. THE TRANSFORMATION OF THE CHRISTIAN IN CHARACTER AND CONDUCT (3:5-17)

Paul has repudiated the false asceticism of the Colossian teachers, which sought to bring the life of the believer into subjection to a set of external regulations. Now he proceeds to call for a far more radical denial of self. Instead of regulating the old earthbound life by the observance of particularized prohibitions, his readers are to dig it out by the roots and destroy it altogether, so that the new life may have full dominion. His plea must necessarily take the form: "Be what you are. You have put off the old man: then put it off and have done with it. You have put on the new man: then put it on." There is a superficial appearance of absurdity in such charges; yet this is the only kind of moral exhortation that is at all valid. A bad tree cannot bring forth good fruit; and neither law nor exhortation can bring forth goodness from a life which has not the principle of goodness already planted within.

Paul here adopts a literary form which is not found elsewhere in his letters; in place of a general catalogue of pagan vices such as he gives in Rom. 1:26-31 and Gal. 5:19-21, he uses here an artificial schema of pentads—two of vices and one of virtues. This is hardly likely to be his own invention; it has no necessary connection with anything in his own thought. Possibly his opponents at Colossae had drawn up similar schemata, based on a correspondence with the five senses as constituting the appetitive nature of man. However, as we find the same form used in I Peter (note the pentad of vices in I Pet. 2:1 and of virtues in I Pet. 3:8), it is probably a convention of Hellenistic moralists.

**5.** This first pentad includes the gross sins of appetite; the second (vs. 8) is particularly concerned with sins of the temper and of the tongue. **Covetousness** (πλεονεξία) is

---

be fulfilled. Christ's victory will be complete. The Christian who lives in Christ now will have fellowship with him and with his faithful forever (see I Cor. 15:22-28) .

**5-8. The Source and Center of the World.—** Having raised their earthbound thoughts to heaven, Paul promptly trains their heaven-directed thoughts on earth. "Give me a place to stand," said Archimedes, "and I will move the universe." Physically speaking, we have no such place to stand. Spiritually speaking, that is exactly what we do have in Christ. Jesus manifested the spiritual Being whose loving will sustains the universe. The eternal Christ is the spiritual source and center of the world and of all true living. Out of the ultimate reality of the divine life, disclosed in Christ, divine energies flow to transform the world. But first God must change the world of men. To do that he

must change the life of *a* man. What he can do for one he can do for all. Through Christ every man can enter into the life and love of God. Dwelling in the life that is Christ, he experiences the spiritual power which can transmute into moral nobility his private universe in all its relationships, inner and outer, spiritual and material, personal and social, Godward and manward. This is what Paul means by his mystical figure of vital union with the self-giving Christ through complete renunciation in the will of whatever is against Christ —"you have put off the old nature with its practices" (vs. 9) —up to the new birth or resurrection of complete identity of the self with everything that is like Christ—you "have put on the new nature" (vs. 10) .

What a contrast to the barren moralism and the vacuous spiritualizing of the Colossian cult,

| 6 For which things' sake the wrath of God cometh on the children of disobedience: | 6 On account of these the wrath of God is |

---

commonly treated by the Stoic moralists as the fountainhead of all evil (cf. I Tim. 6:10, where, however, the narrower term φιλαργυρία, "avarice," "love of money," is used instead); and Jewish teachers had already equated this vice with **idolatry** in order to give pertinence to O.T. warnings which were regarded as needless in the literal sense.

**Evil desire:** p46 omits κακήν, **evil;** this reading, though it has no other support, may be the original; cf. Rom. 7:7-8, where Paul uses ἐπιθυμία without qualification, as summing up the violation of the law (literally, "I had not known desire, except the law had said, 'Thou shalt not desire.' But sin, taking occasion by the commandment, wrought in me all manner of desire").

**6. The wrath of God:** Paul uses this phrase not of an emotion in God, but concretely of the Day of Judgment (cf. Rom. 1:18 and C. H. Dodd's note on the passage in *The Epistle of Paul to the Romans* [London: Hodder & Stoughton, 1932; "The Moffatt New Testament Commentary"]).

The phrase **on the children of disobedience** (KJV), though the text which it represents has good MS attestation, should certainly be rejected as an interpolation from the parallel passage in Eph. 5:6. It is not found in p46 B and the Sahidic, and appears to have been omitted by the first scribe of D.

---

which, after all, was completely failing to challenge or change the spirit of the age! On the one hand, there was this pretentious religious system, long since forgotten—promising a greater salvation than Christ's, (a) by means of superstitious taboos which put a morbid taint upon the innocent relationships of life, and an unholy pride in those who practiced them, and (b) by means of illusory flights of the spirit into supposed alliance with vague and characterless world forces, which left the starry-eyed worshiper as helplessly involved in the materialistic ways of pagan society as he had always been. On the other hand, there was Paul, whose interpretation of Christ has gone into all the world, proclaiming (a) the personal God of the Christian gospel, all-wise, all-loving, and all-good, manifested in Christ, the redeemer of the world by the way of the Cross, the creator of the church, and the transformer of human character into his own image, and (b) the power of men and women who have been re-energized and redirected by the life of Christ in the depths of their personalities, to go out into the world to be the creators, rather than the creatures, of their environment, molding unregenerate surroundings by the robust strength of honest Christian character, and living victorious Christian lives in a discouragingly unchristian world.

*5. Put to Death Therefore What Is Earthly in You.*—The two lists of vices (vss. 5 and 8) include both the sins of the flesh and the sins of the spirit. The first series stresses the sins of the flesh, though not exclusively. Evil desire and covetousness spring from the spirit. The second series lays entire emphasis on the sins of the spirit.

Impurity and covetousness were commonly regarded as the characteristic sins of the pagan world. However, they were not, and are not, confined to the pagan world. While the Pharisees enforced a strict standard of moral purity, our Lord had constantly to warn them against covetousness (Luke 12:13-21; 16:13-14). These sins are not peculiar to any race or culture. They are the sins of unregenerate human nature everywhere.

**Covetousness, which is idolatry.** Pagan worship was dominated by the quest of materialistic goals (see Expos. 2:9). A man worships what he loves, whatever his profession of religion may be. He loves what he covets. If what he covets, loves, and therefore worships, is less than God, he is a practical idolater. "Lay not up for yourselves treasures upon earth, . . . for where your treasure is, there will your heart be also" (Matt. 6:19-21).

*6. The Wrath of God.*—The terrible, progressive, and inevitable demoralization of those who abandon themselves to evil desire is portrayed with awesome thoroughness in Rom. 1:18-32. There is nothing arbitrary or capricious about the increasing degradation that flows with impartial justice from violations of the moral law. We pay the full price for every moral detour from the path that leads to life. So Paul says, "God *gave them up* to a base mind and to improper conduct" (Rom. 1:28), i.e., God permitted them to exercise their freedom to their

7 In the which ye also walked sometime, when ye lived in them.

coming.*f* 7 In these you once walked, when you lived in them. 8 But now put them

*f* Other ancient authorities add *upon the sons of disobedience.*

---

**7.** With or without the omitted phrase, we must continue "in which"; for ἐν οἷς has the same antecedents as δι' ἅ ("on account of these"), above; it refers to the vices mentioned. The Colossian Christians are reminded that they too were guilty of all these vices of pagan life while they **lived in these things,** i.e., while their life was grounded in the sphere of visible things, before it was "hid with Christ in God."

---

own undoing. "He who sows to his own flesh will from the flesh reap corruption" (Gal. 6:8).

The Christian emphasis upon belief in God as a personal will sometimes makes it difficult to understand aright the nature of divine retribution. How can a God of love express "wrath"? On the other hand, how can a God of righteousness condone sin? It is impossible to exaggerate the absoluteness of God's love of righteousness and hatred of iniquity, but it is quite possible to misinterpret the quality of his "wrath." That the divine will is ultimately involved in the way by which sin is punished, and takes responsibility for it, must be believed; but human anger is so prone to the deliberate infliction of unnecessary cruelties that we too easily ascribe the same attitude to the righteous God in his rejection of evil. This is moral anthropomorphism.

It would be well to think of God's attitude to the sinner in terms of the relation of the loving father to the prodigal son. He let the boy go because there was no way of stopping him, short of violating the freedom and integrity of his personality. Furthermore, he did nothing to minimize or turn aside the inevitable denouement of the way of life to which his son still stubbornly adhered. Artificial softening of the consequences by an indulgent father could only have confirmed the son in the contempt for the moral law which was already ruining his life. Nonetheless, the father was there, where the wanderer knew that he could always be found, and always in character, eager to receive him back into a status which he could now neither claim nor achieve for himself, the status of a son who had learned through a father's forgiving love to accept for himself the moral disciplines of life. In fact, when the youth was miles removed from home, and morally worlds away, the decisive influence which brought him to himself and turned his penitent steps toward home was the character of his father, which laid hold of him with the force of love's persuasion. Moral influence crosses space as if it were not there. Love overleaps infinities of spiritual alienation. The boy could not say, "How heartless of my father to let me come to this." He

could only say, "Father, I have sinned against heaven, and in thy sight" (Luke 15:21).

Meantime, until that point is reached we lay the lash of demoralized living and frustration of soul upon ourselves in spite of all that God does to turn us from destruction. We choose our own punishment when we choose immoral ways. **The wrath of God is coming [cometh—KJV] upon the sons of disobedience.** This view of **the wrath of God** does not lessen one whit the tragic reality of divine retribution. It does reinforce the conviction to which the Christian must ever cling when he thinks of the terror in **the wrath of God**—that God in his ultimate and absolute nature is love.

**7.** *Among Whom You Also Once Walked, When You Lived in These Things.*—Pagan society was morally debased, sexually overstimulated and unrestrained, and constantly prompted toward material desire—covetousness —as indeed is the paganism of modern times or of any time.

> On that hard Pagan world disgust
> And secret loathing fell.
> Deep weariness and sated lust
> Made human life a hell.[2]

The Colossians may not have been given to immorality more than others, but it was out of that morally tainted environment that they had been led into Christianity, and in that environment they still lived their daily lives. Both overtly and covertly the pressure of old ways must have been relentlessly ever-present upon them. One wonders whether the religion of harmony with natural forces, which was advanced by the Colossian cult, had much effect on the sins of the flesh. Did their "Do not handle, Do not taste, Do not touch" (2:21) give them any real power to master the immoralities against which Paul warns them?

There can be no doubt whatever that even the thought of Christ shames moral impurity and abashes evil desire in anyone who thinks of Christ and of impurity at the same time. There can be no doubt that the acceptance of

[2] Matthew Arnold, "Obermann Once More."

8 But now ye also put off all these; anger, wrath, malice, blasphemy, filthy communication out of your mouth.

9 Lie not one to another, seeing that ye have put off the old man with his deeds;

all away: anger, wrath, malice, slander, and foul talk from your mouth. 9 Do not lie to one another, seeing that you have put off the old nature with its prac-

8. **Put away:** The same verb should be understood in vs. 5 also as governing **immorality** and the following nouns, which cannot well be taken as in apposition to "what is earthly" (RSV) in vs. 5 ("members which are upon the earth" is the more exact KJV rendering). As these vicious habits are alien to the new nature of the Christian, they must be put "off" or "away," as a garb that is wholly unsuited to the estate of the wearer. **Anger** (θυμός) is the sudden flame of fury; **wrath** (ὀργή) is the settled attitude. **Malice** (κακία) is defined as "the eagerness to harm one's neighbor" (Suidas). **Slander** (RSV) or **blasphemy** (KJV) properly means in this context "reviling." The last of the five words has a similar connotation—"loud abuse," "opprobrious language" (αἰσχρολογία), rather than **foul talk.**

9. To the pentad of vices which flow from a bitter and vengeful disposition toward others, Paul adds a particular injunction against lying. Then he reverts to the thought of the presupposition upon which all these injunctions are based—the transformation of the inward nature. The vices which Paul has named belong to **the old nature** which believers have **put off,** and are incompatible with "the new nature" (see on vs. 10), which has been imparted to them in Christ. **Put off:** The same verb is used as in 2:15, where it is translated "disarmed" (RSV) or "spoiled" (KJV); it brings in the note of triumph won over sinful habit.

---

Christ into the inner control room of the will ennobles natural instincts and affections, not by repressing them, but by fulfilling and perfecting them in the service of morally constructive goals. Countless Christians know what Augustine meant in his classic statement of Christ's conquest over his own impotent and divided will:

But I wretched, most wretched, in the very commencement of my early youth, had begged chastity of Thee, and said, "Give me chastity and continency, only not yet." For I feared lest Thou shouldest hear me soon, and soon cure me.

Then a little later, in the garden at Milan, under great agitation of spirit,

I sent up these sorrowful words; How long? how long, "to-morrow, and to-morrow?" Why not now? why not is there this hour an end to my uncleanness?

So was I speaking, and weeping in the most bitter contrition of my heart, when, lo! I heard from a neighbouring house a voice, as of boy or girl, I know not, chanting, and oft repeating, "Take up and read; Take up and read." . . . Eagerly then I returned to the place where Alypius was sitting; for there had I laid the volume of the Apostle, when I arose thence. I seized, opened, and in silence read that section, on which my eyes first fell: *Not*

*in rioting and drunkenness, not in chambering and wantonness, not in strife and envying: but put ye on the Lord Jesus Christ, and make not provision for the flesh,* in concupiscence. No further would I read; nor needed I: for instantly at the end of this sentence, by a light as it were of serenity infused into my heart, all the darkness of doubt vanished away.[3]

**9-10. *You Have Put Off . . . and Have Put On.*** —The putting to death of the old nature which Paul proclaimed in vs. 5 is thought of now as accomplished. The transformation has taken place (see vs. 1, "If then you *have been raised* with Christ"; the "if then" has the force of "since"). Paul's confidence in the genuine conversion of his Colossian brethren does not waver. Yet somehow the thing accomplished is not complete, and the transformation that has taken place has not come to full fruition. Those who claim for themselves "entire sanctification" are pretty unconvincing, and usually display a woefully limited understanding of what sanctification is.

In this contradiction we are faced with one of those unresolved paradoxes which confront us in life. On such questions experience is a

[3] *The Confessions of St. Augustine,* tr. E. B. Pusey (London: J. M. Dent & Sons; New York: E. P. Dutton & Co., 1907; "Everyman's Library"), pp. 163, 170-71. Used by permission.

10 And have put on the new *man*, which is renewed in knowledge after the image of him that created him:

11 Where there is neither Greek nor Jew, circumcision nor uncircumcision, Barbarian, Scythian, bond *nor* free: but Christ *is* all, and in all.

tices 10 and have put on the new nature, which is being renewed in knowledge after the image of its creator. 11 Here there cannot be Greek and Jew, circumcised and uncircumcised, barbarian, Scyth'ian, slave, free man, but Christ is all, and in all.

---

**10. The new nature** is not static, but is continually **being renewed.** It does not grow old or decay, but takes upon itself more and more **the image of its creator.** As man was made in the image of God, so when he is restored to true fellowship with God in Christ, the divine image which had been effaced by sin becomes ever more clearly visible. The phrase εἰς ἐπίγνωσιν, translated **in knowledge,** means properly "unto knowledge." The thought is that our growing likeness to God leads us onward to the true knowledge of him. Any knowledge that we may have of him comes to us only as his holiness and glory and beauty are mirrored in our lives (cf. II Cor. 3:18).

**11.** Where the image of God is reflected in men, distinctions of race and class and culture lose all significance; the fundamental unity of the human race is restored. **Barbarian** is an unfortunate translation of the Greek word βάρβαρος; when the Greeks called Persians and Egyptians βάρβαροι, they were by no means scorning them as uncivilized peoples. The notion of the raw barbarian is really conveyed by **Scythian;** the inroads of these savage nomads from the northern steppes had left an ineffaceable memory of horror on the peoples of the eastern Mediterranean. **Barbarian** and **Scythian,** then, are contrasted as the cultivated Oriental and the rude savage from the northern wilds. Even these, like the proud peoples of Greece and of Judea, are brought through Christ into the all-embracing unity of redemption.

**Christ is all, and in all:** Cf. I Cor. 15:28, "Then shall the Son also himself be subject, . . . that God may be all in all." The form of expression rendered "all in all" was doubtless framed in the first instance within a pantheistic context, and has been

---

surer guide than logic. The Colossians must still "seek the things that are above" (vs. 1). It is still necessary to exhort them, "Put to death therefore what is earthly in you" (vs. 5), and "put on" (vs. 12) the qualities of the new life. The parallel passage in Ephesians (4:22-24) is also in the imperative mood, rather than in the indicative, as here (vss. 9-10).

Paul seems to switch continually from one to the other. This is because experience switches continually from one to the other. On the one hand, the Christian is conscious of the actual rebirth to the new life in which, potentially, sin and self-will are destroyed. On the other hand, he knows that he must struggle to make the outward life progressively conform to the new nature in which Christ has become the animating center of the heart and will. The classic theology of justification and sanctification fits the facts of experience: first the new status, then the continual process of maturing growth in the new status. There is all the difference in the world between (*a*) striving "on one's own" toward the moral ideal, with the futile resources of a self-centered life, and (*b*) experiencing the change to a Christ-centered life

which is moved from within to its never-ending task of expressing in outward conduct the love of Christ which already reigns in the heart. This is Paul's fundamental distinction between hopeless involvement in the demands of the law, and utter dependence on divine grace. The gospel of redemption transcends mere moralism. The moral quality which the new life is able to express is the outreaching of the life of Christ, who is already in possession of the soul. So the "new nature," still in the old body and bound to the old environment, needs continually to be **renewed in knowledge after the image of its creator** (see II Cor. 4:7-12, 16-18).

Pascal reminded us that we could not seek God unless in some real sense we already possessed him. Our Lord's great teaching of the vine and the branches insists that we cannot express Christ except he first possess us (John 15:5).

**11. *Christ Is All, and in All.***—The personality that is genuinely transformed within moves with the radiant energy of Christ to the outer transformation of society.

The classifications which are listed represent the major separations which shut men out from

**12** Put on therefore, as the elect of God, holy and beloved, bowels of mercies, kindness, humbleness of mind, meekness, long-suffering;

**12** Put on then, as God's chosen ones, holy and beloved, compassion, kindness, low-

---

transferred by Paul from an original application to the divine *Nous* or *Logos* to the Christ, whom he is interpreting in cosmic terms in this epistle. He would not, of course, use it in the Stoic sense, which would involve the absorption of individual personality in the one divine essence; he seizes upon the phrase as a graphic expression of the absolute pre-eminence of Christ. Here it bears especially upon the thought that the relationship of men to Christ transcends all earthly relationships and annihilates the barriers which separate man from his brother man.

**12.** Paul now turns from his warnings against the vices of pagan life to speak of the virtues which belong to the new life as members of the people of God—**chosen, . . . holy, . . . beloved.** All three terms are titles given to the community of Israel in the O.T. scriptures, transferred now to the heirs of Israel's spiritual prerogatives. The appeal is now based, not upon their experience of death and resurrection with Christ, but upon their status before God. The pentad of virtues here given is the counterpart to the second pentad of vices; against the bad temper and self-assertiveness which the pagan shows in

---

brotherhood with their fellow men: **Greek and Jew**—racial differences; **circumcised and uncircumcised**—differences of religious tradition, rather than vital differences of true and false faith; **barbarian, Scythian**—cultural differences; **slave, free man**—social differences. The similar classification in Gal. 3:28 adds, "male nor female"—in affirmation of the principle of equal personal worth which has elevated the status and dignity of women in all Christian lands.

It is not suggested that all differences are to be eliminated in order to achieve a kind of Christian stereotype, but that all unbrotherly discriminations based on human differences are to be cast out in order to achieve a true community, in reverence for life, stemming from love of one another in Christ.

To see Christ *in* a Christian Greek or a Christian Jew, a Christian of one religious tradition or another, a Christian of advanced culture or a Christian of backward culture, a Christian of whatever social and economic status, this is what the "new nature" in Christ makes both necessary and possible. Further than that, to see in one of these, and in all of them, though he be no Christian at all, a brother for whom Christ died, and a potential brother in Christ, this also is enjoined upon Christians, for the true fulfillment of life for all is to realize, i.e., to make real, the kingdom of God in which **Christ is all, and in all.**

This ultimate unity in diversity (see 2:19) is even more plainly declared in Gal. 3:27, "For as many of you as have been baptized into Christ have put on Christ"; and also in I Cor. 12:13-14, "For by one Spirit are we all baptized

into one body, whether we be Jews or Gentiles, whether we be bond or free; and have been all made to drink into one Spirit. For the body is not one member, but many."

In Paul's day this was a tremendous and absolutely new *revelation*. In modern times the elite of the church have gloriously demonstrated it, especially in overseas missions, and in the new churches which have sprung from them. But though in that way we accept the revelation and take it for granted, yet for human society in modern "Christian lands," and for the church as well, a tremendous *task* remains to be done— to conform the communal life of our time to this revelation of the brotherhood of all in Christ to which Christians have long given lip service.

> Already in the mind of God
>   That city riseth fair;
> Lo, how its splendor challenges
>   The souls that greatly dare—
> Yea, bids us seize the whole of life
> And build its glory there.[4]

**12. God's Chosen Ones.**—See Expos. of "the saints and faithful brethren in Christ at Colossae" (1:2) for the universal and progressively inclusive scope of the gospel.

It is only too easy to abandon a great truth in the act of rejecting some misconception of it. The revolt of the conscience against the idea that God arbitrarily chooses some to exclusive privilege, in the spirit of favoritism, has led more than one shallow believer to the sup-

[4] Walter Russell Bowie, "O holy city, seen of John." From *Hymns of the Christian Life*, copyright 1910 by Harper & Bros. Used by permission of the publishers.

217

speech and in disposition toward his neighbor is set the unfailing kindness and gentleness to all in which the Christian character flowers. In substance, and with a certain degree even of verbal resemblance, Paul summarizes in these five virtues the description of Christian love given in I Cor. 13:4-7. All of them are social virtues, bearing upon the Christian's disposition in relation to others.

The metaphorical verb **put on** is altogether inappropriate to its objects, inasmuch as the cultivation of **compassion,** literally, a "heart of pity" (**bowels of mercies,** KJV) is not analogous to the putting on of a garment; it is clearly an *inward* transformation that

posedy advanced conclusion that God does not choose anybody for anything. Yet history and experience uniformly attest a principle of selection in life. It falls to some men to accomplish in this world what is not given to other men to do. The secular mind may be content with explanations based on chance or "the breaks" or native human genius. The Christian sees behind the vagaries of circumstance the ceaseless operation of divine providence.

In a sense Kepler's scientific discoveries were spontaneous, the achievements of one man's creative search. Others can justly say, "He was a great man, the credit is his." Kepler could only make due acknowledgment to the source and giver of all truth, "I think God's thoughts after him." Edison filled the world with new inventions. Frederick Banting discovered insulin, and Archibald Fleming, penicillin, the latter literally as an unexpected by-product of his quest for something else. Why was it given to these men, rather than to some other particular persons, to introduce enriching knowledge to the world? The answer must be that they fulfilled the conditions by which new truth can break in upon the human understanding from its eternal source.

Those conditions include singleness of purpose, intense application to a task, a trained mind, informed, equipped, and disciplined for its work, and an expectancy of new light and leading. In the particular contribution which each made he was "chosen," not primarily or necessarily by the official selection of some human organization or society which commissioned him to make his discovery, but by the creative Spirit who crowns man's sincere aspiring with new truth and creative achievement.

**God's chosen ones,** chosen for the privileged tasks of Christian witness and redemptive action in this world, must look on their "calling and election" in the same way. Their honored place in the mission of the church, which is the saving work of divine providence, is not the reward of merit, nor is it the result of sheer favoritism, implying unjust discrimination against others who might just as well have received the call. So far as the immediate neighborhood of the Christians of Colossae was concerned, many others who remained outside the church did

get the call. True, those who believed were brought into the fellowship of the faith by the grace of God; but the grace of God is ever seeking to bring all men into that fellowship. Being in it they were so situated as to be the most usable instruments of the divine will for his divine work. Their choice—God's call and their response—was to service, not to privilege; their service was to be given for the good of men, not for self-satisfaction; their contribution to the good of men was to be their means of glorifying God, not an occasion for self-congratulation. Jesus said, "Ye have not chosen me, but I have chosen you . . . that ye should go and bring forth fruit" (John 15:16). Paul testified, "I was made a minister, according to the gift of the grace of God given unto me by the effectual working of his power. Unto me, who am less than the least of all saints, is this grace given, that I should preach among the Gentiles the unsearchable riches of Christ" (Eph. 3:7-8).

There is an ultimate mystery which human knowledge cannot fathom. Why some are favored to be born within the Christian heritage, consistently under Christian influence, and therefore privileged at least in their access to a mature spiritual faith, while others, in the very circumstances of their origin, are denied these opportunities, is a question in ultimate justice which the mind of man cannot solve. It reaches back into the agelong record of man's alienation from God. But God is merciful (see Acts 17:30). He "desires all men to be saved and to come to the knowledge of the truth" (I Tim. 2:4). His choice will never be withheld from any man anywhere who fulfills the conditions of humble, seeking faith. His desire that the influences of the Christian community which encourage a saving acceptance of Christ should be extended and intensified in all the world infinitely surpasses the readiness of his church to fulfill "the Great Commission." Upon those who *are* in Christ he firmly places the Christian responsibilities of their Christian privileges. Paul does not congratulate **God's chosen ones** on their selection. He lays upon them the divine summons to give contagious witness to the joy of Christian living.

**12-15. Let the Peace of Christ Rule in Your Hearts.**—As in Gal. 5:19-24, the positive fruits

13 Forbearing one another, and forgiving one another, if any man have a quarrel against any: even as Christ forgave you, so also *do* ye.

14 And above all these things *put on* charity, which is the bond of perfectness.

liness, meekness, and patience, 13 forbearing one another and, if one has a complaint against another, forgiving each other; as the Lord has forgiven you, so you also must forgive. 14 And above all these put on love, which binds everything together in

---

is required. The expression probably derives from a baptismal symbolism, the baptized person being clothed in fresh raiment, typifying a new personality; cf. Gal. 3:27, "As many of you as were baptized into Christ have put on Christ." The mystical experience is now expounded in terms of its ethical significance. There is, however, a good preparation in the LXX for the use of the verb with nouns denoting moral qualities (rendering Hebrew לבשׁ); for example, Job 29:14 (LXX), "I have put on righteousness, and wrapped judgment about me like a doublet." Even in classical Greek there is an approach to this sense in the Homeric phrase "put on strength," and in Aristophanes' phrase (here, however, in a context of women putting on male attire) "putting on so daring a scheme" (*Ecclesiazusae* 288).

13. The sense that the Christian character finds expression within the corporate unity of the fellowship to which we belong is strongly brought out in this verse with its two reciprocal pronouns ἀλλήλων and ἑαυτοῖς. The need of forbearance and forgiveness is mutual; therefore the apostle does not speak of "forgiving others," but of **forgiving one another.** The call to forgive is based not upon any command of Christ, nor upon his example as a pattern of human conduct, but upon our own experience of his forgiveness. **As the Lord has forgiven you** (the weight of textual authority favors ὁ κύριος): This expression occurs only here in the N.T.; elsewhere it is God who is said to forgive for Christ's sake; the new phrase is another indication of how completely the apostle's mind has been seized by the thought that Christ occupies in relation to us the entire sphere of God.

14. The crown of all the Christian virtues is love, **which is the bond of perfectness.** Bond (σύνδεσμος) is the same word as was translated "ligaments" in 2:19. The physiological metaphor is still in Paul's mind; he is thinking of the unity of Christians in "the body." This unity, however, is defined in terms of **perfectness** (τελειότης), which must here have the connotation of the Hebrew תם or תמים (LXX—τέλειος); as in the teaching of our Lord when he sums up his injunctions concerning our attitudes to others in the words, "Be ye therefore perfect, even as your Father which is in heaven is perfect." In this love, **which is the bond of perfectness,** the Christian life reflects most truly its renewal in "the image of its creator" (vs. 10).

---

of the spirit are set over against the destructive sins of the spirit (vss. 8-9). Notable Christians must be noticeably Christian. If the modern reader is somewhat surprised at the stress of so robust a Christian as Paul on the gentle virtues as the differentiae of the Christian life, as he is sometimes puzzled by the similar emphasis of Jesus in the Beatitudes, two things should be borne in mind.

(a) The "manly virtues," courage, determination, aggressiveness, "drive," and the like, so naturally consort with the human ego and so easily serve the ends of crass individualism that they constitute, rather than cure, man's moral problem. Without an overmastering spiritual control they descend into the "anger, wrath, malice, slander, and foul talk" (vs. 8) which

Paul seems to have found so prevalent in pagan society. In fact, an examination of the moral climate of the ancient world [5] reveals only too clearly the gross immorality, open materialism, moral irresponsibility, and unashamed self-seeking which characterized the spirit of that age. One need not turn to former times to realize how the self-regarding instincts can turn the world into a howling wilderness of clashing wills.

It is the virtues which put a curb and rein on crude individualism that really liberate life and make possible a livable community, instilling respect for others, sympathy, understanding,

[5] See T. R. Glover, *The Conflict of Religions in the Early Roman Empire* (11th ed.; London: Methuen & Co., 1927), *passim.*

15 And let the peace of God rule in your hearts, to the which also ye are called in one body; and be ye thankful.

16 Let the word of Christ dwell in you richly in all wisdom; teaching and admon-

perfect harmony. 15 And let the peace of Christ rule in your hearts, to which indeed you were called in the one body. And be thankful. 16 Let the word of Christ dwell

---

**15. The peace of Christ** is clearly thought of as that inward serenity which Christ bestows (cf. John 14:27, "Peace I leave with you; my peace I give to you"). But this inward serenity is related also to the cosmic "peace" (see on 1:20) which God makes through the Cross, in reconciling all things to himself. It can therefore be regarded as the end for which Christians **were called in the one body.** There is here a foreshadowing of the thought which is to be developed in its fullness in Ephesians, that the divine unity of the church of Christ is the pattern, or rather the nucleus, about which the ultimate unity of the redeemed cosmos is even now taking shape. The universal harmony which God ordains to be the final state of his whole creation is to be reflected in the heart of the Christian believer.

Once again Paul calls for thanksgiving in the glad and humble recognition that the love and peace of the Christian fellowship are not our achievement of which we might boast, but God's gracious gift to us in Christ. The same note is repeated twice again in the following two verses, suggesting that thanksgiving is the culminating expression of the Christian's whole life before God (cf. on 1:12).

**16.** The meaning of these apparently simple phrases is not easy to determine with exactitude. It seems best to take the participles (**teaching, . . . admonishing, . . . singing**)

---

patience, tolerance, and self-control. These are the spiritual virtues of humility, forgiveness, and love.

(b) The "Christian virtues" include and fulfill the "manly virtues." There is nothing weak or effeminate about them, though they may be misinterpreted to mean passivity and ineffectiveness. The Christian virtues enlist and use all positive human qualities "unto a perfect man, unto the measure of the stature of the fulness of Christ" (Eph. 4:13).

Look at Christ and see it in perfection. His was the freest life man ever lived. Nothing could bind Him. . . . He acted out the divinity that was in Him up to the noblest ideal of liberty. But was there no compulsion in His working? Hear Him: "I must be about my Father's business." Was it no compulsion that drove Him those endless journeys, footsore and heartsore, through His ungrateful land? "I must work to-day." What slave of sin was ever driven to his wickedness as Christ was to holiness? What force ever drove a selfish man into his voluptuous indulgence with half the irresistibility that forced the Savior to the cross? O my dear friends, who does not dream for himself of a freedom as complete and as inspiring as the Lord's?[6]

"Strong Son of God, immortal Love," exclaims Tennyson in the opening lines of *In Memoriam,* offering adoring tribute to the more than manly love of Christ. The consistent de-

[6] Phillips Brooks, *The Candle of the Lord and Other Sermons* (New York: E. P. Dutton & Co., 1881), p. 197.

termined purpose of good will, which is Christian love (ἀγάπη), takes all that a man has, and the grace of God supporting that. The massive goodness of Christian character is seen not in the hard and self-assertive, but in those who have been mellowed, without being softened, by the love of God which Christ inspires. There is a severity in love that does not let us down but pulls us up. See the demands that the love of Christ lays upon us in the message which the author of Revelation addressed to the church at Laodicea, hard by Colossae, a generation after Paul wrote his Epistle to the Colossians (Rev. 3:14-22). To this church, "neither cold nor hot," which had evidently lapsed into arrogant materialism, is addressed one of the tenderest invitations to loving fellowship with Christ to be found in all scripture, "If any man hear my voice, and open the door, I will come in to him, and will sup with him, and he with me" (Rev. 3:20). But these words are immediately preceded by love's relentless imperative, "As many as I love, I rebuke and chasten: be zealous therefore, and repent. Behold, I stand at the door, and knock" (Rev. 3:19-20). Holman Hunt missed something of this. **Above all . . . put on love.**

**16. Let the Word of Christ Dwell in You Richly.**—A lot of this strange Colossian talk about "thrones, or dominions, or principalities, or powers," "the elemental spirits of the universe," "fullness of life," "worship of angels,"

ishing one another in psalms and hymns and spiritual songs, singing with grace in your hearts to the Lord.

in you richly, as you teach and admonish one another in all wisdom, and as you sing psalms and hymns and spiritual songs with

---

as sharing the imperative force of the governing verb. They are at the same time epexegetic, making clear and specific how the abiding of **the word of Christ** is to express itself in spiritual activities; the presence of Christ in the community is to be manifested in mutual edification as each member contributes to the higher life of all, and in the songs of praise to God that rise from the hearts of all. Ἐν ὑμῖν (**in you**) may mean "in your hearts," or it may be taken in the corporate sense, "among you," "within your fellowship"; the latter seems better suited to the context.

The expression **word of Christ** is not found elsewhere in the Pauline writings (in I Thess. 1:8, "word of the Lord" evidently means "the gospel"). Several interpretations are possible: the phrase may mean "the word which Christ speaks" as a living presence among his people, or as "an inward monitor" in the believer's heart (Lightfoot). W. L. Knox suggests that it may be "a conflation of the Gospel expressing itself in utterance . . . with the thought of Christ as dwelling in the Christian" (*St. Paul and Church of the Gentiles,* p. 176, n. 2). It is perhaps better to see in it an influence of the widespread notion—originating with Heraclitus, adopted by the Stoics as a fundamental dogma, and through them passing into the general mind of the times—of the logos as the divine essence immanent in the universe and present in each individual soul. In the place of this impersonal essence Paul sets "the Logos of Christ," i.e., "the Logos, which is Christ," thus giving to the floating philosophical notion a concrete personal significance. In a measure he anticipates the thought of the Fourth Gospel, that "the Word [Logos] was made flesh, and dwelt among us, . . . full of grace and truth" (John 1:14).

**Teach and admonish one another in all wisdom:** Since the sense of the participles is imperative, omit **as you** here and in the following phrase. Note the parallelism with 1:28. The functions which the apostle there ascribes to himself are here enjoined as a mutual duty upon the whole community. The Christian ideal is that all the members of the

---

"Do not handle, Do not taste, Do not touch," was quite out of Christian context. Much of it could be taught and pondered with scarcely a thought of Christ at all. Get back to your center, urges Paul, in your religious instruction (**as you teach**); in your moral education (**as you . . . admonish one another**); in your quest for culture and a well-stored mind (**in all wisdom**). Abandon this timid aping of the contemporary fashion in thought. Some other philosophy "according to human tradition" (2:8) will be in style tomorrow. Get over the idea that you can find in the realm of secular learning, especially in the pseudo learning which has beguiled you, a more profound understanding of man's destiny in the universe, and of his duty in this world, than is offered you in the Christian revelation. Steep your minds in the drama of our redemption as it is given in the gospel of Christ our Savior. Let the divine light of that revelation suffuse and illuminate the widest researches of human thought with its unique moral and spiritual values.

Modern higher education takes but scant notice of the "perennial philosophy." But it will have its day again, and will, please God,

inspire and undergird a great new "age of faith." Meanwhile, the modern cultivated mind will be not less scholarly, less educated, less intellectually free, but more, for heeding Paul's counsel, **Let the word of Christ dwell in you richly.** One is reminded of Sir William Osler, scientist, scholar, educator, and Christian, who said that he began each day with Christ and his prayer and at night, as he laid off his clothes, he undressed his soul too, and laid aside its sins. In the presence of God he lay down to rest, and wakened a free man, with a new life.

**As you sing psalms and hymns and spiritual songs with thankfulness in your hearts to God.** The Exeg. suggests the imperative—"sing!" Whether or not the Colossian cult sang like this is not known. Their ascetic ritual and their carefully guarded secret rites suggest otherwise. There are hints of something puritanical and overserious, possibly grim, in their preoccupation with "questions of food and drink" (2:16), their regulations "Do not handle, Do not taste, Do not touch" (2:21), and their "rigor of devotion and self-abasement and severity to the body" (2:23). Paul gives, perhaps by contrast, a warm and glowing testimony to the joy and

church should accept, each in his own measure, a share of responsibility for the spiritual welfare of all. The duties of the pastor, even those of a leading apostle, are also the mutual charge of the entire congregation of believers.

The triple phrase **psalms and hymns and spiritual songs** affords a striking indication of the richness of Christian worship at this early time, if a small provincial congregation, without distinguished leadership, could have such diversity in its music. Song, of course, has always been a distinctive feature of our religion: "The Christian church has come singing down the ages." Every revival has been marked by a new expression of faith in song.

**In your hearts** cannot in the context mean that the songs are to be silent; it can only suggest the fervor and sincerity of the singing. The words ἐν τῇ χάριτι, then, are probably best taken not in the unusual sense **with thankfulness** (RSV), nor yet as "in God's grace" (Lightfoot), but with the aesthetic undertone conveyed by **with grace** (KJV), i.e., "with beauty" (a good classical sense from Homer down). The apostle has

---

goodness of believing, and of sharing faith and fellowship in the glad freedom of forgiven men who can say, "I know whom I have believed, and am persuaded that he is able to keep that which I have committed unto him against that day" (II Tim. 1:12). In a community or a company where Christ really reigns there ought to be a noticeable radiance of spirit.

The early Christians impressed the pagan world with the joy of their new life. In the second century the unknown writer of the Epistle to Diognetus gave this testimony.

Christians are not distinguishable from the rest of mankind in land or speech or customs. They inhabit no special cities of their own, nor do they use any different form of speech, nor do they cultivate any out-of-the-way life. . . . But while they live in Greek and barbarian cities as their lot may be cast, and follow local customs in dress and food and life generally, . . . yet they live in their own countries as sojourners only; they take part in everything as citizens and submit to everything as strangers. Every strange land is native to them, and every native land is strange. They marry and have children like everyone else—but they do not expose their children. They have meals in common, but not wives. They are in the flesh, but they do not live after the flesh. They continue on earth, but their citizenship is in heaven. They obey the laws ordained, and by their private lives they overcome the laws. . . . In a word, what the soul is in the body, that is what Christians are in the world.[7]

When the faith ceased to be the religion of the intensely loyal minority and became the official religion of the Roman civilization, some of this was lost. Smaller groups, when knit together by whole-souled Christian purpose, have always showed it.

**With thankfulness in your hearts to God.** The singing of many Christian congregations is flat

[7] T. R. Glover, *Conflict of Religions in the Early Roman Empire* (London: Methuen & Co.; New York: Charles Scribner's Sons, 1927), pp. 159-60. Used by permission.

and lifeless in comparison because so many do not lift their hearts with their voices. Paul's enumeration of the fruits of the Spirit (Gal. 5:22-23) puts "love" and "joy" at the head of the list, and mentions them both as distinguishable qualities. This suggests that correct relationships of love may conceivably be expressed without the spontaneity of joy that properly belongs to them. By coincidence the RSV speaks of "love, which binds everything together in perfect *harmony*" (vs. 14), and the KJV translates Eph. 5:19, "Speaking to yourselves in psalms and hymns and spiritual songs, singing and making *melody* in your heart to the Lord." Great music has both harmony and melody. It seems to be possible for the average Christian congregation to express the harmony of love in correct moral behavior, but with an austere restraint which suggests that the effort to curb the sins of the flesh and of the spirit should never be relaxed to the point of "letting one's self go" lest the "old Adam" get out of control. The spontaneity and abandon of lives that are securely centered in Christ make rich, free melodies of joyous living that do not jar the harmony of Christian fellowship, but enrich and glorify it. They even add obbligatos which turn the sometimes sober harmonies of Christian life and work into hymns of praise that rise and soar on wings of song.

Christians can sing on the eve of Gethsemane (Matt. 26:30); when in prison for the Lord's sake (Acts 16:25); in "the fellowship of kindred minds" as they "teach and admonish one another," in the high worship of the sanctuary, and in the intimacy of the informal meeting (vs. 16); and they shall sing the "new song" in praise of "the Lamb that was slain" with "ten thousand times ten thousand, and thousands of thousands" in the eternal kingdom (Rev. 5:9-14).

Paul's brief references to the Colossian cult worship do not suggest a warmth and goodness

17 And whatsoever ye do in word or deed, *do* all in the name of the Lord Jesus, giving thanks to God and the Father by him.

thankfulness in your hearts to God. 17 And whatever you do, in word or deed, do everything in the name of the Lord Jesus, giving thanks to God the Father through him.

of course no thought of the technical excellence of the music, but of the impalpable beauty which is found in all true worship (cf. Ps. 27:4).

**17.** In this verse the apostle gathers up all that he has to say about the Christian life. The emphasis lies on the cardinal place of Christ; the whole duty of the Christian can be summed up in the injunction to **do all in the name of the Lord Jesus.** This phrase suggests, to begin with, that all the Christian's activities should be undertaken in prayer, that he should invoke the presence and aid of his heavenly Lord in everything; it suggests further that he should act as under the authority of Jesus. Acting in his name we cannot do anything that would be contrary to his spirit. Our thanksgiving to God, which is likewise to accompany all our actions, is offered **through him.** The position of this phrase at the end of the whole passage gives it the greatest emphasis possible, and invites us to remember that he is the only Mediator in our approach to God.

and confident love of Christ that would make outsiders eager to come in out of the coldness and loneliness of an unbelieving world. Formal and conventional Christian worship may do but little better. Where the "peace of Christ" really rules in the heart, and "the word of Christ" dwells richly in a Christian company, the skeptic, the outsider, and the man who has never found a faith cannot fail to sense the enthusiasm and joy of those who believe, longing to share their secret too.

**17.** *Do Everything in the Name of the Lord Jesus.*—One thinks of Augustine's "Love God and do as you please," the opposite of the pagan's, "Do as you please in despite of God."

So much that we do is not **in the name of the Lord Jesus** that Paul's words carry an accusation and rebuke. Who can approach this precept without penitence and a change of heart?

So much that the world does, in social contexts so all-pervasive that they involve us all, is contrary to **the name of the Lord Jesus** that the sensitive Christian can contemplate our "way of life" only in deep penitence for the corporate sin of immoral society, from which he cannot entirely free himself while he lives in this world. The way to heaven, as Bunyan reminded us, is *through* Vanity Fair, not around it. It remains for a modern Bunyan to write a Pilgrim's Progress for Christians who do not merely pass through Vanity Fair on their way to heaven, but live *in* Vanity Fair for threescore years and ten, and take responsibility for Christianizing its spirit and its ways. But the new Pilgrim's Progress will not be half as good as Bunyan's if it leaves Christian at the last buried in Vanity Fair, instead of being received gloriously into the Celestial City.

In Paul's day Christians were not citizens with responsibility for the government of society on every level from the community to the world order, as Christians now are, at least in the self-governing democracies which have arisen under the inspiration of the Christian teaching of the rights and dignities of man as a child of God. Paul's Christian ethics, like the Christian ethics of the N.T. generally, were therefore most specific on the personal level. Social ethics rightly extend, but they do not cancel out, the significance of an individual Christian life.

> There is no expeditious road
> To pack and label men for God,
> And save them by the barrel-load.[8]

In the areas of freedom that are open to him the individual Christian must count, and does count, for good when he sets his sights on this standard. **Whatever you do, in word or deed, do everything in the name of the Lord Jesus.**

What the world today needs is Christian individuals with real depth and power. Such individuals will become the centers of this creative and redeeming fellowship wherever they are. They will become the nuclei of growing and multiplying cells. We need men today whose will to live has been freed from the will to power, to success, to superiority, to social recognition, to possession, and to pretense; and has found its peace and power in the will to love, the will to fellowship, the will to self-giving service, the will to do God's will and be His children.[9]

[8] Francis Thompson, "A Judgment in Heaven," Epilogue. From *Collected Works*, ed. Wilfred Meynell. Used by permission of Burns, Oates & Washbourne, Ltd., and The Newman Press, publishers.

[9] Nels Ferré, *Return to Christianity* (New York: Harper & Bros., 1943), p. 36.

| 18 Wives, submit yourselves unto your own husbands, as it is fit in the Lord. | 18 Wives, be subject to your husbands, |

Thus in this magnificent passage Paul brings us back to the essential simplicity of the Christian life. High as his thought has soared, deeply as he has plunged into the mysteries of God and the universe in his struggle to overthrow the complex speculations of the false "philosophy" which is disturbing the Colossian Christians, he leads them back at last to the simple yet sublime beauty of the Christian character in which the truth of the gospel must flower—purity, kindness, truth, humility, love, peace, joy, thankfulness of heart—the life in which Jesus is Lord of all and his name alone is named.

### B. TABLE OF HOUSEHOLD DUTIES (3:18–4:1)

This passage is unique among the epistles of Paul, though the same literary form is employed in several of the deutero-Pauline epistles (Eph. 5:21–6:9; I Pet. 2:13–3:7; and less directly Tit. 2:1-10; I Tim. 2:8-12 and 6:1-2) and in the writings of the Apostolic Fathers. The form itself is a creation of Hellenistic moral philosophy, devised as a medium of systematic instruction in the duties of life in specific relationships. "There were philosophers who held that the function of philosophy was not to reveal the mysteries of the universe, but to advise mankind as to their conduct in the relations of domestic life. Paul himself may have felt no little sympathy with this point of view" (Knox, *St. Paul*

Someone, when asked what he understood "entire consecration" to mean, replied, "It means that I will consecrate to God everything that I can lay my hands on." The things that are done **in the name of the Lord Jesus** involve the things that are used.

A coin is so much minted grace. A dollar bill is a sacramental thing, not to be handled lightly or irreverently or to be squandered with levity. A bank should be a kind of temple, and the banker a sort of priest, a minister of holy things. There will be such a thing as a sacrament of banking when we admit the Spirit into our banking practice; and eye hath not seen nor hath ear heard nor have entered into the heart of man the things that God hath prepared for bankers that love him. And for merchants that love him. We shall have a real world of business, and not the confused commercial scramble we know, when we have understood that all business is at last the business of God. Our business transactions will then partake of the nature of acts of worship; and indeed, even as it is, for a man, who calls himself a Christian, no business transaction is safe in which he does not worship God. "The true scholar goes to his desk as to an altar," and so should the business man go to his office and the doctor to his consulting room, the cook to her kitchen and the cobbler to his last. That is the spiritual conduct of life.[1]

**Giving thanks to God the Father through him.** Note the persistent stress on the importance to a wholesome Christian life of the spirit of glad thanksgiving (see Exeg. and Expos. of vss. 15, 17; 1:3, 12; 2:6).

[1] Richard Roberts, *The Spirit of God and the Faith of Today* (New York: Harper & Bros., 1930), pp. 125-26. Used by permission.

**3:18–4:1. *A Table of Household Duties.***—The social implications of the gospel have slowly but surely come to light in the intervening centuries, and some of them to realization. The position of women in society has been radically changed and elevated since the days of Paul. Slavery, now rejected in principle everywhere, has been abolished in most quarters of the globe, though new and hidden forms of slavery subtly rise in one disguise or another to revive man's dominance over his fellow man. The family remains, even if vastly changed.

"God hath yet more light and truth to break forth from His holy Word," said John Robinson, who organized the Pilgrims' emigration to America three centuries ago. Even he could not realize the new applications of the gospel, social and personal, which were to come to light as a result of his own pioneering adventure. These changes for the liberation and enrichment of human life under God do not outdate the gospel, but merely the contemporary applications of the gospel to the conditions of first-century life. Christ is as he was and ever shall be. Mankind must still look to him as Savior and guide into the rewarding ways of love and brotherhood.

It is right, and indeed, imperative, that Christians take responsibility not only for bringing individual lives into a saving relationship with Christ, but also for making the institutions of society more serviceable instruments of God's will for all mankind. And through consecrated Christians more conquests of the spirit over the material conditions of life shall come as surely as God is God.

*and Church of the Gentiles,* p. 177). Knox cites Seneca (*Epistles* 15. 2 [94]. 1), who tells us that "some have allowed only that part of philosophy which . . . tells the husband how to behave toward his wife, the father how to bring up his children, the master how to govern his slaves." In all his other epistles, as also in the preceding section of this epistle (vss. 5-17), Paul's exhortations bear altogether upon the conduct and character of the Christian simply *qua* Christian, without concern for his age or civil status. Here for the first and only time his instruction deals with particular areas of social life—with the duties of husbands and wives, children and fathers, slaves and masters. Obviously the one man may be at once husband, father, and master (or slave) ; here he is addressed in all three capacities, and his duty as a Christian in each respect is severally pointed out.

This awakening of concern for mutual relationships within the Christian household has a significance which does not appear on the surface. It is in part a reflection of the decline in the emphasis on eschatology which we have noticed elsewhere in the epistle (see on 3:3-4) ; in part, also, of the more settled conditions of church life at the end of a generation of evangelism. As the thought of the apostle ceases to be dominated by the expectation of the imminent end of history and of human society as it has been known, the settled life of the Christian family gains in importance for religion; the fundamental social institutions are no longer viewed as belonging to the conditions of an era which is swiftly to pass away, but as the enduring sphere of Christian living. The earlier attitude of Paul, as reflected in his discussion of marriage in I Cor. 7, offers a striking contrast to the passage with which we are now dealing.

In this connection we are bound to recall the subordination of family loyalty to the allegiance of the individual to Christ and to God which is forcibly expressed in the teaching of Jesus. He rejects the family tie as supreme or decisive for himself (Mark 3:31-35, with its final "Whoever does the will of God is my brother, and sister, and

---

These things shall be: a loftier race
    Than e'er the world hath known shall rise
With flame of freedom in their souls
    And light of knowledge in their eyes.[2]

Man cannot bring it to pass. But Christians must consecrate themselves to it, because God works his sovereign will in history chiefly through men. If Paul were living in the twentieth century he would not withdraw himself from the campaign for the Christianizing of the social order, even as he did not withdraw himself, like the Colossian cultists, from the duty to Christianize the personal and community life of his time.

Though the ultimate conclusion of things when

    . . . man shall be at one with God
        In bonds of firm necessity [3]

lies beyond the sphere of time and history in eternity, the Christian's duty to work with Christ for God in this world is altered not one whit.

It would, however, be a grave distortion of the gospel to offer to hard-pressed lives only the hope of a far-off salvation when social conditions would be made favorable to living the good life. Multitudes would live through their

[2] J. Addington Symonds, "These things shall be."
[3] *Ibid.*

generation and pass from earth before such a goal was even in sight.

The new life in Christ is a present offer and a present experience in those who accept him. For two thousand years Christians have been living the life of saving fellowship with Christ in an unchristian world, and often in the most unfavorable environment. The heart of the gospel is not that Christ is slowly saving society and wants your help. That is the second step. It stems from the first, viz., Christ has redeemed you; accept him and live victoriously in him in whatever kind of world your lot is cast. That was Paul's message to the Colossians. It is the gospel for moderns as well (see Expos., vs. 17 above, "Whatever you do, in word or deed, do everything in the name of the Lord Jesus").

The society to which Paul addressed his "table of household duties" was very different from ours; but the duty to make one's individual life a witness for Christ, which he impresses upon wives, husbands, children, fathers, slaves, and masters, has lost none of its cogency in the changed conditions of modern times. The practical counsels that follow are all to be read in the light of the joyous, loving, thankful, Christian life which Paul has already described (vss. 12-17).

**18. *Wives, Be Subject to Your Husbands, as Is Fitting in the Lord.*—**Modern ideals of the

19 Husbands, love *your* wives, and be not bitter against them.

as is fitting in the Lord. 19 Husbands, love your wives, and do not be harsh with them.

---

mother"); and he demands that his followers also shall subordinate it to loyalty to himself: "If any one comes to me and does not hate his own father and mother and wife and children and brothers and sisters, yes, and even his own life, he cannot be my disciple" (Luke 14:26). It is clear that the coming of the gospel frequently brought strife into the household, as some believed and others rejected the message; and the believer was frequently obliged to make the harrowing decision between obedience to Christ and loyalty to his family. All too often a man's enemies were those of his own household, as brother delivered up brother to death, and the father his child, and children rose against their parents and had them put to death (Matt. 10:21, 34-39).

The introduction into Christian literature of the table of household duties reflects a time when these family divisions were no longer so general, and when the Christian community tended more to consist of entire households, with parents, children, and slaves. It is worth noting that all the other instances of the use of this form in the N.T. occur in writings of the second generation or later (Ephesians, I Peter, the Pastorals). Its use in Colossians, therefore, lends some weight to the argument against the authenticity of this epistle. On the other hand, it has been suggested that the flight and return of Onesimus and Paul's intercession on his behalf led Paul to deal with the general question of the relations of slave and master within the Christian society, and to preface his discussion with a few words concerning the more intimate relationships of kinship by blood. Some force must be accorded to this suggestion, in view of the disproportionate attention that is devoted to the attitude of the slave.

**18-21.** We cannot fail to be struck by the meagerness of the instruction given to the different family groups, and by the entire lack of appeal to any specifically Christian motive in the exhortations to husbands and to fathers, and the indefiniteness and generality of the Christian motivation adduced in the address to wives and to children. It

---

freedom and rights of women stem directly from the Christian gospel. Paul wrote to those who must perforce live in a social system where women had no rights as they are understood today (see Eph. 5:22-23). There is little evidence that he questioned that system, or could then conceive of a society so radically different from anything that he knew as is our own. Nonetheless, the Christian principle of reverence for persons as persons, which has inspired the social advance that we know, is implicit in the Christian view of life and explicit in Paul's own teaching, "There is neither male nor female: for ye are all one in Christ Jesus" (Gal. 3:28).

Whether in that social context or in ours, the goodness of a noble Christian life, fulfilling and surpassing mere duty, is beyond price, and its influence beyond measure. Without that, the improved social pattern will prove to be a hollow gain. It is the soul, not its surroundings, that counts the most.

Modern marriage vows are identical and reciprocal for man and woman. The obligations of love in the family circle are entirely mutual. They lose none of their inherent sacredness,

their binding quality, or their preserving goodness, for that.

**19. Husbands Love Your Wives, and Do Not Be Harsh with Them.**—Paul evidently observed this to be a familiar fault! When one is secure in his rights over another, he is prone to imperious dragooning. And who or what shall stop him from doing what he likes with that which is his own, especially in the intimacy of his private domain? Only a changed heart and a disciplined spirit will avail—in any kind of social order. In the authoritarian family of Paul's time Christ in the heart could elevate the marriage relationship to the high comradeship of shared responsibility in enduring love. Present-day recognition of the dignity and rights of women in home and community is a needed defense against abuse. It rightly supplements, but can never supplant, the preserving power of an inner love.

The two clauses in Paul's admonition may not be meant as simple alternatives. A man may not love his wife, and therefore be harsh to her. On the other hand, he may love his wife sincerely and still be harsh to her. The correct relations may hold, and all moral obligations

20 Children, obey *your* parents in all things: for this is well-pleasing unto the Lord.

21 Fathers, provoke not your children *to anger,* lest they be discouraged.

22 Servants, obey in all things *your* masters according to the flesh; not with eye-service, as menpleasers; but in singleness of heart, fearing God:

20 Children, obey your parents in everything, for this pleases the Lord. 21 Fathers, do not provoke your children, lest they become discouraged. 22 Slaves, obey in everything those who are your earthly masters, not with eyeservice, as men-pleasers, but in singleness of heart, fearing the Lord.

---

cannot be claimed that any great advance is made toward the formulation of a Christian ideal of family life here. It is impossible to draw any sweeping contrast with the family ethic of the contemporary paganism, for the conditions of family life varied widely in different parts of the empire in accordance with local custom and with the relative degree of stability which was to be found in particular social groups. Nothing specific is known about the position of women in the neighborhood of Colossae, nor does the language suggest that any concrete social condition is envisaged by the writer. There is indeed a curious implication that discipline in the household tends to be unduly severe: men are warned, as **husbands,** against harshness to their **wives;** and as **fathers,** against "provoking" their children by a severity which would cause them to **become discouraged.** "Chafe" would perhaps be a better rendering of ἐρεθίζετε than **provoke;** the thought is certainly of a continual irksome discipline such as causes children to feel that nothing they do can be right.

22-25. The greatest emphasis is laid on the exhortation to **slaves** (RSV, correctly; not **servants,** as in KJV). It is to be noted that in I Pet. 2:18-25 the slaves are again addressed at much greater length than any other group in the household. This emphasis may be due to the fact that slaves constituted a great part—perhaps the majority—of the early Christian communities; even more, it is occasioned by the need to check the tendency to rebellion which the Christian gospel of freedom was bound to quicken in the mind of the slave. Here again, the fading of the eschatological expectation weakened the force of the appeal to endure a situation which was in any case fleeting; some other ground of comfort and of patience had to be found when men could no longer be confident that the time was short. The new motive was found in the acceptance of the lowly status of slave, with all the indignities which it involved, as the sphere of service appointed for one by Christ. Early Christianity was far from accepting the existing social order as

---

be fulfilled, but their union may be jarred by an irritable spirit. "The peace of Christ" can rule within to fill the outward harmony of dutiful demeanor with the inward melodies of attuned spirits.

**20. *Children, Obey Your Parents in Everything, for This Pleases the Lord.*—**In everything needs the qualification for this pleases the Lord. Who, knowing human nature, would care to counsel, "Children, obey your parents in everything, for this pleases the parents"? Ephesians puts the meaning clearly, "Children, obey your parents in the Lord: for this is right" (Eph. 6:1). Unhappy the child, and wretched the parents, when parental influences lead young lives away from God (see Matt. 18:6).

**21. *Fathers, Do Not Provoke Your Children, Lest They Become Discouraged.*—**Severely con-

scientious fathers can frustrate their own good purposes for their children by frustrating the children. On the other hand, Paul would not have regarded as Christian the laxness of parents who fail to curb their children's willful disregard of moral duty, lest they forfeit their affection, and thereby relinquish moral control of the immature, and sometimes wayward, lives for which they are responsible. The exercise of parental authority is a duty for parents. It is the mishandling of it which Paul deplores. Love is the clue to the discipline that does not drive with goads, but leads and guides in mutual respect and cordial partnership.

**3:22–4:1. *Slaves, Obey . . . Your Earthly Masters. . . . Masters, Treat Your Slaves Justly.*—**It is wrong for one man to own another. In the "new nature" there cannot be slave or free

23 And whatsoever ye do, do *it* heartily, as to the Lord, and not unto men;

24 Knowing that of the Lord ye shall receive the reward of the inheritance: for ye serve the Lord Christ.

25 But he that doeth wrong shall receive for the wrong which he hath done: and there is no respect of persons.

23 Whatever your task, work heartily, as serving the Lord and not men, 24 knowing that from the Lord you will receive the inheritance as your reward; you are serving the Lord Christ. 25 For the wrongdoer will be paid back for the wrong he has done, and there is no partiality.

---

satisfactory, but it was conscious of no mission to change it for the better. It taught its adherents neither to conform to the external framework of their time, nor to seek directly to alter it, but to live within it a life rooted in a totally different order. So the slave was encouraged not to rebel against his status, but to govern himself under all its disabilities as one whose supreme loyalty was to Christ. The thought of Paul here is that the obedience of the slave ceases to be an enforced compliance with the authority of his master when he accepts it as the will of Christ for him and seeks to please Christ by doing service to his master with heartiness and good will. His labor as a slave can then be viewed not as something that must be endured because it cannot be cured; nor, in accordance with the earlier attitude, as something that can be endured with patience because the joys of the new age are at hand, but as a service in which he can find fulfillment because it is done for Christ: **you are serving the Lord Christ** (vs. 24).

**Lord** is here used with a kind of double sense: it is a play on the ordinary civil use of *kyrios* as "master" of the slave, and its religious use as the cult title of Christ (cf. 4:1). Such labor is not unrewarded, though the slave does not receive wages; the reward will come to him in a higher sphere—**from the Lord** [he] **will receive the inheritance as** [his] **reward** (vs. 24). The high reward of life, however much materialists may scoff at "pie in the sky," is not to be sought in the material realm; and the slave was not deluded but ennobled when he was taught to seek something higher than earth could hold for him. Every noble soul that ever lived has sought that which grows not on mortal soil; and Paul here teaches the very slave to nourish in his heart immortal aspirations.

The point of the warning in vs. 25 is not clear. It may be written with the case of the slave Onesimus in mind (see on Philem. 18). Paul had somehow made his acquaintance in Rome and had persuaded him to return to his duty, sending a letter of warm intercession to his master Philemon (or Archippus). Some unrest may have been caused among the Christian slaves of Colossae if they felt that Onesimus had not suffered punishment for his flight, but had at Paul's request been received into high favor. They may have been aggrieved at his good fortune and have felt that he had been shown **partiality**

---

man. "Christ is all, and in all" (3:11). "Ye are all one in Christ Jesus" (Gal. 3:28). Christ dethroned slavery when he gave us the gospel. How long it took for the import of his teaching to permeate the mind of man which was conditioned to slavery as a universal social pattern! How long after that to penetrate the ponderous mass of the social and economic order! But there can be no doubt whence the moral guidance came, or whence the spiritual dynamic to honor the guidance in constructive reform. The abolition of slavery was man's obedience to the law and will of God. History will not reverse its verdict. The spiritual principle is clearly seen. Other forms of human exploitation await, and will yield to, the awakened Christian conscience.

Nonetheless, the great reform is sabotaged and spiritually barren if the liberated are hated, despised, and deprived of recognition in the world of free men. Outward status can be an empty blessing when the spirit that makes all one in Christ Jesus is callously withheld. On the other hand, when that spirit is extended, it can enhance the mutual fellowship of the free beyond the highest possible relationship of master and slave. The remedy is not to withdraw the freedom, but to fulfill it in the community of Christian love.

Again, in the social order of Paul's day, which was not ready for what has since come to pass, the personal dedication to Christ of life, possessions, privileges, and powers, by master and by

4 Masters, give unto *your* servants that which is just and equal; knowing that ye also have a Master in heaven.

4 Masters, treat your slaves justly and fairly, knowing that you also have a Master in heaven.

---

in being treated better than they who had never run away from their masters. The incident may also have suggested to other unhappy slaves that the consequences of flight were well worth risking; even if they were caught and compelled to return, the results might be advantageous to them, as to Onesimus. The words might then be taken as a warning against meditating such escapades, taking advantage of the kindliness of Christian masters. It is simpler, however, to take them as the counterpart to the promise of **reward** (vs. 24), especially as impartiality is always attributed to God elsewhere in the N.T. (except Jas. 2:1, which is not a true parallel). As the slave who does his duty faithfully will be rewarded by his Master in heaven, so **the wrongdoer will be paid back for the wrong he has done. Partiality** (RSV) or **respect of persons** (KJV), usually referring to undue privileges granted to the high and mighty, has here the converse reference. The slave will have no special favor shown him at God's judgment merely because of his low estate.

**4:1.** The Christian master is now taught not to regard his slave as a mere chattel. Here again the point of the verse lies in the double sense of *kyrios,* here translated **Master.** Christ holds the same authority over the master as the master holds over his slave; the master must learn to exercise his rights over others in the spirit in which Christ governs him.

The modern reader finds it surprising that no N.T. writer condemns the institution of slavery or even advises Christian masters to free their slaves. It must be remembered, however, that there was little free labor in the world of that time; and the gift of freedom in itself, without some provision for future employment, would have been a doubtful kindness. We hear of occasional freedmen who made a place for themselves in the structure of society; some of the emperors employed freedmen in the highest offices of state. But those who attained such eminence were cordially hated, and they were of course exceptional men. The freedman generally became a hanger-on of some wealthy house, as dependent on his patron's bounty as any slave, or sank into the mass of the urban proletariat, eking out a precarious existence on the public dole of grain. The indiscriminate bestowal of freedom was simply not feasible in the social conditions of the time, and the Christian teachers were wise in their generation when they did not make emancipation a general obligation on their converts. At the same time they struck at the roots of the institution of slavery when they gave the slave full rights in the church. No office was barred to him or made more difficult of access because of his civil status; he came to the sacraments on the same terms as his master and shared freely in all that the fellowship had to offer. The same moral ideal was held before him; and in every way he was regarded, and taught to regard himself, as a person loved by God and made to love

---

slave alike, could demonstrate the power of love to ennoble life and to make it spiritually creative. To that high level of victorious Christian living Paul called both slaves and masters. To that same spiritual quality of living Christ calls us, in whatever social context our lot is cast. The worst situation will yield at last to the man who is committed to serve the Lord Christ. The most favorable situation will overwhelm the man who is not.

**4:1. *You Also Have a Master in Heaven.*—** Note the words of Jesus, which go beyond what Paul states here—**Masters, treat your slaves**

justly and fairly—to declare specifically the equality and brotherhood of all men in himself, "Be not ye called Rabbi: for one is your Master, even Christ; and all ye are brethren. And call no man your father upon the earth: for one is your Father, which is in heaven. Neither be ye called masters: for one is your Master, even Christ. But he that is greatest among you shall be your servant" (Matt. 23:8-11).

In every one of these social relationships that Paul has touched upon, every individual has an obligation to others which he can turn into an opportunity for expressing the creative Chris-

2 Continue in prayer, and watch in the same with thanksgiving;

3 Withal praying also for us, that God would open unto us a door of utterance, to speak the mystery of Christ, for which I am also in bonds:

2 Continue steadfastly in prayer, being watchful in it with thanksgiving; 3 and pray for us also, that God may open to us a door for the word, to declare the mystery of Christ, on account of which I am in

---

and to be loved by all his Christian brethren. The master, for his part, was taught to regard the slave no longer as his chattel, but "as a beloved brother" (Philem. 16), and to look upon his legal relationship to the slave as imposing a responsibility, rather than as conferring rights. It was not practicable to advocate the abolition of the institution, or even its abrogation as between Christians; but a new spirit was introduced into the relationship, as the slave was taught the secret of inward freedom, of responsibility, and of self-respect, and the master learned not humanitarianism alone, but respect for the person of his slave and all the lessons that flowed from fellowship with him in the life of the Christian community.

### C. Exhortation to Prayer (4:2-4)

**2-4.** After the brief series of admonitions bearing upon Christian conduct in the several relationships of the household, Paul now returns to general exhortations which apply to all alike. **Continue steadfastly in prayer:** The verb προσκαρτερεῖτε is strong and picturesque. It is used by the historian Polybius to describe the obstinate continuance of a siege. Prayer is not to be perfunctory or intermittent or halfhearted, but earnest and assiduous; we are urged to besiege the throne of God with our prayers, with the unremitting perseverance which cries, "I will not let thee go, except thou bless me" (Gen. 32:26). **Watchful:** Against temptation; the thought is that the life of prayer is the surest means of guarding against slackness and moral failure (cf. Matt. 26:41). **With thanksgiving:** The phrase need not be taken in dependence on the participle; rather, it is co-ordinate with it. **Thanksgiving** is not especially associated with **being watchful**; it belongs to all

---

tian spirit that conquers sin and strife and all unbrotherliness. There is a victorious Christian way to meet every situation that arises. This teaching is easily enough understood. The harder task is to translate it into life. The power to do it is in Christ, the great reconciler to God, and to one another, of the willful, the frustrated, the defeated, and the estranged (1:10-12, 21-22; 3:3).

**2-4. Continue Steadfastly in Prayer . . . and Pray for Us Also, that God May Open to Us a Door for the Word.**—The theory of the devotional life, the correct doctrine of it, and even an overwhelming initial experience of it will not avail to keep "the new nature . . . renewed . . . after the image of its creator" (3:10). That requires constant practice of the devotional life. Here every Christian is "on his own." The reality of his Christian life fades when he neglects its culture and discipline.

In addition to constant prayer and spiritual alertness, Paul especially commends intercession for the cause of Christ in its world-wide aspects, both as a strength to him who prays and as a channel by which the tides of the Spirit can

sweep with fuller power through the church. Note in the use of "us" and "I" how he urges the intercessions, not in vague and general terms, but for specific persons and specific tasks. **Pray for us also, that God may open to us a door for the word . . . that I may make it clear.**

**That God may open to us a door.** Paul was in prison. His course was nearly run. His restless, active journeyings were ended. One might say that the doors had closed for him—prison doors, at that. But it was not so. When a Christian wants to serve God, God will find a way to use him. When he cannot go forth to find his opportunities, God will bring them to him. Consider what God did with this man in the seemingly hopeless frustration of an imprisonment from which only death released him. Those saints in Caesar's household (Phil. 4:22)—servants in the very palace of the pagan emperor—how many of them owed their knowledge of Christ to Paul? In Phil. 1:12-14 he declares that he is bearing witness "in all the palace," and elsewhere as well, and that his own faith and fortitude in adversity are inspiring many of the Christians in Rome to more resolute witness for Christ

230

| 4 That I may make it manifest, as I ought to speak. | prison, 4 that I may make it clear, as I ought to speak. |
| 5 Walk in wisdom toward them that are without, redeeming the time. | 5 Conduct yourselves wisely toward out- |

true prayer. Prayer guards the inner life against the assaults of temptation; it also expresses our gratitude to God for his past mercies and present grace. To this Paul now adds the element of intercession, prayer for others. High as is his own mission, he desires to be supported by the prayers of the whole church; and he impresses upon all Christians their responsibility to pray for those on whom the heaviest burden of Christian labor falls. It is significant of his mind that he does not ask his readers to pray that his imprisonment may end, but that he may find opportunity to preach the gospel—**that God may open to us a door for the word.** For the significance of **door** cf. I Cor. 16:9, "A wide door for effective work has opened to me." The second ἵνα-clause (vs. 4) is subordinated to the first, and is final, as the first is not; it expresses the purpose for which Paul desires **that God may open . . . a door.** Φανερώσω (**make it clear**) suggests more than **declare** (vs. 3) or **speak** (vs. 4), both rendering the same Greek infinitive λαλῆσαι; it conveys Paul's sense of a mission not only to proclaim the gospel, but also to expound its deeper implications.

### D. On Christian Behavior Toward Pagans (4:5-6)

**5-6.** This is really an appeal to temper enthusiasm with discretion—a warning against ill-timed manifestations of hostility to pagan customs, and an admonition to meet inquiries and criticisms with grace and good humor. Like the table of household duties (3:18–4:1), this passage implies that the Christian group is now a coherent, settled element in the community.

**Them that are without:** Pagan neighbors and associates. **Without** suggests the figure of a walled enclosure; the walls were invisible, but the separation between Christians and the general society of the time was real. The phrase reflects most vividly the Christian

than ever before. His influence reached out by letter and special messenger to Philippi in Greece, to Colossae in Asia Minor, and doubtless to other places near and far. Somehow Paul fell in with Onesimus, the slave who had run away from his master in Colossae. In that encounter he found the opportunity to win the man to Christ, and then to send him back home with the letter to Philemon. Because he was so vital a Christian himself, the seven men whom he mentions in vss. 7-14 voluntarily gathered about him to be multipliers of his own influence, both in Rome and across the seas. The letters which he wrote from prison are sacred scripture, and have kindled countless flames of Christian devotion from that day to this. "Man's extremity is God's opportunity." If he really wants to be used, God opens doors for him where all the doors seem closed. Christ turns his frustrations into triumphs.

**5-6. On Christian Behavior Toward Pagans.**—Having sought their prayers for his own effective witness, Paul counsels them to be personal evangelists themselves—a gloriously constructive conclusion to a letter whose actual purpose was to recall his readers from compromising en-

tanglements with the pagan world. The best defense is offense. If one's faith is shaky, let him take some real responsibility for the faith of others and see it through. Paul leaves with his Colossian brethren not merely a warning, nor even an exhortation, but a task to do—to commend Christ to their pagan neighbors. Before they were through they would doubtless have commended Christ to themselves as never before. The fantastic complexities of the Colossian speculation would fade from view, as a dim light is swallowed up in brightness, and doubtless others would be won to Christ.

**5-6. Conduct Yourselves Wisely Toward Outsiders.**—The outsiders were the non-Christian population, the overwhelming majority of the people among whom they lived, and specifically the friends, neighbors, and acquaintances in business and social life with whom of necessity they had constant daily intercourse. In that situation the unconscious attitudes and habitual practices of Christians assumed the utmost importance. They could exalt or degrade the new life in the estimation of the world. More than that, they could win or repel those who were potential converts.

6 Let your speech *be* always with grace, seasoned with salt, that ye may know how ye ought to answer every man.

siders, making the most of the time. 6 Let your speech always be gracious, seasoned with salt, so that you may know how you ought to answer every one.

---

sense that the church is the true community, from which unbelievers are shut out; there is no feeling of deprivation on their own part, as might be expected in men who were in many respects outcasts from the established social order. The handful of believers do not think of themselves as a minority group, living on the outskirts of society; their imagination sees the picture in reverse, and thinks of the whole surrounding mass of paganism as of **them that are without.**

**Redeeming the time:** The participle is epexegetic, giving point to the counsel to **walk in wisdom. Time** (καιρός) : Not of duration, as the rendering of the RSV would suggest, but of a particular moment or season. The general sense is "making proper use of the occasion." In association with **wisdom** the words are probably in part a warning against unseasonable manifestations of zeal, such as would be more apt to turn men away from, than to win them to, Christ and the church; in part, to be taken positively as an invitation to seize every favorable occasion for testifying to the faith.

---

It is still so as regards the skeptics, the decent pagans, the indifferent multitudes lacking any real belief and often unaware of their lack, who are outside the fellowship but not beyond the reach of the church of Christ. The settled attitudes of individual Christians count either for or against the faith which they profess.

The non-Christians are called outsiders. Christians were to be separatists, and yet they were not to be separatists (cf. I Cor. 7:14-18). Their separation was to be qualitative, not spatial or social. They were not to withdraw from ordinary community life in order to nourish an ingrown spiritual life of their own. No "iron curtain" of exclusiveness was to shut them out from brotherly human relationships with non-Christian neighbors. (Cf. the attitude of Jesus with the attitude of the Pharisees toward the common people who were "without the law." Note also the reference to the Epistle to Diognetus in Expos., 3:16.)

There is an aggressive as well as a defensive purpose behind Paul's words. The defensive purpose was to protect the good name of the Christian community. By their personal conduct they could shield their fellow believers from calumny, abuse, and even persecution. The aggressive purpose was to go after the outsiders and bring them in. This is how the church grew from small beginnings. The average modern Christian has largely lost this urgent sense of personal mission. The disciples of modern revolutionary movements have taken it up with alarming zeal. The church of Christ must recapture it.

Paul gives three directives to those whom he urges to commend Christ to others:

**Redeeming the time** (KJV); **making the most of the time** (RSV) ; "making the proper use of the occasion" (Exeg.).

(*a*) This has been taken to mean not wasting time, but filling it with positive Christian living, possibly with the thought that little time remained before the return of Christ.

> Fill up each hour with what will last;
>    Buy up the moments as they go;
> The life above, when this is past,
>    Is the ripe fruit of life below.[4]

(*b*) Another meaning is suggested in the Exeg. Be alive to opportunities for personal witness. Live "existentially," alert to Christ and for Christ, in the experience of every moment. Seize the critical moment as it comes, the chance encounter, the unforeseen turn in the conversation, the unplanned incident which brings a Christian mind and a pagan mind into momentary contact, "making the proper use of the occasion" for wise and effective Christian witness. Be prepared for such opportunities, expect them to come, and grasp them when they do come. So Paul found his open doors. His meeting with Onesimus is one example. His meeting with Epaphras in Rome is another. It led to this very letter which he is writing.

A slack Christian will go on indefinitely, serenely believing that he never gets a favorable opportunity to "put in a good word for Jesus Christ." A vital Christian will find opportunities on every hand, and will speak in a natural, unforced way of the faith that means so much to him. He will learn when to speak and when to

[4] Horatius Bonar, "He liveth long who liveth well."

**With grace, seasoned with salt: Grace** has here the well-established classical sense of "pleasantness" or "attractiveness." There may be an undertone of the thought that such **grace** is the fruit of divine influence on the character. **Salt:** The point of the metaphor is not certain; perhaps the best interpretation is "good humor." In any case, it must have some connotation of that which does away with the dull, the insipid, the platitudinous. **How ye ought to answer every man:** Each man must be dealt with individually; that is the force of ἐνὶ ἑκάστῳ. The reference is still to **them that are without.** There is no stock answer to jeers, perplexities, idle curiosity, and sincere inquiry; each person is a special case and must be answered as his condition and his character require.

---

keep silent, when his witness would alienate and when it may persuade, "making the proper use of the occasion" for Christ.

**Let your speech always be gracious, seasoned with salt.** Have the right approach to others. This is the second point in Paul's short summary of how to be an effective witness. Note the suggestion of the Exeg. that in the zeal and exaltation of the new faith Christians were likely to break into incessant and fanatical hostility to pagan customs, possibly also into crudely aggressive ways of advocating Christ. **Let your speech always be gracious.** Do not take the short cut of trying to make Christians before you have taken the trouble to make friends. Persistent invasion of the private personalities of other people will set up barriers to the acceptance of Christ which were not there before. *Savoir-faire* can add graciousness to a Christian's social relationships, as well as to a pagan's, and increase his Christian influence as well. A loving spirit makes a lovable character. Behind the graciousness of a Christian's bearing is the divine grace which nourishes his spiritual life.

At the same time, Paul always got his message through. Christians who permit a gracious bearing toward others to absolve them from all responsibility to give a positive Christian witness to their non-Christian friends and neighbors are neglecting the aggressive good will which makes personal evangelism really effective.

**Seasoned with salt.** The idea goes deeper than mere brilliance and liveliness in conversation. Not all are gifted in this way. Paul would not counsel the unnatural pretense of a forced imitation of the salty speech and engaging manners of others. By salt he means the elevating influence of a life rooted in Christ and devoted to his purposes. Religiosity, priggishness, or pious unreality do not commend Christ. But any Christian whose life is firmly established in an honest Christian loyalty can speak convincingly from his own experience. What he says in that spirit will not sound like religious humbug. It will have the ring of reality. (For the meaning of "salt" see Expos., Matt. 5:13 and Mark 9:49-50; refer also to Eph. 4:29.)

**Know how you ought to answer every one.** Speak to the individual. This is Paul's third rule for personal evangelism. Know people, be aware of them as persons, love them as fellow men, and you will be in rapport with them. When it is a single individual with whom you are dealing, you will be in rapport with him. If you respect him, he will come to respect you. If you like him, he will be encouraged to like you. What you say to him will then be addressed to his condition. The faith that he senses in you, or hears you speak about, will have meaning for him in his own unique character and circumstances. He will learn from you, through the understanding of his personal interest or problem which you reveal, the real meaning of Christ for his own life.

Paul founded churches, but they began with individuals. And Paul had learned how to deal with individuals, the individuals who approached him, and the individuals whom God prompted him to approach with the invitation of Christ. Many of his open doors led him straight into the lives of individual persons— Timothy, Silas, Luke, Lydia, Onesimus, and many whose names are now unknown. And he sent them out to repeat in cumulative Christian witness what by the grace of God he himself had done for them.

So, he reminds his Colossian friends, the casual encounters of normal, everyday life can be made the means of (*a*) vindicating their own faith to the pagan world (see I Pet. 3:15), and (*b*) leading others into the Christian life (see I Cor. 9:22).

Having himself taken the initiative in sending to his Colossian brethren this letter of inspiring assurance that they have in Christ the full answer to their own problem, Paul closes his instruction with an open invitation to take the initiative themselves in commending Christ to their fellows, confident that with Christ as guide, they have the spiritual resource **to answer every one.**

| | |
|---|---|
| 7 All my state shall Tychicus declare unto you, *who is* a beloved brother, and a faithful minister and fellow servant in the Lord: | 7 Tych'icus will tell you all about my affairs; he is a beloved brother and faithful minister and fellow servant in the Lord. |

## IV. Introductions and Personal Greetings (4:7-18)

The substance of the epistle is completed. Paul has set forth his great doctrine of the primal significance of Christ in creation and in redemption; and in the light of this he has refuted the Colossian "philosophy," which was seeking to introduce a cult of angelic mediators—"elemental spirits of the universe" (2:8)—as needed to supplement the saving work of Christ. He has then set forth a magnificent ideal of the inward and outward life of the Christian in its freedom, its heavenly aspirations, its purity, its humility, and its love and joy; he has affirmed the application of the loftiest principles of the spiritual life to the pedestrian circle of domestic duties; and he has concluded his teaching with an admonition to prayer and thanksgiving, a request that his readers will aid him with their prayers, and a few words of advice about the way to approach pagans. The remainder of the epistle is given over to personal matters: the introduction of his messengers, greetings to the church at Colossae from friends in Rome, a reference to the sister church at Laodicea, and a subscription in Paul's own hand.

The main interest of this section for us lies in its bearing upon debated critical questions—the date and place of writing of the epistle (see Intro., pp. 134-37), and its relation to other Pauline writings, especially to Philemon. The following comments will be limited mainly to the few phrases which are of permanent significance for the life and outlook of the Christian fellowship.

### A. Introduction of Tychicus and Onesimus (4:7-9)

**7-9.** Tychicus and Onesimus, who were traveling in company from Rome to the cities of the Lycus Valley, are here introduced. Tychicus is known to us as one of Paul's associates whom he chose to include in the representative group of Gentile converts who

---

**7-18. Introductions and Personal Greetings.** —The Epistle to the Colossians is not the easiest book for the general reader, at least in its theological sections. John Oman tells of a devout old farmer who dutifully listened to a long series of sermons based upon it. When he had heard them all he remarked, "The Colossians . . . must have been very clever folk. If, as we were told, the epistle was just a letter written to be read to them, I suppose they would understand it when they heard, while we have been three months at it and don't understand it yet." [5] The original hearers did understand more easily many of the references to contemporary thought and practice which puzzle the modern reader, because Paul does not stop to describe what was known to everybody at that time. Confusing phrases in the original text, and in the KJV, and allusions to a world of ideas quite foreign to modern minds, need to be explained. It is hoped that unlike the British farmer, the reader of the present interpretation in the Exeg. and the Expos. will gain a clearer understanding of the relevance of this

[5] *Concerning the Ministry* (London: Student Christian Movement Press, 1936), p. 236.

message from Paul to the real spiritual problem of the church to which he sent it, and also of the abiding value of his teaching for Christians in every age and everywhere.

A useful summary of the main points which Paul has touched upon in this letter is given in the opening paragraph of the Exeg. of this section. It might well be made the basis of a series of studies or addresses on the great ideas of the Epistle to the Colossians.

Furthermore, if one takes the trouble to trace, through the scattered references in the N.T., what can be learned about the lives of the friends and fellow workers whom Paul mentions in his letters, some rewarding insights into the transmission of Christian influence through individuals come to light (see Expos., 1:7, on Epaphras). Most of their story has been lost but enough remains to repay study. Standard dictionaries and encyclopedias of the Bible give the relevant facts. With the help of a concordance and this Commentary one can make his own survey of what there is to be known about the careers of these men who were real builders of the church, though less than the very great. A valuable compilation of the data and

8 Whom I have sent unto you for the same purpose, that he might know your estate, and comfort your hearts;

9 With Onesimus, a faithful and beloved brother, who is *one* of you. They shall make known unto you all things which *are done* here.

10 Aristarchus my fellow prisoner salut-

8 I have sent him to you for this very purpose, that you may know how we are and that he may encourage your hearts, 9 and with him Ones'imus, the faithful and beloved brother, who is one of yourselves. They will tell you of everything that has taken place here.

10 Aristar'chus my fellow prisoner

---

accompanied him to Jerusalem on his final visit (Acts 20:4), when he was bringing the collection from his Gentile congregations of Macedonia and Achaia to present it to the mother church for the relief of the poor (Rom. 15:25-26). Tychicus himself was a man of Asia, probably of Ephesus, but he had been assisting Paul in the evangelization of Macedonia and Achaia. **Faithful minister:** Paul uses the same word (διάκονος) of Epaphras (1:7) and of himself (1:23). It is not an official title ("deacon") as in the later organization of the church; it simply affirms that Tychicus is engaged in the service of the gospel. Paul affirms his sense of comradeship with him in calling him **fellow servant in the Lord.** Strictly, we should translate "fellow slave." He is a partner in that voluntary bondage to the Master in heaven, which Paul often puts forward as his proudest title (Rom. 1:1; etc.). Paul is entrusting to him the delivery of this letter, and is leaving it to him to tell them of the apostle's situation at Rome.

Onesimus is described only as **the faithful and beloved brother;** no reference is made to his status as a slave, which was a matter of indifference to the Christian community, and no mention is made of the circumstances in which he was returning to his master. **One of yourselves:** A Colossian, not a member of the Colossian church; Onesimus had been converted to Christianity after his flight from home, when he somehow made acquaintance with Paul at Rome.

### B. Greetings from Paul's Associates (4:10-14)

**10-11.** Three Jewish Christians send their greetings. Aristarchus was a Macedonian of Thessalonica (Acts 19:29; 20:4), who had helped Paul during his mission in Ephesus

---

tradition concerning Timothy, Tychicus, Aristarchus, Mark, Barnabas, Luke, Demas, Onesimus, and Philemon has been made by L. B. Radford in his commentary *The Epistle to the Colossians and the Epistle to Philemon.*[6] More imaginative and conjectural reconstructions of the lives of Mark, Barnabas, Luke, Epaphras, Archippus, Onesimus, and Philemon are worked out with great suggestiveness for the teacher in J. A. Robertson's *The Hidden Romance of the New Testament.*[7]

**9. Onesimus.**—From the Epistle to Philemon we know that Onesimus was a slave who had left Philemon, his master, and run away to Rome. Philemon's home was in Colossae; so he would be a member of the very church to which Paul sent the Epistle to the Colossians. Onesimus had been won to Christ by Paul, and had been persuaded by the apostle to return and make amends. Paul's Epistle to Philemon deals with this personal matter.

⁶ Pp. 127-43, 324-26.
⁷ London: James Clarke & Co., n.d.

Note in the present passing reference to Onesimus another instance of Paul's characteristic attitude to believe the best of others, and to speak and act so as to encourage them to rise to it. Not a hint is given in this public letter which is to be read to the whole Colossian church that Onesimus is a slave or that he has been a renegade. Paul simply calls him **the faithful and beloved brother, who is one of yourselves.** He trusts Onesimus to make good. His further assumption that Onesimus will be associated with Tychicus in reporting to the Colossian congregations all the news of Paul in Rome carries an intimation to them all, and especially to Philemon, that Paul has every confidence that they will indeed receive Onesimus with forgiveness and complete reconciliation. Paul trusts also Philemon and the Christians of Colossae.

**10. Mark the Cousin of Barnabas, ... Receive Him.**—Was there a special poignancy in Paul's earnest plea for the restoration of Onesimus to a richer fellowship in the Christian community

eth you, and Marcus, sister's son to Barnabas, (touching whom ye received commandments: if he come unto you, receive him;)

11 And Jesus, which is called Justus, who are of the circumcision. These only *are my* fellow workers unto the kingdom of God, which have been a comfort unto me.

greets you, and Mark the cousin of Barnabas (concerning whom you have received instructions — if he comes to you, receive him), 11 and Jesus who is called Justus. These are the only men of the circumcision among my fellow workers for the kingdom of God, and they have been a comfort to

---

and would thus have a personal interest in the Christian cause throughout the province of Asia. He was with Paul on his voyage to Rome in captivity (Acts 27:2), and may have been himself in custody. **Fellow prisoner,** however, is probably used in the same spiritual sense as "fellow slave" above; the word properly means not "prisoner," but "captive"—it is a word of the military vocabulary. Acts does not suggest that Aristarchus was in the custody of the Romans; and in the letter to Philemon (vs. 23), the same word is used of Epaphras ("my fellow prisoner in Christ Jesus"), clearly in the spiritual, not the literal sense. Paul and his comrades are captives of the world-conquering Christ. The same thought is found in II Cor. 2:14, in a slightly different form, "Thanks be to God, who in Christ always leads us in triumph"; the triumphal procession of captives following in the victor's train "spreads the fragrance of the knowledge of him everywhere." **Mark the cousin of Barnabas** is to be identified with the young companion of Barnabas and Paul who incurred Paul's displeasure by deserting the mission in Pamphylia (Acts 13:13; 15:38); his home was in Jerusalem (Acts 12:12, 25). He had evidently vindicated Barnabas' faith in him, and had regained the confidence of Paul. The **instructions** which the Colossians had received concerning him had not come from Paul; some other Christian group was sending him on a mission to the Asian churches, and Paul co-operates by adding his good word in Mark's favor. **Jesus who is called Justus** is not otherwise known to us,

---

than ever before, because of a painful memory out of his own past? Paul had once refused to take back a young man who had deserted him at a critical time, though the youth had sought another chance to make good. On the eve of the perilous first mission of Paul and Barnabas to Galatia, John Mark had suddenly quit and gone home to Jerusalem. Paul refused to have anything more to do with him. It was Barnabas, the "Son of encouragement" (Acts 4:36), who restored his young cousin to active Christian leadership and led him into a career which had as one of its enduring fruits the writing of the earliest gospel (see Acts 12:12, 25; 13:5, 13; 15:36-41). Paul had been wrong. The great exponent of the forgiving grace of God, who insisted that no man could live up to the moral law by his own striving, did not hold out to John Mark the same assurance that by the grace of God he could rise to his full Christian stature, which in this letter he so magnificently extends to Onesimus and to the Colossians. Through his anxiety for the larger interests of the cause, which are bigger than the interests of the individual man, Paul "laid down the law" to John Mark. Barnabas, largehearted and sympathetic, though perhaps lacking some of Paul's statesmanlike grasp of principle, saw the gospel more

clearly in individual relationships than in its wider aspects, and was most immediately alive to what God's grace could do with that particular young man. In this case Paul had the right theology of grace but failed to apply it. Barnabas, the lesser theologian of the two, put Paul's doctrine of grace into practice. But long since Paul had acknowledged his mistake, for he now numbers Mark among his friends and fellow workers, and commends him warmly to the Colossian church, linking his name with that of his great cousin, Barnabas, and banishing all doubt about him, which might linger in the minds of any who had heard the earlier story, with an emphatic and unreserved **receive him.** Paul learned something from his failure to apply his own gospel to the problem of John Mark's defection. See it in the glorious assurance with which he declares to erring Onesimus, to the misguided Colossians, and to Philemon, who, like Paul in his displeasure with John Mark, was about to face a man who had let him down, that the reconciling love of God in Christ will surely lead them to their Christian best.

**11. The Only Men of the Circumcision Among My Fellow Workers.**—Paul's advocacy of the universality of the gospel brought him

but a simple conjectural emendation allows his name to be included in the list of friends who send greetings to the household of Philemon (Philem. 23-24). **Jesus** was a fairly common Jewish name, being the Greek form of the name Joshua; **Justus** is a Latin surname, probably taken from a Roman patron. There is a pathetic note in Paul's remark that "these are the only comrades in the work of God's realm, belonging to the circumcised, who have been any comfort to me" (Moffatt). Paul felt deeply his alienation from the great body of his own people (cf. Rom. 9:3), and still more the lack of sympathy, often passing into open hostility, shown toward him by most of the Jewish Christians. His words here suggest that even in the days of his imprisonment at Rome, with his very life set at hazard for the sake of the gospel, he was not receiving the sympathetic support of Christians of his own race, except for these three. It is interesting to see that Barnabas is a well-known name even in the interior of the province of Asia, though we have no knowledge of any activity of his in that area.

---

into actual peril in his relations with non-Christian Jews, and into repeated controversy with Christian Jews.

He could hardly expect anything but enmity from the Jews whom he had deserted to go over to Christianity. Soon after his conversion his newly found Christian brethren had to persuade him to leave Jerusalem for his own safety and for the peace of the church (Acts 9:29-30). He went home to Tarsus, where, it seems, he remained for perhaps a decade, out of active leadership in the church. Later on it was an attack on his life by a Jewish mob in the temple precincts that led to his long final imprisonment (Acts 21:20-36).

In addition, Paul also came into strenuous conflict with conservatively minded Jewish Christians who were determined that the new faith must be kept within the bounds of Jewish racial and religious tradition—the Judaizing Christians. The official reconciliation of the Jerusalem church to his Gentile mission is related in Acts 15. The strain and tension of this crucial controversy between Christians is revealed in his letter to the Galatians. Wherever there were Jewish Christians this division in the church must have persisted for some time. Paul's comment about **the only men of the circumcision** indicates that the lines of demarcation were traceable in the church in Rome. There were other Jewish Christians in Rome besides Aristarchus, Mark, and Justus, but they had little to do with Paul. Whether they actively opposed him or not (see Phil. 1:15-18), they evidently carried on a more or less independent Christian work, and had little or no fellowship with him. The loneliness of the Apostle to the Gentiles in his valiant struggle for a universal Christianity comes out in his comment that, out of all the Jewish Christians in Rome, only the three whom he has mentioned are among his fellow workers, **and they have been a comfort to me.**

It is worth noting that Barnabas, Paul's one-time partner in the great team of Paul and Barnabas, if he did not side with the Judaizing party in the church, at least compromised with them. "Even Barnabas was carried away by their insincerity" (Gal. 2:13)—another example of the two types of character represented in these two men. Barnabas, though not so incisive in his adherence to the general spiritual principle, expressed his love of Christ in cordial personal relationships. Paul stood ruggedly by the principle of universality, the equality of all men in Christ, regardless of the personal tensions which he might create. What the church owes to men like Paul! But also, what the church owes to men like Barnabas! For it was Barnabas who saw Christ's man in John Mark. It was Barnabas, too, who saw Christ's man in Saul of Tarsus. In fact, Barnabas first introduced Paul into the Christian fellowship in Jerusalem when the other Christians were too suspicious and too fearful to receive him (Acts 9:26-28). Again, after Paul had been persuaded to go away to Tarsus, it was generous, forgiving, understanding, and lovable Barnabas who made a special journey to that city, and brought Paul back into active leadership in the church after some years of separation (Acts 11:25-26).

Paul's party prevailed at last, to the everlasting good of the world-wide church of Christ. But God had great uses for the more conservative and less pioneering Barnabas as well. Perhaps it was John Mark, friend of both men and now allied with Paul in the Gentile mission, who healed the breach between them. In any case, though Paul never traveled with Barnabas again after they parted company over John Mark, he is now completely reconciled with his old partner in the faith. His reference to Mark and Barnabas (vs. 10) is proof that he loves them both as fellow workers in the service of Christ.

12 Epaphras, who is *one* of you, a servant of Christ, saluteth you, always laboring fervently for you in prayers, that ye may stand perfect and complete in all the will of God.

13 For I bear him record, that he hath a great zeal for you, and them *that are* in Laodicea, and them in Hierapolis.

14 Luke, the beloved physician, and Demas, greet you.

15 Salute the brethren which are in La-

me. 12 Ep'aphras, who is one of yourselves, a servant[g] of Christ Jesus, greets you, always remembering you earnestly in his prayers, that you may stand mature and fully assured in all the will of God. 13 For I bear him witness that he has worked hard for you and for those in La-odice'a and in Hi-erap'olis. 14 Luke the beloved physician and Demas greet you. 15 Give my greetings

[g] Or *slave*.

12-13. In sending the greetings of Epaphras (cf. 1:7), the founder of the Colossian church, who had come to Rome to get Paul's advice and help in the face of the danger to which his converts were exposed through the insidious propaganda of a "Gnostic" sect (2:4), Paul takes occasion to commend him again. He too is **a servant** [properly, "a slave"] **of Christ,** devoted absolutely to his Master's will. As befits "a faithful minister of Christ" (1:7), he does not forget his congregation when he is far away; his solicitude expresses itself in earnest prayer. **Remembering . . . earnestly** (RSV) somewhat weakens the force of ἀγωνιζόμενος (**laboring fervently**—KJV); the same participle is rendered "striving" in 1:29 (see Exeg. on that passage). The verb, originally used of contesting for the prize in games of track and field, had been extended metaphorically by classical writers to describe struggles for the supreme issues of life. Its use in connection with prayer conveys the thought that Christian prayer, especially intercession for others, is no perfunctory motion, but a most strenuous spiritual exercise. This thought is intensified by the expression of the next verse, "he has worked hard for you"—literally, "he has heavy toil on your behalf" (ἔχει πολὺν πόνον ὑπὲρ ὑμῶν). Πόνον ("work," "toil," "trouble") still refers to the prayers of Epaphras, not to some commission which he was charged to undertake at Rome. The object of his prayers—**that you may stand mature and fully assured in all the will of God**—looks back to the danger of wavering under the influence of false teachers (cf. 1:23); Paul's supreme object is likewise to "present every man mature in Christ" (1:28). **Stand** has its full force; it is not a mere copula, but suggests firmness and stability in the face of shocks.

**Laodicea and Hierapolis:** Twin cities of great commercial importance, on either side of the Lycus River, about ten miles below Colossae; Epaphras had evidently carried the gospel to both of them and founded churches there (see Intro., p. 134).

14. **Luke the beloved physician:** Known to Christian tradition as the author of the Third Gospel and the book of Acts. If the tradition is valid, two of the evangelists were in Paul's company at Rome. The reference to Luke's profession suggests that he was attending Paul as his medical adviser, but he is also one of the apostle's "fellow workers" (Philem. 24). Nothing is known of Demas, apart from the mention here and in Philem. 24, and the reference to his later defection (II Tim. 4:10).

C. GREETINGS TO LAODICEA AND FINAL INSTRUCTIONS (4:15-18)

15-16. The greetings to Laodicea and the directions for an exchange of epistles between the two Christian groups indicate that there were close and continuous relations

12. *Epaphras.*—Note Paul's unstinted support and commendation of lesser associates (see Expos., 1:7).

14. *Luke the Beloved Physician.*—This passage is the source of the cherished phrase which has passed into our language. From this casual

reference we also learn what Luke's profession was.

15. *Give My Greetings.*—From these final sentences one would gather that Paul was an old friend and personal acquaintance of the people in Colossae, Laodicea, and Hierapolis,

odicea, and Nymphas, and the church which is in his house.

16 And when this epistle is read among you, cause that it be read also in the church of the Laodiceans; and that ye likewise read the *epistle* from Laodicea.

to the brethren at La-odice′a, and to Nympha and the church in her house.

16 And when this letter has been read among you, have it read also in the church of the La-odice′ans; and see that you read

---

between them, as we might expect. **Nympha and the church in her house:** Possibly the church of Hierapolis, or a rural congregation in the neighborhood. As the Christian "sacrifices" were spiritual and required no temple, there was no haste to erect buildings for the public worship of God, and meetings were commonly held in houses. The Yale University excavations at Dura-Europos on the Euphrates uncovered a house in which one of the rooms had been prepared for use as a Christian church.

As this letter deals with problems of faith and understanding which were not confined in interest to the church at Colossae, Paul wishes it to be read in the neighboring church as well. **The letter from Laodicea** must refer to a letter which Paul was sending by the same messenger. It has sometimes been identified with our Epistle to the Ephesians, but the latter is probably the work of a disciple of the apostle; the identification would be attractive if Colossians also were deutero-Pauline. It has sometimes been suggested that the reference is to the letter to Philemon. We are bound to feel, however, that the delicacy of Paul's approach to the master of Onesimus (Philem. 8-14) would be utterly destroyed by such an attempt to apply the united pressure of the churches of Laodicea and Colossae to him. Paul repudiates the use of any kind of constraint when he writes, "I preferred to do nothing without your consent in order that your goodness might not be by compulsion but of your own free will" (Philem. 14). A number of Latin MSS contain among the Pauline epistles an "Epistle to the Laodiceans," which is clearly translated from a Greek original, though the latter is no longer extant. It is, however, a palpable compilation, of no intrinsic worth, and no one thinks of attributing its composition to Paul or to anyone connected with him. **The letter from Laodicea** had been lost or destroyed before the letters of Paul were collected; it is scarcely possible to doubt that the same fate has befallen many more letters which the apostle wrote in the course of his missionary career.

The verse gives a clear indication that Paul's letters were not conceived so informally as is sometimes supposed. He himself realized that they possessed more than transient and local interest. It might almost be said that we are shown here one aspect of the process which led to the formation of the Pauline corpus. If copies of Paul's letters were

---

able to draw on a firsthand knowledge of their daily life and activity. Yet, as far as is known, he had never been among them (1:4; 2:1). A prisoner in Rome, shut off from the world, he did not repine and shrink into himself, but identified his heart and hope and love with Christians everywhere, not in any merely general sense, but with intense personal interest in particular groups and in particular people. Happy the Christian whom Christ teaches so to triumph over his own disability, whatever it may be. The true measure of life is not in outward circumstance, but in intensity of spirit, in range of interest, in identity of purpose with the work of Christ, and in depth of concern for its prosperity in definite places and in the lives of actual people.

**16. The Letter from Laodicea.**—How many letters of Paul have been lost? How many gospels? How much of the literature of the first-century church? No one knows, though many more writings than we now have must at that time have circulated among the churches. The genuine discovery of any one of these would add rich content to the records of the faith. But would it add any essential that we do not now possess? One cannot believe that it would. The gospel of Christ is complete. All that man needs to enter, live in, and serve the saving fellowship of Christ is available to us. Amid the vagaries of history, divine providence has preserved for all time the authentic gospel of Christ. In the ongoing life of the Spirit in the church the full life in Christ is known and

17 And say to Archippus, Take heed to the ministry which thou hast received in the Lord, that thou fulfil it.

18 The salutation by the hand of me Paul. Remember my bonds. Grace *be* with you. Amen.

¶ Written from Rome to the Colossians by Tychicus and Onesimus.

also the letter from La-odice'a. 17 And say to Archip'pus, "See that you fulfill the ministry which you have received in the Lord."

18 I, Paul, write this greeting with my own hand. Remember my fetters. Grace be with you.

---

exchanged between neighboring churches during his own lifetime and at his own suggestion, it would be only natural that wider exchanges would take place among groups that cherished his memory after his death, so that limited collections would gradually be formed in a number of different churches. The final composition of the corpus was the result of a long period of editorial work, rather than of the fortunes of a single collector (against the hypothesis of Goodspeed, *The Meaning of Ephesians*, pp. 5 ff.).

**17.** The message for Archippus, enigmatic to us, would no doubt be perfectly clear to the Christians of Colossae. Lohmeyer (*ad loc.*) suggests the possibility that after the departure of Epaphras, Archippus had taken over his work as pastor of the Colossian group. John Knox (see on Philem. 2 and the fuller argument in his book, *Philemon Among the Letters of Paul* [Chicago: University of Chicago Press, 1935], pp. 25-34) suggests that Archippus is the primary recipient of the letter to Philemon, and the owner of the "house" where the church meets (Philem. 2); he takes this verse as an attempt to secure the support of the Colossian church for his appeal "for [his] child, Onesimus." Those who ascribe this epistle to the time of Paul's ministry in Ephesus tend to think of the **ministry** of Archippus as connected with "the offering for the saints" (II Cor. 9:1; Rom. 15:25-27; etc.). **Received** (παρέλαβες) suggests a task that has been taken over from someone else; the whole wording seems to imply a specific commission of some kind, rather than a settled function. It is not possible to do more than guess at the nature of this duty, but it is interesting to observe that the whole body of believers at Colossae is asked to share the responsibility for its execution.

**18.** Paul's letters were dictated to a scribe (cf. Rom. 16:22); it was his custom to write a few words in his own hand at the end in "large letters" (Gal. 6:11), i.e., uncials

---

lived, unalterably rooted in history, applied in ever new ways (see Luke 1:1; John 20:30-31; 21:25).

**18.** *Remember My Fetters.*—There are frequent references to Paul's imprisonment in the later epistles (Phil. 1:7, 13; Philem. 9, 13; Eph. 3:1; 4:1; 6:20). It was Paul's practice to dictate his letters, relying on a companion to do the writing, a somewhat laborious task with the materials then in use. Paul would add a brief greeting and signature in his own handwriting (see II Thess. 3:17; I Cor. 16:21). On at least one occasion misleading teachings had been advanced in a letter purporting to be from Paul (II Thess. 2:2). The personal signature served to authenticate Paul's authorship, and also to convey his personal regard in a more intimate way.

Some commentators have suggested that as Paul reached for the pen, he would feel the heavy pull of the shackles on his wrists and hear the rattle of the chains. All his past would

come before him, his visions, his strivings, his sufferings for Christ's sake, and his labors for the churches. His heart would rise in passionate prayer that he might be given grace ever to build up the faith of his Christian brethren throughout the world till his work was done (see 1:24; Gal. 6:17).

As he feels the weight of the chains, his thoughts are suddenly jerked back from far Colossae and Laodicea. **Remember my fetters.** It is the appeal of a friend to friends for the friendship he needs and craves. It means (*a*) pray for me (4:3); (*b*) rise to your own full Christian stature, for I and others have pledged our sufferings for your growth to maturity in the faith (vss. 12-13; 1:9); (*c*) give heed to what I have written, for this is what it has cost me to be true to Christ (1:24; 2:1-2).

**Grace be with you. Amen.** In the KJV the "Amen" occurs at the end of all of Paul's epistles. In the RSV it is found at the end of Romans, I Corinthians, and Galatians. Else-

or "capitals." Perhaps he had never learned to write the cursive hand favored by the scribes of the period. In part this signature was a safeguard against letters that might be sent in his name, but without his authority (II Thess. 2:2; 3:17) .

**Remember my fetters:** The words are in part an appeal to his sufferings for the faith, as reinforcing his claim to a hearing; in part they recall his need of his readers' prayers (cf. vs. 3) . Theodore of Mopsuestia takes it as an encouragement to them also to face persecution fearlessly, "Following my example, do not be ashamed to suffer for the truth."

The epistle ends as it began, with a prayer for **grace** (cf. 1:2) .

---

where it is omitted. In some cases Paul evidently wrote it in himself. In the others it was apparently added in conformity with the devout practice of the churches in which the epistles were read. It is the sign of final and unreserved assent—"So let it be." This is indeed God's word to us through his apostle. So, in the ritual and custom of the church in later ages, the ascription of acceptance, gratitude, and praise is wont to be made, "May God bless to us this reading from his holy Word." The devout but alert and questing mind, having studied the import of these pages of scripture, may well add a thanksgiving for Paul and for his Epistle to the Colossians with its grand affirmations of the reality of the everlasting Christ, "May God bless to us this study of his Word, and to his name be all the honor and the glory. Amen."

The First and Second Epistles to the

# THESSALONIANS

*Introduction and Exegesis by* JOHN W. BAILEY
*Exposition by* JAMES W. CLARKE

# I AND II THESSALONIANS

## INTRODUCTION

When Paul and his companions, Silvanus and Timothy, came to Thessalonica, it was one of the significant cities of the east Mediterranean area. Located at the northeast corner of the Thermaic Gulf, which received its name from the hot springs in the vicinity of Therme, the city was built upon a rising hill overlooking both the gulf and a beautiful and fertile plain. Thessalonica was by natural advantages the leading harbor of Macedonia. The Romans also established there a naval station and docks, and its importance as a port was thus increased. Moreover, the city was located upon the great Via Egnatia, or "Overland Military Highway," from the city of Rome to the countries at the eastern end of the Mediterranean. This highway ran through the city from west to east, with arched gates at the eastern and western limits of the city. The district had been reorganized and the city rebuilt in 315 B.C. by Cassander, brother-in-law of Alexander the Great. He named the new city for his wife, Thessalonica, the daughter of Philip of Macedon, and stepsister of Alexander. When the Romans conquered Macedonia in 167 B.C., and in 166 organized it into a province, Thessalonica became the capital of the second of the four regions into which for administrative purposes the province was divided. In 146 B.C., when Macedonia was consolidated, Thessalonica became the capital of the entire province and the residence of the provincial governor, the proconsul.

After the victory of Octavius and Antony over Brutus and Cassius at Philippi in 42 B.C., Thessalonica was made a "free city" as a reward for its support of the victors through the days of conflict. In the earlier days of the Roman administration Macedonia was an imperial province, requiring the presence of troops and garrison. In 27 B.C. it became a senatorial province, and troops and garrison were removed. But conditions became so unsettled that in A.D. 15 it was again made a military province. In A.D. 44, however, it became a senatorial province once more, and was administered by a proconsul. Garrison and troops were removed, but Thessalonica remained the seat of government. Five ancient inscriptions have been discovered [1]—one on the old west gate arcade, torn down in 1876—which give support to the statements of Acts 17:5-8 that the city was governed locally by politarchs, and had its own "assembly" or "demos."

The city was the home of two of the recognized mystery religions that were to be found everywhere throughout the Hellenic, or eastern, half of the Roman Empire. These were the religion of Dionysus the dying and rising god, and of Orpheus, hero of a kindred and somewhat reformed Dionysiac cult. Both of them were fertility cults, expressing themselves in phallic symbols and sexual indulgences, in wild orgies and extravagant ecstasies. Along with these there was also a primitive cult of the Cabiri (*Kabeiroi*), which was of similar character. Further, at that time emperor worship was being actively practiced in Macedonia. Beroea was the center of this worship and the home of the high priest of emperor worship in the province. From Acts we learn that there was a Jewish synagogue in both Thessalonica (Acts 17:1) and Beroea (Acts 17:10), and that asso-

[1] These and other inscriptions, a total of nineteen, were collected and fully described by Ernest D. Burton, "The Politarchs," *American Journal of Theology*, II (1898), 598-632. For two additional references see J. H. Moulton and George Milligan, *The Vocabulary of the New Testament* (London: Hodder & Stoughton, 1914-19), *s.v.* πολιτάρχης.

245

ciated with these synagogues were a large number of "devout" Greeks.

### I. Paul, Silvanus, and Timothy

When Paul came to Thessalonica, he brought with him his two trusted companions, Silvanus and Timothy. The three of them labored together in the founding of the church; they were also associated in the writing of these two letters to the church. The plural "we," meaning Paul and companions, is found more often in these Thessalonian letters than in any others written by him.

The salutation of the Thessalonian letters is the simplest used in any of Paul's letters. He takes his place by the side of his associates in both the writing of the letter and the establishing of the church at Thessalonica. (Acts 17:4, 10 closely associate Paul and Silas; Acts 17:2-3, 13-14 make clear Paul's leadership.) Paul does not characterize himself in any way as either "apostle" or "servant" of Jesus Christ. In the two Corinthian letters (I Cor. 1:1; II Cor. 1:1), and Colossians (1:1) he is "an apostle of Christ Jesus through the will of God." In Romans (1:1) he is "a servant of Jesus Christ, called to be an apostle, set apart for the gospel of God." In Galatians (1:1) he is "an apostle—not from men nor through man, but through Jesus Christ. . . ." In Philippians (1:1) he and Timothy are associated as "servants of Christ Jesus." Ephesians (1:1) records that he is "an apostle of Christ Jesus by the will of God." Philemon (vs. 1) indicates that he is "a prisoner for Christ Jesus." But here the three persons are simply named. This close association of Paul with his two companions, Silvanus and Timothy, upon somewhat equal terms, and the later emphasis (e.g., I Thess. 2:4) upon their having been approved of God, and consequently entrusted with the gospel, seem to suggest that up to this time opposition to Paul had not been opposition directed primarily against him and his apostleship, but had been a phase of a general resistance, the outgrowth of antagonism on the part of Jews who had "killed the Lord Jesus," and the "prophets," and "persecuted" him and kept on seeking to prevent the proclamation of the gospel to the Gentiles (I Thess. 2:14-16a).

Silvanus [2] is associated with Paul in the writing of both the Thessalonian letters (I Thess. 1:1; II Thess. 1:1) as he had been in the founding of the church (I Thess. 2:1-12; cf. Acts 17:4). Also, II Cor. 1:19 reflects the fact that Silvanus was one of the companions of Paul responsible for the preaching of the gospel among the Corinthians. It is generally agreed that it was from Corinth in A.D. 50 or 51 that these two Thessalonian letters were written (cf. Acts 18:5). We thus have Silvanus associated with Paul explicitly during his ministry in the provinces of Macedonia and Achaia. He does not appear further in the story of Paul's work. [3]

This Silvanus is generally regarded as the Silas of the book of Acts (15:22–18:5), a companion of Paul (see Exeg. on I Thess. 1:1). He was one of the prophets in Jerusalem (Acts 15:32; cf. 13:1) and one of the two bearers of the letter written from the council in Jerusalem to the churches in Syria and Cilicia (Acts 15:22-29, 32-33). [4] He was chosen by Paul as his companion for the second missionary journey in Barnabas' place (Acts 15:39-40), when the two decided to separate. He accompanied Paul throughout the journey from Antioch as far as Corinth. There he disappears from the story. That he and Silvanus are the same man seems to be the meaning of the facts reported to us.

Timothy was one of Paul's constant and most trusted companions. Son of a Jewish mother and Greek father, Paul found him at Lystra as a young disciple, well reported by the brethren in Lystra and Iconium (Acts 16:1-4). Paul selected him as a companion apparently to take the place of Mark, who had gone with Barnabas to Cyprus (Acts 15:39). He appears as coauthor of this Thessalonian correspondence (I Thess. 1:1; II Thess. 1:1) and as emissary of Paul and Silvanus to the Thessalonian church from Athens (I Thess. 3:1-6). He was a trusted messenger of Paul in the period of his Corinthian correspondence (I Cor. 4:17; 16:10; II Cor. 1:1), and was with him at the time of the writing of Rom. 16 (vs. 21). He was also with him when he wrote the letters to the Colossians (1:1), to Philemon (vs. 1), and to the Philip-

[2] The name Silvanus is a regular Latin form. In the Greek papyri the name is spelled "Silbanos," the pronunciation of which would be practically indistinguishable (except that the accented syllable would not be the same) from the pronunciation of the Latin.

[3] I Pet. 5:12 refers to the fact that that letter is being written "by Silvanus, a faithful brother as I regard him." Most interpreters believe that this is the Silvanus who had been associated with Paul.

[4] Two of the most significant of the older MSS of the N.T., Ephraemus Rescriptus and Codex Bezae (C and D), as well as 33, "the queen of cursives," indicate (Acts 15:34) that Silas remained in Antioch at the time Judas, his companion, returned to Jerusalem (Acts 15:33). This is one of the noteworthy "rejected readings" of Westcott and Hort, not found in the most commonly accepted text, and may have been inserted very early upon the basis of the fact that Silas was in Antioch at the time Paul decided upon his "second missionary journey" (Acts 15:40).

pians (1:1). Paul hoped to send him to Philippi very soon after the writing of the Philippian letter, and he expected him to return with good news from Philippi. Timothy was the only one then with Paul who was of "like mind" with him in his concern for "the things of Christ." He had won widespread approval as he had "served . . . in the gospel" with Paul as "a son with a father," as the Philippians themselves well knew (Phil. 2:9-22). Timothy vindicated Paul's confidence in him by his loyal companionship, and by his constant, faithful, and effective service throughout the apostle's missionary career.[5]

### II. Founding of the Church in Thessalonica

Paul with Silvanus and Timothy founded the church in Thessalonica (Acts 17:1-10; I Thess. 2:1-12). They came to Thessalonica from Philippi, where they had suffered persecution and insolent insulting treatment (I Thess. 2:1-2). When they arrived in Thessalonica, they "had courage in God" to proclaim the gospel; and here again they met great opposition. However, they continued their labors, and gave themselves without stint to the work and to the people, who became increasingly dear to them.

During their labors among the Thessalonians the apostles had supported themselves by strenuous manual toil (I Thess. 2:9; II Thess. 3:7b-8). Paul was a tentmaker or tent cloth maker (Acts 18:3). This resort to labor was in part necessitated by economic conditions (there had been a recent famine throughout Greece and Macedonia and things were unsettled economically[6]), but was also an expression of the evangelists' convictions concerning their vocational independence. As messengers of the gospel of God, they might have asked for support by those among whom they labored (I Thess. 2:6, 7, 9; 4:10; II Thess. 3:7-9). According to I Cor. 9:7-12, 14, Paul was convinced that it was not only in accordance with the principles of Christian responsibility, but also the express command of Christ (cf. Matt. 10:10; Luke 10:7-8) that those who received the gospel should support those who gave it to them. However, he was earnest in his conviction that he must maintain his independence so that he could not properly be charged with being in the

gospel service for the sake of the living which it provided (I Cor. 4:11-12; II Cor. 12:13-18). The world of the Greeks was full of strolling teachers and philosophers who sought to live by their wits (cf. Acts 13:6-12; 19:13-20). Paul was careful so to conduct himself that he could not rightfully be charged with any such spirit. As a matter of fact, the Philippian Christians had, at least twice while Paul was in Thessalonica (Phil. 4:16), sent to him some contribution for his own needs; of what sort or how large we are not informed.

Paul, Silvanus, and Timothy had spent sufficient time in their work in Thessalonica not only for the Thessalonians to become well acquainted with their previous experience, but also for the development of mutual affection and loyalty (I Thess. 2:7, 8; 2:11; 3:6; cf. 1:7; 2:19-20). The record in Acts 17:1-9 mentions only three sabbaths upon which Paul appeared in the Jewish synagogue and proclaimed to them the gospel. However, it is clear from the Thessalonian letters that the church was composed very largely of Gentile believers who had turned from idolatry to serve the living God (I Thess. 1:9-10). Precisely how long this work among the Gentiles had been carried on we cannot say. Some (e.g., Moffatt) think in terms of a few weeks, possibly two months; others (e.g., Ramsay) think the period must be extended to some seven or eight months. In view of the statement in I Thess. 1:7-8; 4:10, implying the presence of disciples throughout both the whole of Macedonia and Achaia, and in places beyond, probably we should think in terms of several months for the service in Thessalonica and surrounding areas, though probably not so long as seven or eight months. Into what surrounding areas had the gospel been carried?

Paul says to the Romans (15:19-23) that at the time of writing that letter he had "fully preached the gospel of Christ"—"from Jerusalem and as far round as Illyricum." Further, he says that he had sought not to build upon the foundation of another, but had been a pioneer missionary, and had carried the gospel to those who had not hitherto heard it. There was no longer any place "in these regions" of the East for the proclamation of the gospel and he would make his way to Rome and on to Spain. Illyricum (known fairly soon after the time of Paul as Dalmatia; cf. II Tim. 4:10) lay on the Adriatic Sea directly north of the west coast of Macedonia. Perhaps the mountainous area of Illyricum might be seen from Thessalonica. Whether during his years in the East Paul had actually gone into Illyricum or only up to what he considered the borders of that province is a

---

[5] The references to Timothy in I Timothy (1:3, 18; 4:14) and II Timothy (1:6; 4:19, 21) emphasize the general impression of his significance in relation to Paul, which had come to be a recognized tradition in the church.

[6] See Thomas Lewin, *The Life and Epistles of St. Paul* (London: G. Bell & Sons, 1875), I, 230; this writer refers to *Fasti Sacri* (London: Longmans, Green & Co., 1865), p. 290, No. 1735.

point of differing opinion. The particular phrasing of the apostle is hardly decisive. Possibly this statement in Rom. 15:19 that the gospel had been carried as far as to Illyricum described work that had been done at a time later than this first journey into Macedonia (cf. II Cor. 2:12). In any case, we are not required by the language of the apostle, either in the Thessalonian letters or Romans, to think of extended areas of Macedonia outside of Thessalonica, and of Achaia outside of Corinth and Athens, as having been evangelized before the time of the writing of I Thessalonians (cf. Tit. 3:12, "Nicopolis"). Careful inspection of the record in Acts (see especially 20:17-35; 19:8-10) as well as Paul's letters (e.g., Col. 2:1; 4:7-17) indicates that Paul's policy was to establish himself in the leading centers and work out from there, using helpers in the evangelization of the surrounding territory.

Thessalonica was about one hundred miles from Philippi on the great Egnatian Way, which ran directly west from Thessalonica to Pella, the capital and chief city of the third division of the province. From Pella it ran directly across to the coast of the Adriatic Sea. Just before reaching the coast the road forked, and the north fork touched the sea close to the borders of Illyricum, which lay stretched out along the sea to the north. Thus behind this first extant epistle of the apostle lies an extended missionary career which had carried him from Jerusalem as far west as the Grecian peninsula. How far west in the peninsula cannot be said with certainty. He was a vigorous, deeply earnest, and newly commissioned ambassador of the gospel; he pushed into whatever regions God seemed to open to him. In this first letter he speaks of "all the brethren throughout Macedonia" (I Thess. 4:10). How widely distributed these brethren were we cannot say. But it does seem that the phrase "in all Macedonia" must include at least a wider territory than three cities on the eastern border.

The Thessalonians had heard the gospel with interest. As already indicated, the church was composed largely of Gentiles who turned from their idols to the acceptance of the gospel which Paul and his fellow missionaries proclaimed (I Thess. 1:9; 2:14, 16; 4:5, 9, 10; II Thess. 2:13-14). The record in Acts (17:1, 2, 4a; 18:4) indicates that the response was made by, literally, "some Jews, of devout Greeks a great multitude, and of chief women not a few." When the Gentiles began to respond to the gospel, they were brought under persecution from their own "countrymen" (I Thess. 1:6; 2:13, 14; 3:3-4; II Thess. 1:4-6). Acts (17:5) reports that there were "some wicked fellows of the rabble" who raised a riot. And it is possible that they were stirred to action because Paul had made some impression upon their group. Some of them may have become Christians. (Does this fact help account for the tendency to idleness in the Thessalonian church—II Thess. 3:6-10?) On the whole, however, Paul seems to regard the new church as composed of persons of worthy spirit and character, who had received the message as indeed the word of God itself (I Thess. 1:6; 2:13). Because of their full persuasion of the truth of the message they had endured all the sufferings forced upon them.

Their sufferings had continued after Paul left them. Even at the time of the writing of both these letters there was occasion for him to utter warning against those who were causing the sufferings, and to voice encouragement to the Thessalonian Christians to stand firm and faithful. As a matter of fact, he says they had remained faithful to the gospel (I Thess. 3:6; 4:1, 10; 5:21, 22; II Thess. 1:4)—so much so that their steadfastness had been proclaimed throughout both Macedonia and Achaia and even into regions beyond (I Thess. 1:7; 4:10). Their example was so well known that it was reported to Paul by Macedonians and others. He himself had no need to make mention of it to anyone; it was known and appreciated in many places (I Thess. 1:8).

### III. Occasion of I Thessalonians

The movements of Paul and his companions after they left Thessalonica are very briefly stated by the writers. They had kept in touch with the situation among the Thessalonian Christians, and were made anxious by the information that kept coming. Paul had tried at least twice ("again and again"?) to return to them, but he had been hindered by "Satan" (I Thess. 2:18). When he could endure the anxiety no longer, he had sent Timothy back to them from Athens (I Thess. 3:1-2, 5). He wanted Timothy to encourage them to stand against all temptations and persecution (cf. I Thess. 4:1-8). When I Thessalonians was being written, Timothy had just returned and had brought a very encouraging report (I Thess. 3:6-10). It is possible also, as has been suggested,[7] that Timothy had brought along a letter to Paul from the Thessalonian Christians (I Thess. 2:13; 4:9, 13; 5:1). Either through the verbal report of Timothy, or in the letter which they had written, certain questions and problems before the Thessalonian

[7] See especially J. Rendel Harris, "A Study in Letterwriting," *Expositor*, Fifth Series, VIII (1898), 161-80.

church had been presented for the apostles' consideration and answer.

The feeling of thanksgiving because of Timothy's report seems to be most in evidence and dominates I Thess. 1-3. So distinctive is this element that such scholars as Bernhard Weiss [8] and Theodor Zahn [9] have regarded these three chapters as essentially the letter which the apostles were led to write on Timothy's return, the remaining two chapters being in the nature of appended notes. This view hardly seems warranted; but it is evident that the spirit of thanksgiving is foremost in their thought as they write. The Thessalonian converts had remained steadfast in their "faith and labor of love" even though they had experienced continual opposition and persecution (I Thess. 2:14). The apostles had likewise experienced and endured heavy testing, and were all the more able to understand the strain under which their newly made converts had been living.

But running throughout this first section of the letter there is also an apologetic strain. Timothy had evidently reported that the Jews, who had been persecutors of the apostles when they were at work in Thessalonica (cf. Acts 17:5-8; I Thess. 2:2), had continued their antagonism, and had made serious charges against the motives and character of the missionaries, thinking thus to undermine their influence among Gentile believers.

This apologetic strain is especially in evidence in I Thess. 2:1-12. Here the writers defend themselves against flattery, mercenary motives, impurity; and call both the Thessalonians and God himself to witness that their lives were above reproach, and their interest in the Thessalonian disciples like that of a nurse or a father in the children whom they loved. The missionaries and the disciples had alike suffered conflict and persecution, they had likewise endured together, and together they were to be sustained by hope of God's own approval in the day of vindication at the coming of the Lord Jesus.

On one particular point the new disciples needed special instruction. It appears from the whole course and tone of the two letters that when the evangelists had preached in Thessalonica, they had presented as a part of their message the conception of the parousia of the Lord Jesus in which all believers would participate and which they were to "await" with high

hope (I Thess. 1:10). However, since the departure of the apostles, some of the Thessalonian disciples had died and their fellow disciples were greatly troubled. They were concerned lest the death of these disciples who were awaiting the Lord meant that they would have no share in the glory of his coming, and the consummation that would follow. One paragraph of the letter (I Thess. 4:13-18) is especially devoted to the consideration of this matter. The apostles assure their readers "on the word of the Lord" himself that those disciples who were asleep in death at his coming would be raised from death to share with the living in all the blessings of "that day."

The second portion of the letter (chs. 4-5) contains other instruction and exhortation. The new Christians, coming out of paganism, had in their traditions nothing that set any standards or demands for purity of life, especially in sex relationships. The writers remind them that they had given explicit instructions on this point when they had been among them. Some were weak and fainthearted (I Thess. 5:14), and these were to be helped and encouraged by those who were stronger and more firmly established. The attitude of some toward those who were toiling among them and leading them needed correction (I Thess. 5:12-13). Further, the idlers and busybodies who had been making trouble from the beginning (I Thess. 4:11-12; II Thess. 3:6-15) were in need of admonition, and the apostle would have the faithful attend to that (I Thess. 5:14).

## IV. Authenticity and Relationship of the Letters

The authenticity of I Thessalonians has been so generally recognized by all modern scholarship that it is not necessary to discuss that question here; but the authenticity of II Thessalonians and its relationship to the other letter have been very frequently questioned. The general grounds upon which the question of authenticity has been raised are two. First, the eschatology of this second letter is held to be inconsistent with that set forth in the first letter. In I Thessalonians the day of the Lord is presented as imminent, to be expected at any time, and confidently to be "awaited" by all believers in the Lord. It will come as a thief in the night, and it is highly important that all disciples be expectant and ready. In II Thessalonians two new features are introduced into the discussion —"the rebellion" and the "man of lawlessness." Of them it is said that before the Lord Jesus is revealed, "the rebellion" must take place, and the man of lawlessness must be revealed, but of neither of these events was there any evi-

[8] "The Present Status of the Inquiry Concerning the Genuineness of the Pauline Epistles," *American Journal of Theology*, I (1897), 331-44.

[9] *Introduction to the New Testament*, tr. John Moore Trout, *et al.* (Edinburgh: T. & T. Clark, 1909), I, 215-20.

dence at the time of writing. Thus the day of the Lord is pushed on to an uncertain and indefinite future. This view is held to be quite inconsistent with the imminent and vivid expectation found in the first letter. The two of them could not have been written by any one person in any closely related time. This second letter must then be much later and not an authentic writing of Paul and his companions.

Second, it is held that the second letter is so nearly like the first both in frame of thought and in language that it would not be psychologically probable (if indeed possible) for both to have come from the same writer at nearly the same time. If Paul had written both of them to the same people in practically the same circumstances, there would almost certainly have been more difference between them than there actually is. Hence this second letter must be from a later hand. Only a copyist would have written a letter so nearly like the first.

This view has been intermittently presented since the days of Ferdinand Baur, a century ago. A modern writer expressing this view of II Thessalonians is Morton S. Enslin [10] who is not impressed by the argument from the difference in eschatology (there may have been sufficient reason for both views to be set forth by one author), but does feel that the style and tone of II Thessalonians form a real basis for argument against authenticity. The first letter is warmhearted, full of personal feeling and interest; the second is cool and detached, lacking in personal feeling and the emotional warmth of the first. It could have been written by Paul, but it is more probably to be dated in the early second century, written to meet a need of that time.

A second general view would explain the recognized differences between the two letters in terms of the amanuenses whom Paul used (cf. II Thess. 3:17). Friedrich Spitta [11] held that this second letter was the work of Timothy, to whom Paul left the composition of the letter. Timothy had been brought up as a strict Jew (Acts 16:1, 3; II Tim. 1:5; 3:14-15) and had been closely associated with Paul. This would account both for its close similarity to the first letter and its distinctive Jewish coloring. Akin to this view of Spitta is that of F. C. Burkitt, [12] who thought that the writing of both these letters was turned over to Silas: he wrote them, and read them to Paul, who approved them,

though some of the ideas are not his. The first letter was written to the Gentile element in the church; the second, to the Jewish element. Neither of these views has been given much attention in later discussions.

A third view holds that II Thessalonians is an authentic letter of Paul, but that in reality it is the first of his letters to Thessalonica, and the "first" is the second. This view goes back to Hugo Grotius, and has had the support of some great names in biblical study. It was cogently argued by Johannes Weiss [13] who thought II Thessalonians was a letter of Paul carried by Timothy when he was sent back from Athens to visit the Thessalonian church (I Thess. 3:1-5). Weiss believed that this view would give II Thessalonians a new significance, and would place its authenticity upon a sound footing. A closely related view was expressed by J. S. West, [14] who goes over the ground rather carefully, comparing the two letters in language, ideas, and specific statements, and concludes that the second letter was written by Paul and sent back to Thessalonica from Beroea (cf. Acts 17:14-15). F. J. Badcock [15] likewise holds that Paul wrote and sent the letter from Beroea, and by Timothy. He thinks Paul and Titus (cf. Gal. 2:3; Tit. 1:4) went on to Athens and Corinth. Here Silas and Timothy came to him, and he then wrote I Thessalonians and sent it back by Titus. The statement in I Thess. 1:7-8 that the Thessalonian Christians had become examples to many in widely separated areas demands months of time. This general view has received comparatively little notice from scholars—as Weiss himself explicitly complained. [16]

A fourth view, set out by Adolph Harnack, [17] is that both of the letters were authentic writings of Paul and were written at the same time. The first was addressed mainly to the Gentile branch of the church; the second, exclusively to the Jewish element. Each letter dealt with the specific problems which were of vital moment to the respective element in the church to which it was addressed. This view has received scant attention. Burkitt (as above) thought it probably correct to the extent that the second letter was addressed to the Jewish element in

---

[10] *Christian Beginnings* (New York: Harper & Bros., 1938), pp. 239-44.

[11] *Zur Geschichte und Litteratur des Urchristentums* (Göttingen: Vandenhoeck & Ruprecht, 1893), I, 111 ff.

[12] *Christian Beginnings* (London: University of London Press, 1924), pp. 128-32.

[13] *The History of Primitive Christianity*, ed. F. C. Grant (New York: Wilson-Erickson, 1937), I, 289-91.

[14] "The Order of 1 and 2 Thessalonians," *Journal of Theological Studies*, XV (1914), 66-74.

[15] *The Pauline Epistles and the Epistle to the Hebrews* (New York: The Macmillan Co., 1937), pp. 43-52.

[16] *Op. cit.*, I, 289, n. 16.

[17] *Das Problem des zweiten Thessalonicherbriefs* (Berlin: Georg Reimer, 1910; "Sitzungsberichte der Königlich Preussischen Academie der Wissenschaften").

the church. Kirsopp Lake [18] agreed with Harnack that both came from Paul rather than Silas (against Burkitt), but he believed (against Harnack) that Paul first wrote I Thessalonians, and a little later realized that this letter would not satisfy the Jewish element in the church. Thereupon II Thessalonians was written and sent to them. This view Lake presents, with some hesitation, as the one that will most fully meet objections to Pauline authorship.

Contemporary English and American scholars have held to the authenticity of both letters, and to their origin in the usually assigned time, place, and order. We shall so consider them.

### V. Occasion of II Thessalonians

Sometime after the first letter was sent, probably soon, a new situation arose which called for correction. There had arisen in the Thessalonian church the rumor, or the teaching, that the day of the Lord, for which they had been instructed to be in readiness, had arrived. The missionaries themselves were not sure of the basis of this rumor. It was their thought that it might have been caused by a misinterpreted Christian tradition, or a prophetic utterance, or even by a letter purporting to be from Paul and his associates (II Thess. 2:1-2). But whatever the reason, such an impression had been created. The Thessalonian Christians had been given pretty thorough instruction in this whole field of thought and expectation (I Thess. 5:1-2; II Thess. 2:5), but for some reason not clear to the apostles they had been led astray at this point, and were greatly excited and troubled.

This second letter is written primarily to deal with this matter. Paul reminds his readers of what he had at some length set out to them when among them—that the day would not come "unless the rebellion comes first, and the man of lawlessness is revealed." Only the general outlines of the thinking are here given, it evidently being taken for granted that the fuller instruction which they had already received would be thus brought back to their minds, and would correct and steady them.

But along with this basic need, the apostles had also received information that the idlers and busybodies, who had been making trouble all the while, were still active. Despite previous instruction by the apostles, both by word of mouth when among them, and later by letter (II Thess. 2:15; 3:6, 10, 14), they were still in need of admonition. There is a certain sharpness of tone in the discussion of this particular group which implies its wantonness and persistence.

It appears (II Thess. 3:11) that word on all these matters had been brought to the apostles orally by some of those who were coming and going all the time (I Thess. 1:7, 9; II Thess. 1:4), or by the unknown bearer of the first letter written to them by the apostles (cf. I Thess. 1:1; 3:6); or even by a letter received from them (James E. Frame). We are not sure of the channel or channels of information, but the conditions and needs are themselves fairly clear.

### VI. Outline of I and II Thessalonians

#### I THESSALONIANS

I. Address and greeting (1:1)
II. Personal thanksgiving and apologia (1:2–3:13)
  A. Thanksgiving for the disciples (1:2-10)
  B. Review of the apostle's work (2:1-12)
  C. Gratitude for the success of the gospel ministry in Thessalonica (2:13-16)
  D. Paul's desire to revisit Thessalonica (2:17-20)
  E. The sending of Timothy to Thessalonica (3:1-10)
  F. The apostle's prayer (3:11-13)
III. Exhortation and instruction (4:1–5:28)
  A. The duty of purity and love (4:1-12)
  B. Concerning those who have fallen asleep (4:13-18)
  C. Concerning the sudden coming of the day of the Lord (5:1-11)
  D. Practical exhortations (5:12-22)
  E. Prayer for the church (5:23-24)
  F. Concluding salutations and benedictions (5:25-28)

#### II THESSALONIANS

I. Address and greeting (1:1-2)
II. The thanksgiving (1:3-12)
  A. Faith, love, steadfastness (1:3-4)
  B. The judgment of God (1:5-7a)
  C. The revelation of the Lord Jesus (1:7b-10)
  D. Prayer for God's blessing (1:11-12)
III. The revelation of the man of lawlessness (2:1-17)
  A. False teaching concerning the day of the Lord (2:1-3a)
  B. The man of lawlessness (2:3b-10)
  C. Lovers of error and their punishment (2:11-12)
  D. Thanksgiving for God's call to the Thessalonians (2:13-15)
  E. Prayer for firmness (2:16-17)
IV. Closing appeals, instruction, prayer (3:1-16)
  A. Request for prayer (3:1-2)
  B. Expressions of confidence (3:3-5)
  C. Injunctions concerning idlers (3:6-15)
  D. Prayer for the disciples (3:16)
V. Closing greeting and benedictions (3:17-18)

---

[18] *The Earlier Epistles of St. Paul* (London: Rivingtons, 1911), pp. 83-86; and in *An Introduction to the New Testament* (New York: Harper & Bros., 1937), pp. 131-36.

## VII. The Text

The Revised Standard Version is usually followed in the Exegesis of Thessalonians. This text agrees essentially with the Greek text of Westcott and Hort, but there are six passages in these two letters where the Revised Standard Version does not follow the Westcott and Hort text.

In I Thess. 1:2, WH, with Nestle, edits the text so that the word "constantly" is associated with the word "remembering," instead of with the word "mentioning," as in RSV.

In I Thess. 1:5 the word translated "among" by RSV is omitted by WH; their text would be translated "to you"; the Nestle text agrees with RSV.

In I Thess. 2:7, WH reads "babes"; RSV, with the Nestle text, reads "gentle."

In I Thess. 5:4, WH reads "that the day come upon you as thieves"; RSV follows Nestle, who reads "that the day come upon you as a thief [comes]."

In II Thess. 1:10 WH reads the verb "was believed," with Nestle and RSV, but regards it a primitive error for a very similar verb, "was confirmed."

In II Thess. 3:6, WH, with Nestle, reads "the" instead of "our" in the phrase translated in RSV, "our Lord Jesus Christ."

## VIII. Message of the Letters

The total Thessalonian correspondence is dominated by two great emphases. One of them is the note of thanksgiving. The apostle, with his fellow authors of the letters, reflects upon the call which God had extended to these Thessalonian Christians in the presentation to them by his approved messengers of the gospel of the Lord Jesus Christ. They had heard this gospel; they had received it; they had become obedient to it; they had remained faithful in all their trying experiences. They had become examples not only in the two areas of the Grecian peninsula, Macedonia and Achaia, but also in communities beyond. They brought joy to the heart of the apostle and his associates. They were the evidence of the fruitage of their labors in the gospel. In the power of the Spirit of God, in endurance under difficulties, in abiding hope for the consummation, they remained true and loyal in their devotion to Jesus Christ.

The second emphasis is that of yearning and prayerful desire on the part of the writers that these new and harassed disciples would not only continue steadfast but would abound more and more in all Christian virtues and graces. A great tradition had been delivered to them. It was a tradition in the truth of the gospel, the

gospel of God in the gift of the Lord Jesus. In their obedience to the call of God they had entered upon the Christian way. It was not a way with a "blind end"; it was a way opening more and more into larger and fuller experience and power. It was a way whose consummation would arrive with the arrival of the Lord himself, who would come in glory and would bring all those who remain faithful into the fellowship of his kingdom.

Some from the beginning had not entered fully into the understanding of, or obedience to, the new way of life and fellowship. Of these some were persistent in their failure and their inadequacy; some became meddlesome and troublesome; some became a burden upon the faithful of the fellowship. All of these are told that they must change their attitude and their ways. They should fall into line with the great tradition of truth and life which had been delivered to them. Their responsibility could not be evaded. If they refused finally and definitely to show themselves worthy members of the fellowship, they were to be left to themselves. This was to be done not as a final abandonment of them, but in hope that such treatment would bring them to realization of themselves, to shamefaced change of life and a return to a worthy place in the fellowship.

Because the Thessalonians had come out of a pagan background, many things in this Christian message were difficult to understand and appreciate. With painstaking care, with much repetition, the writers seek to instruct, to correct, and to clarify their understanding. Particularly difficult for them to get was the total picture of the parousia. Here repeated and painstaking instruction was needed. This the writers sought to give. They had discussed this subject so fully when at Thessalonica that they took much for granted in their writing. Precisely what they had said is difficult to recover, but the general lines of thought are clear.

A second area where Christianity confronted these converts from paganism with something new and difficult to grasp was the sphere of practical moral living, particularly as regards relations of the sexes and fidelity to one's tasks. Paul sets forth with clarity and force the manner in which they should conduct themselves in both areas. Again he had said more to them when among them than these letters repeat. He had apparently talked in very plain and simple and direct language. Because he and his fellow workers had done so, they can speak now with less detail. But the substance of what they had had to say is again abundantly clear. It is a part of the great Christian tradition that converts should become not only obedient to the truth in the gospel, but responsive and obedient to the high challenge of Christian living. To this the writers call them. They themselves grow strong in heart and courage as these newly won disciples respond to the challenge. It is their abiding hope and prayer that they may all so live that they will be unblamable in the day the Lord comes for his own. To this high destiny they are called. That they may fully enter into it is the yearning of those whom God used as his messengers to bring them into obedience to his message and abiding fidelity to his will.

### IX. Selected Bibliography

For those who must do their work mainly in English, the following commentaries are likely to be found of most value:

DIBELIUS, MARTIN. *Die Briefe des Apostels Paulus: die neun kleinen Briefe* ("Handbuch zum Neuen Testament"). Tübingen: J. C. B. Mohr, 1913.

ELLICOTT, CHARLES J. *A Critical and Grammatical Commentary on St. Paul's Epistles to the Thessalonians.* Andover: Warren F. Draper, 1864. Characterized by sound scholarship and grammatical interests.

FINDLAY, GEORGE G., ed. *The Epistles of Paul the Apostle to the Thessalonians* ("Cambridge Greek Testament"). Cambridge: University Press, 1904. The work of a leader in the interpretation of Paul, with special interest in textual discussions and careful interpretation.

FRAME, JAMES EVERETT. *A Critical and Exegetical Commentary on the Epistles of St. Paul to the Thessalonians* ("International Critical Commentary"). New York: Charles Scribner's Sons, 1912. Justly recognized as one of the best of the volumes in this well-known series.

LIGHTFOOT, J. B. *Notes on Epistles of St. Paul from Unpublished Commentaries.* London: Macmillan & Co., 1895. Material all in English. The work of one of the greatest names in New Testament study.

LÜNEMANN, GOTTLIEB. *Critical and Exegetical Hand-Book to the Epistles of Paul to the Thessalonians* ("Meyer Commentary"). Tr. Paton J. Gloag. Edinburgh: T. & T. Clark, 1880. One of the justly celebrated older commentaries with ample presentation of varying views on all important points.

MILLIGAN, GEORGE. *St. Paul's Epistle to the Thessalonians.* London: Macmillan & Co., 1908. The work of one of the best-known scholars in papyri and New Testament lexicography. Many quotations from classical authors and papyri.

MOFFATT, JAMES. *The First and Second Epistles of Paul the Apostle to the Thessalonians,* in W. Robertson Nicoll, ed. *Expositor's Greek Testament.* London: Hodder & Stoughton, 1910. Vol. IV. Sound historical scholarship; keen appreciation.

NEIL, WILLIAM. *The Epistle of Paul to the Thessalonians* ("Moffatt New Testament Commentary"). New York: Harper & Bros., 1950.

STEVENS, WILLIAM ARNOLD. *Commentary on the Epistles to the Thessalonians* ("American Commentary on the New Testament"). Philadelphia: American Baptist Publication Society, 1890. The work of a recognized leader in New Testament interpretation.

WOHLENBERG, GUSTAV. *Der erste und zweite Thessalonicherbriefe* ("Kommentar zum Neuen Testament"). Leipzig: A. Deichert, 1909.

# I THESSALONIANS

## TEXT, EXEGESIS, AND EXPOSITION

1 Paul, and Silvanus, and Timotheus, unto the church of the Thessalonians,

1 Paul, Silva'nus, and Timothy, To the church of the Thessalo'ni-

### I. ADDRESS AND GREETING (1:1)

**1:1.** This is the characteristic form of salutation used by the apostle in nearly all his letters. In the light of the total content of the letter, and of the clear indications here

**1:1. The Heroic Triumvirate: Paul, Silvanus, Timothy.**—This opening sentence of the epistle has hidden within it the evangelical daring of the early disciples of Christ. Thessalonica was a city of pagan corruption and idolatry. What a challenge to the early church! How swiftly accepted! "We had courage . . . to declare to you the gospel of God in the face of great opposition" (2:2). And so, out of the dark and stubborn substance of this evil society, the evange-

and there of a specific personal responsibility of Paul for some special word or advice on some particular point, we should probably understand that the apostle himself is the real author, but that those named with him share in his general concern for those to whom he writes, and assume with him responsibility for the message which the letter contains. Silas and Timothy had helped in the founding of the church (Acts 17:2, 4) and had been the messengers of Paul to the churches of Macedonia after he himself had left the area (Acts 17:4, 10, 14-15; 18:5). In 2:6 apparently, though not all interpreters accept this suggestion, they are included in Paul's reference to "apostles of Christ." In his salutation Paul does not include any descriptive term (such as "apostle" or "servant"), as he does everywhere else except in the letter to Philemon. Some have held that this omission implies that these letters were written very early before any formal claim to apostleship had been made. Others believe that the absence of any such descriptive reference implies that his apostleship was fully recognized and needed no affirmation. They point out that in Galatians and I and II Corinthians he is thinking of the attacks which Judaizers had made upon him; in Romans he is writing to a community which he has never visited and which he would forewarn and forearm against Judaistic attacks; Phil. 3:2-6 distinctly carries a warning against unbelieving and interfering Jews; Colossians and Ephesians attest his right to vouch for the Christianity which has been proclaimed by his associates to these communities. Whatever the explanation, there is a tone of personal naturalness and intimacy not only at this point but running through these two Thessalonian letters.

Silvanus is quite generally regarded as the same person as the Silvanus of I Pet. 5:12 and, despite the difficulty of the form of the name, the Silas of Acts, a prophet from the church in Jerusalem (Acts 15:27, 32), a Roman citizen (Acts 16:37), and chosen by Paul as a companion for this missionary journey (Acts 15:40; 17:4, 10). He seems to have replaced Barnabas, who probably also was of the prophetic rank, as was Silas (Acts 4:36; 13:1; cf. I Cor. 12:28). Timothy was a young man of high reputation in two of the churches founded by Barnabas and Paul (Iconium and Lystra), son of a Jewish mother and Greek father, selected by Paul (Acts 16:1-2) to take (along with Silas) the place of Mark who had been the companion of Barnabas and Paul on their missionary journey into Asia Minor (Acts 13:5c; 15:37-38; 17:15). He is more frequently named as an associate of Paul in his varied journeys and labors than is any other person in the apostle's letters.

This letter is addressed to **the church of the Thessalonians in God the Father and in the Lord Jesus Christ.** The term used by Paul which we translate **church** was employed for various kinds of assemblies and really means a group of people "called out" to form

---

lists drew a Christian congregation which became their joy and crown.

Courage has ever been a feature of the faith. It is (a) a basic virtue. Unless we have it, we have no foundation for any other. It is the rock quality on which temperance, truth, purity, faith, patience, and endurance are built. It is (b) a Christian virtue. The steady courage of Jesus has fired the imagination of history. Courage is dual in nature—the courage to suffer and the courage to do. Jesus had both. He endured hardship, pain, desertion, misunderstanding, and loneliness, not with the grim pride of Stoicism, but with the passionate surrender of faith; and when he saw that the enemies of the kingdom, of himself, and of his ideas were centered in Jerusalem, he set his face like a flint and went toward it. In Jerusalem he would encounter Pilate, the representative of violence and the totalitarian dictatorship of Rome; Caiaphas, the representative of ecclesi-

astical vested interest and hoary religious tradition, and the fierce enemy of anyone who might imperil them; Herod, the representative of vice —dissolute and savage—the moral corrupter of the youth of Judah. This combination of evil men and powers Christ challenged, and died, as it were, upon their spears. His heart knew no recoil, and a great company has followed in his train—Paul, hounded, defamed, imprisoned, beaten with many stripes; Savonarola, the mighty preacher of Florence, who went to the stake of burning "walking lightly, singing softly, while Machiavelli looked on"; Francis Xavier, the gentleman of the Lord, who ranged from Rome to the Sea of Japan, with the cry upon his lips: "On to the bound of the waste; on to the city of God"; Bunyan, whose dungeon door would have swung open had he but agreed not to preach in public; and Livingstone, missionary and explorer, whose motto was "I push on." It is (c) a required virtue. Christianity has lost

*which is* in God the Father, and *in* the Lord Jesus Christ: Grace *be* unto you, and peace, from God our Father, and the Lord Jesus Christ.

ans in God the Father and the Lord Jesus Christ:

Grace to you and peace.

an assembly. Paul distinctly indicates, in a phrase found only here and in II Thess 1:1, the character of the assembly of Thessalonians: it has its reality and meaning in God and in Jesus Christ. Paul addresses his letters to a church (I and II Corinthians, Philemon), or churches (Galatians), or the saints (Romans, Colossians, Ephesians), or the saints with bishops and deacons (Philippians), in a given place. Here he speaks of the people who compose the church; the same form is used of the "church of the Laodiceans" in Col. 4:16. It has been suggested that the reason for this difference in form of address is that the work in Thessalonica was so new that as yet no church organization had been effected, and Paul naturally thinks of the persons, not the group (but see on vss. 6-7). If, however, Acts 14:23 represents the regular procedure of the apostle, this seems not to be a valid explanation. Add to this his reference to "those who are over you . . . and admonish you" (5:12), and we seem to have specific indication that there were accepted officers and leaders of the church. Possibly no labored explanation of the difference in form of address is needed; it may be merely a matter of mood and of chance.

It may be observed that to Paul God is **Father** and Jesus Christ is **Lord**. This represents his basic religious heritage and conviction from his Jewish background and his new experience in the fellowship of Christ. The Shemoneh Esreh, the eighteen (later nineteen) prayers of the Jewish liturgy supposed to be recited daily, include petitions to "our Father"; the fifth asks that he lead his people again to "thy law," and the sixth, that he forgive us for "we have sinned." Throughout the N.T. period, from the first sermon of Peter recorded in Acts 2:36 on, the designation of Jesus as Lord was constant in Christian thinking.

The greeting which Paul extends to the Thessalonian church is the briefest in any of his known letters. His greetings are not duplicated in any other letters we know. The nearest approach to them is found in I Peter and the letter of Clement of Rome. Greek letters reflect a variety of greetings, the simplest—and at the beginning of our Christian Era the most frequently used—form of which is found in the single word χαίρειν in the epistle of James and in Acts 15:28-29. II John 10-11 twice mentions this same word as a possible personal greeting. Many combinations with this simple one-word greeting are found in the Greek letters of the N.T. period. The Jewish form of greeting was the word "peace." It is found specifically mentioned as a personal greeting in Luke (10:5; 24:36) and John (20:19, 21, 26), and as a closing personal greeting in III John (vs. 15). It is the greeting in a number of letters dating from the pre-N.T. period of Jewish history

many of its battles, not in conflict but in default. It has denied its Master by fleeing the field. Even such a man as Martin Niemöller, who so bravely fought the Nazi regime in Germany, had to make this confession:

In 1933, when the Communists were imprisoned, I did not lift my voice. I did not say to my congregation, "Be on your guard. There is something wrong happening here." And when the feeble-minded were murdered, I said to myself, "Am I to be the guardian of the feeble-minded?" I could not even claim that I was ignorant of the persecution of the Jews, but I did nothing. I only started speaking out when the faith of the Church was persecuted. For this neglect I am greatly to blame. I have sinned.[1]

[1] Quoted in *Expository Times*, LX, 228.

If the church had been courageous and alert, would the acids of unbrotherliness have so dispersed through the arteries of the world that war has succeeded war? Would drunkenness and gambling be the social poisons which they are now? Would Sunday be virtually lost to the community as a day of worship, quiet, and religious education? Would the life of the nations be so widely secularized? As Christians we should remember we "are the body of Christ" (I Cor. 12:27). He must have interpreters. The heroism that flashed out in the cry "In the world you have tribulation; but be of good cheer, I have overcome the world" (John 16:33) should be in us, for the world needs the moral, intellectual, and physical power to combat the sin, enlighten

2 We give thanks to God always for you all, making mention of you in our prayers;

2 We give thanks to God always for you all, constantly mentioning you in our

---

(e.g., Dan. 4:1; 6:25) ; it is also found in combination with various other words. Some of the letters coming from the centuries immediately preceding the time of Paul contain some form of Greek greeting in combination with a Jewish greeting.

Many scholars believe that the combination of Greek and Jewish greetings forms the basis of Paul's distinctive salutation. Others (e.g., Stevens) believe that he has in mind the priestly benediction given in Num. 6:24-26. But whatever its sources, the distinctive Pauline greeting is his own coinage—a special form into which he infused the very essence of his Christian thought and conviction. **Grace . . . and peace** from God and the Lord Jesus Christ were at the very heart of his Christian experience.

## II. Personal Thanksgiving and Apologia (1:2-3:13)

The opening section of the letter is concerned almost exclusively with Paul's personal relations with the Thessalonian Christians. The entire passage is permeated with the note of thanksgiving. Interpreters are divided as to whether an apologetic or self-defense note is also present. Some (e.g., William A. Stevens) believe that such a note nowhere appears in the letters; others (e.g., James E. Frame), that an apologetic interest runs throughout this portion of the letter. This latter opinion is supported by the specific affirmations which the apostle makes concerning himself and the specific denial of certain attitudes and motives which would hardly be a point of discussion with him if he were not speaking to charges that had been definitely made against him. Not all parts of these chapters carry the same measure of apologetic. It is especially prominent in ch. 2.

## A. Thanksgiving for the Disciples (1:2-10)

**2-3.** Here Paul sets forth his thanksgiving to God as he reflects upon the total response of the Thessalonians to the gospel which he and Silas and Timothy had

---

the ignorance, expose the superstition, uproot the bigotry, and quell the hatred of our time. The first sacrament is that of gallant men and women who by their sacrificial courage become the body of Christ their Lord to their day and generation. An incarnation of Christ's spirit is Christianity's supreme persuasive.

**2-10. A Paean of Praise.**—Paul frankly exults in the Thessalonian church, and in this paragraph speaks with gratitude for the creative things he sees in its members—faith, love, enduring helpfulness, high Christian character, evangelical zeal, and personal friendship. **We give thanks to God always for you.**

Here is an emphasis too often missing in the conception which Christian ministers convey to their congregations concerning the church that is the body of Christ, of which those congregations ideally are part. Christian leaders publicly criticize, exhort, and sometimes scold the church, but seldom publicly rejoice in it. They ought; for a dispassionate and comparative examination shows it to be the unique institution. Admitting its many failures, it is nevertheless the purest institution. What fraternal order, economic group, or political party is as clean? It is the noblest institution, for it is the only one that

deals solely with ideal aims and spiritual objects, and worships steadily in the name and around the Person who is the most sublime figure of history. It is the tenderest institution, for it is based on the yearnings and aspirations of the human heart. It is the most persistent institution, for it has not died. Its enemies have persecuted it and seemingly slain it, yet on the third morning it has always risen. Empires, dynasties, and systems have had their day and ceased to be, but it has pursued the difficult tenor of its way. It is the most courageous institution, for while dictators and tyrants found it possible to bend education, the press, radio, art, literature, politics, capital, labor, and fraternal societies to their wills, the Christian congregation has been the anvil upon which their hammers have broken. It is the most redemptive institution, for no other agency can match its good works and creative deeds, and most of the great ameliorative and philanthropic agencies are rooted in and inspired by it. It is the most universal institution, for while the great world wars rived asunder the internationalism of finance, trade, government, and education, the Christian congregation maintained its unity and world-wide ministry. It is the only international society able

3 Remembering without ceasing your work of faith, and labor of love, and pa-

prayers. 3 remembering before our God and

---

proclaimed among them. Perhaps because it is most vivid in his mind, he refers first to the continuing manifestation which the Thessalonians had given to the power of the gospel. He expresses his thanksgiving to God **for you all.** He and his fellow writers of the letter not only remember constantly these Christian friends, but make mention of them always at the time of their prayers. The word translated **without ceasing** (KJV) and **constantly** (RSV) should apparently be associated with **mentioning you in our**

---

to overcome permanently the differences of language, culture, race, and history. It is entitled to and should be given, at least occasionally, a resounding vote of thanks.

We should remember its three elements: (a) It is a fellowship. It was born in a world divided racially, culturally, and socially, but was strikingly different, for while it was poor in money it was rich in friendship. Brotherliness was not merely a characteristic, but its essence. Its fellowship transcended rank, wealth, color, and culture. (b) It is a fellowship around a Person. "I am the vine, you are the branches" (John 15:5). Fellowship in the congregation is dependent upon fellowship with its Head. A Christian congregation is where two or three are gathered together, with Jesus in the midst. It is not constituted by numbers or organizations, but by the spirit of the members and their relationship to its Leader and Lord. (c) It is a fellowship around a Person who can give it the shepherd heart, the serving hand, the burden-bearing back, the questing mind. Its concern is with all of life. Its responsibility is for all the world. It can be the sympathizer and champion of every good cause, and the unrelenting, intelligent, and powerful enemy of every evil one.

2. *The Love that Is Boundless.*—The significant word in the phrase **for you all** is the final and emphatic **all.** As the later parts of this epistle indicate, no one knew better than Paul that there were problem people in the Thessalonian church, and he addressed them with blistering forthrightness. But his candor never declined to scolding, bitterness, or enmity of any individual. He is the shepherd of all the sheep of the flock—white, gray, and black. His love is nonselective. Few leaders can honestly meet this high standard. It is easy to give thanks for the lovable and responsive members. What of the inconsistent, the renegades, who, when they took the solemn vows of Christian discipleship, were merely "blowing bubbles"? What of the indifferent? Their names are on the membership roll, but Christ, the Bible, the church, their fellow members, mean little or nothing. What of the hostile? Why they ever related themselves

to a Christian congregation is a mystery, for they exhibit a discouraging eagerness to dredge up every piece of scandal reflecting on the church in general and its ministry in particular. What of the unlovable? The members who are brusque, hard, unpleasant, whom Spurgeon described as being built on "uncomfortable principles"? When Daniel Poling was very young in the ministry, he complained to S. Parkes Cadman about the hypocrites and spiritual loafers in his congregation. The older man looked at him with a twinkle in his eye and said, "I know, I know. But if you want to keep them and save yourself, you'll have to learn to love them, my boy!"

3. *Three Work Horses.*—Here Paul's great trinity of virtues goes into action. They are not likened to the usual three female graces, but to three heavy truck horses. Each is associated with something toilsome and hard, not with the state of poesy and passivity found in some of the popular hymns: **work ... labor ... steadfastness.**

**Work of faith.** The long centuries of history have produced religions in variety and number, but in final analysis they can be divided into religions of works and religions of faith. The former teach that man can secure the favor, forgiveness, or power of Deity by doing something —making a pilgrimage, performing a rite, bestowing a gift, undergoing a penance, offering a sacrifice, or maintaining a moral code. The latter teach that man cannot secure the favor of Deity by a price he may pay, a labor he may do, or a pilgrimage he may make. It is not what he does, but what God does that counts. Christianity is such a religion. "For by grace you have been saved through faith; and this is not your own doing, it is the gift of God—not because of works, lest any man should boast" (Eph. 2:8-9).

But Christian faith is not confined to intellectual or spiritual belief. It has expressions without which it cannot be Christian (Jas. 2:17). Observe: (a) Its seeming foolishness. It is intangible and imponderable, for it cannot be elucidated like a philosophical argument or demonstrated like a geometrical theorem. It is to start with a hypothesis and trust the unseen even in a century when the issues and problems

tience of hope in our Lord Jesus Christ, in the sight of God and our Father; | Father your work of faith and labor of love and steadfastness of hope in our Lord

---

**prayers** rather than with **remembering.** The word is found in the N.T. in Paul only, and there always in connection with his prayers (cf. 2:13; 5:17; Rom. 1:9). Paul and his associates are thinking of the general moral conduct, the fruit of the faith of these Christians. They are aware also of the irksome toil which attests the reality and quality of their love. The toil may include physical as well as spiritual activity (cf. 2:9; 3:5; II Thess. 3:8). The apostle is grateful also for their endurance or **steadfastness,** their

---

are so fiercely practical, so terrifyingly immediate that faith seems an invitation to madness and credulity. (*b*) Its inevitableness. It is an ingredient of life. No man lives on the basis of knowledge. We must have a faith that goes beyond what we know. We might as well try to hear without ears, see without eyes, breathe without lungs, as live without faith. Subtract it from the departments of life—business, science, family life, politics, religion—and what is left? The temple of history is not built on the foundations of mathematics, but on the unseen foundations of faith (Heb. 11:1). Life is a great adventure of belief. No faith, no life. (*c*) Its varieties. There is the faith of the child, of which Thomas Hood sang so wistfully, which is based on the say-so of others; and the faith of the man, based on experience and the long search of the spirit. There is good faith, because it is intelligent and creative, manifested by such men as Grenfell, Schweitzer, Kagawa; and bad faith like that of Nazism, which sent tens of thousands of young Germans singing to their deaths. There is the faith that is feeble, spineless, and pale; and there is the faith strong, upright, and vital. (*d*) Its necessity for achievement. Two things there were to which Jesus set no limit—the love of God and the power of faith. Faith to him was not a speculative idea to be interestingly discussed but a practical idea to be acted upon. His greatest deeds were prefaced with "If you have faith." Paul is here lauding and rejoicing in such a faith—that which strikes out for goals, quickens the mind, and nerves the arm. Without faith life is paralyzed; with faith life is energized. It is only on this basis that we can explain such a group as the Thessalonians, or such men as Paul, Chrysostom, Francis of Assisi, Bunyan, and John Wesley.

**Labor of love.** Paul declared love to be the supreme virtue—greater than faith or hope (I Cor. 13:13). Without it, he says, the finest organization is a cipher. The greatest preacher without it is but sound, signifying nothing. The greatest generosity without it is profitless. Even dying a martyr's death is a worthless gesture. This is not the rhetoric of the orator but clear-

eyed truth. It is what Jesus put at the very center of his teaching (Mark 12:31; John 15:12). It is what he exemplified in his life and demands in the lives of his disciples. It has been defined in a variety of ways, e.g., "glowing good will." But definition and analysis are insufficient; for like the rose, it is greater than the sum of its parts. It is best understood in its practical expressions—patience, friendliness, magnanimity, humility, courtesy, unselfishness, good temper, guilelessness, and sincerity (I Cor. 13:4-7).

It is a difficult virtue. The word **labor** in this clause makes that clear, with its connotation of strenuous, sweating effort: "Your love has meant hard work."[2] The Thessalonians were spending themselves in the task of loving a community and individuals whose delight was their annoyance and persecution. This was indeed "hard work," for it entailed the constant exercise of love's noblest attribute—forgiveness. In this they were following in the footsteps of their Lord, for he both taught and practiced it. The way to win an enemy, he said, is to forgive him; the way to destroy evil is to pardon it (Matt. 18:22). No other teaching of Christ receives less response from his alleged disciples. We give it lip service only, for we believe in our hearts that it is out of touch with reality. It is the most unpopular virtue. But Christianity is love, which includes forgiveness, so there is no recourse for us but its practice. It is a spiritual imperative for our own sakes. Our personal salvation depends upon it. The only conditional petition in our Lord's prayer is "Forgive us our debts, as we forgive our debtors." Forgiveness is a spiritual imperative for the world's sake. Look at its confusion, division, and impoverishment. It is literally dying for lack of friendship. The machine gun and bomb may be able to restrict, restrain, and repress evil aggressors, but they can never produce good will and good resolves in the present and for the future. A certain attitude and atmosphere are required which only forgiveness can provide. "Love or perish" is the ultimatum of a moral universe to

[2] J. B. Phillips, *Letters to Young Churches* (New York: The Macmillan Co., 1948), p. 127.

4 Knowing, brethren beloved, your election of God.

Jesus Christ. 4 For we know, brethren be-

---

"manly constancy" under the trials and afflictions which they have had to undergo—constancy born of the **hope** which they have in the Lord Jesus Christ (cf. II Thess. 1:4). This hope is directed especially to the consummation in which they are to share before God their Father at the time of the "manifestation" (parousia) of the Lord Jesus.

**4-5.** Paul's thought now takes a new turn. His Christian friends in Thessalonica are addressed as **brethren,** a term frequently used in that time (as shown by the papyri) to refer to members of the same guild, or those closely associated in some form of activity. The word reflects Paul's feeling of close and sympathetic fellowship with these new disciples. They are also addressed as **beloved by God,** and are reminded of their **election;** they have been **chosen** by God to be participants in the blessings of the gospel. It is quite possible (Frame, with Calvin, says it is "certain") that Paul is here thinking of election in the same basic way as in the letter to the Romans (9:11; 11:5, 7, 28), a view supported

---

mankind. If this ultimatum is not acceded to, what is before our world? A fearful waste of personality, because of the permanent isolation of man from his kind, and the destructiveness of atomic warfare; the loss of friendly relationships with their warmth, color, and joy; the continuance of sullen distrust between nations; the overlordship of tyrannies, with bitter insurrectionary feelings and actions on the part of repressed groups; the end of everything answering the description of civilization; and life under an ever-present threat of death, for life without love destroys itself.

Of course it is a **labor!** It was a labor for Jesus to forgive the craftiness of the scribes, the hypocrisy of the Pharisees, the brutality of the Roman power, the cold indifference of the populace, and the shameful cowardice of his disciples; but looking down on them from the cross, he said, "Father, forgive them." If it was not easy for him, why should we expect it to be easy for us? "The disciple is not above his master, nor the servant above his lord" (Matt. 10:24). The **labor of love** is a high and difficult challenge.

**Steadfastness of hope.** The N.T. has given the most resolutely honest reading of life, man, and God the world has ever received. It has shirked no fact, however ugly, and colored no truth, however strong the temptation; yet it has given hope a higher place as a virtue than any other religion. It says not merely, "While there's life there's hope," but "Beyond life there is hope." The N.T. is the most hopeful book in the world. The positive note sounds in it from beginning to end like the tone of a mighty bell. It opens with the story of a tiny group of quiet-eyed people, gathered in the temple for prayer, living in hope of liberation, and of the birth of a Savior who would carry upon his shoulders the government of the world, redeem mankind, and be set for the rising and falling of the nations.

It continues with the story of a band of lowly people, living in a delinquent, dissipated, and disenchanted world, yet traveling through it radiant of heart and glorying in the hope of the coming day of righteousness, peace, and joy. It ends with a vision of the throne of God, and the sound of great voices in heaven saying, "The kingdom of the world has become the kingdom of our Lord and of his Christ, and he shall reign for ever and ever" (Rev. 11:15). "That by steadfastness and by the encouragement of the scriptures we might have hope" (Rom. 15:4).

The steadfast, unflagging hope possessed by the Thessalonians is rich in fruitage. It is the hope which saves, because it liberates, energizes, stabilizes (Heb. 6:19) and protects (I Thess. 5:8). This quality of hope is not something that can be worked up. No man can say, "Go to now; I shall hope." It is a religious virtue, established on the solid basis of something greater than itself—faith. "So faith, hope, love abide" (I Cor. 13:13).

First the faith, then closely pursuing, the hope. There can be no change in the order. The Christian hope rests on the Christian faith. It is the only real way to live. The Christians of the early centuries were tonic men because they rejoiced in hope. The golden age of the pagan world in which they lived was behind it, and its literature was full of nostalgia for the days of innocence and joy that were no more; but the Christians' faces were toward the sunrise. Their hearts were not gloomy with regret, but eager with expectation of the coming reign of Christ, when every knee should bow and every lip confess his glory. Do we follow in their train? If not, why not?

**4. God's Elect.**—Here is the reason for the apostles' thankfulness, intercessory prayer, and the remembering of the Thessalonians before the Father for their work of faith, labor of love, and steadfastness of hope—God has chosen

5 For our gospel came not unto you in word only, but also in power, and in the | loved by God, that he has chosen you; 5 for our gospel came to you not only in word,

---

by II Thess. 2:13; but inasmuch as the immediately following sentence indicates that the apostle had in mind very definitely the response of these Thessalonians to the gospel which was preached among them, he is apparently thinking of election primarily in the sense of the call which they had not only heard but responded to (cf. I Cor. 1:26-28).

Paul reminds the Thessalonian leaders that the gospel which he and his companions had preached had come to them not only in word (of their preaching), but also in the

---

them. And this choice has been validated by the manner of their lives, their good works, and their response to the efforts of the evangelists. Their election is first and foremost a personal act of God. It is his love operating in life. They are **beloved by God,** therefore **he has chosen** them. William Neil states it this way:

The Thessalonians have been chosen by God, not because it is a necessary stage in some theological system he [Paul] has devised, but because of what he has seen among them and heard about them (vers. 5 ff.). Obviously they had not chosen God. Their Christian witness was only possible because God had first selected them, a tiny handful in a pagan city, to be among the first to embody His Kingdom in Europe. They had responded finely; but the initiative was the grace of God. Election for Paul is inseparably connected with love. God calls because God loves.[3]

The final why of God's election is beyond our ken. The mists lie thick and heavy on our minds when we try to explore this vast problem. Why did God elect Israel from all the nations of the earth to reveal his truth and bring his light to the Gentiles? Why did the early church feel that God had elected it to follow in the succession of Israel, to be, as the Epistle of Peter puts it "a chosen race, a royal priesthood, a holy nation, God's own people, that you may declare the wonderful deeds of him . . ." (I Pet. 2:9)? Why have individuals over the centuries been convinced they were set aside by God for specific high purposes? We cannot tell. The undeniable truth is he has called, and he does call. Sometimes we can see a reason for election in extraordinary spiritual sensitivity as in the Jewish people, or in the rare gifts of persons like Paul, Augustine, John Wesley, or Henry Drummond. But we know only in part and peer through the glass darkly. We can thank God, however, that election is not related to any whim or caprice, but to the divine love.

**5. Fidelity with Originality.**—In several places in his letters, Paul speaks of **our gospel** (II

Thess. 2:14), "my gospel" (II Tim. 2:8), "the gospel" (II Thess. 1:8). As no two men are alike, so it is with interpreters of the gospel. They are distinctive individuals, with distinctive backgrounds, temperament, culture, approach, and utterance. Also, each one has a dominant mood, a mood that comes to him oftener than any other, and so is the ruling expression of his life, which he inevitably shares with disciples. So each has, in a deep and true sense, his own gospel. This truth shines like a beacon from the N.T. pages. Study the four evangelists: the towering fact and radiant glory to each of them was Jesus Christ, but observe the varieties of approach, style, and interpretation. Matthew, having in mind his own race, preaches him as the Messiah—the fulfillment of the wistful dreams and high prophecies of a thousand years. Christ to him was the One who was to come. Mark presents him as the One touched with the infirmities of his people, a worker of gracious and miraculous deeds in their behalf. Luke, the Greek physician, presents him as the ideal for whom for centuries his people has been searching—the complete personality, the perfect man. John, mystical in his nature, presents him in terms of the Incarnation (John 1:1). His gospel is that Christ is the eternal purpose, the complete incarnation of Deity. Now, hard on their heels (but before them in his writing), comes Paul, the most vivid, mystical, and erudite personality in the early church. With the evangelists he shared Jesus Christ and the great truths and experiences in God's revelation of his Son; but like them, he sees and rejoices in those truths from his particular viewpoint and need. So again and again he speaks of "my gospel," "our gospel." Any man of worth has "my gospel"; otherwise he speaks only with "authorities," not with the authority of a distinctive approach. Preaching is truth through a personality to personalities. Saul must wear his own armor, and David likewise.

But "my gospel," "our gospel," must conform to, be obedient to, and be checked by "Christ's gospel." This truth Paul and all true apostles of the Word have recognized. No mental or spiritual exercise will bring more productive results

---

[3] *The Epistle of Paul to the Thessalonians* (New York: Harper & Bros., 1950; "The Moffatt New Testament Commentary"), p. 14.

Holy Ghost, and in much assurance; as ye know what manner of men we were among you for your sake.

but also in power and in the Holy Spirit and with full conviction. You know what kind of men we proved to be among you

---

power of the Holy Spirit. The word translated **much assurance** (KJV) or **full conviction** (RSV) is found infrequently in the N.T. with a somewhat varying meaning. Paul uses it only here and in Col. 2:2, where it is associated with "riches . . . of understanding." Here Paul is doubtless thinking of the **full conviction** of himself and his companions that the gospel they preached to the Thessalonians was in very truth the gospel. He calls it **our gospel** (cf. Rom. 2:16; 16:25; II Cor. 4:3; II Thess. 2:14; II Tim. 2:8), but in this same letter it is "the gospel of God" (2:2, 8, 9), the personal and ultimate source of it, and the gospel of the Lord Jesus, the personal center of it (cf. 3:2; II Thess. 1:8).

In the latter part of vs. 5, explicitly, and in vss. 6-7, implicitly, the character of himself and his fellow preachers of the gospel is brought into the picture. The apologetic note which is still more vividly and amply presented in the first part of ch. 2 is noticeably

---

than a constant comparison of "my gospel," "our gospel," with Christ's gospel. There is so much meagerness, stridency, immediacy, and so little penetration, dimension, and range in present-day preaching. These would soon disappear if we preached the fullness of the gospel of our Lord with our own distinctive approach and emphasis.

**5. The Dry Bones Live.**—"Our Gospel came to you not as mere words, but as a message with power behind it—the effectual power, in fact, of the Holy Spirit." [4]

There were not many wise men "according to worldly standards, not many . . . powerful, not many . . . of noble birth" (I Cor. 1:26) in the ranks of the early church, but they exercised a power out of all proportion to their culture and numbers. They were confronted (a) by the Roman Empire, the mighty social, military and political power, whose story was one of expansion and colonization, and whose laws governed or influenced the government of every land; (b) by an awful day, in which society was corrupt; a filthy world was becoming filthier still. It was the day of the beast, the scarlet woman, the seven vials, the pit and martyrdom. Yet the Christians brought to bear against these grim and tremendous forces a power greater than themselves—"the effectual power . . . of the Holy Spirit."

In this century we are lovers of power. With all this vast acquisition of might, are we happy and serene? No! Our successes may become Dead Sea fruit and our mouths be filled with ashes and bitterness. The civilization of which we have so vauntingly spoken may be blown to pieces, and mankind revert to the squalid and barren ferocity of primitive days unless we can discover a spiritual force which will direct the vast physical powers under our command. The ulti-

matum of modern scientific knowledge is addressed to neither communism nor democracy, but to man. It says, "Discover spiritual power or be wrecked! Be good or be dead!" The power we need is that possessed by the Thessalonians, "the effectual power . . . of the Holy Spirit"; which is God on the spot alongside his people, getting inside them, and so imparting himself that the whole man is vitalized and illuminated.

Thus the Jesus of history is not a figure in an ancient story, but a living being today. The church can, if it only will, repeat the victory of its early centuries if, confronted in many ways by a similar secularized world, it confronts it with a similar living Christ. It must go further by convincing a skeptical generation, not by argument but by incarnation, that Christ lives. All the resources of modern Christianity, its closely woven organization, elaborate techniques, stately edifices, impressive services, liturgies, and more or less eloquent preaching, are insufficient. The evidence must come from life. The church must be ablaze with the divine nature, and the living Christ must spring into attractive vitality in the lives of its members. In them the vision must be verified, the Word made flesh. "Christ who lives in me" (Gal. 2:20).

**5-10. No Other Name.**—And with full conviction. There was no "maybe" or "perhaps" in Paul's mind concerning Christ and his gospel. For him there was "no other name under heaven given among men by which we must be saved" (Acts 4:12). There was no hesitation in his mind or stammer on his tongue. In his heart he was a believer in the supremacy and uniqueness of Jesus.

To many this high dogmatism smacks of intolerance, but Paul saw clear as the blazing sun in the sky that Christianity by its very nature is intolerant; that the moment it ceases to be intolerant it ceases to be Christian. He was

[4] Phillips, *Letters to Young Churches*, p. 127.

6 And ye became followers of us, and of the Lord, having received the word in much affliction, with joy of the Holy Ghost:

7 So that ye were ensamples to all that believe in Macedonia and Achaia.

for your sake. 6 And you became imitators of us and of the Lord, for you received the word in much affliction, with joy inspired by the Holy Spirit; 7 so that you became an example to all the believers in Macedo′nia

---

present here. **You know,** he says, what **kind of men** we were as we were preaching **among you;** and you know, despite anything that may be said to the contrary, that our ministry was carried forward in your behalf.

**6-7.** The apostle now moves to a slightly different point as he reflects upon the acceptance of the gospel by these Thessalonian Christians. You not only received us, he says, and our message; you also **became imitators** (not **followers**—KJV; cf. 2:14) **of us and of the Lord** himself in that **the word** of truth which we preached **you received . . . in much affliction.** It had cost, and was still costing, these Thessalonians something to become Christians and to maintain their Christian lives among their fellows (2:14; 3:2-5, 7; II Thess. 1:4). It had cost Paul and his associates to become Christians and to be Christian evangelists (2:2, 15-16; 3:7), just as it had cost the Lord Jesus to carry forward his ministry. It is of value in understanding just what Paul had brought into his message at Thessalonica to observe that he here assumes some acquaintance of his readers with the life and death of the Lord Jesus. This is in keeping with the total impression of the letters. The affliction which his readers had suffered had been accepted, not in regret and sad resignation, but in the joy that was the manifestation of the Holy Spirit in their hearts and lives.

The church had become **an example** (singular, not plural) for all **believers in Macedonia and Achaia,** the two provinces of Greece, for their **faith in God** had **gone forth everywhere.** The **everywhere** must refer to areas outside of Greece, apparently in Asia Minor and its borders, in which the gospel had been preached before Paul arrived in Macedonia. Paul's statement further implies that Paul (then at Corinth; Acts 18:1) is in frequent contact with these various centers. Travelers—older commentators thought

---

the advocate not of *a* faith but of *the* faith. No religion has a real gospel unless it believes it has the best gospel. The central point of tension between the early church and the Roman Empire was here. The latter had no objection to Christianity as one more religion operating within its vast borders, and was blithely willing to add the Christian God to those already in its Pantheon. Its only demand was a simple annual recognition of the supremacy of Caesar. To him all other knees must bow. To such a man as Paul this was the rankest blasphemy and sacrilege. To him Christ, and Christ only, was Lord. His full conviction was that the starting and finishing point of Christianity is Christ Jesus. It is this full conviction that too many present-day laymen and clergymen lack. How many believe, really believe, the gospel is the answer for the moral weakness, fierce misery, spiritual delinquency, and social sin of our time? A just criticism of our culture is its lack of soul or enthusiasm. The same judgment can be pronounced on our religion. Many favorable things can be said of the average Christian congregation, but where are the fervor and passion which

distinguished the congregations of the first century? Are the hearts of its members afire? Does their faith excite them? Are they eager to witness? Does the wonder of their Lord so possess them that it shines in their eyes and vibrates in their voices? To ask such questions is to answer them. They are serious but not excited; conventional but not adventurous; decent but not ardent. Their baptism is into a cautious and respectable repentance. What of the pulpit? Are the clergy such believers, so possessed by their truth, so inflamed of soul, that they communicate their burning conviction to the people? No! They do not convey the impression that they are in the grip of, or are gripped by, a great something. Too often they talk of heaven, hell, salvation, the tragedy of sin, the grace of God, the sacrifice of Calvary, and the immortality of the soul without any seeming rise in bodily temperature, exultation, or heartbreak.

Many of us are afraid of emotion in religion, but we should remember that as Christians we are humanity's suffering servants, the agents of the divine Compassion and the liege men of the

8 For from you sounded out the word of the Lord not only in Macedonia and Achaia, but also in every place your faith to God-ward is spread abroad; so that we need not to speak any thing.

and in Acha'ia. 8 For not only has the word of the Lord sounded forth from you in Macedo'nia and Acha'ia, but your faith in God has gone forth everywhere, so

---

perhaps traveling merchants—were coming and going, and Paul was repeatedly meeting Christians from a great number of places. It has been suggested (e.g., by Lünemann, Wieseler, Milligan) that Aquila and Priscilla, who had recently come from Rome to Corinth, may have reported that the reputation of the Thessalonian Christians had reached Rome (cf. Acts 18:2-3). Paul has no need to give these travelers any information about the state of affairs in Thessalonica. They not only know the story, but are continually declaring to the apostle what is common knowledge among them in the localities from which they come.

**8-9a.** Still another aspect of the Christian career of the Thessalonians is now brought to attention. There had **sounded forth** from them the word of the Lord (the gospel) not only in Macedonia (cf. 4:10, "the brethren throughout Macedonia") and in Achaia, but also in **every place** (cf. the hyperbole, "whole world," Col. 1:6; "every creature under heaven," Col. 1:23). This had happened as a result, not of missionary work or of propaganda, but of Christian living. The word translated **sounded forth** is not elsewhere found in the N.T. Originally it suggested a great variety of loud sounds. Joel 3:14 (LXX) retains this association. Ecclus. 40:13 uses it of loud thunder. A noun of the same root is used by Paul in I Cor. 13:1 to mean a "noisy gong." Luke uses the same word in speaking of the "roaring of the sea" (Luke 21:25), and of the "report" that went forth about Jesus "into every place in the surrounding region" (Luke 4:37). Heb. 12:19 uses it to designate the sound of a trumpet; and Chrysostom thought that Paul is here thinking of the trumpet. Lightfoot thought the implied simile was that of thunder. The basic

---

Man of Five Wounds. The emotive forces of man are not in his head but in his heart. We bleat about "pure reason." There is no such thing, for there has never been a disembodied mind. The fact is that what we feel deeply is more vital than what we think. We may think for a long time and do nothing. It is feeling that spurs us to action. All creative preaching has an emotional quality. Call the biblical roll of those who have left an abiding impression on history. Jeremiah finds the burden of his message almost greater than he can bear.

There is in my heart as it were a burning fire shut up in my bones (Jer. 20:9).

Amos strides down from the hills of Tekoa incandescent with the sorrow and indignation of his truth. Isaiah's message rolls forth in sonorous and blazing sentences as he sees the vanity, drunkenness, and duplicity of the people and rulers. Jesus is moved with compassion as he looks on the people who are as sheep without a shepherd. John is a burning as well as a shining light. Apollos preaches "with ardour and accuracy" (Acts 18:25 Moffatt). Paul is the God-intoxicated Jew. In the true preacher there

is always something that glows and burns, for he is inflamed by the love of Christ, is not separated from the pain and struggle of human life, and has ever before him the vision of the New Jerusalem coming down from God out of heaven, possessed by William Blake, who sang:

> Bring me my bow of burning gold!
> Bring me my arrows of desire!
> Bring me my spear! O clouds unfold!
> Bring me my chariot of fire!
>
> I will not cease from mental fight,
> Nor shall my sword sleep in my hand,
> Till we have built Jerusalem
> In England's green and pleasant land.[5]

The apostles were ever conscious of a new interior power. Its effects were shown in such transformations of attitudes, deeds, and speech as to amaze not only those around but themselves. They believed that Christ dwelt in them, and the manifestations were so convincing that others felt compelled to follow in their way. **You became imitators of us and of the Lord** (vs. 6). Moffatt states the idea more emphatically, "You started to copy us and the Lord."

5 "Milton."

9 For they themselves show of us what manner of entering in we had unto you, and how ye turned to God from idols to serve the living and true God;

that we need not say anything. 9 For they themselves report concerning us what a welcome we had among you, and how you turned to God from idols, to serve a living

---

meaning is clear: Paul is thinking of the fargoing report of the character and spirit of the Thessalonian disciples. In II Thess. 3:1 Paul asks for the prayers of the Thessalonian Christians "that the word of the Lord may speed on and triumph," an indication of his freedom in the use of symbolic language.

9b-10. The apostle's attention now moves from the reports constantly coming to him to the basic facts themselves. The reports tell not only of the entrance or reception (welcome) Paul and his companions had at Thessalonica, but also of how those who constituted the Thessalonian church had turned to God from idols, to serve a living and true God. This characterization of God is found only here in Paul, though it is a part of the agelong Jewish thinking concerning the God of Israel. The idols from whom these Thessalonians had turned are not named. The fact of the change from idolatry to the one true God means that Paul's readers came not from the Jewish community but from among Gentiles and pagans. Implicit in the statement of the apostle about God is the centuries-long tradition of his people as they contrasted their God with the many idols round about. A notable expression of this thinking is found in Isa. 40:12-26. The Thessalonians not only had turned from idolatry to God, but also had responded to the proclamation of the gospel of the parousia of the Lord Jesus, God's Son, and were awaiting his coming, and the deliverance he would bring.

In these verses we thus have not only a reflection of the turning of these Thessalonians to the gospel, but also a condensed outline of that gospel which Paul, Silas, and Timothy had proclaimed to them. It is the apostle's own personal declaration (I Cor. 15:3-11) that these were basic common elements in the gospel which he preached and in the gospel of an apostolic group who were preachers before him. Further, careful

---

Without minimizing the value of other influences, the shining fact is that we are changed by beautiful incarnations, whether evil or good. There is the dynamic power of beautiful wickedness. The worn strumpet of the streets, with her lusterless eyes, hard face, and harsh voice evokes our pity, but the well-educated siren of fashion, attractively clothed and of voluptuous form, exercises a subtle enticement. The coarse vulgarian grates on our sensibilities, but the suave Chesterfield, with his polite and whimsical depravity, fascinates us. The blatant atheist who rants and raves against religion has little appeal, but the brilliant professor with his knowledge, sophistication, and uplifted eyebrow makes unbelief glow like a jewel. The uncouth cynic, with his open and loud-voiced disdain for everything good, true, and beautiful, repels us, but the polite, polished misanthrope, with his three genteel sneers for everybody, charms us.

There is the dynamic power of beautiful goodness. The strength of truth, the high-mindedness of honor, the loveliness of gentleness, the glow of joy, the challenge of courage, the sereneness of peace, are hard to resist. The basis of power over others lies in character. Goldsmith's parson

was poor in purse, but because of what the villagers saw in him he "Allured to brighter worlds, and led the way." [6]

A. J. Cronin puts this agelong truth in the mouth of the Chinese scholar who for so long had remained aloof and had turned aside all the efforts of Father Chisholm, the simple missionary priest, to convert him to Christianity: "The goodness of a religion is best judged by the goodness of its adherents. My friend . . . you have conquered me by example." [7]

We can state the arguments for Christianity, and all of them can be argued against or scoffed at, excepting one—the life it can and does produce. A Christian character cannot be confuted. Few are preached into the faith; they are won when they see it in an incarnation. There is a compulsion in true goodness which cannot be gainsaid. The lives of such men as Francis of Assisi, Brother Lawrence, George Whitefield, Leo Tolstoy, Henry Drummond, Wilfred Grenfell, Toyohiko Kagawa, and others, confirm this truth.

[6] "The Deserted Village," l. 170.
[7] The Keys of the Kingdom (Boston: Little, Brown & Co., 1941), p. 320.

10 And to wait for his Son from heaven, whom he raised from the dead, *even* Jesus, which delivered us from the wrath to come.

and true God, 10 and to wait for his Son from heaven, whom he raised from the dead, Jesus who delivers us from the wrath to come.

---

comparison of the letters to the Thessalonians with the reports in the book of Acts of the message of the preachers in the early church indicates that the message of these preachers and the message of Paul to the Thessalonians were on essentially the same lines. There was agreement that the Lord Jesus, who in the counsel of God had been put to death (Acts 2:23), had been raised from the dead, and had been exalted to the right hand of God, as Son of God with power (Acts 2:33-35; Rom. 1:4). Him the heavens must receive until the time of the restoration of all things (Acts 3:21; the "regeneration" of Matt. 19:28), when he would come from heaven (I Thess. 4:16; II Thess. 1:7) for both judgment and deliverance (Acts 17:31). Those who had not received the gospel and given themselves in faith to the Lord Jesus could expect only the manifestation of the wrath of God upon them (cf. Rom. 2:5; 5:9). All those who had turned to the Lord Jesus and to the living God would share in the redemption by the Lord Jesus from the coming wrath. These Thessalonian disciples were among those who had this hope of deliverance.

The raising of Jesus from the dead was God's designation and vindication of him as such a deliverer. The term **delivers** is thought by some interpreters to refer to the Lord Jesus as the "continual deliverer"; others hold that the Greek word is "timeless" and is essentially equivalent to an adjective. In view of the whole eschatological mold in which Paul's thought at this point is cast, the latter is the preferable interpretation. The expression virtually means that at a given time in the future, Jesus the Son (of God) will be our deliverer from the wrath which is to fall on those who have not accepted him.

---

The apostle saw this winsomeness in the faith of the Thessalonians and rejoiced in it. **You became an example to all the believers (vs. 7). Your faith in God has gone forth everywhere (vs. 8). You turned to God from idols, to serve a living and true God (vs. 9).**

These decisive testimonies to the attractive and redemptive power of incarnated Christianity inspire us and at the same time make us uneasy in spirit. Halford E. Luccock asks:

Has anyone been forced to ask questions about us? Has there been anything in our lives concerning which men ask in wonder, How does he do it? Is there anything in us not easily explained without calling in divine resources? It is a crucial matter, for Christianity has spread and endured largely because, beneath all the fluctuations of time and circumstance, this impression has been made on men by Christian lives.

There are two sorts of wonder about lives and their achievements. The first is caused by what persons *are;* the second by what they *do.* Genuine Christianity has a question-compelling power in both these respects.[8]

We must show that the love of Christ works within us, and that such great chapters as I Cor.

13 are not merely lessons written in a holy book, but can be translated into lovely attractiveness in a holy life. People openly or secretly long for this quality of life to be held up before them. "For all creation, gazing eagerly as if with outstretched neck, is waiting and longing to see the manifestation of the sons of God" (Rom. 8:19 Weymouth).

This winsome quality grows in us as we live in communion of both mind and spirit with our incarnated Lord. Our goodness has then a warm, spontaneous quality. We do not labor to be good; we are good. But so much "goodness" is stiff and unnatural, like a singer straining her voice so distressingly that her audience travails with her. The goodness of the Thessalonian Christians was unlabored. They did not seem to work at it. The inner light just shone through them to the pagan world around. They were joyful and radiant, and the secret of that was their intimacy with the living Christ, stated so clearly by Paul in his letter to the Corinthian church. "And we all, with unveiled face, beholding the glory of the Lord, are being changed into his likeness from one degree of glory to another" (II Cor. 3:18). We grow like those we live with. If we lived with him, we too would be **an example to all the believers.**

8 *The Acts of the Apostles in Present-Day Preaching* (Chicago: Willett, Clark & Co., 1938), I, 97.

2 For yourselves, brethren, know our entrance in unto you, that it was not in vain:

2 But even after that we had suffered before, and were shamefully entreated, as

2 For you yourselves know, brethren, that our visit to you was not in vain; 2 but though we had already suffered and been

## B. Review of the Apostle's Work (2:1-12)

**2:1.** Paul here takes up the thought of 1:9b and reminds his Thessalonian friends of what they already well know, that his **visit** to them **was not in vain.** The "welcome" of 1:9 and the **visit** of 2:1 represent the same Greek word (**entrance**) and tie the thought here into that of the closing part of ch. 1. The word translated **in vain** is used to declare either that a thing is without content, or that it is without result. Some of the older interpreters (e.g., Stevens, with stress on the Greek verb) thought that both ideas are included here. Others (e.g., Moffatt) have believed that Paul meant to say that his work was not fruitless. Some of the older, and most of the recent, interpreters (e.g., Lünemann, Milligan, Findlay, Frame) observe rightly that this phase of the matter is not taken up until vs. 13, and that in the intervening discussion (vss. 2-12) the apostle gives attention to the character of the workmen and their work. Thus he is here expanding the statement made in 1:5. The Thessalonians themselves know "what kind of men" Paul and Silas and Timothy had "proved to be" in their ministry among them.

**2.** Paul begins by reminding his readers of what, probably soon after his arrival, they had come to know, viz., that he had come to Thessalonica from Philippi, and that there he had **already suffered and been shamefully treated.** Philippi was a Roman colony, the first city and administrative center of one of the regions (*Macedonia Prima*) of the Roman province of Macedonia (Acts 16:12), and Thessalonica was from 146 B.C. the

---

**2:1-12. A Noble Defense.**—As stated in the Exeg., this paragraph is an expansion of "You know what kind of men we proved to be" (1:5). The characterization is given not in any spirit of self-glorification, but as known facts in the record of their stay among the Thessalonians. In addition to courage (1:2-12), they had wisdom, purity, candor of speech, unselfishness, humility, gentleness, love, industry, independence, and appreciation. This frank self-proclamation was required because of the savage attacks of the local Jews and pagans, who accused Paul and his associates of mental delusions, libertinism, cupidity, and cold-blooded deception ("a wandering sophist making money out of his followers"[1]).

Here we see the severity of the demands of the Christian ministry in Paul's day, and the quality it requires. Attitudes to the gospel and its proclaimers vary in different times and parts of the world. Some of our twentieth-century missionaries labor under similar conditions, receive similar treatment, and require the same qualities as Paul. The overwhelming majority of Christian leaders, however, are not confronted with such open and physical violence. The opposition is subtler and deadlier in its nature. (a) There is the superior mind. No other foe is

[1] A. S. Peake, *A Commentary on the Bible* (London: Thomas Nelson & Sons, n.d.), p. 877.

so irritating and difficult to handle. Its possessor is not vulgar or bitter but is perched complacently on Mount Olympus. His looks and conversation are so lofty and impressive that the average man is overawed. He admits religion was a good thing once upon a time, when people were savage, ignorant, and superstitious, but now it is a relic mankind has long outgrown. Then with repulsive modesty he adds that while he will not speak of himself, he knows many others who never step over the threshold of a church, but who are just as decent, generous, clean-living, honest in their dealings, kindly, and industrious as any deacon who ever sat in a pew. Here and there the latter statement is true, but in proportion to numbers it is a flagrant falsehood. On the whole, the best people in the community are within, and the worst without, the church.

Where the statement is true, is it not fair to ask where those good nonchurchgoers received their moral equipment and respect for ideals? Where did they get their ideals of monogamous marriage, the present status of womanhood, concern for childhood, respect for morals, sensitiveness of conscience, conception of the state? Did they create them, or were these transmitted to them? If the river of their lives is so pure in its stream, it is worth while following it to the source. The good nonchurchgoer is usually the

ye know, at Philippi, we were bold in our God to speak unto you the gospel of God with much contention.

shamefully treated at Philippi, as you know, we had courage in our God to declare to you the gospel of God in the face of great

---

capital and administrative center of the entire province. The writers imply—what Acts 17:1 apparently indicates—that they had gone directly from the one center to the other, passing by the intervening towns. At Philippi they had suffered some physical violence (cf. Acts 16:22-24). The Greek word for **shamefully treated** implies wanton, insulting mistreatment, or some form of indignity. It was this which they so deeply felt and remembered. The language here lacks the detail of the report in Acts 16:19-29. Precisely what the mistreatment was they do not say. However, out of this experience of suffering and insult they had come to Thessalonica, and in spite of all, they had been emboldened (**had courage**) to declare **the gospel of God.** The phrase **had courage** should be connected not with their coming, but with their proclamation of the gospel. The word is used elsewhere in the N.T. only of Paul (Acts 9:27, 29; 19:8; 26:26), of Paul and Barnabas (Acts 13:46; 14:3), and of Apollos (Acts 18:26). It seems to have been one of the characteristic features of Paul's preaching. This ministry had been carried on **with much contention** (KJV), or **in the face of great opposition** (RSV). The apostles did not need to describe to the Thessalonian Christians just what the experience among them had been; this was well known. Acts 17:5-9 describes a general reaction against the Thessalonian Christians, but does not relate any overt act against Paul and his helpers themselves. The word for **opposition** here used is found in I Tim. 6:12; II Tim. 4:7; and Heb. 12:1 of inner struggle or endeavor. It is used by Paul in Phil. 1:30 of external conflict, and some scholars (e.g., Milligan, Stevens) think that is the meaning here. In Col. 2:1 it is used of inner struggle, and others (e.g., Frame, hesitantly) so understand it here also. Chrysostom thought both external and internal struggles were in mind. The context seems to suggest outer opposition as the basis of any inner conflict that might have arisen. Paul's usage of the term does not suggest any actual overt violence; it rather points toward some strenuous or energetic opposition or "moral resistance." Perhaps the **opposition** consisted

---

product of religious parents or ancestors. How often he will say with unctuous pride that while he does not go, his father and mother never missed a Sunday at church, were officers of a congregation, and took him regularly to public worship in his boyhood. The striking fact is that all the best in his present moral outfit is rooted in his parents, who secured their ideals from the Bible, Jesus Christ, and their religious forebears. He has a decent character because they kept the faith. So this superior-minded man is living on the spiritual capital and traveling on the moral momentum of others. He is a parasite, and a very troublesome one at that.

(b) The secular mind. This is the mind which threatens all the world's Christian opinions, practices, and emotions. It is hard to define but easily seen in its expressions on any Main Street. It is frivolous and irreverent, for it recognizes no sanctities, has no belief in spiritual realities and no regard for the great veracities. It fails to see God in the past or present of history. It is cheap, brittle, wise-cracking, bereft of any sense of awe. It is worse than the pagan mind, for the latter believes profoundly that there is spiritual power of some kind focusing benefit or

evil forces on every area and activity of human life—crop growth, the birth of children, the marriage of youth, the issue of battle, bodily health, and daily toil.

The secular mind is also materialistic and carnal, for it reduces man to the level of a mere planetary being—a stiffly-bound prisoner within the narrow boundaries of life and death. It clips man's wings and makes him a crawling insect of the earth, robbing him of any total perspective and ultimate frame of reference. Gaius Glenn Atkins declares the secular mind is literally "this age-ism," and our own age has it acutely. Its possessor is obsessed with the paraphernalia and baubles of life and is engaged in the unclean worship of gold. His motto is "Let us eat, drink, and be merry; for tomorrow we die." The senses to him are the realities. He is concerned with activity, not with thought. Life can be lived by wealth alone, pleasure alone, comfort alone, power alone, brains alone. Happiness is therefore dependent upon the acquisition of things and the satisfying of the passions of the flesh. Life comes through the thrill of a nerve. A clever cartoonist summed up the irreverent cynicism of the secular mind in a single

3 For our exhortation *was* not of deceit, | opposition. 3 For our appeal does not
nor of uncleanness, nor in guile: | spring from error or uncleanness, nor is it

mainly in malignant perversions of the motives of the missionaries in their work. At any rate, the discussion following seems to indicate just that kind of situation.

**3-5.** Despite the strenuous experience through which Paul and Silvanus and Timothy had passed at Philippi, and again at Thessalonica, they had been given courage in God to speak **the gospel of God.** This particular phrase is found in this chapter three times (vss. 2, 8, 9) and elsewhere in Paul in II Cor. 11:7; Rom. 1:1; 15:16. It is based in the thinking of the apostle that the God of his fathers, "the living and true God" to whom the Thessalonians had turned from idolatry (1:9), was the one from whom the message of the gospel had come. He was its source and author. He had commissioned Paul as his messenger. The apostle further affirms what lay at the very base of his apostolic career: He had been tested and approved (old English, **allowed**) by God to be **entrusted with the gospel.** This exact statement is not found elsewhere. Paul speaks in Galatians (1:12, 15) of having his call from God, and by direct revelation; in Romans (1:1, 5) of his being "separated unto the gospel of God," through revelation of Jesus Christ. The word "approve" means to prove by testing. This is the word translated "test" in 5:21 and is the word in Luke 14:19, "I go to prove them." Having been tested, one may be approved. It is also true that having been tested, the apostle speaks not **to please men,** but **God who tests our hearts** (cf. Jer. 11:20; 17:10). Elsewhere in Paul we find his affirmation of having been **entrusted** with the gospel "of uncircumcision," just as Peter had with the gospel "of circumcision" (Gal. 2:7). This all means that the apostle's preaching grew out of a deep consciousness that he had been commissioned by God to become an apostle, that he had accepted the responsibility, that in an abiding sense of obligation under his commission he sought to be true and well pleasing unto the God who had commissioned him. To God he owed all that had come to him in his personal experience, in his call to apostleship, and in the gospel which he had been commissioned to proclaim. It was not his concern that he should be pleasing man. His first allegiance must ever be to God. As

drawing: "A New York apartment on a summer's Sunday afternoon. A pair of well-dressed sophisticates leaning from their lofty window ledge to gaze at an open window across the court. The girl remarking: 'Those people must be drunk. They're singing hymns!' " [2]

(c) *The respectable mind.* It is tragically true that this may seem the predominating power inside the Christian church. When one thinks of the average congregation of any of the major denominations and seeks a truly descriptive word, the one that pops to the surface of the mind is "respectable." The church is a respectable institution, for it is decent, decorous, cautious, conventional, and tolerant. It is full of honest, moral-living and worth-knowing people. Its spiritual temperature is well below the boiling point. It pronounces few judgments upon the world and stays carefully within certain bounds. It is so geared to the political and economic systems, and has given so many hostages to the civilization around it, that it has become indulgent of many dubious things. Its pride in its "tolerance" is calamitous, for it for-

gets it cannot abate by the faintest shade its original unrelenting idealism without failing its King and Head.

However, to describe the church as respectable is not unduly to disparage it. In a rash, nondescript, and intolerant world we need the respectability of the church with its decency, coolness, caution, and convention. Respectability makes certain demands and presents certain definite goals of conduct. It takes effort to attain and represents definite ethical achievement. But it does not go far enough. It is a plane, not a height: a goal, but a near one. Its demands are limited, its range narrow, its span but a handspan. It has interests, but they are related to its own family, business, and community. It has givings, but they are conservative, shrewd, and carefully estimated. One can be as stingy as Shylock, yet be thoroughly respectable. Its deadly weakness is that it makes no heroic demands. Respectability did not lift civilization to its present level. If the world had always been respectable, it would have permanently congealed, for respectability has no quest or biological thrust. It conforms, and does not question. It accepts existing standards, seldom asking

[2] Cf. Arthur L. Swift, Jr., "Irreligion and the Churches," *Social Progress,* XL (1950), 8.

he puts it elsewhere, he was an ambassador in behalf of God (II Cor. 5:20; Eph. 6.20) ; he was a steward "of the mysteries of God" and must be faithful (I Cor. 4:1-2) .

The writers now take up for consideration and for utter repudiation certain charges that had been made against them by the opponents. They had been accused of speaking out of a background of **error** and **uncleanness** and in a spirit of deceitfulness. The use of the word **error** here, in II Thess. 2:11, and in Rom. 1:27, carries the suggestion not of guiltless, harmless and unintentional, or excusable error, but rather of wrongness which has moral meaning and quality. It is not simply lack of correctness due to honest but inadequate understanding; it is wrong-mindedness. The **uncleanness** which the apostles repudiate is seen from 4:7; Gal. 5:19; Rom. 1:24; 6:19; Col. 3:5, to be associated with sexual indulgence and impurity. They feel called upon to repudiate this as a possible motive in their work among these Thessalonians. We should perhaps bear in mind that the city of Corinth, from which the letter was probably written, was notorious for sexual degeneracy; and at Thessalonica, the home of his readers, there was notably

---

if they are right. A community completely respectable would be a study in still life—like some churches.

Respectability is not enough. This was the solemn judgment of Jesus. The Pharisees were the eminently respectable people of his day. But Jesus said, "Unless your righteousness exceeds that of the scribes and Pharisees, you will never enter the kingdom of heaven" (Matt. 5:20) . If respectability was not enough in his simple, agrarian, and camel-speed civilization, how much less is it in our intricate, urban, and airplane-speed day? A merely respectable church is inadequate for its interior and exterior tasks. This was the conviction of the Master who was hounded and finally crucified by it.

(d) The ignorant mind. Paul in his letter to the church at Corinth commands, "Do not be children in your thinking; . . . be mature" (I Cor. 14:20) . In the modern church spiritual illiterates are in almost every pew; people who, with a lifetime of attendance, have not yet learned the A B C's of their religion, and carefully avoid the pain of thought. They are childish in their ideas of God, his Son, the church, salvation, heaven, hell, immortality. Who is to blame? What are the causes of this ignorance? Among them are:

(i) The religious collapse of the home. An ignorantly minded church is rooted in an ignorantly minded home. The great betrayal is that by parenthood. The trouble, to a major extent, with the young people is the old people. Sir John McClure, headmaster of the famous Mill Hill School, bitingly said, "The more I see of the average parent, the more I respect the average schoolboy." The family altar is almost completely dismantled. The father is no longer the high priest of his home, gathering his family around him at morning or evening for the reading of the Scriptures and prayer. How much Christian conversation is there around the din-

ner table? How many religious books are in the library? How much time is given to quiet and contemplation? Is there not an overoccupation with business and social activities? The home is too often a dormitory attached to a garage. As the dyer's hands take the color of the fluid with which he works, so the knowledge and attitudes of our youth are colored by the homes in which they daily live.

(ii) The practical absence of religious teaching in the public schools. Almost universally religious teaching is considered as outside the educational process and as an addendum to life instead of being integral to it. Man's religious sense is as much a part of him as his intellectual, emotional, recreational, or esthetic sense. Education that denies or ignores this fact is not education but an unsightly truncation, for it leaves out that apart from which personality cannot come to its full stature and completion.

(iii) Overemphasis on specialization. The average student does not go to the university to acquire culture, but to become a doctor, lawyer, engineer, dentist, or chemist. He learns little of the humanities, so has little breadth of knowledge or depth of culture. Take him outside his specialty and he is a child. The average college man is not opposed to religion; he is ignorant of it. His knowledge of Christianity is of the sketchiest kind, for he has no grip on its central doctrines, little familiarity with the Bible, and the products of the reverent scholarship of the past fifty years are a closed book to him.

(iv) The failure of the pulpit. Central in the preaching of Jesus was the teaching function. Dotting the gospels are such statements as "He began to teach them many things" (Mark 6:34) . The first command to Peter after Christ's resurrection was "Feed my sheep" (John 21:16) . The minister is ordained "for the equipment of the saints, for the work of ministry, for building up the body of Christ" (Eph. 4:12) . Yet of many clergymen it may be said as of the dis-

4 But as we were allowed of God to be put in trust with the gospel, even so we speak; not as pleasing men, but God, which trieth our hearts.

made with guile; 4 but just as we have been approved by God to be entrusted with the gospel, so we speak, not to please men, but

---

present the worship of the Dionysiacs and the Cabiri. The character of both of these is indicated by their phallic emblems. In Rev. 2:20 we are expressly told of a certain Jezebel at Thyatira, who called herself a prophetess and who was "teaching and beguiling my servants to practice immorality." The word "beguile" carries much the same kind of meaning as the word **uncleanness**. In II Cor. 12:16 the apostle expressly refers to the charge that as an evil one he had taken the Corinthians in craftiness and "with guile." In Rom. 1:29 he associates the word **guile** with "envy, murder, strife." The words here describe the general atmosphere and spirit in which Paul and his fellows were charged with having made their appeal to the Thessalonians.

It is very revealing of the character of the time (cf. Rom. 1:18-32; 6:19, "servants of uncleanness"), and of the defaming charges made against them, that the writers felt it necessary to enter such a disclaimer as is here recorded. With conviction, fervor, and bluntness they declare that it was not in any such spirit nor with any such motives that they had made their presentation of the gospel to the Thessalonians. Such teachers might be known, indeed were known. They were common in the religions familiar in all that area, but Paul and his companions were of a wholly different type.

---

ciples, they have "forgotten to bring bread" with them (Mark 8:14).

There is an ignorance from which all suffer and for which they cannot be blamed. The most brilliant and industrious student must say of many things, "I do not know," for the circumference of knowledge is so vast that no single mind can travel it. But there is an ignorance that is culpable because the mind is inactive and unreceptive to study. How many ministers have gone to seed! They do not know the things they ought, so they cannot impart the full gospel of Christ. With this condition existing, there is naturally a lack of systematic biblical exposition. Robert Freeman said: "If you want to attract people to the church, anything will do. If you want to attach people to the church, teach." If expository preaching became the common custom of the pulpit biblical knowledge would increase, continuity of instruction would be assured, stability would be deepened, and a rising interest in the message of the gospel would be guaranteed.

4. *The Supreme Trust.*—Of all the favors bestowed by God on man, is there a greater than to be **approved by God to be entrusted with the gospel?** It is this which makes the preacher the most significant person in the community, for he is the steward of the mysteries of God, the evaluator of the unsearchable riches of Jesus Christ, elected of God to form man's ideals, rouse his conscience, widen his vision, and sharpen his social sense. For him the word of God to Jeremiah is still valid: "The eternal

said to me: 'There! I have put my words into your mouth; here and now I give you authority over nations and kingdoms, to tear up, to break down, to shatter, to pull down, to build up and to plant'" (Jer. 1:10 Moffatt).

We should be constantly awed and inspired by the glory of the gospel. It is the gospel of God—existent, approachable, available, righteous, and loving. It is the gospel of the kingdom; the ideal state in the individual soul; the ideal state in the social order; the beatific state beyond, the kingdom of God is not restricted to this life. It is the gospel of life—happiness is not through sensory but spiritual values. Life must be spiritually interpreted, for a man may be full of bread and starve to death. It is the gospel of man. Personality cannot fully achieve itself apart from religion. Man is a spiritual being whom irreligion destroys, because it denies that which lies at the heart of his nature. It is the gospel of the Cross, for its essence is the deliberate identification of God with the moral tragedy of human life and his inability to stand apart from the pain and pathos of his creation.

That is the gospel committed to our care. It is all the fullness of Jesus Christ. Its commitment to such as we are is one of the startling mysteries of the ages. But it is true. Is it any wonder that there are occasions when, poor creatures as we are, the deep swift-running tides of the gospel sweep through our souls, and we expand and speak with the authority not of the world, nor of man, but of the Father and of the Son and of the Holy Ghost?

5 For neither at any time used we flattering words, as ye know, nor a cloak of covetousness; God *is* witness:

6 Nor of men sought we glory, neither of you, nor *yet* of others, when we might have been burdensome, as the apostles of Christ.

to please God who tests our hearts. 5 For we never used either words of flattery, as you know, or a cloak for greed, as God is witness; 6 nor did we seek glory from men, whether from you or from others, though we might have made demands as apostles

---

In 2:5 the missionaries proceed further in their repudiation of the charges that had been lodged against them. They affirm that at no time had they used any **words of flattery**, as the Thessalonians themselves well know. They had not tried to insinuate their way into the confidence of the Thessalonians. They had been open, candid, honest, and sincere. Nor had they wrought in any **cloak for greed**. To this Paul calls God as witness. The word **greed** is the regular word for **covetousness**. In Col. 3:5 Paul says that covetousness is idolatry. In Eph. 4:19; 5:3 it is associated with sexual impurity. In Mark 7:22 it is named between adulteries and fornications. It thus appears that the charge laid against Paul and his associates was that of cupidity, the desire for gain that it might be spent upon personal indulgence.

6-8. It is further affirmed that at no time had the three of them sought **glory from men, whether from you** [Thessalonians] **or from others.** They might indeed **have made demands** [the expression is found only here] **as apostles of Christ.** But on the contrary, they had been **gentle** and affectionate in their attitude, **like a nurse taking care of her children.** The Westcott and Hort Greek text reads **babes** instead of **gentle.** Most modern commentators prefer to read **gentle.** The only difference between the two words in the Greek is that the word **babes** has an initial ν in the spelling, the word **gentle** being ἤπιοι, and the word **babes,** νήπιοι. It is agreed by all that the word **babes** is the better-attested reading. There is difference of opinion as to whether this word fits the context as well as the word **gentle.** (Stevens has a good note on the point.) Paul uses the word **babes**

---

5. *In the Great Taskmaster's Eye.*—Few men in history have been so God-conscious as Paul. "God-intoxicated" is not too strong a description. He passionately believed he had been converted by God, called by God, entrusted with the gospel by God, was daily being tested by God, and must live a life worthy of God (vss. 4-5, 8-9, 12). God to Paul was God. This is not surprising, for he was reared in a strict Jewish home where the great monotheistic doctrine was as much a part of life as the air its members breathed. His heritage was one of reverence. The awe of the Eternal was in his heart, and he carried it into his new life in Christ. He demonstrated "how the most unqualified monotheism and the loftiest Christology could go hand in hand." [3]

This lofty conception is rare in the church and in the life of the average Christian. It is a sad loss. Our grandfathers had narrow and rigorous conceptions of Deity, but there was nothing dwarfish or feeble in their ideas concerning him. To them he was "awe-ful," "almighty," and they constantly reminded themselves of this fact by use of such adjectives as infinite, eternal, omniscient, incomprehensible, and transcendent. They had not all the truth

[3] James S. Stewart, *A Man in Christ* (New York: Harper & Bros., 1935), p. 40.

about him, but they had one great truth which provided them with a commanding, sustaining dynamic for noble and dignified living.

This generation has left God his name but taken away his character. He is the God of love, but our interpretations of human love have emptied it of its strength, so that it has been reduced to a puling, mawkish, sentimental thing, meaning anything from the singing of a ballad to the degeneracy of pornography; from the self-sacrifice of motherhood to the invitation of a streetwalker; from the smoking desires of the flesh to the loneliness of a lad dying in the sky in the cause of human freedom. There has been an inevitable mental carry-over. Our ideas of the divine love have followed in the sorry wake of our thoughts of human love. We have immersed God in the enervating, tepid mists of sentimentalism and shabby thinking. Thus the prevalence of the notion of an easygoing God modeled in the shape of Mr. Pickwick—genial, expansive, tractable, who can be trusted to deal leniently with both sin and the sinner; one who can be easily wheedled from his purpose, whose moral judgment will swerve when confronted by our dark idolatries, who has no more backbone than a jellyfish and the persuadable disposition of a half-wit, and from whom all judicial ele-

| 7 But we were gentle among you, even as a nurse cherisheth her children: | of Christ. 7 But we were gentle[a] among you, like a nurse taking care of her children. |
|---|---|

[a] Other ancient authorities read *babes*.

in I Cor. 13:11 and Gal. 4:1 in its natural sense; in Gal. 4:3; I Cor. 3:1; Rom. 2:20; Eph. 4:14; Heb. 5:13-14, it is used in a figurative sense of the immature in mind and understanding. The word **gentle** is found elsewhere in the Greek Bible only in II Tim. 2:24. The authors certainly do not intend to speak here of their immaturity. The contrast is with the "arrogant demands" which they as apostles might have made. On the contrary, they were **like a nurse** [nursing mother?] **taking care of her children.** If the apostles originally wrote **babes,** they may have had in mind a comparison which they never completed, such, e.g., as is found in Gal. 2:3-5, and is common in Paul.

The peculiar phrasing of the words **made demands** is found only here. The noun is used in Gal. 6:2, where Paul enjoins the Galatian Christians to "bear one another's burdens." In II Cor. 4:17 he speaks of an "eternal weight [fullness] of glory" using the

ments have been removed. In brief, we have made God after our own image, indeterminate, a respecter of persons, and altogether such a one as ourselves. We speak glibly of the "general mercy of God." There is no such thing. It is always specific and conditional. We receive God's mercy so as to obey God's commands. We are saved as we believe. We are guided when we ask. We are redemptively used when we accept the discipline of the cross—"The gate is narrow and the way is hard" (Matt. 7:14).

A revival of awe and reverence is the prime requirement of our time. It is not an academic question but a practical issue; for everything results from our ideas of Deity—our manners, deeds, thoughts, industry, and use of leisure; our ideas of the rights of man, patriotism, religion, culture, and life. A majestic God produces majestic men; a sentimental God, mawkish men. To be adequate for our time we need a fresh awe-struck sense of the unsearchable, divine majesty, and a realization of the transcendent Deity who is altogether other than ourselves. To bow before God in reverence bordering on trembling is not religious obscurantism but a recall to reality and Christian theology.

**7. A Real Sea Change.**—Here is conversion in great might. It is easy to think of Paul as the missionary who made Europe and Asia his parish and lifted Christianity out of its Palestinian cradle; as the warrior who fought the good fight of faith, and whose sword seldom rested in its scabbard; as the statesman who conceived vastly and executed daringly; as the theologian who handled the huge imponderables and the grand particularities of the faith with ease and judgment; as the personality, powerful and decisive, who cut his signature deeply into the life of his time, and beside whom his contemporaries were but dwarfs; as the mystic who

beheld the faraway hills of silence and wonder, and whose great theme was "union with Christ." But it strains the imagination to picture him, who was so imperious, in the gentle and tender role of nursemaid. Truly, there is no limit to the converting power of God in Jesus Christ.

It was in this power Paul constantly gloried (Rom. 1:16, 18; etc.). It was this power that the Roman world, so delinquent, degraded, disenchanted, needed. It was this power his fellow men yearned after, for they were religiously panic-stricken, fleeing from one cult to another; standing today under the taurobolium with the hot blood of bullocks dripping down upon them that their sins might be washed away, and tomorrow indulging in the base rites of the ground gods. It is this power which is needed today.

Stare intently at the human situation and what is seen? Devitalization, with its loss of ruggedness and inability to stand up to life. Suspicion, with its cynicism concerning the motives and conduct of others. Fear, with its hesitation, avoidance of issues and independent action. Lovelessness, with its contempt, indifference, and unpleasantness. Materialism, with its lack of idealism and emphasis on money, first, last, and all the time. Discontent, with its peevish restlessness and surly resentment toward things and people. Moral weakness, with its low behavior, futile resolutions, and lost self-respect. Power over ourselves and exterior circumstances is the dire and urgent need of our time.

The Christian church proclaims itself to be the possessor of the power of God which enables men to be more than conquerors. But from how many churches is it intelligently expounded and forthrightly offered? Sir Robertson Nicoll, editor of the *British Weekly*, once made a tour of churches in the south of England. He participated in dignified services of worship, listened to sermons delivered by thoughtful and sincere

**8** So being affectionately desirous of you, we were willing to have imparted unto you, not the gospel of God only, but also our own souls, because ye were dear unto us.

**9** For ye remember, brethren, our labor and travail: for laboring night and day, because we would not be chargeable unto

**8** So, being affectionately desirous of you, we were ready to share with you not only the gospel of God but also our own selves, because you had become very dear to us.

**9** For you remember our labor and toil,

---

word "burden." In the light of the discussion that follows in this chapter it is apparent that Paul and his associates are thinking in the same terms as are reflected in I Cor. 9:6-14. They might have asked the Thessalonians to support them in their work, but instead of doing so, they themselves were so **affectionately desirous of you** that they were entirely **ready to share . . . not only the gospel of God but also our own selves, because you had become very dear to us.** The depth of their affection for the Thessalonian Christians took away entirely any desire to receive from them; their deepest desire was to give them not only the gospel but also all the meaning, energy, and service of their own lives.

**9-12.** Paul continues the "apology" by reminding the Thessalonians of what they well knew—that the missionaries had worked night and day that they might not have to

---

men, and then gave as his mature conclusion that not one of them would have converted a titmouse.

The truth of God's power to save must be continuously preached, and must blaze into undeniable light in the lives of Christians. It was a convincing reality in Paul, the brutal persecutor who became gentle like a nurse; in Augustine, who turned from his chambering and wantonness to purity and rightness of conduct; in John Newton, the profane captain of a slave ship, who became a minister of the gospel and writer of hymns; in John Wesley, prim, austere, and sick of soul, whose heart was strangely warmed by God's spirit so that he became a leader of a great host of converted folk; in Charles G. Finney, the proud, cold-minded lawyer, who became mighty in prayer and the exposition of the Scriptures. And what more can be written? The pen of the writer would fail to tell the story of the innumerable company who followed in their train.

**8. A Two-Handed Giver.**—Here is an apostle who does not stand apart from his people—objective, cautious, and cool—handing his gospel to them like a benevolent dowager bestowing a favor. With the delivery of his message he delivers his heart, for they are truly dear to him. To hear him must have been an experience of uplift and sharing.

How many of us follow in his way? We have many things—a fair education, general sincerity, a few ideas churning around in our minds, a veritable genius for criticism and analysis (there is hardly a Sunday when preachers do not lug a problem into the pulpit to exasperate further an already problem-ridden people) ; but how

much of the self is given with the sermon? Is the sign over us a tongue of fire? Is our speech warmed and charged by obvious love for the congregation? How many of its members have the heart-warming knowledge that the preacher deeply cares for them? All changers of lives have been men who have mingled themselves with their truth. Jesus was moved with compassion as he spoke to the people who were as sheep without a shepherd. John was a burning as well as a shining light. Apollos "preached and taught about Jesus with ardour and accuracy" (Acts 18:25 Moffatt) . John Chrysostom so mingled his heart's blood with his great discourses that his vast congregation bowed to his truth as the grain before the breeze. Father Damien was so filled with the pity of God that he was carried on its tide to a leper colony and, accepting leprosy as his glad lot, died there to the great glory of God and man. Savonarola, in the marble pulpit of Florence Cathedral, cried with streaming eyes, "Wilt thou have Jesus to be thy king?" And so the story goes down the years. We want no painted fire, no imitation enthusiasm. no spurious feeling, but an emotion which is fresh and authentic because it comes from within. Then our gospel will, like Paul's, have about it a sense of the inevitable; the listeners will know that we are giving with both hands, and sense that in our inmost hearts we are affectionately desirous of them.

**9-12. Life's Highest Level.**—Here is the hoped for result of all Paul's labors and loving: **To lead a life worthy of God.** Set before the Thessalonians is a spiritual goal which might well daunt the most mystical and ardent spirit. The exhortation is not to be worthy of a great tradi-

any of you, we preached unto you the gospel of God.

10 Ye *are* witnesses, and God *also*, how holily and justly and unblamably we behaved ourselves among you that believe:

brethren; we worked night and day, that we might not burden any of you, while we preached to you the gospel of God. 10 You are witnesses, and God also, how holy and righteous and blameless was our behavior

---

call upon the Thessalonians for help. He apparently meant that they began work even before daybreak and worked on into late evening (cf. William Ramsay, *The Church in the Roman Empire* [New York: G. P. Putnam's Sons, 1893], p. 85 n.). We are told in Acts 18:3 that Paul was by trade a "tentmaker," or a weaver of the cloth used in making tents. He was at the time of the writing of this letter following the same procedure in Corinth (I Cor. 4:12; 9:6) that had been followed in Thessalonica, and which is also enjoined upon the Thessalonian Christians themselves (4:11).

The Thessalonian disciples were also able to testify—and God was witness to the same fact—that the missionaries had lived among the Thessalonians in a **holy and righteous and blameless** manner. Further, not only had they been **righteous and blameless** in their behavior, but they had also been concerned, **like a father with his children,** for their Thessalonian converts. They had **exhorted** them and **encouraged** and **charged** them to lead a life (**walk** KJV; so used fifty times in the N.T.) worthy of the God (cf.

---

tion, of a great man, or of a great institution. It goes far beyond and above any and all of these—to be **worthy of God.** To have a clear conception of the discipleship to which we are urged, we turn to the thought of God in Christ Jesus: the Incarnation—"He who has seen me has seen the Father" (John 14:9). God is Christlike. **To lead a life worthy of God** means:

(a) Quality of life. The life of Jesus is the supremely fertilizing one of history. In creativity it has never been matched. Its impression upon the conscience and conduct of mankind is unique. Its influence, contrary to the usual impression made by the world's great, has been in constant acceleration. The centuries have but increased its command. When we think of greatness of personality we must think of him. When we think of flawless morality we must think of him. He alone has ever dared to challenge the world with such words as "Which of you convicts me of sin?" (John 8:46). In him there is such beauty of character, such innocence of heart, and such delicacy of nature that the coarse thumb and finger of time could not sully him. He is humanity's perfect articulation, "The Word was made flesh" (John 1:14). We see in him the qualities we covet at our best—courage, gentleness, chivalry, purity, humility, beauty, naturalness, and sacrifice.

Today he stands revealed against the skyline of our time as the noblest being of history: the only one who ever really lived; gentle, yet brave; confident, yet humble; wise, yet simple; who met life with calmness, trouble with fortitude, hate with forgiveness, disloyalty with magnanimity, and crucifixion with faith. He said, "Follow me" (Matt. 4:19). "You, therefore, must be

perfect, as your heavenly Father is perfect" (Matt. 5:48). This is the quality of life to which we must aspire if we are **to lead a life worthy of God.**

(b) Acceptance of a task. The world to which Jesus came was totalitarian in nature, with a despot on the throne of the empire. The "peace of Rome" lay like a sheet of steel over many lands. The most familiar sight and sound were those of armed men. Jesus took a long look at its tyranny, bigotry, slavery, unemployment, false philosophy, boredom, and life weariness, and declared it was not life according to his Father's intention. So he "came . . . preaching the gospel of God" (Mark 1:14) with its two great imperatives—the new man and the new society: the new man (John 3:3), because he saw the tragedy of the human dilemma with its sin, despair, and overwhelming sense of mortality; the new society, because of the need of a fitting social environment for the new man, if he was to live in mutual effort and brotherliness. These two imperatives are the heart of his gospel and were committed by him to his disciples. "As thou didst send me into the world, so I have sent them into the world" (John 17:18).

The early church accepted this mighty task in the period of the decline of Rome, when its brave day was sinking into night. Degenerate, disillusioned, and disenchanted, Rome's symbols swiftly became the Saturnalia and the Colosseum. John in the Revelation proclaimed that time to be the day of the beast, the scarlet woman, the pit, the four horsemen, the seven vials, and of Satan loosed. Undaunted, the Christians set to work and from that evil world made converts, congregations, evangelists, missionaries,

11 As ye know how we exhorted and comforted and charged every one of you, as a father *doth* his children,

12 That ye would walk worthy of God, who hath called you unto his kingdom and glory.

to you believers; 11 for you know how, like a father with his children, we exhorted each one of you and encouraged you and charged you 12 to lead a life worthy of God, who calls you into his own kingdom and glory.

---

Col. 1:10; Eph. 4:1) whose gospel had been preached to them and who through that preaching had effectively called them into his own kingdom of glory (cf. also 4:7; II Thess. 2:14).

Thus it is clearly seen that in this first paragraph of ch. 2, Paul, with Silvanus and Timothy, is openly and stoutly affirming the integrity, the conscientiousness, the purity, and sincerity of the motives of himself and Silvanus and Timothy, and of their conduct and their service among these Thessalonian believers. This apologia is made necessary by the serious charges which have been lodged against Paul and his companions. These charges he pointedly and utterly repudiates. To the truthfulness of his presentation he calls the Thessalonians themselves as witnesses, and solemnly affirms that God himself, "who tests and knows men's hearts," has tested their hearts and approved them as his messengers. Their record is clear, and God himself would so declare.

---

and scholars. In the fulfillment of the task they crossed deserts, pierced mountain ranges, and sailed seas. The story of their spiritual and social achievements is unmatched in history. On their lips was the prophetic, daring, and eloquent cry of the venerable apostle, "The kingdoms of this world are become the kingdoms of our Lord, and of his Christ" (Rev. 11:15).

This is the mighty task laid upon us. We are committed to the redemption of man and society. For us there can be no rest until individual lives, national governments, the social, political, and industrial sciences are Christian in their structure, culture, ethics, and loyalties. How merciless and glorious it is! We can labor on it from the break of day until the stars ride forth. It challenges every resource of spirit, brain, and body. But only by its acceptance can we lead a life worthy of God.

(c) Fellowship with God. To be worthy of God we must live in intimacy with him, which is secured almost exclusively through Christ. God is brought near to us in Jesus, for he conveys a sense of the unseen and eternal. Brood over the Gospels and you are made conscious of the divine quality of his mind; so intimate was his relationship with Deity that he could say, "I and my Father are one" (John 10:30). In him the temporal and eternal join and interpenetrate.

It is interesting to observe the stages of the apostles' apprehension of him. They saw him first as leader. Something in him they fain would call master. At his quiet word of command "they left everything and followed him" (Luke 5:11). Then they saw him as prophet: the one of insight and foresight. Finally they saw him as Son

of God. "You are the Christ, the Son of the living God" (Matt. 16:16). It is impossible to abide in his company without being beset by a sense that he is greater than we can ever see and vaster than we can ever know. Paul fixes on him his trained, experienced eye and says, "The glory of God in the face of Christ" (II Cor. 4:6). Harry Emerson Fosdick vividly sees Jesus as God's near end.

God has a near end! . . . To believe in the Christian God is to believe that in spiritual life at its best we have touched the hither side of God. Whatever more he may be, he is that. Ask the New Testament what God is, and the New Testament says, "God is love." Say to the New Testament, then, Where do we reach him? and it answers, "He that abideth in love abideth in God, and God abideth in him." That is God's near end.

Of course, this is what the "divinity of Jesus" means. Many people are troubled because they cannot believe that all of the great God was in Jesus. . . . The omnipresence of the great God was not in Jesus. The omnipotence of the great God, swinging the eternal stars, was not in Jesus. No intelligent theology ever meant by the "divinity of Jesus" what some people think is implied in it, but this it does mean, that in the spiritual life and character of Christ we touch the near end of God. There God reaches us. There he washes our island.[4]

The simple truth is that when we see Jesus, we see Deity. Apart from him we could not know more than the elemental facts about God. As far as God can be translated into humanity, so far does Christ reveal the Father. He is not only Son of God, but God the Son.

[4] *The Secret of Victorious Living* (New York: Harper & Bros., 1934), pp. 166-67. Used by permission.

13 For this cause also thank we God without ceasing, because, when ye received the word of God which ye heard of us, ye

13 And we also thank God constantly for this, that when you received the word of

### C. Gratitude for the Success of the Gospel Ministry in Thessalonica (2:13-16)

**13.** These verses are an expansion of the condensed thought of 1:6. First, gratitude is expressed that when the Thessalonians had received the message of the apostle and his companions, they had received it not simply as the word of the men who preached it, but as what it really was, **the word of God.** A number of scholars (e.g., Rendel Harris, Bacon, McGiffert, Frame) believe that Paul implies by the use of the word **also** that the Thessalonian Christians had written him a letter in which they had expressed to him their gratitude for the coming of the gospel to them, and their reception of it. This view has support, so far as the grammar of the sentence is involved, in every other passage (eleven of them) in Paul's letters in which a similar construction is found. Other scholars of high rank (e.g., Lietzmann) think the **also** should be connected with the entire sentence. Even if Paul did have in mind an expressed thanksgiving of the Thessalonians,

So to **lead a life worthy of God** is to live a quality of life, labor at a task, and have fellowship with God through his Son. What a challenge to high-level living!

**13-16. The Steep Ascent.**—The Thessalonian church knew how deep was the bite of the scourge of persecution. As individuals they had opened their minds with readiness to the gospel, but from the first they had to suffer for it (1:6). Paul gives thanks that in so doing they were thus "followers of us." Here he pictures the whole flock under the maltreatment of the oppressors, and declares their pains are sharpened, for to persecution by the Jews there has been added persecution by their compatriots. But again he rejoices that they are standing as the beaten anvil to the stroke. Of course the Thessalonians were not the only group to be beaten with many stripes. All Christians faced a bleak and perilous life because of their faith. Paul constantly emphasized that accepting Christ was a dangerous business. To the Philippians he wrote, "It has been granted to you that for the sake of Christ you should not only believe in him but also suffer for his sake" (Phil. 1:29).

The story of the persecution of the first-century church is a somber one. It began when the winsome and brilliant Stephen alienated the synagogue authorities by denying the permanence of the Mosaic law (Acts 6:14). Hard on his cruel death, for which Saul accepted responsibility (Acts 8:1), there burst on the young church the Jerusalem persecution with its "binding and delivering to prison both men and women" (Acts 22:4). The Christians were indeed the pursued ones. Their principal oppressor, who later repented with tears, said, "I punished them often in all the synagogues; . . . I persecuted them even to foreign cities" (Acts 26:11). Some of the original leaders were mowed down, including James, the brother of John, who fell before the wrath of Herod Agrippa. It is significant that the persecuting band expanded from the inner circle of "the scribes and Pharisees" to the full outer national circumference of "the Jews." The only assaults not stirred by them were related to trade disturbances at two places, Philippi and Ephesus.

For a brief period the Roman government protected Christianity as a Jewish sect, but this shield was soon withdrawn. Persecution became inevitable. Nero used the Christians as scapegoats after the fire at Rome in A.D. 64. The evidences of his malice are revealed in at least three books of the N.T. In his letter to Timothy, Paul declares himself about to be sacrificed and that the time of his departure has come (II Tim. 4:6). In the same letter it is prophesied that "all who desire to live a godly life in Christ Jesus will be persecuted" (II Tim. 3:12). In I Pet. 4:12 the Christians are warned of fiery trials which will beset them, and are encouraged repeatedly to bear them with fortitude and forbearance. In the Revelation there are frequent references to the sharp sufferings of the churches in Asia. The bodies of the saints lie around the altars, "slain for the word of God and for the witness they had borne" (Rev. 6:9). The empire is drunk with their blood (Rev. 16:6).

The basic reason for the hatred aroused against the Christians was that immediately conversion took place they became different. The supreme ethic of the empire was force; their supreme ethic was love. Drunkenness, gluttony, and lust were the frequent pleasures of the populace; they lived in sobriety, restraint, and purity. Emperor worship was a necessity laid upon every citizen by law; they stubbornly proclaimed, "There is no other name under heaven . . . by which we must be saved" (Acts 4:12).

The general mind of man was disaffected and despairing; their mind was loving and hopeful. Thus they were out of step with their neighbors and time, and so a source of confusion and exasperation which swiftly developed into harsh intolerance, which in its turn developed into brutal physical persecution.

But history shows persecution to be creative as well as destructive, enriching as well as impoverishing. This truth applies to all levels and types of people—rich and poor, cultured and illiterate. It also includes in its reach all colors and races. Turn to the shining honor roll in Heb. 11. On it are the names of those who in dark and testing hours proved themselves beyond question and helped rescue their generation from physical and spiritual defeat. There are great names like Moses and Abraham, and dubious ones like Rahab the harlot, and Samson, mighty in muscle but weak in morals. There are historic names which will echo through the centuries, but also there are men so humble they had to be registered anonymously. In its effects persecution is no respecter of persons.

In the history of the church persecution has occasioned three benefits: (a) Identification. Some disciples brave the storm, taking everything that falls. Others flee to shelter, cowering out of sight. But all stand in clear outline. The sheep and goats are separated. Neil writes of the Thessalonian Christians: "The more they suffered persecution from the world, the more is it proof that they are faithful to their Master—as the Churches of the Continent discovered during the Second World War." [5] A man is shown for what he is when life strongly pressures him. John Brown, of tragic memory, in a discussion of the theory of human perfection, said: "We never know ourselves till we are thoroughly tried. As the heating of an old smooth coin will make the effaced stamp visible again, so the fire of temptation reveals what is latent even to ourselves." [6]

(b) Purgation. The timorous and halfhearted are afraid of the pains of persecution, so they desert; the ranks are thinned, but the earnest and heroic remain. The flail and the fan do their work so that only the clean, hard seed is left. Suffering, rightly received, is the great refiner, out of which comes "the peaceful fruit of righteousness" (Heb. 12:11). Of Jesus it was written, "Although he was a Son, he learned obedience through what he suffered" (Heb. 5:8).

(c) Inspiration. When persecution smites, many discover to their joyous surprise resources of endurance and faith never hitherto suspected. The whip of the oppressor scourges them to life, not death. Something lyrical is awakened, and they have a song in the night. The suffering church has always been the singing church. In 1950, W. A. Visser 't Hooft, speaking of a visit to the persecuted Hungarian Reformed Church, declared the only parallel to its members' radiant joy was in the Acts of the Apostles. Never in his life had he witnessed Christians so suffering and yet so rejoicing.

There comes a rare sense of the divine favor, a realization that God is asking us to play a high part. When Britain was standing alone for a period in World War II, and it seemed as if the pagan tyranny of Hitler's might would rule over the tight little island, the indomitable Winston Churchill, after outlining the coming calamities inherent in the situation, cried: "Let us therefore brace ourselves to our duties, and so bear ourselves that, if the British Empire and its Commonwealth last for a thousand years, men will still say, 'This was their finest hour.' " [7]

There comes also a rare sense of faith. How often have the smitten ones walked out to the edge of the last promontory and stepped out and, lo, they have not fallen upon the dark, surf-washed rocks far below, but into the sure strength of the Everlasting Arms. "They looked unto him, and were lightened: and their faces were not ashamed" (Ps. 34:5).

Some people are convinced that, among many things, the American and other churches need a first-rate persecution. Have they not settled down to a comfortable pedestrianism? Have they not become enamored by the trappings of merely formal religion? Pungently was it said: "Well, well, if trouble comes, it'll keep our religion from getting rusty. . . . That's the great thing about persecution; it keeps you up to the mark. It's habit, not hatred, that is the real enemy of the Church of God." [8] If the whips of persecution and deep suffering fell, there would come again, as in days past, its great fruits—identification, purgation, and inspiration. Well may we cry:

Nearer, my God, to thee,
Nearer to thee!
E'en though it be a cross
That raiseth me.

**13-16. The Contrasting Minds.**—The Thessalonians engaged in no long hairsplitting or doubt-filled questioning when the gospel was first brought to them, but took it to their hearts: **You accepted it not as the word of men but as**

---

[5] *Epistle of Paul to Thessalonians*, p. 50.

[6] Clarence Edward Macartney, *Macartney's Illustrations* (New York and Nashville: Abingdon-Cokesbury Press, 1945), p. 400.

[7] *Their Finest Hour* (Boston: Houghton Mifflin Co., 1949), p. 226.

[8] Bruce Marshall, *The World, the Flesh, and Father Smith* (Boston: Houghton Mifflin Co., 1945), p. 6.

received *it* not *as* the word of men, but, as it is in truth, the word of God, which effectually worketh also in you that believe.

14 For ye, brethren, became followers of the churches of God which in Judea are in Christ Jesus: for ye also have suffered like things of your own countrymen, even as they *have* of the Jews:

God which you heard from us, you accepted it not as the word of men but as what it really is, the word of God, which is at work in you believers. 14 For you, brethren, became imitators of the churches of God in Christ Jesus which are in Judea; for you suffered the same things from your own countrymen as they did from the Jews,

that might very well have been conveyed to him orally through Timothy (see 3:1-6, especially vs. 6). Paul was so utterly convinced of the divine origin and authority of his gospel that he expresses (Gal. 1:8-9) an extraordinarily strong condemnation of any who might preach another gospel. As he indicates so explicitly in Gal. 1:11-12, his gospel had come to him by direct revelation from God in Jesus Christ; and he was unwilling, or unable (in the spirit of the old prophets of his people), to concede that it could be subject to any modification at the hands of men. The Thessalonian believers had accepted the message as **the word of God**; and that **word** was even then **at work** energetically in them as continuing believers (cf. Rom. 1:16; Col. 1:29). As the apostle reflects upon these facts he is constantly in the spirit of thanksgiving to God, and Silvanus and Timothy with him.

**14-16a.** They continue with the observation that these Thessalonian believers had become **imitators of the churches of God in Christ Jesus which are in Judea.** As the **churches . . . in Judea** had suffered for their faith at the hands of their own fellow Jews, the Thessalonians had suffered for their faith at the hands of their fellow tribesmen. Why Paul should have referred to the Jews of Judea, when the Jews had continually opposed him all the way (cf. the stories of Philippi, Thessalonica, and Beroea, in Acts 16:12–17:13), does not appear at first reading. However, it was they who had **killed both the Lord Jesus and the prophets** (cf. Matt. 23:37; Luke 13:34). Luke 13:33 and Acts 7:52 suggest that Jerusalem was proverbially known as the killer of prophets. It is recorded in Matt.

**what it really is, the word of God.** True spiritual life immediately began in them. Vital religion was theirs and surged in and through them with such vigor that Paul once again broke into a paean of thankfulness. Opening their minds to the truth, they were made free.

What a contrast to this teachable mind is that of the Jews (vs. 16), who not only refused the word of God for themselves, but purposely hindered its delivery to others. While Paul sweepingly refers to "the Jews," he undoubtedly has in mind the Pharisaic group as the active and relentless persecutors of him and his fellow Christians, for they were the leaders of the people. It was to please them that Herod persecuted the Christians, put James the brother of John to death, and cast Peter into prison. They exercised great influence with both the Romans and their own people. They had many virtues. They had played the primary part in the fight for Jewish freedom; had fought relentlessly against the inroad of pagan religions; and had striven to keep the Jewish blood stream pure. While the Sadducees were primarily a political party, and religion to them a secondary thing, the Pharisees were primarily a religious

party, although they were not averse to the use of political measures to attain their ends. They were the most devout and spiritual people in the Jewish church, stressed religious values as no other group, and placed a spiritual interpretation on the universe and life. They kept before the nation the glowing story of past greatness, and summoned it to be faithful to the noble traditions of the fathers. They were faithful in church attendance; engaged in severe and frequent fasts; were generous, for they were meticulous tithers; had fiery patriotic fervor; and were the most popular and influential of the Jewish parties. But they were guilty of one thing which carried in its train a succession of ugly vices—their minds were closed because of patterns and preconceptions. They knew everything. They were never wrong, but everyone else was. They were the possessors, guardians, and interpreters of God's law. To them he had committed all his truth and told all he knew. Thus they became precise legalists, unyielding bigots, haughty and superior people, who loved the uppermost rooms at feasts and the chief seats in the synagogue. They daily gloried in the meaning of "Pharisee"—"separated one." They

15 Who both killed the Lord Jesus, and their own prophets, and have persecuted us; and they please not God, and are contrary to all men:

16 Forbidding us to speak to the Gentiles that they might be saved, to fill up their sins always: for the wrath is come upon them to the uttermost.

15 who killed both the Lord Jesus and the prophets, and drove us out, and displease God and oppose all men 16 by hindering us from speaking to the Gentiles that they may be saved — so as always to fill up the measure of their sins. But God's wrath has come upon them at last![b]

[b] Or *completely*, or *forever*.

---

23:34 (cf. Luke 17:49) that Jesus said he would be sending the Jews prophets, some of whom they would kill, and some they would "persecute from town to town." Acts (13:50; 14:19; 17:5, 13; 18:6) says that they continually so treated Paul. If we translate ἐκδιωξάντων **drove us out** (RSV), we must suppose that Paul is still thinking of the Jews in Judea. If we render it **persecuted** (KJV), in accordance with the prevailing usage of the LXX, it alludes to the continuing conduct of the Jews. They were constantly displeasing God by their interference with the work of the apostle, and were constantly seeking to hinder the preaching of the gospel **to the Gentiles.** The book of Acts also reflects what Galatians, II Corinthians, and Philippians make so evident, that Paul throughout his ministry was face to face with opposition from the Jews. Both the preachers of the gospel and those who accepted it suffered persecution. Thus the Jews were filling to the full **the measure of their sins.**

The Thessalonian Christians had suffered similar experiences at the hands of their **own countrymen.** It has already been said that they had received the gospel "in much affliction" (1:6), but they had also received it with the joy which was the evidence of the Holy Spirit of God within them. Here the apostle is again in the presence of the suffering Thessalonians, and is expressing his deep sympathy for them in the experience. With this goes also gratitude to God that they had not only originally received the message as **the word of God** but also, under the stress and strain of persecution, had remained faithful.

**16b.** The last sentence in vs. 16 is difficult. It is believed by some (e.g., Moffatt, *The First and Second Epistles of Paul the Apostle to the Thessalonians,* in *Expositor's Greek Testament,* ed. W. Robertson Nicoll [London: Hodder & Stoughton, 1910], p. 29) to be a later addition to the apostle's original letter, being added after the destruction of the

---

considered themselves the Simon-pure Israelites, while the residue of the population were simply the people of the land, common persons, the foolish, clucking mass. So they evoked the blazing anger of Christ and wrought their own condemnation (Matt. 23).

Pharisaism has not died. This old bitter weed still grows rank and tall. Pharisees are in every congregation and religious assembly. Religion to them is something long set and static. It is a fetter, not a fingerpost pointing forward to new areas waiting occupation, or to fresh and expanding experiences. It is associated with the straggling, not the struggling, mind. Pharisees are afraid and resentful of original ideas, are incorrigible traditionalists, want to think and do exactly as their fathers did. Their shouted slogan is "The old-time religion is good enough for me!"

One reared in a home where the parents gloried in "the old-time religion" rejoices in its

many virtues. We want much of it, but something more. Parental religion is good, but not good enough. We must have a better one if we are to meet with confidence the chaos of this century.

If at any time we are tempted to Pharisaism, we should remember that: (*a*) The mind of God is not yet exhausted and he did not tell our fathers everything he knows. The hope of advance lies in those who walk humbly with their God and who gladly say, "Speak, Lord, for thy servant heareth." (*b*) The great biblical truths have not yet been completely apprehended. The Eternal has still new revelations to make and insights to give out of his word. We ought to seek a fresh immersion in the Bible, both scholarly and experimentally, and remember that because of the findings of reverent modern students we should see deeper than our fathers did. (*c*) A new age has new eyes and new needs. (*d*) The riches of Christ are un-

17 But we, brethren, being taken from you for a short time in presence, not in heart, endeavored the more abundantly to see your face with great desire.

17 But since we were bereft of you, brethren, for a short time, in person not in heart, we endeavored the more eagerly and with great desire to see you face to face;

---

city of Jerusalem in A.D. 70, with all of the accompanying calamities and terrors. Holtzmann thought the interpolation included all of vss. 14-16; Schmiedel, only vss. 15-16. Others have seen in the statement a reference to the kind of judgment of God which Paul finds in the moral decline and degeneracy of the Gentiles who refused to have God in their knowledge (Rom. 1:18-28); in similar manner the Jews had repudiated the gospel of God in Jesus Christ and were entering into spiritual decline and confusion. Others (e.g., Ellicott, Stevens, Frame) regard it as a prophetic and proleptic reference to the disaster that was to come upon Jerusalem some fifteen years later. On the whole, it seems most natural to regard the last sentence as an interpolation (with Moffatt and others).

### D. Paul's Desire to Revisit Thessalonica (2:17-20)

**17-18.** At this point the apostle enters upon a brief explanation of his extended absence from Thessalonica, after his enforced departure. This defense was apparently made necessary by the charge of Jewish enemies that the failure to return was due to lack of interest. He indicates that his absence, though only **for a short time,** was so deeply

---

searchable. There are treasures of grace and truth still to be discovered in him. He is a flying goal. Our reach concerning him will always be longer than our grasp. Our fathers found meanings in that perfect life which their fathers did not find. Our children will find yet larger meanings missed by us. (e) The "old-time religion" was not good enough for Moses, Abraham, Jesus (Matt. 3:9), and Paul. True religion always sets life in motion; it is a leaving from and a going to (Ps. 84:5 Moffatt). It means new quests, discoveries, and methods. It means the open road, the wider spaces, the great winds, and the vast hinterlands beyond the edge of cultivation. Our God is not the God of the dead but of the living. Our faith is not a fortress into which we coweringly retreat but is an army on the march, whose caissons go rolling along. (f) God's vast work cannot be done and his kingdom brought to pass by the small, the bigoted, or the proud, who say, "We are the people." How constricted and handicapped we are by our ecclesiastical vanity, our crass sectarianism, and our hard intolerance! All of us need the open mind and the humble heart. It is so easy to fall a victim to Pharisaism, with its inevitable destruction of personality, hindrance of truth, reduction of usefulness, and loss of religion. Let us get rid of the narrow mind and the contracted heart. "The sin of making a Christ of our opinions and worshiping it" can come upon us unawares.[9] The word of Jesus should sound loud as a fire bell in our ears. "God opposes the proud, but gives grace to the humble" (Jas. 4:6).

[9] Joseph Fort Newton, *River of Years* (Philadelphia: J. B. Lippincott Co., 1946), p. 80.

**17-20. The Beloved Flock.**—Again glows the pastoral passion of Paul. Only a **short time** (vs. 17) away from the Thessalonian congregation, and yet he is bereft, i.e., "orphaned." He yearns to see them, not at rare intervals, but **again and again** (vs. 18), and he states the reason. **What is our hope or joy or crown of boasting before our Lord Jesus . . . ? Is it not you? For you are our glory and joy.** Paul walked in the footsteps of his Master, who loved all kinds of people, good and bad, well and sick, rich and poor, saint and sinner, friend and foe. That Master loved them when he started his ministry, in its heyday, and at its end. The supreme cry of compassion and forgiveness which broke from his lips on the cross will ever haunt, challenge, and inspire mankind. It will cling in humanity's memory as long as time endures (Luke 23:34).

When we think of Paul's natural imperiousness, swiftness of mind, and forthrightness of speech, this wistful, tender concern is all the more remarkable. To the end of his days certain limitations were obvious to others and to him. When his death appeared to be at hand he wrote to his beloved Philippians, telling them that he had not attained but was pressing on (Phil. 3:14). True, he was far from perfection, but he could never be accused of coldness, disinterestedness, or nonchalance where the congregations he had founded were concerned. As with the Thessalonians, he yearns after them all. They are his **hope, joy, crown of boasting** before the Lord. He visits them and writes encouraging, warning, instructive letters. When he cannot be with them, he sends special messengers, so that he can have firsthand news of

18 Wherefore we would have come unto you, even I Paul, once and again; but Satan hindered us.

18 because we wanted to come to you — I, Paul, again and again — but Satan hin-

---

felt that he seemed to be **bereft** ["orphaned"] . . . **in heart.** (The exact wording seems to say just the opposite, but this is the evident intention, cf. 2:7, "nurse," "gentle"; 2:11, "father.") He had an eager longing to return to them, even as a father to his sons in their need, or as a mother would cherish her own children. Indeed, Paul himself had **wanted to come . . . again and again,** but for some reason which we cannot accurately know, he had been prevented from making such a trip. **Satan hindered us.** The precise form of this hindrance is not told. It is connected with the "distress and affliction" in 3:7. The two words here used are found also in Paul's description of his experiences in II Cor. 6:4. In I Cor. 5:5 (cf. I Tim. 1:20) Paul speaks of turning over one who has gone into sexual sin "to Satan for the destruction of the flesh." In I Cor. 7:5 he enjoins the Corinthians that a man and his wife shall be considerate of each other so that Satan may not tempt them. I Cor. 11:28-30 refers to judgment which has come upon some who have partaken undiscerningly of the Lord's Supper. This judgment is evident in weakness, ill

---

their welfare. This concern and compassion for his fellow Christians leaps out in all his epistles. He wants them to be kind and tenderhearted, and to forgive one another if any disagreement has arisen in their midst (Eph. 4:32). When any of his friends are ill, he is full of solicitude and takes their weakness and pains upon himself. When Epaphroditus recovers from a serious sickness, he thrills with joy and says: "God had mercy on him; . . . but on me also, lest I should have sorrow upon sorrow" (Phil. 2:27). When his fellow evangelist John Mark has let him down badly in an important mission, but later has made a gallant recovery, he urges the Colossians to give him a vote of confidence and the right hand of fellowship (Col. 4:10). Even when he is dealing out a pungent rebuke, as in the case of the Galatian Christians, who had wandered so far astray, the yearning of his heart speaks through his severity and he cries, "My little children, with whom I am again in travail until Christ be formed in you" (Gal. 4:19). This man, who had stood with harsh face while the glorious life of Stephen was being stoned out of him, can weep over the tribulations of the young church at Ephesus as it tries to give its witness in the midst of a lustful civilization. He says that for three whole years he has not ceased to warn everyone "night and day with tears" (Acts 20:31).

Where do we stand in this matter of pastoral concern? How many of us can honestly say that we yearn after people when we are separated from them for even a little while, that we want to see them again and again (vs. 18), and that any parting from them leaves us bereft, orphaned (vs. 17)? Henry Ward Beecher declared that when he looked out on his congregation his principal emotion was measureless compas-

sion. It is time we re-examined our commission. Primarily we are not essayists, analysts, educators, or administrators, but humanity's suffering servants, ministers of the God who could not stand apart from the tragedy of his creation, but "who gave himself," "who came down."

In a time when the individual feels himself as but one in a vast anthill of human beings, when he is overwhelmed by the problems which possess his mind, and is beset by a desolating loneliness of heart, there is great need of true shepherds of the flock of Jesus Christ. Deep in every heart is the desire for and need of care. In John Drinkwater's beautiful book, *Robinson of England,* the author and his friends attend a country church in the Cotswold hills. After the service they are speaking with Old Bob, the shepherd. An airplane, symbol of a new way of life, flies overhead. The grizzled keeper of the flocks looks up at it and says quietly: "That's one thing they can't do away with, though, shepherding. Sheep'll want shepherds 'till doomsday." [1] Sad to say, some men forget this basic truth of human nature. John Oman writes of the sedate, smug parson, who thinks of God as the head of the clerical profession, not as the Father of all men. What are the marks of the true shepherd of souls?

(*a*) He knows his sheep. Human nature is not easy to understand. It has many remote and secret places which are found out only by long and patient search. How well does the average clergyman know his congregation? When he stands in his pulpit and looks out, what do the faces mean to him? What proportion can he name or identify? What have been his relations with them? Can he preach effectively to them without such knowledge? The sheep "do not

[1] New York: The Macmillan Co., 1937, p. 88.

19 For what *is* our hope, or joy, or crown of rejoicing? *Are* not even ye in the presence of our Lord Jesus Christ at his coming?

20 For ye are our glory and joy.

dered us. 19 For what is our hope or joy or crown of boasting before our Lord Jesus at his coming? Is it not you? 20 For you are our glory and joy.

---

health, and in some cases, death. In II Cor. 2:11 Paul exhorts the Corinthians to be careful that they are not overtaken or put to disadvantage by Satan, "for we are not ignorant of his designs." His "thorn in the flesh" (II Cor. 12:7) was a "messenger of Satan to buffet me." It was something that was recurrent or continuous, some bodily condition (cf. Gal. 4:13). II Thess. 2:9 speaks of the coming of the man of sin "by the activity of Satan." From the fact (cf. 3:1-6) that when Paul could not return, Timothy could be sent as his messenger, we may gather that the hindrance, whatever its nature, was not in the external situation but somehow related to Paul personally. In Acts 16:6 Paul and his companions are said to have been "forbidden by the Holy Spirit" to speak the word in Asia. According to Acts 16:7, when they would have gone into Bithynia "the Spirit of Jesus did not allow them" (cf. I Cor. 16:9). Just how Paul determined whether it was Satan or the Spirit who was so intervening as to necessitate a change in his plans is not told us. For him each of them was equally a reality, and for reasons which are not disclosed, the one or the other is judged responsible in a given set of circumstances.

19-20. Paul's statement that the Thessalonians are his **glory and joy** refers to his eager expectancy that they will be received of the **Lord Jesus at his** [second] **coming** (see below on 4:15, 16). They will not only be worthy of such reception, but the worthiness of their character will be a source of gladness for the apostle, and a basis of approval of him as a good workman of God.

---

know the voice of strangers" (John 10:5), and strangers do not know the needs of the sheep. What does it benefit if we are intimate with the prophets of the O.T. and the apostles of the N.T., with the sages of Greece and Rome, with the whole company of ancient and modern theologians, if we know not the men and women who sit before us? Richard Baxter knew every house in Kidderminster. Charles Spurgeon could call by name every member of his vast congregation. Alexander Whyte pursued the pastoral office with steady, unrelenting zeal. S. Parkes Cadman was forever visiting the sick, counseling the disheartened, giving a helping hand to the weak. George A. Buttrick searches our hearts with trenchant words: "The minister who knows the books on his shelves better than the fleshly volumes in his parish will not for long preach with authority." [2] It will be a humbling experience for any minister to go into the pews of his church and ask: "Who sits here? What do I know of him? What am I doing for him? Have I ever visited or been visited by him? Have I ever prayed for him?" Every minister must avoid, as if it were the plague, the heresy that he is such a great man, with so many duties, that he has the time neither to see nor to visit his people.

(b) He loves his sheep. How deep and passionate is the look he bends on his people Sunday morning? What are they to him? Does he really care for them? He cannot be of any permanent use to them unless he does. A surface geniality, a verbose manner, gay backslapping practices, will never take the place of the shepherd heart.

Frank Laubach wrote in his diary: "I am determined to fill every moment full of the thought of God. And I added another resolve— to be as wide open toward people and their need as I am toward God. Windows opened outward as well as upward! Windows especially opened downward where people need most." [3]

The test of the minister's affection is simple but drastic. Does he love his people enough to tell them the truth? Only that can set them free. Does he give them the word whether they bear or forbear, whether it makes them comfortable or uncomfortable? The words of the true shepherd do not bubble up through honey. He is not an ecclesiastical butler serving at the table of expediency with a napkin over his arm; neither is he a currier of popularity. He is the good shepherd who loves his sheep. Ellery Sedgwick said of the great Phillips Brooks: "In the pulpit Brooks's torrential eloquence was all

[2] *Jesus Came Preaching* (New York: Charles Scribner's Sons, 1931), p. 120.

[3] *Letters by a Modern Mystic* (New York: Student Volunteer Movement, 1937), p. 9.

3 Wherefore when we could no longer forbear, we thought it good to be left at Athens alone;

3 Therefore when we could bear it no longer, we were willing to be left behind

---

E. The Sending of Timothy to Thessalonica (3:1-10)

**3:1-5.** These verses connect directly with the closing verses of ch. 2, continuing the discussion of the major point. Referring to his repeated disappointment in his desire to return to Thessalonica, Paul says that he finally could **bear it no longer.** He, with Silas, decided to remain alone (the word is plural in the Greek) in Athens, where they were at the time, and sent Timothy back to Thessalonica. Timothy had been left behind (with Silas) in Beroea when Paul had had to leave there (Acts 17:14). Paul here indicates what Acts 17:15 implies, that Silas and Timothy had come to him in Athens. They had

---

tradition says, but after talking with him I remember wondering whether he did not love everybody too dearly to care especially for anybody." [4]

(c) He feeds his sheep. The ignorance of the average church member is pathetic. He knows little of the faith by which he is supposed to live and hopes to die. The reasons are legion— neglect of the family altar, lack of religious books in the average home, scarcity of theological conversation around the meal table, over-occupation with business and social activities, the divorce of educational and religious instruction in the public-school system, and the partial failure of the church school.

The good shepherd is a teaching shepherd. In this he is a follower of the Great Shepherd (Mark 6:34). His preaching is biblical and expository. His sermons have content, and he delivers them in frequent and progressive series, so that the congregation is given a body of truth. There are Bible classes in his church following regular courses of study, and the midweek service is considered a major opportunity for further instruction. The hungry sheep look up and are fed. All this demands self-discipline, systematic study, regular periods of reflection and concentrated thought, adequate preparation, the reading of great books, and a deep devotional life. To all these imperatives the good shepherd cheerfully responds, for he knows they are the conditions of a solid ministry and the guarantee of a strong framework of ruling Christian ideas. Of G. A. Studdert-Kennedy, the beloved padre of World War I, it was written: "He thought, worried, shook, and wrestled his way through mighty questions. What he said later to his audiences was wrestled through in those times of soliloquy." [5] Do we hear a voice of command saying, "Go, and do thou likewise"?

[4] *The Happy Profession* (Boston: Little, Brown & Co., 1946), p. 58.
[5] *By his Friends, G. A. Studdert-Kennedy* (New York: Richard R. Smith, 1929), p. 187.

**3:1-5. The Cup That Will Not Pass.**—In this paragraph Paul returns to the fact and problem of the Christian's affliction: **We told you before that we should suffer tribulation** (vs. 4). Moffatt puts it in crisper form, "Troubles are our lot, you know that well." Of course, as is pointed out (2:13-16), the difference between the Thessalonians and those around them invited the pains and persecution, but we should never forget that affliction and the Christian faith go hand in hand: suffering is a Christian "inevitable." There are three reasons for this:

(a) The Cross. One of the fine things about the Bible is its fidelity to the facts of life. It describes what it sees without glossing, improving, reducing, or exaggerating. Thus it does not hide the truth that the Cross was reared and preached amid the world's contempt and hate. As the early church lifted it up, it stirred to further fierceness already flaming prejudices and increased the strength of already existing opposition. To the Jews it was "a stumblingblock" (I Cor. 1:23). They shrank from it with shuddering, for in their eyes one hung on a cross was a being accursed of God. The gospel of the cross was a horror, and the religion of the gibbet was an insult. They simply could not make head or tail of a faith which could take such a coarse, repulsive, painful, and disgraceful thing as its central symbol. It was a road block they could neither remove, walk around, nor climb over.

On the other hand, to the Greeks it was "foolishness" (I Cor. 1:23). They sought the ideal man, who would be a worthy human link between God and them. That a man of dubious birth, with the Galilean accent on his tongue, a small group of fishermen as his disciples, who had died a disreputable death, should be the perfection of their dreams, was a mad, crackbrained tale unworthy of their intelligence. To them it was a derision and joke—"foolishness." So trouble was the lot of the early Christians because they preached Christ crucified, and it

2 And sent Timotheus, our brother, and minister of God, and our fellow laborer in the gospel of Christ, to establish you, and to comfort you concerning your faith:

3 That no man should be moved by these afflictions: for yourselves know that we are appointed thereunto.

at Athens alone, 2 and we sent Timothy, our brother and God's servant in the gospel of Christ, to establish you in your faith and to exhort you, 3 that no one be moved by these afflictions. You yourselves know that

---

doubtless brought Paul information as to the state of affairs when they left Macedonia. This information intensified the apostle's anxiety over the Thessalonian disciples; and when he could no longer endure the suspense, he sent his fellow worker, a true servant of God **in the gospel of Christ,** as his messenger and representative to them. Timothy was a brother beloved of the apostle, brought by him into the work (Acts 16:1-3), and used by him frequently as his agent and messenger.

The Thessalonians knew that they were destined to **afflictions,** for when Paul was with them, he had told them that Christians must expect such experiences. Such **afflictions** had been theirs from the beginning, and were continuing; they also knew that the missionaries who had labored among them had likewise suffered **affliction.** In the midst of difficulties themselves, Paul and Silas were deeply anxious to learn how the Thessalonians were conducting themselves under these continuing trials. Therefore Timothy was sent to **establish you in your faith and to exhort you, that no one be moved by these afflictions.** The peculiar word used in 3:3 (σαίνεσθαι), translated **be moved,** found only here in the Greek Bible, meant in older Greek, "to fawn upon," "to beguile or deceive." It was later associated with words implying violent disturbance. If we are to think of the term here as

---

will be ours if we preach with an equal fidelity. A selfish, ease-loving, proud, embittered, and divided world cannot regard the Cross or its advocates with any gladness. To the worldly man we cannot be anything else but a displeasure, a disturbance, and a reproach. He says, "Get and hold"; the Cross says, "Give and serve." He says, "Me and mine"; the Cross says, "God and others." He says, "Self-realization through self-interest"; the Cross says, "Self-realization through self-investment." So the advocates of the Cross must walk the road of pain. "Trouble is your lot."

(b) The gospel of the kingdom—acceptance of a task (see Expos. on 2:9-12). Jesus' vision of the ideal man and the ideal state is the biggest and bravest moral, social, and spiritual concept which ever blazed in the mind of man, for it faces the facts of life and human nature, deals with the individual and the group, compasses time and eternity, embraces present reality and future hope, and uniquely strikes the universal note, for it knows nothing of sex, race, clan, or color, and gathers into its wide embrace men, women, and little children (Matt. 19:14; I Cor. 12:13). It is not the plan of a human architect, but an eternal and divine purpose established from before the foundation of the world.

To the bringing of this kingdom to concrete reality Jesus exhorted his disciples. Human be-

ings were never summoned to greater obligation. They found themselves confronted by stark paganism and dissolute society. Yet they were undaunted, and set themselves to the making of the society wherein love dwells, believing that the kingdoms of this world would become the kingdoms of their God and of his Christ. But as their Lord suffered for his vision of the kingdom, so did they. They were boycotted in business, ostracized by society, cast out of their synagogues, suspected by the government, accused of many evils, and declared to be members of a third race. This doctrine of the kingdom to which we are also committed, therefore, carries within itself the seeds and fruits of pain for us. Conventions, deep-rooted customs, moral attitudes, ethical standards, economic and political systems, cannot be changed without savage resistance. The kingdom will not come without the shedding of blood. "Trouble is your lot."

(c) Humanity's suffering servants. The great doctrine of the suffering servant was first given by Second Isaiah, who set forth the noble and revolutionary principle that good men must take upon themselves the unbelief, thoughtlessness, transgressions, strife, and guilt of the evil men, if the latter are "to be saved." [6] This doctrine came to its fullest and most beautiful ex-

[6] See George Adam Smith, *The Book of Isaiah* (rev. ed.; New York: Harper & Bros., 1927), II, 351 ff.

4 For verily, when we were with you, we told you before that we should suffer tribulation; even as it came to pass, and ye know.

5 For this cause, when I could no longer forbear, I sent to know your faith, lest by some means the tempter have tempted you, and our labor be in vain.

6 But now when Timotheus came from you unto us, and brought us good tidings of your faith and charity, and that ye have good remembrance of us always, desiring greatly to see us, as we also *to see* you:

this is to be our lot. 4 For when we were with you, we told you beforehand that we were to suffer affliction; just as it has come to pass, and as you know. 5 For this reason, when I could bear it no longer, I sent that I might know your faith, for fear that somehow the tempter had tempted you and that our labor would be in vain.

6 But now that Timothy has come to us from you, and has brought us the good news of your faith and love and reported that you always remember us kindly and

suggesting deception, then we are to understand that there were those who were seeking to court the favor of these new Thessalonian disciples, and to lead them astray with guile (so, e.g., Frame). The other meaning is, on the whole, more likely: "to be strongly shaken or to be troubled" (see, e.g., Findlay). The phrase is evidently in contrast with **to establish you.** Paul knew the stress and strain under which these Thessalonian Christians were laboring (cf. 1:8), and he feared that the tempter might have lured them to their fall and his apparently fruitful labor among them would finally prove to have been in vain. Timothy was sent first of all to learn **your faith** and to become acquainted with the total situation. He was then to strengthen and encourage them that they should not be upset or overcome by their temptations. Finally, he was to return to Paul and Silas with the information for which they were so eager. How long Timothy remained in Thessalonica is not said, but he evidently carried out his mission with great effectiveness.

**6-10.** At the time of Paul's writing, Timothy had just returned from his visit to Thessalonica with a very encouraging report. This included several items. First of all, he **brought us the good news of your faith and love;** you are standing **fast in the Lord.** The report on this point was, amid all of the **distress and affliction** of the apostle and

pression in the life of Jesus. He was its incarnation, and he demanded its acceptance as a condition of discipleship. His followers must deny themselves and follow him who "came not to be ministered unto, but to minister, and to give his life a ransom for many" (Matt. 20:28). True progress comes, then, only after sacrifice is made. The blood of the sacrificial victim has fed and watered the growth of history. It has been carried toward its goals when the suffering servants of humanity have been wounded for its transgressions, bruised for its iniquities, and have gathered to themselves the filthiness of the leper, the darkness of the blind, the wandering of the prodigal, the heartsickness of the oppressed, and the fierce misery of the worldling. Souls are redeemed only when others are willing to wrestle like Jacob until the break of day, even though their thigh is flung out of joint. The vicarious element is the center of the Christian ethic. To fire others, the match itself must waste. It is only when the burnt offering is made that the song of the Lord begins.

When will we learn that the cross of Christ is not a date A.D. 32 or 33, but a timeless fact of history; not a piece of wood to which Jesus was

nailed, but his way of living—the way of love—the very nature of which is to insinuate itself into the sins and sorrows of others? If we are his true followers there is no evading humanity's load, for "he laid down his life for us; and we ought to lay down our lives for the brethren" (I John 3:16). "Trouble is your lot."

With the foregoing incontrovertible truths before us, the question which will not down is why the American and some of the other Western churches are unafflicted. The only answer which we can give—a sad and solemn one—is that the Cross is no longer central; we have lost the vision of the kingdom of God, and have no intention of being the suffering servants of humanity. Ichabod!

**6-10. The Under-Shepherd's High Reward.**— Paul's passionate shepherd-heart is again speaking in this paragraph. **We long to see you** (vs. 6). **We live, if you stand fast in the Lord** (vs. 8). **The joy which we feel for your sake** (vs. 9). **Praying . . . night and day that we may see you face to face** (vs. 10). We have dealt with Paul's appreciation of the Thessalonian congregation (1:2-10; 2:17-20). But here his affection becomes almost lyrical, for he is now rejoicing not only in

7 Therefore, brethren, we were comforted over you in all our affliction and distress by your faith:

8 For now we live, if ye stand fast in the Lord.

9 For what thanks can we render to God again for you, for all the joy wherewith we joy for your sakes before our God;

10 Night and day praying exceedingly that we might see your face, and might perfect that which is lacking in your faith?

long to see us, as we long to see you — 7 for this reason, brethren, in all our distress and affliction we have been comforted about you through your faith; 8 for now we live, if you stand fast in the Lord. 9 For what thanksgiving can we render to God for you, for all the joy which we feel for your sake before our God, 10 praying earnestly night and day that we may see you face to face and supply what is lacking in your faith?

---

Silas, a source of great comfort. **For now we live, if you stand fast in the Lord,** so deep is our concern for you, so interwoven our lives with yours, so tied up our hopes in you. The joy **which we feel for your sake before our God** is so great that it is beyond our thanksgiving. **Your sake** means not "in your behalf," but "on account of you." The apostle has in mind their steadfast fidelity in the Lord, which Timothy had reported. There is nothing adequate that can be said to express "our gratitude." Timothy also **reported that you always remember us kindly.** This remembrance of the Thessalonians and the missionaries was mutual, and mutually appreciative (cf. 1:2-3) and abiding. To their kindly remembrance the heart of the missionary responds in glad reciprocation. Timothy further reported that you **long to see us, as we long to see you.** All the while that the missionaries had so ardently desired to return to Thessalonica, their converts and friends there had longed for their return. Paul and Silas are in fact praying constantly and earnestly **that we may see you face to face and supply what is lacking in your faith.** Whether the Thessalonian disciples had informed Timothy of certain things **lacking,** or Timothy himself had observed these needs, is not indicated. That such

---

his attitude to them but in their reciprocal attitude to him. **Timothy . . . brought us the good news of your . . . love and reported that you always remember us kindly and long to see us** (vs. 6).

Apart from the tender ties of home life, is there any bond so beautiful and enduring as that which exists between a faithful minister and a loyal congregation? In its fidelity and joyousness it challenges the power and the passion even of love of country and love of friends. Many disparaging things have been said and written by ministers and observers of congregational indifference, ingratitude, disloyalty, and even cruelty. In some cases the indictment is true, but they are not representative. Sometimes, where they exist, they are traceable to the tactlessness, laziness, or faithlessness of the minister. Generally, the congregational heart responds to an outgoing, strong, and wise love given by its pastor. To be the recipient of such a response is a joy unfeigned. In G. F. Barbour's biography of Alexander Whyte of Edinburgh, there is a tremendous chapter on "Dr. Whyte as Pastor and Friend," with which every minister should be familiar.[7] His joy in the loving attitude to

him of his kirk session, deacons' court, church officers, and congregation was unconfined. He rejoiced in it and was proud of it. In no way, however, was their affection permitted to affect the candor and faithfulness of his dealings with them, for no preacher in Scotland was more frank and scathing than he when necessity demanded; but always his happiness at being the minister of Free St. George's, Edinburgh, was manifest. One Sunday evening when he was beset by a sense of failure in his work, he permitted his low mood to color his sermon. The same night one of his members wrote him a letter, telling what his ministry had meant to her. Immediately he sent this noble and tender reply, "Your letter is a cup of wine to me this morning.—Believe me, Alexander Whyte."[8]

The apostles of today enlarge too frequently on the hardships and problems of their calling. To hear the lachrymose talk of some of them, the listener is given the impression that unceasing labor, want of appreciation, and misunderstanding are their constant lot. Any self-respecting man, no matter what his type of profession, works hard; and a minister knows a dozen men in his church who toil longer hours, carry heavier burdens, and are subjected to more

[7] *The Life of Alexander Whyte* (4th ed.; London: Hodder & Stoughton, 1923), pp. 350-76.

[8] *Ibid.*, p. 366.

11 Now God himself and our Father, and our Lord Jesus Christ, direct our way unto you.

11 Now may our God and Father himself, and our Lord Jesus, direct our way to

---

deficiencies existed is here clearly implied, and their general nature is reflected in the later part of the letter (4:1-12; 5:12-22). In any case, the apostle knows of them, frankly recognizes them, and prays constantly that he and his fellow workers may be able to get back to Thessalonica and **supply** (RSV), or **perfect** (KJV), **that which is lacking.** The Greek word (καταρτίσαι) really means "to put into unified and good working condition"; this is Paul's urgent prayer and hope.

### F. THE APOSTLE'S PRAYER (3:11-13)

**11.** The apostle now gives the third major turn to the argument of the epistle, moving directly into a prayer directed to **our God and Father himself;** and it is impressive to note also that **our Lord Jesus Christ** is associated in his mind and in his prayer with God, our Father. This is the only time in any of his letters that Paul includes Christ in a prayer addressed to God. But he shares the general thinking of the early church that God has "made that same Jesus . . . both Lord and Christ" (Acts 2:36) and that Jesus is now

---

harassment, without the minister's amazing compensations. Think of some of these compensations: the opportunity to preach the good news of the grace of God; an ever-enlarging number of devoted friends, varying according to the size of the congregations and the places in which he serves; service to the whole life span and gender range of human personality; the recipient of confidences given to no other living soul; the general respect of both the congregation and the community in which he lives; the counseling of many people in times of trouble and indecision; and practically every door open to him in sincere welcome. Of course the faithful minister gives much, but how much more he receives! John Watson, better known by his pen name Ian Maclaren, gave himself to his congregation and the city of Liverpool with both hands. As Paul received reciprocal action, so did he. It was said of him at his death that nearly every man on the streets of the city was affected by his loss. A clergyman was returning home late at night when an electric car pulled up, and the driver, white with emotion, leaned over the rail. "Have you heard the news?" he said. "John Watson is dead; it is a bad day for us." [9] It would be wonderful to be loved like that by a people. Each minister can, if he will pay Paul's and Watson's price.

**11-13. *The City of a Grateful Heart.*—**Paul's thankfulness at the good news brought back from Thessalonica overflows in this comprehensive, eloquent, and deeply devotional prayer. Observe four features of it:

(a) Its exaltation of Jesus. **Now may our God**

[9] W. Robertson Nicoll, *"Ian Maclaren," The Life of the Rev. John Watson* (New York: Dodd Mead & Co., 1908), p. 359.

**and Father himself, and our Lord Jesus, direct . . .** (vs. 11). God and Jesus are addressed here as a unity. The singular of **direct** is employed. This exaltation of Jesus is notable in all the Pauline epistles. Paul's favorite designations of Christ are "Son of God," "Lord." All the fullness of the Godhead dwells in him (Col. 2:9). H. A. Kennedy in his article "The Pauline Theology" writes: "This marvellous Person, who had recreated [Paul's] life, who had lived a man among men well known to Paul, stands solitary in the world of being. He has disclosed to Paul the heart and purpose of God." [1]

Theologically, of course, Paul differentiated between God and Christ, but Jesus to him was so complete a revelation that in the practical use of prayer he considered them the same. We can well follow Paul in his exaltation of the Lord, for his uniqueness is not sufficiently stressed. We need a fresh emphasis on the lordship of Christ, delivered without apology or equivocation. Before he is our teacher, healer, leader, or exemplar, he is our sovereign Lord. That is what he considered himself first of all to be (John 13:13). Without social background or acquired prestige, he walked through the world as if he owned it. Among his first words were "Follow me." Without hesitation or apology, he told the accredited teachers of a long-established and revered religion that in many ways they were wrong. He declared that heaven and earth would pass away, but his words would endure (Matt. 24:35). He demanded that men and women turn from some of the ways and teachings of Abraham and Moses, saying, "I am the way, and the truth, and the life" (John 14:6). He confronted history as Commander,

[1] Peake, *Commentary on the Bible*, p. 808.

12 And the Lord make you to increase and abound in love one toward another, and toward all *men,* even as we *do* toward you:

you; 12 and may the Lord make you increase and abound in love to one another

---

reigning "with power" (Rom. 1:4; cf. I Cor. 8:6; 15:25-28), at the right hand of God. It is in God the Father and the Lord Jesus Christ that the church at Thessalonica has its existence (1:1; II Thess. 1:1). It is also of value in finding our way into the mind of the apostle to observe that the verb **direct** is in the singular. The prayer is one; and the apostle's mind moves in but a single direction as he breathes his prayer. His knowledge of the glory of God came to him "in the face of Christ" (II Cor. 4:6). To that God, revealed and present in that Lord, he makes his appeal. It is his prayer that God himself, and the Lord Jesus, may **direct** ("make straight and open") his **way** to the Thessalonians.

**12.** But closely connected with this prayer is a second one. It springs from a more central desire of the apostle's heart, and it is especially directed to **the Lord** (i.e., Christ). As for you, he writes, may the Lord make you **increase and abound** ["overflow"] **in love to one another, and to all men.** Paul's thanksgiving that their Christian love is mutually

---

and his utterances were studded with such imperative verbs as "ask," "come," "go," "seek," "knock," "do." With unparalleled daring he said such things as "A greater than Solomon is here" (Matt. 12:42) and "Before Abraham was, I am" (John 8:58). And when the question was bluntly put, "Are you the Son of God then?" "Certainly," he replied, "I am" (Luke 22:70 Moffatt).

It is worth noting that throughout the whole N.T., the period when Christianity was close to its sources, there is this massive concentration on Christ as Lord. It proclaims him Lord of all. Its triumphant shout is

Bring forth the royal diadem,
And crown him Lord of all.

One of the great problems of our time is the question of authority. No one can deny that we are living in a world which has largely refused it, or accepted it in such form that it does despite to man's dignity and development. Governments and systems, traditions, customs, and laws which have guided and shaped the destinies of nations have been derisively rejected. Political, economic, moral, and spiritual sanctions which have over great spans of time determined human action have been swept out of doors. Individuals and groups seem determined to follow their own sweet or sour wills even if it means running down a steep place, like the swine of Gadara, into the sea of war, famine, insurrection, and misery. What or whose power can provide the supreme persuasive by which nations and men can live in friendship, dignity, and moral strength? There is but one ultimate answer—the authority of Christ. This is the orthodox belief of the Christian church, but it is not the belief it practices. Too often Christ

is made one among many saviors, and this is supposed to be an evidence of tolerance and magnanimity. We actually labor to show how much he has in common with Buddha, Mohammed, and Confucius, and continually emphasize his likeness to other good men. We draw skillful but false analogies between his words of wisdom and those of the world. We give the impression that the difference between him and others is after all a difference in degree, not in nature; of development, not of genus. So we rob him of his uniqueness and sovereignty. We respect but do not worship him; we praise but do not obey him; we admire but do not follow him. He is a fluctuating emotion, not a ruling passion. The plain fact is we have been seduced, beguiled, or browbeaten from the grand centrality of our Christian faith—the lordship of Christ—and so have no adequate authority to offer our lawless, undisciplined time.

The church itself is suffering the inevitable consequences of this somber fact, consequences which we can see in the secularization of our congregational life, the nondescript nature of our church membership, the lapse into materialism and humanism, the loss of redemptive power, the pallid nature of our evangelism, the ill-concealed contempt of the malign forces in our society which believe the church has lost its cutting edge and can therefore be ignored.

Christ is Lord! To that conviction we must return. In him God invaded history with power and great glory. He is the Word made flesh, who lived in the intimacy of the Spirit, and who in God consciousness stands alone, the first to give a complete "Yes" to the agelong willingness of God. In him the temporal and the eternal join and interlock (John 14:9). He is not only Son of God, but God the Son. This is foolishness to the multitude, but it should be glorious truth to

13 To the end he may stablish your | and to all men, as we do to you, 13 so that
hearts unblamable in holiness before God, | he may establish your hearts unblamable
| in holiness before our God and Father, at

---

abounding or increasing is expressed in II Thess. 1:3 (cf. Phil. 4:17; Col. 1:4). Love **to all men** was of special difficulty for the Thessalonians in view of the treatment they were receiving from their fellows, so that this prayer would be a vital challenge to the reality of their Christian faith. In Rom. 13:10 Paul declares love for one's neighbor to be the fulfillment of the law. Such love was difficult, but it was demanded. Incidentally, the writers indicate that nothing is being asked of these Thessalonians which the missionaries themselves are not doing; as we ask of you toward all, so do **we do to you.**

**13.** The ultimate goal toward which the prayer is directed is that the Lord may establish **your hearts unblamable in holiness before our God and Father.** A similar and even more comprehensive prayer is voiced in 5:23. But again nothing is being sought for these new disciples that is not also a part of the very life of the apostle. The Thessalonians knew how holy and righteous and blameless the missionaries had been in their lives among them (2:10). Also, as God himself knew the lives of his messengers (2:10), so it is the prayer of Paul and his fellow writers that these new converts may be known and recognized of God as blameless in their holiness, when they are before him **at the**

---

all who profess Christianity, for it was proclaimed by Christ, asserted by the apostles, set forth in the N.T., declared by the creeds, inset in the liturgies, and made the theme of hymns.

Robert Browning puts it truly:

I say, the acknowledgment of God in Christ
Accepted by thy reason, solves for thee
All questions in the earth and out of it.[2]

(b) Its humility. **May the Lord make you increase** (vs. 12). One of the great temptations of a Christian leader is to forget that while one may plant and another water, it is God who gives the increase (I Cor. 3:6).

The response of the Thessalonians to Paul's message was remarkable. The conversions were many: some Jews, a very large group of Greeks, and a goodly number of the prominent women of the city. He might have been lifted up and have credited himself with the success, for his gifts and abilities were many. But Christ's humility so possessed him that to Christ was given the glory, and as he prays for the further spiritual development of the young church he had founded, he emphasizes that the source of further power is neither in it nor in himself, but in the Lord. This quality is all the more amazing when we remember what he had been—arrogant, imperious, hasty, proud, "a Pharisee of the Pharisees." Christ, however, had wrought such a revolutionary change in him that he was a new creature, and behold, all things had become new! Humility does not mean servility, groveling, or cringing. Neither does it mean becoming a door mat for any overbearing per-

son who feels like tramping on us, or possessing the disposition of a worm. A man can be truly humble and yet have a high opinion of himself based on his capabilities and achievements. Humility, therefore, is basically self-knowledge. Paul is a vivid illustration of this truth. Always before his eyes was the sight of his Lord, "Who, though he was in the form of God, did not count equality with God a thing to be grasped, but emptied himself, taking the form of a servant, [and] humbled himself" (Phil. 2:6-8). But as Christ was never a sycophant, neither was Paul. As Christ was bold and plain spoken, so was he. As Christ made high claims for himself, so did he. There was in him real, not counterfeit, honest, not artificial, humility. Charles E. Jefferson writes: "Paul thought highly of himself, but no more highly than he ought to think. He thought soberly, and took accurate measurement of the abilities which God had given him. He was not wise in his own conceits, but realized he had always something more to learn."[3] Thus he was truly humble, and his humility is shown in his prayer, **May the Lord make you increase.**

Absence of humility has ever been one of man's obvious weaknesses. It was Adam's self-sufficiency which drove him out of the garden, and since then many an Eden has been lost because of it. The present generation will never be given any medals in respect of its humility, for this virtue runs counter to our ideas of success, ambition, and power. Our admiration is for aggressive strength and virility which enable a man to plunge through opposition to his goal. We are in no haste to attribute either to God or

[2] "A Death in the Desert."

[3] *The Character of Paul* (New York: The Macmillan Co., 1923), p. 136.

**coming of our Lord Jesus with all his saints.** The **coming of our Lord Jesus** (παρουσία) was at the very center of the apostle's attention as he was writing the Thessalonian letters. He links to it every phase of his discussion (cf. 1:10; 2:19; 4:15; 5:2, 23; II Thess. 1:7; 2:1, 8).

At his **coming** the Lord will be accompanied by **all his saints.** Who are these saints? Many of the older interpreters, and some modern ones (e.g., Schmiedel, Findlay), have held that the term refers to those who are to be raised "first" (4:16) to meet the Lord and then "will come with the Lord." Supporting this view is the fact that the term "saints," or "holy ones," is used by Paul more than eighty times, and in all other passages it clearly is used of holy men. Frame holds that if it refers to holy men, then these holy ones will come not at the time of the parousia but later, at the time of judgment. Other scholars (Schmiedel, Dobschutz, Dibelius, Moffatt) think the reference is to angels. This view is supported not only by the reference to the archangel in 4:16 and by II Thess. 1:7,

---

to our fellows around even partial "assists" in our achievements. The personal pronoun singular, "I," is a sweet morsel to, and frequent one upon, our lips. Arthur John Gossip tells how Thomas Chalmers, one of Scotland's greatest preachers, was pondering over his lack of spiritual success despite all his efforts and tremendous popularity. His conclusion was that he was trusting his "own animal heat and activity." [4] "Is not this great Babylon, which I have built" (Dan. 4:30) is so often our boast. We are even deliberately transmitting our arrogance to our children, for we are training them that self-assertion and self-assurance are desirable. "Son," we say, "it's all right to be humble, but don't let anyone put it over on you." So we may be launching into the world a generation of go-getters and climbers who will win their desires even if it means trampling on the faces of their fellows. Pride and arrogance creep up on us and we become their victims before we realize it. They invade church groups and try to corral the minister. The indications are many. We take ourselves too seriously, and convince ourselves we are the indispensable men; we are sure the women's association, session, board, or Bible class, cannot succeed if we are not their leaders; if we are not consulted, or our opinions called for, we are ruffled; when we express our viewpoint and others demur, we are highly offended and consider they lack intelligence; if a joke is on us, we writhe inwardly and present a poker-face outwardly; we are pompous and can strut sitting down; we eat up flattery like blueberry pie; and we are unconsciously braggarts.

A return to humility is long overdue, for it is close to being the most imperative requirement of individual, national, and religious life. It will assist our return if we remember: (i) Humility is pleasing to God. This is true, for it is a reflec-

tion of his nature. Is he not the God who came down? A. E. Whitham, whose *Discipline and Culture of the Spiritual Life* is a classic of the soul's quest, says:

> The very method of the Incarnation does suggest that if Jesus Christ is like God, is God, very God of very God, then God is a humble God. If Jesus Christ is God, he does not behave as one who is on top of things. If I were on top, I would look around for a throne on which to sit. He accepted a cross whereon to hang. When I am on top, I think of my rights. He was concerned with his burden. I count success in my servants; he in his service.[5]

(ii) Humility is enjoined and exemplified by Jesus. The first thing he taught his disciples was to be modest and quiet of spirit. Their nation was swallowed up in the empire. They were part of a vast totalitarian regime. There were many mighty and great traveling the land with their beplumed and nodding escorts, to whom swift and cringing obedience was given. Jesus said: "The rulers of the Gentiles lord it over them, and their great men exercise authority over them. It shall be not so among you" (Matt. 20:25-26). When the enraptured populace cried, "Let him be our king!" and would have honored him by force, he withdrew to his favorite mountain retreat for reflection and prayer (John 6:15). So natural and deep was his humility that without any sense of pose he girt himself with a towel and washed the feet of his disciples. Truly his was the stoop of the mighty!

(iii) Humility is a condition of effective prayer. Jesus declared that the Pharisee's prayer was rejected because it reflected pride, arrogance, self-complacency, and contempt of others (Luke 18:9-14), and said that prayer was not to be offered ostentatiously in the synagogues and at the corners of the streets, but in the quietness of the closet (Matt. 6:5-6). "Thus we are met, on the very threshold of prayer, by a

---

[4] *Experience Worketh Hope* (New York: Charles Scribner's Sons, 1945), p. 58.

[5] London: Hodder & Stoughton, 1938, p. 32.

even our Father, at the coming of our Lord Jesus Christ with all his saints.

the coming of our Lord Jesus with all his saints.

---

but also by Mark 8:38; Matt. 16:27; 25:31 (cf. Luke 9:26); and particularly by the declaration of Jude 14, quoting Enoch 1:9. Still others (e.g., Bengel, Ellicott, Lightfoot, Milligan) have held that both holy men and angels are in Paul's thought (note the term all).

The opinion that Paul is thinking of angels seems to have the strongest support. As a matter of fact, Zech. 14:5 (in the LXX) expresses essentially the same idea in much the same wording. It reads, "And the Lord, my God, will come, and the holy ones with him." This conception seems to have been a part of late Jewish and early Christian tradition, with which Paul was so closely connected (see further on 4:13-18).

The first major part of the letter has now been completed; some very old and important MSS recognize this fact by reading here a final "Amen," which may well have

---

moral demand. Friendship with God presupposes the beginnings of genuine humility and of fundamental simplicity of aim. Without humility—that is, without reality—there can be no power in prayer." [6]

(iv) The vain man is the unworthy man, for his center is himself. The humble man is the worthy man, because his center is in other people or in God. The vain man is ec-centric ("off center"); the humble man is centric ("on center"). Vanity is weakness; humility is strength, a stout and soldierly quality, for it demands a sense of reality and proportion. In both John the Baptist and Jesus we see the worthy beauty of humility. They represented opposing forms of religion, one old, the other new; one severe and hard, the other comparatively sunny; one ascetic, the other tender. There was rivalry between their respective disciples, but observe the humility of the leaders to each other. John says: "He who is mightier than I is coming, the thong of whose sandals I am not worthy to untie" (Luke 3:16). "He must increase, but I must decrease". (John 3:30). Jesus pays handsome tribute to John. He asks the multitude if they had trudged into the hot desert to see a reed shaken with the wind or a man clothed in soft raiment. Then he goes on: "Why then did you go out? To see a prophet? Yes, I tell you, and more than a prophet. . . . Among those born of women there has risen no one greater than John the Baptist." (Matt. 11:7-11.)

Many have been captured by the mind of Bernard of Clairvaux. What warriorlike qualities were his! He fought a good fight against principalities and powers and spiritual wickedness in the high places of Europe. His amazing magnetism, philanthropic spirit, and powerful

eloquence brought him much honor and applause. He walked with kings and grandees, but remained simple and humble of mind; so the beauty of his Lord was upon him:

The humility of his heart . . . surpassed the majesty of his fame, so that when receiving the profuse honors and adulation of princes or of peoples, he did not seem to himself to be Bernard, but some one else substituted for him; he only recognizing himself in his proper personality when he resumed familiar talk with the humbler of his brethren. [7]

It is time all of us emerged from the ether of self-sufficiency and pride, particularly teachers of the gospel, who are supposed to be God-centered, but are so often self-centered. Their usefulness to God and the people is dependent on the acquisition of this basic virtue. In 1898, Alexander Whyte in the course of his moderatorial address spoke of "the sunken rocks I have foundered on, and some of the whirlpools which have well-nigh swirled and sucked down my soul." Then he cried, "Fathers and Brethren, did not Augustine and Calvin speak to the point when they said: 'First, second, and third—humility'? And especially in you and me?" [8] A greater than Augustine, Calvin, and Whyte said, "Unless you turn and become like children, you will never enter the kingdom of heaven" (Matt. 18:3). O my soul, remember!

(c) Its emphasis on brotherhood. "May the Lord make you increase and excel in love to one another and to all men (as is my love for you)" (vs. 12 Moffatt). Again Paul rings the changes on what epitomizes the Christian ethic to him—love. In the opening sentences of his letter (1:2-3) he is exuberantly grateful for the fact

[6] E. Herman, Creative Prayer (New York: George H. Doran Co., 1921), p. 23.

[7] Quoted in Albert H. Currier, Nine Great Preachers (Boston: Pilgrim Press, 1912), p. 95.
[8] Barbour, Life of Alexander Whyte, p. 284.

been the original reading. Up to this point the dominant note of the letter has been one of thanksgiving for the reception given to the gospel message by these Thessalonian disciples, for their exemplification of the gospel, and for the true Christian spirit which they have shown under severe testing. A subordinate note of self-defense has been struck regarding the spirit of the writers and the character of their labors among the Thessalonians. In the course of this self-defense they have given also an explanation of their failure to return to Thessalonica as they had continually hoped—and possibly had promised—to do. Vss. 11-12 might very well have closed the letter if there had been no need of admonition and exhortation. These dominate the rest of the letter.

---

of their love to each other. Now they must ascend two steps higher and they must, in Moffatt's words, "increase and excel"; and in Phillips', "increase and overflow." [9] In addition, they must **love . . . all men,** which of course meant loving the fierce-eyed bigots who were persecuting them with such cruelty. Lest they think he is setting them an impossible task, he declares that this is the measure of the love he has for them and others. As the Lord has given it to him, so will he give it to them.

It is interesting to observe how Paul emphasizes this plus quality in his other letters. He tells the Roman Christians they are "more than conquerors" (Rom. 8:37) ; prays that the love of the Philippians may not merely abound, but that it may "abound more and more" (Phil. 1:9) ; and in his great Ephesian benediction he assures them that the Christ who loves them can do "far more abundantly" than they can ask or think (Eph. 3:20) . This liberal use of superlatives is apt to make us conclude that Paul was guilty of rhetorical flourish or poetic license. Not so. The history of the early church declares these things were fact, not fancy. So he is running true to form when he bids the Thessalonians to **increase and abound in love to one another and to all men.**

Lest there still be a reluctance to go along with this "plus" spirit of Paul, we should remember that God never deals in mere sufficiencies, but in magnificent plusses; never in meticulous measures, but in grand generosities. He never skimps, doles, or carefully packets out. Turn to that lyric, Ps. 23, the grand climacteric of the devotional spirit of the O.T. For what does the psalmist give thanks? Is it for a cup filled carefully to the brim? No, it is for one which overflows. He rejoices not merely for the exact bounty of God, but for his unstinted and overflowing generosity. So let us not shrink from the high challenge to excel in love to one another, and to all men, for it is an excellence we urgently need in this time. We can hardly claim to excel in love to one another while Protestantism is still divided into over two hundred and

[9] *Letters to Young Churches,* p. 130.

fifty large and small splinters. Despite the tender and passionate prayer of our Lord, "That they may all be one; even as thou, Father, art in me, and I in thee, that they also may be in us, so that the world may believe that thou hast sent me" (John 17:21), we are a shamefully divided household. For this division we are paying a stern price: the criticism of thoughtful men; the inability to mobilize our resources quickly to repel and attack blatant evils; the lack of a united voice on great social and moral issues; the prodigal waste of men and money in competitive and overlapping efforts; the casual setting aside of the churches in community enterprises, which our fractionalism invites; and the open sneers of the ungodly.

The church ought to be the greatest building organization in the world and be ever so excelling in love to the brethren. Yes, and to all men, for we are living in a riven, suspicious, and armed world, whose clamant and urgent need is the restoration of friendship. How can a divided world be won by a divided church? Is it not past time for the denominations to agree to differ and unite to serve? Are we not fellow citizens with the saints of the household of God, built together for a habitation of God through his spirit? Is not fellowship the cardinal note of all active and living Christian faith? Is not the goal of the gospel the reconciliation of the whole race in Christ?

(d) Its goal. **So that he may establish your hearts unblamable in holiness before our God** (vs. 13). This noble prayer drives to a point. It does not finish, as many prayers do, in broad, vague generalities. It desires the renewal and unification of the whole personality—nothing less. Only thus will the Thessalonians be ready to meet Christ when they stand before him. This quality of character is to be in terms not of man's, but of God's, judgment, **before our God;** and the sturdy foundation on which it is to be built is **love to one another and to all men.**

A man may be morally blameless without being holy, and a man may be ecclesiastically "holy" without being moved by love. But to be blameless in

4 Furthermore then we beseech you, brethren, and exhort *you* by the Lord Jesus, that as ye have received of us how ye ought to walk and to please God, *so* ye would abound more and more.

2 For ye know what commandments we gave you by the Lord Jesus.

4 Finally, brethren, we beseech and exhort you in the Lord Jesus, that as you learned from us how you ought to live and to please God, just as you are doing, you do so more and more. 2 For you know what instructions we gave you through the Lord

---

### III. Exhortation and Instruction (4:1–5:28)

As just indicated, at this point the letter changes in general tone from the spirit of thanksgiving to one of exhortation and instruction, and this combination continues through to the close of the letter. The last verse of the preceding chapter gives the frame and canvas for the first exhortation. The writers have just expressed the hope that the Lord Jesus may establish the hearts of the Thessalonian Christians "unblamable in holiness before our God and Father." This idea of holiness and blamelessness is carried directly into the first paragraph of the second part of the letter.

### A. The Duty of Purity and Love (4:1–12)

This section consists of a series of exhortations in which the Thessalonian disciples are urged to advance still further in the manifestation of Christian virtues which they have already exemplified so notably and nobly. These exhortations are given against a background of pagan life which it is difficult for us, in a society in which Christianity has become somewhat domesticated, to recover and realize.

**4:1-2.** The word **then** (KJV; the word is not found in some ancient MSS; cf. RSV) in vs. 1 expresses what the writers regard as a logical sequence of the hope expressed in the immediately preceding sentence. **Furthermore** (KJV) is better than **finally** (RSV) to introduce a paragraph so far from the end of the letter. The word (λοιπόν) in Gal. 6:17 is translated by RSV "henceforth"; in I Cor. 1:16, "beyond that"; in I Cor. 4:2, "moreover"; in I Cor. 7:29, "from now on." It does not imply that the writers have reached the end of the letter or its closing paragraph. It indicates only that they are making a definite transition in the discussion. They are about to draw an inference from what they have just said. As they reflect upon the progress the Thessalonians have made, the writers are led to make an urgent appeal for still further advance in the way of life concerning which they already have received **instructions.** Findlay thinks that the word **beseech** (ἐρωτῶμεν) carries an interrogative quality, i.e., virtually, "Will you do so and so?" This was the meaning of the word in the classical Greek. However, out of sixty-three occurrences of the word in the N.T., almost exactly 45 per cent carry the apparently simple idea of request or petition. The words **beseech** and **exhort** are several times found together in the papyri with essentially the same meaning. That seems to be the case here. The readers

---

holiness **before God** demands the inwardness of consecrated service—the "heart" must be pure as well as the outward behaviour, and the motive must be love to God and one's neighbour.[1]

Here all of us are inwardly searched as with a candle. We have a certain standing in the eyes of men, but what are we in God's sight? We also have a certain love of others in the eyes of men, but what about the inner affections? Are our motives and actions in accord? We need the love of Jesus Christ in our hearts. "Only God can

make one sincerely loving and wholly selfless in such work. Only the directing love of Jesus Christ can give any worker the right to enter the life of another human being. And, in fact, only such love can gain us the entrance." [2]

**4:1-12.** *Excelsior!*—Paul rejoices in the well-doing of the Thessalonians, but they must do **more and more** (vs. 1), for they have not yet reached the ideal of the life which is in Jesus Christ. If their hearts are to be established "unblamable in holiness before our God," certain

[1] Neil, *Epistle of Paul to Thessalonians*, p. 73.

[2] V. C. Kitchen, *I Was a Pagan* (New York: Harper & Bros., 1934), p. 141.

3 For this is the will of God, *even* your sanctification, that ye should abstain from fornication:

4 That every one of you should know how to possess his vessel in sanctification and honor;

Jesus. 3 For this is the will of God, your sanctification: that you abstain from immorality; 4 that each one of you know how to take a wife for himself in holiness

---

are addressed as **brethren,** and the exhortation is given in friendly and kindly spirit. Cordial reception of the appeal is assumed. No new request is being made; only an exhortation to a yet fuller realization of that to which they have given themselves.

**3.** A part of the instructions already given, described as **the will of God, your sanctification,** is that the readers **abstain from immorality. The will of God** here means the desire and purpose of God. The word **immorality** (πορνεία) refers to any kind of illicit sexual indulgence. It may seem as if disciples who had already been congratulated upon their fidelity to their Christian calling would hardly need this particular appeal. However, we must remember that the Thessalonian Christians had come out of a background in which sexual freedom and promiscuous indulgence were regarded as natural and to be expected, if not indeed as normal; and practice was in conformity with this idea (see Vol. VII, pp. 81-82). The Jewish people from whom the missionaries had come were a much more moral people both in thinking and conduct; and the specifically Christian requirements were even higher. It is this Christian level of living that the writers here have in mind.

**4-6a.** Two special applications of the general truth are immediately presented. The assumption that advice is needed on these two points suggests that special information had been received through Timothy, either orally or by letter. The first application of the principle is that **each one of you know how to take a wife for himself in holiness and honor** (as apparently some had not; cf. I Cor. 5:1-2; 7:1-7, 36-38). The word translated **wife** (σκεῦος) is the word "vessel." Some older interpreters (e.g., Tertullian, Chrysostom, Calvin) and some moderns (e.g., Stevens, Milligan, R. L. Knox) have believed that the reference is to one's body as his "vessel." Beginning with Augustine, however, many older and most modern interpreters, in company with nearly all modern English translations, adopt the meaning **wife.** The **Gentiles** (KJV; **heathen** RSV) **which know not God** is an O.T. expression describing the pagan peoples whose idolatry was the

---

moral goals must be attained, and Paul again throws behind his exhortation the authority of **the Lord Jesus.**

**3-8.** *The Strength of Ten.*—In these verses Paul states precisely what he means by walking so as "to please God" (vs. 1). He begins by definitely relating morality to religious faith. Christian truth and Christian behavior must walk in step together. **This is the will of God, even your sanctification.**

The Thessalonians cannot be Christians and be sexually loose, says their great leader. Their new faith entails chastity in the unmarried, and fidelity to their vows in the married. This was revolutionary and stern teaching, for the religion from which they had been recently turned had as its center phallic rites. Also, polygamy was the rule rather than the exception, and concubinage was widely prevalent. Immorality was not a matter for shame, rather of pride, for it was a part of the ritual of temple worship.

"In some religious societies sacramental fornication was part of the worship."[3] Thus religion and sexual indulgence were tied together. Vice was a consecrated thing. Paul demanded consecration to holiness. The difficulties of this rigid demand were further increased by the fact that Thessalonica as a cosmopolitan seaport, and as part of a pagan society in which the Christians did their business, reared their families, and found their pleasures, was drenched with sex. But Paul will have no compromise, and backs his demands with three grave reminders: (*a*) Their call is to holiness. "God's plan is to make you holy, and that entails first of all a clean cut with sexual immorality."[4] (*b*) Impurity is a grave sin and the judgment of God is upon it. **The Lord is an avenger in all these things.** (*c*) Impurity in the final analysis is a despisal of God.

3 Neil, *op. cit.,* p. 78.
4 Phillips, *op. cit.,* p. 130.

5 Not in the lust of concupiscence, even as the Gentiles which know not God:

6 That no *man* go beyond and defraud his brother in *any* matter: because that the

and honor, 5 not in the passion of lust like heathen who do not know God; 6 that no man transgress, and wrong his brother in

---

basis of their vicious conduct (see, e.g., Jer. 10:25). Paul reflects the same idea in Rom. 1:21-25; cf. also Eph. 4:17-19. Repudiating all this lustful thinking and living, the Thessalonian disciples, in the spirit of consecration to God and with a feeling of their responsibility to respect and honor the women whom they individually choose to marry, should sanctify the relationship, and not desecrate and degrade it to the level of merely passionate lust.

The second application of the general truth is that a man should not **transgress, and wrong his brother in this matter.** This appears to be an injunction against an adulterous marriage either by taking away from a fellow Christian the wife to whom he is married (cf. I Cor. 5:1), or by committing adultery in violation both of one's own marriage and that of his brother. The fact that the possible wronging of a Christian "brother" is spoken of does not of course open the door to such conduct affecting a non-Christian.

Some great names in biblical interpretation (e.g., Calvin, Lünemann, Dobschütz, Zahn) have held that in vs. 6 the apostle leaves the question of sexual conduct and turns to the realm of **business,** forbidding one to take advantage of or **defraud his brother** (see especially W. A. Stevens, *Commentary on the Epistles to the Thessalonians* [Philadelphia: American Baptist Publication Society, 1890; "American Commentary on the New Testament"], pp. 47-49, and RSV mg.). But the large majority of interpreters, older and recent, think that sexual conduct is still under discussion. The evidence for this view is very strong. Note particularly the summary in vs. 7, which seems to imply all but conclusively that the thought to this point can be summarized in the one contrast— **not . . . for uncleanness, but in holiness.** The fact that such instruction should have been necessary not only when the gospel was preached among the Thessalonians, but again at this time of writing, is an impressive testimony to the challenges which early Christian teachers had to meet. In particular, Thessalonica was a center of the "mysteries" of both Dionysus and the Cabiri (see Intro., p. 246), and the phallic symbolism of both these would be often in evidence. The Thessalonians were not in the dark as to the pertinence of this particular appeal.

---

The moral demands of Paul, the relationship between religious truth and personal conduct, and his three grave reminders are certainly pertinent to our day with its low standards and frank paganism. There is little recognition of what our fathers termed "the exceeding sinfulness of sin." It is neither clearly identified nor feared. It is not merely willful wrongdoing or naughtiness, but something that stains and corrodes the whole nature and throws life out of line. It is the oldest and most terrible mystery of mortal life. Yet despite its menace and destructiveness, there is no general sharp and biting conscience on it, and little realization of its momentousness. We sin easily, and live in terms of our lower urges. We can do wrong, look slyly around, wipe off our lips, and ask, "How does God know?" Something has atrophied inside us.

We further domesticate our conscience by covering up guilt under such fancy names as

"neurosis," "psychosis," "action of the subconscious," "moral delinquency," "maladjustment," "complex," "frustration." But despite all our callousness and evasiveness, guilt will not down. Continually it breaks through our toughness, or rises up before us in all its stark ugliness and fearful consequences. It exposes and condemns our generation as it did Judah.

Judah's sin is printed with a pen of iron,
  with a point of adamant
plain on the tablets of their heart,
  on the very knobs of their altars,
on every spreading tree, upon the heights,
  upon the hills of the open country (Jer. 17:1-2 Moffatt).

Impurity, of which Paul warned the Thessalonians, is one of sin's worst expressions in our time. Many do not consider their bodies as temples of the Holy Ghost (I Cor. 6:19), but live for the thrill of their nerves. Sensation is

Lord *is* the avenger of all such, as we also have forewarned you and testified.

7 For God hath not called us unto uncleanness, but unto holiness.

this matter,*c* because the Lord is an avenger in all these things, as we solemnly forewarned you. 7 For God has not called us for uncleanness, but in holiness. 8 There-

*c* Or *defraud his brother in business.*

6*b*-8. Again, as several times previously (vss. 1-2; 3:4), the apostle refers to the fact that he had given advice and testimony in this matter at an earlier time. He had **solemnly forewarned** that the Lord was **an avenger in all these things.** The words seem to suggest that there had been ample discussion of the whole field of sexual conduct, and that the apostle's point of view was then so new to these new disciples that the instruction had been given with great emphasis and earnestness. Formerly, as again here, the apostle had solemnly impressed upon them that God took account of all such conduct, that it was sinful in his eyes, and that he would require full accounting for it (cf. 3:13). This conception of God is constant in O.T. thinking, and was a part of the religious inheritance of all Jews. Still further, Paul reminds the Thessalonian disciples that God had called them not to the freedom of sexual indulgence, **but in holiness.** Therefore, anyone who sets aside or disregards the truth and the teaching which the missionaries as messengers of God had given is indifferent not simply to some legislation or instruction of man; he is setting aside the will of God himself. It is the God who has given his own **Holy Spirit.** In the joy inspired by the Spirit the Thessalonians had originally received the gospel message of the apostles. In the midst of persecution from their fellows they had, because of their faith, remained steadfast. They must not now set aside the will of the very God whose gospel they have received, whose Spirit has inspired and empowered them and still works within them. God has given his word as the gospel (2:4); as such they have received it (2:13); this teaching is a part of that gospel; abide in it now.

J. E. Frame (*A Critical and Exegetical Commentary on the Epistles of St. Paul to the Thessalonians* [New York: Charles Scribner's Sons, 1912; "International Critical Commentary"], p. 154) identifies the **Lord** who is the **avenger in all these things** with Christ, for "he is the one who inflicts punishment directly or indirectly (cf. II 18)." It seems correct, however, to regard God as the avenging Lord. This is in line with the thinking of the O.T. and of Judaism. II Thess. 1:8 is a part of a total picture presented in 1:5-8, and in this fuller statement God is the judge and arbiter. In Acts 17:30-31 Paul is

the summit of their desire. So chastity, they declare, is old-fashioned and outmoded. Has not nature put within us sex desires? To deny them expression is therefore to create a sense of frustration. To release them is to develop the growth of personality. This specious and false reasoning is the argument of young people who express their adolescent biological pressures in sexual union; in maturer people who are determined to have the physical pleasures of marriage, without its responsibilities; in engaged couples who because of serious matrimonial intentions believe that they may rightly anticipate the marital state, or think it wise to have intercourse to be assured of sexual compatibility; and in married people who indulge in extramarital relations without apology, or rationalize them with a variety of excuses. Every Christian leader with any depth of experience knows that not all such people are outside the Christian churches. The devastating results, both personal

and social, are seen on every hand. Individually there is loss of self-respect or, what is worse, loss of any sense of guilt—the conscience is "seared with a hot iron" (I Tim. 4:2); slyness, because of the secrecy involved in their "affairs"; fear of discovery entailing reproach; often physical and mental ill-health; and frequently disgust and anger with the other involved.

Socially, impurity's most devastating hurt is upon the home. The family is the oldest human social unit. From the beginning "God setteth the solitary in families" (Ps. 68:6). Christianity was given by our Lord in family terms, "Pray then like this: Our Father who art in heaven" (Matt. 6:9). "One is your master . . . ; all ye are brethren" (Matt. 23:8). "Unless you . . . become like children, you will never enter the kingdom of heaven" (Matt. 18:3). It was in a home in Emmaus that Jesus found the conditions and atmosphere wherein he could manifest himself after the Resurrection. It was in the

8 He therefore that despiseth, despiseth not man, but God, who hath also given unto us his Holy Spirit.

9 But as touching brotherly love ye need not that I write unto you: for ye yourselves are taught of God to love one another.

10 And indeed ye do it toward all the brethren which are in all Macedonia: but we beseech you, brethren, that ye increase more and more;

fore whoever disregards this, disregards not man but God, who gives his Holy Spirit to you.

9 But concerning love of the brethren you have no need to have any one write to you, for you yourselves have been taught by God to love one another; 10 and indeed you do love all the brethren thoughout Macedo′nia. But we exhort you, brethren,

---

reported to have told the Athenians explicitly that God would "judge the world in righteousness by a man whom he has appointed," viz., Jesus. The association of God and the Messiah, his chosen, in the judgment was one of the elements of thought in current Judaism, and a part of the inheritance of the apostles. That is almost certainly the thinking here. (See especially Enoch 37–71; cf. George Milligan, *St. Paul's Epistles to the Thessalonians* [London: Macmillan & Co., 1908], pp. lxvii, 51-52.)

9-10. At this point the writers leave the general area of sexual conduct and turn to a series of other practical matters, the first of them being **love of the brethren** (RSV), better, **brotherly love** (KJV; cf. 3:12). This was one of the recognized Christian virtues (Heb. 13:1; I Pet. 1:22; II Pet. 1:7). The word (φιλαδελφία) is almost absent in the Greek of the pre-Christian period, and where found, refers to love for a natural brother. In the N.T. it is always love for a Christian brother (cf. Rom. 12:10; I John 3:14-17). The writers say that there is no need that anyone should write the Thessalonian disciples about such a subject as this, for they themselves had **been taught by God to love one another.** This love was not their natural disposition; they had been "God-taught." The apostle doubtless is thinking of their understanding of their relationship to each other before they accepted the gospel. This love was not theirs before, but it came to them with their Christian experience. It is further remarked that because they have been so **taught by God,** they do in fact **love all the brethren throughout Macedonia.** Thessalonica, being capital and seaport, would naturally have contact with people coming and going all the while; and the new Christians would have many opportunities to manifest their Christian regard. The writers urge upon them that as opportunity may offer, they **do so more and more.** (Note the combination of "brotherly love" and "hospitality" in Heb. 13:1-2.) It is worthy of notice that even at the time of this letter there were **brethren**

---

homes of the early disciples that the Christian congregations were organized. The home is the social unit upon which the church builds, because it exposes the whole range of human personality: the working father, the brooding mother, and the developing child. It is the only enduring and healthy foundation on which national life can be built. No nation has been able to survive its loss. When the family goes, the nation goes. Anglo-Saxon civilization rests upon it. Historically, it is the base upon which the United States has been built, and the unit around which it has revolved. It has been our sanctuary from the hunt of life, our harbor from the storms of life, and the center of our noblest and purest loyalties. It has been the nuclear germinal cell which has provided the dynamic of our national career.

But because of widespread impurity and mari-

tal infidelity, something has happened to the American home. Its permanence and unity are being distorted, as the frequency of divorces and separations prove beyond question. Long-established loyalties are being surrendered, so husbands and wives are discovering they are unfit for the adventure in stanch comradeship and mutual help that marriage demands. The romantic element is dying, so harmony is being broken, enchantment is being destroyed, and something once alive and glad is passing away.

What must the church do to save the people, the home, and the nation? It must (a) emphasize Paul's three truths: the Christian is called to holiness; there is a judgment of God on impurity, which in the final analysis is a despisal of God himself; (b) present fearlessly its position on divorce; (c) teach the necessity of righteousness in national life; (d) center its own

11 And that ye study to be quiet, and to do your own business, and to work with your own hands, as we commanded you;

11 to do so more and more, 11 to aspire to live quietly, to mind your own affairs, and to work with your hands, as we charged you;

---

**throughout Macedonia.** Acts (16:11–17:14) mentions three places in Macedonia (Neapolis, Philippi, Beroea), in addition to Thessalonica, but there must have been others. The precise limits of the region covered by the missionaries at this time cannot be given (cf. above on 1:7-8).

**11-12.** Still another series of three very practical, and, it might seem to us, quite incidental and unrelated matters now receive attention. They are tied in closely with what precedes, as they are included in the preceding main exhortation. On close examination an inner relationship with the manifestation of "brotherly love" (vs. 9) may be seen. The appeal is first that the readers **aspire to live quietly.** In Rom. 15:20 the word here used for **aspire** (φιλοτιμεῖσθαι) is translated "making it my ambition." The word for **live quietly** (ἡσυχάζειν) is found only here in Paul. The related noun is found in II Thess.

---

program in the family; (e) encourage its members to spend more time in the home, make it a center of pleasure, re-erect the family altar, and reoccupy the family pew; (f) hold instructional classes in marriage for its youth.

**11-12. Minding One's Affairs.**—Paul urges three virtues upon the Thessalonians: quietness, attendance to their own affairs, and industry. (a) **Aspire to live quietly.** "Make it your ambition to pursue your ordinary avocations with a quiet mind." [5] If they had been country dwellers, this admonition would have been comparatively easy to practice, for the outer environment might have communicated itself to their inner spirits. But they were dwellers in a rowdy, bustling, largely-populated city, where noise, confusion, and haste were the constant expressions of the community's mood and life. It is a summons to deliberate calmness, peace of mind, disciplined self-control, and inner guidance, achievement of which would be secured only by the spiritual means of prayer, reflection, and regular daily periods of appointed silence. This is a sentence in season for us. We live in a noisy day and in a noisy way. Ruskin spoke of the London of his time as "talking, growling, roaring"—a London that never knew a pneumatic riveter, an overhead train, a twenty-ton truck, a radio's blare, a screaming tire, or a moaning siren. What adjectives would he apply to this day with its blare, screech, yelp, clatter, honk, and mechanized grating activity? We have little sense of repose or inner stillness, for we identify life with motion and so are constantly going from here to there, doing this and that. We are hyperactivists, suffering from the dread disease of doing something always. We are under the lure of speed, ever in a sweaty haste, worshipers at the shrine of the great god "Whirl," and continually breathing hotly down

[5] Peake, *Commentary on the Bible*, p. 878.

the neck of the man ahead of us or under us, saying, "Hurry up," or "Get out of my road."

We also identify life with commotion. Motion is physical; commotion is of the mind. So we suffer explosions, are torn with warring winds, and split by inner divisions. Our souls are storm-swept when misfortune, bereavement, or severe sickness comes upon us. We rebel against God, government, and social groups because of the problems and perplexities which stare so threateningly at us. We are under the harassment of a mosquito swarm of impending duties, are nervous, restless, and distracted. We are also very vocal, which is not to say we are either articulate or reasonable. We have too much to say and too little to tell.

As indicated above, there are several ways by which quietness can be secured. There is an additional one, and perhaps the most useful of all—deliberate reflection on, and contemplation of, the quietness of God. Think of its expression in the physical nature around us. There God rings no bell, beats no drum, blows no trumpet. He is not heard in the great and strong winds which rend the mountains, or in the quakes which make the earth shift and stagger like a drunken man, or in the lightning fires that flash out of the thunder clouds, but in "a still small voice" (I Kings 19:11-12). When last did we hear the footsteps of the approaching dawn or evening? The sound of the rising or setting of the sun? The changing phases of the moon? The cycles of the seasons? The ebbing and flowing of the mighty tides? What values would come to us if we possessed true quietness! We would have a greater knowledge of God, for he demands silence in us if we are to know him (Ps. 46:10). We would have a nobler dignity, for how often we have lost it in garrulousness and protestation. We would have greater knowledge, for philosophy and wisdom are bred in

12 That ye may walk honestly toward them that are without, and *that* ye may have lack of nothing.

12 so that you may command the respect of outsiders, and be dependent on nobody.

---

3:12. The verb is used but few times in the N.T. (twice in Luke, twice in Acts, and here) and is variously translated. It seems always to carry the idea of controlled quietness. Secondly, there is the injunction not to be busybodies interfering with the affairs of others but to **mind your own affairs** (cf. II Thess. 3:11). Further, they are enjoined **to work with your hands.** Paul himself had not only given them such an example (2:9; II Thess. 3:7-8); he had also, when first among them, charged them to do likewise. In view of the reference here to this original instruction, and the attention which is given the matter in the second letter (3:9-12), it is evident that the problem was a persistent one. Some among them were disposed to become idlers—turbulent and meddlesome. In consequence, they created a very unfavorable impression upon outsiders. This affected adversely the standing of the entire church in the community. It is important that they

---

the stillness of the spirit. We would have deeper understanding and insight, for these come only to the quiet heart which waits and searches for them.

If our vociferous and loquacious generation could be quiet, it might take its first step away from the fields of battle with their clangor and shoutings and move along the road which leads to peace and friendship. The citizens of the ancient city of Shechem had a traditional belief that in the silence of the night there could be heard the fascinating music of the deeply buried streams flowing under the city. Let us aspire to live quietly, so that we may hear and be helped by the deep things which belong to our peace.

(*b*) **Mind your own affairs.** There is a question as to what or whom Paul is after here. Was the church being pestered by a few busybodies who felt it was their inalienable right to manage the affairs of other members, or was he laying down a principle for happy usefulness in living? Some scholars are of the opinion that because of belief in the near return of Christ, the Christians were neglecting their regular daily work and spending their time looking up into the heavens expecting them to open, or chattering about the whys, wherefores, and whens of the tremendous event.[6] But while this idea may have been in the back of Paul's mind, in its forefront was his desire to see the Thessalonian Christians not only examples of pure living and brotherly affection, but outstanding in modest self-effacement and strict attention to their daily business.

In one sense the Christian's business is the other man's business. We believe it is our appointed duty to say something on his behalf if he is being exploited, tyrannized, tempted, or corrupted. Yet it is so easy to become a busybody: to serve on too many committees, get

involved in too many activities, be concerned about what other people are doing, spend a good portion of our time setting others to rights, and telling them how to do their work and conduct their lives. Moffatt speaks of man's busy life becoming "an empty ado" (Ps. 39:6). It is so easy, but the results are so dreadfully calamitous. The story of the busybody is nowhere better illustrated than in the familiar story told in I Kings 20. The unknown prophet relates it in the first person. No other words can match his: "Thy servant went out into the midst of the battle; and, behold, a man turned aside, and brought a man unto me, and said, Keep this man: if by any means he be missing, then shall thy life be for his life, or else thou shalt pay a talent of silver. And as thy servant was busy here and there, he was gone" (I Kings 20:39-40). "He was gone." If we are busybodies, what do we lose? (i) Opportunities for service and friendship. Flitting here and there, and having time only for temporary influence and casual acquaintanceship, we but touch the surface of events and people. No depths are penetrated; no enduring results are achieved. Our hearts are good. We fully intend really to help this good cause or that piece of community work which clamors for someone to take hold of it, and we do mean to sit down with our neighbor who is in deep trouble, but we just cannot find the time, for we have so many other irons in the fire. What happens? We lose opportunities of service and affection. (ii) Our finest ideals. Most busybodies are basically fine persons. They want to be of help, but their overcuriosity causes them to lose their sense of true values. The busybody sooner or later discovers that the things by which he is living are small and foolish. The greater ideals always steal or fade away when we take our eyes off, or are too busy to attend them. (iii) Our Christian witness. Chris-

---

[6] Neil, *Epistle of Paul to Thessalonians*, p. 87.

walk in a way that will **command the respect of outsiders.** It appears also from the closing words in the paragraph that some of them had, because of their idleness, become **dependent** upon others for daily sustenance (cf. Eph. 4:28). The Thessalonian disciples must remove entirely all such stigmas. If they will do as they are so earnestly advised, they will be **dependent on nobody.** The KJV reads **nothing** and is followed by Bible Union and Twentieth Century translations. Some of both the older and the most recent interpreters support this view. The Greek word (μηδενός) may be either masculine or neuter. It is true that the neuter is more frequent than the masculine and that it is more natural to say "have need of nothing" than "have need of nobody." Still, that which would be supplied to meet the need would have to come from somebody, of whom they might then be said to have need, and most recent translations and some interpreters think the rendering **nobody** is preferable.

The first section of exhortation ends here. It has been concerned with very practical injunctions having to do with the standards of Christian living as these were involved in certain specific areas of life. The areas particularly mentioned were those of sexual conduct, brotherly relations with one another, tranquillity of mind, the prevalent disposition to become idlers and busybodies and to depend, not upon their own work, but upon help from others. The Thessalonian Christians are enjoined to correct all these faults in order to give to the public a more favorable impression of the general character and spirit of the group. They should become examples of good, wholesome, and worthy living.

---

tianity is faith in a person, which produces a certain quality of life. It was said of the early Christians that they were new creatures (II Cor. 5:17), the moral transformation in them was so definite and pronounced. They did all things in the light of the mind of Christ, so they were also "new creatures" as they worked in the field, labored by the bench, or toiled in the bazaar. Their occupations gave them a signal opportunity for demonstrating their new faith's inspiration to thoroughness, concentration, and assiduous work. So their fellow workmen as well as their fellow citizens took knowledge that they had been with Jesus. This is the kind of witness every Christian should, but unfortunately does not, always have. There is no greater occasion for the exercise of influence than is given to the Christian mechanic at his bench, the Christian stenographer at her desk, the Christian housewife in her home, the Christian banker in his office, the Christian doctor in the sickroom, or the Christian politician in the hall of legislation. In the place of their labors they are known and read of all. But suppose they become busybodies, as all too many professors of Christianity do, with inevitable loss of efficiency, garrulousness, interference in others' affairs, and fussers over little matters. What happens? Personal respect goes, regard for what they say departs, and their Christian witness is surrendered. (iv) Our Christian faith. Religion is generally lost through lack of cultivation. The busybody in the beginning may possess it, but he cannot long retain it, for its development requires certain attitudes, peri-

ods of quietness, and consecutive study. But his mien is not that of love but criticism, and his time is largely spent talking about the affairs of others or running between points. The flame of faith has to be carefully guarded, like that which the Russian pilgrims formerly kindled at the Holy Sepulcher and then carried back across many leagues and through wind and weather to light the lamps before the icons in their humble homes. Few things will extinguish it more quickly than attending to everybody's business but our own.

(c) **Work with your hands.** This challenges industry and concentration. God has given each of us a definite assignment, out of which ought to come a definite sense of destiny. Jesus had this when as a lad he said to his parents, "Wist ye not that I must be about my Father's business?" (Luke 2:49). Paul had this when he thrust aside the things which would deflect him with the dedicatory words, "This one thing I do" (Phil. 3:13). Michelangelo had it as he worked with single and unremitting energy on the Sistine Chapel. Hideyo Noguchi, the son of Japanese peasants, who became one of the world's greatest bacteriologists, had this when he wrote, "I have no leisure morning or night, and all night I break my bones writing the record of the day." His fellow workers called him "the twenty-four-hour man." [7] At all times and places we can constantly tend the piece of business in life God has given us to do.

[7] R. M. Bartlett, *They Dared to Live* (New York: Association Press, 1937), pp. 2-3.

| 13 But I would not have you to be ig-nard, brethren, concerning them which are asleep, that ye sorrow not, even as others which have no hope. | 13 But we would not have you ignorant, brethren, concerning those who are asleep, that you may not grieve as others do who |

---

## B. Concerning Those Who Have Fallen Asleep (4:13-18)

At this point the writers move over into a very different phase of discussion. They now proceed to give instruction upon a matter about which they apparently had received an inquiry. The particular problem is that of the destiny of Thessalonian Christians who have already fallen asleep in death. We have no information concerning the way the problem arose except what is implied in this paragraph. So far as we can recover the situation, the Thessalonian Christians had in general anticipated sharing in the blessings which would come with the arrival of the Lord "from heaven" (1:10; 2:12, 19; 3:13). It appears that after Paul had left them, some of the disciples had passed away. This had raised the question of the relation of the dead in Christ to the expected parousia. Paul's answer is that those who have passed away will share equally with those who are still alive at the coming of the Lord.

**13.** At no point in the paragraph do the writers say that they had previously given instruction upon this point; apparently they had not done so, or the problem would not have arisen so sharply. However, they now wish to make very clear the truth in order that the **brethren** may not sorrow concerning **those who are asleep,** as do those **who have no hope.** "Those who are sleeping" would be an accurate translation of the approved reading in this verse; it suggests both the temporary nature of the sleep, and the vivid

---

**4:13-18. Hope Rises on Exulting Wings.—** This passage and the one following (5:1-11) cannot be separated, for they are two halves of a block of eschatological truth. Both raise a vital issue (4:13; 5:1). Both present an answer (4:14-17; 5:2-10). Both conclude with an admonishment to the Thessalonians to comfort one another (4:18; 5:11).

Here the issue is obscured for the average reader and the whole passage made difficult because of Paul's vivid description of the manner of the parousia. The end of the world has come. The clouds of the sky open and the Lord descends **with a cry of command, with the archangel's call, and with the sound of the trumpet of God** (vs. 16). There is a dramatic opening of the graves of the Christian dead, their resurrection, and startling levitation into the clouds. Simultaneously, the living Christians are swept off the earth, there is a joint and rapturous meeting of both of them with the Lord in the air, and an eternal union with him in glory begins (vss. 17-18).

The Christian theology of the first century was built around belief in the speedy return of the Lord, and the early Christians assumed that all who accepted him and received the Spirit would take part in the blessed event. This hope sustained them in their tribulations, nourished their courage, and refreshed their hearts. In its power they faced their bitter trials with quiet faith. It was the morning star in their dark

sky. But the Lord did not come. Time passed and no trumpet of God sounded. They were still being oppressed and harried. The haughty and evil kings of the earth were still on their thrones. So their hearts began to fail and their minds to be disturbed because of two things. First, the inevitable scoffing of the pagans and Jews around them, who ridiculed the Christian hope and pointed out that things were going on just as they always had. If their Christ was going to come, why did he not come when their need was so great? Second, and more important, some of their number had died. What was to happen to them? Had God withdrawn their election? Would they just lie in the ground as the pagans expected to do? Or would they have a glorious resurrection and have part in the parousia? If so, what would be the order of precedence? Would the dead precede the living or vice versa?

These six verses are a glorious reassurance to the troubled. Paul's absolute certainty is that all who die **in Christ** remain **in Christ** (vs. 16) forever, and will therefore have their share in the Second Advent. He undergirds this truth with the rising of Jesus Christ as the validation and guarantee of the resurrection of the saints (vs. 14).

This paragraph has much to say to us in this day. (a) A great man can be in error. Paul was firmly convinced that Jesus would return during his lifetime. This was a tremendous dynamic to him as a missionary and evangelist, for it was his

14 For if we believe that Jesus died and rose again, even so them also which sleep in Jesus will God bring with him.

have no hope. 14 For since we believe that Jesus died and rose again, even so, through Jesus, God will bring with him those who

---

expectation of the "return" of the Lord Jesus. The use of the term "sleep" for death is not intended as a description of the state of the dead. It is a term found in classical Greek writers and other writers who had no particular views as to the state of the dead, and did not believe in resurrection. It was rather a well-known euphemism for death, common in Judaism; and of course it fits well into the thought of Paul and his fellow workers who believe that those who have passed in faith into death shall be raised unto life. Besides this passage, the expression is used five times in I Corinthians (7:39; 11:30; 15:6, 18, 51). It is recorded also as a term used by Jesus (John 11:11), and is found in the book of Acts (7:60; 13:36) and II Peter (3:4). Those **who have no hope** and the "outsiders" of vs. 12 belong to the same general class. They are those who have not come to faith in the Lord Jesus, and consequently are living in the hopelessness of most pagans of the day (cf. Eph. 2:12).

14. It is here affirmed that the resurrection of the believers in Jesus is also involved in the resurrection of Jesus. **If we believe that Jesus died and rose again,** then we may fully and firmly believe in the resurrection of his followers. The form of the Greek sentence—**if we believe** . . . (KJV)—indicates that the condition named is fulfilled. **Since we believe** . . . (RSV) gives the real meaning of the sentence. Such was not only the belief of the early church, but in I Cor. 15:3-5 Paul affirms that it was, literally, "among firsts" preached by him and certain apostolic preachers before him. In I Cor. 15:14-18 he affirms that if the resurrection of Jesus is not true, then there is no gospel at all. Men would in such case be hopeless and miserable. That the **we** who **believe** includes the Thessalonian Christians, though not specifically said, is clearly implied (cf. vs. 13); it is also involved in the statement of 1:10. It is the "living and true God" to whom these new disciples had turned (1:9), who also had raised Jesus from the dead. It is he who is to bring with Jesus those who sleep in him. This, say the writers, is the real basis and ground of our hope—**If we believe** [as we all do] . . . **even so** . . . . The phrase **through Jesus** (RSV; **in Jesus**—KJV) is difficult and has occasioned a variety of opinion. The KJV takes the phrase with **sleep,** reading **them also which sleep in Jesus.** This has the support of the ERV and the ASV, Bible Union Version, the Twentieth Century N.T., and R. L. Knox (from Vulg.); also Chrysostom and the Greek fathers, Calvin, Luther, and many moderns (Lightfoot, Weizsäcker, Stevens, Findlay, Milligan, Frame; see

---

hope personally to present to God the members of the churches he had formed (Col. 1:28); they were to be his crowning glory in the presence of his Lord (2:19). He was wrong in this and changed his views as the years passed. Yet he tenaciously clung to the conviction that the parousia was near at hand (Rom. 13:11; I Cor. 16:22). He was also wrong in this. Still hoping for the coming, he was later forced to accept the possibility that death might cut him down before his hope was fulfilled (Phil. 1:20-25).

Flexibility and humility of mind are qualities all of us can cultivate. To be willing to change a viewpoint on the evidence of incontrovertible facts, and say, "I was wrong," is a very great virtue. It is only thus we can grow in heart and mind. The "meek" are to inherit the earth (Matt. 5:5). The Hebrew word for "meek" connotes "being molded": placing one's self under

the divine will for instruction and in ready obedience. How little there is of this willingness to learn! Our views are formed and opinions set. We can be told—but not much. The streams of new knowledge lap against our mind, but find no entrance. This unteachable spirit both the Bible and history warn against by precept and example. The sage of Proverbs said:

Cease not, my son, to listen to instruction,
and never turn away from a wise teacher (Prov. 19:27 Moffatt).

Paul's mighty mind was a growing mind because it was ever learning and receiving from all quarters. The brooding and humble-minded Abraham Lincoln has left us a noble example in deed and speech. "The dogmas of the past are inadequate to the stormy present. The occasion

15 For this we say unto you by the word of the Lord, that we which are alive *and* remain unto the coming of the Lord shall not prevent them which are asleep.

15 For this we declare to you by the word of the Lord, that we who are alive, who are left until the coming of the Lord, shall not precede those who have fallen asleep.

---

especially Frame's discussion, *Commentary on the Epistles to the Thessalonians, ad loc.*). The RSV reads **through Jesus, God will bring with him those who have fallen asleep.** This reading is supported by Goodspeed, Moffatt, Montgomery, Weymouth, and Verkuyl. The Greek text is ambiguous. Grammatically it may be read either way. The balance of the sentence suggests the construction of the KJV; but that introduces a difficult thought. "Asleep, through Jesus"—what does it mean? Some would make it the essential equivalent of "dead in Christ" (vs. 16) and "those who have died [fallen asleep] in Christ" in I Cor. 15:18 (cf. II Cor. 5:6-8). Kirsopp Lake (*The Earlier Epistles of St. Paul* [London: Rivingtons, 1914], p. 88) thinks the words must be placed with "sleeping" and suggests, with 2:15 in mind, that the reference is to those who have been martyred for their faith. Ellicott thinks the construction "must remain an open question." If we follow the RSV, we have the support of I Cor. 6:14 and II Cor. 4:14, the latter being the closer in thought to the statement here. This interpretation is more nearly in line with what Paul says elsewhere.

The main thought of the passage is clear, whatever precise relation and consequent meaning may be assigned to this phrase. The blessings which came with the Resurrection belong to those who have in faith given their life to Christ.

**15.** At this point the apostle moves on to support the statement about the participation of "those asleep" in the coming of the Lord with a message which has come to him as a **word of the Lord.** Some have thought this means a word found in the Gospels; others, that it refers to a special revelation from the Lord to Paul (e.g., Chrysostom, Ellicott, Lightfoot, Findlay, Milligan, Moffatt); and still others, that it refers to a word which has been transmitted to Paul as a part of the Christian tradition which had its basis in the teaching of the Lord Jesus (e.g., Calvin, Frame). This last view seems to be supported by the general character of the discussion of that Christian tradition in these two letters (see II Thess. 2:15; 3:6).

The first part of Paul's answer is that those who are alive and are left at the time of the parousia shall not anticipate or **precede those who have fallen asleep.** It may be observed that Paul, Silvanus, and Timothy here assume the parousia as needing to be neither defined nor defended (cf. 3:13). They and the Thessalonians together take

---

is piled high with difficulty and we must rise to the occasion. As our case is new, so must we think anew and act anew. We must disenthrall ourselves and then we shall save our country."[8] The wise man is the teachable man, and so is a clean channel for the transmission of the life and wisdom of God.

(*b*) Nothing can separate us from the love of Christ. In vs. 16 the noble Pauline phrase **in Christ,** which is sprinkled through all his epistles, again is used. Greater to him is this doctrine of mystical union with Christ than those of justification, reconciliation, and sanctification. It is the keystone of his whole theological arch. His heart and mind swell and glow as he meditates upon the heights and depths of this sustaining and inspiring truth, and his whole religion comes to its focus in such luminous texts as "We . . . are one body in Christ" (Rom. 12:5); "You are wise in Christ" (I Cor. 4:10); "It is no longer I who live, but Christ who lives in me" (Gal. 2:20); "In Christ shall all be made alive" (I Cor. 15:22); "There is therefore now no condemnation for those who are in Christ Jesus" (Rom. 8:1); "He who is united to the Lord becomes one spirit with him" (I Cor. 6:17); "If any one is in Christ, he is a new creation" (II Cor. 5:17). For Paul believes that the Christian can have a communion with the Lord of the most vital and immediate nature, of such a kind indeed that Christ can live in him and he in Christ. This to Paul is "the fulness of the blessing of Christ" (Rom. 15:29), the alpha and omega of the faith. It was also the truth he emphasized and re-emphasized to the Thessalonian and other churches. No less than

[8] Quoted in Halford E. Luccock, *The Haunted House* (New York: Abingdon Press, 1923), pp. 148-49.

16 For the Lord himself shall descend from heaven with a shout, with the voice | have fallen asleep. 16 For the Lord himself will descend from heaven with a cry of

---

it for granted. This term was commonly employed among Greek writers to refer to the expected visit or arrival of some person in a particular locality. It is so used by Paul a half dozen times (I Cor. 16:17; II Cor. 7:6-7; 10:10; Phil. 1:26; 2:12). The papyri show that the word was often used in a special sense to refer to the visit of an official or some other prominent personage. This usage in the empire in the time of Paul furnishes ample and easy basis for the use of it with reference to the "coming" both of the "man of sin" (II Thess. 2:9) and of the Lord Jesus Christ (2:19; 3:13; 5:23; II Thess. 2:1, 8; I Cor. 15:23). At no point is any explanation of the term offered; it needed no explanation to any Greek-speaking person of that day, any more than we need to explain the word "visit" to any English-speaking person. How it could be applied to Jesus, and what it meant in connection with him, were the points that needed to be made clear. So far as we can know, Paul was the first one to use the word with reference to Jesus, but it became an accepted term in the church. (It is found in Jas. 5:7-8; Matt. 24:3, 27, 37, 39; I John 2:28; and II Pet. 1:16; 3:4, 12. Comparison of Matthew [24:3] with Mark [13:1-4] and Luke [21:5-7] in their reports of the final eschatological discourse of Jesus suggests that the term is here Matthew's; it was not used by Jesus.) No elaborate explanation of the coming of the Lord is given here. From 1:10 it is clear that Paul had so amply presented his conception of this event when he was first preaching among the Thessalonians that it had become a very central element in their faith and hope for the future. This is implied also by the frequent casual references to the matter in these letters.

The writers now proceed to indicate why those who will be living will not **precede** (in 1611 **prevent** [KJV] had this meaning) **those who have fallen asleep.** These last words are a single Greek word in a form almost impossible to transfer to English. Included are those not simply who had fallen asleep at the time of the writing of the letter, but who would have fallen asleep at the time of the parousia. That this would be soon is not here or anywhere else said explicitly; but such an expectation is evident from many passages in the N.T. Paul apparently expected to be alive at the time.

**16. For the Lord himself will descend from heaven. . . . And the dead in Christ will rise first:** This does not mean, as is sometimes thought, that the dead in Christ shall rise before the dead out of Christ shall rise, but that the dead in Christ shall rise prior to other events in connection with his coming. The thought is not related to that of Rev.

---

164 times does "in Christ," or some cognate expression such as "in the Lord," "in him," "through him," appear in his epistles.[9] No condition or bitter experience can daunt the believer who has this relationship with his Lord.

The saints in Caesar's household illustrate this truth. They lived in a citadel of sin, in perils of the city and of betrayal, in painfulness and weariness, yet through Christ they were "more than conquerors" (Rom. 8:37). We need this sense of oneness with Christ. In the great play, *Green Pastures,* as God discusses the forthcoming flood, he says to Noah, "De levees is gonter bust an' everything dat's fastened down is comin' loose."[1] This is a flashlight picture of our time. Loose morals, loose religion, loose

homes, loose politics, loose friendships—personal and national—and loose literature. Vast militarized, mechanized, and materialized powers in both the eastern and western areas of the earth are threatening the very life of mankind. It is grimly said that the future of the world is a blood bath and a fiery furnace. The only hope lies in Jesus Christ—his saving power and his kingdom mediated through his disciples. But are we **in Christ?** Are we doing things "through him" in the mystical union of which Paul so frequently writes? Is he the master light of all our seeing, the power of all our days, the forgiver of all our sins, the hope of all our future years? Until we are so sure of this that we can truly say, "It is no longer I who live, but Christ who lives in me" (Gal. 2:20), there is no true hope for either ourselves or the world. "In him" we need not be afraid of the human situa-

9 Stewart, *A Man in Christ*, p. 155.
1 New York: Farrar & Rinehart, 1929, Part I, scene 8, p. 69.

of the archangel, and with the trump of
God: and the dead in Christ shall rise first:

command, with the archangel's call, and
with the sound of the trumpet of God.

---

20:1-10. Following the rising of the dead, then **we who are alive, who are left, shall be caught up together with them.** The dead shall be raised and they with the then living shall **together . . . meet the Lord in the air.**

This is the essence of the message which the evangelists have to give to these Thessalonian Christians. However, with this are included certain incidental statements which are distinctive and in part unparalleled. First of all, it is said the Lord shall come **with a cry of command, with the archangel's call.** The word for **cry of command** is found only here in the N.T. and is very rare in the LXX. It was used in classical Greek to indicate a command from a general, or a call or summons given by some official. It is the latter idea that is the more prominent here—a call to the dead. There is some uncertainty as to whether this call is independent of the **voice of the archangel,** and the **sound of the trumpet,** or whether these phrases explain the method by which the call is made. The thought is not expressed elsewhere in Paul's letters. But in view of John 5:25, 28, we are probably to think of the summons as that of Christ himself (cf. John 11:45). If so, **the voice of the archangel** is the second accompaniment of the coming. There is an elaborately developed angelology in the Judaism from which Paul came. It had its background in the O.T., particularly in the later books (see especially Zech. 1:2, 14, 19; 4:1-6, 10-14; 5:1-11; Dan. 4:13, 23; 6:22; 7:10). It is elaborated with much detail in the literature of Judaism beginning in the pre-Christian period and running down into the early Christian centuries. It overflows into the N.T. and was a part of the thought background of early Christianity (especially Matt. 13:39, 41, 49; 16:27; 25:31; Mark 8:38; 13:27; Luke 9:26). In all of these passages the angels are associated with the coming of the Lord.

The conception of archangels was a specialized phase of angelology which in Paul's day had had a marked development. It may further be noted that throughout the entire literature of Judaism, wherever the names of the archangels are given, that of Michael always appears. In literature nearly contemporaneous with Paul, Michael is "the chief of the angelic hierarchy," who blows his trumpet and calls the angels to assemble and hear the judgment that God is to pronounce. Michael appears in the N.T. in two passages: in Rev. 12:7 as the leader of a host of angels who with him had cast Satan and his angels out of heaven; in Jude 9 as the "archangel" who disputed with the devil concerning the

---

tion, for he is redeemer of principalities, and of evil powers he can make an open show. Lift up your hearts!

(c) Christianity is the religion of hope. The simple and great truth about the religion of Jesus is hope. That is why it is the gospel—good news. Its declarations are creative and positive. Its emphasis is not sin but grace, not punishment but pardon, not judgment but mercy, not defeat but victory, not death but life, not the temporal but the eternal. The center and ground of this exulting hope is the resurrection truth of which Paul speaks (vs. 14).

In the two thousand years of its history the church has had many differences within itself. It has differed on the nature of God, the person of Christ, the time and manner of his return, the work of the Holy Spirit, the inspiration of the Scriptures, marriage and sacrifice, the Lord's

Supper; but faith in the fact of the Resurrection has been the very essence of Christian belief. Latitude of thought on the other elements of Christianity has been permissible, but none on this. If Christ is not risen, Christian teaching is useless, Christian hope is vain, and we are of all men the most miserable (I Cor. 15:19). We may refuse to eat, drink, and be merry yet after all we shall die as the beasts of the field, and our burial will be like the burial of an ass. But Christ is risen indeed! He is alive now! He does not belong to the past. Neither is he a character in a book of history, a voice whispering out of yesterday, nor an influence once upon a time vigorous and relevant, but now unfelt. He lives now, speaks now, inspires now, redeems now! The indestructible perennial of the ages travels in the greatness of his strength, mighty to save and strong to deliver. He was dead, but

17 Then we which are alive *and* remain shall be caught up together with them in the clouds, to meet the Lord in the air: and so shall we ever be with the Lord.

And the dead in Christ will rise first; 17 then we who are alive, who are left, shall be caught up together with them in the clouds to meet the Lord in the air; and so we shall

---

body of Moses. The suggestion lies close at hand that in the reference to the archangel here Paul has in mind this same identification. This view is frequently expressed, but of course cannot be stated with certainty. Milligan (*St. Paul's Epistles to the Thessalonians,* p. 59) doubts whether any identification is in Paul's mind.

It is further affirmed that the Lord will come with **the trumpet of God.** This same statement is made in I Cor. 15:52, and the thought is found also in Matt. 24:31. The evidence is very ample that **the sound of the trumpet** was a feature of the events of the day of the Lord in the centuries-long tradition of the Jews. The idea is recurrently present in the O.T. (Isa. 27:13; Zeph. 1:16; Joel 2:1; Zech. 9:14). It is found in the literature of Judaism, both before and after the day of Paul. It was included in the tenth of the "Eighteen Benedictions" (Shemoneh Esreh), a part of the daily Jewish prayer ritual. This reads, "Blow the great trumpet for our liberation, and lift a banner to gather our exiles, and gather us into one body from the four corners of the earth; blessed be thou, O Lord, who gathereth the dispersed of thy people." The idea is carried over into Christian tradition and appears in elaboration in the book of Revelation. It is clear that we have here a Judaeo-Christian eschatological conception, which Paul is simply carrying forward as a part of his heritage in the "traditions of my fathers" (Gal. 1:14); it was also part of that tradition which had come down from the Christian preaching prior to his own ministry, and to which he was closely related (I Cor. 15:3-5).

With the accompaniments thus set forth, **the Lord himself will descend from heaven.** This point had been part of the message which had been originally preached to the Thessalonians and they had made it a part of their hope (see 1:10; cf. II Thess. 1:7; see also Acts 1:11; 3:21; Eph. 6:9; Col. 4:1; Heb. 8:1). The dead shall rise at his coming and his call. G. G. Findlay (*The Epistles of Paul the Apostle to the Thessalonians* [Cambridge: University Press, 1904; "Cambridge Greek Testament"], pp. 100-1) thinks that the "sleeping saints" will have already been raised and will come with the Lord. But in I Cor. 15:52 it is explicitly said that "the trumpet will sound, and the dead shall be raised incorruptible, and we shall be changed." Both resurrection and transformation are to take place in connection with the sounding of **the trumpet** that heralds the coming of the Lord.

**17-18.** Following this rising of **the dead in Christ, then we who are alive . . . shall be caught up together with them in the clouds.** No exact parallel to this thought is

---

behold he is alive forevermore. He is the son of God with power by the resurrection from the dead. This is the gospel the world needs today, for it is the gospel of hope, the gospel of the living Christ, whose creative power can lift man to new levels and charge him with new energies.

(*d*) The Christian's attitude to death. **That you may not grieve as others do who have no hope** (vs. 13). The scientist looks at death and sees it as a part of nature's indispensable process whereby the worn-out, ill-fitting parts are removed from the machinery of this ongoing human life of ours. The biologist scrutinizes it and declares it to be a natural phenomenon without character. A person is born, lives, dies, and that is the story. The philosopher concentrates his trained mind upon it and cannot think of it

apart from the nature of the universe in which life exists. He therefore sees in death something more than the removal of a used or weak part or a piece of flesh which has pulsed with vigor for a few years and then faded out through weakness or disease. His mind goes beyond those conditions and declares that man is greater than the sum of his parts and that in a moral universe death simply cannot have the last word. The Christian looks at death and strides ahead of the scientist, biologist, and philosopher. To him, sin and death are in some strange way related; but Christ has conquered both. The triumph over sin on Calvary was completed in the Resurrection by the triumph over death. And in these victories the Christian already shares.

Thus out of the resurrection hope comes a

**18** Wherefore comfort one another with these words. | always be with the Lord. **18** Therefore comfort one another with these words.

---

found in the O.T. or N.T. However, the clouds as mediums of translation to heaven are found in Acts 1:9; Rev. 11:12. The coming of the Lord "on the clouds" or "in the clouds" is reflected as a part of the early Christian thinking (Matt. 24:30; 26:64; Mark 13:26; 14:62; Luke 21:27; Rev. 14:14-16). The disciples heard a voice out of the cloud at the Transfiguration (Matt. 17:5; Mark 9:7; Luke 9:35). II Kings 2:11 speaks of the going up of Elijah in a somewhat similar way.

**To meet the Lord in the air** is a statement not elsewhere known. It seems to imply that the Lord will not himself actually reach the earth but will remain in the air and call the saints to his side. Having in mind the statement of the N.T., occurring about two dozen times, concerning the exaltation of Christ "at the right hand of God"; having in mind further the common conception of "the heavens above," and the "third heaven," where Paul heard that which it was not possible to utter (II Cor. 12:1-4); recalling also Acts 3:21 that "the heaven must receive" the Lord Jesus "until the times of restitution"— in view of all this we are doubtless to see here a reflection of the fact that the apostles are thinking of the heavens as the abode of Christ, as they were of God (cf. Enoch 24; 39–41; 46). The word **meet** is found in the papyri in the sense of an official welcome. In this instance it is the Lord who extends the welcome.

The outcome of all this statement is that both the living who have been "changed," and the dead who have been raised "incorruptible," shall thenceforth and **always be with the Lord.** Neither living nor dead shall be at disadvantage. They shall share alike in the glory and blessing of the parousia. This section contains several items not elsewhere found, but still it is not in either intention or fact a complete presentation of Paul's view. The effort to bring it into line with what is said elsewhere by the apostle and by others should be carefully made, lest we wrest these words and make them express ideas which were wholly absent from the minds of the writers.

This "word of the Lord" is given by the apostle and his fellow writers that the Thessalonian disciples "may not grieve" (vs. 13), but may indeed rejoice in their new hope. Paul's final injunction is that they **comfort one another** with the message they have received. For a strikingly different message one may compare the second-century papyrus letter, often quoted, which having spoken of the death of a friend, continues: "But still there is nothing anyone can do about these things. Hence, comfort yourselves."

---

new attitude to death. Neil rightly points out that Paul's statement **others . . . have no hope** is too inclusive.

Plato taught immortality, the Pharisees believed in the resurrection of the body, and the worshippers of the various mystery religions . . . were guaranteed victory over death. [Paul] is speaking presumably particularly of the rank and file of ordinary pagan working folk of the same social background as the Christians.[2]

The average pagan had a dread of death. There was a deep-rooted fear of "the long sleep." Unafraid of his enemy in savage battle, and bearing his wounds in stoical silence, he had an unutterable horror of the last great enemy, the king of terrors, the final and inevitable happening. It was against the historic fear which had

[2] *Epistle of Paul to Thessalonians,* pp. 92-93.

ruled the lives of their forebears, and theirs until their conversion to Christ, that Paul warns this little group.

This pagan fear still exists. Many modern funerals are evidence of it; instead of being evidences of faith they are revelations of atheism, for that is what fear of death is. The Christian, like other people, is human, and therefore has his feelings. When a loved one dies, he of necessity grieves, but it is not for the departed he should weep. This truth is often forgotten, and many so-called Christian burials are scenes of gloom, despair, and sobbing. The gospel of the Resurrection ought to deliver us as it did the early Christians. Christ was and is the risen Christ, who "brought life and immortality to light through the gospel" (II Tim. 1:10), and thereby the grave has been robbed of its victory and death of its sting. Alleluia!

5 But of the times and the seasons, breth-ren, ye have no need that I write unto you.

2 For yourselves know perfectly that the day of the Lord so cometh as a thief in the night.

5 But as to the times and the seasons, brethren, you have no need to have any-thing written to you. 2 For you yourselves know well that the day of the Lord will

---

## C. CONCERNING THE SUDDEN COMING OF THE DAY OF THE LORD (5:1-11)

At first glance the discussion now seems to shift to a very different focus from that in the immediately preceding paragraph. But closer reading of the two indicates a close logical connection. The **day of the Lord** just mentioned as the time of the consummation of all hopes is carried forward. The uncertainty of the Thessalonian disciples as to the participation of those "fallen asleep" in the consummation at the "coming" of the Lord very naturally leads on to the question: To what may the rest of us look forward? How soon may the Lord be expected? Unless the day comes soon, are we all to be disappointed? This paragraph speaks to that question.

**5:1-3.** First of all, the Thessalonians are reminded that they really have no need that anything shall be said about "times and seasons." **You yourselves know well that the day of the Lord will come like a thief in the night.** No indication is given as to how they have come to this knowledge. The Spirit of God might teach them how to live (4:9), but would scarcely have been expected to inform them thus factually. It has been suggested that Paul is quoting the words of the Thessalonians to him, "Tell us precisely [ἀκριβῶς]." Findlay (*Epistles of Paul to Thessalonians*, p. 108) thinks that Paul may have been speaking in irony, and in effect saying, "You know precisely that we cannot know precisely." It is more probable, however, that Paul, as elsewhere in the letters to the Thessalonians, is referring to his own teachings when he was with them (3:4; 4:2; II Thess. 2:5; 3:10). That he had discussed the parousia at Thessalonica is also implied by their waiting for God's Son from heaven (1:10). The matter of **the times and the seasons** would certainly have been mentioned.

The coming of the Lord is like the coming of **a thief in the night** only as regards its suddenness and unexpectedness. The same comparison is reported as a part of the teaching of Jesus (Matt. 24:43-44; Luke 12:39-40; cf. also Mark 13:28-37; Matt. 24:32-42; Luke 21:29-33), taken up by the church (II Pet. 3:10), and it underlies the warnings in

---

**5:1-11. On Guard.**—This entire paragraph is an imperious summons to alertness and a warn-ing of the penalties of failure: **You yourselves know well that the day of the Lord will come like a thief in the night. When people say, "There is peace and security," then sudden de-struction will come upon them . . . and there will be no escape** (vss. 2-3). **Let us not sleep, . . . let us keep awake and be sober** (vs. 6). **Therefore encourage one another and build one another up** (vs. 11). Paul cannot tell the Thes-salonians when the sky will open and the Lord will emerge. His great concern is, will they be living such lives of faith, courage, love, sobriety, and service that Christ's advent will be an occasion not of fear, but of joy? Will they be awake or asleep? Will they be well-trained sol-diers at attention, breastplated, helmeted, sword in hand, and wits about them, ready to obey instantly the words of command, or will they be unarmed and sprawlingly asleep in barracks?

Jesus commanded his disciples to watch and pray (Mark 13:33). Paul is but paraphrasing and expanding that exhortation in this passage. It is a cogent and urgently needed admonition for the church today: not to be blinded by the wisdom and practices of the secularized society in which it is set, but to be awake to these startling things: (*a*) We are the first genera-tion of the atomic age. The fact, stark and huge, is that man has got his hand on the ulti-mate forces of the universe. War has achieved a new intensity and destructiveness; all previous wars will be but children's squabbles and side-alley brawls compared with the abomination of desolation we can now release. Humanity has been given a new opportunity. By the wise use of what we have we can bring the world fresh energy, leisure, and comfort. We can develop and administer it positively and creatively, and accept it as a fresh revelation of the wisdom and power of God, given for the good of mankind.

**3** For when they shall say, Peace and safety; then sudden destruction cometh upon them, as travail upon a woman with child; and they shall not escape.

**4** But ye, brethren, are not in darkness, that that day should overtake you as a thief.

**5** Ye are all the children of light, and the children of the day: we are not of the night, nor of darkness.

come like a thief in the night. **3** When people say, "There is peace and security," then sudden destruction will come upon them as travail comes upon a woman with child, and there will be no escape. **4** But you are not in darkness, brethren, for that day to surprise you like a thief. **5** For you are all sons of light and sons of the day; we are

---

Revelation (3:3; 16:15). The combination **times and seasons** is found in the N.T. only here and in Acts 1:7; there, as here, the reference is to the times of the consummation. No distinction is intended between **times and seasons,** which are known, and the **day,** which is not and may not be known (Matt. 24:36; Mark 13:32). What Jesus is reported in Acts 1:7 to have said is really, "It is not your prerogative to know. That is something in the mind of God only. Leave it; turn to your own responsibility."

A note of warning is now sounded. If the coming of the Lord is to be so unexpected, then one must be ready and on the watch. The insensitive or oversanguine will be proclaiming **peace and security** even to the very end. Jeremiah (4:10; 6:14=8:11; 28:9) and Ezekiel (13:10, 16) speak of those who cry "peace" when there is no peace. Probably their words are in Paul's mind here. Even while the words are on the lips of these false prophets, **sudden destruction will come upon them as travail comes upon a woman with child.** This was an old simile, a favorite with Jeremiah (6:24; 13:21; 22:23; 30:6; 49:24; 50:43), and it needed no elaboration or explanation. The figure applies only as regards the *suddenness* of the travail. A woman does not know the hour, but she is in an expectant mood as it approaches, whereas it is evident that some of the Thessalonian disciples had been tempted to give up hope. (Others, as soon appears, were too much preoccupied with the expected day of the Lord; cf. II Thess. 2:2.) The statement that **there will be no escape** is emphatic in form (cf. Amos 5:18-20).

**4-5.** By a characteristically sudden turn of thought, Paul's mind moves from the thief coming in the night to the sleep of his victims which makes his coming possible and rewarding (cf. Matt. 24:43-44; Luke 12:39-40). But these Thessalonian Christians are **not in darkness;** they are **sons of light and sons of the day.** Upon them the light has shined "in the face of Jesus Christ" (II Cor. 4:4, 6). They have come into the truth of the gospel and are partakers of the full light of day (cf. I Cor. 4:5; II Cor. 6:14; Col. 1:13; Eph. 4:18; 5:8; and especially Rom. 13:11-13). The writers shift the form of the sentence (vs. 5b) so as to include themselves.

---

We can think of it not in terms of terror and destruction, but in terms of irrigation, electrification, manufacturing power, artistic living, and on our knees say, "Thanks be to God for his incredible bounty." We thus have a fateful decision to make—the nature of the future: whether it is to be beauty or burning, healing or destruction. This is a solemn and challenging truth, something as to which every Christian should be thinking, reaching conclusions, creating a conscience, and decisively acting.

(b) The Bible is being superseded. All agree the Bible is a wonderful book, enriching the mind and inspiring the soul. But that is what we say of Browning's poetry, and give it similar treatment: we seldom read it. There is hardly a Bible interpreter in the land who may assume

biblical knowledge on the part of a congregation. When spiritual allusions and references are made, they must be carefully explained. How many church people read a single chapter of the Bible a day, or even one of the short epistles in a week? This neglect is not confined to the lay folk. How many Christian leaders give one hour daily to an intense, systematic, and open-minded study of the Scriptures? Yet all Christians proclaim that it is by its teachings they hope to live and die! And we need the Bible as never before. We need it for our culture. It is the supreme literature of the ages. Its words, images, symbols, and thoughts have worked their way into the very warp and woof of the mind of mankind, and its sublimity, emotion, and beauty of expression are unabated by

6 Therefore let us not sleep, as *do* others; but let us watch and be sober.

7 For they that sleep sleep in the night; and they that be drunken are drunken in the night.

8 But let us, who are of the day, be sober, putting on the breastplate of faith and love; and for a helmet, the hope of salvation.

9 For God hath not appointed us to wrath, but to obtain salvation by our Lord Jesus Christ,

not of the night or of darkness. 6 So then let us not sleep, as others do, but let us keep awake and be sober. 7 For those who sleep sleep at night, and those who get drunk are drunk at night. 8 But, since we belong to the day, let us be sober, and put on the breastplate of faith and love, and for a helmet the hope of salvation. 9 For God has not destined us for wrath, but to obtain salvation through our Lord Jesus Christ,

---

**6-7.** From the figures of the day and wakefulness, the thought of the writers passes quickly to the idea of remaining **sober.** The **so then** is a combination, peculiar to Paul in the N.T., of two well-known words which, joined in this way, emphasize the logicalness or inevitability of a conclusion. Sexual excesses and drunken debaucheries are often associated by Paul with the coming of the night (Rom. 13:12-13; Gal. 5:19-20; I Cor. 6:9-10; cf. Acts 2:15). Rejecting both sleep and emotional "escapes," the Thessalonian disciples, as sons of the day, are to remain sober and alert (see also I Pet. 1:13; 5:8).

**8.** At this point the figure changes again, to the warrior getting ready for conflict. As "sons of the day," the believers are to put on the armament appropriate for the battles of the day. They are to put on **the breastplate of faith and love, and for a helmet the hope of salvation.** This simile is found in more elaborate form in Eph. 6:14-17. Paul often thinks of the Christian life in terms of a contest, a race (I Cor. 9:24), a prize fight (I Cor. 9:26-27), a battle (II Cor. 6:7; 10:4-6; Rom. 6:13; cf. I Tim. 6:12; II Tim. 4:7).

**9-11.** We are not destined to **wrath** "on the day of wrath" (Rom. 2:5) but **to obtain salvation through our Lord Jesus Christ** (cf. 1:10; see also Rom. 5:9; Col. 3:6). **Wrath** is reserved for those who refuse the proffered salvation and who choose to live as sons of darkness (cf. John 3:18). It was a constant and essential part of Paul's gospel also that **the Lord Jesus** had died **for us.** In his first letter to the Corinthians (15:3-11) he indicates that this had been an element of primary importance in all Christian preaching from the beginning. Through his dying, the Lord Jesus would deliver us "from the wrath to come." Precisely how Christ's death would have this effect Paul does not say at this point. He comes nearer to doing so in the two classical passages, Rom. 3:21-26 and II Cor. 5:14-21. Here he says only that whether we are alive and watchful or are dead in Christ, we shall **live with him** (cf. 4:17).

---

the wisdom and experience of the centuries. We need it even more for our inspiration. What other book can match its creative and uplifting power? It has influenced every area of faith and culture. If it had not been, Augustine's *City of God,* Dante's *Divine Comedy,* à Kempis' *Imitation of Christ,* Bunyan's *Pilgrim's Progress,* Handel's *Messiah,* Haydn's *Creation,* and Mendelssohn's *Elijah* would never have been written or composed. It transcends practically all the boundaries of race and language, for it is now translated into over 950 languages and dialects. It sounds the universal note in its emphasis on God's fatherhood, man's brotherhood, and Christ's saviorhood. It is the Almighty's word to the world of his creation, tells the story of his

search for man and man's response, and is the supreme textbook of moral law. It is the book of reality and of eternally effective power, yet we keep it tightly shut or drowse over its pages. We must awaken to the fact of its supersession.

(c) A strange generation of youth is at the church's door. Not like the youth of the past that went to public and high school, then into college, store, or factory, dated a neighborhood girl, married, and settled down contentedly to father a family and be a steady-going citizen. This is the generation that was plucked out of shop, factory, office, high school, and university not once but sometimes twice. It has experienced the harsh discipline of military training, has been in far-off and strange places of the earth,

10 Who died for us, that, whether we wake or sleep, we should live together with him.

11 Wherefore comfort yourselves together, and edify one another, even as also ye do.

12 And we beseech you, brethren, to know them which labor among you, and are over you in the Lord, and admonish you;

10 who died for us so that whether we wake or sleep we might live with him. 11 Therefore encourage one another and build one another up, just as you are doing.

12 But we beseech you, brethren, to respect those who labor among you and are over you in the Lord and admonish you,

---

In closing this discussion, Paul again asks the Thessalonian brethren to **encourage one another** and also to **build one another up**. He adds **just as you are doing** (cf. 4:1, 10). These new Christians are already seeking to carry out his exhortation; the apostle would give them greater incentive for doing so.

This instruction concerning the coming of the day of the Lord is set out in part as something not yet understood by the Thessalonians and in part as something well known by them. The conception that the day of the Lord was not only to be expected, but to be expected soon, was a part of the gospel from the beginning. Paul and his fellow writers share that general view. Comparison of the two letters to the Thessalonians with the earliest materials in the book of Acts reveals both a common tradition and in general a common understanding of that tradition. So far as we are able to recover the facts, Paul was the first to use the term parousia for the "day of the Lord." But the entire early Christian movement contained this "message of hope."

### D. PRACTICAL EXHORTATIONS (5:12-22)

**12-13a.** In this paragraph we are back in the atmosphere of 4:1-12. The Thessalonians are being urged again to live in every way so as "to please God." First, reference is made to those in places of leadership. These leaders, ministers and teachers, are **over you in the Lord and admonish you** in the ways of seemly and fruitful, wholesome living. They are to be regarded with overflowing **love**. The three terms used to designate these leaders, **labor among you, are over you,** and **admonish you,** refer not to three different groups, but to one (as most interpreters hold). The **labor** of the apostles with their own hands is mentioned in 2:9, and the word is used with similar meaning in I Cor. 4:12 and Eph. 4:28. It is used frequently in Paul's letters of the missionary labors in which he had engaged (Gal. 4:11; I Cor. 15:10; Col. 1:29; Phil. 2:16; cf. also I Thess. 1:3; I Tim. 4:10; and especially I Tim. 5:17). The phrase **are over you** translates a word (προϊστάμενος) used by Paul in Rom. 12:8: "He that ruleth [with KJV] with diligence." The word is

---

fought in deserts, in jungles, on open beaches. It has supped with pain, loneliness, temptation, and strange experiences, and has now returned —although for how long cannot be said—a mixture of good and bad, hope and discouragement, willingness and indifference, faith and doubt. Now its ruling mood is skepticism, its need is understanding, its energy is turbulent, and its questions to the church are both pointed and troubled. On the whole, it wants to renew its former not altogether vigorous connection with the church, but its attitude has changed. It is not prepared to listen to a sissy, one who has neither experimented with nor experienced life; to swallow down strings of insincere platitudes because they are uttered in a holy tone; to

retire to a corner, sit down quietly and be grateful for the privilege; nor to give meek and sycophantic obedience to others because of their old age. This generation compressed a lifetime of experience into a few years, traveled the globe, was forced to think, arrived at some conclusions, achieved a certain dignity, and now demands, and ought to be given, a definite respect and hearing. It stands at the door of the church. Are we awake to its worth, its power, and its future significance? On guard!

**12-22. *Accepting the Yoke.*—**While this is principally a recapitulation of 4:1-11, with a few additional precepts, a significant emphasis is developed. In no uncertain manner Paul urges discipline of a twofold nature—external and

13 And to esteem them very highly in love for their work's sake. *And* be at peace among yourselves.

14 Now we exhort you, brethren, warn them that are unruly, comfort the feeble-minded, support the weak, be patient toward all *men*.

13 and to esteem them very highly in love because of their work. Be at peace among yourselves. 14 And we exhort you, brethren, admonish the idle, encourage the faint-hearted, help the weak, be patient with

---

used in I Tim. 3:4-5, 15 of the ruling of one's household. In Tit. 3:8, 14 it refers to the promotion of good works. It is used in papyri frequently of those who are in some ruling capacity.

In view of the total usage in the N.T. and the direction in which the meaning of the word was developing, it probably should be taken here as referring to those who have leadership or influence, but are exercising it in the interest of those among whom they labor (note RSV in Rom. 12:8). This is in fact the general spirit of the passage (cf. Mark 10:42-44). **Admonish** carries the idea of warning against what endangers the Christian life of the Thessalonian disciples. The spirit in which this admonishing is to be done is indicated by vs. 14 and II Thess. 3:15. In I Cor. 4:14, Paul speaks of admonishing the Corinthians as "beloved children." In Col. 1:28 and 3:16 admonishing and teaching are closely associated. The word itself means "to place in mind." These leaders sought to do just that. The disciples at Thessalonica are urged to have a high regard for the leaders who are serving them in such exemplary spirit and manner. This recognition should be given freely and gladly in love, and not in fear or under compulsion.

**13b.** The Thessalonians are to **be at peace** among themselves. This injunction is given by Paul to the Corinthians (II Cor. 13:11), and he enjoins the Romans (12:18) to be at peace with all men if possible. A like word of Jesus is recorded in Mark 9:50. It seems to have been a widely felt need in the church. Here it is closely tied up with a word about the idlers. Both these Thessalonian letters indicate that strife and antagonism had arisen in connection with idleness (cf. II Thess. 3:11-12).

**14-15.** As the brothers have themselves been admonished, so they also are to admonish (the same word) the **idle** (RSV), or **unruly** (KJV), a very rare word in the N.T. The word means out of rank (of a soldier), or to be out of line with established and standard procedures. In the papyri it is used of idleness and loafing. Idlers who have become "busybodies" (II Thess. 3:11) are apparently in mind.

Encouragement must be given to those who have lost their courage. The word for **encourage** (παραμυθεῖσθε) is not known in classical Greek prior to Christian writing, and this is its only occurrence in the N.T. It is used several times in the LXX. The reason for loss of courage may have been in part the severe suffering some had undergone at the hand of their fellow citizens (2:14-15; cf. especially 2:11-12 for the inner meaning of this exhortation). **The weak** in Thessalonica were probably not afflicted with the identical weakness of those in Corinth (I Cor. 8:7-10), but it was a weakness of faith. Paul recognizes **the weak** in worldly resources (Acts 20:35), in bodily health (I Cor. 11:30), and in faith (Rom. 14:1; 15:1), and asks help for all of them. To **help** was to attach oneself to, and to sustain, by giving one's strength to support another. On the meaning of **patient,** see Rom. 2:4; Matt. 18:26-29; Jas. 5:7. The teaching of vs. 15 is quite

---

internal. The former is urged in his words, **Respect those who labor . . . in the Lord, . . . esteem them very highly. . . . Be at peace among yourselves. . . . admonish the idle** (vss. 12-14); the latter in **be patient** (vs. 14); **See that none of you repays evil for evil** (vs. 15); **pray constantly** (vs. 17); **give thanks in all circumstances** (vs. 18); **abstain from every form of**

evil (vs. 22). Modern Protestantism needs to ponder this passage, for its dual truth is seasoned with salt and addresses our present condition. Historically, the Reformation was both a revolt and an affirmation: a revolt, because it expressed, among other things, the resentment of the people against the rigid and cruel authority of an institution (the Roman Church); an

15 See that none render evil for evil unto any *man;* but ever follow that which is good, both among yourselves, and to all *men.*

16 Rejoice evermore.

17 Pray without ceasing.

18 In every thing give thanks: for this is the will of God in Christ Jesus concerning you.

19 Quench not the Spirit.

20 Despise not prophesyings.

21 Prove all things; hold fast that which is good.

22 Abstain from all appearance of evil.

them all. 15 See that none of you repays evil for evil, but always seek to do good to one another and to all. 16 Rejoice always, 17 pray constantly, 18 give thanks in all circumstances; for this is the will of God in Christ Jesus for you. 19 Do not quench the Spirit, 20 do not despise prophesying, 21 but test everything; hold fast what is good, 22 abstain from every form of evil.

in line with the "golden rule" (Matt. 7:12) and the even more striking word about one's enemies (Matt. 5:43-48). Paul makes the same appeal to the Romans (12:17, 21); and I Pet. 3:9 directs it to the Christians of Asia Minor.

**16-18.** The tone of the exhortation now changes again, from an ethical to a religious emphasis. The word **rejoice** is found in Paul's letters more than two dozen times. He professes joy as a part of his own experience (II Cor. 6:10). A nearly identical appeal is made to the Philippians (4:4), the ground of the rejoicing being given—"in the Lord" (cf. I Thess. 1:6; Phil. 3:1). Note also I Pet. 4:13. The word **always** in vss. 15, 16 is found four other times in this letter (1:2; 2:16; 3:6; 4:17), and with the possible exception of 4:17, carries the idea of "on every occasion" or "in every set of circumstances." In line with this, we find in Col. 1:24 a striking confession of Paul's own rejoicing even in suffering. The readers are also to pray unceasingly and in everything to have the spirit of thanksgiving. Thanksgiving is possible, for God has willed it in the gift of the Lord Jesus. These conceptions—joy, constancy in prayer, thanksgiving—are expressed also in Rom. 12:12; Col. 4:2-3; Eph. 6:18, and belong essentially to the Christian life as Paul lived and taught it.

**19-22.** These injunctions belong together intimately: **Quench not the Spirit** and **Despise not prophesyings.** An examination of the very extended discussion by Paul of the gifts of the Spirit (I Cor. 12–14, especially 12:7-11; 14:1-5, 29-33) indicates that prophecy was one of these gifts; see also Peter's interpretation of the experience of the Spirit on the day of Pentecost (Acts 2:13-18). The exuberance and overflow of the Spirit are suggested by Col. 3:16-17; Eph. 5:18-20; cf. also I Sam. 10:6-13; 19:20-24. The word **quench** is related to the association of the Spirit with fire (Matt. 3:11; Luke 3:16; Acts 2:3; and especially, II Tim. 1:6: "Stir to flame the gift of God in thee").

affirmation, because it exposed and re-emphasized certain religious principles embedded in the N.T. Religious liberty for one third of the people of Europe was thus secured and a return to the simplicity of early Christianity made. The unfortunate thing is that over the succeeding centuries we have used our liberty as an occasion for license. Because the external disciplinary powers of Roman Catholicism were rejected, we have too often rejected all external authority, and in addition have failed to impose upon ourselves any internal authority. It will be well to revisit the rock from which we have been hewed and see the nature of early Protestantism.

When the reformers flung off the autocratic

rule of the Roman institution and broke the theocratic imperialism of the hierarchy they immediately replaced them with other external and inner authorities. Externally they accepted the carefully defined and limited authority of certain church courts. Internally they put themselves under the higher disciplines of conscience, intelligence, and will. They did not think their newly acquired freedom authorized them to do what they liked, but what they ought; not to grasp privileges, but to discharge duties. Beyond any question they were self-controlled and self-obligated men who imposed upon themselves many things—family devotions, regular public worship of God, observation of Sunday,

23 And the very God of peace sanctify you wholly; and *I pray God* your whole spirit and soul and body be preserved blameless unto the coming of our Lord Jesus Christ.

23 May the God of peace himself sanctify you wholly; and may your spirit and soul and body be kept sound and blameless at the coming of our Lord Jesus Christ.

Further, the Thessalonians are to **test everything**. II Thess. 2:2 cautions against being misled by a spirit (of a prophet), and I Cor. 12:10 places together "prophecy" and "discerning of spirits," as is done also with "speaking in tongues" and "interpretation of tongues" (cf. also I John 4:1). When they have tested and approve any prophetic utterance, they are to **hold fast what is good** (cf. Phil. 1:9-10: "Approve things that are excellent"). Finally, they are to **abstain from every form of evil**. This, in view of the pagan life about them, was no easy requirement (cf. Rom. 12:9, "Abhor that which is evil"). It was possible with the help of God (II Thess. 3:3; cf. I Cor. 5:13).

### E. PRAYER FOR THE CHURCH (5:23-24)

**23.** Just as the first major section of the letter closed with a prayer (3:11-13), so this entire section of instruction and exhortation is brought to a conclusion with a comprehensive prayer. **The God of peace** is the one from whom the inward peace comes. He is also the one who has wrought peace between himself and those who have accepted his grace in Jesus Christ (cf. Rom. 5:10-11). For Paul, God is the ultimate, the source of all; and his prayer for his readers is that this one who gives peace may **himself sanctify** them **wholly**. This word **wholly** (ὁλοτελεῖς) is not found elsewhere in our Greek Bible, but its usage in the few instances known in literature leaves no doubt of its meaning. It is formed from ὅλος (all) and τέλος (end), and suggests finality as well as completeness.

The apostle further prays that his readers' **spirit and soul and body** may be **kept sound and blameless**. The spirit is the innermost functioning reality of the personal life

encouragement of education, civic service, effective scientific research, and the carrying forward of the missionary enterprise.

Is the contrast between them and us not to our shame? What external and internal discipline do we accept? So many of us have reduced our religion to sheer individualism, whim, and caprice. We solemnly promised to give all due loyalty in the Lord to those set over us in the church, and to attend regularly on the means of grace. We do neither, for too often we are hypercritical of both the minister's words and presence, and we can refrain from attendance at public worship and other church meetings without any qualms of conscience. We know we ought to teach a church-school class, hold family worship, have regular times daily for prayer and Bible study, give sacrificially to the causes of God throughout the world, but we just do not. We also know that as Christian employers we should take reasonable profits and pay generous wages, and as Christian employees we ought to work faithfully and industriously, but many do not, and so the name of Christ is being dishonored and the whole private enterprise system endangered. We could do worse things than read this passage of command upon our knees. Accept the yoke!

**23-28.** *Parting Blessings and Admonitions.*—Here is counsel in "good measure, pressed down, shaken together, running over" (Luke 6:38). What a magnificent and pointed series lies within it.

(*a*) Consecration—the imperative need of Christians (vs. 23). So many of us are going through life at half or three-quarter pressure. We are thought to be alive, and are partly dead. We make religious affirmations, but are defective in religious conduct and service. We are, like Ananias, keeping back part of the price, for we are split in our enthusiasms, divided in our minds, and faltering in our loyalties. We are akin to the Laodiceans, "neither cold nor hot" (Rev. 3:15). We need reconsecration to God, to the causes of his kingdom, to truth, and to service.

(*b*) Trust (vs. 24). If there is one thing we should have, it is a good relationship with life, for it is in us and we are in it, and no matter how we try, we cannot escape it. Unfortunately few of us have that relationship. One of the principal causes of the disruption is fear. All of us have experienced its pains and penalties—anxiety about things beyond our control; anticipation of troubles and ills for ourselves, our children, our business, our nation; the blowing

| 24 Faithful *is* he that calleth you, who also will do *it*. | 24 He who calls you is faithful, and he will do it. |
| 25 Brethren, pray for us. | 25 Brethren, pray for us. |
| 26 Greet all the brethren with a holy kiss. | 26 Greet all the brethren with a holy kiss. |

(I Cor. 2:11; Rom. 8:15-16). The Greek idea was that soul and body constitute the living person known and observed of all. Paul's prayer is essentially that these Thessalonian disciples may be preserved "intact" in the whole of their personal life; and that they may be so preserved until **the coming of our Lord Jesus Christ.** Thus the parousia is again brought into focus.

**24.** He who calls you is "the living and true God" (cf. I Cor. 1:9; II Thess. 3:3), and it is he who has given all the promises to his people in the gospel. He will faithfully do all that needs to be done to preserve those who fully commit themselves to him.

### F. Concluding Salutation and Benediction (5:25-28)

**25.** The prayer for the Thessalonian Christians is followed immediately by the request that they continue in a spirit of prayer **for us.** The missionaries are conscious of a mutual relationship. Not only are the missionaries interested in their converts, remembering them constantly in prayer, but they assume the interest of the Thessalonian brethren in them. This request for prayer was a phase of a reciprocal relationship between the apostles and the disciples (cf. II Thess. 3:1-2; II Cor. 1:8-11; see also II Thess. 1:11).

**26.** The greeting which is extended to **all the brethren** is a part of the regular closing words in all of Paul's letters. It is not simply that the greeting is given, but that in the name of the apostle the greeting is to be transmitted to the brethren. The **holy kiss** is mentioned in three other letters of Paul (I Cor. 16:20; II Cor. 13:12; Rom. 16:16), and in slightly different and somewhat clearer language in I Pet. 5:14. From Luke 7:45 and 22:48 it is seen to be a regular form of greeting in that world to which Paul belonged. It is implied by Luke 7:45 that one has failed in proper welcome to a guest if one has not given him the kiss of greeting, and from Luke 22:48 it appears that the kiss is a symbol of sincerity of respect and welcome. Taken over into the early church, it became a symbol of cordial Christian fellowship—a *holy* kiss.

up of petty problems out of all proportion to their importance; loss of faith in ourselves, others, and God, so that although we are professing Christians, we become practicing atheists, for basically the nature of unbelief is that it fears circumstances more than the Almighty.

Many methods of securing serenity and trust are offered—good, bad, and indifferent. The certain method is the way of Christ. He saw that fear prevented man from believing in himself, in the coming of his kingdom, in God his father. What was his remedy for it? The substitution of courage, which most people think is fear's counterbalance? His insight was truer. In the place of fear he put faith. To the poor and anxious he said, "Will [God] not much more clothe you, O men of little faith?" (Matt. 6:30). To the brokenhearted ruler of the synagogue, whose daughter was sick unto death, he gave the command, "Do not fear; only believe" (Luke 8:50). To the anxious and dismayed disciples

he said, "Fear not, little flock" (Luke 12:32). Let us ask three questions: Why did he urge faith as fear's remedy? Because it changes basic attitudes; and doing that, changes emotions, thoughts, dispositions, actions, and beliefs. In what did Christ's own faith center? In God's fatherhood and God's omnipotence, i.e., in the love and power of God. Has history vindicated his teaching? Study the story of the centuries.

(c) Intercessory prayer (vs. 25). Paul invites intercessory prayer, which is perhaps the noblest form of prayer. In Isaiah we are told that when the land was in decay, God "wondered that there was no intercessor" (Isa. 59:16). How many of us enter into this great experience of divine and human companionship, sometimes so delightful, other times so painful? Here is an amazing vicarious ministry open to us all, whether we are rich or poor, black or white, cultured or illiterate. Its purpose is not to change the will of God, for his mind is made

| | |
|---|---|
| 27 I charge you by the Lord, that this epistle be read unto all the holy brethren.<br><br>28 The grace of our Lord Jesus Christ *be* with you. Amen.<br><br>¶ The first *epistle* unto the Thessalonians was written from Athens. | 27 I adjure you by the Lord that this letter be read to all the brethren.<br><br>28 The grace of our Lord Jesus Christ be with you. |

**27.** The request that the **letter be read to all the brethren** is expressed in solemn and urgent language and in the first person singular, **I adjure you** (ἐνορκίζω). The reading would naturally be done in a public assembly of the church (cf. Heb. 10:25). Acts 19:13 suggests the solemnity implied by this word **adjure** (ὁρκίζω). Paul does not use the word elsewhere, and the special (active) form in which he here employs it is not found earlier. Inasmuch as he asks that the letter be read **to all the brethren,** we may conclude that it is to be delivered to the leaders in the church. Though addressed to the church as a whole, those who "are over them" in the Lord and "admonish" them (5:12) have special prerogatives and responsibilities.

**28.** A closing benediction was frequently found in ancient letters. It is used in all of Paul's letters, not always in precisely the same language. He ends his letters, as he begins them, with a prayer that the grace of the Lord Jesus Christ may be with his readers.

up on the basis of the divine intelligence and infinite love. To try to change it is to ask him to step down and be less than God. The purposes of intercessory prayer are to make God's mind clear to the one for whom we pray, to ask that his life may be opened to the inflow of the eternal power, to invoke for him faith, patience, cheerfulness, courage, etc. Lacking this element, our prayer life is weakened and restricted, and we fail to see God's will for those around us. It is in the light of intercessory prayer that we see light. When the historical sense fails, when group wisdom is a confusion, and when personal intelligence fails to pierce the veil, this high type of prayer illumines the path. Greatness, humility, and insight are in the apostle's request, **Brethren, pray for us.**

(*d*) Fellowship (vs. 26). The **holy kiss** of greeting in the Western church is a thing of the past, but in the life of the early church it was the outer symbol of the inner affection which made the Christian congregations the wonder and puzzle of the pagan world. We should understand clearly the nature of this fellowship. It is not necessarily of the mind. Christians have many things in common: the N.T., church history, personal and social ideals; but they differ in birth, training, ability, tradition, and temperament, which produce inevi-

table differences in interpretation of religious truth and the manner in which it should be applied to life. We have no right, therefore, to demand unity of mind at all times among Christians. Our Christian unity is of the spirit. "By this all men will know that you are my disciples, if you have love for one another" (John 13:35). In every congregation there is room for honest disagreement of opinion, but there is no room for differences of spirit. The moment bitterness, envy, truculence, carping, backbiting, or gossip enters, that moment it ceases to be a Christian congregation. The test of our Christianity was put in definite terms by the venerable John: "We know that we have passed out of death into life, because we love the brethren. He who does not love remains in death" (I John 3:14). All of us are sending forth projections. Not one of us can confine his life within his own skin. What projection are we sending forth as we walk through the world?

(*e*) Obedience (vs. 27). This is so closely akin to discipline (see Expos. on vss. 12-22) that it needs no further elaboration, excepting the statement that until we learn to obey we disqualify ourselves to lead. Paul used a strong word when he "adjured" that his letter be read to all the brethren. But sometimes strong words are the useful and creative ones.

# II THESSALONIANS

## TEXT, EXEGESIS, AND EXPOSITION

1 Paul, and Silvanus, and Timotheus, unto the church of the Thessalonians in God our Father and the Lord Jesus Christ:

2 Grace unto you, and peace, from God our Father and the Lord Jesus Christ.

3 We are bound to thank God always for you, brethren, as it is meet, because that your faith groweth exceedingly, and the charity of every one of you all toward each other aboundeth;

1 Paul, Silva'nus, and Timothy,
To the church of the Thessalo'nians in God our Father and the Lord Jesus Christ:

2 Grace to you and peace from God the Father and the Lord Jesus Christ.

3 We are bound to give thanks to God always for you, brethren, as is fitting, because your faith is growing abundantly, and the love of every one of you for one another

---

### I. Address and Greeting (1:1-2)

**1:1-2.** The salutation of this second letter follows very closely that of the previous letter. First are named those who are the writers of the letter, Paul, Silvanus, and Timothy; next, those to whom the letter is written, **the church of the Thessalonians.** Here also it is indicated that the church has its existence and its character **in God our Father and the Lord Jesus Christ.** The phrase **our Father** suggests the kinship the writers feel with their readers. The double greeting **grace to you and peace** given in the first letter is the shortest form of greeting found in any of Paul's letters. The Colossian letter contains the second shortest form, viz., "Grace to you and peace from God our Father." The form found here **from God the Father and the Lord Jesus Christ** is essentially that which is found in the remaining seven letters usually assigned to Paul. The real meaning of the double reference to God and Christ is given in I Cor. 1:30: ". . . life in Christ Jesus, whom God made our wisdom, our righteousness and consecration and redemption." I Cor. 3:21*b*-23 and 12:4-6 give other statements of the same essential truth.

### II. The Thanksgiving (1:3-12)

### A. Faith, Love, Steadfastness (1:3-4)

**3-4.** As customary in his letters (all except Galatians), Paul and his associates begin this letter with thanksgiving. In the first letter the writers had mentioned the "faith," the "love," and the "endurance" of the Thessalonian Christians as bases for thanksgiving; now these are mentioned again in much the same way.

---

*The Letter.*—See Intro., p. 249. It may well be, however, that we have here an authentic communication of Paul. If so, it demonstrates that Paul, like many other preachers, could occasionally fall into dull repetition.

**1:3.** *Two Shining Jewels.*—Paul becomes almost lyrical in his praise and gratitude, **because**

For Introduction to II Thess. see pp. 245-53.

**your faith is growing abundantly, and the love of every one of you for one another is increasing.** Not always is a church's growth determined by the measurements of faith and love. Too often others are used. How large is the membership? What number was added to the roll last year? What is the size of the budget? How much is the salary of the minister? How many are on the staff? Is it crowded Sunday mornings? Are

4 So that we ourselves glory in you in the churches of God, for your patience and faith in all your persecutions and tribulations that ye endure:

is increasing. 4 Therefore we ourselves boast of you in the churches of God for your steadfastness and faith in all your persecutions and in the afflictions which you are enduring.

---

The apostles feel **bound to give thanks to God . . . , as is fitting.** The same statement in almost identical words is found in II Thess. 2:13, and not elsewhere in Paul's letters, or in the N.T. The word **bound** indicates a sense of something called for and appropriate, but not an obligation which Paul and his associates are reluctant to grant. On the contrary, they are eager to **give thanks** because the faith of the Thessalonian **brethren . . . is growing abundantly, and the love of every one of you for one another is increasing.** They had been anxious about the faith of these Thessalonian Christians (I Thess. 3:2), and the former letter had been written in part to establish their faith (I Thess. 3:5-7). They had also hoped and prayed that they might have the opportunity of visiting Thessalonica again to supply any deficiencies in faith (I Thess. 3:10). The further information from some unidentified source (3:11) had given them much satisfaction: their prayers and longings had been answered; the Thessalonian Christians were growing in their faith and in love for one another. The love of the brethren for each other was so outstanding and well known that in the earlier letter (I Thess. 4:1, 10) they are told there is no need to write them about it at all. This love which they have manifested so splendidly is still increasing. The language of vs. 4 reflects also the fact that the persecutions and afflictions referred to several times in I Thessalonians (1:6; 2:14; 3:2-5) are still continuing.

The result of the knowledge of all this is that the writers **boast of you in the churches of God.** II Cor. 1:1 refers to the saints "in all Achaia." If Paul, Silvanus, and Timothy were at Corinth at the time of the writing of this second letter to the Thessalonians, the churches in which they did their boasting may well have been those in the province in which they were then at work. However, I Thess. 1:8 implies a much wider contact than any single province. Chrysostom (quoted by Ellicott) thought that this allusion to boasting among the churches shows that considerable time had passed since the first letter was written. This is not necessary. The same phrase **churches of God,** with as much (specifically more) breadth of view as here, is found in the first letter (I Thess. 2:14; cf. I Cor. 11:16). It is thus evident that the general background of this letter is the same as that of the first letter. The report of the fidelity and fellowship of the Thessalonian Christians has gone "far and wide"; according to I Thess. 1:8d-9, the churches were themselves "boasting" about it.

---

the "best people" being attracted? Does attendance help one socially and economically? Read denominational magazines or newspapers which print the annual reports of congregations, usually sent in by the ministers, and take cognizance of the elements stressed. Is much said about souls forgiven, lives redeemed, divided families reunited, new missions established, community responsibilities accepted? The harsh fact is that we have accepted the success standards of the secular society in which the church is set, carried into our boards and committees by sincere but unspiritual men who live by them in the business world. This is not a plea for or defense of slovenliness and inefficiency in the administration of church affairs, but a reminder of the

ease with which we can put second things in first place.

**4. A Noble Word.**—"You are our glory and joy" (I Thess. 2:20) indicates Paul's honest pride in the virtues of the Thessalonians. When he uses the word **boast** he may seem out of character. To the Romans he had declared boasting "is excluded" (Rom. 3:27). To the Corinthians he had declared, "There is nothing to be gained by it" (II Cor. 12:1), and to the Galatians he had solemnly asserted that the cross alone is worthy of glorification (Gal. 6:14). The spiritual achievements of the Thessalonians were evidently of such a nature as to evoke from even the restrained apostle a spontaneous cheer. He says that he boasts not only in their faith and

5 *Which is* a manifest token of the righteous judgment of God, that ye may be counted worthy of the kingdom of God, for which ye also suffer:

6 Seeing *it is* a righteous thing with God to recompense tribulation to them that trouble you;

5 This is evidence of the righteous judgment of God, that you may be made worthy of the kingdom of God, for which you are suffering — 6 since indeed God deems it just to repay with affliction those who afflict

## B. The Judgment of God (1:5-7a)

**5-7a.** At this point the writers turn from their reflection upon the virtues of the Thessalonian Christians to the judgment merited by those who are responsible for their persecutions and afflictions. First of all, the writers see the Thessalonian Christians themselves brought through the discipline of these afflictions into the position of being **made worthy** (RSV) of the kingdom of God in behalf of which they are suffering. The reading of KJV, **counted worthy**, is in line with Pauline usage of the word here employed and is preferable to the reading of the RSV. Although the phrase **righteous judgment** is found in Paul only here—the Greek term in Rom. 2:5 is a combination of the two words here used in a single word of Paul's own coinage—the idea is basic in his thinking. Elsewhere in the N.T. the phrase appears only in John 5:30; 7:24. A similar idea, that of "true judgment," is in John 8:16, and judgment is called both "true and righteous" in Rev. 16:7; 19:2. The verb "to judge" is found several times in Paul in reference to the judgments of men in the present time. It is never used of God except in reference to the future judgment (see, e.g., Rom. 2:16; 3:6; I Cor. 5:11-13; cf. II Thess. 2:12). The term **evidence** (ἔνδειγμα) is found only here in early Christian writings and is rare in classical Greek, where it is used in the sense of "proof." A very closely related word meant

love (vs. 3) but in their **steadfastness** or **patience** (*hypomonē*).

We are apt to think of **patience** as merely endurance under trial or quiet acquiescence to certain conditions. In both the O.T. and the N.T. it means much more. In Isa. 53, while the word itself is not used, patience is a sacrificial force which transforms evil. It is more, for it is the very nature of God. He is the One "merciful and gracious, long suffering" (Exod. 34:6; Num. 14:18). R. Gregor Smith writes:

The patience of man has in it therefore, besides endurance, the quality of expectation, waiting for something to happen, for "someone to help." The message of God's patience in and through the prophets makes for a quickening of patience. God's patience breeds men's patience. In the NT . . . the "patience of God" (Rom. 15.5) has still the same broad sense.[1]

**5-10. *The Stars in Their Courses.***—Paul's rejoicing in the growth and increase of faith and love in the Thessalonians is added to by the knowledge that this happy improvement is in spite of continued vicious persecution. It is then natural that one of his fiery disposition and powerful theological mind should turn to the

[1] Article on "Patience" in Alan Richardson, *A Theological Word Book of the Bible* (New York: The Macmillan Co., 1951), p. 164.

issues of rewards for the gallant group of whose patient endurance under the rods of the smiters he is so proud, and of punishments for the bigots and evil men who have brought such suffering upon them. He draws it to their attention that: (*a*) God has not left them to their own resources. The very fact that they have been able to absorb long punishment and slander with patience and equanimity is powerful evidence that divine power has been given them. "They are proof positive of God's equity" (vs. 5 Moffatt). Their warfare has not been at their own charges, and the consolations of God have been many. (*b*) Out of their persecutions certain creative values will assuredly accrue. **That you may be made worthy of the kingdom of God, for which you are suffering** (vs. 5). (*c*) This is a moral universe; therefore punishment for wickedness and blessing for goodness are inevitable over the long span, **since indeed God deems it just to repay with affliction those who afflict you, and to grant rest with us to you who are afflicted** (vss. 6-7). Neil says that here is not a matter of primitive or O.T. justice, an eye for an eye and a tooth for a tooth, "nor is it a matter of doling out punishments and rewards. It is, like the Wrath of God (Rom. i.18 . . .), inherent in the nature of a moral universe. Because God is ruler of that universe, retribution for sin is a part of life either here or

7 And to you who are troubled rest with us, when the Lord Jesus shall be revealed from heaven with his mighty angels,

8 In flaming fire taking vengeance on them that know not God, and that obey not the gospel of our Lord Jesus Christ:

you, 7 and to grant rest with us to you who are afflicted, when the Lord Jesus is revealed from heaven with his mighty angels in flaming fire, 8 inflicting vengeance upon those who do not know God and upon those who do not obey the gospel of our

---

"indictment." This latter is the word translated "clear omen" in Phil. 1:28, a passage parallel to this one in thought. In that passage, as here, it is said that the judgment of God will be manifested upon both the righteous and the unrighteous—and upon each of them in accordance with their present lives (cf. especially Rom. 2:5-11; see also Rom. 8:19). The endurance of the Thessalonian disciples is the evidence that God is supporting them because they are his. The persecutors are just as manifestly disobedient to the truth (2:12) which God had given his apostles to proclaim.

## C. The Revelation of the Lord Jesus (1:7b-10)

**7b.** This judgment of God will be manifested **when the Lord Jesus is revealed.** This "revelation" is the same event as the parousia, which is mentioned four times in the first letter (2:19; 3:13; 4:15; 5:23) and twice in this one (2:1, 8). The special aspect that is indicated by the term "revelation" is that the one who has hitherto been obscured or concealed shall become openly manifest. There is to be not only his "presence" but a "revelation" of him, and of his glory and his judgment, at the time of his coming (see further on I Thess. 4:13-18).

**8-9. For those who do not obey the gospel of our Lord Jesus** his "revelation" will be a manifestation of **vengeance,** and **they shall suffer the punishment of eternal destruction.** **Vengeance** is mentioned by Paul only here and in two other passages (Rom. 12:19; II Cor. 7:11); Romans joins with Heb. 10:30 in quoting from Deut. 32:35; the verb is also used by Paul in two passages (Rom. 12:19; II Cor. 10:6). The idea in both noun and verb is that God "acts forthrightly in justice," giving to the unrighteous what is the rightful return for their unrighteous conduct. **Destruction** is a Pauline word (I Thess. 5:3; I Cor. 5:5; cf. I Tim. 6:9). So far as he at any point indicates what he means by it, it is **exclusion from the presence of the Lord and from the glory of his might.** The

---

hereafter."[2] Assuredly these are three powerful points. Have they the support of the minds of men and the experience of history? (a) Does God help his children? Can one believe in the Incarnation and the Cross and think anything else? In the Incarnation he is the God who came down, who could not stand apart from the pain and suffering of the family he created, and who must in his Son encourage, heal, and save it. In the Incarnation he identifies himself with humanity, becomes bone of its bone, flesh of its flesh, and heart of its heart, and so enters with it into similarity of experience. In the Cross we see God taking to himself man's sin, weariness, and sorrow: the eternal conscience being wounded for our transgressions, the eternal innocence being bruised for our iniquities, and the eternal holiness gathering the chastisement of our indifference to himself. But we see yet more, for in it man receives forgiveness, redemption, sympathy, strength, inspiration, and constant incitement to fresh moral striving. Man's

experience from the beginning is that God is his helper. The patriarchs declared it, the prophets experienced it, the psalmist sang it, the disciples rejoiced in it, the martyrs evidenced it, and in the succeeding days men and women of every kindred and people and tongue have cried with those who have marched the rugged way before them: "God is our refuge and strength, a very present help in trouble. Therefore will not we fear" (Ps. 46:1-2).

(b) Is suffering creative? It all depends on how we meet it, and what we do with it. The Stoic accepts it with grim resolution and absorbs it. The Mohammedan says, "Kismet," everything is the will of God, and submits to it. The Buddhist turns the thought of it over in his mind and decides to evade it by escape to Nirvana. The Hindu traces it back to previous incarnations and sees it pursuing him in this and subsequent life, so feels the futility of submission, combat, or flight. The O.T. righteous Jew considered that, so long as he remained righteous, he was excused from it (Ps. 91:7).

[2] *Epistle of Paul to Thessalonians*, pp. 144-45.

9 Who shall be punished with everlasting destruction from the presence of the Lord, and from the glory of his power;

Lord Jesus. 9 They shall suffer the punishment of eternal destruction and exclusion from the presence of the Lord and from

---

Greek word used here for **destruction** (ὄλεθρος) prevailingly carries a literal idea in the classical Greek, as distinguished from the word more common in the N.T. (ἀπώλεια), which has a more ethical connotation. I Tim. 6:9 joins the two words, probably for emphasis. The language of this passage is more vivid than that in I Thess. 5:3, even though the general idea is the same. The word **eternal** applies to the age to be, following the revelation of the Lord. Paul uses it with reference to God (Rom. 16:26), invisible reality (II Cor. 4:18), future glory (II Cor. 4:17; cf. 5:1), God-given comfort (II Thess. 2:16), and life (Gal. 6:8). In the N.T., the word occurs forty-three times in this last connection, as over against twenty-three times in all other connections. The conception of **exclusion from the presence of the Lord** is a part of Paul's inheritance from the religion of his fathers and is expressed in language reminiscent of the prophets Isaiah and Jeremiah (e.g., Isa. 2:10, 19, 21; 66:4, 15; Jer. 10:25).

The accompaniments of the revelation of the Lord Jesus from heaven are derived in part from the apocalyptic literature of Judaism, and belong with the inherited thinking of the apostle. The O.T. speaks of the manifestation of God in fire (Exod. 19:18; 24:17; Deut. 4:11-13; Isa. 66:15; Jer. 4:4; 5:14; Ezek. 1:4; 5:4; 8:2; etc.). The **flaming fire** is to be associated with the "revelation" (as in RSV), and not with **taking vengeance** (as in KJV). Dan. 10:2-9 is especially valuable as background for this passage (cf. also the vivid description of the glorified Lord in Rev. 1:13-16). The **mighty angels** or "angels of his power," the **flaming fire, the glory of his might** all belong to the tradition of Judaism. Frequently the language of quotation is employed in the N.T. more fully than the particular thought of the writer in a given passage requires. By this "drapery of language" the major concept is set forth vividly, forcefully, and feelingly (Acts 2:16-21 is a good illustration). The reward of the righteous is the most constant element included in the outcome of the parousia, for it was to vindicate his people that

---

But the Christian believes with Jesus and Paul that it can be used. He is not exempt from it, but when it comes he can employ it to fertilize his character, as the pond lily does with the mud in which it is rooted.

Trouble nobly used can open up within us deep interior resources of spiritual power. Listen to Cardinal Mercier himself. "Suffering," he wrote, "accepted and vanquished, . . . will give you a serenity which may well prove the most exquisite fruit of your life." That is a strange thing. Suffering bring out serenity? [3]

When Paul thought of the pains inflicted upon himself—accusations of hypocrisy, cowardice, greediness, usurpation, lying, beatings, stonings, imprisonment, and shipwreck—he said they had taught him serenity and had actually furthered the gospel. Much of the great literature of the world would never have been written but for the dungeon and prison cell. It was in loneliness and twilight that Boethius composed *The Consolation of Philosophy*, Grotius wrote his commentary on Matthew, Buchanan composed the *Paraphrases of the Psalms of David*, Bunyan

wrote *The Pilgrim's Progress*, Sir Walter Raleigh wrote his *History of the World*, and Nehru wrote *Glimpses of World History*. Is there any scene more moving than that of Dostoevski falling on his knees on the wild Siberian steppes and amidst "those stern and awful solitudes" giving thanks "that [there] he found the road that leads to the Father's home"? [4] And have we not found affliction creative? We are average side-street men and women, relatives of Mr. Jones and Mr. Smith; but obscure and limited in experience as we are, we also have learned by the things we have suffered, and out of them have piped our little songs.

(c) Is this a moral universe? The poet and mystic often discern what the philosopher and historian miss. In the book of Judges there is a wild, tumultuous ballad by Deborah, the Joan of Arc of her time. Jabin, king of the Canaanites, for twenty years had been a whiplash on the back of Israel. His strength lay in his possession of nine hundred chariots. At the summons of Deborah a young captain of Israel,

[3] Fosdick, *Secret of Victorious Living*, p. 18.

[4] F. W. Boreham, *A Faggot of Torches* (Philadelphia: Judson Press, 1951), p. 103.

10 When he shall come to be glorified in his saints, and to be admired in all them | the glory of his might, 10 when he comes on that day to be glorified in his saints,

---

the Lord would be revealed. The reward here promised for the believers **who are afflicted, is rest with us.** Thus again the writers remind the Thessalonian converts that they, preachers and disciples, are all suffering together, and that they all together shall receive release from their afflictions **when the Lord Jesus is revealed** (cf. Rom. 8:18-20). This release is to be in the "kingdom of God," which is to be established in fullness at the consummation of the revelation of the **glory of his might.**

**10a.** It is also said that when the Lord comes he is **to be glorified in his saints, and to be marveled at in all who have believed.** There is a difference of opinion as to the exact meaning of the phrase **to be glorified in his saints.** The phrase is found only here, and the word **glorified** (ἐνδοξάζω) occurs in Paul only here and in vs. 12. The word in 3:1 (δοξάζω) is the common one and is the root of this term. It is used many times in the N.T. of the present glorifying of God in the acclaiming of him in speech, and also by deeds wrought (e.g., Matt. 5:16; John 17:4). It is used also of the exaltation of Christ to glory (John 7:39; 17:5). Paul uses it of the future glorification of believers by God (Rom. 8:30; cf. II Thess. 2:14), in what precise manner he does not say. Findlay (*Epistles of Paul to Thessalonians,* p. 151), referring to Isa. 4:2-3 and Ezek. 28:22, seems to think the glorification will be based in what the Lord will do in his saints. Ellicott and Milligan suggest that his own glory will be reflected in his saints. Moffatt thinks that vss. 7b-10 are a quotation from an early Christian hymn (cf. Col. 3:16), and finds the glorification in the character of the saints. Most modern interpreters reflect this same opinion; Frame compares Gal. 1:24, "They glorified God in me." Lünemann thought it was a possible reverberation of Psalm 89:8 (LXX), and that the Lord will be glorified in the glorification of the saints (cf. Heb. 2:10; Rom. 8:18, 21; I Cor. 2:7; Eph. 1:12, 14; Phil. 1:11; 2:11; I Pet. 5:1). The whole tenor of the passage favors the identification of the **saints** with **all who have believed;** and 1:12 explicitly states the mutual and reciprocal glorifying of the Lord and his saints.

The phrase **to be marveled at** is not used elsewhere. The only other passage in Paul's letters in which the word "marvel" is found (Gal. 1:6) reflects the same kind of usage as is general in the N.T.—our ordinary use of the word "to wonder" or "to marvel." Two questions need to be asked: (a) What is the basis of the wondering? and

---

Barak, went out against his nation's tormentor at the head of the men of Naphtali and Zebulun. Jabin's charioteers were led by a great warrior, Sisera. On the face of things the Israelites were doomed to defeat. But as the battle is joined, the poetess pictures the God of Israel descending in anger on the wings of storm and tempest against the enemies of his people. The agents of his wrath—thunder, lightning, earthquake, and torrential rain—strike fear into their hearts, the plain of Esdraelon is turned to a bog in which many of the chariots are mired, and those who manage to get back to the river discover that the fords are flooded. Panic, rout, slaughter, and drowning are their portion. Then comes the spiritual insight and summing-up of the poetess:

The very stars in heaven were fighting,
  fighting Sisera from their spheres (Judg. 5:20
    Moffatt).

Turn to the N.T. for a similar flashing insight. In Rev. 12 the mystic writer tells the story of the persecution of the early church and its deliverance, under the form of a woman, about to give birth to a child, suddenly confronted by a fearful dragon which waits to devour the infant at birth. She is given "two wings of a great eagle" (Rev. 12:14) and escapes. She is again attacked, this time by a serpent, who vomits water from his mouth to drown her, but here the poet says, "The earth came to the help of the woman" (Rev. 12:16).

Ponder these two statements, "The stars in their courses fought against Sisera," and "The earth came to the help of the woman." What are they both saying? The universe is moral. In the struggle between right and wrong there are other forces at work which we cannot see but which are against wrong. Heaven and earth combine to secure the ultimate triumph of the right. The universe is not neutral but takes a

that believe (because our testimony among you was believed) in that day.

11 Wherefore also we pray always for you, that our God would count you worthy of *this* calling, and fulfil all the good pleasure of *his* goodness, and the work of faith with power:

and to be marveled at in all who have believed, because our testimony to you was believed. 11 To this end we always pray for you, that our God may make you worthy of his call, and may fulfill every good re-

---

(*b*) Who does the wondering? As to the first question, nearly all interpreters regard this phrase as parallel to the preceding one. The glorifying and the wondering belong together, the one being the ground of the other. Charles J. Ellicott (*A Critical and Grammatical Commentary on St. Paul's Epistles to the Thessalonians* [Andover: Warren F. Draper, 1864], p. 112) speaks for many in saying that the wonder is at the glorification which has been wrought in all who believe. As to those who wonder, Stevens (*Commentary on Epistles to Thessalonians*, p. 79) says that the "manifested glory of the saints will elicit the wonder of all the beholding universe." Moffatt is uncertain, but refers to Ezek. 39:21, where the nations are in mind, and to Eph. 3:10, where the heavenly "principalities and powers" are mentioned. Milligan refers to Ps. 68:36 [LXX], where Israel, the people of God, is to be in wonder. Findlay and Frame imply that any beholder will wonder, and suggest no identification. This is probably the interpretation closest to the mind of the writers; it is the one who is glorified and marveled at who is in the focus of thought, and the spectators do not need to be identified.

**10*b*.** Parenthetically, and in an intimate aside, the brethren are reminded that the gospel testimony of the writers had been **believed** by them. Moffatt and Goodspeed agree with Westcott and Hort, and a couple of later MSS, in thinking that **was believed** should read "was confirmed." Hort thought the usual reading was not logical or clear. But nearly all Greek MSS, all the versions, nearly all interpreters, and most modern translations follow the reading, **was believed.** The difference between the two Greek words involved is very small (ἐπιστεύθη and ἐπιστώθη).

"That day" is of course the day of the revealing of the Lord Jesus (vs. 7) as identified by the context. It is hardly as yet a technical phrase for "the last day" (cf. II Tim. 1:12, 18; 4:8; I Cor. 3:13).

### D. PRAYER FOR GOD'S BLESSING (1:11-12)

**11-12.** It is the prayer always of the apostolic writers that **God may make** the Thessalonian readers **worthy of his call,** which they have received and heartily answered

---

hand, for goodness and badness are not merely local and earthly. Do not the solid facts of nature substantiate this? If I want health, what I need to do is keep step with the universe around me, breathe its air, expose my body to its sun's rays, eat its fruits with their cleansing and vitalizing juices and meats, sleep in its dark and soothing night, open my mind to its color and beauty. But what happens to me if I turn against its air, sun, fruit, night, color, and light? My skin becomes pale and mottled, my body becomes emaciated, my nerves become disordered; I sicken and die. I have turned against the law of the universe.

Study the moral history of the world. Has hate, greed, cruelty, falsehood, tyranny, impurity, or slavery ever finally triumphed? Are not Egypt, Assyria, Persia, Greece, and Rome vivid

illustrations of the truth that things are weighted on the side of love, sacrifice, sympathy, truth, peace, purity, and liberty? Fight against these and you fight against the stars in their courses. God is not mocked. His law cannot be flouted. "Though the mills of God grind slowly, yet they grind exceeding small." [5] There comes the day when the books are opened and judgment is pronounced. It may be near, it may be far off, but it comes. "Hear, O heavens, and give ear, O earth: for the LORD hath spoken" (Isa. 1:2).

**11-12. *A High Summons.*—**In vs. 10 the apostle impresses on the Thessalonians the blessing which the return of Jesus with the angels of his power will mean to them. It "will mean

[5] Longfellow, "Poetic Aphorisms: Retribution." From the *Sinngedichte* of Friedrich von Logau.

12 That the name of our Lord Jesus Christ may be glorified in you, and ye in him, according to the grace of our God and the Lord Jesus Christ.

solve and work of faith by his power, 12 so that the name of our Lord Jesus may be glorified in you, and you in him, according to the grace of our God and the Lord Jesus Christ.

---

(cf. I Thess. 5:24). The KJV reads **count you worthy of this calling.** The word is used six times in the N.T. in addition to this passage. In five of those six the meaning is clearly that given in the KJV. In the other, Acts 28:22, ἀξιόω is translated "desire"—a well-recognized meaning from classical Greek. In no other passage known is the meaning "to make worthy," but always "to deem worthy." Paul prays that God may deem them worthy because of that purpose and faith which he sees in them. It is also his constant prayer that God may by his dynamic power bring to fulfillment **every good resolve and work of faith.** It is these, then present in them, which form the ground of his judgment of their worth and their due. The writers express also the deep desire that **the name of our Lord Jesus may be glorified in you.** The relationship between the Lord and his followers is mutual: he is to be glorified in them, and they in him. This is in line with the idea expressed in 1:10 and supports the interpretation given of that verse. This is all in accord with **the grace of our God,** which has been manifested through the Lord Jesus Christ. God has set him forth as his own free gift. Those who have heard the message and believed in him share his glory (cf. Rom. 8:16-17).

There is thus reverberating through ch. 1 a combination of the ideas of certain portions of the first letter. These ideas are in new combination; they are expressed in somewhat different language; and they manifest a somewhat less exuberant, a more restrained feeling. The writers are handling the same general situation and are doing so in substantially the same way, but their mood and emotion are at a lower level of vibrancy. The reasons for this will become evident as consideration of this second letter proceeds.

---

splendour unimaginable, . . . a breath-taking wonder to all who believe." [6] With this magnificent prospect before them, Paul feels he must constantly pray **that our God may make you worthy of his call.** Once more we have emphasized the value he places on intercessory prayer (Phil. 1:9; Col. 1:9; I Thess. 5:23, 25) and the call to Christian discipleship (Rom. 1:1, 7; I Cor. 7:22; Eph. 4:1).

Much debate has taken place on what constitutes God's call to the Christian fellowship. To Paul it is an eternal act of God (I Thess. 2:12), begins when a man knows he is face to face with God, effects a definite change in his character (I Thess. 4:7), and is a continuing and expanding experience. This was the nature of his own call and was to him the great decisive hour of his life. He knew it was initiated by the divine Being, but it was so wonderful that language could not express it (II Cor. 9:15). "To me, says Paul in effect, it was . . . sheer miracle, a word proceeding out of the mouth of God, a creative act of omnipotence. . . . This conversion experience was far and away the most vital and formative influence of Paul's

life." [7] Here he pictures the culmination of the Thessalonians' call—the glorification of God in the kingdom of Christ, at his return, and forever after. This culmination, however, can be effected only if **every good resolve and work of faith** is fulfilled. It is not enough that the Thessalonians have good intentions and plan to do acts of kindness. The intentions must be translated into actions, and the noble plans must become realities by God's power. One hallmark of the Christian is moral and ethical. The dynamic of this new quality of life is from above. Thus will the **name of our Lord Jesus Christ . . . be glorified.** In the Bible **name** is used not merely as a means of identification, but as descriptive of personality and character (Isa. 9:6). So the faith, love, and steadfastness of the Thessalonians glorify the Lord's **name** in them now, and will do so on the great day of his return.

These verses challenge us sharply. How often do we kneel in intercessory prayer for our home, churches, fellow workers, nation, and the world? How deep is our realization of the wonder of our call to the Christian fellowship? Is our

[6] Phillips, *Letters to Young Churches*, p. 135.

[7] Stewart, *A Man in Christ*, p. 82.

2 Now we beseech you, brethren, by the coming of our Lord Jesus Christ, and *by* our gathering together unto him,

2 That ye be not soon shaken in mind, or be troubled, neither by spirit, nor by word, nor by letter as from us, as that the day of Christ is at hand.

2 Now concerning the coming of our Lord Jesus Christ and our assembling to meet him, we beg you, brethren, 2 not to be quickly shaken in mind or excited, either by spirit or by word, or by letter purporting to be from us, to the effect that the day of

### III. THE REVELATION OF THE MAN OF LAWLESSNESS (2:1-17)

In this paragraph a very different aspect of the subject which has been central in the immediately preceding discussion is given attention. It is not now a matter of the vindication of the believers in the kingdom; nor is it a question of the accompaniments of the parousia. Attention is now focused upon the disturbance of mind in the Thessalonian church because at least some of its members have been led to believe that the **day of the Lord has come.** The KJV reads **is at hand;** but the Greek word is found six other times in the N.T. and always with the idea of "present." Here it means "has set in." Along with the excitement about the "coming of the Lord" is included also what is involved with it— **our assembling to meet him.** This is something of special interest to both the apostles and the disciples, and something of which the apostles had already spoken (vs. 5), and written (I Thess. 4:17; 5:10). It is closely related to the idea reported by Matt. 24:31 and Mark 13:27 as included in the teaching of Jesus.

The teaching here given is intended to quiet their disturbed minds. In the course of the discussion we are given a vivid picture of some of the features of the eschatological event as Paul thought of it. He now writes in earnest and brotherly sympathy, with the hope that when the Thessalonian disciples get a true view of the whole matter, they will be restored to quiet mind and orderly and fruitful living.

### A. FALSE TEACHING CONCERNING THE DAY OF THE LORD (2:1-3a)

**2:1-3a.** The Thessalonian church is in a distressing state. The word for **shaken** always implies violent unsettling; in Acts 16:26 it is used of the shaking of the foundations of the prison by an earthquake (cf. also Acts 17:13, where it is used of the disturbance of a crowd). To be "shaken from their minds" implies that they were not mentally stable. The word for **excited** is used in the N.T. only here and in the apocalyptic discourse of Jesus (Matt. 24:6; Mark 13:7; and in Luke 24:37, in MSS B and 1241). In classical Greek it meant "to cry aloud," "to be violently disturbed," and was used mainly in tragedy. We are to understand that there was great excitement in Thessalonian church circles.

Precisely the source of the false rumor or teaching is not given. Apparently it was not clear to Paul and his associates. They mention as possibilities, **spirit or word** or **letter purporting to be from us.** Spirit refers to a prophetic utterance, probably from one of the prophets in Thessalonica. Already at the time of the writing of the first letter a word of caution about "proving" such utterances seemed advisable (I Thess. 5:19-21). **Word** as a possible source is given various interpretations. Some have thought it referred to a word of Jesus; others, to some apocalyptic reckoning on the basis of Daniel (cf.

Lord's character revealed in us? Is his cause benefited or handicapped by our witness? Is the **name** of our Lord glorified in us?

**2:1-12. *Man's Enemy Number One.*—**This is the bizarre passage on antichrist. Chickens come home to roost. A whole flock of them are at rest on Paul's windows and roof tree. His first epistle put the Thessalonians in a state of anticipation, for he definitely told them the

parousia would be soon; not in the coming days of their children, but in their own. As the weeks passed by with each one bringing its crop of rumors, prophecies, and forebodings, on their heels came angry debate, nervousness, disappointment, replacing Christian conversation, serenity, and courage. Paul is distressed and irritated. They should know better, for has he not told them that certain things must first

3 Let no man deceive you by any means: for *that day shall not come,* except there come a falling away first, and that man of sin be revealed, the son of perdition;

the Lord has come. 3 Let no one deceive you in any way; for that day will not come, unless the rebellion comes first, and the man of lawlessness[a] is revealed, the son of

[a] Other ancient authorities read *sin.*

Matt. 24:15; II Esdras 12:11-12); others still, to some teaching discourse from a teacher in the church (cf. I Cor. 12:28; Acts 13:1). It is generally agreed that it refers to some oral message. **Letter . . . from us** is understood by Frame, Moffatt, and others to refer to a possible misrepresentation of some passage in the first letter (Frame thinks this is certain), or to a lost letter of Paul, or even possibly to a forged letter purporting to be from Paul (as apparently RSV). This last view seems best to fit the entire tone of the passage and the specific form of words in which the letter is mentioned. The request that the readers are to **let no one deceive** them **in any way** clearly indicates, as Paul understands it, that someone (or ones) has been spreading false teaching among them. As Paul uses ἐξαπατέω (**deceive;** he alone in the N.T. uses it), it carries the idea of willful deception; so probably here.

### B. The Man of Lawlessness (2:3b-10)

This section (and through vs. 12) has been the object of endless speculation and discussion. There are several radically differing schools of interpretation; and within each school individual interpreters reflect greatly differing opinions. In referring to this whole body of opinion F. W. Farrar (*The Life and Work of St. Paul* [New York: E. P. Dutton, 1880], I, 617) speaks of "that vast limbo of exploded exegesis—the vastest and the dreariest that human imagination has conceived." Inasmuch as Paul had given to the Thessalonian Christians very extended instruction in this area when he and his fellow missionaries were first preaching among them, he can and does take much for granted here which was well known to them, but of which we are entirely ignorant. It is clear enough, however, that the passage centers in the teaching concerning **the man of lawlessness.** The term appears here for the first time in any known writing, just as the term antichrist is first known in I John (2:18-19), where he is identified with certain teachers who have been associated with the Christian group but did not really belong with it (I John 2:22; 4:3; II John 7; on the general character of the apocalyptic pattern, many features of which appear in this paragraph, see Intro. to Revelation in Vol. XII of this Commentary).

**3b-9.** The apostle calls to the mind of the Thessalonian Christians some matters about which he had given instruction earlier. **I told you these things.** The disturbed disciples are reminded that **that day will not come** until after the **rebellion** (RSV; a **falling away**—KJV) and **the man of lawlessness is revealed, the son of perdition.** There is no identification of either the **rebellion** or **the man of lawlessness** at any point in the discussion, and in order to attain any real understanding of the teaching here we must pay close attention to the smallest details of the description. The fact that already the Thessalonians had been told these things means that all this had been a part of Paul's thinking when he and his companions arrived in Thessalonica. Taking into account the

occur (vs. 6)? He again reminds them: (*a*) There will be a great **rebellion** (vs. 3 RSV), **a falling away** first (KJV). No clear indications of its nature are given, but it is generally agreed that the apostle has in mind a far-flung and active defiance of God's rulership. (*b*) At the height of the rebellion the **lawless one** or antichrist is to appear, and he will be the personification of all wickedness. He is not **Satan,** for vs. 9 shows

he is under Satan's direction. He will bestride the earth and will make vast claims, even attempting to seat himself on the throne of God. He will possess powers to do miracles, but their object will be evil, will deceive many, and will be the incarnation of all wickedness and falsehood. At the present he is being held in check by a power Paul does not indicate, but the day of his revelation will come. That day will also

4 Who opposeth and exalteth himself above all that is called God, or that is worshipped; so that he as God sitteth in the temple of God, showing himself that he is God.

5 Remember ye not, that, when I was yet with you, I told you these things?

perdition, 4 who opposes and exalts himself against every so-called god or object of worship, so that he takes his seat in the temple of God, proclaiming himself to be God. 5 Do you not remember that when I

---

references to "traditions" in vs. 15 and 3:6, one may understand that Paul's views here were shared by Christian teachers generally at the time and that both they and the preachers before them (cf. I Cor. 15:3-11) were inheritors of the traditions of Judaism. The eschatology of apocalyptic Judaism and that of early Christianity are of the same general pattern.

The man of lawlessness is here closely associated with the rebellion; but he is not identical with it, as most interpreters now agree. He is described as one who opposes and exalts himself against every so-called god or object of worship. Further, he takes his seat in the temple of God, proclaiming himself to be God. If we observe that the singular God and not "gods" is used in the latter clause, it must be evident that reference is being made to the temple of Israel in Jerusalem. The rebellion is in Greek ἀποστασία, our word "apostasy." This term, with variant spelling, was used in classical Greek of a political revolt; and it has been suggested that the writers in this passage might be thinking of the revolt of the Jews from Rome. However, the idea of a religious falling away is more likely. The word is used in the LXX (Josh. 22:22; II Chr. 22:19; 33:19; Jer. 2:19) always in that sense. It is also so used in I Macc. 2:15, where the agents of the king, Antiochus Epiphanes, are seeking to force the Jews to Hellenize. The idea of a great religious defection is characteristic of Jewish eschatology (see, e.g., II Esdras 5:1-13). It passes over into early Christian thinking and appears in varied forms. It is reported as a phase of the teaching of Jesus (Matt. 24:4-5, 10-13; Mark 13:5-6, 22; Luke 21:8). The writer of Hebrews (6:4-6; 10:26-29) knows of such apostasy in his day; and I Tim. 4:1, citing some prophetic utterance, uses the verb to predict such a falling away from the faith. Frame holds that in the present passage the event is conceived as taking place in the non-Christian world, and Stevens (with most scholars) is just as positive that it is something within the church itself. As a matter of fact, the total tradition includes both the falling away from faith, and the world-wide expansion and increase of the power of evil. The rebellion is, strictly speaking, within the church, but the outcome affects the world outside; and evil becomes blatant and dominant in the whole of the inhabited world. This apostasy was one feature of the picture of the future which Paul had drawn for the Thessalonians.

The man of lawlessness is the very embodiment of this evil (cf. John 8:44; the devil "is a liar and the father of lies"). The term son of perdition is a Hebrew idiom and is concerned with the ultimate doom of this lawless one. This same term is used of Judas (John 17:12). Further, the man of lawlessness demands that all other gods and objects of worship be set aside and he only be given recognition. Indeed, he insists that he is God and that he only is entitled to the worship accorded God. This he does in connection with taking his seat in the temple of God. When we remember that Paul and

---

be his day of certain doom, for the Lord Jesus will slay him with the breath of his mouth and destroy him by his appearing and his coming (vs. 8). With such a fabulous figure of evil, and with such a lack of specific identity and time of arrival, is it any wonder that so many zealots and theorists, as well as others of sober mind, have made this prophecy of Paul a three-ringed circus on the tanbark of which they have disported themselves in terms of their own particular interpretations? As dwellers in the twentieth century, with its deliverance from much theological ignorance and medieval superstition, we feel superior to any such conception of antichrist as possessed Paul and the Thessalonians. But let not our sophistication blind us to the

6 And now ye know what withholdeth that he might be revealed in his time.

7 For the mystery of iniquity doth already work: only he who now letteth *will let*, until he be taken out of the way.

8 And then shall that Wicked be revealed, whom the Lord shall consume with

was still with you I told you this? 6 And you know what is restraining him now so that he may be revealed in his time. 7 For the mystery of lawlessness is already at work; only he who now restrains it will do so until he is out of the way. 8 And then the lawless one will be revealed, and the Lord

his fellow workers were Jews and that though they recognized there were many so-called gods and lords (I Cor. 8:5-6), they knew that for all Christians, as well as all Jews, "there is but one God, the Father, . . . and one Lord Jesus Christ"—when this is remembered it seems almost certain that **the temple** intended here is the temple in Jerusalem.

**6-7.** The Thessalonian disciples **know** not only that **the man of lawlessness** is being restrained **now**, but also **know what is restraining him.** This had been explained to them when they received the original instruction in these matters. Vss. 6-7 both speak of this restraining power or force as **already at work.** In vs. 6 the "restrainer" is referred to in the neuter gender; in vs. 7, in the masculine gender. Thus it is something which can be thought of both as an abstract force and a personal figure—probably two phases of the same power and authority. If the restraining power may be conceived either as impersonal or personal, it was probably an authority or an institution which could be regarded as embodied in a personal agent. The authority would be the neuter, and the personal agent the masculine. But again, there is no identification of this restraining force, or power, or authority. The **mystery of lawlessness** is already at work. This again is a neuter and is parallel to the restraining force as described in vs. 6. In Paul's letters a mystery is either something that has hitherto been hidden or unknown, but has now been revealed (Rom. 16:25; Eph. 3:3, 9; 6:19; Col. 1:26), or something which lies too deep in nature or history or life to be understood by ordinary human understanding (I Cor. 13:2; 14:2; Col. 2:2; 4:3). We must suppose, then, that at present the force of lawlessness is working invisibly and in ways unknown or unappreciated. But for the time being there is a restraining power holding this lawless power or energy in check. This is to continue for a limited time—**until he is out of the way.**

Precisely what this clause means is difficult to determine. It is prevailingly and probably correctly understood to mean that the time is coming when the "restrainer" is to be removed. The verb used does not imply that he (or it) is "removed," but rather that he (or it) removes himself, literally, "becomes out of the midst." This phrase "out of the midst" is employed in Paul's letters elsewhere three times (I Cor. 5:2; II Cor. 6:17; Col. 2:14); and in each instance the removal of something evil, or the separation of oneself from evil, is being enjoined. According to the usual interpretation of this present passage, the evil is being restrained or held in check, and the restraining one, and not the evil, is to "become out of the midst." In what manner or by what means the restraining one is to be removed or takes himself out of the situation is not said. Our understanding of this particular point is ultimately related to our conception of the identification of both "the man of lawlessness" and the "restrainer" (see below, on vss. 8-10).

**8-10. Then the lawless one will be revealed.** This **coming** will be a manifestation of the **activity** [ἐνέργειαν] **of Satan.** And it will be attended **with all power and with**

truth at the core of this prophecy—there are antichrists in our present world: forces of evil, concentrated, intelligent, determined, and deadly, opposing God and everything he represents in life. Here are but three of them: (a) War with its scientific capacity for the destruction of the body, the mind, the faith, the ideals,

the savings, the homes, the places of employment, the culture, and the future. This is a raging, foaming, mighty antichrist. (b) The secular mind. Its nature has already been described (see Expos. on I Thess. 2:1-12). Its results are already tasting bitter in our mouths— the loss of Sunday, with its opportunities for

the spirit of his mouth, and shall destroy with the brightness of his coming:

**9** *Even him,* whose coming is after the working of Satan with all power and signs and lying wonders,

**10** And with all deceivableness of unrighteousness in them that perish: because they received not the love of the truth, that they might be saved.

Jesus will slay him with the breath of his mouth and destroy him by his appearing and his coming. **9** The coming of the lawless one by the activity of Satan will be with all power and with pretended signs and wonders, **10** and with all wicked deception for those who are to perish, because they refused to love the truth and so be saved.

---

**pretended signs and wonders, and with all wicked deception.** The words **power** and **signs** and **wonders** which are employed here are those used of the powers and signs and wonders of the Lord Jesus "which God wrought through him" (Acts 2:22). The manifestation of **the lawless one** will be accompanied by the doing of miraculous deeds similar to those wrought by the Lord Jesus. His **coming** is also designated by the same term (parousia) as is used of the "coming" of the Lord Jesus. These signs of **the lawless one** will have effect primarily, if not exclusively, upon those "who are perishing" (τοῖς ἀπολλυμένοις), because they had no love of the truth, and indeed no disposition toward it (cf. Col. 1:21; Eph. 4:17-19; Rom. 1:25). They will be deceived by the pretensions of the lawless one because they have no moral discernment: the "light" that is in them is "darkness" (Matt. 6:23). But when the lawless one is thus revealed, the Lord Jesus will himself become manifest in his own parousia. He will destroy the lawless one **with the breath of his mouth** and bring him to naught by (literally) "the manifestation of his coming." **The breath of his mouth,** found only here in the N.T., probably reflects Isa. 11:4; cf. also Job 4:8-9.

Who is **the lawless one?** And who, or what, is restraining him? It is safe to say that those who see here simply a discussion of principles or forces of righteousness on the one side and unrighteousness on the other are not following Paul. He is not thinking simply of principles; personages are involved. It is equally certain that all who think of Paul as pointing to some modern historical figure or institution, as, e.g., the papacy or Mussolini or Hitler or Stalin, are deplorably astray. Nor is Paul thinking simply of some legendary figure coming down in the stream of tradition from old Babylonia. The thought here must be understood in terms of essentially contemporary figures and affairs. There are two leading general conceptions of Paul's meaning. On the one side are those who believe that **the mystery of lawlessness** represented to Paul the Roman Empire, and **the man of lawlessness** a Roman emperor. Over against the two are the "restraining power" and the "restrainer," which are not so readily identified. It is certainly true that to many Jews of Paul's day Rome was the embodiment of evil. The apocalypses of Baruch and II Esdras deal with the future and final destiny of the Jews under Roman tyranny. The Revelation of John deals with the same problem, set in the same frame, for Christians suffering persecution. But Paul lived before the years when these books were written, and it is difficult to place the thinking reflected in Rom. 13:1-7 in any such context as this view implies.

A second view, the opposite of the other, is that for Paul **the mystery of lawlessness** is Judaism; and **the man of lawlessness** is some leader in that faith, e.g., the high priestly house or some high priest yet to be. The "restraining force" would then be the Roman Empire, and the "restrainer" would be the emperor. But the man who wrote Rom. 9:1-5 could hardly have thought in this way.

---

public worship and religious education; the breakdown of law and order; the increase in divorce and separation, with consequent collapse of home life, etc. (*c*) Racialism, manifested in the United States in two forms: (i)

Anti-Semitism: the scandal of history, which has broken out with new violence, so that the lot of Israel is once more groans and tears, the wandering foot, and the weary breast. This black infection is virulent in American life. (ii) Anti-

11 And for this cause God shall send them strong delusion, that they should believe a lie:

12 That they all might be damned who believed not the truth, but had pleasure in unrighteousness.

11 Therefore God sends upon them a strong delusion, to make them believe what is false, 12 so that all may be condemned who did not believe the truth but had pleasure in unrighteousness.

---

The evidence is ample that the conceptions of Daniel (9:27; 11:36-37; 12:11) passed into the thinking of Judaism (see especially II Esdras 12:11-12) and became a part of the heritage of Paul. It is also evident that early Christian tradition reported such thinking to be characteristic of Jesus (see especially Matt. 24:15; Mark 13:14). With this early Christian tradition Paul was familiar. Also, about a dozen years before the writing of II Thessalonians, Caligula (A.D. 39 or 40) had tried to have his statue set up in the temple in Jerusalem as an object of worship (Josephus *Antiquities* XVIII. 8. 2-6; *Jewish War* II. 10. 1-5). It is almost certain that the horror of Daniel at Antiochus Epiphanes and the horror of the Jews at the attempted blasphemy of Caligula gave background and color to the thinking of the apostle. **The man of lawlessness** would be a personal figure who would have all the characteristics of these two historical figures who had sought to destroy or desecrate the holy of holies in Judaism. Paul as a Christian still held the basic convictions and emotions which were his as one zealous for the traditions of his fathers (Gal. 1:14). As he looked toward the future consummation, he followed the pattern of both his Judaism and primitive Christian thinking. Whether he precisely identified these figures is doubtful. If he did do so, it is certain that we are not in position to recover what he said or thought.

### C. Lovers of Error and Their Punishment (2:11-12)

In the closing part of vs. 10, Paul has spoken of those who do not "love the truth," and are to be deceived by the manifestations of signs and wonders which will be wrought by "the lawless one." Here he carries that point still further. Because these have "refused to love the truth," there has come **upon them a strong delusion, to make them believe what is false.** This delusion has come from God. It is not only what we might call the moral result of their attitude; it is a punishment from God. This was a thoroughly Jewish way of thinking and to be expected of Paul (Gal. 1:13-14). God hardened Pharaoh's heart (Exod. 4:21; 9:12; 10:20, 27; 11:10; 14:4, 8, 17) and those of the inhabitants of Canaan who opposed the coming in of Israel (Josh. 11:20); he sent "a lying spirit" to the prophets of Ahab (I Kings 22:19-23). In Rom. 1:20-28, Paul describes the judgment of God on those who had him in their knowledge and refused to hold him there. God turned them over in judgment to unclean desire, reprobate mind, degenerate affections. Persistent refusal to hear the truth and pleasure in evil bring the inevitable result—a natural outcome, but only because God has placed us in a world of moral meaning and order. It is the world of his making, and its laws are the expression of his mind and will. Those who believe not the truth, but find pleasure in unrighteousness, "receive the reward of what they have done" (II Cor. 5:10). In the present case not only does the judgment of God appear in their present blindness, but it will also appear as the final judgment of God upon them in the day of his wrath (cf. I Thess. 5:9-10).

---

Negroism. This is racialism's main expression in our land. It is not a simple problem to solve and will take both time and wisdom. But the blunt fact is that the Negro is now sharply aroused to the anomaly of being asked to give, work, fight, and die for democracy in all parts of the globe, yet being denied participation in it at home. We brought him here, enslaved and released him, and since have been exploiting him. In parts of his own country he is denied sleep in our hotels, food in our restaurants, education in our universities, work in our factories, residence in our districts, recreation at our beaches and resorts, membership in our unions and churches, justice in our courts, healing in our hospitals, and enfranchisement at

13 But we are bound to give thanks always to God for you, brethren beloved of the Lord, because God hath from the beginning chosen you to salvation through sanctification of the Spirit and belief of the truth:

13 But we are bound to give thanks to God always for you, brethren beloved by the Lord, because God chose you from the beginning[b] to be saved, through sanctification by the Spirit[c] and belief in the truth.

[b] Other ancient authorities read *as the first converts.*
[c] Or *of spirit.*

---

### D. THANKSGIVING FOR GOD'S CALL TO THE THESSALONIANS (2:13-15)

**13.** Having dealt with the disturbing problem of the day of the Lord, the writers express again their thanksgiving to God for these new converts. The beginning sentence is almost identical with the opening clause of 1:3. They feel **bound to give thanks to God always.** The disciples are **beloved by the Lord;** they were chosen by God unto salvation. **From the beginning** is the reading followed by both our versions, but "as first fruits," i.e., **as the first converts** (RSV mg.) is also well attested. **Salvation** was to be theirs because of their **sanctification by the Spirit and belief in the truth.** Most commentators think **sanctification by the Spirit** should be understood as referring to the sanctifying power of the Holy Spirit. Findlay and Frame see a reference to sanctification of the human spirit (cf. RSV mg.). This latter view is supported by the fact that in II Cor. 7:1, another passage in Paul concerned with the idea of sanctification, the word **spirit** clearly means the "spirit" of the person (cf. also I Thess. 5:23). This **sanctification** is in sharp contrast to the "energy of error" in those "who believed not the truth" (vss. 11-12) and find their pleasure in evil. They are facing destruction.

---

our polls. But these antichrists will our Lord Jesus destroy. Our cry is, "How long, O Lord, how long?"

**13-17. *Lift Up Your Hearts.*—**When one lives in a valley, it is a profitable experience to be taken up occasionally to the mountaintop from which one can get a look at the whole scene and get a breath of winelike air. The Thessalonians had had a rough time. They had been living right up against many difficult things and were still bleeding from the wounds of the persecutors. The artificial and strenuous excitement of the hope of Christ's immediate return, and their disappointment at his delay, had left their minds fatigued. The irritation in their midst caused by a few incorrigible busybodies and confirmed loafers had left their nerves frayed. They needed uplift, so Paul takes them up to a high place where they can have a conspectus of their own state, the religion in which they believe, and God's purpose for them in the present and future. It is a dazzling and encouraging scene unrolled before their entranced eyes. We too shall be entranced as we peer intently at a few of its features, for Paul, the theologian, with his flashing insight and compact statement, is here at his best; he puts his theology in a nutshell.

(a) The greatness of God and the love of God. Away back in the far reaches and silences of eternity, God had planned their place, and their final glory is Jesus Christ. Alexander Whyte continually urged his congregation, fellow ministers, and seminary students to brood upon the magnificence of God. This we seldom do, for the dust and fire of our overbusy, hurrying, and unreflective lives are upon us. If God is magnificent he should be reverenced and worshiped. We should never revert to O.T. theology in its completeness, but we ought for our own good to revert to some of its particulars, one of which is its awe-struck sense of God's greatness. "Enter into the rock, and hide thee in the dust, for fear of the LORD, and for the glory of his majesty" (Isa. 2:10) is the commanding and sobering summons of the young prince, Isaiah. "O come, let us worship and bow down: let us kneel before the LORD our maker. For he is our God; and we are the people of his pasture, and the sheep of his hand" (Ps. 95:6-7) is the stately and eloquent appeal of Israel's sweetest singer. These sonorous and solemn words seem remote from our mood and attitude. When the average apostle proclaims the gospel, does he by his bearing, voice, and message convey the profound conviction to the hearts of his hearers that he lives daily in the presence of the Eternal and has just come forth from it? When the minister looks out upon the average Christian congregation, do its members impress him as people living daily in God's sight, and as now engaging in the greatest act of which the human soul is capable—the public worship of the God and Father of our Lord Jesus Christ? Life offers us many electives. We

14 Whereunto he called you by our gospel, to the obtaining of the glory of our Lord Jesus Christ.

15 Therefore, brethren, stand fast, and hold the traditions which ye have been taught, whether by word, or our epistle.

14 To this he called you through our gospel, so that you may obtain the glory of our Lord Jesus Christ. 15 So then, brethren, stand firm and hold to the traditions which you were taught by us, either by word of mouth or by letter.

14-15. The Thessalonians had been called into this experience through the **gospel** which had been preached among them and which they had received in glad response and confidence. They were destined to come into the possession of **the glory of our Lord Jesus Christ** himself. As these disciples share in the power of the gospel of Christ, they would share also in his victory. If we "suffer with him," we shall also be "glorified" with him (Rom. 8:17).

Because of the richness and the fruitage of their experience through the acceptance of the gospel, they are urged as a logical consequence to **stand firm and hold to the traditions** which they had received. These **traditions** are referred to again in 3:6. At that point the reference is to what had been transmitted to them concerning the proper conduct of those who had newly become Christian disciples. Here the term would appear to be used in a more inclusive sense, to designate the whole body of teaching, practical and doctrinal, which Paul shared with others and had conveyed to the Thessalonians. The relation of Paul to early Christian thinking was close and vital (cf. I Cor. 11:2; 15:3-11).

The Thessalonians had been taught these traditions **either by word of mouth or by letter.** The reference to **letter** implies that already they had been given written instructions through at least one letter. This one might well be our first Thessalonian letter (so Frame and others); however, the possibility of more than one letter is not excluded.

can dress this way or the other, be carnivorous or herbivorous, drink wine or water, study or remain ignorant, save or spend—but worship is not an elective. It is an imperative, for without it our conception of the eternal Being will be distorted and untrue.

He is our Father and should be loved. The O.T. reveals a growing and expanding conception of God, but its highest understanding of him is in the words of the psalmist: "Like as a father pitieth his children, so the LORD pitieth them that fear him" (Ps. 103:13). Then Jesus came and said God is not *like* a father, God *is* a father. To the discouraged and needy he spoke, "Your Father knows what you need" (Matt. 6:8). To his disciples he counseled, "Pray then like this: Our Father . . ." (Matt. 6:9). When he himself prayed, he said, "My Father . . ." (Matt. 26:39). Our wonderful Lord took our noblest idea of character, refined and purified it of all dross, and then addressed it to God. Fatherhood means self-giving, sacrifice, discipline and order, wisdom rooted in experience, and individual concern for each member of the family. All these are in our heavenly Father. Should we not love him? He is not merely the great I Am or the great It, he is the great Heart.

He gives us a great conception of ourselves, and should be thanked. The truth of God's fatherhood immediately gives us the noble status of sons—sons of God. It is the reaffirmation of the primal truth in Genesis that we are made in his image. We are not merely a little better than the beasts of the field; we are but a little lower than the angels. He who was before the innumerable worlds of the universe began to roll; he who is the source and maintainer of all the laws by which life is directed; he who is our creator, the life of all lives, the omnipotent, the eternal, the all-wise, is our Father. Then we are his sons. Should we not fall upon our knees in wonder, love, and praise?

(b) **The glory of our Lord Jesus Christ.** This, exclaims Paul, is God's objective for us (vs. 14). The very thought bedazzles us. Like him? Will there ever dawn the hour when people or angels will exclaim about us, "How like Christ he is!" Jesus said, "I am the light of the world" (John 8:12). That is what he is. The great artists, philosophers, scientists, prophets, and poets have brought us light. We owe them a debt we can never repay, for their swinging lamps have illumined dark and shadowed paths which but for them would have remained in primal obscurity and mystery. But with all their giving, not one has been able to give us a philosophy whereby we are enabled to select true values by which we can live in honor and

16 Now our Lord Jesus Christ himself, and God, even our Father, which hath loved us, and hath given *us* everlasting consolation and good hope through grace,

17 Comfort your hearts, and stablish you in every good word and work.

16 Now may our Lord Jesus Christ himself, and God our Father, who loved us and gave us eternal comfort and good hope through grace, 17 comfort your hearts and establish them in every good work and word.

### E. Prayer for Firmness (2:16-17)

**16-17.** This section of the letter ends with a prayer that **our Lord Jesus Christ himself, and God our Father, who loved us and gave us eternal comfort and good hope** may give comfort to the hearts of these Thessalonian readers. Observe again the close relationship of God and Christ in this prayer (cf. the prayer in I Thess. 3:11-13, and the Exeg. there). II Cor. 13:14 contains a closing benediction which is a condensed expression of the relations of God, Christ, and the Holy Spirit in the life of a Christian disciple (see also I Cor. 12:4-6). When both God and Christ are mentioned together, God is usually spoken of first. Perhaps the fact that the letter has had so largely to do with "the coming of our Lord Jesus Christ" accounts for the present unusual order. The phrase **God our Father** calls attention to the **grace** of God in Jesus Christ. He has shown his fatherly care for all, including the Thessalonians; and they may be strong in their confidence in him. The death of Christ is mentioned only twice in these letters (I Thess. 4:14; 5:10) and that casually. In the latter passage it is said that his death was "for us," and it is clearly indicated that through his death we obtain salvation. That idea is not here stated, but it can hardly be wholly absent from the mind of the writers. **Comfort** does not need to mean only release from grief; it may mean the presence of a great hope. The Thessalonian Christians have suffered for their faith; they have remained steadfast; they may look forward to the fulfillment of the hopes they have in the gospel of the Lord Jesus, which God has manifested to them in his **grace.** Paul further prays that Christ and God may establish these much harassed disciples **in every good work and word.** Though he is deeply grateful for the strong witness they have already given to the meaning of the Christian gospel, he desires that they may abound more and more in the fruits of Christian faith and experience.

---

die in peace; not one has been able to give us the spiritual power whereby we can resist temptation, uproot deep-seated habits, and be inspired to follow the upreaching ideals of our souls. They can show us new worlds through their telescopes, present new ideas from the fertility of their minds, reveal new beauties through their seeing eyes and skillful brushes, place new inventions at our disposal; but they cannot endow us with generosity, self-control, wisdom, and plant in us the desire to use them aright. Nor can they answer the questions which have been nagging at the heart and teasing the mind of endless generations. Whence? Why? Whither? Whence am I come? Where is my root and beginning? Why am I here? What are the purposes for which I am so fearfully and wonderfully made? Whither am I going? Have I an eternal home and dwelling place? Is the grave a goal or a thoroughfare? Is there One beyond?

But **the glory of our Lord Jesus** is that he can do all these things and answer these questions. It seems unabashed and overwhelming egoism for him to say, "I am the light of the world," but human experience says it is not boasting but fact. Two thousand years have come and gone, yet not one of his claims has been reduced or flung out of court by the march and test of the centuries. No one has ever been able to say truthfully, "Here he erred," "There he is wrong," "In this he failed." He is the Savior of men, the declarer of the kingdom, the seer of the centuries, the guide of the human soul, and is now the final hope of a discouraged, brutalized, ashamed, aspiring, and yearning world. How glorious is he who was made manifest in the flesh, vindicated by the spirit, seen of the angels, preached among the nations, believed on throughout the world, received up into glory. And his glory is to be ours!

(*c*) *The power of gospel preaching.* To God's wonder and Christ's glory, the Thessalonians have been called **through our gospel** (vs. 14). Here is the divine-human co-operation again set forth and re-emphasized in **hold to the traditions which you were taught by us, either by**

333

3 Finally, brethren, pray for us, that the word of the Lord may have *free* course, and be glorified, even as *it is* with you:

2 And that we may be delivered from unreasonable and wicked men: for all *men* have not faith.

3 Finally, brethren, pray for us, that the word of the Lord may speed on and triumph, as it did among you, 2 and that we may be delivered from wicked and evil

---

IV. CLOSING APPEALS, INSTRUCTION, PRAYER (3:1-16)

A. REQUEST FOR PRAYER (3:1-2)

This brief letter is being brought to a close. The word **finally** introduces not a conclusion from the preceding discussion, but a new phase of discussion which will be the closing one. As is his custom, Paul asks that the readers may pray for the success of his further labors in the gospel. He asks them to join him in prayer that the word which he preaches **may speed on.** This figure of speech is apparently taken from the race course; and one would expect Paul to add "and be crowned." Actually, however, instead of holding to the figure, he moves over into the realm of his religious hope—that the word of God may be, not "crowned" but **glorified** (KJV; **triumph**—RSV). It will be glorified in the glorified life it gives to those who obey it. It will repeat elsewhere what it has accomplished in Thessalonica. The labors among them of himself and his fellow missionaries had, as they well knew, been successful. They were a part of the fruitage of the gospel, and the prayer is that this gospel may be equally successful elsewhere. He and they (cf. I Thess. 2:1-2) knew perfectly well that the way he and his helpers had already traveled had been one of difficulty and persecution; so the way before him would be.

Hence the further request that the readers should also pray that the missionaries **may be delivered from wicked and evil men.** The phrase here used to describe these men (ἀτόπων καὶ πονηρῶν) is unique in the Greek Bible. It is vivid and forceful. Such men were to be found in every community, and wherever Paul and his fellow preachers might go, he expected again to face them. **For not all have faith.** There are those, both Jews and Gentiles (I Thess. 2:14-16), "who disbelieve the truth" (2:10-12) and are hostile to those who preach it. The book of Acts and Paul's letters furnish abundant evidence of this

---

**word of mouth or by letter** (vs. 15). There is a tendency in many quarters to minimize the power and place of preaching, which we should decisively reject as both untrue historically and in the present world situation. "Preaching," said a would-be pundit, "is just words." As foolish and vague a statement as could weary the patient ear! For anyone in this century to decry words, when through their eloquent use by such men as Hitler, Churchill, and Roosevelt, its direction has been changed, millions of lives transformed, and many geographic boundaries moved, approaches stupidity. There is no such thing as "just words," for it is through them man thinks, articulates his soul, conveys his mind, and moves his fellows. Paul searchingly asks: "How are they to believe in him of whom they have never heard? And how are they to hear without a preacher?" (Rom. 10:14.) And words are ours to learn and use aright to tell of God, of his Son, of his kingdom which has foundations, of heaven's joys, of hell's terrors, of sin life's final shame, of salvation life's noblest glory. Let us not deceive ourselves. The

minister of the word should be able to preach with persuasiveness and effectiveness. To that he is first of all called, and he should be willing to pay its high price and accept its stern disciplines. It is still God's good pleasure "by the foolishness of preaching to save them that believe" (I Cor. 1:21).

3:1-17. *Repetitions.*—There is little in this chapter not already dealt with by Paul in his first epistle and in the two previous chapters of this one. He again solicits the prayers of the Thessalonians, for himself, for his message, and for deliverance from the plottings of his enemies; assures them that God will not fail them, and that he is certain of their continued loyalty to him, his associates, and God; commands that the idlers be not only refused bread but fellowship, and again urges them to persistence in good deeds; reiterates the obligation of obedience to his words, and pronounces a blessing upon them.

1-2. *Feather the Arrow.*—Paul is still being harried by the bigotry of the Jews, the hatred of his former associates of the Pharisaic order, and

3 But the Lord is faithful, who shall stablish you, and keep *you* from evil.

4 And we have confidence in the Lord touching you, that ye both do and will do the things which we command you.

5 And the Lord direct your hearts into the love of God, and into the patient waiting for Christ.

6 Now we command you, brethren, in

men; for not all have faith. 3 But the Lord is faithful; he will strengthen you and guard you from evil.[d] 4 And we have confidence in the Lord about you, that you are doing and will do the things which we command. 5 May the Lord direct your hearts to the love of God and to the steadfastness of Christ.

6 Now we command you, brethren, in

[d] Or *the evil one.*

---

fact. In Corinth such opposition was experienced—perhaps even while this letter was being written (see Acts 18:5-6). It was Paul's habit to ask for the prayers of those to whom he was writing (cf. I Thess. 5:25; II Cor. 1:11; Rom. 15:30-32*a*; Col. 4:3, 18). Intercession for others was equally a habit with him (1:11; 2:16-17; 3:16; I Thess. 3:11-13; 5:23; Phil. 1:4, 9; Philem. 4).

### B. Expressions of Confidence (3:3-5)

**3.** Over against all this opposition and antagonism from wicked men is the Lord, who is himself **faithful.** He has expressed and committed himself in the gospel. He will not only deliver his messengers, but will also strengthen and guard these Thessalonians from **the evil one** (RSV mg.) whose spirit is manifested by those who may persecute them.

**4.** Confidence in the Lord extends to confidence in the disciples. Because the writers are persuaded of the faithfulness of the Lord in his helping of the much belabored and persecuted disciples at Thessalonica, they are also persuaded that the disciples not only are doing, but will continue to do, those things which they have been enjoined to do. The word **command** (παραγγέλλομεν) receives content from 2:15 and, more explicitly, from 3:6-15. They are to continue in the great tradition which has been delivered to them. They will live as Christians should live who have faith and love and hope (I Thess. 1:3), who live in Christ.

**5.** Again Paul expresses himself in prayer. He (with Silvanus and Timothy) now asks that the Lord may **direct** their **hearts** (get them well straightened) into the way that brings them **into the love of God** and **to the steadfastness** which may be theirs because of their commitment to Jesus Christ. This prayer catches up in spirit and tone what reverberates constantly in both these letters—a great longing that the good work which has been begun may be brought to completion (I Thess. 3:11-13; cf. Phil. 1:6).

### C. Injunctions Concerning Idlers (3:6-15)

**6.** A part of **the tradition** which the Thessalonians had received from the apostles had to do with a very practical everyday matter. Some of them were living in a disorderly

---

the malevolence of the pagans whose commercialized idolatry his truth threatens. In I Thess. 5:25 he merely asks for prayer. Here he asks for prayer at two specific points: **Pray for us that the word of the Lord may speed on and triumph, . . . and that we may be delivered from wicked and evil men.**

On analysis many a "pastoral prayer" appears as a sad example of disorder, prolixity, vagueness, and meagerness.

> Prayer is the soul's sincere desire,
> Uttered or unexpressed.[8]

[8] James Montgomery, "What Is Prayer?"

But its expressions should be intelligent and purposeful. There would be fewer vague and disorderly prayers if we knew the parts of prayer: The address, adoration and thanksgiving, confession (some liturgists say confession should precede adoration and thanksgiving), petition, intercession, conclusion. Quietly kneeling with a large sheet on which these headings are written in order, we will be able to pray with a new definiteness, orderliness, and effectiveness.

**6-15. *Off Come the Gloves.*—**Paul never hesitates to bid the members of the churches he established look to him as an example. He has

the name of our Lord Jesus Christ, that ye withdraw yourselves from every brother that walketh disorderly, and not after the tradition which he received of us.

7 For yourselves know how ye ought to follow us: for we behaved not ourselves disorderly among you;

8 Neither did we eat any man's bread for nought; but wrought with labor and travail night and day, that we might not be chargeable to any of you:

9 Not because we have not power, but to make ourselves an ensample unto you to follow us.

10 For even when we were with you, this we commanded you, that if any would not work, neither should he eat.

the name of our Lord Jesus Christ, that you keep away from any brother who is living in idleness and not in accord with the tradition that you received from us.

7 For you yourselves know how you ought to imitate us; we were not idle when we were with you, 8 we did not eat anyone's bread without paying, but with toil and labor we worked night and day, that we might not burden any of you. 9 It was not because we have not that right, but to give you in our conduct an example to imitate. 10 For even when we were with you, we gave you this command: If any one will

---

manner. They were not giving themselves steadily to any task and were becoming a source of confusion and difficulty for others. Paul, Silvanus, and Timothy had given specific instructions concerning this point during their ministry there (I Thess. 4:1; 5:14), and they feel called upon again to emphasize it because of the serious disturbances resulting from its being ignored. They speak as brethren to **brethren,** but they also speak **in the name of our Lord Jesus Christ,** whose messengers they were (cf. I Thess. 2:13), and under whose authority they set forth this message. The Thessalonians are commanded to avoid **any brother who is living in idleness.** A similar caution with regard to another kind of group is expressed in I Cor. 5:9-11. Jude 11 and 22 also reflect something of the spirit of this injunction. It is intended to work for the good, not the evil, of the one who is shunned.

**7-9.** The evangelists again refer to their own conduct and remind the readers that they should imitate their example. When they were at Thessalonica preaching the gospel, they did not live in idleness or disorder. The KJV has the more accurate translation here, **we behaved not ourselves disorderly.** The verb is found only here in the N.T. It really is a military term and here might well be translated "we did not break ranks" among you (cf. I Cor. 14:40, which may be rendered, "Let all things be done presentably and according to the proper 'line up' or order"; also Col. 2:5, the "good order and the firmness of your faith"). They did not eat anyone's bread "gratuitously" (cf. II Cor. 11:7, "without cost"), but toiled and labored by night and by day in order that they might **not burden** anyone (cf. I Thess. 2:8-9). They had toiled with their own hands, not because they did not have the right to expect support in their work of proclaiming the gospel (cf. I Cor. 9:4-6; 9:14-18), but because they would give **an example** of what was the right way of life for all. Paul frequently refers to himself as an illustration or example of that which he enjoins upon others (cf. Phil. 3:17; I Cor. 11:1; I Thess. 3:12). He seeks to make his own life conform to that which he believes to be the Christian standard of conduct, the standard to which he would call others.

**10.** When the missionaries were in Thessalonica, they had laid upon the believers there the injunction: **If any one will not work, let him not eat.** Adolf Deissmann (*Light*

---

a sanctified knowledge of his own character and activity. In the previous letter he congratulates the Thessalonians on their emulation of him and does not hesitate to link his conduct with

that of Christ. "You became imitators of us and of the Lord" (I Thess. 1:6). This sounds sacrilegious, but it is not. Paul is so sure of his own sincerity and intelligent discipleship, so certain

11 For we hear that there are some which walk among you disorderly, working not at all, but are busybodies.

12 Now them that are such we command and exhort by our Lord Jesus Christ, that with quietness they work, and eat their own bread.

13 But ye, brethren, be not weary in well doing.

14 And if any man obey not our word by this epistle, note that man, and have no company with him, that he may be ashamed.

not work, let him not eat. 11 For we hear that some of you are living in idleness, mere busybodies, not doing any work.

12 Now such persons we command and exhort in the Lord Jesus Christ to do their work in quietness and to earn their own living. 13 Brethren, do not be weary in well-doing.

14 If any one refuses to obey what we say in this letter, note that man, and have nothing to do with him, that he may be

---

*From the Ancient East,* tr. L. R. M. Strachan [New York: George H. Doran, 1927], p. 314) thinks this may have been a piece of well-known workshop morality. Others regard it as a Jewish proverb. Statements somewhat akin have been brought from later Jewish tradition. It is said by some (e.g., Findlay, Milligan) that the proverb was based on Gen. 3:19. Nothing in any of these sources gives to work the moral meaning here assigned it.

**11-12.** The writers use here a play on words which we cannot very well transfer to English. These idlers were doing no work, but were "working" with great zeal over the affairs of others. The apostles hear of this, probably by word of mouth: **We hear . . . .** Someone had carried the first letter to Thessalonica, and had probably returned at the time this second letter was being written. Information had also come about the other point with which this letter is most concerned (cf. 2:1-12). It is not unlikely that Christians were coming and going often between these two important centers, Corinth and Thessalonica (cf. I Thess. 1:8-9). But however the news may have reached them, the writers sternly rebuke these **busybodies,** commanding and beseeching in the Lord Jesus that they work **in quietness** and eat the bread which they themselves have earned by their own toil.

Probably there is an element of truth in the suggestion, frequently made, that expectation concerning the early coming of the Lord had led these "loafers" into idleness and meddlesome living. However, inasmuch as the apostles had felt it necessary to refer to their own example even when first among them, and had given so strict a command as that if they would not work they should not eat, we should probably look for a deeper cause. The habit of idleness seems to be a part of the background of some of the members of this church. It was not something induced by their new outlook but something which held on into their new experience.

**13.** In this paragraph the apostles shift back and forth between these whom they are censuring for their disorderly and meddlesome lives, and those whom they are commending for their fidelity. They now ask the latter not to become weary in their right living. They are surrounded by those who annoy them and make it difficult for them to persevere. However, they are enjoined to continue steadfast and faithful in their daily lives.

**14-15.** Attention is again given to those who have fallen under censure. The Thessalonians are told that if anyone refuses to become obedient to what has been

---

that he must and does represent Christ to this group of young Christians, that he can say, "Look at me and imitate me." He is particularly insistent that they copy him in hard work (I

Thess. 2:9). He has already rebuked the busybodies who do everyone's work but their own. He is hard on them, but even more so on the drones in the congregational hive. If they will

15 Yet count *him* not as an enemy, but admonish *him* as a brother.

16 Now the Lord of peace himself give you peace always by all means. The Lord *be* with you all.

17 The salutation of Paul with mine own hand, which is the token in every epistle: so I write.

ashamed. 15 Do not look on him as an enemy, but warn him as a brother.

16 Now may the Lord of peace himself give you peace at all times in all ways. The Lord be with you all.

17 I, Paul, write this greeting with my own hand. This is the mark in every letter

written in this letter, they are to have nothing to do with him at all. Some MSS read "your" (ὑμῶν) rather than our (KJV) and this fact leads a considerable number of expositors to think that the letter here mentioned should be understood as a letter to be written by the Thessalonian disciples in which they would report on the reaction of the idlers. Our (ἡμῶν) has the stronger MS support, however. The Thessalonians are to "avoid" the busybody not because they are to look upon him as an enemy; they are to think of him as a brother. They are to admonish him and seek to bring him into the right way. If he will pay no attention to what is said, then they are to have nothing to do with him (cf. Matt. 18:15-17). The word here used is found also in I Cor. 5:9; it carries the same idea there as here. The attitude that is enjoined is intended to bring such a one to a consciousness of his condition and relation to others and make him ashamed of his conduct.

### D. Prayer for the Disciples (3:16)

**16.** Again the writers express themselves in a prayer—that the Lord of peace may give the Thessalonians peace at all times in all ways. This peace will not be a gift from afar, for it is Paul's prayer that the Lord himself will abide with them and in them.

### V. Closing Greeting and Benediction (3:17-18)

**17.** At this point Paul takes the pen from his amanuensis and writes a word of greeting with his own hand. Just what peculiarity (mark) there was in his writing he does not say. Gal. 6:11 refers to "large letters" with which Paul writes. Apparently he wrote a large and bold hand, possibly a natural reflection of his own bold, forthright spirit. He tells the Thessalonians that this writing with his own hand is a mark of identification in every letter which they may receive. Perhaps this is a sidelight upon his suggestion in 2:2 that they are not to be disturbed "by letter purporting to be from us." Paul had reason to believe that others had written counterfeit letters in his name, and he takes care to say that they may test every letter received as from him by reference to his own handwriting, which he will put into every letter he writes. It is the way I write. The identical wording of this letter, "Greeting with my own hand," is found also in I Cor. 16:21 and Col. 4:18, probably for a similar reason.

not get out in the morning, put their hands to an honorable task, and come home at evening with the sweat of honest toil still on them, then let them starve. He has said they are to be admonished (I Thess. 5:14). Now he goes one drastic step farther—they are to be isolated: **Keep away from any brother who is living in idleness.** This seems not only too drastic but definitely unchristian, and a negation of the central ethic of love. But it is not so. Christianity is finally dependent, for its influence on and growth in the world, upon the character of its disciples. The most real instruction in the Chris-

tian way is always the Christian himself. Paul knew that a few notorious lazybones in the congregation of Thessalonica would undo much of his teaching, so they must be publicly exposed and separated from the brethren.

It is example the world is crying out for. A radiant life of Christian service can never be argued away. There it stands and who can deny it? Is that not the force of the Incarnation? "I have given you an example" (John 13:15). When men ask, "What is God like?" we can say, "Look at Jesus. See him and you see the Father" (cf. John 14:9). There is a valley in northern

**18** The grace of our Lord Jesus Christ *be* with you all. Amen.

¶ The second *epistle* to the Thessalonians was written from Athens.

of mine; it is the way I write. **18** The grace of our Lord Jesus Christ be with you all.

---

**18.** The final word of this letter is almost the same as the closing word of the first letter. It is a prayer that **the grace of our Lord Jesus Christ,** which had been manifested to them and in them, may continue to abide and sustain them. So the writers began the correspondence; so they close it. This is their prayer always; it is at the heart of their gospel.

---

Manitoba which was opened up by a Presbyterian minister named Johnson. He was not a strong preacher nor impressive in person, and often traveled in overalls; but he covered the valley and the mountains by his labors, like a light. No shack was too remote, no camp too distant for him. It is no extravagance to say he was revered. Ten years after he left, his name was still as ointment poured forth: witness the fervent sentence of a humble woman, as with shining eyes she said, "He's just like God to me!"

The First and Second Epistles to

# TIMOTHY

and

The Epistle to

# TITUS

*Introduction and Exegesis by* FRED D. GEALY
*Exposition by* MORGAN P. NOYES

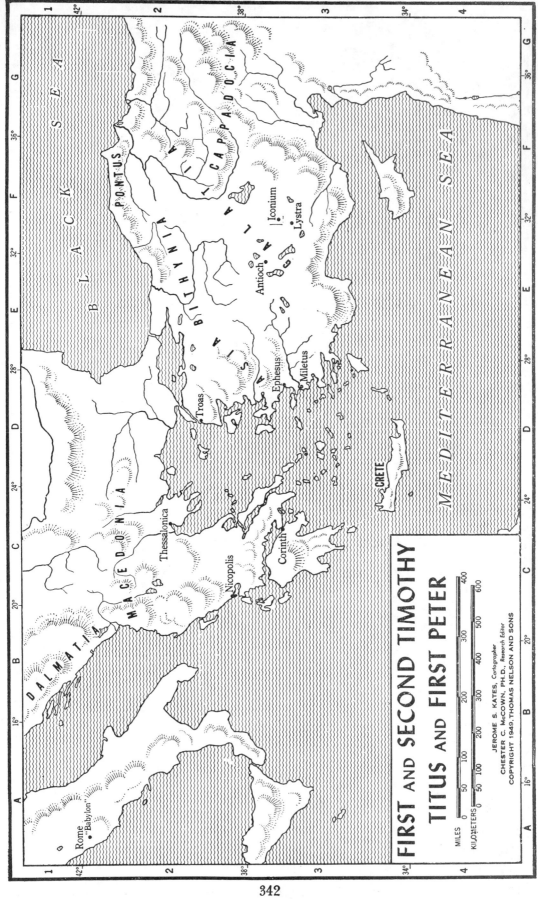

# FIRST AND SECOND TIMOTHY
# TITUS AND FIRST PETER

JEROME S. KATES, Cartographer
CHESTER C. McCOWN, PH.D., Research Editor
COPYRIGHT 1949, THOMAS NELSON AND SONS

MILES
KILOMETERS

# I AND II TIMOTHY

# TITUS

## INTRODUCTION

The interpreter of the Pastoral Epistles finds himself immediately and at every point confronted with a set of historical problems of great importance for our knowledge of early church history, but to which only tentative and conjectural solutions can be offered. The ultimate question is of course that of authorship and date. Did Paul write the letters as they themselves allege, and as church tradition has for the most part held through the centuries; or are they in whole or in part pseudonymous, that is, written not by Paul but later by a Paulinist? Obviously the meaning of the letters as a whole and in detail depends in the main upon the answer given to this question.

Since this is true, and since difference of opinion as to author and date persists, conceivably an interpreter might strive after strict neutrality and offer a double interpretation of the text, setting forth in one column its meaning if it is taken as genuinely Pauline, and in a parallel column its meaning as a pseudonymous writing of, say, the middle of the second century. Obviously, however, such a procedure is not practical. Furthermore, it is on other grounds preferable that a commentator weigh the evidence as honestly as he can, and on the basis of his conclusions choose the hypothesis which seems most adequately to explain the texts; whereupon he must relate the documents in question to the larger processes of growth and development which clarify and are clarified by them.

This study is frankly based on the theory that the Pastorals, in large part at least, are pseudonymous; that they belong to a later generation than Paul; and that in the main they are to be explained out of the historical context of the first half of the second century. Where details of the text do not easily fit into this theory, they will be honestly faced. Nevertheless, every attempt will be made to explore the significance of the second-century context for the texts, and to show that they yield their most fruitful meanings if interpreted as belonging to this later setting. The reasons for the belief in the pseudonymity of the epistles, while not presented in formal array, will emerge clearly as we proceed, as will the principal arguments of those who still insist upon Pauline authorship. Attention will also be paid from time to time to the possibility that genuine fragments of Paul's correspondence were used by the second-century writer.[1]

### I. To Whom Addressed

**A. Who Were "Timothy" and "Titus"?**—In contrast to all other New Testament letters which carry Paul's name, the Pastorals appear to be addressed not to churches, but to individuals. These are named—and indeed within the body of the text as well as at the beginning (I Tim. 1:2, 18; 6:20; II Tim. 1:2; Tit. 1:4) —as Timothy and Titus. Since, however, in the view of this study the letters are pseudonymous and belong to a period later than either Paul or Timothy and Titus, Timothy and Titus here cannot really be regarded as the men who worked with Paul: rather they stand for the (higher?) clergy who in this later generation stand to the writer as Timothy and Titus stood to Paul in the apostolic age. As the writer regards his own ministry as being in the true line of succession from Paul, so likewise he is careful to insist that the Timothys and Tituses of his own day—his "children" as well as Paul's—must regard themselves as fully accredited churchmen apostolically commissioned to establish and maintain faith and order in the church.

[1] In 1900 B. W. Bacon (*An Introduction to the New Testament* [New York: The Macmillan Co.], p. 128) could write: "Critics generally admit . . . that fragments at least of genuine letters of Paul to Timothy and Titus are here present." This statement is by no means as true now as when Bacon wrote it. In spite of the array of scholars who have held the "fragments theory" (e.g., Harnack, von Soden, Clemen, von Dobschütz, McGiffert, Moffatt, Streeter, Harrison, E. F. Scott), the present tendency is for those who reject Pauline authorship of the Pastorals as a whole to reject also any "fragments theory" (so Jülicher, Enslin, Goodspeed, Dibelius, etc.). B. S. Easton is cautious: "On the possibility of genuine Pauline fragments in the Pastorals . . . no final decision seems possible" (*The Pastoral Epistles* [New York: Charles Scribner's Sons, 1947], p. 16; see also pp. 75-78, 106). So far as the interpretation of the epistles is concerned, the point is not important, since the "fragments" are not extensive or important in content.

The Pastorals are thus distinguished from all other New Testament letters in that they are addressed not to "all God's beloved" (Rom. 1:7) nor to the "church of God," whether at Corinth, Galatia, or Thessalonica, nor to the totality of "the saints and faithful brethren in Christ" as at Colossae (see also Jas. 1:1; I Pet. 1:1; II Pet. 1:1), but to a special functional class within the church, namely, the professional ministry. Thus these letters occupy the unique distinction of being not simply the only letters in the New Testament to be addressed primarily to clergymen, but also of being in this sense the first extant pastoral letters—that is, letters written by a pastor to pastors—in the history of the church.

**B. Ecclesiastical Status of "Timothy" and "Titus."**—The status or rank in the church of "Timothy" and "Titus" is likewise problematic. At first glance the tone and temper, the form and content of the letters, suggest that the author was an old man, an "elder" both in age and function, a ruling elder, even a bishop, and that "Timothy" and "Titus" stand for the younger clergy: (a) The writer assumes a position of high authority in the church with the right and duty to command "Timothy" and "Titus." If he does not, by writing under Paul's name, intend to claim to be himself an "apostle" (see II Tim. 1:11), nevertheless he does regard his authority as apostolic and his rank in the church as superior to that of "Timothy" and "Titus." (b) The letters frequently speak of the addressees as younger persons: they are Paul's "children" (I Tim. 1:2; II Tim. 1:2; Tit. 1:4); "Timothy" is his "son" (I Tim. 1:18; II Tim. 2:1), is to shun "youthful passions" (II Tim. 2:22), must allow no one to "despise" his youth (I Tim. 4:12; see also I Tim. 5:1-2). Since subordinate position and youthfulness often coincide, and because particularly of I Tim. 4:12, and of the authoritative position assumed by the author in the letters, it is tempting to suppose that "Timothy" and "Titus" stand in the main for the younger clergy. Nevertheless, there are weighty arguments against the supposition: (a) "Timothy" and "Titus" occupy positions of responsibility and authority in the church next to "Paul." The functions assigned to them are the most important duties which can be prescribed, and in this period they surely cannot generally have devolved on young men. They are indeed historically the functions of bishops. As Easton has well observed,

It is evident that "Timothy" and "Titus" are much more than elders like the other elders. It is they who appoint elders—or at least control their appointment—"Titus" in places where the organization is still incomplete, "Timothy" (in 1 Timothy) to fill vacancies or enlarge the number (with similar authority as regards the deacons). "Timothy" (again in 1 Timothy) determines when extra compensation is due elders, receives charges against them, decides whether or not charges shall be entertained, inflicts penalties on the guilty and restores those who have repented. But, more than all, it is "Timothy" (or "Titus") who is responsible for the instruction and discipline of the flock. Other elders too may "labor in the word and the teaching" but this labor, voluntary for them, is his primary duty; it is he who teaches, exhorts, reproves and repels heresies; it is he who must make himself the "pattern" for others to imitate. . . . In "Timothy" and "Titus," therefore, the Ignatian bishops are actually found in everything but the title.[2]

B. H. Streeter writes:

The author of the Pastorals, we infer, takes the monarchical episcopate for granted. To him the figures of Timothy and Titus are of interest, not as historical personages, but as affording him an opportunity of portraying two different types of the ideal bishop. Timothy is the ideal bishop in his relation to his own church in a province like Ephesus, where organised churches already existed in all the principal towns. Titus, on the other hand, is the ideal of the Missionary Bishop—the bishop of some outlying province, where the churches outside the bishop's own headquarters are weak and discouraged.[3]

(b) Furthermore, "child" and "son" are terms which can be used affectionately to indicate subordinate position rather than age. All that the words need signify here is that "Timothy" and "Titus" are younger than and subordinate to the author or indeed to Paul. And further, the emphasis on the youthfulness of the addressees may well be a way of saying that second-century ministers belong to a later generation than that of Paul.

C. Ecclesiastical Status of the Author.—It follows, then, that if "Timothy" and "Titus" are (monarchical?) bishops, at the head of bodies of (local) presbyters composed of presiding presbyters (=bishops) as well as of non-overseeing elders and deacons, the author himself is akin to an archbishop in the more comprehensive sense. He certainly regards himself as having high authority over them. That he writes in Paul's name shows in itself what status he claims. Nor can such nomenclature for "Paul" and "Timothy" and "Titus" be regarded as invalid if the Pastorals were written well into

the second century, even though not clearly applied in the Pastorals themselves: (a) the author writing pseudonymously in the name of Paul would naturally use Paul's functional title "apostle" rather than his own title; (b) the Pastorals naturally take for granted the orders of clergy current at the time of writing and also knowledge of those orders on the part of their readers. If they are not concerned to distinguish between "bishops," "elders," and "deacons" it is because both they and their readers knew well enough what the terms meant.

D. Conclusion.—The probable conclusion, then, is that "Timothy" and "Titus" are more than presiding elders (=local bishops); rather, they are metropolitans, men of wider authority yet subordinate to the author, who will assert his jurisdiction over the whole of Asia, of Crete, and indirectly—since he writes in Paul's name—over the entire church.

If "Timothy" and "Titus" are merely symbolic names, it is gratuitous to interpret the "Timothy" and "Titus" of the Pastorals on the basis of the Timothy and Titus of Acts and the Pauline letters, and we are thereby relieved of the necessity of trying to harmonize closely the two sets of persons. To what extent pseudonymous writers in general, or this author in particular, felt themselves under necessity of assimilating the characters and events of contemporary persons addressed under the guise of ancient names to the characters and events of their historical prototypes can hardly be known. That such assimilation would take place at certain points is to be expected. On the other hand, the evidence here is against the supposition that any persistent or consistent effort was made to present "Timothy" and "Titus" in conformity with what Acts and Paul tell us of them.

## II. Background and Purpose

A. Church Organization. 1. The Problem: Status and Functions of Bishops, Elders, and Deacons.—Although the Pastorals are written to pastors by a pastor who takes it for granted that his readers know full well the functions and status of bishops (ἐπίσκοποι), elders (πρεσβύτεροι), deacons and perhaps deaconesses (διάκονοι), and widows (χῆραι), the letters themselves furnish a distressingly small amount of information relative to forms of organization, and much of that is ambiguous and inexact. That the "office of bishop" is "a noble task" is stressed in a "sure saying" (I Tim. 3:1). That it is the bishop's responsibility to "care for God's church," that is, to manage it as he does his own household, is made clear in I Tim. 3:4-5. In a special sense he is "God's steward" (Tit. 1:7). It is his function "to give instruc-

[2] The Pastoral Epistles (New York: Charles Scribner's Sons, 1947), pp. 176-77. Used by permission.
[3] The Primitive Church (New York: The Macmillan Co., 1929), pp. 118-19.

tion in sound doctrine and also to confute those who contradict it" (Tit. 1:9). The position carries prestige and its occupant may easily "be puffed up with conceit" (I Tim. 3:6). Since he stands between the church and the world, "he must be well thought of by outsiders" (I Tim. 3:7). Yet in the two cases in the Pastorals where "bishop" is mentioned (I Tim. 3:1-7; Tit. 1:7-9) the primary interest is in his character qualifications, not in the details of his status and work. Further, the lists of virtues and vices (see Exeg., ad loc.) are too formal to supply any precise information about the office.

The situation is equally perplexing with regard to elders. In the series mentioned in I Tim. 3:1-13, only "bishop" (in the singular), "deacons," and "the women" (deacons' wives or deaconesses?) are listed. The order of widows follows in ch. 5. Then, first, comes the mention of "elders who rule well" (5:17), some of whom, at least, also "labor in preaching and teaching." That the elder is in a position in which "charges" may readily be brought against him is suggested by 5:19. Possibly 5:22 may be taken to mean that elders are authorized to lay on hands, that is, to ordain (see Exeg., ad loc.).

The Pastorals contain only one further reference to elders, viz., Tit. 1:5, where Titus is charged with the responsibility of appointing elders in every town in Crete. But again the character qualifications listed for elders are essentially the same as those listed for bishops and deacons. Furthermore, the abrupt transition from elders in vs. 5 to bishop in vs. 7 seems evidence that in the Pastorals "elder" and "bishop" are synonyms for the same official (see Exeg., ad loc.). In the author's time there may have been elders in the church who were not ruling elders, but in these letters he is not concerned with them.

The same situation obtains with regard to deacons, mentioned only in I Tim. 3:8-13: the same stereotyped list of character qualifications recurs, but without hint of function or of status relative to the elder or bishop. That the office of deacon is mentioned only once in the Pastorals, and that, in contrast to elder and bishop, the abuses to which it was subject are not regarded as perilous enough to deserve mention, probably may be taken as evidence that the office was subordinate to that of elder or bishop. As for "deaconesses" and "widows," see Exegesis on I Tim. 3:11; 5:3-16.

Since, then, the Pastorals provide so little direct information concerning church orders, their establishment, differentiation, and functions, the problem of determining the presuppositions of the letters or the status of the various ministers in the churches is complex and difficult. This must remain a matter of great regret, for the Pastorals are the only letters in the New Testament devoted to the person and work of pastors. If the author had been interested in the matter he could easily have clarified the whole situation, and have settled problems which must be debated as long as history continues.

2. *Interpretation of the Evidence.*—Since according to the point of view of this study the Pastorals are best understood against the background of the second century, the evidence in the letters relative to church orders, both direct and indirect, may be interpreted as follows:

(*a*) The Pastorals clearly reflect a time when apostle and prophet have been succeeded by bishop (and archbishop?) and/or elder in a stabilized church organization fully committed to an authorized succession of ordained ministers. The local churches are no longer lay churches, nor are their needs now taken care of simply by itinerant missionaries. There is obviously hierarchical organization both in the local and ecumenical church. The chief function of the bishop (or archbishop?) is to transmit and maintain the true faith: as "Paul" is to Paul, so are "Timothy" and "Titus" to "Paul," and so are the local elders to "Timothy" and "Titus." An unbroken chain of ordained ministers may be regarded as already established.

(*b*) Since the sketchy and somewhat perfunctory description of "a [or the] bishop" in I Tim. 3:2-7, of "elders who rule well" in I Tim. 5:17-22, and of elders and "a [or the] bishop" in Tit. 1:5-9 are so similar as to seem parallel accounts characterizing the same sort of official, the common impression is that the terms "bishop" and "elder" are equivalent in the Pastorals. Those who hold to this interpretation explain the variation in terms (i) out of geography: so, for example, Goguel and Jeremias, who think *episkopos* may have been preferred in Asia, and *presbyteros* in Macedonia; (ii) or by suggesting (so Bultmann) that when the author of the Pastorals writes himself he prefers *presbyteros*, but that his written source(s) may have preferred *episkopos* (I Tim. 3:1-7; Tit. 1:7-9).

(*c*) Although the texts may not exclude the possibility that *episkopos* and *presbyteros* are exact synonyms, nevertheless they suggest that differentiation of terminology, as well as function, was taking place—perhaps very definitely had taken place—within the official ministry of the church. If "elders who rule well" are also *episkopoi*, it is still true that not all elders are ruling elders (see on I Tim. 5:17). Also *episkopos* is always used in the singular (I Tim.

3:2; Tit. 1:7) ; *presbyteros,* never. Although it may be admitted that the singular number in itself is not enough to prove that at the time the Pastorals were written the monarchical bishop was established at the head of the presbytery or elderhood, it may yet be said that there is no way of proving that the definite article before *episkopos* (I Tim. 3:2; Tit. 1:7) must be interpreted generically. Since the texts are ambiguous, everything depends on the date of the Pastorals and on the state of organization of the ministry at the time and place of writing.

(*d*) That the Pastorals assume a more advanced and highly differentiated type of church organization than the relevant texts themselves suggest is to be argued (i) from the fact that they are written to "Timothy" and "Titus," who, whether actual individuals or symbols, are regarded as persons of high official authority (see above, pp. 344-45), themselves superior in rank to elders; (ii) from the fact that the author ("Paul") stands yet above "Timothy" and "Titus" as a person of more than local authority. There can be no doubt but that the total context in which the Pastorals are best understood requires us to suppose that the church of the time was characterized by a more clearly defined system of hierarchical orders than the texts themselves reveal. Streeter writes:

The epistles might be entitled, "Advices to those who are, or who aspire to become, Bishops." And the advice is exactly what we should expect of an author who wrote *after* the monarchical episcopate had been established in Ephesus and the principal towns of the neighbourhood. He wrote to supply what the time needed; and what the time needed was, not a defence of episcopacy, but good bishops.[4]

### 3. The Pastorals and the Ignatian Letters.—
The problem of church orders in the Pastorals cannot be dismissed without some consideration of the situation in the letters of Ignatius of Antioch, seven letters written on the way from Syria to martyrdom in Rome, A.D. 110-17, one each to five churches in Asia—Ephesus, Magnesia, Tralles, Philadelphia, Smyrna—one to Rome, and one to Polycarp, bishop of Smyrna. The church as reflected in these letters, both as regards doctrine and organization, seems already fully "catholic." Indeed, the phrase "the Catholic Church" first appears here. The primacy of the Roman church is recognized. The hierarchy of bishops, priests, and deacons is again and again insisted upon. Indeed, the organization of the church seems so finally established as to make the descriptions in the Pastorals seem primitive by way of contrast, and even to require a dating much earlier than 110.

[4] *Primitive Church,* p. 121.

That the differences between the Pastorals and the Ignatian letters are great and important, and that the Ignatian letters from the standpoint of church orders constitute a formidable objection to dating the Pastorals as late as 150, must be admitted.[5] No entirely satisfactory solution of this problem is yet available. The most attractive suggestion has been made by Walter Bauer.[6] It is his thesis that as a result of the triumph of "orthodoxy" over "heresy," extant early Christian writings (*a*) conceal the real strength of heretical movements in the various areas of the ancient church, and (*b*) represent the orthodox patterns of faith and order as both older and more widespread than they actually were. Therefore Bauer asserts that contrary to the impression created by Ignatius, in his time Syria and west Asia Minor cannot be supposed to have had a monarchical episcopate. The real fact that is concealed behind Ignatius' constant insistence on episcopal claims is that he is the frantic leader of a minority group in intense struggle with a determined majority stubbornly refusing obedience to him. In insisting on the claims of the hierarchy, then, he describes less an established order than one which he will move heaven and earth to establish. As is generally the case when a minority group is at its wits' end, in desperation it puts forward the man of power with determination to dictate. If, then, Ignatius can effectively assert the claim to authority of *one* bishop, himself that bishop in Antioch, he might well hope by a Herculean effort climaxed in martyrdom to turn his minority into a majority, and to establish as orthodoxy the faith and order championed by himself.

If Bauer's analysis of the situation is correct, the argument for a pre-Ignatian date for the Pastorals, derived from the supposedly more advanced pattern of church orders in the Ignatian letters, is at least weakened. The differences, then, between the Pastorals and the Ignatian letters at this point are to be explained less by the differences in church organization prevailing at the time than by the difference in purpose between the writer of the Pastorals and Ignatius: Ignatius, concerned to rehabilitate his personal authority and to establish his own minority "sect" as orthodoxy, projects a hier-

[5] Kirsopp Lake, as he lets us know in a review of Harrison's work on Polycarp (see below, p. 369), continued to believe that the journey-to-martyrdom framework of the Ignatian letters is not convincing, and that they are therefore spurious. If this should be so, of course they would present no problem for a late dating of the Pastorals (see *Journal of Biblical Literature,* LVI [1937], 74).

[6] *Rechtgläubigkeit und Ketzerei im ältesten Christentum* (Tübingen: J. C. B. Mohr, 1934).

archy ideally calculated to force the antagonistic majority into submission; "Paul," concerned primarily to exclude and destroy the powerful heretical sects of his time, takes for granted the bishop-elder-deacon triad as the official form of the hierarchy. The need for him is not so much to defend the form (but see I Tim. 3:1) as to secure able Christian men as officers.

**B. The Functions of the Ministry.**—The essential function of the bishop and, by extension, of the lesser ministry in the Pastorals is supervision and control of the transmission of Christian doctrine. If "sound doctrine" is to be maintained in the churches, (a) heresy must be repudiated; (b) the true (Pauline) Christian faith must be preached in Paul's own spirit and tireless devotion; (c) ministers, professional Christian workers, including "widows" and perhaps deaconesses, must be carefully chosen with regard to their faith as well as their moral conduct; (d) discipline must be maintained; and (e) finally both form and content of the public worship must be strictly controlled.

**1. To Establish and Maintain Orthodoxy.**—More than any other writings in the New Testament, the Pastorals are concerned with the establishment of a Christian orthodoxy, and that in terms of the Pauline gospel.[7] Obviously the Christian faith is now well started on its way to becoming a fully integrated, clearly formulated body of thought and practice structurally stabilized in the hierarchically co-ordinated institution of the church, "the pillar and bulwark of the truth" (I Tim. 3:15). Indeed, so far as the author himself is concerned, orthodoxy is in theory already an accomplished fact. The problem is to secure general recognition of and obedience to it.

That the word "doctrine" or "teaching" should occur fifteen times in the Pastorals as against six times in the rest of the New Testament; that the adjective "sound" (see Exeg. on I Tim. 1:10), meaning "correct" or "orthodox," should be used frequently and exclusively in the Pastorals—these facts well indicate the extent to which at the time these letters were written church leadership was determined to solidify the Christian faith in a rigid orthodoxy. Likewise, the word "to teach a different doctrine" (ἑτεροδιδασκαλεῖν; in N.T. only in I Tim. 1:3; 6:3), absolute and unqualified as it is, reveals how fixed in form the Christian teaching is in the author's mind. Characteristically, then, the chief function of the minister is as teacher, that is, as transmitter of the deposit

---

[7] "What you have heard from me" (II Tim. 2:2); "as preached in my gospel" (II Tim. 2:8); "the glorious gospel of the blessed God with which I have been entrusted" (I Tim. 1:11).

of (the) faith or of (the) truth: I Tim. 4:6, 16; 6:3-5, 14, 20; II Tim. 1:13; 2:2, 14-16, 23; 3:14-17; 4:1-5; Tit. 1:9-11; 2:1.

Moreover, to urge a true faith is to combat a false one. Therefore he must be on constant alert to prevent persons wherever possible from getting a hearing for "different doctrine" (I Tim. 1:3). All teachers and preachers who have access to Christian congregations must be held in strict obedience to the received form of the faith. Those who remain obstinate in error must be "sharply" rebuked (Tit. 1:13); at any cost "they must be silenced" (Tit. 1:11). "The Lord's servant must not be quarrelsome but kindly to everyone, . . . forbearing, correcting his opponents with gentleness" (II Tim. 2:24-25). Nevertheless, he must be fully aware of the fact that these are the last days, the times of stress, and that therefore "proud, arrogant, abusive" men (II Tim. 3:1-5), "corrupt and unbelieving" (Tit. 1:15), "impostors" and "deceivers" (II Tim. 3:13), "liars whose consciences are seared," under domination of "deceitful spirits and doctrines of demons" (I Tim. 4:1-2), have greatly increased in number and power. Where possible, he must "avoid such people" (II Tim. 3:5). Yet when confronted with them he must not flinch in his duty to rebuke them, and if after admonishing them "once or twice," they remain "factious," he "must have nothing more to do" with them (Tit. 3:10). And if worst comes to worst, such persons must be "delivered to Satan" (see on I Tim. 1:20).

**2. To Preach with Tireless Devotion.**—To oppose heresy when presented by vigorous and commanding men is no easy task. First, then, adequately to discharge his duties the minister must look to himself as well as to his teaching (I Tim. 4:16). He must himself "follow the pattern of sound words" which he heard from Paul, he must "guard the truth" entrusted to him (II Tim. 1:13-14). He must do his best to present himself to God "as one approved, a workman who has no need to be ashamed, rightly handling the word of truth" (II Tim. 2:15). And to handle the word of truth rightly is to keep the Christian teaching intact and transmit it unaltered. Thus, "nourished on the words of the faith and of the good doctrine," he must train himself in godliness (I Tim. 4:6-7). He must "set the believers an example in speech and conduct, in love, in faith, in purity" (I Tim. 4:12). He is to "aim at righteousness, godliness, faith, love, steadfastness, gentleness" (I Tim. 6:11; see also II Tim. 2:22, 24-25). He shall show himself "in all respects a model of good deeds," and his teaching must be marked by "integrity, gravity, and sound speech that cannot be censured" (Tit. 2:7-8).

In addition to disciplining himself in godliness, the minister shall always keep in mind that his work is the positive preaching of the true (Pauline) Christian faith. If he tends faithfully to the public reading of scripture, to the preaching and teaching of the deposit of faith, and to his proper pastoral work, he will have no time for any "morbid craving for controversy and for disputes about words" (I Tim. 6:4). Controversies are "stupid" and "senseless," only breeding quarrels (II Tim. 2:23), and therefore "unprofitable and futile" (Tit. 3:9). Disputes "about words" do no good, but rather lead people further into irreligion (II Tim. 2:14, 16). The purpose of true Christian preaching is practical, not speculative. "The aim of our charge is love that issues from a pure heart and a good conscience and sincere faith" (I Tim. 1:5). Just as the purpose of Jesus Christ in coming into the world was eminently practical—to save sinners (I Tim. 1:15)—so it is the one business of the minister to seek godliness and to instruct others in the way of salvation: "to this end we toil and strive" (I Tim. 4:10). The minister who is aware that scripture is given not for speculation, but for instruction in salvation, and that its usefulness is "for teaching, for reproof, for correction, and for training in righteousness" is already completely "equipped for every good work" (II Tim. 3:15-17). He has no further need of "myths" or "speculations." Therefore he is resolutely to avoid the vain discussions of speculative theology.

In a time when the orthodox pattern of faith and order is yet in the making, when an important variety of interpretations of Christianity clamor for pre-eminence, and when the Christian finds himself at many points in conflict with contemporary religions and philosophies, even with the state, the minister must expect to endure suffering and persecution. Since religion strikes so deeply into life, religious disputes are usually insistent and intense, and frequently unreasoning, acrimonious, harsh. Nevertheless the minister must stand up to his faith in spite of all opposition. He must take his "share of suffering as a good soldier of Christ Jesus" (II Tim. 2:3; cf. II Tim. 4:5). In his hour of trial let him remember "Christ Jesus who in his testimony before Pontius Pilate made the good confession" (I Tim. 6:13). Above all, he should remember Paul, who languished in prison, who for the gospel suffered and wore fetters like a criminal (II Tim. 2:8-9). Having observed Paul's teaching, his conduct, his aim in life, his faith, his patience, his love, his steadfastness, his persecutions, his sufferings, indeed his deliverance from them all (II Tim. 3:10-11);

looking back upon his triumphant life, "I have fought the good fight, I have finished the race, I have kept the faith" (II Tim. 4:7); looking forward to sharing in Paul's coronation on Judgment Day and to a permanent place in the heavenly kingdom (II Tim. 4:8, 18)—thus remembering Paul, the minister is assured that just as surely as "all who desire to live a godly life in Christ Jesus will be persecuted" (II Tim. 3:12), so surely "our Savior Christ Jesus, who abolished death and brought life and immortality to light" (II Tim. 1:10), will rescue him from every evil (II Tim. 4:18).

*3. To Exercise Care in the Selection of Professional Workers.*—Fixity and uniformity of doctrine are most easily and effectively secured through a hierarchically ordered officialdom. Therefore the impulses to clarification of Christian teaching, to its definition in terms that could be accepted everywhere, always, and by all, and the need for assurance that having once for all been delivered it could be transmitted intact—these factors naturally produced a professional ministry with rules for its governance, a body of men carefully selected with reference to their faith as well as to their moral conduct. "Timothy" and "Titus" obviously are charged with great responsibility here. Since it is they who "lay on hands" in ordination (I Tim. 5:22), whose duty it is, under "Paul," to "appoint elders in every town" (Tit. 1:5), and to apply the churches' rules of faith and order, it is they who are made responsible for the character and work of the ministry and for the transmission of the faith. They must see to it that the bishop, in addition to possessing certain basic but elementary moral qualifications, holds "firm to the sure word as taught, so that he may be able to give instruction in sound doctrine and also to confute those who contradict it" (Tit. 1:9). To this end he must be well established in the faith, and not "a recent convert" (I Tim. 3:6) who might too easily introduce innovations. Deacons too, it is insisted, "must hold the mystery of the faith with a clear conscience" (I Tim. 3:9), that is, they must not be "picking at it" to modify it but must take it as it is.

Also, according to the author, professional opportunities for women in the church have got out of hand and should be very much restricted. The freedom granted them in the apostolic age to exercise the gifts of the Spirit, even Paul's insistence that in Christ there is neither male nor female, had brought them into quick and widespread public activity. This will not do at all, the writer urges. Since "the woman [Eve including her daughters] was deceived and became a transgressor," she is permanently disqualified as a public teacher and must be given no authority over men (I Tim. 2:12-14). As "weak" (II Tim. 3:6), women are easily captured by glib heretical propagandists; and in any case, they talk too much (I Tim. 5:13). So far as public professional work for women is concerned, it must be limited to the order of "widows." And the rules, here the author insists, must be revised and rigorously applied to limit the numbers as far as possible (see on I Tim. 5:3-16).

*4. To Provide Adequate Ministerial Support and Discipline.*—Regulations for ministerial support and discipline are likewise important. If on the one hand ministers are warned against being lovers of money (I Tim. 3:3; 6:6-10) or "greedy for gain" (I Tim. 3:8; Tit. 1:7), nevertheless they are entitled to support (I Tim. 5:17-18), that is, "food and clothing" (I Tim. 6:8). "Elders who rule well," in addition to preaching and teaching (local bishops?), may appropriately have double salary or at least be entitled to special recognition (see I Tim. 5:17).

"Timothy" is also instructed to receive complaints against ministers in maintenance of discipline. In discharge of such legal duties he must be both cautious and judicious, strictly impartial, neither shielding evil-doing nor punishing it hastily. Once the minister is found guilty and yet persists in sin, he must be rebuked publicly. As for heretics, whether minister or layman, if they remain obstinate and unconvinced they are to be excluded from the fellowship as perverted and sinful (Tit. 3:10). The author himself has delivered two of them to Satan (I Tim. 1:20).

*5. To Supervise Services of Worship.*—Finally "Timothy" is charged with liturgical functions. He is to be responsible for public worship, both in form and content. Of special importance in the public prayers is that "all men," including "kings and all who are in high positions," be prayed for (I Tim. 2:1-2). The prayer position advocated is "lifting holy hands" (I Tim. 2:8), that is, standing with hands upifted, palms turned upward. Particular emphasis is laid on the rule that only men shall be allowed to participate in the public prayers, or in teaching or conduct of public worship. Women shall by no means lead in prayer or teach or in any way be put in a position of authority over men in the church (I Tim. 2:8-15). They may attend public worship, but inconspicuously and in silence.

Scripture [8] is to be read as part of the service and explained in preaching and teaching (I

[8] Since for the author, Paul is the standard interpreter of Christian orthodoxy, "scripture" in the Pastorals may include Paul's letters as well as the O.T. (See II Tim. 3:16.)

Tim. 4:13; II Tim. 3:16; 4:2); and although no instructions are given to "Timothy" and "Titus" with regard to liturgical professions of faith, creeds, hymns, and doxologies, no New Testament writings quote so freely from them (I Tim. 2:5-6; 3:16; 6:15-16; II Tim. 2:11-13; etc.).

*C. The Heresies.*—The author's primary purpose in writing the Pastorals was to combat the powerful heresies which he saw corrupting the faith and practice of the church and thereby casting a dark and hostile shadow across its future, and against which he will initiate a countermovement by tightening the lines of faith and order and by stirring up the ministry of the church into action against the dangerous forces of evil aggressively active among them. Every paragraph—indeed almost every detail—in the letters directly or indirectly functions to refute heresy, to confound the heretics, and either to reduce them to conformity or to drive them out of the church. Whether discussing true and false patterns of belief, true and false courses of action, clarification and validation of church orders, or exhibiting Paul as the model Christian, imitation of whom is essential to sound faith and practice, the author's one concern is to purge the church of what he is sure is alien, un-Pauline, and therefore unchristian belief and practice.

In the intensity of his opposition the author flings an accumulated heap of epithets at his opponents, denouncing them with scathing and scorching language. They profess to know God, but actually know nothing. Their minds are corrupt and depraved. They have rejected the truth. Their knowledge is falsely so called. Their wrangling is only godless chatter, disputes about words, godless and silly myths. Their craving for controversy is morbid; their discussions vain. They do not understand what they say or about what they say it. Having rejected conscience, their minds have become corrupted, seared over. Having departed from and missed the mark as regards faith, being disobedient, insubordinate, and unbelieving, they have become subject to deceitful spirits and doctrines of demons, caught in the devil's trap. And although they are evil men and impostors, deceivers and deceived, liars, yet they are puffed up, swollen with conceit. And as if this were not enough a vice list of eighteen terrific items is catapulted at them in one shot: "Lovers of self, lovers of money, proud, arrogant, abusive, disobedient to their parents, ungrateful, unholy, inhuman, implacable, slanderers, profligates, fierce, haters of good, treacherous, reckless, swollen with conceit, lovers of pleasure rather than lovers of God, holding the form of religion but denying the power of it" (II Tim. 3:2-5).

**1. Who Are the Heretics?**—And yet with all this name-calling the letters give no systematic account or reasoned refutation of the heresy or heresies involved. No sect or party names are applied. No major heretic is named. Obviously the author is less concerned to analyze or refute specific heresies than to combat "different doctrine" as such, to which he is opposed on two grounds. (*a*) It promotes "speculations," "vain discussion," "craving for controversy and for disputes about words," "godless chatter." (*b*) All such wranglings destroy conscience, sincere faith, and replace the Christian virtues with conceit and quarrelsomeness. They are therefore unprofitable and futile, even ruinous, plunging people only deeper into irreligion. Although, indeed, two of the "certain persons" are named, Hymenaeus and Alexander, we are told nothing about their ideas or actions, only that by "rejecting conscience," they had "made shipwreck of their faith" and had been "delivered to Satan."

**2. The Background of the Heresy-Orthodoxy Problem.**—In attempting to identify the heresies we should bear in mind the complex character of life and thought in the Mediterranean world of these early centuries. Religious ideas and practices from every quarter, Jewish and pagan as well as the more distinctly Christian, were freely circulating and seeking amalgamation into the vigorous and commanding new religious movement becoming known as Christianity. Made up as the church was of an increasing multitude "from every nation, from all tribes and peoples and tongues" (Rev. 7:9), it was inevitable that every significant religious point of view in the ancient world should attempt to assert itself and achieve for itself a dominant and determinative position within the Christian movement.

It should further be remembered that even in their most precisely developed forms "heretical" and "orthodox" Christianity are not at every point mutually exclusive. The difference will frequently be essentially a matter of emphasis, or a difference in some one or more details. Such differences of course may be of far-reaching significance, and if pursued to a logical conclusion may result in an entirely new orientation toward religion and life. "Heresies" become "orthodoxies," a new emphasis in religion becomes a new religion, only when sociological factors unite with ideological to separate by fission a new movement from the old, thereby elevating an emphasis to a basic principle or major integrating factor which in turn forms a "school," a sect, a church. In the Pastorals the author is determined to define and consolidate the faith and order of the church as over against, on the one hand, certain lingering and tenacious Jewish practices which Jesus, and particularly Paul, had rejected, and on the other, against a variety of religious ideas which may be broadly termed Hellenistic because derived from the peculiar interests of the Greek mind, but which would be at home anywhere in the Greek-Oriental-Roman culture complex of the Mediterranean world.

The problem of Christianity as the heir of Hebrew-Jewish faith and culture was how to release the prophetic, ethical element of Judaism from that complex of accumulated ideas and practices which confined its effective functioning to an ethnic group—how to release this element without at the same time losing it in the vigorous but essentially nonprophetic alien religious patterns of Hellenism. Christianity, under one aspect, was Judaism transplanted to and sustained by a Hellenistic soil. As a Jewish heresy, Christianity never thrived on Jewish soil; transplanted to Hellenistic soil, however, it flourished so luxuriantly in the new climate that it seemed at times to have wholly lost its Jewish identity and to be completely transformed by its new environment into a wholly Hellenistic thing. Although the historic church may never have been quite sure—nor is it indeed now—as to just what proportion of Jewish and Hellenistic ingredients may most healthfully be mingled in its faith, its leaders have recognized that it thrives best when neither Jew nor Greek is allowed to exclude the other, when tension is maintained between them, but when the Jewish prophetic ethical spirit is recognized as pre-eminent.

Since then, as polemical writings, the Pastorals seek to maintain Christianity as a middle way, rejecting with intensity extreme Jewish or Hellenistic beliefs and practices; and since the pressures of both systems have always been persistent and relentless upon the church, we are ill-advised to seek wholly Gentile sources for the heresies attacked in the Pastorals. Even after the membership of the church had become predominantly Gentile, even after the break between synagogue and church had become irreconcilable, the pressures of Judaism continued to exert themselves upon the church, particularly through the medium of the Old Testament scriptures. As the New Israel, as the heir to the promises, the church as a matter of course (notwithstanding Marcion) retained the Jewish scriptures. This meant not only that Christianity was to remain a religion of an older written revelation, but that it was to be prompted to produce a new collection of writings which in turn would come to be regarded as authoritative and binding on all Christians.

Now a written revelation, related as it must be to time and place, lays a heavy burden on believers who follow after. Sincerity demands that the text be accepted literally; yet the changing years often make such acceptance impossible. The result is the practice of the allegorical or typological method of solving problems of scripture interpretation, a method widespread in ancient and modern times alike. The allegorical method of interpretation, however, furnishes no objective controls to the imagination of the interpreter, and to the plain man rightly seems overingenious if not actually dishonest. Teachers of true prophetic type, like Jesus and Paul for whom devotion to God was scarcely distinguishable from devotion to human welfare, could find ways of splitting the hard and inflexible crust of literalism, although on occasion they too, and particularly Paul, were compelled to resort to methods of scripture interpretation which seem to us tortuous and involved. The fact is that not until modern times saw the development of the historical method of Bible study did any adequate key to the problem of interpreting an inherited written revelation become available. Given a written word held to be infallible and sufficient, the sincere religious man of all times feels the constant pressure of its literal or hidden meaning, and this at every point without discrimination. The very fact that the church retained the Old Testament as its revealed authority meant that the battles which Paul fought against Judaism were not—indeed could not be—permanently won. In an inspired moment a Christian might affirm that "the letter killeth," yet all Christians found necessary and happy refuge in the formula "it stands written." Furthermore, a radically non-Jewish Christianity is scarcely possible, since Christianity is so surely derived from, rooted in, and constantly refreshed by the religion of the people of Israel, especially in its literary expression, the Old Testament. And just as in all Christianity, whether "orthodox," Gnostic, or Jewish, there would be some Jewish element or elements, so surely were there always present in Christianity elements to tempt even Gentile Christians to heresy of a Jewish stripe.

In the history of interpretation of the Pastorals, and at the present time, the heresies combated have been variously identified as Jewish, Jewish-Christian, Gnostic, or Marcionite. Those who hold to Pauline authorship naturally reject any Marcionite references and greatly minimize Gnostic ones. Those who regard the Pastorals as pseudonymous, but as late first- or early second-century writings, must likewise reject any Marcionite reference. They tend also to minimize any Jewish character of the heresies and see them as essentially Gnostic. Those who date the Pastorals at 150 or later do so because they are sure that the letters are given their proper place in the history of early Christian apologetic only if viewed as anti-Marcionite documents. In this latter case Jewish ingredients in the heresies are in the main denied, and while Gnostic elements are admitted as part of the general background, they are believed not to occupy the center of the target aimed at.

Probably the best solution of the problem, both in view of the complex ferment of ideas active in the process in which what we call the orthodox pattern of the Christian faith was formulated, and in view of the incoherent variety of "heretical" ideas and practices combated in the Pastorals, is to admit that no one heresy alone can account for all the descriptions or allusions in the letters. To admit a plurality of heresies is not merely to do better justice to the texts; it is also to become aware of the variety of inadequate but vigorously defended views over against which the church had to work out its better formulation of its faith.

**3. Proposed Identifications.**—We may now consider the three most important types of heresy which have been proposed.

*a) As Jewish-Christian Heresies.*—A determined effort to show that the false teachers were Jewish Christians has been made by C. Spicq,[9] who, because he regards the letters as Pauline, is compelled to identify the heretics with groups active in Paul's time. He finds three types of errors indicated in the letters, all of which he regards as Jewish mixed with Greek or native elements: (*a*) "myths" and "genealogies," (*b*) magic, and (*c*) asceticism, both in food and marriage.

(*a*) Since Tit. 1:14 speaks of "Jewish myths," Tit. 3:9 of "quarrels over the law," and Tit. 1:10 of "the circumcision party," Spicq concludes that "myths and endless genealogies

---

[9] *Saint Paul: les Épitres Pastorales* (Paris: J. Gabalda, 1947), pp. lii-lxxii; following F. J. A. Hort, *Judaistic Christianity* (Cambridge: Macmillan & Co., 1894), pp. 135 ff. Martin Dibelius writes: "The connection of our gnostics with Judaism is not absolutely certain, but seems probable" (*Die Pastoralbriefe* [2nd ed.; Tübingen: J. C. B. Mohr, 1931; "Handbuch zum Neuen Testament"], pp. 42-43). Hans Lietzmann, *The Beginnings of the Christian Church* (tr. Bertram Lee Woolf, New York: Charles Scribner's Sons, 1937), p. 289, calls the heretics "Jewish gnostics"; Rudolph Bultmann, *Die Religion in Geschichte und Gegenwart* (2nd ed.; Tübingen: J. C. B. Mohr, 1928), IV, 995, uses the term "Jewish-syncretistic gnosis." See also Eduard Meyer, *Ursprung und Anfänge des Christentums* (Stuttgart: J. G. Cotta, 1923), III, 587-91.

which promote speculations" (I Tim. 1:4) must be interpreted as referring to allegorical interpretation of the Old Testament developed according to methods used in the Haggada or Mishnah. A typical example of such midrashic method is the book of Jubilees, written between 135-105 B.C. Just as the Chronicler rewrote Samuel and Kings to represent David and his successors as observing all the precepts of the law in the spirit of the priestly code, so Jubilees rewrote Genesis to make it show that the law, at least in its major prescriptions such as sabbath and circumcision, was eternally ordained, observed even in heaven by the archangels, and was of course rigorously observed by the patriarchs. Similarly, Spicq concludes, the false teachers of the Pastorals are Jewish Christians who insist upon rabbinical minutiae in exegesis, and in whose interpretation of Christianity the Old Testament is given a place of importance which dims the luster of the Pauline gospel of salvation by grace through faith in Christ as Savior.

It is further probable, he argues, that these teachers were familiar with the methods used by Greek philosophers and rhetors in the interpretation of Homer, and applied them to the Old Testament, thus representing a fusion of rabbinical and Hellenistic practices.[10] Spicq concedes that such persons may be regarded as "Gnostic," but only in the sense that their orientation is intellectualist, not practically religious.

(b) Likewise the allusions to magic which Spicq sees in the Pastorals he attributes to converted Jews. The magi-astrologers claimed to be the heirs of Zoroaster. From the Chaldeans of Mesopotamia they learned divination by astrology, by means of which they became influential in Greece, particularly among the Pythagoreans. The magi practiced also sorcery and occult sciences: incantations, exorcisms, charms, which procured the aid of heavenly powers against the spirits of darkness. Informed in the natural and physical sciences, they disclosed the secrets of nature, read minds, and practiced hypnotism. Knowing medicine, they could ward off pests, protect against evils, make rain, drive off harmful animals (cf. Simon Magus [Acts 8:11], Bar-Jesus [Acts 13:6], the seven sons of Sceva [Acts 19:14]). This combination of biblical cosmogony with Mazdean chiliasm could perfectly well qualify as μῦθοι Ἰουδαϊκοί (Jewish myths). The heretics of II Tim. 3:6-9 may well have been magicians, judging from their success with the women, their comparison with Jannes and Jambres, and the parallel with Acts 13:6-12. The term γόης is a term of scorn current for magicians, who seem to have claimed knowledge of special secrets which they would reveal only insidiously in homes (II Tim. 3:6). And this in turn would give point to the insistence in the Pastorals that Christianity is the true mystery.

(c) Asceticism in food (I Tim. 4:3), drink (I Tim. 5:23), and marriage (I Tim. 4:3) is here likewise of Jewish derivation, urges Spicq. The distinction between "clean" and "unclean" foods is typically Jewish. The prohibition of marriage could be of Essene origin.

If the Pastorals were Pauline and were written in the sixties of the first century, the a priori probability that the teachings combated were basically of Jewish-Christian origin would at least be stronger. Since, however, the letters are almost certainly pseudonymous and second century, and since the thought world reflected in them is so surely Hellenistic, Spicq's (and other) attempts to identify the heretics as Jewish Christians are as unwarranted as they are unsuccessful. This does not mean that Jewish elements can with certainty be completely excluded from the heresies, as is sometimes done by interpreters who see the heresies as solely (Gentile) Gnostic. For example, it is sometimes proposed that such Jewish language as "teachers of the law" (I Tim. 1:7), "Jewish myths" (Tit. 1:14), "quarrels over the law" (Tit. 3:9), "the circumcision party" (Tit. 1:10) should be interpreted as having nothing to do with any ultra-Jewish form of Christianity but only with problems the church faced in (Gentile) Gnosticism. From such a point of view, "teachers of the law" has been interpreted as purely figurative, the equivalent of scholars or professional religious teachers, without any actual reference to the Jewish law as such (so Dibelius). Or, it is urged, if the author uses a Jewish term here, it is because as a Paulinist second-century churchman he naturally combats even Gentile Gnostics in the name and with the weapons of Paul.[11] Likewise the adjective "Jewish" (Tit. 1:14) has been regarded simply as an abusive epithet signifying nothing as to the actual origin or nature of the "myths."

While conceivably it is possible to purge the terms "teachers of the law" and even "Jewish" of any literal Jewish connotation, the additional expressions, "the circumcision party" (see Exeg., Tit. 1:10), "quarrels over the law" (Tit. 3:9), and the extended discussion of "the law" in I Tim. 1, make any such procedure seem forced and overingenious. Such language in any early

[10] Following F. H. Colson, "'Myths and Genealogies'—A Note on the Polemic of the Pastoral Epistles," *Journal of Theological Studies*, XIX (1918), 265-71.

[11] Walter Bauer, *Rechtgläubigkeit und Ketzerei im ältesten Christentum*, pp. 92-93.

Christian writing is most naturally taken as referring literally to Jewish institutions, of course with depreciatory intent.

It is true that when heretical ideas or practices are specified—such as forbidding marriage, abstinence from foods (flesh?) and wine, belief that the "resurrection is past"—they are not obviously Jewish (vs. Spicq). And unfortunately in I Tim. 1:7-11, the author neither indicates the specific points at which the heretics appeal to the "law" nor does he cite the "law" against them in refutation. Instead he trots out a stock and not too apt reply. As an orthodox Christian, he affirms that "the law is good" in principle. Then he proceeds to cut the ground from beneath the heretics by stating a (Pauline) view of "law" which makes it irrelevant for "the just," that is, for Christians.

There is no evidence in the Pastorals, however, that the false teachers wanted to reintroduce such Jewish practices as circumcision or the Levitical food laws into the church. They were not in this sense literalists. And surely Paul had won that battle for the church. Rather, what was now taking place was that in the process of the Hellenization of Christianity, elaborate syncretistic religious and philosophical speculations were capturing the imagination of Christian thinkers. Under the influence of Greek-Oriental forms of thought the Christian faith was being transformed from a practical prophetic religion centered in moral redemption to a theosophy concerned to protect the transcendent purity of God as over against the inherently evil world of matter, and to offer men release from the charnel house of corrupt flesh by a mystical experience of enlightenment. And it is entirely reasonable to suppose that this reinterpretation of Christianity was being related by some Christians, honestly enough no doubt, to the Old Testament.

It should be remembered that even after the formation of the New Testament, Christians have commonly believed that only as the Christian faith could be found or foreseen in the Old Testament could its truth be fully accredited. How much more, then, in the days when the Old Testament only was fully established scripture, would Christians with advanced views—Marcion was the great exception—seek to ground them in the Old Testament and claim the authority of revelation for them. Thus the conclusion that the heretical teachers, whatever the actual source and content of their teachings, believed that they arrived at them in conjunction with their study of Jewish literature is entirely credible. They would then have insisted that their doctrine was not "different," but was the true form of the Christian faith, that it was authorized, indeed required, by (Old Testament) revelation. Logically, Gnosticism is thoroughly incompatible with Judaism and should radically exclude it together with its scriptures. Still, many (Christian) Gnostics did not think of themselves as *rejecting* the Old Testament but as furnishing the true interpretation of it.

Nevertheless, it is against all such "modern" interpretations that the author of the Pastorals stands adamant. Such speculations, inherently secular and silly, he scorns as a form of irreligion. He will not admit for a moment that such absurdities have anything to do either with common sense or with revealed religion. Rather they are but "commands of men" (Tit. 1:14). The "sound doctrine" of the church is Paul's "glorious gospel of the blessed God," and beyond it one cannot go. What the Christian faith means and is, had been perfectly revealed in Paul's redemptive experience, clearly described and interpreted in I Tim. 1:13-16.

*b) As Gnostic Heresies.*—Even though it may be admitted that at least some heretical teachers sought to ground their "myths" and "genealogies" in the revealed scriptures, the "law," thus giving a Jewish tinge to the heresies, nevertheless the content of the myths was not really Jewish, but Greek-Oriental-Gnostic. The essential context within which alone the meager descriptions of the heresies combated in the Pastorals and the concerns of the writer can be adequately interpreted is the complex, confused, yet pervasive and fascinating Gnostic movement of the second century.

It is unnecessary for our present purposes to engage in detailed discussion of the origins of Gnosticism in relation to the beginning of Christianity. Briefly, two differing points of view have been proposed. (a) The movement, it is urged, is of pre- and non-Christian origin, and was essentially from beginning to end a non-Christian, indeed an unchristian, amalgam of ideas and practices. A turbid and turbulent stream, its confused waters poured out of Asia into the Roman Empire during the first two centuries of the Christian Era, mingling Oriental dualism with Hellenistic world weariness and "loss of nerve," offering men both a rational explanation for the facts, as they were believed to be, of a God wholly good and a world wholly evil, and a salvation (for certain select persons) from the finite world of matter, change, evil, ignorance, and sin, effected by means of a mystical rebirth into the higher world. According to this point of view, Gnosticism stood over against and apart from Christianity, a competitor, not a form of it. For example:

Gnosticism . . . is non-Christian in essence and fundamentally alien to the Christian scheme. . . . The primitive Gnostics, therefore, cannot be justly called Christian heretics. . . . No Gnostic leader ever acknowledged himself a Christian: no Christian writer of the first four centuries ever asserted that the Gnostics were Christian. A Gnostic cannot, therefore, be called a heretic.[12]

(b) Since Gnosticism and Gnostics are known for the most part from Christian sources and by way of Christian reaction, the movement, in its most developed forms at least, has been regarded as a true heresy. F. C. Burkitt quite bluntly states:

"The Gnosis" . . . does not precede Christianity but is a new formulation of Christianity. . . . Without Christianity, without the growth and success of the Christian Church, there would have been no Gnosticism. The various forms of Gnosticism are attempts to reformulate and express the ordinary Christianity in terms and categories which suited the science and philosophy of the day. . . . In my view the systems were invented to explain Jesus in terms of the science of the day by Christians who were dissatisfied with the Old Testament, or rather with that view of GOD and the Universe, which the Old Testament seems to set forth.[13]

Harnack's position is similar to that of Burkitt. The Gnostics he regarded as

the first to transform Christianity into a system of doctrines. . . . The majority of Gnostic undertakings may also be viewed as attempts to transform Christianity into a theosophy, that is, into a revealed metaphysic and philosophy of history, with a complete disregard of the Jewish Old Testament soil on which it originated, through the use of Pauline ideas, and under the influence of the Platonic spirit.[14]

[12] Paul Stevens Kramer, "The Sources of Primitive Gnosticism and Its Place in the History of Christian Thought." Unpublished dissertation, University of Chicago Libraries, 1936, pp. 122-23. See also Richard Reitzenstein, *Poimandres* (Leipzig: B. G. Teubner, 1904), and *Die hellenistichen Mysterienreligionen* (3rd ed.; Leipzig: B. G. Teubner, 1927); G. H. C. Macgregor and Alexander Purdy, *Jew and Greek: Tutors unto Christ* (New York: Charles Scribner's Sons, 1936), pp. 309-16. These statements may be contrasted with those of Schmidt: "The Gnostics most emphatically claimed for themselves the title 'Christian.' For the most part they sought by their brisk propaganda to win adherents from members of the church proper in which they formed cells. Their special teachings they eulogized as the higher stages of Christianity. Pagan apologists such as Celsus, Plotinus and Porphyry reckoned them as Christians. On the other hand the church proper fought the Gnostics with the utmost energy as arch-heretics." (*Religion in Geschichte und Gegenwart*, II, 1276-81.)

[13] *Church and Gnosis* (Cambridge: Cambridge University Press, 1932), pp. 57-58, 88. Used by permission.

[14] *History of Dogma*, tr. Neil Buchanan (Boston: Roberts Bros., 1895), pp. 227-28.

Since Harnack saw in Gnosticism "the acute secularising or hellenizing of Christianity, with the rejection of the Old Testament, while the Catholic system . . . represents a gradual process of the same kind with the conservation of the Old Testament,"[15] obviously in his opinion Gnostic Christianity *might have become orthodox Christianity* had it been able to prevail over the Catholic system—that is, had it not moved too quickly and too far from the Jewish element in Christianity, had it been able to persuade the church to exchange its philosophically naïve Jewish prophetic ancestry for the involved, abstruse, even occult Hellenistic metaphysics congenial to the age.

No one would now maintain that in its origins Gnosticism was a Christian heresy. That it became one, however, there should be no doubt. The statement of Samuel Angus is correct: "Gnosticism is a comprehensive term for a phase of religion which appeared in Paganism, Judaism, and Christianity, but it was in Christianity that it grew most aggressive."[16] And we may be sure that it was only because Gnosticism was an attractive and powerful heresy, dangerous because it was vigorously at work within the church as it tried to define and determine the nature and pattern of Christian faith and life—only so is it possible to account for the intense and persistent opposition to it on the part of the author of the Pastorals and other Christian leaders.

The main concerns of Gnosticism may be briefly outlined: (a) Both religiously and philosophically all forms of Gnosticism are rooted in dualism. The basic assumption is that God as Spirit is wholly good, the world as matter wholly evil. God is thus radically separated from the world, which, because it is in essence evil, cannot have been created by him. Both the transcendence and perfection of God are protected by a theory which accounts for the world as the end product of a series of emanations (called aeons), generally thought of in pairs, male and female. As manifestations of the transcendent God these aeons constitute the pleroma, the "fullness" of God. Eventually, as a result of progressive degeneration, one of them (sometimes called Sophia) "fell," dragging a fragment of spirit into matter and thereby calling the world into being, either with or without the aid of an inferior creator god, a Demiurge, now identified with the God of the Old Testament, now less concretely with angels or "rulers" (ἄρχοντες).

(b) Salvation is thought of as the release of the spirit from its prison house of flesh and

[15] *Ibid.*, pp. 226-27.

[16] *The Religious Quests of the Graeco-Roman World* (New York: Charles Scribner's Sons, 1929), p. 377.

restoration to its heavenly sphere. Since the spirit in man has been contaminated by its lodgment in matter, salvation can be effected only by a savior sent from the aeon world. As a heavenly aeon, Christ could not really touch matter. Hence Gnostic Christology was commonly Docetic—that is, Christ only seemed to have a body. Sometimes he was thought of as only loosely joined to Jesus at baptism, and as quickly separated from him before the Crucifixion. Sometimes it was supposed that he had a body assembled from the upper air, passing through Mary but not really born.

Salvation is effected by means of "gnosis," knowledge indeed, but in the sense of supernatural illumination bestowed upon the initiate in sacramental and magical rites, secret teachings, mystical experiences. Not all men are thought of as capable of salvation, however. Rather, there are three groups: the ὑλικοί, the "material" persons, who are hopeless; the ψυχικοί, the "psychical," who may expect a moderate salvation; and the πνευματικοί, the "spiritual," who are by nature so constituted as to be capable of receiving the full saving knowledge which will entitle them at death to rise into the pleroma to take their place among the planetary powers. Of course Christian Gnostics regarded their doctrines as a superior form of Christianity, and themselves as alone the truly "spiritual," the true "knowers."

(c) Logically, then, the Old Testament with its creator God was regarded as the revelation of a lower divine being. Affirming as it did that the created world is good, and concerned with the history of a particular people, the Jews, the Old Testament was either radically rejected as revelation of the highest truth, or radically allegorized in such a way as to find Gnostic meanings in it. The concern was no longer with God in history. Rather, history, whether that of the Old Testament or in the case of Jesus, was sublimated into dramatic myth.

(d) Since only spirit, "light-stuff," is capable of ascending into the heavenlies, or of union with God, since the flesh as matter is inherently evil, a radical revision of early Christian eschatology is called for. The very idea of the resurrection of the flesh becomes abhorrent. Since the "knower," the illuminated, is already immortal, he awaits only separation from the body. There is really no need for any parousia or second coming of Christ or for a future general resurrection and Last Judgment. At the time of death the soul rises into the pleroma among the planetary powers in heaven. Of course not all Gnostics consistently drew all these inferences. For instance, the resurrection of the flesh might be denied, and yet a place retained for a Last Judgment. The church proper, too, modified its earlier eschatology without intending to abandon it.

(e) Gnostic ethic was logically inclined to asceticism. Since the material world was evil the saved man should shun it as far as possible. Hence marriage as creating new bodies was avoided; so also the more "material" foods such as meat and wine. However, antinomianism or libertarianism was also congenial to the Gnostic way of thinking. Since salvation was thought of as cosmological rather than moral, the "spiritual" man might think of redeemed spirit as quite unaffected by anything the flesh did, and thus give free rein to physical impulses.

Even so brief a description of the main concerns of Gnosticism indicates how complex and comprehensive a movement it was: It sought speculative answers to the problems of philosophy as currently felt; it advanced both a theory and technique of salvation; it urged an ethic. And in its Christian forms it attempted to fashion the orthodox pattern of the Christian faith in terms of its own presuppositions. That it was this movement, perhaps in various forms, which agitated the author of the Pastorals to vigorous reaction can hardly be doubted.

Although caution must be observed in discovering an anti-Gnostic motive under every word in the Pastorals, nevertheless the texts frequently become luminous when seen over against these fashionable religious patterns. And if the evidence is not in every case conclusive, yet it is cumulative. The probabilities are great that the dominant emphases in the letters, together with the terminology in which the Christian faith is set forth, were to a considerable degree determined by way of reaction to the Gnostic conglomerate.

As for the root assumption of Gnosticism, cosmological dualism with its identification of matter as evil and its separation of God from the world, the Pastorals reject it vehemently and decisively. "There is one God" (I Tim. 2:5), who has created the material world. And "everything created by God is good" (I Tim. 4:4). The problem of evil here is not cosmological: it is rather the problem of sin. Christ came into the world not to release men from the body as a prison house, but "to save sinners" (I Tim. 1:15). Indeed, he was himself "manifested in the flesh" and (even so) "vindicated in the Spirit" (I Tim. 3:16). Christians are not to aim at an experience of illumination or mystical union, but at "righteousness, godliness, faith, love, steadfastness, gentleness" (I Tim. 6:11).

The content of the "myths and endless genealogies which promote speculations" (I Tim. 1:4; Tit. 3:9), the "godless and silly myths" (I

Tim. 4:7; II Tim. 4:4; Tit. 1:14), products of "a morbid craving for controversy and for disputes about words" which produce "dissension . . . and wrangling" (I Tim. 6:4-5; II Tim. 2:23), are most meaningfully interpreted as referring to the curious, fanciful, and involved attempts of the riotous Gnostic imagination to fashion a myth adequate to account for the paradox of a good God and an evil world. All such attempts to elaborate an angelic hierarchy of mediators, aeons, or emanations, as intermediate causes, are nonsense to the author of the Pastorals, to whom the Gnostic putting of the problem is basically false. Since for him God created the world, evil is not a cosmological problem but a moral one. The creator God is therefore not a morally inferior God, and the need for any series of protective emanations vanishes.

Since to the author of the Pastorals God the Creator is also God the Savior, the Gnostic theory and scheme of salvation is rejected at four points: (a) There are not two gods, a lower creator God and a higher savior God. With almost equal frequency in the Pastorals God and Christ are both described as Savior. If there is one God, there is also but "one mediator between God and men" (I Tim. 2:5). If it is "the living God, who is the Savior of all men" (I Tim. 4:10), it is also "our Savior Christ Jesus, who abolished death" (II Tim. 1:10). (b) Salvation is not effected by "knowledge," that is, supernatural or mystical illumination, but by faith and obedience. Most characteristically, Christianity in the Pastorals is described as (the) faith, not as knowledge (gnosis), and Christians as believers not "knowers." Hence also the persistent emphasis on good works. (c) Insistence that "God our Savior . . . desires all men to be saved and to come to the knowledge of the truth" (I Tim. 2:1-6; see also I Tim. 4:10; Tit. 2:11) seems to be a direct repudiation of the Gnostic classification of men into the three types, only one of which is capable of salvation. To the author all men are sinners and all are capable of devoting themselves to good deeds. Therefore whether they are *pneumatikoi, psychikoi,* or *hylikoi* is beside the point. And (d) a Docetic Christology is unnecessary and impossible. The mediator is "the man Christ Jesus" (I Tim. 2:5), "manifested in the flesh" (I Tim. 3:16).

Further, the Pastorals reject the Gnostic interpretation, disparagement, or rejection of the Old Testament. I Tim. 4:3-5 presents an argument drawn from Genesis. "The public reading of scripture" (I Tim. 4:13) refers to the Old Testament. And II Tim. 3:15-16 certainly insists that Christians regard the Old Testament as sacred scripture (see Exeg., *ad loc.*).

Likewise, the writer rejects at least the most radical Gnostic modifications of early Christian eschatology. To hold that "the resurrection is past already" is to "have swerved from the truth" (II Tim. 2:18). And although the author and the second-century church themselves had necessarily to make some adjustments as to the "time of his coming," nevertheless they still believed that the Lord would come. "The appearing of our Lord Jesus Christ . . . will be made manifest at the proper time" (I Tim. 6:14-15; see Tit. 2:13), "to judge the living and the dead" (II Tim. 4:1, 8). How else could history be brought to a close? Yet the very phrase "at the proper time" (lit., "in his own times") indicates a cooling in expectancy of an immediate coming.

It is certainly Gnostic asceticism in the form of prohibition of marriage and of abstinence from certain foods which is so vehemently opposed in I Tim. 4:3. That bishops (I Tim. 3:2), elders (Tit. 1:6), and deacons (I Tim. 3:12) should be married is standard practice in the church; and as for widows (I Tim. 5:4, 9, 14), the younger ones indeed should be married more than once if necessary. Therefore to oppose marriage is a doctrine of demons (I Tim. 4:2). Food asceticism is likewise rejected. Anything created to be food should be eaten if consecrated (I Tim. 4:3-5). And since wine is medicine, it should not be refused when health requires it (I Tim. 5:23).

That Gnostic asceticism is combated in the Pastorals seems obvious. Are there also evidences that antinomian or libertarian trends were present among the heretics? It has been urged that such is the case, (a) on the ground of the vice lists (I Tim. 1:9-10; 6:4-5; II Tim. 3:2-9; etc.); (b) it is contended that the author's determined attempt to put women in their place (I Tim. 2:8-15; 5:3-16), to keep slaves submissive (I Tim. 6:1-2), even his concern that the clergy exemplify model behavior (I Tim. 3:1-13; etc.), are to be taken as evidence that the heretics were promoting a feminist, slave, layman's movement in insubordination to the established hierarchy of the church. If we are not to regard the author as a pure propagandist refuting arguments by blackening characters, it must be admitted that his opponents not merely held different opinions, but also in certain cases at least, or at certain points, had abandoned the Christian ethic. Unfortunately the letters do not make plain why their author denies the heretics' good faith. And one must remember that in history religious conflicts are frequently characterized by recrimination and unprovable moral accusations.

*c) As the Marcionite Heresy.*—In the consideration of the Gnostic background of the Pastorals in the preceding section no attempt was made to identify the heretics with any particular Gnostic sect or sects. The fact that the letters themselves name no such groups, the fact that the complex of ideas and practices combated do not easily form a coherent or consistent whole, stands as a formidable obstacle to any such identification. Nevertheless, from the time of F. C. Baur (1835) on, it has been from time to time vigorously maintained that it was the Marcionite schism which evoked the Pastorals. If such could be shown to be probable, the pseudonymity of the letters would be proved and a date not far from 150 assured. We must therefore consider the arguments.

(*a*) Marcion [17] was the most interesting and important heretic of the second century. Sincere and determined, he was an incisive dialectician, the tireless advocate of a clear and challenging interpretation of Christianity which, it could plausibly be urged, had every right to claim to be the only authentic form of the faith. Also an able organizer, Marcion was the most versatile, the most enterprising, the most planful, and therefore the most annoying and dangerous heretic in the second century. This is clear from the fact that "no other single man had called forth such a volume of anxious apologetic from the Church." [18] That followers of Marcion were many and widespread is attested by Justin Martyr, writing about 150: "Assisted by the demons, he has caused many men of every country to blaspheme." [19] At the end of the second century Marcionism threatened the church in all the provinces: "It was combated by Dionysius at Corinth, Irenaeus at Lyons, Theophilus at Antioch, Philip of Gortyna in Crete, Tertullian at Carthage, Hippolytus and Rhodon in Rome, and Bardesanes at Edessa." [20] The sheer prominence and aggressiveness of Marcion make for a priori probability that he would be in the target of any Christian antiheretical writing written in mid-second century —perhaps if earlier, certainly if later—and particularly if it concerned Asia Minor. For it should be remembered that Marcion was born in Sinope of Pontus and spent his formative years in Asia Minor. According to credible tradition he grew up in the church, his father being a bishop. The nature and extent of Marcion's pre-Roman activity is not known; [21] however, active and aggressive as he later was in the dissemination of his gospel, it can hardly be supposed that in his earlier adulthood he was indifferent to it. [22] He may indeed have left Asia for Rome (*ca.* 138 or 139), hoping to find a more cordial reception for his faith and better to secure its world-wide acceptance. In any case, he joined the church at Rome, sought favor by a large gift of money, and urged his case. Nevertheless, both he and his theories were rejected, probably in 144. The rest of his life he spent in establishing and promoting the Marcionite church, the first truly schismatic church of importance, it would seem, in Christian history. A tireless traveler, he journeyed throughout the empire winning converts and organizing them into churches.

(*b*) Of particular importance is the fact that previous to Marcion, so far as the evidence goes, promulgators of divergent or unusual interpretations of Christianity which might ideologically be designated as heresies made no effort to form organized churches constituting separatist sects and seeking to displace other points of view and impose their patterns of faith upon the whole church. "Before him there was no such thing [as a church] in the sense of a community, firmly united by a fixed conviction, harmoniously organised, and spread over the whole world." [23] And although evidence as to the form of organization in the Marcionite churches is uncertain, [24] it is nevertheless probable that Marcion himself introduced bishops, presbyters, and deacons. He seems also to have permitted women to hold office. Intensity of opposition to heresy in the Pastorals is best explained if directed against some such organized movement. The author's concern with bishops, presbyters, and deacons, even his antifeminist emphasis, have special point if the letters were directed

[17] On Marcion see especially Adolf von Harnack, *History of Dogma,* I, 266-86; *Marcion: Das Evangelium vom fremden Gott* (Leipzig: J. C. Hinrichs, 1924); *Neue Studien zu Marcion* (Leipzig: J. C. Hinrichs, 1923); R. S. Wilson, *Marcion: A Study of a Second-Century Heretic* (London: James Clarke & Co., 1933); Walter Bauer, *Rechtgläubigkeit und Ketzerei im ältesten Christentum,* pp. 224-30; Hans Lietzmann, *Beginnings of the Christian Church,* pp. 333-53; Martin Rist, "Pseudepigraphic Refutations of Marcionism," *Journal of Religion,* XXII (1942), 39-62; John Knox, *Marcion and the New Testament* (Chicago: University of Chicago Press, 1942), especially pp. 73-76; Jules Lebreton and Jacques Zeiller, *The History of the Primitive Church* (New York: The Macmillan Co., 1949), II, 641-53; E. C. Blackman, *Marcion and His Influence* (London: Society for Promoting Christian Knowledge, 1948).

[18] Blackman, *op. cit.,* p. ix.
[19] *First Apology* XXVI.
[20] Lebreton and Zeiller, *op. cit.,* II, 651.

[21] On the possibility that Marcion may have been active in western Asia Minor as early as 110 or 120, see Knox, *Marcion and the N.T.,* pp. 8-12.
[22] "It is very probable that Marcion had fixed the ground features of his doctrine, and had laboured for its propagation, even before he came to Rome" (Harnack, *History of Dogma,* I, 266, n. 1).
[23] *Ibid.,* I, 281-82.
[24] See Blackman, *op. cit.,* p. 5.

against a movement similarly organized. Men of action are more commonly feared than men of thought. The whole tenor of the Pastorals—in spite of their hostility to "speculations"—seems to require as object of attack some such type of person as Marcion, less a metaphysician or cosmologist than a practical organizer industriously organizing a competitive church according to a clear, if radical, simplification of Christianity, and urging at the same time a rigorous, even ascetic, discipline. Gnosticism, it may be urged, was at the time too loosely organized to warrant the intensity of opposition displayed in the Pastorals.

(c) Marcion's basic assumptions appear to have been (i) an essential dualism according to which the created world is inherently evil; (ii) Christianity, given adequate expression by Paul alone, should be clearly, decisively, and dramatically separated, as *sui generis*, both from Judaism and from Hellenistic-Gnostic-Christian sects of any sort. If Marcion refused to countenance the speculative technique of the Greek philosophers of religion, he likewise refused to allegorize the Old Testament. The only alternative left to him was to reject the Old Testament—indeed, all portions of the "New Testament" also which seemed to him to "Judaize." Thus naturally his thought fell into "antitheses": law and gospel, wrath and grace, works and faith, flesh and spirit, sin and righteousness, death and life, which—it is urged—is the probable reference of I Tim. 6:20 (see Exeg., *ad loc.*). Marcion's dualism further expressed itself in two ways: (i) rejection of belief in the resurrection (see II Tim. 2:18), and Docetic Christology with abandonment of belief in the return of Christ; and (ii) asceticism.

We know of no Christian community in the second century which insisted so strictly on renunciation of the world as the Marcionites. . . . Those who were married had to separate ere they could be received by baptism into the community. The sternest precepts were laid down in the matter of food and drink. Martyrdom was enjoined.[25]

Since much of the precise polemic in the Pastorals is directed against (a) a dualistic conception of God (I Tim. 2:5); (b) the rejection of the Old Testament (II Tim. 3:14-17); (c) the belief that the resurrection is already past, that is, that it will not take place (II Tim. 2:18); (d) asceticism in food, drink (I Tim. 4:3-4; 5:23), and sex (I Tim. 3:2; 4:3; 5:14)—for these reasons it would fit most pointedly the basic tenets of Marcionism.

Although it is admitted that not all the polemic in the Pastorals is applicable to Marcion as we know him, nevertheless it is urged[26] that it was none other than Marcion and his movement which furnished the author with the primary incentive to write. One of the most annoying problems of the second-century church was how to reclaim Paul from the heretics—Gnostics as well as Marcionites and the later Manichaeans. As a Paulinist himself, the author was particularly well equipped to spearhead this effort. In certain respects more Jewish in type than Paul, and certainly than Marcion, he could by representing Paul as stressing "good works" and "sound teaching" honestly represent him as softening the antithesis between works and faith without denying it, and could permit him plainly and vigorously to denounce Marcion's dualism with its theological and ethical implications. Marcion's scripture was Luke and Paul: our author's scripture was the Old Testament and (at least) Paul (see II Tim. 3:16); Paul's scripture was the Old Testament. If Marcion rejected Paul's scripture as a consequence of consistently carrying through Paul's doctrine of justification by faith, the writer of the Pastorals was here loyal to Paul's practice, although not to Paul's theory as sharpened by Marcion. He did not reject the "law" for the "gospel" as Marcion did. Rather he gave it a permanent if subordinate place, thereby weakening the Pauline principle but conserving the values of an ancient tradition.

Those who although regarding the Pastorals as pseudonymous yet exclude Marcion from consideration as the chief object of attack do so primarily on the grounds (a) that the dominant heresy (or heresies) attacked in the letters is Gnosticism, and Marcion was not a Gnostic, and (b) there is in the Pastorals no adequate isolation of nor organized argument against Marcion's peculiar doctrines.[27] These objections cannot be answered with complete satisfaction. They are a part of the problem discussed above on pp. 354-57. We may agree that the variety of "heretical" details combated is too incoherent to belong exclusively to any one "heresy." A partial reply, however, might be as follows: (a) If Marcion, like the author of the Pastorals, was opposed to Gnostic speculation concerning the pleroma, aeons, syzygies, and the like, nevertheless the basic dualistic philosophy which determined his ideas of God, the world, and salvation, was Gnostic. (b) Second-century opponents of Marcionism did not draw as clear a distinction between Marcionism and Gnosticism as might be supposed. (c) Even if Marcion was the author's chief stimulus to writing, letters

[25] Harnack, *op. cit.*, I, 277.

[26] So, e.g., Baur, Bauer, Goodspeed, Rist, Riddle, Knox, Barnett.

[27] See Easton, *Pastoral Epistles*, pp. 7-8.

of the sort might well be expected to cast a wide net with a view to bringing into the sphere of condemnation every variety of heresy rampant. (d) It may be recalled that "the great Gnostic crisis . . . was at its height from c. A.D. 150-180." [28] Valentinus, whose sect was the most numerous and powerful of all the heretical sects of the period, was active in Rome and elsewhere both contemporaneously with and subsequently to Marcion. If, then, the Pastorals are to be dated about the middle of the second century, with Marcionism flourishing and Gnosticism on the increase, an "orthodox" polemic could hardly have avoided attacking either. Indeed, the more advanced and better-organized Gnostic sects could well have been regarded by the church as blood brothers of Marcionism, in the sense at least that both were offspring of the rejection of tradition, Marcion interpreting the Old Testament literally and therefore rejecting it, the Gnostics turning it into myth and allegory and likewise really rejecting its literal meaning under the guise of reinterpreting it.

There remain finally the problems related to Marcion's collection of Paul's letters. That Marcion's canon did not contain the Pastorals is certain.[29] Why? Did Marcion not know them? Or did he reject them as representing in his opinion a compromised Paulinism or even as being spurious? Or had they not yet been written? And is the inference such as to increase the probability that the Pastorals were anti-Marcionite in origin? The whole matter is of course complicated by the circular problem of author and date. Many have held (a) that Marcion knew the Pastorals but rejected them (so the patristic writers, Goguel, Bacon, Moffatt, etc.). The assumption here is usually that the Pastorals are Pauline, or if not, were in existence early enough to be part of a late first-century thirteen-letter Pauline corpus (so Blackman). Or, it is urged that as known to Ignatius and Polycarp (see below, p. 369), they cannot have been unknown to Marcion, and if known, they must have been rejected, probably as spurious (Bacon, etc.). Others argue (b) that Marcion did not know the Pastorals. Either (i) the Pauline collection he used in Pontus did not contain them or they lay neglected in the churches until after Marcion's heresy exploded, when, if not written expressly as part of the anti-Marcionite campaign, they were edited and added to the ten to give an anti-Marcionite slant to the whole Pauline corpus (so Loisy).

Or more commonly, (ii) if the Pastorals had been in existence, Marcion would have known them. If he had known them, he would have amended them, not rejected them. Therefore the Pastorals must be post-Marcion and must have been produced to combat Marcion by making Paul a catholic churchman (so Riddle, Walter Bauer, etc.).

Evidence is not at hand to bring these problems to final settlement. Nevertheless it can be concluded that the Pastorals find their most meaningful place in the history of early Christianity if interpreted in a Marcionite-Gnostic context.

## III. Language and Style

A. The Linguistic Facts.—Even the casual reader of the New Testament is aware of the fact that the Pastorals contain numerous important words or expressions which, although they are highly characteristic of the language and thought of these letters, do not occur at all in the ten Paulines, and indeed nowhere else in the New Testament. As early as the first chapter of I Timothy there leap to the eyes such new expressions as "to teach any different doctrine," "sound doctrine," "the saying is sure," to mention only a few. It is no wonder, then, that careful students of the text should have been led to penetrating investigation of the some 902 words of the Greek text.[30]

It is not possible here to reproduce the elaborate statistical tables which Harrison has published in his linguistic comparative analyses of the vocabulary of the Pastorals. The basic fact is that of the 902 words, of which 54 are proper names, 306, or more than one third, are not

[28] Gregory Dix, "The Ministry in the Early Church," in K. E. Kirk, ed., *The Apostolic Ministry* (London: Hodder & Stoughton, 1946), p. 203.

[29] See Knox, *Marcion and the N.T.*, pp. 40 ff.

[30] The most complete study of the vocabulary of the Pastorals in any language is the well-known monograph of P. N. Harrison, *The Problem of the Pastoral Epistles* (London: Oxford University Press, 1921). The reader may be referred also to Walter Lock, *A Critical and Exegetical Commentary on the Pastoral Epistles* (New York: Charles Scribner's Sons, 1924; "International Critical Commentary"), pp. xxvii-xxx, and to R. St. John Parry, *The Pastoral Epistles* (Cambridge: Cambridge University Press, 1920), pp. cxi-cxxvi. Lock, who holds to Pauline authorship, quite frankly says: "The conclusion is difficult. . . . The argument from style is in favour of the Pauline authorship, that from vocabulary strongly, though not quite conclusively, against it." Parry argues quite positively that the linguistic peculiarities may be understood without rejecting Pauline authorship. Another interesting attempt to prove the same thing is in Montgomery Hitchcock, "The Latinity of the Pastorals," *Expository Times*, XXXIX (1928), 347-53. The best modern summary of the problem, presented in support of the conservative conclusion, is in Spicq, *Saint Paul: les Épitres Pastorales*, pp. cvii-cxix. Spicq, too, is quite frank to say that "the only argument of worth against the authenticity of the Pastorals . . . is that *of style and especially of vocabulary.*" Nevertheless he believes himself able to turn, or at least to blunt, the edge of the argument.

found in the ten Paulines. According to Harrison, 175 of these (171 according to H. J. Holtzmann) do not occur elsewhere in the New Testament; 131 words occur in the Pastorals and other New Testament books, but not in any Pauline letter. The total number of words shared by the Pastorals with one or more of the ten Paulines is 542. Of these only 50 may be described as exclusively Pauline in the sense that they do not appear in the other books of the New Testament. Of the few among these which may be regarded as distinctively or characteristically Pauline, practically all form an integral part of phrases which (according to Harrison) were taken over bodily by the author of the Pastorals from the Pauline epistles before him.

Furthermore the language of the Pastorals manifests a kinship with that of the Apostolic Fathers and Apologists that is quite unexpected. "The outstanding fact here is that one word in every four throughout the Pastorals, 211 out of 848, while foreign so far as we know to the vocabulary of Paul, is now proved to form part of the working vocabulary of Christian writers between the years A.D. 95 and 170." [31] Of the 634 words used by Paul in his ten letters which have disappeared entirely from the current speech of second-century Christendom, as represented by the Apostolic Fathers, no less than 595 are absent from the Pastorals. And finally, the residue of words in the Pastorals not found elsewhere in the New Testament or in the Apostolic Fathers, or in the Apologists—that is, in no Christian writing previous to A.D. 170—find their linguistic affinity for the most part with the non-Christian writings of the first half of the second century: Epictetus (ca. A.D. 60-120), Dion Chrysostom (ca. A.D. 40-115), Dioscorides (ca. A.D. 100), Plutarch (d. A.D. 120), Arrian (ca. A.D. 100-170), Marcus Aurelius (A.D. 121-180), and so forth.

**B. The Significance of the Facts.**—That linguistically the Pastorals stand in a group by themselves is admitted by all. However, the significance of the linguistic facts for authorship remains in debate. The arguments may be summarized:

(a) The most striking group of words in the Pastorals are such expressions as "the saying is sure" (five times), "godliness" or "religion" (εὐσέβεια; ten times, plus cognates), "sound" (teaching, words, in the faith; nine times). These are only some of the most conspicuous examples of the 306 words in the Pastorals not found in the ten Paulines. Equally unusual, however, is the variety of compound words made up in different fashion from Paul's pre-

ferred compounds and used consistently in place of them. Notable too is the absence of particles prefacing or connecting clauses, so characteristic of Paul. Such Latinisms as the frequent omission of the article, circumlocutions such as "for which cause" (quam ob rem or causam) instead of "therefore" (διό; II Tim. 1:6; etc.), or "to lead a . . . life" (διάγειν βίον=vitam degere; I Tim. 2:2), or "to give thanks" (χάριν ἔχειν= gratium habere; I Tim. 1:12; etc.), and so forth, need to be accounted for.

(b) Of equal importance with the presence of such important non-Pauline words, phrases, and turns of language, is the absence of the commonplaces of Pauline language, as well as of words which are particularly dear to Paul and which express the genius of his interpretation of Christianity. For example, although "Spirit" is used about eighty times by Paul, it occurs in the Pastorals (i.e., in the sense of the Holy Spirit) only three times, once in each letter, and there in citations. Nor does Paul's language of mystical union with Christ find any place. The word "justify" occurs only once, in Tit. 3:7 (excluding the quotation of I Tim. 3:16). "Righteousness" (δικαιοσύνη) is an ethical quality rather than a religious relationship (I Tim. 6:11; II Tim. 2:22).

Or when Paul's words are used, they are used with a different meaning. For example, where Paul uses "revelation" and "reveal" (ἀποκάλυψις, ἀποκαλύπτω), the Pastorals use "appearing," and "appear" (ἐπιφάνεια, φανερόω). Paul uses "lord" (κύριος) over against "slave" (δοῦλος); the Pastorals, "master" (δεσπότης). In Tit. 3:1 "rulers" (ἀρχαί) means political authorities; in Paul, never. The meaning of "faith" (πίστις), too, has shifted to mean *the* faith, that is, what is believed. And in keeping with this shift "good" (καλός), used by Paul almost exclusively as substantive (τὸ καλόν, καλά, καλόν ἐστιν), is used twenty times as an adjective, especially with "works" (ἔργα), certainly an un-Pauline emphasis. And quite in harmony with the above usages, the author of the Pastorals never uses "gospel" as Paul used it, "for he does not teach what to Paul was the height of 'good news,' that men are accepted not because of their works but because of their faith." [32]

Complete lists of the relevant Greek words may be found in the references cited, especially in Easton. [33] The illustrations given above may serve to indicate the nature of the problem.

(c) Of further importance is the fact that whereas the language of Paul is that of the popular koine, that is, middle-class Greek, the

[31] Harrison, op. cit., p. 73.

[32] Easton, Pastoral Epistles, p. 12.
[33] Ibid., pp. 171-237.

language of the Pastorals is Hellenistic Greek of a higher literary level, similar to that of Hebrews and I and II Peter.

As many-faceted and as formidable as is the linguistic argument against the theory of Pauline authorship of the Pastorals, nevertheless those who follow the tradition make reply:

(a) Paul was quite capable of modifying his vocabulary under the influence of his own reading of Hellenistic literature. For example, of the forty-six *hapax legomena* in II Timothy, not a single Greek word requires a date later than Paul.[34]

Nothing prevents us from supposing that the studious Paul, who certainly spent the four or five years of his captivity at Caesarea and Rome in reading and meditating, assimilated a richer and more literary vocabulary, and that this cultivated mind should express itself in a language more and more correct, that of profane hellenistic literature.[35]

Parry,[36] on the contrary, observes that the higher literary words in the Pastorals need not have been derived from any acquaintance with the Hellenistic literature of the period. It is obvious from the earlier letters that Paul was familiar with the manner and methods of the diatribe, or popular lectures by professional teachers of the period. A large proportion of the new words, as listed by Theodor Nägeli,[37] express ethical ideas, just the area in which we should expect Paul to use words belonging to the literary stratum, considering the vogue of popular philosophy of an ethical cast.

(b) The importance of the *hapax legomena* has been misinterpreted, and their extent overestimated. As a matter of fact, *hapax legomena*, however many there may be, are not important as such.[38] Each word must be considered in itself. In any case, their total may be effectively reduced by excluding from the list cognate forms of words used in Paul, that is, words which do not appear in Paul in the forms occurring in the Pastorals, but of which he uses words from the same root. Spicq lists thirteen such.[39] Two other groups of words which rate as *hapax* may be eliminated as without importance for the problem of authenticity, continues Spicq: words or phrases current at the time, but which Paul

had not yet had occasion to use (some sixteen are listed) and biblical terms which Paul knew by heart from the Septuagint and which one day or another would come to his pen (about two hundred).

(c) Every Pauline letter presents notable linguistic peculiarities.[40] And it should further be recognized that the Pauline letters comprise four groups distinct in language, content, figures of speech, and circumstance: I and II Thessalonians; I and II Corinthians, Galatians, Romans; the epistles of the captivity; and the Pastorals. Spicq therefore urges that it is no more reasonable to deny the Pastorals to Paul because the language differs from that of the other three groups than it would be to deny I Thessalonians and Colossians to the writer of I Corinthians.

(d) Montgomery Hitchcock[41] endeavors to trace all the stylistic and linguistic peculiarities of the Pastorals to Latin influence. He proposes that as soon as Paul made plans to evangelize Spain he began to study Latin, since according to Strabo, the Spaniards spoke only that language. One may suppose that during the two years of his Roman captivity he studied Latin with his Praetorian Guards, educated men and of "pure Latin race." During his long stay in Rome, Paul's tastes must have been modified and his vocabulary enriched by the ascendant Roman culture of the time. Indeed, at more than one point the mentality of the author of the Pastorals is Roman: the emphasis on *gravitas* and *pietas,* the desire for peace with dignity, *otium cum dignitate.* The prescriptions concerning church organization reflect Latin influence, and recall Cicero.[42] The virtues stressed in the Pastorals are those exalted in Valerius Maximus, contemporary of Tiberius, in his *Nine Books of Facts and Memorable Words:* dignity, gravity, modesty, chastity, moderation in authority, humanity, clemency, steadfastness, patience, liberality. Hitchcock counts 160 words or phrases in the Pastorals that are specifically Latin, in addition to seeing Latin influence on the formation of compound words peculiar to the Pastorals. The thirty imperative verbs of II Timothy, he thinks, reflect Latin as a language of conquerors, apt in giving commands. Likewise the short, concise sentences, piling up one after another.

(e) In addition to pointing out that the Pastorals are separated by at least seven years from the latest of the earlier epistles which are assumed to give the normal Pauline style, Parry insists that the distinctive address of the letters

---

[34] Spicq, *Saint Paul: les Épitres Pastorales,* p. cx.

[35] *Ibid.,* p. cxiii.

[36] *Pastoral Epistles,* p. cxvi.

[37] *Der Wortschatz des Apostels Paulus* (Göttingen: Vandenhoeck & Ruprecht, 1905), pp. 85-88.

[38] Spicq's acute comment is: "The statistical method . . . confuses history and psychology with logic and arithmetic" (*op. cit.,* p. cxvii). Dibelius also, who rejects Pauline authorship, concedes that the statistical method of contesting authenticity is not adequate (*Pastoralbriefe,* p. 2).

[39] *Op. cit.,* p. cx.

[40] See F. Torm, "Über die Sprache in den Pastoralbriefen," *Zeitschrift für die Neutestamentliche Wissenschaft,* XVIII (1918), 225-43.

[41] "Latinity of the Pastorals."

[42] *Laws* III. 3-5.

to intimate and trusted individuals sufficiently accounts for the main characteristics of style, and the new subject matter explains the fresh vocabulary: "The question of vocabulary really resolves itself into a question of subject: we have not to ask whether S. Paul was likely to use these particular words or clauses of words: but whether he was likely to deal with these subjects." [43] The rule is that vocabulary follows subject. Parry then submits lists of words peculiar to the Pastorals to show that vocabulary is determined by subject: some thirty have to do with false doctrines, twenty-nine with the church ministry and its qualifications, sixty-one with the duties and virtues appropriate to Timothy and Titus, ninety with church order and discipline, and so forth.

In conclusion, we may allow Spicq to plead the case for the conservative point of view in his eloquent summary of the argument:

It must be recognized, then, that the language of the Pastorals is not of such a character as to exclude their Pauline origin. The evolution of the Apostle's style may be due to his more matured Greek and Roman culture, his new vocabulary to subjects which he treats for the first time, his tone and exhortations to his age and to the fact that he is addressing his disciples. It must be further affirmed that there does not exist any canon of the vocabulary, style, and theological thought of Saint Paul to which all of his literary products must be compared and reduced. To define the authentic Apostle exclusively by the language and the doctrine of the *Hauptbriefe* would be to mutilate the rich personality of the thinker, the writer and the man. Nothing is so academic, so arbitrary and so artificial as this a priori application of the principle of the static fixity of thought and its means of expression in an Apostle at home in the most diverse situations with a prodigious vitality, whose concern and regulations extend to all the churches of the universe, who produces a masterpiece of eloquence before the wise men of Athens, lets himself go in the most spontaneous outbursts with his intimates, elaborates daily a new theology, receives his illuminations directly from the Holy Spirit, and does not disdain to rule on the most concrete questions such as feminine toilet. [44]

The only concession Spicq will make is that Paul may have written through the hand of a secretary, perhaps Luke (II Tim. 4:11). [45]

Yet after as much allowance as possible is made for the element of probability in the ingenious counterarguments advanced to neutralize the force of the linguistic argument against Pauline authorship, we must agree with Dibelius that "the burden of proof is on him who derives these words and phrases from Paul." [46] The words of the author of the Pastorals are not the words of Paul.

**C. Style.**—If the vocabulary is strikingly un-Pauline, the style of writing is equally so. The spirited energy and emotional intensity which drive Paul to impassioned and sustained, even tortuous and involved, argument; the vivacity of spirit which runs faster than words; the wide range of mood as in humility he pleads, in boldness he commands, in love he yearns, in anger he sears, now soaring in ecstasy of hope and faith, now overwhelmed in frustration and despair; the richness of thought together with fecundity, incisiveness, and aptness of image and metaphor—all these dramatic qualities of the Pauline style are conspicuous by their absence in the Pastorals. Here the language is slow, diffuse, incoherent, repetitious, and on the whole lusterless.

Those who defend Pauline authorship in spite of stylistic differences do so on three grounds: (*a*) The subjects treated and the persons addressed determine style in any given case. Paul is not here concerned to demonstrate a thesis or argue a case, but to regulate and exhort. The letters should therefore not be compared with the argumentative parts of earlier letters written under strong personal provocation (II Cor. 1–7; 10–13), but with more quiet sections of the letters such as Rom. 10–15; II Cor. 8–9 (so Lock). (*b*) It is further urged that letters written to individuals, fellow workers and friends of Paul, would naturally be more restrained than letters to churches or groups. And (*c*) there is always recourse to the suggestion that Paul, now an old man, had quieted down. In some detail, Spicq has attempted to show that on every page the Pastorals reflect the psychology of an old man. [47]

Nevertheless, in spite of the ingenuity which has been employed to deflect the argument from vocabulary and style from striking full force against the theory of Pauline authorship, it must be insisted that to make the writer of the Pastorals simply a desiccated and senescent Paul with fires burned out and creative vigor abated is to commit injustice to both men, as well as to the Pastorals themselves. Once the author of the Pastorals is seen as a separate individual, and not as a depleted or altered Paul, he assumes a new position of importance in the New Testament and in the history of the ancient church. The New Testament thereby becomes enriched with an important type of

---

[43] *Pastoral Epistles*, p. cxv.

[44] *Saint Paul: les Épitres Pastorales* (Paris: J. Gabalda, 1947), p. cxviii. Used by permission.

[45] But see Harrison, *Problem of Pastoral Epistles*, pp. 52-53.

[46] *Op. cit.*, p. 3.

[47] *Op. cit.*, pp. lxxxix-xcii.

personality distinct and different from any of the other great figures delineated therein, a type without which the origin of the catholic church is inexplicable.

### IV. Form and Content of Doctrine

*A. The Literary Sources.*—Since the author has an administrative, not a creative, mind, and since like Ignatius he is concerned to establish and maintain a church loyal to its received (Pauline) faith and obedient to its ministry, the Pastorals are naturally dominated by a hortatory, moralizing mood. The writer will confront the world with a stabilized rule of faith and doctrine, a stabilized organization and ministry, a stabilized form of worship, in which common-sense virtues will demonstrate to all men the soundness and worth of the church. He is the type of person who by nature protects the old and rejects the new. And just as his interest in the heresies does not extend to the religious and philosophical problems involved in them but exhausts itself in a fury of repudiation, so likewise he makes no attempt to present a systematic account of orthodoxy. Entirely in accord with such a mentality is the fact that the glimpses we obtain of the content of his faith are not original phrasings but are derived (a) from counterstatements evoked by the heresies, (b) from the frequent conventional summaries or quotations from hymns or other liturgical forms, (c) from the glowing statements of faith in which the personal experiences of Paul are narrated, and (d) from the paraenetic or advice sections.

The writer's ideas are thus more practical than profound. Unlike Paul, he does not himself rise to lyrical heights of religious expression: rather, he quotes, now snatches of liturgical lines, now more or less extended passages from hymns, baptismal confessions, or other well-formulated church materials. The extensive use of liturgical materials suggests that he may have borrowed further from a larger number of written sources which, because they are prose—lacking the more easily distinguishable diction and rhythm of poetry—cannot be easily detected. The Old Testament is cited explicitly as scripture only in I Tim. 5:18 (Deut. 25:4); however, Old Testament passages are clearly referred to in I Tim. 1:9-10 (the Ten Commandments); 2:13-14 (Gen. 3); 4:3-5 (Gen. 1); 5:19 (Deut. 19:15); with short phrases occurring in II Tim. 2:19 (Num. 16:5?); 4:14 (Ps. 62:12?); 4:17 (Ps. 22:21); Tit. 2:14 (Ps. 130:8; Deut. 14:2). A Jewish apocryphal writing is drawn on in II Tim. 3:8 for the Jannes and Jambres illustration (see also II Tim. 2:19).

As for the Gospels and Acts, only Luke 10:7 is quoted (I Tim. 5:18). Some form of Mark 7:15 lies behind Tit. 1:15. Acts 13:50; 14:5, 19 are summarized in II Tim. 3:11 (see also II Tim. 4:19-21). Harrison [48] tabulates two pages of phrases as common to I Peter and the Pastorals, but direct literary relationship is not proved.

Of course the Pastorals show thorough acquaintance with the Pauline letters. For lists of Pauline phrases see Harrison,[49] and A. E. Barnett.[50] See also above, pp. 360-61.

The lists of virtues and vices, so frequent in the Pastorals, are not to be regarded as strictly original, although it is not possible to trace them to definite sources. Such lists were easily available for use when the occasion demanded: virtue lists for praise or admonition, vice lists for sticks with which to beat an opponent; see the excellent note on "Ethical Lists," in Easton.[51]

Hellenistic epigrams have been detected in I Tim. 1:9; 3:1; 4:8; 5:4; 6:7-10; II Tim. 2:4-6, 20; 4:7; Tit. 1:12, 15.

More complex is the question of the origin of the "church order" sections. Easton is quite sure that

in all the "Church Order" sections . . . the style is that of an author writing these rules for the first time and relying largely on contemporary commonplaces for his material; if these codes had been drawn up separately we should expect rather the succinct clarity found in the true Church Orders.[52]

It is of course obvious that the rules in these sections are not worked out or organized with the completeness or detail of the later church orders as found, for example, in the *Apostolic Tradition* of Hippolytus or the *Apostolic Constitutions*. Nevertheless it cannot be denied that not all the rules regulating the form of worship (I Tim. 2), bishops and deacons (I Tim. 3:1-13), widows (I Tim. 5:3-16), elders (I Tim. 5:17-22), and slaves (I Tim. 6:1-2) appear to have been formulated for the situation at hand. In part, at least, the material was assembled by the author from previously formulated regulations.

*B. The Author's Piety Essentially Jewish.*—It is completely in accord with his conservatism that the temper and the pattern of his Christian faith should be basically Jewish or Jewish-Christian. In the first place, as has been pointed out, he is thoroughly antispeculative, anti-intellec-

[48] *Problem of Pastoral Epistles,* pp. 175-77.
[49] *Ibid.,* pp. 167-75.
[50] *Paul Becomes a Literary Influence* (Chicago: University of Chicago Press, 1941), pp. 251-77.
[51] *Pastoral Epistles,* pp. 197-202.
[52] *Ibid.,* p. 17.

tualist in temper. He is a practical-minded man whose life is absorbed in the care of the churches. Completely satisfied with the (Pauline) Christian faith as he has received and interpreted it, his one concern is to remain faithful to it and to secure its transmission "unstained and free from reproach until the appearing of our Lord Jesus Christ" (I Tim. 6:14). The truth is a "deposit" (I Tim. 6:20), a "confession of faith" (I Tim. 6:12), a "common" faith (Tit. 1:4). If we accept C. H. Dodd's description,

For the Hebrew, . . . to know God is neither (primarily) an intellectual exercise nor an ineffable mystical experience. It means rather to acknowledge God in His ways with man, to recognize His claims upon man, to understand His Law with the intention of obeying it,[53]

then the author's piety is essentially Hebraic. To the speculation which he condemns he does not oppose speculation which he regards as true. Such expenditure of energy he regards as fruitless, indeed harmful. Obedience and discipline are his constant theme: "Train yourself in godliness" (I Tim. 4:7); "practice these duties" (I Tim. 4:15); "keep the commandment" (I Tim. 6:14); "follow the pattern of the sound words" (II Tim. 1:13); "continue in what you have learned and have firmly believed" (II Tim. 3:14); "a bishop . . . must hold firm to the sure word as taught, so that he may be able to give instruction in sound doctrine" (Tit. 1:7-9); "show yourself in all respects a model of good deeds, and in your teaching show integrity, gravity, and sound speech" (Tit. 2:7-8); "good deeds . . . are excellent and profitable to men" (Tit. 3:8); "let our people learn to apply themselves to good deeds" (Tit. 3:14). The writer accepts the (Pauline) Christian faith as the Jew accepts torah and insists that it shall be as rigorously obeyed.

Likewise, in his attitude toward women he holds an essentially Jewish point of view. Women shall have no part in public worship except to attend in silence. They must keep themselves inconspicuous by adorning "themselves modestly and sensibly in seemly apparel, not with braided hair or gold or pearls or costly attire" (I Tim. 2:9). Their service to God shall be through "good deeds, as befits women who profess religion" (I Tim. 2:10), not as teachers or administrators in the church. That Eve was created second to Adam, and that she, not Adam, "was deceived and became a transgressor," proves her natural incapacity to teach, preach, or administer. Her place is in the home.

[53] *The Johannine Epistles* (New York: Harper & Bros., 1946; "The Moffatt New Testament Commentary"), p. 30.

She "will be saved through bearing children, if she continues in faith and love and holiness, with modesty" (I Tim. 2:13-15). Since woman is by nature weak (II Tim. 3:6), a temptress, frivolous, prone to be a gossip and a busybody (I Tim. 5:13), she must be restrained from public life where that is possible. Marriage and the family are her true vocation. Only when this is not possible is she to be enrolled by the church in the order of widows. So insistent is the author that no one shall be accepted as a "widow" except as a last resort that he requires that the applicant be quite without kin, therefore without any means of support (I Tim. 5:3-8), and that she be sixty or more years of age and therefore presumably not liable to marriage (I Tim. 5:9-14). The younger widows must remarry and establish families. Only women who are too old to find a vocation in the home and who are quite without material support may be provided with a vocation by the church.

Insistence on the importance of the family, also Jewish, is supported in the Pastorals on two grounds: (a) The true vocation of woman is in the home. Normally, her very salvation depends on her performing adequately her duties as wife and mother. When wives love their husbands and children, and are "sensible, chaste, domestic, kind, and submissive to their husbands," the word of God is not discredited (Tit. 2:5). Rather, it is magnified, for Christian women like Lois and Eunice (II Tim. 1:5) communicate their faith to their children, and the church lives and grows. Therefore the order of marriage must be protected. Those who forbid it (whether to clergy or laity?) are prompted by "deceitful spirits and doctrines of demons" (I Tim. 4:1-3). And although the text does not tell us on what grounds the heretics forbade marriage, those alleged grounds, whatever they were, could not but be false because they ran counter to the divinely ordered institution of the family.

(b) The family is recognized as the training ground of the churches' ministers: "If a man does not know how to manage his own household, how can he care for God's church?" (I Tim. 3:5; see also I Tim. 3:12). It is quite taken for granted that ministers (bishops, elders, deacons), like all other adult men, will be married; indeed, marriage is thought of as so inevitable as to be almost a requirement. Nowhere in the Pastorals is there any suggestion of hesitancy to undertake marriage such as occurs in I Cor. 7. The writer's reactions here are those of a man in settled society. He is not anxious about "the impending distress" (I Cor. 7:26), nor is he even troubled about the possibility that the married man will be "anxious about worldly affairs, how to please his wife" (I Cor. 7:33). The only uncertain note is the problem posed by the repeated phrase, almost a formula, "husband of one wife" (I Tim. 3:2; Tit. 1:6), or in the case of "widows," "wife of one man" (I Tim. 5:9), understood by RSV to mean "married only once." For discussion of this phrase, see on I Tim. 3:2. However this difficult phrase is understood, the author seems here to have stepped slightly out of bounds from "normative" Judaism. Although he clearly does not object to a second marriage as such, as in the case of the younger widows (I Tim. 5:14), yet once widows have become "enrolled," their desire to remarry is described as growing "wanton against Christ" and as "having violated their first pledge" (I Tim. 5:11-12). It is quite possible also that the author in applying this formula to ministers will exact a stricter morality from them than from laymen.

In regard to the matter of food and drink, the author clearly represents a nonascetic, and therefore a Jewish, point of view. He rejects the demand for "abstinence from foods" (flesh?) as a doctrine of demons (I Tim. 4:1, 3). Likewise, he does not require of ministers that they shall be total abstainers. In fact, he forbids them to be "water-drinkers" (I Tim. 5:23) for that would mean renunciation of wine as a medicine as well as a beverage. His advice is to be temperate (I Tim. 3:2), no drunkard (I Tim. 3:3, 8, 11; Tit. 1:7), not slaves to drink (Tit. 2:3). The point of view is basically Jewish in that it reaffirms the Genesis account declaring that "everything created by God is good, and nothing is to be rejected if it is received with thanksgiving" (I Tim. 4:4). It is un-Jewish in that it has rejected the Levitical distinction between "clean" and "unclean" foods, and insists that there is nothing which a Christian may not eat provided it is sanctified "by the word of God and prayer."

Again, in his attitude toward scripture the author represents the middle path of a modified Judaism. Although he uses the Old Testament sparingly, citing it as "the scripture" only in I Tim. 5:18, it is obvious that he regards it as authoritative for Christians. It stands as a bedrock of revelation. When he appeals to it, whether formally or informally, literally (I Tim. 5:19 [Deut. 19:15]; II Tim. 2:19 [Num. 16:5; Isa. 26:13]) or analogically (I Tim. 2:13-15 [Gen. 3:1-6]; 4:4 [Gen. 1]; 5:18 [Deut. 25:4]; II Tim. 4:14 [Ps. 62:12; Prov. 24:12]; II Tim. 4:17 [Ps. 22:21]; Tit. 2:14 [Ps. 130:8; Ezek. 37:23; Deut. 14:2]), it is with the assumption that the reference affords indisputable proof. Moses, too, stands on the side of truth (II Tim.

3:8). When the heretics advance an interpretation of "the law" which the author regards as erroneous, his defense is not rejection of the law as such. Rather, he reaffirms it—"we know that the law is good" (I Tim. 1:8)—but he insists that it shall be interpreted as Paul interpreted it. And whatever the full meaning of II Tim. 3:15-16 may be (see Exeg., ad loc.), "the sacred writings," "all scripture," will include the Jewish Bible; the text will assert the validity of (at least) the Old Testament scriptures for the church (as over against Marcionism?). The attitude of the author toward the Scriptures is basically the same as that of Paul and Jesus: on the one hand, it insists on their adequacy and finality; on the other, it radically reinterprets them, on occasion even to the point where reinterpretation actually means rejection. If, as is probable under the theory of pseudonymity, "scripture" in II Tim. 3:15-16 includes the writings of Paul, then of course the author has already advanced to the Christian conception of "scripture" as including Christian as well as Jewish literature.

Again, the author's eschatological ideas, although not outlined in any detail, veer to the Jewish rather than to the Greek side. In the usual Jewish view the resurrection was to come—it could not be "past already" (II Tim. 2:18). Since the scene of the final consummation was thought of as the earth or some sort of materially conceived place, belief in the resurrection of the body was a common presupposition of all forms of rabbinical belief in the future life. Whether it was supposed that the dead were summoned to life directly from the grave, or that in the resurrection the soul at death having left the body in the grave to depart elsewhere would then be reunited with it, or that a new and different sort of body would be given to the soul—always in rabbinical theology, the body was thought of as an element essential to a human being. A resurrected body, whether naïvely conceived as grossly material or in a more refined sense as half material, half spiritual, whether thought of as the same body that was laid in the grave or a newly fashioned one—in every case a body was believed necessary to complete existence.[54] To deny the resurrection as future event was to reject the basic framework of Jewish eschatology with its clear distinction between the present (evil) age and the (good) age to come, and to substitute for it the Greek view of cycles, a repetitious round without the possibility of any permanent good time coming. In this view salvation is the soul's lib-

[54] See Paul Volz, *Die Eschatologie der jüdischen Gemeinde im neutestamentlichen Zeitalter* (Tübingen: J. C. B. Mohr, 1934), pp. 249-55.

eration from the prison of matter, its union with or absorption in the Divine through some supernatural enlightenment or birth from above, through some mystical initiation into knowledge, in the sense of "gnosis."

All of this Hellenistic alternative to Jewish eschatology the author rejects. For him Christians are "heirs in hope" (Tit. 3:7). Although the Christian has been regenerated and renewed (Tit. 3:5), he looks forward to "that Day" (II Tim. 4:8), he awaits "our blessed hope, the appearing of the glory of our great God and Savior Jesus Christ" (Tit. 2:13; I Tim. 6:14-15). Therefore those "who have swerved from the truth by holding that the resurrection is past already" (II Tim. 2:18) are a poison. For as surely as there is a present life, there is a life to come (I Tim. 4:8). The Christian looks forward.

*C. Some Important Differences Between Paul and "Paul."*—That the writer is basically of a conservative temper is further seen in his affection for dogmatic rather than experimental or mystical religion. Here faith is not faithfulness or trust or commitment; rather, it is *the* faith—what is believed. The Christian is not one who has committed himself to Jesus Christ, who has "put on" Christ, or who is "in Christ," or who has been buried with Christ in his death and raised with him in his resurrection; rather, he is one who believes and is loyal to the received faith, the dogmatic deposit which the author regards as long since formulated and of unchanging validity. Thus in contrast to Paul's teaching, faith in the Pastorals is not the condition of redemption, but its consequence (I Tim. 1:14; II Tim. 1:9; Tit. 3:5-7). The concept loses its Pauline warmth because it now signifies not an intimate interpersonal experience, but "the pattern of the sound words" (II Tim. 1:13).

Quite in accord with this concern for orthodoxy in faith and order are the regularization and virtual disappearance of the Spirit, which is now regarded not as a creative power but as a conservative one (II Tim. 1:14). The Spirit does not now manifest itself spontaneously and unpredictably: it is conferred by a rite, the laying on of hands (I Tim. 1:18; 4:14; II Tim. 1:6). Church officials thus derive their authority from their appointment by authorized churchmen, not as in Paul from the gift of the Spirit. The most striking difference between the Pastorals and the Paulines at this point is that whereas Paul is profoundly mystical, the writer of the Pastorals is rigorously ecclesiastical. A stabilized faith and order is his chief concern.

Further in character is the absence of the important Pauline idea of grace, so distinc-

tively Christian, and yet here crowded out by the writer's moralizing mood and insistence on good works. Only once does the true Pauline usage of grace appear, and that in a quotation from an early Christian confession formula (II Tim. 1:9-10). Surely Paul would not have stressed a piety grounded so exclusively in good works, reward, conscience, and reputation. Absence of "grace" means also the absence of "gospel" as "good news" in the Pauline sense that men are accepted by God because of faith (that is, commitment as an experience of union with Christ), not because of works. Likewise, such important Pauline terms as "righteousness" and "justification" are denuded of their peculiar Pauline content, when they appear at all (see I Tim. 6:11; II Tim. 2:22; 3:16; 4:8; Tit. 3:5, 7). And as little is made of reconciliation between man and God as effected by the death of Christ, so "love" is retained formally in conventional lists of Christian virtues (see I Tim. 2:15; 6:11; II Tim. 2:22; Tit. 2:2), but without the Pauline warmth or centrality.

As devoted to Paul as the author is, we are compelled to conclude that he is in temper and type nearer to common sense rabbinical Judaism, nearer to a sober Roman pattern of piety, nearer even to a non-Gnostic form of Hellenistic piety than Paul was. His constant kinship with Hellenism will be observed throughout the epistles.

## V. Place and Date of Origin

*A. Place.*—That the author was geographically separated from "Timothy" and "Titus" during the writing of the letters need not have been the case in the usual sense. It is of course true that most letters, whether individual, circular, or general, are necessitated by the fact that geography prevents oral communication. It is also obvious that since the Pastorals were written generally to the clergy in Asia Minor the writer could not have been immediately or simultaneously present with them all. Nevertheless, the intent of I Tim. 1:3 to suggest that the letter is simply a written reminder and re-emphasis of counsel previously given orally by the author on the eve of his departure for Macedonia must be regarded as the stage setting of pseudonymity, a literary device intended to ensure both the authenticity of the letter and the necessity for writing it. The similar pattern of Titus, "This is why I left you in Crete" (1:5), is likewise schematic. Such geographical details, therefore, in pseudonymous letters, cannot be taken at face value.

The situation is the same with regard to the prison motif. Only II Timothy appears as a prison letter (1:8, 12; 2:9; 4:6-7; perhaps such is the inference also of 1:15-18; 2:3, 10-13; 3:1-5, 10-13; 4:16-18). Obviously the prison motif, or martyr pattern, is of no value in determining the place of origin of a pseudonymous letter. Here the author (who may himself be in peril of death, possibly himself in prison) employs the martyr pattern to steel the spirits of the clergy to utter consecration to the true (Pauline) Christian faith by bringing to bear upon them the full weight of Paul's perfect martyrdom. The whole church knew that Paul was the great sufferer (1:12), that he had gladly borne his share of suffering for the gospel (1:8; 2:3). They had observed his persecutions and sufferings (3:11) and they knew that out of them all the Lord had rescued him (3:11; 4:17) and that his crown in the heavenly kingdom was assured (4:8, 18). As a martyrology, II Timothy is concerned not with the *place*, but with the *fact*, of Paul's imprisonment. The letter may even take it for granted that there was only one really important imprisonment of Paul—in Rome (1:17)—at the end of which Paul was "sacrificed" (4:6). But even so, it cannot be argued from this basis that the letter was written in Rome. The descriptions of Paul as martyr do not require—indeed, do not even suggest—any particular place of imprisonment or form of martyrdom. If pseudonymous, the letter might even have been written in Ephesus or Asia Minor without any necessity of postulating an Ephesian imprisonment as the setting. Indeed, even if there are genuine Pauline fragments in the letters deriving from one or more imprisonment experiences, it is no longer possible to determine from what prison they were written (see II Cor. 11:23). The conventions of the practice of pseudonymity make it unnecessary to conjecture either an Ephesian or a second Roman imprisonment as time and place of writing. There is a problem only if we suppose the letter is authentically Pauline. Then a second Roman imprisonment must be conjectured to provide an interim of freedom to pursue the sort of missionary work suggested in the Pastorals and to furnish a setting in which Paul's martyr confession is appropriate.

Having made such observations, one may hazard the guess that the letters were written in Asia Minor, perhaps in Ephesus. Such phrases as "remain in Ephesus" (I Tim. 1:3); "all who are in Asia" (II Tim. 1:15); "you well know all the service he rendered at Ephesus" (II Tim. 1:18); "this is why I left you in Crete" (Tit. 1:5), suggest that the letters were written primarily for the churches of Asia, and therefore were written in Asia.[55]

[55] This point of view is held, among others, by Maurice Goguel, *Introduction au Nouveau Testament* (Paris:

However, the opinion that the Pastorals were written in Rome has been maintained by some scholars who reject their authenticity, from F. C. Baur to Goodspeed and Barnett:

The regulative tone of the letters with their definite statements of the requisite qualifications for church superintendents, assistants, assistants' wives, I Tim. 3:11, and dependent widows suggests the atmosphere of Rome rather than that of Ephesus. The conflict with the sects seems to have been hottest at Rome. . . . There, too, the feminism which was advancing in the province of Asia . . . would be sternly repressed.[56]

However, all of these arguments may also be used to support the theory of Ephesus. On church orders in Asia see Streeter.[57] Asia was a hotbed of heresy and syncretism: did not Marcionism begin and probably end there? Feminism, too, continued to increase in Asia, as Goodspeed, referring to Thecla in the Acts of Paul, about A.D. 160-70, and Priscilla and Maximilla in Montanism, well knows. Asia, probably Ephesus, therefore remains the most probable place of origin.

*B. The Date.*—The difficulty of establishing the date of the Pastorals, already obvious from previous discussions, is further evident in the fact that different scholars variously assign them to a time anywhere between A.D. 61 and 180. Even when Pauline authorship and the earlier datings are rejected, considerable disagreement remains. An important group of scholars suggest a date around 110; [58] a second group, not too much impressed by the arguments which would hold the figure near to A.D. 100, would extend the time somewhat farther into the second century; [59] a third group, who see the

Ernest Leroux, 1922-26), IV², 553-55; Adolf Jülicher, *Einleitung in das Neue Testament* (7th ed. rev.; Erich Fascher, Tübingen: J. C. B. Mohr, 1931), p. 183; Hans Lietzmann, *Geschichte der alten Kirche* (Berlin: Walter de Gruyter, 1932), I, 229; Streeter, *Primitive Church*, pp. 109-12; Easton, *Pastoral Epistles*, p. 22: "For the place of writing neither Egypt nor Rome is a possibility, for neither church had a single head comparable to 'Timothy' until many years later. The alternatives are Syria or Asia Minor." Dibelius, *Pastoralbriefe*, p. 79, thinks the names in II Tim. 4:10 ff. speak for Caesarea as the place of composition of II Timothy.

[56] E. J. Goodspeed, *An Introduction to the New Testament* (Chicago: University of Chicago Press, 1937), pp. 342-43; so also A. E. Barnett, *The New Testament, Its Making and Meaning* (New York and Nashville: Abingdon-Cokesbury Press, 1946), p. 284.

[57] *Op. cit.*, pp. 109-21.

[58] E.g., Goguel, Harnack, Streeter, Moffatt, Harrison, *ca.* 90-110; Ropes, Scott, Easton, F. C. Grant, *ca.* 95-105.

[59] Jülicher-Fascher, J. Weiss, *ca.* 100-125; so Enslin, who adds that "a date fifty years later is not impossible"; Bultmann, *ca.* 100-150; Dibelius, whose approach favors a somewhat late view, refuses to name a figure and cautiously suggests that "the composition of the Pastorals

Pastorals as anti-Marcionite documents, set the time between A.D. 140-180.[60]

Since the problem of Marcion and the identification of the heresies has already been discussed on pp. 358-60, nothing further need be said here. Naturally scholars who do not see in the letters any reference either to Marcion or to any well-developed form of Gnosticism, and who regard the form of church organization reflected in the Pastorals as more primitive than that of Ignatius (see pp. 347-48), incline to a pre-Ignatian date. Such a dating seems further confirmed by the traditional interpretation of the apparent points of contact between the Pastorals and certain of the Apostolic Fathers, which affirms that the Pastorals were known to and either assumed or quoted by I Clement, Ignatius, and Polycarp in his letter to the Philippians. In I Clem. 2:7 (ca. 95) occurs the expression "ready for any good work," which with slight variation is identical with Tit. 3:1. Moreover, the phrase "ready for any good work" recurs like a refrain twice more in the Pastorals: II Tim. 2:21; 3:17.

Although the points of contact found between Ignatius and the Pastorals are numerically greater, they are generally too vague and uncertain to merit confidence in any theory of literary dependence. Only one recurrent expression is impressive, the frequent characterization of Jesus as "our (common) hope": Ign. Eph. 21:2; Ign. Mag. 11; Ign. Trall. 2:2; Ign. Phila. 11:2=I Tim. 1:1.

With the letter of Polycarp to the Philippians, however, the parallels become both closer and more extensive. Among them particularly Polyc. Phil. 4:1=I Tim. 6:10, 7; and Polyc. Phil. 9:2= II Tim. 4:10 seem important, although Spicq will add also Polyc. Phil. 5:2=II Tim. 2:12; I Tim. 3:8; Polyc. Phil. 11:4=II Tim. 2:25; Polyc. Phil. 12:3=I Tim. 2:1-2. Polyc. Phil. 4:1 reads "the beginning [ἀρχή instead of ῥύξα, "root"] of all troubles [χαλεπῶν instead of κακῶν, "evils"] is the love of money," and "we brought nothing into the world and we can take nothing out of it." That the second clause should be introduced by "knowing therefore" suggests that it is treated by Polycarp as a quotation. And curiously enough, the conjunction introducing the second clause, although different from that in I Tim. 6:7, is equally obscure (see Exeg., ad loc.).

The second parallel always noted, Polyc. Phil. 9:2=II Tim. 4:10, is the phrase "loved this present world."

Without considering in further detail the resemblances between Polycarp and the Pastorals, it is sufficient for our purposes to note that in the judgment of many scholars the passages indicated are sufficient to require a date for the Pastorals prior to the writing of Polycarp's letter to the Philippians, that is, according to the usual accepted dating, A.D. 110-17.[61]

However, as interesting as are the resemblances between the Pastorals and I Clement, Ignatius, and Polycarp, they are too fragmentary, imprecise, and uncertain to be allowed to determine the date of the Pastorals. Words and phrases used in common are either epithets like "Christ our (common) hope," a phrase which might well have circulated freely among Christians in the second century, or proverblike sayings such as "the love of money is the root of all evil" (see Exeg., ad loc.). In both cases the proverbs are quotations, but neither author need have quoted the other. Dibelius properly writes: "Dependence of the letter of Polycarp on I Tim. 6:7, 10 is not provable. . . . However, it may perhaps be supposed that the section in Polycarp goes back to an older Christian homily from which also our author ["Paul"] has drawn." [62]

If the Epistle of Polycarp (chs. 1–12) was written about 135, as is argued at length by P. N. Harrison,[63] the theory of its dependence on the Pastorals would not require a date for them earlier than, say, 130. However, in any case, if, as argued in this study, the Pastorals as a whole are best understood in a mid-second-century context, the parallels between Polycarp and the Pastorals would have to be explained either by the use of common sources or by the use of Polycarp by the author of the Pastorals. Taking the parallel texts in themselves, there is no more reason to suppose that Polycarp is dependent on the Pastorals than the Pastorals on Polycarp. Once again the problem is the problem of the total situation.

Arguments from language and style which weigh against Pauline authorship (see pp. 360-

---

does not seem to belong too far in the second century" (op. cit., p. 6).

[60] E.g., Goodspeed, Knox, Barnett.

[61] E.g., Moffatt, Jülicher, Goguel, Scott, Streeter, M. S. Enslin. Easton, too, is reasonably positive: "Patristic citation of the Pastorals appears to begin with Polycarp. His passage in 4.1 . . . seems all but indubitably to be a reminiscence of 1 Tim. 6.10 and 6.7. . . . Equally probable, . . . Polycarp 9:2 . . . is a recollection of 2 Tim. 4.10. . . . The total number [of instances] is impressive and makes a dependence of Polycarp on 1 and 2 Timothy seem reasonably certain." (Pastoral Epistles, pp. 30-31.)

[62] Op. cit., p. 54; so also Bultmann, Religion in Geschichte und Gegenwart, IV, 996.

[63] Polycarp's Two Epistles to the Philippians (Cambridge: Cambridge University Press, 1936). Burkitt (1933) and Streeter (1929) accepted Harrison's arguments. Kirsopp Lake (Journal of Biblical Literature, LVI [1937], 73) stated, "This is by far the best suggestion which has yet been made."

64) also support a date later than Paul. However, they can hardly provide confidence for determining on which side of A.D. 125 the letters should be dated. That the Pastorals did not stand in the first Pauline collections, and that they echo all the other Paulines including Ephesians,[64] likewise indicate a later but uncertain date.

The absence of the Pastorals from Marcion's canon (see pp. 359-60) probably argues for a somewhat late date. Indeed, their status in the ancient canonical lists suggests that they were regarded as supplementary material: the Muratorian fragment (*ca.* 190?) puts them at the end of the Paulines. The Michigan Beatty Codex of Paul (*ca.* 250) probably did not contain them at all.[65] Yet Irenaeus, who wrote his important *Against Heresies* between 181 and 189, quotes from all the thirteen chapters of the Pastorals except Tit. 1. Easton therefore insists that they could not have appeared within the memory of Irenaeus; otherwise he would not have used them so unquestioningly.

Arguing for a date of 160 or later, Barnett[66] urges the importance of the martyrological tone: such terms as "confess" and "witness," the martyrological use of the trial of Jesus, the comparison of Jesus and the emperor, the use of Paul as model martyr find their context in the times of Antoninus Pius (138-161) and Marcus Aurelius (161-180) and are parallels to the Martyrdom of Polycarp, the Acts of the Scilitan Martyrs, and the Acts of Justin. However, this argument should not be pushed too far. The Gospels themselves are martyrologies. Indeed, at any time during the first three centuries the Christian summons was to a heroic stand, if not to actual martyrdom. Already in I Clem. 5 (*ca.* 95) Paul is exhibited as setting a splendid example in bearing a martyr's witness before rulers. No later Paulinist writing in Paul's name or in his defense at any time could have failed to make use of Paul's martyrdom as his chief crown of glory. For precise dating, therefore, the motif is of uncertain value.

If a date must be suggested, A.D. 130-150 would seem to be a reasonable conjecture.

### VI. Sequence and Number

**A. Sequence.**—No agreement has been reached as to the order in which the Pastorals were written. Naturally in our New Testament the two Timothys are put together, with Titus last.[67] Since, however, no one supposes Titus written last, two possible orders remain. First: I Timothy—Titus—II Timothy. As would be expected, those who regard the letters as Pauline commonly accept this order, primarily on the ground that in II Tim. 4 there is the solemn and poignant anticipation of imminent death on Paul's part. His warfare is over; he now reluctantly but formally bids the world farewell, clinging to a few friends but certain only of God. For example, Meinertz[68] conjectures that in A.D. 64 Paul went from Spain to Ephesus, thence to Colossae (Philem. 22), thence to Macedonia (I Tim. 1:3), perhaps as far as Corinth. On this trip I Timothy was written. The next year Paul went to Ephesus, and early in 65 to Crete. Shortly he again returned to Miletus (II Tim. 4:20), then to Troas (II Tim. 4:13), on through Macedonia to Corinth (II Tim. 4:20), where he may have written Titus. Wintering in Nicopolis in Epirus (Tit. 3:12), he went to Rome in 66, wrote the second letter to Timothy, and suffered martyrdom in 67.

However, among scholars who reject the Pauline authorship of the letters and date them in the second century there are those who regard the same order, I Timothy—Titus—II Timothy, as probable; for example, Dibelius is impressed with the personal tone of II Timothy, in which Paul is set forth as model of suffering and endurance for the encouragement of Timothy. "The character of II Timothy," he writes, "is perhaps best explained by the assumption that I Timothy (and Titus?) had already been written when II Timothy was composed."[69] Then the character of Paul, which in I Timothy and Titus is primarily administrative and conservative, is in II Timothy given a deeper dimension. And in Jülicher's words the author grows before our very eyes to become more like Paul in expression, ideas, and attitudes.

Nevertheless, the majority of critics support the second order: II Timothy—Titus—I Timothy. Indeed, in 1926 Goguel could write that "critics are almost unanimous" in considering

---

[64] See Harrison, *Problem of Pastoral Epistles*, pp. 167-75.

[65] See H. A. Sanders, *A Third-Century Papyrus Codex of the Epistles of Paul* (Ann Arbor: University of Michigan, 1935), pp. 10-11.

[66] *N.T.: Its Making and Meaning*, pp. 283-84.

[67] Who originally decided which letter should be designated as "I Timothy" and which as "II Timothy" cannot be known. Perhaps I Timothy was so designated because it is longer; or perhaps the farewell scene in II Timothy made it appear to be the second letter.

[68] *Op. cit.*, pp. 2-8; see also Wilhelm Michaelis, *Einleitung in das Neue Testament* (Bern: BEG, 1946), p. 262, and Spicq, *Saint Paul: les Épitres Pastorales*, pp. lxxxiii-lxxxviii.

[69] *Op. cit.*, pp. 5, 45; see also Jülicher, *Einleitung in das N.T.*, p. 184, "II Timothy may most easily be understood as the last trump card which the author plays as he permits the dying apostle to hand over his will and testament to a successor in the service."

the order as II Timothy—Titus—I Timothy.[70] The arguments advanced may be summarized as follows:

(a) The opposition to heretics becomes progressively more intense as one moves from II Timothy to Titus to I Timothy. In II Timothy disputatiousness appears as a probable consequence of heresy; in Tit. 3:9, disputes have come to be an essential element in heretical propaganda which has become more definitely polemic. In I Timothy the heresies are more harshly characterized than in II Timothy and Titus. Likewise, heretics are more severely handled in I Timothy than in II Timothy and Titus: in II Tim. 2, Hymenaeus and Philetus make shipwreck of their faith but they are still in the church. Tit. 3:10-11 insists that every "factious" man must be rejected. In I Tim. 1:20, Hymenaeus and Alexander have been "delivered to Satan," that is, excommunicated.

(b) It is also urged that development in church polity can be clearly seen to move from II Timothy to Titus to I Timothy, and this in two ways: (i) II Timothy orders the selection of "faithful men" to be made tradition-bearers with sphere of authority undefined. Titus first names them elders, commands their installation everywhere. In I Timothy the third-century form of polity is taken for granted, and rules are given for remuneration and discipline. The addressee is clearly a bishop, monarchic head of a local church. There is a council of elders, deacons, enrolled widows.[71]

(ii) In II Timothy 1:6, ordination is by an apostle. This, it is argued, is an earlier practice than ordination by the elderhood (I Tim. 4: 14) which is the catholic revival of Jewish precedent.[72]

(c) Further, the presence of the personal elements in II Timothy has been interpreted (in contrast to the interpretation offered by Jülicher and Dibelius) as evidence that II Timothy is prior to I Timothy. A progressive lessening of the purely personal Pauline elements in the letters, urges Easton, is only natural in a pseudonymous author.

At his first attempt he would take pains to preserve the Pauline atmosphere, to use authentic materials—written or oral—where available and to avoid palpable anachronisms. The success of 2 Timothy called for a sequel that would deal more directly with contemporary difficulties; for the "recipient"

of this he chose Timothy's companion. Finally in 1 Timothy the method was so well known that the pseudonymity is a bare convention; it is only in 1.3 (copied from Tit. 1.5) that any attempt is made to put the situation back into the past. And as Paul had no third noted disciple, the Pastor addressed it to Timothy once more.[73]

P. N. Harrison is also of the opinion that the author used up all his genuine Pauline materials in II Timothy, and that when I Timothy was written, no more were available.

(d) And finally, Easton is quite sure that Tit. 1:1-4 is a condensation of II Tim. 1:1-10, that I Tim. 1:1-2 uses both II Tim. 1:1-2 and Tit. 1:1-4, and that I Tim. 3:2-5 is a revised version of Tit. 1:5-8.

However, as attractive as any argument or arguments for a particular order may be, they must be entertained with caution. The evidence is certainly ambiguous. For example, Dibelius, following Eduard Schwartz,[74] regards ordination by the elderhood in I Tim. 4:14 as "relatively historical" and that by an apostle in II Tim. 1:6 as corrected to correspond with the "apostolic tradition," thereby rejecting its value as evidence for the order II Timothy—I Timothy. The differences between I Timothy-Titus, and II Timothy at this point he will explain not by a certain sequence in composition, but by difference in their character: I Timothy and Titus contain church regulations; II Timothy personal advice with emphasis on epistolary form.[75]

***B. Number.***—If we could be certain why *three* letters were written, or where they were written, or to whom they were first sent, we should be in a better position to know the order in which they were written. Evidently the author was a persistent and determined church administrator. He may have thought three letters on the same subject addressed to different men, and perhaps circulated in different areas, would be more effective than one. Or they may have been issued to the same groups, one after the other, serving as successive reinforcements. It is perhaps possible, as Barnett argues, that "instead of being three distinct communications, the Pastorals were probably a single epistle whose threefold form was a literary artifice contributing to the purpose of the author."[76]

---

[70] In support of the position he named Moffatt, Baur, Holtzmann, von Soden, von Harnack, Pfleiderer, Schmiedel. In addition may be named Harrison and Easton.

[71] See Easton, *Pastoral Epistles*, pp. 17-19.

[72] *Ibid.*; see also Exeg., *ad loc.*

[73] *Ibid.*, p. 19.

[74] *Über die pseudsapostolischen Kirchenordnungen* (Strassburg: K. J. Trübner, 1910), p. 1.

[75] Dibelius, *op. cit.*, p. 45.

[76] *N.T.: Its Making and Meaning*, p. 277; so Goodspeed, *Introduction to N.T.*, p. 339: "It is a mistake to approach the Pastorals atomistically and seek to determine which is earlier and which later. They are to be understood as a unit. . . . It was as a corpus that they were produced and put forth."

This seems improbable, however. Being the dogged and determined man he is revealed to be in the letters, it is most unlikely that he would have been content to fire only one salvo of ammunition in defense of the faith he held with such intensity. The three letters will represent a broadside attack, more effective if discharged one after the other.

### VII. The Nature of Pseudonymity

The use of an assumed or pen name is a literary practice so widespread as scarcely to need explanation. Yet in its special form known as pseudonymity—the use of a "false name"—that is, a name of historical importance to confer special authority on a contemporary writing by a person of lesser prestige, the practice among Jews and Christians deserves some comment. The large collection of Jewish apocalyptic literature put out under such names as Enoch, Daniel, Baruch, Tobit, is easily available and well known. In the early Christian centuries there was similar production among Christians, such as the Gospel of Nicodemus, the Gospel of Peter, and so forth, not to mention possible examples in the New Testament. Obviously a literary convention practiced over so many centuries cannot be dismissed simply as a pious fraud. Nevertheless the question must remain as to the extent to which a particular author was concerned to fashion and wear a guise which would conceal him as effectively and consistently as possible. It has been urged [77] that in the case of the writer of the Pastorals there was no element of deception at all, that in fact his readers knew full well who wrote the letters. If this is so, however, it is not easy to see the point of pseudonymity. Given the literary convention and its common acceptance within the moral pattern of the times, the guise may be effectively assumed without our having the right to pin the ugly word "forger" upon our author. The problem is not moral; it is historical.

It is at least clear that the author writes as he thinks Paul would if he were living and working in the writer's situation. One would not expect him to be overcautious in avoiding anachronism at every point, or to be at too great pains to make the disguise complete.

In addition to the usual purposes of pseudonymous practice, three reasons may be suggested why he wrote in Paul's name: (a) Paul was for him truly the greatest Christian who had ever lived. In sincere humility, then, he would hide himself underneath his great hero. With complete effacement he would forever conceal his own name, and allow Paul to speak in his stead.

(b) Paul was indeed a doughty warrior for Christ. He too engaged heretics in battle. When he struck, he struck hard. He was good to have on one's side. The author was sure that if the great apostle, so surely commissioned to be an apostle, were in his position, he would speak again his wonted word of power, he would slay the enemies of the church with the breath of his mouth, he would summon men back to his faith, and he would so organize the church against its heretical enemies that henceforth his doctrine would be kept pure and transmitted without variation. And (c) by making Paul the champion of the "catholic" point of view, of orthodoxy, the author reclaims Paul forever from the heretics, from Marcion and the Gnostics, whose constant appeals to his letters in support of their tenets had brought him into bad repute with the church.[78]

If these suggestions are admitted as valid, the very use of pseudonymity must itself be regarded as a most important service rendered by the author both to Paul and the church, a service which in the times could not have been rendered otherwise.

### VIII. The Importance of the Pastorals

Although the rather elementary and somewhat stereotyped, if basic, advices to deacons and bishops in the Pastorals have become an established part of the ordination liturgies of many churches, and although certain other texts such as I Tim. 1:15; 6:10; II Tim. 1:12; 2:15; 3:16; 4:7-8 are frequently quoted, the Pastorals have never been regarded as standing on the highest level of New Testament inspiration. The modern man, indeed, is not likely to see in the author too congenial or attractive a person. The genius of Protestantism has called for emphasis on the prophetic or creative spirit rather than on the priestly or transmissive spirit in religion. Likewise, the concern of Protestantism with the religion of the inner life, with religion as feeling and as "a way of life," has tended to weaken the sense of the importance of dogma and of the institutional aspects of the church. Furthermore, the recent important centuries of exploration and discovery, of endless production of marvelous inventions, of belief in progress and evolution, have conditioned us to conceive of educational process in dynamic rather than in static, in creative rather than transmissive, terms. The educated man of our time who is trained in the liberal arts, who cherishes an open and inquiring mind, who honors originality and creative genius, repudiates the very idea of heresy. When he is told

[77] See Easton, op. cit., p. 19; Harrison, Problem of the Pastoral Epistles, p. 12.

[78] On this point see Walter Bauer, Rechtgläubigkeit und Ketzerei im ältesten Christentum, pp. 227-28.

that he must submit to "sound doctrine" or yield to an orthodox tradition, that all speculation, argument, and debate, on any question whatever, are but "godless chatter, . . . disputes about words, . . . stupid, senseless controversies, . . . unprofitable and futile" and that those who engage in them are "liars . . . evil men and impostors . . . empty talkers and deceivers . . . detestable, disobedient, unfit for any good deed," he is both chilled and angered. He is inclined to discard the author and the Pastorals together to the dustbin of dead enthusiasms. Yet a better justice than this may be secured for the writer.

In attempting to appraise the importance of "Paul" in his time, it may be said quite frankly that in the New Testament, after Jesus, there are but two great and seminal minds who were able to translate one religious tradition (Judaism) into another (Hellenism) in such a way as to create a genuinely new religion (Christianity) —Paul and the author of the Fourth Gospel. Both of them were men of such spirit, imaginative insight, and religious intensity, so bold and expressive in language and metaphor, that between them they have practically determined what Christian language is. In contrast to these two giants, the author of the Pastorals, and indeed most other later New Testament writers, seem without originality— sincere and devoted, it is true, but without fresh ideas. Our author is best described as a priest devoted to transmitting that which he has received, not a prophet or creative spirit illuminating the Christian faith with his own genius, not restating it or reinterpreting it to include whatever of value there may have been in the presentations of the heretics. He is a churchman, fanatically loyal, intense, intolerant, yet able in administration. Concerned that the church shall be respected in its pagan environment, that is, concerned with what we should call public relations, he advocates virtues which are as pagan as they are Christian. They represent what we should call a common-sense, middle-of-the-road, conservative point of view— the point of view of a church which will minimize the difference between itself and the world so that it may the more easily win the world.

That the author is intellectually unadventurous is obvious on every page.[79] He is here af-

flicted with what seems to be almost an occupational disease of administrators. Just as large denominations tend to smother alike their more radical and their "fundamentalist" groups, so the author will tolerate nothing but a middle-of-the-road position between Judaism and Hellenism, or better, between extreme forms of Jewish Christianity and Hellenistic Christianity, between asceticism and libertarianism, between a fully stabilized and a prophetic religion, between an ultraliteral obedience to tradition and the unbridled and fantastic speculations of Gnosticism.

Yet this author's importance to the church is derived from the very nature of his limitations as well as from his own gifts and temper. If on the one hand he was unable to cope intellectually with contemporary problems of thought, on the other hand it should be remembered that the "modern mind" which formed the religious-philosophical background of his time is best exemplified by Gnosticism and Marcionism, both of which, if they had been allowed to triumph in the church, would have destroyed Christianity as a historical, ethical, prophetic religion. When Gnosticism in its various forms was the prevailing philosophy, the transformation of Christianity into its terms could only have done irreparable harm. From this standpoint we must regard the writer as the prototype of those who have saved the church in the only way it can at times be saved, by tightening the lines that hold it together, by forging bands of loyalty that would anchor it fast when the powerful and recurrent waves of syncretistic-Oriental-Greco-Roman thought on the one hand and the pagan social and political power of the Roman Empire on the other should beat against it. Perhaps there will always be times when the church cannot express its faith adequately in terms of a prevailing philosophy, when the best it can temporarily do is to reaffirm its traditions and to witness to the life-giving power of its naïve, unpretentious, but self-evidencing insights. Given the situation in hand, the author's only possible service to the church was to consolidate its tradition, its ministry, its forms of worship, that is, to initiate a counteraction in which practical religious interests would be set over against the speculative fantasies of Gnosticism, and against which the Gnostic dualisms might be broken.

In defense of the author's emphasis on sobriety, seriousness, temperance, and such elementary virtues, B. S. Easton insists that they were the virtues most needed at the moment.

[79] Of the third-century church Charles Cochrane, *Christianity and Classical Culture* (Oxford: Clarendon Press, 1940), p. 231, writes: "Morally bold and vigorous, it was still intellectually timid or weak; and, victorious as a way of life, it was still philosophically deficient." Neither were there any intellectual giants in the second-century church. For the church to work out the elements of a philosophy in keeping with its own distinctive first

principles was to be a long and arduous task, which, it would seem, needs to be done all over in our time.

As B. W. Bacon has said, the apostles went out into the highways and hedges and compelled men to come in—and the post-apostolic Church had to contend with the result. Those enemies of the cross of Christ over whom Paul wept had increased in number and influence until they threatened to wreck everything; they made easy converts among the multitudes of well-meaning but utterly bewildered believers whom missionary efforts were bringing in. . . . The times called for orthodoxy, not for inspiration. . . . The demand at the moment was for rules in black and white. Naturally this meant a return to "laws"—even, if one will, to "legalism"—but for children laws are a necessity and in this regard many good men never outgrow their childhood. . . . Such rules would not produce great saints and were not intended to produce them. They were designed for the thousands of men and women who were finding in their new faith a life incomparably higher and purer than they had lived in the past, incomparably higher and purer than men and women were living in the world outside the Church.[80]

We should further gladly remember that though the common sense of the author sometimes seems commonplace, yet it is not unheroic. It summons men to an utter loyalty to their faith, and to the institution which cherishes and transmits it—a loyalty which in a hostile world may well mean suffering and even death. The Pastorals, too, call men to martyrdom.

It is almost true to say that the great revivals of religion which have taken place in the history of Christendom have been returns to Paul. Although our author may not have understood Paul in any profound way, he was truly Paul's champion. And in helping to reclaim and establish Paul and Paul's interpretation of Christianity as central in the church, he has contributed in an important way to putting the great apostle and the true father of evangelical Christianity in the dominant position which he has held throughout the subsequent history of the church.

### IX. Outline of the Epistles

#### I TIMOTHY

I. The salutation (1:1-2)
II. The charge to maintain sound doctrine (1:3-7)
III. The Christian and the law (1:8-11)
IV. Paul, the ideal preacher (1:12-17)
V. Timothy, Paul's loyal successor (1:18-20)
VI. The universality of the Christian faith (2:1-7)
VII. Rules for public worship (2:8-15)
VIII. The character of bishops (3:1-7)
IX. The character of deacons (3:8-13)

[80] *The Pastoral Epistles* (New York: Charles Scribner's Sons, 1947), pp. 23-29. Used by permission.

X. The church, the guardian of the Christian mystery (3:14-16)
XI. False teachers and demonic doctrines (4:1-5)
XII. The good minister of Christ Jesus (4:6-10)
XIII. The minister as example (4:11-16)
XIV. The conduct of the minister toward various groups (5:1-2)
XV. The church and the order of widows (5:3-16)
XVI. The remuneration and discipline of elders (5:17-25)
XVII. The Christian slave (6:1-2b)
XVIII. The importance of sound doctrine (6:2c-5)
XIX. The contented Christian (6:6-10)
XX. The obedient Christian warrior (6:11-16)
XXI. True riches (6:17-19)
XXII. A concluding appeal for faithfulness (6:20-21)

#### II TIMOTHY

I. The salutation (1:1-2)
II. Timothy, the ideal minister (1:3-7)
III. The true minister is loyal to Paul's gospel (1:8-14)
IV. A personal appeal (1:15-18)
V. The minister as Christ's soldier (2:1-7)
VI. To die is to live (2:8-13)
VII. The good minister keeps the received faith (2:14-19)
VIII. The good minister teaches correct doctrine in love (2:20-26)
IX. Warning against corrupt and heretical teachers (3:1-9)
X. Remember Paul's selfless devotion (3:10-13)
XI. Hold fast to inspired scriptures (3:14-17)
XII. Fulfilling the ministry (4:1-5)
XIII. The coronation of Paul as model minister (4:6-8)
XIV. Paul and some personal relationships (4:9-18)
XV. Concluding greetings (4:19-22)

#### TITUS

I. The salutation (1:1-4)
II. On elders and bishops (1:5-8)
III. The bishop's function: to maintain sound doctrine (1:9-16)
IV. The duties of the minister to his congregation (2:1-10)
V. Working and waiting (2:11-15)
VI. Christian conduct in a non-Christian world (3:1-7)
VII. Christian faith manifest in works, not words (3:8-11)
VIII. Concluding personal instructions and greetings (3:12-15)

### X. Selected Bibliography

DIBELIUS, MARTIN. *Die Pastoralbriefe* ("Handbuch zum Neuen Testament"). 2nd ed. Tübingen: J. C. B. Mohr, 1931. The best recent commentary in German. Dibelius not only rejects Pauline authorship, but after considering the matter very carefully, decides against Pauline sources also.
EASTON, BURTON SCOTT. *The Pastoral Epistles.* New

York: Charles Scribner's Sons, 1947. Of exceptional value. In addition to its compact and incisive analysis of the text, it offers a series of word-studies of unusual importance. Pauline authorship is decisively rejected, although it is conceded that "on the possibility of genuine Pauline fragments in the Pastorals . . . no final decision seems possible" (p. 16).

HARRISON, P. N. *The Problem of the Pastoral Epistles.* London: Oxford University Press, 1921. May be read as the most painstaking attempt to show that although the Pastorals are not Pauline they contain five genuine fragments from Paul.

JEREMIAS, JOACHIM, ed. *Die Briefe an Timotheus und Titus* ("Das Neue Testament deutsch"). Göttingen: Vandenhoeck & Ruprecht, 1935. A good recent commentary in German defending Pauline authorship.

LOCK, WALTER. *A Critical and Exegetical Commentary on the Pastoral Epistles* ("International Critical Commentary"). New York: Charles Scribner's Sons, 1924. One of the two best twentieth-century defenses in English of Pauline authorship.

PARRY, R. ST. JOHN. *The Pastoral Epistles.* Cambridge: Cambridge University Press, 1920. One of the two best twentieth-century defenses in English of Pauline authorship.

SCOTT, ERNEST F. *The Pastoral Epistles* ("The Moffatt New Testament Commentary"). New York: Harper & Bros., 1936. A similar point of view to that of Harrison is represented in this very readable commentary.

SPICQ, C. *Saint Paul: les Épitres Pastorales.* Paris: J. Gabalda, 1947. Certainly the most adequate and comprehensive defense in print of Pauline authorship.

---

# I TIMOTHY

## TEXT, EXEGESIS, AND EXPOSITION

1 Paul, an apostle of Jesus Christ by the commandment of God our Saviour, and Lord Jesus Christ, *which is* our hope;

1 Paul, an apostle of Christ Jesus by command of God our Savior and of Christ Jesus our hope,

---

### I. THE SALUTATION (1:1-2)

**1:1.** Greek letters normally begin with the name of the sender, followed by that of the receiver, to whom greetings are sent. Sometimes the salutation is very brief, such as "Apollonius to Zenon greeting." Or there may be added a more or less conventional formula of well-wishing: "If you are well, it would be excellent. I too am in good health." Sometimes the greeting is more intimate: "I suffered anxiety when I heard of your protracted illness, but now I am delighted to hear that you are convalescent and already on the point of recovery. I myself am well." Or again it may contain a religious note: "I give thanks to all the gods if you are in good health yourself and everything else has been satisfactory."

Formally, the N.T. letters fit well the ancient letter pattern. They differ from the ordinary Greek letter in that (*a*) they are generally, if not always, written to a group of people rather than to an individual; and (*b*) as Christian letters written by church leaders,

---

**1:1. The Divine Commission.**—Here is a writer who speaks with authority.[1] Whoever he

[1] This Expos. assumes that the Pastoral Epistles contain fragments of letters written by the apostle Paul, which have been combined by a later editor with material which reflects conditions in the Christian church at a date subsequent to the time of Paul. For a discussion of authorship and date see pp. 367-70. Because of the difficulty in identifying the Pauline and non-Pauline passages, however, the Expos. follows the common practice of referring to the writer as Paul.

may have been, his message is that of an **apostle of Christ Jesus,** who writes **by command of God.** An apostle does not undertake a commission in obedience to his own whim. Literally, he is "one sent." In the N.T. sense he is one who has been commissioned to bear witness to the gospel revealed in the life, cross, and resurrection of Jesus. He speaks in obedience to the command of God. That note of assurance is too often lacking in contemporary Christianity. Who has a

they possess a religious interest and intensity which break through the simple letter form and expand it to resemble the tract, the homily, the rhapsody.

In the N.T. letters the interest is no longer in physical health or well-being, nor yet in prosperity. No N.T. writer uses the familiar formula, "I myself am well." Indeed, of the two words commonly used in papyrus letters to mean "to be well" (ῥώννυμι and ὑγιαίνω) the former does not occur in the N.T. letters at all (but ἔρρωσθε, meaning "farewell" is found in Acts 15:29 and, according to some MSS, in Acts 23:30) ; the latter in reference to physical health occurs only in III John 2, "I pray that all may go well with you and that you may keep well" (see also Luke 5:13; 7:10; 15:27). Likewise, it is only III John 2 among N.T. letters which includes a prayer for prosperity. The N.T. writers are concerned only with the spiritual welfare of their readers.

Paul is called **apostle** also in II Tim. 1:1; I Cor. 1:1; II Cor. 1:1; Gal. 1:1; Eph. 1:1; Col. 1:1. He describes himself as "slave" and "apostle" in Rom. 1:1; Tit. 1:1. In the letters in which Timothy is included as joint author, he is carefully excluded from the category of apostle. In II Cor. 1:1 and Col. 1:1 Paul designates himself as "apostle" and Timothy as "brother." He likewise separates himself from "our brother Sosthenes" in I Cor. 1:1. In Phil. 1:1, where Paul is not concerned to appeal to his authority, he is free to begin with "Paul and Timothy, servants." In Philemon his self-designation is "prisoner," and for obvious reasons. In the Thessalonian letters, presented as of triple authorship, "Paul, Silvanus, and Timothy," there are no epithets at all, and Paul does not separate himself from the other two men. Obviously the term **apostle** now has official significance; it indicates status, a position of primary authority in the church. Paul as apostle has the right to command and to be obeyed. In his own churches he is first, under God.

In the Pastorals also the title is limited to Paul; it is distinguished from "preacher" (κῆρυξ) and "teacher" (διδάσκαλος) : I Tim. 2:7; II Tim. 1:11. The authoritative rank of apostle as standing above bishops, presbyters, and deacons, comes to frequent expression in the letters of Ignatius (*ca.* A.D. 110), who though a bishop, writes, "Do not think that I . . . should give you orders like an apostle" (Ign. Trall. 3:3).

Of N.T. letters which go by the name of Paul, there are five which begin with the same impressive words, **Paul, an apostle of Christ Jesus:** I and II Timothy, II Corinthians, Ephesians, Colossians. And of the eleven which contain the name in the opening line, according to the best texts, only Titus uses the order "Jesus Christ." In the ten Paulines (excluding the Pastorals) "Jesus Christ" appears sixty-seven times as against sixty-three times for "Christ Jesus." Even if we regard "Christ" generally in the N.T. as a proper noun, and not simply a verbal adjective meaning "the anointed one," its almost equal distribution before and after the name need cause no perplexity. In any case the double usage would derive from the originally adjectival quality of "Christ" and out of the Greek idiom which allows the adjective to precede or follow the noun it modifies. But if the ten Paulines do not present a problem here, I and II Timothy do (as against Titus, which uses "Jesus Christ" and "Christ Jesus" each twice). They use "Christ Jesus" twenty-three times, and "Jesus Christ" three. This is not the Pauline proportion; it remains a mystery if it is assumed that Paul wrote the letters.

**By command of God our Savior:** The consistent language of Paul refers his apostolic commission to the will (θέλημα) of God (so I Cor. 1:1; II Cor. 1:1; Gal. 1:4; Eph. 1:1;

---

right to the conviction that he is under divine orders? No doubt this writer is thinking of himself as set apart by the church for his special task. But in a large sense the command of God comes to every man who has responded to the summons of God in Christ and has found saving power in God and unquenchable hope in Christ. How does the divine command come to men? No doubt in a variety of ways, as men differ in temperament, background, training, and experience. But any man who has made a loyal response to the revelation of God in Christ, who sees a human need confronting him, is aware that he possesses resources and capacities with which to serve that need, and is constrained by an inner compulsion to give himself to the task—that man stands in the great succession of those who labor by command of God.

II Tim. 1:1), not to his command. The word **command,** however, seems peculiarly suitable to the Pastorals with their interest in ministerial "orders." A more vigorous word than "will," **command** suggests that since Paul is under God's command, he should be obeyed. Furthermore, those whom Paul establishes as officials in the church may similarly command obedience. The Greek word for **command** (ἐπιταγή) appears in inscriptions especially in connection with royal or divine commands. If the ultimate right to command belongs to God alone, those whom God commands are thereby placed in authoritative positions.

In the language of Christian devotion, Christ, not God, is the **Savior.** Although the N.T. is well on the way toward this later usage, yet out of twenty-four occurrences of the word in eleven N.T. writings, eight refer to God. Of these eight, six are in two of the Pastorals (1:1; 2:3; 4:10; Tit. 1:3; 2:10; 3:4). II Timothy has the title only once (1:10); and then it refers to Jesus. Titus uses **Savior** six times, its reference alternating deliberately, it would seem, between God (1:3; 2:10; 3:4) and Christ (1:4; 2:13; 3:6). What is more noteworthy than the fact that the Pastorals show a greater preference for attaching the epithet **Savior** to God than is characteristic of the rest of the N.T. is the fact of their preference for the word itself. Of the twenty-four N.T. instances of the word, ten are in the Pastorals. Surprisingly, **Savior** does not occur at all in the earlier Paulines (but see Phil. 3:20; Eph. 5:23, of Jesus). It occurs in Luke 1:47; 2:11; Acts 5:31; 13:23; John 4:42; I John 4:14; II Pet. 1:1, 11; 2:20; 3:2, 18; Jude 25; and, except in Luke 1:47 and Jude 25, always in reference to Jesus.

As is the case with so many important Christian words, to trace the tributaries of savior to their sources is a complex and difficult undertaking. It is at least clear that in its Christian uses the word is the result of the flowing together of two streams of thought and language, Jewish and non-Jewish. While in the Greek O.T. "savior" is on occasion used of men (e.g., Judg. 3:9; Neh. 9:27), it is most frequently used of God. God may have given the people of Israel saviors (i.e., deliverers in the sense of victorious military leaders), yet it is God who gives saviors and is therefore himself *the* Savior. In the devotional language of the O.T. God as "our Savior" or "my Savior" runs like a refrain. It is frequent in the psalms; it occurs in the wisdom literature; especially in Isaiah among the prophets; and in the Apocrypha. Also, here and there in later Jewish literature the Messiah is called "Savior" (Enoch 48:7).

In the light of O.T. and Jewish usage it is strange that in the Gospels the word never falls from the lips of Jesus. How could he not have used this meaningful word of the psalmists and prophets? Paul likewise never calls God Savior (outside of the Pastorals). Indeed, only twice (outside of the Pastorals—Phil. 3:20; Eph. 5:23) does he use the word of Jesus.

So far as the silence of Jesus is concerned, it may or may not be historical. In the primitive Christian community, at least by the time the later Gospels were written (the word does not appear in Mark), Jesus himself had come to almost exclusive possession of the title. Since those who gave literary form to the Gospels regarded Jesus as their Savior and "the Savior of the world," they would not naturally have thought of Jesus himself as using the term of another, even of God. The silence of the Gospels here may therefore conceivably be a reflection of the Christology of the church.

---

Obedience to the commandments of God is the pathway to (*a*) freedom, for the inner life is chaos until it is directed by some loyalty great enough to gather up and channel its energies; to (*b*) fellowship, for it is only in God that life meets life on the deepest level; and to (*c*) power, for there are hidden resources in every man which are released only by the love of God in Christ accepted and made dominant. The Bible is full of the stories of men who were led

through obedience to God into freedom, fellowship, and power, e.g., Moses (Exod. 3–4); Jeremiah (ch. 1); Isaiah (ch. 6); Paul (Acts 9).

The fact that God is at work in his world, commissioning men and women for his service and empowering them in it, is the world's great hope. The forces of evil often seem insuperable. The mystery of evil is always deep and dark. How can we hope for a better life for mankind? How can we hope that evil will not be too much

2 Unto Timothy, *my* own son in the faith: Grace, mercy, *and* peace, from God our Father, and Jesus Christ our Lord.

2 To Timothy, my true child in the faith:

Grace, mercy, and peace from God the Father and Christ Jesus our Lord.

---

Why Paul, to whom Jesus was certainly Savior, uses the term so sparingly is best explained by the fact that in the Greco-Roman world and among the Gentiles who made up the majority of his church members, too many secular and pagan associations clustered about the word. It was too soon for a title which was commonly associated with the adoration of emperors and mystery-gods to be applied to Jesus as a matter of course. However, the persistent direction of the flow of all high language was toward Jesus. Out of the O.T. Savior came to him from the Godward side; out of Hellenism it came to him from the manward side—from heroes, rulers, healing divinities, and savior-gods. Henceforth in Christian language it is most naturally used not of God, nor of man, but of the God-man.

The usage of Savior in the Pastorals is certainly not Pauline. Neither is it characteristic of the language of later Christian devotion. It can be described only as peculiar to the author of these writings, an unusual combination of Jewish and Hellenistic-Christian usage (see also II Tim. 1:10).

The phrase **God our Savior and . . . Christ Jesus our hope** is fashioned in the elevated rhythmical parallelism of liturgical language. Therefore **Christ Jesus our hope** may be used more or less formally, and without any very precise meaning in the author's mind. Col. 1:27, "Christ in you, the hope of glory," is doubtless the source pattern for all later formulas in which Christ is designated **our hope.** In the most general sense, to speak of Christ as **our hope** means simply that he is the ground of our hope of salvation. This will be the meaning of the recurring Ignatian formula, "Jesus Christ our [common] hope" (Ign. Eph. 21:2; Ign. Mag. 11; Ign. Trall. 2:2; Ign. Phila. 11:2). The language here, however, could well be interpreted to include the idea that Christ Jesus is not merely the one *in* whom we hope but the one *for* whom we hope. He is our hope in that it is his "appearing" (6:14) for which we wait. In the N.T., however blessed life with God in Christ may be in this present world, it cannot compare with the fullness of salvation that is yet to come. Although in the language of Paul the Christian is "in Christ" and Christ in the Christian, yet the great Christian event, the final and perfect consummation, is still to take place. Hope will become full fruition only when he who was "manifested in the flesh" and "taken up in glory" (3:16) will again "be made manifest at the proper time" (6:15). The world began in God; it must have an appropriate ending in him.

**2.** Ostensibly the letter is written **to Timothy.** More accurately it is written through Timothy to church officials, to ministers in charge, with a view to establishing certain standards of church order and administration (see Intro., pp. 344-45).

**My true child in the faith:** Paul found Timothy, already a disciple, at Derbe and

---

for us as individuals? How can we hope for anything beyond the dissolution of physical life for ourselves or our planet? Short-range hopes for individual and social life can be built upon a better use of human intelligence, upon better social organization, and upon a truer sense of values among men. It is no part of the Christian task to disparage these secular objectives. But none of them is adequate without a new life deep in the hearts of men, and none of them has anything to say in the face of the ultimate mysteries. The ultimate basis for hope is the saving power of God which has been revealed

and is revealed in the reality **of God our Savior and of Christ Jesus our hope.** As Christina Rossetti wrote,

> None other Lamb, none other Name,
>   None other Hope in heaven or earth or sea,
> None other Hiding-place from guilt and shame,
>   None beside Thee.[2]

**2. From One Generation to Another.**—This entire epistle is written from the point of view of an older friend addressing a younger man.

[2] "None other Lamb, none other Name."

Lystra and made him a traveling companion and responsible fellow worker (Acts 16:1). That Paul regarded him as a thoroughly mature person is evidenced by the fact that in II Cor. 1:1; Col. 1:1; Phil. 1:1; I Thess. 1:1; II Thess. 1:1, Timothy is included with Paul as one of the senders of the letter and is described as "brother" (II Cor. 1:1; Col. 1:1) or "servant" (Phil. 1:1). In Rom. 16:21 Paul calls him "my fellow worker," in I Thess. 3:2, "our brother and God's servant [διάκονος] in the gospel."

And although Paul himself speaks of Timothy as "my beloved and faithful child" (τέκνον, I Cor. 4:17), and states in Phil. 2:22 that Timothy has served with him "as a son with a father" (τέκνον), it remains a question both in these passages and in the present text (see also II Tim. 1:2; Tit. 1:4) just what the precise inferences from the word **child,** and particularly the phrase **true child,** are.

The expression is frequently taken to mean that Timothy was Paul's convert. However, Acts 16:1-2 seems to be against this. Or a reference has been seen to the event of II Tim. 1:6 (which see), according to which "the gift of God that is within" Timothy came to him through the laying on of Paul's hands.

A somewhat subtle interpretation points out that since Timothy's mother Eunice, although a Christian, had been a Jewess, and since his father was a Greek, the marriage was illegal according to Jewish law, and Timothy an illegitimate child. The text, then, may wish to suggest that Timothy's illegitimacy of birth has been set aside by the legitimacy of his spiritual rebirth: Timothy is a **true child in the faith.**

On the assumption that the Pastorals are pseudonymous and were written after the death of both Paul and Timothy, we may suppose that Timothy was chosen as the name of the addressee because of the high regard which Paul had for Timothy, particularly as expressed in Phil. 2:19-22 and I Cor. 4:14-17. Indeed, it may have been these very passages which gave the author the idea. In the Corinthian passage Paul speaks of all the Christians as "my beloved children" and of himself as their father. It is not a matter of age differences, but of obedient discipleship. In the East the chief virtue of the son of whatever age is "filial piety." And although there is an affectionate note in the greetings in the Pastorals, that is not the primary emphasis. **My true child** is the address of a superior official or person in authority to a subordinate, a younger official (see Intro., pp. 344-45).

**In the faith** is literally "in faith" but should probably be interpreted to mean in the Christian faith as taught by Paul as well as by the author of the Pastorals.

**Grace, mercy, and peace from God the Father and Christ Jesus our Lord:** Striking, indeed, is the fact that the greetings or opening blessings in both I and II Timothy are

---

It may have been written to a younger man who owed to the older man his understanding of the Christian faith and his loyalty to it. It was inscribed **to Timothy, my true child in the faith.** There is no more sacred relationship. Christian faith is not something into which one man argues another, although frank and honest discussion of the grounds for faith is important. Essentially, Christian faith is communicated from one life to another, as the man who knows its reality and power shares life with the man in need of faith by which to live. The great days of Christianity are the days when Christians are so communicating faith to others. In this case the relationship had been deepened by partnership in the Christian cause, and by that process of education which goes on when an older friend shares his experience and deepest insights with a younger colleague. There are dangers as well as satisfactions in this relationship. Some-

times the older man attempts to dominate the younger, exhibits him as a sort of trophy for the gratification of his pride, seeks to make the younger man a second edition of himself, and so stunts the growth of the younger man for whom God has some unique call. This epistle reveals an older friend who is content that Christ rather than he should be the Master of the new disciple. This is a grace which every minister, every teacher, every parent, and every friend of youth needs. George Herbert Palmer once said: "Every teacher knows how easy it is to send out cheap editions of himself, and in his weaker moments he inclines to issue them. But it is ignoble business." [3]

As the Exeg. points out, it was the Christian faith to which Paul referred when he spoke of Timothy as his child **in the faith.** This reminds

[3] *Ethical and Moral Instruction in Schools* (Boston: Houghton Mifflin Co., 1909), p. 44.

precisely identical, and yet differ markedly from the characteristic form used in all the Pauline letters, and also from Titus. "Grace to you and peace from God our Father and the Lord Jesus Christ" is the preferred Pauline form, employed in the four great earlier letters—Romans, I and II Corinthians, Galatians—and in Ephesians, Philippians, II Thessalonians, Philemon. Colossians reduces the greeting to "Grace to you and peace from God our Father"; I Thessalonians to "Grace to you and peace." Titus varies significantly both from the usual Pauline form and from that of the other two Pastorals. In agreement with Paul it is two-membered, "grace and peace"; in contrast it offers a unique phrase, "Christ Jesus our Savior." It is only in the greetings in I and II Timothy that we have the order **Christ Jesus our Lord.** In the genuine Paulines it is always "our Lord Jesus Christ."

Only II John ("grace, mercy, and peace") and Jude ("mercy, peace, and love"), in addition to I and II Timothy, have three members. And only in these four does the word **mercy** occur.

Paul's own use of **mercy** is scanty. James Moffatt writes: "His favorite conception is that of the divine power which deals with the situation of man, either as freely providing reconciliation or as releasing the prisoners from their captivity. 'Charis' [grace] was better for this purpose than mercy; it denoted power no less than pardon. The ordinary connotation of mercy limited it to pity for the unfortunate, and even although the pity of a great God acted graciously, it did not call up before the mind the same active and spontaneous intervention as 'grace' did. What moved God, in Paul's mind, was not the silence or the sighing of mortal misery in a short-lived life which had to face death and the judgment before long, but the initiative of God's loving purpose which would no longer wait." (*Grace in the New Testament* [New York: Harper & Bros., 1932], p. 120. Used by permission.)

---

us that the Christian faith is a historic faith. God has new light for each generation, and each generation may have its new, creative insights. But it is based upon historic facts, God's disclosure of his love and purpose in Christ. An essential element in the preaching of the gospel consists in making these facts known. The Christian faith is a redemptive faith. In Christ, God is seeking to find and to save the lost. Through Christ, God's power invades our world to transform aimless men into his servants, to lift wasted lives to new heights of power and victory, to give life to mankind dead in selfishness and sin, and to draw lonely, godless folk into his eternal fellowship. The Christian faith is a challenging faith. It is God's demand as well as his promise. It claims priority over all other loyalties. It says, "Seek first his kingdom and his righteousness" (Matt. 6:33). Henry Drummond used to challenge students to put Christianity first or to leave it alone, saying that it would make them miserable if they put it in second place in their lives. The Christian faith is also a rewarding faith. It is the narrow way that leads to life. It is the pearl of great price for which a man gives all he has. One of the paradoxes of the gospel is that while Jesus cautioned his hearers against serving him for the sake of reward, the promise "your Father who sees in secret will reward you" (Matt. 6:3, 6, 16-18) runs through it all. Even the command to "seek first his kingdom"

is followed by the assurance "and all these things shall be yours as well" (Matt. 6:33).

It was in the fellowship of this historic, redemptive, challenging, and rewarding faith that Paul and Timothy became comrades. This is the deepest and most invigorating of bonds. There are innumerable other associations into which men enter: business associations, social relationships, educational ties, common interests based on tastes, racial backgrounds, national loyalties, and geographical proximity. All have their place, but none can satisfy the deep need for community and spiritual fellowship which a broken and divided world craves. This must be fellowship **in the faith.**

2. *A Benediction.*—*Benedictus benedicat* is a favorite grace said at the table in Oxford halls. So the N.T. epistles, as here, commonly begin with a petition that the Blessed One may bless: **Grace, mercy, and peace from God the Father and Christ Jesus our Lord.** Grace, mercy, and peace are words of ocean depth. They

> split the sky in two,
> And let the face of God shine through.[4]

As used here, they offer three suggestions which have a bearing on our life: they suggest the unlimited goodness of God; they suggest what

[4] From "Renascence." Copyright, 1912, 1940, by the author, Edna St. Vincent Millay. Used by permission.

| 3 As I besought thee to abide still at Ephesus, when I went into Macedonia, that thou mightest charge some that they teach no other doctrine, | 3 As I urged you when I was going to Macedo'nia, remain at Ephesus that you may charge certain persons not to teach |

The threefold benediction, **grace, mercy, and peace** is a rich and meaningful symbol of the Christian interpretation of life. For sinful man harassed by sinful men in a temporal order infected by ingrown sin there can be peace only under the grace and mercy of God.

## II. THE CHARGE: MAINTAIN SOUND DOCTRINE (1:3-7)

**3.** In the travels of Paul, as they are known to us, he first set sail for Europe as a result of his Macedonian vision at Troas (Acts 16). Timothy, who had just been made Paul's traveling companion, accompanied him as far as Beroea, it would seem, where threats of violence made it necessary for Paul to proceed posthaste to Athens. And here, although Acts 18:5 says otherwise, Timothy seems to have joined him (I Thess. 3:1 ff.).

After more than a year and a half in Corinth, a quick trip to Jerusalem, Antioch, and through the region of Galatia and Phrygia, and then two years in Ephesus, Paul decided to go again to Macedonia. This time he sent Timothy on ahead (Acts 19:22). Where in Macedonia Paul may have met Timothy, Acts does not say. In any case, on the return trip, Timothy with others proceeded to Troas, where Paul joined them after some days.

Clearly, Acts recounts no such journey to Macedonia as the verse here suggests. If, then, such a journey took place, it might have been during Paul's two-year stay in Ephesus. This is at least theoretically possible. Acts narrates only one brief chapter of incidents out of this two-year period. Spending so much time in travel as Paul did, it seems doubtful that he should have remained away from the Macedonian churches for some four years. Also it is known on other grounds that the account in Acts of Paul's activities is notoriously incomplete. Nevertheless, any trip to Macedonia within the two-year stay in Ephesus would necessarily have been a short one, and a brief absence from Ephesus furnishes no explanation as to why Paul communicated so much and such important material by letter and through Timothy when shortly he himself could have communicated it directly.

God is ready and eager to give to men; and they suggest the gifts of the Spirit by whom God seeks to transform human life through dedicated men and women who accept his gracious life and become the instruments of his creative and redemptive power.

**3. Stay Where You Are.**—So Moffatt translates the phrase **remain at Ephesus.** There are times when the command of God is clearly to move out into new and perhaps undiscovered country. The Epistle to the Hebrews represents Abraham as the pioneer who "went out, not knowing whither he went. . . . For he looked for a city which hath foundations, whose builder and maker is God" (Heb. 11:8b, 10). An essential aspect of the Christian life consists in having a share under God in the work of the pioneers who are seeking a new international order, more fraternal dealings between people of different races, a business and industrial society in which brotherhood can be a greater reality than it is at present. God is always saying to his people, "Get thee out of thy country . . . unto a land that I will show thee" (Gen. 12:1). But there are also times when the commandment of God is "Stay where you are." Some task which has lost the luster of novelty needs to be completed. The new is not always the better and sometimes it is "the homely beauty of the good old cause" [5] that needs to be maintained. Distance lends enchantment, and there is a romance about setting out to some far-off duty which the common round near at hand may lack. Macedonia may have called to Timothy with an appeal which Ephesus lacked at the moment. But it was apparently in Ephesus that he was needed. Mr. Standfast in *Pilgrim's Progress* is the type of the man who does not run away from the immediate obligation for the remote adventure when the order of the day is clearly to stand.

**3. No Other Faith.**—Timothy is told to **charge certain persons not to teach any different**

[5] Wordsworth, "O Friend! I Know Not Which Way I Must Look."

Therefore, and because on any theory the letter requires late dating, it is more commonly supposed that the journey took place between the Roman imprisonment of Acts 28 and a conjectural second and final Roman imprisonment. Unfortunately this is to ground the unknown in the uncertain.

The fact is that although the silences and the inconclusive ending of Acts can in no way be regarded as excluding the possibility, even the probability, of some such Macedonian visit as is here mentioned, yet there is no historical evidence to verify it other than the statement itself. If Paul wrote I Timothy, obviously the journey took place; if Paul did not write the letter, the journey may or may not have taken place. But in either case nothing can be known about it. Those who regard I Timothy as non-Pauline may suppose either that the writer refers to a Macedonian journey of Paul's not known to or differently described by Acts, or that the Pauline framework of the letter is purely fictitious, the journey motif being a literary device to create a situation in which a letter is appropriate—a device not too convincing, it may be urged, since Paul's return is expected soon (3:14; 4:13), making a letter not really necessary.

**Remain at Ephesus:** On the assumption that Paul wrote the letter, the text has meaning only if Timothy was reluctant to stay on in Ephesus, wanting rather to be traveling with Paul or on his own account. If the letter is pseudonymous the phrase will serve only to indicate destination.

Ephesus was the chief city of Asia Minor, the seat of the governor or proconsul of the province. The western terminus of a great system of roads, it was a center of wealth. The city was also of unusual religious importance. It was a chief seat of the worship of the deified Roman emperors, the location of the famous temple of Artemis, or Diana (Acts 19:23 ff.), the home of various magic arts and cults, and therefore must have furnished lively resistance to the growth of the church even as it attracted and challenged many of the greatest Christian leaders. Paul, Apollos, Aquila, Priscilla, and Timothy too, labored there. There are two letters to the Ephesians in the N.T.—four if the Timothys may be so described—one purporting to be by Paul, the other in Rev. 2:1-7. The first letter of Ignatius (*ca.* 110) is to the Ephesians. The Johannine literature, too, probably emanated from this city. And tradition says that Timothy, John, and Mary the mother of Jesus, were buried there.

As might be expected, all the literature we have reflects the syncretistic nature of Ephesian religion. When the Pastorals present the problem of heresy—i.e., of chaotic conglomerations of Jewish, pagan, and Christian ideas and practices offensive to the church officials but championed by vigorous and effective teachers—as their basic problem, we may be sure that they reflect accurately the anguish of the church in that period when it was seeking to define and standardize its faith in the midst of a bewildering bedlam of insistent and inconsistent voices. It is always well to remember that in its creative periods the church has achieved its most significant statements of faith, not in unawareness of the thought currents of the time, nor yet in meek conformity to them, but in reaction to and interaction with them.

**That you may charge certain persons not to teach any different doctrine:** In a genuinely personal letter not intended for public reading there would have been no need

---

doctrine. The Exeg. points out that the church in Ephesus was surrounded by pagan religions and was in danger of diluting its testimony by accommodating itself to them. The N.T. insists upon the uniqueness and indispensability of Christ. "There is salvation in no one else, for there is no other name under heaven given among men by which we must be saved" (Acts 4:12). Every age presents Christianity with its rivals. The twentieth century has seen Nazism, communism, the worship of power, the cult of

success, the pursuit of comfort, and other loyalties challenge man's supreme loyalty to God in Christ. All fail to meet man's deepest needs. Jesus Christ is unique in his life and character, his message and teaching, his revelation of God, his power to win and transform, his divine mission to bring men home to God. No other faith will do for this age or any age.

**3-7. Speculations that Go Astray.**—Timothy was urged to keep the church on the main road of Christian faith when it was in danger of

4 Neither give heed to fables and endless genealogies, which minister questions,
rather than godly edifying which is in faith:
*so do.*

any different doctrine, 4 nor to occupy
themselves with myths and endless genealogies which promote speculations rather
than the divine training[a] that is in faith;

[a] Or *stewardship,* or *order.*

---

to conceal the names of these **certain persons;** in fact, names would seem to be required
if the charge was to be effectively transmitted. And although the text has a knowing air, as
if "Timothy" would understand exactly just who these persons were, the probability is
that the indefinite pronoun (τισίν) has other significance. Its vagueness may rather
intend to suggest that **different doctrine** was being taught by a larger number of persons
than any list of names could encompass, and that wherever heresy appeared the minister
should attack it.

The Greek word meaning **to teach a different doctrine** (ἑτεροδιδασκαλεῖν) occurs
only here, in 6:3, and in later Christian literature. It implies a normative or standard
rule of faith, approved not only by the writer of the letter but also by the larger church
body. Although the chief problem in the Pastorals concerns heretical teaching, no clear
or concise statement is given describing either the standard rule of faith or the precise
nature of the rejected teachings. Since Paul is set forward as the writer, we may suppose
that our author is urging the Ephesians to remain loyal to Paul's gospel. And although
the language of the paragraph is not Paul's usual language, nor is the form of Christianity
presented in the Pastorals characteristically Pauline as we know Paul from his major
epistles, the author certainly believes it to be Pauline. It is his purpose to apply the
apostolic authority of Paul to the church in Ephesus—a church with which Paul had had
so much to do—in order to hold its members, and those of Asia too, in line with the
accepted (Pauline) faith. **A different doctrine** is doctrine different from that which Paul
taught.

**4. To occupy themselves with** (προσέχειν) : This usage occurs frequently in I Timothy
(3:8; 4:1, 13; 6:3; cf. Tit. 1:14), but is not found in Paul. The admonition assumes
that to turn one's attention toward ideas is to be captivated by them, or at least to run
the risk.

**Myths:** The Greek word "myth" (μῦθος) occurs only twice in the LXX, and both
times in the Apocrypha (Wisd. Sol. 17:4[A]; Ecclus. 20:19). In the N.T., excepting II Pet.
1:16, it occurs only in the Pastorals (1:4; 4:7; II Tim. 4:4; Tit. 1:14). Myths are always
assumed to be purely imaginative, fictitious, and therefore false and untrue accounts of
religious reality which misrepresent and conceal what they would reveal.

Whatever the precise meaning of "Jewish myths" (Tit. 1:14) may be, the Christian
who here writes can turn the condemnatory epithet against anyone who teaches a **different
doctrine,** whether the source of the difference is Jewish or Gentile. The letters thus
presuppose a Christian orthodoxy, the contents of which must have been measurably
clear to the writer, although they are only sketchily outlined in the letters themselves.
What is most baffling in the letters is that they do not adequately define either the
orthodoxy which they champion or the heterodoxy which they combat. This may be due
to the fact that the author is a practical-minded church administrator who enjoys
orthodoxy because it is taken for granted and deplores heterodoxy because it is conducive
to controversy, and who sees no particular need to define either.

---

going off into byways that allured those given to
**speculations rather than the divine training
that is in faith.** There were those among them
who would have turned the church into a fruitless debating society, spending its time and
energy wrangling over trivialities of belief while
the world perished in its need for Christ's gos-

pel. What a man or a church believes is of
inestimable importance. The modern world has
learned to its bitter sorrow that there are creeds
which make people heartless, ruthless destroyers.
Genuine belief in Christ issues in love which
finds its source in **a pure heart and a good
conscience and sincere faith.** The preliminary

5 Now the end of the commandment is charity out of a pure heart, and *of* a good conscience, and *of* faith unfeigned:

5 whereas the aim of our charge is love that issues from a pure heart and a good con-

---

**Endless** (ἀπεράντοις) : In the N.T. only here; it may qualify **myths** too. **Myths** and **genealogies** are **endless** in that such forms are rank as jungle growth and as extravagant as unrestrained fancy (on myths and genealogies see Intro., pp. 352-53, 356-57) .

The root meaning of the Greek word for **speculations** (ἐκζητήσεις, not in LXX; only here in N.T.; "controversy" [Goodspeed]; "quarrels" [Easton]; see also ζητήσεις— 6:4; II Tim. 2:23; Tit. 3:9; Acts 15:2, 7; 25:20; John 3:25) is "research," "investigation." From this meaning the word developed to connote speculation, then disputation and even quarreling. Our author would assume that **speculations** inevitably result in quarrels. As inconclusive as they are beyond control, **speculations** distract the Christian from his true course and should be repudiated. To church administrators religious speculation usually seems only to create ferment, instability, and even weakening of loyalty. With difference of opinion there often comes disputatiousness and with it dilution of concentration on or application to a task. At the very beginning of his appeal, therefore, our author warns church leaders against independent religious thinking. Let them hold fast to the received faith—i.e., Christianity as the author conceives Paul to have interpreted it.

The meaning of **the divine training that is in faith** is obscure. It probably does not mean "the divine system which operates through faith" (Goodspeed) . **In faith** probably equals "in the faith," i.e., "Christianity." The contrast is either between two views of religion, i.e., between non-Christian (Jewish or pagan) speculative philosophy and the Christian revelation or plan of salvation; or between two types of activity, i.e., between indulging in religious speculation on the one hand, and on the other, devotion to the practical work of church administration, which, according to the letter writer, is the divinely appointed function of the church official. The obscurity of the passage may be due to the fact that the word "economy" (οἰκονομία) faces two directions: it may mean God's economy or plan of salvation; it may mean the administrative responsibility for carrying out his plan which God delegates to those whom he summons. Church officials are stewards of a received faith; they are not to search out a strange one. And stewardship of faith includes the proper conduct of administrative duties, which, it is inferred, would leave neither time nor interest for controversies.

**5.** The real purpose (τέλος) of the charge—both "Paul's" and "Timothy's"—to the false teachers is not to antagonize them or drive them out of the church, but rather to call forth the **love that issues from a pure heart and a good conscience and sincere faith.** The purpose of preaching is practical, not speculative. "Timothy" is not to increase disputatiousness by his **charge,** i.e., he is not to debate the heresy issue on philosophical or theological grounds. Rather, he is to counsel conformity as the only way to secure and maintain love among Christians.

**Pure** (καθαρός) occurs six other times in the Pastorals (3:9; II Tim. 1:3; 2:22; Tit. 1:15, three times) , but only once in Paul (Rom. 14:20) . In the Pastorals **pure** qualifies **heart** twice (here and II Tim. 2:22) and **conscience** twice (3:9; II Tim. 1:3) . The expression **pure heart** is Semitic (see Gen. 20:5, 6; Pss. 24:4; 51:10; also Matt. 5:8; I Pet. 1:22) .

---

statement to the *Form of Government of the Presbyterian Church in the U.S.A.,* adopted in 1788, says that "truth is in order to goodness; and the great touchstone of truth, its tendency to promote holiness." In that statement the Westminster divines were echoing Paul's counsel. The discussion of religious beliefs is not an intellectual pastime for those who enjoy the game. It is a serious dealing with vital truths which when accepted make for righteousness and good will among men. Timothy was to warn the church in Ephesus against those who would distract their attention from the essentials of the faith which bear the fruits of the Spirit and entangle them in endless argument about other matters, to the detriment of the gospel.

**6** From which some having swerved have turned aside unto vain jangling;

**7** Desiring to be teachers of the law; understanding neither what they say, nor whereof they affirm.

science and sincere faith. **6** Certain persons by swerving from these have wandered away into vain discussion, **7** desiring to be teachers of the law, without understanding either what they are saying or the things about which they make assertions.

---

**Conscience** does not occur in the Gospels. It does occur in Paul to indicate the moral sense or the innate faculty of judging between right and wrong (Rom. 2:15; 9:1; 13:5; I Corinthians, eight times in chs. 8; 10; II Corinthians, three times). It occurs six times in the Pastorals, twice without qualifying adjective (4:2; Tit. 1:15); twice as **good conscience** (here and vs. 19); twice as "pure" or "clear conscience" (3:9; II Tim. 1:3). The expression "good" or "pure conscience" does not appear in the genuine Pauline letters. **Sincere faith:** This combination of words likewise is found only in the Pastorals in the N.T.

In this context the members of the triad, **pure heart, good conscience, sincere faith,** mean essentially the same thing (Easton). Christian love is the fruit of simple unquestioning sincerity in acceptance of the received faith. Disputation and argument only destroy the fellowship. Timothy is summoned to command heretical teachers to cease speculating and to devote themselves with single-minded loyalty to the approved teaching and program of the church.

**6. Swerving** (ἀστοχέω) occurs in the N.T. only here and in 6:21; II Tim. 2:18; lit., "miss the mark." Certain teachers in centering their interests in intellectual rather than practical and moral concerns have been "sidetracked" (ἐκτρέπομαι, elsewhere only 5:15; 6:20; II Tim. 4:4; Heb. 12:13) **into vain discussion,** empty argument (ματαιολογία; only here in N.T.; cf. ματαιολόγος, Tit. 1:10). Both words belong to the higher koine.

**7.** The word for **teachers of the law** (νομοδιδάσκαλοι) does not appear in the Greek O.T. or in profane Greek; in the N.T. it occurs elsewhere only in Luke 5:17; Acts 5:34. Strictly speaking, Christians could not be **teachers of the law** since such a functionary belongs only to Judaism. Either, then, the term is used ironically to suggest that the heretics are vainly trying to revert to a position in Judaism which as Christians they have necessarily forfeited, or that their failure to understand the law from the Christian standpoint has disqualified them from being teachers of it in the church. In the light of vss. 8-9, **the law** most naturally means the Pentateuch or Torah. Otherwise νομοδιδάσκαλος could conceivably be the equivalent of scholar or professional religious teacher without reference to the Jewish law as such. Dibelius suggests that the author of the Pastorals uses the term to indicate a value judgment after the manner of Paul rather than to specify a religious-historical category. Paul had already given his judgment on such persons and the author will strike the heretics with Paul's weapons. In any case, the

---

There is, however, a danger in this counsel, if the Exeg. is correct in interpreting it to mean a plea to avoid all "research" and "investigation" as leading inevitably to disputation and quarreling. Jesus' invitation was, "Come and see" (John 1:39). He asked men to follow him with their eyes and minds open. The whole question of authority and freedom is involved in the interpretation of this passage. Men in positions of authority in the church have frequently insisted that their particular views of the meaning of Christian truth should be regarded as binding upon all Christians. That would close the door against all new revelation. On the other hand, there have been those who have had

no respect for the Christian tradition as commonly received, but have insisted upon the superiority of their own ill-considered opinions. That means loss of the richness and breadth which come from the communion of the saints. To combine honest, fearless thought with respect for tradition; to keep an open mind and still to recognize the authority of tested experience; to be supremely loyal to Christ alone and at the same time have a decent regard for what others have known of him; to have faith that God has new truth yet to be revealed, never forgetting that in times past he has spoken through the apostles and the prophets—this is the hard way that leads to Christian knowledge.

8 But we know that the law *is* good, if a man use it lawfully;

9 Knowing this, that the law is not made for a righteous man, but for the lawless and disobedient, for the ungodly and for sinners, for unholy and profane, for murderers of fathers and murderers of mothers, for manslayers,

8 Now we know that the law is good, if any one uses it lawfully, 9 understanding this, that the law is not laid down for the just but for the lawless and disobedient, for the ungodly and sinners, for the unholy and profane, for murderers of fathers and

---

heretics are chided for their overweening ambition to set themselves up as authoritative teachers, an ambition grounded only in ignorance, unconcealed by the hollow vehemence of their assertions.

Unfortunately the author only denounces the heretics; he gives us no account of **the things about which they make assertions.** This leaves us almost in the dark as to the precise issues involved and at a definite disadvantage in appraising either his arguments or those of his opponents.

### III. The Christian and the Law (1:8-11)

**8.** What is the function of **the law** in the Christian faith? Obviously the problem is the persistent one. In both synagogue and church **the law** had the status of revelation and therefore a priori had to be held to as "holy and just and good" (Rom. 7:12, 16). In the Christian experience of redemption, however, "the righteousness of God has been manifested apart from law, . . . the righteousness of God through faith in Jesus Christ" (Rom. 3:21-22). This problem of dualism the church wisely did not solve by rejecting the old revelation outright, nor yet by insisting on full literal obedience to it. It labored rather with principles of discrimination and reinterpretation. The rejection of the food laws and circumcision by liberal or Gentile Christians constituted virtual abandonment of the law in the eyes of Jews and of many Jewish Christians. This, together with insistence that no man could be saved by works of the law, could only make the church appear to be acting in cavalier fashion with regard to the divine revelation, to be picking and choosing, and professing only a hypocritical faith in scripture. But no matter how much of O.T. law in detail the church abandoned, and even though it asserted insistently and impressively a nonlegalistic conception of religion, nevertheless it insisted that **the law is good, if any one uses it lawfully**—i.e., law has certain functions and its use is valid with reference to them alone. It is not a substitute for the gospel.

**9-11.** There is no need to probe for some mysterious hidden meaning which the law may hold for Christians: the law is for bad people, not for good. It was **not laid down** for Christians and therefore it has no real importance for them. It does not reach to the level on which they live. Its function is negative, not positive: it will restrain the vicious and the criminal. Since the Christian has advanced beyond any such need for law, any further concern with it is a falling away from the gospel. The sinners for whom the law is said to have been **laid down** are those who are guilty of the most heinous offenses imaginable. Although the list follows in general the Decalogue, the command-

---

**8-11. *The Constructive Uses of Law.*—**This passage obviously thinks of the law in a much wider sense than Paul usually does when he refers to the Mosaic law. The reference here is to outward authority which restrains men from wrongdoing. No wise freedom has ever been able to get completely away from such authority. The purpose of moral training is to build up within an individual the inner motives and restraints which will make legal restraints un-

necessary. But who can look within himself and not be grateful for some of the compulsions, positive and negative, which have kept the channel of his life within certain clearly defined banks? **We know that the law is good, if any one uses it lawfully.** There is a point at which law becomes tyranny. There is a point at which law cripples the development of individual initiative. Home, school, and state need to be on guard against these abuses of authority. Law

**10** For whoremongers, for them that defile themselves with mankind, for men-stealers, for liars, for perjured persons, and if there be any other thing that is contrary to sound doctrine;

**11** According to the glorious gospel of the blessed God, which was committed to my trust.

murderers of mothers, for manslayers, **10** immoral persons, sodomites, kidnapers, liars, perjurers, and whatever else is contrary to sound doctrine, **11** in accordance with the glorious gospel of the blessed God with which I have been entrusted.

---

ments are paraphrased and made more specific, and the sins named are the grossest possible, e.g., "Thou shalt not kill" is elaborated to refer to the worst forms of murder, the murder of fathers and mothers. Adultery is expanded to include **immoral persons** and **sodomites.** Kidnaping is specified as the worst form of stealing. Since Christians are not guilty of such misconduct, obviously the law has no meaning for them. To seek within it hidden meanings in order that the law may be re-established as relevant is to follow a wrong track and to engage in "speculations" and "vain discussion."

Vs. 10*b* might more logically have continued, "whoever else acts contrary to the correct teaching of the Christian faith." The present text is awkward.

The word **doctrine,** or teaching (διδασκαλία), occurs fifteen times in the Pastorals as against six times in the rest of the N.T. The use of the word **sound** in connection with Christian teaching occurs only in the Pastorals in the N.T. Its frequency in such phrases as **sound doctrine** (II Tim. 4:3; Tit. 1:9; 2:1), "sound words" (6:3; II Tim. 1:13; Tit. 2:8), "sound in the faith" (Tit. 1:13; 2:2), further indicates the emphasis which these letters put on correct or orthodox doctrine. **Sound** here does not mean "healthful" or "health-giving"; it means "correct" and "right," "normative" and "reasonable." Christianity is not here a spirit religion: it is a settled established body of teaching. Christianity has become for this writer a new law and a religion of obedience. Nothing could be more un-Pauline.

**11.** The law as given for the wicked and as superseded by the gospel is without luster; **The . . . gospel of the blessed God,** however, is **glorious** (cf. II Cor. 4:4-6; Col. 1:27). As the writer witnesses to his own faith he becomes radiant.

In the Pastorals **gospel** occurs elsewhere in II Tim. 1:8, 10; 2:8. It stands for the (Pauline) Christian faith as the author understands and teaches it.

**The blessed God** (cf. also 6:15): The expression is unique in biblical Greek, and is purely Hellenic. In the Greek tradition the divine nature is perfect, therefore unchanging and unaffected by any outside cause. The gods are blessed in that, being in this sense perfect, they are perfectly happy. The common Semitic term ascribing blessedness to God (in Greek εὐλογητός; frequent in Paul but nowhere in Pastorals) means "worthy of being praised," something very different from the meaning of μακάριος here.

As a devout liturgical-sounding phrase, "the gospel of the glory of the blessed God" (thus the Greek) need not be original coinage of our author, but may have been current language in the church in Asia Minor in his day.

---

can never redeem or re-create the inner man. Only **the glorious gospel of the blessed God** can do that. The training of children involves discipline and restraint, but they do not become mature persons in the Christian sense until a voluntary loyalty to God in Christ makes restraint superfluous. The peace of the world demands international law, agencies of justice, and instruments for international co-operation, but the greatest need is for the proclamation and acceptance of Christ's gospel which can create the spiritual life essential to peace and freedom.

**11. The Gospel a Sacred Trust.**—Having been confronted by Christ, Paul was never able to live as though he had not seen that light. The revelation carried with it a responsibility. No one born in the Christian Era can evade some share in that obligation. Something has been done in Christ as the result of which the world can never look the same again. No man or woman need be without God and without hope in the world since God made his own love manifest in Christ. This is **the glorious gospel** with which we are entrusted, and the acceptance of

12 And I thank Christ Jesus our Lord, who hath enabled me, for that he counted me faithful, putting me into the ministry;

12 I thank him who has given me strength for this, Christ Jesus our Lord, because he judged me faithful by appoint-

---

**With which I have been entrusted: I,** in contrast to the false teachers, and as "Timothy's" chief pastor. The feeling of responsibility for the preservation and communication of the gospel which prompted the writing of the letters here comes to high expression.

### IV. PAUL, THE IDEAL PREACHER (1:12-17)

**12. I thank him who has given me strength for this** is strikingly different from the normal Pauline thanksgiving, wherein Paul always thanks God for the Christians to whom he is writing.

The Greek expression used here and in II Tim. 1:3 for **I thank** (χάριν ἔχω) does not appear as a thanksgiving formula in the genuine Pauline letters. Paul uniformly uses εὐχαριστέω, a verb that does not occur in the Pastorals. The Pastorals as handbooks of church order and administration, rather than true letters, naturally have no place for a formal thanksgiving in the usual Pauline style.

Since one purpose of the Pastorals is to nerve ministers and church leaders to stand firm against any defection from the received teaching, the writer will exhibit Paul as the splendid example of the minister fully endowed with divine power for the accomplishment of this work. As **Christ Jesus our Lord** strengthened Paul when he **judged** him **faithful** or trustworthy enough to appoint him **to his service,** so does he give strength to all ministers whom he approves and appoints.

As pseudonymous, the paragraph is more meaningful if the author is here not merely entering sympathetically into Paul's religious experience, but is also giving expression to his own. He may be here confessing his own sins as well as Paul's. Perhaps his devotion to Paul is due to the fact that he owes his conversion to Paul, if not personally, then through Paul's letters. In any case, he too is charged with a high and difficult mission.

---

Christ involves responsibility for this great trust. Christianity is more than a philosophy. It is more than an optional course in life's curriculum, planned for those of a special taste or interest. It is a cause which comes as an inescapable challenge to every man who has had a glimpse of "the light of the knowledge of the glory of God in the face of Jesus Christ" (II Cor. 4:6). No Christian can avoid his share of the responsibility for carrying forward Christ's cause. We have this gospel in earthen vessels, but we have it in our keeping as a sacred trust.

This suggests some of the other trusts committed to us to be used in the service of God. Our time, our talents, our money, our knowledge, our church, the treasures of the earth, the heritage of ideals and faith—all are entrusted to us to be used for God's purposes.

**12-17. Gratitude for a Mission.**—The reason for a man's thanksgivings are a searching test of the quality of his inward life. Some men are thankful when they can escape responsibilities, dodge hardships, find some measure of immunity from sacrifice. Here is a man who is grateful that he has been called to a hard, dangerous

mission in which with all his heart he believes. There are a number of strands in his thanksgiving. He is thankful that he has been given strength for his ministry. **I thank him who has given me strength for this, Christ Jesus our Lord.** Whatever attempts are made to explain it away, this experience of spiritual vitality adequate for life's demands given to the man who accepts life's challenges with Christian faith is an element in Christian experience completely convincing to every man who has shared it. The fear that some future day may confront him with a situation to which he may not be spiritually equal is often the anxiety which saps a man's vitality and makes him inadequate for the tasks in hand. Any man who has discovered a source of spiritual power in Christ Jesus has grounds for thanksgiving.

This man is also thankful that he has been entrusted with his high calling in spite of his earlier activity in opposition to the Christian cause. **He judged me faithful by appointing me to his service, though I formerly blasphemed and persecuted and insulted him.** His past mistakes had been due partly to ignorance. Every

**13** Who was before a blasphemer, and a persecutor, and injurious: but I obtained mercy, because I did *it* ignorantly in unbelief.

ing me to his service, **13** though I formerly blasphemed and persecuted and insulted him; but I received mercy because I had

---

He too is one in authority. He too has been empowered, judged faithful, appointed. He too has the right to command and the right to be obeyed. Perhaps the word **service** is chosen here as broader than apostleship and as more suitable to the author's own situation.

**13.** Of course Timothy would not need to be informed about Paul's conversion and the events preceding it. All this was widely known in the church. And although Paul's cruel and relentless persecution of Christians before his conversion haunted him to the end, and although he must have told the story of his conversion many times in his preaching, the language here is more meaningful if framed by a devoted admirer who sees in Paul's conversion God's most momentous act of mercy, an act in which the mercy of God for all sinners was openly manifested and made completely available.

**But I received mercy because I had acted ignorantly in unbelief:** Paul is gently shielded from the full impact of his pre-Christian wickedness by the attributing of it to unbelief as a result of ignorance. This defense sounds more like a friend in court than like Paul himself. Would Paul have recognized human ignorance as a ground of divine mercy? (Cf. Rom. 1:18 ff.; 9:15 ff.; 10:3.) And particularly, would he have excused himself on such a basis? One may see (with Dibelius) **in ignorance** (ἀγνοῶν) as an example of the intellectualistic interpretation of Christianity which characterizes the Pastorals, and as derived from the Stoic conception of natural religion (Epictetus *Discourses* II. 22. 22) ; or one may remember that the O.T. regards "unwitting" sins as less culpable (Lev. 22:14; Num. 15:22-31) than "presumptuous" sins (cf. also Luke 23:34; Acts 3:17).

---

man can look back on certain decisions in which with the best of intentions he was wrong, and on certain occasions when he did wrong to other people though that was the last thing he wanted to do.

> These clumsy feet, still in the mire,
>   Go crushing blossoms without end;
> These hard, well-meaning hands we thrust
>   Among the heart-strings of a friend.
>
> .    .    .    .    .    .    .
>
> Our faults no tenderness should ask,
>   The chastening stripes must cleanse them all;
> But for our blunders—oh, in shame
>   Before the eyes of heaven we fall.[6]

The risk of being wrong is part of the price we must pay for any decisive action, for we must frequently act on incomplete knowledge when we cannot see all the implications of what we are doing. Theodore Roosevelt once said that the only man who never makes mistakes is the man who never does anything at all. Here is one man's testimony that the grace of God covers even the wrongs done in ignorance. Saul the blasphemer can by the grace of God become Paul the apostle. **I received mercy because I had acted ignorantly.**

[6] Edward Rowland Sill, "The Fool's Prayer."

In dealing with the sins of ignorance the N.T. makes three things clear. First, God's forgiveness does not obliterate the consequences of the wrongs men do. Nothing can change the fact that millions of innocent people have suffered because evil ambitions have plunged the world into wars. The man who has wrecked his health and his fortunes through reckless living may become a new man spiritually, but he must still live in the wrecked world he has made for himself. Charles Morgan echoes the point of view of Greek tragedy in saying of his hero, who had with good intentions committed a great wrong,

> What he had done . . . had not been wrong within the limits of his knowledge, and there was, he knew, a rational argument that would pronounce him to be, therefore, guiltless; but it was an argument that he could no longer apply to himself. Absence of knowledge was not an acceptable plea of innocence. . . . I did not know! I did not mean it! was a cry to which Fate was deaf. . . . The requirements of its compassion were inexorable: that a man bear responsibility for the wrong that came through him and be purified by it.[7]

[7] *The River Line* (London: Macmillan & Co., 1949), p. 195.

14 And the grace of our Lord was exceeding abundant with faith and love which is in Christ Jesus.

15 This *is* a faithful saying, and worthy of all acceptation, that Christ Jesus came

acted ignorantly in unbelief, 14 and the grace of our Lord overflowed for me with the faith and love that are in Christ Jesus.

15 The saying is sure and worthy of full

---

**14.** The verb **overflowed** (ὑπερεπλεόνασεν) appears neither in the LXX nor in profane Greek. In Rom. 5:20 Paul stated in unforgettable form the idea that "where sin increased, grace abounded all the more." Beyond all reckoning and expectation the Lord endowed Paul with that fullness of faith and love which is known only to those in union with Christ Jesus.

Although **faith** occurs thirty-three times in the Pastorals (I Timothy nineteen times; II Timothy eight times; Titus six times), it never means faith as the justifying principle in the full Pauline sense. In the present passage, **faith** and **love** are results of justification, not its condition. Here **faith** is both belief and trust (see II Tim. 1:13).

**15.** The citation formula, **the saying is sure**—i.e., wholly trustworthy, absolutely certain—appears five times in the Pastorals (here; 3:1; 4:9; II Tim. 2:11; Tit. 3:8) and nowhere else in the Bible. Twice is added **worthy of full** [i.e., wholehearted or universal]

---

There is nothing distinctively Christian about this observation of fact. But the N.T. affixes its grim seal that whether or not his enemies knew what they were doing, Jesus was crucified. Second, there is a limit to justifiable ignorance. Speaking on the Areopagus in Athens, and referring to the worship of false gods, Paul said, "The times of ignorance God overlooked, but now he commands all men everywhere to repent" (Acts 17:30). Third, God forgives such sins. Jesus prayed from the cross, "Father, forgive them; for they know not what they do" (Luke 23:34). In this case Jesus prayed for the forgiveness of his murderers before there was any evidence of penitence on their part. His prayer must have involved a plea that they might understand what they had done, repent of it, and be led into new life with God.

But the deeper problem was that of sin—wrong motives, desires, ambitions, purposes at the very heart of his life. Even here God had made all things new. **And the grace of our Lord overflowed for me with the faith and love that are in Christ Jesus.** Grace means graciousness. When Jesus spoke, men "wondered at the gracious words which proceeded out of his mouth" (Luke 4:22). Some people do good grudgingly or awkwardly or self-consciously. Jesus had the capacity for doing good gracefully. Grace, however, means more than that. It refers to an overflow of kindness which goes far beyond the recipient's deserving. Justice deals with people according to their deserts. Grace does not stop there. Jesus taught that it is characteristic of God's love never to be limited to nicely calculated merits. "He makes his sun rise on the evil and on the good, and sends rain on the just

and on the unjust" (Matt. 5:45). It is common for people to complain when misfortune strikes them, saying, "What have I done to deserve this?" It is not so common for people to stop in the midst of all the blessings of ordinary life and ask, "What have I done to deserve this?" But in the N.T. grace means even more than that. It means the power of God touching human life through Christ to save and to redeem. Grace found its highest expression in the Cross. "While we were yet sinners Christ died for us" (Rom. 5:8). In Christ God has come and comes into human life, drawing to himself those who have been estranged from him by their own self-will, empowering those who have been defeated by their own weaknesses, redirecting those who have been living without purpose or for the wrong purposes, and giving himself to those who have felt themselves lonely pilgrims in a universe where no heart cared for them.

Some Christians believe that this grace is communicated only through the sacraments rightly administered. Others believe that in the sacraments of the church, and in every other act of life which is dedicated to God in the spirit of Christ, the grace of our Lord is given to men. Paul suggests here that the evidence of grace is the **faith and love that are in Christ Jesus.** Moffatt translates this "the faith and love that Christ Jesus inspires." Whatever else may be regarded as evidence of grace, life inspired by the kind of faith and love which Christ inspires is its authentic mark.

**15-16.** *To Seek and to Save.*—From a well-stored mind Paul brings out a familiar saying, or perhaps a line from a hymn familiar to his readers, to the effect that **Christ Jesus came into the**

into the world to save sinners; of whom I am chief.

**16** Howbeit for this cause I obtained mercy, that in me first Jesus Christ might show forth all long-suffering, for a pattern to them which should hereafter believe on him to life everlasting.

acceptance, that Christ Jesus came into the world to save sinners. And I am the foremost of sinners; **16** but I received mercy for this reason, that in me, as the foremost, Jesus Christ might display his perfect patience for an example to those who were

---

**acceptance** (also 4:9). The form is probably "a fixed preaching expression of Hellenistic origin" (Falconer).

In Tit. 3:8 alone does the formula follow the quoted material; however, see Exeg. on 3:1; 4:9.

**Saying** is frequently connected with **sure:** Rev. 21:5; 22:6 (also with "true," ἀληθινός). For examples, see Walter Lock, *A Critical and Exegetical Commentary on the Pastoral Epistles* (New York: Charles Scribner's Sons, 1924; "International Critical Commentary"), *ad loc.*

**Christ Jesus came into the world to save sinners** is obviously a quotation, although its source cannot be determined. The statement is as rhythmical and as compactly phrased as a proverb; and the frequency with which it is still quoted bears witness to its epigrammatic character. The language is certainly not that of Paul, who nowhere speaks of Jesus as "coming into the world." Nor does the expression **to save sinners** occur elsewhere in the N.T. The general idea is common enough on the lips of Jesus (Mark 2:17; Luke 5:32; 19:10), although Jesus does not say he came to *save* sinners, but to *call* sinners to repentance. That Jesus **came into the world** is the language of John (5:43; 7:28; 8:42; 9:39; 10:10; etc.).

**And I am the foremost** [=greatest=worst] **of sinners:** Although Paul may be credited with saying, "I am the least of the apostles, unfit to be called an apostle, because I persecuted the church of God. But by the grace of God I am what I am" (I Cor. 15:9-10), objections are raised both to the form and temper of the present passage; so, e.g., E. F. Scott (*The Pastoral Epistles* [New York: Harper & Bros., 1936; "The Moffatt New Testament Commentary"], p. 14): "We cannot but feel that the self-abasement is morbid and unreal; it suggests a type of piety which is out of keeping with the manly sincerity of Paul." Easton, too, believes both the language and the logic of the verse are "purely formalized." Paul does not here speak with the emotion of a sinner redeemed but rather as "Exhibit A." This giving way of emotion to logic and illustration is best explained if we suppose the language was framed not by Paul but by another who was concerned primarily with the illustrative and demonstrative value of Paul's remarkable transformation.

**16. Foremost** includes both "worst" and "first." If God's mercy was extended to him although he was the worst of men, it was not for Paul's own sake; rather it was in order

---

**world to save sinners.** This is one of the many instances recorded in the Bible where a man is helped by remembering something which he has learned perhaps long before. Verbal memorization of scripture texts does not automatically produce Christian character. But many a man is helped by some truth which has been stored away in his mind long before the occasion for its use arose. Jesus himself found strength in the words of the O.T. in the Temptation (Matt. 4:4, 7, 10); on the threshold of his mission (Luke 4); and on the Cross (Mark 15:34; Luke

23:46). Paul here remembers the words of others affirming the saving power of Christ Jesus. Then very simply he writes his own name at the top of the sorry list of sinners. The difficulties involved in the interpretation of this passage are discussed in the Exeg. Perhaps Paul felt that he was a sort of test case. If the grace of God could save him, there was hope for all. The implication that he was selected merely as a demonstration of the power of Christ is unacceptable to us. Surely the Father who is eager to seek and to save every misdirected life was concerned

17 Now unto the King eternal, immortal, invisible, the only wise God, *be* honor and glory for ever and ever. Amen.

to believe in him for eternal life. 17 To the King of ages, immortal, invisible, the only God, be honor and glory for ever and ever.[b] Amen.

[b] Greek *to the ages of ages.*

that Christ Jesus might display his "entire unlimited, ever-patient patience" (Lock) with evil men, and that he might establish Paul as the first and perfect example, the prototype, of all subsequent believers for whom Christ is the ground of faith, and eternal life its goal. If, for the writer, Paul was not the first Christian he was the first important one.

**17.** There are two doxologies in I Timothy, here and in 6:15-16. The terms are the established language of liturgy, framed to assert the sole supremacy of God as over against and above all earthly kings and emperors, and probably derived from the liturgical prayers of the pre-Christian, Hellenistic synagogues.

In the N.T. God is elsewhere described as **King** in Matt. 5:35; Rev. 15:3, as "King of kings," in 6:15; Rev. 17:14; 19:16. For **King of** [the] **ages**, see Tob. 13:7, 11; Enoch 9:4; I Clem. 61:2; Ps. 145:13; Exod. 15:18; III Macc. 5:35; Josephus *Antiquities* 1:272; 14:24; Rev. 15:3. "To Jews 'aeons' means 'universe,' not 'ages,' but here the latter translation is necessary because of (literally) 'aeonic life' that precedes and 'aeons of aeons' that follows. This shift in meaning that occurred when the phrase passed from Judaism into Hellenism resulted in a certain vagueness in 'King of the aeons,' but the sense is presumably 'eternally King.' " (B. S. Easton, *The Pastoral Epistles* [New York: Charles Scribner's Sons, 1947], p. 115.) In the Jewish liturgies God is commonly addressed as "King," "King of the universe," or "King eternal," "King of kings" (Dan. 2:37). The idea of **the ages** goes back ultimately to the Babylonian idea of world periods or thousand-year cycles, which in the heavenly order correspond to our earthly years.

**Immortal** or "imperishable" (cf. 6:16; Rom. 1:23; Epicurus in Diogenes Laertius *Lives of Eminent Philosophers* X. 123; Philo *Moses* II. 171), and **invisible** (cf. 6:16; Rom. 1:20; Col. 1:15; John 1:18; Philo *On Abraham* 75-76; etc.) are both Greek, not Jewish, attributes of God. Pure being as opposed to process, God is not subject either "to the enhancement or ruin of time."

**The only God** (cf. I Cor. 8:4-5) is thoroughly Jewish. While **honor and glory** are frequently joined in the N.T. (cf. Rom. 2:7, 10; Heb. 2:7 [Ps. 8:5]; 2:9; I Pet. 1:7; II Pet. 1:17; Rev. 4:9, 11; 5:12, 13; 7:12; 21:26) only here are they ascribed to God in a benediction and in this order (but see Rev. 5:12). The usual order is "glory and honor." Paul does not use the combination in either order in his benedictions.

with this man for his own sake. At any rate he knew what had been done for him, and his heart overflowed with thanksgiving. The most majestic phrases at his command come naturally to his mind when he thinks of what God has wrought in him. **To the King of ages, immortal, invisible, the only God, be honor and glory for ever and ever.** We share this spirit of thankfulness when we enter sincerely into the words of Walter Chalmers Smith's great hymn:

Immortal, invisible, God only wise,
In light inaccessible hid from our eyes,
Most blessed, most glorious, the Ancient of Days,
Almighty, victorious, Thy great Name we praise.[8]

[8] From *Enlarged Songs of Praise.* Used by permission of Oxford University Press.

Of the author of that hymn, George Adam Smith said:

It was a great ministry he achieved in Glasgow and Edinburgh. For over thirty years his preaching was one of the strongest spiritual forces among the educated men of both these cities. It was Biblical and expository; it was ethical, and with strong insight into human nature. . . . But its chief quality was a strenuous and solemn engagement to win men and women from the world and from themselves for Christ; an anxiety, sustained from first to last, to feed the flock committed to his charge, and to guide their characters through the perils of the time.[9]

Like the author of the Pastoral epistles, he praised God not only with his lips but in his life.

[9] Quoted by Alexander Gammie, *Preachers I Have Heard* (London: Pickering & Inglis, 1945), p. 105.

18 This charge I commit unto thee, son Timothy, according to the prophecies which went before on thee, that thou by them mightest war a good warfare;

18 This charge I commit to you, Timothy, my son, in accordance with the prophetic utterances which pointed to you, that inspired by them you may wage the

## V. TIMOTHY, PAUL'S LOYAL SUCCESSOR (1:18-20)

**18.** After the brief explanatory digression in which he clarifies the meaning of the law by limiting its application to "the lawless and disobedient," thereby rendering it irrelevant for Christians (vss. 8-11); and after a glowing personal testimony to the fully adequate saviorhood of Christ and to the epoch-making importance of Paul's conversion brings into high light the worthfulness of the "glorious" Christian gospel, the author returns to re-emphasize the **charge** to "Timothy" to hold faith and to insist that others do likewise.

In the summary providing transition from 1:3-17 to 2:1 **this charge** refers both backward and forward. Remembering how "by rejecting conscience, certain persons have made shipwreck of their faith" (vs. 19), "Timothy" is charged to **wage the good warfare, holding faith and a good conscience.** But the charge does not look backward alone. The letter is a series of charges, one leading to another.

These repeated charges are incomprehensible if thought of as delivered to Paul's tried and true co-worker Timothy. There is surely no reason to suppose that during the years of his mature ministry Timothy was in any danger of apostasy. The advices are therefore most meaningfully interpreted as addressed to all the "Timothys," he ministers who are under "Paul's" authority. Them he will hold in line.

**Commit,** or entrust (see 6:20; II Tim. 2:2), is the language not of creative but of transmissive activity. For the author the Christian faith and practice have already been established. It is now the Christian's duty not to modify or try to improve, but to transmit it.

**18-20. Close Up the Ranks.**—The Exeg. suggests that **this charge** cannot have been addressed to the Timothy who was Paul's fellow worker, since there is no reason to believe that he was ever in danger of apostasy. But is any Christian ever beyond the need of such an appeal as this? Discouragement, weariness, lethargy, faintheartedness sometimes assail the most devoted disciples of Christ, and a stirring summons like this fills a need. Even if Timothy never stood in need of such an exhortation, none of us is likely to be beyond the range of its appeal. **This charge I commit to you, Timothy, my son.** Like a runner in a relay race, Paul passes on the torch. The new runner or runners are inevitably reminded of what they owe to those who have run before them. This is something that all Christians need to remember. No man can ever measure his personal debt to the Christian faith and life of those who have gone before him. In countless ways beyond his knowing his life has been inspired, enriched, deepened, and strengthened by influences which have come out of the Christian loyalty and missionary zeal of an earlier day. It is often said that the present generation is living on spiritual capital bequeathed by a previous age of faith, and the query is raised as to how long it will be before the inheritance is dissipated. Here an

older generation charges a younger to maintain and pass on the faith. A man grown old in the service of Christ sees in the not distant future the time when another must carry on his work. To some people that is a bitter thought from which they shrink. They make no plans for handing on to younger leadership the responsibilities which they have carried. This Christian apostle, with no self-pity or regret, summons the future to close up the ranks and march forward when he has fulfilled the mission which had been entrusted to him.

Evidently divine guidance had been sought in the selection of the younger man to whom this charge was to be committed. **Prophetic utterances** had pointed to him as one divinely appointed for the task. We may assume that Timothy had given evidence of his sincerity, ability, and fitness for this responsibility. As a young man in Lystra, as well as on journey with Paul, he had displayed the gifts which qualified him for leadership. He had become a marked man and, when his older friends were consulted and the choice was committed to God in prayer, no doubt the conviction became clear in the minds of all that he was the man for this work. The epistle says that he was chosen **in accordance with the prophetic utterances which pointed to you.** God often guides the choice of

19 Holding faith, and a good conscience; which some having put away, concerning faith have made shipwreck:

good warfare, 19 holding faith and a good conscience. By rejecting conscience, certain persons have made shipwreck of their

---

A term of affection, **my son** (see 1:2; II Tim. 1:2; 2:1; Tit. 1:4) signifies age less than it does the relationship of pupils to teacher or of a subordinate to one in authority.

"Timothy," or the Christian minister, is confirmed in and for his **good** or noble **warfare** by the fact that he is not self-appointed. He is a minister less because of any decision which he has made than because he has been called by God and designated by the church. The Spirit has previously **pointed** him out, designating him for his task through **prophetic utterances** of Christian prophets. If the plural, **prophecies,** is taken literally, and the writer has the real Timothy in mind, it could mean either that at Timothy's consecration and appointment there were a number of prophets present and prophesying, as in Acts 13:1-3, or that there were various occasions when prophetic guidance was sought and found by Timothy. If the author has in mind the group of ministers to whom the letter was written, the plural may suggest to each one his own prophetic designation for the ministry. The occasion uppermost in mind may be the equivalent of our "ordination" (cf. 4:14; II Tim. 1:6). If so, the text would suggest that to the author the most important element in ordination was **the prophetic utterance,** as in Acts 13:1-3.

The use of the military metaphor to set forth the strenuousness and seriousness of life is everywhere attested (see in N.T. especially Eph. 6:10 ff., also II Tim. 2:3-4). The use is also characteristic of the language of the mystery religions and of Greek philosophy. Early Christian use of the figure, particularly where it is used almost proverbially, as here, I Cor. 9:7; II Tim. 2:3-4, was probably influenced by the popular philosophy of the time (Dibelius). To be a Christian is to be engaged in **warfare.**

19. To the author right belief, i.e., the received faith and a good conscience, belong together. Their relationship is reciprocal: to reject the faith is to reject conscience; to reject conscience is to make shipwreck of faith.

---

a man for a work through the lips of those who have seen the man in his unguarded moments.

Timothy was charged that in his Christian service he must **wage the good warfare.** Military metaphors appear frequently in the N.T. They are frankly metaphors, and cannot legitimately be used as arguments for or against participation in modern war. They recognize the inescapable fact that the Christian life involves conflict with evil. There is something in man which rises to the challenge of conflict. When that capacity is employed for selfish or unworthy ends it brings untold sorrow and misery into human life. Employed in the age-old conflict against the entrenched wrongs in the world, and against the evil in every man's heart, it is a source of power for the prophet, the reformer, the builder, the servant of the kingdom of God. In one of its aspects the Christian life stresses inner peace, contemplation, quiet fellowship with God. Here is another aspect which never can be overlooked, calling for heroic courage, the determination to stand against wrong, the will to contend "against spiritual wickedness in high places" (Eph. 6:12). William James's

essay *The Moral Equivalent of War*[1] urged that man's fighting instincts be directed into the struggle against ignorance and disease, to overcome nature and to make its waste places fruitful, to rid the world of injustice and wrong. Here is a call to every man to put his belligerent nature to constructive uses. In such efforts man may find one aspect of the experience of fellowship with God. Hence, "fight the good fight," as Moffatt has translated this phrase.

Two essentials for the warfare against evil are **faith and a good conscience.** Faith in general is needed, for morale is essential to success in any high endeavor. A man who is to contend stoutly against any evil must have faith in himself, faith in his cause, and faith that he lives in a universe in which he and his cause have significance. In other words, he needs faith in God. As the Exeg. points out, however, it is right belief and not merely faith in a more general sense which Paul seems here to have in mind. He is referring to what we would express in the words "the faith." He has in mind the body of beliefs which have been accepted

[1] New York: Association for International Conciliation, 1910.

20 Of whom is Hymeneus and Alexander; whom I have delivered unto Satan, that they may learn not to blaspheme.

faith, 20 among them Hymenae'us and Alexander, whom I have delivered to Satan that they may learn not to blaspheme.

20. In what way Hymenaeus and Alexander **have made shipwreck of their faith** is not stated. Therefore it must have been known to the first readers; otherwise the mention of the names would be meaningless. The offense of Hymenaeus is more explicitly stated in II Tim. 2:18, but nothing further is known about him. He and Alexander may have rated as archheretics in the Ephesian church in Paul's time and their names have become proverbial; or they may have been the leaders of the opposition in the time when the letters were written. If the latter is the case, the writer may have handled the situation as he believed Paul would have (after I Cor. 5:5). A coppersmith by the name of Alexander is named in II Tim. 4:14 as having done Paul great harm. Inasmuch as the letters were written by the same author to the same destination, the two Alexanders are probably the same person (see on II Tim. 4:14; also Acts 19:33).

Since the disposition of Hymenaeus and Alexander in the present verse is so much more final than that in II Tim. 2:17 and 4:14, this detail is frequently taken as evidence that II Timothy was written before I Timothy. In II Tim. 4:14, punishment of Alexander is left to the Lord. In II Tim. 2:25 gentleness is suggested in dealing with opponents (of whom Hymenaeus has just been named as one) for "God may perhaps grant that they will repent and come to know the truth, and they may escape from the snare of the devil."

In the present verse, however, "delivery to Satan" is a last resort, and in spite of **that they may learn not to blaspheme,** the very crisp finality of statement indicates that the author does not really expect a repentance.

"Delivery to Satan" recalls Job 2:6, where Job is handed over to Satan to suffer any misfortune including bodily suffering but short of death. In I Cor. 5:5 punishment includes "destruction of the flesh" (not of the spirit). Here, however, death is not clearly indicated, but could be intended in spite of **that they may learn not to blaspheme.** Certainly more than excommunication is meant: misfortune or sickness would be included.

and held by the Christian church. In the light of what he has said in vs. 4, we can be sure that he is not encouraging Timothy to become an argumentative hair-splitter about minute points of doctrine which make no vital difference in the conduct of life, but "promote speculations rather than the divine training that is in faith." He is recognizing the fact that faith is something more than an individualistic venture. Beyond the faith of the individual there is "the faith" which represents the corporate convictions of the church of Christ. When a man is trying to fight the good fight there is strength in the knowledge that he is not a lone contender, but stands in a fellowship of faith. To this writer **faith and a good conscience** belong together. The idea that faith is an intellectual feat unrelated to the moral life meets with no encouragement here. **By rejecting conscience, certain persons have made shipwreck of their faith.** Christian believers are sometimes accused of "wishful thinking." They are accused of believing in God because they want the reassurance of that belief. However that may be, there is a negative type of "wishful thinking" which does not believe in the Christian God because

of reluctance to face the ethical demands which such belief involves. "If your heart does not *want* a world of moral reality, your head will assuredly never make you believe in one," wrote William James.[2]

Hymenaeus and Alexander are types of disbelievers who first lost their right to a good conscience and then gave up their faith in a God who is concerned about righteousness. They were **delivered to Satan that they may learn not to blaspheme.** This probably meant that they were excommunicated, although the implication of the concluding phrase is that the action was disciplinary and tentative, not final and destructive, as the church in later times sometimes regarded such removal from membership in the church. In Protestant churches of our day ecclesiastical discipline is seldom invoked, and wisely so, for the dangers in it are subtle and colossal. But we may discern in this ancient disciplinary action a recognition of the fact that sometimes the hard experiences which follow in the train of moral irresponsibility may be used by God for the education and reformation of

[2] *The Will to Believe* (New York: Longmans, Green & Co., 1917), p. 23.

2 I exhort therefore, that, first of all, supplications, prayers, intercessions, *and* giving of thanks, be made for all men;

2 First of all, then, I urge that supplications, prayers, intercessions, and thanks-

---

What actually happened to Hymenaeus and Alexander we do not know. If the readers knew that they had suddenly or violently died (see Acts 5:5, 10: Ananias and Sapphira), the plural subject of **they may learn** could be not Hymenaeus and Alexander, but others among the "certain persons." Hymenaeus and Alexander would then be cited as a pointed warning to the opponents to show what happens to unrepentant heretics.

Rituals of "cursing" or curse formulas are widely attested in both Jewish and pagan practice. Calamity would automatically follow the pronouncement of the curse, it was believed; often a threat would be sufficient to bring the recalcitrant person into line.

Both heresy in belief and opposition to church authority would be blasphemy against God.

### VI. THE UNIVERSALITY OF THE CHRISTIAN FAITH (2:1-7)

**2:1. First of all, then,** is more naturally taken as transitional introduction to the first section of practical advices (which begins here and runs to 3:13) rather than as stressing the primary importance of prayer in worship.

The keynote of vss. 1-7 is the universal relevance of the Christian faith; it is **for all men,** even **for kings and all who are in high positions.** Vs. 1 is grounded in vss. 3-6: since "there is one God, and there is one mediator between God and men, the man Christ Jesus, who gave himself as a ransom for all," and since God "desires all men to be saved," the churches should pray (publicly) **for** [the conversion of] **all men,** including royalty.

The heaped-up language—**supplications, prayers, intercessions, and thanksgivings**—indicates the centrality of prayer in Christian worship. Yet there is no need to try to establish precise distinctions between the various terms. Synonyms add fullness and emphasis. Frequently this is their only function.

---

those who have played fast and loose with conscience; and in the reconstruction of their moral values and loyalties they may find their way back to a righteous God in whom they can have faith. The conclusion of the Exeg. that "the author does not really expect a repentance" seems to give insufficient weight to the words **that they may learn.**

Henry Sloane Coffin once preached a moving sermon on this text, drawing from it the suggestion that sometimes God permits individuals or society to go their evil ways in order that through the suffering incurred they may be moved to repent and turn to God. He added that such instruction may teach **not to blaspheme,** but that more positive lessons must be learned from another Teacher. Modern counterparts of Hymenaeus and Alexander are found in meetings of Alcoholics Anonymous, where no testimony is more frequent than the statement, "I was in hell until I found God."

**2:1-4. Duty and Privilege of Public Worship.** —Paul takes it for granted that every church will be a worshiping fellowship. From the beginning that has been the distinctive function of a Christian church. The church has rendered

many other services to mankind, but its unique and supreme privilege has been to unite people of faith in the worship of God. This privilege is insufficinetly appreciated even by those who believe in the church, and this duty is too often neglected. William Temple once said in an address to students at Oxford: "The most effective thing that the church of Christ can do in the world, and the most effective thing that any individual Christian can do, is to lift up his heart in adoration to God." [3] True worship is delightful. "Delight thyself . . . in the LORD" (Ps. 37:4) is the key to a richness of inner experience unknown to the hectic multitudes who are exhausted and disappointed in a feverish pursuit of a happiness which they never find. But worship is also a duty. Human beings grow to new heights as their lives are refreshed and enriched through fellowship with God and they find themselves equipped for new undertakings in his service. Human fellowships take on new meanings as realized fellowships in God. Human experience bears witness that God does new things through men and women who in fellow-

[3] *Basic Convictions* (New York: Harper & Bros., 1936), p. 19.

2 For kings, and *for* all that are in authority; that we may lead a quiet and peaceable life in all godliness and honesty.

givings be made for all men, 2 for kings and
all who are in high positions, that we may
lead a quiet and peaceable life, godly and

---

That the author finds it necessary to urge prayer **for all men** presupposes some sort
of exclusiveness. It could be that because of the struggle which the church was having with
Judaism and paganism on the outside, with problems relating to faith and order and
to the various syncretisms and gnosticisms which threatened to destroy it from within,
the church was turning in upon itself and becoming separatist and more concerned with
consolidation than with expansion. As Judaism abandoned its missionary activity in
order to save itself, so the church in the empire may have been tempted to shield itself
from a hostile paganism by withdrawal into itself. But exclusiveness, the author says, is a
basic betrayal of Christianity. The Christian must actively seek the salvation of all men,
not excluding **kings and all who are in high positions.**

2. If the theme of vss. 1-7 is the universal relevance of Christianity, and if vs. 1 is
grounded in vss. 3-6, then vs. 2 seems like an intrusion. Easton assumes as much and
proposes that vs. 2 is a quotation from an actual Christian prayer and therefore is only
loosely connected with its context. However, the entire paragraph may be interpreted as
a unity if we suppose its central problem to be: What shall the attitude of the church be
toward kings and those in authority? Shall public recognition of the secular authority
be made in the public prayers? We should not suppose that the continuation of the
Jewish practice of prayer and sacrifice for heathen rulers (see Jer. 36:7; Baruch 1:10-13;
Ezra 6:10; I Macc. 7:33) would be maintained by the church as a matter of course.
Christianity had come into widespread conflict with the emperor cult. The book of
Revelation shows with what horror the empire and its rulers were viewed in some circles
in the church. And it may well be that in the churches to which these letters were written
the question of public prayer for the emperor was a burning one.

The answer given is that (public) prayers shall be made for secular rulers (*a*) because
thereby Christians will be at least partially relieved of suspicion of disloyalty to the state
and will be permitted to **lead a quiet and peaceable life,** and (*b*) more importantly,
because kings are men too, and God **desires all men to be saved** (vs. 4). If Christians
are summoned to pray for kings, kings are thereby summoned to become Christians. In
the emperor cult people prayed *to* emperors; for Christians to pray *for* them removed
emperors from the savior class and made them, like others, subjects for Christian salvation.
The author has here advanced a bold and positive point of view which was held by the
church until emperors did become Christian (see also I Pet. 2:13-17; Rom. 13:1-7; Tit.
3:1-3, where submission to, not intercession for, rulers is the dominant theme).

The expression **kings and all who are in high positions** is so phrased as to include
emperors, local or petty kings, and all superior government officials. In the Orient "king"
meant emperor; among Greeks it designated sovereignty in general. Whether or not the
clause is an actual quotation from an early Christian prayer, it is used in the context to
formulate a principle for universal application.

---

ship worship him. Note the strength of the
English verbs used in the various translations
of Paul's admonition to common prayer: **I
exhort** (KJV); **I urge** (RSV); "My very first
counsel is" (Moffatt). Here is a matter regarded
by the writer as of central importance.

It is significant that the main emphasis here
seems to be upon prayer for others. **I urge that
supplications, prayers, intercessions, and thanksgiving be made for all men.** This is a problem
for many people who recognize the subjective

benefits resulting from prayer but find it difficult to believe that prayer has efficacy beyond
the interior life of the person who prays. In all
prayer there is mystery. How God meets man
in his inner life is as much beyond our comprehension as are God's activities in the world beyond the praying individual. Christian prayer
begins in Christian faith in a personal God
who is concerned with individuals and is also
active in his world. All prayer reaches up into a
realm where human understanding fails and

**That we may lead a quiet and peaceable life:** Taken by itself, vs. 2 could easily be viewed as suggesting that the easiest way to get rid of the annoyance of the emperor problem was to pray for him and thus be done with one's duty to the empire. However, elsewhere in the N.T. obedience to rulers is commonly enjoined. And furthermore, it is insisted that Christians are in prayer to seek the salvation of all men. By being "submissive to rulers" (Tit. 3:1) and praying for them, Christians believed they were rendering to Caesar in full the things that were Caesar's, and that they would receive in exchange the unhindered right to render to God the things that are God's.

**Godly and respectful in every way:** **Godliness** or "religion" (εὐσέβεια) and **honesty** or "seriousness" (σεμνότης) are the Hellenic counterpart to the Hebraic "holiness" (ὁσιότης) and "righteousness" (δικαιοσύνη; see Luke 1:75). Both words illustrate the Hellenistic speech-and-concept character of the Pastorals. In the N.T. godliness (religion) and its cognate forms (εὐσεβέω, εὐσεβής, εὐσεβῶς) occur only in Acts (3:12; 10:2; 17:23), II Pet. (1:3, 6, 7; 2:9; 3:11) and in the Pastorals (thirteen times), all writings with a noticeable Hellenistic vocabulary. **Honesty,** or, better, "seriousness," "respectfulness," "gravity," is likewise a Greek concept.

In a valuable note Dibelius points out how important this passage is as indicating the type of piety which characterizes the Pastorals, and how different it is from that of the Pauline letters. Paul lived in tension between the two worlds. The author of the Pastorals, on the contrary, is concerned to establish himself and the church in this world. His ideal is civic, practical, and rational. He lives on the brink of no catastrophe from

---

where precise definition of results is presumptuous. Two things are clear. One is that prayer in the name of Christ must have larger scope than the self-centered concerns of the man at prayer. The other is that Christian prayer is incomplete without intercession, in which the praying individual is gathered into a community in God. Elton Trueblood speaks of the church as a "Fellowship of the Concerned." [4] There can be no true Christian life without this concern for others which is offered to God in prayer, and there can be no true church which is not a fellowship in such articulate concern.

Says Eric Hayman:

All souls are deeply interconnected. . . . This interdependence is truly known only in God, in whom we all find our life, and on whom we all depend. . . . Intercession is the supreme activity of that living society—this fabric of praying souls. The power of our intercession is not our isolated pressure on a God remote from us. It is the action of His Spirit in and through our little souls, self-offered to the purpose of His will. So our intercession depends on our keeping open both to the perfect will of God and also to the need and suffering of the world. That openness must always make of intercession a prayer blended of great joy and great pain. For so the intercessor learns to share the Cross. [5]

Intercessory prayer is the supreme affirmation of the Christian faith in a God **who desires all**

[4] *Alternative to Futility* (New York: Harper & Bros., 1948), p. 58.

[5] *Prayer and the Christian Life* (London: Student Christian Movement Press, 1948), pp. 122-23. Used by permission.

**men to be saved and to come to the knowledge of the truth.** A penetrating Norwegian novelist makes one of her characters say in reply to his wife who scorns the church on the ground that she can pray just as well alone:

But one can do that *too,* Björg. I can worship God as much as I like when I'm alone. But I'm not sure that what I *most* need to learn at present isn't this—that God is everyone's God, and that what I wish God to be for me, God Himself wishes to be for *all.* Without respect of persons. So I ought to rejoice in every human being who pays Him adoration, and I ought to be grateful to anyone who may say to me, come, let us worship—. [6]

**Prayer is enjoined for kings, and for all that are in authority.** Christians face a serious problem when they live under governments of which they do not approve, as Christians discovered in the first century, and as Christians have tragically discovered in land after land in the twentieth century. Christians frequently differ as to their duty under such circumstances. On one duty and opportunity there is no disagreement. All Christians can and should pray for those in power.

Various attempts have been made by commentators, following Augustine, to tone down the sweeping assertion that God **desires all men to be saved and to come to the knowledge of the truth.** But there seems to be no reason to assume that this writer did not mean what he says: that the pursuing love of God knows no

[6] Sigrid Undset, *The Burning Bush* (tr. Arthur G. Chater; New York: Alfred A. Knopf, 1932), p. 133.

3 For this *is* good and acceptable in the sight of God our Saviour;

4 Who will have all men to be saved, and to come unto the knowledge of the truth.

5 For *there is* one God, and one mediator between God and men, the man Christ Jesus;

respectful in every way. 3 This is good, and it is acceptable in the sight of God our Savior, 4 who desires all men to be saved and to come to the knowledge of the truth. 5 For there is one God, and there is one mediator between God and men, the man

---

which faith alone saves. His position is a moderate, not a heroic, one. Asceticism is rejected. Moderation is the keynote: of foods, wine, marriage, riches.

3. Christians should abandon their hesitancy to pray for rulers: such prayer is right and proper; it is truly in accord with God's own character as Savior.

4. Even kings come within the concern of God. **Knowledge of the truth** is a technical term in the Pastorals (II Tim. 2:25; 3:7; Tit. 1:1; elsewhere in N.T. only Heb. 10:26). It is the equivalent of **to be saved** or "to become a Christian." The phrasing is Hellenistic in that it uses the language of intellection to express religion. Its use of **truth** is similar to that of John. The Greek words however seem carefully chosen. **Knowledge** here is not the familiar "gnosis," but a special compound word, ἐπίγνωσις, perhaps used to avoid a word with such heretical connotations as "gnosis." And **truth** here is almost the equivalent of the Christian faith. **Knowledge of the truth** in this sense is arrived at less by intellection than through repentance and faith. It is knowledge by acquaintance or experience rather than knowledge by description. It is less abstract than personal. Thus **knowledge of the truth** really amounts to the acceptance of a revelation of the received faith which is truth. The phrase thus presupposes a clear and established rule of faith.

5. These five compact, rhythmical, liturgical, clauses of vss. 5-6, obviously not in the style of the Pastorals, may well be part of a baptismal confession. In any case, they contain an exceptionally precise and clear statement of the basic pattern of the Christian faith: one God, one mediator, Christ Jesus, who is both God and man, and who on the Cross gave himself to be the world's Redeemer. The use of the citation here is to ground the command to pray for all men, even kings, in the very rule of faith which all Christians learned when first they became Christians. The Christian faith, the writer will urge, has never been ambiguous in its universalism. Christians should never have been in any doubt about this. The catechism which they early memorized told them that **there is one God, and there is one mediator between God and men, the man Christ Jesus, who gave himself as a ransom for all.**

---

exceptions, and that there is no man, even a tyrannical oppressor, whom God does not seek to save from his evil ways and bring into the saving knowledge of the truth revealed in Christ. A young minister once asked Lyman Abbott what he could say to a mother who mourned the wasted life of a prodigal son. "Say, 'His mercy endureth forever,'" replied Abbott.

**5-7. *A Creed for Life.*—**These lines, couched in a rhythm quite distinct from the prose of the epistle, may well be the quotation of a creed familiar to the first readers of the letter. It consists of two majestic affirmations. **For there is one God.** That is the fundamental basis of all intercessory prayer. We bring to God our concern for others because he is our common Father. For many moderns the creed needs to be-

gin on an even more elementary level, "There is at least one God." Too many people have no God at all to whom they give allegiance. But it is also important to say, "There is only one God." Too many people serve many gods: mammon, success, prestige, power—all claim loyalty, and the poor soul that tries to serve them all is torn asunder. Our age also needs to learn to say, "There is one God for all mankind." One God for all races, for all nations, for the adherents of all faiths—in that lies our hope for the world. Explosive ideas can generally be stated in very simple terms. When men first learned to say, "The earth is round" or "Heat expands" or "Government exists for the people," human thought and life turned new corners. The belief in the unity and the universal-

**6** Who gave himself a ransom for all, to be testified in due time. | Christ Jesus, **6** who gave himself as a ransom for all, the testimony to which was

---

In the N.T. mediator is applied to Christ only here and in Hebrews. In ascribing this function solely to him, the text excludes Jewish and Gnostic mediators, whether Moses or the law, high priest or angel, or any "aeon," from the central position of mediatorship.

In the Greek there is no definite article before **man,** thus stressing the category man, perhaps as over against Docetism or Gnosticism, or perhaps with reference to the Incarnation, as later reflected in the creeds, "and was made man."

**6.** As the one mediator, Christ **gave himself as a ransom for all.** Thus one must pray for kings and all men; otherwise they cannot be saved at all.

Almost certainly the verse is a reminiscence of Mark 10:45. "To give his life as a ransom for many" (λύτρον ἀντὶ πολλῶν) is here interpreted as **who gave himself as a ransom for all** (ἀντίλυτρον ὑπὲρ πάντων) .

---

ity of God is the most revolutionary of all ideas, and when it is really accepted mankind will face a new day.

J. E. Lesslie Newbigin, bishop of the United Church of South India, has written graphically of the problem presented to new Christian communities by the ancient traditions of caste. Christianity faces one of its severest tests in churches made up of people who have been separated into diverse groups by caste. But he describes the children in one village as singing while they danced:

There is one true God who made the whole world.
He is the only God, there is none like Him,
And He is the Father of us all,
All the world is His dear family;
He is the dear Father,
And so we are all brothers and sisters. . . .

This [says the bishop] is the foundation on which anything else worth doing will have to be built. This is what has frightened the caste people, because this must in the end mean a revolution.[7]

**And there is one mediator between God and men, the man Christ Jesus.** That is the second affirmation of this creed. When labor and management or two hostile nations have reached a deadlock, a mediator is sometimes called in. He is usually someone with no personal interest involved who tries to find some common ground on which the two sides can meet. That is not what is meant when Christ Jesus is spoken of as the mediator between God and men. God does not need to be reconciled to man. When there is estrangement it is a one-sided disloyalty. It is man who needs to be brought back to God.

[7] *A South India Diary* (London: Student Christian Movement Press, 1951), p. 92; published in the United States under the title, *That All May Be One* (New York: Association Press, 1952; "A Haddam House Book"), p. 94. Used by permission.

God is always seeking to win man to himself. Christ, the mediator, is not a disinterested third party. He cared enough about this difference to lay down his life to reconcile man to God, and the Cross is the measure of his involvement in the tragic predicament of man. The central problem of life is how to overcome something that lures men away from God, which means away from the true ends of life, and so away from peace and power. The man Christ Jesus has overcome sin, and to generations of Christians he has brought God's power to overcome sin. "This is the victory that overcomes the world" (I John 5:4) .

There are two key words in this second affirmation: **One mediator.** The modern world likes to say that there are many roads which lead toward God, which is true. But Christ is the unique revelation of God, the unique way to God, and the unique reconciler of man to God. "I am the way, and the truth, and the life; no one comes to the Father, but by me" (John 14:6) . The other key word is **the man Christ Jesus.** In the writer's mind this probably was a protest against the belief of heathen cults that redemption could be wrought only by a heavenly being completely dissociated from human life in this world. Orthodox Christianity insisted upon the full humanity of Jesus. The Epistle to the Hebrews glories in this: "He had to be made like his brethren in every respect, so that he might become a merciful and faithful high priest in the service of God, to make expiation for the sins of the people. For because he himself has suffered and been tempted, he is able to help those who are tempted. . . . We have not a high priest who is unable to sympathize with our weaknesses, but one who in every respect has been tempted as we are, yet without sinning. Let us then with confidence draw near to the throne of grace, that we may receive

7 Whereunto I am ordained a preacher, and an apostle, (I speak the truth in Christ,

borne at the proper time. 7 For this I was appointed a preacher and apostle (I am

---

The phrase translated **the testimony to which was borne at the proper time** is in Greek so cryptic as to be almost unintelligible. It seems to mean that the Christian faith or the Christian redemption as summarized in vss. 5-6 was fully revealed and certified by God when and as the sovereign and unconditioned will of God determined. The Christian faith is true because God has validated it of his own unconditioned will. Perhaps the chief item in this **testimony** to God's desire to save all men is thought of as the self-giving of Christ; however, the **testimony** should not be limited to this meaning. God's "times" are many. Oscar Cullmann (*Christ and Time* [tr. F. V. Filson; Philadelphia: Westminster Press, 1950], pp. 40-41) proposes the interesting interpretation and translation, " 'as a witness to appropriate *kairoi*' still to come." The text would then say that the decisive *kairos,* that point of past time in redemptive history when Jesus **gave himself**, stands as **testimony** and surety for all future *kairoi,* particularly for the final redemptive event.

7. After years of intimate association in work and travel, Paul would not have needed

---

mercy and find grace to help in time of need" (Heb. 2:17-18; 4:15-16). Christianity is not primarily a theory or a philosophy of life. Christianity bears witness to an event—the life, ministry, death, and resurrection of Jesus. It was to bear witness to the saving power of God mediated through **the man Christ Jesus** that Paul had been ordained a preacher. Christian truth had been validated in history, **the testimony to which was borne at the proper time.**

Donald M. Baillie makes this helpful comment:

The New Testament does not speak of God being reconciled to man, but of man being reconciled to God, and of God as the Reconciler, taking the initiative in Christ to that end. . . . There is in the New Testament a remarkable identification of the love of Christ which led Him to the Cross and the love of God which sent or gave Him. The identification is the more striking because it is made so tacitly. It does not appear as a theological consequence of an actual identification of Christ with God, for St. Paul's Christology had hardly got so far as that in express formulation. But when he is speaking of the great reconciliation, he runs ahead of his Christology and speaks of the love of Christ and the love of God almost interchangeably. . . . There was no distinction: the two were one and the same thing. In discoursing of the love that was shown in the Cross of Christ the New Testament is never able to stop short of tracing it up-stream to the eternal love of God dealing sacrificially with the sins of the world.[8]

Lesslie Newbigin has recorded a significant conversation with a wealthy Hindu cloth merchant who admired but did not follow Jesus, although his wife had found great joy and power in the Christian faith.

[8] *God Was in Christ* (New York: Charles Scribner's Sons; London: Faber & Faber, 1948), pp. 187, 189. Used by permission.

"Why do you not accept Christ as your Saviour?" I ask, "You have seen what He has done for your wife. You have read His words and His deeds. Is there any to compare with Him? Why do you reject Him?" "I don't reject Him. On the contrary I admire Him very much. But why should I not admire others also? Why Jesus only?" I open the Bible and read to him. "Thomas said [*sic*] unto Him, Lord, we know not whither thou goest; and how can we know the way? Jesus saith unto him, I am the way, the truth and the life; no man cometh unto the Father but by me." There is silence. . . . "Don't you see that the Man who said things like that forces you to a decision? If this claim was true, then, of course, you must accept it; if it was false, then the man who made it was a rank imposter [*sic*], and you ought not to admire him at all. He will not leave you to be a mere admirer." . . . When we kneel for prayer he gets up to go out, then stops in the doorway, and stands there till the prayer is finished—undecided.[9]

At Amsterdam in 1948, speaking at the conference which launched the World Council of Churches, Miss Saroe Chakko, of Isabella Thoburn College, Lucknow, said that

she felt that one of the most important matters in evangelism was to bring home the uniqueness of Christ. Surrounded by Moslems and Hindus, and those who have made nationalism a religious cult, Indian Christians are convinced that only Christ came to reveal God to man and only He can serve as a means of our redemption.[1]

**7. A Varied Ministry.**—Here is an echo of Paul's oft-repeated defense of his credentials as

[9] J. E. Lesslie Newbigin, *A South India Diary* (London: Student Christian Movement Press, 1951), pp. 115-16; published in the United States under the title, *That All May Be One* (New York: Association Press, 1952; "A Haddam House Book"), pp. 117-18. Used by permission.

[1] James W. Kennedy, *Venture of Faith* (New York: Morehouse-Gorham Co., 1948), p. 59.

| *and* lie not,) a teacher of the Gentiles in faith and verity. | telling the truth, I am not lying), a teacher of the Gentiles in faith and truth. |

either to assure Timothy that he had been appointed apostle to the Gentiles, or to asseverate that he was not lying. **I am telling the truth, I am not lying** is too intense to be well in place in this context. We may suppose that the author is allowing Paul to speak with his wonted vehemence (see Rom. 9:1; II Cor. 11:31; Gal. 1:20) in order to secure the great apostle's most vigorous affirmation of the universalism of the gospel, of which Paul was the chief witness and ablest defender.

**Preacher** (κῆρυξ): In the N.T. only here; II Tim. 1:11; II Pet. 2:5. The Greek word (κηρύσσω) "preach" always conveys the idea of an authoritative, solemn, public proclamation which demands respect.

Paul is called a **teacher** elsewhere in the N.T. only in II Tim. 1:11. He never refers to himself as a **teacher** in the earlier epistles. He uses the verb "to teach" of himself in I Cor. 4:17; Col. 1:28; cf. Acts 20:20. The verb is used of him in Acts 11:26; 15:35; 18:11; 21:21, 28; 28:31. That Paul is called **teacher** is in accord with the stable, ordered, non-charismatic type of Christianity which characterizes the Pastorals.

The language of **a teacher of the Gentiles in faith and truth** is ambiguous. Moffatt translates "to teach the Gentiles faith and truth," a meaning which best fits the nature of the Pastorals, where **faith and truth** are characteristically synonymous and objective in meaning. Christianity is "the true faith."

The triad **preacher, apostle, teacher** occurs in the N.T. only here and in II Tim. 1:11. In the N.T. groupings "apostles and prophets" are always coupled together, either alone (Eph. 2:20; 3:5) or with "teachers" (I Cor. 12:28) or, in the longer list of Eph. 4:11, with "evangelists, pastors, teachers." Paul never designates himself as a prophet, evangelist, pastor, or teacher (except in this verse and in II Tim. 1:11).

an interpreter of the Christian faith, of which the Epistle to the Galatians is a conspicuous example. Controversies over the validity of orders weakened the Christian witness in the early days of the church, as they do today, standing as the chief barrier in the way of the unity of Christ's church. When we grow impatient with these differences, we need to remember that there are two important issues involved. On the one hand, we need to guard against supposing that God is limited to working through those who bear a particular ecclesiastical stamp of approval. On the other hand, we need an orderly way of making sure that those who speak for the church are qualified to do so. Hence the importance of an ordained ministry.

Whether or not the author of this epistle intended to emphasize the threefold nature of his ministry, there is a deep significance in the terms which he uses. **I am ordained a preacher, and an apostle, . . . a teacher of the Gentiles.** The preaching of the Word of God is one of the essential functions of the church. The gospel must be proclaimed, and it must be proclaimed in the light of each generation's need. But the preaching must not be confined to those already within the fold of the church. The church has a mission to those without, and its servants must be apostles—messengers sent out to bear witness

in the spirit of the Great Commission (Matt. 28:19). The church's messengers must also be teachers, interpreting the meaning and the application of the Christian faith. In our day the importance of Christian teaching cannot be exaggerated. When rival religions like Nazism and communism seek to extend their influence, they set to work to teach their doctrine to young and old. By common consent the Christian church has for a generation failed adequately to teach its faith. As a result, multitudes of nominal Christians are ignorant of the history of Christianity, of its basic convictions, of the lives of its saints, of what it is doing, and of what it is called to do in the world today. Here is a challenge to laymen as well as to ministers. What are the marks of the good teacher? (*a*) He must be a person of Christian faith and character; (*b*) he must care about other people, young and old, and must be eager to share Christian faith and knowledge; (*c*) he must be willing to learn the art of teaching, one of the most difficult of all the arts; (*d*) he must have courage, patience, persistence, and love; (*e*) he must be ready to give his best and leave the results with God.

**Preacher, apostle, teacher**—these three words convey a good picture of a well-rounded ministry.

| 8 I will therefore that men pray every where, lifting up holy hands, without wrath and doubting. | 8 I desire then that in every place the men should pray, lifting holy hands with- |

---

### VII. Rules for Public Worship (2:8-15)

**8.** After validating universal prayer by expounding the Christian doctrine of one God and one Mediator, that true faith to which the Apostle to the Gentiles devoted his life, the author now turns to the problem of women in worship.

**I desire** (βούλομαι) is used in the Pastorals in the sense it normally has in Hellenistic Judaism: it is the courteous form for giving expression to the decree of a legislator or ruler. It is a strong word, indicating (a) the position of authority which the writer holds in the church, and (b) the urgent need of the legislation which is to follow. Even against opposition the author asserts his will and expects it to be obeyed.

The author's insistence that **in every place the men should pray** suggests that in some churches the conventional synagogue practice in which men alone recited the prayers was being modified to admit participation of women. The unusually prominent part which women played in the early church, together with the freedom from tradition encouraged by a religion of prophecy and the Spirit, not to mention the fluidity in form which always characterizes the "sect" or the schismatic religious group deprived of the traditional equipment for worship, architectural and otherwise—these factors must have made the old restraints excluding women from active participation in the services seem both irksome and meaningless. The church began as a laymen's organization; everyone was expected to have some part in the service (I Cor. 14:26). And the Spirit, we should suppose, would descend without regard to sex, even though the prophets doubtless exceeded the prophetesses in number. This enthusiasm in early Christianity and the sheer numbers of women active in the faith, seeking release, vocation, and status, could not long have allowed the old ways to go unchallenged. And some men were agreeing to it. This feminist trend our author will oppose. It is the men only who shall participate in the public prayers.

**In every place** most naturally means "throughout the church." If the phrase is a direct quotation from some older source like Mal. 1:11 (Dibelius, Easton, Lock, etc.), such modeling of style after scripture would confirm the impression that the author will legislate for the whole church in authoritative fashion. The reference is of course to public worship. The writer can scarcely have known a problem here so far as home and family devotions were concerned. As is always true in societies where women are excluded from public life, in the family they were given larger responsibilities than in synagogue or church. They were expected to "rule their households" (5:14), a responsibility which would surely include religious functions. Nor would there be the likelihood in the home

---

**8. The Moral Prerequisite to Prayer.**—To his recapitulation of his plea for unceasing, universal prayer the author adds a direction regarding the spiritual conditions for effective prayer. **Lifting holy hands without anger or quarreling.** Both in the O.T. and in the N.T. emphasis is laid upon the right heart as essential to the prayer which is communion with God. "Who shall ascend into the hill of the Lord? or who shall stand in his holy place? He that hath clean hands, and a pure heart" (Ps. 24:3-4). Jesus put it in even more searching language. "If you are offering your gift at the altar, and there remember that your brother has something against you, leave your gift there before the

altar and go; first be reconciled to your brother, and then come and offer your gift" (Matt. 5:23-24). Coleridge caught the spirit of the Sermon on the Mount in *The Rime of the Ancient Mariner:*

> He prayeth best, who loveth best
> All things both great and small;
> For the dear God who loveth us,
> He made and loveth all.[2]

William Law pointed out that there is a two-way influence in this matter: one must love his brother before he can effectively pray, but pray-

[2] Part VII, st. xxiii.

9 In like manner also, that women adorn themselves in modest apparel, with shamefacedness and sobriety; not with braided hair, or gold, or pearls, or costly array;

out anger or quarreling; 9 also that women should adorn themselves modestly and sensibly in seemly apparel, not with braided

---

that Christian wives would be ambitious to take over the prescribed religious duties assigned to the father as head of the house.

**Lifting holy hands:** The most widely accepted form of prayer posture was standing with hands uplifted, palms upward; kneeling and prostration signified unusual intensity or anguish (Mark 14:35), and were symbols of abasement scorned by Greeks as barbarous. **Holy hands** in an older time would presuppose a washing ritual. In the text **holy** is interpreted ethically, meaning **without anger or quarreling.** The practice of cleansing in "holy" water may or may not be taken for granted. Both in and out of early Christianity the language of ritual purity was not infrequently interpreted ethically and metaphorically. But whatever the case may be with regard to a ritual act, the author is enough of a Paulinist to know that what makes hands holy is not water but a sincere and gentle spirit. **Without anger or quarreling** reflects Matt. 5:23-24; 6:14. It is the consistent emphasis of the Bible that prayer is efficacious only if one is at peace with his brothers. Only men who forgive can be forgiven.

9. In Greek the connection between vss. 8 and 9 is rough. The writer takes it for granted that women should be present at public worship and prayer. However, since the explicit statement of vs. 8 is that (only) men shall pray, i.e., read the public prayers, and since the insistence of the paragraph is that women must remain silent in church, it is scarcely possible to suppose that the author meant to say, "I desire also the women to pray in modest apparel," etc. (But see I Cor. 11:4-16; 14:34-35.) The text should rather be taken to mean, "I desire also that women attending [public] prayers should adorn," etc. In the paragraph "Paul" is less concerned with the duties of women to pray than with their dress and behavior at prayer. The topic sentence of the section is vs. 11: "Let a woman learn in silence with all submissiveness." The lack of coherence in the paragraph is due to the fact that the content of vss. 9-10, 13-15 extends beyond the needs of the immediate issue. It being admitted that modest apparel is congruous with silence and submissiveness, the sheer elaboration of vs. 9, the admonition to good deeds in vs. 10, and the argument of vss. 13-15 suggest that the writer has gathered together certain general advices to women and a certain appraisal of their function, which just because they were of traditional and broader reference could be the more effectively used to keep women in their place.

**That women should adorn themselves modestly and sensibly in seemly apparel:** In the context the form of dress advocated has reference primarily to that worn in church. In public worship women should dress with simplicity and reserve, not concerned to display their physical charms. However, it is not necessary to infer from the text that Christian women came to church dressed ostentatiously and in bad taste. Ancient moralists (usually men), whether Christian or pagan, regularly inveighed against women's devotion to fashion. And probably our author has here picked up a weapon which was lying conveniently at hand and with which he could effectively strike: a woman who

---

ing for a brother makes one love him. "There is nothing that makes us love a man so much as praying for him; and when you can once do this sincerely for any man, you have fitted your soul for the performance of everything that is kind and civil towards him." [3]

**9-15. The Place of Women in the Church.—** There are few passages in the Bible which have

[3] *A Serious Call to a Devout and Holy Life,* ch. xxi.

aroused more heated discussion than these verses. Taken literally as authoritative commands, they would exclude women completely from all leadership in the church. Obviously such an interpretation does not square with the universal practice of the N.T. churches. The epistles of Paul contain the names of many women who were prominent in the work of the church in various ways: Lydia, Dorcas, Priscilla.

10 But (which becometh women professing godliness) with good works.

11 Let the woman learn in silence with all subjection.

12 But I suffer not a woman to teach, nor to usurp authority over the man, but to be in silence.

hair or gold or pearls or costly attire 10 but by good deeds, as befits women who profess religion. 11 Let a woman learn in silence with all submissiveness. 12 I permit no woman to teach or to have authority over

---

would want to pray in public, he supposes, would be guilty of almost any kind of lewdness, irregularity, or insubordination. She might even wish to remove her veil (see I Cor. 11:4-16).

**Not with braided hair or gold or pearls or costly attire.** If these details are not merely those of the traditional Greek or Latin moralist, if they reflect truly the situation in the church, they furnish evidence for the presence of some, perhaps considerable, wealth and "nobility" in the church of the time.

**10.** "It is strange that in the Pastorals 'good works' are always named as signs of genuine Christianity, whereas the genuine Pauline letters know only the singular form and correspondingly another meaning of the expression" (Martin Dibelius, *Die Pastoralbriefe* [2nd ed.; Tübingen: J. C. B. Mohr, 1931; "Handbuch zum Neuen Testament"], *ad loc.*). This conception of **good works** belongs to the second Christian generation, as Eph. 2:10 and Heb. 10:24 show. **Good deeds** are sufficient ornamentation for a Christian woman.

**11.** This verse is crisp and epigrammatic in form. In church women are learners, not teachers; they must **learn in silence with all submissiveness,** neither speaking nor asking questions, but listening quietly to what the men say. The first **good work** (vs. 10) of women is to keep still (Spicq)! The advice here agrees with I Cor. 14:34-35, which is even more vehement. I Cor. 11:2-16, on the contrary, does not question woman's right to pray or prophesy in church, but only insists that she be veiled when doing so. If I Cor. 14:34-35 is a marginal gloss (so J. Weiss, Easton), and if I Cor. 11:2-16 conveys the true Pauline point of view, then the present passage would represent a later and more conservative position with regard to women in church than that of Paul or than is represented in the book of Acts (see also Phil. 4:2-3; Rom. 16:3-5; Acts 18:26; 21:9). The Pastorals are characterized by a type of stabilized piety in which Spirit phenomena are for the most part quenched, perhaps entirely so as far as women are concerned. In regard to the place of women in church, the writer has reverted toward the older Jewish practice. In part this may have been caused by extravagances resulting from the primitive Christian "emancipation" of women, in part by a natural masculine reluctance to yield historic prerogatives to women.

**12.** Here the author is severely dictatorial: **I permit no woman to teach,** i.e., in public. **Or to have authority over men:** The unusual verb αὐθεντέω (only here in the Bible) is obscure. Dibelius translates "interrupt"; Moffatt, "dictate to." A meaning opposite to "keeping silent," such as "contradict," would suit the context well. If the meaning **to have authority over** is retained, the prohibition can only mean that women shall under no circumstance be placed in administrative positions in the church.

---

Tryphena and Tryphosa, Persis, Julia, Euodia, Syntyche, and others. This epistle is explicit, however, in forbidding women to speak in the churches, and in subordinating them to the authority of men. No doubt its position was influenced by the customs of the day, in the light of which Christian women would have been subject to criticism had they been conspicuous in public. In some churches in the Far East it has been necessary for women to exercise a

voluntary self-restraint in the matter of public appearances in order to avoid misunderstanding in localities where women have been traditionally secluded in the home. The argument of the epistle, based on a reference to Adam and Eve, seems far-fetched and unconvincing. In actual practice, while the churches have for the most part declined to ordain women as ministers, the great gifts of women have been employed as teachers, missionaries, and in a multitude of

13 For Adam was first formed, then Eve. 14 And Adam was not deceived, but the woman being deceived was in the transgression.

15 Notwithstanding she shall be saved in childbearing, if they continue in faith and charity and holiness with sobriety.

men; she is to keep silent. 13 For Adam was formed first, then Eve; 14 and Adam was not deceived, but the woman was deceived and became a transgressor. 15 Yet woman will be saved through bearing children,[c] if she continues[d] in faith and love and holiness, with modesty.

[c] Or by the birth of the child.
[d] Greek they continue.

13. Priority means superiority: the first is the best. The argument rests on the widespread belief that creation began in perfection and that history is progressive degeneration. Also, according to the Genesis story, woman was created for man, not man for woman.

14. Secondly, **Adam was not deceived, but the woman:** "The point made is that Adam was not deceived by the serpent but sinned with his eyes open; Eve, on the other hand, succumbed blindly to the serpent's wiles. And from this reading of Gen. 3.1-6 is deduced that women are by nature so easily deceived that they can never be trusted to teach" (Easton, *Pastoral Epistles,* p. 124). This one all-important time when woman taught man proved fatal: everything was lost. Since it was now obvious that she was not worthy of the status of equality, it was necessary that she should be subjected to her husband (Gen. 3:16) and deprived of the right to teach men.

The cogency of the argument rested upon the interpretation of Genesis, widely held in both synagogue and church, that Adam and Eve were not just two individuals but were archetypes in whom the whole history of the race was foreshadowed, delineated, included, and determined. When the text reads not "Eve," but **the woman,** it means to say that it is feminine nature to be easily deceived. What Eve did all women still do. Eve's daughters are of necessity just like their mother. They must therefore be permanently denied teaching or liturgical functions in the church.

15. Strictly, the unexpressed subject of **will be saved** is Eve. However, the transition in thought to the Christian woman is already made in vs. 14, where ἡ γυνή is properly translated **the woman,** not "his wife"; and to Christian women in the shift to the plural in the verb **if she continues,** lit., **if they continue.**

These irregularities in the language and structure of the Greek text, together with the brevity of the statement, have made for obscurity of meaning and have through the

ways. The movement to recognize complete equality between men and women in the work of the church grows with each passing year, and the usefulness of the church is increased by the larger place given to women.

The National Council of the Churches of Christ in the United States of America published a report on "Women in American Church Life," prepared under the guidance of a counseling committee of women representing national interdenominational agencies. The conclusion of the report says:

Women are, it is clear, carrying on an enormous variety of activities within the church. . . .

Yet certain questions must still be raised. . . . Are the women using their abilities to the full in their church work? . . . If women's abilities are to be fully used, there must be an opportunity for both the "Marthas" and the "Marys"—one might add,

for the "Martha" and the "Mary" in every woman. . . . The grave situation in the world today with mounting secularism can only be met by a truly unified church that uses all the talents of all its members, whether clerical or lay, male or female. Perhaps what is really needed is to give new meaning to the basic Protestant concept of "the priesthood of all believers." [4]

Obviously the disposition of this epistle to limit the service of women in the churches does not accord with Jesus' attitude of complete respect and chivalry toward women. It is not in keeping with the modern attitude which moves steadily toward the equality of the sexes in so far as rights and privileges are concerned, and does so under the pressure of the spirit of Christ.

[4] Inez M. Cavert, *Women in American Church Life* (New York: Friendship Press, 1949), pp. 81-82. Used by permission.

3 This *is* a true saying, If a man desire the office of a bishop, he desireth a good work.

3 The saying is sure: If anyone aspires to the office of bishop, he desires a noble

---

centuries provoked a variety of interpretations, many of them oversubtle or even fantastic. The simplest and probably the best interpretation is that woman's salvation depends upon her devotion to the purpose for which she was created, viz., to bear children, and of course upon her faithfulness to a chaste Christian life. Her divinely ordained place is in the home; her function, the bearing and rearing of children. Our author will assure Christian women that even though woman was responsible for man's first disobedience and must therefore bear the guilt of having brought death into the world and all our woe, nevertheless **woman will be saved** if she does her duty. Only, because of woman's primal sin, her nature as easily deceived, and her function as childbearer, she is forever unfit to be a teacher or administrator in the church.

### VIII. The Character of Bishops (3:1-7)

**3:1.** Interpreters remain disagreed (*a*) as to whether **the saying is sure** belongs with 2:15 or with 3:1, and (*b*) as to whether the original text read as above or "the saying is popular."

The problem is that although this conventional citation formula of the Pastorals normally precedes its quotation (yet see 4:9; Tit. 3:8), vs. 1*b* has seemed less a quotation than 2:13-15. If we suppose that the formula must precede its quotation (so Dibelius), then vs. 1*b* will of necessity be the quotation indicated. However, the Pastorals evidence the use of the phrase both before and after a quotation. And if it may be taken to mean "this argument is valid," it could refer to the statements immediately preceding it (2:13-15). The phrase then becomes the writer's own certification of the involved if not far-fetched argument in 2:13-15. This interpretation would require the text **the saying is sure.**

Moffatt (so Easton) regards **sure** as the "easier" reading, the original "popular" having been altered to "sure" for the sake of uniformity with 1:15, etc. More probably, however (Dibelius, Scott, Spicq, with the mass of textual evidence), an original "sure" was changed to "popular" as a result of construing the formula with 3:1 and feeling its unsuitability to what seems so banal a remark. Problems (*a*) and (*b*) are both complicated because it is difficult to determine the overtones or the points of view which gave currency

---

It does not meet the needs of the world which could not afford to be without the special gifts which women bring to the leadership of the churches. Here is a case where an early Christian's understanding of the will of God needs to be corrected by the further light which God has caused to break forth from his holy Word.

The Exeg. aptly refers to this attitude as an instance of "stabilized piety," a rigid loyalty to older Jewish practice and unreadiness to recognize the call of the Spirit to new ways. This is a constant temptation in other matters in addition to the question of the place of women in the church. "Stabilized piety" for generations defended slavery, child labor, slums, racial discrimination, and other evils, and claimed divine sanction for them because of their antiquity. What are the entrenched wrongs which "stabilized piety" maintains in being today? Robert Frost in his poem "Mending Wall" speaks of

the New England farmer who insisted on keeping in repair a stone wall the usefulness of which was a thing of the past, and justified his care in mending the wall by repeating his father's saying, "Good fences make good neighbors."

He moves in darkness as it seems to me,
Not of woods only and the shade of trees.
He will not go behind his father's saying,
And he likes having thought of it so well
He says again, "Good fences make good neighbors." [5]

Not stabilized piety, but dynamic, creative piety is the fruit of the Spirit.

**3:1. *A Noble Task.*—**We may well draw from vs. 1 a plea for the right kind of ambition in the church. We would like to think of a Chris-

[5] "Mending Wall," from *Complete Poems of Robert Frost.* Copyright, 1930, 1949, by Henry Holt & Co. Used by permission of the publishers.

to such a saying as vs. 1*b*, a saying which may have been intended to function less in relation to itself than as transitional to the new material of vs. 2.

**If anyone aspires to the office of bishop, he desires a noble task** is obviously a quotation. But what its original meaning was or just why it is quoted here is uncertain. It may be (*a*) simply a current proverb, having originally nothing to do with an ecclesiastical office and used here without overtones merely as introductory to vss. 2-13. Then it should be translated as in Moffatt: " 'Whoever aspires to office is set upon an excellent occupation.' Well, for the office of a bishop," etc. Ἐπισκοπή, then, would mean rulership in general, the position of inspector, manager or administrator, rather than episcopacy or **office of bishop** in the church sense. The saying would then reflect a situation in which civic offices were such a source of expense and trouble that volunteers were few. "In Christianity the saying would be doubly true, for the compensation must have been negligible, the duties . . . onerous and often embarrassing" (Easton, *Pastoral Epistles,* p. 130). As used here, the saying could reflect a problem faced by the church in the period of transition from a lay ministry to a professional one. Capable men—such as Paul, whose own hands ministered to his necessities (Acts 20:34)—who were well established economically, might hesitate to offer themselves for full-time service when there was no well-ordered tradition or plan in the church for ministerial support.

(*b*) It is possible that the verse reflects a situation in which the office of bishop lacked prestige or was regarded as less than **a noble task,** and that it is the writer's purpose to encourage qualified men to aspire **to the office.** In the list of church functionaries named in I Cor. 12:28, "administrators" (κυβερνήσεις) come next to the last. In the apostolic age the most highly esteemed gifts of the Spirit were those given to apostles, prophets, teachers, workers of miracles, and healers. That this attitude persisted into the second century is clear from Did. 15, which finds it necessary to plead, "Do not despise them [bishops and deacons], for they are the honored men among you along with the prophets and teachers." Our author will then say that although the functions of the bishop are administrative and liturgical, and although there may be more exalted "gifts," yet the office is not to be looked down upon: it is indeed **a noble task.**

(*c*) Further, since the bishop was the head and representative of the local church,

---

tian church as quite free from the selfish ambitions from which the church tries to purify the world. But the church is made up of human beings who are still struggling with human weaknesses, of which egotistical pride is one of the most insidious and disastrous. Thomas Hardy called this "mundane ambition masquerading in a surplice." [6] Jesus faced among the twelve a dispute as to which would be counted greatest (Matt. 18:1), and Paul faced factions in the church at Corinth (I Cor. 3) which may perhaps not have been altogether unconnected with the ambitions of individual leaders. Here the emphasis is put where it belongs, on the **noble task** which leadership in the church involves. The best cure for ecclesiastical pettiness is a sense of vocation in a great work. Ignatius of Loyola's prayer voices the ambition of the true disciple of Christ: "Teach us, good Lord, to serve thee as thou deservest; to give and not to count the cost; to fight and not heed the wounds; to toil and not to seek for rest; to labor and not ask for any reward, save that of knowing that we do thy will. Amen."

[6] *Jude the Obscure,* Part III, ch. i.

**1. The Office of Bishop.**—The Exeg. points out the difficulty in translating the Greek word ἐπίσκοπος and the changing character of the office to which it refers. This suggests that there was variety in the organization of the early Christian churches. B. H. Streeter writes:

Whatever else is disputable, there is, I submit, one result from which there is no escape. In the Primitive Church there was no single system of Church Order laid down by the Apostles. During the first hundred years of Christianity, the Church was an organism alive and growing—changing its organisation to meet changing needs. Clearly in Asia, Syria, and Rome during that century the system of government varied from church to church, and in the same church at different times. Uniformity was a later development. . . .

It is permissible to hint that the first Christians achieved what they did, because the spirit with which they were inspired was one favourable to experiment. In this—and, perhaps in some other respects—it may be that the line of advance for the Church of to-day is not to imitate the forms, but to recapture the spirit, of the Primitive Church.[7]

[7] *The Primitive Church* (New York: The Macmillan Co., 1929), pp. 267-68. Used by permission.

2 A bishop then must be blameless, the husband of one wife, vigilant, sober, of good behavior, given to hospitality, apt to teach;

task. 2 Now a bishop must be above reproach, married only once,[e] temperate, sensible, dignified, hospitable, an apt

[e] Greek *the husband of one wife.*

---

in times of persecution he would be singled out first. Perhaps because of this arduous responsibility of standing between the church and a hostile world, men were reluctant to offer themselves for the task. There is not much support in the paragraph for this interpretation; however, the emphasis on the bishop's being above reproach, not violent but gentle, and well thought of by outsiders may be regarded as pointing in that direction.

(d) H. B. Swete ("The Faithful Sayings," *Journal of Theological Studies,* XVIII [1916], 3) offers an ingenious interpretation. Vs. 1b, he thinks, may in origin be the apology of an Ephesian Christian who loved the pre-eminence of the bishop's office and sought to justify his episcopal ambitions by pleading, "I desire a noble task." With a bit of irony "Paul" then picks up the saying, affirms its truth (the saying is sure), but, to the probable discomfiture of the aspiring brother, outlines the high qualifications requisite to the office. Theoretically possible, Swete's interpretation is too esoteric to warrant confidence.

(e) Finally, vs. 1b may be taken simply as a somewhat platitudinous introduction to the list of virtues which follows. We may suppose that the writer himself is a bishop who thinks well of his work. He finds in the saying, whatever its origin, both an expression of humility and of appreciation for his noble task. He himself doubtless exemplifies the virtues he enumerates. He is fervently concerned that his fellow bishops measure up to the standard. "Timothy" and his fellow clergymen are to see to it that all candidates for the high office are fully qualified.

2. In Greek the text reads "the" bishop. However, the definite article and the singular number need not mean that at the time the letter was written there was only one bishop in the community. The singular indicates a category. This is the justification

---

One of the barriers to Christian unity is the idea that there was one fixed form of organization in the early church and one definite pattern of orders for the ministry which should be reproduced today. If those interpreters are correct who find evidence for the belief that different churches had different forms of organization, then it ought to be possible to find a way to Christian unity which recognizes diversity of forms within a unity of spirit. Reflection on the difficulties involved in distinguishing between bishop and presbyter in these epistles might well lead to a new emphasis upon such convictions as these: (a) The N.T. envisages one church; (b) it is unity in Christ rather than uniformity that is important; (c) a united church is needed to heal a broken world; (d) the mission of the whole church is to lead the whole world to God in Christ. It is a tragedy when the essential function of the church is impeded by controversies over matters of lesser importance.

A foretaste of what the united church of Christ will mean is given in J. E. Lesslie Newbigin's account of the service in Madras Cathedral at which the United Church of South India was constituted:

We are praying again: "Thou hast heard the prayers of Thy people and blessed the labors of Thy servants, and hast brought us to this day for the glory of Thy name. In obedience to Thy will and led by Thy Spirit, as we accept one another as fellow members and fellow ministers, do Thou strengthen the bonds between us and unite us and make us one body, Thyself, O Christ, being its Head. Make us all of one heart and of one soul, united in one holy bond of truth and peace, of faith and charity." . . . A great peal from the organ breaks in upon the words and in a moment four thousand voices burst into the *Te Deum* in one tremendous shout of praise. All the long-frustrated desires of these last painful years have burst through the dam and are flowing in one irresistible flood. We look at each other with a kind of wonder; we are no longer friendly strangers but brothers in one household. With God all things are possible.[8]

**2-7. The Responsibility of Church Officers.—** In the light of all the uncertainties as to the meaning of the word translated bishop, to which the Exeg. refers, we are justified in considering

[8] *A South India Diary* (London: Student Christian Movement Press, 1951;), p. 23. Published in the United States under the title, *That All May Be One* (New York: Association Press, 1952; "A Haddam House Book"), p. 25. Used by permission.

for the translation **a bishop.** Yet the contrast with the plural **deacons** in vss. 8-13 is noticeable. The variation may be (*a*) purely stylistic and without further meaning; (*b*) due to the source or sources from which the author drew the advices, and therefore accidental; or (*c*) the singular number may indicate a growing concentration of power and authority in the office, which produced the "monarchical" episcopate and finally the papacy.

The difficulty of determining the precise meaning of "bishop" in the Pastorals is due (*a*) to the fact that the letters are more concerned with his character qualifications than with his official functions, and (*b*) to the uncertainty of the date of writing. The later the letters the more highly developed will be the office as presupposed by them. Therefore the proper English equivalent of the Greek ἐπίσκοπος is a moot question. Among modern translators, the term "bishop" is retained by Moffatt and Dibelius; Goodspeed translates "superintendent"; Easton selects "ruler" as the least inadequate translation. The translation should be determined by the date assigned to the letters.

Since the task is a **noble** one, the **bishop** should be a paragon of virtue. He should be **above reproach** (ἀνεπίλημπτος: elsewhere in N.T. only 5:7; 6:14), in the sense of being not liable to public criticism, or "chargeable with no misconduct" (Easton).

**Married only once,** lit., "a husband of one wife" (also 5:9; Tit. 1:6). The meaning of this ambiguous phrase has been debated from ancient times. It has been taken (*a*) as prohibiting (i) concubinage, (ii) polygamy, (iii) remarriage after divorce, (iv) digamy, i.e., a second marriage after the death of the first spouse; or (*b*) as (i) insisting that the bishop shall be a married man, or (ii) more generally, that he shall be an example of strict morality, without more specific denotation (so Dibelius, Scott). In behalf of (*b*) (i) it may be urged that in 4:3, the author contends against those "who forbid marriage" (to the clergy?) and that he urges the marriage of "bishops" and "deacons," among other reasons, as a demonstration to the false teachers that "everything created by God is good" (4:4). While it is obvious that marriage as such is no Christian problem to the author, whether for clergy or laity, and indeed that he takes it for granted (vss. 4-5), this interpretation hardly does justice to **one** (μιᾶς). The basic problem is: What is the force of **one** in the phrase **one wife?**

We may exclude as possible interpretations concubinage, polygamy, and remarriage after divorce, as defined by the church, because these were prohibited to all Christians alike. From its inception, however, the church was confronted by Roman law under which Christians lived and by pagan practices out of which Christians emerged with certain practical problems which made decision difficult in concrete cases. Paul himself ruled that in the case of mixed marriages, "If the unbelieving partner desires to separate, let it be so; in such a case the brother or sister is not bound" (I Cor. 7:15). Would remarriage to a Christian after such separation be considered by the church as the first real marriage? Among adult converts from paganism there would be a good many instances of marital offenses against the Jewish-Christian ideal of strict monogamy, e.g., Hippolytus *Apostolic Tradition* XVI. 24*a* rules concerning new converts: "If a man have a concubine, let him desist and marry legally." Otherwise, he should put her away. But suppose he had more than one concubine and married none of them, but yet another: how would the church count such premarital experiences? The matter was further complicated in the case of slaves, whose marriages, whether the partner was free or servile, were not accorded

---

the possibility that the word applies to lay leaders in the church as well as to the clergy. This passage is a striking illustration of the impossibility of appealing to the practice of the N.T. churches for an authoritative example of church organization, for it is impossible to say whether the word bishop here refers to a lay leader of the church, after the pattern of the elders who made up the Sanhedrin in the Jewish synagogue, or to an ordained minister in charge of a local congregation, or to the later practice of selecting an ordained minister as an overseer of a group of churches. In view of the possibility that the first interpretation is the correct one, we may legitimately draw from these verses helpful suggestions for laymen chosen to office in the church as elders, vestrymen, members of official boards, etc.

First of all, the author exalts the importance of such leadership. No man ought to be re-

the status of *matrimonium* (full marriage) by Roman law. Since the state did not recognize such marriage as indissoluble, should or did the church? As a way of cutting through such a maze of complexity, should the church rule (*a*) that since "by the washing of regeneration and renewal" (Tit. 3:5) the Christian had become a new creature, such offenses before baptism did not count? (*b*) Should it define marriage in such a way as to exclude from the category all unions not validated by the church, whether sanctioned by the state or not? Or (*c*) should it accept as "marriage" any formal union declared by state or society to be such, although not consummated by the church? Or (*d*) should it regard sexual union as in itself constituting marriage? Obviously (*d*) is impossible to manage; (*c*) has been acceded to by the church grudgingly and only where necessary. At one time and place or another, the demands of strict monogamy have been simplified in practice by resort to (*a*) and (*b*), e.g., in the Eastern Church, marriages before baptism were not counted as disqualifications to the priesthood.

The complexity of the background situation, and the ambiguity of the phrase **married only once,** make it difficult if not impossible to decide whether the writer means "not divorced before the present marriage (of course from an unbeliever)" or "not married a second time after the wife's death"—i.e., digamy—or whether he even forbids both. This last view is by and large that of the patristic period, of Thomas Aquinas, and of course of contemporary scholars in the Roman Catholic Church, e.g., Meinertz, Spicq. If the logic of monogamy is "once only," the growth of asceticism with its accompanying ideal of celibacy aided in giving it cogency.

Easton (see his valuable note, "Married only once," *Pastoral Epistles,* pp. 212-15) rejects the meaning "not a digamist" on the grounds (*a*) that as post-Pauline the Pastorals are not to be interpreted out of Paul's advice to the unmarried and the widows of Corinth that if possible they should "remain single as I do" (I Cor. 7:8), or that although a widow "is free to be married, . . . she is happier if she remains as she is" (I Cor. 7:39-40). On the contrary, the author of the Pastorals vigorously denounces those "who forbid marriage" (4:3) and insists that the younger widows (under sixty?) be practically compelled to remarry. If remarriage was desirable for widows, it was equally if not more so for widowers. And (*b*) that as the apocalyptic hope waned, the high Jewish estimate of marriage reappeared in the church. The Pastorals should be read in the light of the later N.T. wholehearted appreciation of the family as seen in the symbolic use made of it in Eph. 5:22–6:4, and in its glorification in John 2:1-11.

To these arguments may be added the unlikelihood that the nonascetic, middle ground, at-home-in-the-world type of piety which characterizes the Pastorals would hold so severe an attitude toward second marriage as to make it a disqualification for church office.

If these arguments have weight, **married only once** will exclude from office all divorced persons, even those whose divorces were sanctioned by the church and allowed to be followed by a second marriage.

It must be admitted, however, that these arguments are not conclusive. Since the phrase **married only once** stands absolutely, without qualifying explanation, it would, given the persistent trends toward celibacy of the clergy in the ancient church, be understood almost immediately to refer to a second marriage quite as much as to a previous one. Indeed, to permit one marriage to the clergy in the circles in Asia where our author

---

garded as too busy with other responsibilities to bear some share of responsibility in the church. The church needs the leadership of its best laymen. Leadership in the church should never be regarded as an alternative to other forms of service, for the church needs on its lay boards men who are capable of carrying responsibility in any line of work and who regard the church as a first claim upon their time and abilities.

Church officers should be people of unquestioned character. There is no support here for the theory that God works through the office regardless of the character of the incumbent. The writer says nothing here about the importance of a particular method for choosing and consecrating church officers. He puts all his emphasis upon Christian life as the prime essential in one chosen to lead in the church of

3 Not given to wine, no striker, not greedy of filthy lucre; but patient, not a brawler, not covetous;

teacher, 3 no drunkard, not violent but gentle, not quarrelsome, and no lover of money.

---

lived may have seemed, if not actually liberal, a moderately generous working rule. That sexual asceticism was appreciated in N.T. times may be seen from Acts 21:9; Rev. 14:4; I Clem. 38:2; Ign. Polyc. 5:2; and of course I Cor. 7. In the end the church honored marriage for the laity and refused it to the clergy.

Since "no drunkard" occurs in vs. 3, **temperate** (νηφάλιον: elsewhere in N.T. only 3:11; Tit. 2:2; νήφω: I Thess. 5:6, 8; II Tim. 4:5; I Pet. 1:13; 4:7; 5:8) should probably be taken here in its wider sense of "sober minded," unless the list of vices is composite and the author indifferent to duplication of ideas.

**Sensible:** See Exeg. on II Tim. 1:7; the word here means "poised," "balanced," "self-controlled."

**Dignified** (κόσμιος) means "well bred"; "well behaved" (Easton); "unruffled" (Moffatt). **Sensible** (σώφρων) and **dignified** are frequently associated in profane literature, e.g., Plato *Gorgias* 508A.

**Hospitable** (φιλόξενος): The necessity of hospitality for the early church is well known. Inns were few and badly equipped. Travel was frequent, for evangelistic and other purposes. Christians were members of one family. Then, too, the homes of Christians were the first meetinghouses (Rom. 16:5; I Cor. 16:19; Col. 4:15). Church officials would have to bear a heavy burden of hospitality; they may at times even have been chosen in part because they were financially able to share their homes in this way.

**An apt teacher** (διδακτικός: elsewhere in N.T. II Tim. 2:24 only). However 5:17 suggests that preaching and teaching were not functions of all ruling elders. Why is nothing said about skill in preaching? Is the idea of teaching as over against preaching evidence of a date or locale when or where the charismatic ministry has given way to a teaching ministry, when the minister was an expositor of doctrine rather than a prophetic preacher?

**3. No drunkard** (πάροινος: only Tit. 1:7 elsewhere in N.T.): In regard to the use of wine, the author takes a middle course: he is opposed to total abstinence on the one hand (5:23), although he there justifies the use of wine only as medicine. On the other hand, he is opposed to drinking to excess. Unless we suppose that the list of virtues here, including **not given to wine,** is on the whole a conventional list not of Christian origin and therefore not to be applied too closely to the actual Christian situation, bishops must have been addicted to drink frequently enough to warrant admonition against it.

**Not violent** or **quarrelsome:** The *Apostolic Constitutions* thought it necessary to decree that "a bishop, elder, or deacon who strikes believers when they sin or unbelievers when they do wrong, desiring by such means to terrify them, we command to be deposed; for nowhere has the Lord taught us to do such things. On the contrary, when he was struck, he did not strike back, 'when he was reviled, he did not revile in return; when he suffered he did not threaten'" (VIII. 47. 28 in Alexander Roberts and James Donaldson, eds., *The Ante-Nicene Fathers* [New York: Charles Scribner's Sons, 1899], VII, 501; VIII. 47. 27 in F. X. Funk, *Didascalia et Constitutiones Apostolorum* [Paderborn: Ferdinand Schoeningh, 1906], I, 570).

**And no lover of money** (ἀφιλάργυρος: only Heb. 13:5 elsewhere): See Luke 16:14; II Tim. 3:2; and Exeg. on 5:17; 6:6-10.

---

Christ. The characteristics which he selects are no doubt reflections of problems known to the early churches, but they have their point always. Note what he considers important: a high ideal in marriage, a serious disposition, self-control,

ability to get along harmoniously with other people, freedom from an obsession with getting money, some demonstration of ability to exert a good influence in his own family, some experience in the church to qualify him for leader-

4 One that ruleth well his own house, having his children in subjection with all gravity;

5 (For if a man know not how to rule his own house, how shall he take care of the church of God?)

4 He must manage his own household well, keeping his children submissive and respectful in every way; 5 for if a man does not know how to manage his own household, how can he care for God's church?

---

**4. Respectful in every way** is best construed with the participle **keeping:** "controlling his children with complete dignity" (Easton). The bishop should not merely keep his children under control and manage the church well, but he should do it with dignity, not resorting to violence to achieve his ends. That the capacity to manage the "great family" well should have been widely recognized as the best credential for official position, whether church or state, is easily understood. Older than either church or state, the family has functioned as both. The patriarchal family is an apt symbol of the church because it too is hierarchical and depends for its smooth functioning on the sincere recognition of assigned and appropriate duties by its various members. The relationships were father and son, husband and wife, elder brother and younger brother. Daughters and sisters were subordinate both to their mother and to all the male members of the family. And of course servants or slaves would be at the base of the system. The system works best when each is content with the station in which he is born. The "great family" approximates its ideal when inferiors are happily submissive and superiors exercise their authority firmly but gently and inconspicuously. Since the father stands at the apex of the system, its success or failure both depends on and tests his ability.

That our author takes it for granted that the bishop will be a married man and the head of a family shows how Jewish and nonascetic the piety of the Pastorals is.

**God's church** (here and 3:15 in the Pastorals) without the definite article in either term (in contrast to Paul's usage) may mean "a (local) church" (Goodspeed, Spicq) or "the church" (Moffatt).

---

ship, freedom from pride, and the respect of the outside world. None of these qualities is without its importance today.

**4-5. *The Christian Family.***—The Christian home is one of the finest flowers of the Christian life, and there is no greater service that a Christian leader can give than to establish and guide such a home. The Christian vocabulary is derived from the family relationship, calling God "Father," Jesus "the elder Brother," a Christian society a "brotherhood," and heaven our "eternal home." One difficulty today in interpreting the richness of the Christian life lies in the fact that these terms have been debased in common usage, and their full meaning is unknown to people to whom the Christian family relationship is unfamiliar. The terms need to be revitalized by convincing demonstrations of their deep meaning.

Today we would amplify Paul's desire that children should be **submissive and respectful in every way.** Obedience and respect for authority are important. But sometimes the submissive child is the repressed child whose quietness gives evidence not of strong character but of an unhealthy mental state which bodes ill for the future. The dynamic energies of children, instead of being dammed up, need to be directed toward worthy ends. The difficult art of Christian education consists in surrounding young people with influences which will enable them to combine (a) obedience to God with the glorious liberty of the children of God; (b) conformity to the mind of Christ with freedom to express the distinctive gifts with which God has endowed each of his children; (c) knowledge of Christian facts and Christian history with receptivity to the more light which God causes to break forth from his holy Word for each new generation; (d) reverence for the revelation of God in times past with the courage to believe that God speaks to every man who has ears to hear and the will to obey; (e) gratitude for what God has done in other days with faith that God has greater things for his people to accomplish in the future; and (f) respect for the experience of an older generation with a purpose to seek first the kingdom of God and his righteousness. Christian education must transmit the knowledge gained by experience and must at the same time release the creative powers of those who are called to press forward

6 Not a novice, lest being lifted up with pride he fall into the condemnation of the devil.

6 He must not be a recent convert, or he may be puffed up with conceit and fall

---

**6.** The word **recent convert** (νεόφυτος) occurs only here in the N.T. Literally, "newly planted," its figurative use is confined to Christian literature. The verse seems to reflect a situation in which new converts in numbers were pressing into the church and with the energy and enthusiasm of converts were crowding the more staid members of long standing for official position. The writer of the letter insists that the episcopal office is to be arrived at in due process of time. Newcomers therefore are not to be permitted to step into line out of turn. How much time would need to elapse before a **recent convert** would cease to be reckoned as **recent** is an unanswerable question. In the early years of the Pauline mission officials would necessarily be recent converts. The advice here given seems better suited to a period later than the Pauline. It may in fact have been prompted by an actual case of a new convert's having been made a bishop and through conceit meeting his downfall.

**The condemnation of the devil** is obscure. The term **the devil** is not used by Paul (but see Eph. 4:27; 6:11). It occurs six times in the Pastorals (here; also vss. 7, 11; II Tim. 2:26; 3:3; Tit. 2:3), three of them being the only plurals of the word in the N.T. (3:11; II Tim. 3:3; Tit. 2:3). In the plural the word is uniformly translated in its usual secular Greek sense, "slanderers." Although in the N.T. outside of the Pastorals διάβολος invariably means opponent or chief opponent in the sense of chief evil spirit (**the devil**), it has been proposed that the word should be interpreted consistently in the Pastorals as **slanderer** (RSV mg.) or human enemy. Then **condemnation** would mean "criticism," and **devil**, a "malicious gossip." While this is linguistically a possible interpretation both here and in vs. 7, the usual translation, **devil**, is better: (a) the obvious meaning of διάβολος in the singular in a Christian writing would be **devil**; (b) to interpret **condemnation of the devil** as "criticism by a gossip" is both too secular and too weak as a motive or as a warning; (c) vs. 7a is mere repetition if vs. 6b simply refers to malicious criticism: "moreover" (vs. 7) signifies "in addition to," not "in other words."

The question still remains: Is **of the devil** subjective or objective genitive? Does it mean that the inflated bishop will fall under the condemnation which the devil has

---

into new knowledge and to greater achievements.

The virtues stressed in this passage are not the heroic, spectacular virtues, but they are essential ones. Writes Ernest F. Scott:

It may be granted that from the Pastoral Epistles we should never guess what Christianity has meant to the saints and mystics. The precepts of the Gospels, the aspirations of Paul and John, are transposed into a lower key. But it may truly be said of this writer that while he compromises he does not abandon anything that is essential. . . . The religion of these Epistles may not be the highest, but in the men and women who have honestly practised it the Church in all time since has found its strength. Because he thus made Christianity a working religion for ordinary men, the author of the Pastorals may justly be ranked among the great Christian teachers.[9]

[9] *The Pastoral Epistles* (New York: Harper & Bros.; London: Hodder & Stoughton, 1936; "Moffatt New Testament Commentary"), p. xxxviii. Used by permission.

**6-7. The Snare of the Devil.**—Without repeating the exegete's discussion of the belief behind the references to the **devil**, two practical considerations may be involved. First, in ancient legends Satan was a fallen angel whose downfall was the result of pride, through which he set himself against God. These legends contain a true insight into the insidious and destructive results of human pride, when man attempts to set himself up as a god and to worship the work of his own hands rather than his Creator and Redeemer. Second, the moral inadequacies of laymen and clergy who make up the church are an asset to the forces of evil that work against the church of God. The most common criticism of the church by **outsiders** is directed against the so-called "inconsistencies of Christians." No one will ever in this world be a perfect Christian. The church is, as F. R. Barry has written, "the home and school both

7 Moreover he must have a good report of them which are without; lest he fall into reproach and the snare of the devil.

8 Likewise *must* the deacons *be* grave, not double-tongued, not given to much wine, and not greedy of filthy lucre;

into the condemnation of the devil;*f* 7 moreover he must be well thought of by outsiders, or he may fall into reproach and the snare of the devil.*f*

8 Deacons likewise must be serious, not double-tongued, not addicted to much wine,

*f* Or *slanderer.*

received or will receive? Or does it mean that he will be handed over to Satan for punishment? The second interpretation accords with 1:20 and is preferable.

**7.** There was constant concern in the early church that the behavior of Christians should be such as to "command the respect of outsiders" (I Thess. 4:12) and to "give no offense to Jews or to Greeks" (I Cor. 10:32; see also Col. 4:5; I Pet. 2:12; 3:1). Ecstatic and unconventional religion is always regarded with disrepute by outsiders; a new religion is always suspect; and Christianity particularly was on trial because of the nature of its origin, its cohesiveness, exclusiveness, and its repudiation of the "world." Christians always had to be concerned about securing the right to survive.

The meaning of vs. 7*b* is obscure. At first glance it seems to mean that the bishop who is a target for hostile criticism from those outside the church is thereby put into a position so delicate and so difficult that he may be tripped up to his own downfall. Just how this might happen is not intimated. Perhaps he might retaliate in kind and thus intensify the opposition of outsiders to Christians. The consequent deterioration of public relations would require the church to depose him. But probably the text is less concerned with the bishop as such than it is with the fact that he stands to the world for the church. To appoint bishops, then, who invite hostile criticism is to fall into the trap which the devil has laid to prevent the growth of the church. Candidates for the office should be carefully screened from the standpoint of skill in public relations.

The repetitiousness in vss. 6-7, **condemnation of the devil** and **reproach and the snare of the devil** (see II Tim. 2:26), suggests composite origin.

## IX. The Character of Deacons (3:8-13)

**8.** As was the case with "bishops" in vss. 2-7, so with **deacons** in vss. 8-13; no definition of duties is given, and the character qualifications are essentially the same. What

of saints and sinners,"[1] but whenever the hostile critics of the church can use the moral failures of church leaders as ammunition against the church, such churchmen have fallen into what this writer calls the **snare of the devil.**

At the close of his autobiography, as he reflected on the stirring times through which he had lived, and looked ahead to the future, John Buchan (Lord Tweedsmuir) observed:

Today the quality of our religion is being put to the test. The conflict is not only between the graces of civilisation and the rawness of barbarism. More is being challenged than the system of ethics which we believe to be the basis of our laws and liberties. I am of Blake's view: "Man must and will have some religion; if he has not the religion of Jesus he will have the religion of Satan, and will erect a synagogue of Satan." There have been high civilisations in the past which have not been Chris-

tian, but in the world as we know it I believe that civilisation must have a Christian basis, and must ultimately rest on the Christian Church.[2]

**8-9. Basic Virtues and High Adventure.**—The Christian church was engaged in a magnificent adventure. It was undertaking to capture the world for Christ. Leaders in such an enterprise must be men whose heroic spirit was founded on character in which the basic virtues of honesty and sobriety were unquestioned. **Deacons likewise must be serious.** The writer of the epistle does not say that they are to be gloomy men or men who have lost all zest in life. "Rejoice in the Lord" (Phil. 3:1) is a characteristic admonition of the great apostle. But just as the highest form of humor is that which finds laughable incongruities in the midst of life's impor-

[1] *The Relevance of the Church* (New York: Charles Scribner's Sons, 1936), p. 67.

[2] *Pilgrim's Way* (Boston: Houghton Mifflin Co., 1940), p. 297. Used by permission of the Tweedsmuir Trustees and the publishers.

importance is to be given to the fact that deacons are not required to be hospitable **or apt teachers** (vs. 2) is uncertain. Not only is real difference of function between bishop and deacon not indicated in the text, but also there is no indication as to which office is superior, unless we are intended to infer superior rank for the bishop because he **is** named first, and because of the greater emphasis on the need for maturity in vss. 6-7. Indeed, the two paragraphs seem almost like doublets, or as if lists of virtues, originally unconnected with any specific office, were applied indiscriminately. Easton thinks the direct source of vss. 1-7 is Tit. 1:6-9, with the awkwardness of wording corrected. The poor arrangement of vss. 8-13 he takes as evidence that the paragraph is the writer's composition, not an extract from a church order.

The vices listed in vs. 8 could easily be acquired by ministers engaged in pastoral visitation. Wine would frequently be served by their hosts; drinking could easily stimulate conversation to the point of gossip, and the pastoral call end in triviality and frivolity. Therefore deacons must be **serious,** i.e., dignified and earnest, **not double-tongued,** saying one thing to one person, something else to another, "not heavy drinkers" (Easton), **not greedy for gain.** Although the church insisted that the laborer was worthy of his hire, yet the common view in antiquity was that the teacher or preacher who accepted money for his services was unworthy. Further, since deacons would collect funds, live from them, and distribute them, it would not always be easy to avoid the temptation to pilfer or the appearance of having done so.

---

tant concerns, so the joy of the Christian is found not apart from but in the thick of Christianity's serious demands. "They are not to be tale-bearers" (Moffatt). Leaders in the church, both lay and clerical, are entrusted with knowledge of the personal affairs of many church members. This is to be kept in the strictest confidence. They are not to be peripatetic gossips, regaling the homes of the congregation with information about other members which the other members do not wish publicized. Nor are they to use information so gained as illustrations in public addresses in ways that would be distasteful to those involved. "Nor addicted to drink or pilfering" (Moffatt). These seem like unnecessary counsels for church officers, but are they? Modern scientific studies of alcoholism show that with people of certain emotional types indulgence in alcoholic beverages easily becomes "compulsive drinking," a habit so gripping and so crippling that only the grace of God, as the Alcoholics Anonymous say, can effect deliverance. No one has yet been able to determine in advance in the case of an individual whether or not he is of the type for whom alcoholism may become a horrible disease. In such a situation a leader in the church will be concerned that he shall not expose other people to the risk of so devastating a calamity. **Not greedy of filthy lucre** is translated by Moffatt as "pilfering." Church leaders are not likely to become shoplifters or petty thieves, if that is the meaning of the word. But in more subtle ways every Christian faces the temptation to something less than strict honesty in matters of money and property—to be careless of truth

in buying and selling, to practice legal but questionable methods of getting something for nothing, to expect special privileges not accorded other people, to deal in black markets in times when goods are rationed, to pay less for services received than they are worth or to demand more for services given than they deserve. Church officers and members should be above question in such basic matters. These fundamental virtues are the foundations on which a Christian society must rise.

The specific virtue which is here demanded of deacons, however, is sincerity. **They must hold the mystery of the faith with a clear conscience.** There is always an element of mystery in "the faith," the body of Christian belief to which the writer refers. We know in part. "Faith," says Theodore M. Greene, "may be defined as whole-hearted belief on the basis of evidence, but not wholly conclusive evidence, and of interpretation which is reasonable, but which falls short of absolute proof." [3] Honest men shrink from presuming to claim to know more than they actually do about the mystery of God and his dealings with men. Such intellectual honesty is the first essential to the gaining of more knowledge. But intellectual honesty equally requires the courage to face the facts that we do have clearly before us. Chief among them is the fact of Christ, in whom God has revealed light on the mystery of his own being and purpose. Having seen the light of the knowledge of the glory of God in the face of

[3] "Christianity and Its Secular Alternatives," in Henry P. Van Dusen, ed., *The Christian Answer* (New York: Charles Scribner's Sons, 1945), p. 76.

9 Holding the mystery of the faith in a pure conscience.

10 And let these also first be proved; then let them use the office of a deacon, being *found* blameless.

11 Even so *must their* wives *be* grave, not slanderers, sober, faithful in all things.

not greedy for gain; 9 they must hold the mystery of the faith with a clear conscience. 10 And let them also be tested first; then if they prove themselves blameless let them serve as deacons. 11 The women likewise must be serious, no slanderers, but temper-

---

**9. Mystery** (elsewhere in the Pastorals only vs. 16) in Paul carried overtones of awe, wonder, and the hush of imminent disclosure, e.g., "Lo! I tell you a mystery" (I Cor. 15:51). However, it has here become merely a technical term, suggesting not that the Christian faith is a revelation to be marveled at, but that it is a body of revealed doctrine to be accepted unfeignedly, **with a clear conscience**. The combination of **faith** and **conscience** is characteristic of this letter (see also 1:5, 19). The reference is simply to the unquestioning acceptance of the received faith.

Although a similar requirement of orthodoxy is not made of the bishop in vss. 2-7, it is found in Tit. 1:9 ff. One may infer that even though no mention is made of the necessity that the deacon be "an apt teacher" (vs. 2), nevertheless the duties of deacons, as Acts makes clear, included teaching or preaching as well as "serving tables."

**10.** Candidates for the diaconate must be examined as to character qualifications before they are approved for the office. Strangely enough, how or by whom the examination is to be given is not said. Whether the examination indicated was a formal one is not clear. It could refer to some sort of questioning at an "ordination" ceremony, or even to some period of probation.

**Blameless** (see Tit. 1:6, 7) may mean "above reproach" or free from the faults named in vss. 8-9; or simply "if no one raises an objection to them."

**11.** Unless we suppose that vs. 11 is totally unrelated to its context, either as a badly integrated interpolation or as material abstracted by the author from a longer source in which change of subject was clearly motivated, **the women** (there is no article in Greek) cannot mean women in general. It must mean either deaconesses or deacons' **wives** (so KJV)—as to which, commentators are well divided.

In support of deaconesses (so Wohlenberg, Lock, Meinertz, Scott, Falconer, Spicq, *et al.*) it may be urged that (*a*) the Pastorals are primarily concerned with church officials; (*b*) the adverb **likewise**, as in vs. 8, introduces a new category parallel to "deacons," etc.; (*c*) the parallel if not identical list of virtues suggests parallel officials; (*d*) it is strange that requirements should be made only of deacons', and not of bishops' wives; and (*e*) the writer would have made his meaning clear by using the personal pronoun "their" with the noun "women" (γυναῖκας αὐτῶν).

In support of "deacons' wives" (so B. Weiss, von Soden, Moffatt, Goodspeed, Jeremias, Easton, *et al.*) it may be urged that (*a*) if deaconesses had been meant, a more specific word would have been used; (*b*) the description of qualifications is too

---

Jesus Christ honest men can hold the mystery of the faith with a clear conscience.

**9. Faith and Conscience.**—Again, as in 1:16, the author of this epistle links faith and conscience as partners not to be separated. Conscience may be unreliable unless it is sensitized by faith in Christ. Conscience may be merely the voice of custom or tradition or social approval or timidity or ambition. It is the man whose deepest motive is faith in Christ whose conscience can be trusted to point to the truth, as a magnetic needle can be trusted to point to the pole. On the other hand, the truest con-

science may be ineffective if it lacks the dynamic of a strong faith. It was such feeble folk that Matthew Arnold described:

Light half-believers of our casual creeds,
  Who never deeply felt, nor clearly willed,
Whose insight never has borne fruit in deeds,
  Whose vague resolves never have been fulfilled;
    For whom each year we see
Breeds new beginnings, disappointments new;
  Who hesitate and falter life away,
  And lose to-morrow the ground won to-day.[4]

[4] "The Scholar Gypsy," st. xviii.

12 Let the deacons be the husbands of one wife, ruling their children and their own houses well.

13 For they that have used the office of a deacon well purchase to themselves a good degree, and great boldness in the faith which is in Christ Jesus.

14 These things write I unto thee, hoping to come unto thee shortly:

ate, faithful in all things. 12 Let deacons be married only once,ᵍ and let them manage their children and their households well; 13 for those who serve well as deacons gain a good standing for themselves and also great confidence in the faith which is in Christ Jesus.

14 I hope to come to you soon, but I am writing these instructions to you so

ᵍ Greek *husbands of one wife.*

---

brief to refer to a category of officials; (c) women officials are treated at length in 5:9-16; (d) the sequence of thought is less awkward if wives rather than deaconesses are meant. Then the subject matter of vss. 8-13 is deacons—deacons' wives—deacons' married and family life; (e) deacons' wives would often accompany their husbands in pastoral visitation and would have the same temptations to gossip and drunkenness. They therefore should be characterized by the same virtues as their husbands.

12. See on vss. 2, 4.

13. **Standing** (βαθμός: only here in N.T.), lit., "base," "foundation," "pedestal" of a statue, "step" or "stair"; figuratively, **degree** or "rank." The word is used to indicate the steps in gnosis (Clement of Alexandria *Miscellanies* II. 9), or steps on the journey to heaven (*Corpus Hermeticum* XIII. 9). In philosophy it is a technical term for a step toward a goal. **To gain a good standing,** then, may mean simply that deacons who do their work well are making steady progress in the Christian faith (**the faith which is in Christ Jesus;** see 1:14), and will find increasing joy and confidence in it. As they gain increased boldness or liberty in preaching, they become the more sure of their salvation.

The verse has been interpreted to mean that the good deacon in serving well gains a good reputation in the church, or may hope thereby to become a bishop. Both of these interpretations, however, seem foreign to the spirit and intent of the text. Easton believes that "in the third century—and doubtless in the second as well—deacons were more highly regarded than elders" (*Pastoral Epistles,* p. 134).

### X. The Church, the Guardian of the Christian Mystery (3:14-16)

14-16. This passage is without grammatical or doctrinal connection with the material which immediately precedes or follows. The verses serve a triple purpose: (a) they reaffirm the personal interest of the writer in the recipients of the letter, furnishing a moment of relaxation and heart warming in the midst of admonitions and arguments; (b) they remind the reader that all practical rules and regulations find their validation

---

Albert W. Palmer has written:

By faith I obviously do not mean mere blind uncritical credulity. . . . No, faith is rather "reason in a courageous mood" as L. P. Jacks has somewhere defined it. It is "betting your life there is a God," to use the words of Donald Hankey, "the beloved captain." Or, as Josiah Royce once put it, "faith is the soul's insight or discovery of some reality that enables a man to stand anything that can happen to him in the universe.⁵

Such faith is the source of power.

⁵ Stanley I. Stuber and Thomas Curtis Clark, eds., *Treasury of Christian Faith* (New York: Association Press, 1949), p. 273.

13. *A Tested Faith.*—The word "deacon" comes from the Greek verb meaning "to serve." The reward of Christian service is **great confidence in the faith which is in Christ Jesus.** Moffatt translates this "great freedom in the faith," and the KJV has **great boldness in the faith.** There is mystery involved in the Christian faith, but to the person who lives a life of Christian service on the basis of the Christian faith there comes increasing confidence in the revelation of truth made in Christ, for it so completely meets his own need and so obviously meets the need of mankind. Thus Paul, in speculative mood, wrote "Our knowledge is imperfect" (I Cor. 13:9), but when he spoke out of his

15 But if I tarry long, that thou mayest know how thou oughtest to behave thyself in the house of God, which is the church of the living God, the pillar and ground of the truth.

that, 15 if I am delayed, you may know how one ought to behave in the household of God, which is the church of the living God,

in the function of the church, which exists to support and protect the truth as revealed in Christ. Although the regulation of behavior in the household of God may seem very matter of fact, even dull and irksome, yet all is transfigured in the light of the great revelation, **the mystery of our religion;** (c) the exalted lyrical statement of the faith in vss. 16 provides a foil in contrast to which the folly of the "doctrines of demons," the "godless and silly myths," denounced in 4:1-8 seems only the more foolish.

Vss. 14-15a are strange at this stage in the letter and can hardly be regarded as indicating adequate motivation for the writing of such a letter as we have. Neither can the real Timothy be supposed to have been so ignorant of church matters as the verses imply. They are best understood as a literary fiction, a device directed to the purposes above outlined (see I Cor. 4:19; Phil. 2:24).

**These instructions** most naturally refer to chs. 1–3, but need not exclude the advice which follows.

Of course Paul was **delayed!** However, in these very words his presence must have seemed very near: he must have seemed about to appear. The word for "delay" (βραδύνω) occurs in the N.T. only here and in II Pet. 3:9.

While **behave** is a comprehensive word covering all the conduct of life, "behavior" here refers primarily to the rules and regulations according to which the church should be ordered, and then to the proper conduct of members of **the household of God,**

own experience, he was more confident: "I know whom I have believed, and am persuaded that he is able to keep that which I have committed unto him against that day" (II Tim. 1:12).

> Whoso has felt the Spirit of the Highest
> Cannot confound nor doubt Him nor deny:
> Yea with one voice, O world, tho' thou deniest,
> Stand thou on that side, for on this am I.[6]

**15. Behavior in the House of God.**—This letter obviously has to do with Christian conduct in all the relationships of life. But when the writer says it is written so that **you may know how one ought to behave in the household of God,** he clearly includes the relationship existing among the members of the church. The church ought to be a demonstration of the spirit of Christian fellowship which the church prays may become the spirit of all human life. If the church seeks to promote in the world at large a spirit of co-operation, absence of self-seeking, mutual burden-bearing, freedom from class and race distinctions, generous sharing of resources, and respect for honest differences, the church must bear a convincing witness to its belief in these virtues in its own fellowship.

[6] Frederic W. H. Myers, *Saint Paul.*

When Paul wrote to the church at Corinth, he had searching criticisms to make of the behavior of church members in their gatherings for worship, even at the Lord's Supper (I Cor. 11:18-22). "Let all things be done decently and in order" (I Cor. 14:40) was his summary of the matter. Modern congregations sometimes need to be reminded that reverence is becoming in the house of God. In nonliturgical churches especially there is need for an occasional sermon interpreting the meaning of worship, and why a service of public worship follows the pattern of adoration, confession, thanksgiving, petition, intercession, and dedication. This is a good text for a children's sermon on "What We Do in Church"—we bow in silent prayer when we enter, we praise God together in hymn and prayer, we hear the Word of God from Scripture and sermon, we offer our gifts and ourselves to God, and we bow or kneel again in silent prayer for God's grace as we leave the house of God.

What such worship demands from its participants has been finely stated by William Temple:

[Worship] calls for all your faculties. It is the use of your mind to work out the revelation of himself that God has given. It is the opening of your imagination that it may be filled with pictures of his glory and of his love. It is the submission of your conscience that it may be quickened and enlightened by his perfect holiness. It is, because of

particularly of church officials. The Greek word translated **household** (οἶκος) holds the meaning "house" as well as "family" (vs. 5). Since the letter gives instructions for the conduct of public worship (2:1-15; 4:13), **house of God** may in the first instance refer to the church as a sanctuary, i.e., "in a church." However, a church is not just a worshiping place, it is a worshiping people. **The house of God** is the household of God, God's family. God's family is not just a family. It is a congregation, a church. And as there is only one church, it is **the church of the living God.** Not only the church in Ephesus is in mind, but the church throughout the world, that church which is **the pillar and bulwark of the truth.**

**The truth** is identified with the Christian faith, which, the writer believes, it is the function of the church to protect and maintain against, e.g., those in 4:1 who have departed from the faith "by giving heed to deceitful spirits and doctrines of demons." The Pastorals stand at the beginning of that long period in Christian history when the church can almost be said to have regarded its chief task as combating heresy. I Clement (end of first century) begins with denunciation of the "abominable and unholy schism" in the church at Corinth. Ignatius (A.D. 98-117) likewise is ever concerned to insist on obedience to the bishop as the most effective way to "shun schisms" (Ign. Mag. 6; Ign. Phila. 7; Ign. Smyr. 8). The historical importance of this concern with correct doctrine can hardly be exaggerated. It was in its pursuit of uniformity in faith that the church wrought out its hierarchy of ecclesiastical orders, its canon of scripture, and its creeds.

---

all these, the subjugation of your will, that he may take you and use you. And you become glad to be used even though you cannot see the purpose for which he is doing it. Sometimes he lets us know but often not. What we should be sure of is that if we truly open our hearts and submit our wills to him, he is working his purpose through us whether or not we ever come to know it.[7]

**15. The Church of the Living God.**—The names by which local churches designate themselves are interesting but often not very significant. Sometimes they are geographical— "Central Church," "Broad Street Church," "Hillside Church," etc. Sometimes they are chronological—"First Church," "Second Church," etc. Sometimes they are personal—"Smith Memorial Church," "St. James's Church," etc. Sometimes they are descriptive—"The Brick Church," "The Stone Church," etc. Sometimes they emphasize Christian virtues—"Grace Church," "Faith Church," "The Door of Hope," etc. Sometimes they are doctrinal—"Trinity Church," "The Church of the Holy Spirit," "The Church of the Redeemer." Here is a description of the church which goes to the heart of the matter—**The church of the living God.** When a church is concerned only with its history, or becomes the slave of a static interpretation of doctrine, or is tempted to become a mildly religious club of congenial people, it needs to be recalled to the worship of **the living God,** who is present and active in his world, who has more truth yet to break forth from his

[7] *Basic Convictions* (New York: Harper & Bros., 1936), p. 20. Used by permission.

Word, and who is summoning his church to partnership in a great task for which he inspires and enables his people.

**15. Pillar and Ground of Truth.**—B. S. Easton renders this, "pillar and support of the truth." Truth is of God, and from one point of view needs no human defense or support. But just as God, who needs no help from men, in the mystery of his providence has made men his fellow workers in the world, so he has entrusted the truth revealed in Christ to his church. Historically it has been the church through which Christ's truth has been transmitted from generation to generation. Actually it is the church which is the **bulwark of the truth** in the world today. Those who wish to see the truth as it is in Christ prevail, and at the same time ignore the church which is the **pillar and bulwark of the truth,** are defying history and closing their eyes to present fact. There are many disagreements among Christian churches as to the exact nature of the truth of which the church is the bulwark but at Amsterdam in 1948 Clarence T. Craig listed seven points of basic agreement:

We all believe that the Church is God's Creation, not man's; that the redemption of this people centers in God's act in Jesus Christ; that the Church is marked by the presence of the Holy Spirit; that the Church has been set apart in holiness as a worshiping community; that the Church is related to two worlds—of forgiven sinners who are at the same time heirs of the Kingdom of God; a ministry which is equipped by God with various gifts of the Spirit; that the Church is one in very nature.[8]

[8] Kennedy, *Venture of Faith*, p. 41.

16 And without controversy great is the mystery of godliness: God was manifest in the flesh, justified in the Spirit, seen of angels, preached unto the Gentiles, believed on in the world, received up into glory.

the pillar and bulwark of the truth. 16 Great indeed, we confess, is the mystery of our religion:

Heh was manifested in the flesh,
vindicatedi in the Spirit,
seen by angels,
preached among the nations,
believed on in the world,
taken up in glory.

h Greek *Who;* other ancient authorities read *God;* others, *Which.*
i Or *justified.*

**16. Mystery** here does not mean "mysterious." It means revealed truth: **Great indeed . . . is the** [revealed truth] **of our** [lit., "the"] **religion** (see vs. 9).

**We confess:** Not just "admittedly great," but "as we confess or declare in public." **Great is the mystery** . . . is the Christian counterpart to the pagan "Great is Artemis of the Ephesians!" (Acts 19:28). The formula was in common use in invocations and confessions of faith.

The six lines which follow are obviously a quotation from a liturgical confession or hymn: (a) vs. 16a is a citation formula; (b) there is no grammatical connection between these lines and vs. 16a. The preferred Greek text reads **who** (RSV)—the unacceptable variants being **God** and **which** (KJV)—thus introducing the hymn with a relative pronoun for which there is no antecedent and showing that we have here a fragment broken off from a longer hymn. (c) The vocabulary used is not characteristic of the Pastorals (φανερόω, πιστεύω, ἀναλαμβάνω). (d) The compact rhythmical phrases, closely parallel in construction, are the language not of prose but of poetry. Each line of the six begins with a verb in the aorist passive third person singular; therefore with identical accent and sound patterns. Five of the six end in similar prepositional phrases—ἐν (in) with the dative—and all without definite articles. The syllables run 8.9.6:8.7.7. The RSV reproduces the style of the Greek perhaps as adequately as it is possible to do.

A precise interpretation of the hymn is not possible because (a) it is a fragment and without a context adequate to clarify its meaning; (b) as poetic, cryptic, liturgical language, it cannot with certainty be translated back into the prose concepts of which it is a distillate. We are not in a position, therefore, to say just what the hymn meant to its author or even to the letter writer. Yet an attempt at analysis must be made.

**He was manifested in the flesh:** The life of Jesus was an "appearing," an epiphany or theophany, God manifest in **flesh,** in human nature and form (see 6:14; II Tim. 1:10; 4:1, 8; Tit. 2:13; John 1:14; 2:11).

**Vindicated in the Spirit:** Both terms of this phrase are perplexing. Taken in its normal Christian sense "justify" or "vindicate" means "to declare or pronounce upright

**16. An Ancient Hymn.**—The rhythmic character of this passage suggests that it may have been part of one of the earliest hymns of the Christian church. From the beginning the Christian church has had a singing faith. This was no doubt due in part to the fact that early Christian worship was patterned after that of the synagogue, in which the chanting of the psalms was an integral part. The hymn sung by Jesus and his disciples at the Last Supper (Mark 14:26) may well have been one of the Passover psalms (Pss. 113–18). But aside from

precedent there was every reason why the Christian community should have sung its faith. The Christian faith is a joyful faith, too joyful for the cold prose of ordinary speech. There was a spirit of unity in the Christian fellowship which was naturally expressed and deepened through music, which touches depths of feeling beyond the reach of words alone. The early church was a missionary church and, as has been often observed, a great cause marches to music and enlists recruits by its songs. Pliny's famous letter to Trajan describing the practices of the Chris-

421

or righteous." Also, in a Christian writing "spirit" is usually the (Holy) Spirit. Taking the two terms in these senses, and interpreting the phrase in immediate connection with the preceding clause, it may mean that although Christ appeared in (sinful) flesh, he was not himself sinful; rather, he was declared righteous by the Spirit. When such a declaration or vindication may have been thought to take place is obscure. Possibly the reference is to the test put to Jesus in the wilderness, whither he "was led by the Spirit," and after which he returned victorious "in the power of the Spirit" (Luke 4:1-14). In Mark 1:13, "the angels ministered to him." However, it seems more suitable to conjecture an event at the end of his life, viz., the Resurrection, as interpreted in Rom. 1:4, where Jesus is "designated Son of God in power according to the Spirit of holiness by his resurrection from the dead." "Vindication" would then be the equivalent of "resurrection," which took place through the Spirit (Rom. 8:11). Quite possibly, however, the connotation of **Spirit** uppermost here may be simply its meaning as opposite to **flesh**. As Christ was manifested in "a physical body" (I Cor. 15:44) =**in the flesh,** he was vindicated or "raised a spiritual body" (I Cor. 15:44) =**in the Spirit.** Dibelius proposes that we should understand **vindicated** (ἐδικαιώθη) as exaltation into the sphere of spirit, the divine sphere of δικαιοσύνη. This would be a use of the Greek word δικαιόω foreign to Paul but similar to usage in Ign. Phila. 8:2 (Heinrich Schlier, *Religionsgeschichtliche untersuchungen zu den Ignatius-briefen* [Giessen: A. Töpelmann, 1929], p. 171), *Corpus Hermeticum* XIII. 9; Odes of Solomon 17:2; 25:12; 29:5; 31:5; cf. Richard Reitzenstein, *Die hellenistischen Mysterienreligionen* (3rd ed.; Leipzig: B. G. Teubner, 1927), pp. 257-58; Rudolf Bultmann, "Die Bedeutung der neuerschlossenen mandäischen und manichäischen Quellen für des Verständnis des Johannesevangeliums," *Zeitschrift für die Neutestamentliche Wissenschaft,* XXIV (1925), 128 ff.

Equally perplexing is the third line, **seen by angels.** It probably does not simply mean that the "vindication" of Jesus by the Resurrection was guaranteed to the church by the testimony of "two men . . . in dazzling apparel" (Luke 24:4) or "two men . . . in white robes" (Acts 1:10). Nor does one seem to do full justice to the phrase by supposing that Christ appeared merely to the angels around the throne, who number "myriads of myriads and thousands of thousands" (Rev. 5:11-12), whose pleasure is all to adore the Lamb. Rather, the exaltation of Christ appears to be set forth in terms of triumph over the spirit world: Phil. 2:9-10; Col. 2:15. Having ascended gloriously to heaven, he is presented to the heavenly hosts, whose superior he is (Heb. 1–2). Perhaps in the background of thought, angels are conceived as beings of decidedly lesser rank, if not indeed the "principalities" and "powers," the "world rulers of this present darkness," "the spiritual hosts of wickedness in the heavenly places" (Eph. 6:12). Thus, when the Lord of Glory appeared to the angels, it was as their conqueror and lord.

The incarnate and exalted Lord was **preached among the nations,** i.e., to all the world. The language is chosen to emphasize the universal extent of Christian preaching. And **believed on in the world** will indicate that the preaching was met with faith on the part of the people.

The concluding refrain, **taken up in glory,** seems chronologically out of place. The phrase naturally refers to the Ascension, but this took place before the mission to the Gentiles, not after. No really satisfactory solution to this problem of arrangement

---

tians in Bithynia in the second century included among other descriptive comments the statement that "they sing a hymn to Christ as God." [9] There are references to the singing of hymns in I Cor. 14:26; Eph. 5:19; Col. 3:16. Other rhythmical passages in the N.T. which may have been early Christian hymns are I Tim. 6:15-16; II Tim. 2:11-13; Eph. 5:14; Rev. 5:13. The

[9] Pliny the Younger *Letters* XCVI.

Bible and the hymnbook have gone together through Christian history as the springs from which the devotional life of the church has drawn. The singing of hymns is an act of devotion, not simply an aesthetic experience. But hymns should be appropriate to the worship of God. The text of hymns should be good English, good poetry, and good doctrine, expressing religious experience in simple, clear, devout terms

is available. Scott (*Pastoral Epistles,* p. 42) proposes that **taken up in glory** should be interpreted to refer not to the Ascension, which has already taken place, but to the time of the final consummation "after the harvest is fully gathered in," when Christ "will enter on His eternal Kingdom with His whole work gloriously accomplished." Since, however, **taken up in glory** is a technical term in the N.T. for the Ascension, Scott's interpretation here is most unlikely.

Perhaps too much emphasis should not be put on the temporal sequence of the lines. **Taken up in glory** may function simply as a proper poetic parallelism to the previous refrain **seen by angels,** as in Hebrew poetry, and without concern for time sequence.

In form the hymn may have been patterned (unknowingly) after the ancient Egyptian enthronement ceremony (so Jeremias, Spicq), consisting of three acts: First, Exaltation: the new king receives divine attributes in solemn ceremony (the incarnate Lord was exalted by the Resurrection to the divine mode of being). Second, Presentation: the now deified king is presented to the circle of the gods (the announcement of Christ's lordship was made to angels in heaven and peoples on earth). Third, Enthronement: to him is given the rule (Christ was enthroned at the right hand of God, in glory, Lord of those who believed).

It is further possible that the content of the hymn was phrased to contrast the Christian Lord with Artemis of Ephesus (so Spicq). It is known from the inscription that there was a hymnode of the great Artemis. It was the function of such singers, as well as those of the imperial cult, to fashion and to sing, particularly on festival occasions, adulatory hymns in honor of their cult gods. The church claimed all high epithets for Christ alone. Not only vs. 16*a*, but other details may be in intended contrast to the worship of Artemis: **flesh** and **Spirit** contrast strikingly with the stone fallen from heaven, the origin of the Artemisian cult; that Christ should be worshiped by angels, peoples, the world, emphasizes the universalism of Christianity as over against the pretended universalism of the Artemis cult (Acts 19:27); and if Ephesus is "temple keeper of the great Artemis, and of the sacred stone that fell from the sky" (Acts 19:35), the Christian's Lord is glorious in heaven.

---

in which congregations can join sincerely and heartily. The music should be dignified, not too difficult for ordinary groups of people to sing, and possessed of a religious quality hard to define but not hard to recognize. Words and music should be such that a congregation can join in them in the spirit of Paul's counsel, "Singing with grace in your hearts to the Lord" (Col. 3:16).

In the early eighteenth century, when the chanting of psalms was the prevailing form of religious singing in the Church of England, William Law advised everyone to begin private devotions with a psalm:

You are . . . to consider this chanting of a psalm as a necessary beginning of your devotions, as something that is to awaken all that is good and holy within you, that is to call your spirits to their proper duty, to set you in your best posture towards heaven, and tune all the powers of your soul to worship and adoration.

For there is nothing that so clears a way for your prayers, nothing that so disperses dulness of heart, nothing that so purifies the soul from poor and little passions, nothing that so opens heaven, or carries your heart so near it, as these songs of praise.

They create a sense and delight in God, they awaken holy desires, they teach you how to ask, and they prevail with God to give. They kindle a holy flame, they turn your heart into an altar, your prayers into incense, and carry them as a sweet-smelling savour to the throne of grace. . . .

A man's singing of a psalm, though not in a very musical way, may yet sufficiently answer all the ends of rejoicing in, and praising God. . . . Our blessed Saviour and His Apostles sang a hymn; but it may reasonably be supposed, that they rather rejoiced in God, than made fine music.[1]

This particular hymn (vs. 16) was a creed set to music. Without analyzing it in detail, we can identify here three main affirmations which need continual reaffirmation: the revelation of God's truth in the man Christ Jesus; the universal validity of Christ's gospel for all mankind; and the eternal supremacy of Christ in the unseen world.

[1] *Serious Call to a Devout and Holy Life,* ch. xv.

Now the Spirit speaketh expressly, that in the latter times some shall depart from the faith, giving heed to seducing spirits, and doctrines of devils;

2 Speaking lies in hypocrisy; having their conscience seared with a hot iron;

Now the Spirit expressly says that in later times some will depart from the faith by giving heed to deceitful spirits and doctrines of demons, 2 through the pretensions of liars whose consciences are seared,

## XI. FALSE TEACHERS AND DEMONIC DOCTRINES (4:1-5)

**4:1.** Once again, and more specifically than elsewhere in the letter, the author takes up the cudgels against heresy. Although the text does not specifically say the prophecy **that in later times some will depart from the faith** is already being fulfilled, that is his meaning. The **later times,** in which he believes he is living, are the "last days" of apocalyptic (II Tim. 3:1; Mark 13:5, 6, 22, 23). The usual N.T. form is "last" (ἔσχατος). The use of the comparative **later** (ὕστερος; its superlative ὕστατος does not occur in N.T.) may be interpreted as revealing the intention of the author to suggest that the "last times" are later than Paul's time, but this is probably oversubtle.

The apocalyptic view of history is pessimistic, i.e., the world is to become progressively worse until the great catastrophe which ends it. The last days are the worst days. Within such a frame of reference apostasy was expected and, when observed, was regarded as evidence of the nearness of the end.

There is no need to ask where or when the **Spirit expressly** predicts apostasy; such predictions are characteristic of most apocalypses (Mark 13:22; II Thess. 2:4; I John 2:18; etc.).

The heretical teachings have a demonic origin. Man is subject either to God or to the devil: there is no neutral ground on which he may stand. To **depart from the faith** is therefore to fall from the realm of God into the domain of **deceitful spirits.** Since doctrines derive either from God through true prophets or from demons through false prophets, heresies can be only the **doctrines of demons. The faith:** the Pastorals assume that Christianity is a well-defined body of teaching; anything contrary to it is demonic doctrine.

**2.** Not only are the heretical teachers under demonic control, but they are themselves **liars,** hypocrites, who feign the truth. They cannot be excused from responsibility—even though they are in the devil's power. They are inveterate liars because their **consciences are seared,** i.e., burned into insensitivity to the difference between truth and error.

---

**4:1. *Seducing Spirits.***—With an honest realism the epistle recognizes the fact that some who have accepted Christian faith will fall away, **giving heed to seducing spirits.** The particular danger in mind is that which comes from false teachings undermining the faith. These are discussed in succeeding verses. This general statement, however, may well suggest other **seducing spirits** that lure Christians from their faith: the secular spirit, which assumes that the world of things is an end in itself, with no spiritual meaning, and no spiritual goal; the spirit of pride, which prompts a man to put himself first in the universe, so blocking his vision of God; the spirit of greed, which sells out the great causes for the immediate material rewards; the fearful spirit, which prefers safety to achievement and will take no hazard for the sake of the thing not seen with the eyes.

Writing of the attempt to climb Mount Everest, and of the gallantry of the mountaineers who have made the venture, Hugh Rutledge has said:

The mere healthy materialist has no place in such company, and I think Everest will have none of him. When the real strain comes, his appetites will hold him back while the men of ideals go forward, supported at the last by that power of the spirit which surpasses the physical.[2]

So likewise with men seeking the kingdom of God, who seek high goals in life. Only a spiritual faith can hold them fast when the **seducing spirits** tempt them.

**2. *Conscience Which Does Not Function.***—Again the writer returns to the problem of faith and conscience, indicating that true faith

[2] Quoted by James Ramsay Ullman, ed., *Kingdom of Adventure: Everest* (New York: William Sloane Associates, 1947), p. 370.

3 Forbidding to marry, *and command-ing* to abstain from meats, which God hath created to be received with thanksgiving of them which believe and know the truth.

3 who forbid marriage and enjoin absti-nence from foods which God created to be received with thanksgiving by those who

---

It is tempting to translate the Greek verb meaning **seared** as "branded" like criminals or runaway slaves: the heretical teachers really belong to Satan and, if not outwardly on their foreheads, are so branded on their consciences (so Lock, Dibelius, Scott, Easton; *vs.* Goodspeed, Moffatt). Picturesque as this interpretation is, the transla-tion of the RSV fits the text more closely.

3-4. Although the author of the Pastorals nowhere gives a detailed account of the heretical teachings against which he is exercised, the question of marriage or celibacy and of enjoyment of or abstinence from foods stands as the chief symbol of the conflict. The intensity with which abstinence from marriage, food (flesh?), and wine is repudi-ated, indicates an important underlying although not fully explicit religious and philosophical disagreement.

In regard to the enjoyment of sex and foods three distinct points of view asserted themselves: The common mind of the Greco-Roman world assumed in a form which we should regard as somewhat crude a psychophysical dualism of mind-matter, soul-body, spirit-flesh. The higher values then as now were associated with the mind-soul-spirit term. Since salvation was a function of soul or spirit, thought of generally in the Greek tradition as immortal, the body or the "flesh" was demoted to an inferior status as belonging to the world of change and decay, and frequently as evil or as the nexus through which evil and corruption enter man to destroy him. The interpretation of salvation as the soul's redemption from "this body of death" prompted many earnest Christians to an intense and single-minded affirmation of God and the soul through utter renunciation of the "flesh" with its demands and desires. When such a radical dualism was carried to its logical conclusion in a cosmology according to which the good God could not have created the material evil world, repudiation of the latter seemed required if one was to be certain of full salvation. One practical result of this type of religious earnestness was to renounce marriage and to abstain from foods, particularly flesh and wine, so far as abstinence was possible, i.e., to sever connections with the material world to the extent that life permits.

A second point of view seems to have attributed neither religious value nor disvalue to the natural world. Religion had to do essentially with the inner man; the Christian, assured of salvation in the church, could do what he wished without sin. The problems in Corinth which excited Paul seem to have had their origin in this point of view. The "strong," who believed that all things were lawful, not only ate without scruple but got drunk at the Lord's Supper. The sexual aberrations also indulged in would be justified

---

and sensitive conscience go together. This time he refers to those **whose consciences are seared.** Just as the nerves of a part of the body may suffer injury so that they lose all feeling, so the conscience may be dulled and cease to be an inward monitor. Sometimes it is in a specific area that the conscience is dead. John Newton, who wrote the hymn "How sweet the name of Jesus sounds," was during part of his life cap-tain of a ship engaged in the slave trade, and is said to have sat in his cabin reading his Bible and singing hymns while the slaves were herded like cattle in the hold below decks. The history of God's dealings with men is the record of the progressive awakening of conscience in new

areas—the position of women and children, the rights of labor, the relationship of nations to each other, the equality of races, etc. Sometimes all moral sense seems to be deadened by a de-graded faith or a self-centered life. Henry Sloane Coffin quotes a Chinese official in the early days of the republic as saying, in reply to an inquiry, that the distinctive quality about Jesus seemed to him to be his "power to create a more deli-cate conscience." [3]

3-5. *The Right Use of Creation.*—Every gen-eration faces the problem of the misuse of things which, good in themselves, when abused disrupt

[3] *God Confronts Man in History* (New York: Charles Scribner's Sons, 1947), p. 33.

4 For every creature of God *is* good, and nothing to be refused, if it be received with thanksgiving:

believe and know the truth. 4 For everything created by God is good, and nothing is to be rejected if it is received with thanks-

by the belief that the spiritual man is not judged by any man, that religion has nothing to do with "morality." This point of view, to the extent that it was honest, might rest either upon the belief that whatever is, is good, or that the power of the Spirit working in man is so great that no matter what a man does, his inner life cannot be contaminated by anything external or material. To the pure all things are pure.

The third point of view, which may be regarded on the whole as the normal Christian view, stands between the first two, and is essentially the view of the Pastorals. It is basically Jewish in that it affirms the goodness of the created world as described in the sevenfold refrain of Gen. 1, deriving that goodness from God as creator, and in that it accepts God's words, "I have given you every plant . . . and every tree . . . for food" (Gen. 1:29); and "every moving thing that liveth shall be food for you" (Gen. 9:3). It is un-Jewish in that it has rejected the Levitical distinction between "clean" and "unclean" foods, and therefore insists that there are no foods from which a Christian need abstain: **For everything created by God is good, and nothing is to be rejected** ("tabooed," Moffatt). The world was **created to be received with thanksgiving by those who believe and know the truth,** i.e., by Christians.

The Christian, then, should live affirmatively, enjoying life as God made it. He should neither renounce it nor abandon himself to it, but by wise and moderate use of

character. The particular questions raised here have to do with sex and food, but man's attitude toward the whole physical world and its products is involved. The extreme naturalist says that all natural appetites and inclinations are good and are to be indulged. The extreme ascetic says that all natural appetites and inclinations are bad and are to be repressed. Both are wrong. Evidently it was the ascetic attitude which had appeared in the early church, and it was against this mistaken view that the writer of the epistle set himself. **Everything created by God is good, and nothing is to be rejected if it is received with thanksgiving; for then it is consecrated by the word of God and prayer.** He refers to the custom of using words of Scripture and prayer as a blessing before partaking of food. This should be man's attitude in the use of all God's gifts. To receive them with thanksgiving to God, to govern their use by the teaching of God's Word, to ask for God's blessing upon our use of what he has created, is to follow the path of self-control, consideration for others, and intelligent recognition of the personal and social consequences of what we do.

This takes us into the central problems facing modern civilization. Nothing less than the survival of civilization depends upon the right use of God's creation. Shall man's discovery of the means for sending messages through the air carry the impulses of friendship or of ill will? Will the radio and the television set make the human mind trivial, kill the imaginative faculties that see pictures on a printed page, and

produce a generation of morons? Will the conquest of the air result in speedy relief for the suffering, deeper understanding among distant peoples, and a world becoming a spiritual neighborhood, or did Orville Wright's achievement simply constitute the prelude to the bomber and the destruction it can leave behind? Is the release of the energy stored in the atom to mean a better life for the submerged masses, or is it to mean the wiping out of all that we call civilization? We need a new acknowledgment that these are all the gifts of God, to be **received with thanksgiving** and **consecrated by the word of God and prayer** to uses in accord with his purpose revealed in Jesus Christ.

Emil Brunner has pointed out that

every invention is an increase in power, and every increase in power within society is a danger to its balance and order. . . . Where the means become more important than the end, where technics becomes autonomous, a social disease develops, which is analogous to cancer. . . . The perversion of the order of means and ends was caused by the decay of the consciousness of personality. And this in its turn was the consequence of the decay of Christian faith. . . . You cannot cure a demon-ridden technical world with moral postulates. In contrast to mere ethics and morality, Christian faith has the dynamic of passion, of surrender and sacrifice; it is capable of turning men to the eternal end, of unmasking demonic sin and thereby banning it, which no enlightened education is capable of doing.[4]

[4] *Christianity and Civilisation* (London: James Nisbet; New York: Charles Scribner's Sons, 1949), II, 11, 13, 15. Used by permission.

| 5 For it is sanctified by the word of God and prayer. | giving; 5 for then it is consecrated by the word of God and prayer. |

it consecrate both himself and it. "Give me neither poverty nor riches" is his prayer. "If we have food and clothing, with these we shall be content" (6:8).

**5.** And yet, **good** although the created world is, it is not absolutely good: before it is truly good for the Christian, it must be **received with thanksgiving,** i.e., it must be **consecrated** or made holy **by the word of God and prayer.** The good becomes the holy when it is dedicated to God's service and when the blessing of God hallows it.

**Thanksgiving** (on Jewish "thanksgivings" see the valuable note of Easton, *Pastoral Epistles,* pp. 141-43) refers primarily to "giving thanks" before eating, although Jewish marriage thanksgivings are extant, and we may suppose that Christians used similar forms. Is **the word of God** the prayer uttered over the food (Moffatt)? Or does it mean "through God's utterance," "with God's blessing upon it," referring directly to Gen. 1 (Lock; Easton after Gen. 1:31)? Or does it refer to some scripture verse used in giving thanks (Dibelius, Scott)—e.g., Ps. 24:1; I Cor. 10:26?

Since, as we have seen, marriage and foods are the chief symbols of the conflict between the writer and the heretical teachers, we should not expect the author to weaken his affirmation of them by qualifying their use beyond the general statement of the necessity of their consecration; e.g., the propriety of fasting does not come into view. Nor should any importance be attached to the fact that the author does not appeal to Mark 7:15 (cf. Rom. 14:14) or to the arguments of Col. 2:20 ff. This may account, too, for the complete absence of any suggestion of Paul's special problem with regard to food offered to idols (I Cor. 8). The appeal to Genesis, however, suggests a different and more fundamental problem than either the Jewish-Christian problem of the Jewish food laws or the Jewish-Gentile problem of eating food "offered to idols." The error which the writer will combat is that of the radical (Gnostic) dualism as outlined above (see on vss. 3-4).

Likewise, if the writer does not here state in any comprehensive way his views about marriage, it is because he does not want to weaken by qualifying statements his affirmation that marriage is ordained of God. That he regards marriage as the normal state is clear from his expectation, if not insistence, that the bishop, and various others, be married (2:15; 5:14; Tit. 2:4). There is no indication that the Pauline view, as expressed in I Cor. 7, that it is better, "in view of the impending distress," for the unmarried and widows to remain single if they can exercise self-control, is shared by our author. The apocalyptic motive for remaining unmarried is completely absent. On the contrary, younger widows are encouraged to marry (5:14), not, it must be admitted, because marriage is regarded in itself as the more desirable state, but for fear that if they are enrolled as widows, they will "grow wanton against Christ" and "desire to marry," thus incurring condemna-

One of the false teachings which disturbed this Christian teacher was the forbidding of marriage by those who had accepted the idea that the physical life is inherently evil and only the spiritual life good. There are branches of the Christian church today which hold that the celibate life is on a higher plane than the marriage state. There is no justification for this in the teaching of Jesus (see Matt. 19:4-6). The problem today, however, is not so much that of people who dishonor marrage by preferring celibacy as it is that of people who dishonor marriage by taking its obligations lightly, treating this relationship entered into before God as though it were a trivial and unimportant bond

of union. There are some fundamental Christian truths about marriage which are brought into high relief by the paganism of our times: Marriage is a lifelong union entered into by a man and a woman before God, to whom vows of loyalty are reverently given. Marriage is a spiritual and physical union, the sharing of all life in love. Marriage is a partnership of equals, in which each partner finds his highest joy in the other's happiness, and doubles his own wealth by all that he gives the other. Marriage finds its natural setting in a home, and its abiding satisfaction in children in whom the spirit of the home is re-created. Marriage is a partnership of human beings and therefore de-

**6** If thou put the brethren in remembrance of these things, thou shalt be a good minister of Jesus Christ, nourished up in the words of faith and of good doctrine, whereunto thou hast attained.

**6** If you put these instructions before the brethren, you will be a good minister of Christ Jesus, nourished on the words of the faith and of the good doctrine which

---

tion (5:11-12) by abandoning their religious vocation. Whether or not our author would have opposed Paul's recommendation of celibacy in certain cases is not clear. He probably would not have done so. What he is insisting upon in the letter is that the Christian (bishop?) should not be denied the privilege of marrying—once—if he wanted to, the implication being that most men wanted to and did.

If the statement in *Apostolic Constitutions* VIII. 47. 51 is not an accurate expression of our author's view, it is not too radical a development of the logic of it: "If any bishop, elder or deacon or anyone of the clergy abstains from marriage, meat, or wine, not through self-discipline, but through abhorrence of them as evil in themselves, forgetting that 'all things are very good' and that 'God made man male and female,' and thus blasphemously repudiating creation, either let him amend or be deposed and cast out of the church; likewise for a layman also." What we may call the standard view of the church is that nothing is good or evil in itself, but only with reference to function or use or end; whatever may be truly consecrated to the service of God is holy. This point of view provides for, even requires, both self-denial and the enjoyment of the natural world.

### XII. The Good Minister of Christ Jesus (4:6-10)

**6. These instructions** (ταῦτα) occurs frequently in the Pastorals (vs. 11; 3:14; 5:7; 6:2; 6:11; II Tim. 2:14; Tit. 2:15). Although the word indicates a summary, its reach is somewhat vague. It will always include at least the immediately preceding paragraph. The **instructions** are those of vss. 1-5, reaffirmed in vss. 7-10. The author again addresses "Timothy" (see 1:18; 3:14; 5:21), thus personalizing and pointing the advices. Are **the brethren** church officials, clergymen, or Christians in general, including women?

Is **minister** (διάκονος) a technical term or simply "servant" (Scott, Goodspeed, Easton)? If the letter is really directed to church officials through "Timothy," the verse will mean that all ministers (deacons) who insist on the rejection of the heretical doctrines and hold fast to the received faith will be good ministers.

The verb for **nourished on** is present participle, "being nourished on," and is practically synonymous with "living in" (Dibelius) or "on" (Goodspeed). Since "Timothy" throughout the letters is in character as a young man of devout Christian family (vs. 12; II Tim. 1:5; 3:15), the phrase may refer to his bringing-up; the present participle, however, may be adequately interpreted by Chrysostom: "For as we set before us day by day our bodily nourishment, so, he means, let us be continually receiving

---

mands mutual adjustments, forgiveness, understanding, and new beginnings. Marriage is a bond which at its best grows stronger when difficulties must be met and the rosy dreams of youth become the realities of the years. Christian marriage is not adding together two selfish people in the vain hope that together they can find the happiness they have missed alone; it is plighting the troth of two people who have previously committed themselves to Christ and now give themselves jointly to him, to be used by God in the service of his kingdom. In Christian marriage God's good gift of life abundant reaches its finest and noblest manifestation.

**6-8. Going into Training.**—It is the function of the **good minister of Jesus Christ** to "lay all this before the brotherhood" (Moffatt). This applies equally to the ordained minister and to the lay leader in the church. It is not clear which the writer had in mind. In either case, the "good servant of Christ Jesus," as Easton translates the phrase, must "train for the religious life" (Moffatt). Just as an athlete trains for a contest, building up his body by nourishing food and strenuous exercise, so the contender for the Christian cause must keep himself spiritually fit. He must be **nourished on the words of the faith and of the good doctrine.** As the Exeg.

**7** But refuse profane and old wives' fables, and exercise thyself *rather* unto godliness.

**8** For bodily exercise profiteth little: but godliness is profitable unto all things, having promise of the life that now is, and of that which is to come.

you have followed. **7** Have nothing to do with godless and silly myths. Train yourself in godliness; **8** for while bodily training is of some value, godliness is of value in every way, as it holds promise for the pres-

---

discourses concerning the faith, and ever be nourished with them" (*Homilies on Timothy* XII).

**The words of the faith:** "The principles of the faith" (Goodspeed); "the truths of the faith" (Moffatt). By daily feeding upon the received faith and the **good**, i.e., approved, **doctrine** which he has diligently studied and perseveringly practiced, "Timothy" will continue to be a **good minister.**

**7-8.** Repudiation of false teachings recurs almost like a refrain in these letters. On **myths,** see Exeg. on 1:4. The **myths** in which denial of marriage and abstinence from foods are grounded are **godless,** i.e., secular or **profane.** They pretend to be religious but actually have nothing to do with religion. They are **silly,** like **old wives' fables,** and deserve no credence whatever. Instead of listening to such absurd chatter, "Timothy" shall discipline himself **in godliness,** religion. **Train** originally meant to **exercise** physically, but in Stoic and other writings it is used metaphorically for any kind of training or discipline. The emphasis is characteristic of the Pastorals: Religion is not speculation; it is discipline.

Vss. 7*b* and 8 are closely connected through the idea of **training,** though just how is not certain. If vs. 8 is the **sure saying** of vs. 9 (so Lock, Dibelius, Goodspeed, Scott), and is thus a quotation, vs. 7*b* will have been prompted by the desire to integrate the quotation into the paragraph. In its original Hellenistic form the saying would reflect the Cynic-Stoic opposition to the excessive bodily training of athletes, over against which would be set some spiritual activity such as philosophy (Dibelius). Vss. 8*b* and *c*, however, indicate that in its present form the saying is Jewish or Christian. **Godliness** would be a Christian substitute for, say, philosophy. The phrase **for the present life and also for the life to come** is obviously Jewish or Christian (Pirke Aboth 4:22; Luke 18:30). The quotation need not have included more than vs. 8*ab*; vs. 8*c* could be the interpretative comment of the letter writer.

The text is not really interested in affirming the value of athletic training. The point is that since bodily training is of such slight value, men ought to devote themselves to religion, which is **of value in every way,** i.e., **it holds promise for the present life and also for the life to come. Bodily training** has to do only with the present life.

It has been proposed (so Easton) that **bodily training** here really refers to the ascetic discipline rejected in vss. 1-5, and that "of little value" really means "of no value at all." But such an interpretation of **bodily training** is most unlikely: (*a*) the expression

---

indicates, the participle is present and denotes a continual process: "being nourished on." The Christian must feed his mind and spirit on the Word of God as a steady diet. William R. Inge once wrote:

It is quite natural and inevitable that if we spend sixteen hours daily of our waking life in thinking about the affairs of this world, and about five minutes in thinking about God and our souls, this world will seem about two hundred times more real than God or our souls.[5]

[5] *Religion and Life* (New York: D. Appleton & Co., 1923), p. 4.

The older translation seems to indicate a depreciation of physical exercise hardly borne out by the athletic metaphors which star Paul's epistles, revealing either an interest in games on Paul's part, or a recognition of such interest as a legitimate attitude on the part of his readers. The more recent translations make it plain that what is intended here is simply an affirmation of the greater importance of spiritual training. **While bodily training is of some value, godliness is of value in every way.** Man is more than a body. Life is more than threescore years and ten. A man who recognizes the importance

**9** This *is* a faithful saying, and worthy of all acceptation.

**10** For therefore we both labor and suffer reproach, because we trust in the living God, who is the Saviour of all men, specially of those that believe.

ent life and also for the life to come. **9** The saying is sure and worthy of full acceptance.

**10** For to this end we toil and strive,*j* because we have our hope set on the living God, who is the Savior of all men, especially of those who believe.

*j* Other ancient authorities read *suffer reproach*.

---

is the normal one for exercise in the games; (*b*) if vs. 8 or part of it is the **sure saying**, **bodily training** could not have had any other than an athletic reference in an epigram; (*c*) the writer has just denounced Gnostic asceticism too vehemently to permit him to encourage the thought that it is "of some value" or "of little value," or to permit him to allow an ambiguous quotation to weaken the force of his repudiation. The problem of **bodily training** is best solved not by denying to it its normal meaning, but by regarding the sentence as a quotation, the **sure saying** of vs. 9, somewhat incoherently introduced into the section.

**9.** For reasons given above, the **sure saying** is probably all or part of vs. 8 (see on 1:15; 3:1).

**10.** The Christian toils and strives, or wrestles—continuing the athletic figure—not for "a perishable wreath" (I Cor. 9:25), but for life, now and in the age to come.

---

of physical fitness should see the value of being fit for the larger life.

This spiritual training holds promise **for the present life and also for the life to come.** The linking of life on earth and the future life is significant. Often the two are set in sharp contrast. In a sense that is inevitable, as is suggested by the words finite and infinite, temporal and eternal, the world and heaven. But they are two parts of one whole, and each demands the other. Agnosticism looks at this world without a dynamic faith in the eternal world. "One world at a time" was Thoreau's comment when a friend spoke to him of life after death. Otherworldliness looks upon this world as a vale of tears to be endured for the sake of a heavenly reward. But here godliness is represented as the way to abundant life in this world as well as the way to eternal life. Jesus spoke of eternal life in the present tense, as well as in the future. "This is eternal life, that they know thee the only true God, and Jesus Christ whom thou hast sent" (John 17:3). Eternal life is often regarded as having only one dimension, length. But mere existence of infinite duration is not eternal life. In the Christian sense it is four-dimensional. It has breadth—wide outlooks, far-ranging interests, inclusive sympathies. It has depth—deep and solid foundations, resources which go below the surface of life and tap the inexhaustible springs of God. It has height—fellowship with God, "a house not made with hands, eternal in the heavens" (II Cor. 5:1). It has length—eternal life can begin now and never end. Our present life is the richer because of this prospect. The

future life is credible because we can know the eternal Love from which neither death nor life can separate us.

**10.** *The Motive of Sacrifice.*—Get at the motives from which a man's conduct springs, and you are getting near to the real man. When people throw themselves into apparently impossible tasks and accomplish them there must be some adequate dynamic behind their effort. The miracle of the first century was the expansion of Christianity across the Mediterranean world. It did not come about by accident, but under God by the deliberate intent of the little company of Christians who set out to bring the whole world under the lordship of Christ. Why did men dare to undertake a task apparently so impossible? **For to this end we toil and strive, because we have our hope set on the living God.** Wrote Elton Trueblood:

Once there were a few unlettered men in an obscure province, and their movement was obviously a failure; for their Leader had been executed! Yet something so remarkable happened that, within a generation, these men and others like them were beginning to make a difference in the entire Hellenic-Roman world. They brought to a civilization suffering from a sense of futility a genuine lift and, finally, when the Roman power fell into decay, they provided the main structure of faith upon which civilization could be rebuilt.[6]

This is well called the "alternative to futility."

**10.** *The Universal Savior.*—Who is the **Savior of all men** obviously indicates a belief in God's concern for the salvation of men of

[6] *Alternative to Futility*, pp. 28-29.

11 These things command and teach.

12 Let no man despise thy youth; but be thou an example of the believers, in word, in conversation, in charity, in spirit, in faith, in purity.

11 Command and teach these things.

12 Let no one despise your youth, but set the believers an example in speech and

---

His hope of life is sure and secure because God as a living God alone is life and alone can bestow it. Only such an assured hope warrants the arduous training endured and the effort expended by the Christian.

The emphasis on **all men** reaffirms the note of universalism of 2:1-6, and as there, so here it is polemical. **Especially of those who believe** is safeguard and protection: all men may be saved; only Christians will be.

Easton regards vs. 10 (except the last "ungraceful" phrase) as the **sure saying**, which he thinks may have been "a watch-cry in times of trouble." By taking the verse as quotation, Easton is free to entertain the possibility that the textual variant **suffer reproach** is original. Although not suitable to the present context, "in the citation it could be perfectly relevant to the omitted portion of the hymn but was changed by copyists (influenced by Col. 1.29?) to adapt it to 1 Timothy. The thought of the citation is perfectly Pauline, but Paul would not have added the ungraceful 'especially of believers.' " (*Pastoral Epistles*, p. 148.) But see Rom. 8:28-30.

## XIII. THE MINISTER AS EXAMPLE (4:11-16)

**11.** The frequency of these connecting clauses shows them to be editorial, perfunctory, schematic. The commands to "Timothy" form a sort of thread on which the material of the letter is strung (cf. vs. 6; 1:18; 3:14; 5:7; 6:2; II Tim. 2:14; Tit. 2:15). How far backward **these things** reaches need not be asked, but since all of vss. 11-16 are addressed to "Timothy," the paragraph seems to be a general conclusion to chs. 1–4.

**12.** The historic Timothy need not have been born before A.D. 30. Paul, around thirty at the time, is called "a young man" in the account of Stephen's death in Acts 7:58. **Youth** (νεότης) is known to have been applied to full-grown men of military age, up to forty (Irenaeus *Against Heresies* II. 22; W. M. Ramsay, "Historical Commentary on the First Epistle to Timothy," *The Expositor,* Ser. 7, Vol. 9 [1910], p. 327, and *The Cities and Bishoprics of Phrygia* [Oxford: Clarendon Press, 1895-97], I, 110n). Similarly, there is the well-known passage in Ign. Mag. 3:1, "It is your duty not to take advantage of the youth of your bishop, but to render him all reverence in accord with the power of God the Father." However old a bishop might have been in Ignatius' time and still be called youthful, or however flexible the term **youth** may have been at the time our letter was written, the text obviously requires that "Timothy" be young enough to be

---

all nations, kindreds, and races. If Easton is right in assuming that the qualifying clause **especially of those who believe** is a later addition, this may indicate differences of opinion in the early church as to the meaning of salvation. Or it may mean that God wants to be the Savior of all men, but because he has given freedom of choice to men he is in a full sense the Savior only of those who believe. This is the conviction on which the Christian mission to the world proceeds.

**11-16. *A Call to Youth.*—**Charles E. Jefferson once preached a sermon at the ordination of a group of young men to the Christian ministry. His text was **Let no man despise thy youth.** His plea was that however young in years a min-

ister might be, he had a great gospel to preach. Age always finds it difficult to give responsibility to youth. Youth sometimes asserts its independence by ignoring the experience of age. This writer evidently believed that the best way for youth to win the confidence of an older generation is to **set the believers an example in speech and conduct, in love, in faith, in purity.** A young man who sets out deliberately to be an example to his elders will end up as a prig. But a young man who tries to deserve the confidence of those older and more experienced than he is on sound ground.

The young Christian is urged to **attend to the public reading of scripture, to preaching, to teaching.** Here is a three-sided ministry. God

13 Till I come, give attendance to reading, to exhortation, to doctrine.

14 Neglect not the gift that is in thee, which was given thee by prophecy, with

conduct, in love, in faith, in purity. 13 Till I come, attend to the public reading of scripture, to preaching, to teaching. 14 Do not neglect the gift you have, which was

---

treated with contempt, say not much over twenty-five (Easton). Those who regard the Pastorals as Pauline and as written in 65-66 hold that Timothy was between thirty and forty years old at the time, and Paul above sixty. Those who regard the letter as pseudonymous will see here indication that the addressees are the clergy subordinate to the writer.

**13. Till I come:** The pronoun **I** designates the writer of the letter who thus indicates his authority over "Timothy." The phrase does not mean that when he (the bishop?) comes he will take over the work of (public) reading, etc., entrusted to the clergy; it is a gentle reminder that "Timothy" is being held responsible for careful discharge of his duties.

Only men of more than ordinary education could qualify for the ministry. As was Judaism, so was Christianity a religion of a written revelation. Both religions were therefore literary-minded and were extraordinarily creative in the written word. The minister would be constantly engaged in reading both old and new scriptures, the O.T., apocalypses, writings of apostles and teachers, letters of officials, hymns and devotional lyrics composed by prophets, accounts of the early beginnings of the church such as came to form the Gospels and Acts. His most solemn public reading would be before the congregation assembled in regular worship, but since many could not read, and since books (rolls) were scarce, as parish visitor he would need to do much informal reading. As preacher he would interpret the scripture he had read, as Jesus did in Luke 4:16-30. Since the synagogue was both church and school, it was natural that preaching and teaching should continue side by side in the church. The preaching would be expository and hortatory, sometimes prophetic, sometimes consoling in style, like the speeches or sermons in Acts. Teaching would be not too dissimilar. One tends to preach in a formal situation, to teach in an informal one. The difference between them would have more to do with style and setting than with content (cf. Acts 13:15; I Cor. 14:3).

**14.** In the context the verse seems to mean simply: Do not neglect the ministerial duties, particularly the preaching and teaching for which you have been properly ordained. Ordination is not the end; rather it is the beginning.

---

speaks to every age through the Bible. Coming to the Bible as to an unknown book in a time of personal crisis, Katherine Mansfield wrote: "I feel so bitterly I should have known facts like this: they ought to be part of my breathing." [7] God speaks through preaching. Said James Stewart to the divinity students of Scotland:

The Gospel is not for an age, but for all time: yet it is precisely the particular age—this historic hour and none other—to which we are commissioned by God to speak. It is against the background of the contemporary situation that we have to reinterpret the Gospel once for all delivered to the saints; and it is within the framework of current hopes and fears that we have to show the commanding relevance of Jesus.[8]

[7] *Journal of Katherine Mansfield*, ed. J. Middleton Murry (New York: Alfred A. Knopf, 1927), p. 54.

[8] *Heralds of God* (New York: Charles Scribner's Sons, 1946), p. 11.

And God speaks through teaching. The disciples sometimes called Jesus "teacher." He went up onto a mountain and taught them. He sent them out to teach and preach and heal. Today a generation which has been brought up in a nominally Christian society still needs to be taught what the Christian faith and the Christian life are.

Most people have latent powers, physical, intellectual, and spiritual, which they do not usually employ. Emergencies reveal them, but often in ordinary life they are dormant. They are called out when challenged. Sometimes they are evoked by the confidence which other people have in them. Sometimes it is the example of someone else who has done the apparently impossible which stirs up buried talents. The Christian meets such challenge, confidence, and example in Christ. The particular young Christian referred to in the epistle had the additional

the laying on of the hands of the presbytery.

15 Meditate upon these things; give thyself wholly to them; that thy profiting may
appear to all.

given you by prophetic utterance when
the elders laid their hands upon you.

15 Practice these duties, devote yourself to
them, so that all may see your progress.

---

The use of **gift** (*charisma*) to apply to an office shows a virtual displacement of the
ecstatic element in the word—an element uppermost in the thought of the Corinthian
church (I Cor. 12:4) and in the concept of the Spirit in Acts, where a gift is a special
endowment bestowed directly by the Spirit, such as prophetic utterance, power to heal,
speaking with tongues, etc. It is true that Paul tried to stabilize the Spirit experiences, so
to speak, as over against the ecstatic gifts, but he did not pursue his logic to its extreme.
In the Pastorals the Spirit is virtually "quenched," the term occurring indisputably only
in 4:1; II Tim. 1:14; Tit. 3:5, of which the first is the conventional language of scripture
citation, the second reminiscent of the indwelling Spirit of Rom. 8:9, and the third a
probable citation. The **gift** here is not directly referred to the Spirit, although the phrase
"in you" is a survival of Spirit language. Likewise, the phrase **which was given you by**
[lit., and better, "through"] **prophetic utterance** (cf. 1:18), is a survival of Spirit language,
and means that "Timothy" was pointed out and set apart by the Spirit through prophetic
utterance just as were Barnabas and Saul (Acts 13:2). After the pattern of Acts 13:3-4,
the "standard" view of the church was that the gift of authority to perform and of the
"power" necessary to accomplish his commission was bestowed upon the minister or
missionary when he was designated by the Spirit in prophetic utterance, and when the
hands of the elders (elderhood or presbytery) were laid upon him (on laying on of
hands, cf. Scott, *Pastoral Epistles, ad loc.*). Not so very much later it was frankly recognized
that the congregations themselves "elected" their bishops and deacons (Did. 15:1)
without, we may suppose, even the formality of the "prophetic utterance."

Once again, the verse is not really applicable to the historic Timothy. At this late
date Paul would hardly have needed to urge Timothy not to neglect his pastoral duties.
If Timothy was formally ordained, it was by Paul alone and not by any presbytery. Acts
16:2 makes it clear that prophecy had nothing to do with Paul's choice of Timothy.
That our text is not concerned to attribute "Timothy's" **gift** to Paul (despite II Tim.
1:6, which see) is best explained by the supposition that "Paul" here has in mind the
many "Timothys" who were ordained by the various elderhoods in Asia.

**15. Practice** (μελετάω): A strong word meaning "to be diligent in" or "to prosecute
diligently," or to practice as an athlete does. **These duties** (ταῦτα) refers to public
reading, preaching, and teaching. **Devote yourself to them,** lit., "be in them," i.e., "sink
yourself in them" (Easton), or "let them absorb you" (Moffatt), "live in them" (Dibelius). **Progress** (προκοπή; cf. Phil. 1:12, 25) is a favorite word among Stoic writers to

---

incentive in the action of the elders who had
set him apart for his work by the laying on of
hands. Paul bids him make the most of every
power with which he has been endowed. **Do
not neglect the gift you have.**

Paul expected the young Christian to grow
through practice and devotion. **Practice these
duties, devote yourself to them, so that all may
see your progress.** He did not expect maturity
by a miracle, nor did he look to see youth becoming a full grown man overnight. That had
not been the great apostle's history. "When I
was a child, I spoke like a child, I thought like
a child, I reasoned like a child; when I became
a man, I gave up childish ways" (I Cor. 13:11).

He looked forward to spiritual progress for all
Christians, "Until we all attain . . . to mature
manhood, to the stature of the fullness of
Christ" (Eph. 4:13). Timothy was to "learn by
doing," and to grow in fidelity.

The Fourth Gospel records Jesus as saying of
his followers, "For their sakes I sanctify myself"
(John 17:19). The writer of this epistle appeals
to a similar sense of responsibility in the concluding sentence of this chapter. **Take heed to
yourself; . . . for by so doing you will save both
yourself and your hearers.** No man, minister or
layman, can confine the results of his life and
work to himself. He must be sobered by the
realization that more people than he can ever

16 Take heed unto thyself, and unto the doctrine; continue in them: for in doing this thou shalt both save thyself, and them that hear thee.

5 Rebuke not an elder, but entreat *him* as a father; *and* the younger men as brethren;

2 The elder women as mothers; the younger as sisters, with all purity.

16 Take heed to yourself and to your teaching; hold to that, for by so doing you will save both yourself and your hearers.

5 Do not rebuke an older man but exhort him as you would a father; treat younger men like brothers, 2 older women like mothers, younger women like sisters, in all purity.

---

indicate advance in ethical or philosophical achievement. The verb form is used six times in the N.T., the three in the Pastorals (II Tim. 2:16; 3:9, 13) all, oddly enough, signifying progress in the wrong direction. Young ministers should discipline themselves with such planfulness and ardor that all may **see** their **progress.**

**16.** The teacher must not be concerned with his **teaching** to the point of unconcern with his own spiritual welfare, nor yet must he be concerned with himself only. The two are one, and if he heeds both he will fulfill his ministry: he will **save** both himself and his hearers.

**Hold to that:** "Stick to your work" (Moffatt); "Persevere in your work" (Goodspeed). **That** (αὐτοῖς) probably refers to "these duties" of vs. 15.

## XIV. The Conduct of the Minister Toward Various Groups (5:1-2)

**5:1-2.** The word translated **rebuke** is a strong word meaning harsh or violent reproof such as anyone in authority might be tempted to employ. On the other hand, the word translated **exhort** (παρακαλέω) is a kindly, many-sided, Christian word. It includes the ideas of exhortation, admonition, and comfort. In Greek these two verbs are the only ones in the verses and are to be taken with all four groups: "Timothy" is not to govern harshly; whether those under his supervision are young or old, men or women, he is to remember that the church is the family of God (3:15); all are fathers and mothers, brothers and sisters. The parallel with Plato is striking, "He [the Guardian] must regard everyone whom he meets as brother or sister, father or mother, son or daughter, grandchild or grandparent" (*Republic* V. 463C). Only, our text adds the characteristically Christian caution that "Timothy's" affection for the younger women be displayed with perfect propriety and chastity.

---

know are influenced for weal or woe by what he is and does.

**5:1-2. *The Church as a Family.*—**The O.T. concludes with the prophecy: "And he shall turn the heart of the fathers to the children, and the heart of the children to their fathers, lest I come and smite the earth with a curse" (Mal. 4:6). Each generation is impatient with that which went before. Each generation as it becomes older is critical of that which follows. Each needs the other, and the world needs the characteristic contributions of youth and age. Youth brings a tired world new enthusiasm, fresh eyes with which to behold familiar facts, eagerness to try new ways, a spirit of adventure, faith in the future.

"O youth! The strength of it, the faith of it, the imagination of it!" wrote Joseph Conrad.[9]

[9] *Youth* (New York: Doubleday, Page & Co., 1927), p. 12.

The peculiar temptation of youth is to allow early disappointments to turn all this into cynicism, bitterness, melancholy, and despair. There is a pessimism of youth which is generally a shallow optimism turned sour. Experience belongs to age, as do the sense of reality born of success and failure, the wisdom that can be gained only by meeting the world, the stability which comes from surmounting crises, the appreciation of what present privileges have cost, and the faith that has been tested and vindicated. On the other hand, older people are sometimes defeated spirits because they have striven much and accomplished little; they are sometimes timid because so many new experiments have turned out badly; they sometimes cling to old ways long after the time has come for something better. Older people have been known to develop pride in supposedly superior knowledge with slight foundation. "A man finds

3 Honor widows that are widows indeed.
4 But if any widow have children or nephews, let them learn first to show piety at home, and to requite their parents: for that is good and acceptable before God.

3 Honor widows who are real widows.
4 If a widow has children or grandchildren, let them first learn their religious duty to their own family and make some return to their parents; for this is acceptable in the

---

## XV. The Church and the Order of Widows (5:3-16)

**3.** To honor means both to show respect for and to reward or give financial support to. Here a **widow** is not just a married woman bereft of her husband; she is a married woman bereft of all kinsfolk whose relationship obligates them to support her. Only such widows are **real widows.**

Thus one may translate: "Look after widows who are really dependent" (Goodspeed), or "widows in real need" (Moffatt), or "if they are actually in need." Only **real widows** are to be supported by the church. It is "Timothy's" problem to judge who of the group of widows may be advisedly employed by the church as **widow.**

**4.** A **real widow** is one without children or grandchildren (lit., "descendants") who can support her, and who devotes herself entirely to religious exercises (vs. 5).

The Greek of vs. 4 is rough, the subject of the sentence changing from the singular (**widow**) to an unexpressed plural subject in the third person imperative (**let them learn**). This has caused some perplexity, and it has been proposed that the understood subject is "widows," i.e., if any widow has dependents, let her learn that her first religious duty is to them: she shall therefore not seek work from the church. The context, however, certainly requires that **children** should be understood as the subject of **let them learn.** The duty of children to care for their parents, or of relatives for near kinsmen, was accepted as a **first** religious duty in Judaism (Ps. 68:6; Deut. 10:18; 24:17; Isa. 1:17; Luke 2:48; Acts 6:1; Jas. 1:27), and indeed in all patriarchal societies. The writer is not here concerned with the duties of widows but with the duties of their dependents toward them. He wants to reduce the number of widows supported by the church to cases of absolute need; he therefore insists that children or near relatives must make every attempt to support widows before appeal is made to the church.

To **make some return to their parents** means that children who support a widowed mother thereby make some recompense for the care and effort bestowed upon them by those who brought them up. Thus the demand is both reasonable and has religious sanction. It was God who said, "Honor thy father and thy mother."

---

he has been wrong at every preceding stage of his career, only to deduce the astonishing conclusion that he is at last entirely right," wrote Robert Louis Stevenson.[1] Sometimes older people stop learning long before they stop trying to impose their views on others. (Michelangelo's motto at ninety was "Still learning.") Youth is on the whole inclined to be pioneering; age, conservative. Wrote Stevenson:

The true wisdom is to be always seasonable, and to change with a good grace in changing circumstances. To love playthings well as a child, to lead an adventurous and honorable youth, and to settle when the time arrives, into a green and smiling age, is to be a good artist in life and deserve well of yourself and your neighbour.[2]

[1] "Crabbed Age and Youth" in *Virginibus Puerisque and Other Papers* (London: Chatto & Windus, 1913), p. 104.
[2] *Ibid.*, p. 101.

The writer of the epistle urges that in the Christian church the relationships between older and younger men should be that of a family, which is an indication that in the Christian community family life had already reached a high level of understanding and sympathy.

**3-16. Family Obligations.**—In the midst of a discussion of the treatment of widows, much of which has no particular relevance to our day, the writer stresses three obligations which are never out of date: (*a*) The church as a family has an obligation to care for the material wants of those of its own number who are in need. This is implied in the whole passage, especially in vs. 16. (*b*) In a Christian family younger people have a special obligation to **make some return to their parents.** Under modern conditions this frequently presents great difficulties, especially when young people face the alternative between care for parents and furthering

5 Now she that is a widow indeed, and desolate, trusteth in God, and continueth in supplications and prayers night and day.

6 But she that liveth in pleasure is dead while she liveth.

7 And these things give in charge, that they may be blameless.

8 But if any provide not for his own, and specially for those of his own house, he hath denied the faith, and is worse than an infidel.

9 Let not a widow be taken into the number under threescore years old, having been the wife of one man,

sight of God. 5 She who is a real widow, and is left all alone, has set her hope on God and continues in supplications and prayers night and day; 6 whereas she who is self-indulgent is dead even while she lives. 7 Command this, so that they may be without reproach. 8 If any one does not provide for his relatives, and especially for his own family, he has disowned the faith and is worse than an unbeliever.

9 Let no one be enrolled as a widow who is under sixty years of age, or who has

---

**5-6. She who is a real widow, and is left all alone,** has no one but God, the sole center and ground of her hope. And since **night and day** she is busied with his work, she has a right to claim the protection and support of the church. Perhaps the subtle suggestion of vss. 5-6 is that there were only two possible vocations for a **real widow:** either within the church, or as a prostitute; that unless the young widow, at least, spent much time in prayer, she might easily be tempted to plunge "into dissipation" (Moffatt) or "take up an immoral life" (Easton); that therefore the church should be greatly concerned to "honor" **real widows,** that they may truly live while they live and not be **dead** to God.

**7.** "Timothy" must set these regulations and admonitions plainly before both the widows and their families, so that both will be above criticism.

**8.** One last thrust is made at people who do not make proper provision for their relatives and thereby add to the burdens of the church. Whatever profession of faith they may make, they are really unbelievers—even worse, because non-Christians themselves teach and practice this commonplace virtue (for similar appeals to heathen morality cf. Rom. 2:14; I Cor. 5:1; Phil. 4:8).

**9.** This passage is the oldest evidence (along with Ign. Polyc. 4:1; Polyc. Phil. 4:3) of an order of widows in the church. The word **enrolled** (καταλέγω) is a technical term indicating an official order, and shows that a list or catalogue of such full-time workers was kept. "Elders were ordained following the Jewish form (4.14), but lack of precedent in Judaism for the dedication of women to religious work perhaps explains why widows were simply 'enrolled.' This, however, may have taken place with solemnity in the presence of the assembled congregation" (Easton, *Pastoral Epistles,* p. 153).

Obviously strenuous efforts were made to keep the number of **enrolled** widows small. They would of course be selected from the larger body of widows, being (a) **real widows** in the sense of vss. 3-6; (b) sixty or more years old; and (c) committed to life service, in addition to having the character requirements of vs. 10 and to being married only once (see 3:2).

Since younger widows are refused enrollment because they will probably remarry (vs. 11), the regulation, "no one under sixty," may be prompted by the supposition that by this age the danger of remarriage would have passed. For other reasons Plato (*Laws* VI. 759D) prescribes that in the ideal state both priests and priestesses "must be not less than sixty years of age" (cf. Ramsay, "Commentary on I Timothy," *The Expositor,* IX [1910], 439).

In spite of the fact that these older women were supposed to be beyond the age when they would be tempted by worldly pleasures, and would be without other obligations than their church duties and might therefore be expected to devote themselves wholly to Christian work, such a regulation hardly seems to have been prompted merely by requirements of efficiency. Obviously in the section vss. 3-16 there is an undercurrent

10 Well reported of for good works; if
she have brought up children, if she have
lodged strangers, if she have washed the
saints' feet, if she have relieved the afflicted,
if she have diligently followed every good
work.

been married more than once[k]; 10 and she
must be well attested for her good deeds,
as one who has brought up children, shown
hospitality, washed the feet of the saints,
relieved the afflicted, and devoted herself to

[k] Greek *the wife of one husband*.

of problem. There are too many widows on the church's hands, enrolled or not enrolled.
The order itself has grown too large. Apparently younger widows had been enrolled
and then had grown **wanton against Christ** (vs. 11). There were too many women
with official privileges **gadding about from house to house, . . . gossips and busybodies**
(vs. 13). The best way to deal with this increasingly prominent influence of unattached
women in the church, the writer believes, is to have the younger widows marry, bear
children, and stay at home (cf. 2:8 ff.). Further by excluding those under sixty, the
wings of the order would be clipped, and those enrolled would be pretty well tested
with reference to the qualifications stated in vs. 10. Finally, persistent pressure must be
put on families to support their widowed members so that the church would not be
burdened beyond necessity, yet have the financial resources to **assist those who are real
widows** (vs. 16).

How long or how widely an order of sixty-year-old widows maintained itself in
the church is uncertain. That some texts of the Didascalia (3:1) changed "sixty" to
"fifty" indicates that "sixty" had come to be regarded as impracticable (see R. H. Con-
nolly, *Didascalia Apostolorum* [Oxford: Clarendon Press, 1929], p. 103; Funk, *Didascalia
et Constitutiones Apostolorum*, I, 182; the Greek text in Migne, *Patrologie Greco-Latine*,
I, 760, and the English translation in *The Ante-Nicene Fathers*, VII, 426, read "sixty").
In the end, the order of widows was absorbed by the regular religious orders for women.

**10.** All the requirements here are practical. Nothing is said about "sound teaching."
Women were probably less inclined to religious speculation than men. In any case, they
were not entrusted with the teaching office (see 2:11-15). The widow who aspires
to enrollment must be proved qualified in good works:

(*a*) She must have **brought up children.** While, strictly speaking, "to rear children"
does not require that they must be one's own, yet this is the normal expectation of the
word. According to vs. 4, however, such a widow is not a "real widow," and could not
be enrolled. If vss. 3-16 are a genuine unity, we must suppose either that the widow's own
children are dead, or that they are unable or unwilling to support her, or that the
children she has reared are orphans. Since the care of orphans was committed to the
widows, the latter interpretation may be correct. But probably most sixty-year-old
widows would have had children of their own at one time or another; the rule of
childlessness can hardly have been strictly enforced. In any case, the passage need mean
only that the widows must have had some apprenticeship in taking care of children.
In antiquity there would have been few women of sixty who had not "brought up
children."

(*b*) **Shown hospitality:** See 3:2. Hospitality was a virtue required of all church
officials, men or women, indeed of all Christians. Christianity was a traveling religion,
the church a traveling church, and adequate care must be given to members of the

their own careers or, even more perplexing, the
choice between the support of parents and the
establishment of their own homes. There is
much to be said for the argument that society
should provide widows' pensions and old-age
pensions to relieve young people of crippling
burdens. But the basic obligation and privilege
remain. Obviously there is an obligation to care

for parents in other ways, even if there is no
economic necessity. (*c*) There is a Christian
obligation to show hospitality, which is pictured here in the description of the widow who
has **shown hospitality, washed the feet of the
saints, relieved the afflicted, and devoted herself
to doing good in every way.** The particular circumstances referred to had to do doubtless with

11 But the younger widows refuse: for when they have begun to wax wanton against Christ, they will marry;

12 Having damnation, because they have cast off their first faith.

13 And withal they learn *to be* idle, wandering about from house to house; and not only idle, but tattlers also and busybodies, speaking things which they ought not.

doing good in every way. 11 But refuse to enroll younger widows; for when they grow wanton against Christ they desire to marry, 12 and so they incur condemnation for having violated their first pledge. 13 Besides that, they learn to be idlers, gadding about from house to house, and not only idlers but gossips and busybodies, saying

---

Christian family on journey. It is assumed that those who seek hospitality will generally be on Christian business, but even Christians who traveled on other business were Christians and must frequently have sought out those of the faith in strange cities. The text does not suggest that the churches had hostels in charge of the widows; simply, a widow must be a hospitable person.

(c) **Washed the feet of the saints: Saints** ("God's people") for Christians occurs only here in the Pastorals. On foot washing cf. John 13:5; Luke 7:44. This lowest of menial tasks was performed for guests by a slave if there was one, otherwise by the wife. It is therefore a test of humility. The widow must not be above any necessary work.

(d) **Relieved the afflicted:** Details are not specified, but care of the sick and the poor would be included.

(e) **And devoted herself to doing good in every way:** A final generalization. The widow must have shown herself devoted to every sort of good work.

**11-12.** Younger widows would be those under sixty. Evidently vss. 11-15 reflect difficulties which the church had had with younger women who, prompted as they supposed by sincere devotion, were consecrated to the order of widows, but when the opportunity to get married came, took it, abandoning their church work. Whether the widow at the time of enrollment took a vow not to remarry but to remain in the service of the church for life is not clear. Vs. 12 seems to suggest as much. And the phrase **grow wanton against Christ** seems to imply that Christ was a Bridegroom to whom the widow now belonged. Since marriage carried with it necessity of withdrawal from the office, the **desire to marry** meant infidelity, a sort of spiritual adultery (**their first pledge,** lit., **their first faith;** see II Tim. 4:7). The result of widows' remarrying is that both they and the church (vs. 14) are criticized as faithless. The best way to handle this problem, the writer urges, is not to allow widows of marriageable age to be enrolled at all, thus preventing from the outset the possibility of defection.

**13.** The text seems to mean that as these younger widows (the writer may have in mind some real persons!) visit from house to house (the verb need not have the depreciatory connotation of **gadding about**), all serious religious purpose becomes dissipated; they learn from the parish visitation only to be **idlers, tattlers, busybodies**

---

entertaining itinerant Christian teachers. The timeless truth is the warning against a selfish home. A home can be a place where the family shuts itself in with itself and bars the doors against the needs of others. A Christian home needs to have its doors and windows open, so that it can be a center of shared helpfulness as well as a center of shared comfort and pleasure. The happiest homes are those in which families have common interests which reach out to people beyond the family, and make common sacrifices to relieve the needs of others who are homeless.

**13. The Sin of Gossip.**—Not only widows but all Christians need to be on their guard against being **gossips and busybodies, saying what they should not.** As every sin is the misuse of some good attribute, gossip is a personal interest in other people gone wrong. Some people do not gossip because they are shut up within themselves and are not concerned about the affairs of others. Sympathy is a loving "feeling with" other people. When love is absent, concern for other people becomes malicious and even cruel. Four verses in the Bible constitute a sort of antidote to gossip: (a) "Give . . . thy servant

14 I will therefore that the younger women marry, bear children, guide the house, give none occasion to the adversary to speak reproachfully.

15 For some are already turned aside after Satan.

what they should not. 14 So I would have younger widows marry, bear children, rule their households, and give the enemy no occasion to revile us. 15 For some have al-

---

peddling gossip. Of course such is the trivial end of much parish visiting, whether by men or women. But that the younger widows should be regarded as particularly liable to gossiping appears to be a faulty argument; older ones enjoy it quite as much. The writer may assume, however, that the sixty-year-olds have been adequately tested by previous experience.

**14.** "I wish" (**I would**) here means "I command." The problem of the younger widows will be got rid of with one stroke. They must marry, have children, and stay at home. E. F. Scott (*The Pastoral Epistles* [London: Hodder & Stoughton; New York: Harper & Bros., 1936; "Moffatt New Testament Commentary"], p. 62) writes:

> The position here adopted is different from that of Paul in I Cor. vii. 25 f. Although Paul does not forbid marriage, he holds that it is better for the unmarried to remain so, in view of the great crisis which is imminent. When the Pastorals were written, the hope of the Parousia had failed; Christians are now advised to adapt themselves to ordinary conditions and to provide for the continuance of the Church as part of the present order. On the other hand, there is a striking difference between the position here and that of the later Church. In the course of the second and third centuries, as a result of the ascetic ideas which had become prevalent, an increasing value was placed on celibacy. Here, the state of marriage is deemed preferable to the other. The ascetic attitude has been condemned in [an] earlier passage (iv. 3), and now even widows who are of suitable age are advised to follow the course which is more natural. The common sense which is a feature of these Epistles is nowhere more apparent.

The **enemy** (RSV) might be **the adversary** (KJV), i.e., Satan, as he is mentioned in vs. 15, or any human opponent. The writer is always concerned that the church shall stand well in the opinion of the outside world. Christian women must therefore not be allowed to fall into situations which will bring them into disrepute. The ancient mind, however, would not so sharply distinguish between a human opponent and Satan. Man was an instrument: in the hand of God for good, in the hand of Satan for evil. What man did, at bottom, God or Satan did.

**15. For some have already strayed after Satan:** Either by violating their first pledge and marrying again, or by using the parish visitation as an opportunity to stir up scandal, making for tumult if not for schism.

---

an understanding heart" (I Kings 3:9). When we understand why other people are what they are, why they do what they do, we are likely to be charitable in our judgments. What we criticize in other people is often the result of health, home conditions, financial worries, frustrated hopes, or inadequate education. (b) "Love . . . does not rejoice at wrong, but rejoices in the right" (I Cor. 13:6). It is our own pride which tempts us to feed our sense of superiority by gloating over the moral failures of others. If we find ourselves glad when we discover the weak points in the armor of other people, we need to offer a prayer of confession and a petition for a right spirit. (c) "Whatever is true, whatever is honorable. whatever is just, whatever is pure, whatever is lovely, whatever is gracious, if

there is any excellence, if there is anything worthy of praise, think about these things" (Phil. 4:8). There are times when we need to be realistic in appraising the faults as well as the virtues of other people. In giving employment, in writing recommendations, in choosing officers for a church, and in countless other situations fidelity to our responsibilities demands that we take account of all the facts. But in our personal relations with other people we often see the faults magnified and overlook the virtues. A little more thought given to the constructive aspects of character might result in a truer appraisal. (d) "Speaking the truth in love" (Eph. 4:15). The insincerity which plays fast and loose with the truth because it may be unpleasant is generally transparent. Social relations

16 If any man or woman that believeth have widows, let them relieve them, and let not the church be charged; that it may relieve them that are widows indeed.

17 Let the elders that rule well be counted worthy of double honor, espe-

ready strayed after Satan. 16 If any believing woman[l] has relatives who are widows, let her assist them; let the church not be burdened, so that it may assist those who are real widows.

17 Let the elders who rule well be con-

[l] Other ancient authorities read *man or woman;* others, simply *man.*

16. This verse is perplexing both in itself and in relation to its context. That it has always been so is evidenced by the textual variations, some texts offering **believing man or woman,** or **believing man** instead of **believing woman.** The easiest text to interpret is **believing man or woman.** Then the verse is one more repetition of, one more insistence on, the refrain of vss. 4 and 8: relatives must aid in the support of their widows if at all possible.

The best-attested text, **believing woman,** has prompted the question: Why should the support of widows (with relatives) fall on (Christian) women only, and not on the family as a whole? As a means of avoiding this problem it has been proposed that **believing woman** here really means the younger widow (vs. 14) who is compelled to marry and be denied a religious vocation. Such persons could still be of service to the church and to the order of widows by supporting their own widowed relatives, thus relieving the church of a burden and permitting the church to use its needed funds to support widows who are really destitute. This, however, is too devious an explanation to merit credence. Perhaps the best explanation is that **believing woman** stands for the Christian family. It would naturally be the wife and mother under whose care and protection the needy widow would fall. The burden and the problem of a second woman in the home would fall most heavily on her. "No house is large enough for two women" is not a recent proverb. And vs. 16 may reflect the reluctance if not the refusal of some believing women to accept the responsibility of adding widowed kinsfolk to their households. If the verse is awkwardly introduced into its context (and is not a later gloss), it may be because our author will make one more thrust at reducing the number of widows on the roll. His concern in the section is to assert (*a*) that although obligated to support **real widows,** the church cannot support all who come for aid; and (*b*) that the widow order has created other than financial problems for the church, and the number of enrolled widows must be reduced.

### XVI. The Remuneration and Discipline of Elders (5:17-25)

17. Taken at face value, the passage indicates that although all elders ruled, not all ruled well; and only some elders labored in preaching and teaching. As intimated in

built upon such insincerities are generally unstable. But the truth spoken in love need never be feared. Gerald Kennedy says:

There is a kind of man who prides himself on speaking frankly at all times, who needlessly hurts people and is nothing but a boor and a sadist. Perhaps the little girl had this in mind when she prayed, "O Lord, make all the bad people good, and all the good people nice." If we must speak the word of judgment, it will be a good thing if, like Jeremiah, we weep as we speak.[3]

Alexander Whyte a few months before his death in 1921 penned a postscript to a letter to

the churches of Great Britain and Ireland which might well be a postscript to all human relations:

Truth often separates:
Love always unites.
"Love me" says Augustine, "and then say anything to me and about me you like."
And Richard Baxter's people were wont to say, "We take all things well from one who always and wholly loves us."[4]

**17-18. The Ethics of Reward.**—Here the writer touches on one of the most vexed questions of our day. Paul's practice was evidently to

[3] *With Singleness of Heart* (New York: Harper & Bros., 1951), p. 41.

[4] G. F. Barbour, *The Life of Alexander Whyte* (New York: George H. Doran Co., 1923), p. 615.

cially they who labor in the word and doctrine.

sidered worthy of double honor, especially those who labor in preaching and teach-

this text, the essential function of the elder was as ruling or presiding elder; he was an administrative officer rather than a preacher or teacher. If, however, he ruled well, and if in addition to his administrative work he preached and taught, he was to be recompensed beyond the ordinary. **Double honor** means "double pay." That material recompense is meant is clear from vs. 18 (see vs. 3). It is possible that "double pay" was not meant to be interpreted literally: Moffatt translates "ample remuneration"; Goodspeed interprets the passage rather metaphorically: "Elders who do their duties well should be considered as deserving twice as much as they get." In this case the words are only a kindly wish, a word of encouragement and praise for the more able and energetic elders, not a wage scale. Vs. 18, however, demands that "double pay" be taken quite literally. The assumption is that the elder who takes seriously his duties of administration and who adds the duty of preaching and teaching is really a full-time Christian worker, and is not to be treated as a layman who earns his living by handcraft or trade. Further, the verse need not be legislation before the event; it may describe and justify a practice which already obtained but was grudgingly recognized and which was under criticism as discriminatory. Ancient opinion generally favored the lay teacher or preacher, and only reluctantly admitted his right to stated money recompense (I Cor. 9:3-4). Ministers might be the recipients of tithes of first fruits or of alms, but they were expected to be satisfied with as little as possible. Vss. 17-18 are prompted by the reluctance of the church to compensate its elders, and particularly by its reluctance to give adequate support to those who served full time. Although the principle of unequal salaries for unequal work is a just one, administrators are normally reluctant to apply it because it makes for invidious distinctions. It never can have been pleasant or easy to decide which elders ruled well and which should therefore have **double honor;** nevertheless, our author recommends the practice.

support himself by his work as a tentmaker (Acts 20:34) while he engaged in missionary activity. His example is sometimes cited as authority for an unpaid ministry, or for missionaries who go out to the field without assured basis of support. Here the argument is that those engaged in preaching and teaching should constitute a paid ministry. Moffatt translates the quoted words of Jesus from Luke 10:7, "A workman deserves his wages." The word **double,** which Easton translates "additional," seems to imply the belief that those who discharge their tasks well should receive increased remuneration.

The problem raised here is of much wider application than the isolated question of adequate recompense for church workers. R. H. Tawney's early book, *The Sickness of Acquisitive Society,*[5] contended that the profit motive has undermined the health of the modern world. The best work in any field is never done for the sake of material reward. The acquisitive impulse is insatiable and demands more and more, never satisfied. The competitive struggle for gain is at the heart of most of the conflicts of

[5] Later incorporated in *The Acquisitive Society* (New York: Harcourt, Brace & Co., 1920).

our times. Too much concentration on material things disrupts character. On the other hand, a high standard of living may mean freedom from the grinding struggle for mere existence and freedom for intellectual and spiritual development. It may mean freedom from anxiety, which results in better work and larger service. There are detailed questions involved here which may never be fully answered. Better answers than we now have must be worked out experimentally. A few Christian principles seem to be apparent:

(a) A Christian's primary motive is service rather than profit. Jesus drew a distinction between the good shepherd and the hireling, the difference being in the degree of loyalty to a task. "The good shepherd lays down his life for the sheep" (John 10:11). The hireling "flees because he is a hireling" (John 10:13). A man who cares for the sheep will do for them what he could not be hired to do. In the family, in art, in the profession of healing, in teaching, and in other callings it is generally recognized that the best work is done by those who have a motive of service that goes deeper than thought of material reward. When all work is brought under the power of this motive, the world of in-

18 For the Scripture saith, Thou shalt not muzzle the ox that treadeth out the corn. And, The laborer *is* worthy of his reward.

ing; 18 for the scripture says, "You shall not muzzle an ox when it is treading out the grain," and, "The laborer deserves his

---

18. The first quotation, a stock quotation for the purpose (I Cor. 9:9), comes from Deut. 25:4 (LXX). The second is identical with the saying of Jesus in Luke 10:7 except for the unimportant omission of "for" (γάρ). See Matt. 10:10, which has "food" instead of "wages" (so some texts here). The saying in the Matthaean form occurs in Did. 13:1-2, and is doubtless in the background of I Cor. 9:4 ff.

Unless we suppose the saying of Jesus is only loosely attached, it is here designated as **scripture.** If we take the verse at face value, the author did not quote either saying as a floating proverb; both are quoted as embedded in and deriving their authority from the (sacred) scripture. Furthermore, it is striking that Jesus is not summoned to add the weight of his authority to the saying which, epigram though it is, is found only in the

---

dustry and commerce will have a better chance of building men as well as producing and distributing goods.

(b) There is a social obligation to see that every man is adequately rewarded for his work. Jesus' parable of the laborers in the vineyard was probably meant to teach the overflowing generosity of God, and not to lay down rules for regulating wage scales. But it is significant that the master of the vineyard was concerned about those who had least opportunity to work, and seems to have been concerned that every man should have a living wage. Modern legislation specifying a minimum wage is in line with the Christian conviction that industry has an obligation not only to produce goods which society needs, but also to provide an adequate living for those who invest their lives in its enterprises.

(c) Competition for gain should be replaced by co-operation in service. Christianity cannot be identified with capitalism, socialism, or any other particular economic system. There is a place for competition in human life, as evidenced by the fact that if men do not compete for profit they compete for prestige, power, or pleasure. In a society of unredeemed men competition for gain may be necessary as an incentive for their toil. But to the extent that they are captured by the spirit of Christ, such competition ceases to be the central motive, and co-operation in service becomes as natural as breathing. William Temple appended to his little book, *Christianity and Social Order,* this statement:

I should give a false impression of my own convictions if I did not here add that there is no hope of establishing a more Christian social order except through the labour and sacrifice of those in whom the Spirit of Christ is active, and that the first necessity for progress is more and better Christians

taking full responsibility as citizens for the political, social and economic system under which they and their fellows live.[6]

He had previously defined the basis of a Christian social order as follows:

Freedom, Fellowship, Service—these are the three principles of a Christian social order, derived from the still more fundamental Christian postulates that Man is a child of God and is destined for a life of eternal fellowship with Him.[7]

Kipling's whimsical picture of the ideal state of things is Utopian but suggestive:

And no one shall work for money, and no one shall work for fame;
But each for the joy of the working, and each, in his separate star,
Shall draw the Thing as he sees It for the God of Things as They Are![8]

Dorothy Sayers pleads for the recognition that all work is a vocation, and interprets the Christian understanding of work in three propositions:

Work is not, primarily, something one does to live, but the thing one lives to do.
When a man or a woman is called to a particular job of secular work, that is as true a vocation as though he or she were called to specifically religious work.
The worker's first duty is to serve the work. . . . It is the duty of the Church to see that the work serves God, and that the worker serves the work.[9]

[6] New York: Penguin Books, 1942, p. 76.
[7] *Ibid.,* p. 55.
[8] "L'Envoi." From *Rudyard Kipling's Verse.* Used by permission of Mrs. George Bambridge; Methuen & Co.; The Macmillan Co., Canada; and Doubleday & Co.
[9] *Creed or Chaos?* (New York: Harcourt, Brace & Co., 1949), pp. 53-62. Copyright 1949 by Dorothy L. Sayers. Used by permission.

19 Against an elder receive not an accusation, but before two or three witnesses.

20 Them that sin rebuke before all, that others also may fear.

21 I charge *thee* before God, and the Lord Jesus Christ, and the elect angels, that thou observe these things without preferring one before another, doing nothing by partiality.

wages." 19 Never admit any charge against an elder except on the evidence of two or three witnesses. 20 As for those who persist in sin, rebuke them in the presence of all, so that the rest may stand in fear. 21 In the presence of God and of Christ Jesus and of the elect angels I charge you to keep these rules without favor, doing nothing from

---

Gospels. Unless, then, the writer thinks he is quoting the O.T., and has neglected to verify his references, the conclusion seems irresistible, in spite of certain objections, that he thought of the Gospel of Luke as scripture. Since the author almost certainly knew Acts (see II Tim. 3:11), he may well have known Luke too.

**19.** Being in administrative positions, elders are naturally subject to persistent criticism. They therefore need protection from malicious and unfounded charges. This has already been provided by Deut. 19:15 and reaffirmed in the church (see Matt. 18:15-17; II Cor. 13:1). No elder may be brought to trial unless the charge is supported by a minimum of **two or three witnesses.**

**20. Them that sin** (KJV) means sinning elders. The present participle (τοὺς ἁμαρτάνοντας) may mean either "those who *do* sin"—i.e., those against whom charges are legally sustained—or **those who persist in sin** (RSV). If the disciplinary procedure in mind here is based on that of Matt. 18:15-17, the public rebuke would not be the first, and **persist in sin** would be the correct translation. However, the writer may be urging a more rigorous point of view, particularly as regards elders. Charges against elders are indeed not to be lightly admitted; however, once an elder is found sinning, he is to be dealt with severely: he is to be rebuked **in the presence of all**—i.e., all the elders—so that **the rest** (of the elders) may be afraid to do wrong. The rule is general; what constitutes "sin" in the mind of the writer is not indicated. There is apparently no thought of anything serious enough to warrant expulsion from office, or worse.

**21.** The verses which follow seem to be thrown together rather haphazardly, a series of postscripts requiring for their elucidation a wider context than is available.

If vs. 21 is to be taken with vss. 19-20 alone, and is not just one of numerous instances where our author injects a charge to "Timothy" to keep **these rules** or instructions, the

---

**19-25. Dealing with Offenders.**—Evidently some men who have been chosen for leadership have proved unworthy of their trust. Here are some bits of homely advice for dealing with such a situation, which are applicable wherever one man is trying to exercise supervision over others in the spirit of the Christian faith: be slow to believe evil reports and demand convincing evidence (vs. 19); when wrongdoing has been proved, be clear-cut and decisive in dealing with it (vs. 20); be absolutely impartial (vs. 21); be slow to put responsibility on others, and be yourself above reproach (vs. 22); recognize the extreme difficulty of judging other people (vss. 24-25). Sometimes one can see in advance that a man is going wrong, but sometimes it is a shock to discover that one who has been above suspicion has actually been at fault. The same thing is true about good work. It speaks for itself. In case of doubt, wait. Goodness will

eventually prove itself. Good deeds cannot remain hidden. This is faith in the ultimate justice of God's moral order, needed by all who live in a world where truth is so often on the scaffold, wrong so often apparently on the throne.

The seemingly irrelevant admonition to use **a little wine** is not a proof text for or against the use of alcoholic beverages. The argument for abstinence rests upon the social consequences of the use of alcohol in modern life and upon the new knowledge of the psychology of alcoholism.

**21. The Elect Angels.**—To make more compelling his plea that Timothy shall be impartial, Paul refers to **the presence of God and of Christ Jesus and of the elect angels.** The Exeg. refers to other N.T. passages which speak of **the elect angels** or "the holy angels" (Mark 8:38). Revelation speaks frequently of the angels who sur-

22 Lay hands suddenly on no man, neither be partaker of other men's sins: keep thyself pure.

partiality. 22 Do not be hasty in the laying on of hands, nor participate in another man's sins; keep yourself pure.

---

solemn oath, **in the presence of God and of Christ Jesus and of the elect angels,** suggests not simply the importance of maintaining discipline among the elders, but that there had been actual cases of discrimination, perhaps some flagrant ones, where evil men had been shielded or innocent men abused. Hence "Timothy" is commanded to observe the regulations (of vss. 19-20) without partiality. On the one hand, judgments are not to be formed without all the facts being known; on the other, decisions are not to be bent by personal bias.

The threefold reference **God, Christ,** and **the elect angels,** is liturgical language ultimately derived from the belief that these will be present at the Last Judgment (see Mark 8:38; Luke 9:26; Matt. 25:31; Rev. 14:10). **Elect angels:** See Odes of Solomon 4:8; Test. Levi 19; II Esdras 16:66 (cf. R. H. Charles, *A Critical and Exegetical Commentary on the Revelation of St. John* [New York: Charles Scribner's Sons, 1920; "International Critical Commentary"], on Rev. 14:10).

**22.** The incoherence of the section leaves the meaning ambiguous. Two interpretations are advanced: (*a*) **Laying on of hands** in these letters is connected with ordination. What the text says, then, is, "Never ordain anyone hastily" (Goodspeed, Moffatt, Scott, von Soden, all Greek commentators). The argument is that since the disciplinary problem, whether in the case of bishops, elders, deacons, or widows, is difficult, "Timothy" shall exercise great caution in ordaining people into office. If he mistakenly inducts bad men into responsible church positions, he becomes himself a participant in their sins. "Timothy" can keep his own life **pure,** can maintain his own integrity, only if he treats the high offices of the church with the utmost seriousness and consideration and rigorously excludes all unworthy men from them.

(*b*) Against this interpretation, it is urged that although at first sight the words seem to mean ordination, actually they are better taken to refer to the restoration of penitents to the Christian fellowship, a rite which also was accompanied by laying on of hands in blessing (cf. Cyprian *Epistles* LXXIV. 12; Eusebius *Church History* VII. 2; *Apostolic Constitutions* II. 18; so Lock, Dibelius, Falconer, Easton). The point would then be that once an elder has been convicted of sin, one must not be too hasty in revoking the judgment and readmitting him to the fellowship. If "Timothy" should accept a feigned repentance, he would be held as sharing in the sin. The arguments are: (i) The context is concerned, not with ordination, but with discipline. Throughout the chapter, indeed, the author is distressed over problems of wayward church officials. Nor is the problem merely theoretical: vss. 19-21 show that there had been scandals among the

---

round the throne where Christ sits upon the right hand of God. Without attempting to turn the poetry of such passages into prose, we can find in them the truth that life draws one of its greatest inspirations from the Christian assurance of continued fellowship with those who have passed into the unseen world to be with Christ in God. At the end of his chapter on the exploits of mighty men of faith, the writer of Hebrews draws this inspiration from that recital: "Therefore, since we are surrounded by so great a cloud of witnesses, let us also lay aside every weight, and sin which clings so closely, and let us run with perseverance the race that is set before us" (Heb. 12:1). John

Henry Newman concluded his hymn "Lead, kindly Light" with this figure:

And with the morn those angel faces smile,
Which I have loved long since, and lost awhile!

A poet of World War I, Alan Seeger, put a similar thought into the lines:

And we shall brave eternity as though
Eyes looked on us in which we would seem fair—
One waited in whose presence we would wear,
Even as a lover who would be well-seen,
Our manhood faultless and our honor clean.[1]

[1] "Liebestod." Used by permission of Charles Scribner's Sons and Constable & Co., publishers.

23 Drink no longer water, but use a little wine for thy stomach's sake and thine often infirmities.

24 Some men's sins are open beforehand, going before to judgment; and some *men* they follow after.

23 No longer drink only water, but use a little wine for the sake of your stomach and your frequent ailments.

24 The sins of some men are conspicuous, pointing to judgment, but the sins of others

---

elders. Problems of discipline are always difficult: it is easier to be too lenient or too severe than it is to strike a proper balance. If on the one hand "Timothy" is to maintain complete impartiality, on the other, he is not to become involved in any man's sins by being too lenient.

(ii) As addressed to "Timothy," the text, if interpreted as ordination, stands in contradiction with 4:14, where ordination is performed by the presbytery—by the body of elders—not by "Timothy" alone, and in contradiction with the practice of the church at the time.

So far as the latter argument is concerned, it cannot be regarded as formidable if we regard "Timothy" as a symbol of the elderhood rather than as an individual person. Nevertheless, it is better to leave the decision indeterminate. The section is so incoherent as to make it impossible to be sure that any one verse is to be interpreted by its context. Moffatt divides the material from vss. 17-25 into four paragraphs (omitting vs. 23 as either a marginal gloss or misplaced); Easton, into six. Obviously in this section neither the thought nor language is direct or well articulated.

**23.** If the section were more orderly, or if the author were more skilled in the literary art, one might (with Moffatt, Falconer, etc.) regard the verse as interpolated or misplaced. However, it is quite in character with both the literary procedure and the religious interests of our writer if we interpret the passage as a qualification of vs. 22c, prompted by the author's concern to repudiate Gnostic asceticism at every opportunity. Purity, he will say, neither requires nor warrants ascetic abstinence from wine. Since at the time wine was regarded as medicinally useful in healing a variety of ailments, the practice of total abstinence meant renunciation of wine not only as a beverage, but also as a medicine. This practice is wrong, the author says. When "Timothy" has stomach trouble or his **frequent ailments,** he should not scruple to **use a little wine.**

To reconstruct the exact thought context which lies behind vs. 23 is difficult. Literally, the first two words of the sentence may be translated, "Stop being a water drinker." The compound word ὑδροποτέω means more than ὕδωρ πίνειν, and suggests our phrase "total abstainer" (Moffatt); i.e., it indicates a persistent and principled drinking of water as opposed to alcoholic beverages. If the verse is interpreted out of the same background as 4:1-5, total abstinence from wine is rejected by the writer on the religious ground that "everything created by God is good" (4:4). Since here, however, the advice to **use a little wine** is grounded in the practical consideration of health, probably the heresy rampant in Asia advocated healing by spiritual means only and refused the use of medicines. "Paul," seeing that the health of some ministers was being impaired by such procedure, will have none of it.

The verse well illustrates the common-sense, middle-of-the-road point of view of the author. He holds no brief for wine as pleasure. Religion is too serious for that. But when it comes to refusing medicine, he draws the line. Good religion includes good health and approves all easily available means of obtaining it.

Total abstinence was not normally observed by Jews, although it was held by both Jews and Greeks to belong to a life of self-denial (see Dan. 1:12; Pirke Aboth 6:4; Epictetus *Discourses* III. 13. 21; Testament of Our Lord 22; 31).

**24-25.** Our author may here be moralizing in general on the basis of proverbial observations relative to the problem of detecting good and evil, which often at the time seem so intangible and even indistinguishable. Or again, the verses may be thought of

25 Likewise also the good works *of some* are manifest beforehand; and they that are otherwise cannot be hid.

6 Let as many servants as are under the yoke count their own masters worthy of all honor, that the name of God and *his* doctrine be not blasphemed.

appear later. 25 So also good deeds are conspicuous; and even when they are not, they cannot remain hidden.

6 Let all who are under the yoke of slavery regard their masters as worthy of all honor, so that the name of God and the

---

in close connection with the discipline problem of elders. In any case, "Paul" will afford comfort to "Timothy" by assuring him that good and evil are forever different, and that sooner or later their true nature will be manifested. Although not all sins are so conspicuous as to "seem almost to drag" men before God for judgment, and although not all good deeds are likewise conspicuous, yet even when evil is fully disguised or good wholly concealed, in the end they will be seen as they are. Some men may be worse than they seem, others better; but ultimately appearance and reality will be one.

## XVII. THE CHRISTIAN SLAVE (6:1-2b)

**6:1.** Only a slaveholder can have known how unsatisfactory slave labor was. Without civil or religious rights, almost inevitably the slave would be lazy, inefficient, dishonest, and insincere. If the master was a hard man, he could be brutal with impunity. If he was kindly disposed, his slaves, knowing the paternalistic obligations which slavery placed upon superiors, might frequently take advantage of their master's gentility. If either or both of the parties was a Christian, there would be added problems. Should a Christian slave seek liberation from a non-Christian master, who would of course have the right to exact duties which no Christian as a Christian could perform? Did the church grant to the Christian slave a dispensation to sin when commanded to do so by this non-Christian master rather than to bring the church into disrepute by refusing obedience and seeming

---

**6:1-2. Christians in an Imperfect World.**— There are two ways of attacking social wrongs, the direct and the indirect methods. Both are necessary. The direct method consists in a head-on opposition to a specific evil. The indirect method consists in cultivating an attitude toward human life which undermines the evil. Paul used both methods. We cannot doubt that he was opposed to the institution of slavery, but as the Exeg. points out, the N.T. records only his indirect opposition to it. This may be because some of the members of the Christian churches were slaves who, in spite of their hatred of human slavery, had to live under an institution in which they did not believe. In the Epistle to Philemon Paul urged an attitude of Christian brotherhood on the part of both master and slave. So in this passage he urges that **all who are under the yoke of slavery regard their masters as worthy of all honor,** and that **those who have believing masters . . . must serve all the better since those who benefit by their service are believers and beloved.** In an imperfect world the Christian has two duties: to help transform the world until it more nearly reflects the mind of Christ, and to live in the imperfect world in the Christian spirit. Zealous reformers are tempted to throw themselves into

the first effort, and to neglect the latter. A. N. Whitehead has argued that it was the indirect attack which was most disastrous to the institution of slavery in the British Isles. It was, he says, the Methodist revival of the eighteenth century which "produced the final effective force which hereafter made slavery impossible among progressive races. . . . The Methodist preachers aimed at saving men's souls in the next world." But "they made the conception of the brotherhood of man and of the importance of men, a vivid reality," and under the impact of the faith which they proclaimed slavery in the British Isles was undermined and prepared for the final blow dealt by Wilberforce and the abolitionists.[2]

Everyone finds himself involved in an organized society, certain aspects of which fall far short of the Christian ideal. The world of industry and commerce, the international scene, the relationships between people of different races, the social customs of many groups, all need reformation. There are three attitudes which people take toward an imperfect world. The pagan attitude simply accepts it as it is and tries to enjoy it. The monastic attitude tries to

[2] *Adventures of Ideas* (New York: The Macmillan Co., 1933), pp. 27-28.

to be fractious and rebellious? On the other hand, if his master was a Christian, did the Christian slave have the right to expect manumission? And was the Christian slave-holder on his part obligated to set his slaves free, particularly his Christian slaves? Since in Christian assemblies master and slave met on equal terms, and were both slaves of Christ, how in secular life could one be the slave of the other? The persistence of these problems is frequently reflected in the N.T. and early Christian writings (see Tit. 2:9-10; I Cor. 7:21; Eph. 6:5-9; Col. 3:22–4:1; Philem. 10-17; I Pet. 2:18-25; Did. 4:11; Ign. Polyc. 4:3; etc.).

The institution of slavery as such is hardly questioned in the N.T. The insistence, rather, is on integrity and brotherliness within the pattern. That slavery is a real bondage is frankly recognized. This will be the meaning of the double expression, "slaves under yoke." Slavery means just that, and even the Christian slave should not forget that obedience is his first virtue. It cannot have been easy advice to give, certainly not to take, that the Christian slave should regard his master as deserving **all honor** ("perfect respect," Moffatt; "complete respect," Easton) when in fact, sometimes if not often, he was altogether unworthy. But our author is interested here in only one side of the question. He is not concerned about the slave's own conscience, or about whether or not the behavior commanded by the master is Christian: he is concerned only that **the name of God and the teaching may not be defamed** by any (non-Christian) master because he has a disobedient Christian slave. In contrast to Paul in I Cor. 7:22, the slave here is not given status as "a freedman of the Lord," nor is he comforted by the assurance (Col. 3:22-24) that when he serves his master he is "serving the Lord Christ," and that from his Lord he "will receive the inheritance" as his reward. He is simply told his duty.

withdraw from the world, never a wholly successful attempt, for the world is within us as well as without. The Pauline attitude seeks to change the world, seeks to enlist individuals in a loyalty to Christ which changes them, and calls for the exercise of Christian grace on the part of those caught in an unchristian society.

The reference to the **yoke of slavery** calls attention to what slavery essentially means: a denial of the dignity and worth of the individual. It is interesting to contrast this phrase with Jesus' haunting invitation: "Come to me, all who labor and are heavy-laden, and I will give you rest. Take my yoke upon you. . . . For my yoke is easy." (Matt. 11:28-30.) To be yoked with Christ is to find partnership, help with the load, a new sense of the meaning of the task, and a vision of the goal and the reward and of rest after labor. The yoke of slavery is exactly the reverse of all that. The slave is regarded not as a person but as an impersonal unit of labor. (This is the essence of the master-slave relationship, despite the fact that friendship and affection sometimes creep in.) One of the disturbing facts of American history is that when slavery was legally abolished after the Civil War the impersonal attitude toward human beings, which is the **yoke of slavery,** did not disappear but appeared in new forms in other relationships. In the family, in commerce and industry, in schools and colleges, in the attitude of government toward the citizen, and in other aspects of our life today, we need to guard the dignity and the worth of the individual.

This respect for the worth of the individual as a child of God is the foundation of democracy, as the dictators instantly recognized. Said Hitler:

To the Christian doctrine of the infinite significance of the individual human soul and of personal responsibility, I oppose with icy clarity the saving doctrine of the nothingness and insignificance of the individual human being and of his continued existence in the visible immortality of the nation.[3]

Christianity cannot be identified with democracy or any other political or economic system, but democracy at its best owes its basic conviction of the worth of the individual to the Christian heritage. Barbara Ward, of the *London Economist,* recognized this:

The Western idea is a dynamic force based upon the belief in the godlike destiny of man, the supreme value of the human personality, the perfectability of the social order and the vision of a society based on justice, brotherhood and peace. This is the tremendous heritage of our Christian and classical tradition, and if we claim less for our culture, we deny the very sources of its vitality.[4]

[3] Konrad Heiden, *Der Fuehrer* (tr. Ralph Manheim; Boston: Houghton Mifflin Co., 1944), pp. 773-74.
[4] *Policy for the West* (New York: W. W. Norton & Co., 1951), p. 40.

**2** And they that have believing masters, let them not despise *them,* because they are brethren; but rather do *them* service, because they are faithful and beloved, partakers of the benefit. These things teach and exhort.

**3** If any man teach otherwise, and consent not to wholesome words, *even* the words of our Lord Jesus Christ, and to the doctrine which is according to godliness;

teaching may not be defamed. **2** Those who have believing masters must not be disrespectful on the ground that they are brethren; rather they must serve all the better since those who benefit by their service are believers and beloved.

Teach and urge these duties. **3** If any one teaches otherwise and does not agree with the sound words of our Lord Jesus Christ and the teaching which accords with god-

---

**2ab.** It is taken for granted that a Christian slave who has a Christian master is in a privileged position. However, he should not take advantage of the fact that he and his master are brothers in Christ to become insolent or indolent. On the contrary, he must **serve all the better,** knowing that the one who benefits by his service is a fellow Christian and a friend—or is the meaning "dear to God" (Dibelius)? Christians, even slaves, must live affirmatively. "The equality of men before God is one thing; hierarchical orders in society another. In the church there are only brothers; in the world there are masters and slaves, rich and poor" (C. Spicq, *Saint Paul: les Épitres Pastorales* [Paris: J. Gabalda, 1947], p. 183).

### XVIII. The Importance of Sound Doctrine (6:2c-5)

**2c. Teach and urge these duties:** See 4:6. For the last time in the letter the writer uses **these duties** or instructions, now to conclude the whole letter and to introduce the final advices.

**3.** Once again the author cudgels the heretical teachers, taking up the ideas and words of 1:3-7. It is urged by some that the phrase **words of our Lord Jesus Christ** refers to a collection of the sayings of Jesus (Schlatter, Scott, Falconer; Spicq thinks it the Gospel of Luke). If in 5:18 the writer knowingly quotes a word of Jesus as scripture, it would add support to this interpretation. As against it, Easton (also Dibelius) urges that even though the sayings of Jesus were authoritative in the church, "they bear only

---

**2. *These Duties.*—**Again the writer summons the reader to fidelity to duty, which Wordsworth called "Stern Daughter of the Voice of God." As Scott points out, he means the ordinary, humdrum, workaday virtues: "All that he insists on is right belief, courage and loyalty and uprightness, seemly behaviour, honourable fulfilment of all obligations." [5] But alongside that statement should be put another of Scott's comments:

Nowhere in the New Testament is the heroic note so unmistakably sounded. Paul is put forward as the great example because he was the soldier of Christ and died in the good fight. The principle is laid down as self-evident that all who follow godliness must endure persecution (2 Tim. iii. 12).[6]

A popular story by Mary Raymond Shipman Andrews bore the title *The Courage of the Commonplace.*[7] To **teach and urge these duties** calls for such courage.

[5] *Pastoral Epistles,* p. xxxvii.
[6] *Ibid.,* p. xxxiv.
[7] New York: Charles Scribner's Sons, 1911.

**3-6. *The Lure of Novelty.*—**The book of Acts says that the Athenians in Paul's time "spent their time in nothing else, but either to tell, or to hear some new thing" (Acts 17:21). They have their counterparts in every generation, people who rush off after every popular teacher who appears on the horizon with a new formula for achieving peace of mind, physical vitality, or financial prosperity. Moffatt indicates that this passage refers to such teachers, and translates vs. 3: "Anyone who teaches novelties and refuses to fall in with the sound words of our Lord Jesus Christ and the doctrine that tallies with godliness, is a conceited, ignorant creature." Open-mindedness to new truth is one of the marks of the Christian. "Ask, . . . seek, . . . knock" (Matt. 7:7) are the indispensable keys to knowledge. But the person who runs after new fads for purposes of personal display or for the sake of controversy is on false ground. The result is **dissension, slander, base suspicions, and wrangling.** The truth as it is in Christ is the **teaching which accords with godliness.** After his experience at Athens, Paul wrote to

4 He is proud, knowing nothing, but doting about questions and strifes of words, whereof cometh envy, strife, railings, evil surmisings,

5 Perverse disputings of men of corrupt minds, and destitute of the truth, supposing that gain is godliness: from such withdraw thyself.

liness, 4 he is puffed up with conceit, he knows nothing; he has a morbid craving for controversy and for disputes about words, which produce envy, dissension, slander, base suspicions, 5 and wrangling among men who are depraved in mind and bereft of the truth, imagining that godli-

---

indirectly on the problems discussed in the Pastorals." Only in 5:18 (possibly) does the writer quote Jesus, and there only somewhat trivially, to justify financial support for elders. **Words** here then means "truths" ("instructions," Goodspeed): "The present phrase is an assertion that the ultimate authority of all 'sound words' is from Christ, and these 'words' are the same as 'the teaching that is in accord with true religion'" (Easton, *Pastoral Epistles*, p. 164). In other words, Jesus taught what "Paul" teaches. Only one teaching accords with "true religion," that teaching which "Paul" has transmitted from Christ.

**4-5.** The intensity with which the heretical teachers are berated indicates the strength of the heresy. Once again the author engages in name-calling without describing the content of the false teachings.

**Puffed up with conceit:** Elsewhere in the N.T. only 3:6 and II Tim. 3:4. **A morbid craving** (νοσέω): Only here; lit., "being diseased," i.e., engaging in **controversy** and **disputes about words** (λογομαχία, only here in N.T.; cf. II Tim. 2:14, λογομαχέω) to the point of disease. The battle is a sham battle: the weapons are empty words. Religious speculation and controversy produce only harm. The end is only **envy, dissension,**

---

the church at Corinth: "I, brethren, when I came to you, came not with excellency of speech or of wisdom. . . . For I determined not to know any thing among you, save Jesus Christ, and him crucified" (I Cor. 2:1-2).

There is a long-standing debate as to what is meant by "the finality of Christ." Does not God have new truth for every generation? Can it be that God spoke his final Word two thousand years ago in the Man of Nazareth? Should not believers in a living God be open-minded to new revelations of his truth? Yes. But "the finality of Christ" does not mean that God ceased speaking in the first century. Through the Holy Spirit he is active in his world always, guiding, reproving, encouraging, and empowering. But what we think are the promptings of the Holy Spirit are to be tested by their conformity to the mind of Christ. Every Christian is tempted to imagine that the promptings of his own selfish ambition are the voice of the Holy Spirit, or that the voice of the people is the voice of God. The historic Jesus portrayed in the Gospels is the touchstone by which the validity of all moral judgments and all questions of faith is to be tested. Each generation must face the problems and perplexities of its own time in the light of the truth as it is in Jesus. He is the Way, the Truth, and the Life.

In 1948, Trinity Congregational Church, in

the London district called Poplar, celebrated its 106th anniversary, although its church building and even the tombstones which had surrounded it had been destroyed by bombs during World War II. The church's most distinguished son, the writer H. M. Tomlinson, came back to speak. Surveying the ruins, he remarked that "the old standards are gone also. We are living in an age of nihilism." But he added,

I have travelled all round the world and through more than fifty years, and I came back here to tell you the simple truth that Christ is the supreme flowering of human life. Let the world turn there for guidance, for there is the ultimate wisdom without which the world will be lost.[8]

George Matheson confessed: "Son of Man, whenever I doubt of life, I think of thee. Thou never growest old to me. Thou art abreast of all the centuries. I have never come up with thee, modern as I am."

"The Gospel can only successfully be defended as it is continually rediscovered," said W. M. Macgregor to the divinity students of Scotland.[9]

**5-10.** *Is Godliness Profitable?*—One of the commonest superstitions which masquerades as

[8] *The British Weekly*, May 13, 1948.
[9] *The Making of a Preacher* (London: Student Christian Movement Press, 1945), p. 41.

| 6 But godliness with contentment is great gain. | ness is a means of gain. 6 There is great gain in godliness with contentment; 7 for we |
| 7 For we brought nothing into *this* world, *and it is* certain we can carry nothing out. | brought nothing into the world, and[m] we |

**slander, base suspicions, and wrangling.** As men argue and wrangle they become depraved and then defrauded of the truth, robbed of the gospel, and end by thinking of religion as just a way of making money.

Judging from the verses that follow, the heretical teachers are concerned with fees, perhaps for their instruction, to a much greater extent than our writer regards as justifiable. They may have been like traveling evangelists who stir up a community into religious wranglings and end by taking out such large amounts of money as to make it appear evident that they really think of religion only as a means of personal gain.

### XIX. THE CONTENTED CHRISTIAN (6:6-10)

This is a little homily in praise of moderation in the desire for money and the pursuit of material goods. Wealth is here not a privilege nor yet an opportunity; it is a peril. The risks to the soul involved in its accumulation are too great to warrant the venture. This point of view is that of Jesus, is broadly Christian and Stoic, and indeed is widespread in the history of religion.

Obviously the homily quickly passes beyond the concern with heretics, by which it is introduced, and is directed to the Christian reader in general. The fact that it leaps beyond the context and that its pattern of reasoning is not specifically Christian, together with the number of possible epigrams it quotes, suggests that the section is a block of Hellenistic material either combined or adapted by the author for his own purposes.

**6.** The usual interpretation of this verse, viz., that religion is profitable provided it goes with a contented spirit, obscures its real meaning. Rather, as over against vs. 5, in which the heretics are accused of making religion into a means of monetary gain, vs. 6 says that religion is indeed a means of **great gain,** but in quite other than a financial sense. What religion does at its best is to create within man self-mastery or self-sufficiency which is incongruous with the desire for wealth. To the godly man wealth is unnecessary; he has no desire for it; he is content with what he has.

**7.** The argument is that since we can neither bring wealth with us into the world nor take it out, it is not essential to our well-being. The pursuit of wealth is thus not a vocation proper to (Christian) man.

In the commonly accepted Greek text the word "because" connecting the two clauses of vs. 7, if taken in its usual sense, would require some such meaning as: we have **brought nothing into the world** because we can take **nothing out** of it. While this is a possible translation, the idea expressed by it is irrelevant to the context. Spicq defends

---

religion is the idea that **godliness is a means of gain.** Honesty, industry, sobriety, the three virtues which used to appear in framed mottoes in New England parlors, undoubtedly do aid the man who wants to get ahead in the world. Because Puritanism in an age of license stressed these virtues, the theory has been advanced in some quarters that Puritanism identified religion with material prosperity. There is a type of Christian who imagines that his prosperity is an evidence of his righteousness, and there is a prudential type of teaching, of which some of Benjamin Franklin's homely maxims are an example, which would encourage young people to cultivate character as a means of getting wealth. The fact is, however, that many a man is not successful in a worldly sense because of his loyalty to principles, and that many a man has made money by his disregard for ethical principles. There are three searching questions to be applied to all wealth: "How is it acquired?" "How is it used?" "To whom does the owner consider himself accountable in its use?"

The question at issue here, however, is one that goes deeper than does the superficial identification of godliness and gain. Paul is thinking of motives. If he had in mind the attitude of certain religious teachers in whose minds fees

8 And having food and raiment, let us be therewith content.

9 But they that will be rich fall into temptation and a snare, and *into* many foolish and hurtful lusts, which drown men in destruction and perdition.

10 For the love of money is the root of all evil: which while some coveted after, they have erred from the faith, and pierced themselves through with many sorrows.

cannot take anything out of the world; 8 but if we have food and clothing, with these we shall be content. 9 But those who desire to be rich fall into temptation, into a snare, into many senseless and hurtful desires that plunge men into ruin and destruction. 10 For the love of money is the root of all evils; it is through this craving that some have wandered away from the faith and pierced their hearts with many pangs.

---

it as setting forth the idea that life is a pilgrimage, and the reason why we bring nothing into the world is because we can take nothing out. The conditions of birth are determined with a view to the conditions of death. Men ought therefore to be content with the minimum indispensables for the voyage between birth and death. It is better to suppose either that the word for "because" (ὅτι) is used in a weakened sense and is the equivalent of "as" or "and," or that the text is corrupt. None of the early textual variations can be accepted as primitive for they are attempts to clarify our text. The saying had become almost proverbial. Easton prints both clauses in quotation marks (see Job 1:21; Eccl. 5:15; Wisd. Sol. 7:6; Philo *On the Special Laws* I. 294-95; Seneca *Epistles* CII. 24-25; Herm. Sim. I. 6).

**8.** Easton prints the verse as a quotation representing "the very essence of Stoicism." The word translated **clothing** includes shelter too. Knowing the unimportance of wealth, the Christian (or wise man in the Greek tradition) is **content** with food and shelter in moderation.

If the idea is Hellenistic, it also reflects the advices of Jesus to the disciples (see Mark 6:7 ff.=Matt. 10:5 ff.=Luke 10:1-7; Matt. 6:25-33=Luke 12:22-31).

**9.** According to the literal statement, it is not the rich but **those who desire to be rich** who fall into temptation. Although there is a point of contact between this emphasis on desire in contrast to the overt act and the similar emphasis in the Sermon on the Mount (see Matt. 5:21 ff.), the language here and in the section is more immediately Stoic. "In itself 'desire' is morally neutral and becomes good or evil only because of the motive (usually discernible in the object desired) . . . . But in Stoicism, with its ideal of 'apathy' and complete self-sufficiency, the four emotions 'desire, pleasure, grief, fear' became cardinal faults against which relentless war must be waged." (Easton, *Pastoral Epistles,* pp. 186-87.) The **desire to be rich** opens the flood gates through which pour **many** other **senseless and hurtful desires** which submerge men in total ruin. It is a **snare** (of the devil? see II Tim. 2:26) to trip men up to their destruction. The Christian reader might remember Luke 12:16 ff.; 16:19 ff., etc., where rich men are deprived by death not only of their accumulated wealth but also of eternal blessedness.

**10.** Vs. 10a is without doubt a quotation of a current proverb. The definite article is lacking in Greek before **root.** That the meaning of the sentence requires it is held by

---

bulked larger than truth, he was echoing the teaching of Jesus about the hireling (John 10:12-13). Here is a perennial problem for religious workers. They must have remuneration for their work, yet they must not work for the sake of remuneration. But the point of this passage has a much wider application than this. There are modern cults, and certain modern movements within the Christian church, which hold out material prosperity as the promised reward for prayer, meditation, and directed thought. This is to distort religion. This is

trying to use God for our selfish purposes instead of offering ourselves to God to be used for his purposes. Jesus did not say, "Seek first all these things and the kingdom of God will be added unto you," which seems to be the teaching of certain brands of perverted Christianity today.

Paul is here arguing for a balanced view of material possessions. Matt. 6:25-34 contains Jesus' plea for freedom from anxiety about material possessions, which seems to be the point made here. There is no condemnation of riches

11 But thou, O man of God, flee these things; and follow after righteousness, godliness, faith, love, patience, meekness.

12 Fight the good fight of faith, lay hold on eternal life, whereunto thou art also called, and hast professed a good profession before many witnesses.

11 But as for you, man of God, shun all this; aim at righteousness, godliness, faith, love, steadfastness, gentleness. 12 Fight the good fight of the faith; take hold of the eternal life to which you were called when you made the good confession in the pres-

the RSV, Moffatt, Scott, Goodspeed, Lock, vs. Easton, Spicq. The emphasis of the section seems to favor the former interpretation, although the absence of the article itself stands against it. **Love of money is the root of all evils** in that there is none to which it may not lead.

Vs. 10b returns to the heretics, whose heresy is attributed in vs. 5 to desire for gain. **Some** may subtly conceal certain individuals definitely known to the writer. With craving for money has come loss of Christian faith and inevitable and repeated anguish of spirit.

## XX. THE OBEDIENT CHRISTIAN WARRIOR (6:11-16)

**11.** Again the author recedes from general advices to direct address to "Timothy," i.e., to the teaching, preaching, ruling ministry of the church. While it may be taken for granted that all Christians will strive to practice the virtues proper to God's men, and that what is written to preachers is written through them to the people, a very special obligation lies on the preacher as **man of God.** While in a sense every Christian is a man of God, the expression is not used in the N.T. in the plural or as the equivalent of "God's people" (οἱ ἅγιοι), and is most naturally taken as it would have been by the first readers, to designate "Timothy" as a peculiarly called, endowed, and obligated person, in the O.T. sense of the word: Ps. 90:1 (Hebrew); Deut. 33:1 (of Moses); I Sam. 2:27; 9:6; I Kings 12:22; 17:24; II Kings 4:7 (of prophets). The expression has an O.T. ring. In the N.T. it occurs only here in direct address; but see II Tim. 3:17.

Once again we have the vague **these things** (all this—RSV; see vs. 2b; 4:6). The list of virtues is neither O.T. nor Pauline. To **aim at** [pursue] **righteousness** or **faith** is not Pauline language. To Paul these are God's gifts, not man's achievements. To our writer salvation is the consequence, not the cause of the good life.

Here not only are **righteousness, faith,** and **love** regarded as specific virtues needing to be combined with **patience** and **meekness,** but they are understood in a Greek sense: righteousness is integrity or right behavior, faith is loyalty to received teaching, as is **steadfastness.** On **godliness** see on 2:2. Lists of virtues, as of vices, are more or less conventional; the words need not be given too precise a meaning, or their exact differences too carefully distinguished.

**12. Fight the good fight,** printed in quotation marks by Easton as an arena saying, became an athletic metaphor applicable to any kind of struggle. However, the adjective **good** (="noble," "splendid") is characteristic of the Pastorals and is the author's way of

as such in this passage. **But those who desire to be rich fall into temptation, into a snare.** It is not money but **the love of money** which **is the root of all evils.** A modern play *You Can't Take It with You* takes its title from vs. 7. Francis G. Peabody in one of his Harvard Chapel addresses told Ruskin's story of a man who tried to swim to safety from a wrecked ship. About his waist he tied a belt containing two hundred pounds in gold, money which he could not bring himself to leave behind. Unable to reach shore with the extra weight, he sank and was drowned.

Ruskin asked, "As he was sinking, had he the gold, or had the gold him?" [1] Two results of **this craving** are wandering **away from the faith,** and a heart **pierced . . . with many pangs.**

**11-14. A Call to Victory.**—Before an athletic team goes on the field it is not unusual for the coach or captain to give a final exhortation rousing the players to a determination to give their best in the effort to win a victory. There is a similar note in some of these stirring im-

[1] *Mornings in the College Chapel* (2nd ser.; Boston: Houghton Mifflin Co., 1907), p. 2.

**13** I give thee charge in the sight of God, who quickeneth all things, and *before* Christ Jesus, who before Pontius Pilate witnessed a good confession;

ence of many witnesses. **13** In the presence of God who gives life to all things, and of Christ Jesus who in his testimony before Pontius Pilate made the good confession,

---

distinguishing the Christian fight from the struggles of the world, or the "word fighting" (vs. 4) of the heretics.

**The faith** is, as usual in these letters, purely objective, i.e., the Christian faith. The prize which is the reward is **eternal life.** Although it is God "who gives life" (vs. 13), the Pastorals particularly emphasize the duty of man to **take hold of** it. As something that can be taken hold of, **eternal life** seems to be thought of as at least in part a present possession, as in the Fourth Gospel. On the other hand, the metaphor of **the good fight** suggests that the prize comes only at the end of the race. It is this for which Christians are called and sealed (at baptism), but they will secure the gift only if they persevere in keeping "the commandment unstained and free from reproach until the appearing of our Lord Jesus Christ" (vs. 14).

"Timothy" was **called** effectively to eternal life when he **made the good confession in the presence of many witnesses.** The **good confession** here referred to is sometimes identified with the profession of faith which "Timothy" made at ordination. This, however, is quite unsuitable. At ordination one was not called to eternal life, one was set apart for a task. Almost certainly the reference is to baptism. **The good confession** is the baptismal confession, "Jesus is Lord" (Rom. 10:9; I Cor. 12:3; Phil. 2:11), or an elaboration of it. Baptism was the time when men were effectively called to eternal life. In the pagan world, as in the non-Christian world today, baptism, as the rite of passage from the world to the church, as rebirth from this present evil world of darkness into the kingdom of the Son of God's love, was an act of public profession effectively separating the Christian from the world and establishing him in the church. The **many witnesses** who both negatively and positively consolidated the new believer in his faith would be the unbelievers whom he had dramatically abandoned and the believers whom he had joined. Although, it may be urged, "Timothy" was a Christian from childhood (II Tim. 3:15), baptized in infancy, the letter has in mind the many "Timothys" who were pagan converts, and for whom baptism as the sacrament of regeneration was the creative event of their lives.

**13.** The reference of **the good confession** in vs. 12 to the baptismal creed would hardly be questioned if it were not for the solemn oath in vss. 13-14, in which "Timothy" is charged **in the presence of God who,** as alone having immortality (vs. 16), **gives life to all things, and of Christ Jesus who in his testimony before Pontius Pilate made the good confession.** It is tempting to regard "Timothy's" good confession as identical with that of Jesus before Pontius Pilate, and to think of both as martyrdom. **The good confession** which Jesus made **before Pontius Pilate** can scarcely be identified with the (somewhat guarded) admission of Jesus that he was "King of the Jews" (Matt. 27:11= Luke 23:3) or even of his "witness to the truth" in John 18:33-37. The language of vs. 13, both *a* and *b*, is liturgical and confessional. If vs. 13*b* is not an actual variation of the article of the creed, "suffered under Pontius Pilate," the latter is an interpretation of vs.

---

peratives which come at the close of this epistle. **Fight the good fight of the faith** borrows the language of a wrestling match. **Take hold of the eternal life** implies contending for the victor's prize. Timothy is called **man of God,** implying that he is not his own, but Another's. Where Jesus said, "Seek first his kingdom and his righteousness" (Matt. 6:33), Paul paraphrases the command to read, **Aim at righteous-**

ness, godliness, faith, love, steadfastness, gentleness. He reminds Timothy that he is under a vow of loyalty. **You made the good confession in the presence of many witnesses** refers to the pledge given by Timothy when he received Christian baptism, at which he probably subscribed to the affirmation that "Jesus is Lord." This is a passage which may appropriately be called to the attention of all who have taken

| 14 That thou keep *this* commandment without spot, unrebukable, until the appearing of our Lord Jesus Christ: | 14 I charge you to keep the commandment unstained and free from reproach until the |

---

13*b*. **The good confession** before Pilate was not so much what Jesus said; it was what he did. He remained loyal in word and deed; he did not flinch or falter, even before the representative of Rome who had power to take his life. Just when the word "witness" (μάρτυς) came to mean martyr is not clear. Very early, however, when used with reference to the self-defense of Jesus at his trial, the word must have come to include the fact of his death (see I Clem. 5:4). And since Jesus' death immediately followed his confession, his death became his confession.

If **the good confession** of Jesus before Pontius Pilate was his martyrdom, and if "Timothy's" **good confession** in vs. 12 is to be similarly interpreted, we should be compelled to suppose that "Paul" writing to "Timothy" after the real Timothy's death, for the moment writes to or about Timothy, not to "Timothy," and presents Timothy's good confession (at martyrdom) as model for all "Timothys." Tradition (see Acts of Timothy) has Timothy martyred under Nerva in 97.

A simpler and probably better explanation, however, will rather integrate vss. 13*a* and *b* into the baptismal liturgy current in Asia. On the one hand, baptism was commonly associated with rebirth and resurrection; hence the relevance of the clause, **God who gives life**, to the baptismal liturgy. Furthermore, at baptism the Christian was reminded that as Jesus was loyal to the death, so the vows which he was now assuming might also lead him before Roman governors and require a similar **good confession.** "Paul," then, charges "Timothy" **to keep the commandment** (vs. 14) by adjuring him with solemn phrases quoted from the confession of faith which he affirmed at baptism.

Dibelius suggests that the original form of the creed as it came to "Paul" lacked the words **the good confession**, and simply said that "Jesus bore testimony before Pontius Pilate," using "to bear testimony" after the manner of I Clem. 5:4, 7. Then, in order to establish a parallel with the baptismal confession of "Timothy," the author introduced into vs. 13 the words **the good confession**, thereby interpreting the testimony of Jesus as a word confession.

**14. The commandment** which Timothy shall keep **unstained and free from reproach** is not to be limited to the charge of vss. 11-12, or to obligations assumed at baptism (such as I Pet. 1:3–4:11), or yet to the entire body of admonitions given in the letter. "The faith" in vs. 12 and **the commandment** here are synonyms. In the Pastorals, the chief duty of the minister is to maintain the received (Pauline) Christian teaching intact and to transmit it unaltered.

---

the vows of membership in the Christian church.

Every church is concerned with the number of people, young and old, who are confirmed or unite with the church and then cease to have any active connection with its work and worship. They make **the good confession** but they do not **fight the good fight of the faith.** Some obvious reasons for this situation are: inadequate training for participation in the life of the church; the fact that some come into the church on the tide of a group movement rather than by personal decision; the mistaken conception of the church as a congenial club rather than as a heroic campaign for Christ; the insidious influences of a secular or pagan society in which the church and the Christian must live; the lack of staying power which leads people to give up when it grows hard what they undertook when it looked romantic; failure to keep up the practices of the devotional life which are the springs of power; neglect of corporate worship which affirms the reality of the body of Christ; inability or unwillingness to find active expression of loyalty to the church in service; lack of evangelistic zeal, born of the conviction that Christ is the answer for every man's need. Once a year every church needs a sermon on some such text as this: I charge you to keep the **commandment unstained and free from reproach until the appearing of our Lord Jesus Christ.**

15 Which in his times he shall show, *who is* the blessed and only Potentate, the King of kings, and Lord of lords;

appearing of our Lord Jesus Christ; 15 and this will be made manifest at the proper time by the blessed and only Sovereign, the

---

When Christ appears, there will be a reckoning: "Timothy" will then be judged as to his faithfulness. The assumption is that he will live until Christ returns, although the immediacy of the appearing is not emphasized. The word **appearing** (ἐπιφάνεια) occurs in II Thess. 2:8 but otherwise only in the Pastorals (II Tim. 1:10; 4:1, 8; Tit. 2:13, all concerning the apocalyptic appearing except II Tim. 1:10, which see). The older Jewish-Christian word for the apocalyptic appearing, "parousia," "presence," occurs in the N.T. with an apocalyptic meaning seven times in Paul, ten times elsewhere; in a nonapocalyptic sense, seven times in Paul, but nowhere else in the N.T. That our writer should have replaced it with ἐπιφάνεια indicates how far he has moved from the apocalyptic point of view.

15. Although the church generally continued to maintain belief in the (re-)appearing of Christ, as the years passed it became quietly adjusted to the delay. The "appearing" will surely happen; yet there is no need to get excited about it. It will take place **at the proper time**, i.e., in God's own time. The author's mind is essentially nonapocalyptic. For him the church is being organized and established, not to wait, but to work.

The doxology which follows (vss. 15-16) is one of the finest in Christian literature. Its language is characteristic of Hellenistic Judaism, and may be a Christian adaptation of liturgical material used in the synagogue. On this Hellenistic use of **blessed**, cf. on 1:11. That God alone is **Sovereign** is thoroughly Jewish, although the word (δυνάστης) is applied to God only in the later Jewish literature (II Macc. 15:3; Ecclus. 46:5), and in the N.T. only to human rulers (Luke 1:52; Acts 8:27). So also, **King of kings and Lord of lords** (see Rev. 17:14; 19:16; II Macc. 13:4; III Macc. 5:35; Ezek. 26:7; Dan. 2:37; Ezra 7:12. Philo *On the Cherubim* 99; *On the Special Laws* I. 18). Since the titles were used with bombast by powerful rulers, it is natural to see in their Jewish-Christian use an intended contrast and counter assertion to king and emperor worship.

---

**15-16.** *Another Christian Hymn.*—Here is another rhythmical passage which may well have been a hymn familiar to those who first read the epistle. Like other N.T. hymns (Luke 1:46-55, 68-79; 2:14, 29-32; II Tim. 2:11-13; Eph. 5:14; Rev. 5:13) this is a doctrinal statement which was probably set to music and chanted. There is sometimes a notion that a creed is a lifeless thing, a prison for thought, an instrument of oppression, a club in the hand of ecclesiastical authority. But the affirmation of a great belief should be a shout of joy, a song of freedom, a hymn of praise. In vs. 13 Paul has just affirmed belief in God the creator, and in the real humanity of Jesus. Now he goes on to affirm the lordship of Christ, and the majesty of God who is eternal, transcendent, and invisible. Before such a deity man's appropriate attitude is one of awe, praise, and reverent worship.

The title **King of kings** was used to describe Nebuchadrezzar in Ezek. 26:7, and is used with reference to Christ in Rev. 17:14; 19:16. For the early Christians the highest title was not too high to give to Jesus. For our own day we need to recognize him as lord in our personal life,

in our homes, in business and commerce, and in international affairs. We need to make him lord of thought, conscience, and action. This is the belief which Matthew Bridges celebrated in the hymn "Crown him with many crowns." And Francis Thompson used these metaphors in the lines:

" 'Twas on a day of rout they girded Me about,
  They wounded all My brow, and they smote Me
    through the side:
My hand held no sword when I met their armèd
    horde,
  And the conqueror fell down, and the Conquered
    bruised his pride."

. . . . . . . . . . .

What is *Thy* Name? Oh, show!—"My Name ye may
    not know;
  'Tis a going forth with banners, and a baring of
    much swords:
But My titles that are high, are they not upon My
    thigh?
  'King of Kings!' are the words, 'Lord of Lords!'
It is written 'King of Kings, Lord of Lords.' " [2]

[2] "The Veteran of Heaven." From *Collected Works*, ed. Francis Meynell. Used by permission of Burns, Oates & Washbourne, Ltd., and The Newman Press, publishers.

| | |
|---|---|
| 16 Who only hath immortality, dwelling in the light which no man can approach unto; whom no man hath seen, nor can see: to whom *be* honor and power everlasting. Amen.<br><br>17 Charge them that are rich in this world, that they be not high-minded, nor trust in uncertain riches, but in the living God, who giveth us richly all things to enjoy; | King of kings and Lord of lords, 16 who alone has immortality and dwells in unapproachable light, whom no man has ever seen or can see. To him be honor and eternal dominion. Amen.<br><br>17 As for the rich in this world, charge them not to be haughty, nor to set their hopes on uncertain riches but on God who richly furnishes us with everything to enjoy. |

16. The statements that God **alone has immortality** and **dwells in unapproachable light** are paralleled by many utterances in Jewish literature (see H. L. Strack and Paul Billerbeck, *Kommentar zum Neuen Testament aus Talmud und Midrasch* [München: C. H. Beck, 1922-28], III, 656; cf. also Ps. 104:2; Job 37:23; II Cor. 4:6; I John 1:7; Rom. 1:23; Acts 7:2).

**Whom no man has ever seen or can see:** Cf. John 1:18; 6:46; Acts of the Scilitan Martyrs.

### XXI. TRUE RICHES (6:17-19)

17. That so superb a doxology as vss. 15-16 should be followed by the "painful anticlimax" (Easton) of vss. 17-19 has prompted the suggestion that these verses are an interpolation (so Falconer; also see Adolf von Harnack, *Der Chronologie der altchristlichen Litteratur bis Eusebius* [Leipzig: J. C. Hinrichs, 1897] I, 482), or were added by a

Dorothy Sayers has written an essay entitled "The Greatest Drama Ever Staged Is the Official Creed of Christendom." In it she says:

We are constantly assured that the churches are empty because preachers insist too much upon doctrine—"dull dogma," as people call it. The fact is the precise opposite. It is the neglect of dogma that makes for dullness. The Christian faith is the most exciting drama that ever staggered the imagination of man—and the dogma is the drama.[3]

After a brief review of the life and death of Jesus, she comments:

If this is dull, then what, in Heaven's name, is worthy to be called exciting? The people who hanged Christ never, to do them justice, accused Him of being a bore—on the contrary, they thought Him too dynamic to be safe. It has been left for later generations to muffle up that shattering personality and surround Him with an atmosphere of tedium.[4]

It was this excitement which the early church must have felt when it sang its creed.

The discovery of such a rhythmic creedal statement in an epistle like this throws some light on the reasons for the repetition of his-

toric creeds in church services. The difficulties with such repetition are that sometimes the creeds lose their vitality through frequent repetition, sometimes worshipers have difficulty with specific statements in the creeds, and sometimes their use in weekly worship gives the impression that the church is founded upon intellectual statements of belief rather than upon dynamic faith in Christ. On the other hand, the historic creeds constitute a bond which unites Christians of many lands, many communions, and many centuries. There is an experience of "the communion of saints" in their use. They represent the distilled essence of the faith of the church, not the particular conclusions of a lone follower of Christ, however worthy. It is the church which voices its affirmations in the timeless and universal phrases. Just as in many a hymn there are expressions which do not in every detail express the convictions of all the individuals who sing them, so there may be differing interpretations of the meaning of particular statements in the creed. But it is an awesome moment when the church, caught in the midst of a temporal and secular life, rises and with united voice affirms its faith in the God who creates, redeems, and will preserve, the God made flesh in Jesus Christ, saying, "I believe"!

17-19. *The True Riches.*—Again Paul returns to the theme of the transitoriness of earthly

[3] *Creed or Chaos?* (New York: Harcourt, Brace & Co., 1949), p. 3. Copyright 1949 by Dorothy L. Sayers. Used by permission.

[4] *Ibid.*, p. 5.

18 That they do good, that they be rich in good works, ready to distribute, willing to communicate;

19 Laying up in store for themselves a good foundation against the time to come, that they may lay hold on eternal life.

18 They are to do good, to be rich in good deeds, liberal and generous, 19 thus laying up for themselves a good foundation for the future, so that they may take hold of the life which is life indeed.

---

later editor when there were enough "rich" Christians to warrant consideration as a special class (Easton). Von Soden thinks the verses have been accidentally misplaced and should come after vs. 2; Lock, after vs. 10. Scott regards the awkwardness as only "apparent" and as due to the long parenthesis of vss. 11-16. The subject of riches, begun in vss. 6-10, is held in suspense while life devoted to material things is contrasted with the true and eternal life. "Now he returns to his main subject, and as he has spoken before to those who are seeking for riches he proceeds to offer a warning to those who are already rich" (Scott, *Pastoral Epistles,* p. 80).

In this sort of writing, however, there is no need to labor to discover logical order or subtle lines of thought supposed to provide coherence. Rather, admonitions are typically introduced with abruptness, in part because traditional material is at hand ready for use and may be introduced without careful editing; in part because the author's purpose is not to produce fine literature, but by repeated hammering to drive his points home.

The phrase **the rich in this world,** lit., "in the present age" (only in Pastorals: II Tim. 4:10; Tit. 2:12; cf. Rom. 12:2; I Cor. 2:6; II Cor. 4:4) is itself depreciatory. Since the present age will pass away, true riches are not to be found in it; true riches are treasures in heaven. Yet the appraisal of riches here is much less severe than in vss. 7-10 or in Jas. 1:10-11; 5:1 ff. or frequently in the Gospels: Luke 12:16-21; 18:18-30; Matt. 6:19-20; Mark 10:17-26. The rich are not here condemned for being rich or told to renounce their wealth. Rather, they are told **not to be haughty, nor to set their hopes on uncertain riches.** The temptations of the rich, our author says, are to illicit pride and to an unwarranted sense of security. Only God is a safe repository for one's hope.

Wealth may be enjoyed if the Christian remembers that it is **God who richly furnishes us with everything to enjoy.** This is the same antiascetic idea which 4:4-5 presents, but is in another tone than 6:7-10.

**18. Rich in good deeds** is a common idea in the Pastorals (see 2:10; 5:10, 25; II Tim. 2:21; 3:17; Tit. 1:16; 2:7, 14; 3:1, 8, 14).

**19.** A literal translation would be, "Treasuring up for themselves a good foundation." However, the Greek word θεμέλιον has a double meaning, either "fund" (="capital") or **foundation;** and to the Greek reader the text may well have meant "treasure." This meaning is possible without emending the text after a striking parallel in Tob. 4:9-10 so as to make it read "right good treasure" (Moffatt) or "valuable treasure"

---

possessions, and the durability of spiritual treasure. This passage should be read with Luke 12:13-34 as background. Paul reiterates the conviction that the things of this world are the gifts of **God who richly furnishes us with everything to enjoy.** But material possessions are to be judged by the use made of them, and by the extent to which they are made to serve spiritual life which is **eternal life** or **the life which is life indeed.**

Francis Thompson's tribute to Henry Edward Manning is a noble description of what it means to appraise correctly **uncertain riches** and being **rich in good deeds:**

He lives detachèd days;
He serveth not for praise;
    For gold
    He is not sold.

.   .   .   .   .   .

He measureth world's pleasure,
World's ease as Saints might measure;
    For hire
    Just love entire.

He asks, not grudging pain;
And knows his asking vain.[5]

[5] "To the Dead Cardinal of Westminster." From *Collected Works,* ed. Francis Meynell. Used by permission of Burns, Oates & Washbourne, Ltd., and The Newman Press, publishers.

20 O Timothy, keep that which is committed to thy trust, avoiding profane *and* vain babblings, and oppositions of science falsely so called:

21 Which some professing have erred concerning the faith. Grace *be* with thee. Amen.

¶ The first to Timothy was written from Laodicea, which is the chiefest city of Phrygia Pacatiana.

20 O Timothy, guard what has been entrusted to you. Avoid the godless chatter and contradictions of what is falsely called knowledge, 21 for by professing it some have missed the mark as regards the faith. Grace be with you.

---

(Goodspeed). But either "treasure" or **foundation** is terminology which reflects the words of Jesus in the Sermon on the Mount.

**For the future** means "for the world to come."

**So that they may take hold of the life which is life indeed:** On **take hold of life** see vs. 12. By "doing good" and "being rich in good deeds" Christians are assured of life in the world to come, which is the real life.

### XXII. CONCLUDING APPEAL FOR FAITHFULNESS (6:20-21)

**20-21.** The closing verses of the letter reiterate the concern with which the letter began: above all, and as a last word, "Timothy" must **guard what has been entrusted** to him. As a churchman and official, a preacher and teacher, his task is to maintain and propagate the Christian rule of life and to protect the inherited faith from becoming contaminated and distorted by the variety of religions and philosophies with which it is being confronted. Particularly must he **avoid the godless chatter and contradictions of what is falsely called knowledge.**

As in 4:7; II Tim. 2:16, the religious language of the opponents is scathingly characterized as nonsense having nothing to do with religion, as both secular and meaningless. Since the word **contradictions** ("antitheses") later came to have technical meaning in Gnosticism (the heretic Marcion wrote a book so entitled, having to do probably with the "contradictions" between law and gospel), and since these heretics are Gnostics of some sort, it is tempting to see in the word a reference to some form of Gnostic dialectic critical of or hostile to the Christian faith as championed by the author. Since the word is not defined in the text, the possibility that it holds some such technical meaning must be left open. However, it need mean no more than that the teachings of the heretics, **falsely called knowledge,** stand over against or contradict the Christian faith and are therefore to be let alone, or that such teachings are a tissue of inner contradictions, a hodgepodge of unresolved "pros and cons" without the clarity and certainty of the Christian faith.

It is important to note that in vs. 20 only is *gnōsis* (γνῶσις) used for **knowledge.** In an important study of the phrase "knowledge of the truth" (ἐπίγνωσις ἀληθείας), Spicq (*Saint Paul: les Épitres Pastorales,* pp. 362-65) points out that whereas in the earlier Pauline letters Paul is himself the apostle of Christian *gnōsis,* in the Pastorals *epignōsis* has been exclusively substituted for *gnōsis* to refer to Christianity, thereby abandoning the word *gnōsis* to the false knowledge of Gnosticism.

It has been argued that vss. 20-21a are an anti-Marcionite gloss, *ca.* 150 (Baur, Harnack), or are for other reasons the addition of a later editor (Falconer; possibly

---

**20-21. The Final Word.**—How much feeling can be crowded into a word of one letter! All Paul's deep concern is poured forth in the **O Timothy,** with which the concluding appeal of the letter begins. In one swift sentence he recapitulates what he has been saying at length in six chapters. The Christian faith is a trust to be guarded. Vagaries and trivialities are not to be permitted to obscure the central realities of the faith. The believer is not to be intimidated by the parade of what passes for science or knowledge. The example of those who have missed the truth is to be heeded. The grace of God is to be the strength and stay of all believers.

Easton, etc.). This is a possible but by no means necessary conclusion in a letter which is not well organized from the literary standpoint, and which is concerned with certain practical matters of faith and order. It is entirely in the character of the writer that he should end not in a paean of praise, but with a final thrust at his opponents.

The letter closes with the simplest form of benediction: **Grace be with you. You** is plural, as is traditional in church letters. It may further be taken to show that "Timothy," to whom the letter is addressed, is not just a single person but stands for the younger ministry, and through it, for the church.

# II TIMOTHY

## TEXT, EXEGESIS, AND EXPOSITION

1 Paul, an apostle of Jesus Christ by the will of God, according to the promise of life which is in Christ Jesus,

1 Paul, an apostle of Christ Jesus by the will of God according to the promise of the life which is in Christ Jesus,

### I. The Salutation (1:1-2)

**1:1.** The opening lines differ from those of I Timothy in that instead of "by command of God our Savior," we have the more normal Pauline expression **by the will of God** (I Cor. 1:1; II Cor. 1:1; Col. 1:1; Eph. 1:1), and instead of "Christ Jesus our hope," we have **according to the promise of the life which is in Christ Jesus.** The meaning of the preposition here translated **according to** is obscure (see Tit. 1:1). In this text it is best interpreted to mean "with reference to," "in the service of" (Moffatt), "entrusted with" (Dibelius), i.e., the writer's mission under God is to declare to mankind that "in union with Christ Jesus" (eternal) life is (assuredly) promised.

Easton urges that the characteristic Pauline phrase **in Christ** is never used in the Pastorals in the Pauline mystical sense, "enveloped by" or "in union with." In instances where the phrase appears (here; vss. 9, 13; 2:1, 10; 3:12, 15; I Tim. 1:14; 3:13) "in" means either "given by," or "by the fact of Christ's existence," or "Christian" (1:13; 3:15; I Tim. 1:14; 3:13). It is true that the author of the Pastorals was no

---

**1:1. The Promise of Life.**—This epistle, like I Timothy, begins by stressing the Christian hope. To serve **the will of God** is not to obey a dread summons but is to venture forth **according to the promise of the life which is in Christ Jesus.** The N.T. is shot through with this note of promise. Paul applies to the followers of Christ the term "children of promise" (Gal. 4:28), which he took over from the O.T. Standing before Agrippa he claimed that it was "for hope in the promise made by God to our fathers" (Acts 26:6) that he was called in question. He cited Abraham as one who "staggered not at the promise of God through unbelief" (Rom. 4:20). On the day of Pentecost Peter called upon his hearers to be baptized: "For the

promise is unto you, and to your children, and to all that are afar off, even as many as the Lord our God shall call" (Acts 2:39). The Epistle to the Hebrews speaks of those "who through faith and patience inherit the promises" (Heb. 6:12) and recognizes it as a supreme mark of faith that some "died in faith, not having received the promises" (Heb. 11:13).

Christianity is not a shallow optimism. It does involve a mighty hope based on the revelation of truth which God has made in Christ. He is God's promise of a new life for every man, and of a new life for a society of men united in him. He is the promise of eternal life.

As the Exeg. suggests, there are wide differences of opinion as to the exact meaning in the N.T. of the phrase **in Christ Jesus.** Four prac-

For Introduction to II Timothy see pp. 343-74.

2 To Timothy, *my* dearly beloved son: Grace, mercy, *and* peace, from God the Father and Christ Jesus our Lord.

3 I thank God, whom I serve from *my* forefathers with pure conscience, that without ceasing I have remembrance of thee in my prayers night and day;

2 To Timothy, my beloved child: Grace, mercy, and peace from God the Father and Christ Jesus our Lord.

3 I thank God whom I serve with a clear conscience, as did my fathers, when I re-

---

mystic. Easton's interpretation is therefore possible. Nevertheless, a Paulinist can hardly have been unaware of the importance of this phrase in Pauline language or of its Pauline meaning. And if Col. 1:1-2 was a model (so Easton) for this greeting, **in Christ** may well have the same meaning in both places. Goodspeed's translation, "in union with," may then be accepted here, even though the phrase had a less pregnant meaning for the author than for Paul.

The formal solemnity of the greeting suggests public rather than private letter style, and emphasizes the authoritative position of the author as over against those addressed. To write to a body of subordinate clergy in this way is intelligible; to write so to a co-worker of years' standing would be insufferable bombast.

**2. To Timothy, my beloved child:** See on I Tim. 1:2, "my true child in the faith"; Tit. 1:4, "my true child in a common faith"; I Cor. 4:17, "my beloved and faithful child in the Lord."

**Grace, mercy, and peace from God the Father and Christ Jesus our Lord** is identical with I Tim. 1:2*b*, which see.

### II. Timothy, the Ideal Minister (1:3-7)

**3-4.** In contrast to I Timothy and Titus, but in accord with the Pauline letters except Galatians, II Timothy begins with a thanksgiving, which is interestingly similar

---

tical responses, however, seem to be called out by these significant words. (*a*) Gratitude: They sometimes refer to what God has done for men through "the grace which he gave us in Christ Jesus" (vs. 9). (*b*) Faith: Sometimes they refer to Christ Jesus as the adequate object of man's faith. Paul speaks of "the sacred writings which are able to instruct you for salvation through faith in Christ Jesus" (3:15). (*c*) Brotherhood: Men do not become brothers in a vacuum. They find a common bond in some shared loyalty. An officer in the French Air Force during World War II, Antoine de Saint-Exupéry, wrote:

I understand the origin of brotherhood among men. Men were brothers in God. One can be a brother only *in* something. Where there is no tie that binds men, men are not united but merely lined up. . . . The pilots of Group 2-33 are brothers in the Group. Frenchmen are brothers in France.[1]

"Brethren in Christ" (Col. 1:2) is the Christian promise. (*d*) Reconciliation: "If any one is in Christ, he is a new creation" (II Cor. 5:17). Here the phrase reaches ocean depth and we shall probably never plumb its profundity. But if we read this promise in the light of what fol-

[1] *Flight to Arras* (New York: Reynal & Hitchcock, 1942), p. 239.

lows, we may infer that Paul understood being **in Christ** to mean being reconciled to God through Christ. "All this is from God, who through Christ reconciled us to himself and gave us the ministry of reconciliation" (II Cor. 5:18). **The life which is in Christ Jesus** is a life of gratitude, faith, brotherhood, and reconciliation with God.

**2. *A Gracious Benediction.*—**The words of this verse are often used today as a benediction at the close of a church service or a religious gathering. In the Christian tradition, when a minister pronounces a benediction he speaks as an ambassador of Jesus Christ and as a representative of the universal church, blessing a particular congregation. It is appropriate therefore that this function should be reserved for ordained clergymen, and that when lay people lead services they should close with a prayer in the first person plural rather than with a formal benediction. This particular benediction is a reminder of God's marvelous gifts to his church, of the spiritual gifts which the church is called to mediate to the world, and of the character of God as he is revealed in Jesus Christ.

**3-5. *From One Generation to Another.*—**Paul remembers what he owes to the faith of his fathers, and then goes on to remind Timothy

| | |
|---|---|
| 4 Greatly desiring to see thee, being mindful of thy tears, that I may be filled with joy; | member you constantly in my prayers. 4 As I remember your tears, I long night and day to see you, that I may be filled with joy. |

to and different from the usual Pauline thanksgivings. The expression used here for **I thank** (χάριν ἔχω) is never used by Paul (cf. II Cor. 1:15), who uniformly employs εὐχαριστέω. The temporal adverb **constantly** occurs three times in Paul (Rom. 1:9; I Thess. 1:2; 2:13), but again with a slight difference: here the Greek word is in the adjective form. Only Rom. 1:10 has the conjunction "when" (ὡς) before the adverb "constantly." Nor does Paul ever use the idiom "have memory" (μνείαν ἔχειν) in this connection, but always "make memory" (μνείαν ποιεῖσθαι). Further, the usual Pauline expression for **in my prayers** is ἐπὶ τῶν προσευχῶν μου, not ἐν ταῖς δεήσεσίν μου. When δέησις is used in Paul (Phil. 1:4; II Cor. 1:11), it is always in the singular. Although the usual Pauline pronoun object phrase, "for you (all)" after "give thanks" is omitted here, the Pauline causal participial clause followed by a final clause occupies vs. 4. Thus of the seven syntactical units making up the Pauline thanksgivings (cf. Paul Schubert, *Form and Function of the Pauline Thanksgivings* [Berlin: A. Töpelmann, 1939]), six occur here; but within the six, the variations from typical Pauline usage are as striking as are the similarities.

**Whom I serve** has a parallel in Rom. 1:9, but **with a clear conscience, as did my fathers** is characteristic of the Pastorals, not of Paul. While conceivably Paul as a Christian might have said that he served God **with a clear conscience,** e.g., where he was defending himself before Jews who accused him of treason (Acts 23:1), he would scarcely have boasted to Timothy in such fashion. Nor could Paul ever have admitted that his Jewish fathers had **a clear conscience** (Rom. 7). The clause is most meaningfully interpreted if we suppose that the Paulinist author is here primarily concerned to show how Paul, the father and founder of the Asian churches, is the true pattern of the Christian minister. The details of faith are forgotten; it is enough that Paul's upbringing and family were sincerely religious. Indeed, the author may here have slipped out of character: **my fathers** may be his own fathers, who may well have been Christians. After all, the purpose of the pseudonymous writer is not to deceive; in any case, we should not suppose that he was at every point utterly concerned to conceal himself beneath the likeness of Paul, even though we cannot at every point distinguish the historical Paul from the "Paul" of this letter. The appeal in the paragraph is to continuity in faith, and to the parallel between the religious backgrounds of "Paul" and "Timothy." The

that he stands in at least the third generation of faith. If, as may be assumed, Timothy caught from Paul a broader vision of the kingdom of God as a world-embracing fellowship than Lois and Eunice had, he was prepared for that daring adventure of faith by his heritage. How many people have caught the faith by which they live from an older generation, and then expressed it in new ways! John Buchan (Lord Tweedsmuir) wrote of his boyhood home in the Scottish border country and of his minister father:

My father was a man of wide culture, to whom, in the words of the Psalms, all things were full of the goodness of the Lord. . . . He was conscious of living in a world ruled by unalterable law under the direct eye of the Almighty. He was a miserable atom as compared with Omnipotence, but an atom,

nevertheless, in which Omnipotence took an acute interest. The words of the Bible, from daily family prayers and long Sabbath sessions, were as familiar to him as the story of Jack and the Beanstalk. A child has a natural love of rhetoric, and the noble Scriptural cadences had their own meaning for me, quite apart from their proper interpretation. The consequence was that I built up a Bible world of my own and placed it in the woods.[2]

It is sometimes argued that children should be taught only those portions of the Bible which correspond to their own experience. It has no doubt been a healthy thing that religious education in modern times has learned to take a new interest in the child himself and his prob-

[2] *Pilgrim's Way* (Boston: Houghton Mifflin Co., 1940), pp. 5-6. Used by permission of the Tweedsmuir Trustees and the publishers.

5 When I call to remembrance the unfeigned faith that is in thee, which dwelt first in thy grandmother Lois, and thy mother Eunice; and I am persuaded that in thee also.

5 I am reminded of your sincere faith, a faith that dwelt first in your grandmother Lo′is and your mother Eunice and now, I

Christian faith is now no longer new, an affair of one generation: as the author's **fathers** were Christians, so Timothy had a Christian background. Since the faith has stood the test of more than one generation, "Timothy" is summoned not to an untried, but to an established, loyalty. "Timothy's" loyalty to the Christian faith is thus at the same time loyalty to his family, to Paul, the greatest of the apostles, and to the authentic and authoritative tradition. Devoted as the (aged?) author is to the historic faith and church, he cannot think of the younger "Timothy," now taking over his responsibilities, without thanking God for such a worthy successor and son in the gospel.

**As I remember your tears:** The author's devotion to "Timothy" was fully reciprocated. If the statement is a reference to the moving account of Paul's farewell at Miletus, particularly to Acts 20:37, it assumes that Paul and Timothy had not met each other since that time. Or the tears may be "Timothy's" tears because Paul or the author is in prison. Or, indeed, no specific reference need be intended. In Acts 20:19, 31 Paul twice tells how he served the Lord **with tears.** The **tears** of "Timothy" which our author remembers may have been tears like Paul's: tears shed in the anguish of Christian service, even tears transmuted into joy, because in the fellowship of weeping, men are sacramentally joined to one another. As the chief pastor, now inactive because in chains, remembers the tears of the younger "Timothy" as he labors in the service of Christ, his own memories are stirred; he longs **night and day** for the fellowship of his sons in the active ministry.

**5.** On **sincere faith,** see I Tim. 1:5. "Timothy's" **sincere faith** is his unquestioning acceptance of and commitment to Pauline Christianity as understood and cherished by the author, a faith which was held by and transmitted through his family for three generations. Since **Lois** is not mentioned elsewhere in the N.T., nothing is known of her except the uncertain inferences from this verse. Timothy's mother (although not named) is described in Acts 16:1 as a convert from Judaism. Since in the same passage Timothy's father is "a Greek," necessitating Timothy's being circumcised if he was to travel with Paul, and since the present verse mentions neither father nor grandfather, it may be thought that neither became a Christian (yet see p. 463). Since **Eunice** was born a Jewess, it may be supposed that both of her parents were Jews. Since Paul's background (**as did my fathers**), obviously Jewish, is here paralleled with Timothy's pious heritage, likewise Jewish, it is frequently urged that the purpose of the writer is to show that Christianity is the legitimate continuation of Judaism (Dibelius, Easton) or simply that

lems, and has turned to the Bible for light on the resources by which these problems may be effectively met. However, the argument has two sides. A man was once compelled to spend several months in a war situation in a strange land after his baggage, containing his Bible, was lost. He was grateful for certain psalms and other passages from the Bible which he had memorized in his youth. Some of them had little meaning for him when he learned them. Others took on new significance in the new life into which circumstances had thrust him. He discovered that there was a good deal of biblical material stored away as "Luggage to Be Called For" in the hold of his mind, which was of priceless value when he needed it. Like bonds which cannot be cashed until they mature there are great Christian convictions which ought to be the heritage of every child, even though the realization of their practical value is deferred until maturity. Jesus in the great crises of his life—his baptism, temptation, transfiguration, and crucifixion—fed his spirit with passages from the O.T. which he had learned in the synagogue school at Nazareth. The creative education of our time is a great tool in the hands of all who would teach religion to the coming generation. But it is supplementary to

6 Wherefore I put thee in remembrance, that thou stir up the gift of God, which is in thee by the putting on of my hands.

am sure, dwells in you. 6 Hence I remind you to rekindle the gift of God that is within you through the laying on of my

---

Paul and Timothy both had devout religious backgrounds (Scott). It is assumed, then, that Lois remained a Jewess.

What the facts were, however, in the case of Timothy's family, must remain uncertain. Taken at face value, the text certainly supposes that both Lois and Eunice were Christians. Acts 16:1 does not exclude this possibility. Since Eunice married a Greek, she cannot have been a devout Jewess. Her marriage is perhaps more intelligible if prior to it she had been converted to Christianity. That her parents consented to her marriage with a Gentile, or were not estranged from her because of it, argues that they too, or at least Lois, were at one time or another converted to Christianity. If on the other hand the author had known a tradition according to which Lois and Eunice were converts of Paul, he could hardly have avoided making use of it, concerned as he is to relate Timothy's faith to Paul's.

Whatever the precise situation in the historic Timothy's family may have been, the text, as post-Pauline, is best interpreted as showing the writer's great confidence and joy in third-generation Christian ministers, and the security he feels in the case of those who in the home have been rooted and grounded in the received (Pauline) form of Christianity. New converts are not to be trusted too far: they bring too many alien ideas and attitudes with them (see I Tim. 3:6). And even for "Timothy" the closing words of vs. 5, **and now, I am sure, dwells in you,** veil an admonition in addition to expressing a faith. Not even the young minister of excellent family background can take his faith for granted.

**6.** Since "Timothy's" faith is so securely grounded in an assured line of transmission, he should have complete confidence in his ministry; at the same time, confidence should not weaken resolve. Faith is not just an inheritance. It is a fire which God strikes in the soul. It is as if the years of "Timothy's" instruction and preparation for ordination were a laying of the kindling; in the rite of ordination God strikes the fire: **through the laying on of my** [Paul's or the writer's] **hands, the gift of God** had been mediated to the well-instructed "Timothy," i.e., through this rite "Timothy" was fully accredited and empowered to preach the faith which he had received. There is then a double reason why he should exert himself to the utmost in his ministry: he has been both well instructed and supernaturally endowed. Family and church have converged to equip him fully, the family to transmit the received faith (3:14-15), the church to mediate **the gift of God** in the name of Paul himself.

While the Greek verb may mean **rekindle** or "relight," it also may mean "agitate," **stir up** (KJV) or "fan into flame," and should be so understood here. It is not a

---

and not a substitute for the handing on from age to age of the spiritual heritage which God has provided for us in the Word. As Willard L. Sperry put it: "We lay the altar in these lives with classical accounts of the Christian life which will light up when life itself kindles them with sudden insight or vision." [3]

**6. Stir Up the Gift!**—Paul has already urged Timothy not to neglect the gift that is in him (I Tim. 4:14). Now he repeats the exhortation, with the variation **rekindle the gift of God that is within you through the laying on of my**

[3] *Reality in Worship* (New York: The Macmillan Co., 1925), p. 200.

**hands.** The reference here is to the gift of the Spirit at ordination, and suggests that even after a man has received the quickening of the Spirit he himself has a responsibility for keeping the flame burning. The exhortation is applicable to a wider circle than the ordained ministry. Every Christian knows the temptation to discouragement over the progress of the Christian cause and over his own progress, to lethargy as Christian service becomes an old story rather than a novelty, and to a shrinking from the sacrifices involved in a thoroughgoing Christian loyalty. The loyalty and devotion which are at the heart of Christian faith need

**7** For God hath not given us the spirit of fear; but of power, and of love, and of a sound mind.

hands; **7** for God did not give us a spirit of timidity but a spirit of power and love and self-control.

---

question of relighting a dead fire; it is a matter of agitating a slow flame to white and living heat. God's gift at ordination is neither static nor automatic. It is a fire which may be allowed to burn low or die out, or which may be kept a living flame.

In contrast to I Tim. 4:14 (which see), where "Timothy" receives **the gift** through the laying on of the hands of the elders or presbytery, the writer alone is here mentioned as mediator or ordainer. This difference may be explained as due (*a*) to the more personal character of II Timothy, in which the author is concerned to provide a personal-historical background for the general church ordinances of I Timothy by showing the effective and authoritative role which "Paul" played in the ordination of "Timothy" (Dibelius). There may then be no deliberate attempt to exclude the elderhood from participation in "Timothy's" ordination, but simply indifference to its presence. Or (*b*) I Tim. 4:14 may reflect the earlier and established corporate form of ordination, and the present verse its later modification to make history conform to the idea of apostolic succession. Or (*c*) the author may here be "thinking historically; if the real Timothy was formally ordained, the rite would have been performed by Paul alone" (B. S. Easton, *The Pastoral Epistles* [New York: Charles Scribner's Sons, 1947], p. 148), whereas in I Tim. 4:14 it is "Timothy" who is in the writer's mind, and in his time ordination by the elderhood was the normal practice. Or (*d*) if we regard the letter as pseudonymous, perhaps the best interpretation is that in this verse the author is concerned to show how vitally "Timothy" is related to both himself and the apostle Paul. Doubtless the writer had had a prominent part in the ordination of many "Timothys." As authoritative successor to Paul and the apostles, perhaps indeed as a bishop, our author might easily, even naïvely, have written as if the laying on of his hands alone mattered.

**7.** Since the Christian minister is to maintain his faith and zeal at fervent heat that he may witness boldly to the truth and power of the gospel, God has provided him with adequate endowment for his work. Not **a spirit of timidity** was God's ordination gift, **but a spirit of power and love and self-control.** Henceforth the **spirit** of the minister, i.e., the inner core, the abiding essence of his life is characterized by **power and love and self-control.** Although **spirit** is here properly printed with a lower case letter as

---

to be constantly rekindled through prayer, corporate worship, and unceasing Christian service. The Christian cause in every generation is crippled and handicapped by the dormant gifts of its adherents.

There is also the suggestion here that every Christian has latent gifts of which he is only partially aware. Laboratory tests, as well as the experiences of people in emergencies, show that the ordinary person has physical energies which in the usual events of his life he does not call into play. Similarly there are gifts of intellect and spiritual capacities often unsuspected in young men and women. These are awakened and released when life is committed to the Christian cause, and new purpose, new enthusiasm, and new sense of responsibility come into being. Young people and old people need to

count on these hidden gifts, and to stir them up. And they need to be constantly rekindled. John Buchan wrote of his father:

He believed profoundly in the fact of "conversion," the turning of the face to a new course. But, the first step having been taken, he would insist upon the arduousness of the pilgrimage as well as upon its moments of high vision and its ultimate reward. His religion was tender and humane, but it was also well-girded. He had no love for those who took their ease in Zion.[4]

**7. *The Conquest of Fear.***—If Timothy was afraid, his fears are understandable. He was undertaking an apparently impossible task and may have feared failure. He came from Lystra, where Paul had been stoned by the Judaizers

[4] *Op. cit.,* p. 250.

referring to the inner and abiding quality and character of Christian man, yet this spirit is not native to man, nor is it his achievement. It is God's gift. The spirit of Christian man is really God's Spirit.

**Spirit** and **power** are commonly associated in the N.T. (Acts 1:8; I Cor. 2:4; Gal. 3:5; I Thess. 1:5). Athough the Greek word for **timidity** occurs only here (cognate forms, John 14:27; Matt. 8:26; Mark 4:40; Rev. 21:8) in the N.T., the contrast between fear and love appears in classic form in I John 4:18: "There is no fear in love, but perfect love casts out fear." The Christian minister requires boldness and courage, the **power** which derives from a confident faith; yet the exercise of power is Christian only when fully joined with **love,** and these two with **self-control.**

**Self-control** or "sober good sense" (Spicq; σωφρονισμός, only here in N.T., not in LXX; σωφροσύνη, I Tim. 2:9, 15; Acts 26:25; σωφρόνως, Tit. 2:12; σώφρων, I Tim. 3:2; Tit. 1:8; 2:2; 2:5; σωφρονίξω, Tit. 2:4; σωφρονέω, Tit. 2:6; Mark 5:15; Luke 8:35; Rom. 12:3; II Cor. 5:13; I Pet. 4:7) is as un-Pauline as it is a characteristically Greek idea. Ten out of the twelve occurrences of the various forms of the word in the letters ascribed to Paul are in the Pastorals. One of the four cardinal Greek virtues, usually translated "temperance," it is interpreted by Plato as "a kind of orderliness, a control of certain pleasures and appetites" (*Republic* IV. 431E), as suggesting concord or harmony, the mastery of man's worse nature by his better, the guidance by reason and right belief of the simple and moderate desires characteristic of superior people. Aristotle (*Nichomachean Ethics* II. 7. 2; 9. 2) offers a noteworthy parallel to our passage, in which he associates fear, confidence, and "temperance." In discussing courage (ἀνδρεία), a word which does not appear in the N.T., Aristotle writes that "the man who exceeds in confidence is rash, and he who exceeds in fear . . . is a coward. With regard to pleasures and pains, . . . the mean is temperance, the excess self-indulgence." "Temperance" is, then, "a mean between two vices, the one involving excess, the other deficiency." To discover just what "temperance" involves, continues Aristotle, is difficult: "It is no easy task to be good. For in everything it is no easy task to find the middle, for instance, . . . anyone can get angry—that is easy—or give or spend money; but to do this to the right person, to the right extent, at the right time, with the right motive, and in the right way, *that* is not for everyone, nor is it easy; wherefore, goodness is both rare and laudable and noble." The triad before us, then, **power** (boldness, confidence in contrast to **timidity**), **love** and **self-control** (life ordered harmoniously, in balance between extremes) is an excellent example of the fine fusion of Hebraic, Christian, and Greek virtues which characterizes the Pastorals. **Power** stands for intensity of life, **love** for the warm affection of a self-giving life, and **self-control** for a reasoned, disciplined, well-ordered life. It is this spirit which God bestows upon every minister at ordination.

who felt that he was undermining the Jewish faith. Timothy may well have feared their opposition. Moreover, he was the follower of a Lord who had been crucified by imperial power that wanted no popular movements exciting the people. It would have been only natural if Timothy and his fellow Christians had moments of misgiving when they heard the tread of the marching feet of Roman legions, even though there was no active hostility to Christians at the time this epistle was written. Fear is for many people one of the central problems of life—fear of their own inadequacy, fear of the unfavorable opinion of other people, fear of disease, fear of financial insecurity, fear of the unknown. Such fears sap strength, para-

lyze initiative, and poison the atmosphere. Faith is the best weapon for the conquest of fear. **God hath not given us the spirit of fear; but of power, and of love, and of a sound mind.** The gift of the Spirit was sometimes misinterpreted as meaning merely an ecstatic emotion. Here it is understood as conveying adequacy to meet life effectively, practical helpfulness, and healthy-mindedness or self-control. Fear is often the evidence of inner weakness, self-centeredness, and an undisciplined mind. Faith in God which is expressed in commitment of life to the cause of Christ is the great antidote to fear. "Now when they saw the boldness of Peter and John, . . . they took knowledge of them, that they had been with Jesus" (Acts 4:13).

8 Be not thou therefore ashamed of the testimony of our Lord, nor of me his prisoner: but be thou partaker of the afflictions of the gospel according to the power of God;

9 Who hath saved us, and called *us* with a holy calling, not according to our works,

8 Do not be ashamed then of testifying to our Lord, nor of me his prisoner, but take your share of suffering for the gospel in the power of God, 9 who saved us and

---

### III. The True Minister Is Loyal to Paul's Gospel (1:8-14)

**8.** The Christian minister is called to testify to a crucified Lord and to preach a faith for which men are put in prison. But this should not daunt "Timothy." He has been endowed with a spirit of power; therefore he should be bold to declare before men his witness or testimony to his Lord, and also to Paul who is the Lord's prisoner. The writer is such an ardent devotee of Paul that for him loyalty to Christ includes also loyalty to Paul. Indeed, in his mind the two loyalties are so interrelated that his appeal to "Timothy" never loses sight of either. **Testimony** here may be merely a synonym of **gospel** (Easton). Yet the emphasis in the paragraph on **suffering** as a normal accompaniment of preaching suggests that true Christian testimony (μαρτυρία) is martyrdom (see I Clem. 5:4, 7; also Exeg. on I Tim. 6:13). **Testifying** is not only speaking; it is suffering, even dying. "Timothy" must be careful lest shame for Paul as a prisoner, or fear of imprisonment for himself, makes him **ashamed** of the gospel. The Christian in prison is in prison for Christ's sake; he is therefore Christ's **prisoner.** Suffering and in prison, he is still within the sphere of the power of God, which is both within him and around him and is completely adequate to his every need.

The verse would have increased meaning if, just as Paul had been made a prisoner because of his boldness in testimony, i.e., in the preaching of the gospel, we could suppose that the author himself had followed in Paul's footsteps, and writing "Timothy" from prison urges him also to that boldness in preaching which will bring him into this fellowship, this apostolic succession of suffering.

**9.** Vss. 9-10, introduced here to encourage "Timothy" to take his share of suffering, furnish us one of the finest early Christian statements of the meaning of the Christian

---

**8. A Share of Suffering.**—There are two temptations which confront each generation of Christians. One is to try to accommodate the gospel to the spirit of each age, so that there will be no friction between Christians and the world. George Santayana has pointed this out as an ever-present temptation. He says that "the adaptable spirit of Protestantism may be relied upon to lend a pious and philosophical sanction to any instinct that may deeply move the national mind." [5] That is an extreme overstatement, but it is healthy for Christians to be reminded that they constantly face the temptation of trying to use the gospel to add a veneer of respectability to things as they are instead of proclaiming the gospel as God's saving power to make all things new. The second temptation, confronted by a more restricted group, is to seek suffering for its own sake. The so-called martyr complex is a subtle temptation besetting all adherents of minority movements. It is an inverted form

of egotism, a pride in moral superiority, an expression of an unrecognized desire to be conspicuous. Paul charts for his younger colleague a course which avoids both temptations. He is to bear his testimony without hesitation or fear of consequences, and if the consequences are bitter he is to regard them as his partnership with others who have paid a price for the sake of the gospel. **Take your share of suffering for the gospel in the power of God.** John Woolman wrote of a journey in Virginia in 1746, on which he shared the hardships of pioneering Friends, that "we . . . were, in some degree, baptized into a feeling sense of the conditions of the people." [6] Some such baptism is part of the cost of a Christian loyalty.

**9. According to His Purpose.**—Here again we are confronted with the mystery of the divine initiative. "God . . . has saved us and called us to a life of consecration—not for anything we have done but because he chose to do it himself" (Moffatt). The Bible is full of men and women

[5] "The Genteel Tradition at Bay," *Saturday Review of Literature*, VII (1931), 502.

[6] *Journal*, March 12, 1746.

| but according to his own purpose and grace, which was given us in Christ Jesus before the world began; | called us with a holy calling, not in virtue of our works but in virtue of his own purpose and the grace which he gave us in |

faith. Since the two verses (a) form a discursive parenthesis, (b) are composed of a formally arranged series of participial phrases naturally falling into three stanzas, giving expression to three sets of antitheses, (c) and are written in a special vocabulary, technically Hellenistic, liturgically elevated, compact, and balanced, it is probable that they are a citation. Their source may have been a hymn, or a confession of faith, used perhaps at baptism or even at ordination. If these verses formed part of the public confession made by "Timothy" at ordination, their use here would be especially appropriate.

**Who saved us and called us with a holy calling:** Christians are already saved. In a N.T. writing this does not mean that salvation is to be thought of without regard to a future fulfillment or that it is automatically secured to the believer apart from his continuance in obedience and faith. It means that the decisive act in the Christian's salvation has been done once and for all, and God may be depended on to finish what he has begun.

The exact meaning of **called us with a holy calling** is uncertain. There are several possible interpretations: (a) "save" and "call" may be synonymous. God has **saved** men in that he has effectively **called** them out of the world. The **calling** is **holy** in that it is God who has issued the summons; therefore it is "omnipotent and irreversible" (Rom. 11:29; Easton). The dative case (κλήσει ἁγίᾳ) would then be dative of means or instrument, and **calling** would have its usual N.T. meaning: God's effective summons to salvation. Or (b) the word "save" may signify the objective provision which God has made for the salvation of men; "call" may signify God's summons to individuals to accept the salvation provided for them (Dibelius). (c) Moffatt translates the second half of the phrase, "and called us to a life of consecration"; Goodspeed, "to a consecrated life."

who are unable to understand why they have been called to some particular task. Moses complained that he was "slow of speech, and of a slow tongue" (Exod. 4:10) when the call to leadership came to him. Jeremiah shrank from the role of a prophet. "Ah, Lord God! behold, I cannot speak: for I am a child" (Jer. 1:6). On the Damascus road Paul heard a voice saying, "It is hard for thee to kick against the pricks" (Acts 9:5), indicating his resistance to the pressure of the divine purpose on his life. It is part of the deep mystery of grace that God trusts fallible and unworthy men to be partners with him in the fulfillment of his purpose. If men had to wait until their own deeds justified God's confidence before responding to his call, who would dare enlist in his service? Great living springs not from men's pride in what they themselves have done but from the faith which responds to God's inexplicable call to men, trusting that the purpose and the grace which were revealed in Jesus will not fail.

The good purpose of God which Jesus revealed is an eternal purpose. As the Exeg. says: "Both the will for man's salvation and the means for its accomplishment lie beyond the reach or ruin of time; the Christian's salvation is already laid up in heaven." This brings us face to face with the problem of how human effort is related to the fulfillment of God's eternal purpose. Four basic truths may be pointed out in this connection: (a) The N.T. teaches that we "receive" or "enter into" the kingdom of God—we do not build it. "It is your Father's good pleasure to give you the kingdom" (Luke 12:32). (b) We are called to seek and serve the kingdom. "Seek first his kingdom and his righteousness, and all these things shall be yours as well" (Matt. 6:33). (c) God gives both the will and the power for such service. "Work out your own salvation with fear and trembling; for God is at work in you, both to will and to work" (Phil. 2:12-13). (d) God's kingdom is the enduring reality which cannot be shaken. "Hallelujah! For the Lord our God the Almighty reigns" (Rev. 19:6). In other words, God seeks and effects fellowship with men by calling them to serve his kingdom. Men may accept or reject the challenge and the promise of God. Man's freedom is limited but real. God's purpose includes the possibility that men may refuse his grace. But for the everlasting purpose of God which Jesus revealed there can be no ultimate defeat.

10 But is now made manifest by the appearing of our Saviour Jesus Christ, who hath abolished death, and hath brought life and immortality to light through the gospel:

Christ Jesus ages ago, 10 and now has manifested through the appearing of our Savior Christ Jesus, who abolished death and brought life and immortality to light

---

Christians are saved in order that they may live consecrated lives, that they may be holy as God is holy. **Calling** is then interpreted in the sense of a way of life or vocation, a meaning less Semitic than Greek. (d) On the assumption that the Pastorals are post-Pauline, and that vss. 9-10 are liturgical material, perhaps regularly used in the ordination ceremony—in any case cited here to remind "Timothy" of the gospel he was ordained to preach—the **holy calling** may well be interpreted by the author in a technical sense to mean the Christian ministry. "Timothy" was called to be a witness, perhaps even a martyr. In support of this meaning of **calling** is the remarkable parallelism of language and idea in Epictetus *Discourses* I. 29. 33-49, where the Stoic is "a witness [μάρτυς] called [κεκλημένος] by God" with a mission to bear witness to him. To grumble at life is to "dishonor the calling that he has given you, in that he honored you thus and counted you worthy to be brought forward to bear such weighty witness."

**Not in virtue of our works but in virtue of his own purpose and . . . grace:** Only here and in Tit. 3:5 do the Pastorals speak against "justification by works," but even here faith is not set over against works. The text is concerned solely to affirm that the Christian's salvation and election are not due to anything the Christian is or does. They are due wholly to the gracious purpose of God who willed to save men **in Christ Jesus ages ago.** The Christian's salvation is absolutely secure because (a) it is grounded solely in the gracious will of God, purposed "before times eternal," i.e., before time was, before the creation of the world, and thus before man's sin. It is therefore unconditioned by anything that has happened in history; and (b) Christ Jesus through whom the saving purpose of God is effected likewise existed from before creation. Thus both the will for man's salvation and the means for its accomplishment lie beyond the reach or ruin of time; the Christian's salvation is already laid up in heaven.

**10. And now has manifested through the appearing of our Savior Christ Jesus.** Although the gracious purpose of God was established **ages ago,** it has **now** been made

---

Jesus' revelation of the purpose of God comes to us in three aspects. (a) It is challenge. Wrote a youth to Herbert Gray:

I am beginning to see that I can and must believe in God, and I am simply frightened. I have grown accustomed to life without Him to a certain extent. If I admit to myself that He is real, I know I shall have to do something about it, and I feel my whole life may be upset. From these unknown but possible changes I shrink.[7]

(b) It is also the secret of abundant life. In another connection George Bernard Shaw once said: "This is the true joy of life, the being used for a purpose recognized by yourself as a mighty one, instead of being a feverish, selfish little clod of ailments and grievances, complaining that the world will not devote itself to making you happy." [8] (c) It is the source of inner security.

[7] *Finding God* (New York: Ray Long & Richard R. Smith, n.d.), pp. 38-39.

[8] Quoted by James Reid, *The British Weekly*, Sept. 8, 1949.

To a ministerial friend Charles W. Eliot once wrote: "Life would look intolerable to me if I lost faith in the God that Jesus describes in the first three Gospels; or in the Creator of a boundless universe of order and beauty." [9]

**10. Life and Immortality.**—The appearing of Christ the Savior has revealed the eternal purpose of God. Death is not the goal of creation; the goal is everlasting life. The meaning of life and its deathless character have been brought **to light through the gospel. Life and immortality** are linked together as two aspects of one reality.

Here are two enormous words which we ordinarily tend to keep apart. We say that life has to do with this world, immortality with another. Life is present, immortality future. We assume that we can understand life but that immortality is incomprehensible. Sometimes we speak of life as a certainty but of immortality as a hope. Paul says that Christ has bridged the

[9] Henry James, *Charles W. Eliot* (Boston: Houghton Mifflin Co., 1930), II, 297-98.

clearly known to men in that **our Savior Christ Jesus,** so long concealed within eternity, has "appeared" in time. His purpose in **appearing,** i.e., in becoming incarnate, was that he might "abolish death"—illuminating life as with a flare, demonstrating through his resurrection its essentially immortal and incorruptible nature, its sovereignty over the temporal world of change and death. This is what **the gospel** really means and is—the proclamation of the good news that life is freed from death and all that belongs to the sort of world in which death is the last enemy to be overcome.

Both in language and idea vs. 10 is one of the most Hellenistic in the N.T. It is an excellent illustration of the way in which the living church, rooted in Hebrew-Christian language and thought forms, has nevertheless made use of, given place to, and incorporated into itself current religious concepts and terminology.

**Appearing** (ἐπιφάνεια) : On the apocalyptic use of the word see Exeg. on I Tim. 6:14. Notable, indeed, is its use here in contrast to its other occurrences in the Pastorals, to indicate the Incarnation, or the First Coming—more accurately, **appearance**—of Christ. The assumption is that before he was born, Christ existed with God. Birth in his case did not mean the beginning; it signified rather the appearance in history of the divine Savior previously existing but until now concealed. In N.T. times the word "epiphany" had high significance because it was used in the language of Hellenistic religion, and particularly of the emperor cult, with the connotation of divinity. It might refer to the birthday of a god or to some miraculous action in which the god displayed himself to the worshiper or showed forth in startling fashion his divine power. Used of the emperor, it might signify the day of his birth or of his coronation, or it might designate a royal visit, or the king's return from a journey in a foreign land. It is this latter usage which is nearest to the Christian use of the word to refer to the Second Coming or the eschatological return (4:1, 8; II Thess. 2:8; I Tim. 6:14; II Clem. 12:1; 17:4). Nonapocalyptic as Greek religion was, it furnishes no parallel to the Christian eschatological use of "epiphany." Conversely, the essentially apocalyptic nature of Christianity is shown by the persistence with which even the Pastorals, although making use of this important Hellenistic term, in every case but the present instance, give it apocalyptic meaning.

**Our Savior:** See on I Tim. 1:1. Savior gods were legion in the Hellenistic religions.

---

gap between these two aspects of man's experience.

As a matter of fact, we do not begin to understand life until its meaning is brought to light for us in Christ. To one man life is

> a tale
> Told by an idiot, full of sound and fury,
> Signifying nothing.[1]

To another it is a struggle for power, to another a contest in acquisition, and still others take what William James called "the nightmare view of life." [2] Jesus did not answer all the riddles about life, but he revealed its deepest meaning as fellowship with God. Mere existence is not life. Life is found in the will of God.

Jesus also brought to light the meaning of immortality. He revealed the fullness of life, which makes men want immortality. Emerson once asked what use immortality would be to a man who had not learned how to live half an hour. On the whole, it is in those who have

discovered the richness of life in Christ that the desire for eternal life is keenest.

I look forward to the Great Adventure, which now cannot be far off, with awe, but not with apprehension. . . . Always I have stood in the bow looking forward with hopeful anticipation to the life before me. When the time comes for my embarkation, and the ropes are cast off and I put out to sea, I think I shall still be standing in the bow and still looking forward with eager curiosity and glad hopefulness to the new world to which the unknown voyage will bring me.[3]

Whether or not we want it for ourselves, when we have seen the spirit of Christ in other lives we cannot help feeling that the universe would be irreparably poorer if they ceased to be.

Moreover, Jesus made immortality credible. He did so in part by revealing a quality of life which is the finest flower of all creation, so that it seems reasonable to believe that such character is the enduring reality in the universe. But Jesus made immortality credible chiefly

[1] Shakespeare, *Macbeth*, Act V, scene 5.
[2] *The Will to Believe* (New York: Longmans, Green & Co., 1917), p. 40.

[3] Lyman Abbott, *Reminiscences* (Boston: Houghton Mifflin Co., 1915), p. 493.

11 Whereunto I am appointed a preacher, and an apostle, and a teacher of the Gentiles.

12 For the which cause I also suffer these things: nevertheless I am not ashamed; for I know whom I have believed, and am persuaded that he is able to keep that which I have committed unto him against that day.

through the gospel. 11 For this gospel I was appointed a preacher and apostle and teacher, 12 and therefore I suffer as I do. But I am not ashamed, for I know whom I have believed and I am sure that he is able to guard until that Day what has been

---

And there were always the demands of empire rooted in the religious authority of the emperor cult. As over against all other saviors there stands for Christians one Savior, **our Savior Christ Jesus.**

In Greek religion "savior" was used with so great a variety of meanings that it came to be "virtually a divine title in itself, with little or no reference to any specific 'deliverance' from anything" (Easton, *Pastoral Epistles,* p. 230). We should therefore not attempt to fix too precisely the exact connotation of the word here. Nevertheless, in the context the meaning is clearly less Jewish than Greek. In contrast to Paul's emphasis the gospel here centers in incarnation, not in atonement. As **the appearing** here refers to the Incarnation, not to the Second Advent, and as the deliverance effected by the Incarnation is not in the first instance from sin to righteousness, but from death to life and immortality, the term **Savior** here is best interpreted not as deliverer at the Last Judgment, but in the sense in which "savior" is used in the mystery religions, to describe the one who gives the initiate life and new birth. Christ is **Savior** in that he **abolished death and brought life and immortality to light.** The quite non-Hebraic character of this statement of the function of saviorhood with its Greek use of **life** and **light** and **immortality** further suggests that we are here dealing with the language of the mysteries.

**11.** (See Exeg. on I Tim. 2:7.) This is not Paul writing to Timothy, but "Paul" writing to "Timothy." If Paul is set forth as the model of devotion to (Pauline) Christianity as it is, not too accurately, understood by "Paul," the latter has likewise given himself to **this gospel** with the same fullness of consecration. Therefore he has the right to charge "Timothy" to follow the same pattern (vss. 13-14).

**12.** It is taken for granted that appointment to preach such a gospel in such a world includes the call to suffer. **As I do** (RSV; lit., **these things,** KJV) remains purposely indefinite. To the extent that the sufferings of Paul or the writer are known to the readers, there is no need to relate them. Also, leaving the text vague not merely suggests their multiplicity but provides room for every "Timothy" to relate his own sufferings to his own call.

**I am not ashamed** (cf. I Pet. 4:16): "What is desired of Timothy, is asserted of Paul" (Dibelius). For a minister to suffer persecution, even imprisonment, for his faith and work is not shameful. Rather, it is an honor. **For I know whom I have believed,** i.e., "in whom I have placed my confidence or trust." It is true that the Christian minister

---

because he revealed God as a loving Father. No one can believe in the God and Father of our Lord Jesus Christ and imagine that he permits the extinction of the children whom he has created for fellowship with himself. Life is a fellowship of purpose and activity with the Father. Immortality is a continuation and enrichment of that fellowship. Both have been **brought . . . to light through the gospel.**

**11-12a. Preacher, Apostle, Teacher.**—Again Paul reverts to the threefold description of his

commission which he has outlined in I Tim. 2:7. To proclaim the gospel, to represent Christ, and to instruct in the Way—this is the work to which he has been appointed, with special reference to the outreach of Christianity to those beyond the confines of Judaism. **And therefore I suffer as I do.** Such a ministry was a costly one, as it is in every generation.

**12c. A Safe Deposit.**—This is one of the great affirmations of confident trust on which Christians through the centuries have stayed them-

risks everything, and without visible vindication or reward. His whole life is staked on the trustworthiness of God. Fortunately, the one thing the Christian knows is that God whom he trusts is trustworthy. This he has learned from repeated experience. The Greek perfect (**have believed**) indicates action begun, even completed, in the past and continued in the present; it is repeated, persistent, and therefore tested belief or trust. And so **I am sure that he is able**. God both will and can.

Unfortunately the text of the remainder of this confident and meaningful statement of faith is ambiguous. Literally translated "my deposit," the genitive may be either subjective or objective genitive, i.e., the meaning may be either **what has been entrusted to me** or (as in RSV mg.) **what I have entrusted to him**. Known to us best in the KJV, the established interpretation of the text has been that although suffering and tribulation, even mortal peril, are the common lot of mankind, yet the souls of Christian men are in the hand of God: no one trusts God in vain. In behalf of this interpretation it may be said that taken by itself vs. 12 does seem to be concerned with the problem of suffering. Why should one who is **appointed a preacher and apostle and teacher** of the one gospel of salvation be called upon to endure personal affliction, and even more, to languish in prison, prevented by men from accomplishing the work to which he is appointed by God? Vs. 12*a*, then, seems to require that vs. 12*b* provide vindication for the suffering which the Christian minister must of necessity endure, and assurance that God will not allow it to be his final recompense. Come Judgment Day, the Christian will discover that having committed himself and his fortunes to God's keeping, God will protect him and deliver him.

Nevertheless there are weighty objections to this interpretation. It offends both against the meaning of the word "deposit" (παραθήκη) and against the context. In the first place, it does scant honor to the author to attribute to him so much concern with his own personal welfare in a paragraph (and letter) which is almost exclusively devoted to concern for the transmission and preservation of the Christian faith in pure and unadulterated form. Furthermore, since "deposit" occurs again almost immediately, in vs. 14 and in I Tim. 6:20 (not elsewhere in the N.T.), and in both cases clearly refers to the "deposit of faith"—i.e., to the received form of the gospel or of the Christian

---

selves. **I know whom I have believed** is the classic statement of assured knowledge which is the fruit of experimental faith. The change in tense is significant. Present knowledge vindicates past trust. This is the text that John Oxenham put into verse which stresses the personal relationship between the believer and God:

Not what, but WHOM, I do believe,
That, in my darkest hour of need,
Hath comfort that no mortal creed
To mortal man may give;—
Not what, but WHOM! [4]

The figure of speech here is that of a man who has deposited a treasure for safekeeping with someone whom he trusts absolutely. There is a confident ring to the words **I am sure**. Confidence in God's sufficiency breathes through the words **he is able**. A realistic sense of the Christian's need for eternal vigilance is revealed in the words **to guard**. The treasure which Paul had in mind was probably the Christian faith

[4] "Credo," from *Bees in Amber* (New York: American Tract Society, 1917). Used by permission.

which he had been appointed to proclaim. There is a significant suggestion in the two translations of the clause which follows: that **which I have committed unto him** (KJV) suggests that it is God's cause, and that while his servants are called to costly partnership, the ultimate victory is in his keeping; **what has been entrusted to me** (RSV) emphasizes man's responsibility to proclaim the gospel, in the assurance that he who gave the task will secure the outcome. Whichever translation is correct, both emphases are needed.

Although Paul probably had in mind the specific task of proclaiming the gospel, this passage has usually been given a wider application by the sound intuition of generations of Christians. Men and women in critical situations have drawn a sense of personal security from it. People looking forward to the mystery of life after death have confirmed their faith in these words. Parents have committed their children to God's keeping, idealists have entrusted to God's providence causes in which they have deeply believed, and churchmen, perplexed by problems connected with the future of the

13 Hold fast the form of sound words, which thou hast heard of me, in faith and love which is in Christ Jesus.

entrusted to me.[a] 13 Follow the pattern of the sound words which you have heard from me, in the faith and love which are

[a] Or what I have entrusted to him.

---

faith as understood, accepted, and taught by the author—we are compelled to interpret "deposit" similarly here. The preferred translation then will be **what has been entrusted to me.** Those who regard the letter as Pauline may interpret "my deposit" to mean "my gospel," i.e., the gospel of the uncircumcision as against that of the circumcision (cf. Rom. 2:16; 16:25; Gal. 2:7). Those who regard the letter as post-Pauline and the controversy over circumcision as no longer an issue in the Christian church will think more generally of Pauline Christianity as understood and championed by the author, perhaps as summarized in vss. 9-10.

In any case, the verse gives expression to the great sense of responsibility which the writer feels in being entrusted with the preservation and transmission of the (Pauline) Christian faith, and to his great confidence that God is fully able to protect that faith even though his preachers and teachers are imprisoned or otherwise prevented from bearing effective witness to it. Ministers should not allow their faith in the gospel or their devotion to it to grow weak because the preaching of it involves them in suffering. They should rather be assured that their knowledge of God is true and right and that, in spite of the obstacles to the spread of the gospel in the form in which it was once for all delivered, God can be counted on to guard this deposit of faith and keep it intact until the Judgment Day when dangers will be past and all its enemies destroyed.

**13.** The word translated **pattern,** used in sculpture and painting, meant an outline sketch or rough draft; in literature, a summary account giving a general idea of a subject but not a complete exposition. While there is probably no reference here to a formulated creed or catechism, the insistence which lies behind the phrase was already active in producing such convenient and handy devices for grasping and presenting the essence of the Christian faith. The text here means: "As a model or example of correct preaching and teaching, take what you have heard from me." "Timothy" is urged to hold strictly to the received form of the faith and to continue to preach in the church **the sound words** (see I Tim. 1:11) which he heard from "Paul," and which "Paul" is sure came from Paul.

The construction of **in the faith and love which are in Christ Jesus,** loosely attached at the end of the sentence, is obscure. The phrase may be taken with **follow,** meaning either that although orthodox doctrine is the first requirement for a preacher, yet he must preach the correct faith in the spirit of Christian faith and love; or, Timothy must not reluctantly or halfheartedly devote himself to the Pauline gospel: "All Timothy's teaching must express a faithful and loving reliance on Paul" (Easton, *Pastoral Epistles,* p. 45).

---

church, have gained new confidence from these immortal words of assured trust.

Herbert H. Farmer once said that part of the wisdom of the Christian is to be able to distinguish between what God has committed to him and what he ought to commit to God. To each is committed his task, to be discharged faithfully, imaginatively, loyally. But this is God's world, and it is the part of faith to leave the ultimate issues with him. The anonymous paraphrase of Ps. 55 is good counsel always:

Cast thy burden on the Lord,
Only lean upon his word,
Thou wilt soon have cause to bless
His eternal faithfulness.

**13. How to Hold the Creed.**—A creed is important. Strong action comes from strong beliefs, and right conduct springs from right convictions. But it is possible to hold a creed in such a way that it produces evil results. The temptation to persecute those who do not hold our beliefs is not merely an echo from the past. The temptation to assume an attitude of superiority toward those of differing beliefs is a common problem. The temptation to permit creedal loyalty to become a source of bitterness and rivalry has dogged the church through the centuries. **Follow the pattern of the sound words, . . . in the faith and love which are in Christ Jesus,** says Paul. Here is a twofold loyalty

| | |
|---|---|
| 14 That good thing which was committed unto thee keep by the Holy Ghost which dwelleth in us. | in Christ Jesus; 14 guard the truth that has been entrusted to you by the Holy Spirit who dwells within us. |

The location of the phrase in Greek makes also possible its construction with **you have heard,** meaning that since "Timothy" has so graciously listened to the author's instruction, there should be no hesitancy in his regarding these **sound words** as a model for preaching. Or, the phrase could be construed with **me,** to mean that Paul preached in Christian faith and love, and therefore "Timothy" should follow this true pattern. Dibelius suggests still another meaning in his translation: ". . . which you have heard from me (and so remain) in faith and love as they are (contained) in Christ Jesus." On **faith** and **in Christ Jesus,** see Exeg., I Tim. 1:14.

**14. Guard the truth that has been entrusted to you:** Lit., "guard the good ["splendid," Dibelius, Scott, Easton; "noble," Parry; "precious," meaning "authentic," "complete," Spicq] deposit." "Timothy's" most solemn responsibility and obligation is to protect—i.e., to preserve and transmit unchanged—the (Pauline) Christian faith as he has received it from "Paul."

**By the Holy Spirit who dwells within us** may be a reminiscence of Rom. 8:9, 11 where the Spirit is regarded as indwelling in all Christians, but if the phrase looks back to vss. 6-7, "us" in this context may mean "us who have been ordained." Obviously in this letter, and generally in the Pastorals, the author is concerned primarily with ministers or church officials whom he regards as especially endowed with Christian graces; yet this does not mean that he would deny them to the laity.

"These last two verses furnish the foundation of the Catholic teaching relative to the tradition. The apostles have received the Christian truth from the Lord; they themselves have transmitted it orally, especially to their co-workers and successors in the ministry; but these latter have the duty to conserve it in all its purity and to communicate it in their turn only to men tested and capable themselves of assuring a further transmission. But this conservation and this transmission cannot be sufficiently guaranteed by human forces. It is the Holy Spirit which preserves them from all alteration and all deviation, and, according to vs. 7, one may specify that this action of the Holy Spirit is exercised with peculiar efficacy in the members of the ecclesiastical hierarchy" (C. Spicq, *Saint Paul: les Épitres Pastorales* [Paris: J. Gabalda, 1947], p. 320). Easton correctly states that "the Pastorals agree wholly with the usual second-century doctrine of the preservation of 'the faith once and for all delivered to the saints' by an orderly succession of approved teachers" (*Pastoral Epistles,* p. 47), as, e.g., in I Clem. 42:2-4; 44:2: "Christ . . . comes with a message from God, and the Apostles with a message from Christ. . . . And so, after receiving their instructions . . . they went forth, equipped with the fullness of the Holy Spirit, to preach the good news . . . from land to land, . . . and from city to city, . . . and from their earliest converts appointed men whom they had tested by the Spirit to act as bishops and deacons for the future believers, . . . and afterwards laid down a rule once for all to this effect: when these men die, other approved men shall succeed to their sacred ministry." (Tr. Jas. A. Kleist.)

As surely as this is the point of view of the ancient catholic church, so surely is it not the point of view of the ancient church in its formative or prophetic period when the emphasis was rather creative than transmissive. The anxiety here expressed for the preservation of the tradition unchanged is not the anxiety of Paul. This is the language

---

—loyalty to the creed and loyalty to Christlike love. Without both loyalties, life goes astray.

**14. Guard the Trust.**—This is banker's language. Paul says in effect: "You are the guardian of a deposit. A trust has been committed to your keeping. Guard it scrupulously." So also now.

Communism, secularism, and indifferentism challenge Christianity today. The motion picture of Shakespeare's *Henry V* makes a good deal of the fact that when the French army was called upon to defend its country against invasion and conquest, those who should have

15 This thou knowest, that all they which are in Asia be turned away from me; of whom are Phygellus and Hermogenes.

15 You are aware that all who are in Asia turned away from me, and among

---

of the priest, not of the prophet. Neither the language nor the temper is that of the great apostle.

### IV. A Personal Appeal (1:15-18)

**15.** The appeal to Timothy for utter loyalty is made poignant by setting it against a dark background of disaffection and abandonment. Paul ("Paul"?) is utterly lonely, in prison, neglected, even repudiated. He clings pathetically and appealingly to the few friends whose devotion has held steadfast.

**All who are in Asia turned away from me:** The remark, though hyperbole, appears to evidence widespread disaffection on the part of Christians in the province of Asia with its important capital Ephesus. This statement is indeed surprising because the area was one in which Paul had won notable successes (Acts 19–20), and which as a consequence had become the chief center of Hellenistic Christianity (see on I Tim. 1:3).

The problems of interpretation here root (a) in the imprecise nature of the language which appears to take for granted detailed information as known to the readers, and (b) in the even more perplexing problems of pseudonymity. How large a group is contemplated in **all who are in Asia?** Does the phrase really mean the entire body of Asiatic Christians? On any count this seems most unlikely. And in what sense did they "turn away" from Paul (or "Paul")? In the Pastorals, which are so concerned with orthodox doctrine, it is a natural conclusion to suppose with Easton that "the opposition to Paul was of course an opposition to his theology," and that "turn away from" means to repudiate doctrinally. Then **all who are in Asia** would be taken rather literally as evidence that there was (during Paul's lifetime? or at the turn of the century?) in Asia a general abandonment of the Pauline position. "This statement would never be made without a basis in historic fact" (Easton).

Nevertheless, it is also possible to interpret vs. 15 out of vss. 16-18 and 4:10-18, i.e., personally rather than theologically. **Phygelus and Hermogenes,** named only here in the N.T. and quite unknown to us, would then not be thought of as the leaders of some sort of theological revolt, or as being particularly prominent or distasteful heretics, but as persons who abandoned Paul in his hour of need. As names or persons they must have been known to "Timothy." Otherwise there is no accounting for the author's naming them. But it is idle to speculate as to whether "Timothy" is here being informed for the first time of their disloyalty, or had already associated their names with some misfortune, interpreted as punishment, which had happened to them and which made the mere mention of them carry a warning. But whatever their offenses may have been, taken with the context the two men appear simply as a foil to Onesiphorus (vs. 16). In contrast to him we may suppose they were "ashamed of Paul's chains."

Reasoning backward, from this point of view **all who are in Asia** would refer to the smaller group of those who were personally attached to Paul, some of whom are named in vss. 15-18, others in 4:10-18. Perhaps on his arrest Paul sought witnesses in Asia for his defense but was disappointed in the response. Or it may be that of those who

---

been on fire in a great cause were taking their ease and arguing about the rituals of chivalry. The church must resist the temptation to take its ease, arguing about secondary matters, and must guard its sacred trust.

**15-18.** *A Bracing Friendship.*—Phygelus and Hermogenes are types of the fair-weather Christian, whose loyalty to Christ and whose friend-

ship for Paul failed when the test came. Against the background of the defection of the Asians, the loyalty of Onesiphorus is all the more striking. **For he often refreshed me** is translated by Moffatt in the vigorous words, "Many a time he braced me up." In Ephesus Onesiphorus seems to have been able to do practical things for Paul, but in Rome it was simply his evident

16 The Lord give mercy unto the house of Onesiphorus; for he oft refreshed me, and was not ashamed of my chain:

them Phy'gelus and Hermog'enes. 16 May the Lord grant mercy to the household of Onesiph'orus, for he often refreshed me;

---

set out with him for Rome, some became tired of the journey and left him en route (Demas? 4:10) ; others, after his first appearance for trial, believed his case hopeless and started back home (4:16). Or perhaps the expression "those in Asia" is a Hebraism for "those from Asia" (Spicq, after Chrysostom), meaning Christians from Asia, either travelers or dwellers in Rome, who might have been solicitous for and helpful to Paul the prisoner, but who whether from fear or indifference left him to his fate.

Regarding the letter as pseudonymous, it is tempting to suppose that it is not Paul's but the author's situation that is here described. If **Phygelus and Hermogenes**— Onesiphorus too—were known to "Timothy" at, say the end of the century at the earliest, they could have had nothing to do with Paul. At this date the writer's concern with the inner feeling of Paul during his imprisonment is best explained if we suppose that "Paul" himself was at the time in prison and was himself quite literally retracing Paul's footsteps. Then the anguish and its causes would be "Paul's," not Paul's.

**16.** In contrast to the faithlessness of Phygelus and Hermogenes, the loyalty and devotion of **Onesiphorus** are fervently and appreciatively acknowledged in vss. 16-18. Onesiphorus is not otherwise known to us except that his family lived in Ephesus (4:19). According to the Acts of Paul and Thecla, he had been converted by Paul at Iconium and had extended his hospitality to Paul on his first missionary voyage. According to the same source, his wife's name was Lectra. It is curious that whereas all the other persons mentioned in the letter are mentioned simply as individuals, **the household of Onesiphorus** is twice not (cf. 4:19). Does the phrase mean "Onesiphorus and his family," or does it intend to exclude Onesiphorus himself, the assumption being that he was dead? So far as the phrase itself is concerned, the language permits either meaning. Quite possibly **the household of Onesiphorus** may intend to indicate that Onesiphorus was already dead, or it may have been prompted by the fact that Onesiphorus' family had shared in some special way in Onesiphorus' services to our author, and have thereby become so intimate that even in sending greetings he always thought of the family as a whole and had no thought of excluding Onesiphorus from his own household.

Assuming the letter to be pseudonymous, there are three possibilities of interpretation: (a) the author may have consistently projected himself back into Paul's time, as he seems indeed to have done in the case of the names mentioned in 4:9 ff. In this case Onesiphorus could then have been thought of as living, quite as much as, e.g., Luke and Mark were so thought of (4:11). In favor of this interpretation is the fact that so far as we can check the personal names given in the letter, they were contemporaries of Paul. It is therefore unlikely that the writer would have slipped this one time and would unwittingly have stepped out of character to the point of distinguishing between (now-deceased) Onesiphorus, a contemporary of Paul, and Onesiphorus' family of a later generation, contemporaries of "Paul." (b) It has been frequently urged—most recently by Easton—that "Onesiphorus was certainly no longer alive when the Pastor wrote" and "that the present passage assumes his [Onesiphorus'] death can hardly be questioned" (*Pastoral Epistles*, pp. 48, 46). In support of this interpretation is the insistence with which the author speaks of the family of Onesiphorus, the absence of any personal

---

loyalty which warmed Paul's heart. He was not ashamed of Paul's imprisonment, hunted him up in Rome and came to see him. Paul, the great apostle, seems more human in the light of this record that he took new courage and strength from the loyalty of this otherwise unknown fellow Christian.

There are people whom we would like to

help, but for whom there seems to be little that we can do. There are a good many people who feel that their days of active usefulness are over. In every situation, however, there is the opportunity to be a bracing friend. Some people drain strength from all whom they meet. By self-centered concentration on their own problems they demand sympathy and attention, and

17 But, when he was in Rome, he sought me out very diligently, and found *me*.

18 The Lord grant unto him that he may find mercy of the Lord in that day: and in how many things he ministered unto me at Ephesus, thou knowest very well.

he was not ashamed of my chains, 17 but when he arrived in Rome he searched for me eagerly and found me — 18 may the Lord grant him to find mercy from the Lord on that Day — and you well know all the service he rendered at Ephesus.

---

greeting to him at the close of the letter, and especially the prayer for Onesiphorus only, not for his family, at the Last Judgment (vs. 18). (*c*) The interest of the author in Onesiphorus and his family, as well as the fervor of expression, is difficult to explain on any ground other than that it was "Paul," not Paul, who was often "refreshed" by Onesiphorus. If "Paul" is here attributing his own experiences to the apostle, then as a matter of course both Onesiphorus and his family would be contemporaries of "Paul." Even so, of course Onesiphorus might already have died. Vss. 16-18 sound like a brief word of condolence, perhaps prompted by the recent death of Onesiphorus.

**May the Lord grant mercy** may or may not reflect some special need on the part of Onesiphorus' family. It may simply express the pious wish that those who have been merciful may obtain mercy. To "refresh" (ἀναψύχω) means to revive with fresh air, to cool, to allay fatigue or alleviate a wound, whether of body or soul. The text does not state how Onesiphorus **refreshed** Paul ("Paul"?) **often,** although the words **he was not ashamed of my chains** suggest that it was by frequent visits to prison. Furthermore, since prisoners who had resources or were provided for by their friends were not ordinarily compelled to live so restricted a life, Onesiphorus may well have supplied some of the funds required to modify the severity of Paul's imprisonment.

**17.** Onesiphorus went to Rome, apparently on his own business, but he immediately set out to search for Paul. The implication that Paul could be found only with great difficulty is in contradiction with the account in Acts 28:16 ff., according to which Paul's lodging place was common knowledge among Christians, who came and went quite freely. This is explained by those who regard the letter as Pauline by the supposition that in his second imprisonment in Rome Paul was guarded much more strictly than in the first, was put in the "inner prison" to which the public was not admitted, and that not even the church knew where he was imprisoned. If "Paul" is writing about his own prison experience, there is no problem. Christians in Rome could not know where every Christian prisoner was incarcerated.

**18.** There is probably wordplay in the repetition of **find** in vs. 18 immediately after its use in vs. 17: "May the Lord grant him who found me to find mercy."

The identification of **the Lord** is problematic. If it is a Hebraism, repeating the noun where we should use a pronoun, both terms could refer to the same person, God or Christ. It has been argued that **the Lord** (in Greek only the first **Lord** has the definite article) is God, and that in the second case, **from the Lord** (in Greek there is

---

leave other people tired and depleted after casual contacts. There are others, like Onesiphorus, who brace people up. Usually such a refreshing influence is unconscious. The person who goes about deliberately and vociferously bracing people up seldom succeeds in doing anything but wearying them. Whenever anyone is discouraged or fatigued the most refreshing experience possible is friendship with a person of clear purpose, firm faith, and contagious enthusiasm. Such a friend Paul evidently had in Onesiphorus.

A person who braces other people up is likely to be a person who is interested in things outside himself, who is doing things worth while,

who has a clear purpose for which he lives and works, who has spiritual reserves, who is himself reinforced by strengthening fellowships and lives by a great trust in God. An Oxford student once interviewed Samuel A. Barnett at Toynbee Hall in London. Long afterward he wrote: "I remember so well the mixture of enthusiasm and clearheadedness with which one left his study at Toynbee. I felt . . . that the whole world ought to be conquered, and could be conquered."[5] He had been in contact with a bracing personality.

[5] Henrietta Octavia Rowland Barnett, *Canon Barnett, His Life, Work, and Friends* (Boston: Houghton Mifflin Co., 1919), I, 316.

2 Thou therefore, my son, be strong in the grace that is in Christ Jesus.

2 And the things that thou hast heard of me among many witnesses, the same

2 You then, my son, be strong in the grace that is in Christ Jesus, 2 and what

---

no article here), **Lord** means Christ the judge. Since, however, the more common Christian tradition regards Christ as interceding with God for men (Matt. 10:32-33), more probably **Lord** is applied first to Christ, then to God.

If Onesiphorus was dead at this time, this would be a unique instance in the N.T. of prayer for the dead. There is Jewish precedent for this in II Macc. 12:43-45. That Christ or the church may intervene to secure a blessed eternity for the dead appears to be supposed by I Cor. 15:29; I Pet. 3:19-20. Since Onesiphorus was a Christian, however, there should have been no anxiety with reference to him. It may be that we should see in the prayer—it is not in the form of direct address—merely a gracious fervent wish or expression of hope.

**You well know** [or, "you know better than I"] **all the service he rendered at Ephesus** is a last lingering tribute. In this context it should mean all the service which Onesiphorus rendered Paul's cause before leaving Ephesus for Rome, and not his services to the Christian community in general or to Timothy in particular.

### V. The Minister as Christ's Soldier (2:1-7)

**2:1-2.** The conclusion of the matter thus far is that since "Timothy" is a child and heir of faith (1:5), since he has been called by God, ordained by "Paul," endowed with a

---

**2:1. Warning Signal!**—Having seen that it is possible for good men to fall away, Timothy is urged to remember the source of power in Christ. **Thou, therefore, my son, be strong in the grace that is in Christ Jesus.** In these epistles an interesting study can be made of Paul's habit of drawing the inevitable conclusions from facts which he lays before his readers. He points out that there is a logical basis for prayer. "I will therefore that men pray every where" (I Tim. 2:8). "Therefore" refers back to the fact that "there is one God, and one mediator between God and men" (I Tim. 2:5). There is a logical basis for sacrificial Christian service. "Therefore we both labor and suffer reproach." Why? "Because we trust in the living God" (I Tim. 4:10). There is a logical basis for courage. "Be not thou therefore ashamed of the testimony of our Lord" (1:8). The fact on which that exhortation is based has just been stated. "For God hath not given us the spirit of fear; but of power, and of love, and of a sound mind" (1:7). There is a logical basis for endurance. "Thou therefore endure hardness, as a good soldier of Jesus Christ" (vs. 3). "Therefore I endure all things for the elect's sake" (vs. 10). In between these two references to endurance is the fact from which stamina comes: "Remember that Jesus Christ . . . was raised from the dead according to my gospel" (vs. 8). There is a logical reason for preaching. "I charge thee therefore before God, and the Lord Jesus Christ, . . . preach the word" (4:1-2). "Therefore" links this command with the fact that "from a child

thou hast known the holy Scriptures, which are able to make thee wise unto salvation through faith which is in Christ Jesus" (3:15). So here, **Thou therefore, my son, be strong in the grace that is in Christ Jesus** is the logical conclusion of the whole of ch. 1, with its account of the gift of power from God through Jesus Christ.

The use of power presents ethical problems which are very pressing. The term "strong man" has come to have an invidious connotation, because so often the strong man is selfish, domineering, and unfeeling. In highly organized modern life economic power in new dimensions is vested in corporations and in labor unions, and on the right use of this enormous power depend whatever justice and peace can be achieved in the world of commerce and industry. Nations with natural resources, wealth, and man power find themselves in positions of gigantic responsibility, able to influence human history for weal or for woe. The fission of the atom has placed in human hands a power which can be used for healing and for all manner of services to human welfare—or it can be used for destruction on an unprecedented scale. It is a commonplace that the human race has achieved power more rapidly than it has grown in grace. Like the trained bear riding a motorcycle, man is using more power than he understands or is ethically prepared to be let loose with. Here is the Christian answer to the problem of power: **Be strong in the grace that is in Christ Jesus.**

**2. Pass on the Torch!**—There is a contagion about Christian faith and life. Young people

477

commit thou to faithful men, who shall be able to teach others also. | you have heard from me before many witnesses entrust to faithful men who will be

---

spirit of power and love and self-control (1:6-7), encouraged by the matchless devotion of Paul to the gospel (1:11-12), and of Onesiphorus to Paul (1:16-18)—i.e., by a succession of Christians consecrated to the true pattern of the received faith—it is incumbent on "Timothy" for his part to rise fully to the responsibilities which are laid upon him as a Christian minister. Strength for this work is richly available **in the grace that is in Christ Jesus.** At ordination "Timothy" has already been endowed with this "spirit of power" (1:6-7); and in this gift of grace, given and renewed by Christ, he should remain strong.

"Timothy's" chief function as minister and administrator in the church is to transmit intact and unchanged **what he has heard** from Paul to other **faithful men** who in turn **will be able to teach others also.** The deposit of faith is a living word which one generation communicates to another. The minister as preacher and teacher is the key figure upon whom rests full responsibility for receiving the truth and holding fast to it, for selecting qualified successors, and for communicating to them in turn "the pattern of the sound words" and the duty of guarding "the truth that has been entrusted" to them (1:13-14).

As clear as is the intent of the passage in general, there is some obscurity as to the precise reference of the phrase **what you have heard from me before many witnesses.** Since the "what" or the content of the teaching is taken for granted rather than outlined or stated in the text, it is impossible to determine whether or not the body of teaching referred to is thought of as having been given at a particular time, e.g., at ordination. A part of this problem is the difficult phrase **before** [lit., "through"] **many witnesses.**

The translation **before many witnesses** is based on the interpretation of "through" (διά) as "before" or "in the presence of," the assumption being that Timothy was officially instructed in the presence of numerous witnesses who could corroborate the accuracy of the instructions and correctness of the doctrine. Sometimes the instructions are thought of as having been given at ordination, and the **many witnesses** as including the presbyters (I Tim. 4:14; 6:12). However, the whole phrase seems too general and imprecise to refer to ordination. The witnesses have therefore been more widely interpreted to include such as Barnabas, Timothy's mother and grandmother, indeed, all others who have professed the true faith. Scott thinks "through" should be taken in its natural sense, interprets it as "under the attestation of" (so Spicq also), and regards the witnesses as Christians before Paul, including the personal disciples of Jesus, from whom he had received the fundamental Christian truths to which he in turn bears witness.

However, none of the translations which avoid the plain meaning of "through" as mediation can be regarded as satisfactory—and this includes the most of them: KJV and ASV, **among;** Goodspeed and RSV, **before;** Moffatt, "in the presence of."

Easton is exactly right in saying that "all difficulty vanishes . . . when it is remembered that the Pastor is addressing 'Timothy,' who had never actually heard Paul: the witnesses are the various sources—above all the Pastor himself—through which the

---

are won to Christian life and belief in the first instance by coming in contact with people in whose lives Christian faith and conviction are realities. But Christianity must also be taught. Part of the commandment of Jesus was to love God with the mind. Christians must be ready to give a reason for the faith that is in them. An intelligent member of the Christian church should know the history of Christianity, what it teaches, how great Christians have answered some of its basic questions, how the faith has spread, and what it has accomplished in the world. One of the weaknesses of modern Protestantism is that too many Protestant Christians have not been well instructed in their faith.

Paul here pleads for a succession of the teachers, passing on Christian knowledge from generation to generation, as runners in a relay race pass on the torch or the wand. Paul has taught Timothy, who is urged to teach other **faithful**

3 Thou therefore endure hardness, as a good soldier of Jesus Christ.

able to teach others also. 3 Take your share of suffering as a good soldier of Christ

---

various 'Timothys' learned the Tradition. Among these sources Paul's Epistles would take a high place—but only as interpreted in 'orthodox' circles." (*Pastoral Epistles,* p. 49.) The first link in the tradition is Paul, the last link before "Timothy" is "Paul." And in between are **many witnesses,** to whom the deposit has been safely committed and through whom it has been communicated. In this context the phrase **what you have heard,** intentionally vague, will not refer to any compact rule of faith or creed, nor yet to a baptismal or ordination charge, but to the fundamental body of tradition, as it was gradually being formulated in prayer and praise, in hymn and liturgy, in preaching and teaching, perhaps even in Gospel and Epistle, i.e., to the whole deposit of faith as understood and taught by our author.

Although "we have here the earliest hint of an apostolic succession" (E. F. Scott, *The Pastoral Epistles* [New York: Harper & Bros., 1936; "The Moffatt New Testament Commentary"], p. 101), the succession is one of teachers whose only credentials are trustworthiness and competency in transmitting and teaching the faith which they have learned. No passage in the Pastorals is more revealing of the type of piety which characterizes these letters and the churches of Asia at this time. In the earlier prophetic, ecstatic, Spirit-dominated period, administration was ranked among the lesser gifts. But with emphasis on the importance of the preservation of the received faith in its purity and the reappraisal of the teaching function in relation thereto, the administrative function likewise assumes ever greater importance until the administrator-teacher becomes the highest functionary in the church.

**3.** The admonitions in 1:3–2:2 to utter loyalty and devotion to the received Christian faith are driven home in vss. 3-6 by three illustrations from everyday life: the soldier, the athlete, and the farmer. In general the illustrations stress the fact that if one wants to achieve success in any profession, he must devote himself to it completely.

**Take your share of suffering:** Lit., "suffer hardship with." The addition of "me" (Goodspeed: "share my hardships") undesirably narrows down the wider connotation of the absolute use of the verb in Greek. Its force is that the call to the ministry is a call to a fellowship of suffering (1:8, 12). Paul is thought of as indeed the most distinguished example of those who have suffered, but suffering is expected of every **good soldier of Christ Jesus.** Indeed, that is the normal business of the soldier.

The term **good soldier,** frequent in the language of Hellenistic mysticism, occurs only here in the N.T. Military metaphors, however, are common, e.g., Eph. 6:10-17. Among peoples of military prowess the soldier has always stood as the model of unhesitating obedience, of perfect loyalty, of single-minded and heroic devotion, and of the ultimate in self-sacrifice. It is these virtues which are transferred to the realm of spirit in the phrase **a good soldier of Christ Jesus.**

---

**men,** who in turn are to **teach others.** There is a healthy emphasis in modern education on creative teaching which builds on the actual experience of the learner, who learns by doing. This is not exclusive of nor a substitute for the transmission of Christian knowledge from life to life.

Because every church has its problems in the recruiting and training of lay people as teachers, Paul's suggestions in this matter should be noted. Christian teachers are to be first of all those willing to learn what is committed to them. Second, they must be **faithful,** an indispensable quality, as every church-school administrator knows. Third, they must be **able.** No enthusiasm for the task can take the place of genuine capacity, and the teaching task of the church is so important that it should command the services of the ablest. Fourth, they must be concerned about **others also,** eager to share with others what means most to them, zealous to present every man perfect in Christ.

**3-7. Soldier, Athlete, Farmer.**—Three metaphors follow in quick succession as illustrations of what it means to be a Christian teacher. Like a **soldier,** he must be ready to endure hardships. Like an **athlete,** he must keep the rules. Like a **farmer,** he must work hard if he is to get results.

4 No man that warreth entangleth himself with the affairs of *this* life; that he may please him who hath chosen him to be a soldier.

5 And if a man also strive for masteries, *yet* is he not crowned, except he strive lawfully.

6 The husbandman that laboreth must be first partaker of the fruits.

Jesus. 4 No soldier on service gets entangled in civilian pursuits, since his aim is to satisfy the one who enlisted him. 5 An athlete is not crowned unless he competes according to the rules. 6 It is the hard-working farmer who ought to have the first share

---

**4.** The minister is engaged in a perpetual warfare, and like the soldier on duty, he has neither time nor interest for ordinary **civilian pursuits.** His one **aim is to satisfy the one who enlisted him,** i.e., Christ. It must remain a question just how far the writer meant to push the application of his metaphor. Inevitably it came to be interpreted in the church as implying not only complete abstinence from secular trades on the part of the clergy, but even from marriage on their part. That a strictly professional as over against a lay ministry should have developed within the church is intelligible enough, but the present text is not concerned with such details. Epigramlike, it will affirm graphically and pointedly that the minister shall be as wholly consecrated to his warfare as the soldier is to his.

**5.** The professional **athlete** who breaks the rules is disqualified. Again the application of the metaphor to the minister is in detail not clear. The **rules** may be taken as meaning (*a*) those by which the contest is actually waged, or (*b*) those which specify the nature and extent of the preliminary training; e.g., at the Olympian games athletes had to swear before the statue of Jupiter that they had been in training for six months. In a proverbial statement of this sort, however, it is unwise to press such distinctions or to seek too detailed an application. The point is that if the minister is to be a good minister, he must practice arduous self-discipline. He knows what the requirements are; let him wholeheartedly obey them.

**6.** Although the stress here is clearly and wholly on the **hard-working** [lit., "working"] **farmer,** the third illustration appears less impressive than the other two because of its concern with the personal reward due the farmer. It is true that reward or recompense is assumed in the military and athletic figures: the soldier is provided with livelihood; the athlete is crowned. Yet in neither case is the idea of personal gain so prominent as in vs. 6. However, strict parallelism of illustration would have called for something like "A farmer who does not work hard will not get good crops," or "It is only a hard-working

---

Whether or not Paul was quoting popular proverbs, as B. S. Easton suggests,[6] these pictures carry their obvious suggestions.

The military metaphors in Paul's writings cannot be deleted in the interests of peace, and need not be, for they are frankly metaphors. The Roman soldier was part of the landscape in the Mediterranean world. There is no militarism implied or suggested in Paul's not infrequent use of military terms for illustrative purposes, as in Eph. 6:11-17. Christianity was a spiritual warfare against evil in the world. If a Roman legionary could be expected to exercise self-restraint and to undergo discipline, how much more the Christian! Charles Wesley paraphrased Paul's military metaphor in one of his

greatest hymns, "Soldiers of Christ, arise," as did Sabine Baring-Gould in "Onward, Christian soldiers," and Reginald Heber in "The Son of God goes forth to war." The church needs this stirring note of battle against wrong, and it is a pedantic literalism which would banish these hymns from the worship of the Prince of Peace because of the figures of speech employed in them.

The Roman games also followed imperial power, as ruined colosseums in the south of France and along the eastern Adriatic testify. Was Paul himself sometimes a spectator at the races, or was he merely using athletic terms which had become part of the speech of the people? Easton[7] points out that the analogy between the Christian and the runner (both in

[6] *The Pastoral Epistles* (New York: Charles Scribner's Sons, 1947), p. 51.

[7] *Ibid.*

7 Consider what I say; and the Lord give thee understanding in all things.

8 Remember that Jesus Christ of the seed of David was raised from the dead, according to my gospel:

of the crops. 7 Think over what I say, for the Lord will grant you understanding in everything.

8 Remember Jesus Christ, risen from the dead, descended from David, as

---

farmer who deserves success." The awkwardness of the present text may be due to the fact that the agricultural metaphor was so consistently used in the church as defense of the right of the minister to claim support from the laity (cf. I Tim. 4:17-18; I Cor. 9:3-14) that it could scarcely be bent to any other purpose.

If one supposes (with Dibelius, Easton) that the writer is here quoting three popular proverbs, the imperfect parallelism may be attributed to the fixed form of the sayings introduced without editorial improvement.

7. This verse is generally taken as appended to the preceding three illustrations in lieu of an exposition of them. If "Timothy" will ponder well these pregnant sayings, the Lord will open up their deeper meanings to him. Easton interprets the verse as beginning a paragraph, taking what I say very generally to mean "everything I say." Then "if Timothy ponders Paul's teaching deeply enough, Christ will give him understanding of its depths" (*Pastoral Epistles*, p. 51).

### VI. To Die Is to Live (2:8-13)

8. If the burden of the epistle down to this point may almost be said to be "Remember Paul" as the chief bearer of the Christian tradition, "Timothy" and all ministers

---

this passage and in I Cor. 9:24-25) is imperfect, since in the race only one athlete is crowned as winner, while it is the Christian faith that God rewards all who run well. However that may be, Paul's plea for a disciplined Christian life is not impaired. Philip Doddridge used these passages as a background for his hymn:

> Awake, my soul, stretch every nerve,
> And press with vigor on;
> A heavenly race demands thy zeal,
> And an immortal crown.

It may well be that Paul is here contrasting the hard-working farmer with some neighboring farmer who has been indolent. The man who has prepared his field well may expect to have earlier and better crops. In the light of the subject under discussion, Christian discipline, that makes more sense than to assume that Paul is here justifying a gradation of reward in proportion to labor. In I Cor. 9:7-13, which seems to have been the background of this passage (for these same three metaphors are used in that chapter), Paul was defending the right of a Christian teacher to maintenance in his work. No doubt he did not intend these metaphors for too strict an analysis. He was emphasizing the fact that Timothy had been set apart for a hazardous mission which would require courage, self-discipline, and hard work. But the reward for faithful service would be great.

In all three metaphors Paul is calling for

complete consecration to the Christian cause, for readiness to face hardships, and for self-denial. Three rewards are suggested: the approval of a commander, the victor's crown, and fruit from the labor expended. There is a paradox in the Christian teaching about the rewards of Christian life and faith. In Matt. 6 Jesus is recorded as setting in sharp contrast those who seek for earthly rewards for the religious life and those whom God rewards. He goes even so far as to conclude the Beatitudes with the strange formula for happiness: "Blessed are ye, when men shall revile you, and persecute you. . . . Rejoice, and be exceeding glad: for great is your reward in heaven" (Matt. 5:11-12). Jesus seems to indicate that to follow him for the sake of reward is self-defeating, but that to those who are ready to take up the cross, deny themselves, and follow him, great rewards are given. Three of those rewards are hinted at in this passage: the approval of God, victory over evil, and fruit from labor. These pictures could be followed by the exhortation with which Paul concluded his discussion of eternal life in I Cor. 15:58: "Therefore, my beloved brethren, be ye steadfast, unmovable, always abounding in the work of the Lord, forasmuch as ye know that your labor is not in vain in the Lord."

8. *The Memory that Redeems.*—No words in the Bible have been more frequently wrenched from their context than the three words **Remember Jesus Christ**. They can stand alone,

are now summoned to **Remember Jesus Christ** as the true heart and center of Paul's gospel, as the one in whom alone is salvation.

> **Jesus Christ,**
> **Risen from the dead,**
> **Descended from David,**

should be regarded as a fragment of a preaching formula or of a primitive creed summarizing in balanced phrases for purposes of memory the basic articles of the Christian faith. Why these two qualifying phrases only are here reproduced, and in the order in which they appear, cannot now be clearly seen. If, as is possible, this statement of the Pauline gospel is derived from Rom. 1:3-4, the mention of these two articles is accounted for, but not the order in which they appear, which is the reverse of that in Romans. Paul in Romans follows the chronological order, as do the creeds of the church.

Interestingly enough, none of our present creeds carries the clause **descended from David,** although the Davidic descent of Jesus was generally held in the church, and although its occurrence here and its frequent recurrence in Ignatius (Ign. Eph. 18:2; Ign. Trall. 9; Ign. Rom. 7:3; Ign. Smyr. 1:1; cf. Did. 9:2) argue that it was used in some early professions of faith.

There is the further problem that while Paul certainly believed that Jesus "was descended from David according to the flesh" (Rom. 1:3; here only in the genuine epistles), he scarcely made sufficient use of the teaching to warrant its being made one of two items selected to summarize Paul's gospel.

The presence of the article here is commonly explained as laying emphasis on the humanity of Jesus, either as an anti-Docetic or anti-Gnostic touch, or as suggesting that Christ, being both God and man, is able to bestow upon men that same heavenly glory which he enjoys as **risen from the dead.**

That **risen from the dead** comes first is in accordance with logical, if not chronological, order. In the experience and preaching of Paul, as of the whole church, belief in the resurrection of Christ was first and fundamental in importance. The church began with the Resurrection and reasoned in both directions. It reinterpreted the total past and projected the total future in the light of this event.

The use to which this faith is put in the present context is to remind ministers in their suffering that Christ is risen and that as in his case the Via Dolorosa became a Via Gloriosa, so for them too suffering will bring a crown of glory.

**As preached in my gospel:** Once again the writer insists that loyalty to Paul's gospel is the only way to Christ.

---

for they bring us back to the magnetic pole from which all Christian faith and life take their directions. They remind us of the humanity of Jesus who "was in all points tempted like as we are, yet without sin" (Heb. 4:15). They remind us that Christian truth is not a vague abstraction but has been revealed in a Person (cf. I John 1:1-2). In the midst of a secular and semipagan world they remind us of a Life in whom the light and life and love of God were made manifest. A fine litany entitled "A Recollection of Jesus" begins:

Let us remember Jesus:
Who, though he was rich, yet for our sakes became poor and dwelt among us,

and ends with the petition,

Let us remember Jesus:
Who humbled himself and carried obedience to the point of death, even death on the Cross, and endured faithful to the end.

The people's response is:

May this mind be in us that was in Jesus Christ.[8]

The reader is reminded of two aspects of the life of Jesus: the earthly life, **descended from David,** and the eternal life, **risen from the dead.** In our own time, as in early Christianity, there is a tendency in some quarters to forget the historic Jesus, to the neglect of the ethical principles which his life and ministry revealed in

[8] *The Kingdom, the Power, and the Glory* (New York: Oxford University Press, 1928), pp. 5-6. Used by permission.

9 Wherein I suffer trouble, as an evil-doer, *even* unto bonds; but the word of God is not bound.

preached in my gospel, 9 the gospel for which I am suffering and wearing fetters, like a criminal. But the word of God is not

---

**9. The gospel for which,** lit., "in which," meaning "in my work for which." The text is not concerned to specify just what the charges against Paul were which resulted in his suffering "even up to fetters," and although not a bandit or brigand, suffering like one. Its one point is that Paul (or "Paul"?), as model for other ministers, is a model in the suffering which is necessarily involved in the pursuit of Christian work (vs. 3; 1:8, 12). The emphasis of the letter on the necessity of suffering on the part of church officials is best explained if the letter dates from the period in which the Christian church was regarded as an illegal association, membership in which was in itself a crime, i.e., when Christians might be punished for the "name itself." It is suggestive that the word **criminal** occurs elsewhere in the N.T. only in Luke 23:32-33, 39, referring to the brigands crucified with Jesus; perhaps the reader is expected to discern how closely Paul's ignominy parallels that of his master.

**But the word of God is not fettered:** The fervor of faith here leaps into high flame. Men may be fettered, but not the gospel. The word leaps and runs. No human power can circumscribe its freedom.

The precise connotations of **the word of God** (see Tit. 2:5) are difficult to establish. In the context it seems to be the equivalent of "the gospel" or God's message or the Christian preaching. Cadbury has suggested that in Acts, where the phrase is of frequent occurrence, it seems to mean "not merely the preaching but the whole Christian enterprise" (F. J. Foakes Jackson and Kirsopp Lake, eds., *The Beginnings of Christianity* [London: Macmillan & Co., 1933], V, 391). Although such a comprehensive meaning is not required by the present passage, it is quite possible. The work of the church, which of course centers in preaching, cannot be brought to a stop by the imprisonment of its leaders.

---

power and beauty. On the other hand, there is also a tendency in other groups to think of Jesus only as a good man, to the neglect of his revelation of the eternal love of God. The gospel includes both truths. **Remember Jesus Christ, risen from the dead, descended from David, as preached in my gospel.**

**9. The Unfettered Word.**—We are familiar today with rays and sound waves which pass through solid walls. Paul believed that the Christian gospel has like penetrating and expansive power. He himself was a prisoner of Rome. **But the word of God is not fettered.** In the Epistle to the Philippians Paul had pointed out two things: even as a prisoner he had been able to bear witness to the Christian faith and make it persuasive to those around him; and because of his imprisonment, others had been "more bold to speak the word without fear" (Phil. 1:12-14). It was said of Eivind J. Berggrav, imprisoned by the Nazis during World War II, that it was necessary to change his guards from time to time because the bishop so profoundly impressed them with his contagious Christian faith. Time and again when the Christian gospel has seemed to be confronted by insuperable barriers of hostility, in-

difference, rivalry, and materialism, it has burst its bonds and gone on its conquering way. As Moffatt translates the phrase, "There is no prison for the word of God."

**9. The Prisoner of the Lord.**—This verse may refer to Paul's actual imprisonment on a trumped-up charge, or as Scott suggests,[1] the sentence may refer to conditions at the end of the first century when it was regarded as a crime to profess oneself a Christian. There is a long roll of honor made up of those who have yielded their freedom rather than deny their faith: Paul and Silas at Philippi; Peter in Jerusalem; Savonarola in Florence; Martin Luther in the Wartburg; John Bunyan in Bedford jail; Martin Niemöller at Sachsenhausen; the churchmen in Yugoslavia, Hungary, Czechoslovakia, and China who have suffered imprisonment rather than conform their message to communist orders. When civil authority has demanded the allegiance of conscience which belongs only to God a long line of martyrs have replied, "We must obey God rather than men" (Acts 5:29). It is a grave step when any man makes this

[1] E. F. Scott, *The Pastoral Epistles* (New York: Harper & Bros., 1936; "Moffatt New Testament Commentary"), p. 104.

10 Therefore I endure all things for the elect's sake, that they may also obtain the salvation which is in Christ Jesus with eternal glory.

11 *It is* a faithful saying: For if we be dead with *him,* we shall also live with *him:*

fettered. 10 Therefore I endure everything for the sake of the elect, that they also may obtain the salvation which in Christ Jesus goes with eternal glory. 11 The saying is sure:

> If we have died with him, we shall also live with him;

---

**10.** Since it is impossible that the gospel should be hindered from accomplishing its destined work, **I endure everything.** Suffering now has positive meaning, for unless ministers have patience and endurance in it, those whom God has chosen for himself will not be saved. As the apostle's suffering was part of the plan of salvation, so is the suffering of "Paul" and all "Timothys."

As in the Jewish tradition the Israelites were thought of as the chosen people or God's elect, so in the Christian tradition the term was transferred to mean Christians, either actual members of the church or yet to become such. The emphasis here is on those who are yet to be saved as the direct result of endurance in suffering on the part of Christ's ministers.

Christian salvation, the specific content of which is not here set forth, will be indeed a glorious one, in contrast to the present suffering. It **goes with**="is accompanied with"= "is characterized by" **eternal glory.** Eternal glory for the Christian would be understood to mean life no longer subject to sin and death, frustration and loss, but permanent and unhindered participation in the rich, warm, triumphant, secure life of God himself.

**11-13.** The "sure saying" is obviously a quotation of some liturgical hymn or solemn confession used in the formal services of the church. Introduced by the familiar citation formula, composed of four couplets, rhythmically and structurally parallel, and only in part germane to the context, vss. 11-13 are in whole or in part an adaptation or a fragment of some longer and more complete, although not now extant, statement of faith. That the quotation is fragmentary is evidenced (*a*) from the initial **for** (in the Greek), omitted in the RSV as meaningless apart from the antecedent clause on which it originally depended; and (*b*) from its inconclusive and unexpected ending, making it impossible to be sure just how much of vss. 11-13 is quotation and how much is comment on or modification of it by the author.

The material is best explained as derived from the liturgy of baptism, a part of a more extended statement which would be well familiar to first readers, who had themselves uttered the whole of it in the ceremony according to which they were baptized. It is useless now to try to conjecture the larger context in which this present fragment stood. However, such a statement would have more than one interest or emphasis, and it

---

affirmation, and it requires deep searching of heart to be sure that it is God and not his own pride of opinion that he serves. But modern history is tragically replete with instances where Christians have had to choose between being free spirits behind iron bars or remaining physically free while spiritually slaves to tyranny.

**10. Love as a Motive.**—The Gospel of John records Jesus as saying in the prayer at the Last Supper, "For their sakes I sanctify myself, that they also might be sanctified through the truth" (John 17:19). Paul speaks in somewhat similar terms of what he endures: **Therefore I endure everything for the sake of the elect, that they also may obtain the salvation which in Christ Jesus goes with eternal glory.** To put it in its

simplest terms, the gospel means so much to him that he is ready to endure anything to share it with others. This has always been the heart of the missionary motive. "What do all the disagreeable features (the meagerness of means, the exile, the unhealthful conditions) count for," wrote Albert Schweitzer from Africa, "compared with the joy of being here, working and helping?"[2]

**11-13. The Faithfulness of God.**—Here in three verses is another creed or hymn, probably familiar to the readers of the epistle, celebrating the faithfulness of God. **If we have died with him, we shall also live with him.** The Exeg.

[2] John Dickinson Regester, *Albert Schweitzer* (New York: Abingdon Press, 1931), pp. 78-79.

| | |
|---|---|
| **12** If we suffer, we shall also reign with *him:* if we deny *him,* he also will deny us: | **12** if we endure, we shall also reign with him; if we deny him, he also will deny us; |

should not be spoken of simply as a "triumphant hymn," thus by definition excluding from it vss. 12b-13 as too filled with foreboding to be in place in a triumph song.

Vs. 11 is almost an exact quotation of Rom. 6:8, which in turn is explained by Rom. 6:3-5. Just as the Christian has already died with Christ—in baptism, in which "we were buried . . . with him . . . into death" (Rom. 6:3-4), i.e., have actually died with Christ in his death—so the Christian is as surely united with the risen Lord ("we shall certainly be united with him in a resurrection like his" [Rom. 6:5]) and lives, or better, **shall also live with him.**

**If we endure, we shall also reign with him:** In spite of the assurance which baptismal death and resurrection bring, the Christian's blessed future is wholly contingent upon his perseverance; baptism is the beginning, not the end. Only if he endures will he share in that glorious kingdom where the saints "shall reign forever and ever."

If the prospects and privileges of those who remain loyal to the faith are glorious, somber warnings are always in place for the faithless. **If we deny him, he also will deny us** (cf. Matt. 10:33). The newly baptized, even in the ecstasy of his rebirth into eternity, is well advised to remember that if he should prove disloyal, the Christ with whom he might have reigned will deny him before his Father who is enthroned in heaven.

Vs. 13a (**if we are faithless, he remains faithful;** cf. Rom. 3:3; 11:30-32) begins in strict parallelism with vs. 12b as warning, but suddenly in midverse turns back on itself, deflecting a threat into a promise and necessitating an explanatory appendage, **for he cannot deny himself,** and thus breaking down the rhythmical language pattern. On the supposition that the liturgical source was regularly rhythmical, that the couplets were composed according to a consistent scheme of parallel lines of similar length; further, on the ground of the sudden turn in thought in vs. 13a and the consequent reflective prose in vs. 13b, it is argued that vs. 13b, or the whole of vs. 13, or even vss. 12b-13 were not part of the source but modifications of it.

This literary problem cannot with certainty be solved. (a) Since the liturgical source is not now extant, we cannot be sure that its rhythmical scheme was uniform throughout, or that it was consistently modeled on the rhythm and structure of vss. 11-12a. Liturgical phrases are commonly of differing lengths, depending upon the ideas expressed in them. (b) A single literary source may lie behind the entire paragraph of vss. 8-13, including the two obvious quotations, vss. 8 and 11-13, transcribed freely and with comments by

points out the reasons for believing that this whole hymn may have been sung on baptismal occasions, and that this particular phrase may refer to being "buried . . . with him by baptism into death, so that as Christ was raised from the dead by the glory of the Father, we too might walk in newness of life" (Rom. 6:4). However, it would be equally applicable to those who faced the possibility of martyrdom for their faith. Still another possible meaning is the death of the old self to find a new life in Christ, as in Paul's assertion to the Galatians, "I have been crucified with Christ; it is no longer I who live, but Christ who lives in me" (Gal. 2:20). Here is an echo of the words which John attributes to Jesus, "Because I live, you will live also" (John 14:19). To the Christian, whether in this world or in the world to come, life means fellowship with Christ. **If we endure,**

**we shall also reign with him.** No doubt this reflects the current belief in the imminent return of Christ in glory to establish the new age. But beneath that particular conception lies the conviction which Paul expressed in the words, "I consider that the sufferings of this present time are not worth comparing with the glory that is to be revealed to us" (Rom. 8:18). A man was once struck by the apparent incongruity of a company of men in a rescue mission, tattered, bleary-eyed, and unkempt, singing a gospel hymn which concluded,

And when the battle's over, I shall wear a crown
In the new Jerusalem.

The mental picture of crowns on those tousled heads was ludicrous. But the gospel promises a redemption which means unimaginably glorious

| 13 If we believe not, *yet* he abideth faithful: he cannot deny himself. | 13 if we are faithless, he remains faithful — <br> for he cannot deny himself. |
|---|---|

the writer. We cannot reconstruct by conjecture the omitted material, nor can we be sure at every point of the "Pauline" additions. Obviously vss. 8c-10 with the possible exception of **the salvation which in Christ Jesus goes with eternal glory** are "Pauline." In vs. 13 the source may have been both telescoped and modified, leaving the verse intelligible in itself but without much point in the context. Indeed, it is the unrelatedness of the thought of vs. 13 to the context which prompts Dibelius to include it in the citation.

The problem of vs. 13 remains whether it is thought of as a part of the source or as "Pauline." After the severe warning of vs. 12b, the reader is unprepared for the swift shift in attitude which hurries to unsay what has just been said and to make faithlessness seem not too sinful at the very time—whether at baptism or in reference to the situation here—when the emphasis falls on summons to rigorous loyalty. Vs. 13 is as incompatible with the sternness of vss. 14-19 as it is with vs. 12b. The verse can be integrated into the context only if we interpret it as strictly parallel in meaning with vs. 12b, concealing irony in its second clause: if we prove untrustworthy, Christ will prove trustworthy; i.e., he can be depended on to hold men accountable and to bring them to judgment. He has said that he would deny faithless men at the judgment, and he will, **for he cannot deny himself** (so Lock, *et al.*).

If this exegesis is not valid, we are left with the devout but ill-fitting interpretation that in case the baptized—or the clergy here—fail to keep their vows, even so, Christ

possibilities for just such wastrels. Vachel Lindsay caught this authentic note of the gospel in his poem "General William Booth Enters Heaven."

**If we deny him, he also will deny us.** The Exeg. points out the similarity between this stern saying and Matt. 10:33. We find it also in Luke 9:26, "Whoever is ashamed of me and of my words, of him will the Son of man be ashamed when he comes in his glory." This is the note of judgment, which is inseparable from the gospel. Shallow people sometimes say that if God loves us, he will overlook our moral lapses, gloze them over, and pretend that they do not exist. The gospel says that just because God loves us, he makes great demands of us, he cannot overlook or pretend, he sees the truth, and judges us in righteousness. When by our deliberate choice or manner of life we deny that we are followers of Christ he cannot falsify that fact. Milk-and-water philosophies teach that sin does not matter very much. But the gospel is of sterner stuff and has iron in it. Sin is a denial of the righteous Lord, a rebellion against God, and judgment is inevitable. **If we are faithless, he remains faithful.** Here the hymn reaches its climax. The Exeg. points out the difficulty of reconciling this statement with the harsher one which immediately precedes it. But this is the familiar paradox of judgment and grace. A possible interpretation is that these two lines represent the conviction that however

far man may go in his sin, the redeeming love of God is unchanged and the Father waits for the return of the prodigal. He does not call black white, or evil good. **He remains faithful** as our Judge, but also as our Redeemer. This should be read in the light of I Tim. 1:12-13, "He judged me faithful by appointing me to his service, though I formerly blasphemed and persecuted and insulted him." Perhaps I Tim. 2:3-4 is also necessary background for the interpretation of this hymn: "God, our Savior, who desires all men to be saved and to come to the knowledge of the truth." So long as we deny him, he cannot do other than deny us. But **he remains faithful** to his purpose of redemption.

**If we are faithless?** Who is not? One result of our faithlessness is widespread loss of confidence in ourselves. The cocksure optimism of an older day has been shattered. Multitudes have lost confidence in themselves, and at the same time have lost faith in any Reality greater than themselves. F. R. Barry says:

Some of our insecurity we *make* by having no fixed spiritual anchorage. . . . After all, we believe in God, the eternal and undefeated Goodness who is working out a purpose in history, in a righteousness and truth which are imperishable and in a Kingdom which shall be established beyond the horizons of these tortured years; and it is our business to live in the courage and steadfastness of those convictions.[3]

[3] *Convictions* (London: Nisbet & Co., 1939), pp. vii-viii.

| | |
|---|---|
| 14 Of these things put *them* in remembrance, charging *them* before the Lord that they strive not about words to no profit, *but* to the subverting of the hearers. | 14 Remind them of this, and charge them before the Lord[b] to avoid disputing about words, which does no good, but only |
| | [b] Other ancient authorities read *God*. |

will be merciful. "Man's faith in God is not the measure of God's faithfulness to man" (J. H. Bernard, *The Pastoral Epistles* [London: Macmillan & Co., 1906; "Cambridge Greek Testament"], *ad loc.*). "The rhythm of the hymn should require 'If we are faithless, he himself will be faithful,' but this would be blasphemy; the omnipotent God cannot perform acts contrary to his holiness. Now, by nature he is 'the faithful God' (Deut. 7:9); and here, his faithfulness is to be understood . . . as the divine immutability in good. . . . Thus the love of the Savior breaks the logic of the construction and prevails over a strict justice which would demand a rigorous reciprocity." (Spicq, *Saint Paul: les Épitres Pastorales*, p. 350.)

Ill-fitting to the context as is this kindly interpretation of vs. 13, it may be exactly the point of view of both the author and his source. The fact is that the N.T. cannot think of God as other than a forgiving God. That Christ is judge, and a rigorous one, it has no doubt; but if rigorous, he is also righteous (4:8). Therefore he can be depended on. "Christian teaching has often opposed the justice of God, which demands that sin shall be punished, to His mercy, which remits the punishment. . . . The opposition is not recognized in the New Testament. For 'John' as for Paul [and we may add, 'Paul'] . . . the mercy or forgiveness of God is a function of His righteousness; and so far from forgiveness being a kind of breach in His self-consistency, it is both possible and actual only because God is completely 'faithful,' completely to be relied upon in all circumstances" (C. H. Dodd, *The Johannine Epistles* [New York: Harper & Bros., 1946; "The Moffatt New Testament Commentary"], pp. 22-23).

Although the original source of vss. 8-13 was from the baptismal liturgy, the material is here used by the writer to encourage ministers to maintain their vows inviolate, assuring the faithful of a glorious recompense, and the faithless of utter rejection.

## VII. The Good Minister Keeps the Received Faith (2:14-19)

14. **Remind them of this** (RSV; lit., **these things**, KJV), i.e., the importance of holding fast to the (Pauline) gospel, of transmitting it uncorrupted, of the glorious

---

This ancient hymn expresses the conviction that when man is about played out, God is not played out. God does not cease to exist when men cease to believe in him or trust in him.

His sovereign power, without our aid,
    Made us of clay, and formed us men;
And, when like wandering sheep we strayed,
    He brought us to his fold again.[4]

God is! Pygmy men may deny his reality or flout his sovereign will, for he has endowed them with freedom to do just that if they choose. **He remains faithful.**

It is good to remind ourselves of some of the implications of the faithfulness of God. We can count on God to respect the dignity of every man. We can count on him to be at work through the spirit of Christ drawing men together into fellowship. We can count on him to

[4] Isaac Watts, "Before Jehovah's awful throne."

be the Savior of his children. Our task is to be faithful to him, even when we cannot see in advance how he will lead us. We are to commit to him in faith this world which so sorely needs saving. **He remains faithful—for he cannot deny himself.**

14. *Unprofitable Words.*—Occasionally one hears a discussion of some religious theme which reminds him of a brilliant tennis match. It is a good game, interesting to watch or fun to play. The players drive hard and volley, bring out artful drop strokes, employ cunning strategy to lure their opponents into exposed positions, and test out each other's endurance. But it is only a game. When it is all over, nothing of vital importance has been decided. **Avoid disputing about words, which does no good, but only ruins the hearers** (RSV), says Paul. **Strive not about words to no profit** (KJV). Life is not a game. Athletic metaphors have their place in the interpretation of religion so long as they are

15 Study to show thyself approved unto God, a workman that needeth not to be ashamed, rightly dividing the word of truth.

16 But shun profane *and* vain babblings: for they will increase unto more ungodliness:

ruins the hearers. 15 Do your best to present yourself to God as one approved, a workman who has no need to be ashamed, rightly handling the word of truth. 16 Avoid such godless chatter, for it will lead people

---

salvation which is the reward of those who persevere through suffering, and of the perdition which awaits the faithless. **Them** is unexpressed in Greek, but since the letter is a pastoral letter addressed to "Timothy" as representing the ministry of the church, the word is properly supplied in English, and means ministers. It must be made clear to them that their religious duty forbids **disputing about words** (lit., "word fighting"; see I Tim. 6:4), the scornful term with which the author cudgels the heretical teachers. In their expositions of Christianity they never strike reality; they merely mouth words; their battles are sham battles, "sound and fury, signifying nothing." Such sermons serve only one end: the ruin of those who hear them. They are not merely useless: they are positively destructive.

15. The minister must not allow his energies to be sluiced off into vain and subversive wranglings. Rather, he must exert himself to the utmost to demonstrate before God that he is a competent workman. Thoroughly proved and approved, and without any **need to be ashamed** of his competency as a preacher, because he knows how to "handle"— not words—but **the word of truth** (see Col. 1:5; Eph. 1:13, "the word of truth, the gospel"), the Christian revelation, the pattern of sound words, the deposit of faith, as believed and preached by "Paul." The competent minister is one who expounds this gospel just as he has learned it.

The Greek word for "handle" originally meant to "cut straight"; hence the KJV **rightly dividing.** According to Theodoret it is a metaphor inspired by the farmer who drives (cuts) a straight furrow, or a tailor who cuts a fabric according to a pattern. It has been proposed that "to cut the word of truth straight" means to preach it straightforwardly and not beat about the bush. There is evidence, however, that in later Greek the suffix "cut" in compound words had lost its literal meaning, the compound word "to cut straight" coming to mean quite generally, "to handle rightly or correctly." Certainly to the author, **rightly handling the word of truth** is to guard it (1:14), to preach it (1:8), to follow it (1:13), to suffer for it (vs. 3).

16. The good minister will hold strictly to the received faith, avoiding the **godless chatter** (see I Tim. 4:7; 6:20), the worldly nonsense of the heretical teachers. Presuming

---

metaphors. The hymn which Paul has just quoted deals with issues of life and death. Religion does not have to be always solemn, but it is always serious. The temptation to make an intellectual game out of religion is not the only way in which people fail to take religion seriously. There are others. Sometimes religion is made an aesthetic indulgence. Sometimes it is used to give a moralistic veneer to a predatory life. Sometimes it is treated as one of the minor interests of life. Don't use the great words of Christian faith unless you mean them, says Paul. Take religion seriously or not at all.

15. *A Workman Unashamed.*—Again Paul pleads for the sincerity which is concerned with the approval of God rather than of men, "with no need to be ashamed of the way you handle

the word of the Truth" (Moffatt). **Do your best to present yourself to God as one approved.** The common ways in which it is easy to handle the word of truth shamefully are obvious: to neglect the Word of God and treat it casually; to seek comfort in the Word and to ignore its challenges; to try to make the Word say what we want to hear rather than to be receptive to God's message; to deceive ourselves into imagining that hearing the Word of God is equivalent to obeying it. Study (KJV), **do your best** (RSV), "give diligence" (ASV) to handle **the word of truth** rightly.

16. *A Plea for Reverence.*—Moffatt renders this verse, "Avoid all that profane jargon," and Easton has it, "Avoid the jargon used in the world; for they who indulge in it will go on

| 17 And their word will eat as doth a canker: of whom is Hymeneus and Philetus; | into more and more ungodliness, 17 and their talk will eat its way like gangrene. Among them are Hymenae'us and Phi- |

---

to expound religion, they emit only empty noises, which so far from having anything to do with religion lead men farther and farther away from it.

The "profane jargon" (Moffatt), or "jargon used in the world" (Easton), against which the writer inveighs should not be thought of as merely the secular philosophy of the time as practiced outside the church, but as referring to speculative philosophical efforts within the church to relate the Christian faith to current technical (profane) philosophical concepts and interests. The result, says our author, of restatement, reinterpretation, and adjustment of the traditional and true (Pauline) form of the faith in terms of the dominant secular philosophy is to reduce the primacy of Christianity and to subordinate it to secular thought, thereby substituting one faith for another, a secular faith for a revealed. In the guise of religion such men move progressively toward irreligion. "Their devotion to 'deep' matters results in bottomless folly" (Easton, *Pastoral Epistles*, p. 56).

The word translated **it will lead** is, lit., "they will advance" or "progress." The word may be used ironically: such people advance, yes, but backward!

**17-18. And their talk** [i.e., teaching] **will eat its way,** both spreading and destroying, **like gangrene.** Like a repulsive and fatal disease it will destroy the church itself if tolerated. It does not feed the souls of men; it feeds upon them.

Medical metaphors are common in the Pastorals: I Tim. 4:2; 6:4; Tit. 1:15; also "sound" teaching, etc., I Tim. 1:10. To emphasize the fact that such unsound teachers actually exist the writer names two of them, **Hymenaeus and Philetus,** with a brief description of the heretical teaching with which **they are upsetting the faith of some.** Philetus, known only here, remains a mere name. Hymenaeus appears elsewhere only in I Tim. 1:20 (which see). That Hymenaeus and Philetus are named, and with such severity, suggests that they are no longer members of the church, but are still making trouble.

**By holding that the resurrection is past already,** Hymenaeus and Philetus **have swerved from the truth,** i.e., have quite missed the point of the Christian doctrine of the resurrection and thereby falsified the whole Christian faith. According to the text itself, the chief point of contention between the author and his opponents has to do with the question when the resurrection is to take place. Neither side denied the fact of the resurrection. What conclusions Hymenaeus and his friends drew from their interpretation of the resurrection as **past already,** we are not told. Yet obviously the meaning of the word and its content for faith are radically different, depending on whether it is dated wholly in the past or has predominantly a future reference.

---

further into irreligion." This is a repetition of previous warnings against the empty talk about religion which characterized contemporary cults, in contrast with the new life which is the fruit of Christian faith. But this warning goes further in that it points out that to use the sacred truths and practices of religion merely as the material for verbal combat is a form of profanity. This is the peculiar temptation of those whose calling takes them into the service of the church today. To let familiarity with scripture and hymns lead to flippancy in their use; to forget what great doctrines mean for life and to think of them only as texts for debate; to develop pride of

opinion in religious matters until one is constantly defending oneself instead of pleading for loyalty to Christ; to use the language of religion until all its vitality is squeezed out in the routine of professionalism—these are temptations which beset laymen and clergy alike in the service of the church. We must still be on guard against "profane jargon" which leads to irreligion.

**17-18. *Hymenaeus and Philetus.*—**Here are two men who have come down through history with the unenviable distinction of being associated with an ugly metaphor. **Their talk will eat its way like gangrene.** As a spreading sore

18 Who concerning the truth have erred, saying that the resurrection is past already; and overthrow the faith of some.

le'tus, 18 who have swerved from the truth by holding that the resurrection is past already. They are upsetting the faith of

---

Within the N.T. there are points of contact with both views, reflecting the variety of opinions current at the time. According to Paul (Rom. 6; Col. 2-3), when men enter the Christian life (in baptism) they die with Christ and are raised up with him, becoming alive to God. They have been set free from the law of sin and death. They are no longer in the flesh but in the spirit. They have died and their lives are hid with Christ in God. Of course this is only half of the Pauline teaching on the subject but it was a congenial half to the Greek mind which believed in immortality and indeed in judgment after death (see Plato *Apology* XLI; *Republic* X. 614), but which believed that death was "a journey to another place" which the soul made after leaving the body. Within this view there was no place for a general resurrection when the Lord himself would descend from heaven with a shout, when the trumpet would sound, the graves give up their dead, and those who had fallen asleep would be joined to their physical bodies, or in the more refined view of Paul, to spiritual bodies, imperishable and immortal, that they might stand before the judgment seat of Christ to receive good or evil, according to what each had done in the body. To the Greek the soul is of itself indestructible and immortal (Plato *Republic* X. 608-11), but its real nature cannot be understood while it is "flustered and maddened by the body" (Plato *Cratylus* 404A), or "marred by association with the body and other evils" (Plato *Republic* X. 611C). Only when the soul is contemplated in its original purity, uncontaminated by contact with the body, "is its beauty revealed." Since salvation consisted precisely in the liberation of the soul from the body, the idea of the revivification of the flesh or the reanimation of the body could only be an intolerable offense. This is why the Athenians "mocked" when they heard Paul speak of the resurrection of the dead (Acts 17:32). It was not that they did not believe in immortality, but that they thought the resurrection form of the hope to be incredibly vulgar and misplaced in that it desired to perpetuate that part of personal existence which is by nature subject to decay and death, being both corruptible and evil.

It should not be supposed that Paul and the Greeks were utterly at variance in their appraisal of the moral and religious value of the body. Paul too was sure that flesh and blood cannot inherit the kingdom of God. He used such language as the "sinful body" (Rom. 6:6); "sinful flesh" (Rom. 8:3); "I know that nothing good dwells within me, that is, in my flesh" (Rom. 7:18); "Those who are in the flesh cannot please God" (Rom. 8:8). Nevertheless, although Paul thought more meanly of the "flesh" than was normally characteristic of rabbinical Judaism, and by the same token was on this point more in accord with Greek thought than was the average Jew, yet at two points the thought of Paul was radically different from that of the Greeks. (*a*) The body, he

---

corrupts healthy flesh, so their influence, exerted through their teachings, makes everything that it reaches unhealthy. The Exeg. discusses in detail the heresy of these men **who have swerved from the truth by holding that the resurrection is past already.** Why was such teaching regarded as so corrupting? Because the Resurrection is both a historic fact and a glowing hope. In preaching the doctrine of the Resurrection today there are three truths to be emphasized: (*a*) the resurrection of Jesus, which revealed the power and love of God, whose Son could not be holden of death; (*b*) the resurrection of the believer, who becomes a new creature in Christ,

whether by baptism or by some other expression of his surrender to Christ; (*c*) the future resurrection of those who are yet to pass through the gates of death into the larger life of the unseen world. It is sometimes said today that this third emphasis on the future is unnecessary or even undesirable. But to omit it or deny it robs life of its larger perspective, robs human fellowships of their richest meaning, takes away from living its most far-reaching incentive, destroys for sufferers and the lonely their greatest comfort, and denies the Christian faith that God is a loving Father. The Christian church was founded on the doctrine of the Resurrection. The church's

believed, was an integral and indispensable element in personal life, whether here or hereafter. He contemplates with anxiety the possibility of being "naked," "unclothed," between death and the resurrection, and is sure that God will not allow such a sorry state to come to pass (II Cor. 5:1-5). With exquisite passion he pleads with the Corinthians to believe that the dead must and do come with a body, even though qualitatively it is utterly different from the physical body. (b) Since the body is both essential and, as we now know it, subject to the law of sin and death, the redemption of the soul must embrace the redemption of the body. And so Paul's doctrine of redemption labors to show (i) that "if the Spirit of God really dwells in" men, they are not "in the flesh" but "in the Spirit," i.e., the power which sin and death secure over men by way of the flesh is broken, even in this life, and although redeemed men still walk in the flesh, they no longer walk according to it (Rom. 8); and (ii) that when full and final redemption takes place, when the trumpet sounds and the dead are raised, "we shall all be changed." The perishable, dishonorable, weak, physical body will be raised an imperishable, glorious, powerful, spiritual body (I Cor. 15).

Both of these Pauline emphases established themselves as orthodoxy in the historic church. Yet neither of them had meaning for persons reared according to Greek categories of thought. Basic in Greek thought was the belief that matter and spirit were two opposing principles. The salvation of the soul required release from the body. That the body should be redeemed was thought neither possible nor desirable.

Hymenaeus, Philetus, and their companions, then, we may suppose, were teaching a form of Christianity which was essentially Greek rather than Jewish in its eschatology, which accepted only half of Paul's doctrine, rejecting belief in a general resurrection and insisting that the only valid meaning which the word "resurrection" could have would relate to the baptismal experience when the Christian mystically emerged from the waters of regeneration, having been buried with Christ and raised again to newness of life. This supernatural endowment with the Spirit meant that the Christian had already achieved victory over death.

Such spiritualizations, reinterpretations, or "modernizations" of sacred texts and teachings are of course a widespread practice in all religions. As a rule they are sincere attempts to retain traditional language patterns regarded as sacred, by attributing to them meanings congenial to contemporary points of view, meanings which the interpreter honestly believes to be true because the truth must agree with the truth.

**They are upsetting the faith of some:** Not merely are these teachers having some (considerable?) success in undermining the traditional belief in the resurrection, but disbelief at this point carries with it complete apostasy from **the [Christian] faith.** To touch the faith at such a vital spot is to upset it completely.

---

worship was set on Sunday, the day of the Resurrection. The Eucharist, the sacramental meal, was both an act "in remembrance of me" (I Cor. 11:24), and an act of faith in a future fellowship with Christ. "You proclaim the Lord's death until he comes" (I Cor. 11:26). To regard the Resurrection merely as a past event and to repudiate its significance for the future is to destroy the basis of the Christian faith.

We should remember, however, that there are other contemporary kinds of talk which undermine faith: talk based on the assumption that right and wrong are merely personal preferences; talk which assumes that life has no meaning beyond the pleasure of the moment; talk which robs other people of all confidence in themselves, of hope for the future, and of faith in God; talk which holds nothing sacred, makes light of the spiritual ends for which life has been greatly lived, and by innuendo and sarcasm takes the foundations out from under hard-beset folk. The Epistle of James uses a strong metaphor also: "The tongue is an unrighteous world among our members, staining the whole body, setting on fire the cycle of nature, and set on fire by hell. For every kind of beast and bird, of reptile and sea creature, can be tamed and has been tamed by humankind, but no human being can tame the tongue." (Jas. 3:6-8.) But even a destructive tongue can be converted by the grace of God in Christ.

19 Nevertheless the foundation of God standeth sure, having this seal, The Lord knoweth them that are his. And, Let every one that nameth the name of Christ depart from iniquity.

some. 19 But God's firm foundation stands, bearing this seal: "The Lord knows those who are his," and, "Let every one who names the name of the Lord depart from iniquity."

19. **But** is a strong adversative. In spite of the fact that there are some defections, the foundation which God has laid—i.e., the church—**stands** secure, in contrast to "ruin" (vs. 14) and "upsetting" (vs. 18). The Greek perfect is very effective here: the verb means "has stood and still stands."

In the metaphor the **foundation** is probably the foundation- or corner-stone; the **seal,** the inscription which authenticates or identifies the building and indicates its function and nature. In spite of heretical teachers the church stands bold and unambiguous on its received faith; it cannot be upset because God has certified and established it.

**The Lord knows those who are his** is almost an exact quotation from Num. 16:5 (LXX), varying only in the use of **Lord** instead of **God. Let every one who names the name of the Lord depart from iniquity** has contact with Ps. 6:8; Lev. 24:16; Josh. 23:7; Isa. 26:13; 52:11; Matt. 7:21-22; Luke 13:25-28, but is not a precise quotation from any extant scripture. Both "inscriptions" are introduced as quotations, and if they are not loosely quoted by memory from scripture, one or both of them may have been derived from early Christian poetry (Dibelius) or from some early gospel (Lock, Spicq), or be a Jewish or Christian proverb (Easton).

Since "Timothy" was well "acquainted with the sacred writings" (3:15), almost certainly he would be aware of the O.T. setting of the first quotation and be reminded of how the earth opened its mouth and swallowed up Korah, Dathan, and Abiram and their families because they rebelled against the leadership of Moses and Aaron. In Jude 11, too, unorthodox Christians are threatened with Korah's punishment. Obviously the name and the narrative had become the typical illustration of the fate of heterodox and insubordinate Christians.

If **the Lord knows those who are his,** he also knows those who are not his. And as in the presence of Moses he showed "who belongs to him and who is holy" (Num. 16:5, Amer. Trans.), so, the inference is, in the church God will expose the false teachers and will cast them out. The church is secure not because men know God, but because God knows men. In the light of this knowledge which God has, vs. 19b becomes a warning

19. *God's Firm Foundation.*—The N.T. refers frequently to foundations. Jesus stressed the necessity for a solid foundation for life in the story at the end of the Sermon on the Mount. "It did not fall, because it had been founded on the rock" (Matt. 7:25). Paul speaks of Christ as the only foundation. "No other foundation can any one lay than that which is laid, which is Jesus Christ" (I Cor. 3:11). The Epistle to the Ephesians links pioneer Christians with Christ as the foundation of the Christian community. "You are . . . members of the household of God, built upon the foundation of the apostles and prophets, Christ Jesus himself being the chief cornerstone" (Eph. 2:19-20). The Epistle to the Hebrews peers into the future and sees God as the guarantee of eternal life. "For he looked forward to the city which has foundations, whose builder and maker is God"

(Heb. 11:10). The seer on Patmos saw by faith a heavenly city with a twelvefold foundation: "And the wall of the city had twelve foundations, and on them the twelve names of the twelve apostles of the Lamb" (Rev. 21:14). So in this passage a similar note is struck. Paul has been speaking of those whose faith has been undermined. Scott observes:

This "foundation" has sometimes been identified with Christ Himself, or with the true Christian teaching, or with God's eternal law, but, in view of the words which follow, it appears to be the group of genuine Christians who form the rock on which Christ will build His Church.[5]

That group is the foundation of our highest human hopes, as well as the solid foundation on

[5] *Pastoral Epistles,* p. 112.

**20** But in a great house there are not only vessels of gold and of silver, but also of wood and of earth; and some to honor, and some to dishonor.

**21** If a man therefore purge himself from these, he shall be a vessel unto honor, sanctified, and meet for the master's use, *and* prepared unto every good work.

**20** In a great house there are not only vessels of gold and silver but also of wood and earthenware, and some for noble use, some for ignoble. **21** If any one purifies himself from what is ignoble, then he will be a vessel for noble use, consecrated and useful to the master of the house, ready for any

---

to all Christians, especially ministers, **to depart from iniquity,** meaning in the first instance to avoid the sin of "swerving from the truth" and, like Korah, persisting in insubordination to the church authorities. As Korah, Dathan, and Abiram could not effectively resist Moses and the congregation of Israel, neither can Hymenaeus and Philetus harm our author and the church.

### VIII. The Good Minister Teaches Correct Doctrine in Love (2:20-26)

**20-21.** Here we have an answer in allegorical form to the question: Why are there such wicked persons in the church? In plain language the answer is that it is just that way, although no one has to be or remain wicked. The possibility of repentance and of coming to know the truth is always present (vs. 26).

Although the meaning of vss. 20-21 is clear, the metaphorical language employed to convey it makes sense only if completely allegorized. Things do not well symbolize persons; of necessity, therefore, the figure of speech used here is fancifully developed.

Just as in **a great house** there are utensils of varying worth, their use corresponding to their value, so in the church there are all kinds of ministers. But immediately the figure of speech begins to break down and is pushed aside. In a house utensils of wood and clay may be put to humble use, but they are not evil; indeed, such vessels are useful and necessary. In the author's mind, however, the utensils of wood and clay are men like Hymenaeus; and they are definitely neither useful nor necessary. And this leads to vs. 21. No one needs to be a second-rate, not to say a positively useless, minister. If he **purifies himself** (see vss. 22-23), he will be **ready for any good work.** Obviously the writer has here quite jumped over the traces of his metaphor. He is unconcerned with the fact that "a vessel designed for a base use does not, by being washed, become fit for a higher one; much less does a vessel made of earthenware change into gold. There is also an abrupt transition from household utensils to sacrificial vessels in a temple, and from that again to serviceable tools." (Scott, *Pastoral Epistles,* p. 114.)

Owing to obscurity consequent to dissolving the metaphor in its applications there is some uncertainty as to the meaning of the Greek word **these** (things or persons), translated in the RSV **what is ignoble.** Grammatically it should refer to the ignoble vessels, meaning, if allegorized, that one should keep clear of heretical teachers like

---

which God builds. **God's firm foundation stands.** As inscriptions for such a foundation two mottoes are suggested: one emphasizing God's concern for his people, the other his demand for righteousness. The ethical demand of religion is nowhere more crisply stated than here: "Let everyone who names the name of the Lord give up evil" (Moffatt). This is obviously an echo of the words of Jesus: "Not every one who says to me, 'Lord, Lord,' shall enter the kingdom of heaven, but he who does the will of my Father who is in heaven" (Matt. 7:21).

**20-21.** *Meet for the Master's Use.*—It is not necessary to try to find close analogies for the

confused metaphors of these verses. The argument is clear, and it is in line with the intent of the whole chapter. Just as in a house some vessels are finer and more useful than others, so in the Christian cause there are degrees of loyalty and fruitfulness. Timothy is urged to be a vessel **meet for the Master's use, and prepared unto every good work.** Who is prepared to be used by the Master? Here and there among Jesus' sayings we find hints, although never a full description, and the hints are surprising. Those who are fit to be used in Christian service are the penitent (Luke 18:14); the childlike (Matt. 18:3); the spiritually discerning (Matt.

22 Flee also youthful lusts: but follow righteousness, faith, charity, peace, with them that call on the Lord out of a pure heart.

good work. 22 So shun youthful passions and aim at righteousness, faith, love, and peace, along with those who call upon the Lord

---

Hymenaeus and Philetus. If one has to find a specific reference for "these [things]," the context suggests the "godless chatter" of vs. 16 (von Soden, Spicq).

22. See I Tim. 4:12 and Intro., pp. 344-45. In the context **youthful passions** might be disturbing and unmanageable tendencies such as impatience with the status quo, aversion to rule and routine, grudging obedience to authority, love of argument for its own sake, an exaggerated interest in theoretical rather than practical religion, premature acceptance of novel ideas and procedures, insistence on restatement of the tradition in the language and patterns of contemporary thought.

Such **passions** as these are set over against **righteousness, faith, love, and peace** (see I Tim. 6:11), virtues which unite and consolidate the church in a common loyalty, keeping it a closely knit, effective working organization integrated in an established faith, undisturbed by controversy, untorn by schism.

**Aim at righteousness**, i.e., good conduct, particularly as set forth in vss. 14-16, 23-24. **Faith** is fidelity to "the word of truth." **Love** is that genuine, glad, warmhearted devotion which binds men inseparably together in enthusiasm for a common task. **Peace** is absence of confusion and turmoil within the soul and within the church; it is the presence of a quiet radiance which brightens and heals, which provides soil and climate in which the things of the spirit grow.

---

6:19-20, 33); the wholly committed (Luke 14: 26); the loving (Matt. 22:36-39); those who have faith (Matt. 17:20).

As the Exeg. points out, the confusion in this metaphor arises from the inference that by being purified, ignoble vessels can become fit for noble use, wood and earthenware can become gold and silver. Only a miracle could accomplish this. Perhaps, however, the very confusion of the figure of speech strengthens the message here, for in human life this miracle actually takes place through the power of Christ's spirit. Saul of Tarsus had become Paul the apostle. Simon the impetuous fisherman had become Peter the rock. To the skeptical mind, which insists that "human nature cannot be changed," it is no more possible to make a saint out of a sinner than it is to turn a wooden pail into a golden vase. But such miracles are the métier of the divine grace which touches human life in Christ. **If any one purifies himself** [which means if anyone repents, receives the grace of God, is regenerated by the power of God] . . . , **then he will be a vessel for noble use.**

22. *The Perils of Youth.*—Paul has urged Timothy to let no man despise his youth (I Tim. 4:12). The enthusiasms, capacities, and potentialities of youth are incalculable assets too often overlooked by mature religious leaders. But youth has its perils also. Easton translates vs. 22: "Shun the desires common to young men; strive instead for righteousness,

faith, love, peace, in company with those who call upon the Lord with a clean heart." The energies of youth require direction. The passions of youth demand self-control. The loyalties of youth cannot be satisfied without an adequate object. These are to be found **along with those who call upon the Lord from a pure heart.** While prime minister of Great Britain, Ramsay MacDonald once said in an address to a gathering of British young men and women, "Youth is a terrible thing. It can be used to build heaven or hell." Marianne Farningham's paraphrase of Charlotte Elliott's evangelical hymn captures the spirit of this verse:

Just as I am, thine own to be,
Friend of the young, who lovest me,
To consecrate myself to thee,
    O Jesus Christ, I come!

Just as I am, young, strong and free,
To be the best that I can be
For truth, and righteousness, and thee,
    Lord of my life, I come! [6]

That this hymn is the prayer of multitudes of modern youth is evidenced by the topics which the speakers were asked to discuss at the 1950 general assembly of the United Student Christian Council, made up of fourteen American student Christian movements. The topics were:

[6] Used by permission of James Clarke & Co., Ltd., London.

23 But foolish and unlearned questions avoid, knowing that they do gender strifes.

24 And the servant of the Lord must not strive; but be gentle unto all *men*, apt to teach, patient;

from a pure heart. 23 Have nothing to do with stupid, senseless controversies; you know that they breed quarrels. 24 And the Lord's servant must not be quarrelsome but kindly to every one, an apt teacher, for-

---

**Along with those who call upon the Lord from a pure heart:** "Timothy" is to remain loyal to the main body of Christians, and not to be misled by such troublemakers as Hymenaeus. **A pure heart** is an orthodox one.

**23.** This verse is the topic sentence or theme of which the entire letter is an exposition. The church of the writer's time is violently agitated by controversy. So disgusted and impatient is he with all of it that he has no concern to air it in detail; he will not honor his opponents by giving a reasoned answer to their arguments; he will simply be done once and for all with **controversies,** "researches," "speculations."

They are **stupid, foolish** (KJV), and **senseless,** i.e., ignorant and uninstructed, in the sense that their basic assumptions and interests lie outside the Christian faith and therefore cannot attain to the truth. Useless in themselves, they only **breed quarrels** (cf. Tit. 3:9); and quarrels are always bad.

**24-25. The Lord's servant,** or slave, has here the technical sense of minister. The phrase, though common in the O.T., appears only here in the N.T., which regularly has "God" or "Christ" instead of "Lord." The passage may reflect the "servant" passages of Isa. 43:1-3; 53 (see on Tit. 1:1).

By refusing to become involved in arguments and controversies, the minister avoids the danger of losing his temper and quarreling, thus bringing the cause he cherishes into disrepute and turning his opponent against both him and it. Better than argument is kindliness, which attracts, not repels, calms, not irritates, which shifts to a higher level the plane on which thinking takes place. **An apt teacher** is not one who is impatient, harsh, and intolerant before ignorance, slowness of comprehension, or even antagonism; he is not one who nags and scolds and lashes with sarcasm and scorn. On the contrary, he is **forbearing.** He accepts insult and injury without resentment. He does not strike back.

---

"The Situation in Which We Proclaim the Gospel"; "Who Is Jesus Christ?"; "The Urgency of the Proclamation of the Gospel"; "The Mission of the Church"; "The Work of the Holy Spirit and the Task of the Student Christian Movement"; and "The Cost of Discipleship." Here is a company of **those who call upon the Lord from a pure heart.**

**23-24. Controversy, Good and Bad.**—The Exeg. calls vs. 23 the "topic sentence or theme of which the entire letter is an exposition." **Stupid, senseless controversies** breed quarrels because they involve no important issues, are carried on in a spirit of pride and faction, and result in no betterment of life. Paul rightly warns his readers against such wordy warfare. **The Lord's servant must not be quarrelsome but kindly to everyone.** But it is worth noting in this connection that there is another kind of controversy without which human life would be impoverished, the creative controversy which is the matching of honest, sincere minds to determine the truth when good men differ as to what is right. Most of the gains in human life have been achieved through controversy. Galileo

was engaged in controversy which defined the law of gravitation. Columbus had to argue with those who doubted the spherical shape of the earth. There have been fruitful controversies over the theory of evolution, over the rights of the individual, over the legitimacy of child labor, over the responsibilities of government for human welfare, over the practicability of international law, and many similar questions. Controversy carried on with mutual respect, in honesty and good faith, with courtesy and humility, is democracy's way of making up its mind. It is not to be shunned but welcomed. The story is told of Charles W. Eliot that long after his retirement from the presidency of Harvard University he was about to go out one evening to take part in a debate on an important public question. His family, wishing to guard him against excessive excitement, cautioned him about becoming involved in controversy, to which the ninety-year-old educator replied, "What would life be without controversy?"

**24-25. The Skilled Teacher.**—The servant of the Lord must be **apt to teach.** But in teaching

25 In meekness instructing those that oppose themselves; if God peradventure will give them repentance to the acknowledging of the truth;

26 And *that* they may recover themselves out of the snare of the devil, who are taken captive by him at his will.

bearing, 25 correcting his opponents with gentleness. God may perhaps grant that they will repent and come to know the truth, 26 and they may escape from the snare of the devil, after being captured by him to do his will.[c]

[c] Or *by him, to do his* (that is, God's) *will.*

He is infinitely patient with those who resist or contradict the faith, instructing them **with gentleness** and in humility. For it is only in this kind of teaching and learning situation that he can expect that **God may perhaps grant that they will repent and come to know the truth.** The end of Christian teaching is not to win an argument but to win a person. The teacher does not originate the revelation which he declares; neither does he initiate repentance in those who hear. All is of God, who may or may not **give them repentance.** The teacher's concern should be not to stand in the way of God's activity.

On **know the truth,** cf. I Tim. 2:4.

26. **Escape** is a colorful word in Greek, meaning "to become sober again" or "come to one's senses." On the figure of the **snare,** see Exeg. on I Tim. 3:7; 6:9.

Obscurity in the use of pronouns in the last phrase has given rise to endless discussion as to the meaning of the verse. In Greek **him** is the personal pronoun of the third person (αὐτός) **his** is the demonstrative, "that one" (ἐκεῖνος). In spite of the frequent suggestion that "him" means either God (Moffatt; RSV mg.) or the "Lord's servant" (Falconer, Lock, ASV mg.), both interpretations are most unlikely. In the context the antecedent of "him" is most naturally taken to be the nearest personal noun, which is **the devil.** Also, the word **captured** means "captured alive" and is too rough a word to be used of God's rescue work. Surely the clause means to speak of the "opponents" as captured by the devil in his snare.

A more difficult problem is the reference of ἐκείνου (**his;** lit., "that one's"). That we have here a true demonstrative intending to indicate someone other than **him,** and meaning God, is held by some (J. Weiss, Wohlenberg, Bernard, Falconer, Scott, *et al.;* ASV mg., RSV mg.). Then, however—unless both pronouns are taken to mean God (so Moffatt)—the prepositional phrase **to do his** [God's] **will** would have to be construed with **they may escape,** which is separated from it by too great a distance. It most naturally belongs to the participial clause near it, **after being captured.** We may best suppose, then, that, as often in late Greek, the classical distinction between these pronouns is disregarded, "that one" being weakened almost to **him,** and used here to avoid a repetition of the same word (Dibelius, Easton, Spicq), both pronouns referring to the devil. Thus the translation as in the text of RSV, ASV, KJV (so Goodspeed, Dibelius, Easton, Spicq,

the way of Christ the spirit of the teacher is no less important than his technique. Pride of position, a patronizing attitude toward the learner, the disposition to argue down an opponent, the assumption of omniscience, the tendency to take pleasure in putting the other person in the wrong—these attitudes make it impossible for one person to make Christ's way persuasive to another. A skilled Christian teacher must have more than a master's degree from a teacher's college. He must also be master of the arts of humility, gentleness, patience, forgiveness, and faith. Then he will be not so much the teacher as the instrument through whom God teaches. **God may perhaps grant that they will repent and come to know the truth.**

26. *The Glorious Liberty of the Children of God.*—Here in another somewhat obscure metaphor the central fact of the Christian gospel is reiterated. Men who are slaves to habit and self can be made free for a new life in Christ. The man so enslaved is caught in a trap, from which Christ is the way of escape. Moffatt, translating the phrase which describes this release, renders it, that "they may come to their senses," indicating that life apart from Christ is irrational. So the prodigal, "when he came to himself" said, "I will arise and go to my father" (Luke 15:17-18). In the far country, he was out of his senses. Moffatt's translation of vs. 26 also describes this change as a transition from death to life, "As they are brought back

3 This know also, that in the last days perilous times shall come.

2 For men shall be lovers of their own selves, covetous, boasters, proud, blas-

3 But understand this, that in the last days there will come times of stress. 2 For

---

*et al.*) is preferable. This interpretation fits most easily into the context: the opponents have been captured by the devil to work his will, but if they repent, they may escape.

### IX. WARNING AGAINST CORRUPT AND HERETICAL TEACHERS (3:1-9)

**3:1.** If "Timothy" understands why there are so many wicked and faithless men in the world, and even in the church, who pervert the received and true (Pauline) Christian faith, he will be better able to be on his guard against them and he will not become discouraged or fall into despair "when people will not endure sound teaching" (4:3) and "turn away from listening to the truth" (4:4). The reason is that "Timothy" is accomplishing his ministry **in the last days,** and as everyone knows, **the last days** mean terrible times.

The familiar apocalyptic expression, **the last days,** meaning the period just before the return of Christ in power and great glory and the end of the present age or world, occurs in the Pastorals only here (but see I Tim. 4:1, "in later times"). In the genuine Pauline letters it does not appear at all; however, see Acts 2:17 (from Joel 3:1); Jas. 5:3; II Pet. 3:3; also I John 2:18, "the last hour." The most complete lists of "apocalyptic woes" in the N.T. are those in Mark 13; Matt. 24; Luke 21. In these full lists "the end" is preceded by the appearance of a horde of religious impostors, false Christs and false prophets, by apostasy and sacrilege, persecution, wars, earthquakes, famines, pestilences, and confusion in the solar system. In the present passage, however, the author is not interested **in the last days** as such, nor is he really concerned with any future cosmic catastrophe. (The future tense **will come** "is used because post-Pauline conditions are being described by 'Paul' " [Easton].) He uses the apocalyptic pattern only to provide a setting for, to identify, and thereby to expose in all their wickedness the "evil men and impostors" (vs. 13) who **oppose the truth** (vs. 8) and try to deceive the faithful (vss. 6, 7, 13) and persecute them (vs. 12). These evil teachers are a necessary part of the unfolding scheme of this wicked world. This does not make them any the less wicked; rather, it makes them more so. They are part and parcel of a universal corruption. "Timothy" should therefore not be surprised at their prevalence and power. He should only "avoid" them (vs. 5), and the more intently confirm himself in what he has "learned" and "firmly believed" (vs. 14).

**2. For men will be . . . :** The assumption is of mass corruption. It should not be supposed that the vices here catalogued are intended in detail to be a precise characteriza-

---

to life by God to do his will." This, too, parallels the story of the prodigal. "This my son was dead, and is alive again" (Luke 15:24). The practical interest of the Pastoral epistles is indicated again here by the fact that the purpose of Christian freedom is **to do his will.**

Wrote W. E. Hocking:

A life lived on the plan of getting along without God, without a sense of the cosmic demand, is already, whether it knows it or not, sick, off from normal, its values infected with the dry rot of mortality, intrinsically unhappy because unreal, driven subconsciously by a need which some day it is bound to recognize and define.[7]

[7] *Science and the Idea of God* (Chapel Hill: University of North Carolina Press, 1944), p. 49.

When that day comes, "they are brought back to life by God to do his will" (but see Exeg.).

**3:1.** *Character Revealed by Crisis.*—More than a decade before the discovery of the atom bomb, a popular play, *Wings Over Europe,* represented the reactions of members of a cabinet to the news that a man had learned a sinister secret which would enable him, if he chose, to destroy the earth. Face to face with that appalling fact, each individual revealed his real character, strong or weak, courageous or timid, altruistic or self-centered, faithful or faithless. More recent events have demonstrated on a worldwide scale the truth that a present or impending crisis tends to strip away all veneer and to reveal the character of individuals and groups

phemers, disobedient to parents, unthank- | men will be lovers of self, lovers of money,
ful, unholy, | proud, arrogant, abusive, disobedient to

---

tion of the false teachers in the time of "Paul" and "Timothy." The list was a floating list of vices currently available and easily adaptable to the writer's purposes, a whiplash of stinging words of the sort that any orator of the time well understood where to get and how to use.

The description of vss. 2-5 is applicable to any revolutionary period in history when belief in the mores or traditional restraints is weakened, when there is widespread repudiation of tradition and law, whether of God, parents, society, or natural affections, in favor of an arbitrary and extreme individualism. **Lovers of self** comes first; **lovers of God** last. Self-love is the fundamental sin and the source of all others because it substitutes sinful man for God. The truly religious man puts God at the center of his life. **Lovers of self** are naturally **lovers of money,** which is the "root of all evils" (I Tim. 6:9-10). They thus become only the more deeply entrenched in godlessness. Rich, they become **proud,** ostentatious; the Greek word includes the idea of making false pretenses. The braggart always overstates his case. Being **proud,** they are **arrogant,** overbearing, disdainful, insolent, and **abusive (blasphemers** [KJV] in the N.T.=**slanderers** [RSV], "scoffers").

**Disobedient to their parents:** In a patriarchal society, where paternal authority is absolute, disobedience is a particularly heinous sin. Where the family assumes the functions of both home and state, disobedience to parents comes next to disobedience to God in gravity of wickedness. Although it is the young, adolescents and older, who are most appropriately accused of disobedience to parents, nothing can be here inferred about the age of the false teachers. The rebellious spirit in religion is easily accused of every kind of insubordination.

---

for what it actually is. In this passage Paul voices the belief so frequently found in the N.T. that **the last days** are near, days which in one way or another will bring a cataclysmic end of an age and the ushering in of a new era. The Exeg. points out that in other N.T. predictions of such events the appearance of religious impostors and of terrible moral evil in the world was to be expected in advance of the great crisis. In modern times relatively few people hold apocalyptic views like those of the first century. But it is still true that the appearance or the threat of a crisis brings out into the open the strength or the evil that in calmer times may be hidden beneath the surface of human lives.

It is not only some world-shaking event or cosmic disaster which so reveals what people are. There are innumerable challenges in ordinary life which break through all shams and pretenses and serve as revealers of the truth. A new position entailing new responsibilities, the loss of health or economic security, the death of a loved one, being a victim of injustice or cruelty, a new awareness of the injustices and cruelties to which other people are subject, the discovery in one's self of resources with which other people can be served—any one of these experiences may constitute a personal crisis in

which one's strength or inadequacy may be suddenly or gradually revealed. There are other inner experiences which are even more critical —when a man discovers that God's will is concerned with him and that he must obey or betray, when he sees in Christ the manifestation of that truth for which every man is called to live, and when he learns that his life has implications in the eternal purpose of God which sets everything in a new perspective. To go through such experiences as these is to come out into the light where the shabbiness or the goodness of life is made plain; but it may also be to come into fellowship with God in Christ, who transforms, renews, and redeems.

Paul's epistles to the Thessalonians dealt with the problems of people who believed that a cataclysmic end of an age was near. Some of them were tempted to stop working, to relax ethical standards, and to live only for the moment. Paul counseled them to live at their best every moment, leaving "the times and the seasons" to God in whose keeping they were (I Thess. 5:1). So in this chapter the Christian is urged to walk in the ways of righteousness and truth, even though **in the last days there will come times of stress.**

**2-4. The Sins that Beset Us.**—Most of the sins mentioned here are the common faults of

3 Without natural affection, truce-breakers, false accusers, incontinent, fierce, despisers of those that are good,

4 Traitors, heady, high-minded, lovers of pleasures more than lovers of God;

5 Having a form of godliness, but denying the power thereof: from such turn away.

their parents, ungrateful, unholy, 3 inhuman, implacable, slanderers, profligates, fierce, haters of good, 4 treacherous, reckless, swollen with conceit, lovers of pleasure rather than lovers of God, 5 holding the form of religion but denying the power of

---

**Ungrateful:** Either to God or man. **Unholy:** Profane or irreligious, counting nothing sacred.

**3.** Further, they are **inhuman,** i.e., unfeeling, callous, **without natural affection.** Their hearts are hard and dry. **Implacable,** irreconcilable, lit., "without a libation or drink-offering"; then, "without a truce," which was ratified by a libation; then "admitting of no truce," or **implacable,** refusing to break hostilities. **Slanderers,** communicating lies and promoting quarrels. **Profligates,** without self-control, licentious. **Fierce,** wild or savage, brutal, cruel. **Haters of good,** lit., "not loving the good," i.e., without affection for good in any form.

**4. Treacherous,** betrayers of their friends and not to be trusted; **reckless,** rash, stopping at nothing to gain their ends; **swollen with conceit,** lit., "wrapped up in conceit and folly," blinded by the sense of their own importance.

**5. Holding the form of religion but denying the power of it:** "Here the catalogue of vices loses its traditional character: the following words contain a real reproof against the heretics" (Martin Dibelius, *Die Pastoralbriefe* [2nd ed.; Tübingen: J. C. B. Mohr, 1931; "Handbuch zum Neuen Testament"], *ad loc.*). They are accused of a fundamental insincerity. They hold to **the form,** the outward semblance of religion; i.e., they profess to be orthodox Christians, perhaps even insist that they are not making innovations but are only reinterpreting the tradition to meet current needs. Perhaps they even use the old language, so that only an exceptionally keen person could detect that actually they had concealed a whole set of new ideas under the familiar words. Yet they deny **the power of it.** The exact meaning of this phrase is obscure. It is usually taken to mean that their religion is formal and conventional, without life and power, and that their preaching is sterile. However, this does not fit the context very well. The false teachers seem to be very active and fairly successful (vs. 6); in fact, so much so as to stir up the author to write letters against them. It is true that "they will not get very far" (vs. 9); but that is not because they are not energetic but because "their folly will be plain to all" (vs. 9). It is tempting to see in vs. 5*b* a reference to the heresy of 2:18, denial of the resurrection. In the N.T. **power** frequently means miraculous power.

---

ordinary men. There is nothing dated about them. Everyone today is tempted to be selfish, **lovers of money, proud, ungrateful,** irreverent, headstrong, conceited, **lovers of pleasure rather than lovers of God.** These are the temptations which are common to man, of which Paul wrote in I Cor. 10:13, from which God had promised a "way of escape." Scott groups these moral failings in four categories: " (1) sins against God [**ungrateful,** irreverent]; (2) want of natural affection; (3) wrongs to society [**slanderers,** treacherous]; (4) vices of disposition [**proud,** dissolute, savage]." [8] Here is a mirror in which to some extent the average man can see himself, or before which he can say, "There but for the grace of God go I."

[8] *Pastoral Epistles,* p. 119.

**5. *Religion Without Power.***—Those whom the preceding phrases have described are not people who make no profession of religion, or who repudiate religion. Nominally they are religious folk, **holding the form of religion but denying the power of it.** They go through the practices which are associated with religion but neither experience nor expect to experience any transforming power. "If any man be in Christ, he is a new creature: old things are passed away; behold, all things are become new" (II Cor. 5:17). That central fact of vital Christianity is beyond their ken.

It is said that in an English churchyard the tombstone of a squire of former days bears the inscription: "He was not a religious man, but in all other respects he was an ideal church-

| 6 For of this sort are they which creep into houses, and lead captive silly women laden with sins, led away with divers lusts, | it. Avoid such people. 6 For among them are those who make their way into households and capture weak women, burdened with sins and swayed by various impulses, |
| --- | --- |

To the primitive church in general, and to the writer of the Pastorals in particular, the resurrection was *the* miracle par excellence, *the* power. Perhaps, then, the writer will say that in refusing to acknowledge the resurrection—in the orthodox sense—these men are undermining the foundations of the faith. Its form, its superstructure may stand for a while, but in the end, down it will go (see Phil. 3:10; I Cor. 15:12-19).

**Avoid such people** stands in formal contradiction with "be . . . kindly to everyone" (2:24-25). The difference in temper may be due to the employment of different sources; or one may note that 2:20-26 gives the impression of having been written from a somewhat detached point of view, no specific opponents being in mind. At such a time it is easier to be mild-mannered. On the other hand, **avoid such people** is advice which would arise spontaneously after such a detailed list of dreadful sinners as vss. 2-5 bring, and in anticipation of the base tricksters of vs. 6.

**6-7.** The torrential stream of sins and sinners channeled in vss. 2-5 now narrows its dark waters to certain zealous evangelists who, either not daring to preach their false doctrine openly, or having been forbidden to do so by the authorities, insidiously and under false pretenses worm their way into the homes, and by stooping to **capture weak women** (lit., "little women," a diminutive of contempt; KJV **silly women**) establish a foothold from which they hope to capture the whole church. Women are here thought of as by nature fickle, as not knowing their own mind, and easily induced to run after novel ideas. Since they must keep still in church (I Tim. 2:11-12), the purveyor of

man." Authentic Christianity speaks a different language. "I don't know where they are getting it, but they are getting something from somewhere," said a raw young hospital intern to a minister as together they watched a brokenhearted but undaunted father and mother leave a room where a life in which all their dearest hopes were bound up was slipping away. "To all who received him, who believed in his name, he gave power to become the children of God" (John 1:12). The most dangerous heresy which has ever weakened the Christian church has been this error which crops up in every generation, deluding men with the idea that right form, right doctrine, right ritual constitute the whole of religion, and denying the reality of the power of God, which can loose men from their sins and make them new creatures in Christ. The Exeg. suggests that it was the Resurrection as the manifestation of divine power which was in this case denied.

**Avoid such people,** says this letter to Timothy. One might have expected that Paul would have said, "Seek out such people, and take to them the power of the gospel." Jesus had been known as the friend of sinners, and the whole evangelistic career of the great apostle was a mission to bring all men under the sway of the power which Paul described in Rom. 8. This admonition cannot mean that Christian people should

withdraw into monastic seclusion and have no dealings with the unredeemed. But Timothy was to be choosing leaders for infant churches. These leaders should be men who knew the power of God in their own lives. There was no place among them for men who held to the forms of religion but denied the power of God to make all life new.

**6. Fads and Fancies.**—When Paul spoke on Mars' Hill in Athens he addressed a population of whom it was said that they "spent their time in nothing except telling or hearing something new" (Acts 17:21). Every generation has its seekers after intellectual and religious novelties. Most of the cults which spring up and command temporarily large followings before they die away have one thing in common: they promise a great deal to those who go through the right forms, but they demand little in the way of commitment of life to the will of God. This epistle indicates that religious faddists find easy prey among well-to-do women who are dissatisfied with idle and empty life. Easton translates the verse: "It is men of this sort who worm their way into houses and make slaves of silly women filled with sin, ruled by desires of all kinds." Religion becomes a fad when we try to use it as a device for getting what we want, even when what we want is something good like peace of mind, happiness, or contentment. True

**7** Ever learning, and never able to come to the knowledge of the truth.

**7** who will listen to anybody and can never

---

strange doctrines flatters them by seeking them out at home, and preferably, one may suppose, during leisure hours and when their husbands are not present. It could be imagined that it was when Adam was away that Eve was seduced by the serpent.

Of course, to the author such women were despicable: (*a*) they were **burdened with sins,** i.e., heaped up with them, utterly wicked; (*b*) **swayed by various impulses,** at the mercy of chaotic and imperious desires, "wayward creatures of impulse" (Moffatt), without a shred of moral stability; (*c*) they **will listen to anybody** [lit., "always learning"] **and can never arrive at a knowledge of the truth.** The text does not intend to suggest that women are by nature more religious than men, or that their consciences are more tender, or that it is their spiritual sensitivity which makes them hospitable to visiting preachers. Rather it is just because they are so wicked, inconstant, and erratic, not knowing right from wrong, good from evil, error from truth, or the established form of the Christian faith from its perversion, that they are such an easy mark for these mischievous teachers. Since they are "always learning," i.e., cannot make up their minds, they can never arrive at that **knowledge of the truth** which is Christianity (cf. I Tim. 2:4).

Unfortunately the writer does not tell us any detail either about the **sins** of the women or the teachings to which they succumbed. One must suppose either that "Timothy" knew, or that the author thought it safer to denounce in general than to be specific.

---

religion is the giving of ourselves to God to be used for his purposes, even though such self-giving is costly and painful for us.

One of the religious phenomena in the United States is the growth of a multitude of spiritual movements outside the organized churches. In many cities they fill the ballrooms of hotels, occupy store fronts on side streets, and stand ready to take over the building of any church whose dwindling congregation has closed its doors. Appealing to a wide variety of people, in so far as economic status and degree of sophistication are concerned, they all have a basic appeal in common. They provide emotional excitement and color for people to whom life has become monotonous. They promise peace of mind and freedom from anxiety to people for whom the complexities of modern life have increased anxieties almost beyond the limits of endurance. They make few moral demands upon their adherents, are totally ignorant of the language of sacrifice, and invest the universe with a spirit of benevolence which has more characteristics in common with a thin fog than with a purposeful Will. They constitute a challenge to the Christian church which proclaims the good news of Christ—the most exciting message ever known when its true nature is understood. The church offers the only peace of mind which thinking men want, the peace which comes from faith that the issues of life are in the keeping of the God whom Jesus

revealed. The church makes rigorous ethical demands, holds before men the Cross as the price of discipleship, and worships the austere God and Father of Jesus Christ. This is the old, old story, but it comes like a great discovery to every man who hears and accepts the gospel.

**7.** *Learning and Knowing.*—This verse is a classic description of a combination of intellectual curiosity and flabby will which is common in every age. Educational institutions are familiar with the student who wants to go on after graduation taking more and more courses but lacks the courage to do anything with the training he has had. Occasionally there is a scholar who is expert at amassing facts but powerless to draw conclusions from the information he has garnered. American communities which offer extensive cultural advantages sometimes develop lecturegoers who rush frantically from one address to another without taking time to assimilate and digest knowledge from any. Here the reference is to a religious curiosity which does not issue in the religious knowledge which can be gained only by living out religious principles. William Temple, on a visit to the United States while archbishop of York, told the students at Union Theological Seminary in New York that "the purpose of an open mind is to close it on something." That is the point at which they fail **who will listen to anybody and can never arrive at a knowledge of the truth.**

8 Now as Jannes and Jambres withstood Moses, so do these also resist the truth: men of corrupt minds, reprobate concerning the faith.

9 But they shall proceed no further: for their folly shall be manifest unto all *men,* as theirs also was.

10 But thou hast fully known my doctrine, manner of life, purpose, faith, longsuffering, charity, patience,

arrive at a knowledge of the truth. 8 As Jannes and Jambres opposed Moses, so these men also oppose the truth, men of corrupt mind and counterfeit faith; 9 but they will not get very far, for their folly will be plain to all, as was that of those two men.

10 Now you have observed my teaching, my conduct, my aim in life, my faith, my

---

**8-9.** Although **Jannes and Jambres** are not named in the O.T., Philo, or Josephus, they are mentioned rather widely in late Jewish, pagan, and early Christian literature. The two names are reputed to be those of the Egyptian magicians at Pharaoh's court who tried to prevent the liberation of the Israelites by performing countermiracles to those of Moses. At least as early as the first century A.D. there was in circulation some sort of Jewish book probably ridiculing and exposing them and making them into a typical example of the way in which the wisdom of "wise men" who **oppose the truth** is revealed for what it is, **folly.** The fate of "Paul's" opponents will be exactly that of Moses' opponents. In spite of some successes (vs. 6; 2:16, 18), **they will not get very far.** Their madness will be fully exposed, just as was that of Jannes and Jambres.

### X. Remember Paul's Selfless Devotion (3:10-13)

**10-11.** In contrast to the false teachers, "Timothy" is thoroughly qualified to teach the true faith. His intimate acquaintance with the entire career of Paul, his careful observation and analysis of Paul's interpretation of Christianity, of his behavior, of his self-effacing, steadfast, heroic devotion to the faith, of his conduct in repeated persecution and suffering, of which some was shared by Timothy in fact, and all by "Timothy" in his sympathetic imagination—all of this has given the latter complete assurance in, sound understanding of, and loyal devotion to Paul's Christian faith. Remembering Paul (vs. 14), how can the Christian minister help continuing in what he has learned and firmly believed?

The Greek word for **observed** (lit., "to follow," "to follow with" or "by the side of") is a word of rich connotation. As a technical term meaning follower or disciple, it may mean "to accompany"; "to follow in spirit," or "to comprehend a teaching"; to observe either in the sense of "note well," "pay continued attention to," or "to act on the basis of,"

---

**8-9.** *Jannes and Jambres.*—These two men have probably not been the subject of many sermons, but they are types of the reputedly wise who have actually fought against the truth. (See Exeg. for the legends concerning them.) Christian people need to be reminded that again and again the cultured and educated groups have been dull of conscience in the face of social wrongs, while people of simpler background but more sensitive conscience have been God's instruments in overcoming evil. It is possible to have a sophisticated mind and no capacity for faith in anything. Paul was impressed with this fact by his visit to Athens, after which he wrote to the church in Corinth: "Where is the wise? where is the scribe? where is the disputer of this world? hath not God made foolish the wisdom of the world? For seeing

that in the wisdom of God the world through its wisdom knew not God, it was God's good pleasure through the foolishness of the preaching to save them that believe." (I Cor. 1:20-21 ASV.) Here it is pointed out that there is a judgment of God which in the long run vindicates the truth. As Jannes and Jambres were exposed as false guides, so the righteousness of God can be counted on to prevail. Superficial leaders may seem to succeed for a time, **but they will not get very far, for their folly will be plain to all, as was that of those two men.**

**10-13.** *A Bit of Biography.*—It has been said that there is nothing which so helps a man facing difficulties as to hear someone whom he trusts say, "I have been through all that." If we have here an authentic passage of the autobiography of Paul, it is instructive to recall that

11 Persecutions, afflictions, which came unto me at Antioch, at Iconium, at Lystra; what persecutions I endured: but out of *them* all the Lord delivered me.

patience, my love, my steadfastness, 11 my persecutions, my sufferings, what befell me at Antioch, at Ico'nium, and at Lystra, what persecutions I endured; yet from them

---

"to imitate." It could also include the idea of sharing, joint participation; or even of following in the sense of reading after, possibly suggesting that "Timothy" had read Paul's epistles and the book of Acts.

**Teaching** and **conduct:** The juxtaposition of these two words reflects the typical concern of the N.T. church for both theory and practice, theological reflection and ethical admonition, as may be seen in the structure both of the Gospels and of the Epistles. **My teaching:** Either *how* I taught or *what* I taught, probably the latter. **Conduct,** meaning way of life, behavior, may also mean way of guiding, leading, or conduct of affairs. **You have observed . . . my conduct,** then, might mean, "You have accepted my leadership and adopted my methods of church organization and management." **Aim in life,** lit., "purposes," may mean intentions, convictions: "You have understood and shared my intentions and convictions" (Easton translates "firm resolution").

**Faith, patience, love, steadfastness,** are four Christian virtues which Paul notably exemplified, enriched, and adorned by the splendor of his life. They are not less but more meaningful because they both issued in and survived **persecutions** and **sufferings.**

Oddly enough, reference is made only to **persecutions** at **Antioch, Iconium,** and **Lystra** (Acts 13–14), the first persecutions of Paul to be narrated by Acts, and all of them happening on his first visit to these cities and before Timothy had joined him (Acts 16). Although Timothy does not figure prominently in any persecution narrative in Acts, his intimate relationship to Paul after Acts 16 makes it entirely likely that on more than one occasion he suffered with Paul and that his "observations" of Paul's sufferings would be very much more direct after he had become one of Paul's traveling companions than before. Why, then, does our author name these three cities, and these three only? The commonest conjecture is that since Timothy's home was in Lystra and he was well known in Iconium too (Acts 16:1-2), these first persecutions of Paul may have some special significance for him; they may have resulted in his conversion. Possible in itself, there is no direct evidence in support of such a conjecture. The difficulty vanishes if we suppose that the writer is drawing his illustrations of Paul's sufferings straight out of the book of Acts. Nor is he in the least concerned to make the life of "Timothy" correspond at every point with the life of Timothy. Rather, he unreflectively selects and lists in the order therein named the first cities mentioned in Acts in which Paul met violent opposition. These were the beginnings of persecution, not the end. That Timothy had nothing to do with them is beside the point; "Timothy" had something to do with them for he had read the book of Acts and had entered "spiritually" into all of Paul's suffering. The loosely connected repetitive phrase, **what persecutions I endured,** seems intended to extend the scope of sufferings from those just specifically mentioned to the totality of Paul's sufferings, and would then mean, "whatever sort of persecutions I endured anywhere."

---

he had endured all the hardships for the Christian faith which could be visited upon one man. He had been driven out of Pisidian Antioch (Acts 13). He fled before an enraged populace from Iconium (Acts 14:1-7). He was stoned and left for dead by the highway outside Lystra (Acts 14:8-20). Nothing daunted, after a sojourn in Derbe, Paul and his companions "returned again to Lystra, and to Iconium, and Antioch" (Acts 14:21). John Henry Jowett once preached

a famous sermon on that theme, pointing out how the man of faith must sometimes win his victories by going back to the very spot where he has previously met hardship and defeat.[1] The recollection of these events must have been very moving to Timothy, for this was his native region (Acts 16:1-3), and it was there that he became Paul's companion in faith and service.

[1] *God Our Contemporary* (New York: Fleming H. Revell Co., 1922), p. 123.

12 Yea, and all that will live godly in Christ Jesus shall suffer persecution.

13 But evil men and seducers shall wax worse and worse, deceiving, and being deceived.

14 But continue thou in the things which thou hast learned and hast been assured of, knowing of whom thou hast learned *them;*

all the Lord rescued me. 12 Indeed all who desire to live a godly life in Christ Jesus will be persecuted, 13 while evil men and impostors will go on from bad to worse, deceivers and deceived. 14 But as for you, continue in what you have learned and have firmly believed, knowing from whom

---

**Yet from them all the Lord rescued me:** A pious parenthesis, reflecting the spirit of the psalmist (34:18, 20). Of course in the end Paul perished for his faith; yet there was always the miracle of "dying, and behold we live; as punished, and yet not killed" (II Cor. 6:9).

**12.** Lit., "All who want to live religiously in Christ Jesus." Scott paraphrases, "All who resolve to be Christians in real earnest." The writer is here preaching to "Timothy" with Paul's life as his text. The credentials of the true Christian are his scars. The minister must expect to be persecuted if he is really in earnest.

**13.** One might expect here the completion of the paradox begun in vs. 12: good men will be persecuted; bad men will enjoy ease and prosperity. But no Christian could have allowed any such statement to stand. The underlying thought is that although good men will suffer persecutions, yet God will rescue them from them all; **evil men . . . will go on from bad to worse,** but there will be no one to rescue them. **Deceiving,** they are themselves **deceived.** Therefore they are both intentionally and unintentionally wicked, and are virtually without hope. Their progressive degeneration is a part of the inevitable increase of evil in "the last days."

**Impostors:** A contemptuous word meaning "magicians," "sorcerers," "quacks," perhaps intended further to blacken the reputation of the false teachers by relating them to Jannes and Jambres, Egyptian magicians. Perhaps they too claimed to work miracles. Most prominent religious teachers did (see Acts 13:8-12; 16:16-18; 19:11-20; Mark 13:22). Without establishing himself as a miracle worker, no religious teacher could expect the highest success.

### XI. Hold Fast to Inspired Scriptures (3:14-17)

**14.** In contrast to the "deceived deceivers" who "go on from bad to worse" "Timothy" is to "remain fixed" in what he has **learned** and has **firmly believed.** The

---

Thus when Paul speaks of the persecutions he endured there, and adds with touching simplicity **out of them all the Lord delivered me,** he is refreshing Timothy's memory of what Timothy already knows. There is a moving force to the personal character of this testimony concerning **my teaching, my conduct, my aim in life, my faith, my patience, my love, my steadfastness, my persecutions, my sufferings, what befell me at Antioch, at Iconium, and at Lystra, what persecutions I endured; yet from them all the Lord rescued me.**

There are three ways of facing a future bristling with difficulties. One is to close one's eyes and pretend that the difficulties do not exist. For such simplicity there is bound to be a rude awakening. Another way is to cringe before the difficulties and to acknowledge defeat

in advance. The outcome of such cowardice can be nothing but defeat. The third way is the Christian way, which confronts difficulties with the faith that God can make his servants able for anything. Such faith finds strong support in the testimony of those like Paul who look back on difficulties from which God has provided deliverance. Such faith is no guarantee of a painless existence. Paul himself faced the executioner's block in the end. But that too he confronted with the faith that neither life nor death could separate him from the love of God which had been made manifest in Christ Jesus his Lord.

**14-16. *Faith Rooted in Tradition.*—**This passage is sometimes quoted as a proof text for a particular theory of the verbal inspiration of the Bible. Such an interpretation reads into the

15 And that from a child thou hast known the holy Scriptures, which are able to make thee wise unto salvation through faith which is in Christ Jesus.

you learned it 15 and how from childhood you have been acquainted with the sacred writings which are able to instruct you for salvation through faith in Christ Jesus.

---

aorist tense of these two verbs expresses the idea that "Timothy" learned at a definite time, and once and for all, what the Christian faith is. As a revelation and a deposit it cannot change or be changed; it is to be learned, held intact, and transmitted.

"Timothy" may always derive assurance of the validity of his faith from the knowledge of who his teachers were. The plural **whom** may indeed include his mother and grandmother or other Christians; yet of primary importance to the author is the fact that "Timothy" stands in the direct line of transmission of the apostolic preaching.

**15.** If the purity of the Christian faith is guaranteed by an approved and authorized succession of teachers, it is established beyond the possibility of change on an unalterable bedrock of authoritative **sacred writings.** In these, "Timothy" has been rooted and grounded from infancy (see 1:5). His whole life has been encased, as it were, in the true Christian tradition. What he has received is sufficient for salvation, and there is no need of running after new ideas or of getting mixed up with the fads of the hour. The Christian's scriptures are completely adequate **to make . . . wise,** i.e., to convey the knowledge, theoretical and practical, which leads to salvation.

**Through faith in Christ Jesus** seems to be a stereotyped phrase (I Tim. 3:13) which is added more or less automatically. As a Christian catchword, too much weight should not be laid upon it. Since it is taken for granted that Christian salvation is received **through faith in Christ Jesus,** the whole clause simply means "which are able to instruct you in saving faith," or "bring you into a saving relationship to Christ Jesus."

The Greek expression **sacred writings** (ἱερὰ γράμματα), lit., "sacred letters," for the scriptures, does not appear elsewhere in the N.T., but is found in Jewish writings, e.g., Test. Levi 13:2; Philo *Moses* III. 39; Josephus *Antiquities* XX. 11. 2; *Against Apion* I. 10. It need not be other than a synonym for "holy scriptures" (ἅγιαι γραφαί). "It is the name for the holy scriptures of the Old Testament in Greek-speaking Judaism" (Dibelius). It is unlikely that any qualitative distinction is intended between **writings** in vs. 15 and **scripture** in vs. 16. It has been proposed that the author avoids the usual N.T. expressions for scripture because he is thinking less of the books themselves than of the maternal teaching and oral tradition, i.e., of Timothy's religious education (Lock); or to present an antithesis to the myths and genealogies of the oral teachings of the false teachers and to the Ephesian books of Acts 19:19 (Lock, Scott, Spicq). Additional suggestions are offered by Scott, *Pastoral Epistles,* p. 126. It is enough, however, to point out that in vss. 15-16 the emphasis is on the fact that the faith stands written. The "knowledge of the truth" is readily and unmistakenly available in **sacred writings,** writings which God has written and which can be read by anyone. There is no need to look for any hidden meaning in the unusual term **sacred writings.** Like so many of the words in the Pastorals it is peculiar to the author, but without significance other than that it reveals him to be an individual with his own vocabulary.

Of more importance and of greater difficulty is the question, What books are meant by **the sacred writings?** They are commonly believed to be the O.T. (Lock, Dibelius,

---

text more than it actually says. Timothy is urged to hold fast to his own tested convictions, to remember who his teachers have been, and also to remember the tradition of faith embodied in the sacred writings on which he has been nurtured. This is the well-rounded attitude toward religious truth which is always essential if religious folk are to avoid mistaking a partial truth

for the whole truth (which is fanaticism), or are to escape the vagueness which makes religion into a formless optimism based on no clear-cut convictions (as a certain type of liberalism is sometimes accused of doing). **Continue in what you have learned and have firmly believed** —that recognizes the individual's obligation to think for himself. "Remember who your teach-

16 All Scripture *is* given by inspiration of God, and *is* profitable for doctrine, for reproof, for correction, for instruction in righteousness:

16 All scripture is inspired by God and[d] profitable for teaching, for reproof, for correction, and for training in righteousness,

[d] Or *Every scripture inspired by God is also.*

Easton, Grant, *et al.*). That the terms "sacred writings" and "inspired scripture" (vs. 16) definitely will include the O.T. scriptures, no matter when or by whom the Pastorals were written, there can be no doubt. However, if the theory of this Exeg. is true, viz., that the letters were written in the second quarter of the second century by an ardent Paulinist who knew Paul's letters well, who virtually identified orthodox Christianity with its Pauline form, and who will by all means establish Paul in the church, then it is incredible that in his mind the writings of this "preacher and apostle and teacher" (1:11) should not be thought of as sacred writings. Conceivably the description, **which are able to instruct you for salvation through faith in Christ Jesus,** might be appropriate to the O.T. reinterpreted from a Christian standpoint. Nevertheless, it is much more suitable to a collection of writings which include Christian documents, even Gospels as well as Epistles. We may be sure that wherever our writer exercised authority, Paul's letters would be part of the curriculum of religious education, and that all "Timothys" born in Christian homes would have known them from childhood on. If, then, in vss. 15-16, the author is trying to secure the place of the Pauline literature in Christian instruction and in the church, the verses are very much in order, and vss. 10-17 are fully coherent in their plea to Christians to remain loyal to Paul and Paul's faith.

In support of the extension of the meaning of sacred writings to Paul's letters (if not also Gospels or other Christian writings), it may further be urged that the churches generally held to the O.T. as their treasury of proof texts. Ordinarily its inspiration was taken for granted. Only if we suppose that vss. 15-16 are directed primarily against Marcion's radical attempt to discard the O.T. is it possible to find an adequate ground for limiting "scripture" here to the O.T. Quite possibly vss. 15-16 are anti-Marcion (see Intro., pp. 358-60). Nevertheless, in the context this can hardly be their sole or even main purpose. At this late date (A.D. 125-50) it is not reasonable to suppose that the author could have regarded the O.T. as the sole literary source of Christian truth. Vss. 15-16, then, have most meaning in the context if interpreted as an effort to secure authoritative recognition or "canonicity" for Paul's letters as part of all scripture. In II Pet. 3:15-16 Paul's letters are quite unreflectively spoken of as "scriptures." Indeed, the very devotion of the writer to Paul, his rugged insistence that true Christianity is Pauline Christianity, was doubtless one of the most powerful factors in establishing the place of the Pauline corpus in the emerging N.T.

**16-17.** The precise meaning and translation of vs. 16a are notoriously difficult. The Greek permits the adjective **inspired by God** to be taken either as attributive or predicate. Also, **all scripture** is literally "every scripture," with emphasis seemingly on the distributive rather than on the collective idea. The difficulty is that although either alternative may be made to yield meaning, neither is quite smooth or satisfying, and the context is not of decisive help.

ers were" (Moffatt)—that recognizes how knowledge of God can be transmitted from one life to another. "Remember how you have known from childhood the sacred writings that can impart saving wisdom by faith in Christ Jesus" (Moffatt)—that recognizes the great tradition of faith to which learners and teachers are alike indebted. **All scripture is inspired by God and profitable for teaching** in a variety of ways. This obviously refers to the written tradi-

tion through which God has spoken and speaks to those who approach him in faith. Through these sacred writings into which God has breathed his spirit not only does there come teaching or enlightenment, but also they are **profitable . . . for reproof, for correction, and for training in righteousness.**

The Exeg. reminds us that **all scripture** is, lit., "every scripture." This does not mean the whole Bible, nor in all probability does it in-

17 That the man of God may be perfect, thoroughly furnished unto all good works.

4 I charge *thee* therefore before God, and the Lord Jesus Christ, who shall judge the quick and the dead at his appearing and his kingdom;

17 that the man of God may be complete, equipped for every good work.

4 I charge you in the presence of God and of Christ Jesus who is to judge the living and the dead, and by his appearing

---

In any case, the main point is that the writer is concerned to emphasize the fact that the Christian faith is guaranteed by its inspired scriptures. Once written down, these become for all time the standard **for teaching, for reproof, for correction, and for training in righteousness.** The minister finds here correct doctrine whereby he may refute false opinions, correct and restore those who are in error, theoretical or practical, and train men in the way of the moral and religious life.

**The man of God** (see I Tim. 6:11) here is the minister—the type or class ("Timothy") for whom the letter is written. With the scriptures—including Paul's letters—the minister is completely equipped to be God's man, to speak for him and make him known. He does not need to read other books or be concerned with religious speculation. He has work to do, and for this the scriptures are sufficient.

## XII. FULFILLING THE MINISTRY (4:1-5)

**4:1.** After the author has outlined the critical times in which "Timothy" is to exercise his ministry, with evil men and impostors rampant and seeking to destroy the faith; after he has reminded "Timothy" of the heroic devotion of Paul to the Christian cause, and has assured him that the Christian gospel for which he, "Timothy," is called to suffer is fully guaranteed by virtue of its being adequately recorded in writings which are wholly inspired by God, "Paul" once again charges "Timothy," most solemnly as with an oath, and for the last time (see 1:6, 8, 13; 2:1-3, 8, 14; 3:14), to do his unstinted duty. **In the presence of God and of Christ Jesus** (see also I Tim. 5:4) to whom all Christian ministers stand under responsibility, "Timothy" is adjured to fulfill his ministry. Christ Jesus is now on his way **to judge the living and the dead.** The reckoning is sure to come and at no distant future. **At his appearing** (see 1:10; I Tim. 6:14; Tit.

---

clude the writings of Paul (but cf. Exeg. for a different view). The conventional view that this refers to the O.T., at the time the Bible of the church, seems more plausible. Nor does this sentence require a theory of verbal inspiration. The "inspiration" of the Bible means that God speaks to man through the book. The Bible is unique as the Word of God, but it is not unique in being free from error in all matters of scientific interpretation and historical accuracy. One of the significant facts about this passage is that it takes a practical view of inspiration, which is attested by the **profitable** value of the scriptures for the guidance and amendment of life.

**17. Thoroughly Furnished for Good Works.—**Here in a few words is the ideal for everyone, layman or one set apart for the ministry, who is engaged in Christian service. He is to be a **man of God,** a fine title which indicates not a sanctimonious manner but a central loyalty. He is to be **complete,** a whole man developed intellectually, spiritually, and practically in the way of his service. He is to be **thoroughly fur-**nished unto all good works, able to draw on the resources of his own experience of God and of the Christian tradition for guidance and strength in the tasks to which he is called of God in the service of the everlasting kingdom. W. M. Macgregor paraphrased the passage in Isa. 61 as follows:

The Lord has anointed me to bring good news to poor people, to proclaim release to captives and sight to the blind, to send the crushed on their way with their troubles left behind them, and to announce that God's time for doing all this has arrived.[2]

To be so inspired is to be **equipped for every good work.**

**4:1. Under Observation.—**The final charge in which Paul's message is summed up is made solemn by the reminder that Timothy is not a lone wayfarer accountable only to himself for the conduct of his pilgrimage. He is **in the presence of God and of Christ Jesus who is to**

[2] *The Making of a Preacher* (London: Student Christian Movement Press, 1945), p. 70.

2 Preach the word; be instant in season, out of season; reprove, rebuke, exhort with all long-suffering and doctrine.

and his kingdom: 2 preach the word, be urgent in season and out of season, convince, rebuke, and exhort, be unfailing in

---

2:13) he will personally inaugurate the judgment. And in **his kingdom** there will be gathered those who have remained faithful.

Vss. 1-2, 5 have a liturgical ring, as if derived from an ordination charge. The phrase "who is about to judge the living and the dead," present in the historic creeds, may already have been part of some formula of faith (see Acts 10:42; I Pet. 4:5).

**2.** The essential function of the minister is to **preach the word** of God (2:9), i.e., the gospel. He is to be at it incessantly, **in season and out of season,** whether the occasion is favorable or not, i.e., "whether men will listen or not" (Easton). Vs. 3 indicates that the time is not a favorable one for preaching: it is the latter days, when men "will not endure sound teachings." To **convince** is to convince anyone that he is in the wrong, to refute and to reprove; to **rebuke** is to censure or admonish. Both verbs assume that the people who are not Christians have wrong opinions and correspondingly wrong conduct. To **exhort** is to urge to repentance and to become Christians.

**Be unfailing in patience and in teaching:** The phrase belongs with the four preceding imperatives. No matter what provocations or discouragements the minister faces, he should never lose patience, but should suffer willingly the indignities which men

---

**judge the living and the dead.** He is reminded of Christ's appearing and his kingdom. A superficial view of life claims that one is accountable to no one but himself for his discharge of responsibility. This view is expressed in a multitude of common expressions. "I have a right to be happy." "I can do as I please with my own life." "It is nobody's business but my own what I do with my money." "No one will ever know what I do." "I follow the dictates of my own conscience." Paul probes deeper in his charge to Timothy. He reminds Timothy that he lives in the sight of God, who is both observer and judge. The present is under the judgment of God, and eternity also is subject to his decrees.

In one of the most moving spiritual autobiographies of modern times Norman Goodall makes this confession of faith:

As the years have passed, my sense of the ultimate mystery of the Godhead has deepened. The mystery has a luminous centre—Jesus. . . . Although I find in the Bible, as a whole, compelling justification for putting my trust in God as a Person, it is the Risen Christ alone who enables me to discern something of the lineaments of that Person. . . . In Him I come as near to seeing the Face of God as mortal man can ever do in this world, and I believe it will be in Him that I see whatever more of that Face will be granted me to see in the next.[3]

One only sees life in its true perspective against the background of God disclosed in Christ, who sees, judges, and determines the ultimate destiny of all things.

[3] *One Man's Testimony* (New York: Harper & Bros., 1949), pp. 27, 127.

**2. Preach the Word.**—When Lord Robert Cecil was asked to say what he considered the most useful thing the churches could do to aid the cause of world peace, he replied, "Preach the gospel." There is a popular prejudice against the word **preach.** "Don't preach at me," young people sometimes say to their elders. When critics wish to write off a play or a poem as bad art, they say that "it preaches." To preach is with some people equivalent to being dull. That is because people imagine that preaching means talking down from a sense of moral superiority to folk on a lower level, voicing pious moralisms without the deep conviction born of experience, or droning out as a matter of routine what ought to be the most exciting news that ever greeted the ear of man. When Paul talked about the foolishness of preaching he meant something very different from all that. Preach the good news of God revealed in Christ. Life is not a meaningless tragedy but a glorious fellowship with the Father. Duty is not a dull drudgery but a chance to be a fellow worker with God. Sin need not be endless slavery to evil, for Christ came into the world to save sinners. Death is not defeat for the spirit, for the gift of God is eternal life. "This is the victory that overcomes the world, our faith" (I John 5:4). An essential element in the fulfillment of all our highest hopes is the proclamation of this word.

**2. Seasonable and Unseasonable Persistence.** —Moffatt translates this verse, "Keep at it in season and out of season." Easton puts it, "Be at your task whether men will listen or not." There are elements in the gospel which com-

3 For the time will come when they will not endure sound doctrine; but after their own lusts shall they heap to themselves teachers, having itching ears;

4 And they shall turn away *their* ears from the truth, and shall be turned unto fables.

patience and in teaching. 3 For the time is coming when people will not endure sound teaching, but having itching ears they will accumulate for themselves teachers to suit their own likings, 4 and will turn away from listening to the truth and wander into

---

may inflict upon him as he persists in rebuking them for their sins and in teaching them the full Christian faith.

**3-4.** Actually **the time** is here. "Timothy" is already confronted with people who are no longer content to hear the **sound teaching** of Paul but who, **having itching ears,** always wanting to hear something new and different, are not content with one teacher, however great he may be, or with the authorized teaching ministry of the church, but must summon teacher after teacher, in great numbers—teachers without ecclesiastical accreditation, who will "pander to their desires by telling them what they long to hear" (Easton).

---

fort and cheer. They are always popular. There are elements which challenge and rebuke. They also are needed. There are times when enthusiasm for the Christian cause carries a man along as though on a mighty stream. There are other times when it is a steep, uphill way, and one is tempted to give up. Sometimes the results of Christian service are visible. At other times nothing seems to happen, and the Christian must live and labor by faith that God is using his dedicated service. Consecrated persistence in good weather and foul is part of the price of Christian service. **Be urgent in season and out of season.** Matthew Arnold wrote:

We cannot kindle when we will
The fire which in the heart resides;
·   ·   ·   ·   ·   ·   ·   ·   ·   ·
But tasks in hours of insight willed
Can be through hours of gloom fulfilled.[4]

A man whose actions are the victims of his fluctuating moods is an unstable worker in any cause. In efforts to advance the kingdom of God it is the unresponsiveness of other men which is often the baffling factor. The minister must be faithful in "refuting, checking, and exhorting men" (Moffatt), appealing to their minds, their consciences, and their wills. He must not be discouraged by slow results. "Never lose patience with them, and never give up your teaching" (Moffatt).

**3-4.** *Hireling Teachers.*—From the days of the earliest prophets some men have wanted to hear only pleasant things. They have applauded those who have said what the people wanted to hear and have stoned the prophets of unpalatable truth. "The prophets prophesy falsely,

and the priests bear rule by their means, and my people love to have it so" (Jer. 5:31). So Paul warns Timothy that sometimes men **will not endure sound teaching, but . . . will accumulate for themselves teachers to suit their own likings.** Sometimes today congregations expect their ministers to say only the things that the people like to hear, and they turn away from the teacher who speaks the truth as he sees it, come what may. Paul warns Timothy that he must be prepared to be so forsaken. But people who insist on having teachers who "pander to their desires by telling them what they long to hear" (Easton) will in the end miss the truth and **wander into myths.** Totalitarian governments have revived the heresy that truth can be made to conform to a political theory, whether it is truth in art, science, human relations, or even cosmology. In the light of such pronouncements it is refreshing to read again John Milton's affirmation of faith in objective truth in *Areopagitica:*

Though all the winds of doctrine were let loose to play upon the earth, so Truth be in the field, we do injuriously, by licensing and prohibiting, to misdoubt her strength. Let her and Falsehood grapple; who ever knew Truth put to the worse in a free and open encounter?

Arthur Hugh Clough's familiar lines are also to the point:

It fortifies my soul to know
That, though I perish, Truth is so:
That, howsoe'er I stray and range,
Whate'er I do, Thou dost not change.
I steadier step when I recall
That, if I slip, Thou dost not fall.[5]

---

[4] "Morality."

[5] "With Whom Is No Variableness."

5 But watch thou in all things, endure afflictions, do the work of an evangelist, make full proof of thy ministry.

6 For I am now ready to be offered, and the time of my departure is at hand.

myths. 5 As for you, always be steady, endure suffering, do the work of an evangelist, fulfill your ministry.

6 For I am already on the point of being sacrificed; the time of my departure

Fascinated by extravagant **myths**, they get so involved in them that the sober truth of the gospel seems insipid and commonplace, and they **turn away from listening** to it.

5. No matter what other people do, "Timothy's" duty is clear: **always to be steady.** The verb literally refers to sobriety in contrast to drunkenness, and then comes to mean sobriety of conduct in general. Here it means to avoid the fantasy and froth of unrestrained speculation and to remain circumspectly within the received and approved tradition. In such times this will mean suffering, but "as a good soldier" (2:3) "Timothy" will be prepared for it. **The work of an evangelist** (Acts 21:8; Eph. 4:11) is to preach the gospel, not myths. **Fulfill your ministry,** i.e., "discharge all your duties as a minister" (Moffatt). The minister who does his proper work will not be tempted—nor will he have time—to dissipate his energies in fruitless alien aberrations.

### XIII. The Coronation of Paul as Model Minister (4:6-8)

6. Vss. 6-8 are the true conclusion of the letter. Here the author has reached his loftiest lyrical flight. Finely phrased and cleanly polished, balanced and rhythmical, the verses rise to the point of sublimity. They are but the more impressive for being "Paul's" (final?) tribute to the great apostle to whom he owed so much and for whose recognition in the church he fought so valiantly.

There is perhaps a double meaning in the opening word, **for:** Since the time of Paul's departure has come and he is no longer able to "do the work of an evangelist" (vs. 5), "Timothy" is summoned to fill the breach and with double devotion to take his place in the great succession of Christian warriors. And as Paul wings his way to heaven to await his coronation, as his task falls into the hands of his "beloved child" "Timothy," there abides with "Timothy," to bless, preserve, and keep him, the perpetual example, even presence, of the triumphant apostle whose award "Timothy" too may dare hope to share if he endures until the great day when **the Lord, the righteous judge** will come.

The detached, almost Olympian calm, the serene confidence, the full comprehension of the meaning of the martyr-death, the assurance of having lived out his life with unsullied fidelity, the certainty of just reward, remind one of the farewell discourses of Jesus in the Gospel of John. Words which are scarcely fitting, if indeed imaginable, on the lips of Paul are completely pertinent as the writer's tribute of love to a great preacher.

---

5. *Four Principles for Churchmen.*—The admonitions in this verse are addressed to one who has made the Christian ministry his vocation, but they are equally applicable to laymen who have accepted the truth that for a follower of Christ all life is a high calling of God. Stability of purpose—the power to "be urgent in season and out of season" (vs. 2); capacity for sacrifice —the readiness to share the experience of the Cross as part of the price of discipleship; evangelistic zeal—eagerness to enlist all men in the cause of Christ, and willingness to **do the work** involved in such enlistment; fidelity to the task —courage and faith to stay with the job against opposition, through weariness and discourage-

ment, and long after all reasonable obligations have been fulfilled to say, "We are unprofitable servants" (Luke 17:10); these are essential ingredients for effective Christian service under any circumstances.

6. *Time to Go.*—Moffatt translates this in the crisp phrase, "My time to go has come." Death, even a martyr's death, was as simple as that—a going home with clear conscience and the knowledge that faithful service has been fulfilled to the end.

The figure of speech used here is that of the unmooring of a ship for a voyage overseas. It is interesting to put alongside this beautiful metaphor some of the other pictures through

7 I have fought a good fight, I have finished *my* course, I have kept the faith: | has come. 7 I have fought the good fight, I have finished the race, I have kept the faith.

---

**I am already on the point of being sacrificed:** The interesting word here used (σπένδομαι; see also Phil. 2:17) means to offer a libation or drink offering to God, or to consecrate a sacrifice by pouring a libation over it. The suggestion is that Paul's life is being poured out as a libation to God. He too is a saving victim whose death is an offering to God for the consecration of those who follow after him.

**The time of my departure has come: Departure,** lit., "release," a euphemism for death. The term was the one used of the loosing of a ship from its moorings, or of a soldier folding his tents and breaking up camp. Death is both a release and a departure.

**7.** Perhaps the language of all three clauses is derived from expressions used in the arena (see I Cor. 9:24-25; Phil. 2:16; 3:13-14). There is some obscurity of meaning due to the fact that the religious sentiments which have been compressed into the metaphors have quite burst through the forms and, overflowing, have concealed them. **The fight** would be a wrestling match or some arena contest. The **good fight** (see I Tim. 6:12) would be a contest waged for good or noble ends—here, that of the Christian missionary or minister.

**Have finished the race:** A long-distance race it was, and an obstacle race too. Yet Paul never wavered but pushed on until he reached the goal, i.e., Paul finished his work, completed the task he was assigned, rounded out his life, fulfilled his mission and his ministry. His death is here not thought of as bringing his work to a halt just at the time when his productive efforts were proving most fruitful, nor yet is it presented as tragedy. Rather, as the writer, from the vantage point of his own later time, contemplates the life and work of Paul, they seem to him to be a wonderfully completed whole: it seemed clear that Paul had done what God intended him to do.

**I have kept the faith:** If this third member of the sentence rests on and clings closely to the imagery of the games, it should be translated "I have kept my pledge" (Easton), referring to the athlete's promise to keep the rules (see on 2:5; I Tim. 5:12 for **faith**="pledge"). In a writing like II Timothy, however, it is difficult to believe that such language can mean anything but that Paul **kept the faith** in the double sense of

---

which the N.T. speaks of death. In one instance death is referred to as a sleep (John 11:11). Again, death is moving from one house to another (II Cor. 5:1). Elsewhere death is closer fellowship with Christ (Phil. 1:23). A little farther on in II Timothy death is represented as a coronation (vs. 8). The N.T. nowhere gives us a literal picture of life after death, but in striking phrases it affirms its faith in a future life too wonderful for cold words to describe.

**7-8. Victory!**—Few passages in the Bible are more frequently quoted than this in which Paul, again using the vocabulary of the games, states without boasting that he has "played the game," as Scott puts it, has **finished the race,** and has **kept the faith.** He is to appear before the judge to be crowned as victor. This victor's wreath is to be given to all others who have "loved and longed for his appearance" (Moffatt).

There is nothing subtle or obscure about this deeply moving affirmation, and what it says to us is crystal clear. It reminds us that the Chris-

tian life is a struggle against evil in ourselves and around us.

Fight the good fight with all thy might;
Christ is thy strength, and Christ thy right.[6]

It reminds us that the race is not won until the finish line has been crossed, and that there can be no slackening of effort along the way. Among Jesus' most penetrating parables were those in which he pointed out the failure of those who started well but were not able to keep it up to the end (Luke 14:25-33; Matt. 13:5-6, 20-21; 25:8-10). It reminds us that we have pledged ourselves to Christ, to whom we owe faithful allegiance. Among the most tragic words in the Gospels are those which Jesus addressed to the twelve when it was apparent that many of those who had called themselves disciples did not keep faith with him, "Will ye also go away?" The Christian life brings its rewards. One of them is "the crown of a good life" (Moffatt).

6 John S. B. Monsell.

8 Henceforth there is laid up for me a crown of righteousness, which the Lord, the righteous judge, shall give me at that day: and not to me only, but unto all them also that love his appearing.

9 Do thy diligence to come shortly unto me:

10 For Demas hath forsaken me, having

8 Henceforth there is laid up for me the crown of righteousness, which the Lord, the righteous judge, will award to me on that Day, and not only to me but also to all who have loved his appearing.

9 Do your best to come to me soon. 10 For

---

being obedient to it and of transmitting it intact. It is in this fashion that "Timothy" has been constantly urged to keep the faith; how could he have understood the phrase otherwise? One must recognize that such language was not Paul's; but it *was* our author's.

**8. Henceforth** (lit., "for the rest") after the perfect tenses means that since Paul's work is now completed, all that remains is the bestowal of the reward. Or in the language of the games, the race is over and the victor stands waiting to be crowned. And just as the victor's wreath of laurel, of pine, or of olive was prepared and waiting for him, so Paul's wreath **is laid up,** stored away for him, in a secure place until the Judgment Day when the final awards will be made.

**The crown of righteousness** is not a crown which consists of righteousness, but is the wreath or crown which is awarded in recognition of and recompense for a righteous life. Its nature is not described. However, as the crown was a symbol of immortality in the Greco-Roman world of the time, **the crown of righteousness** may well mean the gift of eternal life.

The Christian's vindication and reward belong to the future; the present life remains one of faith. Faith is not misplaced, however, for **the Lord** is a **righteous judge.** Paul will receive his due when the time comes. But not only Paul! The same imperishable wreath which will be awarded to him will be given also to all of his successors who devote themselves to the service of Christ with such intensity that they may be said to **have loved his appearing,** i.e., their whole lives would be a looking toward and a yearning for the full and final manifestation, the great **appearing** which would herald the consummation of all things.

### XIV. Paul and Some Personal Relationships (4:9-18)

**9-12.** Suddenly the tone and the mood of the letter change. After the solemn charge to "Timothy" in vss. 1-2, 5, and the eloquent and confident farewell of vss. 6-8, the

---

One of them is the approval of the righteous judge. "Well done, good and faithful servant" (Matt. 25:21). Beyond all that is the eternal reward which staggers the imagination of finite minds, but which we are confident will include the perpetual vision of God, everlasting fellowship with God, ever greater and more richly satisfying service of God, and spiritual communion with all those who "have loved and longed for his appearance" (Moffatt).

**9-10.** *The Lonely Prisoner.*—In modern life there are many people who claim that they cast their vote for Christian life and for Christian faith, but they want and think they need no Christian fellowship. They want their Christian life to be a solo, not a chorus. Paul was humbler. He needed the friendship, the support, the co-operation of others who shared his faith. Whatever may have been the original text,

there is a startling significance about the order of these messages as we have them in their present form. Paul's calm statement that he has faithfully finished his task, and that he looks forward confidently to the victor's crown, is followed immediately by a very human cry for companionship. **Do your best to come to me soon. For Demas, in love with this present world, has deserted me and gone to Thessalonica; Crescens has gone to Galatia; Titus to Dalmatia.** The church is an essential for many reasons. Courageous Christian living is sometimes a lonely business, and the Christian needs comrades of the faith. The Christian task in the world is too great for isolated individuals, and only the banded, united strength of all Christians can be effective. God is not the private possession of any individual but is the Father of all men, and while solitary prayer has its

| | |
|---|---|
| loved this present world, and is departed unto Thessalonica; Crescens to Galatia, Titus unto Dalmatia. | Demas, in love with this present world, has deserted me and gone to Thessaloni′ca; Crescens has gone to Galatia,[e] Titus to |
| | [e] Other ancient authorities read *Gaul*. |

expectation of imminent death seems to vanish, and Paul suddenly becomes concerned about his own immediate affairs.

Obviously there is some fundamental disharmony between vss. 9-22 and the letter which precedes. The difficulty of accounting for the material makes its interpretation difficult. Is the tone one of lonesomeness, perhaps a bit complaining? Or is its fretfulness due to the fact that it has been taken from a context in which Paul was concerned only with urgency in work and need of workers, and related to a situation of personal tragedy?

Only **Luke** is with him, perhaps as companion, secretary, and physician. **Demas, Crescens,** and **Titus** have for various reasons gone away. Luke and Demas were together

---

place, it needs to be supplemented by corporate worship in which we lift our hearts to God as a family of his children. There are some truths about God that we can discover only in solitude, but there are other ranges of the divine life which we can glimpse only when we say "Our Father." Every would-be Christian dissociated from Christian fellowship should send out his S.O.S. for comrades in the faith.

**10. Slave of Things as They Are.**—Most of the rest of this chapter is devoted to fleeting comments and greetings which reveal in lightning flashes some of those who were Paul's comrades in the work of Christ. One of the saddest lines in all literature is the statement that **Demas hath forsaken me, having loved this present world.** Easton translates it, "Demas —who has set his love on the present world— has left me." In another epistle we read: "Do not love the world or the things in the world. If any one loves the world, love for the Father is not in him. . . . And the world passes away, and the lust of it; but he who does the will of God abides forever." (I John 2:15, 17.) To modern men and women that is a puzzling command. When one looks out over a green valley with mountains in the distance on a summer day, is it wrong to love the world spread out in beauty before him? A modern liturgy contains an expression of thanksgiving for "the radiance, mystery and surprise of this dear world,"[7] a prayer which would not have come naturally to the lips of a medieval saint bent on withdrawing from the world and fixing his thoughts on heaven. Christians always face the problem of appreciating the good things which God has created without becoming their slave. Demas may simply have become so absorbed in things that are good but temporal that he had no concern left for the things which are most good because eternal, a temptation of such pe-

[7] *The Kingdom, the Power, and the Glory*, p. 50.

culiar urgency in modern times that the word "secularism" has been coined to describe it.

Demas may have been one of those people who want no changes in the social structure because they are comfortable and content with things as they are, and dislike change. The proclamation of a new way of life such as Paul embodied in I Cor. 13, or in Rom. 12, may have appealed to Demas at first, but perhaps it lost its glamour when it became apparent that it involved a great deal of personal sacrifice for the common good. The cooling off of youthful ideals and the settling down to contentment with things that ought to be changed constitute tendencies with which all Christians have to struggle in middle life and beyond. In a sense John Masefield was describing one aspect of the Christian life when he wrote:

Not for us are content, and quiet, and peace of
    mind,
For we go seeking a city that we shall never find.

. . . . . . . . . .

Friends and loves we have none, nor wealth nor
    blest abode,
But the hope of the City of God at the other end of
    the road.[8]

Browning perhaps mistakenly put Wordsworth among those who like Demas have forsaken the ideals of youth in the comforts of advancing years.

Just for a handful of silver he left us,
    Just for a riband to stick in his coat.[9]

It should be remembered that sometimes people forsake the Christian adventure not because they love the present world, as Demas did, but

[8] "The Seekers," from *Collected Poems*. Copyright 1915, 1928 by John Masefield. Used by permission of The Macmillan Co., Society of Authors, and Dr. John Masefield, O.M.
[9] "The Lost Leader."

with Paul in Col. 4:14 (see Philem. 24), but Demas (a Greek name, probably a shortened form of Demetrius) has proved disloyal and **deserted** Paul to go to Thessalonica.

Why Demas abandoned Paul cannot be known. Was there some sort of disagreement between them? Had Demas wearied of working with a man whose life was a continual round of incredible toil, hardship, and danger (II Cor. 11:23-28), who was looked at as an agitator and a jailbird? Or did Demas have personal affairs to attend to, which seemed to him to require discontinuing his work with Paul? In any case his loss is regarded as permanent; he seems to have left the church to enter business. That Demas, in contrast "to all who have loved his appearing," was **in love with this present world**, is Paul's (or "Paul's"?) judgment against him for having done it. Thessalonica may have been his home or he may have accepted employment there.

**Crescens** (a Latin name only here in N.T.) and Titus also have gone away, but on church business, one may suppose. The best MSS differ as to whether Crescens went to **Galatia** or **Gaul** (Gallia). The problem as to which is original is complex. On the theory that the verse derives from Paul, "Gaul" is improbable. While there were churches in Lyon and Vienne before A.D. 180, there can scarcely have been any churches in Gaul during his lifetime. If the verse is non-Pauline and late, the problem is more difficult: the word "Gaul" then becomes more easily possible, both linguistically and because the church was moving westward. If original, its alteration to "Galatia" would be motivated by the need to make the text conform to Paul's situation. If, however, "Galatia" was original, it might quite properly have meant and have been interpreted to mean Gaul by a later scribe. Until the second century A.D., Greek writers (Polybius, Josephus, Plutarch, etc.) designated Gaul proper as "(Celtic) Galatia," and Galatia as "Galatia in Asia." Therefore, Eduard Meyer may assert that "whether the correct reading is Galatia or Gallia, it cannot be doubted that Gallia, not Galatia in Asia, is meant" (*Ursprung und Anfänge des Christentums* [Stuttgart: J. G. Cotta, 1923], III, 133, n. 3). In any case, the later tradition which made Crescens one of the seventy-two disciples, attributed to him the founding of the church at Vienne near Lyon, and had him martyred in Gaul under Trajan, indicates that the later accepted interpretation of the text was "Gaul."

**Dalmatia**, where Titus went, is in southern Illyricum, on the eastern shore of the Adriatic, named in Rom. 15:19 as the western limit of Paul's missionary activity.

because they fear it, or because they have given up all hope for it. There is a monastic impulse in every age, tempting Christians to withdraw from the common life and to seek Christian perfection in isolation from the world around them. Such a retreat from life may not be to an institution on a mountain, but may be into an attitude toward life which cuts them off from participation in the common struggle of humanity. The Fourth Gospel records Jesus as praying for his disciples on the eve of the Crucifixion: "I do not pray that thou shouldst take them out of the world, but that thou shouldst keep them from the evil one. They are not of the world, even as I am not of the world." (John 17:15-16.) To be in the world, sharing the common lot of one's fellows, but acknowledging a higher allegiance than this world; to see the evil and despair of the world with unclouded eyes, and still to have faith in the ultimate triumph of God; to accept life with its glory and its misery, its beauty and its terror, its successes and its disappointments, and to

find through it all spiritual resources which this world cannot furnish; to feel like giving the world up as a bad job, and still to be salt, leaven, light, and love to a needy world—this is the way of Christian victory, which sees life realistically and at the same time with the eyes of faith. Demas lacked both the honesty and the faith for a persistent Christian witness.

**10. An Almost Unknown Soldier.**—This is the only reference to **Crescens** in the Bible. Later traditions about him grew up in the church, but this brief sentence is all that is said about him in the canonical Scriptures. He serves to remind us of the great multitude of faithful men and women who have advanced the kingdom of God. In the early centuries of Christianity the church designated one day in each year as "All Saints' Day." There were special days for the remembrance of the great names of Christian history. Here was a day for remembering with gratitude all the men and women whose fidelity to duty, loyalty to the right, generosity to other's needs, and persuasive witness to the unsearchable

11 Only Luke is with me. Take Mark, and bring him with thee: for he is profitable to me for the ministry.

12 And Tychicus have I sent to Ephesus.

Dalmatia. 11 Luke alone is with me. Get Mark and bring him with you; for he is very useful in serving me. 12 Tych′icus I

---

**11.** Timothy is to **get Mark and bring him with** him to Paul. Evidently Timothy knows where Mark is, since Paul does not say. From Col. 4:10; Philem. 24, also, we know that Paul and Mark had got over the differences that separated them in Acts 15:36-41. Mark had proved his worth and had become **very useful in serving** Paul. The exact connotation of **in serving** (lit., "for ministering") is uncertain. Scott (also Easton) thinks the phrase is intentionally vague and means in effect, "I want Mark because he can turn his hand to anything." But whether in the author's mind the emphasis falls on personal service to Paul in prison, such as that rendered by Onesiphorus (1:16-17), or on Mark's usefulness in evangelistic work is not clear. Whether or not "for ministering" (εἰς διακονίαν) should be understood as "a perfectly general phrase" (Easton), or technically as **for the ministry,** for serving as a deacon serves, depends on who wrote the sentence, when it was written, and what was the particular stage of development of the words "to minister," "minister," "ministry," represented in the mind of the author. The Pastorals represent generally a more, not a less, advanced stage in the history of words relating to church offices and orders.

**12.** It is commonly inferred that Mark is to take the place of **Tychicus** (Tit. 3:12; Eph. 6:21; Col. 4:7; Acts 20:4), whom Paul had had to send to Ephesus to take Timothy's place. But these inferences are precarious.

---

riches of Christ have made up the onward march of the Christian faith. Crescens may well serve as a type of all those who make up "the communion of saints."

**11.** *The Beloved Physician.*—In two other places in the epistles **Luke** is mentioned with Demas (Col. 4:14; Philem. 24). Now Demas has deserted. One may imagine that Luke's fidelity meant all the more to Paul in view of Demas' defection. In Colossians Luke is referred to as "the beloved physician." In Philemon he is bracketed with others among "my fellow workers." Here was a many-sided man, the author of the Gospel which is distinguished by its humanitarian interest, a practitioner of medicine who may have joined Paul on his second missionary journey as his personal physician, an ardent Christian who shared the evangelistic labors of his chief, an intrepid traveler who told in the first person the story of some of Paul's most hazardous journeys, a cosmopolitan at home in his own Greek world and at home also in the Jewish world to which Paul introduced him. He is a shining illustration of the variety of gifts which can be used in the Christian cause when dedicated to that service.

**11.** *A Wrong Forgiven.*—Behind this simple statement—**Get Mark and bring him with you; for he is very useful in serving me**—lie a moral tragedy and a moral triumph. Mark left Paul in Perga on Paul's first missionary journey (Acts 13:13). We do not know the reason for the separation, but that it went deep we do know, for when Barnabas later suggested that Mark join them on another journey, Paul would have none of it. In fact, a difference developed between Paul and Barnabas so sharp that Paul took Silas and went in one direction, while Barnabas and Mark sailed for Cyprus (Acts 15:36-41). Divisions among Christian workers are always deplorable, but this historic quarrel had been a disaster. Now, however, all that is forgotten. Somewhere between Acts 15 and II Tim. 4, Paul and Mark had been reconciled and had become fellow workers again. This brief line reveals them as bound together in affection, mutual trust, and mutual admiration. What a spiritual victory lies behind the line **he is profitable to me for the ministry!** Would that all disputes among churchmen might have this happy ending! We may hazard a guess as to what brought about this reconciliation. No doubt it was a vivid sense of the world's need for the Christian gospel, an awareness of the unimportance of their differences in comparison with the importance of the faith which united them, a stinging sense that their quarrel was unworthy of those who followed One who had forgiven his crucifiers, and the redeeming work of Christ's spirit in their hearts. Our divided and quarreling world needs so to be made one in Christ.

**12.** *A Bearer of Tidings.*—Tychicus was one of Paul's helpers who made it possible for the

13 The cloak that I left at Troas with Carpus, when thou comest, bring *with thee,* and the books, *but* especially the parchments.

13 When you come, bring the cloak that I left with Carpus at Tro′as, also the books, and above all the

---

**13.** Some time or other (but when?) Paul left **the cloak**—his heavy winter overcoat, a coarse, wool garment without sleeves, with a hole in the middle for the head to pass through, and used as protection against both cold and rain—with Carpus (otherwise unknown) at Troas. With winter coming on (vs. 21) it would be needed, and Timothy en route from Ephesus is to stop and pick it up.

**The books** would be papyrus rolls, containing one wonders what. Although Paul is more interested in **the parchments** than the books, this does not clarify the contents of either. Parchment or vellum, a very expensive writing material, was intrinsically more valuable than papyrus, and it is possible that the preference is due simply to this fact and that neither the books nor the parchments had anything written on them: they were writing materials which Paul had laid by for future use (Kenyon, Spicq). A popular current interpretation of **the parchments** is that they were "pieces of parchment"="documents" (Easton)="papers" (Moffatt), i.e., legal certificates or official documents such as proof of Roman citizenship (so also Scott, Bernard). On the ground that parchment was reserved for precious writings, especially scripture, many have held these were O.T. books (Dibelius, Parry, Lock), or even official collections of the words of Jesus or accounts of his life (Lock) or Paul's letters (Jeremias). But these last are surely improbable conjectures. Vellum codices were very rare in the first century. It is not likely that either Paul or "Paul" would have called the scriptures **the parchments,** nor would they have so designated early Christian writings, including Paul's letters.

---

great apostle to do his work. There is no record that Tychicus himself was conspicuously gifted as an evangelist or leader. But he was indispensable to Paul. On Paul's last journey to Jerusalem Tychicus was one of those who accompanied him as far as the province of Asia (Acts 20:4), and was evidently left there to carry on the work in Paul's absence. He was sent as a messenger to Ephesus, as is indicated here and also in Eph. 6:21. He was so well acquainted with Paul's personal affairs that Paul did not take the trouble to write about them to the Ephesians, but assured his friends there that Tychicus would tell them everything. Tychicus was to render a similar service to the Colossians, and there is a tradition that he carried these two priceless letters to churches for whom they were written. To Paul he was "a beloved brother and faithful minister and fellow servant in the Lord" (Col. 4:7). These references to this inconspicuous but indispensable man remind us again that the Christian cause is served not only by those who make the headlines, but also by those of lesser gifts but equal devotion who make possible the ongoing work of the church. The average Christian may feel a close bond with those like Tychicus who helped to consolidate the gains made by the more gifted Paul.

**13.** *Above All, the Parchments!*—As a companion piece to this appeal Frederic W. Farrar quoted a letter written by William Tyndale, the translator of the English Bible, from his damp prison cell at Vilvoorde:

I entreat your Lordship, and that by the Lord Jesus, that, if I must remain here for the winter, you would beg the Commissary to be so kind as to send me, from the things of mine which he has, a warmer cap. . . . I feel the cold painfully in my head. . . . Also a warmer cloke, for the one I have is very thin. . . . He has a woollen shirt of mine, if he will send it. But most of all, . . . my Hebrew Bible, grammar, and vocabulary, that I may spend my time in that pursuit.—William Tyndale.[1]

The varied speculations as to the nature of the books and parchments for which Paul longed are outlined elsewhere in this volume (see Exeg.). Obviously we have here an insight of extraordinary clarity into Paul's sense of values. He needed a heavy **cloak** to protect him from the cold, and he hoped to receive it before winter came (vs. 21). Perhaps even more he longed for his **books,** to feed his mind during the lonely hours of imprisonment. It is a reasonable conjecture that some of them at least were

[1] *The Messages of the Books* (New York: E. P. Dutton & Co., 1909), p. 392.

14 Alexander the coppersmith did me much evil: the Lord reward him according to his works:

15 Of whom be thou ware also; for he hath greatly withstood our words.

parchments. 14 Alexander the coppersmith did me great harm; the Lord will requite him for his deeds. 15 Beware of him yourself, for he strongly opposed our message.

---

**14.** If there is any connection between vss. 14 and the preceding verse, Alexander would be thought of as being in Troas—"when there visit Carpus but beware of Alexander" (Easton). However, it is not safe to count on such connection. Vss. 9-18 are composed of three sections incoherently joined. The recipient of the letter would know who and where Alexander was, and could supply in thought what is lacking in language. It would be reading too much between the lines to suppose that he played a part in the arrest of Paul at Troas or Ephesus, or that he followed Paul to Rome as an accuser.

In I Tim. 1:20 a heretic Alexander has been "delivered to Satan." If this meant death and II Timothy was written after I Timothy, the two Alexanders could not be the same person. If II Timothy was written first, the two could have been the same. Then by the time I Timothy was written, Paul had become tired of waiting for the **Lord** to **requite** Alexander, and summarily delivered him to Satan. Another N.T. possibility is the Jewish Alexander of Acts 19:33-34, but the account there is too obscure to warrant the supposition that he was hostile to Paul. It is best to admit that Alexander was such a common name that identification is uncertain.

While the Greek literally means **coppersmith,** the word came to have a more general meaning; hence, Goodspeed renders it "metal-worker"; Moffatt, "blacksmith"; Easton, "smith."

**The Lord will requite him for his deeds** is the language of Ps. 62:12. Later MSS changed the verb from the future tense to the optative mood, making it a prayer for vengeance. Dibelius questions whether the line may not be a Jewish curse formula.

**15.** Alexander is still active, and Timothy had better be on guard. "For he has been bitterly hostile" (Moffatt) to **our message. Our** may be taken as editorial; so Moffatt:

---

religious books from which he had warmed and fortified his own faith in other times of need. A young American who spent a long stretch in prison during World War II was allowed to keep his Bible with him. He said afterward that it had been an enriching experience to read the Bible "in large chunks," and that the broad outlook on life from the viewpoint of Christian history and faith had been one of the great compensations for the limitations of prison. There are other prisons in common life which shut us up to a narrow outlook unless we find release from them—the prison of routine, of self-interest, of class consciousness, of jealous nationalism, of secularism, of fear and anxiety. From them all there is release to be had by those who live in the larger world of intellectual and spiritual freedom found in the Bible and the other classics of faith. James Russell Lowell wrote:

This life were brutish did we not sometimes
Have intimation clear of wider scope,
Hints of occasion infinite.

. . . . . . . . . . .

Sometimes at waking, in the street sometimes,

Or on the hillside, always unforewarned,
A grace of being, finer than himself,
That beckons and is gone,—a larger life
Upon his own impinging, with swift glimpse
Of spacious circles luminous with mind.[2]

Just as Paul craved the reinforcement of faith by his friends (vs. 9), so he longed for the strengthening of his own spiritual life by books which are, as Milton said, "the precious life-blood of a master-spirit." [3]

**14-15.** *Dealing with Opposition.*—Without entering into the various guesses as to who **Alexander the coppersmith** was, or as to the nature of the **great harm** which he had done Paul, we may legitimately look for the significance of this personal relationship in the words **he strongly opposed our message.** Greater than any personal injury which Paul suffered was the fact that Alexander had been in opposition to the cause of Christ. Paul advises Timothy to deal with such an opponent with a mixture of realism and charity. **Beware of him.** Alexander

[2] "The Cathedral."
[3] *Areopagitica.*

16 At my first answer no man stood with me, but all *men* forsook me: *I pray God* that it may not be laid to their charge.

17 Notwithstanding the Lord stood with me, and strengthened me; that by me the preaching might be fully known, and *that* all the Gentiles might hear: and I was delivered out of the mouth of the lion.

16 At my first defense no one took my part; all deserted me. May it not be charged against them! 17 But the Lord stood by me and gave me strength to proclaim the word fully, that all the Gentiles might hear it. So I was rescued from the lion's mouth.

---

"to anything I have said"; Goodspeed, "my teaching." Or it may be a real plural including Timothy and the church in general. Actually there is no great difference in meaning between them, because in the Pastorals Paul's message is identified with Christian orthodoxy; to be anti-Pauline is to be anti-Christian. Alexander may have been a Greek or a Jew opposing Christianity generally; he may have been a heretical (Gnostic) Christian of the sort combated in the letter, and then either identical with or the same sort of person as the Alexander of I Tim. 1:20.

**16. At my first defense:** Better, "at my first appearance in court" (Goodspeed), or "at my first hearing" (Easton), i.e., not the trial proper but the preliminary investigation which ended in adjournment and would be followed some time later with the formal trial. This was regular Roman procedure. In case the judge was not satisfied, this *actio prima* was ended with the verdict *non liquet* or *amplius* and an *actio secunda* became necessary (see Acts 24).

**No one took my part:** The verb used is a technical one meaning to be present before a tribunal as an advocate or friend in court. The Christians in the city who might have been counted on to aid Paul lacked courage and deserted him—every one of them. But Paul forgives them in the language of Stephen (Acts 7:60; see Luke 23:34; I Cor. 13:5; II Cor. 5:19).

**17.** In the very hour when men, even Christian men, abandoned Paul, **the Lord stood by** him, perhaps as in Acts 23:11, and once again gave him courage and power to do as he had done many times before, to turn the hour of his peril into an hour of high privilege, an opportunity "to make a full statement of the gospel" (Moffatt). The occasion was such an important one for declaring the Christian message that, as Paul stood in the presence of the imperial court, it seemed to him as if he were preaching to **all the Gentiles.** And the appeal and power of his defense were so great that he himself was thereby **rescued from the lion's mouth,** i.e., he was granted a delay in the trial proceedings, and for the time at least spared from death.

---

should be recognized for what he was, and the church should be on guard against his efforts to undo its work. But **the Lord will requite him for his deeds.** Though Alexander is to be opposed when he opposes the Christian message, there is to be no attempt to avenge the wrong which he has done. "Dearly beloved, avenge not yourselves, but rather give place unto wrath: for it is written, Vengeance is mine; I will repay, saith the Lord" (Rom. 12:19). It is interesting to put Paul's quotation from Ps. 62 in its setting against the background of the mercy of God: "Also unto thee, O Lord, belongeth mercy; for thou renderest to every man according to his work" (Ps. 62:12). Christianity has its opponents, and never more dangerous ones than in the twentieth century. This opposition is never

abstract but always personalized. The movements and ideologies which rival Christianity are made up of men and women. Here is a formula for meeting opposition to the Christian movement and other good causes: realism in facing the facts and in refusing to yield to opposition, while also refusing to seek revenge for wrongs done, remembering that the offenders are brothers for whom Christ died. The Epistle to the Hebrews appeals to the example of Jesus himself. "Consider him that endured such contradiction of sinners against himself, lest ye be wearied and faint in your minds" (Heb. 12:3).

**16-18. Alone but Not Alone.**—The epistle draws near its close with a moving testimony to the comforting and strengthening power of the

18 And the Lord shall deliver me from every evil work, and will preserve *me* unto his heavenly kingdom: to whom *be* glory for ever and ever. Amen.

18 The Lord will rescue me from every evil and save me for his heavenly kingdom. To him be the glory for ever and ever. Amen.

---

The lion's mouth was a proverbial expression for extreme danger (cf. Pss. 22:21; 7:2; 35:17; Dan. 6:20 ff.; etc.). There is no reference here either to Nero, to Satan, or to the wild beasts of the amphitheater.

The clause that all the Gentiles might hear it seems to spill over its context and therefore is problematic. The interpretation given above is an attempt to give meaning to the words within the context. It can be justified, however, only if all the Gentiles is hyperbole, and then only if Paul's hearing was conducted before an impressive assembly of the imperial court in the presence of a great multitude who were constrained to hear by the sheer compulsion of Paul's oratory. It is possible that, longing as he did to preach the gospel in Rome also (Rom. 1:10-15; Acts 23:11; 27:24), Paul regarded this occasion as the crowning event in his career, and that this assemblage of Roman grandees stood to him as symbol for all the Gentiles, not only because of who they were in themselves but because through them his message would filter downward through the masses.

Yet, one must admit, to press the text into the context in this way seems to do it violence. It is possible to see in the purpose clause an expression of faith on Paul's part that since he was saved from the lion's mouth this time, he would be granted full liberty at the final trial, and freedom to fulfill his preaching mission among the Gentiles. This would require Paul to be writing between the trials. Traditionally it has been regarded as evidence that at his "first defense," i.e., at his first trial in Rome, Paul was liberated, and that he pursued a Gentile mission for some years before a second arrest. However, given the obscurities which obtain concerning the events of the end of Paul's life, and also concerning this section of the text, the first interpretation suggested seems the best.

18. From every evil (RSV), from every evil work (KJV). In the context this should mean "from all harm" (Moffatt, Goodspeed, Scott, Easton), i.e., from every attack on the part of his enemies, and not "from all sin" (Spicq). However, in literature of this sort words frequently have religious overtones which enrich them beyond the demands of the events with which they deal, and perhaps the ambiguous translation of the RSV is best. No attack, whether from men or the evil one, can really harm Paul in this world, and he is equally confident of his place in heaven.

On the surface at least, and perhaps at bottom, vs. 18 is in contradiction with vss. 6-8. They can be harmonized only if vs. 18 is taken to mean, "The Lord will rescue me even from my impending death and take me to heaven."

The doxology is exactly that of Gal. 1:5 (IV Macc. 18:24) except that it is ascribed

---

divine companionship. Paul has stood before his accusers without human support. As Jesus had been forsaken by the disciples when he stood before Pontius Pilate, so Paul. At my first defense no one took my part; all deserted me. As Jesus forgave those who wronged him, so Paul. May it not be charged against them! As Jesus communed with God on the cross, Paul was aware of a superhuman Friend from whom he drew strength. But the Lord stood by me and gave me strength to proclaim the word fully. Here again was a demonstration of the fact that "in everything God works for good with those who love him" (Rom. 8:28). Even arrest

and trial provided an opportunity for Christian testimony before the Roman power. The experience was one of his grounds for faith for the future. I was rescued. . . . The Lord will rescue me from every evil. It cannot be pointed out too often that Paul had not been spared hardships (II Cor. 6:4-10; 11:23-28). His past experience was not such as to lead him to expect immunity from suffering in days to come. But he was confident that the Lord would stand by him and strengthen him in any and every emergency, and ultimately save me for his heavenly kingdom. At this thought he breaks forth into a paean of praise. To him be the glory for ever and ever. Amen.

19 Salute Prisca and Aquila, and the household of Onesiphorus.

20 Erastus abode at Corinth: but Trophimus have I left at Miletum sick.

19 Greet Prisca and Aquila, and the household of Onesiph'orus. 20 Eras'tus remained at Corinth; Troph'imus I left ill at

---

to Christ. Only in I Pet. 4:11 in the N.T. is the verb expressed in a doxology, and there it is "is," not "be." On the strength of this, Easton thinks "is" should be supplied here and elsewhere.

## XV. CONCLUDING GREETINGS (4:19-22)

**19. Prisca** (Priscilla) and **Aquila** were very devoted friends of Paul who "risked their necks" for his life (Rom. 16:4). Four out of six times in the N.T. Prisca is named before her husband, either because she may have belonged to a noble Roman family (William Sanday and Arthur C. Headlam, *A Critical and Exegetical Commentary on the Epistle to the Romans* [New York: Charles Scribner's Sons, 1902; "International Critical Commentary"], pp. 418-20) or because she was the stronger personality. Aquila was a Jew of Pontus (Acts 18), who with his wife Prisca had been compelled to leave Rome in A.D. 52(?) by the decree of Claudius. They went to Corinth where their friendship with Paul began. Paul lived with them there for more than a year and a half, and when he sailed for Syria they went with him as far as Ephesus. They were in Ephesus when I Corinthians was written (I Cor. 16:19). The verse now under discussion supposes that they are still there (see Rom. 16:3-4).

**The household of Onesiphorus**: See on 1:16-18.

**20.** In Acts 19:22 Paul in Ephesus sent Timothy and Erastus (not necessarily an Ephesian) ahead of him to Macedonia. Since Erastus is there coupled with Timothy, it is a reasonable inference that **Erastus** here is the same person. In Rom. 16:23 an Erastus is the treasurer of Corinth. Since nothing is known about them except these three brief notices, the three names may or may not be the same person (for a detailed discussion see Henry J. Cadbury, "Erastus of Corinth," *Journal of Biblical Literature*, L [1931], 42-58). It is profitless to guess why **Erastus remained at Corinth**. It is usually supposed that his duties as treasurer kept him there. How he could ever have traveled with Paul, if a city treasurer, one can hardly see—"unless the duties of Corinth's 'treasurer' were largely honorary" (Easton, *Pastoral Epistles*, p. 78). That Erastus is mentioned at all as having

---

**19. A Consecrated Marriage.**—The searchlight falls for a brief moment on a married couple who stand out as a brilliant example of God's use of a dedicated partnership. **Greet Prisca and Aquila.** Their marriage was confronted by great problems. There was difference in racial and cultural background, the wife, according to the Exeg., being perhaps a Roman and the husband a Jew. They were refugees, driven from Rome with other Jews by imperial edict. They never got their roots down very deep anywhere, and are heard of in Corinth and later on in Ephesus. But they serve to show how effective a man and wife can be in Christian service when they share a common devotion. They opened their home to Paul in Corinth, and they worked together as tentmakers. They accompanied him to Ephesus, where they remained to carry on the work when he returned to Syrian Antioch. The church in

Rome at some time met in their house. How great was their service is revealed in Paul's comment at the end of the Epistle to the Romans: "Greet Prisca and Aquila, my fellow workers in Christ Jesus, who risked their necks for my life, to whom not only I but also all the churches of the Gentiles give thanks; greet also the church in their house" (Rom. 16:3-5). The N.T. has its roster of illustrious individuals who served the Christian cause, and of famous churches. Here is a unique team of married partners who together were servants of the kingdom. Their marriage was doubtless richer because of the common faith, the common interest, and the common cause in which they were united. Their service was richer because they strengthened one another in it.

**19-20. Diversities of Gifts.**—If traditions are taken along with the known facts about the people so briefly mentioned at the conclusion

21 Do thy diligence to come before winter. Eubulus greeteth thee, and Pudens, and Linus, and Claudia, and all the brethren.

22 The Lord Jesus Christ *be* with thy spirit. Grace *be* with you. Amen.

¶ The second *epistle* unto Timotheus, ordained the first bishop of the church of the Ephesians, was written from Rome, when Paul was brought before Nero the second time.

Mile'tus. 21 Do your best to come before winter. Eubu'lus sends greetings to you, as do Pudens and Linus and Claudia and all the brethren.

22 The Lord be with your spirit. Grace be with you.

---

**remained in Corinth** may suggest that Timothy expected him either to come to Ephesus or to have gone on to Rome with Paul.

**Trophimus** was an Ephesian (Acts 20:4; 21:29) who had evidently been more closely associated with Paul than we know. According to Acts he met Paul at Troas and sailed with him to Jerusalem, where he was unexpectedly the innocent cause of Paul's arrest. The only occasion in Acts when Paul and Trophimus were in Miletus together (Acts 20:15) was on this trip between Troas and Jerusalem. Obviously Trophimus was not then left behind sick. If vs. 20 has anything to do with Paul's last days, after his arrest in Jerusalem, one could see how he might have regarded Trophimus as a valuable witness of his innocence of the charge preferred by his Jewish opponents and might have wanted him in Rome. However, Paul went to Rome under custody, nor did he pass through Miletus. Even if Trophimus had returned to Asia via Miletus and had got sick there, it is hard to see how Paul could have written **Trophimus I left ill at Miletus.** Thus there is no way in which this detail can be fitted into Paul's life as we know it.

**21. Do your best to come before winter:** Either because Paul will be needing the cloak, the books, and the parchments (vs. 13), or because he is lonely and needs at once the advice and comfort of Timothy and perhaps his help in the trial. To delay until navigation was closed for the winter might mean that Timothy could not reach Rome until the spring, and then it might be too late.

That Paul knows the names of four Christians in Rome and maintains a normal relationship with them is strange after vs. 16; and how could he have sent greetings from **all the brethren** if **all** had deserted him? Yet Paul and Timothy both must have been acquainted with these four if the greetings are to have meaning, even though we do not know how or where. They are not elsewhere named in the N.T. and we know nothing about them.

Not even legend has adorned the name of **Eubulus.** It made of **Pudens** a Roman senator converted by Peter, and of **Claudia** the mother of **Linus,** held to be the bishop of Rome, the first successor to Peter (Irenaeus *Against Heresies* III. 3. 3; Eusebius *Church History* III. 4; Theodoret *Commentaries ad loc.*). Pudens and Claudia are very common Latin names; Linus, a common Greek name meaning flaxen-haired.

**22.** The final benediction resembles those in Galatians, Philippians, Philemon. The first "you" (**your**) is singular, referring to Timothy; the second, plural, includes Timothy's

---

of the epistle, this cluster of names may serve to emphasize the wide variety of persons whose gifts and services God can use in his church. **Erastus,** a city treasurer in Greece; **Trophimus,** an Ephesian who accompanied Paul on one of his journeys; **Eubulus,** utterly unknown; **Pudens,** reputed by tradition to have been a Roman senator; **Linus,** said by Eusebius to have been bishop of Rome for twelve years after the martyrdom of Peter and Paul; and **Claudia,** thought by some to have been the

mother of Linus. The Christian gospel is universal in its appeal—it meets the needs of all kinds of people. The Christian church should be universal in its fellowship—all kinds of people should find common ground in its faith and service. The Christian cause is universal in its claim—whatever any man anywhere has of ability or resource can be dedicated to God and utilized in ways far beyond our imaginings.

**22. *The Grace of God.*—Grace** is one of the great words of the Christian faith which has

associates, if it is not merely conventional. To make this clear the translation should read, "Grace be with you all."

---

been worn so smooth with frequent use that often it does not take hold on our minds when we hear it. We need to be reminded of some of its common meanings: (a) The capacity for doing things gracefully. When Jesus spoke, men "wondered at the words of grace which proceeded out of his mouth" (Luke 4:22 ARV). (b) A spirit of inexhaustible and indomitable good will. When we speak of being in "A state of grace," it means in part being free from ill will. (c) An overflow of kindness which goes far beyond the recipient's deserving. Justice means dealing with people in accordance with what they deserve, while grace goes the second mile, uncalculating. "While we were yet sinners, Christ died for us" (Rom. 5:8) is the ultimate in grace. There can be no richer prayer for anyone than this, **Grace be with you.**

---

# TITUS

## TEXT, EXEGESIS, AND EXPOSITION

1 Paul, a servant of God, and an apostle of Jesus Christ, according to the faith of God's elect, and the acknowledging of the truth which is after godliness;

1 Paul, a servant[a] of God and an apostle of Jesus Christ, to further the faith of God's elect and their knowledge of the

a Or *slave.*

---

### I. The Salutation (1:1-4)

**1:1.** In the genuine Paulines, Paul never calls himself **a servant of God,** but always "a servant of Christ Jesus" (Rom. 1:1; Phil. 1:1). The unusual expression here has only literary importance and may be ascribed to the need for variety in the two-membered phrase, the second member of which is the usual **apostle of Jesus Christ** of I Tim. 1:1; II Tim. 1:1. Both **servant** and **apostle** (see on I Tim. 1:1) are here official titles (see on II Tim. 2:24). Although **servant (slave,** RSV mg.) emphasizes the idea of complete dependence upon and unlimited devotion to God or Christ as master, the term, like "minister" in English, carries with it less the suggestion of a humble or humiliating status than one of honor and dignity. The **servant of God** as God's representative stands

---

**1:1-3. The Great Commission.**—The Gospel of Matthew closes with what has been popularly called "The Great Commission" (Matt. 28:19-20), a command to proclaim the gospel of Christ throughout the world. This epistle, like the others which bear Paul's name, begins with the writer's claim to the authority of such a commission. Here in one rather complicated sentence are gathered together most of the great words which express the Christian faith: servant, apostle, faith, knowledge, truth, godliness, hope, eternal life, promise, word, preaching, command, Savior. Every word is a window opening out on a broad vista, and together they constitute a comprehensive picture of a larger life

For Introduction to Titus see pp. 343-75.

than any which the secularist can ever know. To make the picture complete, the word "love" is needed also, and it is one of the limitations of this epistle that it is not given central emphasis.

The Exeg. points out that while the term **servant of God** connotes dignity and honor as God's representative, the literal translation would be **slave of God** (RSV mg.). This suggests the paradox of Christian freedom, which involves both self-surrender and self-fulfillment. So long as anyone thinks of personal freedom as consisting merely of absence of any restraint upon his individual desires he is in bondage to those desires. He is the slave of greed, of ambition, of lust, or of his own indolence. He is not

in a position of authority over men, just as does the **apostle of Jesus Christ,** and for the same reason: they are chosen and commissioned. Since Paul holds both titles, and since it is "by command of God" that he has "been entrusted" with "the preaching" (vs. 3), he has a divine right to set standards of faith and order for the church.

The exact meaning of the prepositional phrases which follow is perplexing. Literally the text reads, "According to [the] faith of God's elect and [the] knowledge of [the] truth which is according to godliness in [the] hope of eternal life." The obscurity is due (a) to the wide variety of meanings assumed by Greek prepositions in the colloquial language, and (b) to the fact that vss. 1-3 are composed of a series of phrases in liturgical form—compact, condensed, intense—symbols whose first intent is to evoke an emotion rather than to describe or clarify an idea.

The usual meaning of κατά with the accusative, **according to** (KJV), or "conforming to," is not illuminating here; it is better taken as "in view of," **to further** (RSV). Paul

---

free to be his best self, to render his best service to others, or to discover life's deepest satisfactions. The larger freedom is found only in loyalty to something greater than himself that calls out his best self. Such freedom finds its highest expression in loyalty to the God and Father of Jesus Christ, as is indicated by the salutation with which the letter to Titus opens. Wordsworth gave the classic description of the futility of mistaking lawlessness for freedom:

> Me this unchartered freedom tires;
> I feel the weight of chance-desires:
> My hopes no more must change their name
> I long for a repose that ever is the same.[1]

George Matheson caught the spirit of Christian freedom in his fine hymn that begins: "Make me a captive, Lord." The only freedom worth having is that of a slave of God.

The work of **an apostle of Jesus Christ** is **to further the faith of God's elect and their knowledge of the truth.** In I Tim. 2:4 the writer has asserted that God "desires all men to be saved and to come to the knowledge of the truth." We may therefore assume that in his opening sentence to Titus he is stating the missionary purpose of the church. It is an unfortunate fact that this missionary character of the Christian gospel has never been understood or accepted by more than a fraction of those who are members of the church. The objections to the work of missions are threadbare with constant use. It is argued that Christians should see to their own moral improvement and not bother about other people; that if non-Christian peoples prefer other religions, that is their own affair; that it makes little difference to what religion one adheres if only he holds it sincerely; that there is so much need at home that we can spare no resources for the world-wide expansion of Christianity; and that until so-called Christian nations are more Christian, they have no Chris-

tianity to export. All of these familiar objections reveal a deep misunderstanding of the nature and meaning of Christian missions. Christian missions endeavor not to persuade non-Christian peoples to become like the so-called Christian peoples, but endeavor to share with all peoples the Christian gospel which can bring new life to the whole world. Christianity believes in one God, the Father of all mankind, and cannot be true to itself except as it seeks to make known to all mankind the Father who was revealed in Christ. Christianity believes that truth is one, and that there cannot be one truth for Europe, another for Asia, or one truth for Christians and another adequate for non-Christians. The N.T. obviously contemplates one church, and the ecumenical movement has in modern times recaptured the vision of a world-wide church standing together and working together for the faith of the gospel. The basis of the Christian mission was well stated in the message of the International Missionary Conference in Jerusalem in 1928:

> The Gospel is the answer to the world's greatest need. It is not our discovery or achievement; it rests on what we recognize as an act of God. It is first and foremost "Good News." It announces glorious truth. Its very nature forbids us to say that it may be the right belief for some but not for others. Either it is true for all or it is not true at all. . . .
> We cannot live without Christ and we cannot bear to think of men living without Him. We cannot be content to live in a world that is unChristlike. We cannot be idle while the yearning of His heart for His brethren is unsatisfied.[2]

**The truth which accords with godliness** is rendered by Moffatt as "the Truth that goes with a religious life," by Easton as "the truth revealed in true religion," by the KJV as **the**

---

[1] "Ode to Duty," st. v.

[2] Robert E. Speer, *The Crisis Decade* (New York: Board of Foreign Missions of the Presbyterian Church in the U.S.A., 1950), p. 297.

2 In hope of eternal life, which God, that cannot lie, promised before the world began;

3 But hath in due times manifested his word through preaching, which is committed unto me according to the commandment of God our Saviour;

truth which accords with godliness, 2 in hope of eternal life which God, who never lies, promised ages ago 3 and at the proper time manifested in his word through the preaching with which I have been entrusted by command of God our Savior;

---

is sent in order that those whom God has chosen may arrive at (the) faith, even the knowledge of (Christian) truth. **Knowledge of the truth which accords with godliness** is circumlocution for "Christianity." There is one true religion and one religious truth, and God has revealed it fully and clearly in the Pauline preaching.

**2.** Christians believe and hope in eternal life, which indeed is ultimately the meaning of salvation. The apostolic mission is to bring men through faith and the knowledge of Christian truth to eternal life. As the object of **faith** and **hope,** eternal life might seem contingent and uncertain. However, this is not so; the Christian's hope is grounded in the declared word of **God,** who **promised** it **ages ago** and **who never lies.**

**Ages ago** (πρὸ χρόνων αἰωνίων, lit., "before eternal times") here probably means the distant past (in contrast to its meaning in II Tim. 1:9), referring either to the promises in Genesis or in the prophets. Strictly speaking, in ancient Israel there were no promises of eternal life. However, to both Jewish and Christian faith the O.T. was a book of promises. Future events and fulfillment were believed assured only if found **promised.** The allegorical or "spiritual" method of interpretation provided subsequent generations with a method of discovering contemporary forms of faith concealed beneath ancient texts. That **ages ago** God had promised eternal life it would not have occurred to a Christian to doubt, even though no specific reference in the O.T. was designated in support of the statement.

**Who never lies,** lit., "the unlying God." Although in common use in Greek religious language, the epithet "unlying" never occurs in the O.T. or Apoc. with reference to God. Jews and Christians both took the truthfulness of God for granted.

**3.** This verse breaks off the relative clause and introduces a direct sentence: God who promised, **at the proper time** [cf. I Tim. 2:6; 6:15] **manifested in his word** (the **in** is not in the Greek). I.e., at a precise moment in history, which God fixed, he declared **his word;** he spoke. To the Christian reader God's word (λόγος) is his Son (Heb. 1:2; John 1:14). Yet it is **through** [lit., "in"] **the preaching,** i.e., the apostolic preaching **with which I** [both Paul and the writer] **have been entrusted** that the gospel of eternal life has been

---

**truth which is after godliness** and by the ASV as "the truth which is according to godliness." Through this variety of translations the vital connection of truth and righteousness shines clear. Christian faith is more than ethics, and the attempt to reduce Christianity to an ethical system alone results in something that is not Christianity at all. But the attempt to ignore the ethical fruits of Christian faith, concentrating attention exclusively on doctrine, ritual, or tradition, is equally fallacious. To hold the Christian truth with a good conscience means to live the kind of life which is congruous with the truth that the character, purpose, and redemptive power of God were disclosed in Jesus.

**2-3. The Continuity of Creation.**—Paul writes **in hope of eternal life** as he lived and labored in that hope. To attempt to reduce Christianity

to a way of living in this world bereft of any far horizon reaching beyond the visible and temporal is to deny the basic faith of the apostolic church which knew no Christianity without the immortal hope. In this passage that hope is said to be a reality **which God, who never lies, promised ages ago,** or **promised before the world began.** The Exeg. suggests that this refers to the promises made in Genesis and in the Prophets. It might conceivably refer to the Creation. The inevitable and adequate reply to those who say it is inconceivable that life should continue after death is that life and death are both the gifts of God. To the finite mind it is inconceivable that God should have created the universe or have created man for fellowship with himself. But the Creation is historic fact. It is not inconceivable that God,

| | |
|---|---|
| 4 To Titus, *mine* own son after the common faith: Grace, mercy, *and* peace, from God the Father and the Lord Jesus Christ our Saviour. | 4 To Titus, my true child in a common faith:<br><br>Grace and peace from God the Father and Christ Jesus our Savior. |

revealed. What God first promised and then revealed he commanded Paul—and all who follow after him—to preach. **By command of God our Savior:** See I Tim. 1:1. Easton believes that vss. 2b-3 presuppose the hymn of II Tim. 1:9-10, and that the awkwardness of sentence structure and the apparently different meaning of "before times eternal" are due to imperfect adaptation.

**4. Titus:** Chronologically Titus first appears in the N.T. in Gal. 2:1, 3, where, accompanying Paul to Jerusalem as a sort of exhibition of Paul's evangelistic achievements, he is described as a Greek, i.e., a Gentile. In II Cor. 2:12 he is in Europe, having been dispatched by Paul to Corinth (see II Cor. 12:18) both to carry the "severe letter" and to bring back news of Corinthian reaction to it. Paul had hoped to find him in Troas but was obliged to continue into Macedonia before meeting up with him (II Cor. 7:5-7, 13-14). Since Titus was so successful at Corinth Paul determined to send him there again to collect the offering for "the relief of the saints" (II Cor. 8:6, 16-17, 23). Paul's contacts with Titus must have been much more extensive than the N.T. indicates; therefore it is probably accidental that Acts does not mention him.

How widely Titus may have traveled throughout the churches, or what increasing responsibilities he may have carried after having proved himself in the Corinthian trouble and later, after Paul's death, we do not know. Nor do we know enough to say that he could not have had to do with the organization of the churches in Crete or have traveled to Dalmatia (II Tim. 4:10), even though there is no evidence for this in Acts or in Paul's letters. That the letter which our author wrote with reference to the Cretan churches is addressed to Titus may possibly but not necessarily be regarded as evidence that Titus was active in the evangelization of the island. Whether or not Titus was ever replaced in Crete by Artemas or Tychicus or visited Paul at Nicopolis (Tit. 3:12), there is no way of knowing. Paul's letters and the Pastorals run on parallel lines without intersection, so to speak; and nothing the one says about Titus can be inferred from the other, nor can either be held to contradict the other. In the letter to Titus, Titus is simply a name, not a character.

**My true child in a common faith** (see I Tim. 1:1) emphasizes the loyalty of "Titus" to the Pauline faith, in contrast to the "many insubordinate men" of vs. 10. On vs. 4b see I Tim. 1:2b.

having created, should preserve what he has created. The Creation and the Resurrection are acts of God that logically fit together in his purpose. It was the good news of the Resurrection that was the heart of the Christian gospel. The eternal life, the promise of which was inherent in the Creation, was **at the proper time manifested in his word through the preaching with which I have been entrusted by command of God our Savior.** As H. H. Farmer says: "Whatever it is he is doing in his wisdom and love and power, it will only finally be achieved in a kingdom which lies beyond and transcends this observable world of space and time. There is an unfathomable 'beyond' to it all."[3] This Christian faith is simply expressed in the epi-

[3] *God and Men* (New York and Nashville: Abingdon-Cokesbury Press, 1947), pp. 191-92.

taph on the gravestone of an early minister of the church in Old Bennington, Vermont: "He relinquished his office for the sublime employment of immortality." The **preaching** of the Word with which the apostolic church is entrusted includes the doctrines of God the creator, God the redeemer, and God the eternal hope.

**4. A True Child in a Common Faith.**—The friends and fellow workers of Paul are always fruitful subjects for study. The N.T. references to Titus make it plain that he was an unusual person. Paul evidently regarded him as an example of the power of the Spirit. When he wanted to persuade the Jerusalem Christians that the Spirit was not limited to the Jewish community but could be manifested with equal power in Gentile life, he took Titus along as a

5 For this cause left I thee in Crete, that thou shouldest set in order the things that are wanting, and ordain elders in every city, as I had appointed thee:

5 This is why I left you in Crete, that you might amend what was defective, and appoint elders in every town as I directed

---

## II. On Elders and Bishops (1:5-8)

**5. This is why I left you in Crete** should not be understood as a reply to a letter from Titus asking, "Why did you leave me in Crete?" It is a literary device whereby the author brings the authority of Paul (see Acts 14:23) to the aid of "Titus," who is charged with the responsibility of appointing **elders in every town. What was defective** in the churches of Crete was that they were not properly organized to resist and to repel the inroads being made by unorthodox teachers who were "upsetting whole families" (vs. 11). This "Titus" is to remedy by seeing that a body of elders is set up to govern every

---

demonstration (Gal. 2:1-3). Titus was a bracing person in whom Paul found moral support in his difficulties. "When we came into Macedonia, our bodies had no rest, but we were afflicted at every turn—fighting without and fear within. But God, who comforts the downcast, comforted us by the coming of Titus." (II Cor. 7:5-6.) How often when God comforts he uses human channels like Titus to mediate his comfort! Titus was a friend whose well-being meant much to the great apostle. "When I came to Troas to preach the gospel of Christ, a door was opened for me in the Lord; but my mind could not rest because I did not find my brother Titus there" (II Cor. 2:12-13). Titus was a stalwart and faithful minister. "Thanks be to God who puts the same earnest care for you into the heart of Titus. For he not only accepted our appeal, but being himself very earnest he is going to you of his own accord. . . . As for Titus, he is my partner and fellow worker in your service." (II Cor. 8:16-17, 23.) An example of Christian life, a comfort to a friend in need, a faithful minister of Christ—such was Titus as Paul's letters reveal him.

**5-9. Qualifications for Leadership.**—The moral requirements for an important post of leadership in the church seem startlingly low when this passage is first considered. It would seem that it might be taken for granted that **a bishop . . . must not be arrogant or quick-tempered or a drunkard or violent or greedy for gain.** The essentials here seem to be that he should have a blameless family life, that he should be **self-controlled,** and that he should accept and teach **sound doctrine.** What is required of a church leader seems to be a kind of Christian stoicism, avoiding extremes, eschewing fanaticism, exercising moderation and self-control, observing the golden mean as a guiding principle. Obviously the requirements for Christian leadership are stated here in minimum terms, and these statements can furnish little

detailed guidance for churches today in their choice of leaders.

This passage does, however, underscore two facts which the church always needs to bear in mind:

First, the church can use men of ordinary gifts and lead them into greater virtues than their initial endowment includes. As Ernest F. Scott says,

It may be granted that from the Pastoral Epistles we should never guess what Christianity has meant to the saints and the mystics. The precepts of the Gospels, the aspirations of Paul and John, are transposed into a lower key. . . . The religion of these Epistles may not be the highest, but . . . because he thus made Christianity a working religion for ordinary men, the author of the Pastorals may justly be ranked among the great Christian teachers.[4]

Second, the church needs to be on guard against too easily accommodating itself to a less than Christian ethical standard. The virtues which are commended to Titus make a good beginning toward Christian life, but there are few temptations more dangerous than that of supposing that a Christian can regard them as spiritual goals. This has been sharply stated by Hugh Ross Williamson in a modern morality play, *The Seven Deadly Virtues:*

It is customary to say that Jesus was killed by the sins of the world. That is quite true. But they were revealed as sins only because they killed him. What is important to notice is that they were what the world called virtues, and—since there is an unending incompatibility between the standards of Jesus and those of the world—still calls virtues.[5]

Whenever the church tends to grow content with the unadventurous virtues it needs to re-

[4] *The Pastoral Epistles* (New York: Harper & Bros.; London: Hodder & Stoughton, 1936; "Moffatt New Testament Commentary"), p. xxxviii.

[5] New York: The Macmillan Co., 1936, pp. 9-10.

**6** If any be blameless, the husband of one wife, having faithul children not accused of riot or unruly.

**7** For a bishop must be blameless, as the steward of God; not self-willed, not soon angry, not given to wine, no striker, not given to filthy lucre;

you, **6** men who are blameless, married only once,[b] whose children are believers and not open to the charge of being profligate or insubordinate. **7** For a bishop, as God's steward, must be blameless; he must not be arrogant or quick-tempered or a drunkard

[b] Greek *the husband of one wife.*

---

local church. How many towns in Crete may have had churches there is no way of knowing, but **every town** suggests a considerable number.

**As I directed you** again emphasizes the apostolic (Pauline) source of the injunction.

**6. Men who are blameless** (ἀνέγκλητος, as in I Tim. 3:10; in I Tim. 3:2 the synonym ἀνεπίλημπτος is used), i.e., whose character is clear (see I Tim. 3:7). **Married only once:** See on I Tim. 3:2. **Whose children are believers** is a more explicitly Christian expansion of the virtue list than I Tim. 3:4, 11. The Christian family must be a unity. It is not enough for the elder's own life to be **blameless.** To have **profligate or insubordinate** children is to be disqualified for the elderhood.

**7.** The shift from the plural "elders" (vs. 5) to the singular **a bishop** (in Greek "the" bishop, τὸν ἐπίσκοπον, which may be translated "a" or "the," depending on the interpretation given it), together with what seems to be a second virtue list duplicating vs. 6 in its first item, **blameless**—this results in a certain roughness of connection between vss. 6 and 7 and a consequent obscurity in meaning. On the one hand, it is argued that if "elder" and "bishop" here were exactly synonymous, vs. 7 would read "bishops." The implication of **for,** it is urged, which is to be read between the lines of vss. 6-7, is that it is necessary for candidates for the elderhood to be blameless because the bishop is chosen from their number (so Spicq). Others who interpret τὸν ἐπίσκοπον as "the (monarchical) bishop" regard vs. 7 as later interpolation. While possible, however, these interpretations are by no means necessary. The transition from the plural "elders" in vs. 5 to the singular "bishop" in vs. 7 is less rough in Greek than in the RSV translation, for vs. 6 has already moved into the singular number: the text literally reads, "if anyone is blameless" (concealed under the plural "men who are blameless" of RSV). Further, if "elder" and "bishop" are here taken to mean the same thing, "bishop" being the general term indicating function, "elder" the traditional Jewish-Christian term for the same sort of official, vss. 6-7 gain in coherence and the meaning is: Since it is necessary for a bishop to be qualified thus and so, all bishops (=elders) must

---

member that they put Jesus on the cross. Men who have these virtues can grow into effective Christian leaders, but if they do not grow beyond them they defeat the very cause they are called to serve.

One reason why the writer of this epistle was so deeply concerned with the character of these church officers is that Christianity was fighting for its life against the Gnostic heresy. It had to demonstrate its power to produce better men and women. Again in the twentieth century the Christian church is confronted with powerful and persuasive competitors. Nazism, communism, secularism, materialism, and a whole gamut of enthusiastic cults, many of them embodying some of the features of first-century Gnosticism, challenge Christianity's claim to men's allegiance. These challenges cannot be

ignored or taken lightly. Christians believe in the ultimate triumph of God; but the work of the church may be set back for centuries, and millions of persons may never know the blessings of the gospel, if the church in this generation fails to meet the challenges with which it is confronted. The Christian church must outthink, outserve, and outevangelize its competitors. It can do so only as its adherents demonstrate a capacity to outlove and, if need be, outsuffer the adherents of rival religions. Hence the necessity for outstanding Christian character in the church's leaders.

*5. Paul Watered. Who Planted?*—The church at Crete was the result of labors of which no known record exists. There were Cretans among those who received the Spirit in Jerusalem on the day of Pentecost (Acts 2:11). It has been

8 But a lover of hospitality, a lover of good men, sober, just, holy, temperate; | or violent or greedy for gain, 8 but hospitable, a lover of goodness, master of him-

---

be so qualified. The chief function of the elder is, so to speak, as bishop, i.e., as overseer or superintendent. **As God's steward** he administers the church in God's stead.

Since the office of bishop is one of authority and power, the vices named are those to which persons in such positions are tempted: **he must not be arrogant,** despotic, **self-willed,** domineering, **or quick-tempered.**

**Or a drunkard** (πάροινον) : Lock suggests that the word may only imply "blustering," "abusive," like a man who has been drinking. However, see on I Tim. 3:3. On **violent** see on I Tim. 3:3; on **greedy for gain** see on I Tim. 3:8. The connotations of the latter word are hardly rendered adequately by Moffatt in "not . . . addicted to pilfering," nor is Easton's "not fouled by dishonesty" comprehensive enough. If the bishop might be tempted to appropriate too large a share of the gifts of the faithful to his own use, he might also be tempted to engage in lucrative business ventures not becoming a Christian church official. Furthermore, at this time not all bishops would be fully supported by the church, and some might easily be tempted to neglect their church work in order to make money.

B. S. Easton writes: "The secular origin of this list is seen not only by its close parallels in Greek writers but in the very moderate moral standard it sets; the warning that power should not be entrusted to drunkards, brawlers and embezzlers might not be out of place in a Greek city, but such vices ought to exclude a man not only from the Christian ministry but from the Christian church altogether. So no attempt should be made to soften the language; as in other instances, a familiar formula is used without reflecting on the inappropriateness of some of its terms." (*The Pastoral Epistles* [New York: Charles Scribner's Sons, 1947], p. 84.) Nevertheless, traditional though the list may have been, it cannot have seemed absurdly inappropriate to the situation, or it would not have been used.

**8.** This verse lists six virtues. **Hospitable:** See on I Tim. 3:2. **A lover of goodness** (φιλάγαθος: only here in the N.T.) : One who gladly and sacrificially devotes himself to doing and being good. **Master of himself** (σώφρων) : See on I Tim. 3:2, where the word is translated "sensible" in the RSV. It encloses a variety of meanings: prudent, reserved, reflective, serious-minded. **Upright, holy:** "A just man, a religious man" (Moffatt) ; "He will be just toward his neighbor (δίκαιος) and holy or religious (ὅσιος) toward God" (Spicq) , two virtues similarly associated in I Tim. 6:11; I Thess. 2:10; Eph. 4:24.

**Self-controlled:** ἐγκρατής, only here in the N.T. The two virtues **master of himself** (σώφρων) and **self-controlled** (ἐγκρατής) , more Greek than Jewish, are closely related to each other in Stoic thought. Self-control "has small place in biblical religion because the Christian life is determined by God's command, and self-control loses its high position, asceticism being cut off as a method of meriting salvation" (Gerhard Kittel, *Theologisches Wörterbuch zum Neuen Testament* [Stuttgart: W. Kohlhammer, 1935], II, 340) . **Upright, holy, and self-controlled** do not occur in the list of I Tim. 3.

---

thought by some that among them were those who returned to their native island and preached the gospel. **I left you in Crete** suggests that the author of this epistle had labored there, but nothing is known of any such mission. When Paul as a prisoner was on his way to Rome his ship was in port for a time on the island of Crete (Acts 27:7-9) , but it is inconceivable that it was at that time that the church was planted. The church in Crete was probably the fruit of the labors of forgotten men, whose names were not remembered, but whose work endured on an unfavorable soil. The Christian church must always be served by those who are willing to lose themselves in Christ's cause, and have learned to find their satisfaction in the faith that in his providence no such service is ever wasted. Whittier spoke for such self-effacing servants in his poem, "My Triumph." "Blessed are the dead who die in the Lord; . . . that they may rest from their labors, for their deeds follow them" (Rev. 14:13) .

9 Holding fast the faithful word as he hath been taught, that he may be able by sound doctrine both to exhort and to convince the gainsayers.

10 For there are many unruly and vain talkers and deceivers, specially they of the circumcision:

self, upright, holy, and self-controlled; 9 he must hold firm to the sure word as taught, so that he may be able to give instruction in sound doctrine and also to confute those who contradict it. 10 For there are many insubordinate men, empty talkers and deceivers, especially the circumcision party;

---

III. THE BISHOP'S FUNCTION: TO MAINTAIN SOUND DOCTRINE (1:9-16)

**9. Hold firm to the sure word as taught:** "Titus'" preaching must strictly conform to "the teaching," i.e., the received apostolic, Pauline teaching, which is at the same time the teaching of Christ (I Tim. 6:3). Here the bishop's chief function is (a) positively, **to give instruction in sound doctrine;** (b) negatively, **to confute those who contradict it.**

**10.** The appointment of authoritative church officials of unimpeachable character and of unquestioned orthodoxy is necessitated by the alarming number (**many**) of **insubordinate men, empty talkers and deceivers,** who have become active in the Cretan churches. As is usual in dealing with heretics, the author indulges in name-calling rather than in description and analysis.

**Especially the circumcision party** is commonly taken to mean either Jews (so Dibelius, Easton) or Jewish Christians; Moffatt translates, "those who have come over from Judaism" (so Spicq). G. Abbott-Smith (*A Manual Greek Lexicon of the New Testament* [New York: Charles Scribner's Sons, 1929]) observes that the Greek phrase in question here (οἱ ἐκ τῆς περιτομῆς) means Jews in Rom. 4:12, Jewish Christians in Acts 11:2; Gal. 2:12; and here (so also Walter Bauer, *Wörterbuch zum Neuen Testament* [Berlin: Töpelmann, 1937]).

Since the meaning of the phrase "those of the circumcision" is not self-evident, its interpretation here must be determined by the nature of the heresy combated in the letter (or letters) and by whether or not the heretics were members of the church, claiming the Christian name, or were outside of the church, a rival attacking group. Actually, the Pastorals do not give us enough information to provide a final answer to either question. The probabilities are, however: (a) In general, the heresies opposed in the three Pastorals are the same. Even if Titus alone has the phrase "those of the circumcision," and alone qualifies "myths" in vs. 14 with "Jewish," the language used to describe the heresy or heresies in the Pastorals is so similar in the three letters as to make unwarrantable the supposition that the heresy of I and II Timothy is Christian Gnosticism, and that of Titus, Jewish Gnosticism. That in the author's mind the heresies are essentially the same is clear from his description of all of them as "myths" in vs. 14; I Tim. 4:7; II Tim. 4:4. (b) The later the date to which the Pastorals are assigned, the fewer the Jewish Christians would be in the churches, and therefore the less the probability that here "those of the circumcision" are Jewish Christians, i.e., "those who have come over from Judaism" (Moffatt). As church and synagogue became fully consolidated over against

---

**10-11.** *Free Speech in Crete?*—At first reading this seems like dangerous doctrine. Not content with urging the appointment of good men as elders or bishops, Paul points out that confusion is being wrought in the church by **insubordinate men, empty talkers and deceivers, who are upsetting whole families by teaching for base gain what they have no right to teach.** Paul's remedy is a drastic one: **They must be silenced.** This is dangerous doctrine, because the first measure taken by tyranny is always the silencing of the opposition. Freedom of teaching, freedom of the press, freedom of the pulpit are essential to freedom of conscience, freedom of worship, and

freedom to obey God rather than men. As a general rule it is better to allow error freedom to expose itself to public criticism than to create for it an atmosphere of mysterious glamour by trying to bottle it up. Many political and religious absurdities have been talked to death on the soapboxes of Hyde Park and Union Square which would have won multitudes of disciples if driven underground. But there is no such thing as an unqualified freedom, short of complete anarchy. Educational institutions devoted to freedom of research would not knowingly employ teachers who are committed to the destruction of intellectual freedom. The church, which

11 Whose mouths must be stopped, who subvert whole houses, teaching things which they ought not, for filthy lucre's sake.

12 One of themselves, *even* a prophet of their own, said, The Cretians *are* always liars, evil beasts, slow bellies.

11 they must be silenced, since they are upsetting whole families by teaching for base gain what they have no right to teach.

12 One of themselves, a prophet of their own, said, "Cretans are always liars, evil

---

each other in mutual antagonism, the number of Jewish converts would be negligible. (c) Nevertheless, it seems equally clear that the "false teachers," who seemed to our author so great a peril to faith and doctrine that only an out-and-out attack upon them could protect the church against them, were a vigorous group within the church, not outside. It was with reference to its own needs and functions as a religious organism that the young church, confronted within itself with a bewildering variety of religious ideas and practices, was moved to formulate its creed, to establish clarity and uniformity of belief, to stabilize its ministry and to determine what its sacred scriptures should be. (d) The most reasonable conjecture is that, given a later date for the Pastorals, "those of the circumcision" were neither Jews nor Jewish Christians, but Gentile Christians who were attracted to Jewish practices and were concerned to retain as obligatory for Christians a more considerable body of Jewish customs than Paul or "Paul" could admit (see Intro., pp. 352-53).

**11. They must be silenced:** Just how their **mouths must be stopped** (KJV) is not said, but probably the import of the paragraph is that elders must prohibit such teachers from preaching or teaching in the church. Obviously the heretical movement is a popular one since its leaders **are upsetting whole families.**

Like the heretics of I Tim. 6:3, the Cretan heretics are accused of perverting religion in order to make money. Although vs. 12 indicates that the writer knew of the bad reputation for avariciousness which the Cretans had (see Cicero *Republic* III. 9. 15; Livy XLIV. 45; Plutarch *Aemilius Paulus* XXIII; Polybius *History* VI. 46), the weapon has always been a handy one to use in discrediting an opponent.

**12.** This verse savagely attacks the Cretan heretics with a singularly indiscreet quotation which overreaches itself to defame all Cretans. Out of their own mouths they stand condemned: **One of themselves,** no less than **a prophet of their own, said, "Cretans are always liars, evil beasts, lazy gluttons."**

Although unnamed, the prophet referred to is probably Epimenides of Cnossos, a half-mythical sixth-century Greek, variously described as poet, prophet (Aristotle *Rhetoric* III. 17. 10; Cicero *Divination* I. 18. 34), religious reformer to whom the Cretans offered sacrifices (Diogenes Laertius *Lives of Eminent Philosophers* I. 11), one of the seven sages (Plutarch *Solon* XII), and the reputed author of a body of literature extant

---

would not dream of silencing criticism from without, would not choose for its leaders those likely to teach "objectionable doctrine for the base end of making money" (Moffatt). Churches may legitimately have processes for removing from posts of leadership men who use their privileged positions for unworthy purposes. Such powers should be rarely used, and only as a last resort. It may be assumed that the situation in Crete had reached that state.

**12-14. The Truth Shall Make You Free.**—To lead a Christian church in Crete was no easy assignment. **One of themselves, a prophet of their own, said, "Cretans are always liars, evil beasts, lazy gluttons."** The Exeg. refers to the

author of this saying as "probably Epimenides of Cnossos, a half-mythical sixth-century Greek." Scott says, more definitely:

The allusion is to Epimenides, a Cretan, who lived about 500 B.C., and who was numbered among the seven wise men of Greece. . . . On his instruction an altar was raised "to an unknown God," and there is therefore a twofold link between this heathen sage and the New Testament.[6]

At any rate, this is a most unflattering picture of the character of the Cretans. The crux of the criticism is that they are **always liars** and there-

⁶ *Pastoral Epistles,* p. 159.

13 This witness is true. Wherefore rebuke them sharply, that they may be sound in the faith;

14 Not giving heed to Jewish fables, and commandments of men, that turn from the truth.

beasts, lazy gluttons." 13 This testimony is true. Therefore rebuke them sharply, that they may be sound in the faith, 14 instead of giving heed to Jewish myths or to com-

---

in the first century. (On the problem see F. J. Foakes Jackson and Kirsopp Lake, eds., *The Beginnings of Christianity* [London: Macmillan & Co., 1933], V, 246-51, Note XX, "Your Own Poets"; Martin Dibelius, *Die Pastoralbriefe* [2nd ed.; Tübingen: J. C. B. Mohr, 1931; "Handbuch zum Neuen Testament"], *ad loc.*; C. Spicq, *Saint Paul: les Épitres Pastorals* [Paris: J. Gabalda, 1947], *ad loc.*) Although some Greeks held that Epimenides lived 154 or 157 years, the Cretans extended it to 299.

Epimenides, it appears, called the Cretans liars because they claimed to have the tomb of Zeus among them, whereas his devotees said he was not dead but alive and risen. However, the author of Titus may or may not have known a specific context for the quotation. Such sayings quickly become proverbial. As is common enough today, so was it common in antiquity to regard all foreigners as liars. Cicero declared that the Greeks had a genius for lying (*Letters to Quintus* I. 2. 4). A Greek proverb said that the three peoples whose name begins with "C," the Cretans, the Cappadocians, and the Cilicians, were the worst "C's." Just as "to Corinthianize" in Greek meant to live dissolutely, "to Cretize" meant to lie and deceive.

In a real letter addressed to Cretans the quotation would be singularly untactful. And in any case, the elders "Titus" would appoint would have to be Cretan elders. There must have been some good Cretans. Unless the Cretan destination of the letter is entirely fanciful and unreal, and was conceived by the writer in order to blacken the names of his opponents by smearing them with the reputed Cretan depravity, we should have to suppose either that Titus was strictly a private letter to a non-Cretan named "Titus," or that the writer was strangely insensitive to the insult he was inflicting on the Cretan brethren by the use of so devastating a quotation.

**13.** The author's experience with Cretans confirms the judgment of the prophet (vs. 12). A rational or moral appeal is useless in dealing with such depraved people. Only vigorous rebuke will bring them to a sound Christian faith. But whether by gentle persuasion (II Tim. 2:25) or by severe castigation, the persistent duty of the bishop is to protect the church from heresy and if possible to restore the erring to sound faith.

**14. Jewish myths** would be (Gnostic) speculations based on the O.T. scriptures. To describe them as **Jewish** is to designate them as belonging to an old dispensation now superseded; to describe them as **myths** is to brand them as fantasy, not revealed religion. The **commands of men** (see Isa. 29:13; Mark 7:7; Col. 2:22) here refers to prohibition of marriage and proscription of foods (I Tim. 4:3-6). And since the commands in question are those **of men who reject the truth,** i.e., the Christian faith as the writer understands it, they are to be forthrightly rejected.

---

fore, having no respect for truth themselves, are likely to be deceived by other men who **reject the truth.** Titus is told to rebuke such persons sharply. The twentieth century has seen a revival of the idea that there is no objective truth to be respected and served. Naturally, it has been dictators who have taught this false doctrine, for, as F. R. Barry says, "If men once abandon trust in Reason and in the objectivity of Truth, they are playing straight into the hands of tyrants, whether Fuhrers or impersonal

collectives." [7] If men believe that truth is simply what serves their own advantage, politically, financially, or in any other way, the result is chaos. "To believe in God means, at the very least, that there is a Truth to be known and a Goodness to be reverenced and served, that Justice and Love belong to the nature of things and are neither 'relative' nor illusory." [8]

[7] *Recovery of Man* (New York: Charles Scribner's Sons, 1949), p. 11.
[8] *Ibid.*, p. 13.

15 Unto the pure all things *are* pure: but unto them that are defiled and unbelieving *is* nothing pure; but even their mind and conscience is defiled.

mands of men who reject the truth. 15 To the pure all things are pure, but to the corrupt and unbelieving nothing is pure; their very minds and consciences are corrupted.

---

**15. To the pure all things are pure** has the ring of a proverb. Even if its identical form is not found elsewhere in the N.T. (nor indeed outside; but see Philo *On the Special Laws* III. 208-9; Seneca *Epistle* XCVIII. 3), yet the idea is proverbially used as warrant for engaging in practices traditionally regarded as taboo. Jesus was believed to have given expression to the idea in Mark 7:14-15 (cited by Paul in Rom. 14:14) and Luke 11:41, thereby asserting that purity is of the heart, releasing men in principle from the error of thinking that religious purity can be attained by correct performance of specified ritual or by careful avoidance of practices declared (ritually) "unclean," and releasing them in fact from the necessity of observing those precepts in Judaism, whether written or unwritten, which were to be interpreted as ceremonial rather than moral. In the present passage the writer brandishes the familiar saying in his own defense to justify Christian practice of marriage and enjoyment of foods (see I Tim. 4:3; 5:23): to the spiritually pure all (an overstatement) things are (ritually) pure. The reason why **to the corrupt and unbelieving** [with special reference to the false teachers] **nothing** [an overstatement] **is pure,** not even marriage, or "foods which God created to be received with thanksgiving by those who believe" (I Tim. 4:3), is that **their very minds and consciences are corrupted,** i.e., the impurity is in their souls, not in the created world. Since their souls are totally depraved, they think the world is. The heart of the verse is that purity is a matter of the mind and conscience, not an attribute of things.

---

**15-16. *The Secret Places of the Heart.*—**The writer of Proverbs had a saying, "Keep thy heart with all diligence; for out of it are the issues of life" (Prov. 4:23). This doctrine that the outwardly good life flows from the inwardness of right desires, purposes, and loyalties appears in a variety of places in the N.T. It is at the heart of the Sermon on the Mount. "Every sound tree bears good fruit, but the bad tree bears evil fruit. . . . Thus you will know them by their fruits" (Matt. 7:17, 20). It is at the heart of Paul's discussion of the impotence of outward law as compared with life-giving Spirit. "There is therefore now no condemnation for those who are in Christ Jesus. For the law of the Spirit of life in Christ Jesus has set me free from the law of sin and death." (Rom. 8:1-2.) It is echoed in this passage: **To the pure all things are pure, but to the corrupt and unbelieving nothing is pure; their very minds and consciences are corrupted.** It was probably a very restricted application of this truth to which Titus' attention was called in connection with the Christian attitude toward marriage and foods. But there is no reason why in our time the words should not be given the wider application to which they naturally lend themselves. They might be paraphrased simply for modern life as follows: It is possible for a good man to live a good life in an evil world, but

if life has gone bad at the heart everything is bad. Men and women compelled to work under degrading circumstances; people whose eyes and ears are assaulted every hour by suggestions of a life in which they would not for all the world participate; folk who are involved in an economic system and an international order which only partially satisfies their consciences; citizens who by their citizenship support some state actions in which they do not believe; young people whose lives are set in families which do not share the ideals and purposes which have captured the younger generation—everyone in some way or other faces the problem of living in the midst of a life which is ethically and spiritually alien to his own. On particular issues it is sometimes necessary to make a clean break. But no one can resign from society. He must confess that both ignorantly and knowingly he is a partner in much that is wrong, and he must ask for God's forgiveness for his share in the common guilt of mankind. He will never be sinless in this world, but in the secret places of the heart he must fight for singleness of purpose to please God. "Blessed are the pure in heart: for they shall see God" (Matt. 5:8). **To the pure all things are pure.** To the extent that the inner life is cleansed of evil motive, the outer life can be leavened with a right spirit.

16 They profess that they know God; but in works they deny *him,* being abominable, and disobedient, and unto every good work reprobate.

2 But speak thou the things which become sound doctrine:

2 That the aged men be sober, grave, temperate, sound in faith, in charity, in patience.

16 They profess to know God, but they deny him by their deeds; they are detestable, disobedient, unfit for any good deed.

2 But as for you, teach what befits sound doctrine. 2 Bid the older men be temperate, serious, sensible, sound in faith, in

---

16. These ascetics are also Gnostics: **They profess** [proudly and publicly] **to know God,** to have immediate, certain, incontrovertible knowledge of him. Their actions, however, with equal publicity belie their profession and prove their vaunted knowledge false. Indeed, they are **detestable,** utterly abhorrent to God, because **disobedient** to him and his church. Refusing to obey church authority, they have become **unfit for any good deed.**

### IV. The Duties of the Minister to His Congregation (2:1-10)

**2:1.** In contrast to the false teachers, "Titus" is commanded to **teach what befits** [i.e, conforms to] **sound doctrine.** The concern of the writer here, however, is no more with the details of **sound doctrine** as such than it was in 1:14 with the details of the "Jewish myths" or "commands of men," or with what the "empty talkers" of 1:10 said. The discussion is carried on, less on a doctrinal than on an ethical and practical basis. Advices are to be conveyed to five (why five?) groups of people within the church: older men (vs. 2) and older women (vs. 3), younger women (vss. 4-5) and younger men (vss. 5-6), and slaves (vss. 9-10), with a second and special admonition to "Titus" himself (vss. 7-8).

As is typical of the Pastorals, the morality here urged is in no sense specifically Christian, but is a good account of conventional behavior as approved in any patriarchal society anywhere. It is a civil, not a heroic morality, family rules adapted to Christian purposes. The concern here is primarily that the various age, sex, and status groups shall practice those virtues which make for harmony within the church and thereby create respect for the church on the part of those outside.

**2. Older men:** Not "elders" in the sense of church officials. Nevertheless, the virtues listed are essentially the same as those required of officials.

In the patriarchal family old age is a crown of glory. Authority and prestige increase with the years. The qualities admired and expected in both men and women

---

**16. Words and Deeds.**—Here is the note so often struck in the Pastoral epistles, the condemnation of religious profession which does not bear fruit in Christian life. Nowhere is the verdict on such insincerity so scathing. Such people are **detestable, disobedient, unfit for any good deed.** The condemnation is not too strong. Whenever a man who has been a leader in the church is revealed to be involved in corruption, the faith of the community in all virtue is shaken. Conversely, whenever a crisis or the daily round of life reveals character that is Christlike, the faith of the community in all goodness is strengthened. When Dr. Wilson, an Edinburgh minister, died, Robert Rainy spoke "of the value for their whole community of having within it a man whom you could not see

on the street without wondering on what unselfish errand he was hastening." [9]

**2:1. To Every Man His Task.**—But as for you, says Paul, **teach what befits sound doctrine.** There is deep significance in this emphasis upon the second person singular. Titus was a particular man in a particular situation facing particular circumstances. No one else in all the world faced that particular challenge with his unique equipment at just that juncture of place and time and people. This was the task which God had committed to him alone. Every individual finds himself in some unique situation where he has something unique to contribute. This is God's summons to him and to no one

[9] W. M. Macgregor, *The Making of a Preacher* (London: Student Christian Movement Press, 1945), p. 35.

3 The aged women likewise, that *they be* in behavior as becometh holiness, not false accusers, not given to much wine, teachers of good things;

love, and in steadfastness. 3 Bid the older women likewise to be reverent in behavior, not to be slanderers or slaves to drink; they

---

are ripe wisdom, stability, dignity, and poise. Therefore the virtues listed in vss. 2-5 are typical family virtues.

That both older men and women are warned to be **temperate** (νηφάλιος), **not slaves to drink,** may be due to the observation that "many old people are drunkards" (Antiphon *Third Tetralogy* IV. 2). Nevertheless, the same requirement is made of the bishop in I Tim. 3:2 and of the women in I Tim. 3:11.

To be **serious** (σεμνός) is likewise expected of deacons in I Tim. 3:8 and of the women in I Tim. 3:11. **Sensible** (σώφρων) is also in the bishop's list (I Tim. 3:2). Obviously the nucleuses of the various lists were not chosen with particular reference to the category concerned. They have grown from basic conventional lists, and only at certain points do they become specifically Christian or are they pointed toward the category in question.

In the present list the author first clearly shows his hand in the characteristic expression, **sound in faith, in love, and in steadfastness,** in which the unusual triad consisting of the two Christian terms "faith" and "love" plus "steadfastness" (ὑπομονή) is added to an older nucleus. One of the striking differences between the language of Paul and that of the writer to "Titus" is that in the latter the Pauline triad "faith, hope, and love" regularly becomes "faith, love, and steadfastness" (see I Tim. 6:11; II Tim. 3:10). Furthermore, **sound in faith** means correct in doctrine. Likewise **steadfastness** in the context means primarily unwavering loyalty to the received faith. It is required of "Timothy" (I Tim. 6:11), exemplified in Paul (and "Paul"[?]; II Tim. 3:10), and expected of older men here.

**3-4.** The older women likewise must **be reverent in behavior.** The adjective **reverent** (ἱεροπρεπής) suggests the demeanor of those who handle holy things in holy places, of priestesses in a temple (cf. I Tim. 2:10). The responsibility of the Christian

---

else. Christian faith holds that God has a purpose for each individual life, and that the deepest meaning in life is found only in the fulfillment of that purpose. Henry Drummond was once asked how a man could find out what the will of God is for him. He opened his Bible, and from its flyleaf read these directions which he had given to many other people, and undoubtedly had himself followed:

First, pray; second, think; third, talk to wise people but don't regard their judgement as final; fourth, beware of the putting forward of your own will, but don't be too much afraid of it. God never unnecessarily thwarts a man's nature and liking. It is a mistake to think that His will is always in the line of the disagreeable. Fifth, meanwhile, do the next thing, for doing God's will in small things is the best preparation for doing it in great things. Sixth, when decision and action are necessary, go ahead. Seventh, you will probably not find out until afterward, perhaps long afterward, that you have been led at all.[1]

[1] David A. MacLennan, *No Coward Soul* (New York: Oxford University Press, 1948), pp. 31-32. Used by permission.

No better advice was ever given for a man who wants to discover his own task.

**1-10. *A Family Tradition.*—**Here is some counsel for each of the groups who make up family circles—older men and women, young men, and young women, and servants. It is similar to other bits of instruction for families which are found in the N.T. (Col. 3:18–4:1; Eph. 5:22–6:9; I Pet. 2:18–3:7). Quite aside from the particular content of these admonitions, this passage as a whole is a reminder of the value of a family tradition. The Christian family was something new in a pagan world. It was different in kind from the family which had never come under the influence of the spirit of Christ. It was the spirit that was formative and distinctive, but it was inevitable that customs, habits, and principles should have been developed to give expression to that spirit in the life of the group. Today there is a wholesome emphasis upon the place of the individual in the family relationship, because it is apparent that the family, like any other group, can tyrannize over the individual. We think of husbands and wives as equal partners. We believe that children should

4 That they may teach the young women to be sober, to love their husbands, to love their children.

5 *To be* discreet, chaste, keepers at home, good, obedient to their own husbands, that the word of God be not blasphemed.

are to teach what is good, 4 and so train the young women to love their husbands and children, 5 to be sensible, chaste, domestic, kind, and submissive to their husbands, that the word of God may not be

---

matron in home or in church is to set an example of quiet dignity for all who are under her authority. **Not to be slanderers:** The sharp contrast between **reverent in behavior and not . . . slanderers** is even more prominent in Greek, since the word "slanderer" (διάβολος), although regularly meaning such in secular Greek, in the N.T. outside the Pastorals always means devil (see also I Tim. 3:6, 11). Unless the two vices named, **not to be slanderers or slaves to drink,** are to be regarded as a more formal than real listing, we must suppose that elderly Christian women too were quite given to gossip and liquor. Since similar advices are given in I Tim. 3, there is no need to see here any special reference to Cretan bad habits. **They are to teach what is good:** It is the function of the older women to teach the younger women both by precept and example **what is good, and so train the young women to love their husbands and children.** Domestic virtues depend for transmission upon their adequate communication from mother to daughter.

5. The young women must also be trained **to be sensible** [cf. vs. 2; I Tim. 3:2], **chaste, domestic, kind, and submissive to their husbands** (see I Tim. 3:11-12; I Cor. 14:34; Eph. 5:22; Col. 3:18). To the conventional list of wifely duties is added a Christian motivation: **that the word of God may not be discredited** (RSV), lit., **blasphemed** (KJV; cf. I Tim. 6:1). Since Christian women had been granted unusual freedom, it was necessary that they should be unusually careful not to become insubordinate or neglectful at home. Otherwise their actions would scandalize and alienate pagans. To upset the order of the family would be to precipitate social revolution and bring ruin on the church.

---

be respected as individuals, that their unique aptitudes and gifts should be considered, and that they should have their place (the place of children, not adults) in the family councils. But the Christian home today, as in the first century, exists in the midst of a surrounding life much of which is pagan or semipagan. Without permitting the past or present habit to dictate, it is a helpful thing when a family has its own tradition which it has considered and approved. "In our family we go to church." "In our family we give thanks at the table." "In our family we are interested in the work of the church in India." "In our family we are interested in what each member is doing to help other people." Children are fortunate who grow up in a family which has a tradition to which the family is not enslaved but by which each member of the family is stimulated and empowered.

The Exeg. indicates the five groups of people within the church for whom there are special admonitions. At first glance these moral exhortations seem to be uninspiring and humdrum, so obvious as hardly to need mentioning. But

out of them certain principles emerge which were crucial in Paul's day as they are in every age. (*a*) Life can go to pieces in old age as well as in youth (vss. 2-3). It is commonly assumed that if people can weather the temptations of youth, their characters become set and they are morally secure in their later years. But age has its peculiar temptations as well as youth. The sense that they are no longer needed, the realization that they must curtail their activities, the necessity for turning over to younger hands the responsibilities which they have carried, the narrowing circle of friends and contemporaries, the new perspective on past failures and mistakes which age brings, together with the physical and emotional problems which often come with advancing years—these all constitute an invitation to cynicism, bitterness, sometimes to self-indulgence and loss of faith. Hence Paul writes, **Bid the older men be temperate, serious, sensible, sound in faith, in love, and in steadfastness.** Even more startling is the command, **Bid the older women likewise to be reverent in behavior, not to be slanderers or slaves to drink.** Browning gave the world a ringing affirmation

6 Young men likewise exhort to be sober-minded.

7 In all things showing thyself a pattern of good works: in doctrine *showing* uncorruptness, gravity, sincerity,

discredited. 6 Likewise urge the younger men to control themselves. 7 Show yourself in all respects a model of good deeds, and in your teaching show integrity, gravity,

---

**6-8. The younger men,** too, must **control themselves:** The verb (σωφρονεῖν) is the cognate of the adjective "sensible" (σώφρων) used in vss. 2, 5. The virtues urged for all ages, sexes, and stations are the self-effacing and nonaggressive ones.

**In all respects,** which follows immediately in the Greek, may be taken with vs. 6 (Moffatt, Jeremias, Spicq, Dibelius) or vs. 7 (Goodspeed, KJV, RSV).

Vss. 7-8 are, in form at least, an interruption in the advices which "Titus" is to relay to the older men, the older women, the younger men, and the slaves. The writer here abruptly turns to advise "Titus" himself as to his own duties. The purpose of the shift is not clear. The author may think (*a*) of "Titus" as one of **the younger men,** and the advices of vss. 7-8 as really directed to them. Or, (*b*) as a minister, "Titus" must fully sense the responsibility of his office, and fulfill his duty to all groups in the church by showing himself **in all respects a model of good deeds,** and in his **teaching** showing **integrity** and **gravity.** In any case, the integration of the verses into the paragraph is awkward. Obscurity in meaning is due to the fact that in the Pastorals the addressee seems now to be an individual minister as such ("Timothy" or "Titus" as deacon, elder, bishop?), now an individual as type or representative of a group, a collective individual (the diaconate, presbytery or episcopate?), and now certain lay groups within the church. This plurality of ends in view frequently creates obscurity. **A model of good deeds:** A characteristic emphasis of the Pastorals (see I Tim. 5:10). **In your teaching show integrity:** The Greek word (ἀφθορία), meaning "incorruption," occurs only here in the

---

of faith in the possibilities of old age in the lines:

> Grow old along with me!
> The best is yet to be,
> The last of life, for which the first was made:
> . . . . . . . . . . . . .
> Youth shows but half; trust God: see all, nor be afraid! [2]

(*b*) Christians have a responsibility to see **that the word of God may not be discredited** (vs. 5) by their manner of life. In the field of diplomacy it is often said that the good faith of nations must be shown by deeds, not words. So with the faith of Christians. The Christian church must commend its gospel to others by pointing them to Christ, not to itself. Yet it can never escape the fearful responsibility involved in the fact that others will judge the gospel more by what they see than by what they hear. More people have been alienated from Christianity by the unchristian conduct of professing Christians than by intellectual difficulties with the faith. "Ye are our epistle, . . . known and read of all men" wrote the apostle Paul (II Cor. 3:2 ASV). The best apologetic for the Christian faith is always in the lives of those in

whom the redemptive power of the gospel is a visible reality. How to be such a witness without becoming a Pharisee is one of the subtler problems of the Christian life. Paul's solution was to confess that one is always a sinner redeemed by the grace of God in Christ (Eph. 2:8-9). Jesus put the emphasis on the Godward side of grace. "Let your light so shine before men, that they may see your good works and give glory to your Father who is in heaven" (Matt. 5:16).

(*c*) Young men must learn **to control themselves** (vs. 6), or as Moffatt translates the phrase, "to be masters of themselves at all points." This is the Greek virtue of self-control, so highly prized by Stoics, ancient and modern. It must be interpreted in the light of the Christian faith that no man can be master of himself until he acknowledges Christ as his Master. Swinburne missed this essential point in his lines: "Glory to Man in the highest! for Man is the master of things." [3] The tragedy of the modern world is that man is the master of so many things but not master of himself. William Ernest Henley also missed the point in "Invictus":

> I am the master of my fate,
> I am the captain of my soul.

[2] "Rabbi Ben Ezra," st. i.

[3] "The Hymn of Man."

| 8 Sound speech, that cannot be condemned; that he that is of the contrary part may be ashamed, having no evil thing to say of you. | 8 and sound speech that cannot be censured, so that an opponent may be put to shame, having nothing evil to say of us. 9 Bid slaves to be submissive to their masters and to give satisfaction in every respect; they are not to be refractory, 10 nor to pilfer, but to show entire and true fidelity, so that in everything they may adorn the doctrine of God our Savior. |
| --- | --- |
| 9 *Exhort* servants to be obedient unto their own masters, *and* to please *them* well in all things; not answering again; | |
| 10 Not purloining, but showing all good fidelity; that they may adorn the doctrine of God our Saviour in all things. | |

N.T. It is usually interpreted to mean purity of motive, without desire for financial gain, with **sincerity**. However, in the Pastorals, its primary reference is more likely to be to correctness or purity of doctrine. **Gravity:** See I Tim. 2:2; 3:4, 8, 11.

**Sound speech that cannot be censured:** "A wholesome, unobjectionable message" (Goodspeed); "Free from everything to which exception might be taken" (Scott). **Sound speech** in the Pastorals really means orthodox preaching. Confronted by a minister who is **a model of good deeds** and who teaches the truth with sincerity and earnestness, opponents will **be put to shame, having nothing evil to say.** They will not be minded to argue, nor yet to malign; they will be minded to repent. **Opponent,** lit., "he who is against us," i.e., any opponent. The opponents constantly in mind in the Pastorals are first, the false teachers, and second, the non-Christian world in general. Although on the one hand Christians desire to "lead a quiet and peaceable life" (I Tim. 2:2), unmolested by pagan government or people, yet on the other hand they wish to win the heathen world to their faith. To do this they must practice pagan morality at its best. It is such morality, indeed, which "befits sound doctrine" (vs. 1).

**9-10.** (See on I Tim. 6:1-2.) **In every respect** may be taken with "be submissive" (von Soden, Jeremias, Dibelius, Goodspeed, Spicq, Easton) or with **to give satisfaction** (Moffatt, KJV, RSV). **Not to be refractory** means, lit., "not to talk back." Neither is the

No man is the master of his fate so long as he lives in a universe which he did not create, and no man is the captain of his soul so long as there are within him dark forces which need to be redeemed. Paul voiced the paradox of the Christian truth when he wrote: "I have been crucified with Christ; it is no longer I who live, but Christ who lives in me; and the life I now live in the flesh I live by faith in the Son of God, who loved me and gave himself for me" (Gal. 2:20). This is the Christian secret of self-control.

(*d*) A Christian teacher must himself be a model of good deeds (vs. 7), or "an example of good conduct" (Moffatt). This sounds self-righteous and egotistical unless read in the light of basic N.T. teaching. Paul had written to the Corinthian Christians, "Be imitators of me, as I am of Christ" (I Cor. 11:1). They were to imitate his faith in Christ, and good deeds would flow from that faith. So in this passage the Christian teacher is urged to be an example of the kind of faith in Christ which bears the fruits of the Spirit. Wrote Emil Brunner:

When I give myself to God in the obedience of faith, I become free from the anxious intensity of self-absorption, and I love my neighbor as myself. For when I give myself to God, I will what He wills, I love with His love. That is the wonder of *agape*, of that "love of God which is shed abroad in our hearts," when we have found "peace with God."[4]

It is of this kind of faith that the Christian teacher is called to be an example.

(*e*) A Christian should be able to state the case for his faith in intellectually cogent terms (vs. 7). **In your teaching show integrity, gravity, and sound speech that cannot be censured.** Moffatt translates this: "Be sincere and serious in your teaching, let your words be sound and such that no exception can be taken to them." The Exeg. suggests that in this connection **integrity** refers primarily to correctness or purity of doctrine and that **sound speech** means orthodox preaching. It is evident that Paul is pleading for Christians who know what they believe and the grounds on which they believe it, and

[4] *Revelation and Reason*, tr. Olive Wyon (Philadelphia: Westminster Press, 1946), p. 39.

11 For the grace of God that bringeth salvation hath appeared to all men,

12 Teaching us that, denying ungodliness and worldly lusts, we should live soberly, righteously, and godly, in this present world;

11 For the grace of God has appeared for the salvation of all men, 12 training us to renounce irreligion and worldly passions, and to live sober, upright, and godly

---

slave **to pilfer,** a common vice of slaves. Rather, he is to display perfect good faith or **fidelity.** The quality of his behavior is to be determined by the fact that he is a Christian, not by his status as slave, nor yet by the character of his master, whether good or bad. Thus, in everything that he does (or possibly, in the sight of all men) he will **adorn the doctrine of God our Savior,** i.e., the Christian faith.

### V. Working and Waiting (2:11-15)

**11-12.** The Christian ethic, essentially the same for all, whether young or old, men or women, slaves or free men, is grounded both logically and practically in the Christian faith, which is that God as grace has visibly, spectacularly, miraculously appeared, at a precise time and place in history, for the purpose of saving ("offering salvation to," Easton) **all men** (see on I Tim. 2:1-6), and is even now saving us by **training us to renounce irreligion and worldly passions, and to live sober, upright, and godly lives in this world.**

The unusual expression, **the grace of God has appeared,** occurs only here in the N.T. While **grace** always refers to God's lovingkindness, the description of it here as having **appeared** adds to it concrete, even personalized, meaning: **the grace of God** which **has appeared** is nothing less than the Christian gospel or event in its entirety, an event which centers in and revolves about the two "appearings" of the Savior, the first and the final. When God as grace first appeared, it was to give **himself for us to redeem us from all iniquity;** when he again appears, in accord with **our blessed hope,** in glory, it will be to receive us as a purified **people of his own.**

The function of the bishop, "to give instruction in sound doctrine" (1:9), is fully in accord with the purpose of the historical appearance of the grace of God in Jesus, which was to train, to instruct, to educate men, not, it is true, in any merely intellectual,

---

are able to state clearly to others the reasons for the faith that is in them. In many circles there is a tacit assumption that nonbelief is intellectually respectable, and that religious faith requires a gullible mind. Chad Walsh, who was brought up from childhood as an atheist, says that he was a Christian in part because he "gradually became aware of the places where atheism lets you down, both intellectually and emotionally." [5] Three questions in particular confronted him, unanswered by his nonreligious philosophy: Is there such a thing as good and evil? Is there any meaning in life and the universe? Can the individual pull himself up by his own bootstraps? He found a clear-cut answer in the Christian faith. Intellectually, as well as morally and spiritually, Christ is the answer to the world's need. Christians should be able to present him as the answer to a world which has missed the Way.

[5] "Several Roads Lead to Jerusalem," in David Wesley Soper, ed., *These Found the Way* (Philadelphia: Westminster Press, 1951), p. 122.

(f) Even a slave caught in an indefensible economic system can so conduct himself within that system as to **adorn the doctrine of God our Savior** (vs. 10). The problem of the Christian who is a slave has already been discussed under I Tim. 6:1-2. Here three particular obligations are pointed out: **not to be refractory, nor to pilfer, but to show entire and true fidelity.** To be courteous in speech, to be honest, and to be faithful—these are Christian duties anywhere and everywhere. Under totally different systems many people are obliged by their circumstances to work under conditions which do violence to their dignity as persons, and to work under people who are tyrannical and unfeeling. Here is a minimum formula for Christian conduct even in the most unwelcome situations.

**11-13. Grace, Past and Future.**—Two statements seem here to be in contrast. (a) **The grace of God has appeared** speaks of something that has happened. This is the heart of the Christian gospel, the good news of an event which has taken place in history. A preacher at

**13** Looking for that blessed hope, and the glorious appearing of the great God and our Saviour Jesus Christ;

lives in this world, **13** awaiting our blessed hope, the appearing of the glory of our

---

but rather in the practical moral sense, **to renounce irreligion.** . . . If the word "to train" (παιδεύειν) is not used here in its normal Pauline (also LXX) sense of correcting or chastising (I Cor. 11:32; II Cor. 6:9), neither is it used in the Greek sense of the training of the professional as over against the layman. However, Greek education included character formation, and it is with this meaning that the word is used here. Salvation means in the first place, negatively, the renunciation of **irreligion,** i.e., of non-Christian religious ideas and practices; of **worldly** [κοσμικός: see Heb. 9:1; in this sense, only here in N.T., but see I John 2:16; Gal. 5:16; Eph. 2:3; II Clem. 17:3] **passions,** i.e., of all affection for the world outside the church, of all desires not directed toward the spiritual upbuilding of the Christian man; and, positively, a life that is **sober, upright, and godly . . . in this world,** lit., "in the present (evil) age" (see I Tim. 6:17). The Christian who is self-controlled and who does his duty to God and man while he waits the fulfillment of his "blessed hope, the appearing of the glory of our great God and Savior Jesus Christ," is assured of the final full salvation which then begins.

Perhaps the aorist tense of the Greek participle translated **to renounce** (ἀρνησάμενοι) should be taken as referring to a specific event in the Christian's life, such as baptism, when an overt renunciation of the world and the flesh was publicly made.

**13-14.** The Christian's life is one of waiting, of eager and active expectation of the final great event, **the glorious appearing** (see II Tim. 1:10), when the object of the Christian hope, blessed because it rests in God and is therefore certain of fulfillment, becomes a reality, and the Christian sees the **glory of our great God and Savior Jesus Christ,** i.e., he sees God. The descent of Christ is his ascent to the throne of the kingdom of God. His **appearing** is his enthronement.

**Great** is applied to God in the N.T. only here, although it occurs frequently in the O.T., especially in the Psalms, Isaiah, and later writings. It is common in secular Greek as an epithet of gods or kings, and means "powerful." Easton (*Pastoral Epistles,* p. 95) writes: " 'Great' as an attribute of deity belongs rather to Oriental than Greek religious terminology, and it was largely used in Greek to describe Oriental gods (Acts 19.28, 34)."

The Greek of **our great God and Savior Jesus Christ** is ambiguous and therefore capable of being interpreted as referring to two persons rather than one and translated as in the RSV mg., **the great God and our Savior** (so Moffatt, Scott, Jeremias). It is

---

Oxford once remarked that it is the modern temper to cry in despair, "Look what the world has come to!" while the early Christians shouted for joy, "See what has come to the world!" God has revealed his loving purpose "to save all men" (Moffatt). Here is a clear-cut statement of the universalism of the gospel. (*b*) **Awaiting our blessed hope, the appearing of the glory of our great God and Savior Jesus Christ** speaks of something that is yet to be. There is a redemptive work still to be done in this present world as men yield more completely to the spirit of Christ **who gave himself for us to redeem us from all iniquity and to purify for himself a people of his own who are zealous for good deeds.** The modern saying, "Salvation is character," is incomplete, but Paul obviously thinks of Christian character and salvation as being two facets of one reality. This hope, how-

ever, is not limited to the present world. We need not argue about the details of the future life, but implicit in the Christian faith is the blessed hope of the eternal vision of the glory of God and the holiness of the redeemed. "He that has aye something ahead need never be weary," an old Scottish saying has it. The Christian has had the grace of God revealed in Jesus, and looks forward to fuller, never-ending revelations of **the glory of our great God and Savior Jesus Christ.**

Moffatt throws a helpful light on the mystery of grace by his translation of the opening lines of this passage: "The grace of God . . . schools us . . . to live a life of self-mastery, of integrity, and of godliness in this present world" (vss. 11-12). This is a good picture of the Christian life for young people to consider. Self-mastery refers to a man's attitude toward himself. In-

14 Who gave himself for us, that he might redeem us from all iniquity, and purify unto himself a peculiar people, zealous of good works.

great God and Savior[c] Jesus Christ, 14 who gave himself for us to redeem us from all iniquity and to purify for himself a people of his own who are zealous for good deeds.

[c] Or of the great God and our Savior.

preferable, however, to suppose with most commentators, ancient as well as modern, that both epithets refer to Jesus, even though nowhere else in the N.T. is Jesus spoken of as **our great God.** This is the natural construction in Greek of two nouns following one article ("the"). Also, the language here is obviously framed in reaction to that of the emperor cult and of the mystery religions. Ptolemy I was named "savior and god"; Antiochus and Julius Caesar, "god manifest"; Osiris, "lord and savior." In common usage the compound epithet meant one deity, not two. It should therefore not be surprising that a late Christian writer should speak of Jesus in the same twofold fashion, claiming for him the divine titles which others ascribed to their gods. Furthermore, functions ascribed to Yahweh in the O.T., viz., **to redeem us . . . and to purify for himself a people of his own,** are ascribed to Jesus (vs. 14). Identity of function prompts identity in name. Also, while Jewish apocalyptic speaks now of the appearing of God, now of the Messiah, the two are never thought of as appearing simultaneously. Such a double appearance would be unthinkable. And in the N.T. it is always the appearing of Christ which is expected, not of God (II Thess. 2:8; I Tim. 6:14-15; II Tim. 4:1; I Pet. 4:13). Therefore we may accept the translation, **our great God and Savior Jesus Christ.** (On the early use of "God" for "Jesus" see A. C. McGiffert, *The God of the Early Christians* [New York: Charles Scribner's Sons, 1924], pp. 41-88.)

If vss. 13-14 are of liturgical origin, a citation from a Greek-Christian hymn or creed, the unusual language here would be attributable to the source rather than to the writer. In any case, it is certainly true that Hellenistic Christians could speak of Christ as **our great God** without any sense of impropriety or without meaning to substitute Christ the Son for God the Father. For certain purposes God and Christ were thought of as one and the same; for other purposes they were distinct and different.

The paradox of the gospel of grace is that **our great God . . . gave himself for us.** This fact constitutes the noblest and most effective motivation for the Christian life. Obedience to God is now not of grudging necessity but the eager spontaneous response of fervent gratitude.

The words **who gave himself for us to redeem us** are based upon words of Jesus in Mark 10:45 (Matt. 20:28; see I Tim. 2:6; Gal. 1:4; Ps. 130:8). However, the language is commonly used in the church to describe the saving work of Christ. Redemption here means liberation from the state of subjection to the power of sin, which is thought of as holding man captive under its evil domination. After liberation from the power of evil, purification follows. As Moses sealed the people of Israel with the blood of the covenant (Exod. 24:8), so Christ with his own blood purified **for himself a people of his own** (Exod. 19:5; Deut. 14:2; Ezek. 37:23; I John 1:7; Heb. 9:14-22; I Pet.

---

tegrity refers to his relationships with other people. Godliness describes his fellowship with God. Life is incomplete which concentrates on one of these relationships and neglects the other two.

Moffatt also uses a vivid phrase to describe the redeemed when he refers to them as people "with a zest for good deeds" (vs. 14). Goodness is sometimes supposed to be synonymous with dullness. Paul thinks of the doing of good deeds as an exciting pursuit. The world is full of

bored people who have missed Paul's secret of finding zest in life. They look for excitement in novelties, stimulants, possessions, power, and freedom from obligations. On such terms life always palls, and sooner or later boredom and monotony set in. It is life lived for great purposes, life with large vistas of service, life bound up with the needs and concerns of others, life filled with the spirit of Christ that is always fresh, always new, always satisfying. This is what Jesus meant by "the life abundant."

15 These things speak, and exhort, and rebuke with all authority. Let no man despise thee.

3 Put them in mind to be subject to principalities and powers, to obey magistrates, to be ready to every good work,

15 Declare these things; exhort and reprove with all authority. Let no one disregard you.

3 Remind them to be submissive to rulers and authorities, to be obedient, to be

---

1:2), a "special" people belonging to him because redeemed by him. As Israel was formerly God's peculiar people, so now the church; as Israel was zealous for the law (Deut. 26:18; Gal. 1:14; Acts 21:20), Christ's new people are to be **zealous for good deeds:** without good deeds there is no salvation.

**15.** As frequently in the Pastorals, the writer now introduces an exhortation to the addressee to communicate what has been said thus far to those under his charge. With this literary device he brings to a conclusion one section of instruction and admonition, and provides a transition to a new section. The three verbs add force: "Titus" is not only to **declare** his message, he shall also **exhort** men to obey it and **reprove** those who refuse to do so. "Titus" is qualified to act with full authority. His message is from God and his commission is apostolic. Therefore no one shall be permitted to **disregard** him. Similar advice to "Timothy" in I Tim. 4:12 (but with καταφρονείτω instead of περιφρονείτω) is motivated by "Timothy's" youth. According to the scheme by which the Pastorals are written, their author is the aged apostle Paul commissioned by Jesus Christ himself, their addressees are the younger clergy, the Timothys and Tituses, who are being established in the succession. The main purpose of the command, however, is to secure recognition of the authority which inheres in the pastoral position, whether the pastor is young or old.

### VI. Christian Conduct in a Non-Christian World (3:1-7)

After having established regulations for the organization of the church and defined the duties of its members, the author now advises "Titus" how Christians should behave toward civil authorities and in pagan society.

**3:1.** (See Rom. 13:1-7; I Pet. 2:13-17.) The church as here conceived is not just a voluntary association of persons assembled for certain purposes designated "religious." It is a "people," a "special" people elected by God, joined to him and to one another through the redemptive work of Christ and the indwelling Holy Spirit, a remnant redeemed from the perishing world, hoping soon to be removed from it, therefore superior to it and not dependent upon it. Established on such a high church-consciousness, Christians might easily conclude that their status as belonging to the people of

---

**15.** *A Great Task.*—Paul repeats the advice that he gave Timothy (I Tim. 4:12), **Let no man despise thee.** Young men who take themselves too seriously sometimes become bumptious and officious. Young men who do not take life seriously become trivial and futile. Paul is reminding Titus that the task to which he is called is important. The gospel which has been entrusted to him is all-important. The church which he serves is the body of Christ. Dwight D. Eisenhower said at the Yale commencement in 1948, "A man should take his job seriously—himself, never." Within limits that is a useful distinction. If a churchman takes himself too seriously he becomes a pompous ecclesiastic. If he takes the kingdom of God seriously, he becomes a consecrated servant of God and man.

**3:1-2.** *The Church and the World.*—Paul recognized that the effectiveness of the church would depend not only on the truth of its message and the power of its preaching, but also on the Christian life which its members could demonstrate. Especially in their relations with those outside the church, Christians had an obligation to live out the gospel they professed. He calls for no heroic virtues or spectacular actions, but for the homely and indispensable attitudes toward other people which make for good social relations. **Be submissive to rulers.** Christians should be law-abiding. There are occasions, as the American Declaration of Independence asserts, when government becomes tyranny, and Christians must obey God rather than men. But these are rare and exceptional

2 To speak evil of no man, to be no brawlers, *but* gentle, showing all meekness unto all men.

ready for any honest work, 2 to speak evil of no one, to avoid quarreling, to be gentle, and to show perfect courtesy toward all

---

God lifted them above the necessity of obeying civil rulers. Against such an attitude the N.T. letters generally protest. After all, the church was dependent for existence and prosperity on securing toleration from the empire. And in any case the very nature of the Christian faith is such as to oblige Christians **to be ready for any honest work.**

The double nouns and verbs, **rulers and authorities, to be submissive, to be obedient,** stress the unqualified necessity for obedience. The problem, what shall the Christian do if the magistrate commands him to renounce his faith or otherwise commit sin, is not considered, although **honest** may be a subtle reservation against unqualified obedience. In any case, what the writer wishes to emphasize here is that beyond a passive, perhaps grudging, obedience the Christian is **to be ready for any honest** [Goodspeed, "useful"] **work,** i.e., to co-operate actively with the government in its public works for the common good.

2. Christians must not speak evil of, abuse, or insult anyone, certainly not those in political authority over them, or indeed the heathen in general. Since the Greek word used here for **to speak evil of** (βλασφημεῖν) may also mean to speak profanely of sacred things (see, e.g., Acts 26:11; I Tim. 1:20), perhaps the writer will also suggest that Christians should not make fun of, or speak with abuse of, the gods worshiped by their heathen neighbors.

**To avoid quarreling** perhaps means to avoid coming into conflict with the government or getting mixed up in political quarrels, thus bringing the church with oneself into disrepute; or more simply, the meaning may be that in all circumstances the Christian should give way when disputes with heathen neighbors arise. Quarreling makes no converts; rather, it increases animus against the church. It is better **to be gentle,** peaceful, conciliatory, moderate in pressing one's rights, and always **to show perfect courtesy toward all men.** The Greek word translated **courtesy** (πραΰτης; Goodspeed, Moffatt, Easton: "gentleness") is too rich in connotation to be satisfactorily rendered by any one word. In the N.T. it is a characteristic Christian virtue. As the opposite of irritability, harshness, insolence, arrogance, it stands first for trustful submission to God, and then a consequent quiet, modest, kindly, patient demeanor toward men. The Christian's conduct, our author says, must be a perpetual demonstration of his perfect trust in God and regard for all men, high or low, friends or enemies, Christian or heathen.

---

occasions. For the most part it is the duty of Christians to recognize that government is the way people co-operate politically for the common good, and that to support good government is a Christian duty. **Be obedient.** Henry Thoreau's essay "Civil Disobedience" has been widely reread in modern times, as men have pondered their duty under totalitarian governments which violated their consciences and outraged humanity. In general, however, Christians feel that they are called to demonstrate a social conscience in their respect for speed laws on the highways, in honest payment of taxes, in scrupulous regard for the customs regulations when traveling, in observance of laws regulating business practices, and in all other matters where civil law does not raise crucial issues for conscience. **Be ready for any honest work.** To do an honest day's work in one's employment,

or in one's study, or in the home is service to God, as Henry van Dyke wrote in "The Toiling of Felix." Scott thinks that this refers to social services.

It means that, when occasion demanded, Christians should be among the foremost in showing public spirit. There would constantly be outbreaks of fire, plague, calamity of various kinds, when all good citizens would desire to help their neighbours, and Christians must respond to these calls.[6]

In most urban communities the modern equivalents of these services might be volunteer service in a hospital, driving a car in the Red Cross Motor Corps, raising funds for the community chest, helping get relief to war victims, promoting wise legislation for the public welfare, and similar enterprises.

[6] *Pastoral Epistles,* p. 172.

3 For we ourselves also were sometime foolish, disobedient, deceived, serving divers lusts and pleasures, living in malice and envy, hateful, *and* hating one another.

4 But after that the kindness and love of God our Saviour toward man appeared,

men. 3 For we ourselves were once foolish, disobedient, led astray, slaves to various passions and pleasures, passing our days in malice and envy, hated by men and hating one another; 4 but when the goodness and loving kindness of God our Savior appeared,

3. Already in vs. 2 the thought has leaped beyond concern with the behavior of Christians toward "rulers and authorities" to concern with their behavior toward **all men.** Although **we ourselves** [Christians] **were once foolish, disobedient . . . , hating one another,** now everything is different: from all these mistaken and hateful attitudes and practices, Christians have been saved. Therefore, "Titus" shall "remind them" (does "them" mean the clergy? Christians in general? even non-Christians?) that the church is the home of friendship and co-operation, of the affirmative life, of loving and being loved. In contrast to the warm radiance of this new Christian fellowship, the old pagan life is wretched indeed.

The vices enumerated have little reference, if any, to (political) "rulers and authorities." Rather, they are a description of pre-Christian and non-Christian life. **We . . . were . . . foolish:** Without intelligence or understanding, not knowing God or the meaning of life. **Disobedient:** To God's will as known in nature and conscience, and as a natural consequence disobedient to parents and to all rulers. **Led astray:** seeking to be freed from God they became deceived into enslavement to **passions and pleasures** of every sort, prodigals, living riotously under the domination of the violent and baser passions and pleasures, living out their lives in wickedness **(malice),** doing only evil, insatiably envious, wholly loveless, **hating** and being **hated.**

4. For Christians this wretched sort of life came to an end **when the goodness and loving kindness of God our Savior appeared.** When men, blinded by selfish passions, rejected God and hated one another, even then God appeared (in Jesus), unexpectedly and dramatically, before their very eyes, as **goodness and loving kindness,** to save them from their self-inflicted misery. The Greek word for **goodness** (χρηστότης) carries a variety of meanings: kindly generosity, concern to aid those in need, sense of pity (cf. Rom. 2:4; 11:22; Eph. 2:7). **Loving kindness** (φιλανθρωπία) is a synonym frequently joined with **goodness** by philosophers, where it is the equivalent of the Latin *humanitas,* meaning respect for man as man and including the idea of benevolence. Regarded as a

**Speak evil of no one.** A subtle way of building up one's own conceit is to talk other people down. Many artists are hypercritical of other artists, teachers of other teachers, and alas, preachers of other preachers. Jealousy often masquerades as discrimination. "Charity envieth not, . . . thinketh no evil, . . . rejoiceth not in iniquity, but rejoiceth in the truth" (I Cor. 13:4-6). **Avoid quarreling.** A Christian cannot avoid all controversy. There are times when he must differ firmly and resolutely from other people. Two Christians, however, should be able to be on opposite sides of an argument without permitting it to become a quarrel. They should be able to contend stoutly for what they believe without ill will or lack of respect for each other. It was said of one man in public life that no matter how hotly he advocated his positions in debate, he was always ready to meet his opponents on friendly terms when the debate was

over. The worst way to commend Christian faith is to become involved in quarrels about it. **Be gentle.** Easton says this means that the Christian should be considerate of others. If so, it is synonymous with the final admonition, **Show perfect courtesy toward all men.** In sum, the writer of the epistle says that the Christian should show himself to the outside world as a good citizen and a Christian gentleman. There are loftier statements of Christian ethics than this, but none which contradict this elementary truth.

**3-8.** *A Personal Testimony.*—The most persuasive apologetic for Christian faith in every age is the simple, sincere statement of the man who has found his life made new by the power of Christ. Paul's epistles abound in this autobiographical note, not in pride or self-satisfaction, but in humility and thanksgiving. Rom. 7-8 contains the classic statements of this ex-

5 Not by works of righteousness which | 5 he saved us, not because of deeds done by
we have done, but according to his mercy | us in righteousness, but in virtue of his own
he saved us, by the washing of regenera- | mercy, by the washing of regeneration and
tion, and renewing of the Holy Ghost; |

---

noble virtue, it was frequently ascribed to rulers in the Hellenistic Age. Gilbert Murray observes that "in the honorific inscriptions and in the writings of the learned, philanthropy (φιλανθρωπία) is by far the most prominent characteristic of the God upon earth" (*Five Stages of Greek Religion* [Oxford: Clarendon Press, 1925], pp. 189-90). Easton believes that "the terms are deliberately taken from the language of the Emperorcult and may be actually copied from an inscription in honor of Caligula or Nero; not such men as these but God is the true Saviour" (*Pastoral Epistles*, p. 99).

**5, 7.** The initiative for man's salvation lay wholly with God, nor was it prompted by any good deeds that man had done (see Rom 3:24; 9:11). Salvation is not given as due reward for merit; it is bestowed by grace alone, or in the language of the Pastorals, **in virtue of his own mercy.**

Salvation was effected in the rite of baptism, an act of cleansing, of regeneration, of making new, accomplished by the Holy Spirit, which God **poured out upon us richly through Jesus Christ . . . , so that we might . . . become heirs in hope of eternal life.** Although the ideas expressed in the passage are characteristic of the N.T. and of early Christianity, the words by which they are conveyed are unusual. **Washing** as a term for baptism occurs elsewhere in the N.T. only in Eph. 5:26. **Regeneration** (παλιγγενεσία) occurs elsewhere only in Matt. 19:28, where it refers to the messianic age or the age to come, the new world which is to replace this one, and is therefore translated "in the new world" by the RSV, Goodspeed, Moffatt. When God destroys the first world he will create a second. Although the second world was commonly thought of as discontinuous with the first, as a really new beginning, from another point of view it was thought of as a restoration or re-creation of the original uncorrupted world as it first came clean from the hand of God. Since in both Jewish and Greek thought change was equated with decay, and history with degeneration, such words and ideas as regeneration, re-creation, a making new, a new creature, rebirth, second birth, restoration, renewal, came to Christian thought carrying a rich variety of meanings, and furnishing the spirit of man with hope of and faith in a final salvation, with certainty of fulfillment of life in a world which was believed to be irredeemably corrupt and destined to perish without leaving a trace. In these words are clearly mirrored certain basic ancient views of historic process, of man's place in time and eternity, and of the Christian way of restating them. Although natural man was destined to pass away with the corrupt world of which he is a part, a new act of creation, a new begetting has taken place within Christian man so that he is no longer subject to the powers of the perishable world. Christians are now "a new creation" (II Cor. 5:17). As sons of God (Rom. 8:14-23; Gal. 4:5-7; Phil. 2:15; Eph. 1:5), they have been set "free from the law of sin and death" (Rom. 8:2), they

---

perience. Here it is described in vivid, specific terms. To be lost was to be **foolish, disobedient, led astray, slaves to various passions and pleasures, passing our days in malice and envy, hated by men and hating one another; but when the goodness and loving kindness of God our Savior appeared** all that was changed. It is not fear that changes men's hearts, but an apprehension of the love of God revealed in Christ.

> Love so amazing, so divine,
> Demands my soul, my life, my all.

Whether or not, as the phrase **This is a faithful saying** seems to indicate, the rest of this long sentence is the quotation of some well-known creedal statement, it contains the heart of Christian theology. Note the giant affirmations: (*a*) **He saved us,** (*b*) **not because of deeds done by us in righteousness, but in virtue of his own mercy,** (*c*) **by the washing of regeneration and renewal in the Holy Spirit,** (*d*) **which he poured out upon us richly through Jesus Christ our Savior,** (*e*) **so that we might be justified by his grace,** (*f*) **and become heirs in hope of**

no longer live "in the flesh" (Rom. 7:5; 8:9) but "by the Spirit" (Rom. 8:9; Gal. 5:25). The first birth is of the flesh, the second of the Spirit (John 3:6). Christians are born "not of blood nor of the will of the flesh nor of the will of man, but of God" (John 1:13). By God's great mercy they "have been born anew . . . through the resurrection of Jesus Christ from the dead . . . to an inheritance which is imperishable, undefiled, and unfading" (I Pet. 1:3-4). As they have been buried with him by baptism into death (Rom. 6:4), so have they "been raised with Christ" (Col. 3:1), and although the full "revealing of the sons of God" (Rom. 8:19) is yet to take place, it is sure, and "we wait for it with patience" (Rom. 8:25).

Yet further meanings of **regeneration** would be available in N.T. times, e.g., the term is used of the transmigration of the soul in the teachings of Pythagoras; of the mystical rebirth experienced by initiates into the mystery religions; and, among the Stoics, of the periodical restoration of the world after its periodical destruction by fire. It is indeed quite possible that the church adopted the word with polemic intent from the "wise men" (Mazdeans) of Asia Minor (so Spicq), or from the Stoics (Scott). In any case, the term with its rich and varied connotations was one that easily lent itself in Christian language to express the moral and spiritual rebirth of the individual, effected and sealed at conversion or more precisely at baptism, and to confirm Christians in their faith that as reborn in Christ and made new in the Holy Spirit they had truly "become heirs in hope of eternal life" (vs. 7). In the church a new man is being fashioned for the new world, now "kept in heaven" but "ready to be revealed in the last time" (I Pet. 1:4-5).

It is important to recognize that in the Pastorals the experience of regeneration is not a brief ecstasy but a permanent new life, "sober, upright, and godly" (2:12), a moral redemption available to and characteristic of all Christians, making them even while on earth a colony of heaven.

Although there is no evidence to show how commonly in late N.T. times baptism was spoken of as **the washing of regeneration and renewal** [making new] **in the Holy Spirit,** or what the precise connotations of the phrase for any particular Christian might be, the formula undoubtedly reflects the pregnant meaning and central importance of baptism in the early church. As the event in which God's (re-)creative act in man was accomplished, it was the meeting place where cosmology is vanquished by eschatology, the beginning by the end, the temporal by the eternal, sin by righteousness, servitude by freedom, corruption by incorruption, and death by resurrection. Thus baptism became the focal point for the entire pattern of Christian redemption, which in our text is significantly trinitarian: it was God who "saved us" by "regenerating" and "renewing" us **in the Holy Spirit, which he poured out upon us richly through Jesus Christ our Savior.**

---

eternal life. It would be impossible to find a more inclusive or more majestic statement of the things that the Christian church has most surely believed.

A modern version of this testimony is found in Joy Davidman's account of her conversion from communism to Christianity. As a communist she

learned that "love of the people" made it all right for us to lie to the rank and file of the Party; still worse, that in practice our vague "love of the people" turned into quite specific hatred of the people's enemies, and that the enemies of the people were all those of every class and opinion who hap-

pened to disagree with the Party. . . . [After her conversion she acknowledged] the Redeemer who had made himself known, whose personality I would have recognized among ten thousand—well, when I read the New Testament, I recognized him. He was Jesus.

The rest was fairly simple. . . . My beliefs took shape; I accepted the sacraments as meaningful but not magical; I recognized the duty of going to church, while I rejected the claim of any church to infallibility and an absolute monopoly on divine authority. . . . My reward is a happiness such as I never dreamed possible, "In His will is our peace." [7]

[7] "The Longest Way Round," in David Wesley Soper, ed., *These Found the Way* (Philadelphia: Westminster Press, 1951), pp. 25-26. Used by permission.

6 Which he shed on us abundantly through Jesus Christ our Saviour;

7 That being justified by his grace, we should be made heirs according to the hope of eternal life.

8 *This is* a faithful saying, and these things I will that thou affirm constantly, that they which have believed in God

renewal in the Holy Spirit, 6 which he poured out upon us richly through Jesus Christ our Savior, 7 so that we might be justified by his grace and become heirs in hope of eternal life. 8 The saying is sure.

I desire you to insist on these things, so

---

**6.** The Spirit has been **poured out . . .** [see Acts 2:17, 33; Joel 2:28] **richly:** In the apostolic church the Spirit was poured out intermittently and in ecstasy; now as the effective agent in rebirth it permanently transforms the essential nature of the whole man. **Through Jesus Christ our Savior:** On the use of **Savior** in the Gospels see Exeg., I Tim. 1:1. For Christ as mediator of the Spirit see John 15:26; 16:7; Acts 2:33.

**7.** Reborn through the Spirit at baptism, the Christian, cleansed and made new, is thereby **justified,** perhaps both declared and made righteous by God's grace, thought of either as sanctifying power or as God's mercy. The Christian now becomes a true member of God's family, an heir destined for and thus assured of final salvation— **eternal life.** Although in this life Christians are as yet **heirs in hope** only, it is not a fainthearted hope but an assured one needing only patience for its fulfillment.

As is clear from "the saying is sure" (vs. 8; see I Tim. 1:15), at least a portion of vss. 3-7 should be regarded as a quotation, whether from an early Christian sermon (Dibelius), or from a baptismal liturgy (Jeremias, Easton, Spicq, etc.). It remains a question, however, whether the quotation should be thought of as covering the entire section or only a portion of it: Lock accepts vss. 4-6; Moffatt, Meinertz, vss. 4-7; Spicq, vss. 5-7; Easton, Jeremias, vss. 5*b*-7. Since vss. 3-7 are characterized by the use of the first person plural ("we"), less strange in a quotation than in an author who will write as Paul, Dibelius thinks the whole section may belong to the source. However, vs. 3 is less rhythmical in form and liturgical in phrasing than vss. 4-7 and may have been patterned by our author to be an effective introduction to vss. 4-7. Its list of vices would then be intended to serve as the dark shadow against which the light of the Christian gospel shines the more brilliantly. On the basis of liturgical phrasing and balance, and distinctive vocabulary, Easton limits the quotation to vss. 5*b*-7. Obviously the problem of the extent and exact wording of the source cannot be solved with complete certainty.

### VII. Christian Faith Manifest in Works, Not Words (3:8-11)

**8.** In Greek **I desire you to insist on these things** is connected by **and** (KJV) with **the saying is sure.** Therefore **these things** are best taken to refer to vss. 1-7. If Christians— **those who have believed in God**—remember that in baptism they have become new men, they will be certain to practice the virtues named in vs. 1, and they will **be careful to apply themselves to good deeds** (see also vs. 14). The Christian man must live as befits his new nature. **These** [could refer to **good deeds;** however, it is more commonly taken in a more general sense: Goodspeed, "all this"; Moffatt, "such counsels"; Spicq interprets it of the saving truth of vss. 4-7] **are excellent and profitable to men.** (See Spicq, *Saint Paul: les Épitres Pastorales,* pp. 290-97, Excursus XIII, "The Christian Life and Beauty.")

---

**8-10.** *Recapitulation.*—As the letter draws near its close, Paul reiterates what he has said so often before in the Pastoral epistles: The importance of right beliefs is that they provide the incentive to good deeds; Christians should beware of becoming entangled in theoretical arguments which distract the attention and divert energy from the Christian cause; **as for a**

man who is factious, he is **perverted and sinful** and should be avoided. (Note that the phrase **a man that is a heretic** [KJV] is translated in the RSV as **a man who is factious,** while Moffatt uses the term "a factious person," and Easton an even stronger expression, "a man who is obstinately factious.") The Greek word used here is the origin of the English word "heresy"

might be careful to maintain good works. These things are good and profitable unto men.

**9** But avoid foolish questions, and genealogies, and contentions, and strivings about the law; for they are unprofitable and vain.

**10** A man that is a heretic, after the first and second admonition, reject;

that those who have believed in God may be careful to apply themselves to good deeds;[d] these are excellent and profitable to men. **9** But avoid stupid controversies, genealogies, dissensions, and quarrels over the law, for they are unprofitable and futile. **10** As for a man who is factious, after admonishing him once or twice, have nothing

[d] Or *enter honorable occupations.*

The RSV mg., **enter honorable occupations** (also Moffatt), offered as an alternative to **apply themselves to good deeds,** is based upon numerous secular texts in which the idiom is so used. While it is true that in the early church orders Christians were forbidden to practice certain trades such as the making of idols, acting, dancing on the stage, and fighting as a gladiator, the more general meaning of the phrase is better here. It is the business of the Christian to devote himself to doing good. The intensely practical mind of the author reasserts itself here as, after quoting from the liturgy, he returns to his own literary style.

Since faith is not mentioned in the pattern of Christian salvation in vss. 4-7, it is surprising that the writer should speak of Christians as **those who have believed in God** rather than in some such phrase as "those who have been born anew." The passage shows how little he was himself influenced in his own language by the text he quoted. When he is most himself, he thinks of religion in terms of an obedience to the received pattern of faith issuing in **good deeds.** The function of doctrine is to undergird the practical moral life.

**9.** Once again at the close of the letter Titus is admonished to **avoid stupid controversies** (see I Tim. 1:4; II Tim. 2:23), **genealogies** (see I Tim. 1:4; Intro., pp. 356-57), **dissensions** (cf. I Tim. 6:4), **and quarrels over the law** (see I Tim. 1:7-10; II Tim. 2:23). Easton suggests that explicit mention of the (Mosaic) law here may be due, as perhaps in 1:10, 14, to desire for a Pauline coloring; however, for other possible meanings see Exeg. there. Controversies lead to quarrels; both are **unprofitable and futile** because nothing constructive is accomplished by them: they tear down rather than build up the church.

**10.** The Greek word for **factious** (αἱρετικός) occurs only here in the Bible, but the noun form (αἵρεσις) occurs for "factions" in I Cor. 11:19; for "party" (RSV, Goodspeed, Moffatt) of the Sadducees in Acts 5:17, of the Pharisees in Acts 15:5; for "party spirit" (RSV, Goodspeed, Moffatt) in Gal. 5:20; for "sect" (RSV, Goodspeed, Moffatt) of the Nazarenes in Acts 24:5; for "heresies" (RSV, Moffatt; "sects," Goodspeed, Spencer; "ways of thought," R. A. Knox) in II Pet. 2:1. Originally both adjective and noun had a neutral meaning, simply signifying choice. But choice involves both a positive and a negative act. If persisted in and organized, in its positive form it becomes a system or

(cf. Exeg.). Faction is heresy. In Paul's discussion of divisions in the church at Corinth (I Cor. 11:19), where the KJV translators used the word **heretic,** the more recent translations use **factious.** There are deep differences of convictions among Christians which make a united church for the time being unattainable. Factions, however, are not based on principles. They are based upon pride of opinion, personal vanity, love of power, and insufficient grace for co-operation. Many of the divisions among Protestants are in this sense factions. There has

never been a heresy trial in which the defendant was charged with being "a factious person." But faction is a denial of Christ's teaching that "one is your Master, even Christ; and all ye are brethren" (Matt. 23:8), and repudiates the unity which he sought in the prayer "that they may all be one" (John 17:21). Paul's word to Titus concerning the heresy of faction is a stern one. He says that there is no place in the Christian church for the man who cannot be dissuaded from putting petty considerations before the unity of the body of Christ.

11 Knowing that he that is such is subverted, and sinneth, being condemned of himself.

12 When I shall send Artemas unto thee, or Tychicus, be diligent to come unto me

more to do with him, 11 knowing that such a person is perverted and sinful; he is self-condemned.

12 When I send Artemas or Tych'icus

---

school (of philosophy), a party, a sect. Negatively, by rejection of alternatives, it becomes dissent. As destroying unity of fellowship it is thought of as discord; as rejection of the parent pattern of belief, it is thought of as heresy. Since in the history of religions "factions" and "heresies" are so closely related, each being cause and effect of the other, it is not strange that the neutral word "choice" should have developed shades of meaning from light to dark to become progressively evil in connotation: party, party spirit, (dissenting) sect, schismatic or heretical group, even heresy itself. As would be expected in the apostolic age, αἵρεσις means "party"; later, however, when the "rule of faith" had come to be established and the conception of orthodoxy made clear, it meant either "heresy" or "heretics." In II Pet. 2:1 the word clearly means "heresies" as it does in Ignatius (Ign. Eph. 6:2; Ign. Trall. 6:1).

Given a second-century date for Titus, almost inevitably αἱρετικός would include the meaning "heretical." It is true that in vs. 9 it is "controversies" and "quarrels" that "Titus" is to avoid; and that taken closely in its context, αἱρετικός should mean a controversial, quarrelsome, **factious** person. Nevertheless, standing as it does in the place of emphasis at the beginning of the sentence, the **man** suggested by the term seems to be other and more than a quarrelsome person. Also, the concern of the Pastorals with "sound doctrine" suggests that almost certainly αἱρετικός would include its later sense of heretical. The word would then mean a man who was factious because heretical. Such a person is to be warned **once or twice** (see Matt. 18:15-17) and then, if still insubordinate, is to be shunned or rejected. The precise meaning of the verb used for **have nothing more to do with him** is obscure. In I Tim. 5:11 the same word is translated in the RSV as "refuse to enroll." Possibly the word here could mean: Do not receive into church membership any such insubordinate or heretical person. However, almost certainly it is Christians who are being admonished in the letter. Therefore, to **reject** means to excommunicate (see I Tim. 1:20; 3:6-7; 5:20-22). Perhaps the indefiniteness of the word is best explained by taking the verse not as an actual rule of action to be formally applied by "Titus," but rather as an admonitory threat to the reader whom the shoe might fit. As the church sought to ground its unity in a creed, the problem of heresy and discipline became increasingly troublesome.

11. Perverted: distorted, twisted. To persist in disobedience, to continue in schism, to maintain one's opinions after having been admonished to abandon them is to be both **perverted and sinful.** Since such persons sin knowingly and willingly, they are **self-condemned.** And since they have condemned themselves, the church may condemn them with good conscience.

## VIII. Concluding Personal Instructions and Greetings (3:12-15)

12. The mission of Titus to Crete is now assumed to be almost at an end. When either **Artemas** or **Tychicus**—Paul is not sure which he will send—arrives, Titus is to

---

12. *The Delegation of Leadership.*—To the church in Crete, Titus probably seemed like the indispensable man. If, as tradition holds, he was the first bishop of that church, those whom he had led must have wondered how they could get along without his guiding hand. He would have been a little more than human if he had not been tempted to feel that the infant church

was not quite ready to stand on its own feet. Apparently, however, he was to turn over his responsibilities to another. **When I send Artemas or Tychicus to you, do your best to come to me at Nicopolis.** Older church officers today sometimes find it difficult to transfer responsibility to younger men. Churches faced by the necessity of a change of pastors wonder if

to Nicopolis: for I have determined there to winter.

13 Bring Zenas the lawyer and Apollos on their journey diligently, that nothing be wanting unto them.

to you, do your best to come to me at Nicop'olis, for I have decided to spend the winter there. 13 Do your best to speed Zenas the lawyer and Apol'los on their way; see

---

turn over his responsibilities to his successor, and go to Paul at Nicopolis, where by that time he will be spending the winter. **Artemas** is named only here in the N.T. Nothing is known of him, although tradition has made him one of the seventy-two disciples and the first bishop of Lystra. On **Tychicus** see Acts 20:4; Eph. 6:21; Col. 4:7; II Tim. 4:12.

**Nicopolis,** meaning "city of victory," was a name frequently given to new cities founded as a result of or in commemoration of some military victory. Since the **Nicopolis** in question seems to have been a winter resort, perhaps it is best identified with the city of Actia Nicopolis in Epirus on the Adriatic Sea, a city constituted a Roman colony by Augustus in 31 B.C. in commemoration of his victory over Antony and Cleopatra at Actium, and built on the site where his army camped before the battle.

Whether or not Paul actually spent a winter in Nicopolis—in Epirus or elsewhere—cannot be known. If the letter is pseudonymous, the statement of intention is probably evidence of tradition or knowledge that he did. If the section is a genuine Pauline fragment, the decision to winter in Nicopolis may or may not have been realized. Perhaps "Paul" wintered there.

**13. Zenas** is described as a **lawyer** or jurist by way of identification. If Zenas, like Apollos in Acts 18:24; 19:1; I Cor. 1:12; 3:4, 6, 22; 4:6; 16:12, was a converted Jew, he may as a Christian have retained his former Jewish designation as scribe or lawyer. If a Gentile, whether in Paul's time or later, the law he practiced would be Greek or Roman. Nothing further is known about him, although tradition has made him bishop of Diospolis and author of the apocryphal Acts of Titus.

It is natural to identify Apollos with the Alexandrian Jewish Christian associated with Paul in Acts and I Corinthians. It is possible, however, to regard him as a Christian of the same name belonging to "Paul's" own time, and under his supervision.

The text does not say what the mission of Zenas and Apollos was. Frequently it is thought they were the bearers of the letter. This is possible, even though Apollos—if the familiar N.T. figure—was one of the foremost teachers of the church and therefore not likely to be employed as a mere letter carrier. He might have dropped the letter in Crete on his way to Alexandria. However, since the verse does not tell us where Zenas and Apollos were going or for what purpose, it is idle to speculate. The author is concerned

---

they can carry on. The devolution of authority from the older to the younger churches is one of the most pressing strategic problems in the missionary enterprise. But God is not limited in his working to those whom we consider indispensable. Often new leadership appears in unexpected places when the need for it arises. The Christian cause is advanced by a varied fellowship of endeavor, not by brilliant individuals working alone. Sometimes the necessity for delegating authority to new and perhaps untried hands results in a deepening and strengthening of that fellowship.

**12. City of Victory.**—If **Nicopolis** was the city founded by Augustus in Epirus, the reference to it conjures up a strange assortment of contrasted personalities: the Emperor Augustus, in some ways the representative of imperial power at its

best and yet imperial power already containing the seeds of decay; Antony and Cleopatra, gifted and brilliant rulers defeated there, after they had first been defeated by their own personal weaknesses; and strangely enough, Epictetus, who made Nicopolis famous by teaching there after the time of Paul. It is interesting to contrast each of them with Paul, who sought to bring the known world under the rulership of Christ, who found in Christ the power to overcome weakness, and who added to stoic self-control the dynamic of faith in a personal God, devotion to the Lord Jesus Christ, and the hope of the kingdom of God.

**13. Zenas and Apollos.**—Here are two more men whom it is interesting to remember as fellow workers with Paul. They illustrate the variety of gifts employed by the church in its

14 And let ours also learn to maintain good works for necessary uses, that they be not unfruitful.

15 All that are with me salute thee. Greet them that love us in the faith. Grace *be* with you all. Amen.

¶ It was written to Titus, ordained the first bishop of the church of the Cretians, from Nicopolis of Macedonia.

that they lack nothing. 14 And let our people learn to apply themselves to good deeds,*d* so as to help cases of urgent need, and not to be unfruitful.

15 All who are with me send greetings to you. Greet those who love us in the faith. Grace be with you all.

*d* Or *enter honorable occupations.*

---

only to urge "Titus" to do everything possible to make adequate provision for their journey.

**14.** This verse may be interpreted closely with vs. 13 as emphasizing that Christians (**our people**) should always be ready to assist in such necessary acts of generosity as are required by Christian hospitality and the need for help in defraying expenses of traveling missionaries and teachers such as Zenas and Apollos. The church could expand and yet maintain coherence and sense of oneness only if its leaders constantly moved throughout the length and breadth of the land, and if the local Christian groups co-operated fully and gladly in the arduous effort of providing hospitality and requisite travel needs and expenses. Christians who do not share in this work of furtherance of the gospel thereby become **unfruitful** and render the church unfruitful.

It is also possible to separate vs. 14 from vs. 13, to regard the advice of vs. 13 urging aid to Zenas and Apollos as expanding in vs. 14 into general counsel to Christians to practice honest or honorable occupations (RSV mg., Falconer, Moffatt; Easton prints vs. 14 as a separate paragraph). Christians should not be useless members of society, "living in idleness, mere busybodies, not doing any work" (II Thess. 3:11), but should know that it is their duty to earn their living and supply their own necessities of food, clothing, etc. (Dibelius, Easton). In favor of taking vs. 14 as an enlargement of the thought of vs. 13 are the Greek particles with which vs. 14 begins, δὲ καί (translated by Dibelius as *überhaupt* ["in general"]), the idiom translated **apply themselves to good deeds,** which may also mean **enter honorable occupations** (RSV mg.), and the idiom translated **to help cases of urgent need,** which also may mean "for the necessities of life," and is frequently so used in Stoic writings. Unless, however, we are willing to regard vs. 14 as inserted by the writer into a genuine Pauline section (Scott), or regard his style as consistently incoherent, the verse is best interpreted closely with vs. 13 as above suggested.

**15. All who are with me:** Since no names are mentioned, the farewell greeting is probably purely conventional. It is unnecessary to assume that Titus already knew who

---

early expansion. **Zenas,** the lawyer, and **Apollos,** the teacher, had evidently earned the gratitude of the Christian community as lay leaders. Moffatt adds a very human touch with his translation which almost seems to suggest a farewell party for two beloved and trusted Christians, "Give a hearty send-off to Zenas the jurist and Apollos; see that they want for nothing." Modern churches providing for the practical necessities of their missionaries as they set sail (or take their planes) for foreign lands may find inspiration in this sound counsel.

**14.** *By Their Fruits.*—The Exeg. quotes the varying translations made by modern scholars. Whether the correct wording is **enter honorable occupations** (RSV mg.) or **apply themselves to good deeds,** the emphasis upon the

practical expression of Christian faith is the same. The plea for provision for the needs of the traveling saints seems to remind the writer that Christian faith should always bear fruit in thoughtfulness and helpfulness in little things as well as great. Again and again he has insisted that religious discussion does not take the place of bearing the brother's burden. Concern for the vast sweep of the Christian cause must not obliterate the obligation to do the little things that are required in the immediate neighborhood. The letter closes on the practical note, so conspicuous throughout the Pastoral epistles: **And not to be unfruitful**—"You will know them by their fruits" (Matt. 7:16).

**15.** *The Bond of Faith.*—The salutations at the end of the N.T. epistles are lovely insights

Paul's companions were without their being named. **Those who love us in the faith** may mean simply "Christians." However, even if the expression **those who love us** is a conventional Greek formula Christianized by the addition of **in the faith** (so Dibelius), it may still be said that since the author's church-consciousness always stands over against the heretic and the heathen, the term probably means to exclude the enemies of the true faith.

The greetings are sent to "Titus," but grace is invoked for all. Unless the benediction is taken as merely conventional, **you all** means either the entire ministry of the church for whom "Titus" stands, or the churches where the letter will be read.

---

into the realities of Christian fellowship. **All who are with me send greetings to you.** They were probably unknown to each other in the flesh, but they had the deepest things in their lives in common. **Greet those who love us in the faith.** There is a bond which unites those who live by faith in Christ, which overlaps all the usual barriers of race, nation, locality, and custom. The ecumenical church in our time is discovering in new ways the reality of this fellowship which has long existed but has for too long been submerged. **Those who love us in the faith** are closer to us than many others with whom our fellowship exists on superficial levels but lacks the deep center. The reality of this fellowship of faith is the great hope for days to come.

15. *The Last Word.*—**Grace be with you all.** The last word is not on man's duty but on God's gift. No man of himself can show the spirit which can build the kingdom—only the grace of God working through men can do that. No man can save himself from his own sins— only the grace of God in Christ can do that. No man can cherish hopes founded on his own merit or his own deserts—only the grace of God which deals with us not after our deserts but in the fullness of eternal love can give us grounds for hope that cannot be shaken. When Paul had expressed the best wishes that humans can wish each other, there was one word more which reached far beyond everything human into the realms of eternal goodness and love: **Grace be with you all.**

The Epistle to

# PHILEMON

*Introduction and Exegesis by* JOHN KNOX
*Exposition by* GEORGE A. BUTTRICK

# PHILEMON

## INTRODUCTION

The Epistle to Philemon, although a part of the original collection of the epistles of Paul (see Vol. IX, pp. 356-57), is in many ways unique. Not only does its brevity set it apart from the other letters—it is scarcely more than a page long—but also its character and content are quite distinctive. The other letters are addressed primarily to churches and are concerned with what are obviously church problems; this is addressed primarily to an individual and is concerned with what appears at first to be a merely personal matter. It contains no explicit theological or ethical teaching. And yet it is one of the most interesting and illuminating documents in the New Testament, and in some ways one of the most important.

There can be no question of its genuineness. It is certain that it belonged to the collected epistles of Paul from the moment the collection was first made and published; it was unanimously accepted as Paul's in ancient times and, except for a very few almost whimsically radical critics, has not been questioned since. No reputable modern scholar doubts its authenticity. The little letter bears in itself every mark of genuineness. Its vocabulary and style are those of Romans, Corinthians, Galatians, and Philippians; and the personality of its author is unmistakable. Besides all this, the letter brings us a dramatic moment in the life of Paul which no later writer would have had either the skill or the motive to invent.

### I. Occasion

That moment was the occasion when Paul said good-by to a slave named Onesimus, who was taking leave of the apostle to return to his master, a resident of Colossae (Col. 4:9), one of the less important cities in the province of Asia. It is clear that Paul is a prisoner and that Onesimus has been with him for some time. We are not told how Onesimus happened to be with Paul. Any number of explana-

tions are conceivable, but the usual one is that the slave was a runaway. This explanation is supported by an allusion in the letter to the unsatisfactoriness of the slave's previous service (vs. 11) and by a suggestion that he has caused his master some loss (vs. 18). But however that may be, Paul has met the slave, has won him to faith in Christ (vs. 10), has become deeply attached to him, and now that the time has come for Onesimus to return to his master's house, Paul feels that he is parting with his very heart (vs. 12). No doubt Onesimus and Paul had talked often and earnestly as to whether it was morally necessary for him to go back at all. When in the end they had reluctantly decided that it *was* necessary, Paul would have wanted to accompany his protégé on the journey back. Since he could not do this, he did the next best thing: he wrote a letter. The letter was addressed to Onesimus' master, to two other individuals, and to a church which met in the house of one of them. Though brief, it was composed with extraordinary care and, as we shall see, is one of the most skillful letters ever written. Embracing the slave and placing this letter in his hands, Paul starts him on his journey.

We cannot be sure where Paul was when this occurred. Since he was under custody at the time, it has usually been supposed that he was in Rome, where we know he spent two years in prison at or near the end of his life (Acts 28). Caesarea, the other city where, according to Acts (23:32–26:32), Paul passed many months in prison, would have been an unlikely place for a runaway slave from Asia to reach, and there are other objections to locating the "imprisonment epistles" here (see above, p. 136). But in view of the fact that Paul had apparently suffered many imprisonments earlier than either Rome or Caesarea (II Cor. 11: 23 ff.), one must not limit the possibilities too strictly. Much can be said for Ephesus, where there is good reason to believe one or more of these imprisonments occurred (I Cor. 15:32; II Cor. 1:8-9). The number of communications between Paul and Philippi which are referred to or implied in the letter to the Philippians points to a place of imprisonment nearer to Philippi than Rome was. Ephesus becomes the more probable when it is observed that this city was the metropolis of the province of Asia, in which Colossae, the home of Onesimus and his master, was situated. If Onesimus was a runaway slave, what more likely than that he should have headed toward the largest city in that part of the world? And Paul's request for a lodging at Colossae (vs. 22) is more natural if he is writing from a nearby city than if he is writing from Rome, especially as Rom. 15:23-24 would indicate that in Rome Paul's eyes would have been turned in the direction of Spain, even farther to the west, rather than toward this rather unimportant city in the hinterland of Asia.[1]

Although Paul could not go with Onesimus, he did not send him alone. There are many indications that Philemon was written at the same time as Colossians and that Onesimus was accompanied on his journey by Tychicus, the bearer of the epistle addressed to the whole church in Colossae (Col. 4:7-9). If written from Rome, Philemon was one of the apostle's last epistles, since his final imprisonment took place there; if written from Ephesus, it ought probably to be dated somewhere between the Thessalonian and the Corinthian epistles.

## II. Purpose

It has commonly been held that the purpose of the letter was to persuade Onesimus' master to take him back into service without inflicting the severe penalties which the law allowed. Paul pleads that the owner shall welcome the slave as the Christian brother he has now become. Without doubt the principal ground for this view is the prior expectation that a letter written under the circumstances just described is bound to have such a purpose. A runaway slave in the Roman empire of this period was usually summarily dealt with. An owner might legitimately take the life of such a slave. Onesimus, then, will need an advocate. Paul, who cannot accompany him, writes this letter. What

---

[1] There is no opportunity here for an adequate discussion of the complicated problem of the place of origin of the imprisonment letters. See the discussions, above, pp. 5-8, 134-37. The best defense of the Ephesian theory is in George S. Duncan, St. Paul's Ephesian Ministry (New York: Charles Scribner's Sons, 1930). See also Donald T. Rowlingson, "Paul's Ephesian Imprisonment: An Evaluation of the Evidence," Anglican Theological Review, XXXII (1950), 1-7.

will the letter contain? We hardly need to ask. We know before we open it—it will be a plea on behalf of the slave. This seems so reasonable and inevitable that, once we decide that the note was written to the master of a runaway slave, we are likely to feel that we possess the only clue needed for its complete interpretation.

But in doing so we are taking quite too much for granted. Even if Onesimus was a runaway slave (which is by no means certain), it does not follow that Paul's letter was only an appeal on his behalf. And to read the letter with that assumption may mean missing its message or some important part of it. We are fortunate in having among the letters of Pliny a document of about the length of Philemon, the purpose of which is clearly similar to that which is commonly ascribed to that letter. It is addressed to Sabinianus and is as follows:

Your freedman, whom you lately mentioned to me with displeasure, has been with me, and threw himself at my feet with as much submission as he could have fallen at yours. He earnestly requested me with many tears, and even with all the eloquence of silent sorrow, to intercede for him; in short, he convinced me by his whole behaviour that he sincerely repents of his fault. I am persuaded he is thoroughly reformed, because he seems deeply sensible of his guilt. I know you are angry with him, and I know, too, it is not without reason; but clemency can never exert itself more laudably than when there is the most cause for resentment. You once had an affection for this man, and, I hope, will have again; meanwhile, let me only prevail with you to pardon him. If he should incur your displeasure hereafter, you will have so much the stronger plea in excuse for your anger as you show yourself more merciful to him now. Concede something to his youth, to his tears, and to your own natural mildness of temper: do not make him uneasy any longer, and I will add too, do not make yourself so; for a man of your kindness of heart cannot be angry without feeling great uneasiness. I am afraid, were I to join my entreaties with his, I should seem rather to compel than request you to forgive him. Yet I will not scruple even to write mine with his; and in so much the stronger terms as I have very sharply and severely reproved him, positively threatening never to interpose again in his behalf. But though it was proper to say this to him, in order to make him more fearful of offending, I do not say so to you. I may, perhaps, again have occasion to entreat you upon his account, and again obtain your forgiveness; supposing, I mean, his fault should be such as may become me to intercede for, and you to pardon. Farewell.[2]

Now if the reading of this letter is followed by a fresh perusal of Philemon, a note of almost equal elegance and, if possible, of even

---

[2] Letters, ed. F. C. T. Bosanquet (London: George Bell & Sons, 1895), IX. 21.

greater skill, one will be struck with this difference: Given a common purpose, Pliny is more forthright, direct, and explicit than Paul. Pliny says exactly what we should expect such a note to say. Paul, on the other hand, does not say some things we should certainly expect, and says others which seem scarcely relevant. Pliny cites the penitence of his protégé, devoting a full third of his letter to emphasizing it in various ways, while the rest of the note is made up entirely of repeated pleas for the master's indulgence and of arguments for clemency. But Paul says not one word about any repentance on the part of the slave, and there is no explicit appeal for forgiveness or pity on the part of the master. In other words, the terms we should expect such a letter to contain in abundance are simply not there at all. This fact alone should lead us to suspect a rather deeper purpose in the letter than the obvious one generally assigned.

That deeper purpose was to secure the slave for his own service. Paul has not only grown warmly attached to the slave but has also come to rely on his assistance in his own work. He hopes and expects that the owner will send Onesimus back to continue his useful career at Paul's side. For the evidence that this was the true purpose of the letter reference must be made to the Exegesis. Once one's attention is called to this "deeper purpose," it is impossible for one longer to regard this letter as only a charming and generous appeal on behalf of a slave boy in whom Paul had come to feel an interest (like Pliny's letter). It is a terribly earnest appeal. Paul's own affections and purposes are in the balance; he wants Onesimus to be returned to him.

That Philemon has not always been so understood is due to the force of the returning slave stereotype, as well as to our failure to give full value to Paul's own statement that he wants more than he says (vs. 21). Such a statement should warn the interpreter that every term and turn of the letter must be most carefully examined, and that its real meaning may ultimately be found not in what it says unequivocally and definitely, but in what it suggests with some hesitation and indirection. From the standpoint of the writer of such a letter, a measure of ambiguity at every particular point will be desirable, provided the total effect is clear and strong. Paul is making a large and unusual request; he wants to make it forcefully but not bluntly. Only when Paul's purpose for Onesimus is understood somewhat in the way indicated is it possible for the modern person to realize something of the flavor and weight which many of the words and phrases of the letter had to its original readers, especially since they knew, otherwise than by letter, circumstances of which we must be unaware. That we have not misunderstood Paul's primary object in writing Philemon the closest scrutiny of the language of the epistle in the light of contemporary usage will amply demonstrate. As a matter of fact, the constant recurrence in the brief letter of words which had a definitely established legal or commercial connotation is itself enough to suggest that Paul's request had at least a quasi-business character. However informally, or even playfully, he may be using these terms, they occur to him as being appropriate in a letter which concerns the legal ownership or manumission of a slave. (On the general question of Paul's attitude toward the institution of slavery, see above, pp. 229-30.)

### III. Preservation

As to whether or not the owner of Onesimus complied with Paul's request we are not told; but since the letter has been preserved, it is safe to assume that he did. He would hardly have wanted to save the letter if he had rejected the appeal the letter makes. But the fact of the letter's preservation furnishes us with another more striking reason to believe not only that Paul's request was granted, but also that we have properly understood the nature of the request. The perennial problem raised by the Epistle to Philemon—a problem which troubled ancient as well as modern commentators—is how it happened that this personal note (out of hundreds of personal letters Paul must have written) should alone have been preserved as an item among the published epistles of Paul. The other letters are all concerned with the faith and practices of the churches. Why was this letter preserved and published with them?

If Onesimus was on his way back into slavery when Philemon was written, the question seems unanswerable. But if he was on his way *out* of slavery into Paul's service, an answer immediately suggests itself. Paul's successors in the leadership of the church around the Aegean Sea, where he chiefly worked, would naturally have been chosen from the ranks of his assistants —men like Timothy, Titus, and Silas. If Onesimus became such an assistant, he may well have become an important Christian leader in the Pauline churches during the half century just following the apostle's death.

Now it is a most striking fact that one of the epistles of Ignatius, written soon after the beginning of the second century, lets us know that the bishop of the church at Ephesus at the time was a man named Onesimus. Ignatius was the bishop of Antioch in Syria. He had been arrested as a Christian and was being sent to

Rome for trial and, tradition says, martyrdom. On their way to Rome his guards halted for some days or weeks in Smyrna, a city of Asia, and the churches of that section sent deputations to visit this distinguished representative of a sister church, on his way, as Paul had earlier been, to bear witness to his faith and theirs at the capital of the empire. The head of the deputation from Ephesus, we learn from Ignatius' letter to the Ephesians, was their bishop, Onesimus. This bishop had evidently gone to Smyrna to visit Ignatius and had taken with him other representatives of the Ephesian church—Burrhus, Crocus, Euplus, and Fronto are named. Ignatius wants Burrhus, and perhaps Crocus, to stay with him, and all but begins his letter with this request. His whole manner of making it is interesting: "Now concerning my fellow servant, Burrhus, your deacon by the will of God, who is blessed in all things, I beg that he may stay longer, for your honour and that of the bishop." The similarity of this sentence to one of the sentences in Philemon (vs. 13) will be recognized. It is true Paul writes, "I wished," and Ignatius, "I beg"; that Paul speaks of "keeping" Onesimus with him, while Ignatius chooses to speak of Burrhus' "remaining" with him; that Paul writes "in your place" and Ignatius, "for your honor." But these differences are merely verbal. Having been led in this way to think of Philemon, we are not surprised to find Ignatius in the very next sentence asserting that Crocus has relieved him, using the same word, "cheered," as Paul uses in Philemon (vss. 7, 20). Ignatius goes on immediately to express the hope that he may "make something" out of the Ephesians, using the same verbal expression (ὀναίμην, an obvious play on the name Onesimus) which Paul uses in vs. 20. All of these suggestions of the influence of Philemon on Ignatius' style occur in the four sentences of the second chapter.

In the even shorter third chapter this influence is more decisively indicated: "I do not give you commands as if I were someone great, for though I am a prisoner for the Name, I am not yet perfect in Jesus Christ. . . . But since love does not suffer me to be silent concerning you, for this reason I have taken upon me to exhort [the word is the same as for "appeal" in Philemon] you. . . ." The resemblance of this passage to Philem. 8-9 is too clear to need pointing out. Paul had written that although he felt he had ample right to make demands—was he not Paul, ambassador of Christ and now even a prisoner for him?—yet because of love he preferred to appeal. Ignatius denies that he has the right to command, even though he is a prisoner "for the Name," but love compels him to appeal to his readers.

All of these reminiscences of Philemon are found in Ign. Eph. 2–3; but every one of the first six chapters of the epistle contains some expression reminiscent of Philemon. It would be too much to claim that each of these citations represents a clear case of literary influence; perhaps no one of them standing alone would be altogether convincing. All of them taken together, however, particularly in view of their concentration in the first six short paragraphs of a single letter, can be accounted for only upon the assumption of some literary connection. Ignatius is thinking about Paul's letter to Philemon as he writes to Bishop Onesimus and the Ephesian church.

The striking character of this use of Philemon by Ignatius it is impossible to exaggerate. Nowhere in the whole range of extant early Christian literature is it to be matched in any measure whatever. Occasionally, beginning with Tertullian, references are made to the epistle by name, and eventually commentaries begin to be written on it, but nowhere is such acquaintance with its language and style reflected in another composition. One is not surprised at that fact. Philemon is too local and casual and personal to enjoy the use which the more widely significant church letters of Paul soon enjoyed. The phenomena in Ignatius' epistle to the Ephesians which we have cited are, then, altogether amazing. We should not expect Philemon to be quoted, and we find it quoted only in this single impressive exception. Why should Ignatius alone have made use of Philemon, and he such striking use of it? It is hard to escape the conclusion that the same fact which accounts for the neglect of the letter by others explains its use by him—the personal nature of its contents.

When one reaches this point in the consideration of the significance of this evidence, one finds it hard to dismiss as mere coincidence the fact that the bishop of the church at Ephesus, to which Ignatius is writing, was named Onesimus. One is even less likely to do so when one observes that in the first six chapters of Ignatius' letter are fourteen references to Onesimus either by name or by office, and in the other fifteen chapters no reference to him is made at all, and only one to the bishop's office. As a matter of fact, Onesimus the bishop is the real subject of these six chapters, and it is these chapters only which show traces of Philemon's influence.

At this point, can we escape the strong conviction that the Onesimus of Ignatius and of Paul was the same person? Indeed, why not? Paul's Onesimus would not have been too old to be bishop of Ephesus when Ignatius passed through Asia. Paul was quite possibly in Ephesus when he asked for Onesimus' release. Whether he was there or not at the time, Ephesus was a natural place for this Asian Christian to work—it had long been Paul's primary headquarters. That the slave Onesimus was a man of promise is indicated by Paul's great concern to have him with him. It would have been natural for places of leadership in the Pauline churches to be held by the actual companions of Paul himself so long as any of them were living. That some were living when Ignatius wrote is perhaps suggested by the twelfth chapter of his letter, where the Ephesians are described as "fellow priests" or "fellow initiates" of Paul. Why may not the bishop of Ephesus have been primarily in Ignatius' mind when he wrote that?

But in almost conclusive support of this suggestion attention may be called to the opening sentences of Ignatius' letter. Just after the salutation, he writes: "I became acquainted through God with your [lit., "thy"] much beloved name, which you have obtained by your righteous nature, according to faith and love in Christ Jesus our Saviour. You are imitators of God, and, having kindled your brotherly task by the blood of God, you completed it perfectly. For when you heard that I had been sent a prisoner from Syria for the sake of our common name and hope, . . . you hastened to see me. Seeing then that I received in the name of God your whole congregation in the person of Onesimus, a man of inexpressible love and your bishop, I beseech you. . . ." [3] This passage has always given difficulty to the interpreter of Ignatius. Why is the singular pronoun "thy" employed? Why is the church at Ephesus said to have obtained its dear name because of its righteous nature? Does "name" here mean "reputation"? Would it then be natural to characterize it as "dear" or "well loved"? Does it mean "character"? In that case, is it natural to continue with the remark that the Ephesians have secured it by their righteous nature? Besides, the word "name" in Ignatius seems everywhere else to mean "name" in the more ordinary sense. Similar questions make the phrase "your brotherly [συγγενικόν] task" difficult. Lake follows Zahn in translating the adjective "brotherly"; Lightfoot prefers "natural" or "congenial," although he acknowledges that the word really means "congenital." But what could Ignatius mean by the Ephesians' "congenital task"? And what is this "task"? Is

it merely showing kindness to people in need? If so, how can it be said that they have "completed" it? All of these questions, and others, are raised by Ignatius' language when one undertakes to interpret it as applying directly to the church at Ephesus.

But let us suppose that Ignatius is really thinking of the bishop, and of the church only as it was represented by him. This supposition is in no way extravagant. Ignatius loves to exalt the bishop, as the excerpt we have read will have reminded us, and tends to identify the bishop and the church. Besides, in this passage he explicitly says that it was in the person of Onesimus that he thinks of himself as having "received the whole congregation." Thus it is clear that in saying "You hastened to see me," he is really referring to Onesimus' visit. Indeed, does he not plainly say that in the whole of the first two sentences of his letter he is addressing himself symbolically to the church, but actually to its bishop?

But if this is true, the "difficult" passage not only ceases to be difficult; it becomes luminous indeed. *"Thy* well loved name" is "Onesimus," with which Ignatius had already been "acquainted." Onesimus had "obtained" that name "by his righteous nature"; and one remembers Paul's words about a slave: "my own child, whom I begot in my bonds to be Onesimus, for he was formerly useless . . . but now he is useful." And what about the "congenital work"? How appropriate that phrase, if it applied to one who had been "born" to be "useful"—and not only so in a general sense, but useful particularly to a certain prisoner for the gospel, with whom Ignatius more than once compares himself! "You have now," says Ignatius, "brought the work you were born to do to an appropriate consummation, for when you heard that *I* was a prisoner . . . you hastened to visit me." Could we want a clearer indication of the identity of Paul's and Ignatius' Onesimus? The letter to Philemon is the key to the understanding of the cryptic opening sentences of Ignatius' letter to the Ephesians. Archippus' (or Philemon's) slave (see Exeg. on vs. 2) , who became Paul's "deacon," has now become the bishop of Ephesus!

But if Onesimus was bishop of Ephesus about 110 A.D., there is no reason to suppose that he did not hold the same office a score of years earlier. If so, he was at Ephesus when a collection of Paul's letters was published there; indeed, the publication would probably have been done under his oversight. And what better explanation would we need of both the presence of Philemon in the collection and the predominant influence of Colossians upon the maker of

[3] Ign. Eph. 1:1-3. This and the previous quotation from Ignatius to the Ephesians are from *The Apostolic Fathers*, tr. Kirsopp Lake (Cambridge: Harvard University Press, 1930; "Loeb Library"). Used by permission.

559

Ephesians? Philemon is seen to be the signature of the collector!

This hypothesis can never be proved.[4] The evidence is all circumstantial, and it is more than doubtful that anything corresponding to a "confession" or an eyewitness account will ever be found. But if it is not true, we have on our hands a series of coincidences little short of incredible. Besides, the hypothesis confirms other indications as to the place and period of the primitive Pauline letter collection (see Vol. IX, pp. 356-58 and Vol. I, pp. 63-64), and provides a convincing motive for its creation. For Onesimus would have been a lover of Paul and the collection would have been the devoted "service" of a grateful disciple.

The importance of this "service" cannot be exaggerated. With the publication of the Pauline letters the history of the New Testament as a fixed collection of books properly begins. It was Marcion's appropriation of this corpus a half century later and his setting it up as the major part of a new "Bible" which should take the place for his followers of the Hebrew scriptures —which till then had been the only scriptures of the Christians—that gave the decisive impulse toward the formation of the New Testament as a second formal and authorized canon. That the name of Paul stands affixed to fully one third of the contents of that canon is owing to that same fact. If the account here given is true, it is perhaps not too much to say that this brief note, Philemon, often despised and so

---

[4] For the fuller presentation of the case see John Knox, *Philemon Among the Letters of Paul* (Chicago: University of Chicago Press, 1935), upon which, with the publisher's permission, the present brief sketch has freely drawn. See also P. N. Harrison, "Onesimus and Philemon," *Anglican Theological Review*, XXXII (1950), 268-94.

generally ignored in the history of New Testament study, may well be from the standpoint of the history of the canon the most significant single book in the New Testament—the living link between the Pauline career and the Pauline tradition, between the letters of Paul and the New Testament of the church.

In his appeal for the slave, Paul said that Onesimus had been "useful" to him; he could not have dreamed how "useful" he might still prove to be!

### IV. Text

Except at two points the text of Philemon presents no serious problem. In vs. 6 some manuscripts read "in us" and others, "in you," the first reading being on the whole the more strongly supported. In vs. 9 there is some doubt as to whether Paul referred to himself as "aged" (πρεσβύτης) or "an ambassador" (πρεσβευτής). The manuscript evidence favors πρεσβύτης, but much can be said for the other reading. This textual question will be touched on again in the interpretation of the letter.

### V. Selected Bibliography

Harrison, P. N. "Onesimus and Philemon," *Anglican Theological Review*, XXXII (1950), 268-94.

Holtzmann, H. J. "Der Brief an den Philemon," *Zeitschrift für Wissenschaftliche Theologie*, XVI (1873), 428-44.

Knox, John. *Philemon Among the Letters of Paul.* Chicago: University of Chicago Press, 1935.

Lightfoot, J. B. *St. Paul's Epistles to the Colossians and to Philemon.* London: Macmillan & Co., 1875.

Lohmeyer, Ernst. *Die Briefe an die Philipper, an die Kolosser, und an Philemon* ("Meyer's Kommentar"). Göttingen: Vandenhoeck & Ruprecht, 1930.

---

# PHILEMON

## TEXT, EXEGESIS, AND EXPOSITION

*On the Epistle to Philemon.*—Any worthy exposition must honor the unity of the letter. It is so simple and direct as to be its own best interpretation. Its salient truths are momentous in their implications, but the letter itself in its wholeness is the superlative gift: it has drunk deeply of Christ's living water.

This is a personal letter. It would be a private letter but for the fact that it is addressed to a church as well as to the household of Philemon. So it reveals Paul more intimately than a more formal and public utterance. He has been misunderstood, and sometimes condemned, as a man who has fettered the free word of Christ

| 1 Paul, a prisoner of Jesus Christ, and Timothy, *our* brother, unto Philemon our dearly beloved, and fellow laborer, | 1 Paul, a prisoner for Christ Jesus, and Timothy our brother,<br>To Phile′mon our beloved fellow worker |

**1. Paul, a prisoner of Jesus Christ:** The sense might be that Christ has captured him, as when Paul calls himself "a slave of Christ"; but more probably the phrase is a reference to his imprisonment in the ordinary sense. Thus RSV reads: **for Christ Jesus.** Perhaps both senses are in some measure present to his mind: he is a prisoner for Christ's sake and also in Christ's service. The word here is δέσμιος, which means simply one who is in prison or "in bonds" for whatever cause; but in vs. 23 Paul refers to Epaphras as συναιχμάλωτος, which denotes a prisoner of war. This hint that Paul is thinking of himself as engaged in a war for Christ's sake and as being now a battle casualty is confirmed perhaps by his reference to Archippus (vs. 2) as "our fellow soldier."

in dogmatism. What does this letter (doubtless one of hundreds) reveal about its author? Notice its personal affection, its tact and tenderness, its practicality. So it proves the "mind" that "was in Christ Jesus."

This letter is a seed that finally split the rock of slavery. It gives substance to the otherwise weak concept of "democracy" (see Expos. on vs. 16). Did the runaway Onesimus seek refuge in the slave quarter of Ephesus, or (if Rome was the locale) in the notorious Suburra, that honeycomb of crime in Rome? How did Paul find him? Or did some Christian slave bring him to Paul in prison? Runaway slaves, if recaptured, were flogged, and might even be killed. Yet in an age when life was cheap Onesimus was in Paul's eyes a man "for whom Christ died." Democracy at basis is not a political form, but a religious faith. It believes in man not on his own account, but because he is created by God and is potentially God's child. So democracy is not "the rule of the people," for that invites the demagogue, but the rule of the people according to their true nature. True democracy is born of the gospel of Christ.

This letter is the real revolution, for it changes the heart. Other revolutions merely revolve unless they are saved by the grace that saved Onesimus. Here, in this message carried by a runaway slave, is divinely subversive propaganda—or propagation—for it pleads for a world built not on race or rank or learning, or even on "the rights of man," but on human nature held in the redeeming grace of Christ. This grace is not in a vacuum: for Onesimus it worked through the church in the home of Philemon or Archippus. The Intro. (pp. 557-60) suggests that there is some evidence that Onesimus became bishop of the church at Ephesus. It is hard to find reason for the careful preservation of the letter unless Onesimus did become noteworthy in the Christian fellowship. Here,

therefore, is the record of a conversion, perhaps as dramatic as that of Paul himself. If every letter so testified!

**1. *Prisoner of Christ.*—Paul** doubtless means not only that he is in prison for Christ's sake, but that day by day in every circumstance Christ has him in thrall. Mark carefully that he does not say "prisoner of the Romans." They made the arrest, and the Jews brought the charges; but both groups, together with the jailer, were only small-part actors in the drama. Paul's real life was in the hands of Christ. Notice from the Exeg. the two Greek words for prisoner. One means locked in a dungeon like the prisoner of Chillon in the Byron poem; the other means captured in battle. See where each is used in this letter.

Is not every man a prisoner, the captive of some fealty? A scholar such as Browning's "Grammarian" is instance of a man in noble bondage, and a miser or a libertine represents the host of men ignobly bound. Perhaps we are free only to choose our fealty. The man who always does "as I like" is plainly slave to his likes. There is no absolute freedom, for nobody can cheat death or pluck a star from the sky. Freedom is the fulfillment of our nature; and if our nature is made for homage, liberty comes only as a man is in bondage to his true Lord. Thus the question of freedom—that elusive ideal for which thousands die age on age—cannot find answer until a prior question is answered, viz., "What is man's true nature?" (See John 8:36.) If a man is made for God revealed in Christ, as Christian faith avows, the first words of this letter describe the service that is "perfect freedom." Freedom is obedience to the will of God —surrender to him whose grace brings true fulfillment of our nature. Samuel Rutherford headed his letters from prison, "Christ's Palace, Aberdeen," and declared that every stone in the wall shone like a ruby.

2 And to *our* beloved Apphia, and Archippus our fellow soldier, and to the church in thy house:

2 and Ap'phia our sister and Archip'pus our fellow soldier, and the church in your house:

---

**2. To Philemon, . . . Apphia, . . . and Archippus:** It has often been surmised that these three persons were a husband, wife, and son, but there is no real evidence for this. The pronoun in the next phrase is the singular "thy"—not "your," as one might expect if the house of a whole family group were being designated. But this point cannot be pressed; the singular pronoun might refer to the head of the family.

**The church in thy house:** Reference has already been made to the "house churches" in primitive Christianity (see above, p. 239). The particular question here is, "Whose house?" Is it Philemon's house? So we have always supposed. But it is at least worth pointing out that the pronoun "thy" (σου) may possibly refer to Archippus, who is mentioned just before, and that the house may therefore be Archippus' house. In that case, the slave would have been Archippus', not Philemon's, and the reference to Archippus in Col. 4:17 becomes full of meaning, "And say to Archippus, Take heed to the ministry [διακονίαν] which thou hast received in the Lord, that thou fulfil it." Archippus' "ministry" would be freeing a slave to *serve* (διακονῇ) *in his place* (vs. 13). (For an argument in support of this possibility see John Knox, *Philemon Among the Letters of Paul* [Chicago: University of Chicago Press, 1935], pp. 25-34.)

It is important to notice that for all its preoccupation with what would appear to be a personal concern, Philemon is in a real sense a church letter. It is addressed to a church as well as to several individuals (to only one of whom the slave belonged), and there is every indication that it was prepared with great care and was intended to be taken seriously not only by an individual but by the whole Christian community of Colossae, to one section of which, at least, it is specifically addressed. Paul does not make

---

**2. Fellow Soldier.**—Paul led no insurrection against Rome, neither did he serve as Roman legionary. Yet he was a **soldier**. In his prison he was perhaps chained to a Roman soldier. He makes the contrast. He declares that he is conscripted, yet has enlisted, in a nobler warfare. The follower of Christ is *under orders*, and hears an imperious yet gentle Lord say: "Go ye," "Follow me," "Do this." He obeys—with weapons of love gathered in the armory of prayer. He is *under discipline*. The chances are that he will not become a general, for there are few generals. He renounces many of the world's joys—for a higher joy. The world is too deeply marked by hazard and struggle to justify the assumption that we are here for fame or happiness. He brings his body into subjection. He cannot consult his own whims and fancies. His time and talents are not his own, but dedicate to Christ. Ibsen's *Brand* has this:

> But I see a higher Mark
> Than to wield the knightly sabre,—
> Daily duty, daily labor,
> Hallow'd to a Sabbath-deed.[1]

[1] Act II. *The Collected Works of Henrik Ibsen*, ed. William Archer (London: William Heinemann; New York: Charles Scribner's Sons, 1906), III, 74. Used by permission.

The Christian life bears disciplines of prayer and deed more exacting than the disciplines of the athlete or musician. The follower of Christ is *under comradeship*. That fact shines in the love expressed in this phrase of Paul's letter. He and Archippus and all others in the fealty of Christ were made one not only in the danger and grandeur of the crusade, but also in the companionship of their divine Leader. "Ye are my friends, if ye do whatsoever I command you" (John 15:14).

**2. The Home as Church.**—It is evident that the home of Philemon (or should we say Archippus?) was a Christian meeting place. Not until the third century were there church buildings. Apparently the congregation in the first century met in some large room in the house of a wealthy member: there the assemblies were held. But on other occasions—for the Lord's Supper perhaps, or for classes for instruction—the assembly was broken into smaller groups that met in as many different homes.[2] Perhaps the reference here is to one of these church "cells," perhaps to the whole congrega-

[2] Ernest F. Scott, *The Epistles of Paul to the Colossians, to Philemon and to the Ephesians* (London: Hodder & Stoughton, 1930; "The Moffatt New Testament Commentary"), p. 102.

3 Grace to you, and peace, from God our Father and the Lord Jesus Christ.

4 I thank my God, making mention of thee always in my prayers,

3 Grace to you and peace from God our Father and the Lord Jesus Christ.

4 I thank my God always when I remem-

---

his request in secret; he wants the whole church to support him. If Col. 4:17 has the meaning here suggested, Paul explicitly summons the Colossian church to reinforce his request.

**3. Grace to you and peace:** Here is the regular Pauline salutation which has been more fully discussed earlier (see Vol. IX, p. 385). The phrase "grace [χάρις] and peace" takes the place of the conventional Greek letter salutation, χαίρειν, and is apparently a creation of Paul (later adopted by the author of Revelation; see Rev. 1:4). "Grace," a rich word, no doubt means here God's unmerited favor toward us; and "peace," the reconciliation with God, with fellow men, and with ourselves which that grace works in us.

**4-7. I thank my God . . . :** Here begins the "thanksgiving" with which the salutation in Paul's letters is regularly followed. We have noticed its structure in other epistles. Its recurrence here serves to remind us that though Philemon is concerned largely with personal matters, the epistle conforms to the type established by the church letters. Except that it contains no doctrinal section, Philemon is a typical Pauline letter in miniature.

The "thanksgiving" in Paul's letters has a character somewhat analogous to that of the overture of an opera—the themes to be elaborated in the body of the epistle are briefly struck. The function of the "thanksgiving" is to establish such a relationship between the writer and the recipients in each case as to assure the most sympathetic hearing

---

tion. Almost certainly Paul is appealing to the "authority" of the church to reinforce his request concerning Onesimus.

Trace the threats against the modern home: the factory system, the noise and anonymity of city life, the crowd psychology, and war. Yet the home must stand. There everyone is loved; there wisdom comes by trustful give and take; there teaching moves through life situations, as when a man of another race knocks on the door. Jesus showed us God's dealings by comparing them with parenthood and the home (Matt. 7:11).

We may note that the church in our time seems to be returning to this pattern of organization, as witness so-called "cottage prayer meetings." Perhaps the strength of the first-century church was in its homes. A church religion is not enough, if only because it can claim too few hours to make an abiding imprint. The church needs the home, as the home needs the church. The church gives sacramental meaning to birth, marriage, and death, and saves the home from selfishness; but the home, by virtue of parent love, its togetherness of young and old, its intimacies and securities, can best drive deep the message of the church. **The church in thy house** can overcome even the pagan fashion of a pagan age.

**3. Greetings Old and New.**—Notice from the Exeg. that Paul's χάρις (grace) here replaces the customary χαίρειν ("greeting") of Greek correspondence. The Hebrew shâlôm ("peace"), here in the Greek εἰρήνη, was as commonplace as the Greek χαίρειν. But what rich and unwonted meaning Paul pours into the old conventions! The **peace** and **grace** that he prays for his friends are **from God our Father and the Lord Jesus Christ.** The grace is God's free unmerited favor to sinful men through the forgiving Cross and the enabling resurrection of his Son, and the peace is the consequent reconciliation of men with God. Only through this divine peace can any real peace be known on earth. Compare our customary greetings, such as "Farewell" ("May you fare well") or "Good-by" (a contraction of "God be with you"). Have they become merely conventional? Do we invest them with deep meaning? Perhaps they also need redemption, like the salutations "Greeting" or "Peace" that men used in the days of Jesus.

**4-7. The Nature of Christian Thanksgiving.** —The Exeg. reminds us that the salutation in a Pauline epistle is habitually followed by a thanksgiving. Thanksgiving is native. The man who lacks it is a misanthrope, for we live in a bountiful Providence. Stopford Brooke once

**5** Hearing of thy love and faith, which thou hast toward the Lord Jesus, and toward all saints;

**6** That the communication of thy faith may become effectual by the acknowledging of every good thing which is in you in Christ Jesus.

**7** For we have great joy and consolation in thy love, because the bowels of the saints are refreshed by thee, brother.

ber you in my prayers, **5** because I hear of your love and of the faith which you have toward the Lord Jesus and all the saints, **6** and I pray that the sharing of your faith may promote the knowledge of all the good that is ours in Christ. **7** For I have derived much joy and comfort from your love, my brother, because the hearts of the saints have been refreshed through you.

---

possible for whatever Paul may be planning to say in the body of the epistle. Philemon is no exception in this respect. Notice the reference to the **love and faith, . . . thou hast toward the Lord Jesus, and toward all saints;** Paul is preparing to appeal to that same love (vs. 9). Likewise, in vs. 6 the word **communication** (κοινωνία), better rendered **sharing** (RSV) or, perhaps better still, "partnership," anticipates the request (vs. 17) that Paul himself may be treated as a "partner" (κοινωνόν). In the same way and even more clearly, the reference to the fact that **the hearts of the saints have been refreshed through you** prepares the way for the appeal in vs. 20: "Refresh my heart in Christ." The emphasis here undoubtedly ought to fall upon the personal pronoun, "You have cheered the hearts of others; now cheer *my* heart by granting the request I am making in this letter." The word **heart** (RSV) conveys very well the meaning of the archaic **bowels** (KJV). The Greek word here is an unusual one in Paul and connotes the deepest possible affection.

Vs. 6 is difficult and the meaning is not clear. The confusion in the MSS as to whether Paul wrote "in us" or "in you" no doubt grows out of the obscurity of the sentence. As has been indicated, the preferred reading is "in us." Thus the reading, **that the sharing of your faith may promote the knowledge of all the good that is ours in Christ.** The meaning of "partnership" has been touched on above and will be discussed again under vs. 17. The phrase **by the acknowledging** (ἐν ἐπιγνώσει) might be rendered "through the recognition of" or "through coming to know." At least two possible meanings appear: Paul may be saying—not too clearly, lest he seem to be boasting—"that your active participation in the partnership of faith may be stimulated by what you come to know

---

spoke of Carlyle's "incessant barking at mankind." Contrast that prevalent fault with the mood of these verses. Men reveal themselves by their gratitude. Some are grateful for things, and rightly, for we live by the beauty and bounty of the earth; but this gratitude can easily forget God and turn to a carking sense of insecurity. Some are grateful for friends, and with good cause, for we are all carried in a sedan chair on our neighbors' shoulders; but this thanksgiving also can lack the recognition of God's mercy in the gift, and so turn to sadness as friends depart. Some are grateful for God's mercy made known in Christ, and for friends they have in Christ, and for the use they can make of things for Christ's sake. This thanksgiving breaks into song even though things are taken away and friends are lost from sight. Whatever may be the exact translation of the obscure vs. 6, there is no doubt that Paul

here expresses this third and highest form of thanksgiving. This thanksgiving has no insecurity and no sadness, for God is all in all.

**7.** *An Unrecorded Kindness.*—We do not know what Philemon had done to refresh the hearts of the **saints.** Ernest F. Scott conjectures that he may have given food and shelter at the time of the earthquake.[3] Perhaps it is better that we do not know. All of us live by what Wordsworth calls

> . . . that best portion of a good man's life,
> His little, nameless, unremembered acts
> Of kindness and of love.[4]

Jesus laid requirement on us that kindness should be secret, because kindness is easily infected by pride and because friendship with

[3] *Epistles of Paul to Colossians, Philemon and Ephesians,* pp. 105-6.

[4] "Lines Composed a Few Miles Above Tintern Abbey."

8 Wherefore, though I might be much bold in Christ to enjoin thee that which is convenient,

9 Yet for love's sake I rather beseech *thee*, being such a one as Paul the aged, and now also a prisoner of Jesus Christ.

8 Accordingly, though I am bold enough in Christ to command you to do what is required, 9 yet for love's sake I prefer to appeal to you — I, Paul, an ambassador[a] and now a prisoner also for Christ Jesus —

[a] Or *an old man.*

---

of the good we are doing in Christ"; or perhaps the "good" is God's gracious dealing with us: "that your full sharing of yourself with your fellow Christians may be stimulated by a recognition of how much good is ours in Christ." Both Moffatt and Goodspeed understand Paul to be expressing the hope that the reader's *faith* may be shared more effectually *by others,* but except for that agreement they differ as widely from each other as from the interpretations proposed above. The variety of translation is not surprising. The verse is very obscure.

**8. What is required** (RSV) is the meaning here; not **convenient** (KJV). Goodspeed renders the verse, "Although as a Christian I feel quite free to order you to do what ought to be done," and Moffatt reads, "Although in Christ I would feel quite free to order you to do your duty." The basis of Paul's "boldness" is his sense of authority as an apostle, an authority which he expects the members of his churches to recognize.

**9. Paul an ambassador:** The word in the best MSS is πρεσβύτης, but the addition of a single letter gives us πρεσβευτής, which means "envoy" or "ambassador." Many modern scholars (e.g., Bentley, Lightfoot, Goodspeed) conjecture that this was the original reading, particularly as some of the MSS contain it; and the RSV has adopted

---

God is nurtured in the lowly heart. Notice the anonymous "they" in the gospel record of kindness: e.g., "They come unto him, bringing one sick of the palsy" (Mark 2:3). This kindness, born of God's love to men in Christ, is the reason for Paul's thanksgiving.

The thanksgiving does not become insincere because Paul uses it as entrance for the request he is about to make. Common thanksgiving is the proper climate for any worthy plea. Besides, to remind a man of what Christ has done for him, and of what he has consequently been able to do for Christ, is a worthy way to encourage him in continued Christlikeness. Thus the thanksgiving, found not only in Pauline epistles but in many a Greek letter of the period—in the Pauline epistles in profundity, in ordinary letters in conventionality—is here the springboard for the specific purpose of this letter, as set forth in vss. 8 ff.

**9. The Play of Motives.**—Should he, Paul, command Philemon by apostolic authority, or beseech him in the sheer appeal of love? Notice the play of motives: command or appeal. In the early church an apostle was regarded as the very envoy of Christ, and his word was virtual law. So Paul could almost have exacted obedience (vs. 8). But he laid aside authority and pleaded only the love made known in Christ. Motives, by the very word, give motive power to men's deeds. We must ask: In what direction

does this motive move men, and how long does the "drive" last? Authority, even though apostolic, easily becomes pride in the user; and just as easily it breeds resentment in those commanded, as witness the sin of clericalism throughout the years. The plea of love in Christ, on the other hand, ennobles the pleader, and may indeed finally (even though by way of a cross) melt the hearer. Compare Paul here with such an ecclesiastic as Thomas à Becket.

The word πρεσβυτής, **aged,** would reinforce the plea of love—not in self-pity on Paul's part, but as coming from one who had suffered much for the gospel. If the word is changed to πρεσβευτής (see Exeg.), **ambassador** (see below), it stresses Paul's renunciation of apostolic power. Galsworthy's play *Loyalties* is a study in motives that are good but not best. Every man is caught in the clash of motives. Which motive is purest? Which best serves human destiny? Which is most lasting? Perhaps all these questions are summed up in the question: Which motive is on God's side, and through which can God's power move? Christ left us in no doubt: "This is my commandment . . ." (John 15:12), "By this shall all men know . . ." (John 13:35).

**9. Ambassador.**—If the word is πρεσβευτής, **ambassador,** another window is opened on the deeper meanings of the Christian life. Through the years the peace of the world has crucially depended on ambassadors. Always it de-

10 I beseech thee for my son Onesimus, whom I have begotten in my bonds:

11 Which in time past was to thee unprofitable, but now profitable to thee and to me:

10 I appeal to you for my child, Ones'imus, whose father I have become in my imprisonment. 11 (Formerly he was useless to you, but now he is indeed useful[b] to you and to

[b] The name Onesimus means *useful* or (verse 20) *beneficial*.

this conjecture. (In II Macc. 11:34, the same word, spelled πρεσβύτης, clearly means "envoy.") Paul is appealing **for love's sake**; but that does not mean he is simply appealing to his weakness, as might seem to be the case if the word is rendered "aged." He has the authority of an apostle, an ambassador of Christ, and that authority is even greater because he is now suffering imprisonment for Christ's sake. Paul's statement here would thus correspond with the reference to him in Eph. 6:20 as "an ambassador in bonds."

**10-11. I appeal to you for my child:** Much depends, so far as the meaning of the letter as a whole is concerned, upon the exact force of the preposition "for" (περί). Does it mean "on behalf of" or does it indicate simply the content of a request, as when one asks "for" something? Is Paul appealing *for the sake of* Onesimus or is he asking *for* Onesimus? Either understanding is possible in Greek as in English. The rest of the letter would more adequately support the second interpretation, although Paul may be consciously somewhat ambiguous here. Certainly, however, Paul wants the slave to be returned to him. As Christ's envoy and prisoner he *could* keep him, he is saying; he would have every right. But he prefers simply to ask for him "for love's sake."

He makes this request with the more earnestness and with the greater assurance of being justified in it because Onesimus is his "son": **whom I have begotten in my bonds.**

pends more deeply on the ambassadors of Christ. An ambassador does not speak his own word, but only the message which he receives on instruction from the homeland. The preacher and church member alike declare only the word of Christ: "It shall be given to you in that same hour what ye shall speak" (Matt. 10:19). The essential message of the Christian ambassador is always, "We pray you in Christ's stead, be ye reconciled to God" (II Cor. 5:20). Again, the ambassador is defended by all the powers of the homeland. His person is almost sacrosanct, he has immunities which others cannot claim, and even a potential enemy must afford him protection. Likewise all the defenses of God in Christ encompass his ambassadors, not indeed with swords, but with spiritual powers able always to guard the soul in life or death. Again, an ambassador lives in loneliness, but not in despair, for soon he will be called home. This loneliness is eloquently reflected in the life and letters of Walter Hines Page. All around the Christian ambassador the language is strange and customs are alien, while he longs for home. But home is not far distant, and soon he may be summoned for a shorter or longer time to meet his King. Trace this meaning through the experience of Paul. Whatever the word may be in Philemon (whether **aged** or **ambassador),** Paul used that latter word

clearly in II Cor. 5:20, for he well knew that every Christian is "a legate of the skies."

**9. Prisoner of Jesus Christ.**—See Expos. on vs. 1.

**10. Harvest from Suffering.**—Whom I have **begotten in my bonds.** Notice the Exeg.: "begotten him Onesimus." We may guess that Paul rebelled against his imprisonment (if in his devotion to Christ any measure of rebellion was left), not because of his own pain, but because he was denied opportunity to preach his gospel. But while he was in prison he found this slave, and thus his very fetters became wings. There is no gain or glory in pain itself: it contorts the face—vivid evidence that pain in itself is slow death. But the grace of Christ under the daily and mysterious overruling of God's providence can so change the spirit of the sufferer and so govern events that pain itself becomes an open door. How Paul's bonds deepened his own insight into truth! How they have blessed mankind! Thus *In Memoriam* came because Tennyson dipped his pen in tears. Thus Bunyan's prison was large liberty both for himself and for his fellow men. Thus Paul's bonds served the gospel: this epistle is known and read throughout our world.

**11. Profit and Loss.**—The name Onesimus means "useful" or "profitable." There is here almost a gentle play on words. Industry has in

12 Whom I have sent again: thou therefore receive him, that is, mine own bowels: me.) 12 I am sending him back to you, send-

---

This clearly means that Onesimus has become a believer in Christ under Paul's influence. Perhaps he has received a new name; one cannot tell whether Paul has given him a new name, or made him worthy of his old one. "Onesimus" is the Greek word for "useful," and Paul, after saying that he has "begotten him Onesimus" (ὃν ἐγέννησα ἐν τοῖς δεσμοῖς Ὀνήσιμον), explains the meaning of that somewhat cryptic utterance by saying that whereas the slave had previously been **useless to you,** he has now become **useful to you**—and, he adds, **to me.** "Onesimus" is in the accusative case. Most of the commentators notice that fact and account for it by the attractive force of the relative pronoun "whom." They thus render it as though it were a genitive and in apposition with "my child." But to do so is to miss the whole point of the clause, which involves a play upon the word "Onesimus." "I have begotten him to be 'useful,'" Paul is saying. *"As Onesimus* he is my own child; for before his rebirth he was worthless to you, but now he has value to me as well as to you."

**12. Whom I have sent again:** The word rendered **sent again** is ἀνέπεμψα, an aorist (or past), but the meaning is present (the epistolary aorist). Goodspeed preserves very well the deep feeling of the verse in the rendering: "And now that I send him back to you, it is like sending my very heart." The RSV is very similar. A question, however,

---

some instances found more profit in what was formerly regarded as "waste material" than in its main product, and medicine has discovered healing drugs in common earth. In the Christian view there are no waste men: every man is a "fleshly bundle of infinity." But there are men who through their own folly or "man's inhumanity to man" have become unprofitable. So all the wealth of the gospel is here hinted: the grace of Christ turned a waste into a garden. A runaway slave is dear to God and potentially a blessing to his neighbors. The bruised reed (Matt. 12:20) is not broken, but so restored as to give flute music.

All the power of the gospel finds here its token. The alien "gospels" of our time liquidate the unfit, and exile those who do not share the totalitarian mind; but the gospel of Christ comes in prime concern to seek and "to save that which was lost" (Matt. 18:11). Only so can there be any profit. The stock exchange proverb, "You never lost money by taking a profit," is not necessarily true even on a money level: the United States has suffered financial loss by cutting down her forests to take a profit. On deeper levels the proverb is often false: there is no ultimate profit in profit that breeds pride in the "haves" and resentment in the "have-nots." There is no ultimate profit anywhere except as people become better people. Bank deposits grow in vain and are a threat unless the depositor grows with them. What use skyscrapers if the builders are being dwarfed? This epistle is the story of a man

once **unprofitable** who was made **profitable.** It is therefore a real record of profit and loss.

The profit came from God, but not without human hands and hearts. The farmer gains an increment through the free gifts of earth and sky, yet his own labor is needed. God used not Paul alone, but the church in the house of Philemon. The epistle is a plea to a man through a church. In our time churches do not pay taxes. Granted their faithfulness, they are the real assets of the community. Through them a power works to make profitable people. Jesus used this vital word, "profit": "What shall it profit a man . . . ?" (Mark 8:36.) We must ask of newspapers, schools, factories: Are they really profitable? Do they make better people? The other epistles also use the word: "Though I give my body to be burned, and have not charity, it profiteth me nothing" (I Cor. 13:3); "Godliness is profitable unto all things" (I Tim. 4:8). We see here the true increment. To rearrange unredeemed people in new patterns is no salvation. An infected water supply is not improved by better distribution. The only wealth is a clean heart and a right spirit.

**12-13. Desire Versus Duty.**—The Exeg. evidently leans to a belief that Paul wished not only to restore Onesimus to his master's good graces, but to keep the former slave as his own friend and helper. Onesimus could have been Paul's messenger while the apostle was in prison, and could have filled the prison loneliness with love, for Onesimus had become Paul's "very heart." So Paul "was wishing" to keep

13 Whom I would have retained with me, that in thy stead he might have ministered unto me in the bonds of the gospel: 14 But without thy mind would I do nothing; that thy benefit should not be as it were of necessity, but willingly.

ing my very heart. 13 I would have been glad to keep him with me, in order that he might serve me on your behalf during my imprisonment for the gospel; 14 but I preferred to do nothing without your consent in order that your goodness might not be by compulsion but of your own free will.

can be raised about the words "send back" or "send again." The Greek verb really means "send up," and it was regularly used to indicate the reference of a case from a lower to a higher court. It is used four other times in the N.T. and in every case it has that meaning (Luke 23:7, 11, 15; Acts 25:21). Why do we suppose it means anything else here? Paul uses this term because he has just addressed an appeal to Onesimus' owner. He is referring an issue to the man legally qualified to settle it.

**13-14.** Paul here indicates more clearly just what that issue was: **I would have been glad to keep him with me.** He wanted (ἐβουλόμην: "I was wishing") to keep Onesimus with him that he might serve (διακονῇ—our word "deacon") in the owner's place as one of Paul's assistants. The use of the imperfect tense suggests that Paul not only wanted to keep Onesimus but had actually considered doing so. In the end, however, he had determined (ἠθέλησα) not to do this, lest there might be some appearance of forcing the owner's hand. He preferred that the latter's generous act (ἀγαθόν) should be voluntary and in accord with his own judgment (γνώμη) of what was proper. On the possibility of an echo of διακονῇ in Col. 4:17 see under vs. 2, above.

Onesimus, but *willed* not to keep him except with his master's consent. This is another instance of the immemorial struggle of desire and duty. Paul could have rationalized the keeping of Onesimus. Why should he return him to slavery? Why give him to routine tasks when he might become a herald of the good news? Why send him back when he, Paul, obviously needed the man more than Philemon or Archippus could need him? But conscience cut through all the plausibilities before they could gather. Onesimus had broken faith and (apparently) also had stolen money (vs. 8), and he must square himself; besides, Paul himself must keep faith with the household of Philemon. The conflict of desire and duty is written across our greatest literature. It is the theme of much mythology, e.g., the story of Lorelei. There is a cleft in our nature: the desire of the creature wars against the higher demand.

Paul refused to argue with himself or to deceive himself. He "was wishing," but instantly thrust aside the wish: a sign of the above-named cleft. It is implied in Christ's word, "He that loseth his life . . ." (Matt. 10:39). Paul never evaded that struggle. He did not trust in "evolution." He took his stand and called on God to help him in the desperate battle. So he refused to accept any gain that would spell loss to his neighbor. He was wise enough not to trust his own strength: he carried the struggle

to the place of prayer. He acted promptly, burning his bridges so that he could not return to the lure of his desire. Doubtless he was sad when Onesimus left him, and his prison was a double loneliness. Or was it? He had followed duty for Christ's sake, and therefore knew the nearness of his Lord.

**14. Compulsion or Consent?**—Can goodness ever be by compulsion? Paul could have kept Onesimus, and the household of Philemon thereby could have gained credit for kindness. But a compelled kindness is almost a contradiction in terms: kindness lives only in a man's own free will. Behind the fact that people resent and finally resist coercion, even though it is a beneficent coercion, is a more important fact: a man is free under God, and is therefore outraged when he is treated as if he were a thing.

> I am as free as Nature first made man,
> Ere the base laws of servitude began,[5]

is a romanticism, for liberty is only by a man's growth in God; but the couplet still has its core of truth.

Only God has the right to coerce, for only he is good and only he knows man's need and destiny. Therefore God guides, but does not

[5] John Dryden, *The Conquest of Granada*, Part I, Act I, scene 1.

15 For perhaps he therefore departed for a season, that thou shouldest receive him for ever;

16 Not now as a servant, but above a servant, a brother beloved, specially to me, but how much more unto thee, both in the flesh, and in the Lord?

15 Perhaps this is why he was parted from you for a while, that you might have him back forever, 16 no longer as a slave but more than a slave, as a beloved brother, especially to me but how much more to

---

**15-16.** Paul goes on to suggest that there was a divine Providence in the temporary separation of Onesimus from his owner; now the latter is to have Onesimus back forever. The word used here for "have back" or "receive" (ἀπέχῃς) is rare in Paul, being used only once besides, in Phil. 4:18: "I have all things." It was the word ordinarily employed in writing receipts and clearly has something of that sense in the Philippians passage, where Paul is acknowledging the gift Epaphroditus has brought him. In Philemon the word is apparently intended to suggest completeness and finality of ownership—ownership in a special sense. Paul indicates at once what that sense is. The owner is to receive Onesimus forever—but no longer **as a slave.** We have no right to insert the word "merely" after "slave," as some of the modern translators do. Paul hopes and expects that Onesimus will no longer be a slave; he will be **more than a slave,** a **brother.** He will be dearer than before since he will now be known and loved not merely "as a man" (ἐν σαρκί) but **in the Lord.**

---

coerce! Springtime fields say, "Sow the seed"; and autumn fields say, "Reap the harvest." There are penalties for those who refuse the gentle command, but consent is readily won, so gracious are the dealings of God. Jesus Christ came to earth in the lowliness of our flesh that we might consent to salvation. As he neared Golgotha he did not use "twelve legions of angels" (Matt. 26:53) but died in the appeal of sheer love, that our goodness might not be by compulsion but by our own free will. The fierce reformer and the crowd leader, the bishop and the tyrant, the teacher and the parent alike must learn that at long last life honors only one weapon—the helplessness of Christ's love.

**15. God Moves in a Mysterious Way.**—Perhaps is a frank confession of the finitude of man's mind: Paul did not know, and admitted the ignorance. Human intelligence is always short: it cannot penetrate, much less compass, the range and subtlety of God's providence. Seeming gain proves loss, and seeming loss proves gain; and therefore a man should walk by faith, not forswearing the powers of discernment God has given, but bringing them in lowly trust under the guidance of God's Spirit. The persecution of the early church drove Christians far afield, and thus spread the gospel —like seed carried on the wind. Blessing came from apparent disaster. **Perhaps,** says Paul, in wonder at God's strange yet gracious providence. Who could have believed that an alien

and homespun language (the Greek Koine) would be the instrument of the Christian message, or that an alien empire with its Pax Romana would be its milieu? Who could have prophesied that a Babe born in a stable in a remote and conquered province would be the Savior of the world? Or that pain could be a better teacher than prosperity? Or that the fact of death could reveal everlasting arms beneath the void? Or that a thieving runaway slave could be the herald of the kingdom? Jesus has taught us that tragedy is only for a season, and a vestibule to grace for those who trust:

> All which I took from thee I did but take,
> Not for thy harms,
> But just that thou might'st seek it in My arms.[6]

Stars show only in the darkness. The wine press yields a sacrament. Perhaps this is why pain comes. To follow Christ in lowliness of mind is the best wisdom.

**16. The Banishment of Slavery.**—This sentence is in some regards the heart of the epistle. An encyclopedia gives the facts about ancient slavery. In some areas slaves were not merely manual laborers but poets, musicians, accountants, builders. Generally speaking, the terms for remission of bondage were too severe to be achieved. The life of the ancient world, even

[6] Francis Thompson, "The Hound of Heaven." From *Collected Works,* ed. Wilfred Meynell. Used by permission of Burns, Oates & Washbourne, Ltd., and The Newman Press, publishers.

17 If thou count me therefore a partner, receive him as myself.

18 If he hath wronged thee, or oweth *thee* aught, put that on mine account;

you, both in the flesh and in the Lord. **17** So if you consider me your partner, receive him as you would receive me. **18** If he has wronged you at all, or owes you anything,

---

**17. If you consider me your partner:** This term (κοινωνός) has already been used (see on vss. 4-7). It was a business term, with approximately its modern meaning, and here serves to remind the owner that he and Paul are associates in a supremely important enterprise and must share all they have with each other.

**18. If he has wronged you at all:** It was customary, when the possession of a slave was passed to another, or when a slave was freed, for any debts or penalties outstanding to be assumed by the slave himself or by the new owner. Paul is here assuming Onesimus' debts. The Greek word used here for **wronged** (ἀδικέω) is found again in Col. 3:25 ("he that doeth wrong"), also in a reference to a slave. This confirms other indications that Col. 3:22-25 was written with Onesimus' case particularly in mind (see John Knox, "Philemon and the Authenticity of Colossians," *Journal of Religion,* XVIII [1938], 154-59).

---

in enlightened Greece, even in God-chosen Jewry, as well as in Rome and Babylon, was built on a foundation of slavery. Why did not Paul forthrightly condemn and oppose the whole system? This letter seems the logical place for that protest. But Paul, far from protesting, seems to take the institution of slavery for granted. We can guess some reasons. For one thing, the faith of Christ might have come into ill-repute as a violent and merely external "revolution" had Paul made a frontal attack; and it seems certain that had all slaves rebelled under some demagoguery, the life of the ancient world would have become chaos. For another thing, Paul may have expected an imminent return of Jesus—the signal for the terminus of the then-present order; and he may therefore have counseled every man to be content with his status, and to make ready for the great event (I Cor. 7:20). For yet another thing, we cannot be sure that Paul was *explicitly* aware of the iniquity of the system. That he was *implicitly* aware is clear from this whole letter. But every man is a "prisoner of his date." The noblest minds of ancient Greece accepted slavery as a matter of course; and Christian ministers in the United States, centuries after Paul, defended the institution. The writer and reader of these lines may well be similarly blind to the entrenched evils of their own day. A moving belt in a factory, timed to highest working capacity, is not far removed from bondage. For yet another reason: Paul, like his Lord, knew full well that the inner bondage is the real slavery. To that bondage, in Paul or Onesimus or Philemon, the gospel was directly addressed. If a man is free in soul, he has a vantage point from which to attack external

fetters; if he is a slave in soul, to strike off external bonds may be added curse rather than cure (cf. John 8:33-36).

Yet when all these considerations have been cited, this letter is a landmark of freedom, and Paul, under Christ, is the emancipator. If all men, masters or slaves, depend on Christ for the remission of the bondage of sin—if therefore all men, masters or slaves, are now slaves of Christ who in love calls all men "brethren"—there is no room in the Christian faith for any bondage of man to man. Love for Christ, derived from his prior love for us, is the catalyst that dissolves all our coercions—in home or commerce or statecraft. Without this essential freedom in Christ, "liberty" is a delusion and may become a snare, but with it all coercions among men are under sentence of death. Notice the "transvaluation of all values": **no longer as a slave but . . . as a beloved brother.** Notice the axis on which the change was made: **in the flesh** (in the area of human relations) because **in the Lord.**

**18. Courtesy in Christ.**—Paul says **if he has wronged you . . . or owes you anything,** but probably there was no "if" about the theft. Perhaps Paul wrote that "if" with Onesimus looking over his shoulder. It was more than good manners, unless we say that good

> . . . manners are not idle, but the fruit
> Of loyal nature, and of noble mind.[7]

Courtesy of speech and manners is the savor of life. Oscar Wilde confessed that hope was reborn in him when someone raised his hat to him.

[7] Tennyson, *Idylls of the King,* "Guinevere."

19 I Paul have written *it* with mine own hand, I will repay *it:* albeit I do not say to thee how thou owest unto me even thine own self besides.

20 Yea, brother, let me have joy of thee in the Lord: refresh my bowels in the Lord.

21 Having confidence in thy obedience I wrote unto thee, knowing that thou wilt also do more than I say.

charge that to my account. 19 I, Paul, write this with my own hand, I will repay it — to say nothing of your owing me even your own self. 20 Yes, brother, I want some benefit from you in the Lord. Refresh my heart in Christ.

21 Confident of your obedience, I write to you, knowing that you will do even

---

**19. I, Paul, write this:** Here is a legal bond, written in regular form—followed by a gentle reminder that the slaveowner ought not to ask for it or even to accept it.

**20. I want some benefit from you:** The word is ὀναίμην—the verbal form of "Onesimus"—and a play on words is evidently intended. Paul is really saying, "Let me make a profit from you," and his meaning is ever so much clearer if Onesimus himself is "the profit" he is seeking. Remember vs. 11: Onesimus has become "profitable to me as well as to you." For **refresh my heart** see on vss. 4-7.

**21. More than I say:** Paul has not actually said in so many words that he wants the slave returned to him, but as we have seen, he has come very near to it. There can be no doubt that this is what he has in mind when he uses the words **more than I say.** The use of the word **obedience** in this sentence will remind the readers again of Paul's apostolic authority.

---

But Paul's courtesy went a far greater length: he deliberately assumed the debts of Onesimus (see Exeg.). How was he proposing to pay them? With money left to him by his family, as some commentators assume? Or by the labor of his own hands in his trade as tentmaker? We do not know. But it is clear (see Expos., vss. 19-20) that Paul here proposed and entered into a business transaction, even though he may have guessed that Philemon would not hold him to it. This courtesy at cost Paul had learned of Christ. Did not Jesus say of the grafter Zacchaeus that he was "a son of Abraham," thus paying him a gracious compliment (Luke 19:9)? The world says of wicked men that they are devilish; Jesus says that they are "lost," even though he never glossed the wrong. That "if" is almost the signature of Christ!

**19-20.** *Promissory Note.*—The words **I will repay it** have the meaning and force of an I O U. As such they are written in Paul's **own hand.** Ernest F. Scott says that the legal bond was "meant playfully." [8] But Paul (suffering from eye trouble?) apparently wrote in his **own hand** only the most deeply felt sentences, notably the final benedictions of his epistles. So he was serious in his I O U, as Scott is quick to add. The word translated **joy** (KJV) and **benefit** (RSV) really means "profit," and is almost a pun on the name Onesimus (see Exeg.).

[8] *Epistles of Paul to Colossians, Philemon, and Ephesians*, p. 112.

Why should Paul assume such an obligation? Onesimus had hardly proved himself worthy of the trust. Paul wrote in the awareness of his own unworthiness, well knowing that no man is righteous enough to pronounce final judgment on his fellow man. Paul wrote of Onesimus as a brother in Christ. Charles R. Brown once remarked that the proper answer to the question "Am I my brother's keeper?" is "No, but you are your brother's brother." Paul wrote thus for Christ's sake. Recall our modern custom by which radio operators on transoceanic vessels pause every half hour to listen for the S O S signal, in instant readiness to help, whatever the nationality or business of the vessel in distress. Yet Paul was indulging no slapdash altruism. He and Onesimus had realistically faced the wrong that had been done, and they had sought and found the only true redemption. Is it not the task of the church to assume the social debt—for Christ's sake and in Christ's power? This is a different kind of I O U from that of the business world (cf. Rom. 13:8).

**21.** *The Second Mile.*—A cynic might comment that it is characteristic of our age that "the second mile" has been made to mean, at least in magazine success stories, the willingness of a man to work (for himself?) harder than accepted rules require. Such an interpretation is a far cry from the word originally spoken by Jesus (Matt. 5:41). That original word may have come from the actual instance: Jesus may

22 But withal prepare me also a lodging: for I trust that through your prayers I shall be given unto you.

23 There salute thee Epaphras, my fellow prisoner in Christ Jesus;

24 Marcus, Aristarchus, Demas, Lucas, my fellow laborers.

25 The grace of our Lord Jesus Christ *be* with your spirit. Amen.

¶ Written from Rome to Philemon, by Onesimus a servant.

more than I say. 22 At the same time, prepare a guest room for me, for I am hoping through your prayers to be granted to you.

23 Ep'aphras, my fellow prisoner in Christ Jesus, sends greetings to you, 24 and so do Mark, Aristar'chus, Demas, and Luke, my fellow workers.

25 The grace of the Lord Jesus Christ be with your spirit.

**22. Prepare a guest room for me:** This sentence is perhaps more easily compatible with the supposition that Paul was a prisoner in Ephesus when he wrote this letter than with the usual view that he was in Rome. According to Rom. 15:24, Paul had in mind going on to Spain from Rome, feeling that his work in the East was pretty well done. He may, of course, have changed his mind; but, under any circumstances, this casual allusion to an early visit to a small city in the heart of Asia Minor would be somewhat surprising if Paul was in Rome. It is much more natural coming from an earlier and more temporary imprisonment in Ephesus, which was situated not too far from Colossae.

**23. Epaphras, etc.:** These individuals also greet the church at Colossae (Col. 4:10 ff.). This is one of the evidences that Colossians and Philemon were written at the same time. Epaphras is referred to twice in the companion letter, Colossians (1:7; 4:12), and had apparently been Paul's agent and representative in the establishing of the Colossian church. Mark is John Mark, Barnabas' cousin (Col. 4:10), and the reputed author of the Second Gospel. Aristarchus, besides being mentioned in Colossians, is alluded to three times in Acts (19:29; 20:4; 27:2), where he is identified as from Thessalonica in Macedonia. Demas is referred to in II Tim. 4:10 as having forsaken Paul. Luke, described in Colossians (4:14) as "the beloved physician," is the same Luke to whom the writing of the Third Gospel and the book of Acts is commonly ascribed. All of these are designated, with Philemon himself (vs. 1), as Paul's "fellow workers."

**25. The grace of the Lord Jesus Christ:** This benediction conforms in general to the type established by the closing blessings in the other epistles. An interesting divergence is

very well have been compelled to carry some Roman soldier's baggage the legal mile, only to answer, "I will gladly go two." Compare our rule of work: calculated reward for calculated labor; or our rule under compulsion, even God's compulsion: "I'll get out of this as quickly as I can." Paul asked of Philemon (or Archippus) "the second mile": **even more than I say.** Was that **more** the return of Onesimus that he might be Paul's helper and friend while the apostle was in prison? The Christian deed is never a poor tit for tat—calculated labor for a calculated reward, or grudging gratitude ("Well, I suppose I owe him something"), or a reluctant giving ("It is a nuisance, but I shall look shabby if I do not help"): it overflows all rules, and loves with abandon. Why? "While we were yet sinners, Christ died for us" (Rom. 5:8).

**23-24. The Democracy of the Royal Lord.—** Examine the list of names (see Exeg.). Here is the gamut from wealth to poverty, from edu-

cated to uneducated. If Mark and Luke are the authors respectively of the Gospels that bear their names, they are bracketed with men whose work we hardly know, men who differ in age and nationality at a time when such differences easily became deep cleavages. But Jesus had bridged all the chasms: they were now one in him. Unhappily not all of them remained true (see II Tim. 4:10). Each man's witness was needed. None was obscure even to Paul, let alone to their common Lord. The church fails in so far as it does not cross the lines of prejudice that the world stubbornly tries to keep.

**25. The Grace of the Lord Jesus Christ.—** From epistle to epistle there are slight changes in the essentially unchanged Pauline benediction. There are many meanings of **grace**. There is morning in it, shiningness of person and personality: "Jesus increased . . . in favor [grace]" (Luke 2:52), "And all . . . wondered

the conclusion, found only here and in the epistles to the Galatians and the Philippians; **with your spirit,** instead of the usual "with you" or "with you all." The phrase makes explicit what is always implied: the grace of Christ is always spiritually discerned and spiritually received.

---

at [his] words of grace" (Luke 4:22 ASV). So does the connotation assume a deeper graciousness. There is noontide in it, a pursuing and persistent good will: "Grace and truth came through Jesus Christ" (John 1:17). The story of the good Samaritan is for witness. But there is also sunset in this word, crimson after storm, token of a fair tomorrow. This is the real N.T. meaning. "Where sin abounded, grace did much more abound" (Rom. 5:20); "By grace are ye saved through faith" (Eph. 2:8). Grace in its deepest meaning is God's free and unmerited forgiveness and renewing power. These three meanings are evident in this epistle, but without the third and deepest meaning the epistle could not have been written.

Notice the word **our:** it is both Paul's own joy and the joy of the fellowship. In it is the difference between *"the* house" and *"our* home." The sun is the sun, but it is also the light of *our* eyes and life. The benediction, whether at the beginning or at the end of an epistle, is almost the Pauline trade-mark. It is the signature of his life. And of all life in Christ.

The Epistle to the

# HEBREWS

*Introduction and Exegesis by* ALEXANDER C. PURDY
*Exposition by* J. HARRY COTTON

# HEBREWS

## INTRODUCTION

The Epistle to the Hebrews is today the least known of the major New Testament writings. The common reader knows the stirring chapter on faith, the intriguing name Melchizedek, the priestly imagery, and possibly certain vivid figures of speech such as "the hope set before us, . . . a sure and steadfast anchor of the soul," but he is unaware of the total nature of the author's thought. This is due in part to the closely reasoned and at times somewhat labored character of the argument; in part to the priestly and sacrificial terminology, no longer native to the modern Christian; and in part to the ruling idealism of the writer which does not immediately appeal to contemporary Christian thinkers. The main direction of his thought is not, however, difficult to grasp; his absorption in the priestly sacrifice of Christ is explicitly designed to end all sacrifices; and although he works with "ideas," he develops them in the framework of revelation. While Hebrews will never rival the Gospels or Paul's letters in popularity, it contributes to the richness of New Testament Christianity and merits careful study today.

In approaching the Epistle to the Hebrews it is well to proceed from the known to the unknown. The text reveals the author's religious ideas and his general purpose in writing. We know something about the attitude of subsequent Christian writers toward Hebrews. Beyond that our knowledge must be gained from inference and by hypothesis tested by the text and contemporary literature, for Hebrews does not name its author nor identify the intended readers, nor does it give us any explicit information about the provenance, the destination, or the date of composition. The form in which it

has come down to us is puzzling, for Hebrews begins like a treatise and ends like a letter. The integrity of chs. 1–12 is reasonably sure but whether ch. 13 belongs to the original writing, in whole or in part, is an open question. The larger issue as to the relationship of Hebrews to primitive Christianity and to contemporary Judaism and Hellenism is also debatable.

### I. Argument of Hebrews

The polished and euphonious opening sentence, which translation can exhibit only imperfectly, states the general theme of the writing: the finality of God's revelation in a Son who is the heir and agent of creation, who radiates God's glory because he bears "the very stamp of his nature, upholding the universe by his word of power" (1:3). In keeping with the author's regular literary habit, the unique argument to be developed is only hinted at in a single phrase, "when he had made purification for sins" (1:3); this is to be amplified in his central exposition of the priesthood and sacrifice of Christ. The author's characteristic contrast between the earthly shadow and the heavenly reality is implicit in the opening verses although again this contrast is to become explicit later in his writing. We are prepared also for his rendering of faith as acceptance of the reality of God's complete and final revelation in Christ, and the collocation of scriptural passages which follows the statement of the theme (1:5-14) introduces the reader to the author's formal proof of his thesis which he substantiates throughout from Scripture.

The immediate conclusion drawn from the nature of the Son is his superiority to angels (1:4-14) and to the revelation mediated by them in the law. The angelic Word (Logos) was valid but could not reach home to men who suffer and are tempted. Accordingly, Jesus, "made like his brethren in every respect" (2:17), is superior both in nature and in work, fulfilling the promise of Ps. 8.

But did not Moses, as a human agent of revelation, meet human needs? He was indeed "faithful" (3:5), but as a servant not as a Son; and the Scripture shows that those who received the imperfect revelation mediated through Moses were unable to enter into the promise of "rest" because of unbelief (3:19). Now that the full and effective revelation has been given in a Son, the recipients of it must beware of the disobedience which ruined the wilderness generation (3:11), for no subterfuge can avail to escape "the word of God, . . . living and active, sharper than any two-edged sword" (4:12).

With 4:14 the main thesis of Hebrews is introduced with apparent abruptness: "We have a great high priest who has passed through the heavens, Jesus, the Son of God, . . . who in every respect has been tempted as we are, yet without sinning. Let us then with confidence draw near to the throne of grace, that we may receive mercy and find grace to help in time of need" (4:14-16). Here several of the chief notes of the writing are sounded: the priesthood of Jesus and its effectiveness for men in achieving the *summum bonum* of religion, that is, access to God's mercy and grace in their time of need. The abruptness of this rather full statement of the theme is more apparent than real, however, for the author has been moving steadily toward this point. Angels could not help because of their angelic nature; Moses was a man but not the Son. It is natural that the writer should soon speak of Aaron. The writer's thought thus moves logically toward the priestly principle, and we have been prepared for it by the phrase which summarizes the Son's earthly service, "when he had made purification for sins" (1:3), as well as by the consistent movement of the argument.

The author's exposition of the priestly service of Jesus as Son is introduced by a terse summary of the qualifications of a high priest and how Jesus fulfills them (5:1-10). We are also forewarned that he will develop a priestly concept beyond the limitations of the earthly priesthood, "after the order of Melchizedek" (5:6, 10).

Before he develops this idea, and because he is conscious of the fact that it "is hard to explain, since you have become dull of hearing" (5:11), he prepares the way by an exhortation, psychologically skillful in its movement from rebuke (5:11-14) to warning (6:1-8) to encour-agement (6:9-12) to assurance (6:13-20). There can be no doubt that the author regards his argument as urgently practical, although the exact state of his intended readers remains uncertain to us.

Ch. 7 is the famous Melchizedek speculation in which by an ingenious use of etymology and Scripture the author proves to his own, and perhaps to his readers', satisfaction that although Jesus was not a priest after the Levitical order, he was "a priest forever, after the order of Melchizedek," and that the Melchizedek priesthood, the perfect as contrasted to the imperfect, was destined to supersede it, and with it the law on which it was based (7:12, 18-19). The argument is formal, but a living, timeless note sounds through the artificial structure of the thought, "a better hope . . . through which we draw near to God" (7:19); "he is able for all time to save those who draw near to God through him, since he always lives to make intercession for them" (7:25). The meticulous method of the writer is again indicated as he prepares the reader for the subsequent development of his argument in the words "This makes Jesus the surety of a better covenant" (7:22).

Ch. 8 introduces the next stage in his thought, the ministry of Christ as priest in its sacrificial meaning and as the basis of a new covenant. In 8:1-6 the author brings into the clear the point of what he has been writing and of what he will write, namely, that Christ's priesthood operates in the realm of reality, "the heavenly sanctuary," as over against "the copy and shadow," where earthly high priests officiate. The offering Christ makes must be correspondingly real, and the relationship this offering institutes must be a perfect covenant. Sacrifice and covenant dominate his thought from 8:1 to 10:18, and together they form the heart of his argument.

In 8:7-13 he quotes Jer. 31:31-34 to prove that the first covenant was not final; indeed it "is becoming obsolete and growing old is ready to vanish away" (8:13), for the promise of a "new covenant" ensures the passing of "the first as obsolete." For our author, however, the "new covenant" does not mean the end of the priestly as contrasted with the prophetic conception of religion; it means that sacrifices offered in an "earthly sanctuary" (9:1) which cannot "perfect the conscience of the worshiper" (9:9) have been superseded by the sacrifice of Christ, who has "entered once for all into the Holy Place, taking not the blood of goats and calves but his own blood, thus securing an eternal redemption," the purification of "your conscience from dead works to serve the living God" (9:12, 14).

Is he aware that the Jeremiah citation contains no verbal warrant for the perpetuation of the priestly function? The section following (9:15–10:18) contains his answer to that omission: sacrifice is ended by the perfection of the sacrificial offering of Christ. In the words "For I will be merciful toward their iniquities, and I will remember their sins no more" (8:12=Jer. 31:34c) the continuation of sacrifice is, he assumes, implicit, for "without the shedding of blood there is no forgiveness of sins" (9:22). It is not a question, then, of another and different principle at work in the "new covenant," but only of the perfect sacrificial offering of Christ over against the pathetically inadequate and repetitious sacrifices offered by the earthly priests in the shadowy realm of an outward tabernacle. The author is perhaps not unaware of the incongruity of equating the great passage in Jeremiah with his sacrificial principle, for he hints at other meanings of the death of Christ than are explicit in the priestly-sacrificial analogy. Covenant (διαθήκη) also means will, in the sense of a last will and testament, and no will is in effect until the death of the testator (9:16-17). He hints also at the argument from experience for the "same sacrifices which are continually offered year after year" are a "reminder of sin year after year," for "if the worshipers had once been cleansed, they would no longer have any consciousness of sin" (10:1-3). And in a most significant and all-too-brief passage (10:5-10) he actually cites a famous repudiation of sacrifices (Ps. 40:6-8), interpreting it to mean that the sacrifice of Christ made in the realm of the will fulfills the sacrificial principle. He does not quite draw the conclusion that the sacrifice required of men is of the will, which would lie outside his argument. He rather concludes that "by that will we have been consecrated through the offering of the body of Jesus Christ once for all" (10:10).

From 10:19 to the end of Hebrews the material is predominantly hortatory. After an earnest appeal to confidence, hope, and good works on the basis of the effective priesthood of Christ and as "you see the Day drawing near" (10:19-25), the author states the inevitable conclusion from his argument, "For if we sin deliberately after receiving the knowledge of the truth, there no longer remains a sacrifice for sins, but a fearful prospect of judgment, and a fury of fire which will consume the adversaries" (10:26). He has prepared the way for this stern word (cf. 6:4-8), and the rigorous logic of his position requires it. But as in 6:9 ff., judgment is not his final word; confidence, endurance, and faith, bulwarked by the conduct of his readers in the past and assured by the promise of Scrip-

ture for the future, guarantee that "we are not of those who shrink back and are destroyed, but of those who have faith and keep their souls" (10:32-39).

The appeal to their own past record (10:32 ff.), issuing in an assurance of faith, leads the author to survey the whole sweep of faith as it controlled the record of the past (ch. 11). It is perhaps a mistake to regard these notables as "heroes" of faith; they are rather "witnesses" to the true quality of faith as reliance on the unseen and immaterial reality over against all apparent and tangible goods. The reference of their faith is forward, and specifically to the present moment "since God had foreseen something better for us, that apart from us they should not be made perfect" (11:40). Time fails the author here not only to list all the witnesses, but also to document from scripture the proof that faith was indeed the moving force in their conduct.

The object of faith, but dimly apprehended by the "cloud of witnesses" surrounding them, has been clarified and made real in Jesus "the pioneer and perfecter of our faith, who for the joy that was set before him endured the cross, despising the shame, and is seated at the right hand of the throne of God" (12:2) as the victor and the assurance of victory for all who look to him.

But this victory was wrought out through the discipline of suffering. If Jesus endured this discipline, we ought not to "grow weary or faint-hearted" but to persevere in the struggle against sin "to the point of shedding . . . blood," for discipline is scriptural (Prov. 3:11-12) as administered by human fathers to their own sons—how much more endurable it is when it comes from the "Father of spirits"! It is "for a short time" only and "for our good, that we may share his holiness," yielding "the peaceful fruit of righteousness to those who have been trained by it" (12:3-11).

The chapter closes (12:12-29) with an earnest but rather general exhortation followed by an impressive warning against failing "to obtain the grace of God" and refusing "him who is speaking." The awesome character of the revelation given to Moses on the mountain is but a shadowy reminder of the reality of Mount Zion, the city of the living God, the heavenly Jerusalem, and the eternal verities with which they have to do. These are the unshakable realities to be contemplated in the fear of God. Yet fear is not the author's final word. The acknowledgment that "our God is a consuming fire" ought to issue in gratitude "for receiving a kingdom that cannot be shaken," and ought to induce us to "offer to God acceptable worship, with reverence and awe" (12:28).

The final chapter, as the epistle comes to us (ch. 13), contains sundry exhortations about hospitality to strangers, compassion for those in prison and for the ill-treated, the honor due to marriage, freedom from the love of money, and respect for and obedience to leaders, as well as a warning against "diverse and strange teachings" (13:1-17). After a request for his readers' prayers "that I may be restored to you the sooner" (vss. 18-19) the author concludes with a full and beautiful benediction (vss. 20-21), to which is appended a postscript containing further personalia and a final brief benediction.

The general plan of Hebrews may be exhibited for convenience in the form of an outline, although the thought is so closely knit that no outline can reproduce fully the interrelations of the author's ideas. Decisive forward steps in his argument, such as 4:14, are evident, but it is not possible to suggest the subtle and skillful way in which he prepares his readers for the exposition of Jesus as high priest (in 2:17; 3:1), for the discussion of "God's rest" (in 3:11, 18), and for the Melchizedek speculation (in 5:6, 10; 6:20). No outline can do justice to these and other niceties.

The special difficulty Hebrews presents to the outliner does not lie in an impetuous and rapid movement of thought, as in the case of Paul's writings, but in the author's habit of interweaving massive argument and earnest exhortation. How are we to designate such hortatory passages as 2:1 ff.; 3:7 ff.; 5:11-6:20; and ch. 11? To term them "inserted exhortations" or "digressions" is to beg the question of the author's purpose, inclining the student who takes the outline seriously to regard these passages as incidental, rather than integral, to the main purpose. The question of precisely what is the purpose of Hebrews is closely related to the literary problem and must not be prejudged. An outline, accordingly, should be regarded not as a substitute for the mastery of the text, but as a device for aiding the reader to hold the writer's entire thought in mind as he studies each section of the epistle.

I. Theme: The finality and perfection of God's revelation in a Son (1:1-2a)
II. Argument: Jesus Christ is the final and perfect revelation of God because in his person he is Son and in his work he is Priest (1:2b–10:18)
  A. The personality of the Son (1:2b–4:13)
    1. He is superior to angels as Son, yet able to help men because he "has suffered and been tempted" (1:2b–2:18)
      a) Supremacy of the Son (1:2b-4)
      b) Proof from Scripture (1:5-14)
      c) Warning against inattention and neglect (2:1-4)
      d) Preview of Jesus' work in salvation (2:5-18)
    2. He is superior to Moses as a son is superior to a servant (3:1-6a)
    3. Resultant warning and exhortation based on Ps. 95 (3:6b–4:13)
      a) Introduction (3:6b-11)
      b) Failure of an ancient generation (3:12-19)
      c) Danger of the same failure today (4:1-13)
  B. The work made possible by the personality of Jesus, the Son of God (4:14–10:18)
    1. Jesus is a divinely appointed high priest, "after the order of Melchizedek" (4:14–5:10)
      a) Introduction and transition (4:14-16)
      b) Jesus' qualifications as high priest (5:1-10)
    2. The readers are exhorted to attend to this difficult teaching (5:11–6:20)
      a) By a rebuke (5:11-14)
      b) By a warning (6:1-8)
      c) By an encouragement (6:9-12)
      d) By an assurance (6:13-20)
    3. The Melchizedek priesthood of Christ in its superiority to the Levitical (7:1-28)
    4. The ministry of Jesus as high priest (8:1–10:18)
      a) He ministers in the heavenly sanctuary, not in the earthly copy (8:1-5)
      b) The new place of sacrifice implies a new covenant as the scripture predicted (8:6-13)
      c) The sacrifices of the old and the new covenants are contrasted (9:1-14)
      d) The sacrifice of Christ fulfills the promise of the new covenant (9:15–10:18)
        (1) Theme introduced and established (9:15-22)
        (2) Cleansing of the heavenly sanctuary and the finality of Christ's redemption (9:23-28)
        (3) Failure of the old covenant and the perfection of the new (10:1-18)
III. Application: In view of the perfection of God's revelation in Christ, hold fast by faith, for failure to do so means a fearful judgment (10:19–12:29)
  A. The finality of access to God through Christ also entails a finality of judgment for those who disobey (10:19-31)
  B. The readers' record inspires confidence (10:32-39)
  C. The continuity and solidarity of the faith (11:1-40)
  D. What these leaders witnessed to has been made real in Jesus: let us run our race looking unto him (12:1-2)
  E. Discipline is inherent in sonship, human and divine (12:3-11)

F. Warning of the awful penalty of disobedience, relieved by a final word of assurance (12:12-29)

IV. Concluding exhortations, followed by personal references and benedictions (13:1-25)

## II. Tradition in the Early Church

Tradition gives us direct and indirect information about the title, the author, the date, and to a limited extent about the thought of Hebrews, as these questions were considered in the early church. In this section we shall briefly survey this evidence, reserving a full discussion of these critical questions for later sections.

The title "To the Hebrews," under which the writing is included in the canon, must have been in use at a relatively early date. From the late second century we have two witnesses to this title: Pantaenus (quoted by Eusebius from Clement of Alexandria) and Tertullian. They differ as to authorship, Pantaenus ascribing Hebrews to Paul, and Tertullian to Barnabas; they agree in describing it as written "To the Hebrews." Since the writing never went under any other title in the later church, we must conclude that it was early circulated under that title. This must not be pressed to mean that the title was the work of the author; there are decisive reasons for rejecting that view.

The earliest witness for the existence of Hebrews is I Clement (cf. 36:1-5; 17:1, 5; 19:2; 27:2; 43:1; 56:2-4; etc.), a letter sent from the church at Rome to the church at Corinth, traditionally ascribed to Clement and usually dated in the last decade of the first century. The verbal identities are sufficient to establish the fact of literary interrelationship and the character of the two writings precludes the possibility that Hebrews copied from I Clement. I Clement, although addressed to a church founded by Paul, does not name him as the author of the quotations. Moffatt concludes his survey of the earliest evidences of the existence of Hebrews with the words, "The evidence of the second century upon the whole is sufficient to show that it was being widely circulated and appreciated as an edifying religious treatise, canonical or not." [1]

The most extended discussion of authorship comes from a group of Alexandrian scholars quoted by Eusebius in his *Church History*.[2] Their judgments about the authorship of Hebrews are of interest not only in themselves but as revealing the rise and decline of sound

literary criticism. Pantaenus (*ca.* 185) accepts Pauline authorship without question and explains the lack of the customary Pauline authentication on the grounds that "Paul, as sent to the Gentiles, on account of his modesty did not subscribe himself an apostle of the Hebrews, through respect for the Lord and because being a herald and apostle of the Gentiles he wrote to the Hebrews out of his superabundance." While not questioning Pauline authorship, Pantaenus witnesses to a certain uneasiness about it.

Eusebius records the way in which Clement of Alexandria (died *ca.* 215) dealt with this problem:

He says [i.e., Clement] that the Epistle to the Hebrews is the work of Paul, and that it was written to the Hebrews in the Hebrew language [Aramaic?]; but that Luke translated it carefully and published it for the Greeks, and hence the same style of expression is found in this epistle and in the Acts. But he says that the words, Paul the Apostle, were probably not prefixed, because, in sending it to the Hebrews, who were prejudiced and suspicious of him, he wisely did not wish to repel them at the very beginning by giving his name.[3]

The one sound observation here is that the style of Hebrews is not Pauline, the suggestion of an original text in Hebrew having nothing to commend it, and the naming of Luke as the translator having no basis except that Acts is in better Greek than Paul wrote.

Critical acumen comes to its flowering in Origen (*ca.* 182-251). He writes, according to Eusebius,

that the verbal style of the epistle entitled "To the Hebrews," is not rude like the language of the apostle, who acknowledged himself "rude in speech" [cf. II Cor. 11:6], that is, in expression; but that its diction is purer Greek, any one who has the power to discern differences of phraseology will acknowledge. Moreover, that the thoughts of the epistle are admirable, and not inferior to the acknowledged apostolic writings, any one who carefully examines the apostolic text will admit.[4]

Origen's problem, then, stated with typical scholarly hauteur, is to reconcile un-Pauline style with what he regards as apostolic (Pauline) thought. His solution is as follows:

If I gave my opinion, I should say that the thoughts are those of the apostle, but the diction and phraseology are those of some one who remembered the apostolic teachings, and wrote down at his leisure what had been said by his teacher. There-

---

[1] *Epistle to the Hebrews* (New York: Charles Scribner's Sons, 1924; "International Critical Commentary"), p. xv.
[2] See Hans Windisch, *Der Hebräerbrief* (Tübingen: J. C. B. Mohr, 1931; "Handbuch zum Neuen Testament"), pp. 4-6, where the evidence is conveniently summarized.

[3] *Church History* VI. 14. 2-3.
[4] *Ibid.* 25. 11-12.

fore if any church holds that this epistle is by Paul, let it be commended for this. For not without reason have the ancients handed it down as Paul's. But who wrote the epistle, in truth, God knows [τίς δὲ ὁ γράψας τὴν ἐπιστολήν τὸ μὲν ἀληθὲς θεὸς οἶδεν]. The statement of some who have gone before us is that Clement, bishop of the Romans, wrote the epistle, and of others that Luke, the author of the Gospel and of Acts, wrote it.[5]

Origen's famous words to the effect that God alone knows who wrote the epistle, quoted in all modern discussions, must not be removed from the context. They refer specifically to the literary style of Hebrews, however true they may be of the thought also. There is a curiously hesitant note throughout Origen's comment and one has the impression that he is more concerned to validate Hebrews as apostolic than to establish Paul's role in it.

In the East, from Origen on, critical doubts as to the Pauline authorship decline. Dionysius, bishop of Alexandria (247-64), quotes Hebrews as Paul's without qualification. Eusebius of Caesarea (ca. 325) holds to a Pauline original in Hebrew but thinks Clement of Rome was the translator. He counts fourteen letters of Paul but puts Hebrews among the "disputed" in deference to Roman opinion.[6] After the third century Hebrews is reckoned as Pauline in the Greek and Syrian Orient by all orthodox theologians; only the Arians dispute this, and they do so on theological, that is, christological, grounds.

In the fourth century the Alexandrian tradition began to influence the West, but up to this time, as far as we know, no one there held Hebrews to be the work of Paul. We have noted that I Clement quotes it without ascribing it to Paul. Eusebius knows that "some have rejected the Epistle to the Hebrews, saying that it is disputed by the church of Rome, on the ground that it was not written by Paul," and "unto our day there are some among the Romans who do not consider this a work of the apostle."[7]

It is Tertullian of Africa (died ca. 225) who first names Barnabas in a passage which also reveals why he prized Hebrews. He writes:

For there exists also a writing of Barnabas to the Hebrews, a man sufficiently authorized by God whom Paul placed beside himself in the matter of abstinence: "Or have I alone and Barnabas no right to work?" [I Cor. 9:6], and would that the letter of Barnabas were rather received among the churches than that apocryphal Shepherd of the adulterers. And so admonishing the disciples, leav-

ing all beginnings behind to stretch forward rather to perfection nor again to lay the foundations of repentance from the works of the dead. . . .[8]

And Tertullian continues the quotation about the impossibility of a second repentance, through Heb. 6:8. It is evident that Tertullian desires apostolic authority for Hebrews because of this special teaching; that he rejects or does not know of the tradition of Pauline authorship; and that he names Barnabas as author. There are one or two further traces of the Barnabas tradition, but we know nothing of the source. The validity of the tradition that Barnabas was the author will be discussed later.

In some quarters in the West the situation was not so much that Pauline authorship was rejected as that the writing itself was ignored, as for example, by the Muratorian Canon, Cyprian, and others. It was finally accepted not on the grounds of critical judgment, but by the authority of the churches of the East. Jerome's position, set forth in a letter to Claudianus Postumus Dardanus (A.D. 414), is significant enough to quote in full:

This is to say to our friends, that this epistle which is inscribed "to the Hebrews" is received not only by the churches of the East, but also by all church writers of the Greek tongue before our day, as of Paul the apostle, although many think it is from Barnabas or Clement. And it makes no difference whose it is, since it is from a churchman, and is celebrated in the daily readings of the churches. And if the usage of the Latins does not receive it among the canonical Scriptures, neither, indeed, by the same liberty do the churches of the Greeks receive the Revelation of John. And yet we accept both, in that we follow by no means the habit of today, but the authority of ancient writers, who for the most part quote each of them, not as they are sometimes accustomed to do the apocrypha, and even also as they use rarely the examples of profane books, but as canonical and churchly.[9]

The acceptance of Hebrews as Paul's and therefore as canonical gradually obtained in the West, and the memory of the critical objections was almost lost. For a thousand years no significant discussion is known to us, and it was not until the Reformation that critical doubts about Hebrews were again raised. The Council of Trent (1546) spoke the final word for the Roman church by including Hebrews among the letters of Paul.

The evidence from tradition boils down to the following results: First, Hebrews was known

[5] Ibid. 13-14.
[6] Ibid. III. 3. 5; 38. 1-3.
[7] Ibid. III. 3. 5; VI. 20. 3.
[8] On Modesty 20.
[9] Epistle 129; translated by M. S. Enslin, Christian Beginnings (New York: Harper & Bros., 1938), p. 472. Used by permission.

and prized, especially in the East but also in the West, from the second century on (if I Clement can be dated in the last decade of the first century). Second, so far as our witnesses testify, it bore the title "To the Hebrews" when it came to them. Third, it never named its author. Fourth, the discussion of authorship was involved in the larger question of apostolic authority. Fifth, Pauline authorship, as proposed in Alexandria, made its way against serious critical objections and finally prevailed by authority of the East. It is to be weighed, so far as tradition goes, over against the silence of Western witnesses, as well as against their explicit rejection and against Tertullian's ascription of Hebrews to Barnabas.

Because of the negative character of the evidence from tradition, amounting to ignorance of the origin of Hebrews, questions as to authorship, date, provenance, destination, purpose, and literary form can best be examined against the background of the religious ideas set forth in the writing itself.

### III. Religious Ideas of Hebrews

Hebrews is unique among New Testament writings in style, arrangement, and especially in thought. It is the more important at the outset to note that our author works with a common stock of religious ideas which he can assume as acceptable to his readers from the Christian background which he shares with them. That he and they represent "a small, forgotten circle" in the main Christian movement can be argued, but Hebrews did ultimately win acceptance in the canon not only because it was congenial to Alexandrian thinkers, but also because it presents essentially Christian teaching. It will be of value to summarize the ideas our author shares with other New Testament writers in order to see his unique treatment of these ideas more clearly.

A. Primitive Christian Ideas.—That the person and work of Christ the Son are the final and complete revelation of God is stated rather than argued as an assumption shared by author and readers (cf. 1:1 ff.; etc.). This revelation has been made within humanity and at the point of human need (2:5-18; etc.). The writer repeatedly uses the simple name Jesus, rarely found in the New Testament outside the Gospels, to designate this revealer in his earthly service (2:9; 3:1; 5:7; 7:22; 10:19; 12:2, 24; 13:12). His service focuses in his death (see especially 9:1–10:18); it is foreshadowed in the law (cf. 9:1 ff.; 10:1 ff.; etc.); and was necessary for the forgiveness of sins (see 9:22; etc.). He is "seated at the right hand of the throne of the Majesty in heaven" (8:1) and will "appear a

second time, not to deal with sin but to save those who are eagerly waiting for him" (9:28) and "you see the Day drawing near" (10:25). His death ensures the overthrow of the devil (2:14) and the deliverance of those in bondage (2:15). The response to this revelation required of men is faith (4:2-3; 10:22, 38-39; 11:1-40; 12:2) and obedience (4:6, 11; 12:25) and it inspires hope (6:18-19; 11:1). What they receive is "a kingdom that cannot be shaken" (12:28). They are to "stir up one another to love and good works" (10:24; cf. 13:1 ff.) and not to be "led away by diverse and strange teachings" (13:9). And finally, the author bases his argument on Scripture, which he quotes or refers to in every chapter.

Each item in the above list, which might be enlarged, belongs to the primitive Christian tradition and can be documented from the early New Testament writings. This result has been obtained, however, by rigorously excluding all the unique words and ideas used in Hebrews and by ignoring the omissions, for example, the Resurrection and the sacraments. Perhaps it is unfair to use the argument from silence in view of the author's own words, "Therefore let us leave the elementary doctrines of Christ and go on to maturity" (6:1 ff.), although the Resurrection can be shown to lie outside the structure of his thought (see on 4:14). This one-sided presentation of the thought of Hebrews—it is true but scarcely half the truth—shows the author working with primitive Christian tradition. This must have been apparent to his first readers as it is to us; it must have been equally apparent that Hebrews develops each item in a unique way and that his central argument about the priesthood of Christ does not belong to the primitive tradition as we know it from other New Testament writings. We must endeavor to understand his distinctive contribution against the background of the common tradition he inherited.

B. Dominant Idea.—The author says: "Now the point (κεφάλαιον) in what we are saying is this: we have such a high priest, one who is seated at the right hand of the throne of the Majesty in heaven, a minister in the sanctuary and the true tent which is set up not by man but by the Lord. . . . They [i.e., priests on earth] serve a copy and shadow of the heavenly sanctuary; for when Moses was about to erect the tent, he was instructed by God, saying, 'See that you make everything according to the pattern which was shown you on the mountain'" (8:1-2, 5; cf. 9:11-14, 23-24; 10:1).

He is controlled by a two-story view of reality: on the ground floor the shadowy, transient, fugitive events and institutions; in the upper story the permanent, perfect realm of reality. What men need for their salvation is access to the upper story, i.e., to God, "a new and living way . . . through the curtain" (10:19). This access is only possible through acceptable worship as the divinely instituted priestly sacrifices, in spite of their earthly imperfection, abundantly prove (9:1 ff.). Christ as perfect priest and perfect sacrifice has opened the way for all who will follow him in faith.

This two-story view of reality is not confined to the central argument but controls the entire thought of Hebrews. It explains the high Christology of the opening verses, for no language is too lofty to express the scope and the power of the realm of reality revealed and opened up to us by the word God spoke in Christ. It explains the inadequacy of angels, who do indeed dwell there, but in the role of "ministering spirits" (1:14) and not as sons, and who cannot enter into the suffering and temptation of men. This, Jesus alone can do, "for it was fitting that he, for whom and by whom all things exist, in bringing many sons to glory, should make the pioneer of their salvation perfect through suffering" (2:10), "that he might become a merciful and faithful high priest in the service of God" (2:17). Moses and Aaron qualified in respect to humanity and in faithfulness, but their role was exclusively in the shadowy realm, although the law and its institutions of sacrifice pointed in the direction from which salvation was to come. The Melchizedek argument, labored as it may seem to us, is of the essence of our author's thought, establishing from Scripture the existence of a priest (Christ) whose priesthood is "by the power of an indestructible life" (7:16). The whole meticulous argument about Christ as the perfect priest is designed to prove that his priesthood is the pattern and the Levitical only the copy, and that in obedience to Christ men may walk the way that leads directly to God and "may receive mercy and find grace to help in time of need" (4:16).

We might expect to find our author's treatment of faith closer to primitive Christian teaching, but again it is dominated throughout by his controlling idea. Faith has to do with "things hoped for" and "things not seen" (11:1), and this emphasis persists throughout the famous ch. 11. The merit of the witnesses consists chiefly in their loyalty to values seen only dimly and from afar. If their record is one of stirring achievement, how much more ought we to run our race with perseverance, "looking to Jesus the pioneer and perfecter of our faith, who . . . is seated at the right hand of the throne of God" (12:1-2).

Only the author's eschatology seems conspicuously to lie outside the logic of his thought. If he is really convinced that all earthly things are copies and shadows of the heavenly, and that faith "is the power of apprehension of that which lies beyond the senses," should not the time process itself, and eschatology as depending on it, have been discarded as with Philo or spiritualized after the fashion of the Gospel of John? Actually, eschatological ideas are clear and sharp in his thinking even if they do not hold the central place. It is "in these last days" that God has spoken in a Son (1:2), who "has appeared once for all at the end of the age to put away sin by the sacrifice of himself" (9:26) "now to appear in the presence of God on our behalf" (9:24). "Not yet" (2:8) is the promise of Ps. 8 fulfilled, although Christians "have tasted the heavenly gift, and . . . the powers of the age to come" (6:4, 5). The promise is still promise and not fulfillment (4:1; 6:12; 9:15; 10:36) and they are to hold fast to the end in hope (3:6, 14; 6:11, 18; 7:19; 10:23, 25). "Christ . . . will appear a second time" (9:28) and the "elementary doctrines" the author is leaving behind include "the resurrection of the dead, and eternal judgment" (6:2; cf. 11:35). The judgment will be painful for "the adversaries" but rewarding for those who "please him" (9:27; 10:27; 13:4; 10:35; 11:6, 26). Salvation, in the full sense, is eschatological (9:28), although the "rest of God" is ready for us "today" and we must "strive to enter" (4:3, 6, 11), for the "city" which the ancients sought (11:10, 13-16) confronts us (12:22), yet it is still "to come" (13:14), an unshakable "kingdom" (12:28). "You see the Day drawing near" (10:25) and "you have need of endurance, . . . 'For yet a little while'" (10:36, 37).

The conclusion to be drawn from this strong eschatological emphasis in a framework of alien ideas is obvious: our author was not a philosophic idealist.[10] He was a Christian committed to the historic revelation of God in Christ and he writes with a thoroughly practical purpose: to arouse his readers to a positive Christian stand. Nevertheless, the revelation in history is authenticated for him by the fact that it opens the way into the realm of reality where time gives place to eternity, the copy to the pattern and the shadow to the substance. The dominance of this idea and its application to priesthood differentiates Hebrews from the Synoptics, Paul, and the Gospel of John. It is

[10] "To call him an 'idealist' is the only alternative [to calling him a mystic], and this is misleading, for idealism suggests a philosophical detachment which is not suitable to Πρὸς Ἑβραίους" (Moffatt, *Epistle to Hebrews*, p. lv).

"the epistle of priesthood" and we must examine the author's exposition of priesthood in order to understand his thought. But first let us consider the possible sources of the two-world conception which makes the exposition of Jesus as priest meaningful.

**C. Sources of the Author's Thought.**—Like Melchizedek, the author of Hebrews is "without father or mother or genealogy" (7:3) so far as his personal identity goes. His kinship with contemporary thinkers, however, can be definitely shown. The idea of a realm of reality over against the shadowy realm presented by our senses is clearly Platonic, but, of course, this does not mean that our author had read Plato or that he was a philosopher like Plato. It means that his Christian convictions are presented in the atmosphere of Platonic idealism.

It has long been recognized that Hebrews betrays a close kinship with the thinking of Philo of Alexandria,[11] extending to very striking verbal parallelism. While the author's Christology (see below) is the most impressive evidence of Philonic influence, his use of scripture is almost equally conclusive. Like Philo, he works with the Greek translation of the Old Testament (the Septuagint) and at times his use of a passage depends on a word present in the Septuagint and absent in the Hebrew text (see on 1:10); he presses single words (8:13); employs the etymology of proper names (7:2); stresses the silence of scripture (1:5, 13; 7:3); applies all possible passages to a single figure— the Logos in Philo, Christ in Hebrews (1:5, 6, 8-9; 2:6, 12-13; 10:5-7). Like Philo also, he disregards the historical setting of the scripture passages. His selection of scriptural passages and ideas is also strikingly Philonic. With Philo he mentions the oath of God "by himself" (6:13); what was "fitting" for God (2:10); an estimate of Abel (11:4); the righteousness of Noah (11:7); the faithfulness of Moses (3:2); the obedience of Abraham (11:8); the superhuman significance of Melchizedek (7:1-4); the wandering of the patriarchs as a figure of the homelessness of the pious (11:13-16); the evaluation of deliberate sin (10:26), and the impossibility of repentance in such a case (12:17); the conception of faith as exemplified by Old Testament worthies (11:1-40); and the idea of a heavenly pattern and an earthly copy of the sanctuary derived from Exod. 25:40 (Heb. 8:5).[12]

Again, we are not to conclude that our author

himself was familiar with the writings of Philo; most of these ideas may have been the common property of Hellenistic Judaism. What the parallels do prove is that he worked with a non-Palestinian Jewish tradition and that his interpretation of Scripture was definitely Philonic. He differs from Philo in holding that everything centers in Christ, who has entered into human experience as a priest, and in his retention of the primitive Christian eschatology. Our epistle does not extend the two-world idea to include everything, although this may be implied, but fastens attention on two supersensual realities, the heavenly sanctuary (8:2, 5; 9:11-12, 23-24) and the heavenly city (11:10, 16; 12:22; 13:14), both of which could have been derived directly from Judaism.

The most obvious source of his thinking is the Old Testament institution of priesthood and sacrifice. Even in normative Judaism the validity of the cult was not destroyed, in theory at least, by the destruction of the temple, for the study of the law of sacrifice was to be the surrogate for its literal performance.[13] While our author develops his thinking about priesthood along lines made familiar to us in Philo, his attempt to validate sacrifice as a permanent principle is good Judaism. It is only the absence of this type of thought in other New Testament writings which makes him seem unique. The attempt to discover influences from the mystery religions [14] is less successful than in the case of Paul and the Gospel of John. He does not use the title Savior, although the idea is present (2:10; 5:9); sacraments are not prominent, and most of the other parallels alleged can be shown to spring directly from Judaism and the primitive Christian tradition.

The question of originality is not answered by citing the possible sources of his thought. This author alone of all the writers known to us presented Christ "as the eternal [high priest], by whom the access of man to God is finally and fully assured [and this] may have been a flash of inspiration," which is "not [to be] depreciated by the effort to trace anticipations."[15] It is more important to grasp his idea of the priesthood of Christ than to attempt an evaluation of its relative originality.

**D. Idea of Priesthood.**—The priestly analogy, drawn entirely from the Old Testament, is the source both of the unique contribution and of certain limitations of the thought of Hebrews. The author assumes that the institution of sacrifice is the one divinely appointed way of

---

[11] For a general survey of Philo's life and thought see E. R. Goodenough, *An Introduction to Philo* (New Haven: Yale University Press, 1940).

[12] For the Philonic parallels see Exeg. on the passages cited; also Moffatt, *Epistle to Hebrews;* Windisch, *Der Hebräerbrief.*

[13] G. F. Moore, *Judaism* (Cambridge: Harvard University Press, 1927), I, 505-6.

[14] Windisch, *Hebräerbrief,* p. 135.

[15] Moffatt, *Epistle to Hebrews,* p. xlvi.

dealing with sins, and that access to God, "drawing near" to him, is the *summum bonum* of religion. Accordingly, he asks his readers to think of Christ, God's final and perfect word to men, as priest and offering through whom they may "draw near" to God, "hold fast" in spite of persecution and lethargy, and enter into the promise. As priest, Christ must be divinely called and humanly sympathetic (2:14-18; 4:15-16; 5:1-3); must "make expiation for the sins of the people" (2:17) offering "gifts and sacrifices" (8:3), and above all, blood, for "under the law almost everything is purified with blood, and without the shedding of blood there is no forgiveness of sins" (9:22); and must open the way into the very presence of God for all who have faith in his priestly person and offering (9:7; 10:19-22). Christ has not only fulfilled the requirements of priesthood; he has ended forever all outward priestly rites by achieving the goal they were designed to represent, that is, unhindered access to God. This he has been able to accomplish because of his superior person and work. He is Son and his priesthood is the priesthood of the Son who was called by God for this service (5:4) and authenticated in it by the oath of God himself (7:20-22). Although sympathetic with men because of suffering and temptation, he is not hampered like earthly priests by sin (4:15; 7:26), and so his priesthood is permanent and timeless, "made perfect forever" (7:23-24, 28; 9:14). The earthly rites availed to purify the body; Christ's offering of himself through the eternal Spirit purifies the conscience (9:9-14; 10:4). It is the ultimate and perfect sacrifice which is never to be repeated (10:18), and which terminates all the shadowy rites and ceremonies associated with the Old Testament priesthood.

The logic of the author's analogy leads to the denial of a second repentance (6:4; 10:26-27), to his special view of perfection, and to his exposition of the necessity of Christ's death. The concept of the new covenant, although the passage from Jeremiah which he quotes has no mention of priestly sacrifice, and the idea of a will or testament (covenant and will are the same Greek word, διαθήκη) are both assimilated to his idea of priesthood through the role of death and of blood in covenant and will (9:15-28).

The limitations of this analogy are obvious. In its formal aspects the argument rests solely on the authority of scripture, and the appeal to Christian experience, although not neglected (4:2-3; 6:4-5; etc.), is made in that framework. The author's valiant attempt to sublimate the external and sensual aspects of the sacrificial system has resulted, it may be argued, only in fixing terms like "blood" and "offering," and indeed all the transactional ideas of priesthood, in Christian thinking. Did he succeed, it may well be asked, in sublimating priesthood or only in formalizing and externalizing Christ? And finally, the very logic of his analogy, pressed to the limit, renders his argument somewhat academic in spite of his evident earnestness. In his defense we may point out first that the efficacy of bloody sacrifices was an axiom widely accepted in antiquity, and that the Old Testament institution of sacrifice witnesses to the deep-seated human conviction that sin is a costly thing and can be dealt with only by radical measures. Second, there is no slightest suggestion of the author's intention to reconstitute outward sacrifice of any kind; on the contrary, he is explicit in emphasizing that "it is impossible that the blood of bulls and goats should take away sins" (10:4), and that the sacrifice of Christ ended all sacrifices and did so by cleansing the heart from an evil conscience. And third, while our author is indisputably academic—that is the kind of man he was—he is to be reckoned as perhaps the first Christian known to us who attempted to present the gospel in the form of a philosophy of religion, authenticating it over against another religion, Judaism, as fulfilling the valid ideas imperfectly realized in that religion.

While it is true that Hebrews deals less profoundly than Paul with the moral problem of man's life and with the death and resurrection of Christ and the gift of the Spirit as its solution, the author does speak directly to the universal human longing for fellowship with God through worship as no other New Testament writer does. The institution of priesthood was the answer of antiquity to that quest, and by presenting Christ in his humanity, and especially in his death, as the perfect priest who ended all outward rites by fulfilling their shadowy anticipations, he made a permanent contribution to Christian thought and experience for all who grasp his thought in its entirety.

***E. Christology.***—It is customary to classify I Peter, Revelation, and Hebrews as the three New Testament writings directed to Christians who are suffering persecution, and to say that I Peter meets this situation with an ethical, Revelation with an apocalyptic, and Hebrews with a christological argument. In the case of Hebrews both the nature of the persecution and the meaning of the Christology require examination.

In what sense is Hebrews a christological argument? Obviously in the sense that it is concerned with Christ as priest. The priesthood of Christ is our author's unique contribution to New Testament Christology. His purpose is prevailingly practical and, aside from the priesthood analogy (developed for a practical end), he does not so much argue as assume christological doctrines. Christology in the sense of a reasoned doctrine of the person of Christ is not, indeed, secondary to his practical objective; it is rather prerequisite to the run of his thought. His purpose is not to teach that Christ is the Son, or that as Son he shared human experience from within humanity, but to show how these accepted facts qualified him for perfect priesthood. Both the divine sonship and the human experience of Christ derive directly from the primitive tradition. It is argued that the references to Jesus' humanity are so general (see 2:17-18; cf. 4:15; 5:7 ff.), that they are so dependent upon scripture and the necessities of the priestly analogy, and that there are so many preparations in Philo and in late Judaism for this idea, that no knowledge of the Synoptic tradition was necessary; the author simply spun the whole fabric of his Christology out of the materials present in his own mind. This interpretation violates the principle of economy. We know the author was a Christian and we know that both the idea of Christ as Son and the memory of the human experience of Jesus were integral parts of the primitive tradition. The nature of his argument required scriptural authentication and his knowledge of the Christ tradition would not have served his end. It was the necessity of this human experience which he needed to prove, not the reality of it as a fact. This he could do only by citing scripture.

In what direction did he move out from the primitive tradition? Traces of the Synoptic Christology remain, e.g., 12:28, but Christ for Hebrews is not the anointed agent (Messiah) for bringing in the kingdom; he is the agent through whom God created the world, who "reflects the glory of God and bears the very stamp of his nature, upholding the universe by his word of power" (1:2-3). He is the revealer of God—our author almost, but not quite, uses the term logos (1:1), although the logos idea is thoroughly congenial to him.[16] Pre-existence, existence, and postexistence are not the words, however, for characterizing his Christology because he is less controlled by the notion of a time process than by the thought of a timeless reality revealed within the limits of this world of time and sense. The passage 1:1-4 reminds us inevitably of the prologue of John's Gospel and 2:9 reminds us of Phil. 2:5 ff.; but

[16] In 1:3 and 6:5 he uses ῥῆμα, perhaps because it is less philosophical.

unlike the Gospel, this writer does not use the high Christology to present Jesus' words and deeds as revelatory of God but only as authenticating the priestly ministry of Christ, and unlike Paul, he sees the self-emptying (kenosis) not as a sacrifice which we should emulate (cf. Phil. 2:5), but as a necessary fulfillment of the priestly office.

To say that Hebrews has combined an adoptionist and an hypostatic Christology is not quite accurate, for although these two types seem to be merged, one suspects that our author has inherited rather than created the merger. He seems not to be concerned with such questions as when the Son became priest and how sonship and human experience can be reconciled. The idea of priesthood solves all problems for him, or at any rate the one problem, that is, how men can have immediate and permanent access to God; and this problem he deals with directly. His Christology is therefore further evidence of the practical and religious purpose of his writing.

Anticipations of his Christology are, however, embarrassingly many in contemporary writings. The one explicit source is the Old Testament (Septuagint), and his Christology, including the priesthood of Christ (see 5:6; etc.), is based solely upon the authority of scripture. But we have already noted (see p. 585, above) that his choice of scriptural passages, his method of interpreting them, and on occasion his very words (see on 1:1 ff.) are too close to the thinking of Philo of Alexandria to permit any other conclusion than that Hebrews is in the stream of thought best known to us in Philo.

The parallels between Philo's Logos and Hebrews' Christ are most impressive. Not only does our author set forth the relation of the Son to the Father and to the world in Philonic terms (see on 1:1 ff.) but he presents Melchizedek as typical of the ideal high priest (Christ) precisely as Philo equates Melchizedek with his Logos (see on 7:1 ff.). The sinlessness and the service attributed to Christ as priest (see on 4:15; 2:18) are similarly stressed by Philo in speaking of the Logos. The difference between Hebrews and Philo consists in a different orientation. The Logos for Philo is prevailingly a philosophical concept and can be equated with a "power of God" or "reason in man"; and while Philo has genuine religious objectives and can indeed conceive of an incarnate Logos, he could not have concentrated the Logos in one historic person whose human experience is the one and only source of salvation.

There are striking parallels also with Jewish angelology, especially with the figure of Michael. Passages like Dan. 12:1; 10:13, 21, where Michael is the protector and helper of the people of God, led to speculation about the mediatorial role of angels, although the term "priest" is lacking.[17] Our author begins his argument by proving from scripture that the Son is superior to angels. There is no explicit indication, however, that he is combating angel worship or the trend toward it on the part of his readers. Angels are recognized as in some inferior sense revealers (cf. 2:2), and they, like Moses, are superseded by the Son. The parallels with Jewish angel speculation enforce the conclusion that our author lives, moves, and has his being in the realm of the dualistic world view. As E. F. Scott remarks, "The truth is that this so-called Hebrew Epistle is the least Hebrew book in the New Testament." [18]

Like Paul, and perhaps for the same reason, our author avoids the title "Son of man," although the phrase "son of man" is present in Ps. 8, which he expounds (2:5 ff.). The phrase was meaningless in Greek and only acquired meaning when used as a complement of Son of God to indicate the humanity of Jesus Christ. It is, accordingly, somewhat doubtful if the writings known to us under the name of Enoch should be cited as a possible source for Hebrews. Nevertheless, as Moffatt remarks, "the preexistent Messiah there [that is, in Enoch 37–75] is Son of Man as transcendent and in some sense as human; he must be human, 'Man,' in order to help men, and he must be transcendent in order to be a deliverer or redeemer." [19] To this extent the Enochic conception is like that of Hebrews. It should perhaps be cited as another evidence of the prevalence of our author's basic ideas in the circumambient thought world.

We may sum up our author's Christology negatively by saying that he has nothing to do with the older Hebrew messianic hopes of a coming Son of David, who would be a divinely empowered human leader to bring in the kingdom of God on earth; and that while he still employs the figure of a militant, apocalyptic king (2:8; 7:1-2; 12:28) who will come again (9:28), this is not of the essence of his thought about Christ.

Positively, our author presents Christ as divine in nature, and solves any possible objection to a divine being who participates in human experience, especially in the experience of death, by the priestly analogy. He seems quite unconscious of the logical difficulties of his position, proceeding from the assumption that

Christ is both divine and human, at least human in experience although hardly in nature. It may not be inaccurate to describe his Christology as a kind of modalism, although any academic term fails to do complete justice to his thought, for he is controlled by a profoundly religious need for direct access to God through worship. This way through the curtain of our sin and of our senses has been opened up by Jesus, the one and only perfect priest of God. Preparations for this type of interpretation are many in contemporary thinking, but no one source seems to account for the precise crystallization achieved in Hebrews.

**F. Ethical Teaching.**—There is an earnest note of exhortation throughout the writing, but with the exception of those in ch. 13, the ethical admonitions are quite general in character. The readers are warned against inattention (2:1), disobedience (4:11), dullness of hearing (5:11), and sluggishness (6:12), and are encouraged to earnestness "in realizing the full assurance of hope until the end" (6:11). Sin is deceitful and to avoid being hardened by it they must exhort "one another every day" (3:13). Our high priest is able to "sympathize with our weaknesses" (4:15); yet he is "holy, blameless, unstained" (7:26), "one who in every respect has been tempted as we are, yet without sinning" (4:15). They are to "struggle against sin" to the point of shedding blood if need be (12:4). Holding fast "to the confession of our hope without wavering" implies stirring up "one another to love and good works" (10:23, 24). Their record includes "compassion on the prisoners" and the reckoning of possessions which could be plundered as of lesser value than their "better possession," which is "an abiding one" (10:34). This same note of faith in eternal values as over against tangible and material earthly goods is sounded in ch. 11. The readers are to "strive for peace with all men" (12:14) and to avoid being "immoral or irreligious like Esau" (12:16). Ch. 13 adds specific injunctions about brotherly love, hospitality, remembering prisoners and the ill-treated, marriage, the love of money, and contentment "with what you have."

The sanctions and norms of conduct familiar to us in the Synoptics, Paul, and John are not entirely lacking in Hebrews; for example, God as Father of the Son (1:5; 5:5; both quotations from the Old Testament) and of men, though only in connection with discipline (12:9); love as the Christian ethos (10:24); and the idea that righteousness is the fruit of religion. But these ideas are not controlling. The ethical outlook is determined by the priestly analogy. This precludes any radical proposal of the re-

[17] Windisch, *Hebräerbrief*, p. 13.

[18] *The Varieties of New Testament Religion* (New York: Charles Scribner's Sons, 1943), p. 222.

[19] *Epistle to Hebrews*, p. xlix.

newal or transformation of man's will as the basic necessity for righteousness, for everything depends on a proper priest who makes an effective offering. Man's part is to have faith, confidence, and hope in perfect access to God through the perfect priest. To be sure, the sacrifice of Christ cleanses the conscience (10: 22), which outward sacrifices could not do (9:9), but we miss the note of a radical change effected by the Spirit, as with Paul, or the impact of God's love as determining behavior in the Sermon on the Mount. For the worshiper, gratitude and a sense of awe are the appropriate attitudes (12:28).

It is easy to say that Hebrews is less profound than Paul in the treatment of sin and of ethics; it is better to say that Hebrews is different. Everything depends on one's estimate of the goal of religion—is it "the righteousness of God" (Rom. 1:16-17) or is it drawing near "to the throne of grace" (4:16)? For our author and for all who share his conviction that worship is the root of the matter, the answer is not to be made in terms of relative depth of ideas but in terms of reality of experience.

**G. "Modern" Ideas in Ancient Dress.**—In concluding the survey of the religious ideas of Hebrews it may be well to point out that this writing, so thoroughly "dated" as to form of argument, "of all the New Testament writings, is in many ways the most modern." Ideas which we regard as peculiarly modern are foreshadowed, although never quite in the modern way. For example, the author's presentation of faith as loyalty to unseen values and as the creative power in the past—faith is not for him a uniquely Christian teaching; only the clarification of its object and the realization of its goal are unique—is congenial to many today (see on ch. 11). His cognate idea of the solidarity of history (11:40), and of the continuity of the basic religious hungers of men, typified in the institution of sacrifice and satisfied in the sacrifice of Christ, approaches a developmental idea of history. He did not have the evolutionary concept to work with and, no doubt, would not have accepted it, but his use of symbolism approximates development. E. F. Scott seems to go too far in saying that our author's attitude to other religions is modern in a remarkable degree: "[Hebrews] presents the new religion as the 'perfecting' or fulfillment of those which preceded it. They were not false but only incomplete." [20] The plurals are unwarranted; it was only Judaism, in the direct line of revelation, which was fulfilled. Yet a principle is laid down capable of application to other religions.

[20] *Varieties of N.T. Religion,* pp. 231-32.

This article has avoided the use of the term "mystical," a slippery word; yet it is clear that our author does not follow the Pauline line in setting forth the relation of the Christian to Christ. "In Christ," "in the Spirit," are expressions and ideas foreign to his thinking. His readers are exhorted to "run with perseverance the race that is set before us, looking to Jesus" (12:1). His treatment of the historic reality of Jesus and its essential place in his ministry is appealing to the nonmystical, although it must be remembered that he does not focus attention upon the ethical teaching and the deeds of mercy to be imitated by those who run their race; these historic facts are used to prove that Jesus is a completely qualified high priest.

Perhaps the most significant emphasis from the modern point of view is the insistence upon the utter reality of the revelation in Christ. Other priests were prevented from dealing directly and authentically with the conscience of men by their own sinfulness and by the very paraphernalia and ritual of their office, guideposts to the true worship. Christ's priesthood was a priesthood of personality—although that word is not used—reaching home to men where they live and drawing them to God. It is true that our author never quite says this since his symbolism both suggests the idea and by its externality limits its full expression, yet it is not false to his central thought to say that he presents Christ as drawing men to God by his inherent worth and with an authority which "is not prescriptive but personal."

## IV. Authorship

Attempts to identify the author of Hebrews all rest on tradition or on inferences from the writing itself; it was anonymous when it came to our earliest witnesses. The probability is that Hebrews never bore the author's name, although the hypothesis of an accompanying personal note has been advanced. Only the authorship of the Gospel of John has proved more intriguing to New Testament scholars, but unless fresh evidence comes to light, Hebrews must remain a witness to the richness and variety of thought in the first century among Christians not known to us by name.

The long history of research on authorship has not been fruitless, however, for two solid convictions have emerged: (a) that Paul was not, either directly or indirectly, the author, and (b) that we do know the kind of man who wrote Hebrews in spite of our ignorance of his name.

Evidence against Pauline authorship has been suggested in the discussion of the tradition (pp. 581-83) and of the religious ideas (pp.

583 ff.). Tradition is either negative or contradictory as regards the authorship of Hebrews. But it is the structure and the fabric of the thought which count decisively against Paul. To be sure, a listing of the subjects treated in Hebrews as compared with Paul's letters helps us to understand how a really superb scholar such as Origen could say that "the thoughts are those of the apostle [Paul]." Of the many similarities between Hebrews and Paul, the following are perhaps the most striking: that Christ before the Incarnation possessed divine glory and shared in the Creation (1:1 ff.; cf. I Cor. 8:6; II Cor. 4:4; Col. 1:15-17); that he became truly human (2:14-17; Rom. 8:3; Gal. 4:4; Phil. 2:7); that the death of Christ was the central point of his mission; that the death effected redemption (ἀπολύτρωσις) for our sins (9:15; cf. Rom. 3:24; I Cor. 1:30; etc.); that Christ intercedes for us (7:25; cf. Rom. 8:34); that the law was shown to be ineffective by the revelation in Christ; that faith is the central response required of man, Abraham being an example; that the readers are immature (5:11 ff.; cf. I Cor. 3:1 ff.); and that the heavenly Jerusalem is our possession (12:22; cf. Gal. 4:26).

These similarities, however, are wholly superficial, proving only that Paul and our author worked with a common tradition. The characteristic ideas of Paul are lacking in Hebrews and vice versa. Hebrews knows nothing of the teaching of justification and does not emphasize the Resurrection (it is the Ascension that concerns the author; cf. 4:14), mystical union with Christ, the new life through the Spirit and in the spirit, or reconciliation. Paul does not present Christ as priest, and while the death of Christ is sacrificial, its consequences are described in moral rather than in liturgical terms, that is, in terms of righteousness instead of purification.

The concepts they share are quite differently developed. For Paul the Incarnation is an evidence of the condescension of Christ (II Cor. 8:9); for Hebrews it assures his priestly compassion, fellow feeling, and sympathy (2:17-18; 4:15-16). Paul regards the law as a curse, as introduced because of sin in order to bring home to man the consciousness of sin and his own helplessness, and so to be a tutor to lead him to Christ; Hebrews regards the law as the weak, imperfect foreshadowing of the true priesthood, preparing the way for Christ our great high priest. Paul thinks of the law predominantly under its moral aspects; Hebrews, in respect to its ritualistic requirements. Faith for Paul is receptivity to the gospel; it could

not function under the law, but only, as in the case of Abraham, before the law was given. Faith, for Hebrews, is that loyalty to unseen values which characterized all the worthies of the past who held fast to the invisible realities. The impossibility of a second repentance is not necessarily contrary to Paul's position, but he nowhere states it. In our author's use of Hellenistic ideas, especially the dualistic two-world concept, he has gone several steps beyond Paul who, while he can use language consonant with it, is much more basically eschatological in his thinking.

The author of Hebrews is an independent thinker. His name is not Paul, nor is he a Paulinist. The evidence for this conclusion is cumulative, including style—which the Alexandrian scholars saw and acknowledged—arrangement of materials, the interweaving of long exhortations with the argument in a manner not to be found in any of Paul's letters, and the whole fabric and fashion of the thought.

The one other name assigned as the author by tradition is that of Barnabas. Our information about Barnabas is scanty. That he was a Levite (Acts 4:36) and was associated with Paul may have suggested his as an appropriate name. Actually our author does not draw his analogy from the procedures of the Jerusalem temple but from the ancient tabernacle known to him from the Old Testament; and 7:27 and 9:4 reveal a lack of acquaintance with the temple ritual hardly likely in a contemporary Levite. In Gal. 2:13 Paul records that "even Barnabas" had leanings toward the observance of the food taboo. Our author betrays no such leanings.

Apollos, Aquila and Priscilla, Silas, Aristion, Philip the deacon, Timothy, and Luke are among the many other names suggested. The real or fancied qualifications of these persons amount to little more than ingenious guesses to be balanced against the probability that unknown persons may have been quite as well qualified. Apollos, whose name was transmitted (not first named) by Luther, seems to fit Hebrews best of all those suggested. He was a gifted teacher and an ingenious exegete (Acts 18:24-28; I Cor. 1:12 ff.; 3:6; 16:12), but we have no further knowledge of Apollos, no specimens to compare with Hebrews, and so the most that can be said for him is that there is nothing decisive against the hypothesis that Apollos could have been the author.

We must rest content, accordingly, with the very considerable knowledge to be derived from the study of Hebrews as to the kind of man our author was.

### V. Purpose and Literary Form

The purpose of Hebrews can be stated in general terms but whether it is directed to a specific group of readers to meet their specific situation is a question involving a judgment on the literary form, for references to personal relations with the readers are largely confined to the concluding chapter.

That Hebrews was written to prevent Jewish Christians from falling back into Judaism is the classical formulation of the purpose—a formulation which has obtained through the centuries up to modern times. The title "To the Hebrews," the extensive use of the Old Testament, and the author's explicit argument that Christianity is superior to Judaism might seem to establish this conclusion. It is purely an inference, however, that the readers contemplated a return to Judaism; this is just what the writer does not say or even suggest. What he does say is that they must guard against inattention, sluggishness, disobedience, and dullness resulting in falling away "from the living God" (3:12). His style is not polemical (contrast Galatians); he never suggests that the readers are disturbed by Jewish teaching or a Jewish gnosis; and he assumes a high Christology as the common ground which writer and readers share. The inadequacy of the law is also stated in terse sentences (cf. 7:19; 10:4) which amount to little more than footnotes and do not suggest that any literal performance of its requirements enticed the readers. The title is not original, the use of the Old Testament (Septuagint) shows only that it was the Bible of the first Christians, both Jews and Gentiles, while the author's disregard of the temple in favor of the original specifications for the tabernacle proves, as does his entire argument about priesthood, that it was the idea, not the practice, of Judaism which was in his mind. This is further enforced by his underlying concept of two worlds, derived from Hellenistic and Hellenistic-Jewish thinking. As it stands, then, Hebrews is an argument for the finality of Christianity resting on the valid foreshadowing in the Old Testament institution of sacrifice of the fundamental need for access to God, which has been brought out of the shadows for all men, Jew and Gentile alike, in the sacrifice of Christ. The Jewishness of Hebrews belongs to the form rather than to the substance of its thought.

That the author is combating a type of Jewish-Christian speculation or gnosis has more to be said for it. This must remain a hypothesis until or unless more evidence comes to light, for there is no more explicit warning against this danger than against falling back into normative Judaism. Archeological evidence of the existence of a "Judaism" strongly influenced by Hellenistic ideas is accumulating,[21] and the suggestion that the Roman church—some relation with Rome is indicated for Hebrews—grew out of a Hellenistic-Jewish synagogue[22] is interesting. But again, our writing contains no definite sign of being a polemic against Hellenistic Judaism. It is best to state the purpose of Hebrews in positive terms as an argument for the finality of Christianity intended to arouse the readers from threatening lethargy.

The question of the literary form of Hebrews, one of the unsolved problems of New Testament research, has a direct bearing on the purpose. Was the writing directed to a specific group of Christians with whom the author stood in personal relations, or was it addressed to a larger audience, or even to Christians generally? Three main issues emerge: the absence of an epistolary introduction, the presence of an epistolary conclusion (ch. 13 or 13:18 ff.), and the nature of the exhortations which run through the writing.

As to the first of these points, it seems most probable that Hebrews never had any other beginning than the one we know. The hypothesis that an epistolary introduction was either lost or forcibly excised betrays the tendency to make it conform with the Pauline pattern. It was no more Pauline in this respect than in thought, style, and arrangement. We possess in IV Maccabees, Barnabas, II Clement, and I John writings which lacked formal epistolary introductions. That the salutation of Hebrews was excised because it contained an unapostolic name and therefore could not have secured acceptance in the canon is not an impressive argument because it was valued in Rome where it was not reckoned to be Pauline, whereas in Alexandria, where it was so reckoned, no suggestion of another name is known. The sonorous opening sentence, when it is coupled with the way the writing develops, bears all the marks of being the original beginning of Hebrews.

In ch. 13, especially from vs. 18 to the end, personal relationships between the author and his readers are indicated for which we have not been prepared in chs. 1–12. If Hebrews closed with ch. 12, or even with 13:17, nobody would think of calling it a letter or an epistle. But neither do the terms "treatise" and "homily"

[21] E. R. Goodenough, *By Light, Light* (New Haven: Yale University Press, 1935).
[22] Hans Lietzmann, *The Beginnings of the Christian Church* (tr. Bertram Lee Woolf; New York: Charles Scribner's Sons, 1937), pp. 265-67.

fit completely. The author is, to be sure, concerned with the development of a thesis, but he is too warmly interested in the practical application of his ideas to actual human necessities to be termed a purely academic thinker. There are numerous indications that the writer was preacher and teacher and that the habit of referring to speaker and hearer instead of to writer and reader prevails (cf. 2:5; 5:11; 6:9; 8:1; 9:5; 11:32; 12:25[?]; 13:6[?]). But Hebrews as a whole can hardly be called a homily; it is rather a writing produced by a preacher and teacher who weaves into the whole materials he has often used. Perhaps this writing is quite as unique in literary form as it is in thought when compared with other New Testament books, and the tendency to make it conform to a known type is dangerous.

There are four logical possibilities with regard to the epistolary conclusion: (a) that it is the work of the author who intended his writing for a definite group and wrote the whole of it with them in mind; (b) that it was prepared for one audience and later sent by the original author to another group for whom he added the personalia; (c) that it was sent to a definite group by another than the author, and this other, an unknown person, added the epistolary conclusion; (d) that the conclusion was added by another hand to assist the acceptance of Hebrews in the canon by simulating a Pauline conclusion with Pauline personalia. It must be admitted that no one of these hypotheses is free from serious objections. The first and the fourth seem to raise the real issue, for the personal references in 6:10 and 10:32-34 would have been deleted by so careful a writer if he were sending it to a fresh audience, and the conclusion seems strangely out of place and purposeless as the work of another hand, unless it was intended to simulate Pauline authorship.

Either the author wrote the conclusion as it stands and when he wrote the whole (hypotheses proposing the deletion of this or that phrase or verse are quite arbitrary), or else another hand wrote it for the purpose of making Hebrews seem Pauline. The latter hypothesis seems more probable although it is not wholly convincing. Striking verbal parallels between ch. 13 and Pauline letters, especially Philippians, appear here, and nowhere else, in Hebrews; cf. 13:23 with Phil. 2:19, 23-24; 13:16 with Phil. 4:18; 13:21 with Phil. 4:20; 13:24 with Phil. 4:21-22; and cf. 13:18-19 with Philem. 22; and 13:18 with II Cor. 1:11-12. That 13:19, 23 constitute "a most amazing contradiction"[23] which only another hand could have perpetrated does not seem to be proved, for it

[23] Enslin, *Christian Beginnings*, p. 314.

is not certain that 13:19 requires imprisonment of the writer. It is also somewhat surprising that another person writing ch. 13 for the purpose of authenticating the Pauline authorship should not have gone the whole way by introducing Paul's name as did the author of the Pastoral epistles. Nevertheless, the striking parallels with Paul's letters in the last chapter of an epistle which as a whole is so alien to Paul's style and thought raise very serious doubts as to the genuineness of that chapter.

If, then, the final chapter is suspect, what does this mean as regards the author's purpose? Very little, for except for the references to Timothy (13:23) and to the author's hope to be restored to the readers (13:19), and the thoroughly ambiguous Ἀσπάζονται ὑμᾶς οἱ ἀπὸ τῆς Ἰταλίας (13:24), everything is general rather than specific and might be applied to Christians generally. In other words, the final chapter, even if regarded as genuine, adds little to our knowledge. Indeed, 6:10 and 10:32 ff. are quite as specific evidence of personal knowledge of a definite group and their past history as anything in ch. 13, and it must be admitted that these two passages are hardly more definite than, e.g., I Pet. 4:12 or 5:9.

The upshot of a consideration of purpose and literary form is that the thought and form of this writing are unique in the New Testament. We do not know precisely who the intended readers were nor where they were located. We do know that the author wrote with conviction and with the certainty that what he wrote had a practical relevance for Christians. He was not writing "in the air" or for hypothetical readers, but for Christians who needed to be aroused to a more positive stand, who faced and had faced practical difficulties as well as theoretical doubts, and who will, he believes, respond to his appeal.

### VI. Provenance and Destination

Only the title "To the Hebrews" and the closing salutation Ἀσπάζονται ὑμᾶς οἱ ἀπὸ τῆς Ἰταλίας (13:24) purport to give us information about the place of writing and the destination of Hebrews; both are ambiguous. The title is old, being attested by Pantaenus and Tertullian, independently of each other, and not negated by any witness. "Hebrews" was used to denote Jews and Jewish Christians in distinction from Gentiles (cf. II Cor. 11:22; Phil. 3:5) and possibly Hebrew-speaking in distinction from Greek-speaking Jews (cf. Acts 6:1). The latter meaning does not fit our writing, which cannot be a translation from a Hebrew original since both in thought and in words it depends on the Septuagint. That it was directed to Jewish Christians (it is obviously not for Jews) in distinction from Gentile Christians is nowhere indicated in the text, and, as we have seen, the absence of any polemic against circumcision or the food laws and the presence of a thoroughly Hellenistic cast of thought counts for Gentile-Christian readers or at any rate Christians without reference to racial background. It is not even certain that the author himself was racially speaking a Jew, although most scholars incline to the view that his familiarity with the Septuagint is best explained on that hypothesis. The title represents the effort of a collector to bring the writing into harmony with "To the Romans," "To the Corinthians," "To the Galatians," etc., and has only a negative value for us—it shows that a definite locality as the destination of the writing was not known to tradition.

The closing salutation (13:24), even if it is the work of another hand, may, of course, throw light on provenance or destination or both. The phrase is grammatically ambiguous and may mean Christians domiciled in Italy or Italians away from home who join the writer in greetings to their compatriots in Italy. The RSV reads, "Those who come from Italy send you greetings," without any indication either of the ambiguity of the Greek or of the sharp division of scholarly opinion on this point. If 13:24 is by another hand, and is in a context intended to suggest Pauline authorship, parallels with Pauline letters suggest an Italian provenance (cf. I Cor. 16:19; II Cor. 1:1; and especially "those of Caesar's household" in Phil. 4:22) ; but the parallels are admittedly not exact. There are too many "ifs" in the total situation to permit dogmatism. If Italy is the place of writing, we are left in the dark as to the destination, which might then be any place where thinking like our author's went on. If, on the other hand, the destination is Italy, then the provenance is equally obscure.

All the facts point to Rome or the vicinity as the "home" in some sense of the writing: our first witness is I Clement; the absence in Rome and the West of references to Paul as the author suggests some primitive knowledge of its actual origin; the lack of Pauline ideas suits a region not evangelized by Paul; and the curious blending of primitive and Hellenistic-Christian thinking is natural in cosmopolitan Rome. But would not Rome know the author's name if it was either the place of origin or the destination? This has been variously answered by supposing that the name was unapostolic and so deliberately suppressed, or that the writing emanated from, or was directed to, a small group, perhaps a house church, and so the author's name and the designation of the readers were omitted when his writing was given wider circulation. These are interesting conjectures and little more, for the writing gives no definite evidence in support of them. Actually we are influenced by the fact that Hebrews finally gained a place in the canon to assume that it must have been regarded as an important writing from the first; we are also too little aware of the wealth and variety of Christian literature, only a part of which has come down to us. Hebrews is a valuable witness to this richness. As a matter of fact, however, it survived as canonical only through the mistaken attribution to Paul, in this respect a fortunate error indeed.

## VII. Date

It was once held that Hebrews must have been written before the fall of Jerusalem and its temple (A.D. 70) since there is no indication of that catastrophic event in the writing. Our author, however, is not concerned with what transpired in Jerusalem, but only with the original pattern revealed to Moses on Sinai (8:5) and shows no awareness of Paul's struggle with legalism and with racial dualism in the Christian church. So far as evidence from the type of thought goes, the date depends on how soon thinking like that of Hebrews developed in Christian circles.

There are many signs that Hebrews was "late" as our author regarded lateness. The gospel "was declared at first by the Lord, and it was attested to us by those who heard him" (2:3)—a sentence almost enough in itself to rule out Pauline authorship—showing that author and readers alike are second-generation Christians. This must not, of course, be pressed to mean "the second generation . . . in a chronological sense," [24] but only that they were converts once removed from the original message of the Lord. They are not in the first flush of enthusiasm, but a considerable Christian experience lies behind them. They are in danger of "drifting away" (2:1) ; they need to "hold fast" (10:23) "until the end" (6:11) with "endurance" (10:36) and "perseverance" (12: 1) and not to lose hope which is an "anchor of the soul" (6:19). "By this time" they ought to be teachers (5:12), not requiring elementary instruction (6:1), and the memory of "the former days" (10:32) should stir them to fresh confidence and endurance (10:35-36). The Parousia, although it is postponed (?), is sure (9:28), and they should exhort one another "as long as it is called 'today'" (3:13), for it is later than they think. Whatever doubts the pas-

[24] Moffatt, *Epistle to Hebrews*, p. xxi.

sage of time may suggest, "Jesus Christ is the same yesterday and today and forever" (13:8).

The one certainty is that Hebrews was written before I Clement, who quotes extensively from the writing as authoritative but without naming its author. If we assume that I Clement was written about A.D. 96, Hebrews must have been written before that time. If Hebrews was addressed to Rome, no great lapse of time before I Clement would be required. It is suggested also that the rebuke (to Rome?) in 5:12, "by this time you ought to be teachers," stimulated the Roman church to address Christians at Corinth, where a revolt against the leaders had broken out, and so justify their teaching qualifications. I Clement begins, "Because of the sudden and successive misfortunes and disasters that have overtaken us, we think that we have been too slow to pay attention to the matters under dispute among you, beloved." The "sudden and successive disasters" are taken to refer to a persecution under Domitian (A.D. 81-96); the author is assumed to be Clement, who was head of the Roman church from A.D. 88 to 97; Heb. 10:32 ff. is understood to refer to Nero's persecution, now long in the past, and the present temptation to apostasy (6;4-6; 10:26) is assumed to be the result of persecution under Domitian, which resulted not in the shedding of blood (12:4), but in shame and obloquy (12:2-3), which our author urges his readers to accept as disciplinary (12:5-11). This would date Hebrews in the late eighties or early nineties of the first century.

The argument is ingenious but at every point falls short of being conclusive. I Clement does not name its author, Dionysius of Corinth (ca. A.D. 170) being the first to name him Clement. The opening words of I Clement do not require, although they do not negate, a persecution under Domitian. In fact, a Domitian persecution, while widely assumed, rests on rather slender evidence. It is not certain that Hebrews was addressed to Rome (see above, p. 593); 10:32-34 would fit Nero's persecution, although there is a curious lack of any specific mention of martyrs there; and our author's admonitions, while they do indeed warn against apostasy, cite dullness, lassitude, and the waning of faith and hope as the specific causes rather than overt persecution. Although scholarly pride may be hurt by the admission, the fact is that any specific date for Hebrews is almost as uncertain as authorship, provenance, and destination.

Probably Hebrews was written some time after Paul's letters. There is no reason to suppose that our author had ever read them, although the subjects he treats are known to us from the Pauline corpus as nowhere else in the New Testament, and accordingly, so far as our knowledge goes, presuppose a background of Pauline influence. It is not impossible to date Hebrews as early as the late seventies.

### VIII. Text of Hebrews

The textual history of Hebrews confirms, or rather is an integral part of the evidence for, its acceptance into the canon under the aegis of Pauline authorship. All our early witnesses make Hebrews a part of the Pauline canon, though they differ as to its order in the Pauline list, from a place immediately after Romans to a position at the end of Paul's letters, just before the Catholic epistles. Moffatt thinks that a place between the Pauline church letters and the Pastorals "seems to have been an early (i.e. a fourth century) position in the Eastern or Alexandrian canon, to judge from Athanasius (*Fest. Ep.* xxxix)." [25] This unanimity of ascription to Paul and the inclusion of the writing in the Pauline corpus accounts for the title "To the Hebrews" in conformity with "To the Romans," etc., as we have seen. Further, the judgment that Pauline authorship was not accepted in the West until the time of Jerome and under the influence of the East is confirmed by the fact that there is "almost no patristic evidence for an Old Latin text until that time." [26] Lingering doubts in the West are perhaps reflected as late as A.D. 397 by the Synod of Carthage, which put Hebrews between the Pauline and the Catholic epistles. The lack of independent Western witnesses to the text, reflecting as it does the exclusion of Hebrews from the New Testament canon in that quarter, makes it difficult to ascertain any traditional text for Hebrews.

Codex Vaticanus (B) is usually regarded as our best witness to the text of Hebrews, although it is unfortunately deficient from 9:14 to the end of the writing. The recent publication of a valuable papyrus codex of the Pauline epistles known as p[46], and dated by its editors *ca.* A.D. 200, adds immensely to our knowledge of an early text of Hebrews, and in a few instances may well contain authentic readings of significance for the interpretation. [27] This papyrus codex contains all of Hebrews, placing it just after Romans. It is more than a century older than the earliest of the great vellum uncials, and its readings especially in 10:1 and

[25] *Epistle to Hebrews*, p. lxx, and see pp. lxiv ff. for a survey of the textual criticism up to 1924.

[26] F. W. Beare, "The Text of the Epistle to the Hebrews in P[46]," *Journal of Biblical Literature*, LXII (1944), 381.

[27] *Ibid.*, pp. 379-96, a full and fascinating discussion.

12:1 (see Exeg., *ad loc.*) have large intrinsic probability.

### IX. Selected Bibliography

BRUCE, A. B. *The Epistle to the Hebrews.* New York: Charles Scribner's Sons, 1899.

DAVIDSON, A. B. *The Epistle to the Hebrews.* Edinburgh: T. & T. Clark, 1882.

DODS, MARCUS. "Epistle to the Hebrews," *Expositor's Greek Testament,* ed. W. Robertson Nicoll. London: Hodder & Stoughton, n.d. Vol. IV.

MOFFATT, JAMES. *The Epistle to the Hebrews* ("International Critical Commentary"). New York: Charles Scribner's Sons, 1924.

NAIRNE, ALEXANDER. *The Epistle to the Hebrews* ("Cambridge Greek Testament for Schools and Colleges"). Cambridge: The University Press, 1917.

PEAKE, A. S. *Hebrews* ("The Century Bible"). Edinburgh: T. C. & E. C. Jack, n.d.

ROBINSON, T. H. *The Epistle to the Hebrews* ("The Moffatt New Testament Commentary"). London: Hodder & Stoughton, 1933.

SCOTT, ERNEST F. *The Epistle to the Hebrews.* Edinburgh: T. & T. Clark, 1922.

WESTCOTT, B. F. *The Epistle to the Hebrews.* 3rd ed. London: Macmillan & Co., 1920.

WICKHAM, E. C. *Epistle to the Hebrews* ("Westminster Commentaries"). 2nd ed. London: Methuen & Co., 1922.

WINDISCH, HANS. *Der Hebräerbrief.* 2nd ed. Tübingen: J. C. B. Mohr, 1931.

# HEBREWS

## TEXT, EXEGESIS, AND EXPOSITION

1 God, who at sundry times and in divers manners spake in time past unto the fathers by the prophets,

1 In many and various ways God spoke of old to our fathers by the prophets;

### I. THEME: THE FINALITY OF GOD'S REVELATION IN A SON (1:1-2*a*)

The epistle opens with a full and sonorous sentence which runs to the end of vs. 4. Logically, however, the first part of the sentence, through vs. 2*a*, is a statement of the theme; what follows is the beginning of the argument. The general theme is the finality and perfection of God's revelation in a Son, in contrast to the incomplete and imperfect revelation through other media or agents.

**1:1.** No translation quite reproduces the archaic splendor and rhythm of the opening clause. The RSV, **in many and various ways God spoke of old,** is truer to the order of the Greek words than the KJV, but it misses the rhetorical majesty of the Greek. Probably

**1:1–3:19. The Trustworthiness of Christ.—** There is serious difficulty in these chapters for the interpreter and we do well to face it openly. The task of the interpreter is to mediate between the Word of God and the affairs, the affections, the thoughts, and the world of his hearers. But how can Hebrews be shown to be relevant to our hearers? This is our problem.

The writer of Hebrews was warning of grave dangers. The early glow of the people's faith was becoming a dim memory. Suffering and persecution were at hand. Some would likely renounce their faith. The writer warns against this danger again and again (cf. 2:1; 3:7–4:13; 6:4-8; 10:23-39; 12:25-29). Their bulwark

against that peril was their faith in Christ. To strengthen their faith the writer is concerned to show that Christ was superior to the prophets, to the angels, to Moses, and to the Levitical priesthood. Their confidence in him must hold them fast in time of trial.

People today face similar dangers: sin has a monotonous identity amid its many forms. Hardships are unpleasant and our love of ease is answered by the many gadgets that cushion us against the shocks of pain. People are afraid of standing alone and dislike being isolated from their neighbors. This fear is made respectable because peculiarity and isolation for any reason are now regarded as pathological. Pride

no English translation can better the KJV here, **God, who at sundry times and in divers manners spake in time past.** What the translators cannot reproduce is the fact that five of the first twelve words in Greek begin with the letter π, and that the first and third words are sonorous compounds beginning with πόλυς. It is important to realize that the rhetorical style of Hebrews is a clue to the kind of man our author was. He was not writing down to the man in the street; he was writing up to the highest literary standards he knew. The attempt to bring Hebrews home "to the business and bosom of every man" by translating it into our rapid, formless, nervous English will be less successful than with most N.T. writings because our author was a conscious stylist writing for cultured readers. His message is earnest and simple, but it derives from a closely reasoned argument and is expressed in the best Greek of the N.T.

He is going to center attention on Jesus as high priest, but he begins with the Son, whose relationship to God and the universe is set forth in language so lofty as to bear little resemblance to the words and deeds of Jesus as we know them in the Synoptic Gospels. He does not mention the name Jesus until 2:9. This will strike many as a curious reversal of what must have been the historic process. Was it not the Jesus of history who set in motion the thinking which resulted in doctrines about him? If our

---

is as subtle today as ever, and is made more plausible by the many resources we can summon to buttress our security. Selfishness persists and its guilt is hidden by the complexity of modern social life: we cannot see the victims of our greed, so quickly merged as it is into the collective greed of our day. The very culture in which we live is built on the assumption that God is not relevant, if indeed he exists at all. Moral laxity is commonplace and sin has become half respectable with wide usage. The uncertainty of a skeptical age has weakened the convictions of many church people. The trumpet gives an uncertain sound. The long tradition of the Christian faith has been dulled by custom. It has lost its early luster and many are half embarrassed to be caught in a church.

The answer is still the adequacy, the trustworthiness of Christ, just as our writer sought this answer for his readers. But the modern rivals of Jesus are not the prophets, the angels, Moses, and the Levitical priesthood. To prove Jesus superior to them would leave the average man of today unmoved, if not annoyed. The interpreter must cultivate imaginative insight into the tragic and confused mind of his own time.

What are now the rivals of Christ for the loyalties of men? Rivals that undermine confidence in him? For one thing, we cannot escape meeting the philosophy that makes Christ seem irrelevant. We are preoccupied with this world, and "the world to come" scarcely enters our plans. Many men of science and philosophy will admit as explanation nothing that comes from beyond or above this world of nature. The secrets of life are to be found in the world as it is, and there our search is to be directed. The

search has been remarkably successful. This success fosters the illusion, in spite of our wars, that man is competent to work out his destiny with no help from God. One writer said:

> In the last resort, we ourselves are responsible for our lives. . . . We believe in science, . . . and we encourage it as the most efficient means man has discovered for transforming both nature and human nature toward that end of life which is our supreme faith, and for which all our other faiths exist.[1]

But men have not ceased to serve the gods. With all our jaunty confidence in ourselves, something above and beyond us must rightfully claim our loyalty. Where men have lost the true God, the half-gods have taken over the causes which our generation serves with passionate loyalty. These are the practical rivals of Jesus Christ. They are plausible. They are the half-gods of scientific reason, of the ideal society, of the nation, of race, of class. Yet any human institution erected into an absolute inevitably becomes demonic in its tyranny and enslaves its devotees. Nor can these demigods, however enlightened, serve to answer the deepest and most persistent questions of the human soul. They have no answer for the mystery of death. They cannot forgive sins. They can never bring men to that "rest of God" of which our writer presently speaks. With these precautions in mind we turn to the Exposition.

**1:1. God Has Spoken.**—If God is really God, he contains within himself the ultimate mysteries of nature, of history, and of redemption. If God is in any way personal, his own meaning

[1] Jay William Hudson, in *Religious Liberals Reply* (Boston: Beacon Press, 1947), p. 71.

author intends to validate and to interpret the human experience of Jesus, why does he begin with the cosmic Son of God? Is he to be reckoned among those writers who overlaid the "simple" Jesus with theological speculations?

It is important to think clearly about these questions. Christianity as a separate religion began with belief in the Resurrection. "He lives" was the slogan of the first Christians. That meant many things, but always that Jesus was the key to the total meaning of life and to the destiny of the individual. He was Christ, Lord, Son of God, Son of man, and his human life had its significance only and always in relation to ultimate issues. Every N.T. writing shares with the author of Hebrews this general point of view. Even Mark, our earliest Gospel, which is reputed to give us the most human portrait of Jesus, has as its opening words, "The beginning of the gospel of Jesus Christ, the Son of God." His readers know from the start that the figure whose words and deeds they are to follow is the promised Messiah. First-century man had little difficulty in believing in saviors, redeemers, and revealers who were more than human. The startling and difficult teaching of Christianity was that such a being had lived a genuinely human life within the memory of men, and that he had been tempted, had suffered, and had died on a cross. How was this to be reconciled with faith in One who shared the power and even the nature of God? This question became increasingly difficult to answer as Christianity moved into Hellenistic circles where God was conceived in abstract and absolute terms. The author of Hebrews is dealing with this type of thinking, and he begins where his

---

constitutes final truth. If God is Father, he would seek to impart his meaning to his children, as far as that meaning is needful for our guidance on the way. The answer of the Bible is that God has spoken. If we will not hear, if we scorn all revelation, it is because we fail to think of him as really God. But many men do not hear. They are busy talking to each other. They want to think things through for themselves. They have their own questions to ask and the answers must conform to their own idea of what is reasonable. Is not this man's subtle attempt at mastery over himself and over his world, his sinful refusal to let God be God?

When God speaks, he does not silence our minds: he liberates them. He does not offend our reason: he releases the reason of man by granting the larger perspective of his own meanings. But he does offend our pride of reason which pretends that man is able to answer the central questions of life. Can we be sure that we know enough even to ask those questions? That we even know in what region of life they lie? What are the important questions? Let our daily conversations witness to the variety of human opinion. What is most important—security, food, shelter, health, marriage, family, social position, how to get along with the neighbors, education, literature, entertainment, the political future, war, peace of mind, hope for the future, a task worth doing, the quest of knowledge, the conflict between classes and races? If only we knew how to ask the central questions, we should be much wiser than we are.

Nor can we answer the deepest questions that we do raise. Who is God? Only God can say. What lies beyond the mystery? We do not know, for we live on this side of it. What is the grave? Is it only the bleak destruction of all we hold dear, of all for which we live, of all that gives purpose to our days? Or is it the door to our true home? Only God knows. Does he forgive our sins? If we convince ourselves by reason that it is appropriate for God to forgive us, what have we done but demand our forgiveness? Such an argument eases no burden, frees no conscience, forgives no sins. Only God can speak and convince us. How may we have access to God? Only God can make that clear, for it is an untraveled way into the unknown. If God has spoken, then we had better hear.

How has he spoken? What are his unmistakable accents? **In many and various ways,** as though his purpose to speak would not be thwarted by man's indifferent hearing, as though divine grace had hedged us about on every hand, with a word here and there and there.

How has he spoken? **Of old to our fathers by the prophets.** What did he say by the prophets? Through Elijah he declared himself as the one who alone is God, who alone is worthy to receive the worship of men. Isaiah said that God, who is Lord of all life, is honored by justice and will accept no easy substitute of ceremony, feast days, elaborate ritual. Amos thundered that injustice would lead to the sure doom of the nation, that the coming of that doom was also the working of God. Micah

2 Hath in these last days spoken unto us by *his* Son, whom he hath appointed heir

2 but in these last days he has spoken to us

---

readers begin, with belief in a cosmic Christ, stretching the very bounds of language to express the pre-eminence of the Son, for the meaning of a religion which meets man from within humanity—this is the object he has in view—depends upon the divine reality of its source and sanction.

Three notes which recur later are struck in the statement of the theme: the nature of past revelation; the unique and final revelation in a Son; and that these are the "last days." Past revelation **by the prophets** is not depreciated as if it were not really divinely given. Our author's use of prophetic words—he includes the psalmist and other O.T. writers among the prophets—shows that he regarded them as fully inspired, indeed as organs of the divine revelation in a literal sense. His point is not their human fallibility as imperfect channels of revelation which they can only imperfectly grasp. He seems rather to suggest that revelation in the past was dependent on moments of inspiration and made use of transient forms of expression. The revelation at any time in the past was fully valid but lacked finality and perfection because the prophets were only organs of revelation while the Son was himself, in his very nature and being, the revelation of God. This reminds us of John's Gospel, but as we shall see, Hebrews develops this thought along another line. The one "modern" note suggested is the implied unity and continuity of revelation. That our author regarded Jesus as the culmination of a historic process rather than as an isolated phenomenon is evident throughout his writing. We must not modernize him to mean continuity from the human point of view; the one continuity he proclaims lies in the purpose of God and its outworkings in history.

**2. In these last days . . . by a Son:** The word Son has no article in the Greek. The author means to say that God has revealed himself, not in one who is a Son among other sons, but in sonship incomparable and unique, "a Son who has been made perfect forever" (7:28). The following verses emphasize the unrivaled supremacy of the Son in

---

declared the reign of God both in judgment and in the promise that "they shall sit every man under his vine and under his fig tree; and none shall make them afraid" (Mic. 4:4). Hosea, in one of the most daring figures in all religious literature, likened God to a husband whose wife had been faithless, and who would tenderly woo her. Jeremiah foretold that God would single out the individual, shaken loose from the mass of his fellows, to stand before him; and that a new covenant would be written in the hearts of men. Ezekiel fixed responsibility in the soul of the individual. The second Isaiah gave vivid utterance to the most majestic monotheism.

Our writer clearly included the Psalms among the prophets. He quoted them often. God had also spoken through great deliverances, through repeated mercies. "I have nourished and brought up children" (Isa. 1:2). He had spoken through drought and disease, through harsh rulers and cruel invaders. Only to the prophets was it given to see God at work in the events of history.

**2. *He Has Spoken to Us by a Son.*—**If you want God's clearest Word, study Jesus Christ.

This is the heart of the Christian message. This is the gospel. If we can, let us imagine God contriving by "many and various ways" (vs. 1) to reveal his purpose to man, trying now one voice, then another. He had spoken through the glories and the wisdom of nature (Ps. 19:1; Rom. 1:20). He had planted himself in the conscience of the race. He had spoken through the prophets. If he were to speak through a Man, would not that be his most eloquent, his final word, spoken in the universal language that all men would understand? This seems clearly to have been Jesus' own interpretation of his work (cf. Mark 12:1-12).

No doubt there are other ways and other men through whom God has spoken. God's word is inclusive. But the clear, the persuasive, the complete word is in Jesus Christ. In this sense the word is exclusive. This exclusiveness is an offense to the modern mind. It seems to close doors and we want them left open. It confronts us with a choice and we prefer to delay the choice. The objections to the exclusive revelation in the Son seem plausible until we turn from the other candidates to Jesus. Then the objections seem stale and bookish.

the whole universe. It should be noted that while "Son" is the word he uses, he does not stress the correlative, "Father," in the Johannine fashion. Only twice is God called the Father, even of the Son (1:5; 5:5, both O.T. quotations), and that God is the Father of men only appears in connection with the discipline of suffering (12:9). We must not draw any conclusions from this omission except that the author follows a different line of thought from Paul or John or the Synoptic Gospels. We shall see that his conception of the relationship between God and man is controlled by the approach through worship, and that words denoting the majesty and awe-fullness of God seem to him the appropriate language in which to describe the object of worship. The **last days** are "these" days; the turn of the ages is now. The author shares the view of I Pet. 1:20 rather than holding that the End is still ahead, as in II Pet. 3:3; Jude 18; II Tim. 3:1. His sharply emphasized eschatology seems in contrast to his philosophic type of thought and poses a difficult problem for the interpreter (see Intro.), but we cannot avoid the conclusion that here and elsewhere the author holds to the belief that the End is at hand.

In this terse statement of the theme, then, is presented a conception of the Son which throws into sharp relief the temptations, the sufferings, and the death of Jesus, which are to be the basis of the argument that in him is the final and perfect revelation of God. There is no room for mere intimations of divinity in Jesus' words and deeds; the full and final revelation of God, and nothing less than that, must be made in Jesus. And this is what the author intends to show, for nothing less than uttermost Reality will meet man's need of access to God; it was the shadowy and unreal character of the revelation "of old" that made it unsatisfying. From our point of view the opening words are startlingly bold and the verses that follow serve only to increase the impression of boldness. Can the writer relate this unique Son to the human Jesus in such a way as to meet the needs of human minds and hearts? This is what he undertakes to do.

---

**Heir of all things.** What a claim is this! Perhaps the writer was thinking of Ps. 2:8: "I will give thee the nations for thine inheritance, and the uttermost parts of the earth for thy possession" (ASV). Heir of all things? Then all things really belong to him. He is heir of the wealth of the earth, of its learning and wisdom, of all the achievements of struggling men, of all the glory of the kingdoms of the world (Rev. 11:15), of the powers of nature and the stars in their courses. Heir of all things? Then he is heir also to the shame and the defeat, to the pain and the bitterness, to the abuse and the cruelty, to the ignorance and degradation of men; to the terrors of war and the dread of famine; to the ache of broken lives and the darkness of our hate. This is the tragic insight of the gospel, that he who was to reign must bear our sorrows, must be wounded for our transgressions, must be heir of all the suffering, too (cf. 2:10).

**Through whom also he created the world.** What does this mean? Was not God able to create of himself? Why did it have to be "through" someone, even his Son? Was not the human Jesus just as a man a sufficient Word to all men? Were not his teachings clear, his mighty works, and best of all, the light of the Man himself? Why did our writer have to get

Jesus mixed up with the distant creation? Is not this carrying it too far? What does he mean?

Granted that Philo was the origin of our writer's thought at this point, does he mean that in the very beginning something was put into the nature of the world that called for Christ? That Christ was not an afterthought in the mind of God, but a veritable foundation for the structure of all things? That the whole creation would groan in agony for his coming? That the world was so made that without him it would fall apart? That he was the rightful heir of all things? That only in him and through him and for him would the world and all within it find its meaning fulfilled?

What is the symbol by which the real is to be known? For Plato it was abstract idea. Modern thinkers have tried to reduce all things to matter, to energy, to space-time. The older naturalism is bankrupt. It explained nothing. How could blind matter or energy work itself, by however long a process, into the mind of a Socrates or the character of a Jesus? The newer naturalism recognizes the spiritual dimension, and admits that it was somehow implicit in the process from the beginning. But does it satisfy? Is Christ the key to all things? If he is rightful Lord of all, if he is **heir of all things,** then the course of nature, as well as the long history of

of all things, by whom also he made the worlds; | by a Son, whom he appointed the heir of all things, through whom also he created

---

## II. Argument: Jesus Christ Is the Final and Perfect Revelation of God Because in His Person He Is Son and in His Work He Is Priest (1:2b–10:18)
### A. The Personality of the Son (1:2b–4:13)
#### 1. He Is Superior to Angels as Son, Yet Able to Help Man Because He "Has Suffered and Been Tempted" (1:2b–2:18)
##### a) Supremacy of the Son (1:2b-4)

These verses compress much into a few words. The author sets forth in successive clauses the relationship of the Son to the universe as the heir and agent of creation (2b), to God as reflecting his **glory** and bearing **the very stamp of his nature** (3a), again to the universe as its sustainer (3b), to humanity as having **made purification for sins** only to be exalted to sit down **at the right hand of the Majesty on high** (3c), and finally **to angels**—the only beings who could conceivably challenge his uniqueness.

Everything is keyed to the unrivaled supremacy of the Son as the revealer of God; even the reference to his work of **purification for sins,** which is to be the main theme of the writing, is introduced only casually in order to allay any suspicion that this ministry impaired Christ's unique relation to God.

The condensed form of statement, and the fact that the author does not support the items by scriptural citations, contrary to his usual habit, suggest that he is summarizing teaching acceptable to his readers and not requiring detailed proof (cf. Rom. 1:1 ff.).

Volumes might be written about the theology implicit in these verses. It is best, however, to follow the author's example, pausing only to indicate the major emphases. The first thing to be noted is that he sets forth the unique person of the Son "in borrowed terms." Almost every significant word or phrase can be paralleled from contemporary non-Palestinian Jewish literature, and especially from Philo of Alexandria when he is writing about the Logos. For Philo the term Logos (Word, Reason), including as it does both the thought in the mind and its expression out from the mind, was an appropriate word for solving his problem of how the absolute God could come into contact with the world of matter. Clearly our author is concerned with the same problem, although for him it takes the form not of philosophical speculation, but of a religious issue: how could the divine Son suffer and die? He never uses Logos in the Philonic sense: ῥῆμα is the creative word (cf. 11:3), and Logos is the term for revelation (cf. 2:2; 4:12). Yet he is obviously familiar with the ideas of Philo.

**2b. Heir of all things, through whom also he created the world:** He is heir because he is Son (cf. Gal. 4:7; Matt. 21:38; Ps. 2:8); Philo's Logos is similarly the heir. The idea of the Son as the active agent of Creation (cf. John 1:3), so foreign to primitive Hebrew thinking, appeared in Judaism under the form of Wisdom as the forthgoing power of God, and in Hellenistic circles under the form of the Logos. It is not possible or necessary to assign our author's usage to its exact source, for the idea was in the air he breathed.

---

mankind, needs him as its interpreter. He is not merely the historical Jesus, but the clue to all that is.

> I say, the acknowledgment of God in Christ
> Accepted by thy reason, solves for thee
> All questions in the earth and out of it,
> And has so far advanced thee to be wise.[2]

[2] Robert Browning, "A Death in the Desert."

This tells us not so much about Jesus as it does about the world. Its destiny is to serve as the stage of his redemption. Its suffering, its long history, its cultural ebb and flow will find their climax when "the kingdom of the world has become the kingdom of our Lord and of his Christ, and he shall reign for ever and ever" (Rev. 11:15). What else could be meant by calling Jesus "Lord of all," **heir of all things?**

3 Who being the brightness of *his* glory, and the express image of his person, and upholding all things by the word of his power, when he had by himself purged our sins, sat down on the right hand of the Majesty on high;

the world. 3 He reflects the glory of God and bears the very stamp of his nature, upholding the universe by his word of power. When he had made purification for sins, he sat down at the right hand of the Majesty

---

The translation "world" for the Greek αἰῶνας is probably correct since the thought is of the totality of creation and not of a time sequence as in I Cor. 10:11.

**3ab. He reflects the glory of God . . . word of power:** The word ἀπαύγασμα, used only here in the N.T., can mean either the radiation or the reflection of the glory of God. The latter is more probable since the writer has turned from the Son's creative role to his nature. This too is a Philonic word (and see Wisd. Sol. 7:25 for a striking parallel). The term χαρακτήρ is also unique in the N.T. It means the impression of a seal left on wax or clay. In these two words our author emphasizes the Son's oneness with God without ever quite identifying him with God. He is the outgoing of God into the world, which he sustains by **his word of power.** He bears the **express image** of God and reflects his glory. Glory here is not a word for excellence in an indefinite sense; it carries the connotation of light, for the Son reflects the glory of God. Again we may be sure we are in the realm of contemporary Hellenistic thinking. According to ancient physics, light streams from its source without affecting the source, and is thus an appropriate symbol for the forthgoing of God in creation since it does not imperil the idea of a changeless and absolute Being.

**3c. When he had made purification, . . . the Majesty on high:** These phrases look forward to the author's intended development of thought. They are not a further state-

---

**3. He Reflects the Glory of God.**—Again this tells us not so much about the human Jesus as about God. And what is the glory of God? Is it in heavenly pomp and display? Too often our thought of the glory of God reflects the cheap and vulgar ideas of the "glorious" in our civilization. God is not honored by splendid ceremony, by earthly grandeur, or by any of the trappings by which earthly monarchs—fretful little men!—seek to make themselves impressive.

All this was foreign to Jesus. He renounced the ways of the world in his temptation, the shrewd devices by which men seek power over their fellows. He would not bow to the tempter that "all the kingdoms of the world" might be his (Luke 4:5-7). He walked quietly among men. He had no need to create an impression, for greatness never does. The little children trusted him. The common people heard him gladly (Mark 12:37). Strong men were subdued and mastered by him. A sinful woman poured out her tears in grateful acknowledgment of the new hope he had given her (Luke 7:38). He went to the Cross and died in seeming helplessness. They ridiculed him because he could not save himself (Luke 23:35). This is the glory of God.

The glory of God is found in the eyes of men redeemed and free, in every kindly act

which reflects the mind of Christ, in every patient waiting, in every heroic sacrifice, in every gracious home, in every sincere prayer, in every triumph over sin, whenever "two or three" unite their hearts under the spell of God's grace. This is the glory of God which Jesus reflects. Too often Christian interpreters have sought to make God sound impressive by magnifying his power. The power of God is awesome. But naked power, however complete, degrades its worshipers. The true insight of the gospel is the union of complete power with righteousness and grace. When God's chosen word was spoken, it was not in thunder tones, but in one who came into the world as a helpless infant.

**And bears the very stamp of his nature.** This figure is more accurate than the reflection of glory. It suggests a faithful, and indeed a detailed, reproduction of the nature of God. The long story of man's search for God, the confusing variety of philosophical speculations as to the nature of God, all add weight and meaning to this passage. If you want to know God, look long at Jesus (cf. John 14:6-7). There the character of God is faithfully traced.

It should be added that of course there remain vast mysteries in the nature of God. His thoughts are higher than our thoughts, "as the

| 4 Being made so much better than the angels, as he hath by inheritance obtained a more excellent name than they. | on high, 4 having become as much superior to angels as the name he has obtained is more excellent than theirs. |

ment of the Son's uniqueness as such, but suggest that his service for men has not impaired that uniqueness. They also prepare the way for the contrast with angels who stand and serve, while the Son sits at the right hand. The language is metaphorical; anthropomorphism is far from the author's thought.

Before turning to vs. 4, which introduces the contrast with angels, it is well to consider whether these extreme statements about the unique relation of the Son to God and to the universe do not compromise monotheism. Our author, like other N.T. writers, is not conscious of any threat to monotheism in his Christology. It is God alone who reveals himself in his own nature, glory, and creative power in the Son. The accent is upon God's action and revelation in and through the Son, whose identity in nature with God simply ensures that the revelation is truly from and of God. The real problem the author has set for himself is to explain Jesus' humiliating sufferings and death. In these opening verses he binds creation and redemption indissolubly together. The "purification for sins" is set in the framework of the uttermost and final Reality of the universe. In his own way he is preparing to say with Paul, "For it is the God who said, 'Let light shine out of darkness,' who has shone in our hearts to give the light of the knowledge of the glory of God in the face of Christ" (II Cor. 4:6). The divine creative energy and nature are in the redemptive process.

**4.** Why does our author introduce the contrast between the Son and angels? We

heavens are higher than the earth" (Isa. 55:9). The Bible never promises an answer to all questions, but only to such as are necessary for our salvation.

**Upholding the universe by his word of power.** Here again is the linking of nature to the God of our salvation. The saving purposes of God are not external to the world, foreign to them, but implicit in the world from the beginning. We worship one God, Creator and Savior, in very truth the one who alone exists, and from whom all else has derivative existence. This union is very important. Its bearing needs to be made clear. He who heals the broken in heart is also he who counts the number of the stars and calls them all by name (Ps. 147:3-4).

The voice that rolls the stars along
Speaks all the promises.[3]

**When he had made purification for sins.** Here we are introduced to the major theme of the epistle—Christ as the perfect priest for all mankind. The reference is clearly to sin as contamination, an uncleanness from which no man can purify himself. Lacking purification, he cannot have access to God.

Whatever we may make of the whole Levitical priesthood, and of our author's use of it,

the fact remains that this purification meets a deep and persistent need. Sinners feel unclean. They long for one who can restore to them their lost purity. They find comfort in the promise, "Though your sins be as scarlet, they shall be as white as snow" (Isa. 1:18). The sufferers from mental disease often show pathological fear of uncleanness. Most of the world's religions have rituals of purification. The cry of Lady Macbeth, "What! will these hands ne'er be clean?" is a deeply human cry.

That Jesus suffered and died tells us much about him. But that he rose from the dead, and that **he sat down at the right hand of the Majesty on high,** tells us much about God and the final meaning of this our world. This is what is exalted to the place of honor in the presence of God. The thing for which Jesus stood is of final importance in the world which God created.

The Savior whom the believer worships is not a mere memory, however dear; rather is he a living helper, a present reality. He is alive and makes intercession for the believer (cf. 7:25; Rom. 8:34). Knowing the character of the earthly Jesus, what prayers must even now be on his heart! That he prays for us today, "in the hour of trial," is a sobering and sustaining thought.

**4. Having Become as Much Superior to Angels.**—Why superior to angels? Do not vss.

---

[3] Isaac Watts, "Begin, my tongue, some heavenly theme."

5 For unto which of the angels said he at any time, Thou art my Son, this day

5 For to what angel did God ever say,
"Thou art my Son,
today I have begotten thee"?

know that angels were reckoned as mediators in both Jewish and Christian circles. Col. 2:8, 18 witness to the danger of angel worship in the Christian fellowship, and it has been suggested that a similar danger threatened the readers of Hebrews. While this is not impossible, the evidence is against it. The verses that follow do not sound like a polemic. Not only is there no positive intimation that angels were regarded as worthy of worship or as mediators of the divine salvation, but the writer gives them a high place in 2:2 as the beings through whom the law was delivered, and in 1:14 as "ministering spirits."

Angels are introduced as a necessary link in the chain of his argument. His thought runs like this: Angels, like the Son, share in some sense the divine as contrasted to human nature; yet they are all subservient beings, functioning, as we would say, in the natural order of things, each with his appointed ministry; no divine initiative belongs to them; they can serve only in their places. If men are to be saved, the act of One who shares the divine power will alone avail. The author is quite aware that it is a bold conception to present the Son as entering into human experience. He prepares for it, not by minimizing but by exalting the nature and power of the Son. Only a being who is fully divine could initiate so daring a ministry; it is quite beyond the powers of angels to undertake. The **name**, of course, is Son, with all that name implies, already fully indicated in the preceding verses.

### b) PROOF FROM SCRIPTURE (1:5-14)

A chain of seven quotations is designed to establish from scripture the supremacy of the Son above angels. This scriptural proof is followed in vs. 14 by the author's own conclusion. The angels are not regarded as hostile beings, rivals of God. They do not threaten to "separate us from the love of God" as do the "angels, principalities, and powers" Paul conceives as conquered by Christ (Rom. 8:38-39). They have only to be recognized as fulfilling their proper functions to fall into their proper place in the scheme of salvation. Accordingly, our author can afford to rely on scriptural proof of what that proper place is. We see foreshadowed in these verses the nature of his thought. He knows about "him who has the power of death, that is, the devil" (2:14), but he is not obsessed with a sense of radical moral conflict in man or in the universe. The need of man is no less desperate than in Paul's thought, but Hebrews understands it to be need not for the transformation of man's self, but for the satisfaction of the groping after God which the ancient sacrificial system at once inspires and defeats. Is there real and satisfying access

2-3 clearly establish the position of the Son? And does it not follow that he was superior to angels—in fact, their Creator and their Lord? Why spend so much time laboring the obvious? But the argument does add clarity to the unique position of the Son. As Marcus Dods said, "But when this writer lived the angels may be said to have been in possession, whereas Christ had yet to win His inheritance." [4] Further, it was as the incarnate priest, that the Christ was superior to angels. This was the point to be established.

**As the name he has obtained is more excellent than theirs.** This was not so obvious in

the days of the writer as it is today. It is an interesting fact that in non-Christian lands, where the Christian doctrine is widely attacked, men are careful not to criticize the character of Jesus. Even among the hard-bitten skeptics of our land, who can find no certainty in the articles of our creeds, and who have become skilled in psychological explanations of religious experience, the man Jesus is treated with respect. Excellent name, indeed! Excellent beginning for any Christian message! Excellent center and heart of every sermon and treatise—Jesus, the man, and the Son of God.

**5. *Thou Art My Son, Today I Have Begotten Thee*.**—This passage comes first in the series of seven quotations because it is basic to the others.

[4] *The Expositor's Greek Testament*, ed. W. Robertson Nicoll (London: Hodder & Stoughton, n.d.), IV, 253.

have I begotten thee? And again, I will be to him a Father, and he shall be to me a Son?

Or again,

"I will be to him a father,
and he shall be to me a son"?

---

to God, direct, living, and final? Can he help men in their time of need? This is the question he proposes to answer. Let the "angels keep their ancient places"; they minister faithfully and well. They prove, however, that sharing the heavenly realm is not sufficient equipment for meeting human need. A living way into God's presence must be provided for humanity by One who is adequate to meet the dilemma of man, who is always seeking God, yet always coming short of finding him.

The seven quotations are all taken from the Greek translation of the O.T. (LXX); they are usually exact quotations, although not always from the best-attested text, and in one case (Deut. 32:43) the sentence quoted from the LXX is not in the Hebrew text. Only the third and fourth quotations (vss. 6-7 from Deut. 32:43 and Ps. 104:4) refer directly to angels; the others emphasize the exalted position of the Son, and by implication the inferior status of angels. The quotation from Ps. 102:25-27 (vss. 10-12) might seem to suggest that angels are associated with the material world and will perish with it, while the Son is eternal and immutable. That this is not the author's main point, however, is clear from vs. 14, where he states the conclusion to be drawn from the scripture references, "Are they not all ministering spirits sent forth to serve, for the sake of those who are to obtain salvation?" His interest here and elsewhere is not in cosmological speculation, but in salvation.

What will impress the student of the quotations is that our author is not interested in the original meaning or the original context; e.g., Deut. 32:43 (LXX, cf. Ps. 97:7) is clearly an exhortation to worship God and contains no messianic implication. Many of the quotations, conceivably all of them, may have been messianically interpreted in this time and in the circles in which the author moved, but he assumes a method of scriptural exegesis which is based on the belief that hidden meanings become clear to the reader who has the "key." The "key" is the sonship of Christ, as for Philo it is the Logos. What are we to say about such a method? It is more important to understand than to condemn him. He and his contemporaries reverse the modern developmental approach to the Bible. Without the concept of an evolving, growing revelation of God, he reads back into the ancient scriptures intimations and foreshadowings of the truth as he sees it in Christ. Every passage, as equally inspired, must yield its quota of divine truth to the eye upon which the perfect revelation has dawned. Unjustifiable as this method undoubtedly is for the interpretation of scripture, it yet suggests a valid principle which the historical method tends to obscure, viz., that the prophets were dealing at first hand with God and God with them, and that to regard them as items in a "process" and nothing more is to disregard their essential significance. With this in mind let us briefly examine the several citations and the author's use of them.

**5a. Thou art my Son, this day have I begotten thee:** Ps. 2 was widely regarded as messianic, and our author quotes this verse (vs. 7) again in 5:5. The one difficulty is in the interpretation of "this day." Did it mean before time began (cf. vss. 2 ff.), at the Incarnation (cf. Luke 1:35), or at the Resurrection (cf. Rom. 1:4)? Probably the author is less concerned with this speculative question—he does not seem to make a consistent answer (cf. 1:2c with 1:4)—than with the fact that the verse guarantees the sonship of Christ. That the angels were frequently called "sons of God" in the O.T. (cf. Gen. 6:2;

---

The writer has no ambiguity in his mind. In a unique and exclusive sense Christ is the Son of God, and to him shall divine honors be paid.

**I will be to him a father, and he shall be to me a son.** Men have meant many things by the

words "Son of God." When we have said all that can be said, we must remember that we are using human symbols, even as the writer was using O.T. passages that had quite other meanings at the time of their writing; that "no one

6 And again, when he bringeth in the first-begotten into the world, he saith, And let all the angels of God worship him.

7 And of the angels he saith, Who maketh his angels spirits, and his ministers a flame of fire.

8 But unto the Son *he saith,* Thy throne, O God, *is* for ever and ever: a sceptre of righteousness *is* the sceptre of thy kingdom.

6 And again, when he brings the first-born into the world, he says,
"Let all God's angels worship him."

7 Of the angels he says,
"Who makes his angels winds,
and his servants flames of fire."

8 But of the Son he says,
"Thy throne, O God,[a] is for ever and ever,
the righteous scepter is the scepter of thy[b] kingdom.

[a] Or *God is thy throne.*
[b] Other ancient authorities read *his.*

Job 1:6; 2:1; 38:7) and in Jewish writings is either unknown to our author or is regarded as irrelevant to the sense in which he uses the word son.

**5b.** The word **again** (πάλιν) is this writer's way of introducing additional quotations (cf. 2:13; 10:30; see also Rom. 15:10-12; I Cor. 3:20)—this time from II Sam. 7:14. He never uses the formula "it is written." The words **father** and **son** in the citation are what he needs for his argument, but since II Sam. 7:14 is addressed to David he may have in mind a messianic interpretation although he does not use the Son of David title.

**6.** A quotation from Deut. 32:43 (LXX) and Ps. 97:7. This verse appears only in the LXX translation of Deuteronomy and, inappropriately enough, the LXX has "sons of God." Ps. 97:7 has the required "his angels" and many have assumed that the author is quoting from memory and has mixed the two passages. The **first-born** (πρωτότοκος) must mean "first" in relation to *men* who are called to be sons of God (cf. 2:10; Rom. 8:29) since angels are excluded from sonship. The time reference implied in **when he brings the first-born into the world** is again not to be pressed.

**7.** The Hebrew of Ps. 104:4 may mean, "Who maketh winds his messengers; flames of fire his ministers," which the context of the psalm favors. Our author follows the LXX rendering, but there is no suggestion of depreciation of angels; indeed, in this respect they are superior to men. They are, however, so inferior in nature as compared with the Son that they can be changed into elemental forces.

**8-9. Thy throne . . . is for ever and ever** (from Ps. 45:6-7): The sense in which the author uses this quotation is clear. It means for him that the Son has divine authority

knows who the Son is except the Father" (Luke 10:22); that the mystery of the Godhead is beyond and above all the earth-drawn metaphors of human speech. What the writer meant by the word "Son" the subsequent quotations make clear.

**6. Let All God's Angels Worship Him.**—This clearly establishes the supremacy of the Son over the angels, since they who are the "ministering spirits" (vs. 14) of the Eternal are to do homage to him. **Into the world** emphasizes the incarnate Son in the historic Jesus, the Christ of our worship. For the writer is not concerned with the worship due to him as one who upholds "all things by the word of his power" (vs. 3) but as one who became man. It was on the earthly scene that the heavenly priesthood of Jesus would be validated.

**7. Winds and Fire, Ministers of God.**—The original of this quotation (Ps. 104) is a great hymn to the power of God in nature. Even the wildest forces of nature, winds and fire, which seem utterly brutal and casual in their destruction, are still the ministers of God, and subject to his control. This is a daring thing for faith to say and hard for countless victims of wind and fire to believe. Yet if God is God, the forces of untamed nature are subject to his will. Here the angels are clearly made subject in the same way, being the servants of God.

**8. The Everlasting Reign of Christ.**—The three emphases in this and the following verses are (a) the dominion of the Son which is (b) eternal and (c) founded on righteousness. He is even now actual Lord, although he has not entered into his complete rule. Even now all

9 Thou hast loved righteousness, and hated iniquity; therefore God, *even* thy God, hath anointed thee with the oil of gladness above thy fellows.

10 And, Thou, Lord, in the beginning, hast laid the foundation of the earth; and the heavens are the works of thine hands.

11 They shall perish, but thou remainest: and they shall all wax old as doth a garment;

12 And as a vesture shalt thou fold them up, and they shall be changed: but thou art the same, and thy years shall not fail.

---

9 Thou hast loved righteousness and hated lawlessness;

therefore God, thy God, has anointed thee

with the oil of gladness beyond thy comrades."

10 And,

Thou, Lord, didst found the earth in the beginning,

and the heavens are the work of thy hands;

11 they will perish, but thou remainest;

they will all grow old like a garment,

12 like a mantle thou wilt roll them up,

and they will be changed.*c*

But thou art the same,

and thy years will never end."

*c* Other ancient authorities add *like a garment.*

---

in contrast to the subservient role of the angels. As the opening words stand in our translations, they require the application of ὁ θεός, "O God," to the Son. We have noted that this epistle does not elsewhere give the name "God" to the Son in this unrelieved fashion, and vs. 9 would seem to suggest another rendering. The alternative is to read, "God is thy throne" or "thy throne is God." The usual translation is not impossible, however, in a poetic passage.

**10-12.** Taken from Ps. 102:25-27, these verses originally express the creative power of God and his permanence as against the transient creation. The LXX, however, intro-

---

things, all men, all human institutions are rightfully his; i.e., without him as Lord no man is fully human, ever succeeds in "being himself"; without him as recognized Lord, all human institutions tend to fall apart. His lordship is literally woven into the nature of things. All rebellion against him, all attempts to live without him, are evasions from and sins against reality. The Christ is no alien conqueror. "He came unto his own" (John 1:11). This is a strong claim which the world is denying by its deeds day after weary day. But this whole world view is implied if Christ is rightful Lord and if his throne **is for ever and ever.**

**9. *Thou Hast Loved Righteousness and Hated Lawlessness.*—**These are the strongest words that could possibly be used. To love righteousness is the fulfillment of the fourth beatitude. It is to possess righteousness, to be completely at one with it, to be devoted to it without the least reservation. This is a clear description of Jesus. But it is also the final word about the world in which we live—here is its real ruler. This is the ultimate nature of things. This is the Christian answer to the feeble ethic which sees in the right only a fleeting human custom accepted by the group for a time, and in a tiny

oasis encompassed by a vast moral desert. This is the kind of emphasis the interpreter should constantly make. It rings throughout the Bible. This sturdy faith alone can restore moral backbone to any morally flabby generation.

**The oil of gladness beyond thy comrades.** The comrades referred to are not human beings, but the angels. The interpreter should not miss the incidental insights, the side remarks of the Bible, and especially its momentous "therefores." Here there is a stirring union of righteousness and gladness. Had we eyes to see, we could observe this truth any day and in almost any corner of the globe. Men seek gladness in excitement, in escape, in raucous noise, and in "letting go." Even in our laughter there is a hardness that betrays our fears and our grim joylessness. The biblical teaching is clear. Gladness is not a human achievement. It never admits of direct pursuit. God confers it, **God . . . has anointed thee,** and it is joined to righteousness with a mighty **therefore.**

**10-12. *A Changing World, the Unchanging Son.*—**The writer reaffirms the creative power of the Son. It is possible that he found in the passage here quoted, a psalm which was commonly regarded as messianic on other grounds,

13 But to which of the angels said he at any time, Sit on my right hand, until I make thine enemies thy footstool?

14 Are they not all ministering spirits, sent forth to minister for them who shall be heirs of salvation?

13 But to what angel has he ever said,
"Sit at my right hand,
till I make thy enemies
a stool for thy feet"?

14 Are they not all ministering spirits sent forth to serve, for the sake of those who are to obtain salvation?

---

duces the vocative κύριε, "Lord," which permits our author to apply the words to the Son. The application of the Greek word κύριος to Christ played a great role in early Christian thinking about Christ, but our author does not follow this line elsewhere.

13. Ps. 110, quoted here, plays an important part in our author's thought generally (cf. 5:6, 10; 6:20; 8:1; 12:2), but mainly in the development of the Melchizedek speculation. Here he cites the first verse of the psalm with its militant connotations in order to emphasize the character of the Son as conquering and ruling.

14. The final verse gives the author's point of view in his quotations and introduces what is immediately to follow.

---

the suggestion that the Son was the creator. In any event, the writer is clear that one of the divine functions of the Son was that of being the agent of Creation. This quotation is a graphic way of stating the eternity of the Son's dominion. To human eyes the world of nature is the permanent, especially when in contrast to man's brief span of life. We human creatures **grow old like a garment,** but thou, nature, **art the same, and thy years will never** end. Thus many a modern mind reads the destiny of man. But the Christian revelation is unequivocal. God (and the Son partakes of his nature) is not a victim of time and change. He is their sovereign Lord.

With the speculative questions of time and eternity, and the questions are central for any Christian philosophy, we need not here be especially concerned. But the practical question must be met squarely. We cannot worship a transient process. Something must abide, to which we may cling and by which our way may be guided. That, we seek to worship. For the writer, the Son shared with the Father this transcendence over nature and the unending years belong to him.

Change and decay in all around I see;
O thou, who changest not, abide with me.[5]

13. *Christ as Triumphant.*—This last in the series of quotations is the fitting climax. It is another graphic way of saying that the Son has been "appointed the heir of all things" (vs. 2). The belief in the final and complete triumph of Christ as the goal and horizon of human history is one of the essential elements in the

Christian faith. This faith is often criticized as implying that there are no real battles to be well fought and hard won, no risks to be taken, no momentous decisions to be made, since the issue is already determined and fixed. We have therefore no task to perform, no struggles to endure, but only to sit and wait for God's redeeming action and his appointed time. The criticism has about it the odor of bookishness and can be uttered only by one who is out of touch with the mind of the N.T. For in the N.T., as indeed in Hebrews, this teaching of the assured final triumph is always linked to the decisive choice that must be made now. It introduces an immense urgency and confronts the Christian with imperatives for today (cf. 2:1-4; 4:1-13; 10:19-39; 12:1-2). This is one of the many dual truths of the Bible which, if treated in isolation from each other, lose their excitement, their power, their immense relevance. There is a logic of Christian faith which sometimes confounds the wisdom of the scribe and to which the interpreter must prove faithful.

14. *Angels as Servants of Salvation.*—The writer gathers up the full meaning of his quotations. He never minimizes the importance of angels. They are **all ministering spirits . . . , for the sake of those who are to obtain salvation.** They were the agents of the revelation of old (2:2). Whatever else we may make of them today, and the very idea of angels is foreign to the mind of our time, they are at least symbols of the variety, the accessibility, and the completeness of God's gracious gifts to man. For the writer the angels are servants, never rulers. This royal right is reserved for the Son. In ch. 2 he completes the contrast and introduces us to

[5] Henry Francis Lyte, "Abide with me."

2 Therefore we ought to give the more earnest heed to the things which we have heard, lest at any time we should let *them* slip.

2 For if the word spoken by angels was steadfast, and every transgression and disobedience received a just recompense of reward;

2 Therefore we must pay the closer attention to what we have heard, lest we drift away from it. 2 For if the message declared by angels was valid and every transgression or disobedience received a just

---

### c) WARNING AGAINST INATTENTION AND NEGLECT (2:1-4)

This is an exhortation based on the preceding argument, but it is not really a digression; it is the point toward which the elaborate proof of the Son's superiority to angels has been moving. Angels were "sent forth to serve, for the sake of those who are to obtain salvation" (1:14). What follows is immediately connected with this thought.

**2:1.** We must, with utmost care (περισσοτέρως), hold our minds to (προσέχειν) **the things . . . heard,** i.e., to what God has spoken in his Son in these last days (1:2), **lest we drift away.**

**2-3a.** Lethargy, dullness, and inattention are repeatedly rebuked (cf. 5:11; 6:11-12). This appeal to earnest attention is enforced by an argument from the lesser to the greater. **If the message declared by angels was valid . . . , how shall we escape if we neglect such a great salvation?** What is this angelic message? Apparently the law (cf. Gal. 3:19;

---

the work of the Son, and the Son's superior qualifications to be the priest of all men.

**2:1. Attention or Drifting.**—Hebrews is never far from the business of daily living. We work through the speculative first chapter with its discussion of the mystery of the Godhead and the supremacy of the Son over the angels. Then suddenly the writer says, **Therefore.** Therefore what? Therefore these are the ideas which we must continue to ponder? Therefore you have the correct form of words in your possession to own and handle and manage? **Therefore we must pay the closer attention to what we have heard.** Christian knowledge is always personal and thus differs profoundly from our knowledge of nature. Nature is indifferent to the moral character of the scientist, except in the one vital point of intellectual integrity. Nature will reveal her secrets equally to saint and scoundrel if each knows how to put the right questions. But in the knowledge of divine things the whole man is involved: intellect and conduct, thought and trust, knowledge and the desires of the heart. What you know depends upon the kind of man that you are. Only the pure in heart shall see God (Matt. 5:8).

It is an affront to human pride that with all the brilliance of our thought we cannot by ourselves know God. Knowledge is never minimized in the Bible (cf. John 17:3; I Cor. 14:13-19). But it walks hand in hand with faith if we are to draw near to God. There is nothing arbitrary in this union of knowledge and faith. It is an essential condition of all personal knowl-

edge, including our knowledge of other human beings. And faith walks hand in hand with obedience. The truth of God is never any mere theory to be studied. It confronts us with decisions. We gain and hold divine truth only when it goes to work in our lives. It is plain that if God has spoken, it is the most urgent speaking in the long history of speech. We must listen. And if he has spoken supremely through his Son, then let all else be still, let human talk be hushed, let the babble of the world be silent that we may **pay the closer attention** to what God has to say.

**Lest we drift away from it.** The writer knows his people well enough to recognize that they are in danger. The danger is sad and familiar to every age. There is a strong fascination in the Word of God. When it is clearly and warmly presented, it will hold any audience. But there is that in us which does not want to hear. We will postpone decision. Quietly, at first slowly, almost without our knowing it, certainly without the world's seeing or caring, we drift. Perhaps the best comment on this passage is to be found in the parable of the soils (Mark 4:3-20). The Master early faced the question of the hearer. "He who has ears to hear, let him hear" (Mark 4:9). The warning rings throughout the teaching of Jesus. A resolute act of will, a complete gathering of our strength, is necessary **lest we drift away.**

**2. Old Penalties.**—The reference here is clearly to the law of Moses. It was the common belief among Jews of the day that the law had

3 How shall we escape, if we neglect so great salvation; which at the first began to be spoken by the Lord, and was confirmed unto us by them that heard *him;*

retribution, 3 how shall we escape if we neglect such a great salvation? It was declared at first by the Lord, and it was at-

---

Acts 7:53), since it was under the law that **every transgression or disobedience received a just retribution.** The introduction of the idea of **the message** [or better **the word** KJV] **declared** by angels seems a bit surprising in the light of the supporting citations, none of which indicates such a role for angels until we recall that the theme (1:1-2*a*) is keyed to God's word spoken to us by a Son. We see now that the inferior nature of angels was intended to prove the inferior mediation of the divine word through them. This argument can hardly be directed to Jewish Christians tempted to relapse into Judaism, since it grants too much. Besides, extended proof would be called for by readers of this kind. Our author's identification of the messianic citations 1:5-13 with Christ would also be unconvincing to such readers. He avoids the word law, as indeed he avoids the word gospel. Is it because he is concerned, not to set one over against the other, but to see the perfection of the one in the other?

**3*b*-4.** The greatness of such a salvation is shown in its triple attestation: **declared at first by the Lord, . . . attested to us by those who heard him, . . . God also bore witness by signs and wonders.** Here for the first time the author moves on the plane of historic facts. He seems unaware, however, of any change in the nature of his argument, so completely does he identify the Son with Jesus. **Which at the first began to be spoken by the Lord** (KJV) is not impossible, but the translation in the RSV is more probable in the light of 1:1—the conception of Jesus as the first proclaimer is more consonant with his thought than the idea of Jesus as beginning the proclamation. It is not the teaching of

---

been mediated **by angels.** This law was steadfast. It was the word of God, and its violation brought appropriate suffering as a penalty. These penalties were just, not arbitrary explosions of vengeance, their very justice being a vindication of the law.

**3-4. *New Penalties.*—How shall we escape?** The argument is flawless and convincing. The principle recurs in the Scriptures and in life: the greater the privilege, the greater the penalty. It is a fearful thing to become the favorite of the Eternal (cf. Amos 3:2). If the word of the law and the prophets, here a little and there a little, diverse and fragmentary, carried its penalty, how much more inevitable the punishment for neglect of the supremely clear and final word of God through his Son! Of course this is a hard saying. Like every generation, ours shuns it. Preachers are rebuked because they talk too much of the righteousness of God, not enough of his grace, when the danger of the pew is in the contrary direction. Why does the gospel of grace fail to win a hearing, unless it is because men have forgotten the justice of God? If the danger is minimized, why should we get excited over salvation from that danger? Throughout the Bible the issues of life are sharp and clear. Every ease-loving generation is sooner or later rebuked by some awful judgment which reminds men that life is

not a matter of pleasantry and jest. The gospel of God's grace is precious and persuasive precisely in proportion to the felt severity of life's issues.

**Such a great salvation.** How great was it? And wherein did its greatness lie?

(*a*) **It was declared at first by the Lord.** God himself spoke through the historic Jesus, his words, his deeds, his life, his death, and his resurrection. In Jesus we hear the authentic accents of God himself. There can be no more final word than God speaking.

(*b*) **It was attested . . . by those who heard,** the witness of the living church, pointing beyond itself to its Lord. That God spoke through men, through events, and supremely through his Son, makes the historical witness vitally necessary to the church. God has revealed himself in history. That the central events of this revelation actually occurred is historically necessary to faith. For this assurance we depend on witnesses.

(*c*) **God also bore witness by signs and wonders and various miracles.** The interpreter must make his own decision as to how far miracles go to confirm the gospel in our own day. They were unquestioned in biblical days. But whatever we make of miracles, and faith cannot dispense with them, it is well to remember that they cannot mean to our day just what they did

4 God also bearing *them* witness, both with signs and wonders, and with divers miracles, and gifts of the Holy Ghost, according to his own will?

5 For unto the angels hath he not put in subjection the world to come, whereof we speak.

tested to us by those who heard him, 4 while God also bore witness by signs and wonders and various miracles and by gifts of the Holy Spirit distributed according to his own will.

5 For it was not to angels that God subjected the world to come, of which we are

---

Jesus which is specifically in his mind, although that is not excluded, but Jesus himself as being, because of his nature, the content of God's final revelation. The attestation **by those who heard him** guarantees that the message has come **to us** in its purity and, incidentally, rules out Paul as the author of Hebrews (cf. Gal. 1:1). **Miracles** confirm the authenticity of the revelation in the Son, and **gifts of the Holy Spirit** are grouped with miracles. Our author knows about the role of the Spirit or the Holy Spirit in primitive Christianity (cf. 6:4; 10:29), but in contrast to Paul he makes little use of Spirit. It does not fit into his distinctive teaching of the priesthood of Christ.

### d) PREVIEW OF JESUS' WORK IN SALVATION (2:5-18)

The final stage in the contrast between the Son and angels—the latter disappear after ch. 2—introduces the first presentation of the work of Jesus in salvation. Angels have been considered because they throw into relief the nature of the Son in its superiority. The argument in ch. 1 is not developed as a speculation about angels for its own sake, however, but to show that angels are "ministering spirits . . . to serve . . . those who are to obtain salvation" (1:14), and 2:1-4 drives home the necessity of attention to the salvation fully and divinely attested. The author has now to show why the Son, so superior to angels in his person, must "for a little while" be made "lower than the angels." This necessity leads to a preview of two interrelated themes: Jesus in his human experience of temptation, suffering, and death, and Jesus as a **merciful and faithful high priest** (vs. 17), which are to be the substance of his argument from 4:14 on. His artistic skill in interweaving each stage of the argument with what is to follow appears in this passage.

**5.** Salvation is yet to be obtained (1:14) although its benefits are already present (2:4), and it is **not to angels** that **the world to come** has been subjected by God. The writer is facing his central problem, i.e., how to bring integrally together the Son in his unique supremacy and Jesus in his human suffering and death. The nature of angels

---

to men of biblical times, simply because we believe in the concept of natural law. The Hebrews never met this idea except in rare encounters with the Greeks. In interpreting miracles it is well to recall (i) Jesus' own reticence—"See that you say nothing to any one" (Matt. 8:4); (ii) his own refusal to perform signs for his critics (Mark 8:11-12); (iii) Paul's caution against speaking with tongues, "In church I would rather speak five words with my mind, in order to instruct others, than ten thousand words in a tongue" (I Cor. 14:19); (iv) the central place which the miracle of the Resurrection held for the whole first-generation church; and (v) that the regeneration of every believer is itself miraculous.

(*d*) **Gifts of the Holy Spirit.** The writer does not here refer to the fruits of the Spirit, as Paul did in Gal. 5:22-23, but to the actual imparting of the Holy Spirit to believers. The

Holy Spirit living in men, this was the witness of God. Of course, his living in men leads to the "fruits of the Spirit," by which the presence of the Spirit is known and tested (cf. also Rom. 12:6-8; I Cor. 12:4-11: Eph. 4:7-8). For our day, at least, there is no stronger argument for the Christian faith than one of Christ's noblemen. Such a life is more simple, more complete, more convincing than all the weighty arguments of the learned. It is trite but ever important to remember that all that someone may know of Jesus Christ is what he sees in us. "You show that you are a letter from Christ delivered by us, written not with ink but with the Spirit of the living God" (II Cor. 3:3).

**5.** *God's New Order.*—Here the writer refers to the new order that God would establish and that Jesus came to inaugurate. It was the living hope of the N.T. All human institutions would be transformed and all citizens of the new order

6 But one in a certain place testified, saying, What is man, that thou art mindful of him? or the son of man, that thou visitest him?

7 Thou madest him a little lower than the angels; thou crownedst him with glory and honor, and didst set him over the works of thy hands:

speaking. 6 It has been testified somewhere,
"What is man that thou art mindful of him,
or the son of man, that thou carest for him?
7 Thou didst make him for a little while lower than the angels,
thou hast crowned him with glory and honor,[d]

[d] Other ancient authorities insert *and didst set him over the works of thy hands.*

---

provides him with the link. They are superhuman but on that account disqualified to meet human need.

**6-8a.** It is man's divine destiny to be crowned **with glory and honor** and to have all things put **under his feet,** i.e., to obtain salvation. The author establishes this by quoting from Ps. 8. The formula introducing the quotation **it has been testified somewhere** or "one writer, as we know, has affirmed" (Moffatt) is a literary mannerism much like our "someone has said," and was employed by Philo. The casual sound of the formula is not depreciatory. The identity of the human instrument is unimportant; the inspired message is vitally important both in itself and for its implications. Now Ps. 8 in its original meaning was unsuited to our author's purpose on two counts: it clearly predicts man's conquest of nature under God, and it also clearly states that man in the providence of God is only a little lower than the angels. Our author is not interested in the conquest of nature and so he omits, according to good MS evidence, the words **and didst set him over the works of thy hands.** If the MSS which include those words are correct, then our author regards the entire quotation as applying to Jesus and only in a secondary sense to man. It is not easy to decide this question, for his point is the identity of Jesus with man in

---

purified when **the world to come** became actual. In this new order the angels would not reign. Their subordinate rank would still remain. In the new order Christ would govern. This vision must never be lost. It has kept hearts high in days of discouragement, when it seemed that the church was too feeble for her enemies, that insolent unbelief and pride in high places would cruelly trample the fragile faith. It is this faith which has fostered heroism and enabled even humble Christians to defy the powers of darkness. It has rebuked man's too easy acceptance of things as they are and stirred him from his lethargy.

**6-9. Man's Gifts from God.—What is man that thou art mindful of him, . . . carest for him?** This is a central question for every generation. What momentous issues hang upon the answer! Men complain that human beings are no longer treated with respect. Is it because we have lost sight of that which is respectable in man? Believe of man that he is only an animal, and all logic drives you to treat him as an animal. But Kant, the philosopher, saw that since each man has within him a conscience, you must treat him as a center of dignity. Many see essential humanity in the basic drives

of sex, the lust for power, and the brutal determination to survive at every cost. But others have seen in man the image of God. Many cynically point to man's incurable selfishness and deny that any deed can ever be generous. Its grace is only in its seeming so. Others hear the Savior praying, "Father, forgive them" (Luke 23:34). What you see in man shapes your treatment of him. Here, at least, belief clearly governs conduct. It will be betrayed in your tone of voice, your choice of friends, every dollar you spend, in the work of each day. The degradation of man begins in the mind. Man's labor is a commodity to be purchased in the open market and at the lowest price! A human being is a number on an identification tag, so that when he has been blown to bits the military record may be kept straight. A woman is an object of lust. A competitor is one to be surpassed, no matter by what devices. A home is to be invaded by the endless radio chatter of advertisers. Man's sacred days and prized traditions have commercial value. On and on runs the cheapening, the disfiguring of man.

What is man? The passage contains three answers. First, he is a creature of amazing dignity. Ps. 8 speaks chiefly of man's dominion

8 Thou hast put all things in subjection under his feet. For in that he put all in subjection under him, he left nothing *that is* not put under him. But now we see not yet all things put under him.

8 putting everything in subjection under his feet."

Now in putting everything in subjection to man, he left nothing outside his control. As it is, we do not yet see everything in

---

some real way. Probably through vs. 8 he is thinking of *man,* and from that point on of Jesus as identified with man for his salvation. Βραχύ τι may be rendered either "for a little while lower than the angels" or "a little lower than the angels." The latter is unquestionably the meaning of the psalm in the Hebrew original, but the former is probably the meaning our author gives to it. It is difficult for him to fit into the framework of his thought the idea of a lowering of the Son's nature. A temporary humiliation for the sake of man's salvation is his answer.

**8b-10.** The main movement of thought in vss. 8b-9 is clear: man has not achieved his divine destiny, but Jesus (the first use of the name) has achieved it, and through the suffering of death and the subsequent crowning with glory and honor has opened the way through death—the essentially human experience—to glory **for every one.** Details are less clear. In our author's exegesis of the psalm he makes no use of the phrase "son of man." His thought moves along another line than the heavenly Man or representative Man of apocalyptic thought; he concentrates on the priestly significance of Jesus' suffering and death. Two difficulties appear in vs. 9. What is the relation of the phrase, **crowned with glory and honor,** to the rest of the sentence? Unless the text has been disturbed,

---

over nature, "over the works of thy hands" (Ps. 8:6). Man's puny strength is set in contrast to the vastness of the heavens, "When I consider thy heavens" (Ps. 8:3). Hebrews omits the reference to nature, but enlarges the triumph of man to include **everything, . . . nothing outside his control.** And that is plainly to be consummated in "the world to come, of which we are speaking" (vs. 5). We think of Hamlet's oft-quoted tribute to man, "What a piece of work is a man!" Or we think of Sophocles' celebration of the greatness of man in his *Antigone.* He is master of all in this life except death, which alone can conquer him,

Though skill of art may teach him how to flee
From depths of fell disease incurable.[6]

Or we think of Pascal's quiet word, "By space the universe encompasses and swallows me up like an atom; by thought I comprehend the world."[7]

Surely man's gifts are worthy of praise. He has tamed many of the forces of nature, belittled space, and turned the storm into his instrument. He has built great cities and controls vast interests. He has prolonged human life, eased the curse of drudgery, and opened the door to nature's plenty. There is in man a dimension which escapes the formulas of the

sciences, since man in this dimension creates the sciences. His art, his music, his literature, all refuse to let us discount him. The record of human nobility is inspiring.

Socrates drinking the hemlock,
    And Jesus on the rood;
And millions who, humble and nameless,
    The straight, hard pathway plod,—[8]

and in the Bible every gift of man is a sign of the goodness of the Giver! **Thou art mindful of him, . . . carest for him. Thou didst make him . . . , thou hast crowned him.** In the encounter with God man reaches his greatest height. To hear God speak to him, this is man's fulfillment. Here is his true grandeur, his high destiny.

But declaim as you may on the wisdom and nobility of man, the ghosts of the war dead of our century will rise from their graves and, pointing bony fingers at you, give mute testimony to man's folly and brutality. The second part of the answer to our question is the dark, tragic story of man's failure. Endowed with knowledge, he has invented destruction. Given freedom, he has chosen slavery. Made in the image of God, he has disfigured himself by commerce with the demonic. In magnificent understatement, **we do not yet see everything in subjection to him.**

[6] *Tragedies and Fragments,* tr. E. H. Plumptre (Boston: D. C. Heath & Co., 1912), I, p. 153.

[7] *The Thoughts of Blaise Pascal* (London: J. M. Dent & Co., 1904), p. 133.

[8] William Herbert Carruth, "Each in His Own Tongue." Used by permission of Mrs. William Herbert Carruth.

9 But we see Jesus, who was made a little lower than the angels for the suffering of death, crowned with glory and honor; that he by the grace of God should taste death for every man.

subjection to him. 9 But we see Jesus, who for a little while was made lower than the angels, crowned with glory and honor because of the suffering of death, so that by the grace of God he might taste death for every one.

---

for which there is no MS evidence, it is simplest to take these words as a sort of parenthesis. They would then remind the reader that the humiliation had a glorious outcome, and would not interrupt the flow of thought. The second difficulty arises from the phrase χάριτι θεοῦ **(by the grace of God)** for some of the early church fathers knew a text which read χωρὶς θεοῦ, "without God" or "apart from God." Since such a reading might easily have been changed to χάριτι θεοῦ and so have yielded a text easier to understand, we are bound to consider it. It would probably mean that Jesus tasted death for everyone "except God" (Origen). But the "grace of God" fits well with the opening words of vs. 10 and may well be original. To **taste death** has not our modern connotation of a superficial flavoring of death: it means to experience death (cf. Mark 9:1).

---

He cannot control himself:

We are unable, for example, to suppress many of our emotions; we cannot change a bad mood into a good one, and we cannot command our dreams to come or go. . . . We only believe that we are masters in our own house because we like to flatter ourselves.[9]

Made to be a master, he is a slave to his fears. Made to walk amid the beauties of God's heaven, he wades through the mire. Made for steady peace and abiding joy, his heart is in torment. Made to stand erect with the dignity of God upon his face, his face is brutalized by lust. Made for love, he hates. Made for strength, he is too weak to throw off the shackles of his sin.

This failure to be master in his own house, written large in human institutions, becomes at once his shame and his terror. With all our knowledge and technical skill, our civilization seems to be dissolving, and that in spite of the fact that ours is the first civilization to understand, however darkly, why civilizations grow and decay. The violent hatred between races, the conflict of the classes over power, the threat of economic chaos amid potential plenty, and the horror of recurring wars—how pathetic to say that he **left nothing outside his control!**

**Everything in subjection under his feet?** When all his achievements, all his hopes, all for which he lived, seem destined for universal ruin? The power of death is not merely that we ourselves, one by one, soon or late, come to the end of the road. Its shadow falls upon all we hold fair and dear. All our human institutions, all the human beings that give meaning to our days, all the hopes that ennoble our

lives, all our thoughts, all our heroisms, all our loves, all our loyalties—all are under sentence of death. It seems idle to talk of man's supremacy when man himself is doomed. The "objective immortality" about which Whitehead wrote, the survival of our influence, seems idle mockery when all in which we survive must also be destroyed. "All those . . . through fear of death were subject to lifelong bondage" (vs. 15). It seems clear that this dread of death is the driving power that leads man to assert his own security, to take on sinful pretensions of pride and power. Man's greed for wealth and position, his brutal struggle to obtain them—what are they save his pathetic barricade against fear and death?

Man in bondage to sin and death—this is the second stage of our answer to the question "What is man?"

**But we see Jesus.** Thank God for this final answer! It is our hope in every despairing. It is God's sufficient answer for human failure. No Christian should ever be a pessimist. The pessimist recites the sorry human record and puts a period. God puts a comma. A man has grievously betrayed the good; he has brought heartache and pain to those who are near him. On your knees, man! Make no defense for yourself; have done with these flimsy excuses—your old enemy lurks within those shadows. Pour out the story of your shame to One who knows all about it already. But have a care! Let not this honest penitence turn into a mournful preoccupation with yourself, a fascination over your affairs. "Look away to Jesus." Your penitence is never Christian until it leads you to turn from yourself—that was your trouble all along—and look steadily at your Savior. Hold fast to him. Never lose sight of him. He is your hope.

[9] C. G. Jung, *Modern Man in Search of a Soul* (New York: Harcourt, Brace & Co., 1933), p. 211.

10 For it became him, for whom *are* all things, and by whom *are* all things, in bringing many sons unto glory, to make the captain of their salvation perfect through sufferings.

10 For it was fitting that he, for whom and by whom all things exist, in bringing many sons to glory, should make the pioneer of their salvation perfect through suf-

Vs. 10 begins with a striking reaffirmation of the divine initiative in the Incarnation. This thought is never far from the author's mind. It was **fitting** that God, the God **for whom and by whom all things exist,** should achieve the goal of salvation for men by this means. He alone could do it; he alone did it. The writer gives no proof that the Incarnation was consonant with the divine nature; yet it is apparent throughout his argument that God purposes to reveal himself for the salvation of men (1:1 ff.). Only here and in 12:5 ff. does he speak of men as destined for glory as sons of God. Was he hesitant in using the word son, as applied to men, in view of the uniqueness he has assigned to the one and only Son? The word **pioneer** as a translation of ἀρχηγός is vivid, but not quite accurate, for the idea of a lone hero breaking the trail to salvation is not at all in his mind. Jesus is the completely adequate and completely victorious leader of salvation. We shall have to consider again our author's use of the idea of perfection. Here there is no thought of a moral process leading to moral perfection, but only of a completely adequate qualification for leading men to the final and complete salvation.

One man laments over his wayward children, and for a loving parent this is the bitterest burden to carry. But beyond the sins of your children see Jesus, their Savior and yours. Another complains about the church, its inept and awkward fumbling with the most sacred and urgent task in the world. But look beyond the church to Jesus. Another decries the evil in his world, the growing dishonesty in high places, the breaking homes, the chaos of recurring wars, and declares that our civilization has run its course. It may be so. But you have not told the truth about man and his sorry record until you look beyond to Jesus. He too was man and showed what man could be. He is the ultimate answer to the question "What is man?"

But how does he help? Wherein is he our hope? Because he has already bested our worst enemy, death. He has tasted **death for every one.** This tasting of death is itself the provision of God's mercy. The Savior who has tasted death was not mastered by it. He turned the emblem of shame and defeat into a crown of glory and honor. His death was the defeat of sin, and the promise of saving power to all who believe. But here we are anticipating. For this is the theme which the writer will now develop —Christ as the perfect priest.

**10. *Christ Perfected Through Suffering.*—** The interpreter should stoutly resist the temptation to make this text a basis for the trite theme that suffering perfects. In the first place, it is not so. Suffering sometimes defaces and embitters its victims. In the second place, this interpretation misses the central emphasis of the writer, who was dealing not with the problem of suffering, nor was he enunciating any facile formula about its purifying effects. He was concerned to show that only by enduring the depths of human suffering could the pioneer, or leader of men's salvation, be perfected for precisely this work of salvation.

For Jews and Greeks of that day the suffering of a shameful death was "a stumbling-block" and "folly" (I Cor. 1:23). It was a veritable sign of weakness and of the disfavor of God. Surely the writer is aiming at this offense of the Cross when he writes that **it was fitting that he [God].** . . . This was appropriate to the nature of God. Note carefully that the author was not justifying the suffering pioneer on the very human ground that only a suffering priest could persuade us to trust him with our salvation. This is true and the writer later makes full use of it (cf. 4:15). But here he is saying that the plan is befitting the nature of God. Salvation must originate with God: it must arise from the depths of his own being. Those who despise the sufferings of the Christ show thereby that they are ignorant of the true nature of God. Further, the qualification **for whom and by whom all things exist** is important. It links redemption with creation (see Expos. on 1:2). Redemption was no afterthought with God. It is as primordial as creation itself in the divine purpose. This is the grand emphasis of the gospel which corrects the weakness of all "subjective" theories of the Atonement.

**The pioneer of their salvation.** He is the author, leader, and in their very ranks the captain of their salvation. "He is the strong

11 For both he that sanctifieth and they who are sanctified *are* all of one: for which cause he is not ashamed to call them brethren,

12 Saying, I will declare thy name unto my brethren, in the midst of the church will I sing praise unto thee.

13 And again, I will put my trust in him. And again, Behold I and the children which God hath given me.

fering. 11 For he who sanctifies and those who are sanctified have all one origin. That is why he is not ashamed to call them brethren, 12 saying,

"I will proclaim thy name to my brethren,
in the midst of the congregation I will praise thee."

13 And again,

"I will put my trust in him."

And again,

"Here am I, and the children God has given me."

---

11. Vss. 11-18 deal directly with the question: Why did the Son share human experience "in every respect" (vs. 17) and how does his human experience avail for salvation? The connection is with the preceding verse. The first answer is that **he who sanctifies and those who are sanctified have all one origin,** literally, are "all of one." The "one" is not Adam (cf. Acts 17:26) or Abraham (cf. vs. 16), but God as creator. Jesus, the Son, must share the experience of **many sons** in order to bring them **to glory.** It should be noted that our author carefully avoids identifying the nature of the Son with the sons. The sons are to be glorified, but at present they are also lower than the angels; it is identity of experience which is suggested by **he is not ashamed to call them brethren.** The sanctifier and the sanctified are appropriate terms in the light of the purification for sins (1:3), which is the Son's work, and in the light of the priesthood of Jesus as it will be subsequently developed. The metaphor is sacerdotal.

12-13. This common origin of Son and sons is proved by words of the Lord recorded in scripture. The three citations from Ps. 22:22 and Isa. 8:17-18 are less convincing to the modern reader than presumably to the first readers of Hebrews. The wide use of Ps. 22 as messianic and the presence of the words **brethren** and **children** in the quotations, assuming that Christ is the speaker, make them apt from the author's viewpoint. **I will put my trust in him** seems less obviously apt. Perhaps we are to suppose that the Son also shared with men the attitude of **trust.**

---

swimmer who carries the rope ashore and so not only secures His own position but makes rescue for all who will follow." [1] He has himself opened the way of access to God. He has shown man the way so clearly that he can still say, "I am the way" (John 14:6).

**11-13. On Christ as Our Brother.**—Not ashamed to call them brethren. Well he might be! Look at mankind and see what men have done to their heritage, how they have belied their divine parentage! Look at the ruin they have made of God's order: how they have misused the plenty of the earth; turned the resources of nature into instruments of horrible destruction; used the very gospel to exalt themselves in pride to where they can wield anathemas and enslave the minds of men; put a curse on their God-given freedom—until fear, hunger, disease, and death seem the masters of men. Or more to the point, let us look at our-

selves and see our share in the folly of mankind. And **he is not ashamed to call them brethren!** The interpreter must never lose the wonder and mystery of God's grace, never let it become commonplace and familiar, never let it become a theological package which he can carry about as his own possession.

Have all one origin. They are sons of one Father, although the writer is careful not to blur the distinction between Son and sons. All are of God, and even in their lowest depths men have not completely lost the marks of their lineage. It is this community of origin which makes it possible for the Christ to be unashamed of his brethren.

If we look upon vss. 12-13 as "proofs" that the Christ regards men as his brethren, we shall not make our case. As the Exeg. points out, these quotations are clearly distorted from their original context. Why, then, did the writer include them? Was he not seeking to illustrate

[1] Marcus Dods, in *Expositor's Greek Testament,* IV, 265.

14 Forasmuch then as the children are partakers of flesh and blood, he also himself likewise took part of the same; that through death he might destroy him that had the power of death, that is, the devil;

15 And deliver them, who through fear of death were all their lifetime subject to bondage.

14 Since therefore the children share in flesh and blood, he himself likewise partook of the same nature, that through death he might destroy him who has the power of death, that is, the devil, 15 and deliver all those who through fear of death were sub-

---

14-17. The second answer to the question—Why did the Son need to share human experience?—is in the form of a condensed statement of this necessity from the human point of view and of the outcome in terms of human experience. It is unsupported from scripture because human need arising from human nature does not need to be established by any argument, and because the priestly function of Jesus is to be the main theme of the epistle. Our author does not again discuss the conquest of the devil **who has the power of death** and the deliverance of **those who through fear of death were subject to lifelong bondage.** We must assume that his readers were familiar with the idea that the devil has the power of death—it was current both in Jewish and Christian thinking—and that they will understand how the human experience of Jesus, culminating in his death and exaltation, vanquishes the devil, for the writer does not explain it. Two possibilities occur to our minds: either through the "purification for sins" the devil loses his right to inflict

---

and vivify the complete identification of Christ with man? The Son is not bending a little from the heavens to beckon men thither. Nor is he moving among men "with the kindly superior professionalism of a surgeon who enters the ward of an hospital solely to heal, not to live there." [2] See how graphic the quotations are! Justin Martyr makes the first (Ps. 22:22-23) foretell how Jesus stood in the midst of his disciples singing a hymn to the Father before they started for Gethsemane. Jesus standing in the midst of the assembly, joining his voice with ours in praise to God! He too puts his trust in God, thereby confessing himself a man. And he refers to his disciples as **the children God has given me** (cf. John 17:6). He is in every sense one with us, our elder brother in praise and trust and obedience. He is not ashamed to call us brethren! If that is true, there is hope for all mankind. If that is true, how deep is our shame if we are ever ashamed of him!

14-15. *The Full Humanity of Christ.*—But if he is really our brother, he must share our bitterest defeat. If he is the leader of our salvation, so that through him man is really "crowned with glory and honor" (vs. 9), he must do something about man's greatest enemy, death. Otherwise Sophocles was right, and man, conquering all, is in turn vanquished by death. **To share in flesh and blood** with his brethren is to face death. But here Jesus has proved faithful. This is the supreme evidence of his complete identity with man. He too died.

The fear of death is a **lifelong bondage.** Classical writers were burdened with it. In modern times it is manifest in our reluctance to mention it. Death is taboo in a polite conversation, which betrays our trouble with it. A hidden fear that we may not mention is all the more sinister. The more we love life, the more hateful does death become. The more we give ourselves to other people and see the priceless meaning of life and the high purposes that call for our devotion, the more dreadful does the grim destroyer appear. Robert Browning caught the universal dread of death when he put these words on the lips of Cleon, an imaginary Greek poet of the time of Paul:

Say rather that my fate is deadlier still,
In this, that every day my sense of joy
Grows more acute, my soul (intensified
By power and insight) more enlarged, more keen;

. . . . . . . . . . .

The horror quickening still from year to year,
The consummation coming past escape
When

. . . . . . . . . . .

I the feeling, thinking, acting man,
The man who loved his life so over-much,
Sleep in my urn. It is so horrible,
I dare at times imagine to my need
Some future state revealed to us by Zeus,
Unlimited in capability
For joy, as this is in desire for joy.

. . . . . . . . . . .

Zeus has not yet revealed it; and alas,
He must have done so, were it possible! [3]

[2] *Ibid.,* IV, 266.

[3] "Cleon."

16 For verily he took not on *him the nature of* angels; but he took on *him* the seed of Abraham.

17 Wherefore in all things it behooved him to be made like unto *his* brethren, that he might be a merciful and faithful high priest in things *pertaining* to God, to make reconciliation for the sins of the people.

ject to lifelong bondage. 16 For surely it is not with angels that he is concerned but with the descendants of Abraham. 17 Therefore he had to be made like his brethren in every respect, so that he might become a merciful and faithful high priest in the service of God, to make expiation for the

---

death on those purified, or by inflicting death upon the sinless Christ the devil overstepped his authority and lost his grip on man. Paul is similarly obscure (cf. I Cor. 2:6; 5:5; 10:10). What is striking is our author's affirmation that men are delivered from the **fear of death** through the ministry of Jesus. We are tempted to read this in psychological terms, remembering that this theme plays a great role in classical thought, and there are many "psychological" overtones in Hebrews. These overtones derive, however, from the author's concentration on human experience, especially the experience of worship, and we must not modernize him. He is not concerned with attitudes and emotions as such but with the grounds for them. The fear of death no doubt means for him fear of the consequences that follow death at the Judgment. But unlike Paul, he does not think of the powers of evil in relation to righteousness and sin in a moral sense; his concern is with access to God in worship, and the feelings are much more directly involved.

Although our author never quite asserts that Jesus shared human nature in the complete sense, he is quite insistent that he shared human experience **in every respect.** This he must do in order to **become a merciful and faithful high priest in the service of**

---

The fear of death is aggravated by the thought of what comes after death. It seems clear that Paul at least saw a close connection between sin and death. "The sting of death is sin" (I Cor. 15:56; cf. also Rom. 5:12-14). For our writer death is followed by judgment (9:27). As the life which Jesus came to bring to men was not endless biological existence, but eternal life, so death for the Christian is not a mere ceasing to be alive.

But how did Jesus deliver men from this lifelong bondage? Partly by what he said about death. He treated death almost with a fine contempt. "Do not fear those who kill the body, and after that have no more that they can do" (Luke 12:4). Partly by his own brave facing of it. He did pause at Gethsemane, but when that crisis was past, he moved with steady step. Our writer, however, is thinking of something more. **Through death,** in his own death, Jesus destroyed, brought "to nought" (ASV), **him who has the power of death, that is, the devil, and** delivered **all those who through fear of death were subject to lifelong bondage.** We may not be sure of the author's meaning. But surely he had in mind the demonstration that death did not mean separation from God, but access to him. And he must have been thinking of the Resurrection, that cornerstone of all N.T. faith and hope (see Col. 1:13).

**16. The Descendants of Abraham.**—The word ἐπιλαμβάνεται clearly does not mean "take on the nature of," as in the KJV. But it does mean "take hold of in order to rescue from peril." On this, reliable commentaries agree. The figure is vivid and is lost by the mild translation **is concerned with** in the RSV. It suggests the firm hold which a strong swimmer takes upon a drowning man in order to bring him to safety.

But why introduce the **angels?** Plainly they do not need salvation as man does. The only possible reason is that by excluding the angels from this gift, the lavishing of God's grace upon man is made vivid. And the descendants of Abraham? Is the writer limiting salvation to the Jews? Plainly not. He would have shared Paul's insight that the true seed of Abraham are all the faithful, regardless of racial origin (cf. Rom. 4:16-17; Gal. 3:29). Probably the phrase is used here as an introduction to the priestly work of our Lord which is first mentioned in the following verse.

**17. A Merciful and Faithful High Priest.**—The writer now gathers up the whole meaning of vss. 10-16. **He had to be made,** the very nature of the case required it. In order to be a high priest for the people he had to be one of them, like them **in every respect.** Only so could he be **merciful and faithful.** Only one who knows

18 For in that he himself hath suffered being tempted, he is able to succor them that are tempted.

sins of the people. 18 For because he himself has suffered and been tempted, he is able to help those who are tempted.

---

**God, to make expiation for the sins of the people.** Theodore H. Robinson ventures to call this "atonement by sympathy," using the word sympathy, of course, in its deepest sense (*The Epistle of Paul to the Hebrews* [London: Hodder & Stoughton, 1933; "The Moffatt New Testament Commentary"], *ad loc.*). If we understand the background of our author's thought, it is not inaccurate to use this striking phrase. But in itself the phrase hardly does justice to the sweep of the author's thought. Temptation, suffering, and death as experienced by Jesus are not just evidences of the divine sympathy which shares our lot and helps to slay sins; they are rather the divine necessity, what was "fitting" for him "for whom and by whom all things exist." This is an even more daring thought than the divine sympathy, which is indeed the impact made on man by the divine necessity. Our author's thought is at once more primitive and more potent than the phrase "atonement by sympathy" suggests.

Throughout this initial exposition of the ministry of Jesus the author carefully avoids his special priestly concept, except to indicate that this is to be his theme. He lays the groundwork for his subsequent exposition, however, and prepares the reader for the line of thinking he is to follow.

Jesus has been introduced; his identity with the Son has been maintained; and his service to men has been outlined. The author has moved from the heavenly Son to the earthly Jesus. His approach is not that Jesus in his words and deeds is man's empirical datum for faith in a Christlike God, but that God in his final word to men has spoken in a Son who shared God's nature and was the agent of creation and who, in Jesus the great high priest of the universe, entered into the experience of man when man was neediest—in temptation, suffering, and death.

---

our weakness and our temptation from within, who knows what it means to shrink from suffering, only "one of us" could really be merciful (cf. vss. 18; 4:15; 5:2). He must also be faithful, i.e., trustworthy in the things of God, entirely deserving of all our trust.

The union **merciful and faithful** is fateful and rich. It reminds us of the momentous union of Rom. 3:26 and 11:22, which in both cases is applied to God. Here failure on either count would have disqualified the priest. To be faithful to God, but not to have sympathetic mercy, would have made him another John the Baptist, a prophet denouncing the sins of men, condemning them to yet deeper misery. A merciful priest, tender in understanding, but unfaithful, would end by acquiescing in men as he found them, in consenting to their sins. Such a lenient priest, who made excuses for the sins of men instead of **expiation,** could never win the trust of the sinner. Such a salvation would heal no wounds, forgive no sins. But **merciful and faithful**—this is the union which makes our high priest superior. No angel, however faithful, could know what it is like to be a man.

**To make expiation** is the task of the priest. In its original form the word means that which has its primary effect upon God. As used here,

in the later stages of its long evolution, it applies rather to the removal of **the sins of the people,** as a barrier to fellowship with God.

**18. *Christ's Ability to Help.*—**Βοηθῆσαι is a graphic word. It means literally "run to the cry" of someone in distress. Authorities differ on whether the temptation referred to arose from the suffering, or the suffering from the temptation. It seems reasonable from the construction of the sentence to believe that the writer was thinking of the temptation arising from the suffering, although he had no reason to exclude the earlier temptations of Jesus that had no connection with pain. Jesus had a normal aversion to pain and to death, which was innocent of sin unless it conflicted with the purpose of the Father. The temptation in Gethsemane was to "shrink back." The people to whom this writing was addressed were tempted to "shrink back" (cf. 10:38-39) under hardship and persecution. When the horror of torture and death draws near, and you are tempted to "shrink back," there is One who will "run to your cry" because he knows just what you face.

There is no valid reason for not extending this promise of help to all who suffer from any temptation. We are afraid of danger. This fear becomes sin only when in cowardice we com-

3 Wherefore, holy brethren, partakers of the heavenly calling, consider the Apostle and High Priest of our profession, Christ Jesus;

3 Therefore, holy brethren, who share in a heavenly call, consider Jesus, the apos-

## 2. He Is Superior to Moses as a Son Is Superior to a Servant (3:1-6a)

The connection with what precedes is both formal and substantial, an almost exact parallel with the movement from 1:14 to 2:1. In 1:14 the author summarized the role of angels as "ministering spirits" of the salvation which the Son gives; "therefore" hold fast to the salvation through the Son. Here (2:18) he has summarized the salvation through the Son in its effectiveness for men; "therefore" hold fast to Jesus as over against Moses, who because of his *humanity* might seem to offer what angels could not give. The verbal connection is established through the word "faithful," used of Jesus in 2:17 and of Moses in 3:2.

The role of Moses neither as lawgiver nor as priest is played up, for the mediation of the law has been assigned to angels (2:2) and it is proposed to contrast Jesus' priesthood with the Levitical. Moses seems hardly necessary in the argument, and the author's main purpose in introducing him is to prepare the way for an exhortation based on Ps. 95. This superficial treatment of Moses shows that he is not combating normative Judaism with its strenuous legalism. His readers were not attracted by the kind of Judaism Paul faces. But there is no depreciation of Moses, who **was faithful in all God's house as a servant.**

**3:1.** The full and solemn address, **holy brethren** (cf. "brethren" in 3:12; 10:19; 13:22; "beloved" in 6:9), is the first direct address in Hebrews; in the previous exhortation the author has used "we" and "us" (2:1 ff.). The absence of a direct appeal to the readers up to this point must not be pressed to prove the academic interest of the writer; he is moving from the presuppositions which author and readers share, to the practical consequences which the readers must see and act upon. "Holy" in this writing means the "sanctified" whose sins have been "purged" (cf. 1:3; 2:11).

The idea of **partakers of the heavenly calling** is characteristic of our author. Christians **share** this calling, just as Jesus "shares" human nature (2:14). It is as near as this writer comes to the Pauline "in Christ," "in the Spirit," which is something quite different. Similarly, it would be unlike Paul to urge his readers to **consider Jesus** (cf. "looking to

promise our Christian vocation. In such an hour there is a helper who will "run to our cry." We shrink back from the hard road of humility. Our pride comes easily. We fear the difficult path of the disciplined life. It is easy to let ourselves go. We dread the leap into the dark, committing ourselves completely into the hands of God. It is easy to be safe, to follow the old road, where we keep the controls, make the decisions, have the answers. We would avoid the rough road of pouring out our life in sacrifice for another. A cross, seen ahead of us, is always repulsive. The way of evasion is easy. If in temptation's hour we would only seek every resource of strength, we should suffer no defeats. What can give us more strength and comfort than simply to cry out for him, our high priest, who himself has suffered in temptation and who will therefore "run to our cry"?

**3:1. *Fixing the Mind on Jesus.*—**Much is condensed in this verse. The writer reminds his

people who they are and who Christ is. **Holy brethren** might be equivalent to "Christian brethren." The word translated **holy** literally means "set apart to God in an exclusive sense." Whatever the refinements of meaning introduced into this word by other usages in the N.T., this central meaning is always preserved. The author certainly does not have in view the moral perfection of his people, as is evident from later references. But he reminds them that they are **holy.** A people set apart for God is part of the Protestant emphasis on the priesthood of all believers. This doctrine is a declaration not so much of right as of responsibility. It is not enough to set apart a class for the service of God and to call them "priests." All God's people are consecrated, and whatever their vocation, their service is to him. There is power in this thought. Suppose we really dared to apply it! What if to every Christian, as by his own deliberate choice his membership in

2 Who was faithful to him that appointed him, as also Moses *was faithful* in all his house.

tle, and high priest of our confession. 2 He was faithful to him who appointed him, just as Moses also was faithful in[e] God's

e Other ancient authorities insert *all*.

---

Jesus" [12:2]). In Hebrews this must not be taken superficially as if a mere intellectual consideration of Jesus was meant. We are simply in a different realm of thinking from the Pauline; the imagery and the experience symbolized are controlled by the concept of worship.

**The apostle, and high priest of our confession:** Apostle is a title never applied to Christ elsewhere in the N.T. Why does our author use it here? He has carefully avoided it in 2:3. Son versus angels, Apostle versus Moses, Priest versus priests—is this his thought? But he recurs to Son in the following contrast with Moses. **Jesus, the apostle, and high priest of our confession** suggests to a number of commentators that reference is being made to a creedal statement in which the words "apostle" and "high priest" appeared. But since the writer labors to prove that Jesus is high priest, that part of a "confession" cannot be assumed. We do not have the data for deciding this question, but it is intriguing to find the word "apostle" applied only to Jesus as if there were no other apostles; the author never calls himself an apostle.

**2-6a.** The argument in these verses hinges on the words "faithful" and "house," from the characterization of Moses in Num. 12:7. The writer combines this with the faithfulness of Jesus (2:17) and his role as agent of Creation (1:2) to prove that while Moses

---

the church is ratified, should come that sense of being set apart which normally comes to a minister in his ordination!

**Who share in a heavenly call.** This may mean a call from heaven or a call to heaven, or more probably both. The being set apart to God is no mere human device. It is a call from God himself. Here is a central emphasis that is often neglected. Into the vexed question of election we need not enter. But surely the N.T. is clear that the Christian life never rests merely upon human decision. "You did not choose me, but I chose you and appointed you that you should go and bear fruit and that your fruit should abide" (John 15:16). It is essential to Christian believers that their faith rest in God. They are to understand that their responsibility is personal, that the invitation from God is directed to them as individuals, that God himself is calling them to the life of the redeemed. It is hard to see how a vigorous Christian faith can rest on any other foundation.

**Jesus, the apostle.** Nowhere else in the N.T. is this term used of Jesus, and its use here is evidence of the fresh originality of this epistle. As applied to Jesus the word means one who is sent, "not a mere envoy, but an ambassador or representative sent with powers, authorized to speak in the name of the person who has dispatched him."[4]

[4] James Moffatt, *The Epistle to the Hebrews* (New York: Charles Scribner's Sons, 1924; "The International Critical Commentary"), p. 41.

**Therefore,** seeing that the Christ, superior to angels, was not ashamed to call us brethren, and became "in every respect" one of us, and so, as the **high priest of our confession,** standing before God for us, shows himself able to help us because he had endured our sufferings and trials; **therefore . . . consider Jesus.** The word literally means to "fix the mind upon Jesus." Hold him in your mind; let him live in your thoughts; let him be the major premise of all your syllogisms, the criterion of every judgment. The word **consider** is strong and thorough.

**2.** *The Fidelity of Jesus.*—**He was faithful to him who appointed him.** The writer does not further amplify this terse sentence. The following verses demonstrate not the faithfulness of Jesus, but that he was faithful in a higher office than was Moses, who was also faithful. Faith always carries the note of fidelity, as we shall see in ch. 11. The full comment on the faithfulness of Jesus is written in the Gospels. It governed every word that he spoke. Every healing deed, every purpose, every decision was faithful. The crowning fidelity was his giving of himself, his victorious cry, "Not what I will, but what thou wilt" (Mark 14:36). He had said, "My food is to do the will of him who sent me, and to accomplish his work" (John 4:34).

When He heals the sick, and when He avoids them; when He retreats before His enemies, and

3 For this *man* was counted worthy of more glory than Moses, inasmuch as he who hath builded the house hath more honor than the house.

4 For every house is builded by some *man;* but he that built all things *is* God.

5 And Moses verily *was* faithful in all his house as a servant, for a testimony of those things which were to be spoken after;

house. 3 Yet Jesus has been counted worthy of as much more glory than Moses as the builder of a house has more honor than the house. 4 (For every house is built by some one, but the builder of all things is God.) 5 Now Moses was faithful in all God's house as a servant, to testify to the

---

was faithful as servant in the house, Jesus is faithful as Son over the house. The only real difficulty is with vs. 4, which seems to interrupt the thought. The RSV solves this by making vs. 4 parenthetical. The alternative is to translate, "For every house is built by someone, but the builder of all things is divine" (θεός, here without an article). Since our author's argument does not issue in that conclusion, the RSV translation is probably correct. Whatever "house" meant in Num. 12:7, it means "the household" of God for

---

when He faces them; when He limits His activities to the Jews, as well as when He ministers to Gentiles; when He withdraws to an obscure spot, and when He sets His face steadfastly to go to Jerusalem; when He takes the scourge in His hand, and when He offers the same hand to receive the print of the nails—the same undeviating, consistent will courses through whatever He does, emerging from the depths of His soul, outpouring from the wellspring of His life. . . . And so there resounds through everything Jesus does and says something that seems to come from the deepest recesses of the mystery of the world itself.[5]

We can never fathom the depths of that fidelity. It includes his whole faith, his life of trust in God. It is still the secret of Jesus (cf. Expos. on 10:5-10).

**In God's house.** In the use of this metaphor there is at least a hint of the concept of the family which pervades the thought of the N.T. For **house** suggests father and children, especially when the house is identified with the body of Christian believers (cf. vs. 6). This hint also appears even in such O.T. passages as that to which reference is here made (Num. 12:7).

**3. Jesus and Moses.**—In establishing the superiority of Jesus to Moses we might have contrasted the characters of the two men. We might have sampled the teachings of each of them to show the larger universality, the deeper penetration, the enduring finality of the teaching of Jesus. But our author chose rather to contrast their relative positions in the house of God. **The builder of a house has more honor than the house.** This is a commonplace when applied to a physical house. Any tribute to a house is an honor to the builder. But here the house is

plainly "the household of faith" (Gal. 6:10). By inference Moses was a part of that household. But the builder (cf. 1:2) is God working through the Son. Christ is the Lord of the church, its builder and founder (cf. I Cor. 3:10-15).

**4. God the Builder.**—This verse possibly refers to a favorite argument of antiquity that a building implies a builder. The world is a building, therefore there is a world builder. If so, the argument is weakened today because the growth of the universe is not like the growth of a building. But it is not probable that the author is trying to prove the existence of God by this analogy. The interpreter has no warrant for this use of the text. The point seems to be that since God is the **builder of all things,** he is also the builder of the **house,** the church. Since he made all things through the Son (1:2), the Son himself is the builder of the household of faith and has, therefore, more honor than Moses. This interpretation does connect with what follows.

**5-6a. The Faithfulness of Moses.**—**Moses was faithful . . . as a servant.** The position of servant had a dignity above that of the slave. The servant was free and the position might have honor (Num. 12:7). The point needed no laboring, since the dignity of Moses was acknowledged by all who accepted the law. Throughout Exodus the words "as the LORD commanded Moses" are like a recurring refrain. The crowning fidelity of Moses is recorded in Exod. 32 (or in Num. 14), where Moses refused to be made the father of a nation that would replace a rebellious Israel. "Yet now, if thou wilt forgive their sin—; and if not, blot me, I pray thee, out of thy book which thou hast written" (Exod. 32:32). Yet the work of Moses was to carry out the commandment of God in

[5] Friedrich Rittelmeyer, *Behold the Man* (tr. Erich Hofacker and George Bennett Hatfield; New York: The Macmillan Co., 1929), pp. 49-50. Used by permission.

6 But Christ as a son over his own house; whose house are we, if we hold fast the confidence and the rejoicing of the hope firm unto the end.

things that were to be spoken later, 6 but Christ was faithful over God's*f* house as a son. And we are his house if we hold fast*g* our confidence and pride in our hope.

*f* Greek *his.*
*g* Other ancient authorities insert *firm to the end.*

---

Hebrews, as 6*b* shows. Like the angels, although in a different realm, Moses is a witness to the things that were to be spoken, i.e., the revelation of salvation.

### 3. Resultant Warning and Exhortation Based on Ps. 95 (3:6*b*–4:13)
#### *a*) Introduction (3:6*b*-11)

**6*b*-11.** Our author's concern is not with Moses as a possible rival of Jesus, but with the readers' danger of suffering the fate of the wilderness generation. He skillfully introduces this thought by a transitional sentence (6*b*), **And we are his house if we hold fast,** and follows it by a quotation from Ps. 95 to show that the wilderness generation perished because of unbelief, but that the "rest" promised is still open to his readers as long as it is **today** (6*b*–4:13).

---

God's house. **Christ was faithful over God's house as a son.** Here again the writer is not referring to any particular fidelity of Jesus, but to his superior status as the Son of the house.

**6*b*. *The House of God.*—We are his house if . . . .** The figure is vivid. The company of the faithful, the church, is also called the "house of God" in I Pet. 4:17 and in I Tim. 3:15. We are his house—the home where God delights to dwell. All the sacred associations of a good home are gathered here to their full meaning. In the home of God—that is where the family ties are renewed in joyous fellowship. That is the place of safety, of light, of warmth, of food, of love. That is where others know us most intimately and love us most patiently. That is the source of our strength and peace of mind. Try to imagine how your church would be ennobled if to its members there came the conviction that they are the house of God; that here joyous sacrifice and generous self-giving come naturally; that here the presence of the Father holds the children up to their best; that here men are at rest and at home; that however far they wander, however distant is their business, here is the place to which their hearts turn and are warm with a tender joy. Surely the church would be changed, perhaps beyond recognition, if men regarded it as the house of God.

**We are his house if . . . .** The condition has nothing to do with human ordinances in the church, however useful they are in expressing the inner genius of various groups. There is nothing here about apostolic succession, valid sacraments, a well-decorated clergy, purity of doctrine, a socially correct membership, large endowments, imposing buildings, inspiring music, or brilliant preaching. **We are his house if we hold fast** the faith that never looks back, but resolutely holds and is held by God.

We are to hold fast to our **confidence.** The primary meaning of the word is unreserved freedom in speech. It means the boldness with which the apostles spoke before men (cf. Acts 18:26; 19:8), and with which the Christian is to approach God (cf. 4:16; 10:19, 35; I John 4:17). It is the confidence that is forthright, without bluster and without apology. We are to hold fast our **pride in our hope.** The word **pride** is the same word that Paul uses frequently, variously translated as "glorying," "boasting."

Confidence and pride are essential to a good life. Without them we cease to be men, become mere slaves, the meeting place of forces that happen to play upon us. If we are to be persons, we shall have confidence and pride in something or somebody. The measure of a man is that in which he has confidence. If he puts his confidence in low and mean affairs, he will turn out to be that sort of man. The N.T. never belittles pride. It does not define humility as supine indifference. It does not promise that the spineless "shall inherit the earth" (Matt. 5:5). Pride is one of the highest gifts of man: it is his capacity for loyalty and devotion. But like all his highest gifts, it carries the greatest spiritual danger. Paul is clear that pride of self is the basic sin of man. "Let him who boasts, boast of the Lord" (I Cor. 1:31; cf. also I Cor. 3:21; II Cor. 10:17; 11:16–12:10; Gal. 6:14). Here our confidence (if indeed ἐλπίδος is to be taken with both nouns) and our pride are to be **in our hope.** This hope will hold us steady if we hold to it: our hope in God's triumph

7 Wherefore as the Holy Ghost saith, To-day if ye will hear his voice,

8 Harden not your hearts, as in the provocation, in the day of temptation in the wilderness:

9 When your fathers tempted me, proved me, and saw my works forty years.

10 Wherefore I was grieved with that generation, and said, They do always err in *their* heart; and they have not known my ways.

11 So I sware in my wrath, They shall not enter into my rest.

---

7 Therefore, as the Holy Spirit says, "Today, when you hear his voice,

8 do not harden your hearts as in the rebellion, on the day of testing in the wilderness,

9 where your fathers put me to the test and saw my works for forty years.

10 Therefore I was provoked with that generation, and said, 'They always go astray in their hearts; they have not known my ways.'

11 As I swore in my wrath, 'They shall never enter my rest.'"

---

The introductory formula, **therefore, as the Holy Spirit says,** probably is to be taken with the first verb in the quotation, **Do not harden your hearts** (vs. 8), and not with the author's own exhortation in vs. 12. He would hardly use that solemn formula of his own words.

There are minor alterations of the LXX text as we have it but they do not affect the meaning or our author's use of the passage. The LXX, like the KJV, translated the place names, Meribah and Massah (vs. 8); thus we have **provocation, rebellion** and **temptation, testing.** The most striking alteration of the original Hebrew is the transfer of **forty years** from vs. 10 to vs. 9, i.e., from **forty years I was provoked** to **saw my works for forty years.** Interestingly enough, although our author follows the LXX in this change, he himself attaches the **forty years** to vs. 10 when he comes to apply it (vs. 17). He is now ready to interpret the quotation from the psalm.

---

over sin and death, our hope in the best that is yet to be. Perhaps the best comment on the verse is in the people about us. Some have hope in a turn of fortune, others hope for a victory of their party in an election, for an increase in wages, for a chance meeting with the right people, or for a victory for their particular reform. Their hope is reflected in the kind of people they are. To some earthly hopes we must give ourselves—life requires it. But if our hope is in God, we shall prove steadfast and we shall be the house of God.

**7-11. *On Rebellion and Rest.*—**From this point through 4:13 we have an excellent specimen of an early Christian homily, based on Ps. 95. The point of the sermon is an analogy between the writer's generation and that which of old had wandered in the wilderness.

The purpose of the analogy is clear. The very generation to which the law was given, the people themselves who had been delivered from bondage to Egypt—this was the generation to rebel and complain, to harden their hearts at the sound of God's voice, putting him to the proof (Exod. 17:1-7); witnessing his **works for forty years,** mighty works of judgment and providing mercy, only to perish in the end, doomed for their own disobedience. Signs and

wonders by themselves are not enough to awaken faith (cf. Luke 11:29; Mark 8:11-13). We think of Browning's lines:

How you'd exult if I could put you back
Six hundred years,

. . . . . . . .

And set you square with Genesis again,—
When such a traveller told you his last news,
He saw the ark a-top of Ararat
But did not climb there since 'twas getting dusk
And robber-bands infest the mountain's foot!
How should you feel, I ask, in such an age,
How act? As other people felt and did;
With soul more blank than this decanter's knob,
Believe—and yet lie, kill, rob, fornicate,
Full in belief's face, like the beast you'd be! [6]

The wilderness generation was not saved by mighty works. So, the writer urges, you belong to a generation that is close to still mightier works. God has spoken his clearest word through his Son, through one who is a greater than Moses. The voice of God has come to you, too. Whether or not you hear depends upon your faith (cf. 4:2). You too may harden your hearts. Just as the wilderness generation was condemned to endless wandering, barred from

[6] "Bishop Blougram's Apology."

| | |
|---|---|
| **12** Take heed, brethren, lest there be in any of you an evil heart of unbelief, in departing from the living God.<br><br>**13** But exhort one another daily, while it is called To-day; lest any of you be hardened through the deceitfulness of sin. | **12** Take care, brethren, lest there be in any of you an evil, unbelieving heart, leading you to fall away from the living God. **13** But exhort one another every day, as long as it is called "today," that none of you may be |

The writer interprets and applies Ps. 95:7-11 in two stages: His readers must not harden their hearts as did the wilderness generation, for it was unbelief which caused their failure to enter God's rest (vss. 12-19) ; the promise of the divine "rest" remains open to the people of God and the danger of unbelief is quite as serious now as then (4:1-13).

### b) FAILURE OF AN ANCIENT GENERATION (3:12-19)

The pastoral touch **lest there be in any of you** (cf. 4:11; 10:25; 12:15) individualizes his warning without suggesting that he actually singles out individuals who are trouble-makers. Like the admonition to **exhort one another every day** which follows (vs. 13), it would apply to all Christians everywhere, and tells us more about the author than about his readers. Some commentators (e.g., Zahn) held that the wilderness generation symbolizes the Jews who had rejected Christ and that the **forty years** refer to A.D. 30-70, ending with the destruction of Jerusalem and the temple. On this reading, our author is warning against a relapse into Judaism. The argument against this interpretation is cumulative; here we may note that there is no reference in Hebrews to the destruction of Jerusalem, that the writer is not interested in the temple but in the tabernacle (see on 8:5; 9:1 ff.), and that **to fall away from the living God** (vs. 12) suggests a relapse from religion

the rest of God, so this generation may suffer the same penalty. **They shall never enter my rest** refers to the peace and settled life of the Promised Land in contrast to the nomadic life and constant warfare of the wilderness. For the symbolic meaning of this rest see Expos. on 4:8-11. To the danger of missing it the writer now turns (3:12–4:13).

**12. Our Falling Away from God.—An evil, unbelieving heart.** The epistle is constantly sounding this somber note of warning. **Evil** and **unbelieving** may be synonymous, although the next verse suggests that the one may lead to the other. Is it not as Marcus Dods suggests: "When the heart is hardened through sin, it becomes unbelieving, so that the psychological order might be stated thus: sin, a deceived mind, a hardened heart, unbelief, apostasy." [7] It is an order verified in experience.

Clearly the unbelief is no mere refusal to accept a certain doctrine, any more than faith is the acceptance of a form of words. The interpreter must have a care lest he make doctrinal divergence either a sign or an explanation of evil. For the N.T. faith is not so much belief in a word spoken, as trust in him who speaks. Often the church has been confused at just this point. The peril of unbelief is the breaking of that trust which commits the whole man, thought, feeling, purpose, deed, to God; the trust which depends on him, eagerly listens

to his word, clings to him in joy and sorrow, and earnestly seeks to know and to do his will.

The unbelief of which the writer warns is the unbelief that leads **you to fall away from the living God.** This is the supreme disaster, the central defeat, which may overtake a man. Nothing else really matters. Since we were made for him, since we find our humanity, our destiny, our fulfillment in his service, since "man's chief end is to glorify God and to enjoy him forever," [8] **to fall away from** him is to thwart every good in life and to turn the joy of life into an aching grief. This is life's tragedy and ruin. To see it clearly is to share the author's somber concern over its possibility.

**13. Our Mutual Responsibility.—Exhort:** The word παρακαλεῖτε means to talk to, and has the overtone of entreaty, of comfort, and of encouragement. **One another every day.** This is the preventive of falling away. The teaching is sound. The temptation to be independent of Christian comrades soon becomes the temptation to be independent of God. It is safe to say that the tragedy of every Christian who has fallen away can be traced directly to spiritual loneliness. The pride that pretends that we do not need the comforting, encouraging exhortation of our fellow Christians is one with the pride that we no longer need the grace of God. Safety is found only in a small company where we know each other well enough, trust each

[7] *Expositor's Greek Testament*, IV, 276.

[8] *Westminster Shorter Catechism*, Question 1.

14 For we are made partakers of Christ, if we hold the beginning of our confidence steadfast unto the end;

hardened by the deceitfulness of sin. 14 For we share in Christ, if only we hold our first

---

altogether rather than from Judaism, which claimed allegiance to the living God. The intense seriousness of the warning is emphasized by the danger of hardening of the heart and of falling away from the living God, and by the implication that the readers face a decision which may exclude them from salvation as irrevocably as the wilderness generation was excluded from the Promised Land. The writer will recur to the impossibility of a second repentance (cf. 6:4 ff.; 10:26; 12:15-17, 25), which is based on the perfect and final offering of Christ (cf. 7:27; 9:25-26). This teaching, uniquely stressed in Hebrews, was to play an important role in subsequent Christian life and thought.

14. **Partakers of Christ** (cf. "partakers of the heavenly calling" [3:1]) is, as noted above, characteristic of the writer's thought. It is not as Moffatt says "an equivalent for the Pauline ἐν Χριστῷ," and is one of the many indications that Paul could not have written Hebrews. This and similar expressions derive from the basic outlook of our author, who thinks of religion in terms of worship, the *summum bonum* being access to God through the purification of sins. It is not to be regarded as a lesser but as a different conception of the goal of religion than Paul's.

---

other completely enough, to share our burdens and our temptations. The ideal church is one where every member knows, trusts, and enjoys that living intimacy. The pathos of the church is where exhortation has lost its comfort and encouragement, where the exhorter condescends and is hard of heart himself, and thus destroys the very conditions of fellowship which could have given him, and others too, protection. The N.T. knows no solitary faith. We need **one another.** Here is one of the most serious defects of the church. We have lost confidence in one another, do not trust the saving discipline of a close fellowship. Our fellowship is casual, formal, polite, external (cf. Expos. on 10:25).

**As long as it is called "today."** The writer keeps repeating this word (cf. 3:7, 15; 4:7). By it he clearly means while the opportunity lasts. The present is our opportunity for a deed. It is where we all live. The past lives in us with a grim kind of inevitability. It cannot be undone. The future is the land of our faith (cf. Expos. on vs. 6). But our works belong to the present. It is the place of decision. "Night comes, when no one can work" (John 9:4).

**Hardened by the deceitfulness of sin.** Volumes could be written about this verse. Every generation needs the warning constantly repeated. We can imagine the working of a first-century mind under the temptation to fall away: "I need not be too bold in my witness and perhaps I shall escape persecution. It is just a matter of plain caution. Of course, I shall never waver in my heart's true faith. But discretion is the better part of valor. After all, of what good is a dead Christian?" Sin is always a cheat and a delusion (cf. Gen. 3:4-5). Has God said it?

Will I surely die? Is it really evil, or seen from a broader view is it not really good? Will I not rather profit by this course? Surely the future day of reckoning will not come. Surely I can sow and not reap. Such are the sophistries by which men must deceive themselves before they can do evil (cf. Eph. 4:18). The faithful interpreter will constantly expose this deceit lest people be hardened by it. Once the clear, honest habit of mind is lost, and things are no longer seen for what they are, the self-deceiving knows no end but becomes ingenious. This is a hardening, for to such a mind no gospel can come. Honesty, the faithful dealing with oneself, seeing clearly, these are perhaps the only essential conditions of hearing God's word.

**14. If Only We Hold Our First Confidence Firm to the End.**—The writer has returned to his practical concern about holding fast to the end. It should be noted that he lacks some of Paul's assurance in the doctrine of perseverance (cf. Rom. 5:10; 8:31-39). His is the strenuous kind of faith. But in any case, a strong commitment that will not let go is an essential condition of perseverance. And this strong devotion will not hold unless it is nourished by God. On this both Paul and our author are agreed. What is the reward of holding fast? **We share in Christ.** It is not easy to know what is meant by this clause (see Exeg.). In the light of later passages in the epistle it is at least clear that we share in the benefits that Christ brings: access to God, the comfort of an understanding priest, the forgiveness of sin, and the restoration of our lost humanity (cf. 2:9). That we also share in the joy of Christ, in the fullness of his life, seems to follow.

15 While it is said, To-day if ye will hear his voice, harden not your hearts, as in the provocation.

16 For some, when they had heard, did provoke: howbeit not all that came out of Egypt by Moses.

confidence firm to the end, 15 while it is said,

"Today, when you hear his voice
do not harden your hearts
as in the rebellion."

16 Who were they that heard and yet were rebellious? Was it not all those who left Egypt under the leadership of Moses?

---

15-19. Everything depends on whether it is still "today," and this the author will validate from scripture in 4:1-10. Here he assumes it, for his attention is directed to the fate of the wilderness generation and the implications of their unbelief for his readers. The three questions in vss. 16-18 and the three answers, also in the form of questions, are purely rhetorical. It is obvious that the writer is being here, as often, a conscious stylist. He breaks the monotony of what might seem repetitious by using the form of the familiar diatribe. The thought is subtly advanced, however, by the sequence of questions. **Who were they that heard and yet were rebellious?** Not just anybody, they were those who had experienced the miraculous, epoch-making deliverance from Egypt. And what was the consequence of their rebellion? Not just a temporary and superficial penalty, for

---

15. *On Listening to God.*—**When you hear his voice.** The God who spoke in many and various ways still uses many voices. We go about our day's work unmindful of him. We propose to do this and that before evening comes. Our schedule of appointments may be crowded. With preoccupied mind we turn a corner—and God confronts us. He speaks to us. Do we hear? It may be through the laughter in the eyes of a little child, or the memories of a mother's prayer, or a snatch from a forgotten hymn, or the sudden return of one of boyhood's clean ideals. God may speak through the quiet grandeur of an evening sky, the unpretentious loveliness of a flower, the flight of a bird, or a presence that disturbs us. He may speak through our longing for a better world, our yearning for a more just appraisal of our deeds, or through the blind despair that, when every door seems closed, can only reach upward in helplessness. He may speak his wisdom to the astronomer at night. Kepler once came from his telescope saying that he had been thinking the thoughts of God after him. God may speak through

> a sunset touch,
> A fancy from a flower-bell, some one's death,
> A chorus-ending from Euripides.[9]

Any one of these may be the echo of his clearest word in Jesus Christ.

**Do not harden your hearts as in the rebellion.** The pathetic thing is that many do not hear when God speaks. Perhaps none of us is aware of all that God would say to us. We become preoccupied, our schedule is so tight that neither God nor man can get a word in

[9] Browning, "Bishop Blougram's Apology."

edgewise. We are concerned about our own purposes, our own security, our own program. We may be afraid—most of us are—and so be driven to establish the work of our own hands, to fortify our own security. If any suggest that man's security is not in himself, we become all the more frantic in our efforts to prove them wrong. Is this why so few men ever recognize their own hardness of heart? It wears more plausible names, such as prudence, diligence, and even devotion to duty. Seldom do we recognize in ourselves the rigid obstinacy that, having been deceived by sin (vs. 13), will not acknowledge its own folly and consent to be enlightened.

The task of the interpreter is to help people, not to denounce them. To tell us that we are hard of heart will not help. It will only harden us yet more. Perhaps we can be led to see that our self-centered devotion is a cheap disguise, a pretense that will inevitably exact its penalty. Perhaps we can be led to grow in sensibility to God. To begin the morning in quiet communion with our God, committing our lives again to his keeping and seeking his leading for the day, will help to keep our minds open to his voice for the hours that follow. To practice regular penitence, to be on the alert for the enemy; to use the hours of wakefulness at night, if they come, in meditation on some verse of scripture or in thinking about God: these and many other disciplines will keep us from the danger of hardness. One word of such help is far more priceless than a whole torrent of condemnation.

**16-17.** *A Forfeited Privilege.*—**Who were they that heard?** The style here becomes vivid and urgent. They were not extraordinary sinners,

17 But with whom was he grieved forty years? *was it* not with them that had sinned, whose carcasses fell in the wilderness?

18 And to whom sware he that they should not enter into his rest, but to them that believed not?

19 So we see that they could not enter in because of unbelief.

17 And with whom was he provoked forty years? Was it not with those who sinned, whose bodies fell in the wilderness? 18 And to whom did he swear that they should never enter his rest, but to those who were disobedient? 19 So we see that they were unable to enter because of unbelief.

---

their **bodies fell in the wilderness.** And was physical death the only or the final penalty? No, they received the divine condemnation of exclusion, permanently and irrevocably, **that they should never enter his rest. . . . They were unable to enter because of unbelief.**

This section introduces, largely in negative terms, another ruling idea in Hebrews, the idea of faith and loyalty and its opposite, unbelief and disobedience. This is to be developed in detail in the famous ch. 11. Not all the author means by faith is suggested here. His characteristic understanding of faith as the power of apprehending the unseen, that which lies beyond the senses, is not indicated. But from this passage alone we can gather where he will put the emphasis. Faith is **confidence firm to the end.** Not confidence in a merely psychological sense, of course, but confidence in God, trust in him and in his revelation and his promises. The word loyalty comes close to this author's distinctive thought about faith. The wilderness generation was disloyal, disobedient, rebellious. This understanding of faith is present in the Gospels, in Paul, indeed throughout the N.T., but it is not the typical use of the term in the Pauline epistles, for example. Paul writes of faith as contrary to human reason and human expectation. It is for him that utter denial of self-confidence which opens the mind and heart in complete receptiveness to

---

not vicious folk, not the outcasts and criminals. It was a whole people, a whole nation. The author does not allow for a faithful minority, as Paul did in I Cor. 10:7-10. Further, it was precisely the generation that had been on the scene and participated in the birth of their nation. They had begun with a great venture of faith in following Moses through the seas and into the wilderness. Over their happy throng the song of Moses had rung,

I will sing unto the LORD for he has triumphed gloriously,
The horse and his rider he has thrown into the sea.
The LORD is my strength and my song,
And he has become my salvation;
This is my God, and I will praise him,
My father's God, and I will exalt him (Exod. 15: 1*b*-2).

Later prophets were to look back upon this event as the sure sign of the mercy of God at work in human history. It became almost the identifying mark of God's providence. "I brought them forth out of the land of Egypt" (Jer. 11:4, 7; etc.). But the people who saw this great event, who were led by the hand of no less a person than Moses, these were the people that exasperated God by their hardness of heart.

What was the result of this sin, this provoca-

tion, that according to our writer endured throughout the forty years of the wandering? Their **bodies fell in the wilderness.** What dark tragedy is gathered into these five words! A people destined for a homeland, with peace and a settled life, where God's rest should be enjoyed—and they lived out their days in waste places and were buried in the unmarked graves of the wilderness! They might have known the joy and plenty of the Promised Land—and they chose rather, or were sentenced, to live in homeless wandering and almost unceasing nomadic warfare. Nor were they the only people so to suffer. Analogies leap to the mind. What generations have missed their destiny through disobedience to God! Destined to be the people of God, to be glad in his abundant mercies, to enjoy the bounties of the good earth, they have lived instead at a poor, dying rate, hungry, hating, warring, and have been buried in the wilderness their own sin created.

**18-19. On Unbelief as Inability.—To those who were disobedient.** The crowning disobedience is recorded in Num. 12, where the people of Israel refused to enter the Land of Promise, frightened by the majority report of the spies that the obstacles were too great for them to attempt! The thing was impossible. They counted only their human resources, added them up, and shrewdly observed that these

4 Let us therefore fear, lest, a promise being left *us* of entering into his rest, any of you should seem to come short of it.

4 Therefore, while the promise of entering his rest remains, let us fear lest any of you be judged to have failed to reach it.

---

God's gracious act in Christ, and issues in the believer's being "in Christ" and Christ in the believer. Faith is distinctly Christian in contrast to righteousness under the law, and the O.T. examples, such as Abraham, witness to the precedence of faith over law in God's plan, law being added because of sin. In Hebrews, on the contrary, there is no contrast between faith and the law and no stress on faith as a distinctively Christian attitude; the writer's whole point here and in ch. 11 is rather upon the continuity and solidarity of faith in the whole history of revelation. What is distinctively Christian is the object of faith, which has been clarified in Jesus, to whom we must "look" as we run the race (12:2). Again, this is not necessarily a lesser conception of faith; it is a different conception. And again Pauline authorship is radically impossible.

### c) Danger of the Same Failure Today (4:1-13)

Here is the second stage in the warning and exhortation based on Ps. 95:7-11. The main point is that the promised "rest" is still available; it is promised to us, for the failure of the first recipients of the promise did not destroy the "rest"; it only destroyed the wilderness generation. But to enter God's rest we have to avoid the disobedience which occasioned their failure. Stated in these general terms the logic seems convincing; indeed, in part it is the logic of Ps. 95, for the rebellious spirit of the children of Israel was a classic text for warning against disobedience. But in order to use it for his purpose the writer must subtly change the meaning of the word "rest." Rest for the wanderers in the wilderness certainly meant the promise of settled and peaceful life in Canaan. For once our author pays some heed to the original meaning of the text. He argues that to regard "rest" as equivalent to the conquest of Canaan and its consequences is a misinterpretation of the promise. The "rest" promised was God's own rest as indicated by Gen. 2:2, **"And God rested on the seventh day from all his works"** (vs. 4). This is proved by the psalm, written long centuries after the entrance of the Israelites into Canaan, for the inspired

---

were not enough. They counted not at all upon God. Their disobedience was their lack of faith. To have tried to enter with their unbelief would have led only to military disaster. They did not believe that it could be done, so they could not do it.

Unbelief cripples. The principle is as broad as all human experience. It renders men and nations weak and helpless, an easy prey for their enemies. No significant work was ever accomplished, from the first primitive discovery of fire as a means of cooking to Lincoln's Emancipation Proclamation, without faith as its condition. Every task we undertake today, from the common duties of the daily round to the grand adventures in human brotherhood, rests upon faith.

But faith in what? In a lucky turn of circumstance? In one's own ingenuity? In one's neighbors? Our writer would clearly have little use for faith as such, any kind of faith, faith in anything or in anybody, just so it is faith. He is here talking about faith in God's promises, faith in God who promises. Without that faith we are unable. It is not that God capriciously

bars the way—we are **unable to enter.** Surely we have no need so great and persistent as the recovery of expectation from God. "My expectation is from him" (Ps. 62:5). We kneel in prayer to recite our own words, expecting nothing. We enter God's house to go through the proper forms of worship, with no living hope that perhaps this day he will speak a fresh word, clear away the fog of unbelief, grant us a token of his presence. Nothing happens. We enter on some heroic adventure, not depending upon God. Two young people come to the marriage altar counting on romantic attachment, but not on God. Men seek a better world, relying on committees and a judicious use of public relations, but not on God. Yes, even churches project their missions, expecting much from clever plans, little from God. **So we see that they were unable to enter because of unbelief.**

**4:1. God's Promise of Rest.**—The promise . . . **remains.** Hebrews makes more use of the word **promise** than does any other book in the N.T., although Galatians and Romans are a close second and third. (For a fuller treatment of

2 For unto us was the gospel preached, as well as unto them: but the word preached did not profit them, not being mixed with faith in them that heard *it*.

2 For good news came to us just as to them; but the message which they heard did not benefit them, because it did not meet with

---

writer says, "Today, when you hear his voice, do not harden your hearts" (vs. 7). **If Joshua [Greek: Jesus] had given them rest, God would not speak later of another day. So then, there remains a sabbath rest for the people of God** (vss. 8-9). This ingenious scriptural argument is further guaranteed by two Christian assumptions: we, too, have received the promise (vs. 2) and we do enter that rest (vs. 3*a*). Given the author's presuppositions, we must admit that his argument is neat and cogent.

**4:1. Let us fear:** The tone of severity is not absent from this optimistic passage; the verses which conclude this section enforce the deadly seriousness of the readers' situation. Yet here, and throughout the epistle, warning is never unrelieved by assurance and hope (cf. vss. 2*a*, 3*a*, 9, 10). **Should seem** (KJV) is perhaps better than **be judged** (RSV) for δοκῇ, a curiously tentative statement in view of the vigorous pronouncements of the writer. Perhaps the meaning is "should appear as having come short" or "should be found to have failed." This would be consonant with vss. 12-13, where it is "the word of God" which judges the minds and hearts of men.

**2. For unto us was the gospel preached, as well as unto them:** The KJV has the merit here of placing the emphasis where the Greek puts it, **for unto us.** To translate the verb εὐηγγελισμένοι by **was the gospel preached** is less accurate. Hebrews never uses εὐαγγέλιον, the regular N.T. word for the gospel. Does the writer avoid it because of his strong feeling for continuity between the old revelation and the new, and because he cannot equate the old with the new in spite of this continuity? Probably **good news** represents the thought better than any other English words. The innocent-sounding translations of 2*b*, both in the KJV and the RSV, conceal the very real difficulties in the Greek text which early led to many variants. The main issue is whether the author meant to say with some MSS, "they were not united in faith with those who heard," or with

---

God's promises cf. Expos. on 10:23.) We have here a conditional promise. The promise is faithful, but the conditions of receiving and acting on it will not always be present. God's rest is ample for all who will enter. The door opens to you. The interpreter should not fail to catch the personal note in this verse. The gospel is no mimeographed notice published indiscriminately for all who may chance to read. It is a personal invitation, written and addressed to Henry Jones or Mary Brown. God is a personal God and deals not with humanity in the mass. Individuals are separately known and loved. Duty is not a mere command that floats above us in the air. It seeks out you and me and comes to us with our names inscribed on it. The interpreter should remember that his work is to mediate that personal gospel to individual men and women. The invitation to enter God's rest is never delivered until each man, woman, and child hears it as an invitation to him. The Bible is never God's Word for me until it singles me out, points its finger at me, and declares, "This is for you."

**Let us fear lest any of you.** This is a vivid description of the pastoral concern of the church, the community of Christ, for its individual members. The rest of God is generous and ample. Failure to reach it is life's supreme disaster: **therefore** our concern for you. Many will resent this teaching and for one of two reasons: (*a*) their own touchiness over what they call "private" matters—there are subjects that must not be broached, questions that must not be asked; or (*b*) the officious air of those who are concerned. The leaders of the church should constantly school themselves in humility lest their word of warning embitter those whom they would help. But they cannot neglect their concern for those entrusted to their care. Such neglect is a betrayal and a denial of the gospel they proclaim.

**2. Faith and Hearing.—For unto us was the gospel preached, as well as unto them.** They, the wilderness generation, heard good news from God. So have we, and in a superior way, because the gospel has been proclaimed to us through the Son, God's clearest word. We are under special judgment because we, like them, are a favored generation. They heard the good news, the promise of God's rest, but they did not accept it. We too have the good news, **a**

3 For we which have believed do enter into rest, as he said, As I have sworn in my wrath, if they shall enter into my rest: although the works were finished from the foundation of the world.

4 For he spake in a certain place of the seventh *day* on this wise, And God did rest the seventh day from all his works.

faith in the hearers.[h] 3 For we who have believed enter that rest, as he has said,

"As I swore in my wrath,
　'They shall never enter my rest,' "
although his works were finished from the foundation of the world. 4 For he has somewhere spoken of the seventh day in this way, "And God rested on the seventh day

[h] Other manuscripts read *they were not united in faith with those who heard.*

others, **because it did not meet with faith in the hearers.** A conjectural reading, "They were not united by faith with the things heard" would be the simplest solution, although in 3:16 it is "hearers," not "things heard." The underlying thought is clear, even if we cannot recover the exact shade of the meaning: The word of promise was not enough in itself; it must be joined with faith on the part of the hearers if it was to be a saving word.

3. The accent in *3a* is on the full assurance that we who "have believed" do enter that rest; the author is not at the moment concerned with the question of salvation as present or future but with the present assurance. The grounds for this assurance are, not as in 6:4 ff. the heavenly goods already shared by the Christian, but scriptural evidence that nothing remains to be done by God whose **works were finished.** Not the absence of a prepared "rest" but the presence of unbelief should concern the Christian.

4. The writer could not have been ignorant of the locus of his quotation (Gen. 2:2); the introductory formula is a literary mannerism, for his readers will understand the obvious reference to the creation account and that is all that is necessary, human authors having no significance. The rabbinical interpretation that God rests on every sabbath

more persuasive, a more compelling invitation, given us by the Son. Shall we hear?

Why did they not believe? Because the message was not **mixed with faith in them that heard it.** The word translated **mixed** should not be regarded as implying a mere mechanical mixture, but as an organic union. The only other use of this word in the N.T. is in I Cor. 12:24, "God hath tempered the body together." Any word that has meaning is a living thing. It never carries its whole meaning, but presupposes a background of meaning in the mind of him who speaks as well as in the mind of him who hears. Any word, however common, borrows heavily on that hidden meaning. A word then is a flash of understanding between two minds. It is never a word by its merely being spoken. It is then only a sound. It becomes a word only when it is heard and understood. Further, if it fails to arouse any response, it is still not a word. "A theory is false if it is not interesting: a proposition that falls on the mind so dully as to excite no enthusiasm has not attained the level of truth; though the words be accurate the import has leaked away from them, and the meaning is not conveyed."[1]

All this and more holds for the Word of God. It is "living and active" (vs. 12). It is never a mere form of words to be venerated for its own sake. It never becomes God's Word until it is spoken to and received by individual men and women. Nor is it a complete Word until it is mingled in us with a living tissue of faith. That fact throws an important light on the meaning of the Bible. Had this verse and all it implies been taken seriously, we should have been spared many disgraceful quarrels over the meaning of the Scriptures. The Reformers relied on the work of the Holy Spirit in interpreting the Bible. "For, as God alone is a sufficient witness of himself in his own word, so also the word will never gain credit in the hearts of men, till it be confirmed by the internal testimony of the Spirit."[2] Surely no less is implied in the personal nature of God and in the fact that Christian faith is the most personal of all relations.

**3-5. *God's Rest Is Ready.*—**As evidence that faith is the condition of entry into God's rest, the writer now points to the readers' own experience. **For we who have believed enter that rest.** It is true that rest is not regarded as fully

[1] W. E. Hocking, *The Meaning of God in Human Experience* (New Haven: Yale University Press, 1912), p. xiii.

[2] John Calvin, *Institutes of the Christian Religion,* I. 7. 4.

5 And in this *place* again, If they shall enter into my rest.

6 Seeing therefore it remaineth that some must enter therein, and they to whom it was first preached entered not in because of unbelief:

from all his works." 5 And again in this place he said,

"They shall never enter my rest."
6 Since therefore it remains for some to enter it, and those who formerly received the good news failed to enter because of

---

would not have served our writer, who is concerned to show that the final and perfect rest is indicated. What did the word "rest" mean for him? The inevitable verbal contrast with John 5:17, "My Father worketh even until now, and I work" (ASV), comes to mind. Philo, too, philosophizing on the Genesis verse, cannot conceive of God as inactive in good works; he interprets rest as meaning work without hindrance or tension, the true philosopher's idea of God whose energy flows from him with calm steadiness. Our author does not pause to philosophize. He fills the word with all the goods of salvation assured to the believing through the divine revelation. Only one thing is sure: he is not interested in Canaan, the earthly goal of the wilderness generation. Perhaps we are justified in saying that rest can hardly have meant mere cessation of effort. There is no suggestion of the touching Negro spiritual, "I wish I was in heaven settin' down," reflecting as it does the continuous weariness of a physically oppressed people. More positively, we are justified in filling the word with meaning derived from the writer's dominant longing for a satisfying worship of God. This rest is peace in the assurance of an access to God unhindered by rites that cannot touch the conscience and made possible only by Christ's "purification for sins" that pollute and prevent our reaching the final goal of worship. The longing for Canaan as the place of unhindered worship of God was in the biblical story he uses, and may have been in the back of his mind, but he does not stop to expound it.

5-8. These verses substantiate the assumption already made, viz., that we have a promise, just as had the wilderness generation (vss. 1a, 2a, 3a). The ingenious interweaving of Gen. 2:2, the story of the fate of those who perished in the wilderness because of unbelief recorded in Ps. 95, and the promise of today in the same psalm, together with the application of the whole to the current situation of the church, is a type of argument thoroughly familiar in the first century and not unknown today. We will meet this kind of scriptural interpretation again, notably in the Melchizedek speculation (ch. 7). The fact that no responsible scholar today would juggle scripture in this fashion must

---

experienced in this world (cf. Exeg.), but there is some foretaste of it here. We think of the invitation of Jesus, "Come to me, all who labor and are heavy-laden, and I will give you rest" (Matt. 11:28). The rewards of faith are not all postponed. Even the assurance of future rest confers its rest on the spirit of man today.

**Although his works were finished.** This can refer to nothing but the fact that God's rest was established along with his other works. The rest is prepared, has been prepared, for all who will have faith to enter. "Come; for all is now ready" (Luke 14:17; for a fuller discussion of the meaning of rest see Expos. on vss. 8-11).

That God's rest is prepared for all who will enter it is evident from what the scripture says, **God rested on the seventh day from all his works,** and again from the fact that he excluded the wilderness generation from his rest. Rest is no mere cessation from labor, although it does include that (cf. vs. 10). The

writer can scarcely have conceived God as suffering from fatigue and needing rest. Evidently, then, the rest of God is something much more positive. It is a work to be established, and the writer is taking pains to show that the establishing is accomplished. When God rested from his labors, it was as though he said, "Man is my crowning achievement. The goal of this long process is the coming of a free spirit, bearing my image, and capable of fellowship with me." From the human point of view today this was achieved at almost infinite hazard and represents the wonder of all creation. Yet in a deeper sense God could not rest until man had entered the rest of God.

**6-7. God's Urgent Invitation.**—Since therefore it remains for some to enter it, God's work in preparing his rest will not be in vain. "For such the Father seeks to worship him" (John 4:23). We are reminded of the parable of the banquet. When the first invitations were re-

**7** Again, he limiteth a certain day, saying in David, To-day, after so long a time; as it is said, To-day if ye will hear his voice, harden not your hearts.

**8** For if Jesus had given them rest, then would he not afterward have spoken of another day.

disobedience, **7** again he sets a certain day, "Today," saying through David so long afterward, in the words already quoted,

"Today, when you hear his voice,
    do not harden your hearts."
**8** For if Joshua had given them rest, God*i*

*i* Greek *he.*

---

not be allowed to obscure the underlying thought of the writer. Arguing always in the framework of revealed truth, he nevertheless betrays within that framework his profound interest in history and experience. History, divinely controlled, witnesses to the age-old longing for God, unsatisfied by earthly achievements, even by the conquest of an earthly Canaan. On the other hand, Christian experience witnesses to the assurance of direct access to God through the "living way" revealed in Christ, the perfect and final priest. This is the line the author will follow. "Our hearts are restless till they rest in thee." That **rest** is given in Christ for all who believe in him.

---

jected, the householder said to his servant, "Go out quickly to the streets and lanes of the city, and bring in the poor and maimed and blind and lame. . . . Go out to the highways and hedges, and compel people to come in, that my house may be filled" (Luke 14:21, 23). The writer here overlooks all the righteous (cf. 11:32) that lived between the time of the Exodus and the writing of Ps. 95.

**Saying through David so long afterward.** Centuries passed after the defection of the wilderness. Still the rest of God is open, for the word continues to come, **Today, when you hear his voice.** The rest of God is still open to those who hear. If the argument from scripture seems labored and artificial, we must not miss the point the writer is establishing—that God's benefits are as open today as at any time. It is the interpreter's task to carry the analogy on to his own people and to his own day.

**8-11. Man's Restlessness, God's Sabbath Rest.** —**If Joshua had given them rest.** The word translated Joshua is "Jesus" in the Greek. At this point an objector might interrupt. You speak of the failure of the wilderness people to enter the Land of Promise. But their children did enter. Were they not given the promised rest? Were they not then children of faith and obedience? But, our writer replies, the rest in Canaan was not enough. It was a "shadow" of the perfect rest. For if the comparative ease and peace of Canaan were the only rest of God, God would not centuries later be renewing his appeal, "Today, when you hear his voice" (vs. 7). For the rest of God is a richer heritage than the land that flowed with milk and honey. It is not the comparative ease of a settled life. It is not idleness, with someone else taking on the responsibility of providing food,

clothing, and shelter for our families. Work is not a curse when it is done for love's sake, for the joy of the work done; the pride of craftsmanship, and the good of those who are served by it. Not to have such a work is the real curse of life.

The writer's homily on Ps. 95, which extends from 3:7 to 4:13, centers on this rest. What then is it? He speaks of a **sabbath rest for the people of God.** What is this? What does it mean to be restless? It is not merely the fatigue of the worker whose every muscle cries for rest. It is not only the nervous exhaustion which our complex life brings upon us. What a ceaseless round of duties to be done, committees to be attended, letters to be answered, people to be seen! The confusion of life is a terrible strain. We sometimes wonder why more people do not lose their sanity. But to escape our duties brings no real rest, for then a bad conscience pursues and accuses us. The unrest is in the human spirit. The turmoil is often the conflict of our divided loyalties. We cannot make up our minds to choose between God and mammon, between courage and compromise, between private advantage and the good of others, between asserting ourselves and asserting Jesus Christ. Therefore we are restless. The complexities of our daily work disturb us just because they excite this inner division of spirit.

What does it mean to be restless? Many a man knows persistent, half-covered fears that he cannot quiet. He knows the proud self-security that must ever be on guard against dangers on a dozen fronts and that can therefore never be at rest. To trust himself is to be condemned to an uneasy life of alertness against dangers he must overcome. He knows aimless wandering, without any sense of direction, with the moral stars darkened and no sense of

9 There remaineth therefore a rest to the people of God.

10 For he that is entered into his rest, he also hath ceased from his own works, as God *did* from his.

would not speak later of another day. 9 So then, there remains a sabbath rest for the people of God; 10 for whoever enters God's rest also ceases from his labors as God did from his.

---

**9-10.** The discussion of rest—it does not appear again—has served its purpose. What that purpose was, is here pointed up: **So then, there remains a sabbath rest** [σαββατισμός] **for the people of God.** The word *sabbatismos* is, so far as we know, an invention of the author of Hebrews. Its meaning seems to lie in the positive identification of **rest** with the divine rest which follows the creative activity of God. It is no temporary rest which the Christian is promised, but God's own final and perfect rest, as vs. 10 specifically states.

---

where home lies. He knows the bitterness of defeat when, struggling to be his own master, he loses battle after battle. He knows hatred, that burning pain in the heart that will never let him be at ease. He knows the fearful burden of dishonesty, which condemns the soul to ceaseless fretfulness lest another discover the secret of his weakness, or worst of all, lest he discover that secret himself! As the faithful interpreter knows his people, he will be oppressed by the burden of their restlessness. "The wicked are like the troubled sea; for it cannot rest" (Isa. 57:20 ASV).

Men have been calm in the midst of turmoil; they have kept their judgment when all about them others were in confusion. They have been possessed by a steady hope where others were frantic. They have faced even death with quiet confidence. What is their secret? What is the rest of God? A sabbath rest? The word has lost meaning for our time. There have been folk for whom the sabbath was the best day of the week. One writer could sing,

> O day of rest and gladness,
>    O day of joy and light,
> O balm of care and sadness,
>    Most beautiful, most bright!
>
> . . . . . .
>
> Thou art a port protected
>    From storms that round us rise:
>
> . . . . . .
>
> Thou art a cooling fountain
>    In life's dry, dreary sand;
>
> . . . . . .
>
> A day of sweet reflection
>    Thou art,—a day of love,
> A day of resurrection
>    From earth to things above.[3]

To men for whom the worship of God is the highest privilege of life the sabbath still re-

[3] Christopher Wordsworth, "O day of rest and gladness."

tains its joy and strength. Here we rise to the greatest heights of which we are capable. Here we become truly men and women, reach our full measure. But to many the day, if it is distinguished at all from the others, is one of tedious duties, from which they turn with relief to the round of Monday. It is sad that the privilege of the sabbath could ever have been twisted into the negations of blue laws.

What is it in the sabbath that makes it a foretaste of the heavenly rest? It is more than the very human associations of friends and family. It is our human life, including the family, raised to its highest joy in the worship of God. The soul that has no hunger for God can find no sabbath rest. For that rest is the worship of God.

As for the inner meaning of the rest of God, the great believers have had difficulty in describing what they have found. It was beyond their language. "Eye hath not seen, nor ear heard, neither have entered into the heart of man, the things which God hath prepared for them that love him" (I Cor. 2:9). They do know that above the darkness of man's deceit there is the clear, painful, but healing light of God's righteous judgment. Stronger than man's deepest sin is the grace that "is able to do far more abundantly than all that we ask or think" (Eph. 3:20). For all our aimless wandering there is our own country, our home, in whose service our scattered lives can be woven into strength. Above all our fears that we shall not be able to win our own security, above our flimsy defenses against danger, there is One who can be our "rock" and "fortress" (Ps. 31:3). In that shelter we can fling out Paul's defiance, "Who is he that condemneth?" (Rom. 8:34.) Above "the pulses of desire" are "thy coolness and thy balm." For the fretful little selfishness in which we live there is the joy of the beloved community and its releasing service. Round all our restlessness is the "peace of God, which passeth all

11 Let us labor therefore to enter into that rest, lest any man fall after the same example of unbelief.

12 For the word of God *is* quick, and powerful, and sharper than any two-edged sword, piercing even to the dividing asun-

11 Let us therefore strive to enter that rest, that no one fall by the same sort of disobedience. 12 For the word of God is living and active, sharper than any two-

---

**11-13.** If warning is never unrelieved by assurance, assurance is never without warning, and vs. 11 sounds again the urgent note of the ever-present danger of disobedience. "Today" carries the assurance of opportunity; it also includes the threat of failure. It is better to take vss. 12-13 as enforcing the warning against disobedience than as an interjected apostrophe to the **word of God.** The connection with the argument is immediate: "Let us strive to enter that rest, that no one [again the individualizing, pastoral touch] fall by the same sort of disobedience. For the living God [3:12], i.e., God as active, has revealed himself in promise and warning and his word [λόγος] is living and active in uncovering even the thoughts and intentions of the heart." Nothing is hid from him. The phrase **the word of God** (ὁ λόγος τοῦ θεοῦ) requires consideration. Its verbal similarity to the Logos of John 1:1-18 and, behind that, to Philo's use of the term as the creative Reason, from God and in man, incites the student to find the source of our author's

---

understanding" (Phil. 4:7). All this is included in the rest of God.

> O Sabbath rest by Galilee!
> O calm of hills above,
> Where Jesus knelt to share with thee
> The silence of eternity,
> Interpreted by love!

**Ceases from his labors.** It is hard to imagine any satisfying life in which there is no work to be done. As far as we can see, that would mean no advances to be made, no larger horizons, no new thoughts, no inviting mysteries. What is this but stagnation and death? But to labor without the weariness of a divided heart, so to work with others that we care not for credit in the joy of common achievement, to know that "in the Lord your labor is not in vain" (I Cor. 15:58), this is rest for the soul.

**Strive to enter that rest.** The word **strive** is a strong word. Its basic meaning is to "make haste" and it means "bend every effort" (cf. 12:1). The rest of God being what it is, let us make our entrance into it our constant concern lest we miss it **by the same sort of disobedience.** For the disobedience of an unbelieving heart can as effectively bar us from the rest of God as it did the generation of the wilderness.

**12-13.** *The Word of God.*—What does the author mean? Clearly not the Scriptures, although the word of God is in them. Certainly not the Son, although God's word was supremely in him (1:2). He does mean the word of revelation (1:1-2), the promise of rest with which chs. 3 and 4 are concerned, and here the word of judgment. The word of God, in general, is God speaking. What is said here is clearly

applicable to every word of God, in the Scriptures, in his Son, and wherever he speaks. Our writer marks five qualities in the word of God. The order is significant, for it moves from the general to the individual, and he ends by pointing his finger at us one by one, to the **thoughts and intentions of the heart.**

It is **living,** with the life of God who speaks. It is no dust-covered antiquity, no lifeless record of ancient doings. We never encounter the word of God, whether in nature, in history, in the Bible, or in the Son, until it comes alive for us and becomes, indeed, God speaking directly to us in living conversation. This is the meaning of the Reformation doctrine that the Holy Spirit must interpret the word of God, or it is not yet God's word. A friend once said that when he read the Bible in the morning, he read until one verse leaped up from the page, pointed its finger at him, and said, "You are my man for today." Then he lived with that verse throughout the day, pondered it, let it go to work in his life. The practice is commended to all.

It is **active, powerful,** able to accomplish its work. The best comment here is Isa. 55:11. God's word is strong with the strength of God. When he speaks, things happen. The whole purpose of the interpreter should be to let the word of God come fresh and clear to his people; its power will be quickly and mightily felt.

It is **sharper than any two-edged sword.** The word as a sword is a familiar figure in the Bible (cf. Isa. 49:2; Eph. 6:17; Rev. 1:16; 2:16). It throws light on the prophecy of Simeon in Luke 2:35. The two-edged sword was especially sharp and its user could do more cutting with

der of soul and spirit, and of the joints and
marrow, and *is* a discerner of the thoughts
and intents of the heart.

edged sword, piercing to the division of
soul and spirit, of joints and marrow, and
discerning the thoughts and intentions of

---

thought in this philosophic background. The personification of **the word of God** in these
verses, even if it is largely rhetorical, supports the view that the writer was familiar with
Philonic thought about the Logos. Some familiarity must be assumed, for no one could
use Philonic words and ideas with such freedom and so frequently without being in the
same stream of thinking. This does not mean that our writer must actually have read
Philo's works; his differences from Philo are quite as striking as his similarities (see
Intro., pp. 585-87). He certainly knows that in Philo or the Philonic type of thought
the Logos is the creative power of God. He himself never expressly identifies Christ with
the Logos. In every instance where that identification was ready to his hand (cf. 1:1 ff.)
he avoids making it. The creative role and the divine dignity of Christ are associated
with his sonship. Ῥῆμα, not λόγος, is the word he uses of creation (11:3); λόγος, of
revelation (2:2; 4:12). In our passage there is not the slightest hint of an identification
of the Logos with Christ or Jesus.

---

it in combat. The emphasis of the interpreter
should be on the sharpness rather than on the
sword.

**Piercing to the division of soul and spirit,
of joints and marrow.** Sober interpreters have
abstained from finding any special significance
in the four terms used here, save that the deepest thoughts and most secret intentions of man
are laid bare by the word of God.

**Discerning the thoughts and intentions of
the heart.** This is the point at which the preceding figures are aimed. "There is indeed no
thicker darkness than that of unbelief, and
hypocrisy is a horrible blindness; but God's
word scatters this darkness and chases away
this hypocrisy." [4]

This passage is somber and cheerless—why?
Because there is that in us which dislikes the
light. We are made uncomfortable at the
thought of all the secret places of our thoughts
being exposed. In the Genesis story Adam hid
from God. The story is faithful to life. Perhaps no prospect is so gloomy as the exposure
of our secrets. It is safe to say that one of the
daily driving forces of men is the impulse somehow to escape the notice of God. The point
could be established by a very simple test.
Propose to any group of persons the prospect
that in one hour the old-fashioned picture of
the judgment would be fulfilled. The books
would be open for all to read. All we had ever
done or said or thought—all would be as easy
for the casual observer to see as the outer
clothing that we wear. How instantly all our
jaunty confidence would give way to cringing
shame! Surely this is no way to live, basing

our whole hope for peace of mind on our
ability to conceal and deceive; in daily fear
lest the truth be known about us. If that is our
condition—and who escapes it?—then we are
in a bad state indeed. And this verse, this particular word of God, acting upon us as a two-
edged sword, has exposed the sham of our
outer confidence and revealed secrets we had
scarcely dared admit to ourselves.

For we do not know ourselves. We can never
be sure of our motives, the **intentions of the
heart.** We constantly seek good, or at least
respectable, motives for all that we do. Under
cover of these good motives all kinds of evil
are at work. In this sense every human being
is a hypocrite save he who knows that he is a
hypocrite; and how remote that knowledge is
from all of us! How we love to rationalize our
conduct out of its reach! W. Fearon Halliday
tells a humorous incident of a man who was
subjected to hypnotism. He was given the post-
hypnotic suggestion that when he came out
of the hypnosis he would take a potted flower
from the window, put it on the sofa, and
bow to it three times. When the subject
waked, he carried the suggestion out in detail.
When asked what he was doing, he replied:

You know, when I woke and saw the flower pot
there, I thought that as it was rather cold the
flower pot had better be warmed a little or else
the plant would die. So I wrapped it in the cloth,
and then I thought that as the sofa was near the
fire I would put the flower pot on it; and I bowed
because I was pleased with myself for having such
a bright idea. [5]

The case is typical.

---

[4] John Calvin, *Commentaries on the Epistle of Paul
the Apostle to the Hebrews* (tr. Rev. John Owen; Edinburgh: The Calvin Translation Society, 1853), p. 104.

[5] *Psychology and Religious Experience* (New York:
Richard R. Smith, 1929), p. 75.

13 Neither is there any creature that is not manifest in his sight: but all things *are* naked and opened unto the eyes of him with whom we have to do.

13 And before him no creature is hidden, but all are open and laid bare to the eyes of him with whom we have to do.

---

Accordingly, it is better to say with Moffatt, "Ὁ λόγος τοῦ θεοῦ is God speaking. . . . The free application of ὁ λόγος (τοῦ θεοῦ) in primitive Christianity is seen in I P 1²³ ᶠ·; Ja 1¹⁸ ᶠ·, quite apart from the specific application of the term to the person of Christ (Jn 1¹⁻¹⁸)" (*Epistle to Hebrews*, p. 55). To be sure, the references to I Peter and James show only that the expression could be used in this way; our author's entire cast of thought is much closer to Philo than is that of either of these other writers. It has been suggested that Hebrews is a stage in the development which was to flower out in John's Gospel in the complete identification of the Logos with Christ. But the word "stage" suggests a straight-line development from Hebrews to John. This cannot be proved. It is better to say that the thought of Christ as Logos, while not alien to Hebrews, is irrelevant for our author. God has spoken a final and perfect word, spoken indeed in the Son, who is Jesus. This author is going to show, however, not as the Gospel of John does that every word and deed of Jesus is a window through which the believer may see

---

This is the pathetic plight of all men: we dread the light. It is a dark day when the need comes for hiding anything. Then there are eyes to be avoided, subjects not to be touched, questions that must not be asked. In that day the flower of life is wilted and the joy of life is turned to a heavy grief. We never escape this grief until the word of God exposes us.

To be completely known is one of the deepest needs of the human soul. We cannot find it among our fellow men. Even the members of our families do not really know us, nor do we understand them. When praise comes, we feel that somehow it misses the point, usually in being too generous, often in leaving out of account the thing that really was good. As for the censure of the world, it is safe to say that it never succeeds in putting its finger on the heart of the evil within us. Sometimes the world's blame is not severe enough. But condemnation is almost never just. It reflects too much the weakness and the blind spots of the condemner.

To find One who will know us through and through, who will pass a completely fair judgment upon us and our deeds—this is one of the persistent hungers of the human heart. Every complaint against the rough injustice of the world is really a cry for the perfect judgment of God. This was what Job was seeking when he cried out: "Oh that I knew where I might find him! That I might come even to his seat! I would set my cause in order before him, and fill my mouth with arguments. I would know the words which he would answer me, and understand what he would say unto me" (Job 23:3-5 ASV).

The living word of God which discerns and sees—this is not really a dreadful word, but a word of healing and comfort. Psychologists still say that mental health consists in coming to self-consciousness, in losing our illusions, in exposing all our pretenses, in squarely and openly facing all the facts, in confronting all our fears, in admitting all our failures. Certainly no soul is healthy when its chief concern is a half-hidden fear of discovery, whether by our friends or by God or by ourselves. But to be assured that God, before whom **no creature is hidden, but all are open and laid bare,** knows us through and through, and yet forgives us for Christ's sake, this is health and peace and comfort and joy. But this peace can never come until the word of God has penetrated, exposed, and uncovered us.

Suppose one were to take the truth of this passage in deep earnest. Suppose that one morning you were to rise with the waking thought, "God sees me"; then carry the thought through the day, into every work and every encounter with other human beings. What moral strength and clean joy would be yours! But have a care the moment you begin to wince and wish that you might withdraw from God's presence. There you are in the presence of danger. One thing is certain: if our daily walk were in this manner, we should have a much clearer understanding of what our writer means by the rest of God. **The word of God is living and active.**

What is the bearing of all this on the earlier part of the chapter which urged the people to enter God's rest? Every crisis exposes people. The coming of unexpected joy shows whether we are selfish or unselfish. A sudden bit of financial prosperity exposes men, shows where their true interests lie. Watch what they do with

14 Seeing then that we have a great | 14 Since then we have a great high priest
high priest, that is passed into the heavens, |

---

the divine light and know the divine way and truth and life, but rather that Jesus is the
high priest through whose ministry we may "with confidence draw near to the throne
of grace, that we may receive mercy and find grace to help in time of need" (vs. 16).
The view advanced by some commentators that **the word of God** here means the Scriptures is patently unsatisfactory. Our author regards scripture as divinely inspired, indeed
as the very word of God, but it is God's word as pointing to Christ in whom the final
and perfect revelation was given.

The **word of God** as a **sword** has many parallels (cf. Eph. 6:17; and Philo uses the
figure). Philo has also an almost exact parallel to the closing words of the section, πρὸς
ὃν ἡμῖν ὁ λόγος. Are these words to be translated "with whom [i.e., God] we have to do,"
or as in the Philonic parallel, "of whom we are to speak" (literally, "the word is to
us")? The former rendering would give a closing word of warning; the latter, a rhetorical
conclusion introducing the next step in the argument. Either is grammatically possible,
but the former is more probable because vs. 13a refers to the all-seeing God, before whom
**no creature is hidden,** and the final phrase seems to be a close parallel with 10:31, "It is
a fearful thing to fall into the hands of the living God."

The author now introduces the theme which is to occupy him throughout the rest
of his formal argument. He has presented the Son (Jesus) in the superiority of his
person, hinting at his ministry as priest, and repeatedly exhorting his readers to be
attentive to his message and warning them against the consequences of inattention.

### B. The Work Made Possible by the Personality of Jesus, the Son of God (4:14–10:18)

#### 1. Jesus Is a Divinely Appointed High Priest, "After the Order of Melchizedek" (4:14–5:10)

##### a) Introduction and Transition (4:14-16)

These verses in part form a transition from what has gone before to what follows;
in part they state the theme to be developed. Our author has already indicated that Jesus

---

their new money! A sudden disaster, such as a
shipwreck, ruthlessly sifts the heroes from the
cowards. So every word from God opens us up.
When Jesus came among men, "thoughts out
of many hearts" were "revealed" (Luke 2:35).
He still is doing just that. Let the word of
Jesus be openly proclaimed, let men be exposed
to Jesus afresh, and they will be entirely exposed. He shows where men stand. He brings
hidden things to light. So—and this is the
whole point—the promise of God's rest, his
offer of salvation, uncovers the deeps in man,
shows where his hidden interests lie, reveals
what he really wants. Whenever the promise is
renewed, some will begin to make excuse and
evasion, find reasons for doubting the promise,
falter and then soon forget. But some who
"labor and are heavy-laden" will hear and believe and come and "find rest for" their "souls"
(Matt. 11:28-29).

**With whom we have to do.** To see and know
this as life's first fact is man's best wisdom. The
darkness of sin obscures it. We have to do with

many people and with many affairs. There is
work to be done, there are obligations to be met,
schedules of production to be maintained,
taxes and bills to be paid, enemies to be
watched, and battles to be fought. But God is
an afterthought, an occasional acquaintance, a
possible hypothesis for explaining the world.
This it is to "be hardened by the deceitfulness
of sin" (3:13). When we go about our day's
work we have to do with our duties, but we have
also to do with God. Whenever we meet another person, help him, hurt him, or pass him
by, we have to do with God. When we com-
mune with ourselves, God is there. When we
seek peace of conscience, it is God whom we
seek. When we long for rest, it is God with
whom we have to do. When a child is born into
a home, it is God who is at work. When we
face the end of the road, it is God whom we
meet. "Thou hast beset me behind and before,
and laid thine hand upon me" (Ps. 139:5).

**14-16. Our Sympathetic High Priest.**—It will
be difficult for men and women of our time to

| Jesus the Son of God, let us hold fast *our* profession. | who has passed through the heavens, Jesus, the Son of God, let us hold fast our con- |

is high priest (2:17; 3:1); here he launches the consideration of his priesthood with the full and formal phrase, **a great high priest.** He has also argued at length that the Son is superior to angels and Moses; here he identifies Jesus with the Son fully and formally, **Jesus, the Son of God.** He has shown that the Son must share the experience of suffering and death in order to deliver men from sins and from the fear of death; here he centers attention on temptation as qualifying Jesus to be priest through his experience of temptation and his sinless triumph, ensuring help in human need.

It is significant that these verses are not a full statement of the theme to be developed. Our author knew the rhetorical habit of a careful and complete thematic sentence. But here there is no such exact statement of theme. We have the right to conclude that his purpose was not the academic development of a thesis as such, but a very practical application of a carefully developed line of thinking to meet the needs of Christian readers. This transitional section (vss. 14-16) closes with a warm personal conclusion, genuinely religious in content and intent. This is the purpose of his entire writing. He aims to move men to hold fast to the Christian confession. The academic argument has no other purpose for him.

14. **Passed through the heavens** is not simply rhetorical but is important for the subsequent thought. Of course he believes in the Resurrection (cf. 6:2), but it is not for him the focus of thought as with Paul. It is the necessary prelude to exaltation to "the right hand of the Majesty on high" (1:3), and here as he approaches the theme of priesthood he points to the way which has been opened **to the throne of grace** (vs. 16) through **the heavens,** through all possible lesser realms, directly to the divine presence. The analogy of the holy of holies in the tabernacle is already in his mind. In this context the exhortation to **hold fast our confession** can hardly be limited to the idea of holding fast to a creedal formula. It is not impossible (see on 3:1) that some formula of faith is

understand the priesthood of Jesus if reference is made merely to the Levitical priesthood, its detailed ceremony and meaning. Much there is in this symbolism of rich and abiding significance. But the meaning of priesthood will come alive if we remember that part of the priestly function is to hear confession. A hidden shame is a terrible burden. It weakens every desire for good, consumes precious energy in our suppressing it, infects the whole soul with dishonesty, clouds our moral judgment, and as long as it is unacknowledged is a festering abscess within. What a fearful burden pretense is! How it dulls the joys of life and binds the spirit to sin and death! How much effort men make to keep up appearances not only when they are in company, but when they are alone! Until the word has penetrated our pretenses, torn away the flimsy garments of our self-righteousness, exposed us to the light, every man and woman walks in secret fear. Often they suppress this dread and pretend that they do not have it. With them all seems joyous and free of care. But a suppressed fear is all the more damaging.

For a faithful member of the Roman Catholic Church the institution of the confessional brings relief. There are signs of a Protestant

return to a confessional. To tell the story of our shame, especially if our hearer is to be trusted with our dread secret, brings relief. The evil is out in the open. Another can see it. We are half separated from it already. Every child of a good mother has known such a priest when the mother has listened to the child unburdening himself in perfect confidence. A trusted friend can sometimes give this help merely by being a good listener, by saying little or nothing. But there are some secrets which the most trusted friend cannot penetrate, some judgments of which he is incapable, and the ultimate healing of forgiveness is beyond his power. Can we then unburden ourselves to God? Yes, but God seems far away and too high to be approached. A mediator then? Can Jesus the Christ be our priest?

What are his qualifications? He **has passed through the heavens.** Already our writer begins the contrast with the Levitical priesthood. The high priest once each year went through the curtain to the holiest place, there to make atonement for his own and the people's sins. But Jesus has pierced the ultimate curtain into the presence of God. He is the **Son of God,** God's own nature bending to do the work of

15 For we have not a high priest which cannot be touched with the feeling of our infirmities; but was in all points tempted like as *we are, yet* without sin.

16 Let us therefore come boldly unto the throne of grace, that we may obtain mercy, and find grace to help in time of need.

fession. 15 For we have not a high priest who is unable to sympathize with our weaknesses, but one who in every respect has been tempted as we are, yet without sinning. 16 Let us then with confidence draw near to the throne of grace, that we may receive mercy and find grace to help in time of need.

---

included in his thought; but the parallel is with 3:6, "if we hold fast our confidence" (cf. vs. 16, **confidence**), and the phrase **our confession** means our Christian religion.

**15-16.** Hardly a sentence in Hebrews is packed so full of meaning as vs. 15. Some of these ideas are to be developed later and a discussion of them may be postponed. Here we should note that the formal argument hardly requires such bold language. If our author were concerned only to show that Jesus is a sufficient high priest, he need not have employed such striking phrases as **one who in every respect has been tempted as we are.** Although this thought may be assumed elsewhere in the N.T., it nowhere comes to expression. The temptation account in the Synoptics (Mark 1:13; Matt. 4:1-11; Luke 4:1-13) is not a parallel because there the temptation is to prostitute his messianic calling, a temptation which was not common to men. The writer is implying here—and this is unique in the N.T.—that temptations in every respect like our own were experienced by Jesus, and that his sinlessness was the result of conscious decision and intense struggle (cf. 5:7-9; 12:2-4), rather than the mere formal consequence of his divine nature. It must be remembered that the basis for this author's conviction that such a radical sharing of human experience is necessary for Jesus has been laid by his thought of what was "fitting" (2:10) for God; the conviction is not, of course, an empirical judgment based on the life and words of Jesus as a human being. It is also rooted in the priestly

---

Aaron. But this high priest, who is Son of God, and who has entered the holy presence, is he not too far removed from us? Can he still understand our weaknesses, the easy impulses that come, the quick assaults of the tempter in an unguarded moment, the love of good things, of comfort, and even of life, that may become our sin? He is **one who in every respect has been tempted as we are.** Can this be so? Are not our severest temptations those that grow out of former sins? Do not these former experiences weaken us? Does he realize what that means? We have no way of knowing what he had to endure. But the temptation to avoid pain and death, which so sorely tried the readers, was his also. He knew that well. And for all we can tell, there may be temptations far more severe that attack the sinless soul.

In any event, Jesus is **touched with the feeling of our infirmities.** In his earthly life he had an amazing discernment of people, an exquisite sensitiveness to human need about him. As the author of the Fourth Gospel put it, "Jesus . . . needed no one to bear witness of man; for he himself knew what was in man" (John 2:25). He endured his trials, **yet without sinning.** Surely no man in history has been subject to such careful, critical scrutiny as has the man

Jesus. Men have searched his life and words and still his challenge stands, "Which of you convicts me of sin?" (John 8:46.)

**Let us then with confidence draw near.** The confidence has the overtone of speaking freely (cf. Expos. on 3:6). We are confident and can speak freely because we know that Jesus understands us, is one of us. This is our most solid comfort in time of need. To know that he is afflicted with our sorrows, bears them in patient sympathy, makes it easy to call upon him. It is the most that God could do without destroying our freedom. If we reject this help, we have nowhere else to turn. But we can come to **the throne of grace.** There is beauty in these words. The throne is our human figure for the abode of God, where his presence is most clearly known. But to approach a throne—and such a throne—with the story of our defeats, with our cry for help! We turn away at the mention of **throne.** But it is a **throne of grace,** where kindness, gracious and complete, is seated to reign. There alone we can go in confidence and in safety.

As we read Hebrews, our writer is often severe and we may be tempted to think him an O.T. prophet, untouched by the kindlier elements of the gospel. But in such passages as

5 For every high priest taken from among men is ordained for men in things *pertaining* to God, that he may offer both gifts and sacrifices for sins:

5 For every high priest chosen from among men is appointed to act on behalf of men in relation to God, to offer

---

analogy, as the verses following (5:1-10) show. He must not be robbed of the credit, however, of being the first to ascribe to Jesus full human experience and at the same time full divinity, without, at least from his point of view, compromising either. The thought in the final verse of this transitional paragraph is to run through all his subsequent discussion, explicitly or implicitly.

### b) Jesus' Qualifications as High Priest (5:1-10)

The connection is with 4:15-16: we have a high priest adequate for our human needs; so let us "draw near to the throne of grace" with confidence. The argument has been moving steadily toward this point. Our author is aware that Jesus did not qualify as a priest on the earthly level (cf. 7:14; 8:4), but he is not chiefly concerned here to meet such objections; his concern is with expounding Jesus' qualifications for the heavenly priesthood which is to end the transient institution by perfecting its valid foreshadowings. He moves, accordingly, *from* the "confidence" the Christian should possess in Jesus as priest (4:16) *to* the qualifications of priesthood as required in the earthly official (vss. 1-4) which Jesus fulfills (vss. 5-10), and especially *to* the bitter human experience of Jesus and its significance (vss. 7-10). It is this last emphasis which is to be his main theme. The formal argument here is characteristic of Hebrews and runs smoothly enough, given its presuppositions. **Every high priest** must be sympathetic with men and must be called of God (vss. 1-4). It is unnecessary to document these points from Scripture; they are well known, although the passing reference to Aaron reminds the reader that they can be documented. Christ, the writer goes on to say, was divinely appointed, as Ps. 2:7 shows (cf. 1:5). To be sure, this citation calls him Son, not priest, but it has been indicated in 1:3 that the Son's earthly ministry was to be "purification for sins," and this is followed with a citation from Ps. 110:4 which contains the word priest and indicates that Jesus' priesthood is of a different order **from** the Levitical, **after the order of Melchizedek.** The two qualifications, sympathy and divine calling, are reversed in his discussion of their fulfillment in Jesus. Unless we are to assume that the two are really one—a divine calling to a sympathetic service—we have to conclude that the order is intentional with this careful stylist—an instance of chiasmus. The stress is on the sympathy of the earthly high priest; so he puts that first. The stress is also upon the human experience of Jesus (his divine calling has been amply proved in ch. 1); so he puts that last, as the climax. The really significant point in this section is that vss. 7-9 overflow the formal argument. The two quotations (vss. 5-6) do not require or even permit the bold language that follows. The analogy from vss. 1-4 does not account for it, for although the earthly high priest must indeed **deal gently with the ignorant and wayward** since he is human

---

this the tenderness of God's mercy comes through and warms our doubting hearts.

**Let us hold fast our confession.** This is the conclusion, even though it does not come at the end. With such a high priest, with confident access to the throne of grace, with the abundance of God's mercy at our disposal, we shall hold fast. To turn away from the grace of God, to desert so merciful and faithful a high priest as Jesus, is to come to the ultimate and final loss. Here is rest for the weary spirit of man, God's rest. "Lord, to whom shall we go? thou hast the words of eternal life" (John 6:68).

**5:1-4. The Marks of a Good Priest.**—The writer now sets down the qualifications of a Levitical high priest: (*a*) He is sympathetic and (*b*) he holds his office by divine appointment. The passage has its rich meaning for every minister and indeed for every Christian. It is true that the Protestant churches recognize no priesthood, save that of Christ, and what is commonly called the priesthood of all believers. But there is nevertheless a priestly function in the ministry. For this priestly work there is no better description than that of our writer. He **is chosen from among men[,] is appointed to act**

too, and must offer "sacrifice for his own sins" (a qualification which our author cannot use since Jesus is "without sin," 4:15), nevertheless we are not prepared for the intense and even extravagant terms in which the sufferings of Jesus are described as necessary for his priestly role. The earlier paragraph, 2:14-18, is the true prelude to these verses, but they go far beyond anything written there. We must reckon with this amazingly open and frank description of the agony of Jesus, but first let us look briefly at the more formal argument which leads up to vss. 7 ff.

5:1. The author's skillful characterization of the ideal high priest is a masterly bit of condensed writing. He knows the rationale of priesthood from the scholar's viewpoint. The true priest stands on the Godward side of man; he functions **on behalf of men in**

---

**on behalf of men in relation to God.** He is constantly to be on the Godward side of his people.

His duty in the pulpit is not to proclaim his own opinions, however learned they may be, on the affairs of the day. Nor is he merely to offer good advice to his people, bright and helpful hints on how to be happy, on how to be influential and successful. He is to speak to them on behalf of God. They should enter the church to listen to him as though God himself were speaking. They should have that much confidence in their minister's fidelity as an interpreter of God's word. Their deepest need as they enter the sanctuary is voiced in the question, "Is there any word from the Lord?" How can a man aspire to this high work? How dare he undertake it? It is a fearful responsibility. Yet it is the very source of his joy and power. How can any minister ever be disheartened as long as he keeps this duty clearly in mind? When, therefore, a minister finds himself losing heart, when he is no longer devoured by the zeal of the Lord's house, when he does not enter his pulpit in the eager expectancy that Christ may that day move afresh down the aisles and into the pews among his people, mighty to save, he needs to recall the inner meaning of his work.

His duty in private is to be a priest for his people, to pray for them one by one. In that will lie the secret and source of his growth and power. Many a minister has found that in prayer for a family of his parish some new way of helping them has been revealed, some fresh word to bring them. If his responsibility really weighs on him, he will be driven to his knees— he cannot otherwise carry the burden.

And when you look into their faces on the Sunday, as you lead their worship and proclaim to them afresh the all-sufficient grace of Christ, that background of your hidden intercessions, of your pleading for them name by name, will lift your words and wing them with love and ardour and reality.[6]

[6] James S. Stewart, *Heralds of God* (New York: Charles Scribner's Sons, 1946), pp. 203-4.

His duty in the parish is to study people, to understand why they do what they do, to know the pushes and pulls that govern them. If he has integrity and sympathy within, they will come to trust him with their sorrows, their burdens, their defeats. If he can mediate the forgiveness of God, if he can bring them to appropriate the grace of God, he has done his best work.

**He can deal gently with the ignorant and wayward.** This is never easy. It is relatively easy to be severe with the sins of people. It is comparatively easy to be lenient; while to see the terrible damage that sin always does, and thus to detest it, yet at the same time to be patient and gentle with sinners, is never easy. But it is the priestly work of the ministry.

Many a man has turned tentatively, fearfully, toward the gospel only to be repelled by some hardened saint. His repentance is not sure, his first steps toward Christ are hesitant. But he is sick within and longs for some sure word of hope. If at this time he meets with hardness and scorn, how can he ever come to trust the grace of Christ? The word "grace" will have no meaning for him. But if he by God's grace meets with a sympathetic priest, how open the door to his heart! How powerful is tenderness in dealing with men! Hope is born again. There is a way out of his torment. There is a love that can make him clean.

**Since he himself is beset with weakness.** There is a missing link in this argument. It is quite true that no priest who is not beset with weakness can deal gently with his people. But being beset with weakness does not guarantee gentleness. On the contrary, many a man is hard on others just because of his own weakness. The fact that he has sinned may lead him to condemn others all the more bitterly. In fact, to be able to condemn others rather reinforces his own respectability: it is a cheap and easy way of getting on the side of the angels. What then is the missing link in the argument? When a man really knows his own sin, has frankly admitted it to himself, has asked and received God's forgiveness, then he is prepared to ex-

2 Who can have compassion on the ignorant, and on them that are out of the way;
for that he himself also is compassed with
infirmity.

3 And by reason hereof he ought, as for
the people, so also for himself, to offer for
sins.

4 And no man taketh this honor unto
himself, but he that is called of God, as
*was* Aaron.

gifts and sacrifices for sins. 2 He can deal
gently with the ignorant and wayward,
since he himself is beset with weakness.
3 Because of this he is bound to offer sacrifice for his own sins as well as for those
of the people. 4 And one does not take the
honor upon himself, but he is called by
God, just as Aaron was.

---

relation to God. The present tenses throughout have no bearing on the date of the
writing, for the author betrays no interest in what went on in Herod's temple; his concern
is with the tabernacle as a copy of the "heavenly sanctuary" shown to Moses on the mount
of revelation (cf. 8:5), and other writers after the destruction of the temple use present
tenses in this same way.

2. **To deal gently** (μετριοπαθεῖν) is a word common with the Stoics and witnesses
to our author's culture. It connotes the mean between censoriousness and sentimentality,
and although our author hardly means by it an approach toward that apathy (ἀπάθεια)

---

tend forgiveness to others. In this sense of the
word no man can ever be gracious to others
until God has been gracious to him. "He who
is forgiven little, loves little" (Luke 7:47).
When therefore a Christian finds himself being
hard and unforgiving to another sinner, he
had better look to his own forgiveness. "If you
do not forgive men their trespasses, neither will
your Father forgive your trespasses" (Matt.
6:15).

**He is bound to offer sacrifice for his own
sins.** Any sensitive minister knows what this
means. But it is easy to become insensitive. He
has a full schedule of appointments and even
God finds it hard to interrupt the schedule. He
is preoccupied with the needs of his people
and has little time to think of his own. He is
especially subject to pride, a pride of very
subtle form. His word in any group is important
just because he is a man of weight. He becomes
proud of his position, mistaking it as respect
for his calling. He becomes proud of the achievements of his parish, thinking he is devoted to
his work. He becomes proud of his own institutions, his own denomination, supposing he is
loyal to the kingdom.

Every gift of God carries its correlative peril
and penalty. Every honor, every success, is a
new hazard for a man's soul. Every high office
carries a danger for him who holds it. Many a
youth enters the ministry with true humility, with an oppressive sense of his unworthiness, in deep reliance upon God's calling
and guidance. When we see that same man in
successful middle life as humble as when he
was young, as eager to learn as when he entered
the seminary, as disturbed about his own inade-

quacies as when he was ordained to the ministry, we have seen one of the most difficult
achievements of the faith, and unfortunately a
rather rare one. "Let any one who thinks that
he stands take heed lest he fall" (I Cor. 10:12).
The danger signs are quick resentment at
criticism, being sensitive to our own wounds.
The answer is a life of disciplined prayer and
self-examination. Most ministers need a priest
for themselves, some friend to whom they may
open up their weaknesses and from whom they
can accept searching criticism. The road of
greatest danger is the lonely road.

**One does not take the honor upon himself.**
Self-seeking is the exact opposite of faith. When
any minister jauntily assumes that he is equal
to the demands made upon him, that his task
is his by right rather than by grace, he is un-
fitted for the work of the humblest parish. However small and common his congregation, if
he does not enter his pulpit with a burden, if
he does not at times draw back in reluctance
from his task, he is not qualified for it. The
minister who seeks honors and preferments in
his church casts a shadow upon his church and
doubt upon his gospel. One church in Ohio
had a long tradition that any man in the congregation who let it be known that he wanted
election as an officer in the church became
thereby ineligible for that office. The first requirement was a sense of unworthiness.

**He is called by God.** The "call" comes in
many ways, but unless it issues in humble and
complete devotion it is spurious. The sense of
urgency, of being an ambassador for Christ
(II Cor. 5:20), of being Christ's man, of being
chosen and set apart, is the one source of cour-

5 So also Christ glorified not himself to be made a high priest; but he that said unto him, Thou art my Son, to-day have I begotten thee.

6 As he saith also in another *place,* Thou *art* a priest for ever after the order of Melchisedec.

7 Who in the days of his flesh, when he had offered up prayers and supplications with strong crying and tears unto him that

5 So also Christ did not exalt himself to be made a high priest, but was appointed by him who said to him,

"Thou art my Son,

today I have begotten thee";

6 as he says also in another place,

"Thou art a priest forever,

after the order of Melchiz'edek."

7 In the days of his flesh, Jesus[j] offered up prayers and supplications, with loud

[j] Greek *he.*

---

which was the Stoic goal, it suits his purpose admirably, for the true priest must combine severity toward sin and sympathy for the sinner. He limits the possibility of forgiveness through sacrifice to sins of ignorance and waywardness arising from human weakness, as did the law of sacrifice itself. The day of Atonement, which is in his mind, availed only for such sins, not for deliberate and willful disloyalty. As we shall see, our author finds no place for the forgiveness of such sins (i.e., apostasy) even, indeed especially, in the Christian gospel (cf. 6:4 ff.; 10:26 ff.). Vss. 3-6 need no further comment than has been made above.

7. There is no documentation of this verse or of the verses that follow. Did the author have before him the Synoptic record of the Passion? Is Ps. 22 in his mind? There is no explicit reference to writing of any kind. It seems safe to conclude that an account of the Passion, written or oral, underlies these verses, although an examination will show that this description does not exactly tally with the Synoptic records. The Gethsemane incident (Matt. 26:36-46 and parallels) affords the closest parallel. Perhaps our author's words here indicate the fluid state of tradition about Jesus before it became fully crystallized

---

age in failure, of safety from the temptation of pride, of endurance unto the end.

**5-6. Self-assertion and God-assertion.**—Jesus said, "Every one who exalts himself will be humbled, and he who humbles himself will be exalted" (Luke 14:11). He had no personal ambitions. **So also Christ did not exalt himself to be made a high priest.** It is in keeping with the character of him who could say, "I am gentle and lowly in heart" (Matt. 11:29), yet in so saying carry no hint of boasting, rather making a simple statement of fact. It is significant that Jesus talked little about himself. He claimed lofty prerogatives for himself and his work, calmly assumed that he had a unique mission to accomplish. But Jesus never exposed his inner feelings, never talked about his inner life, except on rare occasions. This freedom from self has baffled the biographers, especially those of a psychological bent.

Jesus owned no property, had not a place to lay his head (Luke 9:58), organized no institution to be his lengthened shadow, marshaled no resources, and at the end committed his gospel to a little group of unpromising men. He is himself the perfect commentary on the text, "Whoever seeks to gain his life will lose it, **but whoever loses his life will preserve it"**

(Luke 17:33). The selflessness of Jesus is worthy of careful study.

What was his secret? How could he move so freely among men without thought of his own prerogatives, with no care for his own security? The answer is that he needed none of these things. Rather he had all things, since he knew and trusted the Father. To love and know God is to be freed from the fretful pursuit of honors, from the restless greed for possessions, from the frantic attempts of little men who must eagerly fortify their own security. This is the perfect freedom. All things were his in God.

**But was appointed by him.** This is the other side of the peace of Jesus. Here is the secret of his poise, his steadiness, his joy. For our writer the important point was that Jesus was a valid priest because God had appointed him. He had therefore no need to be descended from Aaron, since the house of Aaron had also been appointed by God to serve as his priests. The psalms commonly accepted as messianic are taken as the certain signs that God had appointed his Son as priest.

**7-10. The Prayers of Jesus.**—Jesus was appointed by God, so fulfilled one of the requirements of a valid priest. But how could he fulfill the other? How could he "deal gently with

| was able to save him from death, and was heard in that he feared; | cries and tears, to him who was able to save him from death, and he was heard |

in the canonical Gospels. It should also be noted that when our author deals in detail with the life of Jesus (only here), he writes about the Passion. To be sure, it is particularly relevant to his purpose just here, but it supports the modern view that the passion narrative was the first connected form tradition took. The language, **prayers, . . . supplications, . . . loud cries, . . . tears,** is, as already noted, unparalleled in the N.T. in its intensity. These words with what follows suggest that the author has no inhibitions whatever in going the full length of equating Jesus' agony with the uttermost depth of human despair. This is in striking contrast to John's Gospel (cf. John 12:27-28) where "trouble" is little more than the foil for the divine serenity. The language here also strikes our modern minds as difficult to reconcile with the high Christology of the opening chapter. The author himself feels this apparent incongruity (cf. "although he was a Son," vs. 8) but he does not shrink from the identification.

**And he was heard for his godly fear:** Commentators have exhausted their ingenuity in attempting to explain the meaning of this closing phrase of the verse. A prayer that is **heard** regularly means, in the O.T., a prayer that is answered. Now the immediately preceding words, **to him who was able to save him from death,** suggest that this was the content of the prayer, and an answer in that sense, i.e., release from death, cannot be in the author's mind; indeed it would be contrary to his thought here and elsewhere. An ultimate release from death through resurrection is hardly consonant with his thought that Jesus shared the human suffering and agony of death. The suggestion that the original text read, "and he was not heard . . . ," the word "not" (heard) having been stricken from the text on doctrinal grounds, is ingenious and comports with our author's thought that the Son "learned obedience through what he suffered," but this conjecture leaves unexplained the words **for his godly fear.** If we could suppose that our writer has in mind the "thy will be done" (not mine) of Matt. 26:42 and the parallels, then the prayer could be regarded as answered in the sense that Jesus received strength to submit

the ignorant and wayward, since he himself is beset with weakness" (vs. 2) when he was without sin (4:15)? For an answer our author makes his only detailed reference to the earthly life of Jesus, a passage so moving that it reveals how much he was captured by the human Jesus. "No theoretical reflection on the qualification of priests or upon the dogma of messiah's sinlessness could have produced such passages as this." [7] It was through the obedience of such suffering that the Son won his right to be our priest, able to "deal gently" with the sinner.

**Jesus offered up prayers and supplications, with loud cries and tears.** This likely refers to the agony of Gethsemane and the repeated prayer, "Father, all things are possible to thee; remove this cup from me" (Mark 14:36). The loud cry may refer to the desolate word on the Cross, "My God, my God, why hast thou forsaken me?" (Mark 15:34.) In Gethsemane and on the Cross prayer is at its highest. Such prayers are momentous events in the life of the spirit. These are the prayers that lay mighty hold upon God. We do not know the full meaning of the prayer in the garden. It was most

certainly not merely a prayer for more life, although it could well have included the desire to postpone death. His prayer was **to him who was able to save him from death.** Surely if the mind of the Master shrank from what others would do to him in his death, it was primarily because of what they would thereby do to themselves. What darker depths there were in the Cross, what deeper suffering than he even then foresaw in the garden, is beyond us. We can but stand humbly by, knowing that "he was wounded for our transgressions, he was bruised for our iniquities" (Isa. 53:5).

**He was heard.** What can this mean? He was not saved from death. His prayer had been that the cup might pass. He drank it to the last bitter dregs. Yet he was heard. It may be that the calm courage with which he faced his trial and death was God's answer. It may be that our writer was thinking of the Resurrection. Or he may have had something else in mind. But Jesus was heard, his cry did not fall on deaf ears, nor echo back from an unhearing heaven in mocking indifference. Our people need to be reminded that while our prayers may not be granted, they are heard. One bends in grace

[7] Moffatt, *Hebrews*, p. 65.

8 Though he were a Son, yet learned he obedience by the things which he suffered;

9 And being made perfect, he became the author of eternal salvation unto all them that obey him;

for his godly fear. 8 Although he was a Son, he learned obedience through what he suffered; 9 and being made perfect he became the source of eternal salvation to

---

himself to the Father's will and to bear the consequences (cf. Luke 22:43). Actually, we have to admit that we do not know what was in our author's mind when he penned these words.

**8. He learned obedience through what he suffered:** The thought seems to be that "Son though he was," he could learn the inner meaning of obedience only through suffering. Again, we remember the daring suggestion that this line of entering human experience was "fitting" for God (2:10) "in bringing many sons to glory." Did our author even consider for a moment the theological implications of his words, i.e., that they might be taken to mean that a rebellious Son learned obedience through suffering? Or was his mind focused on us men and our salvation? He uses the idea of the discipline of sons as yielding "the peaceful fruit of righteousness" (12:7-11) and applies it to human sons; this suggests that it was the soteriological rather than the christological motive that was uppermost in his mind.

**9-10.** Again we meet the word "perfect" in the same general context as in 2:10. There the context suggests that the word means "completely adequate" to achieve the goal of saving men. Perhaps the word means just that here, although the vivid picture of struggle certainly does not exclude the thought of moral perfection. The writer can

---

to our distress. We may pray for relief from a burden and find instead quiet strength to carry just that burden. But we are heard.

**For his godly fear.** Here again we are walking amid mysteries. The simplest interpretation is that Jesus was heard because he prayed in faith, "Yet not what I will, but what thou wilt" (Mark 14:36). But the full meaning of his submission, of his faith, of his willingness to enter the depths, is still the secret of Jesus. We can but stand in silent wonder.

**Although he was a Son.** Sons have to undergo the discipline of suffering and such suffering is a mark of God's love (cf. 12:6-7). But the Son's suffering is for another reason: **He learned obedience through what he suffered.** The test of obedience always comes when God's will crosses our own inclinations. So long as the way of life is calm and pleasant, so long as we derive spiritual profit from the good that we do, our obedience is not tested. But when inclination pulls back, when our own instincts shrink from the path of duty, then obedience takes on the nature of faith. So Jesus could not learn obedience until he had entered that place where for once his own desires shrank from the results of doing the Father's will. Surely the place where we follow him most clearly is where we offer our dearest idol, the dear self with its pride in its own goodness, and humbly bow in obedience, casting ourselves utterly and finally on the mercy of God, willing to be led as a little child. We never trust God as long as

life is plausible and rational. Only when we cannot see the way, yet walk forth upon it, does trust become strong. We never find God so near as when we have come to the end of our resources, and can only cry out for him. When Jesus said, "It is finished" (John 19:30), the lesson in obedience had been learned.

**Being made perfect.** This is a startling word. Our writer was not thinking of any moral imperfection in Jesus. But the perfection was through his complete obedience and for the work of his priesthood. Unless his obedience had come to this crucial test, he would have lacked sympathy with "the ignorant and wayward" (vs. 2), hence would not have been faithful (3:2).

**He became the source of eternal salvation** through his perfect obedience to God, and by his perfection through obedience. This is the clear meaning of the passage. Suffering is the darkest blot on creation. It seems to argue against the goodness of God. It is the great stumbling block to faith. How can a loving God permit it? This has been the agonized cry of sufferers in every generation, and it is still unanswered. Jesus did not give us a verbal or a reasoned answer. Indeed, his crucifixion constitutes the most poignant statement of the question our long history has ever seen. The darkness of life's mystery becomes thickest about the Cross. He had taught his disciples by word and example the life of complete trust. Consider the depth and simplicity of Matt. 6. "Look

10 Called of God a high priest after the order of Melchisedec.

all who obey him, 10 being designated by God a high priest after the order of Mel-chiz'edek.

hardly have permitted the idea of Jesus as a bad man made good through suffering (cf. "without sinning," 4:15). Does he regard sins—he uses the plural regularly—as no essential part of human experience; suffering, on the contrary, as an integral and inescapable human experience? Did he think this through to its ultimate implications? It is not easy to say, but we are obviously not in the realm of Paul's thought about sin. Although we cannot avoid thinking of the theological overtones of this remarkable passage, we will do well to concentrate upon the writer's own point: Jesus is qualified to be priest, not alone because he fulfilled the formal requirements but also because he is completely fitted to deal with human weakness and human sins in a radical way, having faced these facts from inside humanity itself. This the writer knows is priesthood with a difference, priesthood **after the order of Melchizedek,** and it is this difference which he proposes to expound.

at the birds of the air: . . . your heavenly Father feeds them. Are you not of more value than they? . . . Consider the lilies of the field. . . . Will he not much more clothe you, O men of little faith? Therefore do not be anxious . . ." (Matt. 6:26, 28, 30-31). Couple that faith with the dark mystery of Calvary and the darkness deepens! Seen from the outside, there is no answer but to join the blasphemers at the foot of the Cross. But seen from the vantage point of Gethsemane, of the **prayers and supplications, with loud cries and tears,** Christ's suffering takes on a new splendor. The Son of God, the chosen one, faces the black night where he cannot see the way through, where he almost revolts in anguish, where his perfect trust looks into the torments of hell and cries out, "Is this where faith leads?" He comes to the place where he can only reach up to the Father, cry, "Thy will be done," and drink the bitter cup in blind faith. That faith is the source of our salvation.

Theologians who have argued that God would be satisfied by one perfect obedience as a substitute for the rightful obedience of all, have at least caught the grand dimensions of the Son's obedience. But they have given a curious legal twist to the Atonement. The Father seeks the obedience of all his children. The various theories of the Atonement are usually weak in their negations, valid in their affirmations. This much at least we can affirm: the quality of Jesus' obedience is the pattern for the believer's faith. Saving faith in Christ is like his obedient faith in the Father. Faith is not believing the incredible. Men do not embellish faith by denouncing reason. Thought and trust belong together. But then faith does not at all consist in believing something. Faith believes in some One. And there is an irrational

moment in faith. When we shrink back from the ultimate commitment, when we want to retain some controls for ourselves, some shreds, at least, of our own righteousness, some right to hold up our heads in the presence of God, all reason seems to be on our side. But like Jesus in Gethsemane, we cry, "Not what I will, but what thou wilt" (Mark 14:36). We are plunged into the thick darkness of blind trust, we are "crucified with Christ" (Gal. 2:20), "so that as Christ was raised from the dead by the glory of the Father, we too might walk in newness of life" (Rom. 6:4). To show us this faith, to inspire us with this example, to impart such faith to us, is at least part of what it means to be the **source of eternal salvation to all who obey him.** Any theory of justifying faith which makes it the mere acceptance of a fact, or, worse still, the adoption of a formal theory, distorts the meaning of salvation. The faith that saves means trust, commitment, obedience, even in the darkest hour, even in the renouncing of our own security which is our own righteousness.

**Being designated by God.** The word **designated** is too impersonal to convey the meaning. God addressed him, hailed him, called him a **high priest after the order of Melchizedek.** "When the Son ascended and appeared in the sanctuary on High, God saluted Him or addressed Him as an High Priest after the order of Melchizedek, and, of course, in virtue of such an address constituted Him such an High Priest." [8] "This was His 'ordination' to the priesthood." [9] This was his reward for obedi-

[8] Davidson, quoted by Marcus Dods in *Expositor's Greek Testament*, IV, 290.

[9] S. C. Gaylord in *A New Commentary on the Holy Scripture*, ed. Charles Gore, Henry Leighton Goudge, Alfred Guillaume (New York: The Macmillan Co., 1928), p. 610.

11 Of whom we have many things to say, and hard to be uttered, seeing ye are dull of hearing.

11 About this we have much to say which is hard to explain, since you have become

---

## 2. The Readers Are Exhorted to Attend to This Difficult Teaching (5:11–6:20)

### a) By a Rebuke (5:11-14)

Unlike Paul, our author alternates blocks of argument with blocks of exhortation (cf. 2:1-4; 3:6b–4:13; 5:11–6:20; 10:19 ff.). These exhortations interrupt the argument, but from the point of view of his total purpose they are not digressions, since the writing is intended to be practical throughout. That his purpose is predominantly practical is shown by the intense earnestness with which he drives home his argument, and by the fact, as we have seen, that he fails to expound certain theological implications which are of interest to the student. The exhortation in 5:11–6:20 differs from other similar sections in that it precedes instead of following an argument.

11-14. The writer himself explains this with his remarks that the Melchizedek priesthood is **hard to explain;** that it is to be the subject of an extended treatment **(about this**

---

ence. This was the answer to his prayer when he was heard. This was the vindication of his faith, the clear light on the other side of the thick darkness. The writer does not mention here what lies for us beyond the blind moment in faith. All who know and love the Savior know something of the peace and strength that come from God. The ultimate triumph is beyond heart's desiring, above mind's conceiving.

**11-14. Christian Knowledge and Experience.** —We do not make enough of Christian knowledge. We shun doctrine because it accents differences of opinion, tends to divide the church into camps. Perhaps such "modesty" reflects the uncertainty, the loss of conviction, that characterize the church today. Most laymen are openly embarrassed by the opportunity to express their religious convictions. The force of a hostile skepticism is everywhere present, and church people prefer not to risk their faith in open argument. In the absence of knowledge they propose to have faith as a substitute, meaning by it—and the interpretation is widespread—the belief that certain doctrines are true. This is a perversion of N.T. faith, which always carries the sense of trust, i.e., a complete commitment in Christ. The danger is twofold: the weakening of conviction and the intellectualization of faith.

The N.T. never belittles knowledge. The Fourth Gospel represents Jesus as saying, "This is eternal life, that they know thee the only true God, and Jesus Christ whom thou hast sent" (John 17:3). Jesus' lament over Jerusalem was that it did not know "the things that make for peace" (Luke 19:42). Paul presented Jesus Christ as "the wisdom of God" (I Cor. 1:24), and anticipated the day when he should no longer know "in part," but should "understand fully, even as I have been fully understood" (I Cor. 13:12). So here our writer laments the lack of knowledge in his readers.

Part of our trouble lies in the fact that today we accept mathematical, scientific knowledge as the ideal pattern. We cannot claim that kind of rational certainty for our religious beliefs. The knowledge of which the N.T. speaks is never established by formal argument. To illustrate, our knowledge of persons is never speculative. We hear about a certain man, we hear of things he has done and said, we hear all kinds of opinions concerning him. Slowly we form our own opinion or prejudice about him. But he is at this stage an object, a kind of thing, never a subject or real person. So we do not yet know him. If we are ever to know him as a person, it will be in personal encounter. We shall spend time with him, listen to him talk and answer our questions, have dealings with him, share common concerns with him. If we are ever to know him, our vital interests will become involved in him: we shall have faith in him. We shall indeed love him, or never know him. Here faith is not a substitute for knowledge, but works hand in hand with knowledge.

So all the accumulated speculations of the learned of all ages can never bring us to a knowledge of God. For speculative knowledge, vitally important as it is, always depersonalizes its object; speculative theology makes God an object of thought, a very great and significant object, but an object none the less. To know God in the N.T. sense of the word means a personal encounter, when we as sinful, frail, ignorant creatures meet him as Judge and

12 For when for the time ye ought to be teachers, ye have need that one teach you again which *be* the first principles of the oracles of God; and are become such as have need of milk, and not of strong meat.

13 For every one that useth milk *is* unskilful in the word of righteousness: for he is a babe.

dull of hearing. 12 For though by this time you ought to be teachers, you need some one to teach you again the first principles of God's word. You need milk, not solid food; 13 for every one who lives on milk is unskilled in the word of righteousness,

---

we have much to say); and that **you have become dull of hearing.** Sluggishness, indifference, inattention—it is these faults he combats rather than any specific heresy. If we could suppose that he has received a request from the readers for instruction in **the first principles of God's word,** his reply would run like this: "You say you need a teacher when you ought to be teachers yourselves. The **first principles** are like milk for children, but you have grown up and should be ready for meat. Act like men and take the solid food

---

Savior and Lord, when we commit to him all the concerns of life, even the central concern of that basic security which we try to establish on our own righteousness. All knowledge of God, as indeed all knowledge of human persons, is existential knowledge.

We may talk about forgiveness of sins, but unless we know the bitter experience of penitence, there is an echo of unreality in what we say. We may speak about the grace of God, but unless we have known that grace in our own lives we shall be as "a noisy gong or a clanging cymbal" (I Cor. 13:1). We may discourse at great length on the purgative power of suffering and our audience may suppress a yawn; but if we have known suffering, and by the grace of God have met it in strength, people will listen eagerly to every word, however halting and awkward our speech may be. Nobody ever gets to be an authority in the things of God merely by investigation and inquiry. Sensible folk never belittle theoretical research; but authority comes when men can say, "We speak of what we know, and bear witness to what we have seen" (John 3:11).

If this is true, then true Christian faith should issue in growing knowledge. When our author complains of his readers that they **have become dull of hearing,** he is complaining about the quality of their faith. He is about to launch into the very heart of his epistle, that Jesus is "a high priest after the order of Melchizedek" (vs. 10); but he finds it hard to speak, for his readers will not understand. And they should.

Note the assumptions underlying vs. 12. These readers have been Christians for some years. **By this time you ought to be teachers.** The mere passage of time, if saving faith is at work, should have led them through many experiences of the goodness of God to an advanced knowledge of divine matters. A whole

philosophy of Christian growth is here. Their advanced status implies that they should be taking responsibility for others who are younger in the Christian faith and for those who are entering it, whether their own children or friends or neighbors. Here is a philosophy of Christian responsibility in the church. As it is, his readers need to go back to their Christian A B C's. **You need some one to teach you again the first principles of God's word.** Incidentally, here is a clear case of a N.T. writer who applies the term **God's word** to more than the O.T., although he includes that. But he also includes the word of God through Christ and the body of Christian teaching with which the church surrounded the word through the Son. The trouble with his people is not any intellectual incompetence. Except for a few mentally deficient people, the intellect always is acute enough to serve interests that are alive. Their ignorance betrays their indifference. They have not put their faith to the test of experience. They are children, **unskilled [unpracticed] in the word of righteousness.** Let any Christian leader use this passage as a judgment on the growth of those under his charge, and even more, a judgment upon his program for his church, which in turn reflects his own expectation of the direction Christian growth should take. It is a searching judgment and will make any leader uncomfortable. The judgment begins in the sanctuary, in the church school, in the official meetings, reaches into the homes, goes out to office and store, factory and farm, bank and courthouse. For failure to practice out there roots back in ignorance and uncertainty in the sanctuary. Are Christian laymen inarticulate about their faith? There can be but one explanation: they have not been led to put that faith to the test. They are **unskilled in the word of righteousness.** They are

14 But strong meat belongeth to them that are of full age, *even* those who by reason of use have their senses exercised to discern both good and evil.

6 Therefore leaving the principles of the doctrine of Christ, let us go on unto perfection; not laying again the foundation of repentance from dead works, and of faith toward God,

for he is a child. 14 But solid food is for the mature, for those who have their faculties trained by practice to distinguish good from evil.

6 Therefore let us leave the elementary doctrines of Christ and go on to maturity, not laying again a foundation of repentance from dead works and of faith

---

I am about to give you and which you need." There is no indication, however, that the readers have communicated with the writer, and the very general terms in which the entire exhortation is cast tend to discredit the view that he is addressing a small, select company of Christian teachers with whom he is in intimate personal relationship. The pastoral touch is indeed evident, as elsewhere in Hebrews, but it tells us more about the writer than about the readers. His Hellenistic culture is also apparent in phrase after phrase, for "the entire paragraph . . . is full of ideas and terms current in the ethical and especially the Stoic philosophy of the day" (Moffatt, *Epistle to Hebrews,* pp. 69 ff.).

### *b*) By a Warning (6:1-8)

The first direct rebuke of the readers is followed by a sharp warning. The connection is more psychological than logical, for the writer has admitted the readers' need for "first principles" and now proposes that they leave these behind and **go on to maturity.** They must advance because there is no retreat (vss. 4-8).

**6:1-2.** That this is the author's mood is shown by his terse summary of the "first principles" (1*b*, 2). He subtly reminds his readers of these teachings even as he leaves

---

children, still living on a nursery diet in the church.

Children do not know the difference between right and wrong. They must be told, and it must be explained again and again until slowly a conscience awakens in them. The conscience is sharpened by practice, by growing understanding, and by the feeling, rather than a clear perception, that their parents are governed by these same standards. Many questions will be settled by experience until **for the mature** young man or young woman some suggested evils, at least, are instantly and completely rejected. This is normal and we have a right to expect it. When grown people must be told by authority what is right and what wrong, something is lacking in their experience. This throws light on Jesus' question, "Why do you not judge for yourselves what is right?" (Luke 12:57.) The end of Christian faith is not moral automata, blindly obeying the detailed commands of a superior, but the growth of mature men and women who out of a basic obedience **have their faculties trained by practice to distinguish good from evil.**

Here again failure to understand betrays want of experience. The man whose judgments about honesty are foggy is the man who has played fast and loose with truth. The man who

cannot recognize and distinguish between kindness and selfishness, between fidelity and waywardness, between purity and sensuality, has his judgment distorted by bad practice. Growth in Christian experience means a growing moral sensitiveness to right and wrong, not unlike the skilled eye of the artist or the practiced ear of the musician. Introduce a habitué of the dens of vice into a small company of genuine, mature Christians, and he will be at a complete loss. Let him be ever so brilliant of intellect, he will scarcely understand a word they say. Between him and them is a moral barrier thicker and more impenetrable than a stone wall.

One of the best tests of a question of right and wrong, and of a question of doctrinal theory, is to carry it into the presence of one of Christ's noblemen. What does he make of it? The implications of this seeming commonplace passage are of immense importance for our morally confused and intellectually bewildered generation.

**6:1-3.** *On Getting Beyond the Elementary.*— Faithful interpretation is in part a matter of emphasis. We dare not emphasize that upon which the Scriptures put no accent. Thus the interpreter may be tempted to use some part of these verses for a text on first principles.

2 Of the doctrine of baptisms, and of laying on of hands, and of resurrection of the dead, and of eternal judgment.

toward God, 2 with instruction[k] about ablutions, the laying on of hands, the resurrection of the dead, and eternal judgment.

[k] Other ancient manuscripts read *of instruction.*

---

them behind. To suppose that the author is intent on developing his own speculations, whether the readers need them or not, is to miss the earnestly practical tone of the writing throughout. His summary of elementary doctrines falls into three pairs: repentance and faith, the initial requirements of primitive Christianity; instruction about baptisms and the laying on of hands, the Christian sacraments (?) ; and resurrection and judgment, the Christian teaching about eschatological events. Few sentences in Hebrews, indeed in the N.T., have given rise to more discussion than this brief summary. Is this a reference to a Christian catechism, the earliest we possess? If so, does it presuppose readers whose background was paganism or Judaism? And what does each item connote in the way of teaching? By definition—**the elementary doctrines of Christ**—it is Christian teaching, although each item taken by itself, out of the context, could be discussed without any specific Christian context. It can hardly be a summary of an entire catechism, for that must have included teaching about Jesus as the Christ. On the whole, the evidence favors the supposition of Gentile rather than Jewish readers. To be sure, Christianity had specific teachings about each of the items included, but repentance, faith, resurrection, and judgment—all fundamentals of normative Judaism—would hardly be stated in this way to readers whose background was Jewish. Certainly the older view that the readers were tempted to fall back into Judaism receives no support from this list, for it would be just these fundamentals to which waverers could insist they were returning. It is idle to speculate about the exact content our author gives each word; he simply does not tell us. The omissions also must not be unduly pressed. There is nothing about the Holy Spirit here (but see vs. 4) and nothing about the Lord's Supper, here or elsewhere. It has been pointed out that this list includes only items not repeatable, whereas the Supper was celebrated many times; but the fact remains that Hebrews centers on one "sacrament," the once-for-all-time priestly sacrifice of Jesus. The plural **baptisms,** rendered **ablutions** in the RSV, is puzzling. Scholars have suggested various solutions, such as Christian over against Jewish proselyte baptism, or Jewish ablutions in general, as well as Christian baptism over against the widespread use of water in contemporary religious cults. Again we do not know. The author is too much concerned with his central point to give us the information which we must assume his readers possessed. **From dead works** means

---

But if he wishes to expound **repentance from dead works** or **the resurrection of the dead,** he would better use some other passage. For our writer is hurrying past these points, mentioning them only by way of illustration, to the weightier matters that lie ahead.

Nor is this list of six to be regarded as a complete table of elemental Christian teaching for beginners, or as a reflection of a primitive catechism in the church (see Exeg.). The author might well have said "such elementary doctrines as repentance, etc." It is important to note, however, that at least this much was included in elementary instruction.

These verses are to be read in close connection with 5:11-14, as evidenced by the **therefore.** The implication is important and at first surprising. The writer has expressed fear lest his readers are not ready for the "solid food"

(5:12) which he intends to give them. They are not sufficiently practiced in righteousness easily to grasp what he is about to say. We might expect him then to exhort his readers to a fresh practice of what they already know, a new testing by experience, until they are ready to go on to advanced doctrine. **Therefore, we shall wait until you are ready.** On the contrary, he plunges immediately into the matter of the "solid food." **Therefore** implies that he will give them the higher teaching and for two reasons: intellectual and moral. They need to set their first thought about Christ in a wider context in order to see its true meaning; and the very statement of higher doctrine may stimulate them to more zeal in practice. Knowledge and practice grow together. The emphasis is now on one, now on the other. His readers must advance. If they do not grow, they will go back; there is

3 And this will we do, if God permit.

4 For *it is* impossible for those who were once enlightened, and have tasted of the heavenly gift, and were made partakers of the Holy Ghost,

3 And this we will do if God permits.[1] 4 For it is impossible to restore again to repentance those who have once been enlightened, who have tasted the heavenly gift, and have become partakers of the Holy Spirit,

[1] Other ancient manuscripts read *let us do this if God permits.*

---

works that lead to death, not works of the law in the Pauline sense. Our author grants too much to the law (cf. 9:22)—and note his treatment of the law throughout as foreshadowing the perfect revelation in Christ—and yet disposes of it too summarily (cf. 7:19; 10:4) for us to hold that he is combating legalism in the Pauline sense.

**3. And this we will do if God permits:** What is it we will do?—our author includes himself with his readers in this paragraph. Does he mean that we will develop the fundamentals at some future time, or that we will go on to maturity? If we have been correct in reading his "logic" as psychological, he must mean "go on to maturity," and vss. 4 ff. bear this out. Does **if God permits** mean that progress toward maturity is ultimately dependent on God, or does it mean that the author will develop his thought *deo volente?* The interpretation depends upon one's understanding of the whole tone of the argument and exhortation. If the author is merely a speculative thinker, eager to continue his abstract argument, then the phrase may be formal, hardly more than a pious mannerism. If, as we have held, the whole movement is keyed to a deadly serious and practical crisis, the phrase is to be taken in the former sense.

**4-6.** The impossibility of a second repentance—which is, with the exception of the priesthood of Jesus, the most significant teaching of Hebrews—was to have important consequences in the practice and teaching of the church. The author could not have foreseen that Tertullian, the Montanists, and other rigoristic sects would use his words to oppose receiving back into the church those who had "lapsed" under persecution,

---

no standing still. And if they fall back, they may be tempted to complete apostasy, a danger against which he now gives solemn warning.

**4-8. *The Hopelessness of the Apostate.***—The danger is acute. If they will not advance, they are in danger of apostasy. Once over that cliff, nothing remains but death. This warning is designed to spur the readers to go on to the richer experience and the advanced knowledge of the Christian life. It is one of the soberest words in the Bible. Many a Christian has been afflicted by it. He has sinned after his conversion and wonders if there can be any hope for him. So afflicted, he may be led to deny his faith, to put himself beyond all hope for spiritual recovery. All have sinned in many and grievous ways. Penitence should be a daily prayer. But who can sin without turning back, falling away? Does not this passage close and bolt the door to the kingdom for all men? In the early church it was the occasion of rigoristic attitudes toward penitents who had fallen away under persecution and sought readmission to the church. It led others to question whether or not Hebrews should be included in the canon.[1]

[1] Cf. Moffatt, *Hebrews,* p. 78.

Let us first be clear about the writer's meaning, then see what we can make of it. One thing the writer does not mean. He is not saying, as great and good men have interpreted him, that as long as men keep turning away from Christ they cannot repent. That is obvious and, for the present purpose of the writer, trite. The meaning is much more final and definite.

Note first to whom the word applies. It is **to those who have once been enlightened,** to those who have come out of the darkness of unbelief into the light of God's truth, who have seen and understood the truth of God (cf. John 1:9; 12:35-36). The figure of light appears often in the Bible and in the great prayers of the church. It is vivid and apt. The supreme enlightenment comes but once in a lifetime. "Once for all men enter Christianity, it is an experience which, like their own death (9[27]) and the death of Jesus (9[28]), can never be repeated."[2] The word applies to those **who have tasted the heavenly gift,** who know by experience what it means to be forgiven and to have the peace and joy of Christian faith. It applies to those who **have become partakers of the Holy Spirit,** whose Christian faith has been

[2] *Ibid.*

**5** And have tasted the good word of God, and the powers of the world to come,

**6** If they shall fall away, to renew them again unto repentance; seeing they crucify to themselves the Son of God afresh, and put *him* to an open shame.

**5** and have tasted the goodness of the word of God and the powers of the age to come, **6** if they then commit apostasy, since they crucify the Son of God on their own ac-

---

or that the same words would be interpreted to mean that apostates could be received on repentance but could not be rebaptized, or that the ecclesiastical institution of penance would require rejection of this teaching. It is clear that he meant what he wrote; and that the impossibility of repentance applied to apostasy, the deliberate and willful denial of Christianity, rather than to sins of weakness and ignorance seems certain from the context. What led him to such a rigorous position? While the N.T. nowhere contains an explicit parallel, the essential idea is present in the word about the unpardonable sin (Mark 3:29 and parallels); in Paul's conception of the Christian as a "new creature" (II Cor. 5:17); in I John 3:9; 5:16-17; in every presentation of the gospel as final; as well as in Judaism (cf. 12:17). Our author's position is immediately derived, however, from the whole character of his thought, with its emphasis on the final and perfect revelation in Jesus, his "once-for-all" offering for the purification for sins, the one and only way of access to God through the priestly ministry of Jesus. Is it the writer's thought that repentance is psychologically or objectively impossible? Does the impossibility lie with the decree of God or with the hardening of the human heart? Such a distinction can hardly have occurred to our author. It is true that he stresses the richness of Christian experience as the background on which to see what "falling away" connotes, but it is experience in the framework of revelation, not experience as authentic *per se*. The pastoral instinct

---

genuine, for to no others is the Spirit given. They have shared in the fruits of the Spirit, joy, peace, patience, etc. It applies to those who **have tasted the goodness of the word of God,** who know how pleasant and gracious the gospel is, how it comes as cooling refreshment to one who has thirsted for the living water, how it quiets our fears, renews our life, and sets our feet upon solid ground again. It applies to those who have tasted **the powers of the age to come.** These powers can hardly be confined to the miracles that accompanied the coming of the gospel, although the writer would likely include them. But the powers of the coming age also included the renewal of men, the remaking of all life, and the complete reign of God. These powers are even now at work in the life of the Christian and his joy is more and more to taste and to experience such power in his life. These phrases must not be divided and applied to believers of different classes. They are various aspects of the Christian experience to which all true believers are admitted. These are the beginning experiences that mark the first stages of Christian growth.

Consider now what happens if such Christians renounce what they have seen and known. They turn their backs upon Christ and return to their former life. What are they really doing? **They crucify the Son of God on their own account.**

They join those who drove the nails into his hands and who mocked his suffering. They make the act of crucifixion their own. They say in effect, "Away with him, crucify him! . . . We have no king but Caesar" (John 19:15). To turn away from Christ is to turn against him, to become his enemy. "He who is not with me is against me; and he who does not gather with me scatters" (Luke 11:23). Yet is not this what every sin does? When we neglect human need, it is Jesus that we are despising. What else did he mean by his momentous "inasmuch" (Matt. 25:40)? The wounds of Christ are reopened every day. How else could it be when he was once "wounded for our transgressions" (Isa. 53:5)? They **hold him up to contempt** even more than a deserter dishonors his country. Here is the Savior of men, and the believer who falls away, who denies him, who says, "I have tried him and there is nothing in him," exposes him to the ridicule of all his enemies and makes a laughingstock out of him, even as men did when he was on the Cross.

Now the man who does this closes every door to his own renewal. Clearly our writer was referring to apostasy, and not to any other sin. The attempt to apply this condemnation to all who have sinned after baptism, except the sins of "the ignorant and wayward" (5:2), is vain. For are not all sins done in ignorance and way-

7 For the earth which drinketh in the rain that cometh oft upon it, and bringeth forth herbs meet for them by whom it is dressed, receiveth blessing from God:

8 But that which beareth thorns and briers *is* rejected, and *is* nigh unto cursing; whose end *is* to be burned.

count and hold him up to contempt. 7 For land which has drunk the rain that often falls upon it, and brings forth vegetation useful to those for whose sake it is cultivated, receives a blessing from God. 8 But if it bears thorns and thistles, it is worthless and near to being cursed; its end is to be burned.

---

is revealed in these sharp words. The author is deeply concerned about the readers. No doubt his belief that the End is imminent is implicit in this warning, as it is explicit in 10:25-26. The phrases heaped up in vss. 4-5 are intended to remind the readers of the richness and glory of their Christian experience. **Tasted** (cf. 2:9) means experienced, not sampled. Vs. 6*b* means that they themselves **crucify the Son of God** when they apostatize, not that they crucify him *again* (ἀνασταυροῦντας is a stylistic parallel to ἀνακαινίζειν), for the initial Crucifixion was necessary for his priestly ministry and our author does not regard it as a crime (contrast Acts 2:23).

**7-8.** The agricultural illustration—perhaps the cursing of the ground in Gen. 3:17— adds little to the thought and is not very apt, for as Robinson points out, the burning over of a grainfield did not destroy its fertility but only prepared the field for the new crop. Our author was a man of the study, as Paul was a man of the city, and, in striking contrast to Jesus, they are equally unimpressive when they turn to illustrations from nature (cf. I Cor. 9:8 ff.). This passage stresses the irrevocable fate of apostates, but throws no light on the question whether they are to be eternally punished or to be annihilated.

---

wardness? Does any sinner ever know what he does? We may grant that he ought to know. But are we justified in dividing all sins into two classes: the one forgivable because "ignorant and wayward" and the other unforgivable because "deliberate"? Is there not a deliberate element in all ignorance and waywardness? Who can say? **It is impossible to restore again to repentance** those who so turn back from Christ. The word "impossible" is used in three other places in Hebrews: "It is impossible that God should prove false" (vs. 18); "It is impossible that the blood of bulls and goats should take away sins" (10:4); and "Without faith it is impossible to please him" (11:6). The logic in this passage is unassailable: there is no escaping it. God has done his utmost for such a soul and he will have none of it. Land that has received the favor of God in the form of rain may turn out to be fruitful land and so will continue to receive **a blessing from God.** But other land, enjoying the same favor, brings forth thorns and thistles and is **near to being cursed.** People are like that. God's favors are generously given to all men. Some turn the very gifts of God into a curse.

Such is the clear meaning of the writer. What do we make of it? So far as the question of apostasy under persecution is concerned, the church did not follow our author, but made

provision for the lapsed who later repented, giving the institution of penance its first beginning. In practice the church by-passed this passage.

We can turn it into a hornet's nest of theological argument—to our shame. If a man really falls away, it is because he never really partook of the benefits mentioned in vss. 4-5. If he did actually partake of those benefits, then he has never really fallen away, whatever are the appearances. If after apparent falling away, he returns in penitence and manifests the marks of a faithful Christian life, he never really fell away. All such argument is circular and futile.

What then can we make of it?

(*a*) There is no appeal beyond Jesus Christ. Never can God speak in a clearer, more final word than in his Son. Never can he show his love more fully, more tenderly, than in the Cross. He has no priest yet to come more faithful and more sympathetic than Jesus. God can do no more for us than to forgive our sins, to open the way to his presence, to give us strength for our weakness, light for our darkness, and the Holy Spirit as our faithful guide. If then men refuse the complete gift of God, "there no longer remains a sacrifice for sins" (10:26).

(*b*) There comes a point when the patience of God no longer avails, when the sinner has

9 But, beloved, we are persuaded better things of you, and things that accompany salvation, though we thus speak.

10 For God *is* not unrighteous to forget your work and labor of love, which ye have showed toward his name, in that ye have ministered to the saints, and do minister.

9 Though we speak thus, yet in your case, beloved, we feel sure of better things that belong to salvation. 10 For God is not so unjust as to overlook your work and the love which you showed for his sake in

---

### c) By an Encouragement (6:9-12)

Encouragement and assurance follow the warning of the dire consequences of apostasy. This is our author's constant usage, and in this connection counts against the view that his readers are facing persecution calculated to induce apostasy. The crisis is an inner one; they are in danger of spiritual lethargy, of drifting away (2:1) from their Christian profession. They need to be aroused by strong words to face the possible outcome of this "drift," but the situation is far from being hopeless. For the first and only time he addresses them as "beloved," ἀγαπητοί (Tyndale, "dear friends"), and grounds his affectionate and encouraging words on their conduct in the past and their confidence in God.

**10.** Their loving deeds in the past and indeed in the present will not be forgotten by God. This sentence is not to be pressed to mean that God will save them out of their sluggishness as a reward for their good works, although taken by itself it might suggest

---

committed the sin against the Holy Spirit (Mark 3:28-29). Just where is that point? Never try to find out. When a man is walking near the edge of a high cliff, there is a delicate point where his center of gravity will pull him over to his death below. But who wants to discover where that point in space is? We stay as far away from it as possible. But to call good evil, to prefer darkness to light, to refuse the best that man has ever known, seems to say that a man is bent on his own destruction and that not even the grace of God can deter him.

(*c*) Nothing in this passage should ever lead any man to doubt the complete mercy of God, for then the passage would destroy the gospel. It is true that we abuse Jesus when we sin. But the Lord Christ can stand ridicule. He prayed for those who mocked his suffering at the scene of the Cross, "Father, forgive them" (Luke 23:34). Peter, one of the favored disciples, who certainly would qualify, if any man ever did, for the benefits listed by our author in vss. 4-5, held his Master up to contempt. Yet he was afterward received by Jesus, forgiven, and became the preacher of Pentecost, one of the leaders of the church. God will not turn away from the sincere cry of faith, however much we have sinned. Jesus taught his disciples to forgive until "seventy times seven" (Matt. 18:22). If your brother "sins against you seven times in the day, and turns to you seven times, and says, 'I repent,' you must forgive him" (Luke 17:4). No wonder the apostles cried, "Increase our faith!" (Luke 17:5.) But Jesus

was speaking on behalf of God and God keeps his promises. When therefore any hesitant sinner, no matter how deeply he has fallen, is kept back from penitence by this passage, or by anything else in the Bible, we are not "rightly handling the word of truth" (II Tim. 2:15).

**9-12. The Quality of Christian Hope.**—The quality of his hope is the measure of any man. For what do you hope in and for the people around you? What do you expect to have or see happen to them, in them, and through them? Are your hopes high? You will have an amazing influence over them for good. Do you hope for little or nothing from them? You can do nothing for them. What we hope for others, what we expect from them, and work for in them, often sets the slopes down which the streams of their lives run. The writer has just uttered his most solemn word about a fearful danger in which they stand—the danger of falling back into apostasy. From that fate there would be no release. But he does not leave them there to be hypnotized by that danger. If they have no hope for themselves, they are lost. Faith and hope are twins. A faith that does not expect something from the future is not faith at all.

But what is the quality of his hope? On what is it based? Is it a mere dogged refusal to admit defeat, the kind of clinging to hope that a person feels for a very dangerously ill loved one, for whose recovery the physician offers no encouragement? But such a faith is three parts fear. Or is it the hope that things will be better in a future about which we can do nothing but

11 And we desire that every one of you do show the same diligence to the full assurance of hope unto the end:

serving the saints, as you still do. 11 And we desire each one of you to show the same earnestness in realizing the full assurance of

---

this, for he writes these words in a context of earnest exhortation to action on their part. He means that God is dependable and they need have no concern about the availability of his help. The sentence also suggests some knowledge of the readers by the writer, but does not require specific personal relations, being applicable to any group of Christians deserving the name.

**11.** Kindly deeds, past and present, are not enough; they need, each one of them, **the full assurance of hope until the end.** They need, in other words, the undergirding of a sustaining teaching such as the writer proposes to give them, for the entire exhortation (5:11–6:20) is a preparation for his exposition of the Melchizedek priesthood of Christ. Behavior roots in doctrine and doctrine bears the fruit of behavior as inevitably for the author of Hebrews as for Paul. Our author is fond of the word **hope** and we shall meet it

---

wait and see? That is close to indifference. Or is it a hope anchored in Christ, strong in his promises? Since God has done much, he will continue his work until it is fulfilled. Since the Christ has died for us, will he ever let us go? To hope in Christ, this is the solid hope of the N.T.

The writer expresses his hope for his people, a hope **of better things that belong to salvation.** What are they? In a sense the whole Bible is written about them. All the good that can come, all the gifts of God to man, his forgiveness, his provident care, his mercies, the growing kingdom, these all **belong to salvation.** For the author salvation means steadfastness in all the trials that beset us, together with the rest of God, the peace of conscience he alone can impart. It means love for God and the labor of love for his people.

**Your work and the love which you showed for his sake** [for his name] **in serving the saints.** We have no way of knowing what is meant, any more than we can know all the unrecognized kindnesses that are all about us, whose grace makes the air we breathe fresh and clean. It may have been some sacrificial gift for a poor church, some heroic shelter of a man marked for persecution, some errand of real mercy, some gracious word of encouragement to a doubter (cf. 10:34). Whatever their name, these kindnesses were among the **things that belong to salvation.** They were the work of God's grace. Such graciousness is a sure token of divine grace.

**God is not so unjust as to overlook your work.** The writer would never think of "salvation by good works," of our virtuous deeds as being sufficient to lay God under obligation to **us.** But with all that, God knows well the difference between our doing good and doing evil, **is** pleased with every step in Christian growth.

As John Calvin put it, he recognizes his own gracious gifts in us, and is bound by his nature to acknowledge them. Christian growth is an evidence of grace at work. "You will know them by their fruits" (Matt. 7:16). The writer is encouraged by what they are doing and is wise enough to say so.

While it is not clear that he knew his readers intimately, he had a pastor's eye and heart for the individual. **We desire each one of you to show the same earnestness in realizing the full assurance of hope until the end.** Just as they have shown marked kindness to the people of God, he is eager that they may be kept to the end by hope's strong assurance. Without that hope, that expectancy from God, they could not endure hardship. It is not easy to be a Christian. The first flush of joy may give way to days of low visibility and of heavy going. But hope is an anchor in the heavens. To rely on the triumph of Christ, to expect growth in the things of the spirit, to anticipate the keeping power of God and fresh victories over evil, to look for the final triumph over death, this is to be kept steadfast. To look forward confident in the Christ, that is to have courage.

The message is rich for modern men. When we are tempted to make terms with ourselves as we are, to accept our bad temper, our dishonest practices, our meager prayers, our faltering witness, as inevitable and final, we are really tempted to quit the Christian faith. For who ever told us that those failures were final? None of us has the remotest idea of the man he could be if Christ really had all of him, what fears would be cast out, what kindness would flow through his words, what strong help he would bring to his fellows, what a tower of strength he would become. What Christ could do for us, would do for us, will do for us, if we let him—

12 That ye be not slothful, but followers of them who through faith and patience inherit the promises.

13 For when God made promise to Abraham, because he could swear by no greater, he sware by himself,

hope until the end, 12 so that you may not be sluggish, but imitators of those who through faith and patience inherit the promises.

13 For when God made a promise to Abraham, since he had no one greater by

---

again (cf. vss. 11, 18; 3:6; 7:19; 10:23; 11:1; etc.). Hope is approximated to faith, although he never quite equates the two.

**12.** He closes this paragraph with a challenge to imitate **those who through faith and patience inherit the promises.** This will cure them of sluggishness, their besetting sin. But the word "promises" leads to further emphasis upon the dependability of God, for human effort without divine assistance is not enough, and the reliability of God's promises is sure, however wavering human behavior may be.

### d) By an Assurance (6:13-20)

**13-20.** We can but admire the skill and subtlety with which our author turns his exhortation into a preparation for the Melchizedek speculation, laid aside for the moment because of its difficulty (5:10) and shortly to be resumed (vs. 20). The immediate connection is with the word **promise** and with the call to be imitators of those who inherit the promises (vs. 12). The thought runs thus: **Abraham,** the inheritor par excellence, obtained the promise through patient endurance—the very quality the readers need. And what a promise it was! It was rooted in the very nature of God himself, as the Scripture shows when it states that God **swore by himself.** The universe, so to speak, guarantees it. This should be a sufficient guarantee, but the writer's homiletic instinct leads him to add an *ad hominem* argument. If men reckon an oath by God as final confirmation, how

---

to accept that as the measure of what we shall become is to have **the full assurance of hope.**

Much in our world disheartens us. The spiritual dullness of our age, the illiteracy of many people in the things of faith, the hatred and the strife, the threat of wars and the widespread oppression of men—what a world in which to have hope! But in such a world to lose hope is to lose faith in God. To say that what ought to be is impossible is a complete denial of him. To have faith is to hope for what he can do. And to hope is to expect so strongly that we do all in our power to make it come to pass.

N.T. hope is never idle waiting for God. "There is nothing you can do" is a theological perversion. To have hope is to release all our energies. The writer wants his readers to have this assurance **so that you may not be sluggish.** Hope is the cure for dull lethargy. It stirs us up. The sluggish Christian ought to be a contradiction in terms. The man who has found the pearl of great price, in joy goes and sells all that he has (Matt. 13:45-46). Not to the slothful belongs the kingdom of hope, but to the **imitators of those who through faith and patience inherit the promises.**

A good example is strong medicine for the soul. Nothing quickens hope so much as the sight of another who lives by hope. A soul that

can bid future hope be present fact, who can through hope even now appropriate the gifts of God, is the most powerful argument in the world for the life of hope. We should make more use in the church of the great saints of every age. Let their stories be told, and men, women, and little children will listen.

The promises of God are never unconditional. Before they can be inherited the conditions must be met. We must have **faith** in him who promises and **patience** to wait upon him. Patience to wait through the longest night and never doubt that dawn will break—only to such a person do the promises come, take strong hold, and make themselves believed. To **inherit the promises** is to live by faith and hope and to find them good.

**13-20.** *The Faithful Promises of God.*—Consider the range and variety of the human promises that undergird our lives. Our economic life is daily sensitive to "I promise to pay." The paper currency which we use in trade is, every piece of it, a promise by the government. All the savings by which men prepare for difficult days ahead, all the life insurance policies, are simple promises. Every man does his daily work, receives his daily wage, by faith in promises. Many transactions in the stock or commodity exchanges are concluded by a simple "yes," a

14 Saying, Surely blessing I will bless thee, and multiplying I will multiply thee.

15 And so, after he had patiently endured, he obtained the promise.

whom to swear, he swore by himself, 14 saying, "Surely I will bless you and multiply you." 15 And thus Abraham,[m] having patiently endured, obtained the promise.

[m] Greek *he*.

---

much more immutable the promise of God guaranteed by his oath by himself. But what does God promise? He promises the hope, here almost the thing hoped for. And where is this hope to be attained, the hope which is an **anchor of the soul?** It lies not in the realm of earthly, transient, sensual things, but in the realm of eternal, imperishable reality. It lies in **the inner shrine behind the curtain.** By a quick shift to the imagery of the tabernacle and its Holy of Holies, the author makes the transition to Jesus who has entered that inner shrine **on our behalf,** not as the heir but as **high priest for ever,** and not as an earthly priest but as a high priest **after the order of Melchizedek.** The movement of thought is clear. Perhaps only vs. 18a requires comment. The **two unchangeable things** appear to be the promise and the oath (vs. 18; cf. vs. 17).

This formal argument is thoroughly uncongenial to modern modes of thought. It is a kind of midrash on Gen. 22:16-17, combined with Lev. 16:2 (vs. 19), issuing in Ps. 110:4 (vs. 20) and so tying up the argument with 4:14 and 5:10. Before asking what validity, if any, this method of interpreting scripture may have for us, let us note some points of interest in this strange piece of exegesis. First, it was not strange to the writer's contemporaries. The oath of God by himself had intrigued others, notably Philo. Philo is troubled by the anthropomorphism of the phrase and inclines to regard it as a concession the O.T. writer makes to the human understanding of his readers. The absolute and unchangeable God could hardly have behaved in so manlike a fashion. The author of

---

signal, or a nod of the head—promises all. They reach into every area of life. Even the safety and life of little children rest upon the marriage vows at the altar. A minister takes ordination vows. A soldier and a congressman are alike "sworn in." It is true that many promises are broken. Every broken promise, however cynical the mood in which it was made, is a stab into the vitals of human society. Most promises are kept; otherwise no human society would be possible and we should swiftly sink beneath the level of barbarians. Our human life, every hour of it, rests upon a vast unseen foundation of promises.

A crucial promise is strengthened by an oath. Every high official in the land takes his oath of office. A witness in court binds himself by an oath to tell the truth, the whole truth, and nothing but the truth. In biblical times to swear meant to bind oneself by an oath. It was and is a sacred business. Men bind themselves to fulfill a duty by appeal to a higher, implicitly calling down on their heads punishment from this higher one if they fail in the performance of their sworn duty. **Men indeed swear by a greater than themselves, and in all their disputes an oath is final for confirmation.**

So the life of the spirit rests upon the strong foundations of God's promises. Faith depends upon them. This needs to be made especially

clear to our confused age. Faith is often regarded as a human decision in the face of the world's ambiguity. It faces a whole world of threatening evils and of possible good, and out of its own valor creates the good. It is strong defiance of the forces of darkness. It bets its whole life on the good. Such a faith is really a form of self-assertion (cf. Expos., 11:1-40).

But this is not biblical faith, nor would the writer of Hebrews have accepted it. Faith has its valor, as every age of persecution has testified, as is proclaimed by every heroic triumph of the common Christian man against all but impossible odds. But the appeal of Christian faith is not to the valiant, not to the mighty, but to the weak, to the sinful, to the defeated—yes, to the cowardly. The man of biblical faith rests not on his own courage, but on the promises of God. He does not thank God for his unconquerable soul. Rather he thanks God that God is who he is and what he is. He does not cry, "How brave am I," but "How faithful is God!"

Consider Abraham. His faith rested on a great promise, given him after he was ready to offer his only son as a sacrifice to God. The promise was **Surely blessing I will bless thee, and multiplying I will multiply thee.** This reading (KJV) preserves the strong emphasis of the original better than does the RSV. In Genesis there was an added promise, not mentioned

**16** For men verily swear by the greater: and an oath for confirmation *is* to them an end of all strife.

**17** Wherein God, willing more abundantly to show unto the heirs of promise the immutability of his counsel, confirmed *it* by an oath:

**16** Men indeed swear by a greater than themselves, and in all their disputes an oath is final for confirmation. **17** So when God desired to show more convincingly to the heirs of the promise the unchangeable character of his purposes, he inter-

---

Hebrews apparently feels no such qualms; he is not concerned with philosophical reflections on the nature of God but only with the practical needs of sluggish and wavering Christians. They require an utter assurance of God's trustworthiness. God has gone all the way to give that assurance; he has sworn by himself, as the scripture states. He could do no more; this is the ultimate ground of confidence in his dependability.

Paul's extended use of the example of Abraham (cf. Rom. 4:1 ff.; Gal. 3:6 ff.) invites comparison with this passage. Where comparison is possible—Paul does not use God's oath by himself—the contrast with Hebrews is striking. Hebrews stresses Abraham's "patient endurance" (his faith?) and suggests (vs. 15) that the promise was a reward for this faithfulness. Paul insists that Abraham's faith, contrary to all human reason, was the very opposite of confidence (in the law) and had nothing to do with rewards. The two ideas overlap, to be sure, but the approach is different. Hebrews, in quoting Gen. 22:16, omits the words "thy seed" (vs. 14), although they were present in the LXX. The author has no interest in showing that Christ is the "seed" promised to Abraham. Paul, quoting the promise from Gen. 12:7, interprets it messianically (cf. Gal. 3:16). There is in Hebrews no concern with the Pauline contrast between righteousness under the law and the righteousness of God through faith. Our author betrays no knowledge of the recorded saying of Jesus about oaths in the Sermon on the Mount (Matt. 5:33-37; cf. Jas. 5:12).

---

here, "And in thy seed shall all the nations of the earth be blessed" (Gen. 22:18). This promise becomes one of the dominant notes in the Bible. It is almost the *raison d'être* of Israel as a nation. It became the center of Israel's faith. Paul uses it in Gal. 3–4 to assure the Galatians that as Gentile Christians they have full inheritance of God's saving mercies. The faith of Abraham was his trust in this promise of God and in the God who had made this promise. He **patiently endured,** he was willing to wait the outcome of history. Besides, Isaac, as far as Abraham could see, must never have seemed very promising. He is not the strongest character of the Bible and was usually subject to the plots and plans first of his mother, then years later of his wife. But Abraham believed, he accepted God's word. Did he see the promise fulfilled? Fulfillment came long after his death. There is a larger sense in which he has not even yet **obtained** (cf. 11:13). But neither has God failed.

For Christians, faith centers in the promises. The Bible is full of them. Freedom from anxiety rests on the promise, "I will never fail you nor forsake you" (13:5). The promise of Jesus is explicit, "Ask, and it will be given you; seek, and you will find; knock, and it will be opened

to you" (Matt. 7:7). "Him who comes to me I will not cast out" (John 6:37). "This is what he has promised us, eternal life" (I John 2:25). "By myself have I sworn, the word is gone forth from my mouth in righteousness, and shall not return, that unto me every knee shall bow, every tongue shall swear" (Isa. 45:23 ASV).

Christ is himself the supreme pledge of God. He renewed the promises, rebuilt our faith in them, lived his own life around them. "For all the promises of God find their Yes in him" (II Cor. 1:20). Indeed, the promise of which our writer is here thinking, and which the believers are to find as the **sure and steadfast anchor of the soul,** is the oath by which God promised a priest after the order of Melchizedek (cf. 7:21).

The whole nature of God is involved in his promises. When the promise is reinforced by an oath, we can rely on these **two unchangeable things, in which it is impossible that God should prove false.** It is as though God himself were to say, "If I should break my pledged word, I should cease to be God; my very nature would dissolve." Biblical faith is always trust in the nature of God, his fidelity, his justice, his mercy.

18 That by two immutable things, in which *it was* impossible for God to lie, we might have a strong consolation, who have fled for refuge to lay hold upon the hope set before us:

19 Which *hope* we have as an anchor of the soul, both sure and steadfast, and which entereth into that within the veil;

20 Whither the forerunner is for us entered, *even* Jesus, made a high priest for ever after the order of Melchisedec.

posed with an oath, 18 so that through two unchangeable things, in which it is impossible that God should prove false, we who have fled for refuge might have strong encouragement to seize the hope set before us. 19 We have this as a sure and steadfast anchor of the soul, a hope that enters into the inner shrine behind the curtain, 20 where Jesus has gone as a forerunner on our behalf, having become a high priest for ever after the order of Melchiz'edek.

---

The argument has a validity which lies deeper than the "dated" character of his formal statement. This will appear when we ask how we ourselves would prove the dependability of God. From history? In his own way our author argues from history. For him history is the history of revelation, and he is concerned to present his message in the context of that history, not as an isolated and unrelated fact. The revelation in Christ is the finality toward which all relativities point (cf. 1:1 ff.). From experience? He does not disregard human experience, for God's revelation is constantly related to our saving experience of it (cf. vss. 4-5; 4:3; etc.). But history, humanly conceived, and experience, humanly apprehended, are too uncertain to serve as final guarantees. From reason? Our author employs all his powers within the framework of revelation to substantiate his position. But behind history, experience, and reason there must be, he argues, a surer ground for confidence which these human capacities can only dimly perceive. If God is to be known, he must have revealed himself to the knower. The author assumes that God has so revealed himself. Yet the appeal to revelation, so constantly made in Hebrews, has an overtone that strikes the attentive ear. The ultimate appeal is to the nature of God. The writer's artificial use of scriptural witnesses, by its very disregard of the historical setting and the literal meaning of the passages cited, testifies to his sensitiveness to a

---

This central note must be sounded again and again. We need God. Any form of faith that merely bids us gird ourselves anew and trust our own courage is a betrayal of biblical faith. Faith rests in God. We depend on his word for knowledge about him, not on our own reasoned arguments. We rely on his forgiveness of our sins, not on our own righteousness. We depend on his choosing us, not upon our resolve to follow him. Our faith is in his hold upon us, not in our hold upon him. When men resist this complete trust, want to amend it, draw back from it, it indicates a suspicion of God, a fear that we cannot safely commit that area of life to him.

And we are in danger. The dangers are not chiefly in the physical perils of storm and disease. They are in the realm of the spirit where we are subject to the temptations of our secular age, prone as it is to read life apart from God. We are in danger of our own pride, our own passions, our own weakness. When a man is in danger, he makes for a safe spot quickly. Christian faith runs straight to "the secret place of the Most High" (Ps. 91:1). Christians are those **who have fled for refuge to God.** The

phrase reminds us of the cities of refuge in Num. 35.

We are now ready to return to the Christian hope (cf. vss. 9-12). Hope is faith in the God who has promised, whose very nature is involved in the promise. The readers were in mortal danger of falling away. So are we all. There is one **sure and steadfast anchor of the soul,** which will hold us steady and strong. It is the **hope that enters into the inner shrine behind the curtain,** not the physical representation, the holy of holies of the tabernacle, but into the very heart of God, **where Jesus has gone as a forerunner on our behalf.** To anchor our souls there is to be held steady in every danger.

Why should we seek any other safety? The fears, the bewilderment, the fretful scurrying of men for security, are evidence that they have not found what they seek. The man who does not find his safety **behind the curtain** becomes a victim of worldly forces that play upon him. He is driven from his course. His frail boat changes its direction with the rise and fall of every wave. Even the moral stars are blotted out and he has no landmarks by which to

| 7 For this Melchisedec, king of Salem, priest of the most high God, who met Abraham returning from the slaughter of the kings, and blessed him; | 7 For this Melchiz'edek, king of Salem, priest of the most high God, met Abraham returning from the slaughter of the |

divine Voice speaking through the changing modes of human understanding directly from God to man. This will be apparent in the figure of Melchizedek, whom he will now introduce.

### 3. The Melchizedek Priesthood of Christ in Its Superiority to the Levitical (7:1-28)

The author's treatment of Melchizedek intrigues the modern reader because of the mystic sound of the name, the strange exegesis, and the fact that it is unique in the N.T. Perhaps the two chapters in Hebrews best remembered are ch. 11, on faith, and ch. 7, on Melchizedek. It is accordingly important to see this chapter in relation to the writer's total argument and not to give it a disproportionate emphasis. It is true that he carefully prepares the way for this idea (5:6, 10; 6:20); that he reckons it as "hard to explain" (5:11); and that he makes it the occasion for an extended exhortation (5:11-6:20). But Melchizedek serves only one purpose: to prove the existence of another order of priesthood, older, superior, and so superseding both the Levitical priesthood and the law which rests on it. The author's statement of purpose (4:14-16) and the summary closing our chapter (vss. 26-28) contain no mention of Melchizedek for the very good reason that the scriptural sources (Gen. 14:17-20; Ps. 110:4) afford no basis for his central thesis, i.e., that Jesus is *the* priest for us because of his sympathy perfected through temptation and suffering. He has to show that it is right to call Jesus priest, and indeed that he is the one and only true priest of God. This the Melchizedek speculation enables him to do and it is an important link in his argument. In other words, Melchizedek is used to establish the validity and the dignity of Christ's priesthood, not its nature and function. The writer seems to recognize that to call Jesus priest at all is somewhat daring, at least that it requires detailed proof. Once he has given his proof, he leaves Melchizedek behind, as he has left the angels and Moses behind, and advances to his point. As a matter of fact, Melchizedek plays no explicit role in ch. 7 after vs. 17. (The addition of "after the order of Melchizedek" in vs. 21 in some MSS is probably not original, being designed to complete the quotation, for the author makes no use of this phrase here or hereafter.) Points are introduced (vss. 18 ff.) which are quite foreign to the record of Melchizedek, e.g., covenant and law. Accordingly, there are no sufficient grounds for thinking either that our author

measure his "progress." Clearly to recognize the perils that we face both without and within, and to find our steadfast anchor, our hope in the God who has promised, is salvation for every man, in every circumstance, in every generation.

7:1-3. *Melchizedek the Priest.*—This passage is frankly a stumbling block. Our writer is here using the Alexandrian method of allegorical interpretation, and this means practically to play fast and loose with historical fact. Facts are distorted to comply with the requirements of theory. The most extraordinary claims are made for Melchizedek, claims that have made this passage a happy hunting ground for people who cannot distinguish fancy from fact. Against such thinking all our factual, sober natures, disciplined by the scientific method of historical study, rise up in revolt.

Shall we then dismiss this passage altogether? Before we do so, we need to have a fresh look at what our writer is really trying to do. (a) He is not writing about Melchizedek, but about Jesus Christ. His references to Melchizedek are of use only as they serve to bring us to the perfect priest. (b) He is not here giving us his own reasons for believing in the Christ. Whatever his background of experience, whatever the Christian influences that played upon him, we do not know what it was in the work of Christ that caught and held our writer. But we may be sure that it was not that Christ conformed to the type of Melchizedek. He first knew the work of Christ, saw the effects of his ministry, and was led to claim for Christ the title of high priest, a title that for our writer best fitted the work of Christ. We must therefore remember

**2** To whom also Abraham gave a tenth part of all; first being by interpretation King of righteousness, and after that also King of Salem, which is, King of peace;

kings and blessed him; **2** and to him Abraham apportioned a tenth part of everything. He is first, by translation of his name, king of righteousness, and then he is also king of Salem, that is, king of peace.

---

is combating a Melchizedek worship—in contrast to angels and Moses, Melchizedek is not *inferior* to the Son; he is the prototype of the Son—or that he could have imagined that his words would be used as the basis for a Melchizedek cult, although there is some evidence that they were so used in heretical Christian circles. He has established proof that Jesus is the Son; he must now show that he is Priest. This seems to be the sole purpose of Melchizedek, although he serves to introduce various other matters, as we shall see.

The backbone of the argument derives from a combination of Gen. 14:17-20 with Ps. 110:4, accompanied by the author's interpretation of, and inferences from, the two scriptural passages. He establishes the dignity of Melchizedek, the prototype of Christ, in vss. 1-3; shows his superiority to Abraham and so to Levi and the Levites (vss. 4-10); argues that this superiority involves both a change of priesthood and of the law implementing the Levitical priesthood (vss. 11-14); establishes this change by a quotation from Ps. 110:4, which both proves and is proved by the negative value of the Levitical and the positive efficacy of Christ's priesthood (vss. 15-19); points out, again from Ps. 110:4, that Christ's priesthood is guaranteed by the divine oath and carries with it **a better covenant** (vss. 20-22); contrasts the transitory functioning of earthly priests, who multiply futility by their comings and goings, with the permanent ministry of Christ for men (vss. 23-25); and concludes with a summary of the qualifications of our high priest in his superiority to the Levitical priesthood as **a Son . . . made perfect for ever** (vss. 26-28).

The form of this scriptural argument is quite like the discussion of "rest" (3:6c–4:13) in that the author combines what we would call a historic incident with verses from the psalms, which lift it out of the temporal into the eternal or spiritual realm. We need to remember that this is a legitimate method of interpreting scripture by the standards of the times, and that it is, in fact, quite mild as an example of allegory when compared with the best-known exponent of that school, Philo of Alexandria. Granting the author's presuppositions, we must acknowledge his skill in weaving together the two passages of scripture and drawing from them the conclusions that substantiate his argument. This can best be seen by studying the chapter in detail.

**7:1-3.** He begins by interpreting the Genesis account of the meeting between Abraham and Melchizedek as the former was returning, victorious and laden with spoils, from the battle with the kings (Gen. 14:17-20). **Melchizedek, king of Salem, priest of the most**

---

that every word he utters about Melchizedek is really a tribute to Christ. Unless we can see beyond Melchizedek to Christ, we shall fail as interpreters. (*c*) Plainly our writer discovered Melchizedek in Ps. 110 and found in current interpretations of this mysterious character of antiquity a vivid scriptural background for his argument about the priesthood of the Christ.

**2.** *The King of Righteousness.*—Righteousness and peace had often been joined in messianic expectation. "In his days shall the righteous flourish, and abundance of peace, till the moon be no more" (Ps. 72:7 ASV; cf. also Isa. 9:6-7; Zech. 9:9-10). The words **king of righteousness** as applied to Melchizedek are to be taken to mean "a righteous king," as our writer

would never apply the title "sovereign of righteousness" except to God. In a real sense, however, the title is appropriate to the Son.

To see him as **king of righteousness** is to gain moral perspective. The claim is not exaggeration. Our day is afraid of absolute ethical standards. It seeks a human, and usually a social, origin for all our moral insights. It is impressed by the fact that specific codes of behavior change from generation to generation and from country to country. It seems, therefore, that morals are the work of human minds, the efforts of society to defend itself against destruction from its own members. If so, and men are quick to draw the inference, no moral law is entitled to greater respect than the

**high God,** brought forth bread and wine, **blessed** Abraham, and received a tithe of the spoils from his hand; blessing and tithing serve the writer's purposes and he ignores the bread and wine. Now Melchizedek was a mysterious figure for ancient exegetes, who were under obligation to deal with him because of his relation to Abraham. In the Talmud he is identified as Noah's son, Shem. Other Jewish commentators reckon his lack of a genealogy as evidence of a shameful birth, or hold that he lost his priesthood because he committed the impiety of naming Abraham before he named God (cf. Gen. 14:19), or else simply assume that his priesthood was taken over by Levi in the course of the divinely ordered sequence of events. No typical or normative Jewish writing shows any indication of such an interpretation as we find in Hebrews. Philo, however, identifies Melchizedek as a manifestation of the Logos, who as priest brings peace and righteousness to the soul. Philo derives these qualities by a translation of the name and titles of Melchizedek, just as Hebrews does. Our author is unquestionably familiar with this school of interpretation, but he never explicitly identifies the Son with Melchizedek; on the contrary, he is careful to avoid such an identification, for Melchizedek is "made like" or "resembles" the Son of God (vs. 3) and Christ is a priest "in the likeness of" (vs. 15) and "after the order of," Melchizedek (vs. 16). It would suit neither his purpose nor his own thought to identify Melchizedek with Christ, for then the reader might well ask why is not Melchizedek the perfect priest we seek? Why bring in Christ? This is just the inference the writer wishes to avoid, for Melchizedek indeed witnesses to the perfect priesthood (Christ's), but only Jesus in his tempted, suffering, sympathetic humanity gives the content to priesthood which is required for needy men. Here, as elsewhere, our author betrays his knowledge of the Philonic type of thinking without adopting the thoroughgoing Philonic philosophy. It is vs. 3 that most troubles the modern reader. The silence of Genesis on the genealogy

---

society which has formulated it. This is the price to be paid for making ethics an "empirical science." Such a science tends to be based on current practices rather than upon what ought to be. In the light of the Christian understanding of man, to make natural man the standard of right and wrong is to pervert morality and to exchange light for darkness.

It is quite true that moral standards as well as practices vary from time to time and from land to land. It is also true that any absolute standard, such as the law of perfect justice, or the Christian law of love, must vary in its application from time to time in accord with circumstance. Christian love, for example, will find its fulfillment in one standard at one time and place. But in other times and places the same principle will issue in quite different codes of conduct. That is why Jesus refrained from giving explicit moral instructions, insisted rather upon the inner law written in the heart. The argument from variety of practice and from variety of moral standards is therefore no argument against the Christian absolutes of love to God and love to man.

In order to recover our moral sanity we need to see clearly the bankruptcy of any socially grounded morality. It is true that we are governed by social codes of law. We owe them our obedience and sometimes our criticism. But unless we see these human standards against the background of the divine imperatives, by which

societies themselves are judged, we are reduced to a fearful dilemma. Either we become moral slaves to our society or we become moral rebels, with loyalty to no one for whose sake our rebellion could be saved from self-centered indulgence. Only in Jesus do we find the standard by which we are freed from utter bondage on the one hand, and given a charter of rebellion by which we shall be effective critics of our society on the other.

For human customs invariably tend to become demands for precise moral behavior in prescribed situations. They run out into codes. It is the outward deed that society demands. This has four disastrous consequences. (a) Such laws must invariably become more and more complex to cover an increasing variety of cases, as witness the growing specialization of both civil and criminal law in our own land. In moral matters the tendency is toward finer and finer precision, illustrated by the complexity of rabbinical laws governing the sabbath in Jesus' day. (b) Such laws increase the danger of moral casuistry. They do not get at the heart of the matter. They tend to settle for such minutiae as tithing "mint and anise and cummin," while they neglect "the weightier matters of the law, justice and mercy and faith" (Matt. 23:23). (c) Such laws easily foster the conceit of self-righteousness. The sinner can count the laws he has observed and by the very weight of their number be impressed with his own virtue.

| 3 Without father, without mother, without descent, having neither beginning of days, nor end of life; but made like unto the Son of God; abideth a priest continually. | 3 He is without father or mother or genealogy, and has neither beginning of days nor end of life, but resembling the Son of God he continues a priest for ever. |
| --- | --- |

of Melchizedek is pressed to mean that he had none; he was **without father or mother or genealogy, and has neither beginning of days nor end of life, but resembling the Son of God he continues a priest for ever.** It is tempting to modernize his thought by reading this sentence: "There is no record of Melchizedek's father, mother (i.e., no genealogy); no record of birth, death (i.e., no vital statistics). Now such a record is the *sine qua non* of official priesthood; a man without it is unqualified for priesthood according to the law (cf. Neh. 7:63-64; Lev. 21:18-19). But Melchizedek was a priest (Gen. 14:18*b*). Therefore he proves the existence of priesthood after a different order (Christ's)." This rationalization makes the thought more congenial to the modern mind but misses the force of the original, primitive idea. According to a rabbinical principle, what is not written in scripture is nonexistent. Our author is following this principle. He does really mean what he says; Melchizedek was really the manifestation of a timeless, nongenealogical priesthood. He is under the necessity of "building up" Melchizedek to a superiority sufficient to subordinate the patriarch Abraham and the divinely given law of priesthood, and so to serve as the prototype of the Son as high priest. The danger was that our author should prove too much; and later Christian writers, following his lead, interpreted Melchizedek as a manifestation of all three persons of the Trinity. But he tries to avoid an overvaluation of Melchizedek by his guarded phrases ("resembling," "likeness," "order of," vss. 3, 15, 17) and by dropping the subject when it has served his purpose. We get an insight from these verses into our author's view of history. He regards historical events as valid but

(*d*) Such laws overlook the real source of moral power—in the character of the man himself. It is not outward conformity to a fixed pattern that makes a deed good, but the inner quality of the man who performs the deed. No matter how a transaction conforms to the prescribed standards of honesty, unless the parties love honesty to their innermost, the quality of deceit will stick to everything they do. "Either make the tree good, and its fruit good; or make the tree bad, and its fruit bad; for the tree is known by its fruit. You brood of vipers! how can you speak good, when you are evil? For out of the abundance of the heart the mouth speaks" (Matt. 12:33-34).

It is because Jesus clarified these moral insights that he becomes the judge and standard of every age. You cannot leave him out of account. The flimsiness of much modern moral theory and the squalor of modern practice alike call for him as **king of righteousness.**

But in an even deeper way he is **king of righteousness.** He alone can solve the darkest moral problem of all times and of every place—the problem of guilt. He alone can bring a forgiveness that is at once tender and decent, at once kindly and convincing. Without Jesus the forgiveness of God remains problematic. With him it becomes a pledge, a promise "in which it is impossible that God should prove false" (6:18). He is also the pledge of God that the work of righteousness will be carried to completion; that while we do not know what we shall become, we shall yet "be like him" (I John 3:2). He is the hope in every faithful heart that sin shall finally be conquered. He is, indeed, **king of righteousness.**

**King of peace.** We are reminded of the "Prince of Peace" in Isa. 9:6. It is a hope that will not die. There must be some other way of settling these disputes between nations than the ever-growing horror of war's destruction. But men do not realize how high is the price of peace; that the roots of war go deep; that failure to deal openly and resolutely with these roots will only provoke more wars. The peace for which we seek is not merely the outward absence of open war, for peace may disguise a no less bitter conflict. The peace that we really want is peace of conscience, when we shall be freed from restless torment within. The discovery of that peace alone can make us peacemakers, release our energies to destroy the enmity between men.

**3. Reliance upon Ancestry.**—This verse is the core of the stumbling block referred to above (see on vss. 1-3). Surely the writer does not mean that Melchizedek is an immortal priest!

4 Now consider how great this man *was,* unto whom even the patriarch Abraham gave the tenth of the spoils.

5 And verily they that are of the sons of Levi, who receive the office of the priesthood, have a commandment to take tithes of the people according to the law, that is, of their brethren, though they come out of the loins of Abraham:

6 But he whose descent is not counted from them received tithes of Abraham, and blessed him that had the promises.

4 See how great he is! Abraham the patriarch gave him a tithe of the spoils. 5 And those descendants of Levi who receive the priestly office have a commandment in the law to take tithes from the people, that is, from their brethren, though these also are descended from Abraham. 6 But this man who has not their genealogy received tithes from Abraham and blessed him who

---

shadowy intimations of unseen and timeless realities. He is not prepared to go all the way with Philo and his school in permitting history to evaporate into mere representations of reality, for he focuses attention upon the radical significance of Jesus' human experience; and man's apprehension of the unseen does not depend on any innate potentiality (Logos), but upon an objective living way to God opened up by Jesus as the perfect priest.

4. In vss. 4-10 the interest is not in Abraham but in the Levitical priesthood. The author has already mentioned Abraham (6:13-14), and he will laud his faith with considerable detail in 11:8 ff., 17 ff., both times without depreciation. He begins with a contrast between Abraham and Melchizedek because it is implicit in the Genesis text. **See how great he is! Abraham the patriarch gave him a tithe of the spoils.** Our English translations do not quite reproduce the emphasis of the Greek. The KJV comes closest with its **even the patriarch,** for the idea seems to be, "To whom Abraham gave a tenth of the spoils, yes, I mean Abraham the revered patriarch"; the word patriarch has the place of emphasis in the sentence.

5-6. That the writer is really interested in the Levites appears in vs. 5. The transition is cleverly made. **Tithes,** paid by Abraham in this instance, are the perquisites of the Levites who tithe their brethren, also descendants of Abraham, and this is according to the commandment of the law. The word **tithes** enables the writer to introduce three ideas—Levites, law, and descendants of Abraham—all of which he will amplify shortly. Vs. 6 catches up two points which he will have us remember now that the transition to

---

Yet he seems to say just that. If Melchizedek is the eternal priest, what advantage does Christ have in his eternal priesthood (cf. vss. 24-25)?

But the writer is saying something both profound and pertinent. The Levitical priesthood was validated by its ancestry. No intruder could serve. This would be the principal objection to the priesthood of Christ: he was no Levite (cf. vs. 14). But Melchizedek was a "priest of the most high God" (vs. 1) and was without ancestry of any sort!

Far more significant than ancestry is divine appointment. What God can do and does for a human life is much more fateful than what one receives by inheritance. Heredity is not to be despised. But you cannot explain the greatest characters in history by analysis of their heredity; nor, indeed, by their early training. There is something unpredictable about great men. This is especially true of the servants of the most high God.

We think of John the Baptist's word on this point, "Do not begin to say to yourselves, 'We have Abraham as our father'; for I tell you, God is able from these stones to raise up children to Abraham" (Luke 3:8). Any human institution, however sacred and important in its origin, however it may once have enjoyed the divine favor, may become a center of idolatry. When it no longer serves the purpose of God, when it stands in his way, it is ready for judgment. This is true even of the ministry, even of the church itself. It was true of God's chosen people, of the Levitical priesthood, of the law, of the sabbath. The Bible has many accounts of such judgments. This is the real strength of our writer's argument—it is by God's appointment that our Lord is a priest.

**4-10. *The Priesthood of Levi and Melchizedek.***—The writer now begins the contrast between Jesus and the Levitical priesthood which is to form the heart of his epistle. He

**7** And without all contradiction the less is blessed of the better.

**8** And here men that die receive tithes; but there he *receiveth them,* of whom it is witnessed that he liveth.

**9** And as I may so say, Levi also, who receiveth tithes, paid tithes in Abraham.

**10** For he was yet in the loins of his father, when Melchisedec met him.

had the promises. **7** It is beyond dispute that the inferior is blessed by the superior. **8** Here tithes are received by mortal men; there, by one of whom it is testified that he lives. **9** One might even say that Levi himself, who receives tithes, paid tithes through Abraham, **10** for he was still in the loins of his ancestor when Melchiz′edek met him.

---

Levites has been achieved through the word **tithes:** Melchizedek had **not their genealogy,** i.e., Levitical; and he not only tithed Abraham but *blessed* him, **blessed him who had the promises.** Again the Greek emphasis is on the beginning and the end of the sentence, i.e., a man unqualified genealogically from the Levitical standpoint blessed the man who had the promises. The tithing is here quite incidental to the thought, having been stressed in vs. 5. Robinson reminds us that "blessing" in all primitive thought meant more than a kindly wish; it meant the impartation of a more-than-human power and sanction.

**7.** This verse is perhaps not strictly required by the argument. As in 6:16; 9:16, the writer introduces what every man knows from his own experience, betraying again his earnest, pastoral concern to bring his argument home to his readers. The Greek phrase translated, **and without all contradiction,** or more colloquially, **it is beyond dispute,** was a frequent expression in the papyri, and our "it goes without saying" or "everybody knows" reproduces the thought. **The inferior is blessed by the superior** is also without any difficulty, although, as noted above, blessing does not quite carry for us the force of the primitive idea.

**8-10.** Vs. 8 contrasts the mortality of the earthly priests who receive tithes (Abraham and Levi are long since dead and their successors also die) with the immortality of the one true priest. The point is derived from vs. 3 but looks ahead to the quotation from Ps. 110:4, which will be introduced in vss. 17, 21. The thought is basic to the contrast between Melchizedek (Christ) and the Levites, and its relevance here will be seen as the chapter develops. The author must now definitely commit himself, as he has already done by implication, to the proposition that the priestly acts of Melchizedek when he met Abraham meant that Levi himself, and so the Levitical priesthood, were subordinated thereby. His argument, based on the assumption that an ancestor represents all his descendants, is that since Isaac was yet unborn (Gen. 21:1-3) and therefore all Isaac's descendants, when Abraham gave tithe to Melchizedek, therefore **Levi himself** [the direct descendant of Isaac], **who receives tithes, paid tithes through Abraham.** The phrase which begins this remarkable sentence, **one might even say,** is usually interpreted as indicating that our writer was not unaware of the dubious character of his argument here. But this phrase, like so many others used in Hebrews, was a literary convention frequent with Philo and probably should not be pressed to mean that the writer was unsure of the validity of his argument. He knew, of course, that Levi was not present in the flesh on the historic occasion he is interpreting, and that his argument is of a slightly different kind from that developed directly from the persons in Gen. 14:17-20. It is this shift which is marked by the tentative opening phrase and not any doubts about the cogency of the argument itself.

---

shakes the confidence of those who prefer the Levitical priesthood by reminding them that in their own history there stood one outside their ancestry and superior to the Levites. With apt skill he traces this contrast back as far as Abraham, to whom the promises were given, and in whose ancestry the Jewish people had

such confidence that even Paul had to refer to the Gentile Christians as "men of faith who are the sons of Abraham" (Gal. 3:7). Abraham gave tithes to Melchizedek and in turn was blessed by him. Thus on two grounds Abraham recognized that he was in the presence of a greater than himself. Even the priests of the

11 If therefore perfection were by the Levitical priesthood, (for under it the people received the law,) what further need *was there* that another priest should rise after the order of Melchisedec, and not be called after the order of Aaron?

12 For the priesthood being changed, there is made of necessity a change also of the law.

11 Now if perfection had been attainable through the Levit'ical priesthood (for under it the people received the law), what further need would there have been for another priest to arise after the order of Melchiz'edek, rather than one named after the order of Aaron? 12 For when there is a change in the priesthood, there is neces-

---

11-14. A new step forward is now made. Although the name Melchizedek is to appear again (vss. 15, 17), it is **our Lord** (vs. 14) who now takes the center of the stage. Priesthood and the law are the subjects under discussion here. After his meticulous fashion the author has prepared the way for the introduction of this theme by noting that the Levitical perquisite of tithes was established by "a commandment in the law" (vs. 5). Any other priesthood must reckon, accordingly, with the sacred law itself. His treatment of the law, and the priesthood implemented by the law, is most illuminating. He begins not by challenging the law, but by challenging the legal priesthood. It failed to achieve the goal (perfection), not because it was evil in itself and certainly not because it was other than divinely ordained, but because, as the writer will show in detail, it was a weak, shadowy, imperfect institution by virtue of its earthly character. Here he briefly states that the imperfection of the Levitical priesthood, and incidentally the imperfection of the law as well (for under that priesthood the people received the law), was proved, as anyone can see, by the establishment of another priesthood of a different kind. **For when there is a change in the priesthood, there is necessarily a change in the law as well.** The almost casual way in which the law is disposed of (vss. 18-19) makes it certain that the readers were not in danger of reverting to Jewish legalism; else a more detailed argument

---

Levites who were **still in the loins** of Abraham recognized the superior status of Melchizedek.

11-14. *A New Priesthood, a New Law.*—The author is a man of bold thought, as was Paul. He is challenging the validity of the whole Levitical priesthood and of the law that inevitably belonged to it. He is saying that its day is over and that Jesus Christ, the eternal priest, has now replaced the old covenant. We must never lose sight of the incarnate power which enabled, which compelled him to take this daring step—a step that amounted to nothing less than a thorough religious revolution. Beneath this formal argument, which seems highly artificial to modern minds, we need to see the strong influence and the mighty working of Jesus. That is what is pertinent to our day.

For the devout Jew the law was sacred. It was that which set his people apart from all the Gentiles. It was Israel's reason for existence. Attack the law and you threatened Israel with destruction and disintegration. It is difficult for us to feel the pious horror with which the Jewish leaders must have regarded the growth of Christianity, and the intense bitterness with which they looked on such writers as Paul and the author of Hebrews. It was to add to their political degradation the destruction of that

faith around which all hope of their restoration was gathered. It was the spelling out of their nation's doom.

In almost equally high regard was the priesthood, **for under it the people received the law.** These words can scarcely mean that the priesthood preceded the law, for it was the written law that established the priesthood. But the priests were the guardians of the law, administered its penalties, interpreted it, taught it to the people, and were set aside to fulfill its demands at the altar. Through the law the priests were on the Godward side of the people: they were to bring God and the people together. They were to make sacrifices for the sins of the people and so to remove the stains of impurity that would keep the people from God. All that God meant to the people was vested in the priesthood. Their hopes of what God would do for them lay in this ancient institution.

What had gone wrong with it? Why had it failed? People gathered on the great and solemn Day of Atonement while the high priest entered the holy of holies. It was a moment of hushed expectancy. But when the day's ceremony was over, old sins kept returning, and if a man took his experience in dead earnest, his conscience was more tormented than healed. The

13 For he of whom these things are spoken pertaineth to another tribe, of which no man gave attendance at the altar.

14 For *it is* evident that our Lord sprang out of Juda; of which tribe Moses spake nothing concerning priesthood.

15 And it is yet far more evident: for that after the similitude of Melchisedec there ariseth another priest,

sarily a change in the law as well. 13 For the one of whom these things are spoken belonged to another tribe, from which no one has ever served at the altar. 14 For it is evident that our Lord was descended from Judah, and in connection with that tribe Moses said nothing about priests.

15 This becomes even more evident when another priest arises in the likeness of Mel-

---

would be required. Priesthood is everything for our author and he seems to say that the law itself was given to implement priesthood (vs. 11). He must deal with the law because of its intimate relation to this institution, but the change of priesthood, once established, inevitably means the **change in the law as well.** Paul taught that the law was an episode in the divine dealings with men, and our author's view that the law was neither the original nor the final word of God to men is in harmony, to this extent, with Paul's teaching. But the differences between them are greater than the similarities, for Hebrews views the law solely as enforcing the cult, not in its moral aspects, and as foreshadowing the perfect revelation in Jesus, not as convincing men of their moral inadequacy and their consequent dependence upon faith alone. The priesthood of Christ is therefore not rendered illegal because he came from the tribe of Judah, a tribe which furnished no priests under the law. On the contrary, the legal priesthood is displaced by the new priesthood and the law along with it. The point is that the new order—it was also older— antiquates both the law and the legal priesthood. It is worth noting that the writer knows from Christian tradition that Jesus was reckoned as from the tribe of Judah.

15-19. These verses prepare the way for Ps. 110:4, which has been in the writer's mind from the beginning of the chapter. They add nothing new to the argument but much

---

whole business was too earthly. It was only shadow, not reality. Surely there must be a better way. The writer of Ps. 110 must have realized that. If the old law and the old priesthood were satisfactory, **if perfection had been attainable** by that means, **what further need would there have been for another priest to arise after the order of Melchizedek, rather than one named after the order of Aaron?**

When the priesthood is changed, **there is necessarily a change in the law as well.** What could this mean? That the whole law was set aside? Then why is the argument based on the priesthood of Melchizedek, relying as it had to on Gen. 14:17-20? As Calvin observed, in the law we find "many remarkable sentences by which we are instructed as to faith, and as to the fear of God. None of these were abolished by Christ, but only that part which regarded the ancient priesthood." [4] Jesus himself had said: "Think not that I have come to abolish the law and the prophets; I have come not to abolish them but to fulfill them. For truly, I say to you, till heaven and earth pass away, not an iota, not a dot, will pass from the law until all is accomplished" (Matt. 5:17-18). If the whole law were abolished, why should such

[4] *Hebrews*, p. 167.

pains be taken to establish the validity of Christ's priesthood?

It was the old priesthood that was doomed, and whatever law it required. Divinely ordained though it had been, sacred to the devout as it always was, it came under God's judgment because it had failed his purpose. When the new covenant was given, even the tribe of Levi was passed by. **For it is evident that our Lord was descended from Judah.** The repudiation of the old priesthood was complete.

15-19. *The Revolutionary New Law.*—Another priest arises. This is the tone of all N.T. preaching. Something new has happened. God has spoken, has done a mighty work. The Christ has lived, died, and has risen from the grave. This was the good news which the early church proclaimed. They did not offer primarily a speculation; that would not be good news. Something had happened which was the fulfillment of their age-long faith. "This is that which" (Acts 2:16) became almost a formula of Christian preaching. In Jesus Christ, God has spoken and fulfilled what he began in the days of old.

Our author is in the very center of this movement. He does not say much about fulfillment, however. He emphasizes revolutionary change

16 Who is made, not after the law of a carnal commandment, but after the power of an endless life.

17 For he testifieth, Thou *art* a priest for ever after the order of Melchisedec.

18 For there is verily a disannulling of the commandment going before for the weakness and unprofitableness thereof.

chiz'edek, 16 who has become a priest, not according to a legal requirement concerning bodily descent but by the power of an indestructible life. 17 For it is witnessed of him,

"Thou art a priest for ever,
after the order of Melchiz'edek."

18 On the one hand, a former commandment is set aside because of its weakness

---

to our appreciation of the author, for vs. 16 is one of the great sentences in Hebrews and indeed in the N.T. Limited as he is by the formal and to us rather artificial character of his argument, his thought from time to time overflows it. Christ is **a priest, not according to a legal requirement concerning bodily descent but by the power of an indestructible life.** The authority of this priest is not prescriptive but personal. And this we know from the scripture, witnessing as it does, **Thou art a priest for ever, after the order of Melchizedek.** A rhetorically balanced sentence (vss. 18-19), well translated **on the one hand,**

---

rather than continuity. The law is set aside and the day of the old priesthood is past. This is evident by the mere appearance of a new priest, not after the order of Aaron, but **in the likeness of Melchizedek.** The priest has come and brought with him a new law. When he arrives on this earthly scene, the old custom is dead.

The interpreter may be tempted to reduce this momentous change to an instance of a general law. The general law of course is valid: "New occasions teach new duties, time makes ancient good uncouth." [5] To which the Christian objects that it is God who moves in history. There comes an hour when one can say of the days of "ignorance" that "God overlooked" them—"but now . . ." (Acts 17:30); and these hours come not simply because men grow tired of the old or are idly curious to find some new thing, but because God speaks a new word. A new personality appears and his very coming quietly announces that an old order has passed. Christ's annulment of the old law cannot be reduced to a mere process of moral evolution. This is *sui generis*. It stands unique in human history. Jesus the priest arrives; the old priesthood is ended.

What were the specific weaknesses of the old covenant? These are set forth in a series of vivid contrasts which also serve to enhance the eternal priesthood of the Son. The old priesthood rested on a **legal requirement concerning bodily descent.** The one condition of becoming a priest was to belong to the tribe of Levi and the family of Aaron. It is true that gross infidelities were punished by removal from the priesthood (cf. Lev. 10:1-9; I Sam. 2:12-17, 27-36). But in general, men were admitted by virtue of their birth. The plan had advantages:

[5] Lowell, "The Present Crisis."

a son born in a priest's home was trained from childhood. But it had its serious defects: whatever his inclinations or personal gifts, however far his own heart was from God and however meager his religious interest, he still acceded to the office of priest. What if ministers were chosen on the same basis today? Such are the failures of a law that seeks to prescribe by statute the invisible things of the spirit, the affections of the heart.

But one has come whose validation is **by the power of an indestructible life.** The power of Jesus is no longer a speculation. It is clearly written in history. He said, "I, when I am lifted up from the earth, will draw all men to myself" (John 12:32). And he has been doing just that ever since. Whenever in the long history of the church new reforms have broken the encrusted custom of lifeless men, it has been because someone has had a fresh encounter with Jesus. Whenever new life renovates the church, Jesus is alive and at work. In the name of Jesus what wonders have been wrought! A Francis of Assisi releases the power of unselfish love and the old ways suddenly appear shabby and cheap. A Grenfell goes to Labrador and a Schweitzer to Africa, and all the world of fretful, self-seeking men feel rebuke within themselves. By the power of Jesus men have built hospitals for the sick, provided the homeless with shelter, freed the slaves, established free governments; have left home, comfort, and safety to carry the gospel to unknown lands. By the power of Jesus men of leprous and foul tastes have been made clean, dishonest men have been led to the truth, weaklings have been made strong, hard hearts have been melted into tenderness. See them: a mighty army that no man can number, singing, "All hail the power of Jesus' Name!"

19 For the law made nothing perfect, but the bringing in of a better hope *did;* by the which we draw nigh unto God.

20 And inasmuch as not without an oath *he was made priest:*

and uselessness 19 (for the law made nothing perfect) ; on the other hand, a better hope is introduced, through which we draw near to God.

20 And it was not without an oath.

---

... on the other, serves to sum up the contrast already drawn between the weak and futile former commandment (for the law made nothing perfect) and the better hope through which we attain the goal of all religion, drawing near to God.

20-25. But can we be sure that it is really God to whom this priest gives us access? Yes, we can be sure, for while earthly priests took their office without an oath, our priest has behind his ministry the divine guarantee, as the psalm again proves. This makes Jesus the surety of a better covenant (διαθήκη) . Here is introduced for the first time a word which is to play an important role in the subsequent thought (cf. chs. 8–9) . It would be

---

Paul speaks for all of them, "The love of Christ controls us" (II Cor. 5:14) .

Even those who fly from him cannot escape him. Their frantic efforts to deny him betray that he has become their conscience. Those who blaspheme him find that in their violent hatreds he is still present. Our institutions shake in fear lest they fall, thereby acknowledging his power. His judgment has become the conscience of the race, and however much men love darkness, they can never quite succeed in banishing or forgetting that light. They nailed him to a tree and watched him die. When the last cry was silent, they breathed more easily: this troubler of Israel was now out of the way. But the grave could not contain him. He was strong enough to subdue death.

This was and is the power of an indestructible life. How blind men are when they refuse it and cling instead to a comfortable institution, comfortable because old and familiar! How vastly superior Christ is to an old priesthood whose only claim to office was ancestry!

The former commandment is set aside because of its weakness and uselessness. These are strong words. But in our hearts we have known their truth. A commandment may show us the upward way, but impart no strength for the rugged climb. A commandment may make our duty plain, yet awaken no love to do our duty. A commandment may threaten us with fearful penalties, yet leave our hearts unchanged. A commandment may plunge us deep into despair, and leave us there unaided and alone. A commandment may widen the gulf between God and man. Paul said, "When the commandment came, sin revived and I died" (Rom. 7:9) . It may do nothing to bridge the gap. Even the commandment to love God is weak until there is a self-imparting that kindles our love.

In the same way, the commandment for the

priestly order and the ritual of O.T. sacrifice could not bring men to God. Of course, in the long history of the priesthood there were high priests who must have come from the presence of God dumb with amazement, humbled by what they had seen, and kindled to new love. Certainly among the people who worshiped, many eager hearts could sing, "Oh God, thou art my God" (Ps. 63:1) . But such priests and people were moved by more than earthly symbol. They had by faith passed beyond the shadow to the reality of God's presence. Of and by itself the ritual could cleanse no conscience, impart no peace, bring no soul into the presence of God.

But now we have a better hope ... , through which we draw near to God. No longer need men rely on the blood of slain animals. The priest has offered not a victim but himself, the stainless Son of man. He is able to declare the forgiveness of God, a forgiveness that suffers as it loves; indeed, suffers because it loves. This is a forgiveness that is convincing, that is genuine, that satisfies. With the forgiveness comes the assurance of God's power that we shall not finally fall. "For if, when we were enemies, we were reconciled to God by the death of his Son, much more, being reconciled, we shall be saved by his life" (Rom. 5:10) . Here is not the dreadful ordinance of a God of wrath, but a mercy more tender than a mother's. Christ has enabled weak, despairing men to lift their heads in pride and hope. He has enabled them to say, "Beloved, now are we the sons of God, and it doth not yet appear what we shall be: but we know that, when he shall appear, we shall be like him; for we shall see him as he is" (I John 3:2) . In that hope we can draw near to God.

20-22. *Jesus, the Surety of God's Promise.—* Philo objects strenuously that the unchangeable God may not be conceived of as taking an

21 (For those priests were made without an oath; but this with an oath by him that said unto him, The Lord sware and will not repent, Thou *art* a priest for ever after the order of Melchisedec:)

22 By so much was Jesus made a surety of a better testament.

23 And they truly were many priests, because they were not suffered to continue by reason of death:

---

21 Those who formerly became priests took their office without an oath, but this one was addressed with an oath,

"The Lord has sworn

and will not change his mind,

'Thou art a priest forever.' "

22 This makes Jesus the surety of a better covenant.

23 The former priests were many in number, because they were prevented by

---

better not to translate it here ("covenant" or "testament") because the author uses it, giving us little help as to the meaning he will give it, only in order to pave the way for the later treatment. The connection of thought seems to be that the permanence of Christ's priesthood guaranteed by the divine oath ensures a better διαθήκη. Vss. 23-24 repeat and slightly amplify the points already made in vs. 8. Again the writer is gathering up the

---

oath. He argues that every promise of the Eternal is an oath of the most solemn kind and needs nothing in addition. He therefore regards all reference to the oaths of God as an anthropomorphism. And indeed we may rest content with that explanation. Does it not mean simply that God stoops to our way of speaking in order that we may hear and understand and believe? It is as though he were underscoring what he has to say. It is as though he were insisting, "My words you may not accept. Doubt may infect you and weaken your faith. But this 'oath' you must believe. My very nature is bound up with it."

We are reminded here that priests took their office by heredity. No oath of God lay behind their character or their office. They were not certainly to be depended upon as faithful priests. They might themselves stand in the way of the believer seeking access to God. But in the case of our priest it is different. Relying on Ps. 110, the author argues that the priesthood of the Son was established with an oath. God could depend on Jesus. There was nothing temporary about this priesthood. It would endure to the end of the ages. This was God's pledge.

When a man of modest means takes on a financial obligation and a friend of strong financial position becomes his surety, he is more sure of himself. Others trust him and depend upon him. This is the only use of the word surety in the N.T. The thought is not that Jesus becomes our surety before God. The position is reversed. Jesus is God's surety to us! Certainly the superiority of Jesus as a guarantee does not depend on the interpretation of Ps. 110. By all that Jesus was and is, by all the clean strength of the Man, by all the deep wisdom of his teaching, by all the completeness of his

sacrifice, Jesus is the guarantee of God to man. He is himself God's pledge that the covenant will not be broken. "What more can he say than to you he hath said?" [6]

23-25. *The Eternal Priesthood of Christ.*—The old priesthood was carried on by men under sentence of death: they were prevented by death from continuing in office. But is not this a good rather than an evil? Historically, has not growth depended on the fact that new men come into office? Who would want an immortal Manasseh? His fifty-five evil years were long enough. Let him die. Let Amon have his two years and pass away, that the righteous Josiah may come to the throne. The institution can preserve the strength and wisdom of the past. Let not one man continue in office too long, lest the pride of power corrupt him.

All this the writer must have known. Why, then, did he object to a changing priesthood? Because all priests were weak men in that they were subject to death? But Jesus died too. The contrast between the changing and the permanent is made convincing only by contrasting the character of the Levitical priesthood even at its best with the character of Jesus. What were the advantages of Jesus, the abiding priest?

He holds his priesthood permanently, because he continues for ever. His humanity, the obedience he learned, his sympathy with our sufferings, the temptations he endured, are abiding elements in his nature. The memories of Gethsemane and Calvary are not lost. Once he was able to sympathize with our weaknesses (4:15). That sympathy he keeps, world without end. Any change in office would be a fatal loss. "Jesus Christ is the same yesterday and today and forever" (13:8).

He is able for all time to save. What does

[6] "How firm a foundation."

24 But this *man*, because he continueth ever, hath an unchangeable priesthood.

25 Wherefore he is able also to save them to the uttermost that come unto God by him, seeing he ever liveth to make intercession for them.

death from continuing in office; 24 but he holds his priesthood permanently, because he continues for ever. 25 Consequently he is able for all time to save those who draw near to God through him, since he always lives to make intercession for them.

---

thought to focus it directly upon the ministry of our priest. The permanence of this ministry is the idea (**able for all time . . . , since he always lives**) that runs through these verses. The KJV, **to the uttermost,** is dear to many hearts and is not foreign to the writer's thought, but permanence is clearly central. Because Christ is permanently priest he is able to save those **who draw near to God through him** because **he always lives to make intercession for them.** The function of earthly priests was to bear men up to God in intercession. In the heavenly realm angels, especially Michael, were regarded as intercessors for men. Our author has no place for any figure other than that of the great high priest Jesus, the Son of God.

---

our author mean by the word **save?** Sometimes the great words of our vocabulary suffer an unhappy fate. They have been used so frequently and so thoughtlessly, they have been so batted about, that they have become hard words, the lifeblood of reality long since squeezed out of them. The word "saved" needs to be saved for better use. What does it mean? Safety always implies a danger and the meaning of salvation is strictly proportional to that danger.

He saves us from all that separation from God means. No language can do justice to that danger. To cut ourselves off from all light, and from every hope of light, and to choose darkness, is separation from God. To lose our moral stars, so that we call good evil and evil good, is separation from God. To lose all hope of the triumph of good and to expect the complete victory of evil is separation from God. To live in a world of death, to know the black shadow of futility falling across every sunlit person and deed in our world, to say, "I believe in everlasting destruction and a universal ruin to which the whole creation moves," is separation from God. To live in a loveless world, where the love of the home, the love of neighbor, the love of little children is dead, is separation from God. To be lost in the original sense of the word, lost as a sheep far from the fold not knowing which way home lies, lost as a little child not knowing where shelter is, lost as a sailor at sea with no stars or compass to guide him, not knowing which way port lies, this is what separation from God means. From all this Jesus saves us by providing access to God.

He saves us from the persistent defeat of sin, the guilt and the pollution of the past. Old guilt, the sin that cannot be undone, the "hell of the irrevocable" as Josiah Royce once called

it, is a heavy burden for any man to carry. And we bear that burden whether we are frank enough to confess our sins or not. Old habits have a deadly effect. Some of them can be thrown off: it takes moral heroism and an immense effort of will. But most of them, our prejudices, our evil ways of thinking, the pretensions of our pride, are so much a part of us that we cannot be freed from them until we are thoroughly exposed to a white light. To find real forgiveness, to know the strange power of a love that will not let us go, and to know a new sense of cleanness within, this is what it is to be "saved."

How does he save us? First, by exposing us. Until we drop all our stuffy pretenses, until the rags of our own self-esteem are torn from us, and we stand naked and trembling before the light, we cannot be saved. Second, he saves by bringing to us a forgiveness that satisfies— yes, that satisfies divine justice. Any other forgiveness would not satisfy even us, would not heal our wounds. A lenient forgiveness which passes over the sin in carelessness is really a conniving with evil. And this is precisely what the really penitent sinner cannot accept. No forgiveness will satisfy or cleanse us except it suffer. Someone must be "wounded for our transgressions, . . . bruised for our iniquities" (Isa. 53:5). He saves us, in the third place, by the power of his dwelling in us. If Christ lives in us and we in him, as the vine and the branches live in each other, we can but know the power of his life in us. Finally, he saves us by his intercession (see below).

He saves **those who draw near to God through him.** We need to attend carefully the words **through him.** Certainly some who hear these words become restless. It is all right to **draw near to God through Jesus.** But if people

26 For such a high priest became us, *who is* holy, harmless, undefiled, separate from sinners, and made higher than the heavens;

27 Who needeth not daily, as those high priests, to offer up sacrifice, first for his own

26 For it was fitting that we should have such a high priest, holy, blameless, unstained, separated from sinners, exalted above the heavens. 27 He has no need, like those high priests, to offer sacrifices daily,

---

**26-28.** The concluding verses, "a triumphant little summary" (Moffatt), "a little hymn" (Windisch), serve to emphasize the contrast between Jesus and the Levitical priesthood. It is not his human experience and sympathy which are stressed here (cf. 2:9 ff., 17 ff.; 4:15; 5:7 ff.) but, in contrast to earthly priests, his unsullied, exalted, timeless fitness (cf. 2:10) to function on our behalf. As a matter of fact, the high priest did not offer sacrifices daily (vs. 27), and the double sacrifice is prescribed only for the day of Atonement. Is this one of the errors of our author due to a theoretical knowledge of what went on in the temple? Actually it would be a matter of little importance for his argument. He uses priest and high priest interchangeably. Christ is *the priest, our high priest,* whose suffering was **once for all,** and who ministers timelessly because he is **a Son . . . made perfect for ever.**

---

undertake to come some other way, why try to exclude them? This putting of the question is itself a wrong emphasis. Jesus is not a barrier to any man—not the real Jesus. He breaks down the barriers, opens the way. He is the perfect priest for us only if we accept his services, only if we let him lead us by the hand, only if we take his yoke upon us and learn of him. There is an exclusive aspect in all such strictures in the N.T., but to dwell on the exclusiveness, or even to notice it, is to miss the wide-open door, the clear way, into the presence of God.

**Since he always lives to make intercession for them.** The **since** is important. It inevitably links the saving with the interceding. A Savior who did not follow his saving work with intercession would have forgotten us. It is by intercession that our salvation becomes personal, that we can say with Paul, he "loved me and gave himself for me" (Gal. 2:20).

There is a wide range in the quality of intercessory prayer: all the way from the mechanical prayer list, the prayer said from the sense of duty, to the prayer that wells up from the rich nature of a loving heart, that cares enough to follow prayer with sacrificial deed. The range and quality of our religious life are in part measured by the width and depth of our intercessory prayer.

John G. Paton, the missionary to the New Hebrides, wrote of his father's prayers,

I have heard that, in long after years, the worst woman in the village of Torthorwald, then leading an immoral life, but since changed by the grace of God, was known to declare, that the only thing that kept her from despair and from the hell of the suicide, was when in the dark winter nights she crept close up underneath my father's window,

and heard him pleading in family worship that God would convert "the sinner from the error of wicked ways and polish him as a jewel for the Redeemer's crown." "I felt," said she, "that I was a burden on that good man's heart, and I knew that God would not disappoint *him.* That thought kept me out of Hell, and at last led me to the only Saviour." [7]

"The prayer of a righteous man has great power in its effects" (Jas. 5:16). Consider, then, the power of the prayers of Jesus. There is not an idle word in them. He knows the best that we may become and prays for that. His prayers spring from his profound sympathy with us as men. They are given reality by his complete giving of himself on the Cross. If any of us knew, and many of us do know, that our names were borne in the loving concern of prayer by the best of men and women, would not a strange power be with us? Then how much greater the saving power when our names are borne before the throne of grace by the Son of man with all his clean strength, pleading that we shall not fail him!

**26-28. *The Superior Qualifications of Christ, the High Priest.*—**Our author now summarizes his argument, at the same time giving us hints of new developments which he will carry on in chs. 9–10. This is one of his favorite literary devices.

**It was fitting.** Christ as high priest is fitted to our human need. Study deeply and diligently the spiritual needs of man, and you will be more and more amazed at how Jesus Christ answers those needs. For our pride he is "gentle and lowly in heart" (Matt. 11:29). For our dark ignorance in matters of the spirit he is a

[7] *An Autobiography* (New York: Fleming H. Revell, 1889), p. 21.

sins, and then for the people's: for this he did once, when he offered up himself.

28 For the law maketh men high priests which have infirmity; but the word of the oath, which was since the law, *maketh* the Son, who is consecrated for evermore.

8 Now of the things which we have spoken *this is* the sum: We have such a high priest, who is set on the right hand of the throne of the Majesty in the heavens;

first for his own sins and then for those of the people; he did this once for all when he offered up himself. 28 Indeed, the law appoints men in their weakness as high priests, but the word of the oath, which came later than the law, appoints a Son who has been made perfect for ever.

8 Now the point in what we are saying is this: we have such a high priest, one who is seated at the right hand of the throne

We conclude our study of this famous chapter with a mingled sense of ancient, faraway days, and of intricate and antiquated modes of thought, however masterfully handled, and yet with an underlying conviction that a massive, valid, spiritual truth is wrapped up in these outmoded forms. From the shadowy days of Abraham, we are being told, men have longed for access to God. The institution of priesthood, with all its form and ceremony, its externality and superficiality, bears eloquent witness to the human yearning to draw near to God. Earthly priests stimulate, express, but never quite satisfy, the human hunger for God. But out of the same mists of antiquity a priesthood of personality is revealed. It is a priesthood independent of days and forms and prescribed genealogies, such as can be tabulated in codes of law. This is priesthood "after the order of Melchizedek." And this priesthood, foreseen by divine inspiration, is embodied in matchless reality in Jesus.

### 4. The Ministry of Jesus as High Priest (8:1–10:18)
#### a) He Ministers in the Heavenly Sanctuary, Not in the Earthly Copy (8:1-5)

The brief ch. 8 is important because it introduces the final stage in the argument of Hebrews (8:1–10:18). The author himself indicates the significance of what he now says by the initial word of the opening sentence, κεφάλαιον. In order to grasp the import

clear light. For our weakness he is our strong Savior. For our guilt he brings a convincing forgiveness. For our despair he offers us solid hope because he has gone within the veil.

> Thou, O Christ, art all I want;
> More than all in Thee I find.[8]

He is **holy.** This is not the ordinary word of the N.T. that is used in 3:1, which means "set aside to God" and in the plural is translated "saints" (cf. 6:10). But it means devout, pure, undefiled in his own right. Such a priest has an immense advantage over those who have need to offer sacrifices for their own sins first. He is **blameless,** i.e., innocent of all guilt. He is **unstained** by all his contact with the world. He had no need for ritual cleansing to remove ceremonial defilement, nor is any taint of evil upon him. He is **separated from sinners,** not by his want of sympathy nor by reason of his moral purity, but because he is **exalted above**

[8] Charles Wesley, "Jesus, Lover of my soul."

**the heavens.** He is now above the contagion of sin. **He has no need . . . to offer sacrifices . . . first for his own sins.**

Nor does he need to repeat the sacrifice for sins, for a sacrifice that has to be repeated confesses that it is inadequate. His sacrifice was **once for all when he offered up himself.** Of this more will be said later (cf. 9:11-14, 25-28; 10:11-14). God could not speak more clearly than through the perfect sacrifice of the Son.

**The word of the oath . . . came later than the law.** Ps. 110, where the oath is contained, was written after the giving of the law. It is interesting at this point to remember Paul's argument that the promise, which came first, was not annulled by the law which came later (cf. Gal. 3:17-18). The oath appointed the Son **who has been made perfect for ever,** perfect through his temptation, his suffering, and his obedience (cf. 4:15; 5:8-9).

**8:1-5. The Physical and the Spiritual.**—The interpreter of the Bible often does well to look for the hidden major premise which must be

of the chapter it is well to review briefly the course of his thought to this point, for he looks back as well as ahead, or better, he reveals the underlying "philosophy" of his thought. The Son, although superior to angels, who are ministering spirits to serve those who are to obtain salvation, was made lower than the angels "for a little while" that he might be a faithful and merciful high priest. Therefore hold fast to the Son. Moses was faithful, too, but as a servant, not as Son. Therefore do not fall into unbelief so fatal to the wilderness generation, for the rest promised them was not achieved because of their unbelief; that rest, as the psalm shows, is still available, although unbelief, which thwarted them, may thwart us even though we follow a superior leader. The recognition of the superiority of the Son should be our resource against unbelief, for we have "a great high priest who has passed through the heavens" into the very presence of God, and yet is fully equipped to sympathize with us through the discipline of temptation and suffering. Is it correct to call Jesus high priest? Yes, for he fulfills the requisite qualifications even of earthly priesthood, although his is a priesthood "after the order of Melchizedek." This kind of priesthood will be difficult to understand and to appropriate because the readers are sluggish. They must rouse themselves to full attention of mind and heart. Not to attend will mean irremediable disaster; there can be no second repentance if they deliberately reject the full presentation of salvation and turn their backs upon the values of salvation already experienced. But this is not to be expected, both because their past record is good and because of the divinely guaranteed salvation which assures hope and confidence. While Jesus did indeed fulfill the requirements of priesthood after the order of Aaron and Levi, he was obviously not a Levitical priest but a priest after the order of Melchizedek. This is a superior priesthood, as the Genesis incident shows. As a matter of fact, this superior priesthood sets aside the Levitical, the law which implements it, and the covenant itself. These are antiquated because they are imperfect. Jesus is the timeless, perfect priest.

It would seem that the movement of thought is directed toward the concluding paragraph of ch. 7, i.e., the fact that Jesus is the one and only true priest for us. True, but not the whole truth, says our author. His thought has been directed to another end: the character of the *ministry* of Jesus as priest. In order that he might expound the ministry it was necessary to validate the ministrant. This he has done, but the *ministry* itself has not been out of his mind for a moment. He now proceeds to develop this central theme.

**8:1.** The word κεφάλαιον has been variously translated as **sum,** "chief point," **the point,** and "pith" (Coverdale). It is, of course, from the Greek word meaning "head."

---

assumed if the argument is valid. It is the foundation on which the whole discussion rests. It is usually something that the writer takes for granted in his readers as not needing mention. This habit of bringing hidden assumptions to light is valuable in the study of any literature; it is especially important in the study of the Bible.

In this passage is hidden an assumption quite contrary to our whole modern way of thinking; the interpreter must bring it out clearly into the open. It is involved in the **point,** the nub of the whole argument. Our high priest is superior because he **is seated at the right hand of the throne of the Majesty in heaven** where the **true tent** is. Herein lies his superiority. Earthly priests **serve a copy and shadow of the heavenly sanctuary.** His priesthood is thereby much better than theirs.

What is taken for granted here? That the heavenly is better than the earthly; that it alone is the real; that earthly things have a shadowy, secondary existence; that our true home is in heaven. And this is just what the modern mind will not allow for a moment. We trust the solid realities of earth. We can see them, handle them, and in a measure control them. Our sciences are based upon them, and science is knowledge par excellence. Here is our true home if we are ever to have a home. The heavenly, if it exists at all, is uncertain and shadowy. There may be life after death, but we had better follow the safe course and make the most of life here and now. "One world at a time!" If heaven there is, earth is likely to be the best preparation for it. Many folk are like the character in an early twentieth-century novel who didn't believe any of the nonsense about religion, but went through the forms of it as a kind of insurance, just in case there should

2 A minister of the sanctuary, and of the true tabernacle, which the Lord pitched, and not man.

of the Majesty in heaven, 2 a minister in the sanctuary and the true tent[n] which is set

[n] Or *tabernacle*.

---

Its meaning here must be understood in the light of what has gone before, for the author himself says that the κεφάλαιον **in what we are saying** is about to be stated. **Sum,** in the sense of summary alone, is ruled out, for he does not summarize the preceding argument. He gives what he regards as the gist of it, undoubtedly with reference to what is to come. Is he also conscious of the rather intricate and abstruse nature of the argument just concluded? At any rate, he helps the reader to see what is vitally important in his thought to this point. The first verse repeats 1:3*b* in effect, but that verse was itself a preview of what the author has, in part at least, achieved.

2. It is this verse which points up **what we are saying . . . : A minister of the sanctuary, and of the true tabernacle, which the Lord pitched, and not man.** Again, this sentence does not seem very striking; what follows reveals the philosophy behind these words. We are subtly prepared, however, for the next stage in the author's thinking: the *place* where our priest ministers and the *nature* of his ministry. He is ready to move from the person of the priest to his ministry—this has been his intention from the start (cf. 1:3*b*). We note in passing that he is solely interested in the ancient σκηνή, the tent-tabernacle,

---

turn out to be something in it after all! Indeed, many modern philosophers specifically rule out of their thought any reference to what is beyond our experience. If they acknowledge a God at all, he is a God at work in the world of our experience, where we can study the laws of his working and predict him! Something of this mentality is in all of us, for it is the spirit of our times. It is quite contrary to the basic assumption of Hebrews.

It may well be that here and there through the epistle there are traces of the influence of Plato, by way of Philo; for Plato had taught the relative nonreality of the visible world. But this influence alone cannot explain our author. He belonged to the biblical tradition and biblical writers did not despise the physical, as did some of the Greeks and most of the Hindu philosophers. The latter had taught that evil inheres in matter and that sin is a contamination of the otherwise pure spirit of man by contact with the physical. Salvation was release from the material world, escape from the changing world of shadows to the unchanging world of pure being.

Biblical writers did not despise the material world. It was God's creation and therefore good. To be clothed with material bodies, to have our day set in the world of nature, was not an unhappy fate from which to escape. It was rather the provision of God's wisdom and his mercy. In contrast to some of the religious thought of the Greeks and the sacred books of the East, the Bible is an earthly book. The O.T. is concerned with crops and animals, houses and lands, wars and kingdoms, drought and pestilence, long life and death, having sons

and heirs: in short, with a full earthly life for God's people. The historical books contain not only the record of kings who did good or evil in the sight of the Lord, but stories of intrigue and counterespionage, military tactics, and the treatment of prisoners. In the O.T. we find the tender love story of Ruth, the tale of a captive maid who became queen of an empire; and a love song so unabashed in its imagery that modest churchmen of later centuries felt constrained to interpret it as allegory. Amos talked not merely about the neglect of God, but about injustice, the price of commodities, and large holdings of land. Isaiah condemned not only idolatry, but the foreign policy of his nation, the luxuries of the rich, and the gaudy apparel of idle women.

As for the N.T., our Lord spent little time talking about heaven. He took the commonplace things of small town and rural life and made them the vehicles of divine truth. He talked about stony ground, about pruning grapevines, about sheep that were lost, about the good places to fish, about the signs by which men made weather forecasts, about yeast that women kneaded into dough, about arrogant boys who thought they knew more than fathers, and fathers who waited heavyhearted for boys to return from the far country, about taxes and wages and debts good and bad, about table manners and courtesies to guests, and about a citizen's duty to his government. In not a single teaching of Jesus will you find him despising the physical world. On the contrary, he enjoyed it, used it, was at home in it. His critics objected bitterly to this attitude (Matt. 11:19). Paul dealt not only with faith and doctrine, but with

3 For every high priest is ordained to offer gifts and sacrifices: wherefore *it is* of necessity that this man have somewhat also to offer.

4 For if he were on earth, he should not be a priest, seeing that there are priests that offer gifts according to the law:

up not by man but by the Lord. 3 For every high priest is appointed to offer gifts and sacrifices; hence it is necessary for this priest also to have something to offer. 4 Now if he were on earth, he would not be a priest at all, since there are priests who

---

and that what went on in the temple is a matter of complete indifference to him. That σκηνή was the one commanded by the Lord; men "pitched" the later and derivative temples.

3. Priesthood on the earthly level requires sacrifices; the principle of sacrifice is eternally valid if men would draw near to God. It is not the principle but the performance which is inadequate on earth. And this performance is imperfect because of the weakness of the performers and especially, as will now be shown, because of the shadowy realm in which they perform.

4-5. But first he makes his point negatively. There is no place for Christ's ministry in the priestly system on earth where, according to the law, sacrifice is amply, and always imperfectly, provided by the succession and the multiplicity of priests. If Christ is to minister as priest, it must be in another realm. Here, and here alone, our author might be interpreted to mean that the priestly system was still in operation in the Jerusalem temple, for after A.D. 70, and the destruction of the temple, sacrifices ceased. This single verse cannot be pressed to mean this, however, since here and elsewhere the writer is interested only in the "ideal" of priesthood, not in its historical development. Vs. 5 gives the positive ground, scripturally proved, for **the point** in what he has been saying and is to say. **They serve a copy and shadow of the heavenly sanctuary; for . . . Moses was . . . instructed . . . , "See that you make everything according to the pattern . . . ."** The form

---

the pay of ministers, the attire of women in churches, the relations of husband and wife, and civil suits that Christians brought against each other before pagan magistrates.

To the eye of faith the world was a visible story of God's glory and wisdom. "The heavens declare the glory of God; and the firmament showeth his handiwork" (Ps. 19:1). "Ever since the creation of the world his invisible nature, namely, his eternal power and deity, has been clearly perceived in the things that have been made" (Rom. 1:20). Sin was not contamination by the physical. Sin took place in the spiritual nature of man, in the use of his freedom, where he was most Godlike. It was the physical world that was contaminated by the sin of man. Salvation did not consist in escape from the world, but in the restoration of man as a child of God. Here is at least one profound biblical teaching that sets Christianity apart from all other religions. Sin is the arrogant pretense of self-sufficiency; it dethrones God and sets the mighty little self in his place, so that we try to rule our own lives as well as those about us.

How has the sin of man changed God's order? Man was meant to enjoy the good things of the world, receiving them in humble thanks from

his Father. He was meant to use them in the service of God, to share them with his fellows as instruments of real community, and to honor God in all the conduct of his life. Instead, the sin of man has turned the good things of the world into a curse. The common life of man is enmity against God. When therefore we are warned, "Do not love the world or the things in the world" (I John 2:15), it is the world which man has contaminated that we are not to love. When Paul tells us of the warfare of the spirit and the flesh (cf. Rom. 7), the flesh is the body corrupted by the spiritual sin of man, and the spirit is the man of God's grace.

What, then, shall we make of the assumption that heaven is better, or the explicit assertion that earthly priests **serve a copy and shadow of the heavenly sanctuary?** Heaven is the presence of God; hell is his absence. The earthly tabernacle was deficient not because it was physical, but because God was not fully in it. God was not fully present just because of the sins of the men who ministered and worshiped there. It was **a copy and shadow** not because it was an earthly symbol, but because sinful man could not see what was symbolized; the symbol lost its meaning when it obscured the pattern. The heavenly priesthood and

5 Who serve unto the example and shadow of heavenly things, as Moses was admonished of God when he was about to make the tabernacle: for, See, saith he, *that* thou make all things according to the pattern showed to thee in the mount.

offer gifts according to the law. 5 They serve a copy and shadow of the heavenly sanctuary; for when Moses was about to erect the tent,[n] he was instructed by God, saying, "See that you make everything according to the pattern which was shown

[n] Or *tabernacle.*

---

is still negative, but the inference is positive. Instead of a direct statement that Christ is priest in the pattern sanctuary (he had no direct scripture for that; Christ is exalted and he is priest forever, but no single verse quite combines the two) the author uses Exod. 25:40 to establish the fact that the tabernacle was divinely intended to be patterned after the true sanctuary; but it could never be more than a copy and shadow of the pattern. That true sanctuary exists; every earthly sanctuary is at best a copy; Christ the Son is priest; he cannot function on earth; therefore his ministry is in the true sanctuary. This is the logic of his argument which he presents somewhat indirectly in vs. 5 because he must base it on scripture.

That this is **the point** of the entire argument may not be immediately apparent, but a little thought will show that it does indeed give meaning to the whole. It helps us to see why the writer began by emphasizing the divine person of the Son instead of the human Jesus; why he carried along this emphasis with earnest exhortations to hold fast to Jesus, always coupling the divine person with his human experience; why he interprets faith as the apprehension of unseen reality and as loyalty to it, an idea which will be amplified in ch. 11; why and how he can appreciate the earthly institution of priesthood and yet set it aside together with the law; and why he lays such stress on the mysterious figure of Melchizedek, only to leave him behind. The widespread prevalence of the two-world or two-story idea of reality, which comes to the most explicit expression in vss. 1-5, has been discussed in the Intro. (see pp. 583-87). The precise source from which the author derives it cannot be determined with mathematical accuracy. Plato's doctrine of ideas had permeated the whole Hellenistic world, and almost every type of thought was in some degree colored by it. Philo, whose method of interpreting scripture and whose Logos speculation offer so many parallels to Hebrews, is an obvious source. Yet the conception of the heavenly Jerusalem and the heavenly tabernacle was native to late Judaism, and the one source our author specifically cites is the O.T. Behind Judaism lie sources in Semitic religion which suggest the same concept. The two-world thinking was the atmosphere our author breathed, and we need not suppose any conscious source other than the O.T. passage he quotes. It should be remembered that he does not extend this

---

tabernacle were perfect because God was there. Its ministrant was the sinless Christ, his offering was the perfect sacrifice, the one which alone was well-pleasing in God's sight.

**According to the pattern . . . on the mountain.** In so far as the earthly tabernacle conformed to the pattern, it was not evil but good. It was God's provision. Its deficiency was not to be traced to God, or to the limitations of the physical world. Such an interpretation as this is necessary if we are not to assume that our writer was completely dominated by Platonic (Philonic) idealism, to the exclusion of all influence by O.T. beliefs (cf. Intro., p. 585); and it renders the verse capable of wide application. Not only the tabernacle, but all human achievements are sound only if they conform to

the pattern. The home is a place of happiness when it embodies God's purpose. The Christian ministry is a thing of joy and strength when it is completely sensitive to the guidance of God. Even our virtues turn to vices unless they are guided and informed by the grace of God. In the Sermon on the Mount Jesus was teaching no mere prudential virtue. For example, he did not teach us to love our enemies because that is the only way we can get the better of them, or because that is the only way of creating peace. We are to love our enemies because God is what he is (Matt. 5:45).

Heaven is the presence of God here and now, anywhere, any time. We wait eagerly for the "adoption as sons, the redemption of our bodies," just as "the whole creation has been

6 But now hath he obtained a more excellent ministry, by how much also he is the mediator of a better covenant, which was established upon better promises.

you on the mountain." 6 But as it is, Christ[o] has obtained a ministry which is as much more excellent than the old as the covenant he mediates is better, since it is enacted on

[o] Greek *he*.

---

idea to cover the whole range of sensual as opposed to spiritual reality, though he may well have held such a view. He concentrates on one reality, the heavenly sanctuary, because his purpose is not the development of a philosophy, but the religious significance of the true priest, Jesus.

### b) THE NEW PLACE OF SACRIFICE IMPLIES A NEW COVENANT AS THE SCRIPTURE PREDICTED (8:6-13)

As in ch. 7 the person of the true priest is set over against the persons who function as priests on earth, the Levites, and over against the law sustaining them, so in this chapter the work or function of the true priest is set over against the covenant underlying the whole religion. In chs. 9 and 10, covenant is combined with sacrifice, and the work of the true priest, Jesus, is presented in terms of these two concepts throughout the remainder of the formal argument. The author seems to view covenant in contrast to law just as he views the sacrifice of earthly priests in contrast to the sacrifice of the true priest. He never explicitly equates covenant with law, although he does say that "even the first covenant had regulations for worship and an earthly sanctuary" (9:1). What is clear is the shift in the argument from the person of Christ to the work of Christ as priest.

6. The logical connection of vs. 6 with vss. 1-5 would seem to be: Christ has been exalted to the right hand of the Majesty in heaven; as priest he must function by offering sacrifices, and he could not offer sacrifices on earth where the system excludes him; the earthly system is only a shadow of the heavenly reality, as Exod. 25:40 shows; therefore Christ functions as priest in the true sanctuary. The final clause is what we would expect in vs. 6. The writer has already established the reality of Christ's priesthood, however, and is now concerned with the nature of Christ's sacrifice (vs. 3). In order to validate his sacrifice it is necessary first to deal with the basis of sacrifice in general. Behind the law of sacrifice stood the covenant. Priest to law to covenant is the sequence, and he must show that the imperfection of earthly priests, the earthly law, and the first covenant is matched by the perfection of the true priest and the "more excellent . . . covenant" with its "regulations for worship" (9:1). The logic is a bit subtle, but from the author's point of view and in the context of the entire movement of thought it has validity. What does he mean by διαθήκη? The importance of the covenant idea both in Judaism and in early Christianity can hardly be overestimated. It was the word used (*berîth*) to characterize Judaism as a religion of moral obligations and moral choices. Other religions accepted their gods as a natural and inevitable necessity: Chemosh was the god of Moab, "had never been anything else, and could never be anything else" (Robinson). But Yahweh chose Israel as his people, and the people of Israel freely accepted the divine choice and

---

groaning in travail together until now" (Rom. 8:23, 22). The heaven beyond the grave is desirable only as the fulfillment of that which can never be fully achieved in this world. The hardheaded factualism of the modern mind is wrong, then, not because it is hardheaded and factual, but just because it is not factual enough. It does not deal openly with the fact of man's divine origin, his sin, and his destiny. Therein lies the basic source of our intellectual confusion. Our factualism lives in a world of copies and shadows just because it is incapable of seeing the real significance of our world, our common life, and our destiny as men. The physical world is sacramental. If men will not have it so, then the world becomes the vast graveyard of our hopes.

6-7. *The Old Covenant and the New.*—A better ministry, a better covenant, better promises. Why better? Did God deliberately withhold himself, offer the children of Israel a second best, then condemn them because they did not

7 For if that first *covenant* had been faultless, then should no place have been sought for the second.

better promises. 7 For if that first covenant had been faultless, there would have been no occasion for a second.

---

the obligations involved. Accordingly, Yahweh could disown Israel if they failed to keep his laws (cf. vs. 9c) and they, on their part, could turn from Yahweh and suffer the consequences. This view of covenant was closely bound up with the development of Judaism as an ethical monotheism.

Διαθήκη plays a comparatively minor role in the N.T. (cf. I Cor. 11:25; II Cor. 3:6, 14; Matt. 26:28; Mark 14:24), Hebrews being the writing that uses it most (vss. 6; 7:22; 9:15-17; 10:29; 12:24; 13:20 and in quotations vss. 8-10; 9:4, 20; 10:10), yet it furnished the name for the writings which were to become scripture for Christians, H KAINH ΔIAΘHKH, commonly translated "The New Testament," and the biblical basis for the new religion. In 9:15-17 διαθήκη clearly means will or testament (see below) and some commentators have tried to give it this meaning throughout Hebrews. The words **enacted on better promises** give some semblance of logic to this interpretation, but the emphasis throughout Hebrews—except for the *ad hominem* argument in 9:15-17—is on the divine enactment or provision for a new relationship between God and men rather than upon a last will and testament. The one doubtful point is whether the thought of mutual obligations, implied in covenant as an "agreement" between two parties, is uppermost in Hebrews. On the whole, the thought seems to be of a relationship initiated and carried through by God, which, to be sure, men may break, thus forfeiting their privileges. But the ancient idea of a "contract" or "binding agreement," with all the moral connotations implied, is not prominent. The writer has to set covenant over against covenant, the new over against the old, in terms of the will of God. God's will is gracious and the promises of the new covenant are better, but it is God's will, not man's acceptance of it, which dominates the thought. The word μεσίτης appears also in 9:15 and 12:24. It probably means the agent through whom God deals with men, through Christ as regards the new covenant, through Moses as regards the old. The role of this μεσίτης will depend on the meaning of covenant. If we stress the mutuality of the relationship involved in the covenant, then the μεσίτης might be the one who, so to speak, arbitrates the agreement between God and men. If, as seems more consonant with the writer's thought, the new covenant is revealed and guaranteed by the μεσίτης, then it means something like "surety" (cf. 7:22, ἔγγυος). As guaranteeing the διαθήκη, Christ is not the "middleman"; he is the divine Son who assures us.

7. Our author does not hesitate to brand the first covenant as less than perfect. It was not **faultless**. We are compelled to ask, "Whose was the fault?" Was it not God's fault if a covenant initiated by him was inadequate? The author, of course, does not contemplate

---

accept it? Did the prophets of Israel ever in the least apologize for their God? Was he deficient in his mercy, oversevere in his judgment? Why are these new promises better? Why should Christians discount the law? One O.T. writer could exclaim, "The law of the Lord is perfect, restoring the soul: the testimony of the Lord is sure, making wise the simple" (Ps. 19:7 ERV).

Could the writer mean that the new covenant brought forgiveness? But so did the old. The word "mercy" recurs throughout the O.T. Does he mean that the new covenant is more persuasive, appeals more to the heart, is more plainly written? That the new law was improved only because of its superior literary or artistic

quality? What could be more tender or more moving than the prophecy of Hosea? It is true that mere law does not win the heart and a ritual may become meaningless; but the old covenant warned against those very dangers. One thing is clear: there can be no need of grace without an honest confronting of the fact of our sin. The gospel of grace falls on deaf ears unless men are hungry for it, as witness many in our own day. It then becomes the answer to a question that has not been asked. God's way of reaching men seems to be an alternation between spectacular penalties for evil and the tender pleading of a lover. Both are and always will be essential. But if the stern alternative of the law is essential as the back-

8 For finding fault with them, he saith, Behold, the days come, saith the Lord, when I will make a new covenant with the house of Israel and with the house of Judah:

9 Not according to the covenant that I made with their fathers, in the day when I took them by the hand to lead them out of the land of Egypt; because they continued not in my covenant, and I regarded them not, saith the Lord.

8 For he finds fault with them when he says:
"The days will come, says the Lord,
when I will establish a new covenant
with the house of Israel
and with the house of Judah;
9 not like the covenant that I made with
their fathers
on the day when I took them by the hand
to lead them out of the land of Egypt;
for they did not continue in my covenant,
and so I paid no heed to them, says the
Lord.

---

such a question. The imperfection of the first covenant, like the imperfection of the law and the weakness of the earthly priesthood, was due to its shadowy, transient character; it always pointed to a better, just as a copy proves the existence of a thing copied. Scripture makes this evident in the quotation now to be used from Jeremiah. The writer indicates the primary meaning of the quotation before introducing it—i.e., it proves that the first covenant was not **faultless**—and this is the conclusion he will draw after making the citation (vs. 13).

**8-13.** Jer. 31:31-34 is introduced with the words, **For he finds fault with them when he says,** which seem to refer to **for they did not continue in my covenant** (vs. 9). The author does not relieve the people who proved untrue from responsibility (cf. 3:16 ff.), but his main point is the imperfection of the first covenant. The changes from the LXX—they do not alter the sense nor does Hebrews use them in the argument—are numerous enough to suggest the possibility that the quotation is from memory. As noted above, the idea of covenant as divinely initiated is strongly present in this quotation. The failure

---

ground of our receiving with joy the gospel of our forgiveness; if, as Paul said, "the law was our custodian until Christ came" (Gal. 3:24), is it the law which is now to be regarded as "obsolete," "ready to vanish away" (vs. 13)? Has God modified his moral demands? These are the questions that we must bring with us as in the following verses we find that notable passage from Jeremiah (31:31-34). What are the better promises?

**8-9. Out of Bondage.**—Throughout the O.T. the bondage in **the land of Egypt** is given high significance. It is "the rock whence ye were hewn," "the hole of the pit whence ye were digged" (Isa. 51:1 ASV). It was dramatic evidence of Israel's dependence upon the mercy of God. Repeatedly the prophets identified God as "the LORD thy God, which brought thee out of the land of Egypt, from the house of bondage" (Deut. 5:6). It was against the background of this mercy that the law was given and the tabernacle established. Israel's sin had been that of ingratitude (cf. Isa. 1:2-4). They had violated the covenant of their God, who had by his mercies

established them a nation and had led his people to security and peace. It was the breaking of this covenant that called for a better. It was as though God had said, "What do we do now that Israel has fallen backward?" The new covenant springs out of the resources of God, who does not acknowledge his defeat in human sin.

All of us have our Egypts. For some, Egypt is an unpromising background of home and early training. For others, Egypt is the bondage of an overt, blind betrayal of God. Again, Egypt is the place of defeat and shame. Or it may be a blinding sorrow which seems to close all doors and seal off every way of escape. Had we eyes to see, we too could join the song of Israel, "From Egypt's bondage come." Had we ears to hear, God would still be saying to us, "I . . . brought thee out of the land of Egypt, from the house of bondage" (Deut. 5:6). The mercies of God undergird us even when we know him not. The sin of man is always the sin of ingratitude. God has brought us safely on our way and in folly we leave the way.

**10** For this *is* the covenant that I will make with the house of Israel after those days, saith the Lord; I will put my laws into their mind, and write them in

**10** This is the covenant that I will make with the house of Israel after those days, says the Lord: I will put my laws into their minds, and write them on their hearts,

---

of **the house of Israel** . . . [and] **the house of Judah** to keep the covenant shows that it was not an entirely one-sided enactment from God to man, but involved mutual obligations, yet the new covenant springs from the purpose of God; there is no reason, humanly speaking, why Israel's failure to keep the old should have occasioned the new. This is the author's own idea of the covenant: it was God's plan irrespective of man's action. It was due to God's gracious purpose to give a better covenant "enacted on better promises." This is why he emphasizes only the fact that the new antiquates the old.

What distresses the modern student is our author's failure to make the most of this magnificent passage which is one of the high-water marks of the O.T. Taken by itself,

---

**10. The Better Promise.**—What, then, are the better promises? **I will put my laws into their minds.** An outward command can compel only outward obedience. The word may be spoken in stern tones. We shall then obey simply because the lawgiver is stronger than we are. We dread what he will do to us if we disobey, for he has power over us. But sheer power can never command the consent of the mind nor win the affections of the heart. Being made in the image of God, we are bound to ask the reason of the commandment. Why is it so? Until the commandment is written into our minds, until it wins the consent of reason, it is something foreign, therefore hostile and a thing to be secretly hated.

Robert Browning has drawn a faithful portrait of the worship of a god of sheer power in his sketch, "Caliban upon Setebos." Caliban is a dull, sensuous fellow who lives on a tropical island. His chief pleasure is to lie stretched out on the sand by the sea. There is one cloud on his horizon—his god, Setebos. Setebos has power and Caliban is afraid of him. So when Caliban thinks Setebos is watching, he tries to pretend that he is a very unhappy man, in the hope that his god will not be jealous of his happiness and will thus let him alone. As Caliban lies on the sand, he watches a procession of crabs moving past him to the sea. As he, a willful human being, treats these crabs, so he imagines God deals with human beings:

> He is strong and Lord.
> 'Am strong myself compared to yonder crabs
> That march now from the mountain to the sea;
> 'Let twenty pass, and stone the twenty-first,
> Loving not, hating not, just choosing so.
> 'Say, the first straggler that boasts purple spots
> Shall join the file, one pincer twisted off;
> 'Say, this bruised fellow shall receive a worm,
> And two worms he whose nippers end in red;
> As it likes me each time, I do: so He.

To obey the decrees of mere force is to settle for formal obedience in merely external matters. But no law could possibly prescribe for every human situation. No man can be just by following a code. The law of justice must be written in his mind. Only then will he recognize what is just in the varied new occasions where no ancient pattern will quite fit. No man can love by outward regulation. For love that is outward only is hypocrisy of a vile sort. Love's delight is to discover new modes of expression, new forms of showing itself to surprise and delight the loved one. No code can create an honest man. No man is really honest until integrity is written in his mind. Until that happens he will be concerned only with the show of honesty.

This verse is at the heart of the Reformation. It is not enough that a priest or a hierarchy is the teacher of the law. Moral guidance we deeply need from our church. But when a priesthood undertakes to prescribe details of conduct, the new covenant is betrayed. The inwardness of this new covenant is fulfilled only in individual conscience and in personal responsibility. Jesus himself recognized this truth in the whole method and spirit of his moral teaching. "No longer do I call you servants, for the servant does not know what his master is doing; but I have called you friends" (John 15:15).

**And write them on their hearts.** Even the sinner sees the difference when goodness is "from the heart." We have known courteous folk whose pleasure was in courtesy. It has always seemed hard to imagine them being discourteous, even under the most trying circumstance. We have known men whose honesty sprang from a strong integrity that had become part of the very fabric of their souls. We have known generosity that was glad, kindness that quickened other hearts with its joy. Perhaps the worst exhibition of Christian faith is the grim and joyless goodness that wears the look of

their hearts: and I will be to them a God,
and they shall be to me a people:

11 And they shall not teach every man
his neighbor, and every man his brother,
saying, Know the Lord· for all shall know
me, from the least to the greatest.

12 For I will be merciful to their unrighteousness, and their sins and their iniquities
will I remember no more.

and I will be their God,
and they shall be my people.

11 And they shall not teach every one his
fellow
or every one his brother, saying, 'Know
the Lord,'
for all shall know me,
from the least of them to the greatest.

12 For I will be merciful toward their iniquities,
and I will remember their sins no more.''

---

the Jeremiah passage seems to ignore entirely the priestly system so important for our author, and to present religion, in its purely spiritual aspects. The Mosaic law with its insistence upon code and conduct is set aside for a religion whose laws are written in the mind and on the heart. Obedience, the knowledge of God, and forgiveness of sins are still essential, but they are conceived in terms of inwardness. All this our author seems to ignore in the interest of making his one point: the new antiquates the old. He assumes that the new, like the old, will center in the priestly principle. On his behalf it must be said that he is quite unconscious of any misuse of the quotation. Religion without a priest and a sacrifice was simply unthinkable for him. Forgiveness, which is the final note in the Jeremiah quotation, implies sacrifice to his mind, for "without the shedding of blood there is no forgiveness of sins" (9:22), and although this is a requirement of the law, he never questions its essential validity. As we shall see, he is not proposing a

---

strained effort. The law of God is not obeyed until we can sing with the psalmist, "O how love I thy law!" (Ps. 119:97.) Aristotle once observed with clear insight:

He is perfected in Self-Mastery who not only abstains from the bodily pleasures but is glad to do so; whereas he who abstains but is sorry to do it has not Self-Mastery. . . . (As Plato observes, men should have been trained straight from their childhood to receive pleasure and pain from proper objects, for this is the right education.) [9]

Only when men find their joy in doing the will of God has the law of God been written **on their hearts.**

**I will be their God, and they shall be my people.** This is the fulfillment of the covenant, the purpose of the gospel, the crowning if always conditioned promise of the Scriptures. When this comes to pass, the judgment is stayed, the requirement is met, God's purpose is achieved, salvation is complete, man is redeemed, evil is overcome. This is the goal of all our striving, the fulfillment of our desires and aspirations, the answer to all our prayers.

**11-12. The Christian Knowledge of God.—They shall not teach.** This is not a disparagement of Christian teaching, for that is precisely what our writer is doing throughout his epistle.

[9] *Nicomachean Ethics* II. 3.

Our Lord came teaching and charged his disciples to go and teach. But teaching has its limitations. It can bring a pupil so far and no farther. Let no man think that he knows God if he believes all his opinions about God to be correct. Likely he has a new idolatry, his own correct opinions! Important as clear thinking is, it is not enough. We never know the members of our families merely by thinking about them. Knowledge of persons always involves faith, i.e., a trustful, personal commitment of vital interests to the beloved. Where no vital interests are at stake we do not know a person. So we never know God in abstract terms. However pious the words may sound, the meaning has leaked away from them. We know God only in the immediacy of faith, the faith that commits all our vital interests to his keeping (cf. II Tim. 1:12b). No teaching can impart that knowledge (cf. Expos. on 5:11-14).

Men never know God until the law has been written into mind and heart, until faith has been made inward. Nor can this be done until sin has been forgiven. The faith that receives the forgiveness of sin and the faith through which we know God are one faith. No separation is possible. The works of the Holy Spirit whereby he assures us of our forgiveness, confirm our faith, and clarify our knowledge, are one working. The grace whereby we are

13 In that he saith, A new *covenant*, he hath made the first old. Now that which decayeth and waxeth old *is* ready to vanish away.

9 Then verily the first *covenant* had also ordinances of divine service, and a worldly sanctuary.

13 In speaking of a new covenant he treats the first as obsolete. And what is becoming obsolete and growing old is ready to vanish away.

9 Now even the first covenant had regulations for worship and an earthly sanc-

---

sacrificial system for the new covenant; he is arguing that the sacrificial principle has been perfected in Christ. The sacrificial system on earth is ended, not because it is repudiated, but because it is perfected. In his own way, the way of the liturgist, he presents religion in wholly spiritual terms. Christ's priesthood was perfected because it met human needs in terms of spiritual reality.

*c*) The Sacrifices of the Old and the New Covenants Are Contrasted (9:1-14)

In ch. 8 our author establishes from scripture the promise of a new covenant and argues that the new antiquates the old. Yet the relationship between old and new is that

---

forgiven and the grace whereby we are enlightened are one and the same grace. To understand this clearly is to see at once the limitations of teaching, and the peculiar nature of the knowledge of God which sets it apart from all other kinds of knowing. The blind demand of the world that the knowledge of God be reduced to the level of mathematical knowledge is pure folly.

**From the least of them to the greatest.** That includes all of us. It is as clear a way of teaching the universal scope of the gospel as can be found. This universal scope follows from the nature of the promises. A covenant based on a ritual can be exclusive. It can be limited to one nation or to one class. Any exclusive sect must at once suspect its own inwardness just because it has set up some kind of external barriers, such as circumcision or apostolic succession. Jeremiah was not aware of it, but he was writing the charter for Gentile Christianity. For when faith and knowledge are truly inward, where God deals directly with the human soul, all the man-made barriers of nation, race, cultus, and creed collapse. The doors of the kingdom are thrown open to all men who will fulfill the conditions.

That the greatest should be included is the crowning work of grace. They are under special handicap, especially if they think themselves great. That the least, the lowly, the contrite, the brokenhearted should enter the kingdom is understandable. They see clearly the poverty of their own righteousness, the bankruptcy of their own resources. But they who deem themselves great are far from seeing that all is lost without God. They are visibly impressed by their own knowledge, resources, and virtue. It

is hard for a rich man, a learned man, a powerful man, a man in the public eye, or a naturally "good" man to enter the kingdom. It is hard for a camel to enter a needle's eye. But with God all things are possible, and that the greatest should know him assures us all of hope.

**I will be merciful, . . . I will remember their sins no more.** The forgiveness of sins is the basic condition. Until sins are forgiven the law cannot be written on our minds or on our hearts. Until sins are forgiven we cannot come to a knowledge of God. Until sins are forgiven there is no "new creation" (II Cor. 5:17). Why does the new covenant bring a more convincing forgiveness than the old? This is the question of ch. 9.

**13. *The Old Is Obsolete.*—**We return to our original question. What about the old covenant is now **obsolete**? Everything in it which is more clearly and persuasively stated by the new covenant. Jesus himself said of the law and the prophets, "I have come not to abolish them but to fulfill them" (Matt. 5:17). When the fuller form is available, the partial is obsolete. The demands of the law have not been abolished. But the old externalism, which was exclusive, is done away by the new covenant written on the hearts of men. The old trembling fear of judgment is replaced by a faith that is confident. The old ritual, the old sacrifice, which told of the mercy of God in halting language, is replaced by Jesus, whose offering of himself was God's final word to man. Old striving is replaced by loving faith. Old weakness gives way to the power of God. The old defeats are overcome by the victory of faith.

**9:1-10. *On Evading God and Ourselves.*—**This passage is likely to prove an enigma to the

of copy to pattern, shadow to substance. There is therefore a principle of continuity between them, for the earthly foreshadows the heavenly sanctuary. In the same way the sacrifices made in the old foreshadow the sacrifice in the new since "it is necessary for this priest also to have something to offer" (8:3). Ch. 9, accordingly, moves forward to a discussion of the *ministry* of Christ as high priest in the heavenly sanctuary, interlacing covenant, sanctuary, priest, and sacrifice, with the accent on the sacrifice of Christ. Just as Paul makes faith antedate the law, so our author makes the new covenant with all its regulations antedate the "first," but the similarity is superficial. Paul is dealing with a time sequence while our author is dealing with a "two-world" concept. This is his way of validating the priestly system (the law) by the principle of continuity (copy to pattern). Vss. 1-14 contain a comparison of the "regulations for worship" in the earthly sanctuary (vss. 1-10) with Christ's ministry in the heavenly sanctuary (vss. 11-14). The main point of this comparison is perfectly clear, but a number of questions arise both from the text itself and from the conclusions the author draws from it. We shall first consider the text. A casual reading of these verses may not reveal the meticulous care with which the writer develops his comparison. It can best be shown in a table.

The Earthly Priesthood (vss. 1-10)
1. The *place* where it functions and a description (vss. 1-5)
2. Its *action* and *approach to God* (vss. 6-7)
3. Its *offering* (vs. 7)
4. An *estimate* of the whole institution (vss. 8-10)

Christ's Priesthood (vss. 11-14)
1. The *place* where he functions (vs. 11)
2. His *action* and *approach to God* (vs. 12a)
3. His *offering* (vs. 12b)
4. An *estimate* of the worth of his priesthood (vss. 12c-14)

The greater space allotted to the earthly ministry (ten verses as against four) is due to the fact that points 1 and 2 have been already developed, and points 2, 3, and 4 will be further developed as regards Christ's priesthood. In these verses the reader sees the superiority and finality of Christ's ministry stated in a neat summary form.

**9:1.** The connection of thought seems to be: Although the first covenant "is becoming obsolete and growing old" it had **regulations for worship and an earthly sanctuary,** i.e., there were permanent "principles," as we would say, which must be operative in the new ministry. It was just the failure of the old to perfect the "principle" of sacrifice which

---

modern mind. The details of the ancient tabernacle have only an antiquarian interest. They represent only the curious beliefs of the nomadic Hebrews and reflect what they thought God wanted from them. These ceremonial details were doubtless impressive to the worshiper and likely symbolized in a shadowy way the spiritual truths that men needed to learn. But when the prophets later made explicit the demands of God in terms of justice, mercy, and humility (cf. Mic. 6:8), when they repudiated the elaborate ritual of the temple (cf. Isa. 1:10-14; Jer. 7:22-23), they opened the way for a new understanding of the purpose of God. Why should we who live in this modern age go behind the prophets? In this light is it not, especially from our point of view, highly artificial for the writer of Hebrews to force the atoning work of Christ into the outworn mold

of the tabernacle ritual? Until the interpreter faces these questions, he is not likely to discover the profound meaning of this passage.

But as the enigma is clarified, the offense becomes almost intolerable. For if a man is told that he depends upon the sacrifice of another, that his salvation is a gift that he does not earn, that he is so helpless that he can make no move on his own behalf, that his pride must give way until all he can do is to cry out for God's mercy, then he revolts. Granted that all is not well with him, he is not entirely helpless.

Observe how he tries to extricate himself. There is much wrong in his world, and it has invaded his own life. These disturbing passions that he cannot control are part of his animal inheritance, the law of the jungle in him. His bad moods and his uncontrolled tempers can

2 For there was a tabernacle made; the first, wherein *was* the candlestick, and the table, and the showbread; which is called the sanctuary.

tuary. 2 For a tent*p* was prepared, the outer one, in which were the lampstand and the table and the bread of the Presence;*q* it is

*p* Or *tabernacle.*
*q* Greek *the presentation of the loaves.*

---

led to its obsolescence. The author uses past tenses in referring to the institution as a whole—it no longer existed for him—and present tenses of description, the historical present, when itemizing the furnishings of the tabernacle. The most difficult word in vs. 1 is κοσμικόν, which has a place of emphasis in the Greek sentence. The author's point is: Even the first covenant had valid regulations for worship and a sanctuary which also had a certain validity; what rendered the ministry of the old imperfect was the fact that the sanctuary was κοσμικόν. Our word "cosmic" can hardly represent the meaning intended by the author, despite the etymology. Philo argued that the true sanctuary was the "cosmos" as over against the localized tabernacle. This would not fit the flow of thought here, for the writer is obviously applying the word to the tabernacle, and he is depreciating, not appreciating, what went on there—another indication that he used Philonic ideas without sharing Philo's philosophical point of view. Other meanings of the word, such as "universal," "orderly," and even "ornamented" do not fit the thought, although he will enlarge upon the outward splendor of the trappings in the tabernacle. The KJV translation, **worldly**, carries modern connotations which are not stressed in this context, and probably **earthly** (RSV) best represents the thought in the light of the whole passage, although the word itself remains something of an enigma.

**2-5.** The curiously detailed description of the furnishings of the tabernacle raises the question, Why does the author introduce all these objects only to conclude, **Of these things we cannot now speak in detail?** Is he instructing readers who are ignorant of the arrangements in the tabernacle? Elsewhere he assumes a very considerable knowledge of scripture. Is he suggesting that each item might be allegorized as well as the whole? Or is it the **cherubim of glory** alone which he could develop in its spiritual significance? We can see how he could use this bit of symbolism, representing as it does the presence of God, but he never develops it. The climactic position of 5*b* also makes it probable that περὶ ὧν means **of these things.** Another possibility is that the writer has in mind the **golden** splendor and the rich impressiveness of these outward things as a foil for the spiritual poverty of the entire performance. These rites filled the eye but failed the conscience (9*b*). Such a contrast is implicit but not quite explicit here. What is explicit is the description of elaborate priestly rites and an elaborate priestly paraphernalia, which in spite of, or indeed because of, its elaboration falls short at every point of achieving the divine purpose: free access to God for the worshiper purified by an effective sacrifice

---

be traced to emotional conflicts which he has not yet learned to manage. Some of his evils can be explained by glandular deficiency or improper diet. Others are rooted in corrupt social institutions that can be corrected only by the torch and bomb of the revolutionary. He is the victim of the demands of a highly organized society, which have robbed him of his privacy, disrupted his schedule, and thwarted his nobler purposes. When he does not get along with his wife, his fellow workers, and his neighbors, it is because his infancy was not properly nurtured and the education he received was bad. If things do not go well in the home, his wife is the chief troubler. He has had to work too hard and his jangled nerves need a rest at

the seashore, which he cannot afford, thanks to his wife's extravagance or the failure of his employer to pay him what he deserves. Or perhaps something else is wrong. He needs to do more good works, to make a harder moral effort. Is that all? Then he will roll up his sleeves and get at it! But there is nothing much the matter with him, and nothing that cannot be corrected by a call on the doctor, an interview with a psychiatrist, a good vacation, or a little encouragement from his wife. In our highly complex and interdependent society we have become experts in tracing the causal antecedents of our failure. We have lost our responsibility and therefore our selves.

But this is not especially modern. It is as old

3 And after the second veil, the tabernacle which is called the holiest of all;

4 Which had the golden censer, and the ark of the covenant overlaid round about with gold, wherein *was* the golden pot that had manna, and Aaron's rod that budded, and the tables of the covenant;

5 And over it the cherubim of glory shadowing the mercy seat; of which we cannot now speak particularly.

called the Holy Place. 3 Behind the second curtain stood a tent[p] called the Holy of Holies, 4 having the golden altar of incense and the ark of the covenant covered on all sides with gold, which contained a golden urn holding the manna, and Aaron's rod that budded, and the tables of the covenant; 5 above it were the cherubim of glory overshadowing the mercy seat. Of these things we cannot now speak in detail.

[p] Or *tabernacle*.

from the sins impeding full and perfect communion. Another question concerns the accuracy of the author's knowledge. How are we to reconcile his description with our O.T. sources? Deriving his information from the Exodus account of the tabernacle (Exod. 25–26), he deviates from it in a number of points. **Lampstand, table,** and **bread of the Presence** in the **Holy Place** are accurate enough. The RSV translation, **for a tent was prepared, the outer one,** is interpretation, although unquestionably correct interpretation. The Greek is σκηνὴ . . . ἡ πρώτη and the writer's intention is to say that **the first covenant** provided for a *"first* tent." He proceeds to give a double meaning to the word "first"—he relished this sort of play on words—"first," not only as over against the last, i.e., the heavenly, but also "first" as over against the **second** (vs. 3), i.e., the Holy of Holies. **The second curtain** perhaps is meant to emphasize the progressive difficulty of access to God in the earthly tabernacle. Of course a tent implied an entrance, but the way into the **outer** tent or **Holy Place** was not actually barred against the people's entrance. In describing the contents of the **Holy of Holies** the author emphasizes the **golden** splendor of the **altar,** the **ark,** and the **urn.** Is this a touch of artistry? The Exodus account prescribes that the lampstand and the table should also be overlaid with gold. Our author does not deny this, but he does not refer to it, for the splendor of the Holy of Holies as compared with the Holy Place is his point. The chief difficulty, however, is with his statements that the **altar of incense** was *in* the Holy of Holies, and that the **golden urn** with **the manna** and **Aaron's rod** was *in* the ark. The Exodus account does not accord with either. It has been argued that our author does not quite say that the **altar of incense** is *in* the Holy of Holies; that his use of ἔχουσα instead of ἐν ᾧ means that it "belonged" there but was actually kept out by the veil or curtain. This view is ingenious but hardly convincing. Either the writer has other sources, unknown to us, or else, as is more likely, he was not quite at home here, deriving his knowledge solely from books, and in this case

as the most ancient human records. Indeed, a history of religions might be written as a history of human evasions of responsibility. The story of man's religions might be entitled "The Story of Man's Attempt to Escape God and Himself." Perhaps Dostoevski's Grand Inquisitor was right—we are above all afraid of our own freedom. We prefer to hide ourselves in the forces of nature, to lose our identity in society, to escape ourselves in the tangled business of the world.

Man has always been aware of evil in the world. At first the evil was in forces outside himself. Then it came closer. But as the evil was acknowledged at long last to dwell within, it was always an evil in him, never the self that

was evil. The inner citadel of the self was barricaded. The harm in the primitive world was done by evil spirits that brought storm, disease, drought, and death. Later these troublesome spirits were identified with ancestors, whose burial rites had been improperly performed. Or the wrong in man came from some ceremonial impurity, a taboo that had been violated, and that gave evil magic some power over him. In more sophisticated cultures evil was resident in the physical world which contaminated the otherwise undefiled spirit of man (cf. Expos. on 8:1-5). For many philosophers, and in Buddhism, the evil was in man's attachment to the objects of desire, to the flesh, to honors, to possessions. For many in Israel,

6 Now when these things were thus ordained, the priests went always into the first tabernacle, accomplishing the service *of God.*

7 But into the second *went* the high priest alone once every year, not without blood, which he offered for himself, and *for* the errors of the people:

6 These preparations having thus been made, the priests go continually into the outer tent,*p* performing their ritual duties; 7 but into the second only the high priest goes, and he but once a year, and not without taking blood which he offers for himself

*p* Or *tabernacle.*

using his books carelessly. Nowhere in the O.T. is Aaron's rod or the urn with the manna located in the Holy of Holies, although both are regarded with special reverence (cf. Exod. 16:33; Num. 17:10). That the ark contained "the tablets of the covenant" and was overshadowed by the cherubim is the unanimous testimony of our sources, although the ark and its contents had long disappeared before the Herodian temple was erected. When Jerusalem and the temple were destroyed, the Holy of Holies was found to be empty.

**6-7.** The service of the priests in the earthly sanctuary is described with surprising brevity in view of the extended treatment of the tabernacle furnishings. But this ministry is to be contrasted with Christ's in what follows. In these terse phrases the author packs many of the points essential for his further use: the fact that the Holy of Holies is accessible only once in the year, and then not to the people or the priests in general, but only to the high priest, who must enter with blood offered **for himself and for the errors of the people.** The analogy is a bit involved because the writer has to show that into "the outer tent," the Holy Place, the priests continually go to perform "their ritual duties," but into the second tent, the Holy of Holies, only the high priest ever goes and then only once a year (on the day of Atonement) and even then bearing blood not only for the errors of the people, but also for his own errors. It is not quite a simple comparison. In other words, the analogy becomes more meaningful as the author proceeds, but this is according to his purpose, for the offering of a high priest is the constant factor in both the earthly and the heavenly sanctuary. The daily ritual serves only to show that access into the very presence of God was essential; otherwise it plays no part in the analogy. **Errors,** instead of "sins," means the sins that can be expiated; for, as Lev. 16:14 ff. indicates, there is no provision even on the day of Atonement for deliberate, willful sin such as apostasy, and this the writer has emphasized and will emphasize again with reference to his Christian readers and their Christian confession (cf. 6:4 ff.; 10:26 ff.; 12:25 ff.). The fact that the high priest actually entered the Holy of Holies more than once on the day of Atonement can hardly be counted against the accuracy of our author, for his point is that only on that one day was access possible.

as among other peoples, it was associated with the failure to observe some of the prescribed details of the cultus.

Man has always sought some salvation, an evidence of the restlessness within him. The salvation sought was always a clear indication of man's diagnosis of his trouble. The primitive savage had only one hope—to placate the demons and to enlist the help of friendly spirits. Ancestor trouble led to the worship of ancestors (China) and to scrupulous care for proper burial rites. For the evil magic of impure contacts an elaborate set of ceremonial purifications was devised. For contamination by the physical world asceticism and philosophical contemplation were the twin cures (India). For wrong attachment the remedy came by renounc-

ing desire as such (Buddhism). For a god angered by ritual deficiency the answer was redoubled caution about ceremonial correctness. This would make man well-pleasing to God. For violations of the moral code two remedies were at hand: a clever definition of what was right and wrong in given situations (legalism), and a frantic effort to do good deeds to "make up" for the wrong unintentionally done.

It is as though in all our long human history God had patiently let us try literally every avenue of escape, shutting each off one by one, until we confront God and ourselves, see ourselves as sinners, God as our only Savior, and cry out, "The sacrifices of God are a broken spirit: a broken and a contrite heart, O God, thou wilt not despise" (Ps. 51:17).

8 The Holy Ghost this signifying, that the way into the holiest of all was not yet made manifest, while as the first tabernacle was yet standing:

9 Which *was* a figure for the time then present, in which were offered both gifts and sacrifices, that could not make him that did the service perfect, as pertaining to the conscience;

and for the errors of the people. 8 By this the Holy Spirit indicates that the way into the sanctuary is not yet opened as long as the outer tent[p] is still standing 9 (which is symbolic for the present age). According to this arrangement, gifts and sacrifices are offered which cannot perfect the conscience

[p] Or *tabernacle.*

---

**8-10.** The final estimate of the earthly **sanctuary** and its ministry is presented in two interrelated assertions: it fails to open the way into the presence of God, every act of it symbolizing the obstacles; and it fails to reach home to **the conscience,** purifying the outer man only. This was all an earthly sanctuary and an external ministry could achieve. Vs. 9a **(which is symbolic for the present age)** should probably be in parentheses as in the RSV, for the words can be omitted without interfering with the sense. Unless they are treated as a digression, they can hardly be understood, for the author does not mean to say, surely, that Christians in the **present age** are shut up to the system being branded as imperfect; he is rather reminding his readers that the whole contrast is between the old and the new orders. So understood, these words prepare the way for vss. 11-14.

Before passing from this description and estimate of the earthly priesthood, we should observe that it is made from a Christian point of view and would hardly have proved convincing to readers who were tempted to return to normative Judaism. Normative Judaism would not grant any of the author's points, for the law in its entirety was held to be eternally valid, and it is hardly fair to say that the institution of sacrifice was ever considered, certainly not in late Judaism, to appertain merely to externals. Late Judaism stressed repentance and forgiveness; sacrifice was indeed essential in theory—the practice of outward sacrifice ceased with the destruction of the temple—but it did not avail without an inner change of mind and heart. Our author is to be understood, however, not only as speaking on the basis of Christian experience and conviction, but also as having an understanding of Judaism very different from normative Judaism's understanding of itself. Its priesthood was inadequate because it operated only on the level of the earthly, shadowy copy of a heavenly reality. It could never, in the very nature of the case, effect access to God, permanently and perfectly. And what would he answer to the Jew who said that the repetition of sacrifices was necessary because of the sinful nature of man?

---

According to an old Scottish legend, a farmer thought he was pursued by a monster. His barns were unroofed, his cattle destroyed, his crops ruined, his first-born slain. One night he resolved to find the monster and kill him. So he lay in wait in a ravine. When the monster appeared, he rushed upon it with a cry. He fought it, fell, struggled to his feet, until at length he threw the creature to the ground. He drew his knife to kill it when the moon lit the features and the man stopped dead: the face of the monster was his own! It is a parable of human life.

It is clear that all the foregoing comment was not in the mind of the writer. But something like it was. Any salvation external to man will not avail. Any rite that does not bring man face to face with God is defective. The writer's criticism of the tabernacle worship was

this: **Gifts and sacrifices are offered which cannot perfect the conscience of the worshiper.**

Why, then, did he take pains to describe the structure of the tabernacle and the worship there conducted? Because the details had a profound significance for his argument. After all, the tabernacle was God's provision. But it was meant to point beyond itself; it was symbolic. **By this the Holy Spirit indicates . . . .**

One thing is clear from the tabernacle: **God is not easily approached.** Only one day a year could the high priest enter the Holy of Holies, and that **not without taking blood which he offers for himself and for the errors of the people.** The gap between God and man is not easily bridged. Basically, the gap is the difference between Creator and the created. It is widened by man's sin in which he cannot draw near to God. The very rigors of tabernacle

10 *Which stood* only in meats and drinks, and divers washings, and carnal ordinances, imposed *on them* until the time of reformation.

11 But Christ being come a high priest of good things to come, by a greater and more perfect tabernacle, not made with hands, that is to say, not of this building;

of the worshiper, 10 but deal only with food and drink and various ablutions, regulations for the body imposed until the time of reformation.

11 But when Christ appeared as a high priest of the good things that have come,ʳ then through the greater and more perfect tentᵖ (not made with hands, that is, not

ʳ Other manuscripts read *good things to come.*
ᵖ Or *tabernacle.*

---

This is the very point Paul deals with in a radical fashion by proposing a radical transformation of man through the gracious gift of the Spirit and the inner Christ. Our author never quite faces this issue, except indirectly. He is the liturgist throughout, holding that the cure of man's sin lies in an effective worship. The true priest must have pierced to the very presence of God and also to the heart of man. The author is not unaware of the necessity of a new kind of person. **The conscience,** not just **the body,** must be purified. But worship will accomplish this purification if a proper priest offers an effective sacrifice. How will the sacrifice of Christ avail the sinning worshiper? We shall have to ask this question again as we follow his argument through this and the following chapter.

**11-14.** But Christ, in contrast to all earthly priests, has **entered once for all** the true **Holy Place,** securing through **his own blood** an **eternal redemption;** for if animal sacrifices purified the body, **how much more shall the blood of Christ,** who offered himself, purify

---

worship made it clear that to worship God is a solemn experience. It still is. God is near to each loving heart, but his nearness becomes banal unless we remember that he is the God of infinite majesty. "He healeth the broken in heart," yes, but he also "telleth the number of the stars" (Ps. 147:3, 4). It is the nearness of the majestic God that creates true worship.

But the tabernacle did not make the nearness of God plain. It is not enough that once each year the high priest alone enters the most holy place. God is not properly worshiped until the whole company of believers gathers before him, until the lonely, tempted man has access to him in the moment of his need. **The way into the sanctuary is not yet opened as long as the outer tent is still standing.**

The tabernacle had the advantages and the limitations of a symbol. No religion can dispense with symbols, much less the Christian faith. All the priceless words of the Christian vocabulary are symbols. Take the great words by which God is designated: Father, Creator, Shepherd, Husband, Judge, Holy One of Israel —are they accurate descriptions? They are man's attempt, under the leading of the Holy Spirit, to express in vivid image a meaning that transcends all human thought, just because God's ways are not our ways, and his thoughts are higher than our thoughts as the heaven is high above the earth (Isa. 55:9). Our growth in God's revelation is in part the improvement of the symbols by which we think of him. The

supreme Word which is Jesus Christ is the highest symbol, God clothing himself in human flesh that all might know him. The worship of God is always in symbols. The form of our prayers, the music of our hymns, the structure of our churches, all express something of our belief about God, whether we wish it to be so or not. Sensitive worshipers are constantly seeking to improve their symbols, to make them more worthy of God.

The tabernacle is to be seen in this light. It was **an earthly** [κοσμικόν] **sanctuary.** This was no handicap as long as men looked beyond it to the heavenly. But the eyes of men grow dull because they no longer see with faith. Their ears are heavy so that in the earthly hymns they hear no overtones of the heavenly. The symbol whose very existence is in its meaning, its pointing beyond itself, becomes an end in itself, an idol, and takes to itself the worship that was meant to go through it to God. So it ceases to be a noble thing, becomes instead a thing dull and cheap. Precisely that may happen at any time, among any people, to any symbol. "The Doxology," the "Gloria Patri," the Lord's Prayer, the *Te Deum,* how nobly they clothe the worship of God for those who seek him in spirit and in truth! How dull and tinny they can become! The symbol is alive only when God speaks through it and when the believer hears his God.

**11-14.** *The Difference Christ Has Made.*—But when Christ appeared all was changed. It is

12 Neither by the blood of goats and calves, but by his own blood he entered in once into the holy place, having obtained eternal redemption *for us*.

of this creation) 12 he entered once for all into the Holy Place, taking[s] not the blood of goats and calves but his own blood, thus

[s] Greek *through*.

---

the conscience and achieve the true end of all religion, the service of the living God. The pregnant phrases, making the contrast point by point, raise many questions as to the precise thoughts in the author's mind. We could wish that he were less bound by his comparison and freer to develop each phrase. How does the sacrifice of Christ achieve the result of ridding men of sin and ensuring access to God? The author only hints at answers, for he rests upon the axiom that "without the shedding of blood there is no forgiveness of sins" (vs. 22). This is true in the old and the new dispensation alike; the new achieved what the old foreshadowed because it presented a better priest with a better offering made in a better sanctuary. This is all the logic of his argument requires; with this concise statement he has reached the climax of his thought, and what follows (i.e., after vs. 14) is an exposition of some aspects of the argument and exhortation on the basis of it.

It is now possible to look at the author's presentation of Christ's priesthood as a whole. The Son is priest because he fulfills all the requirements and because he surpasses them. He fulfills them (a) by his human experience ensuring sympathy with man's temptations and sufferings (2:14-18; 4:15 ff.; 5:1-3); (b) by being called of God to this ministry (5:4 ff.); (c) by his adequate offering (vss. 12, 14, 22; 2:17; 8:3); and (d) by bearing this offering through the curtain into the Holy of Holies (vs. 12; 10:19-20). He surpasses the qualifications for priesthood (a) because his priesthood is established by God's oath (7:20-22); (b) because he is sinless (4:15; 7:26); (c) because he remains a priest forever (7:23, 24, 28); (d) because he is priest in the heavenly sanctuary where he continues permanently (vss. 11 ff., 24; 8:1-6); (e) because his sacrifice is "once for all" (7:27; 10:2, 11-14); and (f) because his sacrifice cleanses the conscience (vss. 9-14). The upshot is twofold: the end of the sacrificial system, and the assurance, to those who hold fast their confession, of unhindered access to God.

The word παραγενόμενος is rendered being come (KJV), appeared (RSV), "arrived" (Moffatt). A different word, πεφανέρωται, is used in vs. 26. Older commentators made much of the time relationships in Hebrews, but we must remember that time is a matter of relative indifference to our author, controlled as he is by the "two-world" concept. Perhaps, as Moffatt has suggested, the idea is, when Christ "came on the scene"; for παραγενόμενος is more active than πεφανέρωται. The RSV reads, a high priest of the good

---

worth pausing to see that this was and is literally true. Christ comes on the scene and all life is different henceforth. Christ appears and the old law is embodied in a life, at once more majestic and more tender than Sinai. Christ appears and the forgiveness about which men had long talked is now alive and grips the hearts of men. Christ appears and God becomes at once more majestic than mind can conceive, and nearer than heart can desire. Christ appears and all our old distinctions between race and race, class and class, look shabby and flimsy. Christ appears and the slave lifts his head in hope. Christ appears and woman becomes man's comrade instead of his possession. Christ appears and all the frantic pursuit of wealth and pleasure seems strangely empty. Christ appears and the soul of man can find no rest until it follows him. Aye, Christ appears and the old

symbolism of the tabernacle has lost its luster. Here is the true priest, serving in the real sanctuary, making the one sufficient offering, bringing the one satisfying redemption.

**The greater and more perfect tent.** No man can understand this passage without letting his imagination run. See the earthly tabernacle as clearly as you can. Feel in yourself the hush of awe as the congregation waits while the high priest stands in the Holy of Holies. Let the old tabernacle at its best speak to you, with all its solemnity and dignity, of the God whose service demands man's best and more. Then try if you can to picture the glories of God's presence: all doubts gone, all clouds lifted, all impurities purged away, the song of the redeemed ringing through heaven's cathedral, and you will begin to understand what our writer meant.

**Once for all.** When we understand the perfec-

13 For if the blood of bulls and of goats, and the ashes of a heifer sprinkling the unclean, sanctifieth to the purifying of the flesh;

securing an eternal redemption. 13 For if the sprinkling of defiled persons with the blood of goats and bulls and with the ashes of a heifer sanctifies for the purification of

---

**things that have come** instead of **good things to come** (KJV). It is a question whether γενομένων or μελλόντων stood in the original text. Both have good MS backing and both make good sense when we consider that the author regarded salvation, in the main, as future, but its goods as experienced now, at least in part (cf. 6:4-5). No final decision is possible, but the present context certainly makes **the good things that have come** preferable, since the author is here speaking not of future as contrasted with present goods, but of the goods Christ's priesthood ensures as compared with the "goods" promised by earthly priests. It is true that γενομένων might easily have been written into the text under the influence of the preceding παραγενόμενος; it is equally true that our author was fond of that kind of assonance. In the last part of vs. 11 the Holy of Holies of the tabernacle is actually robbed of its earthly significance. The outer tent symbolizes the earthly; the inner tent symbolizes solely the heavenly sanctuary. But it was closed to men and to priests, except once in the year, and we see how the author uses it as a symbol of the goal never attained by the external system of sacrifice, always pointing to another realm and a better, i.e., a heavenly. Entrance into this Holy Place and access through him into it for all men is the supreme service of Christ as priest. Again we see that the Resurrection, never mentioned in Hebrews except in 13:20 and there in a benediction, plays no role. It is the Ascension which his analogy requires.

It is **his own blood,** not **the blood of goats and calves,** that Christ offers. Why does he specify **the blood** of Christ? Would not his comparison be the stronger if he contrasted bloody offerings with Christ's spiritual offering, i.e., a material sanctuary over against a heavenly, human priests over against the Son as priest, animal sacrifices over against the sacrifice of "a broken and a contrite heart"? He knows the prophetic protest against these animal and bloody sacrifices (cf. 10:5 ff.); yet blood as the recognized seat and the mysterious essence of life itself is the link which binds his comparison together and he cannot avoid its use if he is to press his priestly analogy. Hebrews is the principal N.T. source for the imagery of blood, and this imagery has been stressed in evangelical Christianity, not always without magical and literal interpretations foreign to this author. That he is not unaware of these dangers we shall see in the verses that follow. **Thus securing an eternal redemption:** Although our author emphasizes the temptations

---

tion of the sacrifice of Christ, we see how it could not be repeated. It marked the end of one age, and the beginning of another (vs. 26b; for the author's development see 9:15–10:18).

**Taking not the blood of goats and calves but his own blood.** It is perhaps impossible for the modern mind to recapture the primitive feeling of awe with regard to blood. We know too much about chemistry. But we may have lost something, too. For the primitive man blood stood for life itself, a mysterious business even for us with all our science. Moreover, blood used in sacrifice, coming from the altar, had absorbed and could thus convey to the worshiper some of the hidden powers of the god himself.[1] But there are distinct overtones in the biblical references to blood in sacrifices (cf. vs. 22). The forgiveness of sins is no light matter

[1] See Moffatt, *Hebrews, ad. loc.*

and can be achieved only by the ultimate in sacrificial love, the giving of the life itself. There can be no more powerful evidence of love than this complete sacrifice (cf. John 15: 13).

**How much more:** This is a familiar argument in the N.T. (cf. Matt. 6:30; 7:11; Rom. 5:9, 10, 15, 17; II Cor. 3:9-11). If such and such is true of human affairs—how much more God! It is an argument of faith and will have no meaning except to the man of faith. Here the argument is clear: the blood of Christ is **much more** effective than that of the sacrificial victims in the O.T.

In specifying the superiority of the blood of Christ, our writer provides the proper rebuke to ill-guided interpreters who have made of the blood of Christ almost an instrument of magic. The author of Hebrews would have been

**14** How much more shall the blood of Christ, who through the eternal Spirit offered himself without spot to God, purge your conscience from dead works to serve the living God?

the flesh, **14** how much more shall the blood of Christ, who through the eternal Spirit offered himself without blemish to God, purify your[t] conscience from dead works to serve the living God.

[t] Other manuscripts read *our*.

---

and sufferings of Jesus, he is not here underlining the efforts made, but what they secured or obtained for us. We should like to know more about what he meant by redemption, λύτρωσις. He gives us only hints in what follows, for it is evidently an axiomatic truth for him and for his readers. That this redemption is eternal, needing never to be repeated, is central in his thought and will be stressed again.

In vss. 13-14 the author recurs to his familiar "how much more" type of argument. Possibly there is an additional thought, for **the ashes of a heifer** (not **the blood of goats and bulls**) purified from defilement caused by contact with the dead. Is he suggesting that the death of Christ not only caused no defilement, but that his blood purified even the conscience? If so, it is an overtone, although "from dead works [not bodies]" suggests that this subtle thought may not be absent from a writer who loved such subtlety. **The blood of Christ** offered **through the eternal Spirit** is a vivid juxtaposition of phrases and indeed of realms of thinking. Here we are close to the very genius of our author. He means both phrases to be understood literally, yet not mechanically or magically. The offering Christ made was in the realm of reality, as tangible and real as blood, as central and decisive as life (blood). Yet it was not an offering on the plane of animal existence; it was transmuted into an eternal redemption because it was made **through the eternal Spirit.** At the point of human sin and its consequences in suffering and death, at that point God through his eternal Spirit entered by his Son to rob death of its sting and its victory. The writer does not pursue this thought, although it is implicit, but dexterously turns again to the διαθήκη, which actually stands for the ultimate relationship between man and God, instituted by God, for this is in the framework of his argument.

---

the first to deny that any material thing could purify the conscience. For him the blood of Christ is effectual only because of its spiritual significance. Christ's sacrifice was **through the eternal Spirit**—an uncertain phrase, but at least it signifies that the sacrifice had eternal power. He offered himself **without blemish.** But for his sinless character, how could the offering up of himself avail at all?

> There was no other good enough
> To pay the price of sin.[2]

There was no other who by living or by dying could **purify your conscience from dead works to serve the living God.**

This verse marks the turning point in man's salvation. As long as he loses himself in the crowd, submerges himself in the forces that play upon him, blames his failures on his circumstances, finds his purification in external rites that do not touch the self, he is not a person. He has not encountered God. But when he meets God and sees himself, his inmost self, as the source of his misery, he begins to

[2] Cecil Frances Alexander, "There is a green hill far away."

become responsible: i.e., he begins to be a human person. He now knows that no sacrifice will suffice unless it purifies his conscience. But with this new knowledge comes a new despair. He cannot save himself. However heroic his moral effort, he cannot remove his own self-contradiction, i.e., his alienation from God. However long he may live, however he may multiply good works and penance to "make up for" the evil deeds that he has done, he cannot succeed. For it is not merely his deeds that were wrong, but himself. Not merely his trespasses need forgiving: he himself needs cleansing. Nor can any easy forgiveness satisfy his conscience. The forgiveness must cost a heavy price, must leave him dwelling in the land of moral reality to which he has just become awake. This despair is the human last, beyond which the divine first begins. Completely humbled, he is finally prepared to receive the divine forgiveness. Only in the eternal self-giving of God can his conscience be purified **from dead works.** Only in God's own sacrifice can the believer be restored to his rightful place as a child of God, to find his life, his destiny, his joy in serving **the living God.**

15 And for this cause he is the mediator of the new testament, that by means of death, for the redemption of the transgressions *that were* under the first testament, they which are called might receive the promise of eternal inheritance.

16 For where a testament *is,* there must also of necessity be the death of the testator.

17 For a testament *is* of force after men are dead: otherwise it is of no strength at all while the testator liveth.

15 Therefore he is the mediator of a new covenant, so that those who are called may receive the promised eternal inheritance, since a death has occurred which redeems them from the transgressions under the first covenant.[u] 16 For where a will[u] is involved, the death of the one who made it must be established. 17 For a will[u] takes effect only at death, since it is not in force as long as the one who made it is

[u] The Greek word here means both *covenant* and *will.*

---

### d) THE SACRIFICE OF CHRIST FULFILLS THE PROMISE OF THE NEW COVENANT (9:15–10:18)

#### (1) THEME INTRODUCED AND ESTABLISHED (9:15-22)

**15.** The connection of thought may well be that since the purified conscience (vs. 14) corresponds with the promise of forgiveness in the Jeremiah quotation (8:12), Christ is demonstrated to be **the mediator of a new covenant,** the covenant under which transgressions are actually removed (cf. 10:17). Christ is the **mediator;** he brings God and man into the new relationship. Primitive ideas of placating an angry deity, or of the magical efficacy of blood as averting penalty, may be behind the imagery, but they never come into the foreground and would indeed be alien to our author's main thought.

**16-17.** Since it is a **death** which has had redemptive power, the author is moved to play upon the other meaning of διαθήκη, i.e., will or testament, in order to bring his thought home to his readers. No will is operative while the testator **is alive;** only his death brings it into legal operation. The double use of διαθήκη is not quite so strained as it

---

**15-28.** *The New Covenant of Christ's Blood.* —This passage bristles with difficulties and it is well for the interpreter to face them at the outset. In part, the seeming awkwardness of the writer is due to the fact that the modern mind does not accept his premises. In part, the obstacles lie in the passage itself.

It is a common experience to find in the Bible that which angers us, which questions all our values, which seems to upset even our logic. It is from such passages that irritate and annoy that we have most to learn; for here our whole hierarchy of values faces the judgment of God's word.

For one thing, modern man is not deeply concerned over the world to come. A study estimated that the average life expectancy of the American rose from fifty years of age in 1900 to sixty-seven years of age in 1950, thanks to better medical care, better education, and better food. This fact alone may help to explain our greater indifference to death and the hereafter. Because death is not so immediate a threat, it concerns us less. But however we explain it, the prevailing mood is clear. Even among church members there is a widespread skepticism about the life on the other side of death. Men look back with disdain upon early Christians who were so pre-

occupied with it that they felt no need to concern themselves with the here and now, with economic, political, social, and scientific questions. But our generation knows better. We can be certain about the present, and its demands are urgent enough to occupy all our thought and labor. To multitudes of contemporary folk, therefore, all talk about an **eternal inheritance** seems irrelevant. By their lives as well as by their words they say that they are not deeply disturbed about the judgment after death.

Yet this unconcern is really bravado. The fear of death has not been destroyed. When little ones are taken by death, when the best young men are snuffed out in battle, those old questions return and the old longings are there. "If a man die, shall he live again?" (Job 14:14.) And who knows what dark forebodings come as a man faces the prospect that he too will soon arrive at the end of his days? None but the man who has come face to face with death. On the day when we no longer care to ask these questions, on that day faith is finally vanquished, and the secular view of life has won. On that day, too, love will have vanished; for it is love that keeps asking the question about death. It is one thing to say at the end of life, "I have

18 Whereupon neither the first *testament* was dedicated without blood.

19 For when Moses had spoken every precept to all the people according to the law, he took the blood of calves and of goats, with water, and scarlet wool, and hyssop, and sprinkled both the book and all the people,

alive. 18 Hence even the first covenant was not ratified without blood. 19 For when every commandment of the law had been declared by Moses to all the people, he took the blood of calves and goats, with water and scarlet wool and hyssop, and sprinkled both the book itself and all the

---

seems to the English reader, not only because the same Greek word means both covenant and testament, but also because the covenant was in a sense an **inheritance,** and the use of that word in vs. 15 may have suggested the illustration. It is a playful touch, of which there are few in this serious writing, and the readers would appreciate it without unduly pressing the analogy.

**18-22.** But the illustration of death, in this other connection, carries the author back to the death of Christ and to the life-giving blood in relation to the covenant. The death of Christ, and not just his temptations, sufferings, and sympathy, must be validated. The death of Christ, having its central significance in his blood since he is both priest and offering, must be integrated in the priestly system. This is achieved by a demonstration

---

had my day. I have done my work. I have lived and loved, seen sunset's glow, felt winter's snow, and known the joy of spring's return. What happens to me now does not matter." That sounds impressive, even if it is not quite honest. But stand over the open grave of one you love better than your own life and try to repeat those words, "You have had your day. You have done your work. You have lived and loved, seen sunset's glow, felt winter's snow, and known the joy of spring's return. What happens to you now does not matter." The words will stick in your throat. If men can ever say such words over the graves of those nearest them, love, as well as faith, will have gone from among us.

But we are a long way from that day. Much of our bravado about death wears the air of a none-too-successful conspiracy not to mention a painful subject. Our social taboos against talk of death are evidence of a dark and pervading dread. Hearses are not allowed on boulevards. "Floral tributes" and "soft" music may help to veil the face of reality. Perhaps our frantic attempts to build our own security, to feel confident in our own strength, to depend on our own resources, spring from our hope that we can somehow surmount death. It may be that the greed for possessions is just a pathetic barricade against invading death. While man professes to have outgrown faith in life after death, he all the time labors as though he deeply wanted it. Strange contradiction! Strange penalty exacted for covering over the fear of death with pretense!

On the other hand, when he begins to think seriously about the life beyond, then he is confronted with the N.T. Its message is clear. Because Jesus Christ was bound in the life of God, the grave could not hold him. Because the Christian believer is bound by faith in Jesus Christ with the life of God, he will not be destroyed by death. The soul's deepest question concerning its own destiny cannot be answered apart from faith in the living God, who is also the God of the living.

The modern man's second difficulty is with the principle of sacrifice. If the only obstacle were the principle of animal sacrifice, that would cause little concern. But his trouble goes deeper. He does not like to feel overwhelmingly in debt. He does not want to feel his own moral bankruptcy. Any ultimate sacrifice on his behalf is an embarrassment to him. That he owes his very life to another, that he can never repay his debt to his fellow men, especially to those who have laid down their lives for him, robs him of the comfortable assurance that he can stand squarely on his own two good feet. That Christ should die for him, that he should be a "prisoner of Jesus Christ" (Eph. 3:1), is extremely damaging to his pride. He wants no one to set him free. He does not see that this pretense of self-sufficiency is his fatal sin, and that only God's sacrifice can save him from that guilty pride.

Until the interpreter faces these twin difficulties he is not likely to deal persuasively with this passage.

But other difficulties inhere in the passage itself.

What shall we make of the play on the double meaning of διαθήκη? It was the word which the LXX used to translate ברית, "cove-

20 Saying, This *is* the blood of the testament which God hath enjoined unto you.

21 Moreover he sprinkled likewise with blood both the tabernacle, and all the vessels of the ministry.

22 And almost all things are by the law purged with blood; and without shedding of blood is no remission.

people, 20 saying, "This is the blood of the covenant which God commanded you." 21 And in the same way he sprinkled with the blood both the tent[p] and all the vessels used in worship. 22 Indeed, under the law almost everything is purified with blood, and without the shedding of blood there is no forgiveness of sins.

[p] Or *tabernacle.*

---

that the first covenant was sealed with blood. In the Exodus record (24:3 ff.), which our author seems to be following, there are several differences from his account. There it is **the blood of calves** (he adds **goats**); **water and scarlet wool and hyssop** are not mentioned (cf. Num. 19); **the book** (of the covenant) is read but not sprinkled; nor is there any mention of the sprinkling of the tent and of the vessels used in worship. The author is aware that not everything but **almost everything is purified with blood, under the law,** and he is quite justified in concluding that blood was the *sine qua non* of the forgiveness of sins (vs. 22). This is the principle of continuity between the old and the new, and he unquestionably makes his point as regards the old covenant, whatever may be said about the details of his argument.

It is idle to ask just *how* blood availed to effect forgiveness of sins, for this is precisely the point he assumes as an axiom. Despite protests against bloody sacrifices, the efficacy of blood was axiomatic not only in Judaism, but by and large in the ancient world. He too believed that Christ ended all external sacrifices, but that he did it by

---

nant." But in classic as well as in common speech it also meant "testament." That our writer intended to use both meanings is clear from vss. 16 and 18. But while a will cannot be probated until the death of the testator is established, it does not follow that Christ had to die in order to confer the benefits of the "covenant." All the author had to do was to accept O.T. usage and at once he would remove the verbal necessity for the death of Christ.

He does try to show that the old covenant was in a sense a testament. It was inaugurated by purification with blood. Yet does not the analogy create new difficulties? For the sacrificial death was not that of the testator.

But the crowning difficulty is with purifying **the heavenly things.** From what impurity could they suffer? Are they not beyond the reach of all defilement by sinful man? Moreover, if they were defiled, would they not need a spiritual offering? How could even the blood of Christ, a material substance, serve to purify the spiritual? Is not the attempt made here to have a "shadow" serve in the real world of the spirit? The only solution of this difficulty at the same time makes it impossible, at least within the framework of this epistle, to regard the blood of Christ as in any sense a magical, material power, or as anything less than the symbol of a profound sacrifice within the life of God himself.

**Without the shedding of blood there is no forgiveness of sins.** Why not? (*a*) Did God require the blood of animals to be shed before his forgiving mercy could be awakened? Was there some power in such blood to arouse his otherwise latent compassion? Is grace an afterthought with God? Or was the psalmist right when he said, "His lovingkindness endureth forever" (Ps. 100:5)? Why should God, who had created all living things, need the blood of animals to appease his wrath? (*b*) Moreover, the O.T. cultus is presented as the provision of God himself. Did he devise the blood sacrifices as a pedagogical method? Consider both these points.

(*a*) The natural man tends to minimize the importance of his sin. As long as he must find his security in the pretense of his own decency, he must find some way of averting guilt from himself. He tries to forget his own wrongdoing. He suppresses the memory of his failures, dwells instead on the good deeds that he has done. This suppressed memory of evil is one of the most pernicious effects of sin. "The victim has put all his sins in a box deep down under his heart and he is sitting on the lid. But he finds the box is not air-tight, and the musty smell of boxed-up sins poisons the very air his soul breathes." [3] When he does recall his sins, he minimizes their importance. He gives playful

[3] Leslie D. Weatherhead, *Psychology in Service of the Soul* (New York: The Macmillan Co., 1930), p. 86.

23 *It was* therefore necessary that the patterns of things in the heavens should be purified with these; but the heavenly things themselves with better sacrifices than these.

24 For Christ is not entered into the holy places made with hands, *which are* the figures of the true; but into heaven itself, now to appear in the presence of God for us:

23 Thus it was necessary for the copies of the heavenly things to be purified with these rites, but the heavenly things themselves with better sacrifices than these. 24 For Christ has entered, not into a sanctuary made with hands, a copy of the true one, but into heaven itself, now to appear in the

---

offering himself in his own blood as the answer to unsatisfied hopes and longings expressed through the outpouring of blood on ancient altars. Was Christ's blood propitiatory, expiatory, or merely symbolic? He does not tell us because on the one hand he assumes the necessity of sacrifice and on the other he concentrates on the absolute worth of the person and work of Christ, our high priest.

(2) Cleansing of the Heavenly Sanctuary and the Finality of Christ's Redemption (9:23-28)

The final section of ch. 9 fills out the analogy by re-emphasizing two points already made and by adding an explicit statement of the author's belief in the second coming of Christ.

23-26. If the **copies** had **to be purified,** then the thing copied must be purified by **better sacrifices than these.** Such an understanding seems to be required by the analogy, but we do not see quite what our author means, for the heavenly sanctuary can hardly require purification. His real point emerges in vs. 24, where he repeats what has already

---

names to them. He finds them amusing, the kind of foibles that make him an interesting person. Or he insists that what he does is his own business, as though he ever could contain within himself the consequences of his sin! In order to take the sting out of his conscience, he is driven to obscure his moral judgment. He refuses to confront the moral purity of Jesus. If compelled to accept the seriousness of his evil, he excuses himself by transferring the blame to other people, or to his circumstances, thus losing himself in the forces that play upon him from without. The human mind becomes incredibly subtle and deceitful when it tries to defend itself against an uneasy conscience.

But the shedding of blood was a constant rebuke to this inveterate tendency of the sinner to make light of his own sin. An innocent victim had to be slain for him in order that he might be purified. Something had to shock the insensitive sinner awake. Clearly, the Cross of Christ is in one of its aspects supremely effective at just this point. Here is God's estimate of human sin. Here is what sin really does. It crucifies the Son of God!

The shedding of blood makes it clear that the forgiveness of sin is not a casual matter. Too often God has been presented as an ami-

able, easygoing parent who is quite ready to let bygones be bygones. He picks us up when we fall, gives us a friendly pat on the back, tells us that he will not count this sin against us, and sends us on our way once more with care-free hearts. This is supposed to be his love.

But it is love itself that makes forgiveness hard: the greater the love, the more difficult the forgiveness. We recognize this principle on the human level. Suppose you are driving your car down a quiet city street, past a sign reading "Children at Play." The safe speed is twenty miles an hour. But you in careless haste are driving fifty miles an hour. From behind a parked car a three-year-old boy rushes. You try to stop but you are too late. You pick up a broken body and rush it to the nearest hospital. Hours later you discover that the child's father is a dear friend of yours. The child will live, but he will likely be a cripple his whole life long. You confront the father and ask his forgiveness. He may grant it, but it will not be easy. If he were casual in his forgiveness, it would mean that he did not love his child and cared nothing for you. An easy forgiveness would not forgive you. In that case, you would need two qualities in your friend: a love so strong that he would forgive, and an integrity that would find it hard to forgive, that would

25 Nor yet that he should offer himself often, as the high priest entereth into the holy place every year with blood of others;

26 For then must he often have suffered since the foundation of the world: but now once in the end of the world hath he appeared to put away sin by the sacrifice of himself.

27 And as it is appointed unto men once to die, but after this the judgment:

presence of God on our behalf. 25 Nor was it to offer himself repeatedly, as the high priest enters the Holy Place yearly with blood not his own; 26 for then he would have had to suffer repeatedly since the foundation of the world. But as it is, he has appeared once for all at the end of the age to put away sin by the sacrifice of himself. 27 And just as it is appointed for men to die once,

---

been amply proved, i.e., that Christ has penetrated into the very **presence of God on our behalf.** His service in the heavenly sanctuary is permanent. His sacrifice needs no repetition since it is not only completely effective but also because it has come **at the end of the age.**

27-28. What this means he shows again by a human analogy. **As it is appointed for men to die** *once,* . . . **so Christ, having been offered** *once* . . . , **will appear a second time.**

---

be wounded for your transgression. Do we need less in God?

Men used to work twelve-hour shifts, seven days a week, in the steel mills. Their eyes were dull and they were little better than beasts. It is not easy to forgive that if you care about the light in the eyes of men. When the greedy for the sake of gain prostitute that which is sacred in boys and girls, it is not easy to forgive, not if you prize that which is sacred in youth. When those in public trust use official positions to enrich themselves, thus undermining democratic government, it is not easy to forgive, not if you care about decency in government. Members of the white race often make light of their prejudice against the yellow and the brown and the black peoples. But does God make light of it? We think of a sensitive Negro mother whose joy is just as tender as any white mother's when her first-born son is put into her arms for the first time. Then before long she begins to dread that day, that dark day, when to this growing boy there will come the bitter realization that no matter how hard he tries, no matter how good his education, no matter how faithful to duty he is, some doors will be forever closed to him because his race is reckoned a handicap and his color counted a curse. God must find that very hard to forgive if he loves "colored" people as our gospel says he does. **Without the shedding of blood there is no forgiveness of sins.**

(b) But can blood sacrifice be merely a pedagogical device? Is the long record of such sacrifices merely designed to impress the sinner, to shake him loose from his self-righteous pride? They would fail even as such devices, they would not impress the sinner, unless they pointed beyond themselves to some moral real-

ity in the very life of God. We have not yet fathomed the meaning of our passage. What did our Lord mean in the institution of the sacrament, "This is my blood of the covenant, which is poured out for many" (Mark 14:24) ? And what does our author mean when he writes of the necessity of **the heavenly things themselves** being purified **with better sacrifices?** Does man's sin defile even the presence of God? It befouls everything on earth, besmirches every sanctity that he knows, his conscience, his home, his church, the beauty of the created world. Does it also make heaven unclean?

We need to be very clear on the nature of this defilement. It is primarily moral, ceremonial only in a derived sense. To think of evil only, or chiefly, in a ceremonial sense may become a dangerous kind of evasion (cf. Expos. on vss. 1-10) . In the O.T. passages to which our author refers (vss. 19-22) it is not clear whether the uncleanness is moral or ceremonial. Probably it was a mixture of both, at least in the minds of the people. Clearly Num. 19 refers to ceremonial defilement. Our biblical warrant for the primacy of the moral element in uncleanness is the clear word of Jesus. " 'Do you not see that whatever goes into a man from outside cannot defile him, since it enters, not his heart but his stomach, and so passes on?' (Thus he declared all food clean.) And he said, 'What comes out of a man is what defiles a man. For from within, out of the heart of man, come evil thoughts, fornication, theft, murder, adultery, coveting, wickedness, deceit, licentiousness, an evil eye, slander, pride, foolishness. All these evil things come from within, and they defile a man.' " (Mark 7:18b-23.)

But moral defilement does create ceremonial uncleanness. The evil heart is unfit for the pres-

28 So Christ was once offered to bear the sins of many; and unto them that look for him shall he appear the second time without sin unto salvation.

and after that comes judgment, 28 so Christ, having been offered once to bear the sins of many, will appear a second time, not to deal with sin but to save those who are eagerly waiting for him.

This is the one explicit use of the term "Second Coming" in the N.T. The "parousia" or "presence" is not elsewhere called a "second" coming, although the idea may be present. Our author has combined his dominant idea of Christ as the priest who introduces us to the heavenly sanctuary, i.e., to the true realm of reality, with the primitive eschatology which moves in terms of a time sequence (see Intro., pp. 583-86). The combination would have seemed incongruous to a Hellenist like Philo, but it shows again that the writer of Hebrews was a primitive Christian and never a thoroughly consistent philosopher. What he wants to do is to arouse his readers to a sense of urgency and crisis. The time is short; Christ will return; they must be ready for him. He comes this time as judge, but for those who are ready the judge is the Savior. Again the author shows that he is the skilled pastor who can suggest the terrible consequences of failure to be ready but who also gives expression to the joy with which those who **are eagerly waiting for him** will hail Christ's coming. The words **it is appointed for men to die once, and after that comes judgment**

ence of good. We cannot worship God with unclean hands. "Thou art of purer eyes than to behold evil, and canst not look on iniquity" (Hab. 1:13). "Blessed are the pure in heart, for they shall see God" (Matt. 5:8). The emphasis upon ceremonial defilement is the outward response to a deep and inwardly felt reality (cf. Expos. on 1:3 and 10:2). It suggests with regard to the damage of sin those wider dimensions that a merely moral view is apt to overlook. We owe much to the author of Hebrews, who alone among N.T. writers has preserved this emphasis. He does recognize the moral element in defilement. His complaint of the old sacrifices is that they "cannot perfect the conscience of the worshiper" (vs. 9). The excellence of Christ's offering is that it does "purify your conscience from dead works to serve the living God" (vs. 14). But his failure to make it clear that moral uncleanness is primary, ceremonial defilement secondary, forbids us to read this epistle alone (however, cf. 5:7-10). It should be read along with Paul's letters.

For it is the moral defilement that is acute. How can God receive sinners without acquiescing in their sin, thereby defiling himself? How, unless from himself there comes a sacrifice that purges uncleanness, leaving God and the redeemed sinner dwelling in the clear light of moral reality, with all shadows banished? The satisfaction theory of the Atonement leaves much to be desired. But unless justice itself is satisfied, the penitent and awakened sinner cannot be satisfied. His forgiveness will not be morally convincing. The blood sacrifice of Christ tells us, if it says anything, that God himself sacrifices on our behalf; that, in the words of

Paul, "he himself is righteous and that he justifies him who has faith in Jesus" (Rom. 3:26).

We return now to the question of life after death as the believer must face it. **It is appointed for man to die once, and after that comes judgment.** If the life to come means the presence of God, then judgment is a necessity. For God's estimate of man is the only fair and judicious one. It alone pierces beneath outward appearances and sees us as we really are. God speaks the last and the definitive word about each man, his work and his worth. In a sense, every cry for justice, every revolt against the injustice of our poor human appraisals of each other, is an appeal to the judgment of God. But God's judgment is spoken to the believer in the light of Christ's sacrifice. Herein is our salvation complete.

**Christ . . . will appear a second time.** As a matter of fact, this second appearing of Christ, for all the believers since his day, has been at their death. So little stress is laid here on the final consummation as to furnish no warrant for any of the various elaborate interpretations that are given to that hope. We are interested rather to underscore the latter half of the verse. When he appears, it is **not to deal with sin but to save those who are eagerly waiting for him.**

The interpreter may find his best key to this whole passage in the words **eternal inheritance** (vs. 15) and **will** (vss. 16-17). We are reminded of Paul's usage, "Heirs of God and fellow heirs with Christ" (Rom. 8:17). It is significant that as Paul introduces this thought into the climax of his most complete doctrinal statement, so our writer uses it in the heart of his epistle. The

10 For the law having a shadow of good things to come, *and* not the very image of things, can never with those sacrifices, which they offered year by year continually, make the comers thereunto perfect.

10 For since the law has but a shadow of the good things to come instead of the true form of these realities, it can never, by the same sacrifices which are continually offered year after year, make per-

---

suggest that judgment for each individual follows death immediately, and this interpretation would be consonant with his thought throughout; but the rapid movement of ideas directed to another end makes it dangerous to draw a final conclusion about this.

### (3) FAILURE OF THE OLD COVENANT AND THE PERFECTION OF THE NEW (10:1-18)

The author concludes his formal argument by reiterating his conviction that the single, effective offering of Christ has ended the futile, repetitious offering of animals and has achieved the goal of the new covenant, the forgiveness of sins. While the substance of thought in this section is not new, new shades of meaning are introduced and the tone is more prophetic and decisive than before.

**10:1.** Vss. 1-4 embody the writer's considered and final verdict on the Levitical priesthood and its sacrificial system. The old cult is but the shadow of the new; it failed

---

interpreter should not miss this emphasis. Too often we present religion as an added load of duties which people are to carry. That is not good news. Our business is rather to announce that men have come into a huge fortune, to explain the content of the inheritance, and the terms on which one may enter it. "For you know the grace of our Lord Jesus Christ, that though he was rich, yet for your sake he became poor, so that by his poverty you might become rich" (II Cor. 8:9; cf. also I Cor. 3:21-23). To us Christ offers the clean forgiveness of our sin, freedom from guilt, the abounding and sufficient mercy of God, patient strength for every trying experience, a glorious meaning for this human pilgrimage, the priceless joys of human love, and in the world to come eternal life in the presence of God. Let no man despise such a heritage!

**10:1-4. The Failure of a Recurring Sacrifice.** —This passage is a concise summary of the previous argument (7:11–9:28) and prepares the way for the climactic point of the epistle, the superiority of the sacrifice of Christ. The old sacrifices did not **make perfect those who draw near** because they were **continually offered year after year.** Their very repetition was evidence of their failure. **Otherwise, would they not have ceased to be offered?**

If the worshipers had once been cleansed, they would no longer have any consciousness of sin. The meaning here is far from obvious. The O.T. sacrifices recognized that sin was a constantly recurring affair and that new sins needed fresh sacrifices. **In these sacrifices there is a reminder of sin year after year.** Yet they

did not get at the root of the matter. They did not cure sin or modify the tendency to sin.

But is the Christian sacrifice any better? Did it destroy sin or modify the tendency to sin? Even our writer betrays pastoral concern lest the people who have suffered much for their faith (cf. vss. 32-34) might nevertheless throw away their confidence (vs. 35). He fears that some may not have entered the rest of God (4:1), and warns them against the dangers of disobedience (4:11) and of falling away "from the living God" (3:12). Does he mean that if they disobey and fall away, it could not be said of them that they **had once been cleansed?**

Vs. 2 is a clear indication that in the author's mind the ceremonial element had precedence over the moral in the purification at which the sacrificial system aimed. Only so could he have written without qualification, **If the worshipers had once been cleansed, they would no longer have any consciousness of sin.** To interpreters that have been nourished by the O.T. prophets, by the Gospels, and by Pauline thought, this will seem a strange doctrine. The insights already noted above need to be taken into account. Moral impurity clearly implies ceremonial uncleanness. Sin bars us from the presence of God. The sinner feels himself unclean. But preoccupation with the ceremonial rather than with the moral leads to strange conclusions which can be corrected only by reading Hebrews along with Romans and Galatians (cf. also Expos. on 9:1-10, 15-28).

The whole history of Christian living ought to warn us against any premature claims to sanctification. Sin dies a slow death, even in

2 For then would they not have ceased to be offered? because that the worshippers once purged should have had no more conscience of sins.

fect those who draw near. 2 Otherwise, would they not have ceased to be offered? If the worshipers had once been cleansed, they would no longer have any conscious-

---

to reach the goal, to **make perfect those who draw near,** because it had to be endlessly repeated and because the blood of bulls and goats cannot take away sins. The opening sentence reveals what has been at the center of his thought in his whole argument. The failure of the earthly system is due to its earthliness; it is an inherent failure not to be overcome by scrupulosity. The sacrifices do not **make perfect those who draw near** because they cannot, operating as they do in the realm of the unreal. Here it is the law which **has but a shadow;** elsewhere it is the priesthood. Law and priesthood are identical for our author. The failure of the priesthood means the collapse of the law (cf. 7:11) .

2. This is the author's own inference, unsupported by scripture and resting upon his primary thesis, i.e., the two-world concept. If the sacrifices had been in the realm of reality—they were actually made in the shadowland—they would have achieved the purification of the conscience and therefore would not have been repeated **year after year** (vs. 3) . The author disregards the answer to his argument, which at once occurs to us, as it would have occurred to any good Jew living in the first century. Sacrifices have

---

the believer. Vanquished violently in one area of a man's life, it subtly reappears in another, most likely in the deadly form of self-righteousness. The most advanced saints have warned us that victory is not easy, and that the pride we take in our moral achievements under the grace of God—yes, the pride we take in our humility —is waiting to throw us down from the topmost rung of the ladder.

Self-righteousness is the antithesis of trust in God, whether in the natural man or in the son of grace. It always produces moral blindness. It is easy for anybody, whether converted or not, to be impressed with his own virtue and respectability. He fortifies this sense of his own decency by contrasting himself with his fellows. In this contrast his dear self subtly selects the ground of the comparison so as to be favorable to its own position. If he is short on charity, he can at least talk of his rugged honesty. If he is weak on honesty, he can point to his courage. If courage is not his strong point, he can refer to his fidelity to spiritual exercises. If he has been a notorious sinner, he can point to his very penitence and his complete break with old vices that once held him. But all this leads to a vicious kind of moral blindness, the most serious flaw in the respectable citizen who sees no need of saving grace.

Perfectionists are known to have put their emphasis on moral minutiae, such as tithing "mint and dill and cummin" (Matt. 23:23) . Their morality is often a stern code of negations, with a curious blindness to the Christian law of love, and to their own lack of love for those with whom they daily live. They boast of what they do not do. Even the Christian church

has been infected with this vice. A whole history of Christianity could be written around the theme of the moral blindness of the church to weighty contemporary moral issues. Again and again self-righteous sons of grace have concentrated on moral trivialities rather than upon moral urgencies, just because the former minister to self-respect, while the latter would damage the self-respect of the righteous. As for the actual operating moral standard of the church today, what is it? Not the standard proclaimed and professed, but the working standard by which church members judge one another, and by which the minister often judges his people? It is most certainly not the biblical standard of complete love of God and love of neighbor. That is too high a law for any of us to confront and retain a vestige of satisfaction with ourselves. Rather the basis upon which Christians judge one another is a strange, unholy mixture composed of the Ten Commandments (or at least some of them) , a healthy amount of middle-class bourgeois prejudice, and a good many vestiges of pre-Christian morality from our pagan ancestors, salted by a few maxims discreetly drawn from the Bible.

This is a constant danger for the man of faith, and the danger is not lessened by being told that by one sacrifice sin is destroyed in his life. Rather, our only hope is that we have a **reminder of sin year after year,** nay more, day after day. Frequent self-examination, daily humiliation by confronting Jesus Christ in all his moral grandeur, penitence honest and complete, a persistent **consciousness of sin**—these are the only known safeguards against self-righteous pride. Even the forgiveness of past

**3** But in those *sacrifices there is* a re- | ness of sin. **3** But in these sacrifices there is
membrance again *made* of sins every year.

---

to be repeated because men sin repeatedly. It is the sinfulness of man, not the ineffectiveness of sacrifice, which requires the repetition. Paul understood this and met it by his
message of a gospel that provides radical transformation in man. Paul dealt with the
moral problem more directly and profoundly than the author of Hebrews.

**3.** As if to answer the objection just raised, the writer adds these words. They are
nearer to Paul's view of the law (cf. Rom. 7) than almost anything in Hebrews. Paul,
too, regarded the law as a negative preparation for the gospel, convincing man of his
own guilt and helplessness and leaving him but one alternative, to throw himself in
faith on the mercy of God and his gracious provision in Christ. Hebrews follows a very
different line, arguing that the sacrificial system is a negative preparation for the gospel
in that it points to an effective sacrifice, a way opened through the blood of Christ into
the very presence of God. While Paul sees the gospel as the power to make new creatures,
Hebrews sees it as the revelation of a new and living way of worship whereby men may
have free and perfect access to God. The ultimate goal is the same, but the roads the two
authors travel are different.

---

sins does not destroy their memory. It had better
not! For the memory of these sins, and the wonder of their forgiveness, help to keep us humble
about our own moral abilities. To trust in our
own moral strength is the last citadel in which
original sin takes refuge. Daily to depend upon
the grace of God is the life of faith.

> And they who fain would serve Thee best
> Are conscious most of wrong within.[4]

The man who has no **consciousness of sin** had
better look quickly, honestly, and completely at
himself in the light of the presence of the
Christ.

What, then, can we make of this passage?
Clearly, we have not yet fathomed its meaning.
What does the one sacrifice of Christ do to the
**consciousness of sin** that the repeated sacrifices
of the O.T. cultus failed to do?

(*a*) For one thing, it judges us. The sacrifice
of Christ was superior in that he "offered himself without blemish" (9:14). Let any man
stand in the presence of that unblemished sacrifice and his flimsy pretenses look shabby. He
must cry out for the mercy of God upon his sins
and upon himself. This is the first and the fundamental step. Until the self-regarding ego sees
its own deep need, no salvation will avail.
Until we are persuaded to complete honesty,
until we are willing to be stripped bare, until
we are ready for the Light to search out every
dark area of our life, we still stand aloof from
God. We still depend upon ourselves, we still
usurp the place of God in our own lives. This
is man's basic sin; this is his self-contradiction;
this is his tragedy and his death. It is from this

[4] Henry Twells, "At even, when the sun was set."

pretentious self-trust that he must be redeemed
if he is to be restored to the family of God. To
see the Son of God, perfect sacrifice with no
blemish, suffering the ultimate in human disgrace and shame, this judges and condemns us
as no O.T. ritual, however God-given and impressive, could ever do. For the Cross is a cosmic
affair. All sinners are gathered there to heap
abuse upon the Lord of Love.

> We gibed him, as he went, with houndish glee,
> Till his dimmed eyes for us did overflow;
> We cursed his vengeless hands thrice wretchedly,—
> And this was nineteen hundred years ago.[5]

"I, when I am lifted up from the earth, will
draw all men to myself" (John 12:32). Aye!
But not without repelling them first! For something in us doggedly resists exposure. We are
afraid of the light, the blinding light of Calvary.
We know what it will do to us. Brought to the
moment of crisis, we shrink back. A kind of
primitive terror seizes us. We will agree to any
kind of compromise: we will attend church; we
will give to its support; we will give up this
vice or undertake that duty; we might even
consider giving half our goods to feed the poor.
But not this! The ground shakes beneath our
feet. All our old certainties are tottering. All
the old securities on which we had felt solid
and built our lives are now turning to sand. It
is as though we were being led to a high cliff at
darkest midnight and told to leap, on the assurance that all will be well. Of course we hesitate and draw back.

Augustine has left us an account of his own

[5] Edwin Arlington Robinson, "Calvary," from *Children
of the Night.* Used by permission of Charles Scribner's
Sons, publishers.

4 For *it is* not possible that the blood of bulls and of goats should take away sins.

a reminder of sin year after year. 4 For it is impossible that the blood of bulls and goats should take away sins.

---

**4.** Our author has indicated the verdict he will pronounce on the sacrificial system as a whole, and upon the law implementing it, in a parenthetical remark (7:19), but the words he uses here have a prophetic ring of authority and finality not found elsewhere. Indeed this note of finality is sounded throughout these verses (1-4). Readers attracted by Judaism of the normative type would hardly have been impressed by his argument, for he does not meet the objections a good Jew would raise at every point. He assumes that his controlling concept of shadow and substance, earthly and heavenly, is shared by his readers. If they share it, his argument is really cogent.

Behind the (to us) artificial forms are permanently significant convictions: that men are hungering and thirsting for fellowship with God; that the age-old forms of worship witness to this yearning; that sin is the barrier which prevents man from drawing near to God; that this barrier can be lifted only at a price; that the offering of animals, even flawless animals, is an imperfect substitute for the offering of a flawless person; that blood,

---

final struggle. It began on a day when Pontianus, high in the service of the emperor, told the story of his conversion. He and three of his friends, also in the service of the emperor, had been walking in a garden just outside the city walls when they came upon the simple cottage of some poor Christians. With one of the others he had entered, picked up from the table a life of Antony, the Egyptian monk, and begun to read it. It was so convincing that the two of them, feeling the emptiness of their lives, decided to be baptized. The simple words had their effect on the learned Augustine. He writes:

But Thou, O Lord, while he was speaking, didst turn me round towards myself, taking me from behind my back, where I had placed me, unwilling to observe myself; and setting me before my face, that I might see how foul I was, how crooked and defiled, bespotted and ulcerous. And I beheld and stood aghast; and whither to flee from myself I found not. And if I sought to turn mine eye from off myself, he went on with his relation, and Thou again didst set me over against myself, and thrustedst me before my eyes, that *I might find out mine iniquity, and hate it.* I had known it, but made as though I saw it not, winked at it, and forgot it.[6]

This was the crisis in Augustine's life. That very day in an agony of tears and prayer he was born into the kingdom.

God's love pouring itself out on the Cross, the sinless Christ suffering on our behalf, alone can persuade us to such knowledge of ourselves. It is to his justice and his love that all our secrets are to be bared. It is into his nail-pierced hands that we commit ourselves. No interpreter dare

[6] *Confessions*, tr. E. B. Pusey (London: J. M. Dent & Sons; New York: E. P. Dutton & Co., 1924; "Everyman's Library"), p. 162. Used by permission.

withhold the message of the Cross. It must somehow get through to those whose fears, roused by God's judgment, can be laid only by his tender grace.

(*b*) The forgiveness of sins has been established, and established in the only place where it could be effective, in the heart of God himself. God's attitude toward us as gracious and merciful is both fixed and declared. This is the heart of the Atonement and without it no atonement is possible. For the man whose faith is in God, God is the supreme reality. God is the creator of his world, the Father of his own spirit, his Savior, his heart's true home. For such a believer no mere "moral influence" atonement will suffice. God's attitude toward him is the most central fact in his world. When God has laid hold on him, turned him around, and forgiven him, then the **consciousness of sin** undergoes a radical change. His sins no longer stand between him and God. God has forgiven him. His humble trust in God now becomes his joy. Gone are the old guilty fears, the old despairs. God indeed is God!

(*c*) Again, the perfect sacrifice of Christ slays sin in principle, as we have seen. Sin does indeed die a slow death, but when the sacrifice of the Cross lays hold of a man, sin's death is made certain. It is now a dying sin against which the believer contends, strong even in its death throes, but under sentence of death. We can find illustrations of what this means all about us; e.g., one of the basic characteristics of sinful self-trust is that men must reinforce their self-esteem from every plausible source. We compare ourselves favorably with other people and are careful in our selection of the ground of comparison. This very fact vitiates all human relations. When we are in the pres-

the symbol of life, must be offered; that Christ, the Son of God, was the perfect priest who made the perfect offering, the offering of himself in his sympathetic humanity and in his all-powerful deity; that this offering achieves the promised covenant relationship by assuring the forgiveness of sins and that it opens the way, a new and living way—i.e., a personal way—into the presence of God. Convictions such as these are unquestionably presented in Hebrews. Stripped of the scriptural documentation made applicable by allegory, the author's thought emerges in its true impressiveness. But we need to remember that it is just this "dated" exegesis which serves as the channel for some of his most profound contributions. He sees, perhaps more clearly than any other N.T. writer, a great principle of continuity and solidarity in religion, from its older forms to the new revelation in Christ. He is the first Christian writer to attempt something like a philosophy of religion, employing the two religions he knows best, Judaism and Christianity. It is too much to say that he has developed a philosophy of religion, but he has laid the groundwork for it. Working within the framework of a high doctrine of verbal inspiration of the Scriptures, he nevertheless succeeds in moving steadily from prescriptive to personal

---

ence of a good man or woman, we feel uncomfortable. They rebuke our pride. If we could only find some flaw in them! But we are comforted if we can keep about us some friends who convince us of our moral superiority. When someone whom we have respected suffers a conspicuous moral collapse, we say outwardly, "How dreadful!" But something in us adds, however furtively, "How gratifying!" The pressure is off and we look better. This is one of the most common ways in which pride vitiates every human relationship.

But when the sinner apprehends the meaning of Christ's sacrifice, all this is changed. He no longer must fortify his own self-respect. His trust is no longer in his own virtue and strength. Rather, God has become his defense, his rock, his high tower. Having known the beginnings of grace in his own life, he is prepared to look upon his fellows in the light of what God's grace can do for them. Hence he sees them more fairly and more hopefully. He no longer takes secret pleasure when they do wrong. Love has a chance to work. Perhaps something like this was in the mind of Paul when he wrote: "Love is very patient, very kind. Love knows no jealousy; love makes no parade, gives itself no airs, is never rude, never selfish, never irritated, *never resentful;* love is never glad when others go wrong, love is gladdened by goodness, always slow to expose, always eager to believe the best, always hopeful, always patient" (I Cor. 13:4-7 Moffatt).

The believer thus stands in a truly dialectical position. On the one hand, his very faith in God must keep him on guard against his pride, which dies a slow death. He is humbled by his past sins. He is sensitive to his own wrongs, both past and present. But it is also true that he is no longer subject to guilty fears over his sins. His confidence is in the perfect sacrifice. Humble penitence is something entirely different

from morbid preoccupation with guilt. To keep dwelling on old failures betrays a lack of faith and signifies clearly that the sacrifice of Christ avails not for us. In the death of Christ, God himself has promised, so that "we who have fled for refuge might have strong encouragement to seize the hope set before us" (6:18). Not to accept that promise, not to rest upon it, is not to have faith.

It is important to see that our author never completely disparages the old law of sacrifice, for it provided **a reminder of sin year after year.** The O.T. law provided that on the day of Atonement the people were to afflict their souls (Lev. 16:31). They were not allowed to forget their sin. At least they were reminded of their need, and it is likely that many of the faithful were comforted by the sure mercies of God. But the very rite itself pointed beyond itself to God, and to the necessity for a sacrifice that would purify the conscience.

**For it is impossible that the blood of bulls and goats should take away sins.** This terse sentence echoes the moral grandeur of the O.T. prophets. The material sacrifice, no matter how costly, nor how impressive the ceremony that accompanied it, still could not confer peace of conscience upon the worshiper. Why? Because sin is a personal matter and only a personal power can cleanse. Christianity is supremely the religion that exalts the personal. It has persisted in declaring that personal characters are the worthiest symbols of God. God is to be worshiped as a person, "in spirit and truth" (John 4:24). We encounter him as persons, and it is in this encounter that our personality is established. Revelation is always in personal terms, and the human agents of God's revelation are never suppressed to the level of the impersonal. Christianity today is alike the champion of the personal as against the depersonalizing philosophies that would reduce man to the

5 Wherefore, when he cometh into the world, he saith, Sacrifice and offering thou wouldest not, but a body hast thou prepared me:

6 In burnt offerings and *sacrifices* for sin thou hast had no pleasure.

7 Then said I, Lo, I come (in the volume of the book it is written of me) to do thy will, O God.

---

5 Consequently, when Christ[v] came into the world, he said,

"Sacrifices and offerings thou hast not desired,
but a body hast thou prepared for me;
6 in burnt offerings and sin offerings thou hast taken no pleasure.
7 Then I said, 'Lo, I have come to do thy will, O God,'
as it is written of me in the roll of the book."

[v] Greek *he.*

---

authority in religion. Christ's authority is validated, to be sure, from scripture—even Christ's human experience derives its rationale from this source—yet there is an undeniable movement from the material realm with its outer rites and its animal sacrifices to the spiritual realm with its direct access to God, its purified conscience, its requirement of hope and faith and loyalty. The spiritual realm is not like Philo's, a realm of pure thought; it is a realm of persons. Christ is ultimately a perfect high priest, not the Logos; and his effective priesthood depends upon what he is in himself, upon his personality, as we should say. The prophetic sound of vss. 1-4 leads into a prophetic quotation from Ps. 40:6-8 (vss. 5-7), followed by the exegesis of the citation (vss. 8-10).

5-7. Ps. 40:6-8 is quoted, not as the words of the psalmist, but as Christ's words to God when he came into the world. The psalm in the Hebrew original is a song of praise for God's help. God's wonderful works call for more and other sacrifices than outer offerings; they call for obedience to the will of God. But instead of the Hebrew "mine ears hast thou opened" (i.e., that I may hear and obey), the LXX reads **a body hast thou prepared**

---

mere meeting place of inanimate forces, and the champion of the people against the all-devouring state that would degrade man to the level of an instrument of the body politic. It forever declares that the state is made for man, not man for the state. In its ethics it requires that men treat their fellows as persons. The Christian ethic received one of its most characteristic formulations, although by no means its completest, in that principle of Kant which requires us to treat personality, whether in ourselves or others, as end and never merely as means. We should expect, therefore, that salvation is to be read in personal terms. Nothing impersonal can really change a man or save him. No "overpowering." No "infusion." Such words must always be regarded as figures of speech. The Holy Spirit always treats us as persons.

**5-10. Christ's Obedience as Sacrifice.**—At first reading this passage startles us. It looks like a complete repudiation of the whole sacrificial system. In its place apparently is put ethical obedience as the end and means of the Christian life. That in fact seems to have been the intention of the psalmist. We are reminded of Samuel's rebuke to Saul, "Behold, to obey is better than sacrifice, and to hearken than the fat of rams" (I Sam. 15:22). This is part of the whole

prophetic trend illustrated in such passages as Ps. 51:16-17; Isa. 1:11-15; Amos 5:21-23; Mic. 6:6-7. Indeed, the emphasis upon obedience rather than sacrifice is characteristic of the teaching of Jesus (cf. Matt. 23:25-28). The author seems to be quite in line with the tradition when he writes, **He abolishes the first** [i.e., **sacrifices and offerings**] **in order to establish the second** [i.e., **Lo, I have come to do thy will**]. But if obedience replaces sacrifice, why take such pains to establish the perfection of Christ's sacrifice?

It was an apt scripture to apply to Jesus, this part of Ps. 40. It perfectly summarizes his life and work. No one can understand him without seeing that devotion to the will of God was his very soul. Even as a boy of twelve, he said to his parents, when they found him after long searching, "Did you not know that I must be in my Father's house?" (Luke 2:49.) He met his temptations in the wilderness, one after the other, by clarifying his complete adherence to the Will. "My food [the thing that satisfies hunger] is to do the will of him who sent me, and to accomplish his work" (John 4:34). He had extraordinary poise. He rarely if ever hesitated, never had to retrace his steps, never felt called on to apologize, never showed any fear. What-

8 Above when he said, Sacrifice and offering and burnt offerings and *offering* for sin thou wouldest not, neither hadst pleasure *therein;* which are offered by the law;

9 Then said he, Lo, I come to do thy will, O God. He taketh away the first, that he may establish the second.

10 By the which will we are sanctified through the offering of the body of Jesus Christ once *for all.*

8 When he said above, "Thou hast neither desired nor taken pleasure in sacrifices and offerings and burnt offerings and sin offerings" (these are offered according to the law), 9 then he added, "Lo, I have come to do thy will." He abolishes the first in order to establish the second. 10 And by that will we have been sanctified through the offering of the body of Jesus Christ once for all.

---

**for me.** This word body is essential for the author (cf. vs. 10), and his dependence on the Greek translation is nowhere more obvious than here. It is true that both readings can be reconciled with the main idea of the passage, obedience to the will of God as the true sacrifice, but the Hebrew certainly suggests obedience as the better sacrifice, indeed as the substitute for animal sacrifice. Our author cannot use this thought. He must show that instead of animal sacrifices, Christ offered himself, his own body, as the one acceptable sacrifice to God. The sacrificial principle is thus maintained by the contrast not of sacrifice with obedience, but of *a* sacrifice with *the* sacrifice.

**8-10.** The writer makes this point clear by his interpretation of the psalmist's words. The passage shows, he argues, that God willed a nobler sacrifice than the futile offerings made by earthly priests—offerings made **according to the law**—so that law is set aside with the **sacrifices and offerings** it prescribes. The sacrifice he willed was the offering of the body of Christ. Accordingly, the second abolishes the first; the offering of Christ abolishes the offerings made in the earthly tabernacle. It is by the will of God, then, that Christ's sacrifice of his own body has been made and made **once for all,** and it is by God's **will** that **we have been consecrated.** The author comes close to saying that God willed the sacrifice of the self and of self-will, and that Christ's sacrifice is of that kind.

---

ever he did, wherever he went, whatever he said, he moved with quiet confidence and strength. All of him went into all his words and deeds; and the secret was his complete and unhesitating devotion to the Father's purpose. Even to the last struggle in the garden and on the Cross, when doubts did seem to assail him, one thing he never doubted: that the will of God was good and that he would follow it even to the end (cf. Expos. on 3:2). This fact is not incidental in the atoning work of Christ. How else could God reveal himself than through a man completely sensitive to and devoted to his purpose? The whole doctrine of revelation depends upon the perfect obedience of Jesus. How else could he become the perfect sacrifice "without blemish" and offer himself to God to "purify your conscience from dead works to serve the living God" (9:14)?

Yet our author clearly did not mean that his perfect obedience could take the place of his sacrifice. Rather, by his obedience to the will of God, in offering the body God had prepared for him, he performed the perfect sacrifice that once for all replaced the old sacrifices which **are offered according to the law.** Only by this interpretation can we understand the appar-

ently ambiguous construction of vs. 10, **by that will . . . through the offering.**

Christ did not come into the world to be a good man: it was not for this that a body was prepared for Him. He came to be a great High Priest, and the body was prepared for Him that by the offering of it He might put sinful men for ever into the perfect religious relation to God.[7]

Whenever a teacher of theology, however revered, confronts us with a sharp dilemma and bids us choose one or the other, we have the right and the duty to ask his reasons. Why not both? To interpret the work of Christ as either ethical or religious (sacrificial) may be flying in the face of the plain meaning of the Bible. Certainly, in the light of the prophetic tradition, which culminated in our Lord's teaching, we have no right to interpret our duty to God and man apart from its moral content. The world has long since had enough of religion without morality and we dare not even hint that the Bible gives warrant to any such teaching.

Yet there is danger of overemphasis on

[7] James Denny, *The Death of Christ* (New York: A. C. Armstrong & Son, 1902), p. 234.

11 And every priest standeth daily ministering and offering oftentimes the same sacrifices, which can never take away sins:

11 And every priest stands daily at his service, offering repeatedly the same sacri-

---

We almost expect him to continue the thought by saying that we draw near to God through self-sacrifice and self-denial. Jesus' words, "If any man would come after me, let him deny himself and take up his cross and follow me" (Mark 8:34 and parallels), come involuntarily to mind. But such a thought would be quite outside the author's argument, even if close to his inner meaning. He is held by his priestly analogy to the objective significance of Christ's sacrifice.

**11.** The final section of the formal argument, which begins with this verse and runs to vs. 18, adds nothing new, for it only reiterates the two points already made: Christ's sacrifice was a single offering perfecting **for all time** (vs. 12) **those who are sanctified** (vs. 14), and it achieves the promised goal of the new covenant in the forgiveness of sins. The writer does bring together in vss. 12-13 quotations from his favorite psalm (Ps. 110) and from Jer. 31:33-34 (cf. 8:8 ff.). When we remember that he has based his entire argument on scripture, this final use of two important passages is seen as truly climactic from his point of view. Is vs. 11 slightly ironic in tone? The arduous daily **service,** the endless round of **the same sacrifices,** what does it all mean? Merely the heaping up of futilities, for multiplying sacrifices only multiplies imperfections. They **can never take away sins. Priest** is corrected in some MSS to "high priest." Our author usually speaks of Christ as high priest, except in ch. 7 where he is influenced by the quotation from Ps. 110. In that psalm the reference is to "a priest for ever, after the order of Melchizedek," but since the high priest alone enters the Holy of Holies, and Christ is the true priest who alone enters the heavenly sanctuary, he usually calls Christ high priest.

---

the moral. A religion based entirely on moral grounds tends to issue in the barren outcome of Kant's thought, a "religion within the limits of pure reason." Such a religion tends to be self-centered and self-righteous, and thus becomes the very antithesis of biblical religion. It tends to make even God an instrument of good conduct among men. Some writers, disdaining the sacrificial system as a relic of primitivism, give the impression of not understanding their Bible. The whole doctrine of God's mercy transcends the ethical. The love of God overflows the bounds of justice. It is never unrighteous and we dare not omit the moral from our lives. But there is more in religion than moral calculations. God's mercy accepts us even when we are sinners. **We have been consecrated,** we who have been dead in sin, and in whom sin still works its death struggle. While, therefore, the lifelong obedience of Jesus dare not be excluded from his atoning work, his obedience received its crowning perfection through suffering (2:10). His sacrifice goes beyond the bounds of the purely moral, and achieves that perfect reconciliation of man to God by which sinful man is received and restored. Further, only within the bounds of all that the "sacrifice" means does obedience for us become possible.

**Once for all.** We are now ready to understand the significance of these words. This is their

third appearance (cf. 9:12, 26). All through chs. 9–10, the one sacrifice of Christ has been contrasted with the continual sacrifices of the old law. The farther we penetrate into the author's meaning, the clearer it becomes that the sacrifice of Christ cannot be repeated. Once God showed forth himself completely. He can do no more. Once the complete sacrifice was consummated in the very life of God. It is therefore an eternal sacrifice. The way to God is forever open. God has himself opened it through his Son.

**11-18. The Coming Triumph of Christ.—He sat down at the right hand of God.** This does not picture some agelong idleness. Being **at the right hand of God** suggests that he partakes in all the activity of God as well as in his majesty. The contrast between vss. 11 and 12 indicates only that the sacrificial work of Christ is completed. Since the sacrifice was perfect, nothing remains to be added to it.

**Then to wait until his enemies should be made a stool for his feet,** as though the perfect sacrifice had made the final triumph sure. In our despairing day we deeply need a gospel of hope; only—the Christian hope seems so forlorn, if not ridiculous. The future lies in the hands of the men and the nations of greatest power. The thought of vast atomic energy, the terrifying display of mighty air armadas, the

12 But this man, after he had offered one sacrifice for sins for ever, sat down on the right hand of God;

13 From henceforth expecting till his enemies be made his footstool.

14 For by one offering he hath perfected for ever them that are sanctified.

15 *Whereof* the Holy Ghost also is a witness to us: for after that he had said before,

fices, which can never take away sins. 12 But when Christ[w] had offered for all time a single sacrifice for sins, he sat down at the right hand of God, 13 then to wait until his enemies should be made a stool for his feet. 14 For by a single offering he has perfected for all time those who are sanctified. 15 And the Holy Spirit also bears witness to us; for after saying,

[w] Greek *this one.*

---

The words **daily at his service** would not in themselves exclude the high priest for our author (cf. 7:27), but the phrase **every priest** in this context makes it probable that he means priest *qua* priest, and not the high priest alone. The entire system is antiquated.

**12-13.** Vs. 12 repeats the thought of 1:3, "When he had made purification for sins, he sat down at the right hand of the Majesty on high," but with the added content which the argument has now supplied, **when Christ had offered for all time a single sacrifice for sins.** This is what the author had set out to prove. Christ's service for men is perfected. The priests still stand, ready to repeat their pitifully ineffective sacrifices; Christ sits in triumph waiting the final overthrow of his enemies.

**14.** The perfection achieved is clearly not moral perfection as such, but the perfectly adequate sacrifice on Christ's part and the perfectly assured forgiveness for men. Moral perfection is no doubt implied as a result of this perfect provision for worship, but it is not in the foreground of his thought.

**15-17.** This single offering perfecting worship and the worshiper achieves the goal contemplated by the new covenant, the forgiveness of sins. The author quotes again from the Jeremiah passage (cf. 8:8 ff.)—this time more briefly but at sufficient length to

---

imposing structure of vast industrial systems—these seem the final security. The fragile gospel of suffering love looks absurd to the wise man of the world. What is the ground of our hope?

In the nineteenth century most people believed in automatic progress, "onward and upward forever." That illusion was broken by the disasters of the twentieth. But many of us still retain our confidence in human perfectibility. In one way or another knowledge is to be the savior of mankind. When the scientific method is applied to our social institutions, when we develop our social psychology, our economics, our political science, we shall know how to organize life and to produce the good society. Such plans underestimate the persistence, the perversity, and the power—of sin! Men propose to get rid of it, or at least to restrain its influence. Education and reason are to be the instruments. Goodness will triumph because goodness is at the heart of things and not far from the heart of man. As long as there are victims of this illusion, there will be those who continue to give themselves to sentimental dreams as the solid rock upon which hope is to be built.

At the other pole are the apocalyptic sects, defeatists really, who seem to have taken refuge

from reality in the sheer almightiness of God. After all, they seem to say, the Cross was a mistake. It cannot conquer. They propose in its stead a kind of pagan reliance upon the overwhelming power of God to subdue all his enemies. Force is to be the final argument.

Neither of these extremes is envisaged here. It is the sacrifice itself which assures the final triumph. Its diagnosis of human ills seems foolish, but it is the wisdom of God. The heart of man's evil is his denial of God, the setting up of himself as God, the claiming of prerogatives over his own life and the lives of his fellows that belong to God alone. Hence come fears, cruelty, pride, lusts, greed, wars, and all the desolation that afflict our race. To understand clearly the roots of evil in our revolt against God is the beginning of the interpreter's wisdom. Without it no gospel is possible.

What is to cure these evils? The return to God in faith, love, and obedience. What will induce man to make this return? The showing forth of the righteous love of God. Jesus seemed pathetically weak on the Cross. He seemed powerless to reply to the taunts of his enemies. He even died before the customary time for a crucified criminal. Yet that weakness was and remains the power of God. What the

16 This *is* the covenant that I will make with them after those days, saith the Lord; I will put my laws into their hearts, and in their minds will I write them;

17 And their sins and iniquities will I remember no more.

18 Now where remission of these *is, there is* no more offering for sin.

16 "This is the covenant that I will make with them
after those days, says the Lord:
I will put my laws on their hearts,
and write them on their minds,"
17 then he adds,
"I will remember their sins and their misdeeds no more." 18 Where there is forgiveness of these, there is no longer any offering for sin.

---

remind his readers of the content of the citation. The part he quotes here is what is important for him. A comparison of the two quotations shows several changes from his own rendering. Was he quoting from memory? The slight changes do not alter the thought, although they suggest that he has the present application of the words in mind. The priestly sacrifices on earth were a constant reminder of sin (vs. 3); the perfect offering of Christ resulted not in man's being able to forget his sins, but in the pronouncement of **the Holy Spirit** speaking for God, **I will remember their sins and their misdeeds no more.**

18. The negative form of this verse prepares the way for what is to follow. Forgiveness should give "confidence" (vss. 19-25), yet the fact that **there is no longer any offering for sin** carries with it a terrible warning (vss. 26-31).

---

world calls power is just weakness in masquerade. It is loving grace that is the thunder of God's power (Job 26:14).

Now this will seem stark nonsense to all but the children of faith. But if we have known the beginnings of God's power in our own lives; if our pride has been humbled by the humility of Christ; if our fears have been calmed by the peace that Christ imparts; if our self-centered greed has been softened by the outpouring of Christ's love; if our pretentious self-righteousness has been brought to him who is the light; if this saving work has been begun in us, then we have known by the invincible logic of a living experience the final power that will not fail, the love that will not let us go. This is faith. If faith in the Savior does not lead us to a living hope, it is not genuine faith. A despairing faith is a self-contradiction.

Only by such a living hope can we live and work. The commitments of the Christian are so radical, so complete, so hazardous in an earthly sense, that no man can fulfill them apart from hope in Christ. Not in vain are the wisdom and the power of God. "So shall my word be that goeth forth out of my mouth: it shall not return unto me void, but it shall accomplish that which I please, and it shall prosper in the thing whereto I sent it" (Isa. 55:11).

Robert Browning pictures an Arab physician traveling in Palestine some years after the death of Christ. He meets Lazarus and has a long interview. Now he is writing a doctor's report, trying to make a scientific analysis of the case. At long last he throws caution to the winds and writes excitedly,

The very God! think, Abib; dost thou think?
So, the All-Great, were the All-Loving too—
So, through the thunder comes a human voice
Saying, "O heart I made, a heart beats here!
Face, my hands fashioned, see it in myself!
Thou hast no power nor mayst conceive of mine,
But love I gave thee, with myself to love,
And thou must love me who have died for thee!"
The madman saith He said so: it is strange.[8]

When we have tasted the sacrifice of Christ, we have taken a living hope into our souls.

**Perfected for all time those who are sanctified.** The author can scarcely mean that believers have been morally perfected. If he did, his warnings not to fall into sin would have no meaning. But the essential conditions have been established. The crucial battle in the war against evil has been fought and won. It is now possible for the redeemed to enter the presence of God with confidence (cf. vs. 19). The perfection of the consecrated, once established in principle, will be fulfilled in eternity if not in time. That he has some moral elements in mind is evident from his repetition of the quotation from Jer. 31, **I will put my laws on their hearts, and write them on their minds.** To accept the sacrifice is to have

8 "An Epistle."

| 19 Having therefore, brethren, boldness to enter into the holiest by the blood of Jesus, | 19 Therefore, brethren, since we have confidence to enter the sanctuary by the |

### III. APPLICATION: IN VIEW OF THE PERFECTION OF GOD'S REVELATION IN CHRIST, HOLD FAST BY FAITH, FOR FAILURE TO DO SO MEANS A FEARFUL JUDGMENT (10:19–12:29)

### A. THE FINALITY OF ACCESS TO GOD THROUGH CHRIST ALSO ENTAILS A FINALITY OF JUDGMENT FOR THOSE WHO DISOBEY (10:19-31)

The remainder of Hebrews is keyed to exhortation. His massive argument is finished, although here and there the author adds an argumentative touch to enforce the implications of it (vss. 26-31). After a summary statement (vss. 19-21) he does not even use the word priest again. It is not out of his mind, however, as "high priest" in 13:11 and a phrase like "the sprinkled blood" in 12:24 (and cf. 13:10, 12, 15) indicate. We have noted his skill in dovetailing one stage of the argument into the next. This results in a repetitious style, and accounts, in part at least, for repetition in a commentary on Hebrews. Our author is a seasoned teacher who does not trust the memory and attention of his readers but drives home his thought again and again, moving in a sort of spiral rather than directly to his goal. This characteristic is apparent when he turns at this point to exhortation. Every major note in vss. 19-39 has been sounded before, but he adds something new while emphasizing the old thought. The psychology is precisely the same as in 5:11–6:20, interwoven rebuke, warning, encouragement, and assurance, although here he begins with assurance (vss. 19-24), follows it with rebuke (vs. 25), warning (vss. 26-31), encouragement coupled again with warning (vss. 32-38), and closes with a final word of assurance leading into his great chapter on faith (vs. 39).

**19-21.** This summary weaves together ideas now familiar to the readers. **Great priest,** taken from the LXX, means nothing new or different from "priest" and "high priest."

an internal sanction of the laws of God in the heart and in the mind. The old sacrifices could never achieve this. Now the believer can truly sing with the psalmist, "O how love I thy law! it is my meditation all the day" (Ps. 119:97).

**I will remember their sins and their misdeeds no more.** No merely subjective theory of the Atonement can include this vitally important declaration. Presumably there can be no forgetting with God. Nor can God in strict truth ever treat his children as other than former sinners. But God's attitude toward man is as though he had forgotten our sins. It is the sacrifice of Christ which makes that possible.

**There is no longer any offering for sin.** With these words the account of the priesthood of Christ is completed. The believer has been consecrated by the perfect sacrifice, so that the forgiveness of sins is assured and God no longer remembers them against us. The old sacrifices are no longer appropriate. Nor can we bring any modern equivalent of them. Lifted, set on our feet by the grace of Christ, we may be tempted to believe that we are now fulfilling God's demands. Self-confidence may creep back. Granted that once we needed redeeming grace, we are now able to walk alone.

Surely the deeds of the consecrated are well-pleasing unto God. This is the constant peril of every believer. His moral achievements under the grace of God, however impressive, are still no sacrifice for sin.

> Could my zeal no respite know,
> Could my tears forever flow,
> All for sin could not atone;
> Thou must save, and Thou alone.[9]

The motive of the believer's struggle and of his moral growth is not the re-establishing of his own righteousness. The believer must encounter struggle and must strive for growth; but the motive is no longer self-righteous pride: it is gratitude for God's mercies in Christ.

**19-25.** *Faith, Hope, and Love.*—These three great Christian virtues are now brought together. Such a treatment of them as this is unique in the N.T. Our author shows their theological rootage, their relationship to each other, and their practical importance in the Christian life. His treatment is valuable just because he is not writing about them at all. Having completed his doctrinal argument, he

[9] Augustus M. Toplady, "Rock of Ages."

20 By a new and living way, which he hath consecrated for us, through the veil, that is to say, his flesh;

21 And *having* a high priest over the house of God;

blood of Jesus, 20 by the new and living way which he opened for us through the curtain, that is, through his flesh, 21 and since we have a great priest over the house

---

It is a welcome variation of style. The way Christ has opened is **new and living**. Our author refers to the "living God" (vs. 31; 3:12; 9:14) and to his "living" word (4:12); he also stresses the fact that Christ "lives" after the analogy of Melchizedek and in contrast to mortal priests (7:8, 16, 25); we too are to "live" by faith (vs. 38, LXX), and by accepting discipline (12:9). It is not surprising, therefore, that he calls the way to life **a living way**; it is one of the great N.T. phrases. The immediate reference, no doubt, is to the contrast between dead animals and the living Christ. It carries with it, however, the implication, which is close to the author's thought throughout, that the way is a personal way issuing in full and perfect life. The other fresh touch in this passage is the striking allegorical identification of **the curtain** with the **flesh** of Jesus. Much has been read into these words (cf. II Cor. 5:16), but the context warrants our seeing here only a reference to the necessity of the death of Christ, his physical death, that his redemptive blood (vs. 19) might be available as the effective sacrifice. Mark 15:38 will occur at once to our minds, but the author shows no slightest interest in the Herodian temple.

---

turns to the practical implications in the lives of his readers and almost inadvertently finds himself talking about faith, hope, and love.

Faith is **confidence to enter**. This is surely the most precise definition of saving faith in all literature. Such faith has at least two opposites. One is the self-righteous pride of the natural man, which may become moral jauntiness. It is a fearful peril this, that we may be so blinded by our pride that all modesty and humility are destroyed; that we may even dare to invade the sanctuary of God without falling on our knees; that we may keep our heads unbowed; that we may despise the blood of the covenant. It is the kind of insensitivity to which all self-righteous pride tends.

The other opposite of faith is fear. It is this demonic fear that assails any man who would believe. Seeing his own darkness for the first time in the clear light that is Jesus Christ, he dreads the presence that exposes him. Frankly and objectively to confront our sin is intolerable. It is like trying to put a camel through a needle's eye. Surely every interpreter must be sympathetic with this fear in others because he has known it in himself. Anything but that bright light! Perhaps no man is prepared really to deal in full honesty with his own sin until he is free from its guilt. **Confidence to enter the sanctuary** is never easy. Our fears hold us back. But when God has provided a way **by the blood of Jesus,** then we have the confidence to enter. It is a confidence anchored in the work of Christ, drawing all its life and energies out of the resources of the grace of Christ. To turn away now in fear is a complete denial of the

sacrifice of Christ, an evidence that our trust is not in him. To enter now in confidence, chastened yet eager, humble yet joyful, is to have saving faith. The way is open, nothing need hold you back: this is the good news to all men.

**The new and living way.** There is all the rightful thrill of real novelty in this verse. The word translated **opened** literally means "innovated" or "inaugurated." It is in contrast with the old way of dead sacrificial victims. These words come to us from long ago. Yet for each believer who enters, the way is as new and fresh as it was for the writer of Hebrews or for any of his readers. It is the most glorious and genuine of all novelties. Not our circumstances, nor our friends, nor our work, nor our families are new, but ourselves. And because we are new, all things are made new: our families and friends, our work and circumstances, yes, even the world in which we live. Gone are the old despairs, the old burdens of dishonesty, the old dreariness of the self, the old guilty fears, the old defeats. It is literally into a new world that a believer enters, new because it is the world of God. It is a living way because it is through him who said, "I am the way" (John 14:6), and through him who "always lives to make intercession" (7:25). The way is never impersonal. We do not travel alone. It is by the way which Christ himself is that we travel. It is in his grace that we walk, and with his very life flowing through our members. And it is to him that we strive. All the ways of dead legality, of abstract principle, of repetitive and wearisome sacrifices, stand in sharp contrast

22 Let us draw near with a true heart in full assurance of faith, having our hearts sprinkled from an evil conscience, and our bodies washed with pure water.

23 Let us hold fast the profession of *our* faith without wavering; for he *is* faithful that promised;

of God, 22 let us draw near with a true heart in full assurance of faith, with our hearts sprinkled clean from an evil conscience and our bodies washed with pure water. 23 Let us hold fast the confession of our hope without wavering, for he who

22-25. Four exhortations follow in rapid succession, the first three positive, the fourth negative. Faith, hope, and love, the Pauline trinity (I Cor. 13:13), are enjoined, but love is coupled with the un-Pauline **good works.** The infrequency of our author's use of ἀγάπη has often been noted (only here and in 6:10; contrast φιλαδελφία in 13:1). The verb ἀγαπάω appears twice, both times in quotations from the LXX (1:9; 12:6), and the context shows that our author does not move in the gospel or in the Pauline tradition; neither the love nor the fatherhood of God is central in his thought. The presence of ἀγάπη here, connoting a type of action toward others (cf. 6:10) shows that he knew the nature of the Christian ethic. He did not make larger use of the love imagery or the love motive because it was not relevant to his priestly analogy. The majesty of God and the purification of men from their sins, leading to a sense of awe in worship

with the **living way** opened **through the curtain, . . . his flesh.**

**Priest over the house of God.** This reference to the house of God brings before us again the imagery of the family (cf. Expos. on 3:2).

**Let us draw near with a true heart,** with genuineness. Let us mean what we say. We depend on the mercy of God? Let the reliance be complete. Let there be no unsurrendered areas where the dear self lurks to seize the throne again. Let there be no part of the self that stands aside admiring what the rest of the self is doing. Let the self not be divided, but made one in love and trust. It is never easy to be completely honest. Men sometimes too glibly use the words "absolute honesty." The most that we can do is to cry out with the psalmist, "Create in me a clean heart, O God; and renew a right spirit within me" (Ps. 51:10). There is to be no balancing between judgments, no cautious consulting of our fears, no hesitant, reluctant trust. A little child in danger or in despair literally runs and throws himself into the arms of his mother. This is the **full assurance of faith.** Without it the **true heart** is not possible. Only when faith is assured is the heart kept true. Many men do not run to God. They take a cautious step in his direction, then begin to wonder if it is safe to go farther. The true-hearted man runs.

**With our hearts sprinkled clean from an evil conscience,** i.e., a guilty conscience. We are to draw near to God as men who have been, are, and remain forgiven, with the dread of guilt no longer holding us back. **Our bodies washed with pure water** in baptism. Baptism is an outward washing to signify an inward cleansing of the

heart. When all this has been done for us, there remains nothing for the believer but to draw near with confidence. This is faith.

**Let us hold fast the confession of our hope without wavering.** This part of the verse, taken by itself, is a heartless taunt. It is quite in keeping with the low meaning that has debased the word **hope.** When misfortune overtakes a friend, it is customary to urge him to hope for the best. This is supposed to be Christian comfort. But it is really the opposite of Christian faith. It is akin to the gambler's hope for a better throw of the dice. The law of averages will bring you something better. Such comfort is not Christian; it is idle and cruel. It bids us trust in—nothing.

The loss of solid hope is one of the most tragic aspects of our time. Nicholas Berdyaev has written of modern Western civilization, "We are entering into the realm of the unknown and the unlived, and we are entering it joylessly and without much hope."[1] Without hope, no great culture is possible, no venturesome faith, no noble character. Without hope, we are reduced to a cowardly calculation for our own safety. Without hope, all we can do is to build our own shelter against the oncoming storm, our faith denied, our creative impulses stifled, only the craven instinct of self-preservation dominating us. Without hope, we burrow into the ground, dig bomb shelters, prepare to live the life of a mole, instead of walking freely in God's sunlight. The serious proposal to go underground sounds like the death cry of our civilization.

[1] *The End of Our Time* (tr. Donald Atwater; New York: Sheed & Ward, Inc., 1933), p. 12.

24 And let us consider one another to provoke unto love and to good works:

25 Not forsaking the assembling of ourselves together, as the manner of some *is;* but exhorting *one another:* and so much the more, as ye see the day approaching.

promised is faithful; 24 and let us consider how to stir up one another to love and good works, 25 not neglecting to meet together, as is the habit of some, but encouraging one another, and all the more as you see the Day drawing near.

---

and to forgiveness and fellowship with God as the result of worship—these are the dominant notes for this liturgist. Faith will be discussed at length in the following chapter, and hope has been emphasized already. For a writer who is so steeped in liturgical language and practice, he has surprisingly little to say about the Christian liturgy. If the phrase **our bodies washed with pure water** refers to Christian baptism, it is a passing and rather depreciatory reference. **Our hearts sprinkled clean from an evil conscience** may also be pressed to refer to baptism, but the idea of purity elsewhere in Hebrews is always related to the sacrifice of Christ rather than to sacraments for the believer. As a matter of fact, our author is a sacramentalist on a grand scale. The human experience, the death and the ascension of Christ—this is the supreme sacrament for him. He cannot

---

Contrast with this mood the hope of the American frontiersman. More than one historian has commented on the hope that burned in the common man as he crossed the Alleghenies, settled the Northwest Territory, pressed on across the great plains, followed the Oregon Trail, or joined the California gold rush. A sense of manifest destiny lived in the common man. He had prophetic knowledge that he was sharing in the building of a great nation. It thrilled him in his daily toil, strengthened him amid almost unspeakable hardships. This kind of deed is possible only when a great hope possesses men.

But such a hope is never self-engendered. We do not manufacture it on order. It is always grounded in something or someone. Hope should be a glorious word. Its excellence depends on the person upon whom it rests. Christian hope is the noblest of all, and the most powerful, simply because it rests on the God of the promises, and has faith that **he who promised is faithful.**

It is hard to see how any Christian hope is possible apart from the promises of God. It is established in these promises and in him who promised. The Bible is full of such promises. They are the daily bread of Christian faith and hope. The Bible begins with the promise of redemption and ends with the promise of final triumph.

To what promises is our writer referring? It is probably the promise to Abraham (cf. 6:13-19). If so, it is plain that in that promise are included all the promises of our redemption, since through that promise "we who have fled for refuge might have strong encouragement to seize the hope set before us" (6:18). Pierce beneath the outer shell of noble deeds in any

of Christ's noblemen, go down beneath his opinions and the desires of his heart, and at the very center you will find a confidence in some promise. Many would include such promises as those in 13:6; Isa. 1:18; Matt. 6:33; 11:28-29; John 6:37; Phil. 4:19; Rev. 3:20 (cf. Expos. on 6:13-20). Ask any of the unnumbered faithful, in any land or generation, whether or not God keeps his promises. Their answer is our reassurance. We could ask no stronger evidence.

> Finding, following, keeping, struggling,
>    Is He sure to bless?
> "Saints, apostles, prophets, martyrs,
>    Answer, 'Yes.' " [2]

This is hope.

**Let us consider how to stir up one another to**—what? We are constantly stirring up one another to something. Even the most casual encounter has its unmistakable moral gravitation. I meet a man on the street; we say "Good morning"; we pass on; and something fateful has happened. One man by his very bearing, his tone of voice, the look in his eyes as he passed me in this casual way, has demanded in me honor, confidence, kindness, strength. Probably he was quite unaware of it. It would be better if he did not know. But the gravitation was there. Another man in a similar encounter by his very manner demands in me fear, weakness, deceit, selfishness. If casual meetings have their inevitable influence, how much more fateful the more intimate encounters of the home, the office, the school!

A bitter word stirs up bitterness in another. An honest word provokes thoughtfulness. A kind word awakens kindness. But the hard,

[2] John M. Neale, "Art thou weary, art thou troubled."

**26** For if we sin wilfully after that we have received the knowledge of the truth, there remaineth no more sacrifice for sins,

**26** For if we sin deliberately after receiving the knowledge of the truth, there

---

be regarded as ignorant of or as denying the validity of the Christian sacraments; they simply do not fit directly into the strategy of his argument as a whole. The negative admonition, **not neglecting to meet together, as is the habit of some,** follows naturally and logically after his exhortation to love and good works, for fellowship in worship is the root of right human relations. To draw from these words the conclusion that he was addressing a definite group of readers with whom he was intimately acquainted is unwarranted. Any preacher to any general body of Christians, then or since, might use these words. He closes this section, characteristically and very neatly, by preparing the way for the warning to follow. They are to be diligent in meeting together **all the more as you see the Day drawing near.**

26-31. The "Day" means a **fearful prospect of judgment** for deliberate sinners. Although we have been prepared for this aspect of his thought (cf. 2:2-3; 6:4-8), and he will emphasize it again (12:25-29), the note of punishment is sharper here than

---

unloving word of a virtue impressed with the weight of its own dignity stirs up—anything but virtue. **Let us consider,** that is the work of love. Only love can awaken love, only humility and patience can stir up to good works.

**Meet together.** Some were already drawing away from the Christian fellowship. It was a danger signal. We do not know who they were, nor can we more than guess their motives. Perhaps they were afraid of the danger of open confession. After all, they may have reasoned, we can still hold our faith and preserve our loyalty without risking our necks! The thing literally is impossible. For this verse is a direct transition to the dire warning of vss. 26-31. Let a man break fellowship with the church, and he is on his way to denying the faith. Perhaps there is no more effective denial of all that Christ means than to cut oneself off from the fellowship. Perhaps that is the real tragedy of disunity in the church (cf. Expos. on 3:13).

D. L. Moody once called on a leading citizen in Chicago to persuade him to accept Christ. They were seated in the man's parlor. It was winter and coal was burning in the fireplace. The man objected that he could be just as good a Christian outside the church as in it. Moody said nothing, but stepped to the fireplace, took the tongs, picked a blazing coal from the fire and set it off by itself. In silence the two watched it smolder and go out. "I see," said the man.

**Encouraging one another.** How desperately we all need that! It is the encouragement of a comrade who does not hesitate to point out flaws in our Christian faith and conduct. This finest of encouragement is possible only between two friends who trust each other, and know each other well enough to laugh together at

each other's expense. The creation of this living fellowship is surely one of the most urgent tasks of the church.

And this in the background to give it force— **you see the Day drawing near.** The loss of that sense is surely a weakness. The urgency is real, no matter how long delayed the end of history. "Christ will come for me soon," said a dear old man. He did come in a few months and they found in the old man's pocket a well-worn copy of a poem, "Let the Beauty of Jesus Be Seen in Me." The urgency is real: Jesus began his preaching by saying, "The kingdom of God is at hand" (Mark 1:15). The grace of God may now enter any human heart. The urgency is real: the Judgment Day draws near for our whole civilization. Ask the atomic scientists. The urgency is real: God may yet save his people. "Behold, the Lord's hand is not shortened, that it cannot save; neither his ear heavy, that it cannot hear" (Isa. 59:1). The conclusion drawn from the urgency? Encourage one another. This is the work of love.

26-31. *On Rejecting the Perfect Sacrifice.*— The grace of God is no idle gift. The very wonder of God's provision for man's redemption, the completeness of Christ's sacrifice, the gentle persistence of the spirit of grace, carry with them clear implications which our author now makes terribly explicit.

The sin here is clearly apostasy. The reference in Deut. 17:2-7 is to turning away from the Lord to the worship of other gods, such as the sun or moon. The tense of the word "sin" means "if we keep sinning wilfully." The **knowledge** is complete knowledge. The meaning of this sin is traced out in vs. 29.

There is a stern and inevitable logic in this passage. If we despise the sacrifice of Christ,

27 But a certain fearful looking for of judgment and fiery indignation, which shall devour the adversaries.

28 He that despised Moses' law died without mercy under two or three witnesses:

29 Of how much sorer punishment, suppose ye, shall he be thought worthy, who hath trodden under foot the Son of God, and hath counted the blood of the covenant, wherewith he was sanctified, an unholy thing, and hath done despite unto the Spirit of grace?

no longer remains a sacrifice for sins, 27 but a fearful prospect of judgment, and a fury of fire which will consume the adversaries. 28 A man who has violated the law of Moses dies without mercy at the testimony of two or three witnesses. 29 How much worse punishment do you think will be deserved by the man who has spurned the Son of God, and profaned the blood of the covenant by which he was sanctified, and outraged

---

anywhere else in Hebrews. The emphatic word is ἑκουσίως, **deliberately** or "willfully." Does this terrific warning show that the writer is informed of a danger of apostasy on the readers' part? Certainly his warning here, and elsewhere, envisages nothing less serious than a total and deliberate renunciation of Christian faith. When he directly rebukes them, however, it is for sluggishness, inattention, and immaturity. We are never told that they contemplate apostasy. His point seems to be that a halfhearted adherence to Christianity on their part can have only one end; their "drifting" (2:1) is in the direction of death and destruction. Here, as in 6:4 ff., he heaps up phrases to stress the supreme worth of the saving faith they renounce if and when they deliberately turn their backs on Christianity. Unless we read between the lines meanings which Hebrews nowhere makes explicit, we must interpret this sharp warning as the negative inference from the positive argument: their priest is the Son of God, his blood is the blood of the new covenant, and it is **the Spirit of grace** (vs. 29), not **the law of Moses**, which willful

---

there no longer remains a sacrifice for sins. God has spoken his final word in Jesus. He can say no more. He has revealed the way of salvation. There is no other way. Nor can the revelation be made any clearer.

If men turn away from the Christ, what can they expect? If they will not meet the God of mercy, they will encounter the God of wrath. They are left in their tragic fears, **a certain fearful looking for of judgment.** No man can escape the condemnation of conscience. To be separated from God is itself the **fury of fire which will consume the adversaries.** The fury of this fire men have known in bitter experience in our lifetime. It is the obverse side of the gospel of grace. Without this **fury of fire,** the gospel of grace can have no meaning, make no appeal. The first work of the interpreter is to show men the **fury of fire** which even now consumes them. It should be so announced that men will recognize it out of their own experience. The **fearful prospect of judgment** is deeply suppressed these days and the very suppression is made clear by dread symptoms. The symptoms of fear and hate and bitterness at least can be recognized.

If an apostate under the law of Moses died **without mercy at the testimony of two or three**

witnesses, how much more **punishment . . . will be deserved by the man who has spurned the Son of God,** even as the covenant of Christ is much better than the old ceremonial law of Moses? The higher the privilege, the more severe the penalty: it is the law of scripture and of life.

The reader should ponder the three qualifications of apostasy in vs. 29. The word translated **spurned** means literally to "trample underfoot," and more generally, to "treat with rudeness and insult." The word **profaned** means to "consider common." At whatever cost, evil must disparage Jesus Christ, reduce him, explain him, get him out of the way. When a man has received full **knowledge of the truth,** he can escape that truth only by belittling the Savior. It ought to be obvious to any man that this is the one unforgivable sin. In Mark's account (3:22-30) the scribes came down from Jerusalem to Galilee. They were prejudiced against Jesus. He was popular with the crowd; they were not. He taught with freshness and power; their teaching was dry and sterile. He kept dwelling upon all the grand simplicities of religion; their teaching was all tangled up with trivialities. So they whispered among the people, "He is possessed by Beelzebul, and by the

30 For we know him that hath said,
Vengeance *belongeth* unto me, I will recompense, saith the Lord. And again, The Lord
shall judge his people.

31 *It is* a fearful thing to fall into the
hands of the living God.

32 But call to remembrance the former
days, in which, after ye were illuminated,
ye endured a great fight of afflictions;

the Spirit of grace? 30 For we know him
who said, "Vengeance is mine, I will repay." And again, "The Lord will judge
his people." 31 It is a fearful thing to fall
into the hands of the living God.

32 But recall the former days when, after
you were enlightened, you endured a hard

---

sin outrages. He sums this up in the words **there no longer remains a sacrifice for sins**—
i.e., God has done all that can be done, all that God himself can do. The unspeakable
riches they possess as Christians will be matched by unspeakable dereliction and loss
if they now deliberately reject them. This is not merely the author's opinion; it rests
upon scripture, for if the old covenant punished deliberate offenders by death (Deut.
17:2-6), **how much worse** the penalty for deliberate rejection of the new order.

At this point, it may be said, the author did not catch the full import of the gospel.
His words reveal his passionate eagerness to save his readers from catastrophe, but his
analogy from the old to the new covenant turns out to impose a limitation on the new
rather than a liberation from the old. Can he have known of the record that Peter, who
denied his Lord at a moment of crisis, became a leader in the church?

### B. The Readers' Record Inspired Confidence (10:32-39)

**32-39.** As in 6:9 ff., so here, warning is followed by encouragement and assurance
based on the readers' past record. Their record is referred to in more detail than elsewhere but cannot be pressed to indicate necessarily a small group with which the author

---

prince of demons he casts out the demons"
(Mark 3:22). Their sin was this: they looked
on the best the earth has ever known and they
said, "He hath a devil," and they said it to
preserve their own position and power. It was
then that Jesus gave his teaching about the
unforgivable sin; and Mark adds, "For they
had said, 'He has an unclean spirit'" (3:30).
This is the ultimate moral confusion. When a
man has looked on the best and pronounced it
the worst, he has **outraged the Spirit of grace.**

**Vengeance is mine, I will repay.** This should
be our comfort. It bids us not be cast down
when we are the victims of unfair human judgment. There is a fair judgment where even now
we are justly appraised. It bids us give over
our fretful impulse to pass quick judgments on
our fellows. One there is who looks upon the
heart and judges righteously. Yet the judgment
of God is also a dreadful thing. **It is a fearful
thing to fall into the hands of the living God.**
Before him all our flimsy pretenses drop away.
All hidden things are brought to light. We are
seen through and through. Small wonder that,
facing that prospect, those who have never been
reconciled to God, and so to themselves, "will
begin to say to the mountains, 'Fall on us'; and
to the hills, 'Cover us'" (Luke 23:30). Beyond
God there is no appeal. From him there is no

escape. If he is the sovereign God, and therein
is all our hope, it follows that he is also
sovereign Right, and therein is all our dread.

All this follows with a stern kind of logic
from every kindly, gracious promise in the
Scriptures. We cannot minimize it. We dare
not neglect it. Yet this word must not be misdirected. Its warning is against the sin of
apostasy. It must never deter one timid, fearful
child of God who would like to believe, if he
dared. It is meant to draw men to God in
confidence, not to repel them in dread. Further,
this passage must always be read in the context
of God's grace. While the apostate under the
Mosaic law died **without mercy** at human
hands, it is hard to see how any sinner dies
eternally without the compassion and mercy of
him who said, "As I live, saith the Lord God,
I have no pleasure in the death of the wicked"
(Ezek. 33:11). For the man of faith, for whom
the sacrifice of Christ avails, **it is a glorious
thing to fall into the hands of the living God.**
To whom else can we go?

**32-39. *On Holding the Past in Remembrance.***
—**But recall the former days.** It is good when
memory makes us strong to endure. The appeal
is frequently made throughout the Bible. We
are urged to look back upon what God has
done not only for us, but for our fathers,

33 Partly, whilst ye were made a gazing-stock both by reproaches and afflictions; and partly, whilst ye became companions of them that were so used.

34 For ye had compassion of me in my bonds, and took joyfully the spoiling of your goods, knowing in yourselves that ye have in heaven a better and an enduring substance.

35 Cast not away therefore your confidence, which hath great recompense of reward.

struggle with sufferings, 33 sometimes being publicly exposed to abuse and affliction, and sometimes being partners with those so treated. 34 For you had compassion on the prisoners, and you joyfully accepted the plundering of your property, since you knew that you yourselves had a better possession and an abiding one. 35 Therefore do not throw away your confidence, which has

---

stands in intimate personal relations, for the persecutions endured cover a fairly wide range of troubles. Martyrdom is not in the list (cf. 12:4); obloquy, imprisonment, loss of property, and sufferings in general had been their portion at some time in the past (vs. 32). The assumption is that they are not now facing such persecution; their past record shows they know how to endure it and what they now need is a like endurance (vs. 36) under other circumstances, for they have but **a little while** to wait. The writer enforces

---

"Remember the former things of old: for I am God, and there is none else" (Isa. 46:9). Here the believer is bidden remember his own faith at the beginning of his Christian life. The emphasis is sound. The interpreter will himself remember the eager joy, the strong commitment, the early courage of many whom he knows. Let them also remember. Such experiences are self-validating. They carry their own assurance. We know that then we saw with clear eyes, found our own meaning, set our feet upon the right road to the heavenly city. If now we have wandered, lost our way, dulled the joy of our early faith, we need to **recall the former days.** We are to recall, not to linger in them; for the future is his too who is the God of the past.

**After you were enlightened.** The church has too often surrendered this good word **enlightened** because others have misused it, making intellectual clarity the sole meaning of life, a clarity which men must win by their own resources. Yet the word belongs to our faith. In the deepest sense we do not solve our own problems, cannot penetrate the basic mysteries. The light that comes to us is not of our own devising. Revelation reaches us by the inner illumination of the Spirit that enables us to read and understand the Scriptures, that gives us to see things in sharp perspective. The Christian sees himself clearly for the first time as a sinner deeply in need of grace. He sees his fellows in a new light because he knows what the grace of God can do. He sees pleasures and pains in their right proportion. He sees the evidence of God's goodness in nature, in history, and in his own experience. He sees more clearly the

moral realities and the moral trivialities. "The people that walked in darkness have seen a great light" (Isa. 9:2).

It was not easy to be a Christian. Some of these people had on occasion been exposed to public ridicule and shame. They had been involved with others—**sometimes being partners with those so treated.** This last was perhaps an even more crucial test of their faith. They might have kept a judicious silence. They could have been busy elsewhere. But when their comrades suffered abuse, they boldly took their stand alongside them. That is Christian courage. That is the church fulfilling itself. When some fellow Christian has been exposed to dangers for his faith, do we take our place at his side?

**You joyfully accepted the plundering of your property**—not because they had a pretentious indifference to material possession. Probably very few of them had much, and such as they had was likely essential to a decent and comfortable life. It is never easy to lose that. The assurance that people should never worry over the loss of that which merely costs money may be too bland to carry weight. But these Christians could accept such losses **joyfully** because they knew they **had a better possession and an abiding one.** These enduring things, these "treasures in heaven" (Matt. 6:20), once possessed, transform all other values. To have faith in Christ, the forgiveness of sins, the solid hope that "does not disappoint us" (Rom. 5:5), the love that binds us to our comrades, the light that makes the way clear—to have these is to accept **joyfully** whatever loss may be necessary and to call it gain.

36 For ye have need of patience, that, after ye have done the will of God, ye might receive the promise.

37 For yet a little while, and he that shall come will come, and will not tarry.

38 Now the just shall live by faith: but if *any man* draw back, my soul shall have no pleasure in him.

39 But we are not of them who draw back unto perdition; but of them that believe to the saving of the soul.

a great reward. 36 For you have need of endurance, so that you may do the will of God and receive what is promised.
37 "For yet a little while,
and the coming one shall come and shall not tarry;
38 but my righteous one shall live by faith,
and if he shrinks back,
my soul has no pleasure in him."
39 But we are not of those who shrink back and are destroyed, but of those who have faith and keep their souls.

---

this as usual with a scriptural quotation (Hab. 2:3-4), better known through Paul's use of it (cf. Rom. 1:17; Gal. 3:11). He gives the quotation its original meaning of faithfulness, not Paul's meaning of faith in contrast to a righteousness of works. The last words of the citation enable him both to add a final assurance, **we are not of those who shrink back,** and to introduce with his usual deftness the theme of the next chapter, **but of those who have faith.**

---

**Therefore do not throw away your confidence.** This is the danger. Having achieved, men may grow weary. New and more difficult persecutions were ahead. They were to be severely tested. Looking back from our safe position, it is easy for us to agree with the writer. Of course the people should hold fast, for without their endurance the story would be spoiled for us! But in the midst of danger the scene takes on a different meaning. We can read this passage in our time only if we are in some danger for our faith. Then we can hear truly about the **great reward.**

The interpreter will be aware of the danger of false martyrdom. Men and women may rush upon persecution because they are unbalanced, not because of their faith. There are no mock heroics in the roster of the faithful. The test is Christian love for those who do us wrong. For many the chief hardship of our time will be to love deeply and persistently and to find their love scorned and defeated. To find the place of contemporary tensions between God and man, perhaps in some small community, to find our very destiny there, to fulfill our lives in love and patient hope, we **have need of endurance, so that we may do the will of God and receive what is promised.**

**For yet a little while.** The Greek means "a little, how very, how very." [3] This is needed comfort and wisdom. Men suffer from the tyranny of the present. Goethe's insight was right. If Mephistopheles could show Faust a moment so rich in joy that Faust would say, "Stay passing moment, thou art so fair," then the soul of Faust would belong to the devil. That which pleases is but for the moment. But that which hurts is for the moment also. It is this insight that enables men bravely to endure pain. The time for release will come. To those who wait eagerly for God even the speed of God seems like delay. But **the coming one . . . shall not tarry.** Even while the cry goes up "How long?" God makes haste to come with relief. When the battle is over and the victory is won, we shall see then that the time of hardship was "a little, how very, how very." This is solid comfort and strength in the time of trial.

**My righteous one shall live by faith.** Our author is not here, or in ch. 11, giving us a complete definition of faith. It is important to see the quite different meaning that Paul attaches to this same quotation in Gal. 3:11. Here, as in the following chapter, we are concerned with the faith that endures to the end. The contrast to faith is the man who **shrinks back.** To have tasted the goodness of God, to have known the perfection of Christ's sacrifice, to have seen the light of full knowledge, to have been anchored in faith, and then to **shrink back** in the face of persecution, is to deny the gospel, to profane the blood of the covenant (vs. 29), to repudiate God. In such a person God **has no pleasure.**

The alternatives men face are destruction and keeping **their souls,** losing life or finding it (cf. Mark 8:35). In generous mood the passage ends on the note of assurance that those to whom the author writes join him in holding their faith and keeping their souls.

[3] Dods, in *Expositor's Greek Testament,* IV, 351.

11 Now faith is the substance of things hoped for, the evidence of things not seen.

11 Now faith is the assurance of things hoped for, the conviction of things

## C. The Continuity and Solidarity of the Faith (11:1-40)

This chapter is a rhetorical masterpiece ranking with the great N.T. passages. It speaks directly to the modern reader who finds other aspects of the author's thought difficult to grasp. It is not an inserted exhortation, however, but an integral part of his message; indeed, it is the climax toward which he has been moving, for his purpose is practical. The chapter has neither the radical simplicity of the Sermon on the Mount, nor the poetic beauty of I Cor. 13, nor the passion of the closing verses of Rom. 8, nor quite the sublimity of Revelation. Its force lies in the cumulative and massive testimony of assembled witnesses (12:1)—witnesses from the beginning to the end of history—who surround us, nerving us to a like faith at the moment when faith, theirs and ours, is coming to fruition. Our task is to ask what the author means by faith, and this can best be discovered by following the movement of his thought. Certain general observations about the chapter may well be made before we attempt an answer.

The arrangement of the chapter is roughly chronological, but there is a distinct movement toward faith as exhibited in persecution, suffering, and martyrdom (cf. vss. 32 ff.). After the opening definition there are seven illustrations beginning **by faith**, πίστει (vss. 3-11); a brief summary (vss. 13-16); then eleven more illustrations introduced with **by faith** (vss. 17-31); an extended grouping of witnesses (vss. 32-38); and a final evaluation of their faith as related to ours (vss. 39-40). Why does our author abandon

---

**11:1-40. On Faith and Knowledge.**—The word "faith" has many meanings. It has been observed that a fairly complete history of the Christian church could be written around the varied and successive definitions of that word. There is vast difference between saying, "I believe that the release of atomic energy will bring a greater industrial revolution than any we have thus far experienced," and saying, "I believe in God the Father Almighty, Maker of heaven and earth; and in Jesus Christ his only Son our Lord." Between these wide extremes there are many shades of meaning.

Widespread among believers and unbelievers alike is the notion that faith means believing something to be true where the evidence is not sufficient to establish knowledge. Faith is read in terms of intellectual content. The difficulties that keep men from faith are rational difficulties. It is a commonplace of logic that most knowledge is in terms of probability. A probability of nine tenths is much better than a probability of three tenths. The goal of all knowledge is to increase the fraction of probability toward the number one as a limit. Faith would then be a dogged conviction of some truth the rational probability of which would always have to be represented by a small fraction. The "age of faith" by common consent refers to the time when the intellectual milieu of Western man was essentially the Christian interpretation of the world. That day has long since passed. Now the world view is scientific; and this is supposed to make faith very difficult for everybody, next to impossible for the intelligent person.

The Sea of Faith
Was once, too, at the full, and round earth's shore
Lay like the folds of a bright girdle furl'd.
But now I only hear
Its melancholy, long, withdrawing roar,
Retreating, to the breath
Of the night-wind, down the vast edges drear
And naked shingles of the world.

Ah, love, let us be true
To one another! for the world, which seems
To lie before us like a land of dreams,
So various, so beautiful, so new,
Hath really neither joy, nor love, nor light,
Nor certitude, nor peace, nor help for pain;
And we are here as on a darkling plain
Swept with confused alarms of struggle and flight,
Where ignorant armies clash by night.[4]

A minister was once calling at a home to arrange the funeral of an elderly man who, though not a professing Christian, was highly regarded in his community. Eager to persuade the clergyman of her husband's goodness, the widow said, "Henry was a believer: he believed that there is a God." One can sympathize with this woman, yet she would never have accepted this definition of faith if applied to Henry's

[4] Matthew Arnold, "Dover Beach."

his habit of documenting his points with scriptural quotations? His illustrations are taken in large part from the Scriptures, but he does not rely on the presence of the word "faith" in the record; indeed the word is seldom found in the scriptures he uses. He has completed his argument on the reality and the finality of the revelation of God in a Son. This he has meticulously proved from scripture. But how are men to avail themselves of this perfect revelation? By the same sort of action—the whole chapter is keyed to action— that characterized all the witnesses in the past, for their action and ours are organically related. They did not "shrink back" (10:39) but went valiantly forward toward goals imperfectly seen and goods never fully obtained. That sort of action will avail both them and us now that the reality has come to light. He calls this attitude and action "faith," but it is not faith which gives reality to the unseen; it is loyalty to unseen reality which gives content to the word faith. In other words, the whole chapter is geared to the human response to the divine revelation, and the writer does not feel the same necessity for documenting the word "faith" from scripture as he did when proving the nature and

belief in her. Suppose in the earlier years of their married life she had asked her husband, "Henry, do you believe in me?" Suppose he had replied, "Yes, Mary, I believe that you exist."

It is important to see clearly that faith is not a substitute for knowledge, but an indispensable aspect of all knowledge. If this is true then as Christians we can never look forward to a time when knowledge will replace faith. On the contrary, as knowledge grows, faith will grow. The most complete knowledge will be accompanied by the most perfect faith.

This is apparent when we think of our knowledge of such objects as a hammer, a pen, a sword, a chair, a house. Our ideas of these objects are always accompanied by the use we propose to make of them, our response to them. A hammer is to be used for building, a pen for writing, a chair for sitting. Faith here is the response we intend to make to that which we know.

But this element of faith is essential to all our knowledge. Look at the natural sciences, where knowledge is commonly supposed to dispense with faith completely. Study the methods of any scientist who has advanced knowledge. Of one thing you can be sure, he was never passive in his knowledge. His work involved research, investigation, experiment. He did not sit in an easy chair, innocent of all personal interest, and let the facts pour into his empty, passive mind. Nature maintains a stony silence before all such idle minds. No, he was active, he had an interest, he had a hypothesis to test, he wanted to find an answer to some question. But this active interest, this hypothesis, this desire to know, what are they but expressions of his faith, a faith that always demands a personal response to the known truth? To be sure, his hypothesis is often denied, but the denial is seldom brutal. The negative answer of nature usually carries with it some hints of a better way, a sounder

approach. Thus his personal interest is constantly growing. The growth of knowledge is in part a purification of his purpose, his faith. But without his faith, his active interest, he would gain no knowledge.

Of course his faith always includes beliefs that some things are true. He believes, for example, that nature is uniform. He believes that under the same conditions the same results will follow. Once a certain chemical reaction is established and confirmed by independent observers, it never occurs to the chemist to keep on repeating that experiment in the hope of a still greater certainty. If in performing it some different result should appear, he would at once start looking for some new, disturbing factor that had not been present on earlier occasions. He cannot prove in advance that all nature is uniform. But he acts on that belief and it is verified in his experience. His faith also includes a belief that the future will resemble the past, that unless new, disturbing factors appear, the world of his experiments will not change. But as David Hume pointed out long ago, the not-yet-existent future is certainly not the land of our knowledge. This confidence in the future is a belief. Moreover, the scientist is moved by the belief that the world is rational, at least in part. It progressively uncovers its secrets to rational inquiry. The farther we penetrate into nature, the more of a mind we must have. He believes in one word of the Gospel, "Ask, and it will be given you; seek, and you will find; knock, and it will be opened to you" (Matt. 7:7). He can never prove this in advance; he can only test it in experience. These beliefs of his are never mere ideas in his mind. They are ways of responding to the world of outward fact. They are part of his faith, without which as a scientist he could know nothing.

This faith principle is all the more important in the social sciences. The historian without any

reality of the divine revelation. This becomes clear when he begins his discussion of faith with a formal definition, without any reference to scripture whatever, although he certainly believes his definition to be the inevitable inference from the scriptural record.

**11:1. Now faith is the substance of things hoped for, the evidence of things not seen.** This famous definition of faith will probably long survive in this translation. The ASV and the RSV renderings **assurance** and **conviction** for **substance** and **evidence** are more accurate and guard against any pragmatic understanding of the definition. Obviously our author does not mean that it is human faith which creates the reality **of things hoped for** and is the proof **of things not seen.** His whole argument has been designed to show that the unseen realities have independent and objective validity, and that man's transient life in the shadowland can be redeemed from unreality only by holding fast to such revelations of the eternal as have been vouchsafed to him. How much more ought we to "hold fast" now that a "new and living way" to the heavenly sanctuary has been opened up for us through Jesus. Faith gives *us* **assurance of things hoped for;** it is more,

---

personal interest is a failure. Indeed, history will say nothing to the disinterested mind. Even a prejudice, a theory to establish, a thesis to prove, is of immense help to the historian. It will make him more sensitive to facts, more competent in research. Without any such faith, it is difficult to see how a historian could assemble any data at all. Where would he begin?

If you want an absolute duffer in an investigation, you must, after all, take the man who has no interest whatever in its results: he is the warranted incapable, the positive fool. The most useful investigator, because the most sensitive observer, is always he whose eager interest in one side of the question is balanced by an equally keen nervousness lest he become deceived.[5]

One of the most damaging blind spots in the scientific mind is the pretense of objectivity, meaning the utter absence of any personal, subjective interest. Such objectivity is utterly impossible. The real objectivity of the scientist is to be found in his appeal to other observers to test his findings. His problem, and the problem of all of us, is to check our knowledge and our faith with others. Here, as in every area of life, our most urgent need is that of learning to live with other people. The alternative which men face, whether in the fields of science or elsewhere, is not the choice between faith and knowledge, but a choice between different kinds of faith. There are many unworthy faiths that block the road to knowledge: selfish ease, blind prejudice, worship of tradition. These evil faiths are among the real enemies of science. Faith grows and learns, and the growth of knowledge is always accompanied and conditioned by a purification of faith. Faith is not an alternative to knowledge, but an indispensable condition of knowledge.

Another misunderstanding about faith needs

[5] William James, *The Will to Believe* (New York: Longmans, Green & Co., 1896), p. 21.

to be removed. Faith is supposed to create its own certainties out of the resources of its own valor. It is a heroic defiance of the world of indifferent fact. It refuses to be baffled by a want of evidence, insists that what ought to be true must be true. It proposes to make it true by its own persistence. Such faith is described as a venture or a gamble. It renounces "dead" certainties. It professes to prefer uncertainties, else how could faith have any moral value? Now, there are areas of experience where this kind of faith works. The lover who keeps insisting that his beloved must love him may by his valiant persistence win the heart of his beloved. The salesman who is convinced that his product is superior and that his customer simply must have it is likely to make a successful sales record. But this is not the faith of the N.T. There faith is not impressed by its own valor, but by the faithfulness of God. It does not create its own certainties, but lays hold on the certainties of God's truth. It does not pretend that God's truths are established by its own demands. It believes because God has established his truth.

In general, biblical faith is the response of the whole man to God as he is revealed in Jesus Christ. In the Bible faith means trust as well as belief. The man of faith commits to Jesus Christ his mind and heart, his obedience and destiny, himself. When Jesus said, "My food is to do the will of him who sent me, and to accomplish his work" (John 4:34), that was faith. When a centurion of Capernaum sent word to Jesus that he had a sick slave, asking Jesus to help, but added that since he was unworthy to have the Master enter his house, the Master could say the word and the servant would be healed, Jesus marveled and said, "I tell you, not even in Israel have I found such faith" (Luke 7:9). When a Gentile woman came to Jesus pleading that her daughter be healed, and when she refused to be put off, Jesus answered, "O woman, great is your faith! Be it done for you

2 For by it the elders obtained a good report.

3 Through faith we understand that the worlds were framed by the word of God, so that things which are seen were not made of things which do appear.

not seen. 2 For by it the men of old received divine approval. 3 By faith we understand that the world was created by the word of God, so that what is seen was made out of things which do not appear.

---

then, than hope, because it makes hope operative as a present and sustaining motive for action. Faith gives *us* a **conviction**—and to this extent it is an evidence—**of things not seen.** This idea of faith as our attitude of positive acceptance of the invisible realm dominates the chapter, although other meanings will emerge as the chapter develops.

**2-3.** That faith is the attitude of human response which is divinely acceptable is stated in vs. 2. This is what the chapter is about, and it confirms our understanding of the omission of scriptural quotations. The author must begin with the beginning, with creation (cf. 1:2). Here there were no human witnesses, but faith, as the assurance that the seen came from the unseen, alone enables us to understand the creative act of God. Much can be read into this verse about the author's philosophy, but we will do well to hold close to his explicit thought: even the mystery of creation is to be understood in terms of faith. Man's experience of the divine revelation is to control even the ultimate mysteries.

---

as you desire" (Matt. 15:28). When Thomas the doubter rallied the frightened disciples and said, "Let us also go, that we may die with him," that was faith (John 11:16). When Peter was arrested and replied to his captors, "We must obey God rather than men" (Acts 5:29), that was faith. When Paul could write, "I will all the more gladly boast of my weaknesses, that the power of Christ may rest upon me" (II Cor. 12:9*b*), he had faith.

**1-2. *Faith and Hope.*—**Within this general usage in the N.T. the various writers emphasized now one, now another aspect of faith. The faith that Jesus asked from the sick was simply faith in him as a healer under the power of God. For Paul faith was contrasted with works, and meant that the believer trusted in God's righteousness rather than in his own. So we err greatly when we assume that our author here is giving us a complete definition of faith. He is giving us only the definition which he will use in this great chapter. For him faith means living for future rewards. Without that future the past was futile, the present without meaning. Faith is patient, enduring hope. **Faith is the assurance of things hoped for.** The word translated **assurance** literally means a "thing put under," a "foundation." The Greeks had often used the word as "substance." Hence it came to mean the solid foundation, the "confidence" or "assurance," on which hope rests (cf. II Cor. 9:4; 11:17). Faith is **the conviction** [evidence, proof] **of things not seen.** The unseen things to which our author refers were mostly in the future, and unseen for that reason.

Promised to us is eternal life, but it is promised to the dead; we are assured of a happy resurrection, but we are as yet involved in corruption; we are pronounced just, as yet sin dwells in us; we hear that we are happy, but we are as yet in the midst of many miseries; an abundance of all good things is promised to us, but still we often hunger and thirst; God proclaims that he will come quickly, but he seems deaf when we cry to him.[6]

The mood of faith is that of a son returning to his home after long years. He is nearly there. Familiar landmarks are appearing. Now up this next rise in the road and he will see the old place. In a few moments he will be back again with his parents. Thus a believer, looking forward to his union with God, is assured that God will be there, waiting to receive him. This is the basic meaning here.

It was this willingness to wait for God, this eager expectation from God, that was the faith **of the men of old.** By this faith they **received divine approval.**

**3. *Faith in God as Creator.*—**As the first illustration of faith we are confronted with a proposition. Faith means believing **that the world was created by the word of God, so that what is seen was made out of things which do not appear.** It is likely that our author was thinking here of the creation story in Genesis, since his illustrations in vss. 4-22 are all drawn from that book. That the passing world of sense is not the ultimate reality has been the faith of Western science and philosophy since the time of Parmenides. Men have looked for the real

[6] Calvin, *Commentary on Hebrews*, p. 262.

4 By faith Abel offered unto God a more excellent sacrifice than Cain, by which he obtained witness that he was righteous, God testifying of his gifts: and by it he being dead yet speaketh.

4 By faith Abel offered to God a more acceptable sacrifice than Cain, through which he received approval as righteous, God bearing witness by accepting his gifts; he died, but through his faith he is still speaking.

4. So understood, the transition to human witnesses is at least partially justified. Passing over Adam and Eve, the author cites Abel as the first witness of faith, for he was the first to receive the divine approval (vs. 2). The Genesis account is not clear as to why Abel's offering was acceptable in contrast to Cain's; our author can find no place in his thought for vegetable as against animal sacrifice and he concludes that Abel's faith—the word is not in Genesis—alone explains the divine approval. This is, he believes, substantiated by the record that after Abel's death **he is still speaking** (cf. Gen. 4:10). He disregards the fact that Abel's blood cried out for vengeance (cf. Matt. 23:35; Rev. 6:9 ff.).

in that which does not change. But faith in the Creation is different. We cannot reason our way to it. Even the word "creation" does not have real meaning for us. We do use the word, but the word is our name for a mystery. Faith in God as creator depends upon our belief in God as Savior, the God of future triumph (cf. Expos. on 1:2).

4. *Abel: The Inwardness of Faith.*—**By faith Abel.** We judge each other largely by external circumstance. Among the few persons that we know well, we do try to get behind the outward deed to the inward man. But our attempt is at best a clumsy inference, which more often than not reflects our own prejudices. The inner cost of the struggle to produce a deed that comes easily to us, the deep aspirations that can never be measured by outward performance, the secret prayers that give weight to many an unpromising achievement, all these are hidden from our eyes. Outwardly there may have been little to choose between the sacrifices of Cain and Abel. The Genesis account gives us no reason for God's favor being denied to Cain except the vague "Sin is couching at the door" (Gen. 4:7). Men have speculated on the superiority of animal over vegetable sacrifices, but our author will have none of this.

True excellence is inward. Abel's sacrifice was acceptable because it was brought in faith. This ought to be obvious to every one of us. We know from experience that true courtesy never consists merely in correct form, but is a thing of the heart. We know that the outward gift is no accurate measure of generosity. Without the inner gladness in another's joy, no gift carries weight. We know that courage is an inner fact which no outward valor can fully express. We know that honesty, if it is real, is always the fruit of a deep love for truth and a hatred of all falsehood. We know all that. Yet we pass facile judgment on our fellows based on a hasty survey of their outward deeds.

> Not on the vulgar mass
> Called "work," must sentence pass,
> Things done, that took the eye and had the price;
> O'er which, from level stand,
> The low world laid its hand,
> Found straightway to its mind, could value in a trice:
>
> But all, the world's coarse thumb
> And finger failed to plumb,
> So passed in making up the main account;
> All instincts immature,
> All purposes unsure,
> That weighed not as his work, yet swelled the man's amount:
>
> Thoughts hardly to be packed
> Into a narrow act,
> Fancies that broke through language and escaped;
> All I could never be,
> All, men ignored in me,
> This, I was worth to God, whose wheel the pitcher shaped.[7]

When Samuel went looking for a successor to Saul, he would never of himself have chosen the youthful David, "for man looketh on the outward appearance, but the Lord looketh on the heart" (I Sam. 16:7). Had we been choosing the disciples of Jesus, we should never have selected those twelve unpromising men. The Christian enterprise looked far from safe in their hands. No one noticed the widow's penny except Jesus (Mark 12:43-44).

In all our frenzy for impressive statistics we need to be reminded of the place of faith. No outward excellence can atone for the want of it. Faith may seek noble forms of worship, and should; but God may be more pleased with the rude service of a wayside chapel than with the splendor of a cathedral. God may more effectively use the humble testimony of a simple layman than the scholarly eloquence of a pulpit prince. The gifts of a poor widow may carry

[7] Browning, "Rabbi Ben Ezra."

5 By faith Enoch was translated that he should not see death; and was not found, because God had translated him: for before his translation he had this testimony, that he pleased God.

6 But without faith *it is* impossible to please *him:* for he that cometh to God must believe that he is, and *that* he is a rewarder of them that diligently seek him.

5 By faith Enoch was taken up so that he should not see death; and he was not found, because God had taken him. Now before he was taken he was attested as having pleased God. 6 And without faith it is impossible to please him. For whoever would draw near to God must believe that he exists and that he rewards those who seek

---

**5-6.** The record of Enoch's "translation" (Gen. 5:24) proved to be an inexhaustible source of speculation in late Judaism. Enoch was a favorite figure with the apocalyptists. Our author relying on the LXX (he "pleased" or "satisfied" God, instead of the Hebrew "walked with God") does not speculate, but argues that the record of "translation" is preceded in scripture by the statement that he satisfied God, and that **whoever would draw near to God** in worship and communion **must believe that he exists and that he rewards those who seek him.** Jews would hardly need to be reminded that God exists, but the thought is not philosophical; everything is keyed to worship; **draw near, seek,** and **rewards** must be interpreted in terms of longing for fellowship with God and its

---

more weight with God than the donations of the mighty. The hearty courage of an obscure lad may be more priceless than the bravery that leads an army. Faith that rests its confidence in God, that is sure of his grace, that expects his appraisal and award—this is the true worth of a man.

Yet this worth is often hidden from the eyes of men. No man can judge his own case—even the courts of law recognize this principle. We tend to minimize our faults, exaggerate our virtues, until we are chastened by repeated penitence and learn to trust the judgment of God. Nor can we judge our neighbor's case. We tend to depreciate his virtues, accent his faults, until the grace of God imparts to us the love that "is never glad when others go wrong," that is "gladdened by goodness" (I Cor. 13:6 Moffatt). Our true appraisal is from **God bearing witness.** To know this and to act upon it is the beginning of Christian wisdom (cf. Expos. on 4:12-13). We shall still regard the opinions of men, for to be indifferent to them would be a callous kind of selfishness (cf. I Cor. 4:3-4). But we shall be in a measure independent of them, knowing that

> There the work of life is tried
> By a juster Judge than here.[8]

**5-6. *Enoch: The Faith that Pleases God.*—By faith Enoch** was spared the sufferings of death. The author's argument is something like this: Enoch, being shown this unusual favor, was plainly pleasing to God. His secret must therefore have been faith, since **without faith it is**

[8] John Ellerton, "Now the laborer's task is o'er."

**impossible to please him.** This is an immensely important statement. To paraphrase Paul's chapter on love (I Cor. 13), though I speak in the tongues of men and angels, though I have prophetic powers, and understand all mysteries and all knowledge, though I give away all I have and give my body to be burned, and have not faith, I cannot please God. The faith that finds its solid assurance in "things hoped for," that has a strong "conviction of things not seen" (vs. 1), that rests on the God who has promised, who has spoken through his Son, this alone can please God. Here is basic wisdom for life. Here is man's hope, his safety, his true destiny.

**For whoever would draw near to God.** Throughout the epistle this is presented as the end of human life, the desired goal. The priesthood of Jesus had this as its purpose—to enable us to **draw near to God.** What is the requirement? He **must believe that he exists.** As we have seen above, this is a meager definition of faith and, taken by itself, quite unsatisfactory. It is unlikely, though not impossible, that our author was referring here to speculative atheism. Yet faith in God must include a firm conviction of his reality. Faith has strong metaphysical implications. God is no fiction of our mind to which we impart the weight of our own faith! We cannot trust God unless we believe that he is supreme as being, and **that he rewards those who seek him.**

True faith is marked by expectancy. Those who came to Jesus for healing expected a cure. This was the mark of their faith. Our prayers are often dreary because we expect nothing to happen. The public worship of God is often dull and poor because people enter the sanctu-

7 By faith Noah, being warned of God of things not seen as yet, moved with fear, prepared an ark to the saving of his house; by the which he condemned the world, and became heir of the righteousness which is by faith.

8 By faith Abraham, when he was called to go out into a place which he should after receive for an inheritance, obeyed; and he went out, not knowing whither he went.

him. 7 By faith Noah, being warned by God concerning events as yet unseen, took heed and constructed an ark for the saving of his household; by this he condemned the world and became an heir of the righteousness which comes by faith.

8 By faith Abraham obeyed when he was called to go out to a place which he was to receive as an inheritance; and he went out, not knowing where he was to go.

---

realization. Faith, then, is assurance of "things hoped for," the desired access to the divine presence, and the conviction of "things not seen," the unseen God who *is* and is the *rewarder*.

**7.** The record of Noah contains no mention of his faith, but he too received God's approval as a just man (Gen. 6:9; 7:1), and he acted by building the ark in preparation for **events as yet unseen**—both items illustrate the author's understanding of what faith is. **The righteousness which comes by faith** is a thoroughly Pauline phrase without any of the distinctive Pauline thought. By this faith, the author adds, **he condemned the world and became an heir of the righteousness which comes by faith,** thus reminding his readers both of the peril and of the promise of their own situation.

**8-12.** There follow four illustrations of faith associated with Abraham, the father of the faithful, the third and fourth being interrupted by a summary (vss. 13-16). The primary emphasis is on loyalty to the unseen and unrealized values, although faith is also *venturesome action* (**he went out, not knowing where he was to go**); *obedience* (**Abraham obeyed when he was called**); *trust* (**she considered him faithful who had**

---

ary expecting nothing. What light might shine from the Scriptures! What persistent fears might there be laid! What clear word from God might there draw men unto the way of life! What strength the weak might find! What love might there be kindled! What hope might be awakened! And men enter the worship of God expecting—nothing. "According to your faith be it done to you" (Matt. 9:29).

**7. The Faith that Condemns the World.—By faith Noah.** The thoughtful reader of this chapter will be impressed by one thing: faith conforms to no fixed pattern. It leads one man to offer a sacrifice, another to build an ark, another to become a wanderer in strange lands, another to renounce a royal heritage. The channels through which faith flows are as diverse as men and circumstances (cf. vss. 33-38). There is no predicting into what strange lands and unlikely duties it may lead. There is a unique expression of faith for every duty, for every man and woman. Yet beneath all the diversities is that attitude of the soul which confidently expects great things from God, and by it God himself is pleased.

To Noah faith meant rugged patience. The warning of God had come to him. The world in its unrighteousness was doomed to destruc-

tion. His faith could discern the evil of his day, and we are told that Noah was a righteous man. Faith meant the careful construction of the ark in what seemed pure folly. His neighbors must have ridiculed the clumsy-looking craft, built far from any body of water. But in patient trust Noah kept building. He was confident in the future deliverance of God. For many a believer faith is as simple as that.

Through his faith Noah **condemned the world.** Not that he consciously passed judgment upon the world; that was not his to do. But every faithful confidence in God unconsciously and severely condemns the fretful lives of men who must establish their own security, obtain their own salvation, and work out their own destiny. A good man condemns his evil neighbor. When we confront the man of faith, there follows the inevitable judgment, "Of whom the world was not worthy" (vs. 38).

**8-10. Abraham: Faith in the God of the Future.—By faith Abraham, when . . . called, . . . obeyed.** The order in the Greek text is "By faith called, Abraham obeyed," as though his obedience had been prompt and unquestioning. We read the story at a comfortable distance. We know the outcome of Abraham's obedience. But at the moment the prospect looked **different**

**9** By faith he sojourned in the land of promise, as *in* a strange country, dwelling in tabernacles with Isaac and Jacob, the heirs with him of the same promise:

**10** For he looked for a city which hath foundations, whose builder and maker *is* God.

**9** By faith he sojourned in the land of promise, as in a foreign land, living in tents with Isaac and Jacob, heirs with him of the same promise. **10** For he looked forward to the city which has foundations, whose

---

**promised**); and *confidence* in God's power to do what was beyond reason (**even when she was past the age**) in fulfilling his promises. There is an interesting alternation here, and throughout the chapter, between faith as achieving ends and faith as never achieving the final end. Our author must show that the faith of the ancients was not unrewarded, but that the ultimate reward is yet to come (cf. vss. 39-40). He does this skillfully. Abraham did indeed sojourn in the **land of promise** but **as in a foreign land;** he did become the father of innumerable descendants (vs. 12) but, as the following passage shows (vss. 13-16), this too was but a foretaste of the full fruition of faith. Like Philo and others, our author sees the epic story of Abraham's journey as an allegory of the

---

to Abraham. He had grown up in one of the two great centers of civilization in the world. He would have to leave a land of culture and good living and go out **not knowing where he was to go.** It must have seemed a mad adventure to his friends.

Yet that is just what faith means to any Christian today. We dwell in our fair land, amid things that our hands have fashioned, among surroundings that our minds understand, where our plans have laid out the future, and where our enterprises are flourishing. From this comfortable land of our own security we are called to go—we know not whither.

It is this call that comes to men at the very beginning of their Christian life. They have built their security on the familiar foundation of their own righteousness. Whatever else others may say, I am a decent and respectable man. Now comes the call to renounce all that and the prospect terrifies them. With the first move that they make, the ground seems to be giving way beneath their feet. Small wonder that they shrink back! By this moment of primitive terror let the facile theorists test their view that faith is born of its own valor, conferring its own certainty upon a world of otherwise indifferent fact! No! Faith must rest on a God who speaks in persuasive tones. It must reach out its hand to the Christ who can be seen and heard, who is able "to sympathize with our weaknesses" (4:15). Then faith can move.

Some clear, persuasive word must have come to Abraham, else his faith was folly (cf. 6:13-15). It was more than the will to believe that led and sustained the father of the faithful. Yet the trust is a "conviction of things not seen" (vs. 1). He did not know the land to which he went. There was no prospectus of its beauties,

its rich soil, its good opportunities. His trust was in God. Thus when we give ourselves in faith to God, we know not whither we go. We may be led to do things, to say things, that would have seemed impossible. "Truly, truly, I say to you, when you were young, you girded yourself and walked where you would; but when you are old, you will stretch out your hands, and another will gird you and carry you where you do not wish to go" (John 21:18).

Young Charles McCleary was about to return to West Africa after his first missionary furlough. He had just been married. He was speaking before his home church in Iowa: "When a bridge is built, some foundation stones must be laid beneath the water. If God wills that I should be one of the stones, laid out of sight in his African church, I am ready." Six months after returning to Elat he was dead from fever. But his work lived on. His widow gave her life there, and the Elat church became a flourishing center of the gospel for the whole region. Ahead may be impossible ventures, bitter disappointments, dark defeats, or unspeakable joys. We do not know. Whoever undertakes the journey of faith is like Abraham, who **went out, not knowing where he was to go.**

When Abraham reached the land of promise what happened? He could not call a place his own; he had no permanent house; he could only buy a place of burial for himself and his family. **He sojourned . . . as in a foreign land, living in tents.** It must have seemed that God had not kept his promise. Yet Abraham did not renounce his faith. This is not an uncommon experience. Many a young man has begun his ministry in a fine fervor of consecration, expecting to do great things for Christ. But as the years go by, there are times when his **words**

11 Through faith also Sarah herself received strength to conceive seed, and was delivered of a child when she was past age, because she judged him faithful who had promised.

12 Therefore sprang there even of one, and him as good as dead, *so many* as the stars of the sky in multitude, and as the sand which is by the seashore innumerable.

builder and maker is God. 11 By faith Sarah herself received power to conceive, even when she was past the age, since she considered him faithful who had promised. 12 Therefore from one man, and him as good as dead, were born descendants as many as the stars of heaven and as the innumerable grains of sand by the seashore.

---

soul's search for God. He does not enlarge upon this theme, however, for he is concerned with one aspect alone, the reality of the heavenly city **which has foundations** [in contrast to tents], **whose builder and maker is God.** Here it is the city, not its sanctuary as elsewhere, which he singles out as the goal of Abraham's quest. To this extent he is true to the record as he understands it, although of course the figure cannot be pressed to mean more than the desire for a permanent home. The sentence about Sarah reads smoothly in English; and in view of the Genesis record of the birth of Isaac, her inclusion in the list of witnesses is not surprising (cf. Gen. 17:15 ff.), for the author has already associated Isaac and Jacob with Abraham's faith (vs. 9). The Greek for **received power to conceive** is the more usual form for the male than for the female function, and some commentators have surmised that **Sarah herself** is either a gloss or that it means Abraham "together with Sarah." In vs. 12 it is Abraham again whose faith issues in innumerable posterity so significant for the promise. Abraham throughout is an individual, but there are overtones of the corporate personality of the founder and the descendants in the true people of God.

---

seem idle, his work is thwarted, the expected results do not come, evil is far more deeply entrenched than he had thought. However successful his ministry as a whole may have been, at the end of the road most of what he had hoped has not come about. He has been **living in tents.** This seeming tardiness of God is the most severe test of faith. To come to the promised land, and to end our days there as a stranger, this is hard. Here the real nobility of faith appears. And nowhere else does the comfort of God become so indispensably tender.

How could Abraham endure? **He looked forward to the city which has foundations, whose builder and maker is God.** To what city did he look forward? There is no evidence that the hope of the resurrection was held in Abraham's day. Nor could he foresee any visible city, such as the Jerusalem of Solomon's time. His imagination may have peopled this strange land with his descendants. He did look to the future. But his faith was in the God who would build the city with strong foundations. Faith in God confers no right to draw any blueprints of the coming city. We have our plans and hopes. But they are at best only partially fulfilled. History has an offspring in her womb that we cannot even fancy. But faith in the future rests on faith in God, by whose grace and wisdom the foundations of the coming city will

be laid. What more could Abraham, or we ourselves, ask?

**11-12. Sarah: The Faith of the Hardheaded. —By faith Sarah herself.** The inclusion of Sarah is significant not merely because she is the first woman in our writer's roll of the faithful, but because she was the first skeptic in the list. Hearing the proposal that she become a mother at advanced age, she laughed (cf. Gen. 18:11-15). She is the first in the long line of the hardheaded, honest sons and daughters of fact, who nevertheless belong to the household of faith. When she became convinced that it was God who had promised, her laughter ceased, **since she considered him faithful who had promised.** The homiletic intent of the writer is clear, since he has been commending to his readers this very trust in the faithfulness of God's promise.

This faith of Abraham, who had nothing but the promise of God on which to rest, was a momentous faith. He was to become the father of a great people **as many as the stars of heaven.** Through them God was to make his revelation to all the world. From this people would one day come the Savior of mankind. In God's world the faithful can become the bearers of a momentous destiny. This is part of the reward of those who have "the assurance of things hoped for, the conviction of things not seen" (vs. 1).

13 These all died in faith, not having received the promises, but having seen them afar off, and were persuaded of *them,* and embraced *them,* and confessed that they were strangers and pilgrims on the earth.

14 For they that say such things declare plainly that they seek a country.

15 And truly, if they had been mindful of that *country* from whence they came out, they might have had opportunity to have returned.

13 These all died in faith, not having received what was promised, but having seen it and greeted it from afar, and having acknowledged that they were strangers and exiles on the earth. 14 For people who speak thus make it clear that they are seeking a homeland. 15 If they had been thinking of that land from which they had gone out, they would have had opportunity to return.

---

**13-16.** Before the final illustrations from Abraham and his immediate descendants, the author pauses for a summary which some have held would come better after vs. 19 or even after vs. 22. There is no good reason to suspect a dislocation of the text, however, for the author frequently introduces such sections, and these verses belong here because they emphasize the central point that Abraham and the patriarchs seek a **homeland** and **a better country, a heavenly one;** and that though they did not reach it, it was a reality and not a mirage (vs. 16). The author has spoken of their longing for a city (vs. 10); this city has been prepared for them. It was not in the land of Canaan (cf. 4:8), but in the **heavenly** country. The summary, therefore, belongs just here, before the descendants of Abraham are treated (cf. vs. 12). Vs. 15 adds a salty, almost humorous, touch; they

---

**13-16. Man's Incompleteness, God's Faithfulness.**—These all died in faith, not having received what was promised. This is the riddle of the world, the enigma of our faith. The world's religions and the best literature of the world are full of the incompleteness of human life. It is not merely that we cling to life in the presence of death, that we long for a few more years. There may be nothing noble or noteworthy in this eagerness for more life. But all for which we strive, all that gives meaning or nobility to our days, all is tragically incomplete. Some clue to the world's mystery intrigues us and we set out upon the quest of knowledge. After a life's devotion the work is only beginning. We listen to the high call of duty, and no matter how scrupulous and sincere our moral growth, it calls for a more beyond death. As Kant saw, the moral imperative is so high that only partial fulfillments are possible in this life. But if this life is all that is allowed us, the validity of that imperative is destroyed. We agonize over the meaning of suffering. We see some who by faith turn the black shadows of pain into a pattern of strength and victory. But the compensations are never complete. The suffering of the just is itself a denial of justice in our world. Love's adventure is never complete in this life. There is so much more to know about each other, so much more to do together, that death brings upon love a scoffing ridicule. Faith never receives **what was promised.** It calls for much more, and if the much

more is denied, faith is reduced to an absurdity. Victor Hugo could say to a friend at the age of seventy:

For half a century I have been outpouring my volumes of thought in prose and in verse, in history, philosophy, drama, romance, ode, and ballad, yet I appear to myself not to have said a thousandth part of what is within me; and when I am laid in the tomb I shall not reckon that my life is finished.[9]

He speaks for every man of faith. They never receive **what was promised.**

But it is God who promises. That changes everything. God cannot prove faithless. To know the best in our days, the promise of God inevitably compels us to lift our eyes beyond our time, to see the fulfillment and greet **it from afar.** God and fulfillment go together. Without God, no fulfillment; without completion, no God: such was the simple logic by which biblical men of faith looked at history. To believe in God means trusting him to keep his promises. And what was the promise to the patriarchs? There was no specific reference to heaven or the resurrection. They were promised a better country, many descendants, and that "in thee shall all families of the earth be blessed" (Gen. 12:3). These were the promises they saw and **greeted . . . from afar.** Yet we may not too narrowly circumscribe the bounds of their faith. What they saw was God, who

[9] Alfred Barbou, *Victor Hugo and His Time* (tr. Ellen E. Frewer; New York: Harper & Bros., 1882), p. 254.

**16** But now they desire a better *country*, that is, a heavenly: wherefore God is not ashamed to be called their God: for he hath prepared for them a city.

**17** By faith Abraham, when he was tried, offered up Isaac: and he that had received the promises offered up his only begotten *son*,

**16** But as it is, they desire a better country, that is, a heavenly one. Therefore God is not ashamed to be called their God, for he has prepared for them a city.

**17** By faith Abraham, when he was tested, offered up Isaac, and he who had received the promises was ready to offer up his

---

must have been seeking the heavenly homeland, for if they were disappointed with Canaan they could have gone back home to Mesopotamia.

**17-19.** The final illustration of Abraham's faith is his offering of Isaac (cf. Gen. 22:1-18). The Genesis record is a deeply moving account of what is always reckoned as the supreme test of Abraham's obedience—he obeyed even when the commandment of God seemed to clash with the promise of God. This is the point the author makes (vs.

---

was "able to do far more abundantly than all that we ask or think" (Eph. 3:20), and who would keep his promises. In the centuries that followed, men of faith would see that God's promises called for a coming one. This is the genius of the whole prophetic movement: to link human incompleteness to the faithfulness of God. Hence, with all our historical knowledge we can still say with Calvin:

> Though God gave to the fathers only a taste of that grace which is largely poured on us, though he shewed to them at a distance only an obscure representation of Christ, who is now set forth to us clearly before our eyes, yet they were satisfied and never fell away from their faith: how much greater reason then have we at this day to persevere? If we grow faint, we are doubly inexcusable.[1]

**Having acknowledged that they were strangers and exiles on the earth.** How was Abraham a stranger? This was to be the home of his descendants. But as far as he could see, it belonged to other men. It was the promise of God that made him a stranger and a wanderer (exile). He could not settle down and make terms with things as they were. The patriarchs were condemned by their faith to accept their destiny in the distant future. This is the perennial burden of faith. In our own world of strife, of corrupt institutions and broken lives, of competitive greed and concentrated power, we, as men and women of faith, are **strangers and exiles.** This is not our home.

**They would have had opportunity to return.** We too could settle down in our land of Ur. But when God has promised, to return is to renounce God. For his readers the author's point is clear. To allow persecution or hardship to turn them back would be to surrender all claims on the mercy of God.

The measure of our faith is the intensity with which we **are seeking a homeland.** Our destiny is to embody the tension between what God wants and things as they are, and to keep that tension "so taut that it sings." When we have accepted ourselves and our world as it is, our faith is dead. This tension takes many forms, yet it remains the same. It is the tension between the righteousness of God and the sin of man, between the purity of Christ and the stains of a bad conscience, between the love of Calvary and the enmity that turns our world into a hell, between the peace that passes all understanding and the crippling anxieties of our day, between the communion of the saints and the chaos of our world, between the perfect light of God's truth and the darkness of our ignorance. To embody this tension, to find our very destiny in it, is to **desire a better country, that is, a heavenly one.**

**Therefore God is not ashamed to be called their God.** "I am the God of Abraham, Isaac, and Jacob"; so God introduced himself to the prophets through the centuries. What God wanted from the patriarchs, what he seeks from us, what can make men well-pleasing in his sight, is to become **strangers and exiles,** to seek **a better country,** to live by the promises of God. This is faith in God. Nor will God fail those of whom he is not ashamed. **He has prepared for them a city.** All our hopes for the future, all our confidence in life beyond death, rest in God's word. For the man of faith there can be no higher assurance. God's promise is all he needs or wants.

**17-22.** *The Testing of Abraham's Faith.*—The supreme example of Abraham's faith was in his willingness to offer up Isaac. The command to sacrifice the son of his old age not merely violated every natural feeling and every fiber of his conscience, it destroyed the very

[1] *Commentary on Hebrews*, p. 283.

18 Of whom it was said, That in Isaac shall thy seed be called:

19 Accounting that God *was* able to raise *him* up, even from the dead; from whence also he received him in a figure.

20 By faith Isaac blessed Jacob and Esau concerning things to come.

21 By faith Jacob, when he was a dying, blessed both the sons of Joseph; and worshipped, *leaning* upon the top of his staff.

22 By faith Joseph, when he died, made mention of the departing of the children of Israel; and gave commandment concerning his bones.

only son, 18 of whom it was said, "Through Isaac shall your descendants be named." 19 He considered that God was able to raise men even from the dead; hence, figuratively speaking, he did receive him back. 20 By faith Isaac invoked future blessings on Jacob and Esau. 21 By faith Jacob, when dying, blessed each of the sons of Joseph, bowing in worship over the head of his staff. 22 By faith Joseph, at the end of his life, made mention of the exodus of the Israelites and gave directions concerning his burial.ˣ

ˣ Greek *bones.*

17), suggesting that faith holds fast in crises which threaten to negate the very ends toward which faith is directed. It may seem somewhat surprising that our author makes no use of the sacrifice of a son when *the* sacrifice of *the* Son is his main theme. He has made his point about Christ's priesthood; and Isaac, however significant for the promise, is neither priest nor Son. He shows in vs. 19 that he accepts the orthodox doctrine of resurrection, even though it plays no role in his argument, being displaced by the Ascension.

20-22. The inclusion of Isaac, Jacob, and Joseph in the list of witnesses seems hardly more than formal, for no important deed is recalled. The first two, about to die, show faith in a promise death could not defeat by "blessing" those who were to follow—in the case of Esau it is really a curse (cf. Gen. 27). Joseph's "faith" is shown in his prevision of

promise that **through Isaac shall your descendants be named.** Abraham was **tested,** and was ever testing more severe? It was not only the dread of losing his beloved son, not merely the horror that he himself was to draw the knife, but that in the act the very promise of God would be reduced to emptiness. Yet Abraham obeyed, trusting that God would fulfill his promise, even if he had **to raise men . . . from the dead.**

This heroic example of faith has captured the best in Jewish and Christian imaginations. Martin Luther wrote:

He took two servants and Isaac his son. In that moment everything died in him: Sarah, his family, his home, Isaac. This is what it is to sit in sackcloth and ashes. If he had known that this was only a trial, he would not have been tried. Such is the nature of our trials that while they last we cannot see to the end.

. . . . . . . . . . . .

When they were come to the mount, Abraham built the altar and laid on the wood, and then he was forced to tell Isaac. The boy was stupefied. He must have protested, "Have you forgotten: I am the son of Sarah by a miracle in her age, that I was promised and that through me you are to be the father of a great nation?" And Abraham must have answered that God would fulfill his promise even out of ashes. Then Abraham bound him and laid him upon the wood. The father raised his knife.

The boy bared his throat. If God had slept an instant, the lad would have been dead. I could not have watched. I am not able in my thoughts to follow. The lad was as a sheep for the slaughter. Never in history was there such obedience, save only in Christ. But God was watching, and all the angels. The father raised his knife; the boy did not wince. The angel cried, "Abraham, Abraham!" See how divine majesty is at hand in the hour of death. We say, "In the midst of life we die." God answers, "Nay, in the midst of death we live." [2]

**By faith Isaac invoked future blessings** on his sons. He who had no land of his own, who could scarcely be called a free man, could yet say of one son, "Let people serve thee, and nations bow down to thee" (Gen. 27:29). **By faith Jacob,** who had seen his family transplanted to a strange land, could yet believe in the future enough to distinguish with confidence between the relative positions of Ephraim and Manasseh, giving the position of honor to the younger son. **By faith Joseph,** unimpressed by the political position he had enjoyed, assured his family that God would bring them to the land promised to their fathers, and even instructed them that his bones were to be taken

[2] Roland H. Bainton, *Here I Stand: A Life of Martin Luther* (New York and Nashville: Abingdon-Cokesbury Press, 1950), pp. 369-70. Used by permission.

23 By faith Moses, when he was born, was hid three months of his parents, because they saw *he was* a proper child; and they were not afraid of the king's commandment.

24 By faith Moses, when he was come to years, refused to be called the son of Pharaoh's daughter;

25 Choosing rather to suffer affliction with the people of God, than to enjoy the pleasures of sin for a season;

23 By faith Moses, when he was born, was hid for three months by his parents, because they saw that the child was beautiful; and they were not afraid of the king's edict. 24 By faith Moses, when he was grown up, refused to be called the son of Pharaoh's daughter, 25 choosing rather to share ill-treatment with the people of God than

and preparation for the Exodus. The author's dependence on the LXX is shown in the phrase **the head of his staff** (vs. 21), where the Hebrew has "bed." The consonants of the two words were the same, and the LXX has introduced wrong vowels into the unpointed Hebrew text.

23-29. Five instances of faith are now cited from the career of Moses, whom our author has already declared to be "faithful in God's house . . . as a servant" (3:2, 5). The first illustration is drawn from the conduct of Moses' parents, and the last two (vss.

along when their descendants should return. The pattern of faith is one and the same: confident expectation that God will keep all his promises.

23-28. *Moses: The Faith that Discerns.*—**By faith Moses, when he was born, was hid for three months by his parents.** The writer does not recognize Paul's sharp contrast between faith and the law. Yet it was a brilliant thought to hold the lawgiver up as a superior example of a man of faith. As our author defines faith (vs. 1), he could scarcely avoid mentioning Moses.

The life of Moses began with a daring and well-planned act of faith on the part of his parents. Moses was cradled in faith. Here was a commonplace thing, the birth of a baby boy. Faith, the old story would seem to say, is not reserved for the heroes. It may be the gift of common people, embodied in the duties that confront every parent. In a real sense every child is an expression of faith in the future. As our children grow to maturity we put our hopes in them.

The faith of Moses' parents was kindled **because they saw that the child was beautiful.** The meaning is not clear. All fond parents are notoriously prejudiced about the beauty of their children. In so far as loving hearts clothe the newborn child with high hopes of the favor of God, they are right. As far as the beauty is a reflection of their own love, they see more clearly than disinterested neighbors. Perhaps the parents saw in the unusual comeliness of the infant a sign from God that the child would have an important mission. Faith is attributed to these parents also because **they were not afraid of the king's edict.** In this faith they were not alone. For the Pharaoh had had trouble enforcing his edict; the midwives widely disobeyed his instructions to them because they "feared God" (Exod. 1:17).

**By faith Moses . . . refused to be called the son of Pharaoh's daughter.** This, we say, was admirable! Moses gave up one of the most enviable positions. He had enjoyed the shelter and affection of the royal family. He had received the best education that could be had, in one of the thriving cultural centers of his day. While he may not have been the heir apparent to the throne, he was marked for a position of responsibility and power. All the comforts that heart could desire were his. Menials were at hand to save him from every unpleasantness. He could draw upon the best minds of Egypt for help in any enterprise he wanted to launch. He would have the joy of ruling. Now to renounce all this, to identify himself with a race of slaves, does seem heroic. Yet Jesus would never have held up this choice as an example of heroism. Moses was not impressed with his own valor. Such a sacrifice seems heroic only to minds whose vision of moral realities is distorted by sin, who incline to think that luxury, prestige, and power are excellent in themselves.

It was not heroism but faith that made Moses choose **rather to share ill-treatment with the people of God.** Here is the crowning glory of faith, that Moses could discern in a race of slaves **the people of God.** The evidence was all against his faith. Any wise man of the world would have snorted in derision at his choice. For who were his people? They were brutalized

26 Esteeming the reproach of Christ greater riches than the treasures in Egypt: for he had respect unto the recompense of the reward.

27 By faith he forsook Egypt, not fearing the wrath of the king: for he endured, as seeing him who is invisible.

to enjoy the fleeting pleasures of sin. 26 He considered abuse suffered for the Christ greater wealth than the treasures of Egypt, for he looked to the reward. 27 By faith he left Egypt, not being afraid of the anger of the king; for he endured as seeing him who

---

28-29) include participation of the children of Israel. Faith in vs. 23 is set over against fear of the **king's edict,** although this motive is not explicit in the Exodus account, where mother love motivates the action (Exod. 2:1 ff.). Vss. 24-26 interpret Moses' renunciation of the attractions of Egypt for the **abuse suffered for the Christ,** i.e., the Messiah (cf. I Cor. 10:4) as dictated by faith. Vs. 27 again sets faith over against fear, and again it is fear of an earthly king. In vs. 28 faith is obedience to God's command at a moment of crisis (cf. vs. 7), and in vs. 29 it is trustful action based on reliance on God's power to do what was wholly contrary to human reason and experience. Running through the five illustrations is the thread of allegiance to an **invisible** King before whom earthly monarchs are powerless. This comes to expression in one of the memorable verses of the N.T., **for he endured as seeing him who is invisible** (vs. 27), which is again a statement

---

by slavery. The light of hope, which is the glory of any man, had long since faded from their dull eyes. Their hearts knew only the dark emotions of anger and frustration. Any hidden abilities that may have lain in these people, save the capacity to endure hard toil and suffering, were too deeply covered over for human vision to detect. They themselves, could they have been given even a dim understanding of its meaning, would have laughed bitterly at the phrase **the people of God.** Only faith in the promise of God could have given Moses such discernment.

Here is deep wisdom for every age and for every man. Rightly to esteem our fellow men is urgent business not only for faith, but for the practical decisions of the factory, the office, the market place, and the halls of Congress. But because our scheme of values is confused, we hopelessly misjudge our fellow men. We look almost with veneration upon the "big men," those who hold positions of power and prominence, the political leaders, the heads of large corporations, the leading men of science, the famous men of letters, even those who have been highly honored in the church. We do not see the corruption of conscience that almost inevitably comes to men of power. We fawn over men of large wealth, even in the churches, not seeing the judgment of God that is often pronounced over them, "The name of the wicked shall rot" (Prov. 10:7). We are deeply moved by men of glib tongue, not discerning the forceful eloquence of men whose hearts are honest. We patronize the poor, forgetting one of the most obvious facts of experience, that "God chose what is weak in the world to

shame the strong" (I Cor. 1:27). Like the righteous people of Jesus' day, we take a dim view of the publicans and sinners. We prefer the company of the respectable, forgetting that Jesus once said, "The Son of man came to seek and to save that which was lost" (Luke 19:10). But to see people in the light of what God can do in them, with them, and through them, is solid wisdom.

**To enjoy the fleeting pleasures of sin.** Had Moses chosen to remain in the palace of the Pharaoh, and to spend his days in the governing of Egypt, he need not have succumbed to the evils of court life. Nor does our writer imply that he would. But to choose the position of power and comfort, rather than the destiny of his people, would have been sin for Moses. It is interesting to ask ourselves what we would have done had we been in his place. We can almost reproduce the exact thoughts of some of us. After all, we would have reasoned, I can do more for my people here in the court than out there among the slaves. Someday I shall use my influence to free them. But I can do them that service only if I retain my influence. To renounce the power (and pleasures) of the court is to render myself powerless to help. How good it is when duty directs us to walk in pleasant paths! The power of the human mind to deceive itself on moral questions is simply incredible until we look with complete candor into our own hearts.

**Abuse suffered for Christ.** The abuse which Moses was to suffer—was it **for the Christ?** Did he foreknow the Christ by name? Was he a conscious Christian? Thus to interpret the prophetic temper of the O.T. is a degradation of

28 Through faith he kept the passover, and the sprinkling of blood, lest he that destroyed the firstborn should touch them.

is invisible. 28 By faith he kept the Passover and sprinkled the blood, so that the Destroyer of the first-born might not touch them.

---

of the author's understanding of faith. A careful reading of the Exodus record (Exod. 2 ff.) will show that our author has treated it freely, relying either on his memory or on current tradition. This is especially evident in his interpretation of Moses' flight from Egypt (vs. 27), where the Exodus record (Exod. 3:11 ff.) makes it plain that fear of the consequences (Exod. 3:14) was the occasion of his flight. This can hardly be intended as a reference to the Exodus itself (cf. vss. 28-29), but the suggestion that our author has telescoped the two departures may be the solution. Actually the details would not trouble him, for it is the outcome of Moses' deeds which he regards as illustrating faith, and his eye is on his readers and their needs quite as much as on Moses. The phrase **sprinkled the blood** (cf. 9:19-22) must have tempted him to expatiate, but he moves on without pause.

---

prophecy into a kind of magic trickery with the future. But Moses did have faith in the God who would fulfill his purpose and his promise, a fulfillment which could come, as the events of following centuries were to make progressively clear, only in the coming of the Christ. In this sense it is profoundly accurate to say that Moses discounted the **treasures of Egypt** as of less value than the **abuse suffered for the Christ.** We cannot miss the homiletic turn which the author gives to this verse. He has in mind those who are inclined to "shrink back" (10:39) from **abuse suffered for the Christ** in favor of some kind of security which would be theirs if they followed the way of Moses. If that is your temper, he is saying to them, you do not belong to Moses.

**He looked to the reward.** This could be said with a cynical sneer. We hear this sort of nonsense *ad nauseam.* Your saint finds his pleasure in the worship of God; your humanitarian in the service of mankind; and your sensualist in the lusts of the flesh. All are seeking pleasure, with the implication that this reduces all men to the same moral level! Yet that in which a man finds his pleasure is one of the most certain tests of his character. That which absorbs his attention, quickens his interest, whets his desires, tells us what the man really is. To discern the reward to be found in **abuse suffered for the Christ** is an act of noblest faith. To doubt the reward, to question that God would be faithful to those who suffer such abuse, is to doubt God himself. Even Kant, who was rigorous in insisting on disinterested virtue, the will that chooses good whatever inclination or desire may urge, was driven at the last to see that virtue demanded its appropriate happiness and was content to let his argument for God's existence rest on that demand. It was in

faith that Moses **looked to the reward,** and for that he needs no apology made on his behalf.

**By faith he left Egypt** for the land of Midian. This is the author's clear meaning in spite of the difficulty of reconciling **not being afraid of the anger of the king** with Exod. 2:15. For had the reference been to the Exodus, vs. 27 would not have been put before vs. 28. Moses had renounced his royal position—for what? No instant recognition by his people as their leader! No dramatic stroke for their liberation! Not even the first beginnings of an underground movement that would carefully plan the day of revolt! He went far away and spent long years tending—of all things—a flock of sheep! Long, patient waiting, this is the overtone of the word ἐκαρτέρησε. Here he **endured** while year by year the children of Israel sank more deeply into slavery. Day by day they were dying in bondage, and day by day boys and girls were being born, who would grow up to know nothing but bitter servitude. What misgivings must have been his! Was it for this that he gave up his royal prerogatives? "God does nothing," we are tempted to exclaim.

Writers have often seen the analogy between these years in Midian and Jesus' forty days in the wilderness and Paul's three years in Arabia. The days and years of preparation are often the most severe test of faith. They can easily degenerate into days of idleness unless we endure **as seeing him who is invisible.** Then we can turn them into God's discipline of our souls; we can be remade and refashioned until we are ready to be God's instruments and until God's time is ready. But it is never easy for the impatient man. To wait as seeing him **who is invisible** is one of the noblest deeds of faith.

**By faith he kept the Passover.** Back in Egypt again, the discipline of the desert completed,

**29** By faith they passed through the Red sea as by dry *land:* which the Egyptians assaying to do were drowned.

**30** By faith the walls of Jericho fell down, after they were compassed about seven days.

**31** By faith the harlot Rahab perished not with them that believed not, when she had received the spies with peace.

**32** And what shall I more say? for the time would fail me to tell of Gideon, and *of* Barak, and *of* Samson, and *of* Jephthah;

**29** By faith the people crossed the Red Sea as if on dry land; but the Egyptians, when they attempted to do the same, were drowned. **30** By faith the walls of Jericho fell down after they had been encircled for seven days. **31** By faith Rahab the harlot did not perish with those who were disobedient, because she had given friendly welcome to the spies.

**32** And what more shall I say? For time

---

**30-31.** From the period of the conquest he can cite only the fall of Jericho and the deed of Rahab as illustrations. Strongholds tumble before faith and even the most disreputable are redeemed by it. James brings Abraham and Rahab together (Jas. 2:21-25) as examples in his argument that it is works which justify, rather than faith without works. Evidently Rahab was a classic example of what faith can do with the most unpromising material; and this may be in our author's mind, although he does not place Abraham and Rahab in juxtaposition. Her name is an effective addition to the list of famous and reputable worthies.

**32.** The writer has now concluded the detailed exposition of the faith of great leaders and turns to a brilliant summary of subsequent examples. **And what more shall**

---

the great liberation at hand, faith was still required of Moses. The Passover was observed, of itself a meaningless rite, but as an expression of faith in God's deliverance the most important of Hebrew ceremonies.

**29-31.** *Faith and Foolhardiness.*—**By faith the people crossed the Red Sea.** Faith is not to be confused with audacity. Outwardly they seem the same. It was equally courageous for Hebrews and Egyptians to pass through the Red Sea. Men of faith take risks that seem foolhardy. So do profane men. But the difference between them is profound. Faith is reliance upon God and his word, not a brash disregard of fact. Often interpreters make of it a mere gamble with life. The N.T. would not recognize any such thing. Here a whole people are held up as an example because they believed Moses and followed him into what looked like certain doom.

**By faith the walls of Jericho fell down.** The whole story of the fall of Jericho seems utterly ludicrous. This laughable procession of an ark, with priests blowing their trumpets, and the men marching in silence around the walled city, how pathetic it must have seemed! But if we had eyes to see, we should appear ludicrous in exactly the same way when our pride takes credit for advances in the battle against evil. A victory has been won: some walled prejudice has fallen, some ancient evil has crumbled, a people have been moved to generosity, an un-

likely sinner has come in penitence to his Lord. We review our strategy, recall how carefully we had thought out our plans, how hard we had worked, how brave we had been. We must remember this success; it will fortify us for the next impossible task. The walls of Jericho are falling down before *us.* As though the Spirit of God did nothing! Our work is to be done faithfully, and without it God's purpose can be thwarted. But with all our experience and learning and skill, it is only God's Spirit that can renew the hearts of men. He alone can save. To act on this insight is faith. To forget it is to become ridiculous. "No human being" is to "boast in the presence of God" (I Cor. 1:29). Our faith is not to "rest in the wisdom of men but in the power of God" (I Cor. 2:5).

**By faith Rahab the harlot.** It is a mercy of God that even the most degraded and unpromising may take their place in faith's roster of fame. We know nothing of this poor woman's former life. We know only that she risked death, denied her own people, and gave **friendly welcome to the spies** because she believed in Israel's God and in the future that belonged to the people of God. She and her family were saved and her name was later given a place of honor among the Hebrews (cf. Matt. 1:5).

**32-38.** *The Faith of Warriors and Martyrs.*—To many a modern mind it will seem strange that men known chiefly for their military and political prowess should be included among the

*of* David also, and Samuel, and *of* the prophets:

33 Who through faith subdued kingdoms, wrought righteousness, obtained promises, stopped the mouths of lions,

34 Quenched the violence of fire, escaped the edge of the sword, out of weakness were made strong, waxed valiant in fight, turned to flight the armies of the aliens.

would fail me to tell of Gideon, Barak, Samson, Jephthah, of David and Samuel and the prophets — 33 who through faith conquered kingdoms, enforced justice, received promises, stopped the mouths of lions, 34 quenched raging fire, escaped the edge of the sword, won strength out of weakness, became mighty in war, put for-

---

**I say? For time would fail me to tell of Gideon.** . . . He introduces this summary with conventional literary phrases, betraying the instinct of the orator, although frequently used in writing as well as in speech. The sample names are not arranged in strict chronological order. The most obvious disarrangement, David before Samuel, may be intentional as grouping Samuel with the prophets. Not all those named, notably Samson, would be regarded by the modern reader as conspicuous examples of faith. In this sentence and what follows an intimate acquaintance with the O.T. and with Jewish history is assumed. Elsewhere our author has cited definite passages, but here the reader is expected to depend on his own knowledge. This has been pressed to prove that the readers must have been of Jewish origin. As a matter of fact, however, it shows only that the LXX was their Bible. Did the writer of this treatise, like the modern preacher in many cases, assume a greater knowledge of scripture than his readers actually possessed? We cannot refrain from the attempt to identify the persons to whom the general phrases that follow apply, although the author has just avowed that he does not intend to particularize the record.

33-38. Vss. 33-34 present the deeds of faith in nine compact phrases. The fourth and fifth (**lions, . . . fire**) inevitably recall Daniel and the doughty three, and appropriate names can be suggested for the rest. What strikes the reader is the emphasis on military

---

notables of faith. **Gideon, Barak, Samson, Jephthah**—are these the ideal men we should want our sons to follow? The conquest of territory—what has this to do with the grace of Jesus Christ? The killing of men, women, and little children—how can this be an acceptable service to God? Why should men be included who **conquered kingdoms, . . . became mighty in war, put foreign armies to flight?** It is hard to see in war, even in the relatively harmless wars of antiquity, anything but stark wickedness. To engage in war may be the lesser of two evils, may be necessary for the people of God in particular historical crises. But it is still evil, an awful evidence of the accumulated power of human sin, a judgment of God upon our race. What is to distinguish these men from the long list of bloody conquerors who have afflicted mankind?

They were not men of special virtue. **Gideon** was hesitant and timid. **Barak** had to be shamed into action. **Jephthah** is known chiefly for his rash oath. And **Samson** was a physical giant with the weaknesses of mind and conscience that such men often embody. It is true that at least **Gideon** and **Samson** fought against terri-

fying odds. But so did the Spartans at Thermopylae. So did the Americans at Bataan.

If the phrase **through faith** is in keeping with the usage in other parts of this chapter, it can mean only that these heroes were relying on the promises of God, that they "did not receive what was promised" (vs. 39), that even in battle they were living unto God, knowing that the real significance of their work would never be seen in their own day, willing to wait for the fulfillment that the day of the Lord would bring.

Sensitive Christians will be quick to see that we live in a morally ambiguous world. Evil has infected us and our institutions. There is no human cause, not even the church of Christ, that is a pure cause and that is not infected with sin. If we wait for a morally pure cause to serve, we shall wait out our days in idle futility. In all our choices between human loyalties we must select the relatively good over the relatively evil. That is what it means to live in a world of sin. Yet the Christian will never be content to stop here. He will be faithful in penitence over his own share in the collective sins of his groups. He will let his own witness

**35** Women received their dead raised to life again: and others were tortured, not accepting deliverance; that they might obtain a better resurrection:

**36** And others had trial of *cruel* mockings and scourgings, yea, moreover of bonds and imprisonment:

**37** They were stoned, they were sawn asunder, were tempted, were slain with the sword: they wandered about in sheepskins and goatskins; being destitute, afflicted, tormented;

**38** Of whom the world was not worthy: they wandered in deserts, and *in* mountains, and *in* dens and caves of the earth.

eign armies to flight. **35** Women received their dead by resurrection. Some were tortured, refusing to accept release, that they might rise again to a better life. **36** Others suffered mocking and scourging, and even chains and imprisonment. **37** They were stoned, they were sawn in two,*y* they were killed with the sword; they went about in skins of sheep and goats, destitute, afflicted, ill-treated — **38** of whom the world was not worthy — wandering over deserts and mountains, and in dens and caves of the earth.

*y* Other manuscripts add *they were tempted.*

triumphs, unparalleled in the N.T. While the author unhesitatingly lists these as deeds of faith, it should be noted that they stand in contrast to faith as enabling its heroes to endure martyrdom and incredible sufferings (vss. 35-38), which is the climax of the summary. The source in history for much of this summary must be the Maccabean struggle and its triumph. The contrast between triumph and suffering is most skillfully drawn: they **received promises** (vs. 33; cf. 6:15), but not **what was promised,** i.e., the final promise (vs. 39); they **escaped the edge of the sword,** but **were killed with the sword; women received their dead by resurrection,** but some refused to accept release **that they might rise again to a better life.** Faith achieves results on the earthly plane, but its chief glory lies in its power to link men indissolubly with the heavenly realm, sustaining them to endure all imaginable sufferings and even martrydom. In vs. 37 the RSV omits **were tempted.** Some word having the same assonance as the Greek for **they were stoned** (ἐλιθάσθησαν) and **they were sawn in two** (ἐπρίσθησαν) stood in the original, but

be known. He will keep taut in his own soul the tension between what God wants and what is. And he will endure "as seeing him who is invisible," knowing that he too will not receive the promise, which can be fulfilled only in the world where Christ completely reigns. This is the duty of all Christians to the state and to human society.

**Others suffered mocking and scourging.** It ought to hurt a man to read these lines, for it is a tragic comment on the world in which we live. This is what evil men do to good men. We have seen this in our own day. Even among large sections of mankind that recoil from gross physical cruelty, we have our more subtle cruelties, even more deadly in their working. Our sharp words and vicious innuendoes may hurt more deeply than physical torture. We live and have a share in a world that "was never more clearly itself, never acted more naturally and in character, than in crucifying this good man Jesus Christ." [3]

Yet if we have any imagination, we cannot read these stirring lines without lifting up our

heads in pride and hope. This is what God can do for men, yes, for us. Let all the cheap detractors of human nature, the facile cynics, the naturalists who would reduce man to "nothing but," the forlorn who have lost hope—let them all see the noble army of the martyrs. Let them see what courage faith can engender. Let them behold such steadfastness as keeps our world from becoming uninhabitable, which keeps the fresh clean uprush of hope alive—let them see this and be abashed and silent. No estimate of human nature is adequate, even from the most coldly scientific point of view, that does not make room for the moral heroes of the race, who **through faith . . . won strength out of weakness.**

At this point the author may have raised his head, stared off into space, then added **of whom the world was not worthy.** Here is one of the most notable and poignant asides of the Bible. The fact is that evil cannot tolerate the presence of good. If men of faith would only keep from interfering with evil men, if they would be discreet, if they would keep judicious silence, if they would not notice injustice and oppression, then there would be no persecution.

[3] Norman F. Langford, *The Two-Edged Sword* (Philadelphia: Westminster Press, 1945), p. 150.

39 And these all, having obtained a good report through faith, received not the promise:

40 God having provided some better thing for us, that they without us should not be made perfect.

39 And all these, though well attested by their faith, did not receive what was promised, 40 since God had foreseen something better for us, that apart from us they should not be made perfect.

---

**were tempted** (ἐπειράσθησαν) hardly belongs in this list of violent sufferings, and the MS evidence is uncertain. These destitute, afflicted, ill-treated men "condemned the world" as did Noah (vs. 7). Nowhere is the author's literary skill more apparent than in the brilliant aside, a model of understatement, **of whom the world was not worthy.**

**39-40.** Our author must now show that though the faith of these witnesses was valid, and they received, some of them, earthly rewards, yet our faith is the final faith because it is faith in the heavenly reality revealed in its full glory in Christ. Faith is the same, theirs and ours, and its solidarity across the centuries means not just our privilege, but also our responsibility as will be now shown (12:1 ff.). The privilege, **God had foreseen something better for us,** entails the responsibility, **that apart from us they should not be made perfect.**

Although Hebrews includes trust, confidence, daring, hope, and obedience, the controlling idea is that faith (cf. vs. 1) is the active conviction about unseen realities which moves and shapes human conduct. While the intellectual note is stronger than with Paul, our writing is neither prevailingly abstract nor philosophical, for the reality of this unseen realm has been demonstrated in the temptations, the sufferings, the obedience, and the death of Jesus our high priest, who opens the way into the heavenly sanctuary for all who have faith. Faith means holding fast to Jesus. It is as simple as that; but this holding fast will mean nothing less than salvation.

Our author's unique view of faith arises from his unique conception of religion

---

Or would there be? If good could be secluded and hidden, if it would keep out of sight, if the courage of faith did not rebuke cowardice, if the pure in heart did not bring judgment upon lust, if simple kindness could be darkened so that greed would not look shabby by contrast—then perhaps persecution would cease. Or would it? It is because good still has its weak ally in hearts of evil that the good are persecuted. Without this disturbing echo in the conscience of the wrongdoer, good would lose its power to rebuke evil. So it is really against themselves that they strike when the wicked let fall the blows of torture upon men of faith. They hate because deeply within they hate and distrust themselves.

Yet no Christian dare apply such a judgment as this in self-righteousness. We too are unworthy of the men who have suffered and died for us. There is still that in us which loves darkness rather than light. "None is righteous, no, not one" (Rom. 3:10). Something still lives in us that is rebuked by men of God and takes its pleasure finding flaws in them. We are ourselves part of the world that **was not worthy.**

Here is the sure mercy of God. He sends into our confused and cruel humanity his messengers. He allows them to suffer **chains and**

**imprisonment,** to be **killed with the sword, to** wander **about in skins of sheep and goats, destitute, afflicted, ill-treated,** that we may not be left to our evil ways, that we may feel the sharp pang of shame and turn in penitence. Most of all, he has sent his Son, **of whom the world was not worthy,** whose suffering and death clearly revealed the dark and ugly nature of evil. God's judgment upon an unworthy world is not his final word. He "shows his love for us in that while we were yet sinners Christ died for us" (Rom. 5:8).

**39-40.** *Faith as an Anchor in the Future.—* **All these . . . did not receive what was promised.** Here is applied to all the O.T. heroes of the faith what has previously been said of the patriarchs (cf. Expos. on vss. 13-16). Their trust, and ours, is in the God of fulfillment, whose day is yet to come.

**God had foreseen something better for us.** What is this something better? The "better covenant" (7:22) that Christ had brought? The "better hope" (7:19) that we have through Christ? The "better sacrifices" (9:23) of Christ? It is hard to believe that this is what our author had in mind. For then he would have written, "Without Jesus Christ, they should not be made perfect." In a profound sense this is true. For

12 Wherefore, seeing we also are compassed about with so great a cloud of witnesses, let us lay aside every

12 Therefore, since we are surrounded by so great a cloud of witnesses, let

---

as access to God in worship, made possible in Christ, who has opened the way from the earthly to the heavenly presence. The emphasis is placed on the reality of Christ's revelation of the unseen in terms of our access to it. Faith does not require a change of man's nature or a radical transformation of his attitudes; it is native to man as man. What is required is an adequate object to which man can give his complete loyalty. If the writer can convince his readers that such a perfect object of faith has been revealed in Christ, he is confident that they will be cleansed and transformed by faith into resolute, eager, and unwavering Christians.

### D. What These Leaders Witnessed to Has Been Made Real in Jesus: Let Us Run Our Race Looking unto Him (12:1-2)

**12:1-2.** Vs. 1 picks up the thread of 10:39 with the rich content given to faith and the powerful motivation to its exercise added by ch. 11. The author is now ready for direct

---

the Christ was himself the fulfillment of the central elements of O.T. faith. He was God's answer to their deepest need.

But our author says that **apart from us they should not be made perfect.** Their faith, as we have seen, rested in God, who would fulfill his promises. It was an anchor cast into the future. It counted on God, content to greet the promises from afar (vs. 13); and this was well-pleasing to him (vs. 16). His answer to their faith was the Savior, who alone could provide perfect access through his perfect sacrifice, who alone could "taste death for every one" (2:9).

Yet it was this very faith that also implied the faithfulness of men to come. Abraham's faith would have been in vain had not his descendants entered and possessed the Land of Promise. In the same way, the faith of the heroes would be thwarted if the readers of the epistle did not prove faithful. **Apart from us they** cannot **be made perfect.** Their completion depends on us. It still does. To the roster of the faithful in this chapter has been added a long list of heroic men and women, most of them nameless in human annals, whose perfection waits upon our fidelity. We can fulfill their faith, or we can barter away the priceless heritage they have accumulated in blood, sweat, and tears. We are not to idealize the past, or be blind to its mistakes, or allow it to fasten its dead hand upon us, binding us to outworn ideas, ancient prejudices, old failures. But the principle still holds. Each generation of the faithful cries to its successor,

To you from falling hands we throw
The torch; be yours to hold it high.[4]

[4] John McCrae, "In Flanders Fields." Used by permission of J. M. Kilgour.

Our own generation suffers from conceit over its place in time. We assume that because we date our letters 19——, we are for that very reason better people than those unfortunate souls who had to write 18——, 16——, or 12——. This is a basic dishonesty. We forget our debts to those who have gone before. Every good that we enjoy is consecrated by the bloody sacrifices of the past. In a very real sense it has taken all the living of all the people in the long history of Western civilization, and of the Greco-Roman civilization that preceded it, to produce a single educated man or woman today. The literature, the science, the political insights, the music, the art, the philosophy of the past, all lay us under a heavy debt. Likewise our faith is ours because people in the past proved faithful. So do we in our turn cast our anchor into the future; without those who are to come after us, we shall **not be made perfect.**

The interpreter should note that this chapter is preaching at its best. It is informative, factual, and expert in its craftsmanship. It rests its case on the pride and glory of a noble tradition. Then with high skill the writer links privilege with responsibility and comes to his climax in a mighty "therefore" that begins the next chapter.

**12:1-2. The Cloud of Witnesses.**—Nothing is so disheartening as a lonely struggle. When no one else sees or cares, when no human friend shares the burden, then misgivings begin to plague us. Perhaps we struggle in vain and the issues are not real after all. This principle holds in Christian conflict. If we are to be strong, our strength will come in part from sharing with Christian friends the anxieties and burdens of the battle (cf. 3:12-13). We are never strong when we are alone.

weight, and the sin which doth so easily beset *us,* and let us run with patience the race that is set before us,

us also lay aside every weight, and sin which clings so closely, and let us run with perseverance the race that is set before

---

exhortation. The figure of speech is the most effective in Hebrews. The throng of witnesses who are not mere spectators but, in a sense, fellow participants (11:40), the runner and his preparation, the race itself calling for the utmost concentration and self-discipline, the pacemaker, and the glorious goal—all these are packed into a swiftly moving appeal. The one difficulty lies in the word εὐπερίστατον, translated **the sin which doth so easily beset us** (KJV), and **sin which clings so closely** (RSV). This word has troubled commentators because although universally attested, it seems to have been coined by our author and so we have no clue save etymology to its meaning. Codex p[46] (see Intro., p. 594) has the one variant we know, εὐπερίσπαστον meaning "easily distracting," or "diverting from the course." This fits so well with the figure of a race and with the author's appeal for concentrated attention on Jesus as to be inherently probable in spite of its lack of supporting MS attestation. Our author is aware that the struggle with sin persists; Christians who sin deliberately (10:26) are disqualified even to run the race, but sins such as he is urging them to **lay aside**—inattention, sluggishness, impatience— constantly beset them and have to be constantly resisted so long as life on this plane continues. The vivid translation of ἀρχηγόν, **pioneer** (RSV; see on 2:10), has the advantage of retaining the thought of Jesus as blazing the trail for us, but **author** (KJV) is more accurate, for the accent is on Jesus as the initiator and the perfecter of faith, and it is vs. 2*b* which gives the content of struggle and triumph. Perfection here and elsewhere means achievement of the end in view, and while moral implications are definitely in mind, they are not primary. Our author believes that direct access to God through Christ is the goal of religion, not righteousness as such. Men must be "purified"

---

But in the Christian way we rely not merely on the help of present comrades. **We are surrounded by . . . a cloud of witnesses,** a multitude that no man can number. By the record of their lives they reassure us that endurance is possible, that hardship at its worst is but for the day, that the grace of God will sustain us, and that the joys of faith's rewards are enduring. They show us how to greet the promised fulfillment "from afar" (11:13), how to **run with perseverance the race that is set before us.** Of Abel our writer said, "He died, but through his faith he is still speaking" (11:4). All the heroes of the faith are "still speaking," and that is why they are **witnesses.** When we interpret the **cloud of witnesses** as a massed gallery eagerly watching our race to see its outcome, we miss the main point of the author that they are not mere spectators of our running, but witnesses to the faithfulness of the God who has promised.

There is an immense resource in biography, not only in the Bible, but from the long list of Christian men and women, that we too often neglect in our preaching, in education, and in our private devotional reading. The victories of men and women of old ought not to be forgotten. They are a convincing argument and a constant source of strength.

They may give us strength by first putting us to shame. John Hutton cites Browning, "Bishop Blougram's Apology," how

Blougram tells of Verdi conducting his worst opera in Florence. At the close of the performance, Verdi knowing all the time that it was a poor thing, the audience rose in a body and applauded, throwing roses at the composer, and so on. There he stood drinking in the praise, acknowledging it. until—he looked round to where sat Rossini, patient in his stall! Rossini, a master, looking at him, saying in effect, "Oh, Verdi, Verdi!" Such is the lot of a man who chooses the praise of men, and suddenly catches the eye of some sincere artist or catches the eye of God.[5]

**Let us also lay aside every weight.** The word translated **weight** can mean excess flesh produced by eating rich foods, which the trained runner will not allow. Or it can mean extra things that we carry which impede our running. **And sin which clings so closely.** This likens sin to a flowing garment which tangles the runner's legs. Or, with the Exeg., it means that which distracts or diverts us from the course.

What are these "weights" and "sins"? The author does not specify, and it is good that he

[5] *The Dark Mile* (London: Hodder & Stoughton, n.d.), p. 121. Used by permission.

2 Looking unto Jesus the author and finisher of *our* faith; who for the joy that was set before him endured the cross, despising the shame, and is set down at the right hand of the throne of God.

us, 2 looking to Jesus the pioneer and perfecter of our faith, who for the joy that was set before him endured the cross, despising the shame, and is seated at the right hand of the throne of God.

(1:3) if they are to worship God, and the worship of God results in purification from sins. "For the joy" in **who for the joy that was set before him** could be "instead of the joy," but the context argues against this rendering. Moses (cf. 11:25) chose affliction instead of the false joys of Egypt; Jesus accepted **the cross** and its **shame** because of the true **joy** which lay ahead. The author conceives the sufferings and shame of Jesus not as a renunciation of heavenly joy, but as the way to it for him and for us. It is noteworthy that he recurs to the simple name Jesus, for it is the human Jesus whose human experience fits him to be **author** and **perfecter** for us in our human struggle. The readers will know who Jesus is, the Son of God and our high priest, but lest they should forget, he reminds them that he who endured the cross and its shame **is seated at the right hand of the throne of God** (cf. 1:3; 8:1). It should also be noted that his direct appeal is to run the race **with perseverance;** it is not a short dash to glory but a distance race calling for endurance. Martyrdom did not quench the faith of the witnesses of old, nor did the Cross defeat

does not. To list the things that hinder the runner might sound unduly severe, for they would include for some, at any rate, things that are innocent in themselves and might not impede others in their race. Our moral education often errs at this point. We concentrate on the negative virtues rather than on the race, as though the child, being stripped of these impediments, would at once start the heavenly course! As long as a man or a child is standing still, the "weights" will seem harmless and innocent. But let him begin to run in earnest, and the excess baggage and the clinging garments will soon be thrown aside. Diversions will cease to attract his attention. Set out in line with the promises of God, and conscience suddenly becomes acute.

**Let us run with perseverance the race that is set before us.** Here lies the danger against which the author constantly warns his readers. Men begin in joyous devotion. But the early vision fades; the race is long; obstacles block the way; we notice the diversions at the side; and the race slows to a walk, then to a careless saunter. Paul complained of the Galatians, "You were running well; who hindered you from obeying the truth?" (Gal. 5:7.) The call to perseverance is the only valid call to be a person. Without a goal toward which we bend every energy, we become mere meeting places of the forces that play upon us, not persons at all.

But this danger can be escaped only if we rely on an aid greater than present comrades, stronger than the **cloud of witnesses,** by **looking to Jesus the pioneer and perfecter of our faith.** This does not mean that Jesus instills faith in us, nurtures it, and brings it to perfection.

Elsewhere in the N.T. this imparting and nourishing of faith is the work of the Holy Spirit. Our author's meaning is quite different. The word "our" is not in the Greek text. We are to look to Jesus as one who led the way, who as a man of faith far surpassed all the other heroes of the faith, and who completed, "perfected," his faith.

Men often object to calling Jesus a man of faith or speaking of the faith of Jesus. Paul would not have referred to the faith of Jesus, partly because his "faith" was in contrast to works; it was a confidence in the righteousness of God, a faith which was "in the Son of God" (Gal. 2:20). But as we have seen, faith in this epistle means confidence in the future vindication of God's promises. No N.T. writer holds a higher view of the deity of our Lord than the author of Hebrews (cf. 1:2-3). But he also insists that Jesus was completely human as well (cf. 2:17-18; 4:15-16). For Jesus, faith meant greeting the promises "from afar" (11:13), enduring "as seeing him who is invisible" (11:27), suffering hardship, waiting vindication. To obscure the full humanity of Jesus is to rob the Cross of its shame, and the sacrifice of the Cross of its power.

**Who for the joy that was set before him.** This was a joy that could be fulfilled only by doing the Father's will, by enduring the Cross, by providing full salvation for men whom he loved, and by welcoming them into the Father's presence. In this sense every purposeful action is done **for the joy . . . set before,** i.e., the satisfaction of an objective reached, a purpose accomplished. The key to a man's character, as Aristotle once observed, is that in which he takes

**3** For consider him that endured such contradiction of sinners against himself, lest ye be wearied and faint in your minds.

**4** Ye have not yet resisted unto blood, striving against sin.

**5** And ye have forgotten the exhortation which speaketh unto you as unto children, My son, despise not thou the chastening of the Lord, nor faint when thou art rebuked of him:

**3** Consider him who endured from sinners such hostility against himself, so that you may not grow weary or faint-hearted. **4** In your struggle against sin you have not yet resisted to the point of shedding your blood. **5** And have you forgotten the exhortation which addresses you as sons? —
"My son, do not regard lightly the discipline of the Lord,
nor lose courage when you are punished by him.

Jesus; how much more ought we to fulfill with patient endurance our vocation, which has not called for the shedding of blood (vs. 4).

### E. Discipline Is Inherent in Sonship, Human and Divine (12:3-11)

**3-4.** Why should faith be so difficult? The author answers this question by applying the example of Jesus to his readers' own situation (vss. 3-4) and by interpreting suffering as discipline. What threatens them is weariness and faintheartedness, and the context suggests some kind of persecution as the cause. The cure lies in the imitation of Jesus, who endured so much more than they have to face. **In your struggle against sin you have not yet resisted to the point of shedding your blood.** It has been argued that this excludes Rome (cf. 10:32 ff.) as the destination of Hebrews, for Rome had had its martyrs (see Intro., pp. 592-93); but if the readers were addressed some decades after the Neronian persecution, the words, although not too tactful, would not necessarily be untrue of the Romans. **Who endured from sinners such hostility against himself** shows nothing more than a very general knowledge of the Synoptic tradition.

**5-11.** The familiar argument about parental discipline, based on Prov. 3:11-12, is neither very profound nor specifically Christian. The author has dealt with the sufferings

joy. Let not hedonists be deceived by this passage into saying that Jesus was seeking pleasure. He sought to do the Father's will, salvation for his brethren (cf. 2:10-11), and therefore **endured the cross, despising the shame.**

We often read these words glibly. In retrospect the Cross shines in grace and power. But seen ahead, a cross is a thing of horror. **Despising the shame** is no light thing, not for a man who loves others and whose love makes him sensitive. To be regarded with contempt by a man whose opinions you despise, and for whose character you have a low esteem, is unpleasant but not painful. But for a mother to be held up to reproach by a son or daughter upon whom she has spent special love and sacrifice is as cruel a burden as a human being can be called upon to bear. Our author does not make much either of the love of God or of the love of Jesus, although he did emphasize the sympathy of Jesus in 2:10-18. But it was the love of Jesus for men that made the shame of the Cross the bitterest of all deaths.

**3-11. Our Need of Discipline.**—In our quest of freedom and spontaneity our generation has underrated the place of discipline. Our educa-

tion, led by a superficial psychology, has deified desire, abhorred inhibitions, and put into children's mouths such specious words as "frustration." Impulses are meant to be allowed free rein. We forget some very elemental facts about life. No simple deed is ever performed, such as preparing a meal, reading a paragraph, or writing a letter, without ignoring a thousand allurements. Attention shuts out literally hundreds of distracting sights and sounds, forbids hundreds of inward promptings that would divert us from the task at hand. No significant work or life is possible without discipline. If you want to see the uninhibited life, where people obey their impulses without hindrance, look at the patients in an institution for the feebleminded. There is your undisciplined life par excellence. Whenever they feel like doing anything, they do it! It is significant that some of our most intelligent college students, weary of formless freedom, have rushed eagerly into the arms of totalitarian schemes of reform where their daily work, their opinions and judgments, even their conscience, are all rigidly controlled from above.

Every gift that we enjoy is cradled in a dis-

**6** For whom the Lord loveth he chasteneth, and scourgeth every son whom he receiveth.

**7** If ye endure chastening, God dealeth with you as with sons; for what son is he whom the father chasteneth not?

**8** But if ye be without chastisement, whereof all are partakers, then are ye bastards, and not sons.

**9** Furthermore, we have had fathers of our flesh which corrected *us,* and we gave *them* reverence: shall we not much rather be in subjection unto the Father of spirits, and live?

**6** For the Lord disciplines him whom he loves,
  and chastises every son whom he receives."

**7** It is for discipline that you have to endure. God is treating you as sons; for what son is there whom his father does not discipline? **8** If you are left without discipline, in which all have participated, then you are illegitimate children and not sons. **9** Besides this, we have had earthly fathers to discipline us and we respected them. Shall we not much more be subject to the

---

and temptations of Jesus much more creatively in 2:10 ff. As a matter of fact, our author's thinking along liturgical lines (note **holiness,** vs. 10) prevents him from dealing with the problem of suffering, for he is concerned with the one effective sacrifice and what it means when men have faith. The objective way to God has been opened up for you—walk in that way! When he deals with human suffering as such, he has nothing very profound to offer. The argument here is strictly *ad hominem:* suffering is disciplinary; if

---

cipline that hurts. We might live only for the present, as the lower animals do, unless the pain of the present taught us to plan for the future. No love would be possible without pain. It seems clear that we should never have become aware of ourselves as selves, or of others as persons, except in the conflict of wills and the consequent thwarting of purpose that we underwent as little children. Our very ideas of ourselves and of others are born in conflict that hurts. We should never even glimpse the truth, much less set out in search for it, did we not suffer from the lack of it. All knowledge begins with a "felt difficulty," a "frustration."

We never escape the need of such pain. Without suffering, we tend to settle down in easy nests until the slightest disturbance of the pleasant routine irritates us. Said a wise friend who had been a successful administrator, "Every man is as lazy as he dares to be. The only difference that makes some of us work harder is that we are gifted with imagination to look farther ahead and see doom catching up with us." There is a core of suffering in every joy, every kindness, every grace of life. The larger heart, the clearer vision, the stouter courage, all come at the high price of painful discipline. As Browning once put it:

> Happy that I can
> Be crossed and thwarted as a man,
> Not left in God's contempt apart,
> With ghastly smooth life, dead at heart,
> Tame in earth's paddock as her prize.[6]

[6] "Easter-Day," st. xxxiii.

Indeed, he pictures hell as the place where men have just what they want:

> Hadst thou learned
> What God accounteth happiness,
> Thou wouldst not find it hard to guess
> What hell may be his punishment
> For those who doubt if God invent
> Better than they. Let such men rest
> Content with what they judged the best.
> Let the unjust usurp at will:
> The filthy shall be filthy still:
> Miser, there waits the gold for thee!
> Hater, indulge thine enmity!
> And thou, whose heaven self-ordained
> Was, to enjoy earth unrestrained,
> Do it! Take all the ancient show![7]

This is at least a plausible hint as to the meaning of suffering. It is in keeping with our author's thought. With true pastoral insight he is preparing his people for possible persecution and martyrdom. Martyrdom has not yet come to them. **In your struggle against sin you have not yet resisted to the point of shedding your blood.** This seems the likely meaning rather than that they have not been in deadly earnest in their battle against sin. "He is shaming them, not blaming them. 'Your sufferings have been serious and sharp (10[32]f), but nothing to what others before you, and especially Jesus, have had to bear. Will you give way under a lesser strain than theirs?' "[8]

The Bible does not provide us with a the-

[7] *Ibid.,* st. xxii.
[8] Moffatt, *Hebrews,* p. 199.

10 For they verily for a few days chastened *us* after their own pleasure; but he for *our* profit, that *we* might be partakers of his holiness.

11 Now no chastening for the present seemeth to be joyous, but grievous: nevertheless, afterward it yieldeth the peaceable fruit of righteousness unto them which are exercised thereby.

12 Wherefore lift up the hands which hang down, and the feeble knees;

Father of spirits and live? 10 For they disciplined us for a short time at their pleasure, but he disciplines us for our good, that we may share his holiness. 11 For the moment all discipline seems painful rather than pleasant; later it yields the peaceful fruit of righteousness to those who have been trained by it.

12 Therefore lift your drooping hands

---

you were not sons of God, God would not bother to discipline you; you know this from human parenthood and sonship. Why should you question the divine discipline? It is brief, if painful, and its fruits are good. This sole application of the fatherhood of God to the readers is made in terms of discipline. The love of God as father plays no role in the writer's thinking, which is controlled by a sense of the majesty of God and the corresponding awe of the worshiper.

### F. Warning of the Awful Penalty of Disobedience, Relieved by a Final Word of Assurance (12:12-29)

The very general exhortations which follow his explanation of suffering are thoroughly typical of the author, for once again he reminds his readers of the awful penalty of disobedience, enforcing his warning with scriptural citations and with a splendid and awe-inspiring picture of **the city of the living God.** How much more should the reality of **the heavenly Jerusalem** inspire obedience than its earthly copy! And how

---

oretical solution of the problem of suffering. Certainly the death of Christ is not the answer, but rather the most acute statement of the problem in our long, sorry human story. That the noblest and best the world has ever seen should suffer the most dreadful **hostility** from men and the most shameful of deaths, this alone seems to be a complete denial of God. "He saved others; let him save himself, if he is the Christ of God, his Chosen One!" (Luke 23:35.) Possibly we should have to be God in order fully to understand the meaning of suffering. In the meantime, we have our practical answer in the heroes of the faith, and supremely in Jesus: that faith in the Father who will fulfill his promises is the only way to meet suffering in triumph. It is part of our status as creatures that our vision should be limited. The far-off meaning of our tears can be known only to God. We must believe that "in everything God works for good with those who love him, who are called according to his purpose" (Rom. 8:28). There is no other answer that satisfies the mind and heart.

Our writer reminds his readers of the earthly discipline of fathers, who **disciplined us for a short time at their pleasure,** i.e., as it seemed best to them. But their discipline often erred both in method and purpose, yet **we respected**

them. Why should we not accept the discipline of the **Father of spirits?** When, therefore, hardships come that torment us with anguish, let us look up through our tears to the heart of a loving Father, trusting his good purpose, and we shall be strong. In that hour let it be our joy that God is treating us as sons. Discipline is the mercy of God. Every son receives it, even the Son. **Consider him who endured from sinners such hostility against himself.** If all life were easy and pleasant, it would be a sure token that we **are illegitimate children and not sons.** The purpose of the discipline is high, **that we may share his holiness.** What this means is beyond the mind's imagining, yes, beyond the heart's desiring. True faith is here—so to trust God that we shall be faithful, even "unto death," knowing that the issues of life and of death are safe in his hands who has promised, "I will give you the crown of life" (Rev. 2:10).

In the meantime, we can know that the discipline of pain is **for the moment;** that if borne in faith, it yields fruit, as a seed brings forth its plant. This fruit is **peaceful,** in contrast to the shaking and tossing of difficult days; and it is the **fruit of righteousness.**

**12-13.** *The Spirit of True Church Discipline.* —**Therefore,** since we know that hardship is God's way of preparing us for the heavenly city,

13 And make straight paths for your feet, lest that which is lame be turned out of the way; but let it rather be healed.

14 Follow peace with all *men,* and holiness, without which no man shall see the Lord:

and strengthen your weak knees, 13 and make straight paths for your feet, so that what is lame may not be put out of joint but rather be healed. 14 Strive for peace with all men, and for the holiness with-

---

much more dreadful the rejection of it! **Let us offer to God acceptable worship, with reverence and awe.**

**12-14.** He begins his exhortation in the language of Isa. 35:3, and the prophetic call to strength and courage (Isa. 35:4 ff.) may well be in his mind. Bodily health and vigor, the erect and sturdy strength which walks a straight path, is his figure of spiritual health and confident faith. There is no reason to suppose that he has in mind individuals who need this message. Let him who needs it apply it to himself. The admonition to **strive for peace with all men** sounds like the beginning of a list of short, pithy advices such as we have in 13:1 ff. As the use of "peaceful" in vs. 11, and the collocation of the word with "consecration" or **holiness** in this verse shows, the author has something different in mind from the absence of dissension and quarreling in the brotherhood. He means the quiet security of the dedicated and cleansed life, which will, to be sure, have its social

---

face your hardships with courage. **Drooping hands** and **weak knees** are not for the soldiers of Christ. In the light of vss. 14-17 it is not likely that individuals are so much addressed here, with the exhortation to **lift your drooping hands and strenghten your weak knees,** as is the collective Christian group, in the hope that each will encourage the other. A lonely fighter is not likely to be courageous. Bravery comes by contagion, when men help to remind each other that the pains are short-lived. As Hugh Latimer was being led to the stake in 1555 in Oxford, he greeted his fellow martyr with these words, "Be of good comfort, Master Ridley, and play the man; we shall this day light such a candle, by God's grace, in England, as I trust shall never be put out."

**And make straight paths for your feet.** This is a rich verse and we may put no narrow limits to its meaning. When a man has sinned, he is like one who is lame. Let him make straight paths for his feet, so that the crippled leg will **not be put out of joint but rather be healed.** The weak man had better take no chances. Let him shun the places of temptation; let him flee the region of danger; let him seek the highway (Isa. 35:8). For if he leaves the straight paths, his wound will be made permanent. The church also has a responsibility to its weak members, those who are timid, or who falter, or who are lame. Let no offense be thrown in their way in this hour of danger. Let the road rather be kept clear of any occasion of stumbling.

**14-17.** *Aspects of Church Discipline.*—**Strive for peace with all men,** for it will not come of itself. So habitually do we regard the world and our fellow men through our own eyes, and as

incidental to our self-centered desires, that the conflict of wills seems to be the natural state of man. It is not easy to live among real persons, to see that for my neighbor his life is "as bright a light, as warm a fire, to him, as thine to thee; his will is as full of struggling desires, of hard problems, of fateful decisions; his pains are as hateful, his joys as dear." [9] To live at peace requires the imaginative insight of love. Without this love, the church ceases to be the church. The worst heresy of all is hatred. The test of Jesus is simple. "By this all men will know that you are my disciples, if you have love for one another" (John 13:35).

Yet love without a moral gravitation degenerates into aimless and amiable acquiescence with men as they are. In the church we are to strive **for the holiness** [purification, sanctification] **without which no one will see the Lord.** Such purification, which here has a ritual overtone, is the gift of Christ, through his perfect sacrifice (cf. 9:13-14). Yet we are to strive for it. This is one of the many paradoxes of the gospel that can be resolved only in the life of faith. We strive, yet we receive. All is of grace, therefore **strive.** The church is the company of those who love one another in Christ, and where love has failed by so much as one member, the church does not attain **holiness.** Nor is the pastoral duty assigned to any class or group of officials. It belongs to all, and our author so regards it. He addresses every Christian in these verses.

**See to it that no one fail to obtain the grace of God.** Is it ours, then, to see that others ob-

[9] Josiah Royce, *The Religious Aspect of Philosophy* (Boston: Houghton Mifflin & Co., 1885), p. 158.

15 Looking diligently lest any man fail of the grace of God; lest any root of bitterness springing up trouble *you*, and thereby many be defiled;

16 Lest there *be* any fornicator, or profane person, as Esau, who for one morsel of meat sold his birthright.

out which no one will see the Lord. 15 See to it that no one fail to obtain the grace of God; that no "root of bitterness" spring up and cause trouble, and by it the many become defiled; 16 that no one be immoral or irreligious like Esau, who sold his birth-

---

consequences in a peaceful human relationship. To **see the Lord** has no reference to the beatific vision, which would be quite foreign to his thought. It is the common O.T. expression for "acceptable worship" (vs. 28) which is the key to the entire passage.

**15-17.** This leads the author for the third and final time (cf. 6:4 ff.; 10:26 ff.) to remind his readers of the dire consequences of missing the one way to God. He does this by the use of two analogies, from the fate of Esau (vss. 15-17) and from the fate of those who violated the sanctity of the earthly Sinai (vss. 18-21). Esau was singled out as a **root of bitterness** (cf. Deut. 29:18 LXX) not only because he made the wrong choice between sensual satisfaction and his birthright, but also because he had become the classic example of a fatal and irrevocable decision. The author and his readers would think of the word **birthright** in larger terms than we do, for it included the corporate destiny of all descendants and not merely the disposition of property. This is in the writer's mind when he warns against the example of Esau. He uses strong words to characterize him, **fornicator, profane** (the RSV **immoral, irreligious** are correct and modern but lack the vigor of the KJV), not on account of poor Esau, but because his thought is fixed on the possible apostasy of his Christian readers. **He found no chance to repent, though he sought it with tears** invites a modern psychological interpretation to the effect that Esau had so damaged "the fabric of his soul" that, try as he might, he could not in the very nature of the case achieve true repentance. Our author does indeed

---

tain grace? Is not that gift entirely from God? What have we to do with it? Much every way. There are many people in our world who cannot believe in the grace of God because they see only harsh and hate-filled deeds about them. The flowering of grace into the forgiving spirit of men and women may be the most compelling evidence that God is gracious. Hard legalism may shut the gates of mercy (cf. Luke 7:47). Humility and kindness are twins. To know in ourselves the depth of God's forgiveness is to be prepared to be kindly and gracious to those about us.

**That no "root of bitterness" spring up and cause trouble.** This refers not merely to bitter strife, but to any sin that might spring up among the faithful and **by it the many become defiled.** The glib individualism which boasts, "What I do is my own business," is a denial of everything for which the church stands. Love means that lives are intermingled, and that if my brother goes down to perdition, part of me goes down with him. If my brother is exalted by the grace of God, part of me shares in that exaltation (see Gal. 6:1-2 for the fullest statement of this principle). The callous atomism of city dwellers, where each man scarcely knows his neighbor, has badly infected the churches.

Its result is inevitable weakness and defilement. We desperately need, especially in large churches, to restore the vivid sense of our dependence on one another. The very fact that people shrink from this strong common life is itself a serious symptom.

The writer goes on to specify some of the sins that may become a **"root of bitterness":** **lest there be any fornicator, or profane person.** A strong sense of belonging, of group loyalty and mutual discipline, of living ties to Christian comrades, is the best preventive of sins of the flesh. It is almost inconceivable that a believer should be guilty of such sins until he has first broken, perhaps in the secrecy of his own heart, the ties of Christian brotherhood. We know enough about psychology today to be sure that sexual sins are themselves symptoms of a deeper malady, a sickness of soul which cannot thrive in a beloved community, where hearts and lives are bound together in an intimate loyalty to the Christ.

There is no evidence that Esau was guilty of fornication, although a tradition to that effect grew out of Philo's writing.[1] But he is an example of the **profane person.** To live in the present with no regard to the future, to deify

[1] Moffatt, *Hebrews*, p. 211.

744

17 For ye know how that afterward, when he would have inherited the blessing, he was rejected: for he found no place of repentance, though he sought it carefully with tears.

18 For ye are not come unto the mount that might be touched, and that burned with fire, nor unto blackness, and darkness, and tempest,

right for a single meal. 17 For you know that afterward, when he desired to inherit the blessing, he was rejected, for he found no chance to repent, though he sought it with tears.

18 For you have not come to what may be touched, a blazing fire, and darkness,

---

stress that apostasy in the full light of the heavenly rewards and with complete deliberation is impossible of forgiveness, but he hardly psychologizes in this fashion, for the impossibility of a second repentance, under such conditions, lies in God's will, not in man's (cf. vs. 29).

**18-24.** The second analogy, joined in thought to vss. 14 and 17, is more complex. The main thought seems to be that awe-inspiring and dreadful as the giving of the law to Moses

---

one's own desires and to live for their satisfaction, to believe only in the immediate and the tangible, to regard the world as a collection of things rather than as a veritable sacrament of the sure mercies of God, this is to be **profane or irreligious.**

> Oh, if we draw a circle premature,
>     Heedless of far gain,
> Greedy for quick returns of profit, sure
>     Bad is our bargain! [2]

Esau deeply regretted his bad bargain and sought to regain his birthright. But the bargain was irrevocable: **he was rejected.** When a man barters away the priceless heritage of a good home, of Christian faith, of hope for the years to come, for a brief moment of physical pleasure, the evil can never be undone. Josiah Royce of Harvard once wrote with clear insight about the hell of the irrevocable. Suppose I have betrayed a trust.

I can never undo that deed. If I ever say, 'I have undone that deed,' I shall be both a fool and a liar. Counsel me, if you will, to forget that deed. Counsel me to do good deeds without number to set over against that treason. Counsel me to be cheerful, and to despise Puritanism. . . . Only do not counsel me 'to get rid of' just that sin. That, so far as the real facts are concerned, cannot be done. For I am, and to the end of endless time shall remain, the doer of that wilfully traitorous deed. [3]

But was the door of repentance closed to Esau? Did God refuse his mercy to Esau, **though he sought it with tears?** This seems to be the clear intention. Solemn warning is given about

---

[2] Browning, "A Grammarian's Funeral."
[3] *The Problem of Christianity* (New York: The Macmillan Co., 1913), I, 260-61.

the impossibility of a second repentance (cf. 6:4-8; 10:26-31); yet no more solemn than the word spoken by Jesus of the foolish virgins (Matt. 25:11-12). The faithful interpreter cannot withhold this warning. Sin is no light matter. When a person turns away from the grace of God and deliberately chooses the path of evil, there comes a time when he cannot repent, however bitterly he may lament the disastrous consequences of his sin. He cannot find the **place of repentance, though he** seek **it carefully with tears.**

But valid as is this psychological insight, it was not in our author's mind (see Exeg.). He does not say that God closes the door on one who seriously repents; if he did, he would be in direct conflict with other parts of the Bible.

Repentance here is not to be taken for sincere conversion to God; but it was only that terror with which the Lord smites the ungodly, after they have long indulged themselves in their iniquity. Nor is it a wonder that this terror should be said to be useless and unavailing, for they do not in the meantime repent nor hate their own vices, but are only tormented by a sense of their own punishment. The same thing is to be said of *tears;* whenever a sinner sighs on account of his sins, the Lord is ready to pardon him, nor is God's mercy ever sought in vain, for to him who knocks it shall be opened, (Matt. vii. 8;) but as the tears of Esau were those of a man past hope, they were not shed on account of having offended God; so the ungodly, however they may deplore their lot, complain and howl, do not yet knock at God's door for mercy, for this cannot be done but by faith. [4]

**18-24.** *Mount Sinai and Mount Zion.*—In an eloquent and moving passage the thought of the whole epistle is now gathered up into the

[4] Calvin, *Commentary on Hebrews,* p. 329.

19 And the sound of a trumpet, and the voice of words; which *voice* they that heard entreated that the word should not be spoken to them any more:

20 (For they could not endure that which was commanded, And if so much as a beast touch the mountain, it shall be stoned, or thrust through with a dart:

and gloom, and a tempest, 19 and the sound of a trumpet, and a voice whose words made the hearers entreat that no further message be spoken to them. 20 For they could not endure the order that was given, "If even a beast touches the mountain, it

---

on Sinai was, the true Mount Zion, **the city of the living God, the heavenly Jerusalem,** is so much more awful (and glorious) that to reject the word from heaven's high court is correspondingly more fateful. The contrast carries with it other shades of meaning: awe in the sense of fear over against awe in the sense of holy joy; **darkness, and gloom, and a tempest** over against the **festal gathering** of the angelic and human citizens of the heavenly city; a tangible and terrible **mountain** charged with mysterious and deadly power over against **the heavenly Jerusalem,** wherein dwell **the spirits of just men made perfect** under God, the judge of all, and Jesus, **the mediator of a new covenant.** The author has managed to pack many of his thoughts (cf. the suggestion of the priesthood of Jesus in **covenant** and **the sprinkled blood**) into this climactic figure drawn freely from O.T. sources. It is controlled by his central conviction that the invisible realm of reality, dimly perceived by the men of old and apprehended by their imperfect faith, has been opened up for us through the new and living (i.e., personal) way which Jesus initiated and perfected. If we ask whether Jesus in his earthly life did not partake of the shadowy

---

contrast between Mount Sinai and Mount Zion. We cannot escape the questions. Is our writer quite fair to the O.T.? Is there nothing but somber gloom and dread in the worship of the Old Covenant? What of the psalms of praise, the notes of gladness, and the serene confidence of Ps. 23? Has our author really caught the significant differences between the prophets and the Christ?

It is plain that Hebrews ought to be read in company with the rest of the N.T. Paul has seen other distinctive marks of the gospel. To get something of the force of them one only need turn to the noblest utterances of Isaiah and Jeremiah, holding these up beside the teachings of Jesus in the four Gospels. And even that is not all. It is good to ask ourselves again and again what difference Jesus has made, what faith would be like had he never come, how God and man, destiny and duty, faith and hope, righteousness and grace, would seem to us had not God "in these last days . . . spoken to us by a Son" (1:2).

Yet the passage at hand is worthy of special attention just because it gathers into a swift contrast the whole weight of the epistle. The details are not to be read with cautious accuracy, but as the work of an artist. How vivid they are! **A blazing fire, and darkness, and gloom, and a tempest** [whirlwind], **and the sound of a trumpet.** These are the symbols of God before

he wears a human face. And they still have validity. The God of all creation—how can you conceive him except in terms of awful majesty? Stand alone some night under the stars and contemplate their vastness; or think of the rigorous workings of the laws of nature; or be subdued by the fury of a storm at sea; or watch the sun come up on the grandeur of The Himalaya; or be silent and humble on the rim of the Grand Canyon; or read again the stirring account of nature's wonders in Job 38–41 and cry with him, "I have heard of thee by the hearing of the ear; but now mine eye seeth thee: wherefore I abhor myself, and repent in dust and ashes" (Job 42:5-6).

It were the seeing him, no flesh shall dare,
Some think, Creation's meant to show him forth:
I say it's meant to hide him all it can,
And that's what all the blessed evil's for.
Its use in Time is to environ us,
Our breath, our drop of dew, with shield enough
Against that sight till we can bear its stress.
Under a vertical sun, the exposed brain
And lidless eye and disemprisoned heart
Less certainly would wither up at once
Than mind, confronted with the truth of him.[5]

Then turn to **Mount Zion and to the city of the living God, the heavenly Jerusalem.** The disparity is sharp. The old was tangible, there-

[5] Browning, "Bishop Blougram's Apology."

21 And so terrible was the sight, *that* Moses said, I exceedingly fear and quake:)

22 But ye are come unto mount Sion, and unto the city of the living God, the heavenly Jerusalem, and to an innumerable company of angels,

23 To the general assembly and church of the firstborn, which are written in heaven, and to God the Judge of all, and to the spirits of just men made perfect,

shall be stoned." 21 Indeed, so terrifying was the sight that Moses said, "I tremble with fear." 22 But you have come to Mount Zion and to the city of the living God, the heavenly Jerusalem, and to innumerable angels in festal gathering, 23 and to the assembly[z] of the first-born who are enrolled in heaven, and to a judge who is God of all, and to the spirits of just men made perfect,

[z] Or *angels, and to the festal gathering and assembly.*

---

unreality of all earthly existence, his answer would of course be that Jesus was the Son who leads us out of the shadows into fellowship with God. Our author was not a philosopher like Philo, stressing the inherent capacity of men to apprehend the invisible and to achieve salvation by spiritual discipline and education; he was a Christian, believing that salvation was offered by God in Christ and that men might, through faith in the invisible and timeless reality revealed from within the human and temporal realm by Jesus, be saved to enjoy the complete fellowship with God which the ancient sacrificial system foresaw and prefigured but could never achieve.

While the main import of his analogy is clear, there are obscurities in the details. Vss. 18-21 appear to be the author's summary of the giving of the law on Sinai, although the name Sinai is not mentioned. He has drawn freely on O.T. sources, perhaps again from memory, for the terror inspired by the revelation was not due to the unapproachableness of the mountain as he states in vs. 20 (cf. Exod. 19:12-13), but to the people's awful fear of the revelation emanating from it (cf. Exod. 19:12-22; 20:18-21; Deut. 4:11-12; 5:22-27) as he correctly indicates in vs. 19; and the quotation from Moses comes from another setting than the revelation on Sinai (cf. Deut. 9:19).

The description of the heavenly city, reminiscent of the majestic language of Revelation, is not drawn from O.T. imagery but in the main from the author's own argument. The concept of **the heavenly Jerusalem** was common in late Judaism, especially in the apocalypses (cf. Rev. 21), and Paul refers to "the Jerusalem above" (Gal. 4:26). The writer has prepared the way in 8:2, 5; 11:10, 16, and the concept underlies his thinking throughout. The inhabitants of the heavenly Jerusalem are angels, men, God, and Jesus. All of these are there by inherent right except the men. Who are these men and where

---

fore transient. The new is invisible, spiritual, the land of the real. The old inspired dread. We come to the new with confidence (4:16). The darkness of gloom surrounded the old. Light and peace belong to the new. The old covenant could not assure men of sins forgiven. The new is equal to man's deepest need.

There is sober restraint in the portrait of Mount Zion. The vivid imagery of the Revelation is lacking. We are allowed to infer that much is beyond our power to conceive, remembering that "eye hath not seen, nor ear heard, neither have entered into the heart of man, the things which God hath prepared for them that love him" (I Cor. 2:9). For every phrase actually set down there is good warrant. It is into the presence of the living God that **you have come, . . . to innumerable angels in festal gathering, and to the assembly of the first-born**

**who are enrolled** [as citizens] **in heaven.** This is the company into which **you have come.** You, the humble, the poor, the persecuted, the afflicted, you belong to that noble assembly. Be not downcast or disheartened. The noblest heroes of old are your comrades.

You have come to **a judge who is God of all.** Here is the center of all reality, the one who alone can say, "I am." And do we still wince at the word **judge?** Here is the fair and just estimate of all our deeds and of all the hidden aspirations of our hearts. Here is the One to whom appeal is made, wittingly or not, whenever men complain of the rough injustice of the world's estimate. Here is the One for whom Job cried: "Oh that I knew where I might find him! That I might come even to his seat! I would set my cause in order before him, and fill my mouth with arguments" (Job 23:3-4

24 And to Jesus the mediator of the new covenant, and to the blood of sprinkling, that speaketh better things than *that of* Abel.

25 See that ye refuse not him that speaketh: for if they escaped not who refused him that spake on earth, much more *shall not* we *escape,* if we turn away from him that *speaketh* from heaven:

24 and to Jesus, the mediator of a new covenant, and to the sprinkled blood that speaks more graciously than the blood of Abel.

25 See that you do not refuse him who is speaking. For if they did not escape when they refused him who warned them on earth, much less shall we escape if we reject

---

do they come from and when? That **the spirits of just men made perfect** are men is obvious. While the **first-born** could be angels, the following words, **who are enrolled in heaven,** tend to show that this also refers to men. Were they "perfected" by the sacrifice of Jesus and did they enter **the heavenly Jerusalem** at that time? Were they rescued from Sheol by a descent of Christ into that realm? The author does not inform us. Evidently these **just men**—the list of the faithful in ch. 11 (?)—have escaped the final day of Judgment and are now citizens of the heavenly Jerusalem. Jesus is the last named in the list because he is the speaker whom the readers must not refuse (cf. vss. 24-25). **The sprinkled blood** of Abel cried out for revenge; the blood of Jesus for purification, and so for entrance into the presence of God. This may have been in the author's mind; but he does not say so, and it is best to retain the word **better** instead of **more graciously.** Our author had the opportunity to contrast the efficacy of Abel's sacrifice with that of Christ (cf. 11:4), but he did not use it. The contrast is between Jesus and Abel, not between the redemptive efficacy of Abel's blood and Jesus' blood.

**25-29.** The final warning follows the familiar pattern of what happened on earth and its consequences as compared with the heavenly message and its greater consequences.

---

ASV). It is he that is **God of all,** angels and men, kings and slaves, rich and poor, learned and ignorant, ancient hero and humble sinner.

**And to the spirits of just men made perfect,** men to be honored and trusted, men from whom you have nothing to fear, men of grace who are therefore men you will want to know, men restored to the image of God, men washed clean of every impurity, men with clear minds and warm hearts and generous spirits.

**And to Jesus, the mediator,** him who is the chief of all, to whose grace all are debtors, and in whom your joys are to live forever and ever. To him shall praise be sung, him of the "excellent name" (1:4), him of the perfect obedience (5:8), him who tasted death for everyone (2:9), him who is the pioneer and perfecter of faith (12:2), him whose **sprinkled blood . . . speaks more graciously than the blood of Abel.** The blood of Abel cried for retribution, and justly so (Gen. 4:10). But the blood of Christ cries out for forgiveness and mercy.

The interpreter will find another vivid contrast between Ps. 137 and this passage. The psalm is born out of the dark sufferings of the Hebrew exiles. They are looking back to Mount Zion in sorrow. When their captors bade them provide entertainment by singing one of their

songs, they cried, "How shall we sing the LORD's song in a strange land?" (Ps. 137:4.) Their hearts were bitter and hard. "O daughter of Babylon, who art to be destroyed; happy shall he be, that rewardeth thee as thou hast served us. Happy shall he be, that taketh and dasheth thy little ones against the stones" (Ps. 137:8-9). Here is the answer to the bitterness of that psalm. The Zion whose destruction was once lamented has become the Zion of fulfilled purpose. Mourning has given way to hope and eyes are turned to the joy that is to be.

**25-29.** *A Final Warning: On Refusing the Word of God.*—See that you do not refuse him who is speaking. This is one of the persistent and characteristic emphases of the Bible. God does not keep silent. He spoke "in many and various ways . . . of old to our fathers by the prophets" (1:1). "The word of the Lord came unto . . ."; this is like a constant refrain. He is still speaking in "many and various ways" (cf. Expos. on 3:15). He speaks out of the Mount Zion described in vss. 22-24. To **refuse him** is to turn from our one source of wisdom to complete folly; it is to renounce life, to prefer death. It is to give up the rest of God (4:1) for the restlessness of men. It is to barter the strong peace that comes with the assurance of forgive-

26 Whose voice then shook the earth: but now he hath promised, saying, Yet once more I shake not the earth only, but also heaven.

26 His voice then shook the earth; but now he has promised, "Yet once more I will shake not only

---

It is not entirely clear who the "warner on earth" is, God or Moses, and who the "warner from heaven," God or Jesus. The cosmic language which follows would suggest to us that God must be meant in both cases, but the connection between vss. 24 and 25 would indicate Jesus as **him who is speaking,** and since it is the Son "through whom also he created the world" (1:2), it would be consonant with the author's thought to make Jesus God's agent in bringing it to a close. In any case, it is God speaking through Moses and through Jesus, and not any independent act of either. Using Hag. 2:6, the

---

ness, to return to the tormented conscience that is uneasy just because it knows it can never face the light. It is to renounce the tender joy of Christian love for the bitter hatreds of the world. It is to surrender all solid hopes of what lies ahead (6:11) for the despair that knows no resources beyond our wavering human purposes.

The interpreter should often present sharply and clearly the alternatives of faith and unbelief (cf. Expos. on 7:25). Biblical writers were never afraid of doing so. A repeated vision of these sharp alternatives may well lead to vigorous faith and decisive living.

How swiftly would disaster come down upon us should God cease speaking! How dire was the prophecy of Amos! "Behold, the days come, saith the Lord GOD, that I will send a famine in the land, not a famine of bread, nor a thirst for water, but of hearing the words of the LORD: and they shall wander from sea to sea, and from the north even to the east, they shall run to and fro to seek the word of the LORD, and shall not find it" (Amos 8:11-12). It is not enough that we **do not refuse him who is speaking.** We ought to seek the word of God, to search the Scriptures, to listen to what God has to say, to wait for his word, to be sensitive to it, to cultivate the conditions that will enable us to hear.

Few in our day have seen how vitally dependent we are upon God's Word for many of the common goods that we enjoy. Emil Brunner has written clearly about responsibility as the distinguishing mark of man:

One who has understood the nature of responsibility has understood the nature of man. Responsibility is not an attribute, it is the "substance" of human existence. It contains everything: freedom and bondage, the independence of the individual and our relation to one another and the fact of community, our relation to God, to our fellow-creatures and to the world, that which distinguishes man from all other creatures, and that which binds him to all other creatures. Thus even the knowledge of responsibility is that which makes every human being a real human being—although otherwise he may be and think or believe, what he wills—thus it is the absolutely universal human element. Yet responsibility is at the same time that which no man rightly knows, unless he holds the Christian faith.[6]

Yet responsibility, our essential humanity, comes to us only when we respond to God's Word. Until we meet Christ as our Savior, we dare not be responsible. Standing on our own righteousness, we have to be evasive. We justify ourselves, i.e., we unduly blame other people, and circumstances not of our own making, for our failures. We become responsible only when we reach back into the past and say of an evil deed, "That was mine." But this we cannot do—we are too terrified—until God speaks his love through Christ sufficiently to enable us to cry out even in despair for his forgiveness.

**Much less shall we escape** (cf. 2:3). This warning is repeated throughout the epistle. A better covenant, a better priest, a better hope, these entail a greater responsibility. We cannot be sure of our writer's meaning (cf. Exeg.), but it is likely that he is contrasting Moses and Jesus Christ. God spoke through both of them. But in the word of Sinai it was an awesome, terrifying word. In the word from heaven it was a word of grace and hope.

**When they refused him who warned them on earth.** It is not easy to identify this refusal. For at Sinai the people did not refuse the word of God. They were so terrified by the thunders of God that they simply asked that henceforth God speak to them through Moses. This may have been a very worthy reverence, itself a manifestation of faith. Indeed, God is represented not as blaming but as approving them

[6] *Man in Revolt* (tr. Olive Wyon; London: Lutterworth Press; Philadelphia: The Westminster Press, 1939), pp. 50-51. Used by permission.

27 And this *word,* Yet once more, signifieth the removing of those things that are shaken, as of things that are made, that those things which cannot be shaken may remain.

the earth but also the heaven." 27 This phrase, "Yet once more," indicates the removal of what is shaken, as of what has been made, in order that what cannot be shaken

---

author holds that an ultimate shaking of what is shakable impends. Only visible and heavenly realities will remain.

But far from causing terror, this should evoke only gratitude from those who have received a **kingdom that cannot be shaken.** This **kingdom** (cf. 1:8 [LXX]; 11:33, earthly kingdoms) is not the Synoptic idea of God's rule on a restored earth; it is, as vs. 28 shows, the heavenly realm of **acceptable worship, with reverence and awe** which is to displace

---

for their timidity (Deut. 5:28). But it is likely that our author found in this reticence the first sign of rebellion which came to its full flower later (cf. 3:16-19).

**Yet once more I will shake not only the earth, but also the heaven . . . in order that what cannot be shaken may remain.** By the shaken is clearly meant the transient, the visible, the relatively unreal, which will one day be removed, that the eternal may stand forth in abiding grandeur. In the earthquake of 1923 the Japanese learned some important facts about building materials. The flimsy structures of wood and paper collapsed. Brick buildings tumbled crazily to the ground. The solid buildings of structural steel were relatively undamaged.

The principle is as broad as human experience and divine providence. In this verse at least, we are justified in using the language and thought of the epistle to go far beyond the bounds of their original intention. All of us grow attachments to incidental things: to the pet details of our daily routine, to the familiar devices and conveniences of our ways of working, to our card index and the file of growing sermon outlines, to the tasks regularly assigned to each hour of the day, until almost without knowing it we begin ascribing first importance to trivial things. Then a shaking comes. It may be a fire that destroys our church building and all the dear details go up in flame. Or it may be a sudden demand that one seek a new pastorate, and for a time a man is dumb with bewilderment.

All suffering does that to people. It is easy for us to be lulled into a false sense of security. We attach our affections in the wrong places, to that which is temporal. Our scheme of values gets distorted by our resistance to change and our love of comfort. The shaking is no pleasant process. It tears us and hurts us and we writhe in pain. But it seems to be the only way God can loosen us from our confidence in feeble

devices and bring us face to face once more with the abiding realities that **cannot be shaken.**

Our human history is a story of repeated shakings. The destruction of Solomon's temple, the rape of Jerusalem, and the exile of the people to Babylon seemed to be the supreme tragedy. "How shall we sing the Lord's song in a strange land?" (Ps. 137:4.) What a disastrous shaking that was! Yet any O.T. scholar will tell you that there were some vitalities that the Hebrew faith never knew until after the Exile. Never again were the Hebrews to be guilty of "whoring after the gods of the strangers of the land" (Deut. 31:16). The sack of Rome by Alaric and the Visigoths in 410 shook the morale of the Romans as nothing else had done. It seemed the end of the world. Yet this very disaster called forth Augustine's *The City of God,* which helped to lay the foundations of a new civilization that would one day emerge from the Roman ruins. Wars, in spite of their moral ravages, do this much good: they have sometimes revealed the rottenness in a nation.

In the latter part of the nineteenth century the growing acceptance of the evolutionary theory frightened the church. Countless sermons were preached on the text, "If the foundations be destroyed, what can the righteous do?" (Ps. 11:3.) Robert Speer once quietly remarked that they could go on being righteous! But now we see clear signs that our forefathers' faith had become attached to insignificant and even harmful incidentals, to externals of doctrine rather than to the faith that rests on God alone. Many of the old infallibilities are gone, perhaps forever. But they were at best questionable aids to faith. Perhaps a simpler, clearer, stronger faith will yet emerge from the shaking that modern science has given to theology. In any event, we may be sure that the things that **cannot be shaken** will **remain.**

**Therefore let us be grateful.** "Thanking is the most complete form of thought."[7] It clears our

[7] Brunner, *Man in Revolt,* p. 226.

28 Wherefore we receiving a kingdom which cannot be moved, let us have grace, whereby we may serve God acceptably with reverence and godly fear:

29 For our God *is* a consuming fire.

may remain. 28 Therefore let us be grateful for receiving a kingdom that cannot be shaken, and thus let us offer to God acceptable worship, with reverence and awe; 29 for our God is a consuming fire.

---

all temporal and shadowy things. The final clause, **for our God is a consuming fire,** will seem to the modern reader a tragic misinterpretation of the gospel message of the love of God. It must be admitted that our author does not move in the Johannine (cf. John 4:24; I John 4:13-18) or in the Pauline tradition (cf. Rom. 8:37 ff.). But to do him justice we must interpret these words in the context. They carry, to be sure, the note of warning, but the dominant idea is assurance. We who have received the kingdom that cannot be shaken may rest in confident peace, for God is a God who destroys all transient and temporal things in order that what is timeless and unchanging may emerge in full glory; and we are those who have received this permanent home of the soul.

---

minds. To have faith in God means clearing the mind of lesser attachments, to be willing even to "let goods and kindred go," and to be grateful that God has given us a place in a **kingdom that cannot be shaken.**

**Our God is a consuming fire.** This is a direct quotation from Deut. 4:24. It is pathetic that men should turn in dread from this verse to the loving Father of the gospels, as though there ever could be a love that was not at the same time **a consuming fire.** If this fire were to die out, love would die with it.

There are those who conceive of God as an easygoing old grandfather, who looks down with an indulgent eye upon the faults and failings of men; lets them do as they please, and will somehow make it all right in the end. This thought of God is in part the cause and in part the effect of the careless, self-indulgent lives that many lead.[8]

No human love is worth having unless it burns like a flame of hatred for all that would destroy the one who is loved. If God were not a consuming fire, our salvation would be impossible. If men turn in penitence to him, if they really want to be honest, chaste, generous men of faith, their hope is in the consuming fire. When men seek a better world, a more just economic order, a more democratic society, a more decent international order, their hope is in the consuming fire that is God.

We may see the flames within and without. Unbelief leads to despair. Greed defaces a man. Dishonesty commits a soul to unceasing torment. Sinful lusts of the flesh destroy all physical beauty and a stench follows the man who is guilty. Nations that violate the laws of God sink into rotten weakness. The consuming fire is clearly visible for all who have eyes to see.

**Let us offer to God acceptable worship, with reverence and awe.** This is the real climax of everything that has been said from the beginning. Ch. 13 contains more practical exhortations. But the epistle could end on this note, which has been the dominant concern throughout.

Clearly there can be no genuine worship of God without reverent awe. When one hears the chatty pulpit prayers that sometimes pass for worship, when one sees people saunter gaily into the church, talking with their neighbors about a business deal or about last night's party, when one sees the casual, careless air of many a church service, he feels like stopping the whole business by asking some searching questions, "Just what are you doing? Who is this God you are worshiping? Why should he listen to you, or be pleased with your bad hymns set to even more atrocious music?" Worship is simply not possible until men feel the grandeur, the majesty, the otherness of God.

But reverent awe is not enough. It must be united with confidence in the tender mercies of God. Here we must have the union of "opposites" if we are to worship: majesty and tenderness, holiness and grace, severity and forgiveness, the consuming fire and the loving Father, dread solemnity and holy joy. That the God who is infinite in majesty and in holiness should yet love us with tender grace, seek us to worship him, beset us behind and before with his mercy—to realize this is to worship. To lose this tension between "opposites" is to destroy the heart of acceptable worship.

> Lord of all being, throned afar,
> Thy glory flames from sun and star;
> Center and soul of every sphere,
> Yet to each loving heart how near![9]

[8] J. Ritchie Smith, *The Wall and the Gates* (Philadelphia: Westminster Press, 1920), p. 81.

[9] Oliver Wendell Holmes, "Lord of all being."

13 Let brotherly love continue.
   2 Be not forgetful to entertain strangers: for thereby some have entertained angels unawares.

3 Remember them that are in bonds, as bound with them; *and* them which suffer adversity, as being yourselves also in the body.

13 Let brotherly love continue. 2 Do not neglect to show hospitality to strangers, for thereby some have entertained angels unawares. 3 Remember those who are in prison, as though in prison with them; and those who are ill-treated, since

---

## IV. CONCLUDING EXHORTATIONS, FOLLOWED BY PERSONAL REFERENCES AND BENEDICTIONS (13:1-25)

The final chapter of Hebrews raises the interrelated questions of the purpose and literary form of the writing (see Intro., pp. 591-92); we shall consider here only the thought of the chapter. The total impression (with the possible exception of vss. 8-16) is of fragmentary and rather formal exhortations. The tone is that of traditional moralizing, not all of it specifically Christian, although given a Christian interpretation. It has been suggested that the author began such a list of exhortations in 12:14 only to be diverted to another theme by the warning in the last part of his sentence which is developed in the rest of ch. 12, and that he now goes on with the interrupted list of admonitions. This is a possible but by no means inevitable interpretation (see on 12:14 above).

**13:1-6.** While the subjects of these verses do not have any necessary connection with one another, such groupings were common in lists of moral teaching. The author

---

**13:1-3. The Spirit of Christian Love.—Let brotherly love continue.** The readers have already been commended for their love (6:10; 10:34), although there were signs of the breaking of the Christian fellowship (10:24-25). "We cannot be Christians without being brethren." [1] The first break in Christian faith would likely be a cooling of brotherly love. The pretense that we do not need our brethren is the first step to the boast that we do not need the Christ.

One of the most urgent forms of this brotherly love was the ancient custom of **hospitality.** It is interesting to see how widespread and deep are the religious roots of hospitality. In the case of Christians some of the strangers would be itinerant evangelists; some would be refugees driven by persecution from their homes. **Thereby some have entertained angels unawares.** Literature has many stories of benedictions brought to a home by unknown strangers. We think of the widow of Zarephath and Elijah (I Kings 17:8-24), Paul with Aquila and Priscilla (Acts 18:2-4). We can only imagine how many notable Christians must have been entertained in humble homes during the early centuries, imparting new faith and strength to those who dwelt there. Inns were for the most part poor. Prices were often extortionate and beyond the means of Christians. Frequently these inns were disreputable places. But the highest motive of all is not mentioned by our

[1] Calvin, *Commentary on Hebrews*, p. 340.

writer, the momentous "inasmuch" of Jesus (Matt. 25:40), where Jesus identified himself with the needy and the homeless. **To show hospitality to strangers** may be to entertain Jesus **unawares.**

**As though in prison with them,** as indeed they might well be before long. **Since you also are in the body,** therefore subject to the same ill-treatment as other Christians. The strong solidarity among Christians made a vivid impression upon outsiders.

The spirit in which kindness is shown is important. To serve prisoners as though we were ourselves one of them, to take our place along with the suffering, this is Christian kindness at its best. This is what Christ did for man: he took his place alongside man and let our human burdens fall on himself as well. We have constantly to guard against becoming professional in our sympathy, against patronizing the needy. Josiah Royce once wrote stinging words about such people.

Our hearts may so swell with pride at our own importance as pitiful persons, that we may even long to have somebody of our acquaintance in trouble, so that we can go and pose, in the presence of the sufferers, as humane commentators on the occurrence, as heroic endurers of sorrows that we do not really share. . . . There are people who are always fretful and disconsolate unless they know of somebody who very badly needs consoling. . . . Such people are apt to be intolerable companions

4 Marriage *is* honorable in all, and the bed undefiled; but whoremongers and adulterers God will judge.

5 *Let your* conversation *be* without covetousness; *and be* content with such things as ye have: for he hath said, I will never leave thee, nor forsake thee.

you also are in the body. 4 Let marriage be held in honor among all, and let the marriage bed be undefiled; for God will judge the immoral and adulterous. 5 Keep your life free from love of money, and be content with what you have; for he has said, "I will never fail you nor forsake

---

encourages his readers to **brotherly love** in the Christian fellowship (vs. 1), to **hospitality,** presumably exercised toward strangers who come as Christian travelers (vs. 2), and to remembrance of **those who are in prison,** presumably because of their Christian profession. The limitation to Christians is not explicit, but the author has already mentioned their "compassion on the prisoners" in a context that indicates "fellow Christians" (10:32-34), and we may suppose that brotherly love and hospitality also are thought of as applying to other believers. The motive for hospitality (vs. 2) suggests O.T. stories such as those of Abraham and Sarah (Gen. 18), Lot (Gen. 19), Manoah (Judg. 13), all of whom **entertained angels unawares.** The motive implied in **since you are also in the body** reminds us of Paul's figure of the church as the body of Christ (I Cor. 12:12 ff.; Rom. 12:4 ff.), but since there is no preparation for that thought in Hebrews, it probably means that the

---

for you unless you have a broken leg, or a fever, or a great bereavement. Then they find you interesting, because you are wretched. They nurse you like saints; they speak comfortably to you like angels. They hate to give the little comfort that can be given from day to day to those who are enduring the ordinary vexations of healthy and prosaic life. They rejoice to find some one overwhelmed with woe. The happy man is to them a worthless fellow. High temperature is needed to soften their hearts. They would be miserable in Paradise, at the sight of so much tedious contentment; but they would leap for joy if they could but hear of a lost soul to whom a drop of water could be carried.[2]

The safeguard against such officious kindness is the recognition of our own precarious position. The forgiving spirit is possible only to those who have been forgiven, to men who have confronted their own sin. The spirit of kindness is possible only to men who recognize that it is not their hands that have built Babylon; that they are themselves the recipients of God's mercies. With such an understanding we can remember the prisoners, **as though in prison with them.**

4. *The Sanctity of Marriage.*—Let **marriage be held in honor among all.** There is no evidence that marriage was here being defended against ascetics. But this simple statement is nevertheless a rebuke to later Catholic notions that regarded marriage as an inferior condition, a mere concession to the flesh, and as an unworthy state for the clergy. Protestant wedding ceremonies all contain something like this: "Marriage . . . is instituted of God, regulated by His commandments, blessed by our Lord Jesus Christ, and to be held in honor among

all men." [3] To hold marriage in honor is psychologically the best antidote for immorality of all kinds. Let growing children be given instruction in terms of marriage, the home that will one day be theirs, the love that they will want to hold sacred, and the children that will be given them. That is the core of all sound sex education. It is also the best defense against defilement of **the marriage bed.**

**God will judge.** Any morally sensitive person can discern the awful judgments of God now among people guilty of this vice. The moral flabbiness of both parties, the writhing dishonesties by which they seek to justify their conduct, the secrecies, fears, emotional instability and uncertainties that especially burden the woman involved, the degradation it brings, all are signs of the lesser, preliminary judgment of God upon **the immoral and adulterous.** Who can say what his final judgment is? The Scriptures always sound a clear note at this point.

No society could possibly survive without strong restrictions safeguarding marriage. God has made us for the monogamous family and to revolt against that wise and kindly provision is to rebel against God.

5-6. *On the Love of Money.*—**Keep your life free from love of money.** This warning recurs throughout the N.T., and especially in the teaching of Jesus. It is faithful to our needs. Material necessities cannot be neglected. They are an essential part of the complex social order in which God has set our days. The desire for possessions is very plausible. But the danger is subtle: lest we become more and more de-

[2] *Religious Aspect of Philosophy,* pp. 102-3.

[3] Presbyterian Book of Common Worship, "Order for the Solemnization of Marriage."

6 So that we may boldly say, The Lord *is* my helper, and I will not fear what man shall do unto me.

7 Remember them which have the rule over you, who have spoken unto you the

you." 6 Hence we can confidently say,
"The Lord is my helper,
I will not be afraid;
what can man do to me?"

7 Remember your leaders, those who

---

readers are to recall that they too are living on the physical plane where ill-treatment is to be expected. The appeal to hold marriage in honor (vs. 4) and to maintain sexual purity was always in place, and would be especially necessary for Christians with a Gentile background. Simplicity and contentment **with what you have** over against the **love of money** (vss. 5-6) was also a common Christian and non-Christian admonition, and to link it closely with advices about sexual purity was not unprecedented (cf. I Cor. 5:10 ff.). Both purity and simplicity are God's commands, and he will judge the violator of the one and sustain him who observes the other. The quotation from Ps. 118:6 is the sole instance in Hebrews where the writer uses the words of scripture as a human confession.

7-16. This paragraph, unrelated to what precedes, possesses a possible inner unity. The thought, although by no means clear, seems to run like this: **Remember your leaders**

---

pendent upon things; and lest the pressure of our own greed on the economic life be in reality all too closely linked, partly as cause and partly as effect, with our idolatry of self, which is the basic sin against God. The man whose life consists "in the abundance of his possessions" (Luke 12:15) has made a god out of himself and has denied God.

This truth holds under every system, regardless of the legal and political reforms that may help to ameliorate conditions. We cannot evade our responsibility in matters political and economic. In the complexities of modern life no one can escape his share in the injustices of the current order. Each Christian has a duty to perform in this larger area. But whatever the system, the danger of the **love of money** persists. We have constantly to be on guard against it, as may be seen vividly enough in this way: if every person were paid the wages or salary he thinks he deserves, any economy would go bankrupt in a short time. Perhaps the difficulty with our economy is that we are trying to operate on the principle of satisfying every citizen's greed.

To keep first things first, to love and trust God rather than money, would have its effects on the whole structure of human life. If all men were to practice this teaching, the particular system under which we live would be a question of relative indifference. But the hope is utopian. Certainly we can never expect organized groups to manifest such modesty. Groups as such always seek their own good. The most we can hope is that they will be enlightened in their self-interest. But there is no fixed limit to the gracious influences that would infuse our society were Christians increasingly to be known for the modesty of their economic demands.

**Be content with what you have.** The workers

have often resented this kind of teaching, precisely because the "haves" all too often preach it to the "have-nots." It is not the kind of doctrine that can safely be applied to others until one has first fully tested it in one's own life. Certainly no comfortable man of wealth has any right to apply this verse to the poor, and he would find no support here in doing so. But surely no one will resent our putting this truth to work at home for ourselves.

The warning was of course especially important for the first readers of the epistle. For the times of persecution would soon come, when the pagans about them would plunder their earthly goods. They were not to get entangled then with the business of recovering lost property, for they had God.

**The Lord is my helper, I will not be afraid.** This is the heart of all true courage and liberty of conscience. The record of the strong, who have left a priceless heritage to the race, is the record of those who bowed in reverence before God and therefore stood erect in the presence of men. We think of Socrates making his defense before the Athenian jury, "Men of Athens, I honor and love you; but I shall obey God rather than you." We think of the sturdy sons of faith who laid the solid foundations of our freedom in seventeenth-century England. They feared God and bowed the knee to no man.

7-8. *On Remembering the Heroes.*—The pretense of self-sufficiency ill befits a Christian. Any of us can look back to men and women whose personal influence was decisive: parents, teachers, minister, friends, or a book that we read. What a debt we owe them! It is good to think of them. **Remember your leaders, those who spoke to you the word of God.** We do not

word of God: whose faith follow, considering the end of *their* conversation.

**8** Jesus Christ the same yesterday, and to-day, and for ever.

**9** Be not carried about with divers and strange doctrines: for *it is* a good thing that the heart be established with grace; not with meats, which have not profited them that have been occupied therein.

spoke to you the word of God; consider the outcome of their life, and imitate their faith. **8** Jesus Christ is the same yesterday and today and for ever. **9** Do not be led away by diverse and strange teachings; for it is well that the heart be strengthened by grace, not by foods, which have not bene-

---

who **spoke to you the word of God.** They are gone, but Jesus Christ is timeless. Their message about *him* is your standard for judging all teaching. Do not be led astray, therefore, by **diverse and strange teachings** which have to do with **foods.** Food has no meaning for us. It is grace alone that strengthens the heart. Just as in the ritual on the day of Atonement the bodies of the sacrificed animals were burned **outside the camp,** so Jesus

---

know who these leaders were, but they may include names otherwise unknown in the N.T.

**Consider** [scan carefully, not merely look back to] **the outcome of their life.** The words τὴν ἔκβασιν τῆς ἀναστροφῆς mean literally the manner of their leaving life, or the spirit of their dying. The reference may well be to the heroic examples of martyrdom they left behind. The ending of life often carries its own verdict on what has gone before. Any pastor has known heroic persons who after long suffering went down with all their colors flying. Here is wisdom for the common man. Look to the moment of your own death, whether soon or long delayed. What will then seem important to you? To be governed by that insight is to be wise in daily decisions. In the light of death how foolish will seem many of our fretful cares, how unimportant many of the things once held dear, how truly majestic the things that "cannot be shaken" (12:27).

**Imitate their faith.** This is a discerning word. We cannot imitate all the thought of the past, for our thoughts inevitably reflect our own day. Nor dare we merely copy their deeds, for the same duty prescribes diverse deeds under new occasions. But noble faith is never outgrown. It shines in its own light. Look back upon your leaders, remember the gospel they proclaimed, consider carefully the issue of their life, and **imitate their faith.**

**Jesus Christ is the same.** A thoughtless liberalism objects to anything that is the same **yesterday and today and forever.** All things are in process and all things are relative to their place in time. There are many who do not see the logical contradiction in such assumptions. If all is process, if nothing abides, we could never even know that there is change. Indeed, change itself is not possible without some constancy. If all is relation, if there are no abiding terms

that are related, then relations themselves cease to have any meaning.

The record of Christian thought shows that men's beliefs about Jesus Christ change from age to age. Yet he does not change. Unlike leaders the people remember, those here yesterday and gone today, Jesus Christ is the leader who abides. He is God's Word to man. God's forgiveness does not fluctuate. His mercy is ever sure. The sacrifice of the Christ can never be improved. His intercession abides. Our hope and our faith are in him. It is not a fading memory that we worship.

The Man upraised on the Judaean crag
Captains for us the war with death no more.
His kingdom hangs as hangs the tattered flag
Over the tomb of a great knight of yore.[4]

Such an estimate is belied by every living Christian experience of our day. Our human needs, under changing forms, find in the changeless Christ their full answer.

Nothing is more probable than that he who lived on earth for a few years was the same Christ whom his followers worshipped as Lord, that no new Jesus was created by any syncretistic movement in the first Christian century, that there is a unity in the unsolved mystery of his person which is not only real but the real cause underlying the various interpretations of his life and work, and that later experiences of the Church repeatedly imply a continuity of communion with him which is deeper than any inner or outer change of the faith.[5]

**9-11. False Doctrines.**—Do not be led away by diverse and strange teachings, any doctrine

---

[4] "Stanzas to Tolstoi in His Old Age," from *The Collected Works of Herbert Trench.* Used by permission of the Executor of the Herbert Trench Estate, and G. P. Putnam's Sons and Jonathan Cape, publishers.

[5] James Moffatt, *Jesus Christ the Same* (New York and Nashville: Abingdon-Cokesbury Press, 1940), p. 11.

10 We have an altar, whereof they have no right to eat which serve the tabernacle.

11 For the bodies of those beasts, whose blood is brought into the sanctuary by the high priest for sin, are burned without the camp.

fited their adherents. 10 We have an altar from which those who serve the tent[a] have no right to eat. 11 For the bodies of those animals whose blood is brought into the sanctuary by the high priest as a sacrifice

[a] Or *tabernacle*.

---

**suffered outside the gate.** His physical body has no further significance in our worship, for it was his sacrifice **through his own blood** which consecrated us. We are done with all these outward things, an earthly tabernacle, a temporal city, and the physical sacrifices and rituals (foods?) that go with them. Will this mean dishonor and abuse for us? It meant that for him. Let us go forth to him, bearing abuse such as his, outside the realm of these fleshly rituals, for we seek **the city which is to come,** where true spiritual worship alone is offered. Have we then no sacrifices to offer on earth? Yes, **praise to God** and good deeds to men, for these are the **sacrifices . . . pleasing to God** here and hereafter.

---

that would take you away from Jesus Christ, who is ever the same. Hold fast to him and reject every teaching that obscures your vision of him.

What should be said then of the **diverse and strange teachings** of our day? They are much more distracting to Christians than were the doctrinal novelties of N.T. times. We hear a good bit of cant about the open and the closed mind. A completely open mind could learn nothing, for it would have no interest to direct its search for facts. No intellectual progress of any sort is made without some assumptions, whether axioms or hypotheses. Nor is the mind that is guided by basic convictions a closed mind. The plain fact is that "open" and "closed" are epithets that obscure rather than clarify the problem of truth.

To be guided by Jesus, to have the heart fixed on the Christ who is ever the same, is not to stultify thought, but to liberate it. He broadens our intellectual perspectives. Those who read life purely in material terms, or even merely in human categories, cabin, crib, and confine the mind of man, excluding all those grand dimensions of thought that faith supplies, and that in the past inspired the most profound philosophy, the richest literature, and the noblest art. A philosopher who sees only the flat dimensions of human existence can scarcely be said to release the mind of man. Is not this the missing element of greatness in contemporary literature that clearly sets it beneath the level of Dante, Shakespeare, Milton, Goethe, Browning, and Dostoevski?

All thinking must start with some assumptions, be guided by some polestar. The long history of the race tells us that it is far more fruitful to put Jesus Christ at the center of life than to trust merely in our own rational capacities.

**It is well that the heart be strengthened by grace, not by foods.** The broad meaning is clear. Throughout the epistle it has been argued that the outward and visible ceremonies are defective because they have to do with the transient and relatively unreal. The world of reality is the invisible. The defect of the old priesthood is that "they serve a copy and shadow of the heavenly sanctuary" (8:5). Their sacrifices "cannot perfect the conscience of the worshiper," since they "deal only with food and drink and various ablutions" (9:9-10). Part of the supremacy of the perfect Priest is that he serves in "the greater and more perfect tent (not made with hands, that is, not of this creation)" (9:11). The law had "but a shadow of the good things to come instead of the true form of these realities" (10:1).

**We have an altar.** This altar can hardly refer to the Cross (as Dummelow and others). For the place of slaughter was not the altar. Rather the blood of the sacrificial victim was taken to the altar and sprinkled upon it. Our altar is the heavenly sanctuary where Christ has entered, taking his own blood of purification (9:12).

**Those who serve the tent,** i.e., Christians who serve the heavenly sanctuary, do not eat of the sacrifice. In this respect the sin offering of the old covenant foreshadowed the new in that it was a holocaust (cf. Lev. 4:11-12; 16:27) of which the priests did not eat.

Outward ceremonies and elaborate ritual, in these the human heart delights. It is relatively easy to bring a lamb to the temple, to make a pilgrimage to Mecca or to Rome, to attend a service in the church, to put on the outward trappings of religion. They comfort us with the pleasant thought that here, at least, we have done something which pleases God. They make it easy for us to evade the deeper and more dis-

12 Wherefore Jesus also, that he might sanctify the people with his own blood, suffered without the gate.

13 Let us go forth therefore unto him without the camp, bearing his reproach.

14 For here have we no continuing city, but we seek one to come.

for sin are burned outside the camp. 12 So Jesus also suffered outside the gate in order to sanctify the people through his own blood. 13 Therefore let us go forth to him outside the camp, bearing abuse for him. 14 For here we have no lasting city, but we

---

While the main movement of the thought is not difficult to grasp, we are totally unable to identify the **strange** teaching which is being combated. Do **foods** refer to Jewish ritual meals? To religious sacraments in the mystery cults? Or even to the Lord's Supper? Because Hebrews never refers to the Lord's Supper and because of the language of this passage (vss. 10-12), many have held that this is a protest against it, or at any rate against a materialistic and magical celebration of it. It must be admitted that the argument of Hebrews allows no logical place for the repetition of the Supper. Christ's

---

turbing crisis of a bad conscience (cf. Ps. 50:12-15; Isa. 1:11-20; Amos 5:21-24; Mic. 6:6-8).

But to have the heart **strengthened by grace** is to know that we daily depend on the mercy of God for our forgiveness, for our food and shelter, and for all the common benefits of daily life. This is a spiritual religion.

Such an inward faith must express itself in outward visible form. Against this the author could bring no objection, for he himself has made constant use of symbols throughout. Indeed, he makes worship the central act of faith and the climax of the epistle (12:28). These outward symbols are a human necessity. But daily to be **strengthened by grace** is to give to these symbols their richest meaning and to keep ourselves from debasing them to the level of idolatry.

**12-14. On Sharing the Shame of Christ.**—Another parallel is drawn between the sin offering of the old covenant and the death of Christ. Of old, the animal was slain at the door of the tent of meeting. Only its blood was taken within and sprinkled on the mercy seat (Lev. 16:14). The body of the animal was burned "outside the camp." **So Jesus also suffered outside the gate.** This was the fulfillment of his disgrace. Like all criminals, they took him outside the city to be executed, lest he contaminate the temple, their homes, themselves.

This is the dramatized meaning of human sin. It cannot endure the presence of good. It wants to get the good person out of sight—and thus out of mind. "Away with this man" (Luke 23:18), they had cried. Only when they had seen him die could they breathe easily again. That rebuke to their conscience was silenced. That had finished him. This is the characteristic, frantic gesture of human sin.

It wants to escape from God, just as Adam and Eve hid themselves in the garden (Gen.

3:8). It tries to deny him in whose will is our peace, in whose service is our freedom, in whose truth is our light, in whose purpose is our hope. Sin thus breaks every man in two, sets him in battle against himself; for we sin against our own peace, our freedom, our light, our hope. Part of all those who joined in the condemnation of Jesus was taken outside to the death with him, their best part. That was why they had to mock his sufferings as he hung upon the Cross. Was it also why they set a watch over his tomb?

**Therefore . . . to him outside the camp.** That is where we belong. We have no right to settle down without a word of protest in a city or in a world that drives him out. Our psychological friends are telling us much about the importance of adjustment to our environment, of accepting ourselves and our place in the world. They have an important truth. But it belongs with another truth, the truth of this verse; separated from this context, the talk about adjustment becomes falsehood. We cannot be at home where Jesus was homeless. "Where I am, there shall my servant be also" (John 12:26).

The interpreter will note carefully the words **abuse for him.** There is a kind of Christian who is maladjusted, who prides himself in the abuse that he suffers. He usurps a comfort to which he has no right. There may be no moral heroism involved at all, but only a very bad disposition. We dare not enjoy abuse. The corrective, though not mentioned here, is Christian love. We do not go **outside the camp** to return evil for evil, to give as good as we get, to enjoy our self-righteous feeling that we have broken with the sinners. It is in precisely such a time that our Lord's teaching is most deeply needed, "Love your enemies, do good to those who hate you, bless those who curse you, pray for those who abuse you" (Luke 6:27-28). That

15 By him therefore let us offer the sacrifice of praise to God continually, that is, the fruit of *our* lips, giving thanks to his name.

16 But to do good and to communicate forget not: for with such sacrifices God is well pleased.

seek the city which is to come. 15 Through him then let us continually offer up a sacrifice of praise to God, that is, the fruit of lips that acknowledge his name. 16 Do not neglect to do good and to share what you have, for such sacrifices are pleasing to God.

---

sacrifice cannot be repeated; it was once for all. The evidence is too scanty, however, for any final conclusion, although **diverse and strange** seem hardly the appropriate words to use if the readers were Jews by race, tempted to return to Judaism.

The writer of vs. 8, **Jesus Christ is the same yesterday and today and for ever,** whether our author or another, was a great phrasemaker and this is one of the memorable sentences in Hebrews. The thought, of course, has been expressed before in other words, "Thou art the same, and thy years will never end" (1:12) and "Thou art a priest for ever" (5:6; cf. 7:3, 17, 21, 27; 9:12; etc.).

---

will keep us humble, and it will be **to him** that we have gone forth **outside the camp.**

**For here we have no lasting city.** This is the meaning of faith, as was made clear in ch. 11. This is the spirit in which we are to bear **abuse for him.** Worldliness looks at the temporal city and all its doings as though it were an eternal city. Men live as if they would not die. They greedily appropriate the good things of this life with no thanksgiving to God for his mercy, with no thought of using his gifts to his glory. They settle down in this world of sin, feeling no tension between what is and what ought to be. They are held by no steadfast hope in the promises of God that are to be fulfilled. Paul has set down in reverse order the evolution of the secularist: "Their end is destruction, their god is the belly, and they glory in their shame, with minds set on earthly things" (Phil. 3:19).

To escape the sin of worldliness does not mean despising the physical world upon which God once passed the verdict "very good" (Gen. 1:31). Nor does it mean running away from the responsibilities of our time and place in ascetic defeat. It does mean that we are "strangers and exiles" (11:13), that our real citizenship is in **the city which is to come,** our heart's true home (cf. Expos. on 8:1-5; 11:13-16).

**15-16.** *Two Acceptable Sacrifices: Thanksgiving and Sharing.*—While Christ has made the supreme sacrifice which no man could make for himself and which opened the way of access to God, there remain for us two sacrifices which we can, nay, which we must, make as the spontaneous expression of our faith. **Such sacrifices are pleasing to God.** These verses form one of three notable definitions of Christian service contained in the N.T. The other

two are in Rom. 12:1-2 and Jas. 1:27. The three passages should be studied together and might well be used in a series of three expositions.

**A sacrifice of praise to God.** This **sacrifice of praise** contrasts sharply with the attitude of the man who looks upon the world as an opportunity for plunder. He forgets the many debts which have no standing in a court of law, but which are solemnly his under God. He sees his own success in isolation from the conditions that made it possible. This is to deal dishonestly with life. The events of our lives are not cut off clean and sharp. There are hidden connections and far-reaching relations that our modern boaster cannot fancy even in a dream. But his pride blinds him to these debts to God and man, and he cries out, "Is not this great Babylon, which I have built?" (Dan. 4:30.)

A nationally known American, never noted for his humility, was once lecturing a group of young people on the importance of learning to take steps of accurate length. He boasted, "I became so skilled that I measured the accuracy of maps by my stride!" He and many like him measure all things by their stride. The spirit of self-confident boasting has at times overflowed in the public press and into Thanksgiving Day proclamations. We address Europe and the East on the subject of our own virtues. There are few signs of humility before God. Rather, we congratulate God on our success!

Now to have faith in God is to see the whole world in an entirely different light. **Through him [Jesus] then let us continually offer up a sacrifice of praise to God, . . . the fruit of lips that acknowledge his name.** Redemption throws light on creation and providence. For the natural man all three are at best a speculative conjecture. But once we have been ushered into "the heavenly Jerusalem" (12:22-24), once our

| 17 Obey them that have the rule over you, and submit yourselves: for they watch for your souls, as they that must give ac- | 17 Obey your leaders and submit to them; for they are keeping watch over your souls, as men who will have to give ac- |

**17-19.** The appeal to **obey your leaders**—here their living leaders (cf. vs. 7)—is so like I Pet. 5:1-4, although there it is the leaders, not the followers who are addressed, as to argue literary interdependence. Note the figure of the shepherd in the Petrine passage and in the immediate context here (cf. vs. 20). A somewhat developed conception of

sins have been forgiven, God becomes the heart and center of our world and our vision is cleared so that we can see his work.

His mercies never fail. Even when we do not acknowledge God, he still besets us behind and before with kindness. "He makes his sun rise on the evil and on the good, and sends rain on the just and on the unjust" (Matt. 5:45). To Cyrus he could say, "I girded thee, though thou hast not known me" (Isa. 45:5).

Man cannot exclude me from his little universe; even though he deny my existence and denounce my claim—I am still there. I water the garden of the atheist, and bring his flowers to summer bloom and his fruits to autumnal glory. Men deny me, curse me, flee from me—I am still round about them, and their life is more precious to me than is their blasphemy detestable, and until the very last I will work for them and with them, and if they go to perdition it shall be through the very centre of my heart's tenderest grace.[6]

The vastness of the mysteries of our world, and of our human existence in it, the very fidelity of nature which we understand but a little, though daily we take it for granted, all speak the praise of God. While the crowning mercy is that we, unprofitable servants, rebellious children, poor foolish sinners, should be the objects of divine love, the lost sheep which the good shepherd seeks, redeems, restores to his presence, that our hope in him be not ashamed. This fills the heart of the believer with joy, even when he is "outside the camp" (vs. 13), so that he will **continually offer . . . praise to God.** Thanksgiving can never be fulfilled as a duty, but only as the spontaneous overflow of a glad heart.

> I sing the mighty power of God,
>   That made the mountains rise;
> That spread the flowing seas abroad,
>   And built the lofty skies.
>
> I sing the Wisdom that ordained
>   The sun to rule the day;
> The moon shines full at His command,
>   And all the stars obey.[7]

[6] Joseph Parker, *The People's Bible* (New York: Funk & Wagnalls Co., 1891), XV, 203-4.

[7] Isaac Watts, "I sing the mighty power of God."

**Do not neglect to do good and to share what you have.** This second sacrifice follows the first by the inner necessity of faith. The man who owns no compassion, who looks upon life as a cluster of grapes to be squeezed into his own cup and drained for his own enjoyment, thereby denies his God. If our Christian faith is true, then we are stewards, not owners, of the good gifts of God. To express that faith we must **communicate.** "If any one has the world's goods and sees his brother in need, yet closes his heart against him, how does God's love abide in him?" (I John 3:17.)

This is God's answer to our economic crises. To be sure, we have a Christian duty to promote justice. But whatever the system under which we live, it can be wrecked by godless greed (cf. Expos. on vss. 5-6).

The word translated **communicate** in the KJV is the great N.T. word κοινωνίας. Its primary meaning is to share our material possessions. But it includes all the resources of the Christian community whereby life enriches life, love sustains love, and we "bear one another's burdens, and so fulfill the law of Christ" (Gal. 6:2).

**17-19.** *On Christian Leadership.*—**Obey your leaders and submit to them.** You are to accept the preaching of the word from your leaders rather than to be "led away by diverse and strange teachings" (vs. 9). Their office was to be held in respect, and their discipline was to be received as profitable to the soul. Especially in time of persecution would their burden be a heavy one. Usually they would be the first to suffer imprisonment and death. But if they were spared, they had especially to watch over the members who were inclined to lapse, to encourage and comfort broken families, to fortify those who would soon face great danger. Part of the believer's humble trust in God therefore was to receive the word from his leaders in meekness and faith. **For they are keeping watch over your souls.** The word translated **keeping watch** literally means "to be sleepless," like an alert shepherd. The same word appears in Mark 13:33; Luke 21:36; and Eph. 6:18. It is a graphic account of the solemn responsibility of the men who watch over the souls of their

count, that they may do it with joy, and not with grief: for that *is* unprofitable for you.

**18** Pray for us: for we trust we have a good conscience, in all things willing to live honestly.

**19** But I beseech *you* the rather to do this, that I may be restored to you the sooner.

**20** Now the God of peace, that brought again from the dead our Lord Jesus, that

count. Let them do this joyfully, and not sadly, for that would be of no advantage to you.

**18** Pray for us, for we are sure that we have a clear conscience, desiring to act honorably in all things. **19** I urge you the more earnestly to do this in order that I may be restored to you the sooner.

**20** Now may the God of peace who

---

church order and discipline is implied. The plurals in vs. 18 do not mean that more than one writer is indicated, as the singular of vs. 19 shows. Can we infer from the connection that the writer was or had been one of their leaders (vs. 17)? The connection of thought throughout the chapter is too loose to warrant this inference, and in vs. 17 the writer seems careful to write that **they,** not "we," **are keeping watch over your souls. That I may be restored to you the sooner** does not require the author's imprisonment; it is the close resemblance to Philem. 22 which suggests it. The request for the readers' prayers and the protestation of sincerity on the writer's part need not be dismissed as merely formal, although they do not have the same ring as Paul's similar words about the testimony of his conscience (II Cor. 1:12-13).

**20-21.** A stately prayer and doxology follow, introducing two thoughts not previously mentioned: the resurrection of Christ and the figure of the shepherd. In the body of the writing our author has no place for the Resurrection, since it is the entrance of Christ into

---

comrades, **men who will have to give account.** The writer urges his readers to help them. Make their work lighter. Do not be a burden on their hearts but a strength to their souls. That will make them joyful in their task. There is no profit to you in a minister who goes about groaning or sighing (στενάζοντες).

This is a plain endorsement of the leaders. No fault is found in them. But it is more. It is a succinct summary of the spirit of the ministry in any age. Pastors are to be watchmen over the spiritual welfare of the people. Theirs is a solemn responsibility, for they are men who have to give an account. Failure in fidelity will one day stand out in the presence of their Lord.

**Do this joyfully.** The persistent emphasis on joy in the N.T. is not an accident. For us to do any duty with grim reluctance means that the heart is not in it, that we are not convinced Christians. There is a time when duty is done only by violating wrong inclinations. It belongs to the earlier stages of growth. Without that conflict there is no hope of salvation. Nor does the conflict ever cease in this life. But if inclination never sides with duty, we are "a house . . . divided against itself" (Mark 3:25). The virtuous man who is sad betrays his conviction that sinners have the best of the bargain after all. The grace of God never works long in his heart without a radical change in inclination, so that

one day he comes to sing, "I delight to do thy will, O my God" (Ps. 40:8).

> Since satisfaction and happiness are highly convincing states of mind (understanding by happiness not temperamental gaiety, but the subconscious and hence serious affirmation of life as a whole by the will as a whole),—it follows that children will tend to adopt the beliefs of those whom they instinctively recognize as happy, and of no others.[8]

Faith's contagion can be communicated only by a joyous heart.

**Pray for us,** a very human request that all humble, sincere Christians must often make of their friends. There had apparently been some questioning of the writer's good faith. He assures his readers that he is acting with **a clear conscience.** The word is "I trust" or "am persuaded." By using this word he "partly shews his modesty and partly his confidence." [9] Whereupon he repeats his request for their prayers **in order that I may be restored to you the sooner.** He gives us no inkling of the restraint that is on him, although vs. 23 makes it clear that it was not imprisonment.

**20-21.** *A Pastoral Prayer.*—Now he offers his own stately prayer, every word rich with mean-

---

[8] W. E. Hocking, *Human Nature and Its Remaking* (New Haven: Yale University Press, 1923), p. 236.

[9] Calvin, *Commentary on Hebrews,* p. 355.

great shepherd of the sheep, through the
blood of the everlasting covenant,

21 Make you perfect in every good work
to do his will, working in you that which
is well-pleasing in his sight, through Jesus
Christ; to whom *be* glory for ever and ever.
Amen.

brought again from the dead our Lord
Jesus, the great shepherd of the sheep, by
the blood of the eternal covenant, 21 equip
you with everything good that you may
do his will, working in you[b] that which is
pleasing in his sight, through Jesus Christ;
to whom be glory for ever and ever. Amen.

[b] Other ancient authorities read *us.*

---

the true Holy of Holies which is essential to his analogy. The shepherd figure drawn
from the O.T. (Isa. 40:11; 63:11; Ezek. 37:24; Zech. 9:16; cf. I Pet. 5:4) must be regarded
as a bit of liturgical usage. We would expect something like "our great high priest,"
instead of **the great shepherd of the sheep.** The final clause, **by the blood of the eternal
covenant,** brings the thought into the familiar framework of our writing. In spite of their
beauty, these verses are awkward as a conclusion to Hebrews. The doxology refers to God
who works **through Jesus Christ** (cf. I Pet. 4:11).

---

ing. It should be compared with the prayer of
Paul in Eph. 3:14-19.

Vagueness is no aid to faith. Many a congregation has been afflicted by polysyllabic piety
in prayers that are nebulous and verbose. Such
prayers cost little effort in preparation and
probably are not expected to produce any results. Prayers that come from the heart come
through the mind. They are clean, clear, and
simple in thought. It is true that whenever we
speak the great words of our faith, God, Christ,
grace, salvation, peace, love, we are saying
much more than we can ever know. Yet God,
having spoken in history, has identified himself
with them in very definite ways. We had better
make use of these identifications in our prayers.
Thus they will be clear, therefore sincere.

**The God of peace** refers not to divisions
within the church or yet to strife between men.
This peace is the bliss, the serenity, that comes
from the full triumph over evil. It is the peace
that God knows, when his love seeks sinful
men, is reconciled to them, can and does forgive them because of his own sacrifice for their
sins, and in this grace sees the final triumph of
his people over all the forces of darkness. "For
he is our peace, who has made us both one . . .
that he . . . might reconcile us both to God in
one body through the cross, thereby bringing
the hostility to an end" (Eph. 2:14-16; cf. also
John 14:27). This peace is one of the fruits of
the Spirit (Gal. 5:22), and becomes peace of
conscience, in which the sinner is content to
rest in the grace of God. All the restless, unhappy multitudes of earth cry out for it, and
their cry moves the heart of every faithful interpreter.

God is further identified as the one **who
brought again from the dead our Lord Jesus.**
The Resurrection was necessary to vindicate

the character of God. Had Jesus remained
within the tomb, had death conquered him
who was the Son, the Word, the Sacrifice of
God, then all the blasphemers would have been
right, and men could only have whispered in
despair, "God is dead." Here was a clear working of God.

Jesus Christ is identified as **the great shepherd of the sheep,** the first use of this figure
that our writer makes. The phrase **by the blood
of the eternal covenant** clearly belongs to
**brought again from the dead.** The grammatical
construction will allow no other reading. The
thought is clear. Jesus was raised from the dead
to present his blood as the sacrifice **of the eternal covenant** (cf. 9:11-12, 24-26). Yet it was
our author's genius to bring into close relationship **the great shepherd of the sheep** and **the
blood of the eternal covenant.** The good shepherd not only seeks the lost sheep, watches
over them, cares for them, but sacrifices his life
for them. "I am the good shepherd . . . and I
lay down my life for the sheep" (John 10:14-
15). Here all the tender grace of the word
"shepherd" (cf. Ps. 23) is brought into the
sacrifice **of the eternal covenant.**

The petition is also pointed and clear. **May
the God of peace,** identified as we have just
seen, **equip you with everything good that
you may do his will.** He is asking God to grant
them all they need, every token of his mercy,
that they **may do his will.** Such divine resources
would include a variety of grace suited to
every man in every conceivable circumstance.
To some a warning, a bitter hardship to remind
them that they are true sons and not illegitimate
(12:8). To others the grace of perseverance
through hope, a fresh vision of the Lord Christ
and his patient endurance of suffering (12:2).
To still others a clearer light amid doubts, a

22 And I beseech you, brethren, suffer the word of exhortation: for I have written a letter unto you in a few words.

23 Know ye that *our* brother Timothy is set at liberty; with whom, if he come shortly, I will see you.

22 I appeal to you, brethren, bear with my word of exhortation, for I have written to you briefly. 23 You should understand that our brother Timothy has been released, with whom I shall see you if he

---

**22.** As in I Pet. 5:12-14, a personal note is added to the formal prayer and doxology. **Word of exhortation** correctly and aptly describes the content and the main intent of Hebrews, for if the modern reader is inclined to be chiefly impressed by the subtlety and complexity of the argument, the writer's own purpose is practical. The phrase **I have written to you briefly** is a literary convention which could be justified from the writer's point of view. Brevity is a relative term. Hebrews ranks eighth in length among our N.T. writings and can be read in an hour. The writer has indicated that he could expand his treatment at one point (11:32), and we have every reason to believe this to be true of other parts.

**23-24.** Nothing in these verses is perfectly clear. The usual translation suggests that Timothy has been released from prison, and if he joins the author soon, they will make the trip to the readers together. There is no grammatical impossibility, however, in interpreting these verses to mean that Timothy has set out on his journey to the readers and if he (Timothy) arrives in time, they (the writer and Timothy) will see them together, assuming, of course, that the writer is "restored" to them in answer to their prayers (vs. 19). The former view seems the simpler, perhaps largely because of the Pauline parallels (cf. Phil. 2:19; Philem. 22). Is this the intention of another writer than our author, who adds the name of Timothy and Pauline phrases to suggest the Pauline authorship of

---

warmer heart for their comrades, the spirit of forgiveness that comes from humility, the easing of the fretfulness of pride, the peace of conscience without which no strong work can ever be accomplished.

We often pray for inconsequential goods for those whom we love. But an informed prayer will aim at first things, the fulfillment of our central destiny and of our complete happiness, **that you may do his will.**

The writer also asks that God may work **in you that which is well-pleasing in his sight, through Jesus Christ.** Here is a simple expression of the perennial mystery of faith, "It is no longer I who live, but Christ who lives in me" (Gal. 2:20; cf. also Phil. 2:12-13). When two lives are united in a common task, as a husband and wife are in providing a home and in rearing children, their very love forbids them sharply to divide the credit for the good they do. It was the two working together that produced results which they could never have effected working separately. A man of faith will not take credit for anything he has done, but will attribute all to the grace of God.

This work in us is **through Jesus Christ.** It is Jesus who has brought God's Word to man, made his purpose clear. It is Jesus whose sacrifice brings us to Mount Zion (12:22-24). In the daily graces that we need from God are the

teaching of Jesus for our guidance, his spirit to quiet our restless pride, his love to pervade our dealings with our fellows, his presence to give us peace and hope. All that he has brought to men, all the gifts he has conferred, are the pledge of God to those who believe that he will complete the **working in you** [of] **that which is pleasing in his sight.**

**To whom be glory for ever and ever.** It is impossible in the N.T. to distinguish clearly between the glory of God and the glory of Jesus Christ (cf. Exeg.; cf. also John 17:4). But since Christ has been the central figure of the epistle, it is likely that our author is here giving glory to him. This is the most natural reading. What is the **glory** that is to belong to Jesus Christ? We cannot possibly know it in all its dimensions (cf. Expos. on 1:3). But clearly it is relevant to his **glory** that men should know him, reflect his faith in the Father, his endurance under trials, his forgiving grace, until each can say, "Christ lives in me." Words of praise never ascribe real **glory** unless they come from the heart and are embedded in our deeds.

**22-25.** *Personal Greetings.*—We search these closing verses eagerly for some clue to the identity of our author but find little help. We should like to know this man. But the "I" is kept in the background as in all N.T. writings,

24 Salute all them that have the rule over you, and all the saints. They of Italy salute you.

25 Grace *be* with you all. Amen.

¶ Written to the Hebrews from Italy by Timothy.

comes soon. 24 Greet all your leaders and all the saints. Those who come from Italy send you greetings. 25 Grace be with all of you. Amen.

---

Hebrews? There can be no final answer to this question unless further light breaks on this puzzling ch. 13. **Greet all your leaders and all the saints.** This also is puzzling, for we assume that the writing, if it is a letter, would come first to the leaders, and that they would be enjoined to greet the saints. The chapter, however, reads as if its recipients were addressed over against their leaders (cf. vss. 7, 17). It has been argued that Hebrews was sent to a small group, perhaps a house church, and that this select body was enjoined to greet the leaders of the larger body. Even a small group would have its leader or leaders, however, who would be isolated by such an exhortation to greet them. The very general character of the admonitions in Hebrews hardly warrants the view that a small select body of readers is addressed. Almost everything in ch. 13 raises questions as to its genuineness, although there is no external evidence that it was not always a part of Hebrews. The final ambiguity is in the phrase Ἀσπάζονται ὑμᾶς οἱ ἀπὸ τῆς Ἰταλίας. The translation **those who come from Italy** is interpretive, for the Greek words can be rendered grammatically **they of Italy**, meaning persons domiciled there (cf. I Cor. 16:19), and Phil. 4:22 affords another suggestive although incomplete parallel. As has been often pointed out, if the words convey a greeting from Italians who are abroad, then no other Christians except the absent Italians are included in the greeting. This, of course, might be the case. The one certainty is that the greeting adds another awkward touch to ch. 13. The final benediction, **Grace be with you all,** is Pauline, appearing at the end of all the letters attributed to Paul (except Romans, where in some MSS it comes at the close of 16:20) and nowhere else in the N.T.

---

for the message is the urgent concern. The one exception to this N.T. rule is in Paul's epistle to the Galatians, where validation of his apostleship was an essential part of his argument.

All interpreters face the danger of getting in the way of their gospel, the Christ. To be sensitive to that danger is to be well on the way to overcoming it. It is a hazardous position to occupy—this being a spokesman for God. It carries unique temptations. We see it in the tone of voice, manner, the assumption of dignity, the importance we attach to our opinions on every subject, and the impression we sometimes convey that we have known the really worth-while people, that we are really very learned, and that our insights are uniquely important. How silly is all this egoism in a minister of the gospel of Christ! "Unless the pulpit is the place where you are humblest in giving God's message, it is certain to be the place where you are vainest in giving your own." [1] (See Expos. on 5:5-6.) The test we can apply is our susceptibility to moods. Are we more sensitive to our own wounds than to the wounds of Christ?

**I appeal to you, brethren.** The author is not

[1] John Oman, *Concerning the Ministry* (New York: Harper & Bros., 1937), p. 44.

too certain that his work will have a favorable reception. **I have written to you briefly.** And like all good authors, he has had to leave out much of what he wanted to say. But only such writing carries weight.

**All the saints.** Here is a word in our Christian vocabulary that has been badly misused. We have overidealized the saint, perhaps because in doing so we think to escape the obligation to be saints that rests upon all Christians. Paul wrote to the church at Corinth (of all places!) and referred to the church members as "called to be saints together with all those who in every place call on the name of our Lord Jesus Christ" (I Cor. 1:2). All Christians are "called to be saints." If we could see and know some of the first-century Christians to whom the word saint was applied we should be both encouraged and humbled.

**Grace be with you all.** This was a formal Pauline benediction. But the "form" is a rich one. In this last word of his epistle the writer is calling down upon his people all the abundant, sufficient, though undeserved, favor of God. To leave men nowhere else but in the presence and in the hands of God ought to be the final result of every proclamation of the Word.

Joppa

Bethlehem
2550

Jerusalem
2593

Jericho
820 FEET BELOW SEA LEVEL

DEAD
SEA
1292 FEET BELOW SEA LEVEL

Jordan

PALESTINE
in New Testament Times

© PIERCE & SMITH